South Africa
Lesotho & Swaziland

Simon Richmond
Alan Murphy
Kim Wildman
Andrew Burke

LONELY PLANET PUBLICATIONS
Melbourne • Oakland • London • Paris

Gobabis

WINDHOEK

KGALAGADI TRANSFRONTIER PARK
Discover the stark beauty of the Kalahari
and its fabulous flora and fauna

Central Kalahari
Game Reserve

BOTSWANA

Tropic of Capricorn

Mariental

Kgalagadi
Transfrontier
Park

GABORONE

Kanye

Loba

Zee

Mafikeng

Mmat

Lichtenburg

Tshabong

NORTH-WEST PROVINCE

Kalahari
Desert

Keetmanshoop

Rietfontein

Vryburg

NAMAQUALAND
Come in spring to view the
spectacular explosion of
wildflowers

Hotazel

Bloemhof

Kuruman

NAMIBIA

Fish River Canyon
National Park

B1

B3

Augrabies Falls
National Park

Upington

FREE STATE

Kimberley

Richtersveld
National Park

Orange River

N10

BLOEMFONTEIN

Alexander
Bay

Noordoewer

Prieska

N12

N1

Port Nolloth

Springbok

NAMAQUALAND

SOUTH
AFRICA

Orange River

De Aar

NORTHERN CAPE

Carnarvon

Middelburg

N7

ATLANTIC
OCEAN

Calvinia

Cederberg
Wilderness
Area

Karoo
National
Park

Graaff-Reinet

Crad

Mountain Zebra
National Park

Somerset East

WINELANDS
Sample wines at the lush green
vineyards around Stellenbosch,
Franschhoek and Paarl

Beaufort West

Addo
Elephant
National
Park

St Helena
Bay

N1

Saldanha

CAPE TOWN
Soak up the sights of this
beautiful city nestled between
Table Mountain and the Atlantic

Ceres

Worcester

WESTERN CAPE

Oudtshoorn

Uitenhage

Po

Tsitsikamma
National Park

Elizal

Paarl

Montagu

George

Knysna

Jeffrey's Bay

CAPE TOWN

Stellenbosch

Swellendam

Mossel Bay

Plettenberg
Bay

Cape St Francis

Cape of Good Hope
Nature Reserve

Hermanus

Bredasdorp

De Hoop
Nature
Reserve

Wilderness
National Park

SOUTH COAST
Take in the verdant Garden
Route or head to the surfers'
mecca at Jeffrey's Bay

Cape of
Good Hope

False
Bay

Cape
Agulhas

N2

SOUTH AFRICA, LESOTHO & SWAZILAND

ZIMBABWE

Gonarezhou National Park

MOZAMBIQUE

SUN CITY
Marvel at the world's most kitsch casino resort

Messina

Thohoyandou

Banhine National Park

Louis Trichardt

Limpopo River

Tropic of Capricorn

KRUGER NATIONAL PARK
Watch wildlife in South Africa's premier national park

Ellisras

NORTHERN PROVINCE

Phalaborwa

Inhambane

Pietersburg-Polokwane

Kruger National Park

n City

Pilanesberg National Park

Xai-Xai

Rustenburg

Olifants River

Blyde River Canyon Nature Reserve

Sabie

PRETORIA

Middelburg

Nelspruit

Komatipoort

GAUTENG

N4

Pigg's Peak

MAPUTO

Soweto

Johannesburg

Heidelberg

MBABANE

SWAZILAND
Go white-water rafting on the Usutu River and attend traditional ceremonies

Vereeniging

MPUMALANGA

Manzini

SWAZILAND

Ermelo

Potchefstroom

Klerksdorp

Standerton

Piet Retief

Big Bend

Hlathikulu

Kosi Bay Nature Reserve

N1

FREE STATE

Vrede

Volksrust

Golela

Louwsburg

Mkuze

Sodwana Bay National Park

Kroonstad

Newcastle

Madadeni

Vryheid

Greater St Lucia Wetland Park

Welkom

Bohlakong

Virginia

Harrismith

Dundee

Hluhluwe-Umfolozi Park

Senekal

Bethlehem

Ladysmith

Ulundi

SOWETO
Tour the city at the centre of the new South Africa

Ficksburg

Mtubatuba

Thaba Nchu

Estcourt

KWAZULU-NATAL

Empangeni

Richards Bay

MASERU

Ukhulamba-Drakensberg Park

ZULULAND
Learn about Zulu culture and Anglo-Boer War history

Mafeteng

LESOTHO

Pietermaritzburg

Mohale's Hoek

Durban

Drakensberg

Amanzimtoti

THE DRAKENSBERG
Discover hiking trails and San rock art in this breathtaking escarpment

Aliwal North

Kokstad

N2

J6

Port Shepstone

EASTERN CAPE

Mkamhati Nature Reserve

INDIAN OCEAN

Umtata

Port St Johns

Queenstown

Hluleka Nature Reserve

Dwesa Nature Reserve

LESOTHO
Explore the mountainous heart of the 'kingdom in the sky'

Beaufort

King William's Town

hamstown

East London

Port Alfred

ELEVATION	
	2400m
	1800m
	1200m
	600m
	0

0   100   200km
0   60   120mi

South Africa, Lesotho & Swaziland
5th edition – January 2002
First published – January 1993

Six-monthly upgrades of this title are available free on
www.lonelyplanet.com/upgrades

Published by
Lonely Planet Publications Pty Ltd ABN 36 005 607 983
90 Maribyrnong St, Footscray, Victoria 3011, Australia

Lonely Planet offices
Australia Locked Bag 1, Footscray, Victoria 3011
USA 150 Linden St, Oakland, CA 94607
UK 10a Spring Place, London NW5 3BH
France 1 rue du Dahomey, 75011 Paris

Photographs
Many of the images in this guide are available for licensing from
Lonely Planet Images.
email: lpi@lonelyplanet.com.au
Web site: www.lonelyplanetimages.com

Front cover photograph
Ostriches behind adobe wall in South Africa (Pete Turner Inc., Stone)

Title page photographs
Wildlife Guide: Zebra's mane (Richard I'Anson)
South Africa: Traditional design on wall (Richard I'Anson)
Lesotho: Woman preparing customary good-luck offering for travellers
(Richard I'Anson)
Swaziland: Printed textile with traditional design, Mantenga Craft
Centre, Ezulwini Valley (Richard I'Anson)

ISBN 1 86450 322 X

text & maps © Lonely Planet Publications Pty Ltd 2002
photos © photographers as indicated 2002

Printed by SNP SPrint (M) Sdn Bhd
Printed in Malaysia

Contents – Text

Contents – Maps

The Authors

Simon Richmond
In 30-odd years of travel Simon Richmond had covered fair chunks of the world's continents. He jumped at the chance to explore South Africa from one of its most visually stunning and happening cities. Such were Cape Town's attractions it took some effort for him to actually leave and get on with his research, but the rest of the country did not disappoint. An award-winning author of guidebooks on Japan, South-East Asia, India, South America and Australia, Simon has worked on various projects for Lonely Planet, including *Central Asia*, *Istanbul to Kathmandu* and the Out to Eat series. He calls Sydney home, whenever it's time to clean out the backpack.

Alan Murphy
After relinquishing his dream of cultivating a career in global espionage, Alan decided to tackle dodgy border crossings like everybody else – with a backpack and a fistful of cash. His subsequent adventures to the far corners of the planet convinced him to seek viable employment in a similar vein. Several years and a journalism degree later he landed at Lonely Planet and, after a brief editing interlude, began updating guidebooks. Alan lives in Melbourne, where tight deadlines and nights at the Retreat Hotel have become life when not researching. Alan has also worked on Lonely Planet's *Southern Africa*, *Africa*, *India*, *North India* and *Argentina*, *Uruguay & Paraguay* guides.

Kim Wildman
Kim grew up in Toowoomba, Queensland, with parents who unwittingly instilled in her the desire to travel at a young age by extending the immediate family to include 11 exchange students. Kim graduated from Queensland College of Art, where she studied photography, before packing her backpack and heading to the USA and Bermuda. But it was her next adventure, to Southern Africa, that inspired her to combine her three loves: photography, writing and travel. Kim has a BA in journalism and has worked on Lonely Planet's *Romania & Moldova*, *Eastern Europe*, *Europe on a Shoestring* and *Athens*.

Andrew Burke
Andrew was born and raised in Sydney, Australia, and on finishing school decided journalism would be a good career for an aspiring traveller. He funded several overseas jaunts with a nine-year stint at Sydney's *Daily Telegraph* before heading to London in 1998. For three years, travel to Africa, Asia, the Middle East, Europe and North America was interrupted by work as an editor and writer with the *Financial Times* and the *Independent on Sunday*. Back in Sydney he kept out of trouble at the *Australian Financial Review* before embarking on full-time travel writing. He is now based in Hong Kong.

FROM THE AUTHORS

Simon Richmond

This book couldn't have been completed without the hard work and dedication of my coauthors Alan, Andrew and Kim, who clocked up the kilometres on their respective trails of the country, and the steadying hands of Virginia and Vince back at base.

Virginia Haddon at South African Tourism in Sydney was a great help and gave me a glimpse of the friendliness that would be waiting for me in South Africa. Thanks also to Diana Lyon for some contacts, particularly Anne Wallis Brown and her colleagues. In Cape Town, the dynamic Sheryl Ozinsky and her staff (in particular the marvellous Vicky) pulled out all stops to check details and make arrangements. Andre Vorster gave me an insight into the gay side of the city, Barbara and Barry unveiled its adventurous streak. Donald Paul, Gina Schauffer and Gary de Klerk of SA Citylife and Patricia Davison at the South African Museum were all generous with their time and knowledge. Many thanks to Lee and Toni, Tony and Barbara, and Barry for nights off. On the road it was a particular pleasure to spend time with Janine Taylor and the equally enthusiastic Nic Vorster.

Finally, thanks to two women who more than anything summed up the hopeful, reconciling spirit of the new South Africa: Vicky Ntozini and Tammin Barker. Both put flesh on the Xhosa word *ubuntu* and the Afrikaans word *kuier* – there's little to choose between the meaning of both: hospitality, pure and simple.

Alan Murphy

Firstly, my gratitude and thanks to freelance writer Justine Vaisutis, whose invaluable assistance with research was much appreciated. At Flight Centre it was the effervescent Julie Blythe who once again came through with 'impossible' flights.

In Pretoria, thanks to Algy Vaisutis, wildlife and African arts and crafts expert, for his friendship and his warm hospitality. Around South Africa, thanks to: Fikile in Kimberley for helping me understand the realities of South African life at Galashwe; and in a similar vein, the two artists-cum-caretakers-cum-cultural ambassadors at Lotlamoreng Cultural Village in North-West Province, for their friendly conversation and beautiful artwork. Praise and thanks to Tommy Proudfoot in Graskop and Belinda in Colesburg, for their profound knowledge of their respective local areas; and Lyndyll at Lowveld Travel in Nelspruit for her assistance and patience. A warm thanks to Marc Mcdonald in Kruger National Park for putting his busy schedule on hold to offer his time and assistance in regards to rhino spotting – his expertise in all things Kruger was also invaluable. To the Kalahari Adventure Centre, dogs and all, a big thanks not only for the masses of information but also for enabling backpackers to see South Africa's remote corner.

In Swaziland, I would like to commend and thank the highly organised Mbabane Tourist Office for its excellent information (again!). Also the Lubombo Lobster for salvaging our taste buds from the mediocrity of pub fare. To the Swazi people, whose pride, independence, identity and warmth is comparable only to the beauty of their own landscape, 'ngiyabonga'!

Kim Wildman

My biggest thanks goes to my dear friend Tom Habermann, who put his own life on hold to follow me around one of my favourite countries – I hope my love of South Africa has rubbed off on you.

There are so many others I'd like to thank, but most notably Wynie Botha (Cape Town); Kim and Derek Bredencamp (Jeffrey's Bay); Erica McNulty (Kenton-on-Sea); Beverly Young and Steve Gardner (Port Alfred); Terrance and Nita Gush (Graaff-Reinet); the team from the Marijuana Trail (Cintsa); David Malherbe (Coffee Bay) – I will return for that free surf lesson; Ranni and Viv (aka Mad Dog) for being in every town we visited; Mick Jones (Malealea); Graham, Richard and Meg Chennels (Eshowe); and, special thanks to Greta and Pierre Schoeman (Durban) for opening your hearts and your home to Tom and myself (sorry about the key).

Back home, I'd like to thank Simon Richmond, for expecting nothing but the best, and the Lonely Planet team in Melbourne, without whom this book would not be possible.

And finally, to the people of South Africa – your many, varied, smiling faces will ensure that South Africa will always hold a special place in my heart.

Andrew Burke

There were many people who generously donated their time and expertise during my research in Gauteng, a place where good advice is worth gold. In Johannesburg, those to whom I'm especially grateful include the brothers Baines – Mark, Stephen and Peter – for their hospitality, willingness to accompany me to some of Jo'burg's more interesting nightspots and good grace even when their beloved Cats were beaten; Evan and Muff for their unbending belief in a city that can try even the most faithful; and Gary Bath and Yusoof, whose eye-opening tour of gay Jo'burg was invaluable.

In Soweto, Max Lentsoane, Jabu and Letlela eagerly answered all my questions and proved priceless in reacquainting me with the highs and lows of the township; while in Pretoria the social and culinary directions and all-round good advice of Francois and Marinda and John and Andrea made life much more pleasant.

Thanks also to those research assistants who made looking, eating and drinking a less lonely endeavour: Jason, Andy, Caz, Sarah Way, Charlotte and Elin, among others.

Simon Richmond was the ideal coordinating author and his patience and guidance were greatly appreciated, while the editors and cartographers in LP's Melbourne office, particularly Virginia Maxwell, were the height of professionalism throughout; thanks all for your help.

An extra special thank you goes to Anne Hyland, a woman whose love and understanding sets her apart and without whom this would not have been possible; thanks for being there when I finally get home. And to my family, whose Herculean support is never recognised as much as it should be.

Finally, a big thank you to all the citizens of Gauteng who live in this cauldron of social contrasts; may your futures be brighter.

This Book

The first edition of this book was researched and written by Richard Everist and Jon Murray. The second, third and fourth editions were updated by Jon Murray and Jeff Williams.

The coordinating author of this edition was Simon Richmond, who updated the introductory chapters; Cape Town & the Peninsula; Western Cape; and the peoples, Cape Town architecture and wineries special sections. Alan Murphy updated Swaziland, Mpumalanga, Kruger National Park, Northern Province, North-West Province, Free State and Northern Cape. Kim Wildman updated Eastern Cape, KwaZulu-Natal and Lesotho. Andrew Burke updated Gauteng and wrote the Soweto special section. Sean Pywell compiled the Wildlife Guide, which was based on the previous text by Luke Hunter and Andy MacColl, and the music special section was written by Paul Fisher.

From the Publisher

The editing of this edition of *South Africa, Lesotho & Swaziland* was coordinated by Hilary Rogers; the cartography and design were coordinated by Rodney Zandbergs.

Helping with the editing of this book was a trusty cast of thousands: Susie Ashworth, Kerryn Burgess, Janine Eberle, Hilary Erickson, Justin Flynn, Susan Holtham, Nancy Ianni, Evan Jones, Jenny Mullaly and Isabelle Young. Lara Morcombe compiled the index, assisted by Susie Ashworth and Evan Jones. Yvonne Byron, George Dunford, Evan Jones and Anastasia Safioleas came to the rescue during the final stages of layout.

Tackling all those maps with a vengeance were: Yvonne Bischofberger, Hunor Csutoros, Huw Fowles, Kusnandar, Amanda Sierp, Sarah Sloane and Jody Whiteoak. Hunor also prepared the climate charts. Katie Butterworth and Maree Styles gave Rod a helping hand with layout. Matt King coordinated the illustrations, which were drawn by Jenny Bowman, Clint Curé and Sarah Jolly.

Heartfelt thanks to Emma Koch for her work on the Language chapter, to Jenny Jones for the cover, to Mark Germanchis for all things Quark and, lastly, to Kim Hutchins, Vince Patton, Virginia Maxwell and Katie Butterworth for their indefatigable support and hard work.

THANKS
Many thanks to the travellers who used the last edition and wrote to us with helpful hints, advice and interesting anecdotes. Your names appear on page 664 of this book.

11

Foreword

ABOUT LONELY PLANET GUIDEBOOKS

The story begins with a classic travel adventure: Tony and Maureen Wheeler's 1972 journey across Europe and Asia to Australia. Useful information about the overland trail did not exist at that time, so Tony and Maureen published the first Lonely Planet guidebook to meet a growing need.

From a kitchen table, then from a tiny office in Melbourne (Australia), Lonely Planet has become the largest independent travel publisher in the world, an international company with offices in Melbourne, Oakland (USA), London (UK) and Paris (France).

Today Lonely Planet guidebooks cover the globe. There is an ever-growing list of books and there's information in a variety of forms and media. Some things haven't changed. The main aim is still to help make it possible for adventurous travellers to get out there – to explore and better understand the world.

At Lonely Planet we believe travellers can make a positive contribution to the countries they visit – if they respect their host communities and spend their money wisely. Since 1986 a percentage of the income from each book has been donated to aid projects and human rights campaigns.

Updates Lonely Planet thoroughly updates each guidebook as often as possible. This usually means there are around two years between editions, although for more unusual or more stable destinations the gap can be longer. Check the imprint page (following the colour map at the beginning of the book) for publication dates.

Between editions up-to-date information is available in two free newsletters – the paper *Planet Talk* and email *Comet* (to subscribe, contact any Lonely Planet office) – and on our Web site at www.lonelyplanet.com. The *Upgrades* section of the Web site covers a number of important and volatile destinations and is regularly updated by Lonely Planet authors. *Scoop* covers news and current affairs relevant to travellers. And, lastly, the *Thorn Tree* bulletin board and *Postcards* section of the site carry unverified, but fascinating, reports from travellers.

Correspondence The process of creating new editions begins with the letters, postcards and emails received from travellers. This correspondence often includes suggestions, criticisms and comments about the current editions. Interesting excerpts are immediately passed on via newsletters and the Web site, and everything goes to our authors to be verified when they're researching on the road. We're keen to get more feedback from organisations or individuals who represent communities visited by travellers.

Lonely Planet gathers information for everyone who's curious about the planet – and especially for those who explore it first-hand. Through guidebooks, phrasebooks, activity guides, maps, literature, newsletters, image library, TV series and Web site we act as an information exchange for a worldwide community of travellers.

Research Authors aim to gather sufficient practical information to enable travellers to make informed choices and to make the mechanics of a journey run smoothly. They also research historical and cultural background to help enrich the travel experience and allow travellers to understand and respond appropriately to cultural and environmental issues.

Authors don't stay in every hotel because that would mean spending a couple of months in each medium-sized city and, no, they don't eat at every restaurant because that would mean stretching belts beyond capacity. They do visit hotels and restaurants to check standards and prices, but feedback based on readers' direct experiences can be very helpful.

Many of our authors work undercover, others aren't so secretive. None of them accept freebies in exchange for positive write-ups. And none of our guidebooks contain any advertising.

Production Authors submit their raw manuscripts and maps to offices in Australia, USA, UK or France. Editors and cartographers – all experienced travellers themselves – then begin the process of assembling the pieces. When the book finally hits the shops, some things are already out of date, we start getting feedback from readers and the process begins again …

WARNING & REQUEST

Things change – prices go up, schedules change, good places go bad and bad places go bankrupt – nothing stays the same. So, if you find things better or worse, recently opened or long since closed, please tell us and help make the next edition even more accurate and useful. We genuinely value all the feedback we receive. A well-travelled team reads and acknowledges every letter, postcard and email and ensures that every morsel of information finds its way to the appropriate authors, editors and cartographers for verification.

Everyone who writes to us will find their name listed in the next edition of the appropriate guidebook. They will also receive the latest issue of *Planet Talk*, our quarterly printed newsletter, or *Comet*, our monthly email newsletter. Subscriptions to both newsletters are free. The very best contributions will be rewarded with a free guidebook.

We may edit, reproduce and incorporate your comments in all Lonely Planet products, such as guidebooks, Web sites and digital products, so let us know if you don't want your comments reproduced or your name acknowledged.

Send all correspondence to the Lonely Planet office closest to you:

Australia: Locked Bag 1, Footscray, Victoria 3011
USA: 150 Linden St, Oakland, CA 94607
UK: 10a Spring Place, London NW5 3BH
France: 1 rue du Dahomey, 75011 Paris

Or email us at: talk2us@lonelyplanet.com.au

For news, views and updates see our Web site: www.lonelyplanet.com

HOW TO USE A LONELY PLANET GUIDEBOOK

The best way to use a Lonely Planet guidebook is any way you choose. At Lonely Planet we believe the most memorable travel experiences are often those that are unexpected, and the finest discoveries are those you make yourself. Guidebooks are not intended to be used as if they provide a detailed set of infallible instructions!

Contents All Lonely Planet guidebooks follow roughly the same format. The Facts about the Destination chapters or sections give background information ranging from history to weather. Facts for the Visitor gives practical information on issues like visas and health. Getting There & Away gives a brief starting point for researching travel to and from the destination. Getting Around gives an overview of the transport options when you arrive.

The peculiar demands of each destination determine how subsequent chapters are broken up, but some things remain constant. We always start with background, then proceed to sights, places to stay, places to eat, entertainment, getting there and away, and getting around information – in that order.

Heading Hierarchy Lonely Planet headings are used in a strict hierarchical structure that can be visualised as a set of Russian dolls. Each heading (and its following text) is encompassed by any preceding heading that is higher on the hierarchical ladder.

Entry Points We do not assume guidebooks will be read from beginning to end, but that people will dip into them. The traditional entry points are the list of contents and the index. In addition, however, some books have a complete list of maps and an index map illustrating map coverage.

There may also be a colour map that shows highlights. These highlights are dealt with in greater detail in the Facts for the Visitor chapter, along with planning questions and suggested itineraries. Each chapter covering a geographical region usually begins with a locator map and another list of highlights. Once you find something of interest in a list of highlights, turn to the index.

Maps Maps play a crucial role in Lonely Planet guidebooks and include a huge amount of information. A legend is printed on the back page. We seek to have complete consistency between maps and text, and to have every important place in the text captured on a map. Map key numbers usually start in the top left corner.

Although inclusion in a guidebook usually implies a recommendation we cannot list every good place. Exclusion does not necessarily imply criticism. In fact there are a number of reasons why we might exclude a place – sometimes it is simply inappropriate to encourage an influx of travellers.

Introduction

Listen up. We're going to let you in on a secret that really shouldn't have been kept for so long. South Africa and its enclosed neighbours Lesotho and Swaziland are among the most beautiful and amazing countries you could wish to visit. Rich in wildlife and culture, and boasting a variety of landscapes, each of these countries has a history that can only be described as operatic in its tragedy, and yet a triumphant spirit prevails.

You think we're exaggerating? Let us admit some evidence. Item one is Cape Town, a strong contender for the title of the world's most stunning and hedonistic seaside city. Item two is the host of wildlife conservation zones – stretching from the arid and mesmerising spaces of the Kalahari to the rugged Drakensberg escarpment – where you can see nature close up, bewildering in its diversity, sobering in its fight-for-life savagery.

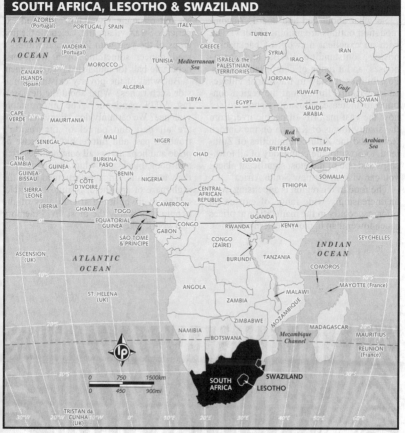

SOUTH AFRICA, LESOTHO & SWAZILAND

Item three is the splendid coastline, graced with gorgeous beaches and surf as if sent from heaven. No wonder whales come to breed here!

Ah, but this is Africa, you say, with its heat and its chaotic infrastructure. Rest assured that on the whole the climate is kind (with the advantage that it is summer here while the northern hemisphere is in the depths of winter); and the transport and communications systems are constantly improving. Whether you're travelling by car, taking the bus or rolling along in luxury on the famous *Blue Train*, most major attractions here are accessible in greater comfort than in other parts of Africa.

So what about bed and board? Accommodation options are nothing if not varied, with an excellent network of backpacker hostels, outstanding B&Bs and guesthouses, and a range of comfortable hotels. Possibilities to stay in traditional villages and townships throughout the region continue to increase, allowing visitors to see how the vast majority of people live, from the shanty towns of Knysna on the Garden Route and the Zulu communities of Zululand, to Soweto, the grandaddy of all townships and one of the most significant places you can visit in the new South Africa.

The food in the region is appetising, with an increasingly wide range of cuisine on offer, especially in the main cities, at prices much lower than in most Western countries.

The shaky rand comes in handy if you plan to indulge in the many activities that South Africa now offers. Long renown for its excellent surfing and hiking, the country is fast gaining a reputation for adventure sports, with opportunities to abseil, dive, mountain bike, paraglide and bungee jump your way around the country.

In rural Lesotho, where time seems to have stood still, you'll be relieved to explore a country not suffering from an apartheid hangover. Rise to the challenge of a tough remote-area hike, while away the afternoon fishing for trout, or embark on a pony trek.

In the tiny, culturally rich Kingdom of Swaziland, travellers with plenty of time can set out on ancient walking trails and experience Swazi village life. Celebrate the first crops of the year with locals, and witness a reed dance, something of a week-long debutante ball for unmarried Swazi women.

But what of the poverty existing alongside such riches? What about the devastating AIDS pandemic? The interminable violence? We certainly don't deny that these are all part and parcel of the region's troubled past and future, but the sense of pride and hope across all communities, rich and poor, black and white, particularly at the way South Africa has emerged from the nightmare of apartheid, is almost tangible.

The overwhelming friendliness of the people is probably the most vivid memory that you'll take home.

South Africa at a glance: The southernmost country on the African continent offers the highlife and the wildlife, traditional fineries and fabulous wineries.

Facts about South Africa

HISTORY

The current national boundaries in Southern Africa are predominantly the creation of competitive European imperialist powers in the 19th and 20th centuries, rather than any geographical, cultural or historical identity. South Africa, Lesotho and Swaziland are, therefore, more usefully seen as a whole until the late 19th century, and will be treated as such in this chapter. For more recent historical events, see the Lesotho and Swaziland chapters later in this book.

For more about history and culture, see the special section 'Peoples of the Region'.

Prehistory

Southern Africa's history before the coming of the Iron-Age peoples is uncertain. However, the discovery in 1998 of the first complete skeleton of a 3½-million-year-old *Australopithecus africanus* in a cave near Sterkfontein (north-west of Johannesburg) should provide new information about human evolution. The site, considered one of the most significant archaeological sites in the world, is still being excavated. (For more information about the discovery of 'Mr Ples', see the boxed text 'Sterkfontein Caves' in the Gauteng chapter.)

Most scientists agree that by about two million years ago, changing climatic and environmental conditions resulted in the evolution of several hominid species. Just over a million years ago *Homo erectus* became dominant and evolved further into *Homo sapiens*.

European Exploration

By the 15th century, the Muslim expansion across North Africa and the Balkans had thrown Christian Europe's trade routes into chaos, prompting the Portuguese and Spanish to search for a sea route to India and the spice islands of South-East Asia.

At the end of 1487 Bartholomeu Dias and his expedition (two tiny sailing ships and a store ship) rounded a cape, which Dias named Cabo da Boa Esperança (Cape of Good Hope). Ten years later Vasco da Gama rounded the Cape and finally reached India in 1498.

The Portuguese showed little territorial interest in Southern Africa. To them, the region was merely a place to get fresh water, since attempts to trade with the Khoikhoi had often ended in violence, and the coast and its fierce weather posed a terrible threat to their ships.

By the end of the 16th century the English and Dutch were beginning to challenge the Portuguese traders, and the cape became a regular stopover for scurvy-ridden crews. In 1647 a Dutch vessel was wrecked in Table Bay, and the crew built a fort and stayed for a year until they were rescued.

In the minds of the directors of the Dutch East India Company (Vereenigde Oost-Indische Compagnie; VOC), this crystallised the value of a permanent settlement. They had no intention of colonising the country but simply wanted to establish a secure base where ships could shelter and stock up on fresh supplies of meat, fruit and vegetables. To this end, a small VOC expedition, under the command of Jan van Riebeeck, reached Table Bay in April 1652.

Europeans at the Cape

Although the settlement traded with the neighbouring Khoikhoi people, there was a

Key Dates in Southern Africa's History

c.100,000 BC	San people settle Southern Africa	**1860**	Indians arrive in Natal
AD c.500	Bantu-speaking peoples arrive in the present-day KwaZulu-Natal area	**1868**	British annex Basotholand (Lesotho)
1487	Bartholomeu Dias sails around the Cape of Good Hope	**1869**	Diamonds found near Kimberley
		1871	Gold discovered in eastern Transvaal
c.1500	Basotho people settle in the present-day Lesotho area	**1877**	British annex the Boer Republic of Transvaal
1652	Dutch settlement in Table Bay (Cape Town)	**1881**	Boers defeat British and Transvaal becomes the South African Republic
1688	French Huguenots arrive at the Cape	**1886**	Gold discovered on the Witwatersrand
c.1690	Boers move into the hinterland around present-day Cape Town	**1893**	Mohandas Gandhi arrives in Natal
c.1750	Nguni people settle Swaziland	**1897**	Zululand annexed by Britain
1779	Boers fight Xhosa at Great Fish River	**1899**	Anglo-Boer War starts
1795	British capture Cape Town	**1902**	Anglo-Boer War finishes
1815	Shaka seizes power – the *difaqane* (forced migration) begins	**1905**	Government commission recommends separate development for blacks, with inferior education
1820	British settlers arrive in Eastern Cape		
1830s	Voortrekkers undertake the Great Trek	**1910**	Union of South Africa created, federating the British colonies and the old Boer republics; blacks denied the vote; Lesotho and Swaziland become British protectorates
1838	Boers defeat the Zulu at the Battle of Blood River		
1852	Boer Republic of Transvaal created		
1858	British defeat Xhosa after the disaster of the Great Cattle Killing	**1912**	South African Native National Congress (forerunner to the ANC) established

deliberate attempt to restrict contact. Partly as a consequence of this, the small number of VOC employees found themselves faced with a labour shortage. Van Riebeeck made two moves to deal with this problem, both with far-reaching consequences. Slaves were imported, mostly from Mozambique, Madagascar and Indonesia, and a handful of burghers (middle-class people) were allowed to establish their own farms.

The burghers were still theoretically subject to VOC control, however, and were forced to sell their produce at prices that were determined by the company. The colony was soon producing fruit, vegetables, wheat and wine so successfully that there was a problem with oversupply. As a result, many farmers turned away from intensive farming to raising livestock.

The number of burghers grew slowly but steadily. The majority were of Dutch descent, but there was also a significant number of Germans. Their church was the Calvinist Reformed Church of the Netherlands. In 1688 they were joined by a group of about 150 French Huguenots, also Calvinists, who had fled religious persecution under King Louis XIV. This small group was more significant than might be imagined: In crude numerical terms it increased the white population by over 15%.

Some trace the Afrikaner idea of a chosen people (and racial superiority) to Calvin's doctrine of predestination, which says that an individual's salvation or damnation is preordained. Surrounded by those whom they considered 'primitive heathens', the whites had no doubts as to which race was superior and who had been chosen.

The Boers

The population of whites did not reach 1000 until 1745, but small numbers of free burghers had begun to drift away from the close grip of the VOC further into Africa. They had crossed the Olifants River to the

Key Dates in Southern Africa's History

1913	Natives Land Act restricts black ownership of land to 8% of the country	1976	Soweto uprisings begin
1928	Communist Party begins agitation for full democracy	1977	Steve Biko murdered
1948	National Party wins government (and retains control until 1994); apartheid laws, such as bans on interracial marriages and sex, begin to be passed	1985	State of emergency declared in South Africa – official murder and torture become rife; black resistance strengthens
1955	ANC adopts Freedom Charter	1990	ANC ban lifted, Nelson Mandela freed
1959	Pan African Congress (PAC) formed	1991	Talks on a new constitution begin, political violence escalates
1960	Sharpeville massacre; ANC and PAC banned	1992	Whites-only referendum agrees to reform
1961	South Africa leaves the Commonwealth and becomes a republic	1993	Chris Hani assassinated; new constitution enacted signalling end of apartheid and birth of new South Africa
1963	Nelson Mandela and Walter Sisulu, among others, jailed for life	1994	Democratic elections held, Nelson Mandela elected president
1966	Basotholand gains independence from Britain and becomes the Kingdom of Lesotho	1996	Truth & Reconciliation Commission hearings; constitution signed into law
1968	Swaziland gains independence from Britain	1997	Nelson Mandela retires as ANC president, succeeded by Thabo Mbeki
1975	South Africa invades Angola; Zulu cultural movement Inkatha is revived by Mangosouthu Buthelezi	1999	ANC wins landslide victory in second democratic elections
		2001	Mbeki rejects calls for the declaration of a state of emergency despite an estimated 4.7 million South Africans thought to be infected with HIV/AIDs

north and were pushing east towards Great Fish River. These were the first of the Trekboers (Wandering Farmers) – completely independent of official control, extraordinarily self-sufficient and isolated.

Many pursued a seminomadic pastoralist lifestyle, in some ways not far removed from that of the Khoikhoi. In addition to its herds, a family might have had a wagon, a tent, a Bible and a couple of guns. As they became more settled a mud-walled cottage would be built, but it would – often by choice – be located days of hard travel away from the nearest European.

Out of this isolated lifestyle evolved courageous individualists, but also a backward people, whose only source of knowledge was the Bible. The Trekboers (later shortened to Boers) were cut off from the great intellectual developments that occurred in Europe in the 18th century: the French Revolution and the associated ideas of liberalism, democracy and religion-free science.

The Boers' lifestyle and culture, both real and idealised, have been the dominant factor in shaping the Afrikaners' view of themselves and their place in Africa.

The Impact on the Khoisan

Confrontations between the Europeans and the Khoisan were inevitable. The Khoisan (a composite term covering both the Khoikhoi and the San peoples) were driven from their traditional lands, decimated by introduced diseases, and destroyed by superior weapons when they fought back – which they did in a number of major 'wars' and with guerrilla resistance which continued into the 19th century.

Most survivors were left with no option but to work for Europeans in an arrangement that hardly differed from slavery. They were exploited for labour and for sex. In time the Khoisan mixed with the imported slaves; the offspring of these unions formed the basis for today's coloured population.

One Khoikhoi group, the Griqua, who had originally lived on the western coast between St Helena Bay and the Cederberg Range, managed to acquire guns and horses. In around 1770 they trekked east and north, in a pattern to be followed 60 years later by the Boers. The Griqua were joined by other groups of Khoisan, coloureds and even white adventurers, and proved to be a formidable military force. They reached the highveld around present-day Kimberley and carved out territory that came to be known as Griqualand. This was forcibly annexed by the British in 1871.

Although a small number of whites did come into tenuous contact with the Sotho-Tswana peoples on the northern frontier in somewhere around 1700, the Xhosa to the west of Great Fish River first met the Boers in the 1770s. The first of nine frontier wars broke out in 1779 between the Xhosa and the Boers.

The Arrival of the British

In 1795, with Dutch mercantile power fading, the British invaded to prevent the Cape falling into rival French hands. They discovered a colony with 25,000 slaves, 20,000 white colonists, 15,000 Khoisan and 1000 freed black slaves.

Power was restricted to a white elite in Cape Town, and differentiation on the basis of race was deeply entrenched. Outside Cape Town and the immediate hinterland, the country was populated by isolated black and white pastoralists whose lifestyles and beliefs were quite antiquated.

The initial British occupation had little impact on society and, in 1803, the colony was handed back to the Dutch. Not long after, however, and in response to the Napoleonic Wars, the British once again decided to secure the Cape against French occupation. In 1806, at Bloubergstrand 25km north of Cape Town, the British again defeated the Dutch. The colony was ceded to the British in 1814.

This time, the British Empire, which was reaching its height in power and confidence at the vanguard of the new capitalist world, firmly took control.

The Settlers

In 1820, 5000 middle-class British immigrants arrived to settle near the eastern frontier of the colony, and immediately found themselves in a heavily contested border region. The Boers were on the western side of Great Fish River, the Xhosa were on the east, and both battled interminably over the coastal plain known as the Zuurveld (Sour Land).

It was hoped that the immigrants would create a buffer of market gardeners between the cattle-farming Boers and the Xhosa, but the Zuurveld was completely unsuitable for intensive cultivation. By 1823 almost half of the settlers had retreated to the towns to pursue the jobs they had held in Britain (see the boxed text 'There Will Always Be an England...' in the Eastern Cape chapter).

As a result, Grahamstown developed into a trading and manufacturing centre, quickly becoming the second-largest city in the country. The relative unity of white South Africa was also fractured – there were now two language groups and two very different cultures. A pattern emerged whereby English speakers were highly urbanised, and dominated politics, trade, finance, mining and manufacturing, while the Boers were largely uneducated farmers.

Despite the fact that settlers did make some positive changes to institutionalised racism (such as the law that gave the Khoisan and free blacks legal equality), the British settlers' conservatism and sense of racial superiority stopped any radical reforms. Apart from anything else, the system served them too well. So while slavery was abolished in 1833, a Masters and Servants Ordinance that perpetuated white control was passed in 1841.

British numbers increased rapidly in Cape Town, east of the Cape Colony (present-day Eastern Cape), Natal (present-day Kwa-Zulu-Natal) and, after the discovery of gold and diamonds, parts of the Transvaal (mainly around present-day Gauteng). Thanks to the British, the border wars with the Xhosa reached new depths of depravity. Traditionally the Xhosa had always spared women and children; the British had no such compunction and pursued scorched-earth policies.

The Difaqane

The *difaqane* ('forced migration' in Basotho) or *mfeqane* ('the crushing' in Zulu) was a time of immense upheaval and suffering among the peoples of Southern Africa.

In the early 19th century the Nguni tribes in present-day KwaZulu-Natal underwent a dramatic change, shifting from loosely organised collections of kingdoms into a centralised, militaristic state. The process began under Dingiswayo, chief of the Mthethwa, a powerful leader who developed disciplined regiments of impis (warriors). When Dingiswayo died in 1818, he was succeeded by one of his commanders, Shaka, born into a small clan called Zulu.

Shaka increased the size of the armies and placed them under the control of his officers rather than hereditary chiefs. He began a massive program of conquest in which his main weapon was terror. The best a conquered people could hope for was slavery, but often whole tribes were wiped out. The impis were subject to similar rigours – failure in battle or a wound in the back meant death.

Not surprisingly, tribes in the path of Shaka's increasingly powerful armies fled, and they in turn became aggressors against their neighbours. This wave of disruption and terror spread throughout Southern Africa, with refugees reaching, and conquering, almost as far as Lake Victoria. Two notable successes among the destruction were the Swazi and Basotho peoples, both of whom used the tide of refugees to their advantage and forged powerful nations.

The Boers, whose Great Trek coincided with the difaqane, mistakenly believed that what they found – deserted pasture lands, disorganised bands of refugees and tales of brutality – was the normal state of affairs. The difaqane also added emphasis to the Boers' belief that European occupation meant the coming of civilisation to a savage land.

Shaka was killed in 1828 by his half-brothers Dingaan and Umhlanga. Dingaan became king, and relaxed military discipline. He also attempted to establish friendly relations with the British traders setting up on the Natal coast, but events were unfolding that were to see the demise of Zulu independence.

For more information about the Zulu kingdom, see the KwaZulu-Natal chapter and also the special section 'Peoples of the Region'.

The Great Trek

From the 1820s, groups of Boers dissatisfied with British rule in the Cape Colony had trekked off into the interior in search of freedom. But the decade of migration known as the Great Trek only really got under way after the banning of slavery in 1833. Most Boers grudgingly accepted that slavery might be wrong, but the British seemed to go a step further and proclaim the equality of races – which was unacceptable to the Boers. This resulted in, for example, servants bringing actions against their masters for not paying wages or for assault.

Reports from early treks told of vast, uninhabited (or at least poorly defended) grazing lands, and from 1836 increasing numbers of Voortrekkers, literally fore-trekkers or pioneers, crossed the Orange River, the Cape Colony's frontier. The Voortrekkers had entered their promised land, with space enough for their cattle to graze and for their culture of anti-urban independence to flourish.

The peoples of the plains offered little resistance to the Voortrekkers. Not only had they been disorganised by the difaqane, but they also lacked horses and firearms. However, the mountains where King Moshoeshoe the Great's Basotho nation (later Lesotho) was melded and the wooded valleys of Zululand were a more difficult proposition, and so began the skirmishes, squabbles and flimsy treaties that were to litter the next 50 years of increasing white domination.

The Battle of Blood River

The Great Trek's first halt was at Thaba 'Nchu, near present-day Bloemfontein, where a republic was established. After a disagreement, the Voortrekker leaders Retief,

Maritz and Uys moved on to Natal (in present-day KwaZulu-Natal), while Potgieter headed north to establish the republics of Winburg (in present-day Free State) and Potchefstroom, before crossing the Vaal River to found the Transvaal (encompassing all of present-day Gauteng and Northern Province and part of North-West Province).

By 1837 Retief's party had crossed the Drakensberg and wanted to establish a republic. Zulu king Dingaan agreed to this and, in February 1838, Retief and some others visited Dingaan's capital Mgungundlovu (near modern Ulundi) to sign the title deed. It was a trap. Immediately after signing the deed Dingaan's men massacred the entire party. There was another massacre at Weenen, and other Boer settlements were attacked.

In December 1838 Andries Pretorius arrived in Natal and organised a revenge attack on the Zulus. Sarel Celliers climbed onto a gun carriage to lead the party, vowing that if they won the battle, Boers would ever after celebrate the day as one of deliverance.

Pretorius' party reached the Ncome River, and on 16 December the Zulus attacked. After three hours of carnage, the river ran red, and was thereafter named 'Blood River' by the Boers. Three Boers had slight injuries; 3000 Zulus were killed.

After such a 'miraculous' victory (the result of vastly superior weapons), it seemed to the Boers that their expansion really did have that long-suspected stamp of divine approval, and 16 December was celebrated by whites as the Day of the Vow until 1994, when it was renamed the Day of Reconciliation.

Perhaps more miraculously, when the Boers pushed on to Mgungundlovu they found the remains of Piet Retief and his party and the deed granting them Natal. With both military success and a title deed, the Boers considered Natal to be rightfully theirs. However, the British annexed the republic in 1843, and most of the Boers moved north into the Transvaal, with yet another grievance against the British.

The Boer Republics

Several short-lived Boer republics sprang up, but soon the only serious contenders were

Orange Free State and the Transvaal. The Transvaal Boers were too far away for the British to do much about, but Orange Free State was more accessible and promised to be a headache because of the Boers' constant encroachment on Basotholand around the Mohokare (Caledon) River.

The years between the Battle of Blood River in 1838, and the conventions of Sand River (1852) and Bloemfontein (1854), which gave independence to the Transvaal and Orange Free State, were full of confusion and conflict. The Boers knew what they wanted: land and freedom. The aims of the black tribes were similar. The British, however, who commanded the strongest forces in the area, were in a political dither, with successive governments holding differing views on whether to expand their power across Southern Africa or consolidate their colony and rein in the Boers.

Britain had nonaggression treaties with many of the peoples with whom the Boers were coming into conflict, requiring the British to send in the army to enforce peace. They knew that any large-scale disturbance had a domino effect, and they did not want to upset their precarious relations with tribes bordering the Cape Colony. However, because of changing policies, their armies and officials often had no idea whether they should be restraining Boers, protecting blacks, enforcing British treaties, revenging Boer losses or carving out new British colonies. Nobody knew what orders would arrive on the next mail boat from England.

Orange Free State was intermittently at war with the powerful Basotho, sometimes with British assistance, sometimes without. At various times, the British placed residents (government representatives) in Bloemfontein and in King Moshoeshoe the Great's court, annexed the Orange Free State, gave it independence, wrote treaties, tore up the treaties, revised borders and supervised a few cease-fires. Finally in 1871, the British annexed Basotholand.

This solved the problem of land for Orange Free State. The settlement terms of the 1865 Orange Free State–Basotho War had been generous, and now there was no chance of Moshoeshoe reclaiming his land. (After South Africa gained majority rule in 1994, Lesotho raised the issue of the stolen land, but South Africa was not interested in negotiations.)

The Transvaal Republic's problems were mostly internal, with several leaders and breakaway republics threatening civil war until Paul Kruger settled the issue with a short, sharp campaign in 1864.

Diamonds Discovered

For a while it seemed that the republics were beginning to settle into stable states, despite having thinly spread populations of fiercely independent Boers, no industry and precious little agriculture. Then diamonds were discovered in 1869 near Kimberley, on land belonging to the Griqua people, but to which both the Transvaal and Orange Free State laid claim. Britain stepped in quickly and annexed the area.

The diamond mines resulted in a rush of European immigrants and a migration of black labour to the area. Towns sprang up in which the 'proper separation' of whites and blacks was ignored. The Boers were disturbed by the foreigners, both black and white, and were angry that their impoverished republics were missing out on the economic benefits of the mines.

Meanwhile, Britain became nervous about the existence of independent republics in Southern Africa, especially as gold had been found in the Transvaal. The solution, as usual, was annexation, and in 1877 the Transvaal lost its independence.

The Anglo-Boer Wars

The Transvaal drifted into rebellion and the first Anglo-Boer War, known by Afrikaners as the War of Independence, broke out in 1880. It was over almost as soon as it began, with a crushing Boer victory at the Battle of Majuba Hill in early 1881. The republic regained its independence as the Zuid-Afrikaansche Republiek (ZAR; South African Republic).

Paul Kruger, who had been one of the leaders of the uprising and had earlier led a delegation to London to argue for an end to

the annexation, became president of the ZAR in 1883.

The British desire to federate the Southern African colonies and republics was growing, and not simply because federation would solve local difficulties. Victoria was now Queen Empress, and her empire builders had visions of a British Africa stretching from Cairo to the Cape. Almost the only obstacle in the path of that imperial dream was the existence of the Boer republics.

With the discovery of a huge reef of gold in the Witwatersrand (the area around Johannesburg) in 1886, and the explosive growth of Johannesburg (Jo'burg) itself, the ZAR was suddenly host to thousands of uitlanders (foreigners), both black and white. Within five years Jo'burg was a city, complete with stock exchange, race course and wealthy magnates and financiers, none of whom were Afrikaners. The influx of black labour to the area was also disturbing for the Boers, many of whom were going through hard times and bitterly resented the black wage-earners. Kruger's government did its best to isolate the republic from the gold rush. The foreigners paid taxes, but were not allowed to vote.

The enormous wealth of the Witwatersrand was an irresistible target for the British imperialists. In 1895 a raiding party lead by Captain Leander Jameson entered the ZAR with the intention of sparking an uprising on the Witwatersrand and installing a British administration. This was a fiasco, but it was obvious to Kruger that the raid had at least the tacit approval of the Cape Colony government and that his republic was in danger. He formed an alliance with Orange Free State.

In 1899 the British demanded that voting rights be given to the 60,000 foreign whites on the Witwatersrand. Kruger refused, demanding that British troops massing on the ZAR borders be withdrawn by 11 October. Kruger threatened that if this didn't happen, he would consider the republic to be at war.

The British were shocked to find that the Boers were no pushover and were, for a time, in disarray. The Boers first invaded Natal, where they won important battles.

They besieged Ladysmith but this, like the siege of Mafeking (now Mafikeng), was a mistake as it gave the British time to bring in more troops and the new commanders Lord Roberts and Lord Kitchener.

The abilities of the Boer *kommandos* (commandoes) were no longer underestimated, and an army of 450,000 men was formed to take them on. The 80,000 Boers from the ZAR, Orange Free State and the Cape gave way rapidly and by 5 June 1900, Pretoria, the last of the major towns, had surrendered.

The Guerrilla War

It seemed that the war was over, but instead it entered a second, bitter phase. Kommando raiders, freed from the now-broken central command, denied the enemy control of the countryside. There was no possibility that the British could be defeated, but the Boers knew that maintaining an occupying army would be an expensive proposition for them.

Faced with such an enemy, the British instituted a policy of reprisals. If a train line was blown up, the nearest farmhouse was destroyed; if a shot was fired from a farm, the house was burnt down, the crops destroyed and the animals killed. The women and children from the farms were interned in concentration camps (a British invention). As the guerrilla war dragged on, the burnings and detentions became more systematic. By the end of the war, 26,000 people, mainly children, had died of disease and neglect in the camps (see the boxed text 'Concentration Camps' in the Free State chapter).

The Boer leaders were facing a dilemma. Their growing hatred of the British deepened their resolve to fight until the end, but the horror stories from the concentration camps compelled them to finish the war quickly. Public feeling in Britain and Europe was swinging against the British government, but it was too late to influence the outcome of the war. On 31 May 1902, the Peace of Vereeniging was signed and the Boer republics became British colonies. Paul Kruger fled to Europe, where he died in 1904.

After the Wars

The terms of the peace agreement were generous, but this was small solace for the Afrikaners, who found themselves again ruled by Britain and in the ignominious position of being poor farmers in a country where big mining ventures and foreign capital rendered them irrelevant.

Nevertheless it was essential for the Boers and British to work together. The blacks and coloureds were scarcely considered, other than as potential labour, despite constituting nearly 80% of the population. The peace treaty did nothing to ensure that blacks and coloureds would be given political rights, in spite of British propaganda during the war that blacks would be freed from 'Boer slavery' – a failure that was regarded as a betrayal by the tens of thousands of blacks and coloureds who had fought on Britain's side.

After the war, the Cape Colony was the only state where political rights were shared between races, but even there only 15% of the registered voters were black and coloured. Political awareness was growing, however. Mohandas (later called Mahatma) Gandhi was working with the Indian populations of Natal and the Transvaal, and men such as John Jabavu, Walter Rubusana and Abdullah Abdurahman laid the foundations for new nontribal black political groups. There was considerable unrest within black communities, which in Natal developed into the Bambatha Rebellion. Bambatha, a Zulu chief, began a guerrilla war of independence, but the rebellion was crushed at the cost of 4000 black lives.

The colonial government, under Lord Milner, spent millions of pounds on reconstructing the country after the devastation of the war, although the primary aim was to get the mines functioning again. By 1907 the mines of the Witwatersrand were producing almost one-third of the world's gold.

Resettlement was less successful, and poor Boers, ill-equipped for urban life, flooded into the cities. There they found a world dominated by the British and their language, and were forced to compete for jobs with blacks on an equal footing. Partly as a backlash to this, Afrikaans came to be seen as the *volkstaal* (people's language) and a symbol of Afrikaner nationhood, and several nationalistic organisations sprang up.

The former republics were given representative government in 1906–7, and moves towards union began almost immediately.

The Union of South Africa

The Union of South Africa was established in 1910. The British High Commission Territories of Basotholand (now Lesotho), Bechuanaland (now Botswana), Swaziland, and Rhodesia (now Zimbabwe) were excluded from the union, and continued to be ruled directly by Britain.

English and Dutch were made the official languages (Afrikaans was not recognised as an official language until 1925). Despite a major campaign by blacks and coloureds, the voter franchise remained as it was in the pre-union republics and colonies, and only whites could be elected to parliament.

At the first election, the South African National Party (which was soon to become known as the South African Party; SAP), a diverse coalition of Boer groups under General Louis Botha and the brilliant General Jan Smuts, won government and Botha became the first prime minister.

The most divisive issues were raised by General Barry Hertzog, who championed Afrikaner interests, advocating separate development for the two white groups and independence from Britain. He and his supporters formed the National Party (NP).

Soon after the union was established, a barrage of repressive legislation was passed. It became illegal for black workers to strike; skilled jobs were reserved for whites; blacks were barred from military service; and pass laws, restricting the freedom of movement of blacks, were tightened.

In 1912 Pixley ka Isaka Seme formed a national democratic organisation to represent blacks. It was initially called the South African Native National Congress, but from 1923 it was known as the African National Congress (ANC).

In 1913 the Natives Land Act set aside 8% of South Africa's land for black occupancy. Black Africans (who made up more than 70% of the population) were not allowed to buy, rent or even be a sharecropper outside this area. Thousands of squatters were evicted from farms and forced into increasingly overcrowded and impoverished reserves, or into the cities. Those who remained were reduced to the status of landless labourers.

In 1924 the NP, under Hertzog, came to power, with an agenda that included promoting Afrikaner interests, independence and racial segregation. The *swart gevaar* (black threat) was made the dominant issue of the 1929 election. In the 1930s, Dr DF Malan's even more radical Purified National Party became the dominant force in Afrikaner political life. The Afrikaner Broederbond, a secret Afrikaner brotherhood, became an extraordinarily influential force behind both the NP and a range of political, cultural and economic organisations designed to promote the *volk* (Afrikaners).

Parity with the English was no longer enough for the Afrikaners. Far right Afrikaner groups pursued a policy of sabotaging the South African effort in WWII. Nonetheless many thousands of South Africans volunteered for military service, and troops fought for the Allies with distinction.

The economy boomed during the war and the black urban population nearly doubled. Enormous squatter camps grew up on the outskirts of Jo'burg and, to a lesser extent, outside the other major cities. Black labour became increasingly important to the mining and manufacturing industries. Conditions in the townships were appalling, but poverty was not only the province of blacks; wartime surveys found that 40% of white schoolchildren were malnourished.

Apartheid & the Republic

The NP fought the 1948 election on its policy of apartheid (literally, 'the state of being apart'). In coalition with the Afrikaner Party, it took control. With the help of creative electoral boundaries, control of the media and vicious propaganda, the NP held power right up until the first democratic election in 1994.

Malan, the leader of the coalition, lost no time in instituting the necessary legal apparatus of apartheid. Mixed marriages were prohibited. Interracial sex was made illegal. Every individual was classified by race, and a classification board was established to rule in questionable cases. The Group Areas Act enforcing the physical separation of residential areas was promulgated. The Separate Amenities Act created, among other things, separate beaches, buses, hospitals, schools and even park benches.

The pass laws were further strengthened: Blacks and coloureds were compelled to carry identity documents at all times and were prohibited from remaining in towns, or even visiting them, without specific permission. This meant even more disruption for black and coloured families. Couples were not allowed to live together (or even visit each other) in the town where only one of them worked; children had to remain in rural areas.

Thanks to the Dutch Reformed Churches, apartheid was given a religious justification:

The separation of the races was divinely ordained and the volk had a holy mission to preserve the purity of the white race in its promised land.

Soon after the Sharpeville Massacre (see Black Action, following), Prime Minister Hendrik Verwoerd announced a referendum on whether the country should become a republic, and a slim majority of voters gave their approval to the change. Verwoerd withdrew South Africa from the Commonwealth, and in May 1961 the Republic of South Africa came into existence.

Black Action

In 1949 the ANC developed a program of action that for the first time advocated open resistance in the form of strikes, acts of public disobedience and protest marches. These continued throughout the 1950s, and resulted in occasional violent clashes.

The Old South Africa

It's useful to have an idea of how the old South Africa operated, if only to understand some of the quirks you'll find in the new South Africa.

South Africa had a Westminster-style system of government, modified several times, from union in 1910 until 1983, when the constitution was rewritten; rather ironically it promised to 'uphold Christian values and civilised norms'.

There were three chambers in parliament representing coloureds, Indians and whites. Blacks could not vote and most were not even considered South African citizens. The state president had enormous power, and since the white chamber was larger than the other two combined, the whites retained control when it counted.

As a result of the compromises made at the time of union, three capitals were created: Pretoria, the administrative capital and capital of the Transvaal; Cape Town, the legislative capital and capital of Cape Province; and Bloemfontein, the judicial capital and capital of Orange Free State. There were four provinces: the Transvaal (covering most of what is now Gauteng, Northern Province and Mpumalanga, and part of North-West Province); Natal (now KwaZulu-Natal); Orange Free State; and Cape Province (covering most of what is now Northern, Eastern and Western Cape provinces). At one time, there were elected provincial assemblies, but after 1986 the provinces were run by authorities appointed by the president.

In addition there were the Homelands, the cornerstones of apartheid. The six 'self-governing Homelands' – Gazankulu, KwaNdebele, KaNgwane, KwaZulu, Lebowa and QwaQwa – had internal self-governments. Transkei, Ciskei, Venda and Bophuthatswana were considered by South Africa (but not by the United Nations) to be independent countries. They had their own puppet presidents, armies, border controls and ludicrous trappings such as 'international airports'.

One of the many fringe benefits for white South Africans was that these 'independent countries' weren't bound by South Africa's puritanical laws. A visit to a Homeland casino, to gamble or see pornographic films, became a popular outing.

In June 1955, at a congress held at Kliptown near Jo'burg, a number of organisations, including the Indian Congress and the ANC, adopted a Freedom Charter. This articulated a vision of a nonracial democratic state, and is still central to the ANC's vision of a new South Africa.

On 21 March 1960 the Pan African Congress (PAC) called for nationwide demonstrations against the hated pass laws. When demonstrators surrounded a police station in Sharpeville (near Vereeniging) police opened fire, killing 69 people and wounding 160. To many domestic and international onlookers, the struggle had crossed a crucial line – there could no longer be any doubts about the nature of the white regime.

Soon after, the PAC and ANC were banned, and security forces were given the right to detain people indefinitely without trial. Nelson Mandela became the leader of the underground ANC, and Oliver Tambo went abroad to establish the organisation outside South Africa.

As increasing numbers of black activists were arrested, the ANC and PAC began a campaign of sabotage through the armed wings of their organisations, Umkhonto we Sizwe (Spear of the Nation; usually known as MK) and Poqo (Pure) respectively. In July 1963 Nelson Mandela, along with a number of other ANC and communist leaders, was arrested, charged with fomenting violent revolution and sentenced to life imprisonment.

The Homelands

Verwoerd was assassinated in parliament in 1966 (there was apparently no political motive) and was succeeded by BJ Vorster, who was followed in 1978 by PW Botha. Both men continued to pursue the Afrikaners' dream of separate black Homelands within a white South Africa.

The plan was to restrict blacks to Homelands that were, according to propaganda, to become self-sufficient, self-governing states on the traditional lands of particular tribal groups. In reality, these traditional lands had virtually no infrastructure or industry and were therefore incapable of producing sufficient food for the burgeoning black population. They were based on the land that had been set aside for blacks in the 1913 Natives Lands Act; just 13% of the country's total area was to be home to 75% of the population.

Irrespective of where they had been born, blacks were divided into one of 10 tribal groups and were made citizens of the Homeland that had been established for that group. Blacks had no rights in South Africa, and could not leave their particular Homeland without a pass and explicit permission.

The Homelands policy ignored the fact that in the 19th century tribes had been in a complete state of chaos because of the difaqane, and that the ethnological grounds for distinguishing 10 tribal groups were extremely shaky. In the meantime, there had been extremely rapid urbanisation and economic integration – blacks had lived and worked on 'white' land and in 'white' cities for generations.

Millions of people were forcibly dispossessed and dumped in Homelands. They were given rations for a limited period, but were expected to be self-sufficient on overpopulated land that was rapidly exhausted. There was intense, widespread suffering – families were fractured as the men were forced to return alone to the cities as guest workers without rights.

To stop the tide of blacks flocking to the large cities, the government banned their employment as shop assistants, receptionists, typists and clerks. The construction of housing in the black 'locations' (dormitory suburbs for black workers) was halted, and instead enormous single-sex hostels were built. Despite this, blacks continued to choose to live in urban squatter camps because life in the Homelands was worse.

The Homelands were first given internal self-government, and were then expected to accept a nominal independence. Chief Mangosouthu Buthelezi, who controlled the KwaZulu legislature with the help of his Inkatha movement, attempted to unite the Homeland leaders in resistance to white South Africa's ploy.

However, power proved irresistible to the leaders of Transkei, Bophuthatswana, Venda and Ciskei. Between 1976 and 1981 the collaborators accepted 'independence', and then proceeded to crush all resistance to their control and to the South African government.

The Siege of South Africa

By 1980 South Africa was the only country in Africa with a white government and a constitution discriminating against the majority of its citizens. The government (and most of the white population) increasingly saw the country as a bastion besieged by communism, atheism and black anarchy.

Growing international disapproval of apartheid meant increasing difficulties in obtaining strategic supplies and new technology. South Africa became very resourceful in circumventing sanctions, using illegal trading or home-grown initiative. The government even developed nuclear weapons (which have since been destroyed).

Negotiating majority rule with the ANC was not considered an option (publicly, at least), and this condemned the government to defending the country against external and internal threats through sheer military might. A siege mentality developed among whites, and although many realised that a civil war against the black majority could not be won, they preferred this to 'giving in' to political reform. Brutal police and military actions seemed entirely justifiable.

From 1978 to 1988 the South African Defence Force (SADF; now called the South African National Defence Force; SANDF) made a number of major attacks inside Angola, Mozambique, Zimbabwe, Botswana and Lesotho. The SADF was (and still is) the largest and best-equipped army in Africa. All white males were liable for national service; thousands of young white South African men were forced into exile to avoid conscription. Thousands more were scarred mentally and physically by their participation in vicious struggles in Namibia and Angola, or in the townships of South Africa.

Paradoxically, the international sanctions that cut whites off from the rest of the world enabled black leaders to develop sophisticated political skills, as those in exile forged ties with regional and world leaders.

The Soweto Uprising

Large-scale violence finally broke out on 16 June 1976 when the Soweto Students' Representative Council organised protests against the use of Afrikaans (regarded as the language of the oppressor) in black schools. Police opened fire on a student march, beginning a round of nationwide demonstrations, strikes, mass arrests and riots that, over the next 12 months, took over 1000 lives.

Steve Biko, the charismatic leader of the Black Consciousness Movement, which stressed the need for psychological liberation and black pride, was killed in September 1977 (see the boxed text 'Steve Biko' in the Eastern Cape chapter). Unidentified security police bashed him until he lapsed into a coma; he went without medical treatment for three days and finally died in Pretoria. At the subsequent inquest, the magistrate found that noone was to blame, although the South African Medical Association eventually took action against the doctors who failed to treat Biko.

South Africa was never to be the same again. A generation of young blacks committed themselves to a revolutionary struggle against apartheid ('Liberation before Education' was the catch-cry) and the black communities were politicised. International opinion turned even more decisively against the white regime.

Recognising the inevitability of change, PW Botha told white South Africans to 'Adapt or die', but then chickened out of full reform when he rewrote the constitution in 1983. The pass laws were repealed, but this failed to mollify the black protesters and also created a white backlash. A number of neo-Nazi paramilitary groups emerged, notably the frightening Afrikaner Weerstandsbeweging (AWB), led by Eugène Terre'Blanche (who was jailed in 2001 for assault).

The violence continued until, in 1985, the government declared a state of emergency, which was to stay in force for five years. The media was censored and, by 1988, 30,000 people had been detained without trial. Thousands were tortured. The fighting was not only between the United Democratic Front (UDF), which had adopted the ANC's Freedom Charter, and the government, but increasingly between blacks themselves, split along political and tribal lines.

Botha's reforms also failed to impress the rest of the world, and economic sanctions began to bite. Foreign banks refused to roll over government loans and the value of the rand collapsed.

Reform
In late 1989 Botha was replaced by FW De Klerk. At his opening address to the parliament in February 1990, De Klerk announced that he would repeal discriminatory laws and legalise the ANC, the PAC and the Communist Party. Media restrictions were lifted, and De Klerk undertook to release political prisoners not guilty of common-law crimes.

On 11 February 1990, 27 years after he had first been incarcerated, Nelson Mandela was released (see the boxed text 'Nelson Mandela').

From 1990 to 1991 practically all the legal apparatus of apartheid was abolished. A referendum, the last whites-only vote held in South Africa, overwhelmingly gave the government authority to negotiate a new constitution with the ANC and other groups.

Free Elections
In December 1991 the Convention for a Democratic South Africa (Codesa) began negotiations on the formation of a multiracial transitional government and a new constitution extending political rights to all groups.

Months of negotiations and brinkmanship finally produced a compromise and an election date, although at considerable human cost. Political violence exploded across the country during this time, particularly in the wake of the assassination of popular youth leader Chris Hani. It's now known that elements within the police and army contributed to this violence. There have also been claims that high-ranking government officials and politicians ordered, or at least condoned, massacres.

Across the country at midnight on 26 April 1994, 'Die Stem' (the old national an-

them) was sung and the old flag was lowered. Then the new rainbow flag was raised and the new anthem, 'Nkosi Sikelele Afrika' (God Bless Africa) was sung – in the past people had been jailed for singing this beautiful hymn. The election was amazingly peaceful and there was an air of goodwill throughout South Africa.

The ANC won 62.7% of the vote, less than the 66.7% that would have enabled it to rewrite the constitution. As well as deciding the national government, the election decided the provincial governments, and the ANC won in all but two provinces. The National Party (NP) captured most of the white and coloured vote and became the official opposition party.

The Truth & Reconciliation Commission
Crimes of the apartheid era were exposed by the Truth & Reconciliation Commission (1994–99). This admirable institution carried out Archbishop Desmond Tutu's dictum, 'Without forgiveness there is no future, but without confession there can be no forgiveness'. Many, many stories of horrific brutality and injustice were heard by the commission, offering some catharsis to people and communities shattered by their past.

The commission operated by allowing victims to tell their stories and perpetrators to confess their guilt, with amnesty on offer to those who made a clean breast of it. Those who chose not to appear before the commission would face criminal prosecution if their guilt could be proven, which is the problem. Although some soldiers, police and 'ordinary' citizens have confessed their crimes, it seems unlikely that the human rights criminals who gave the orders and dictated the policies will present themselves (PW Botha is one famous no-show), and it has proven difficult to gather evidence against them.

The catalogue of crimes committed by the apartheid government and its servants is truly horrific, ranging from beatings, torture, murder and massacre to twisted science experiments such as trying to design poisons that would kill only black and coloured people. Widespread abuses aside, the simple fact remains that apartheid denied tens of millions of people their basic human rights because of their skin colour.

The 1999 Election

In December 1997, Mandela stepped down as ANC president and was succeeded by his deputy, Thabo Mbeki. Jacob Zuma was appointed the new deputy president.

In 1999, after five years of learning about democracy, the country voted in a more normal election. Issues such as economics and competence were raised and debated. There was speculation that the ANC vote might drop, but in fact it increased to put the party within one seat of the two-thirds majority that would allow it to alter the constitution.

The NP, restyled as the New National Party (NNP), lost two-thirds of its seats and lost official opposition status to the revitalised Democratic Party (DP). This party has shifted to the right since the days when the DP's Helen Suzman represented a solitary voice of opposition to the NP during the apartheid years. The new United Democratic Movement (UDM) attempted to exploit disillusionment with the ANC, but fared poorly. The mainly Zulu Inkatha Freedom Party (IFP) lost some support but its leader, Chief Buthelezi, still wields power in the government as home affairs minister.

Since the election in 1999 the NNP and DP have joined together in opposition as the Democratic Alliance, and won control of Western Cape in the provincial elections. The ANC retained all its provincial governments. In KwaZulu-Natal, which was previously held by the IFP, the Democratic Alliance now holds the balance of power.

South Africa Today

Despite the scars of the past and the enormous problems ahead, South Africa today is an immeasurably more optimistic and relaxed country than it was a few years ago.

Economic inequality remains an overwhelming problem. With an economy geared to low wages and a legacy of very poor education for blacks, it will be at least a generation before the majority gain much economic benefit from their political freedom. Finding solutions to the strained living conditions in the townships, including access to clean drinking water and decent sanitation, not to mention decent housing, is what concerns the majority of voters.

Responsible for the day-to-day running of the country for some time before the 1999 elections, Mbeki has proven to be a generally competent president, but in comparison with the almost sainted Mandela, he inevitably suffers. His standing both at home and abroad has not been helped by his refusal to condemn outright the inflammatory politics of Zimbabwe's Robert Mugabe and Mugabe's ill-informed comments on AIDS.

This health crisis, affecting 4.2 million South Africans, seriously threatens to eclipse all of South Africa's other domestic problems. According to the *Economist*, a quarter of a million South Africans were killed by AIDS in 2000. Mbeki has capitalised on the views of the peripheral few Western scientists who question that HIV causes AIDS to justify his slow response to the crisis. However, drugs are sometimes now provided to prevent mother-to-child infection, after high-profile negotiations between African nations

SARAH JOLLY

Chief Mangosouthu Buthelezi, founder of the Inkatha Freedom Party

Nelson Mandela

No other person has been as important in South Africa's recent history as Nelson Rolihlahla Mandela. For a man once vilified by the ruling whites, it is a testament of his strength of character and evident decency and integrity that Mandela helped unite all South Africans at the most crucial of times.

The son of the third wife of a Xhosa chief, Mandela was born on 18 July 1918 in the small village of Mveso on the Mbashe River. When he was very young the family moved to Qunu, south of Umtata, where he grew up in a mud hut. He attended school in the Transkei before going to Johannesburg where, after a few false starts, he became a lawyer and set up in practice with Oliver Tambo.

In 1944 he helped form the Youth League of the African National Congress (ANC) with Walter Sisulu and Oliver Tambo. Its aim was to end the racist policies of the white South African government. He met Nomzamo Winnifred Madikizela (Winnie) and, after receiving a divorce from his first wife, Evelyn, married her in 1958.

In 1956 he was one of 156 ANC and Communist Party members charged with treason; all were found not guilty at the subsequent trial. But in 1964, after establishing the ANC's military wing and having gone underground, Mandela was captured and sentenced to life imprisonment in the infamous Robben Island prison. He remained there until 1981, when he was moved to Pollsmoor Prison on the mainland.

By the time the ANC was declared a legal organisation, Mandela had again been transferred to a house in the grounds of the Victor Vester Prison near Paarl. It was through the gates of this jail that Mandela walked, at last a free man, in 1990. In 1991 he was elected president of the ANC and continued the long negotiations (which had started secretly while he was in prison) to end minority rule. He shared the 1993 Nobel peace prize with FW De Klerk and, in the first free elections the following year, was elected president of South Africa.

The prison years had inevitably taken their toll on the Mandelas' marriage and in 1992, the couple separated, with Mandela saying that he parted from his wife with no recriminations. They were divorced in 1996.

Mandela's contribution to reconciliation was best demonstrated by his famous speech, 'Free at Last!', made on 2 May 1994, when he said 'This is the time to heal the old wounds and build a new South Africa'.

In 1997, Mandela – or Madiba, his traditional Xhosa name which is frequently used as a mark of respect – retired as ANC president and on his 80th birthday in July 1998 he married Graca Machel, the widow of the former president of Mozambique. Despite suffering ailments caused by decades of harsh prison life, Mandela maintains a schedule of international engagements and comments on domestic political and social developments as an elder statesman.

For more information about this charismatic man read his autobiography *Long Walk to Freedom*, the first draft of which was written while he was still on Robben Island, and Anthony Sampson's exhaustive *Mandela, the Authorised Biography*. Also check out the informative Web site of the 1999 PBS documentary series on Mandela (W www.pbs.org/wgbh/pages/frontline/shows/mandela).

Nelson Mandela with his successor, Thabo Mbeki

and the pharmaceutical companies that own the patents to AIDS drugs. These drugs, widely available in the first world but until now far too expensive for African nations, prolong the lives of AIDS patients, but are still too expensive to be offered to all who need them.

GEOGRAPHY

South Africa is a big country, stretching nearly 2000km from the Limpopo River in the north to Cape Agulhas in the south, and nearly 1500km from Port Nolloth in the west to Durban in the east.

There are three major parts to the country's physical geography: the vast interior plateau, or the highveld; the narrow coastal plain, or the lowveld; and the Kalahari Basin. In the east the divide between the highveld and lowveld is marked by dramatic escarpments, notably the Drakensberg.

CLIMATE

Lying just south of the Tropic of Capricorn, South Africa is mostly dry and sunny. The major influence on the climate, however, is not latitude but topography and the surrounding oceans.

Jo'burg is not far south of the tropics, but its altitude (around 1700m above sea level) and its distance from the sea moderate its climate. Its average temperatures are only 1°C higher than those in Cape Town, although it's 1500km to the north.

Western Cape has dry, sunny summers, with maximum temperatures around 28°C. It is often windy, however, and the south-easterly 'Cape Doctor', which buffets the Cape and lays Table Mountain's famous 'tablecloth' (a thick cloud mass that drapes across the mountain), can reach gale force. When it really blows, you know you're clinging to a peninsula at the southern end of Africa, and there's nothing between you and the Antarctic. Winters can be cold, with average minimum temperatures of around 5°C and maximum temperatures of around 17°C. There is occasional snow on the higher peaks. The coast north from the Cape becomes progressively drier and hotter. Along the southern coast the weather is temperate; the eastern coast becomes increasingly tropical the further north you go. Cape Town has what is described as a Mediterranean climate. It can be relatively cold and wet for a few months over winter, between June and August.

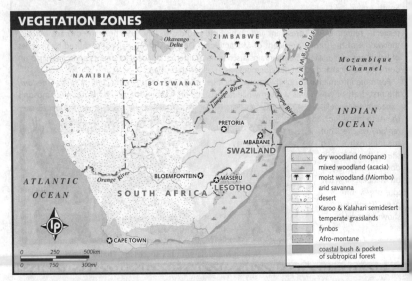

Stallholder, Grahamstown

Dress standards apply: Rickshaws are now a rare mode of transport.

Altar boy, Cradock

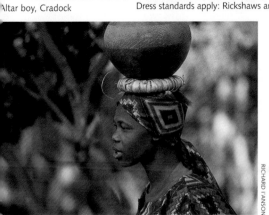

Balancing act: In Zululand, customs and culture influence modern life.

Doorman, Johannesburg

Crafty business: In Southern Africa, art and craft merge into a complex layering of artistic expression

The Cape is the meeting point for the two great ocean currents that have a major impact on the climate of South Africa, and the Cape itself. The cold, nutrient-rich Benguela current from the Antarctic runs north up the western coast, lowering temperatures and severely limiting rainfall. The warm Agulhas current from the tropical Indian Ocean runs south down the eastern coast. Durban is an average 6°C warmer than Port Nolloth on the western coast and receives 16 times more rain (1000mm), although they are on much the same latitude.

The eastern highveld region (including Gauteng and Free State) has a dry, sunny climate in winter (from June to August), with maximum temperatures around 20°C, and crisp nights, when temperatures drop to around 5°C. Between October and April there are late-afternoon showers that are often accompanied by spectacular thunder and lightning; heavy hailstorms cause quite a lot of damage each year.

Temperatures can soar in the Great Karoo (the semidesert heart of all three cape provinces) and the far north (in the Kalahari).

The Transkei area of Eastern Cape and KwaZulu-Natal can be hot and unpleasantly humid in summer, although the highlands are still pleasant; this is a summer-rainfall area.

Mpumalanga and the Northern Province lowveld are very hot in summer, when there are spectacular storms. In winter the days are sunny and warm.

ECOLOGY & ENVIRONMENT

South Africa's environmental issues are similar to those faced by the rest of the world: habitat and wildlife destruction, alien plant invasion, deforestation, soil erosion, water degradation and industrial pollution. None can be addressed in isolation; they are all interrelated and linked to wider economic, social and political situations – on a national, regional and global scale.

Although the richest African country by far, South Africa still has very few public funds to allocate to nature conservation given that its first priority is raising the living standards of the human population – which is increasing at around 60,000 a month.

Increased economic development is the obvious way to provide income for citizens, which in turn leads to a better standard of living. The problem is that it also leads to increased industrialisation, which can cause its own environmental damage such as air and water pollution.

We are all aware that our planet has finite resources, incapable of supporting us at the current, developed-world standards. The need for a global approach is often overlooked, especially by developed countries. Instead, the focus is on the deforestation, overgrazing and pollution levels of the undeveloped world, whose people are often dependent on profits from environmentally harmful activities, ignoring statistics that indicate that it is often the developed countries that are producing greater amounts of pollution.

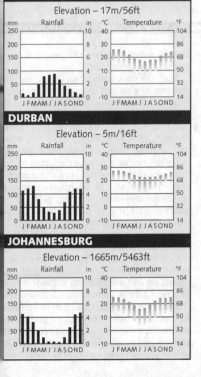

Saving the African Penguin

In June 2000, the fate of the African penguin (formerly known as the jackass penguin) hit headlines across the world when a cargo ship sank 8km off Robben Island, spilling vast quantities of oil into the sea. Over 40% of the penguin population was threatened by the resulting slick, the worst ever suffered along the notoriously treacherous Cape coast.

The penguin colonies at Robben and Dassen Islands received immediate attention from several conservation bodies, the local authorities and even the army, in what turned out to be the world's biggest rescue operation of its kind, affecting over 21,000 oiled birds. Over 28,000 volunteers from as far away as New Zealand, Japan and Canada also took part.

Remarkably, after an extensive rehabilitation process for the penguins, practically all were eventually released back into the wild. The world held its breath as Peter, Percy and Pamela – three of

the penguins removed to Port Elizabeth during the cleanup and released with transmitters on their backs – swam home through shark-infested waters, their progress being monitored on their own Web site.

The cost of the operation nudged the 20-million-rand mark and has pressed the need upon South Africa to toughen up its maritime regulations and penalties for negligent shipping practices.

The Ivory Debate

The issue of elephant conservation is a good example of how environmental matters are never straightforward.

In 1990, following a massive campaign by conservation organisations, a world body called Convention on International Trade in Endangered Species (Cites) banned the import and export of ivory. The closure of this trade, combined with increased funds for law enforcement, was seen as an important step in elephant protection.

Although elephant populations recovered in areas where they'd previously been ravaged, in the well-managed and protected parks of South Africa – where elephants had long been protected – the populations continued to grow. This created another problem: Elephants eat huge quantities of foliage, and a large herd remaining within an unnaturally small area (even though it may be hundreds of square kilometres) will quickly destroy its surroundings. In the past, the herd would have migrated, allowing time for vegetation regrowth, but with the increase in human population

around national parks, this movement is increasingly restricted.

Now the park authorities are facing the problem of elephant overpopulation. Solutions include creating transfrontier parks to allow animals to migrate over larger areas (see National Parks & Reserves later in this chapter), relocating animals to other areas and a pioneering contraception project (whereby breeding cows are injected with a 'pill' equivalent – so no jokes about jumbo condoms please). The alternative is to cull (or crop) elephants, sometimes in large numbers. Killing elephants to conserve them seems a bizarre paradox, but at present other options remain experimental and limited in their effect.

Good management requires money, and in the past, ivory from legally culled elephants could be sold to raise funds. Some Southern African countries, including South Africa, called for the Cites ban to be lifted so that funds from ivory sales could go towards conservation projects to benefit both animals and people. In this way, as unpalatable as it may seem, elephant herds become a resource with tangible value for each country, as do supplies of oil or water, thus giving governments and locals an incentive to ensure the elephants' survival.

In March 1999, Botswana, Namibia, South Africa and Zimbabwe were permitted by Cites to resume strictly controlled ivory exports – this is still continuing under review. Opponents of the ban's lifting say that elephant poaching has increased in other parts of Africa, as poached ivory can be laundered through the legal trade. This argument seems to carry some weight, as an increase in poaching through 1999 was reported Africa-wide, from Kenya to Gabon.

Tourism & the Environment

International tourism is another way in which it is hoped the elephant and other wildlife species can be more highly valued. The idea is that if foreigners pay to come and enjoy the environment and see the animals, some of this money should find its way back to the local people (and to the country as a whole), which will encourage wildlife and environmental protection. This is something that South Africa has embraced with its excellent national parks and its involvement in the transfrontier park movement (see National Parks & Reserves later in this chapter).

Commercial hunting is a form of tourism that, paradoxically, can also have long-term benefits for the wildlife and locals, given the enormous amount of money it generates. In some parts of South Africa, areas of land are set aside for hunting, and big-game hunters are charged 'trophy fees' to shoot the animals. While this may be unacceptable to many people, the trophy fees are significant (thousands of US dollars for an animal such as an elephant or a lion) and can be a valuable source of income for impoverished areas with no other resources to exploit. However, much of the profit invariably ends up in the pockets of big tour companies rather than going directly to locals.

To combat the perception that conservation for its own sake is a luxurious Western notion that the people of Southern Africa simply cannot afford, there are increased moves to involve local people in wildlife conservation schemes. Examples include 'good neighbour' arrangements between South Africa and Namibia in the management of Richtersveld National Park.

Income is also generated by the jobs that hunting and wildlife tourism create, such as guides, game rangers, tour guides and various posts in the hotels, lodges and camps. Further spin-offs include the sale of crafts and curios.

However, tourism itself – one of the largest global industries – has major environmental impacts that are impossible to ignore. You only have to look at the rampant tourist development at Victoria Falls to see the downside of a tourist influx; this is a quandary that South Africa is facing as it ponders how best to manage its immensely popular World Heritage site Robben Island (see Robben Island in the Cape Town & the Peninsula chapter).

A balance has to be struck between tourism growth and environmental destruction – in other words, all development has to be sustainable. Ideally, the principal reason for wildlife and the environment to be conserved is not so that tourists can come and admire, but so locals can enjoy and benefit from their natural environment.

At times, the 'eco' tag is blatantly used to make an activity or organisation feel more wholesome. Even the more specific term 'ecofriendly tourism' is now horribly overused. If you want to support tour companies with a genuinely good environmental record, you have to look beyond the glossy brochures and vague 'eco' claims, and ask what they are really doing to protect or support the environment (and remember that this includes local people, as well as animals and plants). Consider contacting the **South African Forestry Company** (*Safcol*; ☎ *012-481 3615*, @ *ecotour@mail.safcol.co.za*) in Pretoria, which is charged with the management and imaginative development of South African forests; it promotes ecotourism and manages a lot of hiking trails around Mpumalanga.

Also think critically about the type of holiday you're planning. Activities such as camping, wildlife viewing (by car, foot or balloon), or sightseeing trips to remote or fragile areas can be more environmentally or culturally harmful than a conventional hotel holiday in a developed resort.

Perhaps surprisingly, a leading British environmentalist believes that Sun City is one of the best examples of ecotourism in the world: a purpose-built resort complex, creating thousands of local jobs and putting wildlife back onto a degraded piece of otherwise useless veld.

FLORA

In some eyes, Southern Africa's most impressive endowment is its flora. There are more than 22,000 species of flora, accounting for 10% of the world's total – that's more than in the USA, which is seven times larger! The region's flora is not just impressive statistically, it is both fascinating and spectacularly beautiful.

The Cape Floral Kingdom

Of the world's six floral kingdoms the Cape Floral Kingdom is by far the smallest, but is also unquestionably the most diverse. Here you'll find a whopping 1300 species per 10,000 sq km, some 900 more species than can be found in the South American rainforests.

The Cape Floral Kingdom extends roughly from Cape Point east to Grahamstown and north to the Olifants River. These days most of the remaining indigenous vegetation is found only in protected areas, such as Table Mountain and the Cape Peninsula.

The dominant vegetation is fynbos, which literally means 'fine bush', so named because most fynbos species have small, narrow leaves. All told there are nearly 8500 plant species in the fynbos environment, most of which are unique to the area.

Some species have an incredibly small range, with the world's entire supply occurring within a few hundred square metres. Some members of the dominant fynbos families – heaths, proteas and reeds – have been domesticated in other areas and countries, but for many species the clearing of an area the size of a house can mean extinction.

An extraordinary number of domesticated flowers grow in the wild in South Africa: daisies, geraniums, gladiolus, ixias, arum lilies, strelitzias (including the bird of paradise), irises, freesias, proteas, watsonias, African lilies and red-hot pokers, among others, can be found here.

South Africa is the only country with one of the world's six floral kingdoms within its borders. This is the Cape Floral Kingdom, mostly situated in Western Cape, with its characteristic *fynbos* (meaning 'fine bush' in Dutch), which refers to the community of plants found within the area. Many of these plants have small fine stems and leaves and the vegetation has a bushy appearance. Fynbos is characterised by three plant families: Ericaceae (heaths), Proteaceae (proteas) and Restionaceae (reeds). There are over 8500 species – the Cape Peninsula alone has more native plant species than the entire British Isles (see the boxed text 'The Cape Floral Kingdom').

In the drier regions there are weird succulents (dominated by euphorbias and aloes), and annuals, which flower brilliantly after the spring rainfall (see the Namaqualand section in the Northern Cape chapter).

In contrast to this wealth of flowers, South Africa has very few natural forests. Though more widespread in the past, they were never particularly extensive and today only a few remnants remain. Temperate forests occur on South Africa's southern coastal strip between George and Humansdorp and also in the Drakensberg and in Mpumalanga. There is some subtropical forest north-east of Port Elizabeth through the Transkei area and in KwaZulu-Natal.

Large areas in the north are covered by savanna-type vegetation, characterised by acacias and thorn trees. The umbrella thorn and sweet thorn are both found here.

FAUNA

South Africa is rich in wildlife, although most large animals are now concentrated in the national parks (see also the colour Wildlife Guide).

South Africa has the world's largest land mammal (the African elephant), as well as the second biggest (the white rhinoceros) and the third biggest (the hippopotamus). It also boasts the tallest (the giraffe), the fastest (the cheetah) and the smallest (the pygmy shrew).

Conservation of native fauna is an active concern, and although one can only dimly imagine the extent of the loss since the arrival of Europeans, a significant amount remains. The region is home to the last substantial populations of black and white rhinos – with horns intact – and the problem with elephant numbers is not that they are declining but that they are increasing too rapidly (see Ecology & Environment earlier in this chapter).

You probably have a better chance of seeing the Big Five – the black rhino, the Cape buffalo, the elephant, the leopard and the lion – in South Africa than in any other African country. There is also a lesser-known 'Little Five' – the rhinoceros beetle, the buffalo weaver, the elephant shrew, the leopard tortoise and the ant lion – if you are looking for a challenge.

There is also a spectacular variety of birds, with over 900 species recorded, 113 of which are endemic to South Africa. They range from the largest in the world (the ostrich), to the heaviest flying bird (the Kori bustard) and the spectacularly coloured sunbirds and flamingoes. Also here are the extraordinary sociable weavers, who live in huge city-like nests that can have up to 50 chambers and house some 300 birds, including chicks and the pygmy falcon, the world's smallest raptor, which offers the weavers protection from predators in exchange for accommodation.

NATIONAL PARKS & RESERVES

South Africa's national parks and reserves are one of the country's premier attractions. The scenery is spectacular, the fauna and flora are abundant, the facilities are excellent and the prices are extremely reasonable.

In addition to the National Parks Board of South Africa, the various provinces also have conservation bodies. In fact, the provinces control wilderness areas that are sometimes larger and more spectacular than the better-known national parks.

Don't Get Charged!

Only an idiot would want to get up close to a carnivore such as a lion or leopard on the prowl, but you should still remember to keep as low a profile as possible if you see an animal that's obviously hunting. Try to control your excitement and avoid the temptation to move in too close, lest you distract the predator or spook the intended prey.

While many animals will bolt if they spot humans, others can be extremely dangerous. Here are a few to watch out for:

- black rhinos – although very scarce, they will charge just about anything (they're very nervy). White rhino are the opposite, being very docile.

- buffaloes – keep your distance as they will charge if they feel threatened. Never get too close to a herd, particularly if the males start staring at your vehicle.

- lone young bull elephants and cow elephants with young – you'll soon realise if they're jumpy because they'll make fake charges. There will also be a lot of trumpeting.

- hippos – never get between a hippo and its water when it's on land at night feeding. Be careful to get good advice if you go canoeing or boating in water where there are hippos; they're very territorial.

There has also been a recent move within Southern Africa to create 'transfrontier parks' joining neighbouring conservation areas, such as the Kgalagadi Transfrontier Park, which combines the old Kalahari Gemsbok National Park in Northern Province with the adjoining Gemsbok National Park in Botswana. The most ambitious of these projects is the Gaza-Kruger-Gonarezhou Transfrontier Park (to be finished in 2003), which will cover an area larger than Portugal, creating a park of nearly 100,000 sq km across the borders of South Africa, Mozambique and Zimbabwe (see the boxed text 'Conservation the Winner' in the Kruger National Park chapter).

In many national parks (mainly those with dangerous animals), visitors are confined to vehicles. If you don't have a car, the best way to get to and around the parks is to rent a vehicle. If the cost is shared among a group it need not be high, and will probably be lower than the cost of taking a bus tour. A 2WD will serve you fine, but note that if you're in the parks during winter when the grass is high, a vehicle with high ground clearance (such as a 4WD) will enable you to see a lot more.

The quality of the infrastructure and the information in the parks is high. You can often get by without a guide, although with a guide you'll almost certainly see and learn more about what's in each park.

Some of the major parks with dangerous animals (including Kruger National Park and Hluhluwe-Umfolozi Park) offer guided wilderness walks accompanied by armed rangers. You should book these walks well in advance – preferably before you leave home. If you want to do overnight walks in any of the other parks or reserves, it is necessary to get a permit in advance, and you are nearly always restricted to official camp sites or huts. There's no wandering off with a pack on your back whenever you feel like it.

In Kruger and Pilanesberg National Parks there are also guided morning and afternoon walks; these can be booked the day before (subject to availability). During busy times in the park you'll probably need to book a few days in advance.

The national parks have rest camps that offer a variety of good-value accommodation, from self-catering cottages to camp sites. Most rest camps have restaurants, shops and petrol pumps. Advance bookings for camping and cottages is wise – particularly for the more popular parks and during holiday periods – but generally it's possible to get accommodation at short notice.

The entrances to parks and reserves generally close around sunset; check if you think you are going to arrive late.

Private Game Reserves

There are many private game reserves, and while they usually cost more than public parks and reserves (you generally have to stay in the mostly upmarket onsite accommodation), you can usually get closer to the animals and have access to a full program of guided safaris. Before deciding which private reserve to visit, it's worth contacting a specialist travel agent to find out if there are any special deals on offer.

GOVERNMENT & POLITICS

The new constitution of South Africa is one of the most enlightened in the world, which is perhaps not surprising when you consider the people's long struggle for freedom. As well as forbidding discrimination on practically any grounds, the constitution also guarantees freedom of speech and religion, access to adequate housing (which is as yet unrealised, although the government is trying to address this with its reconstruction and development program), reproductive health care and basic adult education, among other things.

There are two houses of parliament: the National Assembly of 400 members; and the National Council of Provinces (NCOP), with 100 members. Members of the National Assembly are elected directly (using the proportional representation method – there are no constituencies) but members of the NCOP are appointed by the provincial legislatures. Each province, regardless of its size, appoints 10 councillors, plus there are 10 more from the South African Local Government Association, representing the six metropolitan districts of Jo'burg, Pretoria, East Rand, Cape Town, Nelson Mandela Metropole and Durban.

The head of state is the president, currently Thabo Mbeki, leader of the ANC. The president is elected by the National Assembly (and thus will always be the leader of the majority party) rather than directly by the people. A South African president has more in common with a Westminster-style prime minister than a US president, although as head of state the South African president does have some executive powers denied most prime ministers.

There are also provincial legislatures, with memberships varying according to population (for example, Northern Cape is the smallest, with 30 members, Gauteng the largest, with 86). Each province has a premier. Provincial governments have strictly limited powers and are bound by the national constitution. There are also the six metropolitan governments, covering South Africa's largest conurbations.

In addition to the Western-style democratic system, there is a system of traditional leadership. All legislation pertaining to indigenous law, tradition or custom must be referred to the Council of Traditional Leaders. Although the council cannot veto or amend legislation, it can delay its passage. In each province where there have been recognised traditional authorities (every province except Western Cape, Northern Cape and Gauteng), a House of Traditional Leaders has similar powers to the Council.

Administratively, South Africa is divided into nine provinces: Western Cape, Eastern Cape, Northern Cape, KwaZulu-Natal, Gauteng, Mpumalanga, Free State, North-West Province and Northern Province. Most of these were formed during the run-up to the 1994 election.

The Homelands no longer exist as political entities, but because of their very different histories and economies it will be some time before you don't notice a marked change when crossing one of the old borders. In this book we sometimes refer to the old Homelands by name because this is what's most commonly used on the ground. Transkei and Ciskei have been absorbed into Eastern Cape

The Legal System

South Africa's legal system is a blend of the Roman-Dutch and British systems. The British influence is seen most strongly in criminal justice procedures. Cases are tried by magistrates or judges without juries, at the instigation of police 'dockets' or private actions. Clients are represented by *prokureurs* (solicitors in Afrikaans) and *advokates* (literally advocates – the equivalent of barristers – in Afrikaans).

While the colony was still under Dutch East India Company rule, *landdrosts* (magistrates in Afrikaans) were appointed; they were essentially governors of their areas. *Drostdy*, the homes and offices of the landdrost, are today some of the earliest and most impressive buildings in the country. The Drostdy Museum at Swellendam (Western Cape) and the various drostdy buildings in Graaff-Reinet (Eastern Cape) are among the best examples.

Unlike a British magistrate, whose decisions are partially influenced by the values of the local community, the landdrost was a company (and later government) official responsible for enforcing policy rather than dispensing an abstract notion of justice. This situation persisted, and until the new constitution came into force in 1994 the judicial system was subservient to the government, in particular the state president, often resulting in politicised decisions.

Now the most important source of law is the constitution, which is interpreted and enforced by the new Constitutional Court. Choosing the members of the court was one of the most crucial post-election tasks for the new South Africa. Although women are under-represented (so what's new?), the court is generally accepted internationally and domestically as an eminent and impartial body.

The Constitutional Court's independence was demonstrated in 1995 when it decided that capital punishment was unconstitutional and banned it. This was despite a large majority of South Africans being in favour of capital punishment (more than 100 people were hanged each year throughout the 1980s).

Judicial independence has had its costs, though. Many perceive the courts' failure to hand down appropriate sentences to offenders, particularly in relation to (the prevalent) sexual crimes against women, as one of the major problems with the new South Africa. The legal system is also reeling from the impact of white professional migration from South Africa, lawyers having flooded out of the country in recent years.

(a small chunk of Transkei has been claimed by KwaZulu-Natal), Venda into Northern Province, and Bophuthatswana into North-West Province (Thaba 'Nchu, an isolated chunk of Bophuthatswana, is in Free State). The smaller Homelands of Gazankulu, KaNgwane, KwaNdebele, KwaZulu, Lebowa and QwaQwa, which were regarded by the apartheid regime as self-governing rather than independent countries, have been more easily reabsorbed into the surrounding provinces.

Cape Town is where parliament sits and is the administrative capital; Pretoria is the legislative capital, where you'll find the government offices and most embassies; and Bloemfontein is the judicial capital. The country's unofficial capital, though, has always been Jo'burg. It lies at the centre of an enormous urban conurbation known as the PWV (Pretoria, Witwatersrand, Vereeniging), and is the largest, richest and most important city in the country.

The provincial capitals are Cape Town (Western Cape), Bisho (Eastern Cape), Kimberley (Northern Cape), Pietermaritzburg (KwaZulu-Natal), Nelspruit (Mpumalanga), Jo'burg (Gauteng), Bloemfontein (Free State), Mafikeng (North-West Province), and Pietersburg-Polokwane (Northern Province).

ECONOMY

South Africa's economy is a mixture of the First and Third Worlds, with a marked disparity in incomes, standards of living, education and work opportunities. On the one hand there is a modern, industrialised and urban economy; on the other there is a subsistence agricultural economy little changed from the 19th century. In the middle are the mainly black and coloured urban workers.

While there is tremendous poverty in South Africa, on an African scale the economy is not only reasonably successful, it dwarfs all others on the continent. The relative success is based, to a large degree, on tremendous natural wealth, First World industrialisation, and an abundance of low-paid black labour.

South Africa accounts for about 50% of electricity produced in Africa, 40% of the continent's industrial output and 45% of mining production. It is also the largest agricultural exporter (by a wide margin).

Within South Africa, wealth is further concentrated in Gauteng, which, it is claimed, accounts for about 65% of the country's gross domestic product (GDP) and no less than 25% of the entire continent's GDP.

South Africa has well-developed infrastructure, with a good transport system linking the interior of the country and the wider region with a number of modern ports. There is great potential for South Africa's economy to facilitate development in the rest of Southern Africa: Wars and trade sanctions have seriously hampered the entire region, and by virtue of its wealth and infrastructure, South Africa holds the key to its recovery.

Until the discovery of diamonds at Kimberley in 1869 and the gold reef on the Witwatersrand in 1886, the economy was exclusively agricultural. Since then, mineral wealth has been the key to development. Mining remains central to the economy, and South Africa is the world's leading supplier of gold, chromium, manganese, vanadium and platinum. Mining accounts for some 40% of exports and 6.5% of GDP. The manufacturing industry grew rapidly during and after WWII, mostly to meet local demand. Oddly, it was the aggressively antisocialist apartheid governments that instituted massive state ownership of industry, and it is the quasi-socialist ANC government that is privatising industry.

Through involvement in the economy, previous governments successfully sought to redirect wealth into Afrikaner hands. The private sector is highly centralised and is dominated by the interrelated De Beers and Anglo-American corporations. Their combined stock-market worth is over four times greater than their closest competition.

Towards the end of white minority rule, international sanctions bit deeper and black mass action destabilised the economy. Add to this a general world economic downturn and a serious drought, and the economy was in serious trouble. The country faced an annual inflation rate running at around 15% and unemployment was rising.

Both inflation (running at 7.8% in February 2001) and massive unemployment remain problems. Moreover, even if the economy recovers to its boom-time peak, almost the only people to immediately benefit will be whites. Blacks and coloureds have never shared in the fruits of their labour and it will be very difficult for the government to ensure that they do so in the future. The economy is still geared to a limitless pool of black and coloured labour (who are paid Third-World rates); restructuring this will be a long and slow process.

The challenges facing a country with a history of institutionalised inequality are not dissimilar to the global issues facing the citizens of the First World, where debate is now being generated about the ethics of multinational companies setting up factories in, for example, South-East Asia, where

HIV/AIDS & the Population Hourglass

Although Africa continues to be a continent afflicted by wars, famines and natural disasters, the effect of AIDS is possibly the greatest problem it has ever faced. AIDS is now the leading cause of death in sub-Saharan Africa – a quarter of a million South Africans were killed by AIDS in 2000. The personal, social and economic costs associated with the disease are already devastating: The US Census Bureau predicts that AIDS-related deaths will mean that, by 2010, sub-Saharan Africa will have 71 million fewer people than it would otherwise; the Joint United Nations program on HIV/AIDS (UNAIDS) estimates there will be 42 million orphans by this time.

The number of women at prenatal clinics testing positive for HIV (24.5% according to a 2000 survey) indicates the pandemic is still growing in South Africa – their babies will most likely also be infected. Of every 10 children living with HIV/AIDS, nine live in sub-Saharan Africa. In KwaZulu-Natal, reported to be the worst-affected province, 36% of pregnant women tested positive to the virus.

There are many possible reasons why AIDS has taken such a hold in Africa compared with the West. Migration of people in search of work and to escape wars and famine, a general lack of adequate health care and prevention programs, and social and cultural factors, in particular the low status of women and their lack of empowerment in many African societies, are all believed to have played a role in the rapid spread of HIV/AIDS. In many African countries there is still a denial of the problem, particularly on the part of governments and some churches.

AIDS starkly highlights the inequities in access to health care between rich and poor. Drug treatments that are available in the West to increase the lifespan of AIDS sufferers and reduce the risk of infection passing to the foetus in HIV-infected women have only recently started being provided to prevent mothers passing the virus to their unborn babies. By the beginning of 2001, the South African government's threats to ignore the patents on HIV drugs persuaded multinational pharmaceutical companies to offer drugs near the price they cost to manufacture. However, these drugs are still too expensive to be offered to all who need them.

Africa isn't uniformly affected by the epidemic. Although no country has escaped HIV/AIDS, some nations are more severely affected than others. Currently, North Africa has a fairly low infection rate, while many of the Southern African nations have alarmingly high rates of infection: One in four is living with HIV/AIDS in Botswana and Zimbabwe, and one in five in Swaziland. In South Africa, which has the largest number of HIV/AIDS sufferers worldwide, one in nine is infected.

In nations with high infection rates, the socioeconomic effects are overwhelming. Unlike many diseases that mostly affect the weak, HIV/AIDS predominantly hits the most productive members of society – young adults. This has a huge impact on family income, and on food production and local economies in general, meaning that Africa faces the loss of a large proportion of whole generations. This is creating a population age profile that will no longer resemble the usual pyramid, but rather an hourglass, representing a generation of orphans and elderly.

Hilary Rogers

labour is cheap and locals are willing to work in conditions considered unacceptable to developed nations.

The government must find a way to both create and redistribute the wealth without alienating the white community (a body of white South Africans recognises the need for this to happen), foreign investors or the many poverty-stricken people. For ways that you as a tourist can help to achieve this goal, see Responsible Tourism in the Facts for the Visitor chapter.

POPULATION & PEOPLE

Of the population of 43 million, 33.2 million are African (or black), 4.5 million are white, 3.8 million are coloured (ie, mixed race) and 1.1 million are of Indian or Asian descent, leaving 400,000 others. There are reported to be several million illegal immigrants from various other African countries.

Aside from the Afrikaners, the majority of white South Africans (around 1.9 million) are of British extraction. There is also a large and influential Jewish population of around 90,000; significant minorities of Portuguese (some 30,000), many of whom are refugees from Angola and Mozambique; as well as Germans, Dutch, Italians and Greeks.

Zulus are the largest Bantu-speaking group in the region (9.9m), followed by the Xhosa (7.3m). The smallest group are the Ndebele (around 200,000).

The Afrikaner heartlands are in Free State and the former Transvaal (now divided into Gauteng, Northern Province, Mpumalanga and much of North-West Province). People of British descent are concentrated in KwaZulu-Natal and Western and Eastern Cape.

Most of the coloured population lives in Northern and Western Cape provinces. Most South Africans of Indian descent live in KwaZulu-Natal.

Although the Homelands system is no longer functioning, it's quite useful to have some idea of where they were and who lived (and still lives) in them. The Homelands and their peoples were Bophuthatswana (Tswana), Ciskei (Xhosa), KwaNdebele (Ndebele), Gazankulu (Tsonga), KaNgwane

(Swazi), KwaZulu (Zulu), Lebowa (Lobedu/ Pedi), QwaQwa (southern Sotho), Transkei (Xhosa), Venda (Venda).

For more information on South Africa's cultural and linguistic groupings, see the special section 'Peoples of the Region'.

EDUCATION

The new South Africa continues to suffer from the educational policies of the apartheid era. There's a whole generation of people who either received little or no schooling because of the colour of their skin. Many black students also took to the streets at the height of the struggle for political freedom chanting 'Liberation before Education'. Nearly one in five South Africans of 20 years of age or older is considered illiterate.

Although education now takes a lion's share of the national budget (21% of government spending in 2000–01), the system remains racked with difficulties. There's a desperate shortage of teachers, particularly in maths and the sciences; violence in schools is a major problem; classrooms are overcrowded; attendance is a problem; and textbooks and other facilities are in short supply. Sexual abuse of girls in schools is another enormous problem, with some teachers believing that sex with students is a fringe benefit of the job, given the poor working conditions and low pay. Even the education minister, Kadar Asmal, admits that 30% of the nation's schools are not fit to be used.

There are some signs, though, of improvement. Results for 2000 showed that 57.9% of pupils had passed their end-of-high-school exams, up from a dismal 48.9% in 1999. In the late 1990s, one school in a poor area of KwaZulu-Natal made an extraordinary leap from a pass rate of 7% to 94%. Also, the proportion of students across South Africa who did well enough to qualify for university rose from 12.5% to 14%. The improvements were attributed to a number of factors, including the sitting of mock exams (previously not done by many pupils) and the allocation of more marks to course work rather than final exams.

ARTS

Artists of all races were involved in the anti-apartheid campaign and some were placed under the equivalent of house arrest. In a society where you could be jailed for owning a painting deemed politically suspect, serious art was forced underground and blandness ruled in galleries and theatres.

For information about the very important role music played during apartheid, and continues to play today, see the special section 'South African Music'.

It is ironic, then, that the political freedom that accompanied the end of apartheid has not been especially kind to local artists on several levels. Firstly there is a lack of government funding, now that there are considerably more serious problems to be addressed in the country. And secondly, with the fight against apartheid won, many artists were initially left floundering for inspiration and expression for their work. Thirdly came the inevitable attack on elitist European arts such as classical music, ballet and opera.

Today the situation is beginning to look a little less bleak. Private companies are starting to fill the funding gap with much-needed sponsorship. Artists are finding their feet with contemporary subjects, or, more excitingly, returning to their roots for inspiration (for example, the theatre of the coloured community in Cape Town). The classical performing arts have fared the worst, but the recent relaunch of the Cape Town Philharmonic Orchestra as well as the continued success of the KwaZulu-Natal Philharmonic Orchestra provide hope for the future.

Visual Arts

South Africa's oldest art is undoubtedly that of the San (see the special section 'Peoples of the Region' for more information about the San), who left their mark on the landscape in the form of rock paintings and subtle rock engravings. Despite having been faded by aeons of exposure these works of art are remarkable; for a fantastic example see the Linton Panel in Cape Town's South African Museum.

While subject to strict conservation regulations, there are a number of rock-art sites that are open to the public and it's worth seeing them (see the Cederberg Wilderness Area section in the Western Cape chapter and the KwaZulu-Natal chapter for some accessible rock-art sites). Today, San motifs are commonly employed on tourist art such as decorative mats and painted ostrich eggs.

The art of the Bantu-speaking peoples is similar to that of the San people due to their prolonged historical and cultural interaction. Their traditional nomadic lifestyle led to their artefacts being portable and generally utilitarian (see the boxed text 'Crafts of the Region'). Snuff containers, headrests, spoons and beadwork are not created as mere commodities: They are individual statements of self and have always entailed long hours of careful labour.

For a good overview of South African art during apartheid, have a look at *Resistance Art in South Africa* by Sue Williamson. Her follow-up book *Art in South Africa: The Future Present* takes a look at the contemporary scene which, as a wander around any of South Africa's major public and private galleries demonstrates, is tremendously exciting and imaginative.

You also can't fail to notice, particularly in the cities, the many examples of public art such as murals, monuments and memorials. It's constantly amazing how many of the old statues and icons of the apartheid era remain, perhaps testament to an acceptance of the past. One such memorial you shouldn't miss is the awe-inspiring Voortrekker Monument in Pretoria. Equally impressive and infinitely more colourful, however, are the many murals that brighten up the townships.

Architecture

The indigenous architecture of South Africa, including Zulu 'beehive huts' and the elaborately painted Ndebele houses and kraals is impressive. In Western Cape you'll also be struck by the distinctive Cape Dutch architecture, which developed from the 17th century (see the special section 'Cape Town Architecture'). For a good overview of 20th-century South African architecture, pick up Christina Muwanga's *South Africa: A Guide to Recent Architecture*, one in the series of pocket-size guides published by Ellipsis.

Performing Arts

There's much breast beating in South Africa about the state of performing arts but, from an outsider's perspective at least, you only have to look at the success of arts festivals such as Oudtshoorn's Klein Karoo Nasionale Kunstefees (Little Karoo National Arts Festival) and Grahamstown's Festival of the Arts to see that the situation is far from bleak.

Theatre was important for blacks during the apartheid era, both as an art form and also as a means of getting political messages across to illiterate comrades. In the 1960s Welcome Msomi had a huge hit with his Zulu version of Macbeth, *Umabatha*, which toured the world. Jo'burg's Market Theatre, where a lot of black theatre was staged, was and still is the most important venue in the country.

Athol Fugard is the country's best-known playwright; his famous works include *Woza*

Crafts of the Region

For decades, African art was dismissed by European colonisers as being distinct from 'real' art. Be prepared to surrender this Western value judgment as you travel around South Africa (and Lesotho and Swaziland): Here art and craft merge into a complex layering of artistic expression.

For information about the colourful rugs and blankets of Lesotho, see the Lesotho chapter.

Pottery

The master potters of the Venda people (see the special section 'Peoples of the Region') are all women. The pots are fashioned from mud by hand on an old potsherd, smoothed with a piece of leather, dried in the sun for about three days (depending on the weather), glazed and fired. Originally the glaze was graphite, but now many different types of paint are added.

Firing is done in a wide, shallow hole. Thin saplings of carefully selected local trees are added to control the rate of firing. If there is too much heat, the pots will crack. Usually the firing takes about four hours.

Traditional pots come in 10 different sizes and designs. Each has a different function, be it cooking, serving food or liquids, or storage. The pots feature brightly coloured geometric designs.

Traditional *zwifanyiso* (clay figures) are, like the pots, fashioned from clay, but are sun-dried rather than fired. These figures may depict a group scene or individuals, such as important tribal personalities.

Woodwork

Venda woodcarvings are also popular. Traditionally, woodcarving was restricted to men, but these days modern female master woodcarvers can be found, such as the talented Noria Mabasa. Carved items include chains attached to calabashes, and bowls, spoons, trays, pots, walking sticks and knobkerries (a stick with a round knob at one end, used as a club or missile). A number of local woods are used, such as mudzwin, mutango and musimbiri.

Beadwork

Zulu beadwork, which takes many forms, is worth looking out for. With the exception of traditional ceremonies, beadwork is now mainly used for decoration. Beadwork ranges from the small, square *umgexo*, which is widely available and makes a good gift, to the more elaborate *umbelenja*, a short skirt or tasselled belt worn by girls at puberty and until marriage. Worn by men and women are *amadavathi* (anklets).

Apart from decoration and as symbols of status (certain designs are reserved for chiefs and diviners), the Zulu people also traditionally used beads as a means of communication, especially as a type of love letter. Messages are 'spelled out' by the colours and the arrangement of the beads. For

Albert and *The Road to Mecca* as well as collaborations with actors John Kani and Winston Ntshona such as *Sizwe Bansi is Dead*, about getting around the hated pass laws.

More recently, Capetonians David Kramer and Taliep Petersen scored an international hit with their jazz musical *Kat & The Kings*, which swept up awards in London in 1999 and received standing ovations on Broadway. Alongside the local success of the Oscar Petersen and David Issacs comedy *Meet Joe Barber* and Oscar Petersen's *Suip!* – a play about the homeless that has toured to Australia and the UK – there's serious talk of an indigenous Cape theatre developing.

Government subsidies for European cultural expressions no longer exist (and they never existed for indigenous cultural expressions). However, collaboration between performing arts companies and business is providing a solution; an example is the annual Summer Festival sponsored by South

Crafts of the Region

example, red symbolises passion or anger; black, difficulties or night; blue, yearning; deep blue, elopement (referring to the flight of the ibis); white or pale blue, pure love; brown, disgust or despondency; and green, peace or bliss. There have always been ambiguities in this system. For example, a 'letter' that is predominantly red and black could be promising a night of passion or it could mean that the sender was annoyed.

Some bead sculptors incorporate social and political comment into their work, often weaving elaborate tableaux; the most famous exponent was the late Sizakele Mchunu.

Also see the special section 'Peoples of the Region' for information about Ndebele beadwork.

Basketwork

The Zulu also have a rich basketwork heritage. The handwoven baskets, although created in a variety of styles and colours, almost always have a functional purpose. The raw materials vary depending on seasonal availability – they could be woven from imizi grass, ilala palm fronds, isikonko grass, ncema grass or ncebe bark. One medium currently in favour is telephone wire. Ncema grass, for example, is used to make traditional *isicephu* (sitting mats), *icansi* (sleeping mats), water-carrying baskets and beer strainers.

The two predominant designs in Zulu basketwork are the triangle, denoting the male, and the diamond design, denoting the female. Two triangular shapes above one another in an hourglass design indicates that the male owner of the basket is married and, similarly, two diamonds so arranged indicates that the female owner of the basket is married.

Many of the finest baskets are displayed in the Durban Art Gallery and the African Art Centre (also in Durban), especially Hlabisa baskets, which are highly sought-after (but are more decorative than functional). A good place to buy baskets is Ilala Weavers in Hluhluwe (see the KwaZulu-Natal chapter for details).

Township Crafts

New and imaginative types of crafts have sprung up in the townships, borrowing from old traditions, but using materials that are readily available, eg, old soft drink tins and cans used to make hats, picture frames, toy cars and planes, or wire and metal bottle tops for bags and vases.

Complex wirework sculptures and mixed-media paintings and collages are common. Printing and rug making are also taking off – the Philani Nutrition Centre projects in the Cape Flats townships of Cape Town are a good example.

Such art has become very popular and can easily be found in both markets and art shops in the main cities – see the relevant Cape Town, Johannesburg and Durban sections for recommendations.

African Airways and held on the Spier wine estate near Stellenbosch. In 2001 the program – performed by an ensemble cast of all races – embraced Bizet's *Carmen*, Brecht's *The Silver Lake*, the Broadway musical *West Side Story* and Fugard's play *Hello & Goodbye*.

Literature

A number of excellent authors have helped unlock something of the region's soul, beginning with Olive Schreiner (1855–1920), whose *Story of an African Farm*, first published in 1883 under a male pseudonym, was immediately popular and established her enduring reputation as one of South Africa's seminal novelists.

Practically anything by Nobel prize winner Nadine Gordimer, who hones in on the interracial dynamics of the country and white liberal consciousness, is worth reading. *The Conservationist* was the joint winner of the 1974 Booker Prize. Her most recent works include the thrilling novel *The House Gun* and a book of essays, *Living in Hope and History: Notes for our Country*.

JM Coetzee's Booker Prize–winning novels, *The Life & Times of Michael K* and *Disgrace*, are grim but excellent. JM Coetzee is another serious writer who is grappling with the white situation in the new South Africa. Among his other most notable works are *The Master of Petersburg*, *Waiting for the Barbarians* and his intriguing memoir *Boyhood: Scenes from Provincial Life*.

Being There, edited by Robin Malan, is a good introductory collection of short stories from Southern African authors, including Nadine Gordimer. *Transitions*, compiled by Craig MacKenzie, is a similar collection covering roughly half a century of South African short stories, and including one by Herman Charles Bosman, the country's most famous exponent of the form.

Bosman, who wrote mainly in the 1930s and '40s, is an accessible writer and is popular for stories that blend humour and pathos, and capture the essence of rural South Africa. His most popular collection is *Mafeking Road*.

Alan Paton's *Cry the Beloved Country* written in 1948, is one of the most famous South African novels, an epic that follows a black man's suffering in white urban society. Paton returned to the theme of apartheid in *Ah but Your Land is Beautiful*.

Among the many recommended works of André Brink are *A Dry White Season* (made into an unusually accurate Hollywood film starring Donald Sutherland), the 18th-century Cape slavery novel *A Chain of Voices* and his most recent book *Rights of Desire*, about an old man in present-day Cape Town who is haunted by the ghost of a slave girl.

Circles in a Forest by Dalene Mathee translated from Afrikaans, is an historical novel about woodcutters and elephants in the forests around Knysna, written from an Afrikaner point of view. It's a good one to read while travelling the Garden Route. Evocative of the Northern Cape, and another fine translation from Afrikaans, is Etienne van Heerden's *Ancestral Voices*, which captures the tangled and tragic history of several generations of a Voortrekker family.

For obvious reasons black writers had a difficult time of it under apartheid. One area they could shine in, though, was the liberal press such as the Jo'burg-based *Drum* magazine, which launched the career of, among others, Todd Matshikiza. Today there is no shortage of black writers to choose from. One to look out for is Zakes Mda, whose *Ways of Dying* is an award-winning tale of a professional mourner in black South Africa and is now a set text in schools. His most recent book, *The Heart of Redness*, a story moving between contemporary themes and characters and the mid-19th-century tragedy of the Great Cattle Killings, has been hailed as the most ambitious work of fiction by a black South African writer in a decade.

The books of Alex La Guma, a coloured writer who died in exile in 1985, are worth reading; they include *A Walk in the Night* a collection of his short stories set in the District Six area of Cape Town. Sindiw Magona is a black female writer whose *Mother to Mother* is a fictionalised account of the correspondence between the mother of Amy Biehl, a white American woman murdered in the Cape Flats in 1993, and the mother of her killer.

In commercial terms South Africa's most successful writer is Wilbur Smith, who's been churning out airport novel blockbusters for decades.

For books about South Africa, including travel guides and reference books, see Books in the Facts for the Visitor chapter.

SOCIETY & CULTURE

For more than 100 years most indigenous people in South Africa have lived in urban areas, on farms owned by whites or (under the apartheid regime) in the tiny and arbitrarily defined Homelands. Loss of land, lack of political power and the need to be part of the economy has radically altered most cultures. Although traditional cultures have survived, very few people are able to live a purely traditional lifestyle. Fortunately, indigenous languages remain strong. Teaching urban children about their heritage has become a growth industry in the new South Africa.

However, cultures are never static and are always evolving in response to the changing environment. During the short recorded history of the black peoples of Southern Africa there have been several significant cultural changes, such as those caused by white invasion and the difaqane. The idea that a people can have an intrinsic and unchangeable cultural identity was one of the racist myths promulgated by the apartheid regime to justify its Homelands policy. For example, if people prefer to live in square brick houses with tin roofs rather than circular mud huts with thatched roofs, it might mean fewer photo opportunities for visitors, but it does mean a more comfortable life for the residents.

Most traditional cultures were suppressed during the apartheid years. To an extent, the Homelands kept alive some aspects of traditional cultures, in an unnaturally static environment. The day-to-day realities of traditional and contemporary cultures were ignored, trivialised or destroyed. The most striking examples of this were the bulldozing of District Six, a vibrant multicultural area

in Cape Town, in the 1960s, and Jo'burg's Sophiatown, where internationally famous musicians learned their craft in an area once graphically described as 'a skeleton with a permanent grin'.

Superficially, today's urban culture in South Africa doesn't seem to differ much from urban life in many Western countries, although there is a proportionately small number of wealthy blacks and coloureds. The difference perhaps lies in the nation's acute awareness of class and race. And yet, whites of Afrikaner and British descent form distinct subgroups, just as distinct from each other as the subgroupings among blacks from different language groups.

Across these groups, marriage customs and taboos differ, though they are always important; in general polygamy is permitted, and a *lobolo* (dowry) is usually paid to the groom's family. First-born males have inheritance rights. Cattle play an important part in many cultures, as symbols of wealth and as sacrificial animals.

The British have always had a slightly equivocal position in South African society, exemplified by the not-so-friendly Afrikaans term *soutpiel*, literally meaning 'salt dick' and referring to a man with one foot in South Africa and one in Britain, his penis dangling in the ocean. The Afrikaners have often felt (rightly in many cases) that Britain's commitment to Africa was less than their own. Apart from anything else, many of the British who arrived in the 20th century can return 'home' if things get really tough.

RELIGION

Over three-quarters of the population of South Africa is Christian, but among the Christians there is enormous diversity. This group includes everything from the 4000 African indigenous churches to the racist sects that have split from the Dutch Reformed Churches.

The indigenous churches are run by and for blacks, independent of the mainstream white churches. They broadly follow either the Ethiopian line, which broke away from the early Methodist missions, or the later Zionist line, which developed as a result of the activities of American Pentecostal missions early this century (see the boxed text 'Seven Million Silver Stars').

The Dutch Reformed Churches cover at least three major groups of Afrikaner churches, all of which are conservative. The largest and most influential is the Nederduitse Gereformeerde Kerk (NG Kerk), sometimes referred to as 'the National Party at prayer'. The Church of England is also represented; it gained a high profile because of the anti-apartheid battles of Archbishop Desmond Tutu.

Approximately 580,000 people, virtually all of Indian descent, are Hindu, and there are about 600,000 Muslims in South Africa. Cape Muslim is the term used to cover all those of Muslim faith who were transported to the Cape Colony during Dutch colonial times.

A minority of blacks follow traditional religions. Among different peoples, beliefs and practices vary, although there is usually a belief in a supreme deity (although the emphasis is still placed on ancestor worship). Magic and folklore play a large part in beliefs and ceremonies, so much so that many blacks combine Christianity with traditional beliefs, in much the same way that Christianity adopted some pagan rituals in its spread through Europe.

LANGUAGE

There are 11 official languages in South Africa – all equal under the law. English comes in at number five in terms of the percentage of the population who speak the language as a mother tongue, but as a traveller you can get by with English alone in all the cities and most towns. In the rural areas, though, you may run into a few communication problems.

The language spoken by the most people in South Africa is Zulu, followed by Xhosa, Afrikaans, Pedi, English, Tswana, Sotho, Tsonga, Swati, Venda and Ndebele.

Forms, brochures and timetables are usually printed in both English and Afrikaans; road signs alternate between the two languages. Most Afrikaans speakers also have a good command of English (coloured Afrikaans speakers far outnumber white ones). It's not uncommon for blacks in cities to speak at least six languages – whites can usually speak two.

With so many languages, melanges are inevitable, particularly in the black townships where all the languages come into contact with each other. The common tongue used in most townships is either a hybrid form of Zulu and Xhosa or some variation on Sotho.

Fanagalo, a pidgin language based on Afrikaans, English and Zulu, was developed for use by black workers. This was once hailed as a future lingua franca, but for many blacks it represents oppression and is rarely used outside the workplace.

For a basic guide to some of the languages that are spoken in the region, and a list of useful words and phrases, see the Language chapter at the back of this book. For details about learning a language in South Africa, see Courses in the Facts for the Visitor chapter.

Seven Million Silver Stars

If you're travelling between Tzaneen and Pietersburg or Polokwane (Northern Province), you might notice a giant Star of David painted on the side of a mountain. This marks the site of Moria, Zion City, home of the Zion Christian Church (ZCC).

You have probably already seen many members of this church: They wear a metal Star of David, often on a green ribbon. There are seven million of them, and they belong to the largest independent church in Africa. Part of the reason for the ZCC's popularity is that it allows its members to also maintain traditional beliefs, most importantly ancestor worship.

Each Easter since its founding (by Edward Lekganyane in 1910), the church has held a huge gathering at Moria, which now attracts around three million people. During the four days of the Easter gathering, participants do not eat, but instead constantly engage in prayer and dancing.

PRIMATES

MITCH REARDON

Bushbabies Greater Bushbaby *Otolemur crassicaudatus* (pictured); lesser Bushbaby *Galago moholi*
Named for their plaintive wailing call, bushbabies are actually primitive primates. They have small heads, large rounded ears, thick bushy tails and the enormous eyes that are typical of nocturnal primates. The greater bushbaby has dark-brown fur, while the tiny lesser bushbaby is very light grey with yellowish colouring on its legs. Both species are often found in family groups of up to six or seven individuals. Tree sap and fruit are the mainstay of their diet, supplemented by insects as well as, in the case of the greater bushbaby, lizards, nestlings and eggs.

Size: Greater bushbaby length 80cm, including a 45cm tail; weight up to 1.5kg; lesser bushbaby length 40cm; weight 150g to 200g. **Distribution:** Greater bushbaby is restricted to far north-east of region; lesser bushbaby to north of South Africa's Northern Province. **Status:** Common but strictly nocturnal.

LUKE HUNTER

Vervet Monkey *Cercopithecus aethiops*
The most common monkey of the woodland-savanna, the vervet is easily recognisable by its speckled grey hair and black face fringed with white. The male has a distinctive bright blue scrotum, an important signal of status in the troop. Troops may number up to 30. The vervet monkey is diurnal and forages for fruits, seeds, leaves, flowers, invertebrates and the occasional lizard or nestling. It rapidly learns where easy pickings can be found around lodges and camp sites, but becomes a pest when it becomes habituated to being fed. Most park authorities destroy such individuals, so please avoid feeding them.

Size: Length up to 130cm, including a 65cm tail; weight 3.5kg to 8kg; male larger than female. **Distribution:** Widespread in woodland-savanna throughout much of the east and north of the region; absent from deserts, except along rivers. **Status:** Very common and easy to see.

RICHARD I'ANSON

Chacma Baboon *Papio ursinus*
The snout of the chacma baboon gives it a more aggressive appearance than other primates, which have more humanlike facial features. However, when you see the interactions within a troop, it's difficult not to make anthropomorphic comparisons. Chacma baboons live in troops of up to 150 animals, and there is no single dominant male. It is strictly diurnal and forages for grasses, fruits, insects and small vertebrates. The chacma baboon is a notorious opportunist and may become a pest in camp sites, which it visits for hand-outs. Such individuals can be dangerous and are destroyed by park officials: don't feed them.

Size: Shoulder height 75cm; length up to 160cm, including a 70cm tail; weight up to 45kg; male larger than female, and twice as heavy. **Distribution:** Throughout the region, except for the heart of deserts. **Status:** Common in many areas and active during the day.

RODENTS

Springhare *Pedetes capensis*

In spite of its name and large ears, the springhare is not a hare but a very unusual rodent with no close relatives. With its powerful, outsized hind feet and small forelegs, it most resembles a small kangaroo and shares a similar energy-efficient hopping motion. The springhare digs extensive burrows, from which it emerges at night to feed on grass and grass roots. Reflections of spotlights in its large, bright eyes often give it away on night safaris. Although swift, and able to leap several metres in a single bound, it is preyed upon by everything from jackals to lions.

Size: Length 80cm, including a 40cm tail; weight 3kg to 4kg. **Distribution:** Widespread in the centre and north of the region; favours grassland habitats with sandy soils. **Status:** Common but strictly nocturnal.

Cape Porcupine *Hystrix africaeaustralis*

The Cape porcupine is the largest rodent native to Southern Africa. Its spread of long black-and-white banded quills from the shoulders to the tail makes it unmistakable. If attacked, a porcupine drives its rump into the predator – the quills are easily detached from their owner but can remain embedded in the victim, causing serious injury or death. For shelter, it either occupies caves or excavates its own burrows. The porcupine's diet consists mainly of bark, tubers, seeds and a variety of plant and ground-level foliage. The young are born during the hot summer months, in litters of between one and four.

Size: Length 70cm to 100cm, including a 15cm tail; weight 10kg to 25kg. **Distribution:** Throughout the region. **Status:** Nocturnal but occasionally active on cooler days; difficult to see.

Cape Ground Squirrel *Xerus inauris*

The Cape ground squirrel is a sociable rodent that lives in a colonial burrow system, usually containing up to a dozen individuals but sometimes as many as 30. The burrows are often shared with meerkats. It feeds on grass, roots, seeds and insects, but readily takes hand-outs from people in tourist camps. The ground squirrel is well adapted to dry surroundings – it does not need to drink, extracting all the moisture it requires from its food. It often stands on its hind legs to scan its surroundings, and erects its elegant fan-like tail when danger threatens. The tail is also used as a sunshade.

Size: Length 45cm, including a 20cm tail; weight up to 1kg. **Distribution:** North-central South Africa. **Status:** Common; active throughout the day.

CARNIVORES

Jackals Black-backed jackal *Canis mesomelas* (pictured); side-striped jackal *Canis adustus*

This jackal relies heavily on scavenging but is also an efficient hunter, taking insects, birds, rodents and even the occasional small antelope. It also frequents human settlements and takes domestic stock. It is persecuted by farmers but is very resilient and can be readily seen on farms. Pairs of black-backed jackals form long-term bonds, and each pair occupies an area varying from 3 to 21.5 sq km. Litters contain one to six pups; they are often looked after by older siblings as well as by their parents. The less-common side-striped jackal is grey in colour with a distinctive white-tipped tail.

Size: Shoulder height 35cm to 50cm; length 95cm to 120cm, including a 30cm to 35cm tail; weight 12kg.
Distribution: Black-backed found throughout region; side-striped only in north-east. **Status:** Black-backed common, active night and day; side-striped widespread but not abundant, active night and early morning.

Bat-Eared Fox *Otocyon megalotis*

The huge ears of this little fox detect the faint sounds of invertebrates below ground, before it unearths them in a burst of frantic digging. The bat-eared fox eats mainly insects, especially termites, but also wild fruit and small vertebrates. It is monogamous and is often seen in groups comprising a mated pair and offspring. Natural enemies include large birds of prey, spotted hyenas, caracals and larger cats. It will bravely attempt to rescue a family member caught by a predator by using distraction techniques and harassment, which extends to nipping larger enemies on the ankles.

Size: Shoulder height 35cm; length 75cm to 90cm, including a 30cm tail; weight 3kg to 5kg. **Distribution:** Throughout western half of South Africa and open parts of Northern Province. **Status:** Common, especially in national parks; mainly nocturnal but often seen in the late afternoon and early morning.

Wild Dog *Lycaon pictus*

The wild dog's blotched black, yellow and white coat, and its large, round ears, make it unmistakable. It is highly sociable, living in packs of up to 40, although 12 to 20 is typical. Great endurance hunters, the pack chases prey to the point of exhaustion, then cooperates to pull down the quarry. The wild dog is reviled for killing prey by eating it alive, but this is probably as fast as any of the 'cleaner' methods used by other carnivores. Mid-sized antelopes are the preferred prey, but it can kill animals as large as buffaloes. The wild dog requires enormous areas of habitat and is one of the most endangered large carnivores in Africa.

Size: Shoulder height 65cm to 80cm; length 100cm to 150cm, including a 35cm tail; weight 20kg to 35kg.
Distribution: Restricted to major parks of the extreme north-east. **Status:** Highly threatened, with numbers declining severely from a naturally low density.

Honey Badger *Mellivora capensis*

Africa's equivalent of the European badger, the honey badger (also known as the ratel) has a reputation for a vile temper and ferocity. While stories of it attacking animals the size of buffaloes are probably folklore, it is pugnacious and very powerful for its size. Mostly nocturnal, it is omnivorous, feeding on small animals, carrion, berries, roots, eggs, honey and especially on social insects (ants, termites and bees) and their larvae. Its thick, loose skin is an excellent defence against predators, bee stings and snake bites. In some parks, honey badgers habitually scavenge from bins, presenting the best opportunity for viewing this animal.

Size: Shoulder height 30cm; length 95cm, including a 20cm tail; weight up to 15kg. **Distribution:** Widespread, although absent from central South Africa and from Lesotho. **Status:** Generally occurs in low densities; mainly nocturnal.

Genets Small-spotted genet *Genetta genetta;* large-spotted genet *Genetta tigrina* (pictured)

Relatives of mongooses, genets resemble long, slender domestic cats and have pointed foxlike faces. The two species in the region are very similar, but can be differentiated by the tail tips (white in the small-spotted genet, black in the large-spotted genet). They are solitary animals, sleeping by day in burrows, rock crevices or hollow trees and emerging at night to forage. Very agile, they hunt well on land or in trees, feeding on rodents, birds, reptiles, nestlings, eggs, insects and fruits. Like many mammals, genets deposit their droppings in latrines, usually in open or conspicuous sites.

Size: Shoulder height 18cm; length 85cm to 110cm, including a 45cm tail; weight 1.5kg to 3kg. **Distribution:** Small-spotted genet is widespread in South Africa, but absent from the central east; large-spotted is common in eastern and southern coastal regions. **Status:** Very common but strictly nocturnal.

Mongoose

Although common, most mongooses are solitary and are usually seen only fleetingly. The slender mongoose *(Galerella sanguinea)* is recognisable by its black-tipped tail, which it holds aloft like a flag when running. A few species, such as the dwarf mongoose *(Helogale parvula)*, the banded mongoose *(Mungos mungo;* pictured) and the meerkat *(Suricata suricatta)*, are intensely sociable. Family groups are better than loners at spotting danger and raising kittens. Social behaviour also helps when confronting a threat: Collectively, they can intimidate much larger enemies. Insects and other invertebrates are their most important prey.

Size: Ranges from 40cm and 400g (dwarf mongoose) to 120cm and 5.5g (white-tailed mongoose). **Distribution:** In most of region there are at least two or three species; the greatest diversity is in northeast. **Status:** Common where they occur; sociable species are diurnal, solitary species are nocturnal.

MITCH REARDON

Aardwolf *Proteles cristatus*

The smallest of the hyena family, the aardwolf subsists almost entirely on harvester termites (which are generally ignored by other termite eaters because they are so noxious), licking over 200,000 from the ground each night. Unlike other hyaenids, it does not form clans; instead, it forages alone, and mates form only loose associations with each other. The male assists the female in raising the cubs, mostly by babysitting at the den while the mother forages. The aardwolf is persecuted in the mistaken belief that it kills stock, and may suffer huge population crashes following spraying for locusts (the spraying also kills termites).

Size: Shoulder height 40cm to 50cm; length 80cm to 100cm, including a 25cm tail; weight 8kg to 12kg.
Distribution: Throughout the region, except for southern and western coast. **Status:** Uncommon; nocturnal but occasionally seen at dawn and dusk.

LUKE HUNTER

Spotted Hyena *Crocuta crocuta*

Widely reviled as a scavenger, the spotted hyena is actually a highly efficient predator with a fascinating social system. Females are larger than and dominant to males and have male physical characteristics, the most remarkable of which is an erectile clitoris (which renders the sexes virtually indistinguishable). Clans, which can contain dozens of individuals, are led by females. The spotted hyena is massively built and appears distinctly canine, but is more closely related to cats than to dogs. It can reach speeds of up to 60km/h and a pack can easily dispatch adult wildebeests and zebras. Lions are its main natural enemy.

Size: Shoulder height 85cm; length 120cm to 180cm, including a 30cm tail; weight 55kg to 80kg.
Distribution: Occurs only in the north-east of the region. **Status:** Common where there is suitable food; mainly nocturnal but also seen during the day.

JANE SWEENEY

Caracal *Felis caracal*

Sometimes also called the African lynx due to its long tufted ears, the caracal is a robust, powerful cat that preys predominantly on small antelopes, birds and rodents but is capable of taking down animals many times larger than itself. Its long back legs power a prodigious ability to leap – it even takes birds in flight. Like most cats, it is largely solitary. Females give birth to one to three kittens and raise them alone. It is territorial, marking its home-range with urine sprays and faeces. The caracal occupies a range of habitats but prefers semiarid regions, dry savannas and hilly country; it is absent from dense forest.

Size: Shoulder height 40cm to 50cm; length 95cm to 120cm; weight 7kg to 18kg; male slightly larger.
Distribution: Throughout the region except for much of Natal and the western and southern coast.
Status: Fairly common but largely nocturnal and difficult to see.

Leopard *Panthera pardus*

The leopard is the supreme ambush hunter, using infinite patience to stalk within metres of its prey before attacking in an explosive rush. It eats everything from insects to zebras, but antelopes are its primary prey. The leopard is highly agile and hoists its kills into trees to avoid losing them to lions and hyenas. It is a solitary animal, except during the mating season when the male and female stay in close association for the female's week-long oestrus. A litter of up to three cubs is born after a gestation of three months and the females raise them without any assistance from the males.

ROB DRUMMOND

Size: Shoulder height 50cm to 75cm; length 160cm to 210cm, including a 70cm to 110cm tail; weight up to 90kg. **Distribution:** Absent from most of region except north-east and mountainous areas of south and east. **Status:** Common, but being mainly nocturnal they are the most difficult of the large cats to see.

Lion *Panthera leo*

The lion spends much of the night hunting, patrolling territories and playing. It lives in prides of up to about 30, the core comprising four to 12 related females, which remain in the pride for life. Males form coalitions and defend the female groups from foreign males. The lion is strictly territorial, defending ranges of between 50 to 400 sq km. Young males are ousted from the pride at the age of two or three, entering a period of nomadism that ends at around five years old when they are able to take over their own pride. The lion hunts virtually anything, but wildebeests, zebras and buffaloes are the mainstay of its diet.

LUKE HUNTER

Size: Shoulder height 120cm; length 250cm to 300cm, including a 100cm tail; weight up to 260kg (male), 180kg (female). **Distribution:** Restricted to major reserves of South Africa's north-east. **Status:** Common where it occurs; mainly nocturnal but easy to see during the day.

Cheetah *Acinonyx jubatus*

The world's fastest land mammal, the cheetah can reach speeds of at least 105km/h. However, it becomes exhausted after a few hundred metres and therefore usually stalks prey to within 60m before unleashing its tremendous acceleration. The cheetah preys on antelopes weighing up to 60kg, as well as hares and young wildebeests and zebras. Litters may be as large as nine, but in open savanna habitats most cubs are killed by other predators, particularly lions. Young cheetahs disperse from the mother when aged around 18 months. The males form coalitions; females remain solitary for life.

JOHN HAY

Size: Shoulder height 85cm; length 180cm to 220cm, including a 70cm tail; weight up to 65kg. **Distribution:** Kgalagadi Transfrontier Park, parts of Northern Province and reserves of South Africa's north-east. **Status:** Uncommon, with individuals moving over large areas; active by day.

UNGULATES (HOOFED ANIMALS)

Aardvark *Orycteropus afer*

Vaguely pig-like (its Afrikaans name translates as 'earth-pig') with a long tubular snout, powerful kangaroo-like tail and large rabbit-like ears, the aardvark is unique and has no close relatives. Protected by thick wrinkled pink-grey skin, aardvarks forage at night by sniffing for termite and ant nests, which they rip open with their astonishingly powerful front legs and large spade-like nails. They dig deep, complex burrows for shelter, which are also used by many other animals such as warthogs and mongooses. Normally nocturnal, they occasionally spend cold winter mornings basking in the sun before retiring underground.

Size: Shoulder height 60cm; length 140cm to 180cm, including a 55cm tail; weight 40kg to 80kg. **Distribution:** Widely distributed throughout nearly the entire region. **Status:** Uncommon; nocturnal and rarely seen.

African Elephant *Loxodonta africana*

The African elephant usually lives in small family groups of between 10 and 20, which frequently congregate in much larger herds at a common water hole or food resource. Its society is matriarchal and herds are dominated by old females. Bulls live alone or in bachelor groups, joining the herds when females are in season. A cow may mate with many bulls during her oestrus. An adult's average daily food intake is about 250kg of grass, leaves, bark and other vegetation. An elephant's life span is about 60 to 70 years, though some individuals may reach 100 or more.

Size: Shoulder height up to 4m (male), 3.5m (female); weight 5 to 6.5 tonnes (male), 3 to 3.5 tonnes (female). **Distribution:** Restricted to a few reserves in South Africa's north-east, east and south. **Status:** Very common in some parks.

Rock Dassie *Procavia capensis*

The rock dassie (also known as the hyrax) occurs practically everywhere there are mountains or rocky outcrops. It is sociable, living in colonies of up to 60 individuals. Despite its resemblance to a large guinea pig, the dassie is actually related to the elephant. It feeds on vegetation, but spends much of the day basking on rocks or chasing other rock dassies in play. Where it is habituated to humans it is often quite tame, but otherwise it dashes into rock crevices when alarmed, uttering shrill screams. Rocks streaked white by dassies' urine are often a conspicuous indicator of a colony's presence.

Size: Length 40cm to 60cm; weight up to 5.5kg. **Distribution:** Throughout the region except the central eastern coast; absent from dense forest. **Status:** Common and easy to see, especially where they have become habituated to humans.

Zebras Burchell's zebra *Equus burchellii* (pictured); mountain zebra *Equus zebra*

Burchell's zebra has shadow lines between its black stripes, whereas the mountain zebra lacks shadows and has a grid-iron pattern of black stripes just above its tail. Both species are grazers but occasionally browse on leaves and scrub. The social system centres around small groups of related mares over which stallions fight fiercely. Stallions may hold a harem for as long as 15 years, but they often lose single mares to younger males, which gradually build up their own harems. Both types of zebras are preyed upon by all the large carnivores, with lions being their main predators.

Size: Shoulder height 140cm to 160cm; weight up to 390kg; mountain zebra smaller than Burchell's zebra; females of both species smaller than males. **Distribution:** Burchell's zebras in north-east of region; mountain zebras in a few reserves in Southern Africa. **Status:** Burchell's zebra common; mountain zebra less common.

Rhinoceroses White rhinoceros *Ceratotherium simum* (pictured); black rhinoceros *Diceros bicornis*

Aggressive poaching for rhino horn has made rhinos Africa's most endangered large mammals. The white rhino is a grazer and prefers open plains, while the black rhino is a browser, living in scrubby country. While the white rhino is generally docile, the black rhino is prone to charging when alarmed – its eyesight is extremely poor and it has even been known to charge trains or elephant carcasses. The white rhino is the more sociable species, forming cow-calf groups numbering up to 10. The black rhino is solitary and territorial, only socialising during the mating season.

Size: White rhino shoulder height 180cm; weight 2100kg to 1500kg; black rhino shoulder height 160cm; weight 800kg to 1200kg. **Distribution:** Restricted to protected areas, occurs naturally only in some reserves of KwaZulu-Natal. **Status:** White rhino threatened but well protected; black rhino endangered.

Warthog *Phacochoerus aethiopicus*

The warthog's social organisation is variable, but groups usually consist of one to three sows with their young. Males form bachelor groups or are solitary, only associating with the female groups when a female is in season. The distinctive facial warts can be used to determine sex – females have a single pair of warts under the eyes whereas the males have a second set further down the snout. The warthog feeds mainly on grass, but also eats fruit and bark. In hard times, it will burrow with its snout for roots and bulbs. It rests and gives birth in abandoned burrows or in excavated cavities of abandoned termite mounds.

Size: Shoulder height 70cm; weight up to 105kg, but averages 50kg to 60kg; male larger than female. **Distribution:** Restricted to the region's north-east. **Status:** Common and easy to see.

WILDLIFE GUIDE

DAVID WALL

Hippopotamus *Hippopotamus amphibius*

The hippo is found close to fresh water, spending most of the day submerged and emerging at night to graze on land. It can consume about 40kg of vegetable matter each evening. It lives in large herds, tolerating close contact in the water but foraging alone when on land. Adult bulls aggressively defend territories against each other and most males bear the scars of conflicts (often a convenient method of sexing hippos). Cows with calves are aggressive towards other individuals. The hippo is extremely dangerous on land and kills many people each year, usually when someone inadvertently blocks the animal's retreat to the water.

Size: Shoulder height 150cm; weight 1 to 2 tonnes; male larger than female. **Distribution:** Restricted to the region's north-east. **Status:** Common in major watercourses.

ARIADNE VAN ZANDBERGEN

Giraffe *Giraffa camelopardalis*

The name 'giraffe' is derived from the Arabic word *zarafah* (the one who walks quickly). Both sexes have 'horns' – they are actually short projections of skin-covered bone. Despite the giraffe's incredibly long neck, it still has only seven cervical vertebrae – the same number as all mammals, including humans. The giraffe browses on trees, exploiting a zone of foliage inaccessible to all other herbivores except elephants. Juveniles are prone to predation and a lion will even take down fully grown adults. The giraffe is at its most vulnerable at water holes and always appears hesitant when drinking.

Size: Height 4m to 5.2m (male), 3.5m to 4.5m (female); weight 900kg to 1400kg (male), 700kg to 1000kg (female). **Distribution:** Restricted to the region's north-east. **Status:** Common where it occurs and easy to see.

ARIADNE VAN ZANDBERGEN

Nyala *Tragelaphus angasii*

The nyala is one of Africa's rarest and most beautiful antelopes. Males are grey with a mane and long hair under the throat and hind legs; they also have vertical stripes down the back and long, lyre-shaped horns with white tips. Females are a ruddy colour with vertical white stripes and have no horns. The nyala browses on trees and bushes. During the dry season they're active only in the morning and evening, but during the rains they more often feed at night. Female nyala and their young live in small groups. The young may be taken by baboons and birds of prey.

Size: Shoulder height 115cm (male), 100cm (female); weight 100kg to 140kg (male), 60kg to 90kg (female); horns up to 85cm long. **Distribution:** Restricted to the region's north-east. **Status:** Common where it occurs, but well camouflaged.

WILDLIFE GUIDE

Bushbuck *Tragelaphus scriptus*

A shy and solitary animal, the bushbuck inhabits thick bush close to permanent water and browses on leaves at night. It is chestnut to dark brown in colour and has a variable number of white vertical stripes on its body between the neck and rump, as well as a number of white spots on the upper thigh and a white splash on the neck. Normally only males grow horns, which are straight with gentle spirals and average about 30cm in length. When startled, the bushbuck bolts and crashes loudly through the undergrowth. It can be aggressive and dangerous when cornered.

Size: Shoulder height 80cm; weight up to 80kg; horns up to 55cm long; male larger than female. **Distribution:** Throughout the region's north-east and eastern and southern coastal areas. **Status:** Common, but difficult to see in the dense vegetation of their habitat.

Greater Kudu *Tragelaphus strepsiceros*

The greater kudu is Africa's second-tallest antelope and the males carry massive spiralling horns much sought after by trophy hunters. It is light grey in colour with between six and 10 white stripes down the sides and a white chevron between the eyes. The kudu lives in small herds comprising females and their young, periodically joined by the normally solitary males during the breeding season. It is primarily a browser and can eat a variety of leaves, but finds its preferred diet in woodland-savanna with fairly dense bush cover. Strong jumpers, greater kudu readily clear barriers more than 2m high.

Size: Shoulder height up to 150cm; weight 200kg to 300kg (male), 120kg to 220kg (female); horns up to 180cm long. **Distribution:** Throughout much of region's north, and with populations in central and southern South Africa. **Status:** Common.

Eland *Taurotragus oryx*

Africa's largest antelope, the eland is massive. Both sexes have horns averaging about 65cm long that spiral at the base and sweep straight back. The male has a distinctive hairy tuft on the head, and stouter horns than the female. The eland prefers savanna scrub, feeding on grass and leaves in the early morning and from late afternoon into the night. It normally drinks daily, but can go for over a month without water. It usually lives in groups of around six to 12, generally comprising several females and one male. Larger aggregations (up to a thousand) sometimes form at 'flushes' of new grass.

Size: Shoulder height 124cm to 180cm; weight 300kg to 950kg; horns up to 100cm long. **Distribution:** Small parts of north-central and north-eastern South Africa and the Drakensberg. **Status:** Naturally low density, but relatively common in their habitat and easy to see.

ROB DRUMMOND

Common (or Grey) Duiker *Sylvicapra grimmia*
One of the most common small antelopes, the common duiker is usually solitary, but is sometimes seen in pairs. It is greyish light brown in colour, with a white belly and a dark-brown stripe down its face. Only males have horns, which are straight and pointed, and rarely grow longer than 15cm. This duiker is predominantly a browser, often feeding on agricultural crops. This habit leads to it being persecuted outside conservation areas, though it is resilient to hunting. The common duiker is capable of going without water for long periods, but it will drink whenever water is available.

Size: Shoulder height 50cm; weight 10kg to 20kg; horns up to 18cm long; females slightly larger than males. **Distribution:** Very widespread throughout the region. **Status:** Common; active throughout the day, except where disturbance is common.

ANDREW VAN SMEERDIJK

Waterbuck *Kobus ellipsiprymnus*
The waterbuck has a bull's-eye ring around its rump, and white markings on the face and throat. It's a solid animal with a thick, shaggy, dark-brown coat. Only males have horns, which curve gradually out before shooting straight up to a length averaging about 75cm. The small herds consist of cows, calves and one mature bull; younger bulls live in bachelor groups. This grazer never strays far from water and is a good swimmer, readily entering water to escape predators. Its oily hair has a strong musky odour – especially with mature males, potent enough that even humans can smell them.

Size: Shoulder height 130cm; weight 200kg to 300kg (males), 150kg to 200kg (females); horns up to 100cm long. **Distribution:** Wet areas in north-eastern South Africa. **Status:** Common and easy to see.

DENNIS JONES

Reedbucks Common reedbuck *Redunca arundinum*
(pictured); mountain reedbuck *Redunca fulvorufula*
The common reedbuck is found in wetlands and riverine areas. The rarer mountain reedbuck inhabits hill country and is the smaller, but is otherwise physically similar, with the underbelly, inside of the thighs, throat and underside of the tail white, and with males having distinctive forward-curving horns. However, their social systems differ: Common reedbucks live in pairs on territories; female mountain reedbucks form small groups, the range of each encompassing the territories of several males. Their whistling call is often repeated when advertising territories, and is also given in alarm.

Size: Common reedbuck shoulder height 90cm; weight 50kg to 90kg; mountain reedbuck shoulder height 70cm; weight 20kg to 40kg; males are bigger in both species. **Distribution:** Common reedbucks in north and east of region; mountain reedbucks in region's east. **Status:** Common and easy to see.

Roan Antelope *Hippotragus equinus*

The roan antelope is one of Southern Africa's rarest antelopes, and one of Africa's largest. A grazer, it prefers tall
grasses and sites with ample shade and water. Its coat
varies from reddish fawn to dark rufous, with white un-
derparts and a conspicuous mane of stiff, black-tipped
hairs from the nape to the shoulders. Its face is distinct-
ively patterned black and white and its long, pointed ears
are tipped with a brown tassel. Both sexes have long
backward-curving horns. Herds of normally less than 20
females and young are led by a single adult bull; other
males form bachelor groups.

Size: Shoulder height 140cm; weight 200kg to 300kg; horns up to 100cm long. **Distribution:** Can be
seen in Kruger NP. **Status:** One of the less common antelopes; although numbers are declining, they are
not difficult to see where they occur.

Sable Antelope *Hippotragus niger*

The sable antelope is slightly smaller than the roan antelope, but more solidly built. It is dark brown to black, with
a white belly and face markings. Both sexes have
backward-sweeping horns, often over 1m long; those of
the male are longer and more curved. It occurs in habitat
similar to, but slightly more wooded than, that of the roan
antelope. Females and young live in herds, mostly of 10
to 30. Mature males establish territories that overlap the
ranges of female herds; other males form bachelor groups.
Both the roan and sable antelopes are fierce fighters, even
known to kill attacking lions.

Size: Shoulder height 135cm; weight 180kg to 270kg; horns up to 130cm long. **Distribution:** Restricted
to extreme north-eastern South Africa. **Status:** Common and easy to see.

Gemsbok *Oryx gazella*

The gemsbok (or oryx) can tolerate arid areas uninhabitable
to most antelopes. It can survive for long periods without
drinking (obtaining water from its food) and tolerates
extreme heat. As a means of conserving water, the gemsbok
can let its body temperature climb to levels that would kill
most mammals. A powerful animal with long, straight horns
present in both sexes, it's well equipped to defend itself and
sometimes kills attacking lions. Herds usually contain five to
40 individuals but aggregations of several hundred can
occur. The gemsbok is principally a grazer, but also browses
on thorny shrubs unpalatable to many species.

Size: Shoulder height 120cm; weight 180kg to 240kg; horns up to 120cm long; males more solid than
females and with thicker horns. **Distribution:** North-central South Africa. **Status:** Common where it
occurs, but often shy, fleeing from humans.

Bontebok & Blesbok *Damaliscus dorcas dorcas & Damaliscus dorcas phillipsi*

Closely related subspecies, the bontebok and the blesbok are close relatives of the tsessebe. The best way to tell them apart is to look at their colour – the blesbok has a dullish appearance and lacks the rich, deep brown-purple tinge of the bontebok. Both species graze on short grass, and both sexes have horns. As with many antelope, males are territorial, while females form small herds. Bontebok and blesbok often stand about in groups facing into the sun with their heads bowed. The bontebok was once virtually exterminated and numbers have recovered to only a few thousand.

Size: Shoulder height 90cm; weight 55kg to 80kg; horns up to 50cm long. Females are smaller than males.
Distribution: Endemic to South Africa; bonteboks confined to south-west; blesboks widespread in central region. **Status:** Bonteboks are rare but easy to see where they occur; blesboks are common.

Tsessebe *Damaliscus lunatus*

The tsessebe is dark reddish-brown, with glossy violet-brown patches on the rear thighs, front legs and face. The horns, carried by both sexes, curve gently up, out and back. A highly gregarious antelope, it lives in herds and frequently mingles with other grazers. During the mating season, bulls select a well-defined patch, which they defend against rivals, while females wander from one patch to another. The tsessebe is a grazer, and although it can live on dry grasses, it prefers flood plains and moist areas that support lush pasture. It is capable of surviving long periods without water as long as sufficient grass is available.

Size: Shoulder height 120cm; weight 120kg to 150kg (male), 75kg to 150kg (female); horns up to 45cm long. **Distribution:** Parts of north-eastern South Africa. **Status:** Common where they occur.

Blue Wildebeest *Connochaetes taurinus*

The blue wildebeest is gregarious, forming herds up to tens of thousands in some parts of Africa, often in association with zebras and other herbivores. In Southern Africa numbers are much reduced and huge herds are a rarity. Males are territorial and attempt to herd groups of females into their territory. The wildebeest is a grazer, and moves constantly in search of good pasture and water. Because it prefers to drink daily and can survive only five days without water, the wildebeest will migrate large distances to find it. During the rainy season it grazes haphazardly, but in the dry season it congregates around water holes.

Size: Shoulder height 140cm; weight 200kg to 300kg (males), 140kg to 230kg (females); horns up to 85cm long. **Distribution:** The region's central-east coast, north-east and central north. **Status:** Very common but mostly restricted to protected areas.

Klipspringer *Oreotragus oreotragus*

A small, sturdy antelope, the klipspringer is easily recognised by its curious tip-toe stance – its hooves are well adapted for balance and grip on rocky surfaces. The widely spaced short horns are present only on the male of the species. The klipspringer normally inhabits rocky outcrops; it also sometimes ventures into adjacent grasslands, but always retreats to the rocks when alarmed. This amazingly agile and sure-footed creature is capable of bounding up impossibly rough rock faces. Male and female klipspringers form long-lasting pair bonds and occupy a territory together.

Size: Shoulder height 55cm; weight 9kg to 15kg; horns up to 15cm long; female larger than male. **Distribution:** On rocky outcrops and mountainous areas throughout the region; absent from dense forests. **Status:** Common.

Steenbok *Raphicerus campestris*

The steenbok is a very pretty and slender small antelope; its back and hindquarters range from light reddish-brown to dark brown with pale underpart markings. The upper surface of its nose bears a black, wedge-shaped 'blaze' useful for identification. Males have small, straight and widely separated horns. Although steenboks are usually seen alone it appears likely that they share a small territory with a mate, but only occasionally does the pair come together. The steenbok is active in the morning and evening. If a potential predator approaches it lies flat with neck outstretched, zigzagging away only at the last moment.

Size: Shoulder height 50cm; weight up to 10kg to 16kg; horns up to 19cm long. **Distribution:** Apart from a large area of the central-east and eastern coast, steenbok are widely distributed throughout the region in all habitats, except desert areas. **Status:** Common where it occurs.

Suni *Neotragus moschatus*

This tiny antelope, which vies with the blue duiker for the title of smallest in the region, is best looked for from observation hides at water holes. It is often given away by the constant side-to-side flicking of its tail (blue duikers wag their tails up and down). Suni are probably monogamous, living in pairs on their small territories, and use secretions from a large scent gland in front of their eye to mark their territories. They nibble selectively on leaves and fallen fruit. When surprised they will freeze, sometimes for prolonged periods, before bounding away with a barking alarm call.

Size: Shoulder height 35cm; weight 4kg to 6kg; horns up to 14cm long. **Distribution:** Wooded areas of the region's extreme north-east; can be seen in Kruger NP and False Bay Park. **Status:** Difficult to see because it is small, shy and lives in thickets; active in the early morning and late afternoon.

RICHARD I'ANSON

Impala *Aepyceros melampus*

Although it is often dismissed by tourists because it is so abundant, the graceful impala is a unique antelope that has no close relatives. Males have long, lyre-shaped horns averaging 75cm in length. The impala is a gregarious animal, and forms herds of up to 100 or so. Males defend female herds during the oestrus, but outside the breeding season they congregate in bachelor groups. The impala is known for its speed and its ability to leap – it can spring as far as 10m in one bound, and 3m into the air. It is the common prey of lions, leopards, cheetahs, wild dogs and spotted hyenas.

Size: Shoulder height 90cm; weight 40kg to 70kg; horns up to 80cm long; male larger than female. **Distribution:** Widespread in the north-east of the region. **Status:** Very common and easy to see.

ARIADNE VAN ZANDBERGEN

Springbok *Antidorcas marsupialis*

The springbok is one of the fastest antelopes (up to 88km/h) and has a distinctive stiff-legged, arched-backed bounding gait called 'pronking', which is commonly displayed when it sees predators. When pronking, it raises a white crest along the back (normally hidden within a skin fold) and the white hairs of the rump. It is extremely common in arid areas, usually in herds of up to 100, whose social structure varies considerably. It can survive for long periods without drinking, but may move large distances to find new grazing, sometimes congregating in herds of thousands when doing so. Both sexes have ridged, lyre-shaped horns.

Size: Shoulder height 75cm; weight 25kg to 55kg; horns up to 50cm long; male larger than female. **Distribution:** North-western and central northern South Africa. **Status:** Very common and easy to see.

LUKE HUNTER

African Buffalo *Syncerus caffer*

The African buffalo is the only native wild cow of Africa. Both sexes have distinctive curving horns that broaden at the base and meet over the forehead in a massive 'boss'; those of the female are usually smaller. It has a fairly wide habitat tolerance, but requires areas with abundant grass, water and cover. The African buffalo is gregarious and may form herds numbering thousands. Group composition is fluid and smaller herds often break away, sometimes rejoining the original herd later. Although it is generally docile, the buffalo can be very dangerous and should be treated with caution.

Size: Shoulder height 160cm; weight 400kg to 900kg; horns up to 125 cm long; female somewhat smaller than male. **Distribution:** Restricted to some reserves of the region's north-east and east. **Status:** Common can be approachable where they are protected.

Facts for the Visitor

SUGGESTED ITINERARIES

It's easy to have a *jol* (good time) in South Africa, especially if you're hooked into the backpacker network. But, if you also want to learn something about the region and its peoples, you'll have to plan a little. For maximum flexibility, and to get easily to some of the best places, including national parks, you'll need your own transport (see the Getting Around chapter).

Breaking out of the, at times, stifling domination of white South African culture is increasingly possible with the proliferation of township tours and the opportunities to interact with black South Africans. Also consider visiting Swaziland or Lesotho, where traditional African cultures hold sway – see those chapters for highlights and possible itineraries.

One to Two Weeks

With just one or two weeks you'll have some tough choices to make. Cape Town and the immediate vicinity alone could happily occupy you for that time, although some people manage to squeeze both this and a lightning visit to Kruger National Park into a week. We don't recommend this: Kruger on its own needs, at the very least, three days.

You may choose to add a week to the one already spent in Cape Town for exploring the Winelands and heading down the Garden Route for the beaches and scenery, which are worth a couple of days. In the right season, whale-watching along the Overberg coastline near Hermanus is also a possibility. An alternative plan may take you along the inland Route 62, where your priorities should be Montagu, Swellendam, the ostrich capital Oudtshoorn, the Little Karoo town of Prince Albert and a series of magnificent mountain passes.

If you fly into Johannesburg (Jo'burg) and want to keep to that side of the country, then consider combining a tour of Soweto (one day) with visits to Kruger (three days),

Blyde River Canyon (two days) and even Swaziland (three to four days), as the south of Kruger is very close to the northern section of Swaziland.

Three to Four Weeks

With time on your hands consider exploring more off-the-beaten-track parts of the country or take extended trips to some of the national parks and reserves.

If you're considering the 'northern park trail' you'll need four days for Kgalagadi Transfrontier Park, two days for Augrabies Falls National Park and at least four days for Richtersveld National Park. This would leave you in Namaqualand, well worth a few days itself, particularly if it's flower season.

Bloemfontein (two days) is a good place to find a bit of nightlife away from the Cape. From here, if you're heading back to Jo'burg, spend a day in Harrismith in the Eastern Highlands and do one of the best township tours in the country.

Golden Gate Highlands National Park is a stone's throw away, so you could spend a day or two here and in the neighbouring QwaQwa Highlands National Park.

It's hard to visit Eastern Cape without following the legendary *Endless Summer* 'surfari trek'. Head the Kombi north along the N2 coastal highway, stopping briefly at Cape St Francis (one day) and Jeffrey's Bay (two days), to Port Elizabeth (two days). If you're a nonsurfer, don't despair – there are great beaches in this area that don't get as crowded as those on the Garden Route.

From Port Elizabeth make a detour inland to the Karoo. Here you'll need at least four days to see the charming settlements of Cradock, Graaff-Reinet and Nieu Bethesda and a day to explore the Karoo National Park. Along this route be sure to allow a day each for Addo Elephant National Park and Mountain Zebra National Park.

Heading back to the coast via Queenstown (one day) take time out to re-energise in mystical, mountainous Hogsback (one day) before resurfacing in East London (two days). From East London continue north to the Transkei region, once an 'independent Homeland' of the Xhosa people, where you could easily spend five days. A hiking trail runs the length of the region's long subtropical coastline, and along it are the small, idyllic and backpacker-friendly town of Port St Johns and the even smaller hamlet of Coffee Bay.

Durban is lively enough to warrant two to three days. West of Durban is the spectacular Ukhahlamba-Drakensberg Park – a magnet for hikers and climbers (two or three days). From the park's southern end you can make a quick side trip to Lesotho (two or three days). However, you will require a good vehicle and a relaxed timetable to penetrate further into 'the kingdom in the sky' from here (most people enter Lesotho from the northwest of the country near Maseru).

If you plan your route north through Zululand allow yourself two days each for Hluhluwe-Umfolozi Park, the Greater St Lucia Wetland Park and Sodwana Bay National Park. From here you can make your way south-west through the Anglo-Boer War battlefields (three to four days) to the misty town of Eshowe (one day) before heading back to Durban.

One Month or More

With a month or longer at your disposal it's possible to do a full circuit of the country taking in most of the highlights mentioned in this book. A possible itinerary would start and finish in Cape Town, following Route 62 or the Garden Route (or bits of both) through to Eastern Cape. Here you could either continue along the coast to Durban, or go inland to explore the Drakensberg and Lesotho. The national parks and Zulu villages of KwaZulu-Natal are next as you approach Swaziland and the neighbouring Kruger National Park. Cut inland to visit Jo'burg, Pretoria and possibly Sun City, then head towards Kimberley as a prelude to exploring the Kalahari. Swing back down to Cape Town through Namaqualand and Cederberg Wilderness Area, and finish up with a relaxing few days in the Winelands.

PLANNING
When to Go

Spring is the best time for wildflowers in Northern Cape and Western Cape provinces and they are at their peak in Namaqualand (Northern Cape) between mid-August and mid-September.

In summer, many places, especially the lowveld, are uncomfortably hot; also expect rain and mist in the mountains. In KwaZulu-Natal (especially on the north coast) and Mpumalanga, humidity can be annoying. The warm waters of the east coast make swimming a year-round proposition.

Winters are mild everywhere except in the highest country, where there are frosts and occasional snowfalls. There is limited skiing in Lesotho and in Eastern Cape.

Waves of South Africans stream out of the cities from mid-December to late January for their annual holidays. Absolute peak time is from Christmas to mid-January. Resorts and national parks are heavily booked, and prices for accommodation (including camp sites on the coast can more than double. Cape Town, the Garden Route and, to a lesser extent, the KwaZulu-Natal coast are packed. Many visitors from Europe and North America, fleeing the northern hemisphere's winter arrive in summer, adding to the crush.

Prices can rise during other school holidays but usually not as steeply. The South African provinces have slightly different dates for school holidays and they all change annually. Roughly, there are two weeks of holidays in April, a month around July, a month around September, and about two months from early December to late January. Contact South African Tourism for the exact dates (see Tourist Offices later in this chapter).

Maps

Good maps are widely available. Lonely Planet's *Southern Africa Road Atlas* is a handy companion to this book. For a sturdy and helpful map of Cape Town see Lonely Planet's *Cape Town City Map*.

Map Studio (W *www.mapstudio.co.za*) with branches in Cape Town, Durban and Jo'burg, produces a wide range of maps and street directories. Michelin maps also cover South Africa.

Map Office (☎ *011-339 4941, ground floor, Standard House, 40 de Korte St, Braamfontein, PO Box 207, Wits 2050, Gauteng; open 7.30am-4pm Mon-Fri*) sells government maps for R30 a sheet. (Drakensberg maps are available only from KwaZulu-Natal Wildlife; KZN Wildlife.) You'll probably get quicker service if you deal with this shop rather than battle with the bureaucracy.

The 1:50,000-scale maps of the KwaZulu-Natal Drakensberg by Peter Slingsby are a must if you are planning on hiking. Trails are shown with detailed information such as dangerous river crossings, distances and difficult sections. KZN Wildlife is currently replacing the Slingsby maps with a new series and these maps cost R25 a sheet, or R45 on plasticised paper. You can buy them at KZN Wildlife headquarters in Pietermaritzburg (see Pietermaritzburg in the KwaZulu-Natal chapter for details). Some bookshops stock them too.

What to Bring

Don't get too stressed about this since you can buy just about anything you need in the major cities in South Africa, often at cheaper prices than at home.

With so much dramatic scenery and so many good nature reserves, binoculars will come in very handy, as will a zoom lens if you're planning wildlife photography.

A sleeping bag is useful, but not essential, in backpacker hostels, in rondavels (circular huts) and in cabins at caravan parks. Camping is an option; again you can buy good-quality equipment and specialised items in South Africa.

RESPONSIBLE TOURISM

The irresponsible tourist in this region is likely to get a fairly drastic comeuppance: Bothering a hippo, swaggering into a Zulu village or disregarding a farmer's fences are all likely to have dire consequences.

There are also a few less obvious points that you should keep in mind. In a country so riven by economic inequality, you might want to make an effort to spend your rands where they'll help most. For instance, take a township tour run by township people, not a big company; stay at one of the township B&Bs; buy your souvenirs from the people who made them, not a dealer; shop for fruit at roadside stalls rather than supermarkets. All such businesses need your support.

Also remember to pay the guys who look after cars in the city centres and towns; in general, they're helping to make the streets safer for everyone. And don't forget to tip waiting and hotel staff – they rely on this income to supplement their low wages.

South Africa's national parks and reserves are well managed, but, in general, environmental laws are weak here, and if you applied the standards of your home country you'd find that some activities wouldn't be allowed. 'Adventure' 4WD tours, shark-diving, sand-surfing and other activities have a potentially deleterious impact on the environment, so try to get a feel for the operators' commitment to treading lightly on the earth.

For details about camping in rural areas, see Accommodation later in this chapter.

One of the most destructive things you can do is spray water onto San rock art in an attempt to make it brighter for photographs. This quickly degrades these incredibly precious pieces of humanity's heritage.

TOURIST OFFICES

The main government tourism organisation is **South African Tourism** (*head office in Pretoria* ☎ *012-482 6200, fax 347 8753, 442 Rigel Ave South, Erasmusrand 0181,* Ⓦ *www .southafrica.net*), formerly known as Satour. It produces useful brochures and maps, mostly geared to short-stay, relatively wealthy visitors. It operates only outside South Africa. Once you've arrived you're at the mercy of the various provincial tourism organisations, some of which are excellent, others of which are distinctly so-so.

Local Tourist Offices

Practically every town in the country has a tourist office. Again, some are extremely helpful, others not. While some of them are obviously for-profit booking offices for tours

Dealing with Racism

In this book we make use of the old apartheid terms of white, black, coloured and Indian. It is impossible to pretend that these distinctions have disappeared from South Africa, as distasteful as it may seem. Many South Africans proudly identify themselves with one or other of these groups – so, for example, you'll meet black South Africans who happily refer to themselves as black rather than South Africans or Africans (which is the African National Congress–preferred collective expression for all people of African, Indian or mixed-race origin).

We have no problem with someone arguing that there are cultural differences, based on language, shared beliefs, ancestry, place of birth, tribe, political beliefs or religion, that sometimes correlate to some degree with skin colour. However, when such differences are used to justify inequality, intolerance or prejudgment, problems arise.

Visitors to South Africa will find that although the apartheid regime has been dismantled, cultural apartheid still exists. To an extent, discrimination based on wealth is replacing that which is based on race (so most visitors will automatically gain high status), but there are still plenty of people (mainly whites) who sincerely believe that a different skin colour means a predictable mind-set. A few believe it means inferiority.

If you aren't white, this will definitely be noticed by white South Africans. The constant awareness of race, even if it doesn't lead to problems, is an annoying feature of travel in South Africa, whatever your skin colour.

Racial discrimination is illegal, but it's unlikely that the overworked and underresourced police force will be interested in most complaints. Tourism authorities are likely to be more sensitive. One or two travellers have complained about not being admitted to caravan parks or B&Bs in rural areas. This is definitely not common, but it can happen. If you encounter racism in any of the places mentioned in this book, please let us know.

and accommodation, you should be aware that even major tourist offices, such as Cape Town Tourism, will only recommend the services of member organisations (ie, those that have paid up) – you may well have to push to find out about *all* the possible options. If the accommodation prices you're quoted at a local tourist office seem high, press the staff about cheaper places; often they don't suggest these as they won't make as much commission on the booking.

Provincial tourist offices include:

Eastern Cape Tourism Board (☎ 040-635 2115, 636 4019, W www.ectourism.co.za) PO Box 186, Bisho 5605

Free State Tourism Board (☎ 057-352 4820, fax 352 4825, W www.fstourism.co.za) PO Box 4041, Welkom 9460

Gauteng Tourism Authority (☎ 011-327 2000, fax 327 7000, W www.gauteng.net) The Rosebank Mall, Rosebank 2196

KwaZulu-Natal Tourism Authority (☎ 031-304 7144, fax 304 8792, W www.zulukingdom .org.za) PO Box 2516, Durban 4000

Mpumalanga Tourism Authority (☎ 013-752 7001, fax 759 5441, W www.mpumalanga .com) PO Box 679, Nelspruit 1200

Northern Cape Tourism Authority (☎ 053-833 1434, fax 831 2937, W www.northerncape .org.za) 187 Du Toitspan Rd, Private Bag X5017, Kimberley 8300

Northern Province Tourism Board (☎ 015-288 0099, fax 388 0282, W www.tourismboard .org.za)

North-West Province Parks & Tourism Board (☎ 018-386 1225, fax 386 1158, W www.tourismnorthwest.co.za) PO Box 4488, Mmabatho 2735

Western Cape Tourism Board (☎ 021-914 4613, fax 914 4610, W www.capetourism.org) PO Box 3878, Tyger Valley 7536

Tourist Offices Abroad

The South African Tourism offices abroad include:

Australia (☎ 02-9261 3424, fax 9261 3414, e info@satour.com.au) Level 6, 285 Clarence St, Sydney NSW 2000

Dealing with Racism

African

If you are of African descent, you may well encounter some white resentment. The lies perpetuated about blacks during the apartheid era are taking some time to wear off. On the other hand, do not assume a special bond with black South Africans. The various indigenous peoples of South Africa form distinct and sometimes antagonistic cultural groups. Pan-Africanism is a force in politics here, but it is not the dominant force. Thus travellers of African descent from France or the USA will not necessarily receive a warmer welcome than anyone else.

White

If you are of European descent, it will be assumed by most white South Africans that you are essentially the same as them. However, if you've saved for your trip by, say, cleaning offices or working in a petrol station, you will get some startled reactions from some white South Africans. You may also find yourself having to listen to some obnoxious racist remarks.

Indian

Although Indians were discriminated against by the whites during apartheid, they were seen as white collaborators by the blacks. If you are of Indian descent this could mean some low-level antagonism from both blacks and whites.

Asian

East Asians were a problem for apartheid – Japanese were granted 'honorary white' status, and people from other East Asian countries are probably indistinguishable from the Japanese to the insular South Africans. Grossly inaccurate stereotyping and cultural ignorance will probably be the main annoyances you will face.

France (☎ 01 45 61 01 97, fax 01 45 61 01 96, **e** satour@afriquedusud-tourisme.fr) 61 rue La Boëtie, 75008 Paris

Germany (☎ 069-92 91 29 0, fax 28 09 50, **w** www.satour.de) Alemania Haus, An der Hauptwache 11, D-60313 Frankfurt

Japan (☎ 03-3478 7601, fax 3478 7605, **e** satour_t@netjoy.ne.jp) Akasaka Lions Bldg, 1-1-2 Moto Akasaka, Minato-ku, Tokyo 107

UK (☎ 020-8971 9350, fax 8944 6705, **e** satour@satbuk.demon.co.uk) 5 & 6 Alt Gve, Wimbledon, London SW19 4DZ

USA (☎ 212-730 2929, fax 764 1980, **e** satourny@aol.com) 500 Fifth Ave, 20th floor, New York, NY 10110

Zimbabwe (☎ 04-746 487, fax 746 489, **e** satour@internet.co.zw) Office 106, Sanlam Centre, Newlands, Harare

VISAS & DOCUMENTS

Visas

Entry permits are issued free on arrival to visitors on holiday from many Commonwealth and most Western European coun-

tries as well as Japan and the USA. You are entitled to a 90-day visa but if the date of your flight out is sooner than this, the immigration officer will use it as the date of your visa expiry.

If you aren't entitled to an entry permit, you'll need to get a visa (also free) before you arrive. These aren't issued at the borders. It's worth getting a visa before you depart for South Africa but allow a couple of weeks for the process. South Africa has consular representation (at the least) in most countries.

If you do need a visa (rather than an entry permit), get a multiple-entry visa if you plan to go to a neighbouring country (such as Lesotho or Swaziland) then return to South Africa. This avoids the hassle of applying for another South African visa in a small town such as Maseru or Mbabane.

On arrival you may have to satisfy an immigration officer that you have sufficient funds for your stay in South Africa. Obviously, 'sufficient' is open to interpretation, so it pays to be neat, clean and polite. We've heard that UK visitors of Indian descent are sometimes given a hard time by immigration officers, and there's general paranoia about illegal immigrants from other African countries, so if you're of African descent (especially if you live in Africa), you might get a chilly reception.

If you arrive by air, you must have an onward ticket of some sort. An air ticket is best but an overland ticket seems to be OK.

Visa Extensions Apply for visa or entry-permit extensions, or a re-entry visa, at the Department of Home Affairs in Cape Town, Durban, Jo'burg or Pretoria. Visa extensions cost about R400.

Travel Insurance

It's worth taking out travel insurance and it's sensible to buy it as early as possible to cover the widest range of eventualities. Work out what you need; you may not want to insure that grotty old army surplus backpack but everyone should be covered for the worst possible case (eg, an accident that requires hospital treatment and a flight home).

It's a good idea to make a copy of your policy, in case the original is lost. If you are planning to travel for a long time, the insurance may seem very expensive; however, if you think you can't afford the insurance, you certainly won't be able to afford a medical emergency overseas. (See Health Insurance under Predeparture Planning later in this chapter for more information.)

Other Documents

To visit South Africa you will need a passport (with a visa, if applicable). Visitors who have travelled through the yellow-fever zone in Africa or South America (including Brazil) must have an international certificate of vaccination against yellow fever. No other vaccinations are mandatory, although there are some you should consider. (See Immunisations under Predeparture Planning later in this chapter.)

All important documents (passport data page and visa page, credit cards, travel insurance policy, air/bus/train tickets, driving

licence etc) should be photocopied before you leave home. Leave one copy with someone at home and keep another with you, separate from the originals.

EMBASSIES & CONSULATES
South African Embassies & Consulates

Diplomatic representation abroad includes the following (for a full list see **W** www .gov.za/structure/samissions):

Australia (☎ 02-6273 2424, fax 6273 3543, **e** info@rsa.emb.gov.au) Rhodes Place, Yarralumla, Canberra ACT 2600
Brazil (☎ 561-312 9500, fax 322 8491, **e** saemb@brnet.com.br) Avienda das Nações Lote 6, Brasilia DF CEP70406-900
Canada (☎ 613-744 0330, fax 741 1639, **e** rsafrica@sympatico.ca) 15 Sussex Dr, Ottawa, Ontario K1M 1M8
France (☎ 01 53 59 23 23, fax 53 59 23 33, **e** 101754.1762@compuserve.com) 59 Quai d'Orsay, 75343 Paris, Cedex 07
Germany (☎ 030-22 0730, fax 22 07 3190, **e** botschaft@suidafrika.org) 4th floor, Atrium Bldg, Friedrichstrasse 60, Berlin 101117
Israel (☎ 03-525 2566, fax 525 3230, **e** saemtel@isdn.net.il) 16th floor, Top Tower 50 Dizengoff St, 64332, Tel Aviv
Kenya (☎ 02-215616, fax 223687, **e** sahc@ africaonline.co.ke) Lonrho House, Standard St Nairobi
Malawi (☎ 265-783 722, fax 782 571) British High Commission Bldg, Capital Hill, Lilongwe
Mozambique (☎ 01-49 1614, fax 49 3029, **e** sahcmap@mail.tropical.co.mz) Avenida Eduardo Mondlane 41, Caixa Postal 1120, Maputo
Namibia (☎ 061-205 7111, fax 22 4140) RSA House, Corner of Jan Jonker St & Nelson Mandela Ave, Windhoek 9000
Netherlands (☎ 70-392 4501, fax 346 0669, **e** info@zuidafrika.com) Wassenaarseweg 40 The Hague 2596 CJ
Sweden (☎ 08-24 39 50, fax 660 71 36, **e** saemb.swe@telia.com) Linnégatan 76, 11523 Stockholm
UK (☎ 020-7451 7299, fax 7451 7283, **e** general@southafricahouse.com) South Africa House, Trafalgar Square, London WC2N 5DF
USA (☎ 202-232 4400, fax 265 1607, **e** safrica@southafrica.net) 3051 Massachusetts Ave NW, Washington DC 20008 (also consulates in New York, Chicago and Los Angeles)
Zimbabwe (☎ 04-753147, fax 757908, **e** sah comm@harare.iafrica.com) 7 Elcombe St, Belgravia, Harare

Embassies & Consulates in South Africa

Most countries have their main embassy in Pretoria, with an office or consulate in Cape Town (which becomes the official embassy during Cape Town's parliamentary sessions), or in Durban, or in both. However, some countries also maintain consulates (which can arrange visas and passports) in Jo'burg. Some have representation only in Jo'burg.

South Africa is a gold mine for travellers hunting visas for other African countries. Some of these can be very difficult to collect as you travel around, so if you're starting in South Africa it makes sense to get as many as you can here. Most African countries have representation in South Africa.

The following list shows some of the more important embassies and consulates; some are open in the morning only:

Australia
 Embassy in Pretoria: (☎ 012-342 3740, fax 342 4222) 292 Orient St, Arcadia
 Consulate in Cape Town: (☎ 021-419 5425, fax 419 7345) 14th floor, BP Centre, Thibault Square, City Bowl
Botswana
 Consulate in Cape Town: (☎ 021-421 1045, fax 421 1046) 4th floor, Southern Life Centre, 8 Reibeeck St, City Bowl
Canada
 Consulate in Cape Town: (☎ 021-423 5240, fax 423 4893) 19th floor, Reserve Bank Bldg, 60 St George's Mall, City Bowl
France
 Consulate in Cape Town: (☎ 021-423 1575, fax 424 8470) 2 Dean St, Gardens
Germany
 Consulate in Cape Town: (☎ 021-424 2410, fax 424 9403) 825 St Martini, Queen Victoria St, Gardens
 Consulate in Durban: (☎ 031-305 5677, fax 305 5679) 2 Devonshire Place, 4001
Ireland
 Consulate in Cape Town: (☎ 021-423 0431, fax 423 0433) 54 Keerom St, City Bowl
Italy
 Consulate in Cape Town: (☎ 021-424 1256, fax 424 0146) 2 Grey's Pass, Queen Victoria St, Gardens
 Consulate in Durban: (☎ 031-368 4388, fax 368 4504) Embassy House, Smith St, 4001
Lesotho
 Embassy in Pretoria: (☎ 012-460 7648, fax 460 7649) 391 Anderson St, Menlopark
Mozambique
 Consulate in Cape Town: (☎ 021-426 2944, fax 418 3396) Pinnacle Bldg, 8 Burg St, City Bowl
Netherlands
 Consulate in Cape Town: (☎ 021-421 5660, fax 418 2690) 100 Strand St, City Bowl
New Zealand
 Embassy in Pretoria: (☎ 012-342 8656, fax 342 8640) Hatfield
Swaziland
 Embassy in Pretoria: (☎ 012-344 1910) 715 Government Ave, Arcadia
UK
 Consulate in Cape Town: (☎ 021-425 3670,

Your Own Embassy

It's important to realise what your country's embassy can and can't do. Generally speaking, it won't help much in emergencies if the trouble you're in is even remotely your own fault. Remember that you are bound by the laws of the country you're in. Embassies will not be sympathetic if you end up in jail after committing a crime locally, even if such actions are legal in your own country.

In genuine emergencies you may get some assistance, but only if you have exhausted other channels. For example, if you need to get home urgently, a free ticket home is exceedingly unlikely – the embassy would expect you to have insurance. If you have all your money and documents stolen, your embassy might assist you with getting a new passport, but a loan for onward travel is out of the question. Embassies generally do not have mail-holding services nor can you expect them to have up-to-date home newspapers for your perusal.

On a more positive note, if you are heading into very remote or politically volatile areas, you might consider registering with your embassy so its staff know where you are; if you do this, make sure you tell them when you come back too. Some embassies post useful warning notices about local dangers or potential problems. The US embassies are particularly good at providing this information and it's worth scanning their notice boards for travel advice about security, local epidemics, dangers to lone travellers etc.

fax 452 1427) Southern Life Centre, 8 Reibeeck St, City Bowl

USA
Consulate in Cape Town: (☎ 021-421 4280, fax 425 3014) Monte Carlo Centre, Heerengracht St, City Bowl

Zimbabwe
Embassy in Johannesburg: (☎ 011-838 2156, fax 838 5620) 17th floor, 20 Anderson St

CUSTOMS

South Africa, Botswana, Namibia, Swaziland and Lesotho are members of the South African Customs Union, which means that their internal borders are effectively open from a customs point of view. When you enter the union, however, there are the usual duty-free restrictions: you're only allowed to bring in 1L of spirits, 2L of wine and 400 cigarettes. Motor vehicles must be covered by a carnet. For information, contact the **Department of Customs & Excise** (☎ 012-284308) in Pretoria.

MONEY
Currency

The unit of currency is the rand (R), which is divided into 100 cents. There is no black market for foreign exchange.

The only old note you might see is the R5 (which has been replaced by a coin) but old coins are still quite common. The coins are one, two, five, 10, 20 and 50 cents, and R1, R2 and R5. The notes are R10, R20, R50, R100 and R200. The R200 note looks very much like the R20 note, so check them carefully before handing them over. There have been some cases of forgeries of the R200 note and some businesses are reluctant to accept them.

Exchange Rates

country	unit	rand
Australia	A$1	R4.08
Canada	C$1	R5.24
Euro zone	€1	R6.80
India	Rs 10	R1.71
Japan	¥100	R6.74
New Zealand	NZ$1	R3.30
Sweden	10 kr	R7.38
UK	UK£1	R11.36
USA	US$1	R8.05

The rand is a shaky currency, and it's likely that you will get more rands for your unit of currency when you arrive than when you leave. However, it's also likely that many costs will rise as the rand falls (see Costs later in this section).

Exchanging Money

Opening a bank account in South Africa is not really possible, as no bank will accept a foreign address from an account holder.

Travellers Cheques Rennies Travel, a large chain of travel agencies, is the Thomas Cook agent. Rennies Travel also changes other travellers cheques; its rates are good and it doesn't charge fees for changing travellers cheques (but does for cash). Thomas Cook has travellers cheques in rands, useful for the countries covered in this book (given the instability of the rand, buy these just before departure), but not for anywhere else.

There are American Express (AmEx) offices in the big cities; these, like foreign-exchange bureaus, don't charge commission but will give you a lower rate of exchange than you'll generally get from a bank.

Most banks change travellers cheques in major currencies, with various commissions. First National Bank is an AmEx agent and its branches are supposed to change AmEx travellers cheques without commission, but some don't seem to know this and you might have to pay a transaction fee anyway.

Keep at least some of your receipts when exchanging money as you'll need to reconvert leftover rands when you leave.

Credit Cards & ATMs Credit cards, especially MasterCard and Visa, are widely accepted. Nedbank is an official Visa agent and Standard Bank is a MasterCard agent – both have branches across the country. Many automatic teller machines (ATMs) give cash advances; if your card belongs to the worldwide Cirrus network you should have no problem using it across the country. However, it pays to follow some basic procedures to ensure safety – see the boxed text 'Beating the ATM Scams'.

Costs

Although South Africa is certainly not as cheap to travel in as many poorer African countries, it is very good value by European, North American and Australasian standards. This is largely due to the collapse in the value of the rand, which gives those converting from a hard currency a major advantage. Don't expect imported or manufactured goods to be cheap, though.

Inflation is high, so the prices in this book can be expected to rise at a corresponding rate. However, the rand is also likely to continue to devalue, so inflation and devaluation may well cancel out each other. For example, hostel beds have stayed at around US$7 for years now, even though the price in rands has more than doubled from R20 to R50.

There is a value-added tax (VAT) of 14% added to most transactions but some of this can be claimed back upon departure (see Taxes & Refunds later). Prices in this book do not include this tax unless otherwise stated.

Shoestring travellers will find that camping or staying in hostels, on-site caravans or bungalows where they can self-cater are the cheapest options. Sit-down meals in restaurants (without getting into *haute cuisine*) consistently cost between R40 and R60 per person (less in pubs). Steak dishes, in particular, are incredibly cheap. Fresh produce is good value.

The distances in South Africa are large, so transport can be sparse and expensive; hiring or buying a car is certainly worth considering, both for convenience and for economy.

Top-end hotels, as well as mid-range places in some popular destinations, have taken advantage of the increased numbers of international visitors by hiking prices up significantly. For example, some places in Cape Town – which has a long history of enticing travellers, showing them a good time and emptying their wallets – can be very pricey. However, there are also plenty of excellent value options both in accommodation and in dining that won't break your budget.

Tipping

Tipping is pretty well mandatory because of the very low wages. Around 10% to 15% is usual.

Beating the ATM Scams

If you are a victim of crime in South Africa, it is most likely to occur at an automatic teller machine (ATM). There are dozens of scams that involve stealing your cash, your card or your personal identification number (PIN) – usually all three. Thieves are just as likely to operate in Stellenbosch as in downtown Johannesburg and they are almost always well-dressed and well-mannered men.

The ATM scam you're most likely to encounter involves the thief tampering with the machine so your card becomes jammed. By the time you realise this you've entered your PIN. The thief will have seen this, and when you go inside to report that your card has been swallowed, he will take the card and leave you several thousand rand shorter. We make no guarantees, but if you follow the rules listed here you stand a better chance of avoiding this and other scams.

- Avoid ATMs at night and in secluded places. Rows of machines in shopping malls are usually the safest.
- Watch carefully the people using the ATM ahead of you. If they look suspicious, go to another machine.
- Use ATMs during banking hours and if possible take a friend. If your card is jammed in a machine then one person stays at the ATM and the other seeks assistance from the bank.
- When you put your card into the ATM press cancel immediately. If the card is returned then you know there is no blockage in the machine and it should be safe to proceed.
- Don't hesitate to be rude in refusing any offers of help to complete your transaction.
- If someone does offer, end your transaction immediately and find another machine.
- Carry your bank's emergency phone number and if you do lose your card report it immediately.
- If you think you might need help using an ATM, seek it *before* arriving in South Africa.

Taxes & Refunds

South Africa has a value-added tax (VAT) of 14% but foreign visitors can reclaim some of their VAT expenses on departure. This applies only to goods that you are taking out of the country; you can't claim back the VAT you've paid on food or car rental, for example. Also, the goods must have been bought at a shop participating in the VAT foreign tourist sales scheme.

To make a claim, you need your tax invoice. This is usually the receipt, but make sure that it includes the following:

- the words 'tax invoice'
- the seller's VAT registration number
- the seller's name and address
- a description of the goods purchased
- the cost of the goods and the amount of VAT charged, or a statement that VAT is included in the total cost of the goods
- a tax invoice number
- the date of the transaction

For purchases over R500, your name and address and the quantity of goods must also appear on the invoice. All invoices must be originals – no photocopies. The total value of the goods claimed for must exceed R250.

At the point of your departure, you will have to fill in a form or two and show the goods to a customs inspector. At airports, make sure you have goods checked by the inspector before you check in your luggage. After you've gone through immigration, you make the claim and pick up your refund cheque – at some airports you can cash it immediately at a bank (in any major currency). If your claim comes to more than R3000, your cheque is mailed to your home address.

To save time, it's possible for you to prepare the paperwork for your VAT claim at the bureau in Cape Town's V&A Waterfront complex.

You can claim at the international airports in Jo'burg, Cape Town and Durban, and at the following local airports: Bloemfontein, Gateway, Lanseria, Mmabatho, Nelspruit, Port Elizabeth and Upington. It's also possible to claim at the Beitbridge (Zimbabwe) and Komatipoort (Mozambique) border crossings and at major harbours.

How Much Is...?

item	cost
cottage, sleeping two	from R150
hostel dorm bed	R50
hostel double room	about R140
two-star hotel room	from R150 a double
five-star hotel room	from R1000 a double
36-exposure print film	R40
36-exposure transparency (slide) film	R50
36-exposure processing	R44
hamburger & chips	R25
steak	from R35
small beer	R6
one-way economy air ticket from Jo'burg to Cape Town	R923
deluxe bus from Jo'burg to Cape Town	R375
minibus taxi from Jo'burg to Cape Town	R240

POST & COMMUNICATIONS

Post

Most post offices are open from 8.30am to 4.30pm Monday to Friday and 8am to noon Saturday. Aerograms (handy prepaid letter forms) and standard-size postcards cost R1.90. Airmail letters cost R2.30 per 10g and internal letters are R1.30.

Internal delivery can be very slow and international delivery isn't exactly lightning-fast. If you ask someone in South Africa to mail you something, even a letter, emphasise that you need it sent by airmail, otherwise it will probably be sent by sea mail and could take months to reach you. If you're mailing anything of value consider using one of the private mail services; Postnet is the one most commonly found in cities and large towns.

Telephone

Local phone calls are timed and you get three minutes for each 70-cent unit. The most expensive domestic calls (for distances greater than 200km) cost R1.24 per minute. If you're calling any government department, expect to rack up several units.

Except in remote country areas, phones are fully automatic, with direct-dialling facilities to most parts of the world.

Phone directories give full details of service numbers and area codes. They also carry long lists of numbers that are due to change. The phone system seems to be being perpetually upgraded so it's possible that some of the numbers (including some area codes) in this book will have changed by the time you get to South Africa.

Area codes must be dialled for all long-distance calls (ie, calls from one region to another). When you are calling within an area, there is no need to dial the code. For example, if dialling a Cape Town number from within Cape Town, there's no need to dial the 021 code; if dialling the same number from KwaZulu-Natal, you would include the area code. In this book, we have listed the area code at the beginning of each city or town section.

International calls are expensive. There are many privately run 'phone centres' where you can make calls without coins. These are more convenient than public phones but are also more expensive. Expect charges for calls from hotel rooms to be outrageous – never less than double what you would pay for a public phone and often a lot more.

The following are some useful directory services:

Inquiries (local and national)	☎ 1023
Inquiries (international)	☎ 0903
Collect calls (national)	☎ 0020
Collect calls (international)	☎ 0900

To make an international call, dial ☎ 09 then your country's access code. International calls are cheaper after 8pm Monday to Thursday and between 8pm Friday and 8am Monday.

To avoid high charges when calling home, dial your Home Country Direct number. This puts you through to an operator in your country. You can then either place a call on your 'phone home' account, if you have one, or place a collect (reverse-charge)

call. Be aware that using these free-call numbers to access the Home Country Direct service incurs a fee at some hotels:

Australia Direct	☎ 0800 990061
Belgium Direct	☎ 0800 990032
Canada Direct	☎ 0800 990014
Denmark Direct	☎ 0800 990045
Ireland Direct	☎ 0800 990353
Japan Direct	☎ 0800 990081
Netherlands Direct	☎ 0800 990031
New Zealand Direct	☎ 0800 990064
UK Direct – BT	☎ 0800 990044
UK Direct Call UK	☎ 0800 990544
USA Direct AT&T	☎ 0800 990123
USA Direct MCI Call US	☎ 0800 990011
USA Direct Sprint Express	☎ 0800 990001

Cellphones The cellphone (mobile phone) network covers most of the densely populated parts of South Africa and the major roads. It operates on the GSM digital system, which you'll need to know if you're thinking of bringing your phone from home. Cellphone ownership is very widespread and although you won't absolutely need a cellphone during your travels here, they can come in very handy, such as when you're out on the town and need to call a taxi late at night.

At the time of research there were two competing networks – MTM and Vodacom – but there was likely to be another in the near future. Hiring a cellphone is relatively inexpensive; we got a deal for R8 a day in Cape Town, including insurance, compared with R13 or R14 a day at Cape Town airport. Some car-hire places also offer deals on cellphones.

Call charges are typically around R2.20 per minute. Prepaid cards for use with your own phone are readily available, from Vodacom and MTM stores in every mall and plenty of other places. Vodacom sells SIM cards for R90, and cards for prepaid services for R29, R55, R110 and R275.

Fax

You can fax most organisations and businesses (phone directories also list fax numbers). You can fax from some Telkom offices, Postnet offices and privately run phone centres.

eKno Communication Card

There's a wide range of local and international phonecards. Lonely Planet's eKno Communication Card is aimed specifically at travellers and provides cheap international calls, a range of messaging services and free email – for local calls, you're usually better off with a local card. To access eKno services in South Africa, call ☎ 0800 992 921 or ☎ 0800 997 285. Check the eKno Web site for updates. You can join on-line at ⓦ www.ekno.lonelyplanet.com.

Email & Internet Access

Internet cafes are pretty well established across South Africa, with the cities in particular being fully wired; you can expect all major hostels to have email facilities and for there to be several cafes in the main shopping and entertainment districts.

Unless you must have a computer (eg, for work) there's no point in bringing anything larger than a palmtop – and given the number of Internet cafes, there isn't a lot of point in bringing this along either.

The easiest way to collect mail is to open a free Web-based email account such as eKno (ⓦ www.ekno.lonelyplanet.com), Hotmail (ⓦ www.hotmail.com) or Yahoo! Mail (ⓦ www.mail.yahoo.com).

However, these free Web-based email accounts sometimes have trouble with large documents, so it pays to have your own Internet service provider (ISP) and email account, and to learn how to access your account directly. To do this you'll need three pieces of information: your incoming (POP or IMAP) email server name, account name and password. Your ISP or network supervisor will be able to provide these. Armed with this information, you should be able to access your Internet email account from any Web-connected machine in the world, provided it runs some kind of email software (Netscape and Internet Explorer both have email modules).

DIGITAL RESOURCES

It's possible these days to plan and book your entire trip using the Internet. There's no better place to start your Web explorations than the Lonely Planet Web site (ⓦ www.lonelyplanet.com). Here you'll find succinct summaries on travelling to most places on Earth, postcards from other travellers and the Thorn Tree bulletin board, where you can ask questions before you travel or dispense advice when you get back. You can also find six-monthly upgrades for many of our most popular guidebooks (including this one), and links to the most useful travel resources elsewhere on the Web.

The Internet has been embraced enthusiastically by South Africans. Listed here are some more useful sites; others are listed throughout the book (eg, see the Getting Around chapter for transport Web sites). It's also worth spending a few hours searching the Web for more.

ananzi South African Internet gateway.
ⓦ www.ananzi.co.za
ANC The official site of the ruling party with daily press releases, plenty of facts and figures and links to other government and useful South African sites.
ⓦ www.anc.org.za
Daily Mail & Guardian Web version of the weekly *Mail & Guardian*.
ⓦ www.mg.co.za/mg
Ecoafrica.com Useful for wildlife information and for making bookings for the national parks.
ⓦ www.ecoafrica.com/saparks
GaySA Listings information with links to other useful sites. Warning! Some links are to explicit erotic images.
ⓦ www.GaySouthAfrica.org.za
iafrica.com South African Internet gateway.
ⓦ www.iafrica.com
Internext South African Internet gateway.
ⓦ minotaur.marques.co.za
South African National Parks All you'll need to know about the country's national parks. Go on an Internet safari with Web cams trained on national park watering holes.
ⓦ www.parks-sa.co.za
South African Tourism New site of the government's international tourism promotion organisation. (For the sites of provincial tourism offices, see Tourist Offices earlier in this chapter.)
ⓦ www.southafrica.net
Womensnet Government-sponsored women's Internet resource.
ⓦ www.Womensnet.org.za

BOOKS

For information on literature by South African authors, see Literature under Arts in the Facts about South Africa chapter.

Lonely Planet

Lonely Planet also publishes the *Cape Town* travel guide with more detail on that great city than this book will allow; *Southern Africa Road Atlas* to help you get around; *Southern Africa*, with information on the whole of Southern Africa; and the classic *Africa on a shoestring* for budget travellers setting out to explore the continent. For novice travellers there is also *Read This First: Africa*, and if you want to stay healthy there's *Healthy Travel Africa*.

Travel

The redoubtable Dervla Murphy comes up with another corker in *South of the Limpopo: Travels through South Africa*, which follows her cycle journeys through the country in the years either side of and during the 1994 elections. More up-to-date, although it lacks Murphy's panache, is journalist Gavin Bell's entertaining *Somewhere Over the Rainbow: Travels in South Africa*.

Booker Prize–winning author Justin Cartwright's *Not Home Yet* is a slim but illuminating study of the expat South African's trips home between 1994 and 1996.

History & Politics

The best general history is Rodney Davenport's *South Africa: a Modern History*, now in its 5th edition. It includes a section on the Truth & Reconciliation Commission (TRC). *South Africa: From the Early Iron Age to the 1970s* by Paul Maylam is a detailed and fascinating book.

A fine introduction to white South African history is *The Mind of South Africa* by Allister Sparks. It's opinionated, readable, insightful and delightfully controversial. Sparks' *Tomorrow is Another Country*, the inside story of the Convention for a Democratic South Africa (Codesa) negotiations, is also a fascinating read. Out of print, but worth searching out, is *The Afrikaners – Their Last Great Trek* by Graham Leach. It gives a detailed analysis of the Afrikaner people and their political development.

The history of the ANC is recounted in *The African National Congress* by Jonathan Ball & Saul Dubow, a concise and up-to-date account. For a disturbing insight into the forces opposed to the ANC, read *A Long Night's Damage: Working for the Apartheid State* by Eugene de Kock & Jeremy Gordon. De Kock was highly placed in the government's Covert Operations Branch, and his story is horrific.

For a passionate but logical reckoning of the evil of apartheid, read *Reconciliation through Truth* by Asmal, Asmal & Roberts. Antjie Krog's *Country of My Skull* is an award-winning and compelling personal account of the TRC hearings.

The *They Fought for Freedom* series of paperbacks features important figures from recent South African history, including Steve Biko, Yusef Dadoo, Ruth First, Chris Hani and Oliver Tambo. For the story (so far) of Winnie Mandela's turbulent life, read *The Lady: The Life & Times of Winnie Mandela* by Emma Gilbey.

If you're at all interested in the political process, read *Election '94 South Africa*, edited by Andrew Reynolds, and its follow-up *Election '99 South Africa*. Anthony Sampson's work, *Mandela: The Authorized Biography*, is a weighty and balanced companion to Mandela's own autobiography.

Culture

Indaba My Children is an interesting book of folk tales, history, legends, customs and beliefs, collected and retold by Vusamazulu Credo Mutwa. *Vanishing Cultures of South Africa* by Peter Magubane is quite a good compromise between a glossy picture book and authoritative text, covering 10 peoples.

Religion in Africa, published by the David M Kennedy Centre at Princeton University, is thick and scholarly but is one of the few books that gives an overview of this subject. More readable is *African Religion* by Laurenti Magesa.

Africa: The Art of a Continent, edited by Tom Phillips, includes an authoritative section on South African art.

Personal Accounts

There can be no more obvious or important book to read before coming to South Africa than Nelson Mandela's autobiography, *Long Walk to Freedom*, which despite its 750-odd pages is a compelling and easy read.

If you want more of Mandela's words, look for the collections of his writings and speeches in *The Struggle Is My Life*. Though pretty dry, they do offer an insight into the steadfastness of this amazing man – and show how he refocussed his message depending on the audience he addressed.

Singing Away the Hunger by Mpho 'M'atsepo Nthunya is a fascinating collection of autobiographical stories by a Basotho woman who grew up in rural Lesotho but also experienced life in apartheid-era South African cities.

For a white perspective on the apartheid years, read Rian Malan's outstanding *My Traitor's Heart*, about his attempt to come to grips with his Afrikaner heritage and his country's uncertain future. Gillian Slovo, novelist and daughter of Joe Slovo and Ruth First, key figures in the struggle against apartheid, writes movingly about her family's turbulent life in *Every Secret Thing*. It's a fascinating book on the same subject covered by the screenplay her sister Shawn Slovo wrote for the movie *A World Apart*, and more far-reaching.

Nobel peace prize winner and former archbishop of Cape Town Desmond Tutu weighs in with his own thoughts on the TRC in *No Future Without Forgiveness*. He was chairman of the commission and clearly describes what was obviously a harrowing but ultimately inspirational experience.

The Lost World of the Kalahari and *The Heart of the Hunter* by Laurens van der Post both chronicle the author's exploration of the Kalahari and give a sympathetic, poetic and thought-provoking interpretation of the nomadic San culture.

Architecture

Phillida Brooke Simons' *Cape Dutch Houses & Other Old Favourites* is a well-illustrated and reasonably priced guide to Western Cape vernacular architecture. Graham Viney's *Colonial Houses of South Africa* is a lavish coffee-table book. Christina Muwanga's *South Africa: A Guide to Recent Architecture* is a handy pocket guide to 20th-century South African architecture.

Astronomy

If you're from the northern hemisphere, you might want a guide to all those unfamiliar stars. The *Struik Pocket Guide to the Night Skies of South Africa* by Peter Mack is a good choice.

Flora & Fauna

Southern African Trees by Piet van Wyk is a handy little guide full of information and photos. *Wildflowers of South Africa* by Braam van Wyk is a pocket-size photo guide covering 260 species.

Mammals of Southern Africa by Chris & Tilde Stuart includes a great deal of information and many excellent photos. *Whale Watch* by Vic Crockcroft & Peter Joyce gives details of whale-watching spots from Namibia all down the Western Cape coast. *Signs of the Wild* by Clive Walker is a field guide to the spoors and signs of South African mammals.

Newman's Birds of Southern Africa by Kenneth Newman is an excellent, comprehensive field guide with full-colour paintings. Ian Sinclair's pocket-size *Southern African Birds* is an excellent guide with colour photos, particularly suitable for the short-term visitor as it does not cover obscure birds.

Surfing

Guide to Surfing South Africa by Steve Pike covers some 300 surf spots, each rated, and has colour photos and maps.

Walking

Although out of print it's worth tracking down *The Guide to Hiking Trails: Exploring Southern Africa on Foot* by Willie & Sandra Olivier. It doesn't cover all the trails (there are so many!) but otherwise this book is simply outstanding.

Complete Guide to Walks & Trails in Southern Africa by Jaynee Levy *does* cover all the trails, but it contains an extraordinary amount of information and is far too heavy to carry. It's not a trail guide but gives you a good idea of what a walk entails in advance.

Lots of small books detail walks in various areas of the country. Look for *Western Cape Walks* and *Drakensberg Walks* by David Bristow, and books on walks in the Cape Town area by Mike Lundy.

Wine
John Platter's South African Wine Guide is updated annually and is incredibly detailed, covering all available wines. It is highly recommended.

FILMS
Foreign movies about South Africa, such as *Zulu*, *Cry Freedom* and *A World Apart*, have found an international audience, but the South African film industry itself has had a more difficult time establishing a reputation. During the apartheid era the only film to make any kind of stir outside of South Africa was the bush comedy *The Gods Must Be Crazy*.

Part of the problem is the lack of support that the film industry receives at home; you'll search in vain at South Africa's multiplexes for any locally made movies. So then what are all those film-makers doing every time you turn a corner in Cape Town? Well, most of them are making commercials and most of those are for overseas clients – they like Cape Town's bright weather, its picturesque and quirky locations, and most of all its high-quality labour and low costs.

At the 2001 Oscars, South Africa was represented, albeit at one remove, by an American documentary, *Long Night's Journey into Day*. This Sundance Film Festival winner follows four cases from the Truth & Reconciliation Commission (TRC) hearings and is very moving.

NEWSPAPERS & MAGAZINES
Major English-language newspapers are published in the cities and sold across the country, although in Afrikaans-speaking areas and the ex-Homelands they may not be available in every little town.

The broadsheet *Jo'burg Star* is a good middle-of-the-road daily. The tabloid *Sowetan* is the biggest-selling paper in the country. Although it caters to a largely poorly educated audience, it has a much more sophisticated political and social outlook than most of the major white papers. The *Nation* and *South* are other black papers that upheld journalistic standards during the apartheid years. The long-running *Imvo* (the title translates roughly as 'My View') is published weekly in both English and Xhosa editions and is sold mainly in Eastern Cape. Cape Town's morning paper the *Cape Times* and afternoon paper the *Cape Argus* are tabloids masquerading as broadsheets, print practically the same news and are not worth worrying about.

The best weekly read, although it can at times take itself too seriously, is the *Daily Mail & Guardian*, which includes excellent investigative and opinion pieces, a good arts review supplement and a week's supply of the Doonesbury cartoon strip. Check out the on-line version at W www.mg.co.za/mg. The *Independent on Sunday* is also worth a look.

The glossy monthly *SA City Life* is one of the better arts and lifestyle magazines available, covering politics and social issues as well as giving decent listing information for the Cape Town, Jo'burg, Pretoria and Durban areas. Also pick up a copy of the *Big Issue*, the weekly magazine that helps provide an income for the homeless – it's a good read and a worthy cause.

RADIO & TV
The South African Broadcasting Corporation (SABC) was the monolithic mouthpiece of previous governments, and although times have changed you'll still find most of its fare bland. There are now some privately owned radio and TV stations but the SABC still dominates.

Most SABC radio stations (AM and FM) are broadcast nationally and play dreary music and stodgy chat, although the hour-long current affairs programs are good and you should certainly tune in to Tim Modise's decent morning talk show on SABC's FM station. Stations broadcasting in African languages other than Afrikaans play the best music.

The BBC World Service is available on short-wave, medium-wave and, if you're near Lesotho (where the transmitter is), FM. If you're about to travel through Africa, then the 'Beeb's' nightly *Focus on Africa* program is essential listening.

The SABC has three TV channels and there's also e-tv, a new, privately owned free-to-air station. Its news services are marginally more international than those of the other stations. Only the cheapest places to stay won't have M-Net, a pay station that shows standard fare and some good movies. CNN is much less widely available than it was. If you're lucky you'll get BBC World. Satellite digital TV is on the way.

Programming is similar to that in any US-dominated TV market: soaps, sitcoms, chat shows and infomercials dominate. On the free-to-air stations 'blasphemy' is edited out, and sudden gaps in the dialogue make you realise how often characters in US sitcoms say 'Oh my God'.

Locally made programs include tacky game shows, some reasonable children's programs, a few music shows and soaps, such as *Isidingo* and *E Goli. Yizo Yizo*, set in a school and reflecting current realities, is one of the better dramas and caused a storm in 2001 when an episode included a male prison rape scene (funnily enough there had been no outcry at the previous episodes' inclusion of violence, sexual or otherwise, to women). Dali Tambo's talk show *People of the South* is worth watching, as is the current affairs program *Agenda*.

English is the dominant language on TV, although there are news broadcasts in several other languages.

PHOTOGRAPHY & VIDEO

Film, cameras and accessories are readily available in large towns. Processing is generally of a high standard. Negative film (24 exposures) costs about R57, plus R37.50 for processing.

Be careful about taking photos of soldiers, police, airports, defence installations and government buildings. It goes without saying that you should always ask permission before taking a photo of anyone, but particularly so if you're in a tribal village.

Travel Photography: A Guide to Taking Better Pictures by Richard I'Anson is a lavishly illustrated Lonely Planet guide that will help you do just what the title says.

TIME

South African Standard Time is two hours ahead of GMT/UTC (at noon in London it's 2pm in Jo'burg); seven hours ahead of USA Eastern Standard Time (at noon in New York it's 7pm in Jo'burg); and eight hours behind Australian Eastern Standard Time (at noon in Sydney it's 4am in Jo'burg). There is no daylight-saving time.

This is a wide region to be covered by one time zone and the sun rises and sets noticeably earlier in Durban than it does in Cape Town.

ELECTRICITY

Most power systems in the region are 220/230V AC at 50 cycles per second. The Pretoria system is 250V and the Port Elizabeth system is 220/250V. This means that appliances rated between 220V and 250V AC will work anywhere.

Plugs have three large round pins. Adaptors aren't that easy to find; we found one at the national camping supply and clothing store Cape Union Mart for around R50. If your appliance doesn't have a removable lead, you can always buy a South African plug and have it wired on (assuming that the appliance takes AC and is rated at the correct voltage).

WEIGHTS & MEASURES

South Africa uses the metric system. See the inside back cover of this book for conversion from other units.

HEALTH

South Africa is facing a terrible health crisis in the form of HIV infection and AIDS, so you must take precautions against this. Otherwise, apart from malaria and bilharzia in some areas, and the possibility of hikers drinking contaminated water, there are few other health problems visitors need be concerned about.

If you're planning to venture into less developed areas of Africa, you might want to read *Healthy Travel Africa* by Dr Isabelle Young, a Lonely Planet guide to staying healthy while on the road in Africa. *Travel with Children* by Maureen Wheeler is another Lonely Planet guide that includes basic advice on travel health for young children.

Predeparture Planning

If you wear glasses take a spare pair and your prescription; there are plenty of optometrists in South Africa where you can get new ones if you run into problems.

If you use a particular medication regularly, take the prescription; better still take part of the packaging showing the generic name rather than the brand (which may not be locally available), as it will make getting replacements easier. In South Africa you can buy drugs over the counter that would require a prescription in some other countries but it's still a wise idea to have a prescription with you to show that you legally use the medication.

Health Insurance A travel insurance policy to cover theft, loss and medical problems is a wise idea. Although there are excellent private hospitals in South Africa, the public health system is underfunded, overcrowded and not free. Services such as ambulances are often privately run and expensive.

If you suffer a major illness or injury in the former Homelands, or in Lesotho or Swaziland, you might want to use your air evacuation cover. Check the small print as some policies specifically exclude 'dangerous activities', which can include scuba diving, motorcycling and even trekking. If such activities are on your agenda, you don't want that sort of policy.

You may prefer a policy that pays doctors or hospitals directly rather than one where you have to pay on the spot and claim later. If you have to claim later, make sure that you keep all documentation. Some policies ask you to call back (reversing the charges)

Medical Kit Check List

Although you'll find well-stocked pharmacies all over South Africa (and in the main towns in Lesotho and Swaziland), consider taking a basic medical kit that includes:

- ☐ Aspirin or paracetamol (acetaminophen in the USA) – for pain or fever

- ☐ Antihistamine – for allergies, eg, hay fever; to ease the itch from insect bites or stings; and to prevent motion sickness

- ☐ Cold and flu tablets, throat lozenges and nasal decongestant

- ☐ Multivitamins – consider for long trips, when dietary vitamin intake may be inadequate

- ☐ Antibiotics – consider including these if you're travelling well off the beaten track; see your doctor, as they must be prescribed, and carry the prescription with you

- ☐ Loperamide or diphenoxylate – 'blockers' for diarrhoea

- ☐ Prochlorperazine or metaclopramide – for nausea and vomiting

- ☐ Rehydration mixture – to prevent dehydration, which may occur, for example, during bouts of diarrhoea; particularly important when travelling with children

- ☐ Insect repellent, sunscreen, lip balm and eye drops

- ☐ Calamine lotion, sting relief spray or aloe vera – to ease irritation from sunburn and insect bites or stings

- ☐ Antifungal cream or powder – for fungal skin infections and thrush

- ☐ Antiseptic (such as povidone-iodine) – for cuts and grazes

- ☐ Bandages, Band-Aids (plasters) and other wound dressings

- ☐ Water purification tablets or iodine

- ☐ Scissors, tweezers and a thermometer – note that mercury thermometers are prohibited by airlines

- ☐ Syringes and needles – in case you need injections in a country with medical hygiene problems; ask your doctor for a note explaining why you have them

to a medical centre in your home country, where an immediate assessment of your problem is made.

Check that the policy covers ambulances or an emergency flight home.

Immunisations Seek medical advice at least six weeks before travel. Some vaccinations require more than one injection, while some should not be given together. Some vaccinations should not be given during pregnancy or to people with allergies – discuss this with your doctor.

Discuss any requirements with your doctor, but vaccinations you might need to consider for this trip include the following (for more details about the diseases themselves, see the individual disease entries later in this section). Carry proof of your vaccinations, especially yellow fever, as this is sometimes needed to enter some countries.

Cholera The current injectable vaccine against cholera is poorly protective and has many side effects, so it is not generally recommended for travellers. However, in some situations it may be necessary to have a certificate as travellers are very occasionally asked by immigration officials to present one, even though all countries and the World Health Organization (WHO) have dropped cholera immunisation as a health requirement for entry.

Diphtheria & Tetanus Vaccinations for these two diseases are usually combined and are recommended for everyone. After an initial course of three injections (usually given in childhood), boosters are necessary every 10 years.

Hepatitis A The vaccine for this disease (eg, Avaxim, Havrix 1440 or VAQTA) provides long-term immunity (possibly more than 10 years) after an initial injection and a booster at six to 12 months. Alternatively, an injection of gamma globulin (a ready-made antibody collected from blood donations) can provide short-term protection against hepatitis A – two to six months, depending on the dose given. Unlike the vaccine it is protective immediately, but because it is a blood product, there are concerns about its long-term safety. Hepatitis A vaccine is also available in a combined form, Twinrix, with hepatitis B vaccine. Three injections over a six-month period are required, the first two providing substantial protection against hepatitis A.

Hepatitis B If you're planning a long trip, and visiting countries where there are high levels of hepatitis B infection, where blood transfusions may not be adequately screened or where sexual contact or needle sharing is a possibility, consider having this vaccination. It involves three injections, with a booster at 12 months.

Typhoid Vaccination against this is recommended if you are travelling for more than a couple of weeks in most parts of Africa. It's available either as an injection or as capsules taken orally.

Yellow Fever If you plan to travel through parts of Africa where this disease is endemic, you'll need vaccination and to carry a document proving so.

Problem Areas

Malaria is mainly confined to the eastern half of South Africa (northern KwaZulu-Natal, Mpumalanga, Northern Province) and to Swaziland, especially on the lowveld. Parts of North-West Province are also malarial. Cases are occasionally reported outside these areas.

Bilharzia is also found mainly in the east but outbreaks do occur elsewhere, so always check with knowledgeable local people before drinking water or swimming in it.

If you find yourself drinking from streams, make sure that there isn't an upstream village, even if there is no bilharzia. Typhoid is rare but it does occur, as does hepatitis A. There was also an outbreak of cholera in the eastern provinces in 2001. Industrial pollution is common in more settled areas.

Medical Problems & Treatment

The number-one rule in a medical emergency or serious illness is to get qualified help as soon as possible.

Sunburn Both on the lowveld and in the mountains you can get sunburnt surprisingly quickly, even through cloud. Use a sunscreen, and take extra care to cover areas that don't normally see sun, such as your feet. A hat provides added protection, and you should also use zinc cream or some other barrier cream for your nose, lips and ears. Calamine lotion or a commercial after-sun preparation are good for easing mild sunburn. Protect your eyes with good-quality sunglasses, particularly when near water, sand or snow.

Heat Exhaustion Dehydration or salt deficiency can cause heat exhaustion. Take time to acclimatise to high temperatures and make sure you get sufficient liquids – don't rely on feeling thirsty to indicate when you should drink. Not needing to urinate and dark yellow urine are danger signs. Carry and drink regularly from a water bottle on long trips.

Salt deficiency can be brought on by excessive sweating; it is characterised by fatigue, lethargy, headaches, giddiness and muscle cramps. Salt tablets may help but much better (and safer) are rehydration mixes, which are available from chemists. Sports drinks are fine for mild cases. Vomiting and diarrhoea can also deplete your liquid and salt levels – this is potentially very dangerous for young children.

Heat Stroke This serious, and potentially fatal, condition can occur if the body's heat-regulating mechanism breaks down and the body temperature rises to dangerous levels. Long, continuous periods of exposure to high temperatures can leave you vulnerable to heat stroke.

Avoid excessive alcohol or strenuous activity when you first arrive in a hot climate.

The symptoms are: feeling unwell, hardly sweating or not sweating at all, and having a high temperature (39°C to 41°C). Where sweating has ceased, the skin becomes flushed and red. Severe, throbbing headaches and lack of coordination will also occur, and the sufferer may be confused or aggressive. Eventually the victim will become delirious or convulse. Hospitalisation is essential but meanwhile get victims out of the sun, remove excess clothing, cover them with a wet sheet or towel and then fan them continuously.

Malaria This serious disease, spread by mosquito bites, is endemic in parts of South Africa, so it is extremely important to avoid being bitten and to take preventative medication. Without treatment malaria can have serious effects and is potentially fatal. Symptoms range from fever, chills and sweating, to headache, diarrhoea and abdominal pain and a vague feeling of ill-health; these may subside and recur. Consult your doctor for advice on the antimalarial medication most suitable for South Africa.

A considerable part of the region's population lives in malarial areas and many more people travel to them, so South African doctors and chemists can offer good information and advice.

Contrary to popular belief, if you contract malaria you will not have it for life. Malaria is curable, as long as the traveller seeks medical help.

When travelling in malarial areas there are two main recommendations. The first is avoid being bitten! Mosquitoes that transmit malaria are generally active from dusk to dawn, so during this period:

- Wear light-coloured clothing.
- Wear long pants and long-sleeved shirts.
- Use mosquito repellents containing the compound DEET on exposed areas (prolonged overuse of DEET may be harmful, especially to children, but its use is considered preferable to being bitten by disease-transmitting mosquitoes).
- Avoid perfumes or aftershave.
- Use a mosquito net impregnated with mosquito repellent (permethrin) – it may be worth taking your own.

The second recommendation is take your antimalarial medication. While no antimalarial drug is 100% effective, taking the most appropriate drug significantly reduces the risk of becoming very ill or dying.

Seek examination immediately if you have any symptoms of malaria.

Bilharzia This is carried in fresh water by minute worms. The disease it causes is called bilharziasis or schistosomiasis.

The worm enters through the skin, and the first symptom may be a tingling sensation and sometimes a light rash around the area where it entered. The worm eventually attaches itself to your intestines or bladder, where it produces large numbers of eggs. Weeks later, when the worm is busy producing eggs, you may develop a high fever. A general feeling of being unwell may be the first symptom; once the disease is established, abdominal pain and blood in the urine are other signs.

Avoid swimming or bathing in fresh water where bilharzia may be present. If you do get wet, dry off quickly and dry your clothes as well. Seek medical attention if you have been exposed to the disease and tell the doctor your suspicions, as bilharzia in the early stages can be confused with malaria or typhoid.

Diarrhoea Simple things like a change of water, food or climate can all cause a mild bout of diarrhoea, but a few rushed toilet trips with no other symptoms is not indicative of a major problem.

The main danger with any diarrhoea, particularly in children or the elderly, is dehydration, which can occur quite quickly. Fluid replacement (at least equal to the volume being lost) is the most important thing to remember. Urine is the best guide to the adequacy of replacement – if you have small amounts of concentrated urine, you need to drink more. Weak black tea with a little sugar, soda water, or soft drinks allowed to go flat and diluted with 50% clean water are all good. With severe diarrhoea a rehydrating solution is preferable, to replace minerals and salts lost. Commercially available oral rehydration salts (ORS) are very useful. In an emergency make up a solution of six teaspoons of sugar and half a teaspoon of salt to 1L of boiled or bottled water.

Gut-paralysing drugs such as Lomotil or Imodium can be used to bring relief from the symptoms of diarrhoea, but they won't cure the problem. Only use these drugs if you do not have ready access to toilets, and note that they are not recommended for children under 12 years. Such drugs should be avoided if you have any of the following symptoms: diarrhoea with blood or mucus (dysentery), any fever, watery diarrhoea with fever and lethargy, persistent diarrhoea not improving after 48 hours, or severe diarrhoea. In these cases a stool test is necessary to diagnose which kind of dysentery you have and you may need antibiotics, so you should seek medical help urgently.

Two other causes of persistent diarrhoea in travellers are giardiasis and amoebic dysentery.

Giardiasis is caused by a common parasite present in contaminated water. The symptoms are: stomach cramps; nausea; a bloated stomach; watery, foul-smelling diarrhoea; and frequent gas. Giardiasis can appear several weeks after you have been exposed to the parasite. The symptoms may disappear for a few days and then return this can go on for several weeks.

Amoebic dysentery is characterised by a gradual onset of symptoms, often with blood and mucus. Cramping abdominal pain and vomiting are less likely than in other forms of diarrhoea, and fever may not be present. It will persist until treated and can recur and cause other health problems.

Cholera is the worst of the watery diarrhoeas and medical help should be sought. Outbreaks of cholera are generally widely reported, so you can avoid such problem areas. Fluid replacement is the most vital treatment – the risk of dehydration is severe as you may lose up to 20L a day. If there is a delay in getting to hospital, then begin taking tetracycline. The adult dose is 250mg four times daily. It is not recommended for children under nine years nor for pregnant women. Tetracycline may help shorten the illness, but adequate fluids are required to save lives.

Hepatitis This is a general term for inflammation of the liver. There are several different viruses that cause this common disease, and they differ in the way they are transmitted. The symptoms are similar in all forms of the illness, and include fever, chills, headache, fatigue, feelings of weakness and aches and pains, followed by loss of appetite, nausea, vomiting, abdominal pain, dark urine, light-coloured faeces jaundiced (yellow) skin and yellowing of the whites of the eyes. Avoid alcohol for some time after contracting the illness, as the liver needs time to recover.

Hepatitis A is transmitted by contaminated food and drinking water. You should seek medical advice but there is not much you can do apart from resting, drinking lots of fluids, eating lightly and avoiding fatty foods.

Hepatitis B is spread through contact with infected blood, blood products or body fluids; for example, through sexual contact, unsterilised needles and blood transfusions, or contact with blood via small breaks in the skin. Other risks include shaving, tattooing or body piercing with contaminated equipment. The symptoms of hepatitis B may be more severe than those of type A and the disease can lead to long-term problems such as chronic liver damage, liver cancer or a long-term carrier state.

Hepatitis C and D are spread in the same way as hepatitis B and can also lead to long-term complications.

Hepatitis E is transmitted in the same way as hepatitis A; it can be particularly serious in pregnant women.

There are vaccines against hepatitis A and B but there are currently no vaccines against the other types of hepatitis. Following the basic rules about food and water (hepatitis A and E) and avoiding risky situations (hepatitis B, C and D) are important preventative measures.

HIV/AIDS Human Immunodeficiency Virus (HIV) may develop into Acquired Immune Deficiency Syndrome (AIDS). Exposure to infected blood, blood products or body fluids may put a person at risk. As in many developing countries, transmission in Southern Africa is predominantly through heterosexual sexual activity, though intravenous drug use, vaccinations, acupuncture, tattooing and body piercing can all be potentially dangerous.

Apart from abstinence, the most effective measure against HIV infection through sexual activity is always to practise safe sex using condoms. It is impossible to detect the HIV status of an otherwise healthy-looking person without a blood test.

UNAIDS, the United Nations' body dealing with AIDS, believes that 4.2 million people in South Africa are infected with HIV; the government's more conservative figure of 2.5 million is still shocking (see the boxed text 'HIV/AIDS & the Population Hourglass' in the Facts about South Africa chapter for more information).

Sexually Transmitted Infections (STIs)
HIV/AIDS and hepatitis B can be transmitted through sexual contact – see the relevant sections earlier for more information. Other STIs include gonorrhoea, herpes and syphilis. Sores, blisters or rashes around the genitals and discharges or pain when urinating are common symptoms. In some STIs, such as wart virus or chlamydia, symptoms may be less marked or not observed at all, especially in women. Chlamydia infection can cause infertility in men and women before any symptoms have been noticed. Syphilis symptoms eventually disappear completely but the disease continues and can cause severe problems in later years. While abstinence from sexual contact is the only 100% effective prevention, using condoms is also effective. The treatment of gonorrhoea and syphilis is with antibiotics. Different STIs each require specific antibiotics.

Women's Health
Gynaecological Problems Antibiotic use, synthetic underwear, sweating and contraceptive pills can lead to fungal vaginal infections, especially in hot climates. Fungal infections are characterised by a rash, itch and discharge and can be treated with a vinegar or lemon-juice douche, or with yogurt. Nystatin, miconazole or clotrimazole pessaries or vaginal cream are the usual treatment. Maintaining good personal hygiene and wearing loose-fitting clothes and cotton underwear may help prevent these infections.

STIs are a major cause of vaginal problems. Symptoms include a smelly discharge, painful intercourse and sometimes a burning sensation when urinating. Medical attention should be sought and sexual partners must also be treated. For more details, see Sexually Transmitted Infections earlier.

Pregnancy Some vaccinations normally used to prevent serious diseases are not advisable during pregnancy (eg, the vaccine for yellow fever). In addition, some diseases (eg, malaria) are much more serious for the mother during pregnancy, and may increase the risk of a stillborn child. But if you're pregnant and considering a trip to, say, Cape Town and Western Cape, you should have few worries.

Most miscarriages occur during the first three months of pregnancy. Miscarriage is not uncommon and can occasionally lead to severe bleeding. The last three months of pregnancy should be spent within reasonable distance of good medical care. A baby born as early as 24 weeks stands a chance of survival but only in a good modern hospital. Pregnant women should avoid all unnecessary medication, although vaccinations and malarial prophylactics should still be taken where needed. Additional care should be taken to prevent illness and particular attention should be paid to diet and nutrition. Alcohol and nicotine, for example, should be avoided.

Water Purification

High-quality water is available practically everywhere in Southern Africa and you need not fear drinking from taps. Hikers drinking from streams might be at risk of waterborne diseases (eg, gastroenteritis or, rarely, typhoid), especially if they take water downstream of unsewered villages.

The simplest way to purify water is to boil it thoroughly for 10 minutes. However, at high altitude, water boils at a lower temperature, so germs are less likely to be killed.

Simple filtering doesn't remove all dangerous organisms, so if you can't boil water you should treat it chemically. Chlorine tablets (Puritabs, Steritabs or other brand names) will kill many but not all nasties, including giardia and amoebic cysts, which are resistant to chlorine. Iodine is very effective in purifying water and is available in tablet form (such as Potable Aqua); remember to follow the directions carefully as too much iodine can be harmful.

If you can't find tablets, use tincture of iodine (2%). Four drops of tincture of iodine per litre of clear water is the recommended dosage; the treated water should be left to stand for 20 to 30 minutes before drinking. Iodine crystals (very dangerous things to have around as they are highly toxic and give off toxic gas when exposed to air) can also be used to purify water, but this is a more complicated process, as you have to first prepare a saturated iodine solution.

WOMEN TRAVELLERS
Attitudes Towards Women

Sexism is a common attitude among South African men, regardless of colour. Modern ideas such as the equality of the sexes have not filtered through to many people, especially away from the cities. Women are usually called 'ladies' unless they play sport, in which case they are called 'girls'.

Fortunately times are changing and there are plenty of women who don't put up with this sort of rubbish, but South African society as a whole is still decades behind most developed countries. Also, ironically, there has been something of an antifeminist backlash without there having been many feminist gains in the first place. The fact that black women were at the forefront in the liberation struggle and that many of them have entered politics may change this, however.

Not surprisingly, there are big differences between the lives of women in the region's various cultures. In traditional black cultures, women often have a very tough time but this is changing to some extent because a surprising number of girls have the opportunity to stay at school while the boys are sent away to work. In South Africa's white communities, however, the number of girls finishing secondary school is significantly lower than the number of boys, which is against international trends.

The practice of female genital mutilation (female circumcision) is not part of the traditional cultures of South Africa (or Lesotho or Swaziland).

There's a very high level of sexual assault and other violence against women in South Africa, the majority of which occurs in townships and rural areas. Given the extremely high levels of HIV/AIDS in the country the problem is compounded through the transfer of infection.

A large part of the problem in South Africa is the leniency of the judicial system that repeatedly lets perpetrators of sex of-fences off with short sentences. This, par-ticularly in recent times, has had women's groups around the country voicing their concerns and demanding that the govern-ment step in and take tougher action.

There have been incidents of travellers being raped, but these cases are isolated, and cause outrage in local communities. For most female visitors paternalistic attitudes are the main problem rather than physical assault.

Safety Precautions

Single female travellers have a curiosity value that makes them conspicuous but it may also bring forth generous offers of as-sistance and hospitality. It is always diffi-cult to quantify the risk of assault – and there is such a risk – but plenty of women do travel alone safely in South Africa.

Obviously the risk varies depending on where you go and what you do. Hitching alone is extremely foolhardy, for instance. What risks there are, however, are signifi-cantly reduced if two women travel together or, even better, if a woman travels as part of a mixed-sex couple or group. But while the days of apartheid have long gone, a mixed-race couple will almost certainly attract attention and receive some antagonistic reactions – old attitudes die hard.

However you travel, especially inland and in the more traditional black communi-ties, it's best to behave conservatively. On the coast, casual dress is the norm but else-where dress modestly (full-length clothes that aren't too tight) if you do not wish to draw attention to yourself.

Although urban attitudes are more liberal, the statistics for sexual assault are horren-dous, particularly in the black townships. Common sense and caution, particularly at night, are essential.

GAY & LESBIAN TRAVELLERS

South Africa's constitution guarantees free-dom of sexual choice and there are small but active gay and lesbian communities and scenes in Cape Town, Jo'burg and Durban.

Things have come a long way since 1990 when Jo'burg hosted a Gay Pride parade with many supporters wearing brown paper bags over their heads to conceal their iden-tity. The parade is still going strong, and there's now a separate annual gay and les-bian film festival, Out in Africa (W www .oia.co.za), with a good selection of inter-national and local films in Jo'burg, Pretoria and Cape Town. In December *everyone* fights for tickets for the popular Mother City Queer Project party in Cape Town.

Despite the liberality of the new consti-tution, it will be a while before the more conservative sections of society begin to accept it. Outside the cities, in both black and white communities, homosexuality re-mains, if not taboo, pretty much frowned upon. Even in Cape Town – the most openly gay city on the continent – there was a public rumpus when a delegation of overseas gay travel agents came to town in 2001. This prompted the local Christian and Muslim communities to band together to denounce the promotion of the city as a gay destination.

Given the constitution, you'd wonder what **National Coalition for Gay and Les-bian Equality** (☎ 011-487 3810, ℮ carrie@ ncgle.co.za) is lobbying for. For starters, same-sex marriages are yet to be legally recognised, there isn't an equal age of con-sent, and the Sexual Offences Act doesn't recognise male rape. On the AIDS front, Cape Town's **Triangle Project** (☎ 021-448 3812) is one of the leading support organ-isations, offering professional counselling, legal advice and education programs.

The country's longest-running gay news-paper is the monthy *Exit* (W www.exit .co.za). The glossy magazine *OUTright*, also a monthly publication, is for gay males and is a little more substantial than similar over-seas lifestyle magazines in this niche. Bet-ter is its lesbian equivalent *Womyn*. Both are available at CNA, Fact & Fiction and Exclusive bookstores nationwide. The Gauteng-based queer magazine *Rush* is also worth looking out for; it's often available at gay venues.

See Digital Resources earlier in this chapter for South Africa's main gay and lesbian Web site.

DISABLED TRAVELLERS

People with limited mobility will not have an easy time in South Africa, and although there are more disabled people per capita here than in the West, facilities are few. Most wheelchair users will find travel easier with an able-bodied companion. The sight- or hearing-impaired traveller should have fewer problems.

There is some good news: an increasing number of places to stay have ramps and wheelchair-friendly bathrooms; many buildings (including safari lodges and huts in the national parks) are single storey; car hire is easy; and assistance is usually available on regional flights. South African Tourism has an accommodation guide with details of disability-friendly accommodation.

For advice on what facilities are available across the country, useful places to start are the **National Council for Persons with Physical Disabilities in South Africa** (☎ 011-726 8040, e ncppdsa@cis.co.za), the **Independent Living Centre** (☎ 011-482 5475, e ilc africa@icon.co.za) and the **Association for Persons with Disabilities** (☎ 021-555 2881, e apd-wc@mweb.co.za).

Carp Diem Tours (☎/fax 027-217 1125) specialises in tours for the physically challenged and the elderly.

Cheshire Homes, an international organisation that works with the disabled, also runs the **Enabled Traveller Program** (W enabled.24.com), which can help you with travel arrangements.

For general information on travelling in the region with a disability try the Web site of **Access-Able Travel Source** (W www .access-able.com). The site lists tour operators that specialise in tours for travellers with disabilities.

SENIOR TRAVELLERS

Much of the tourist infrastructure (which was, until recently, geared to wealthier domestic tourists) caters well to senior travellers. You won't, however, find seniors' discounts, special tours or other 'grey power'-related goodies.

Service in the more upmarket hotels, guesthouses and B&Bs is very good, and even less-expensive hotels have porters. If you're concerned about the logistics of travel, chances are you can prebook and prepay for everything from your own country

TRAVEL WITH CHILDREN

This is a good region for kids, and presents few health problems (although you should seek medical advice on malaria prophylactics for children), an abundance of fast-food 'restaurants', satellite TV (M-Net) great wildlife-viewing opportunities and many other services that children want these days.

Apart from going on safari, there are plenty of things that all members of the family will enjoy, such as riding the *Outeniqua Choo-Tjoe* steam train, seeing some traditional Zulu dancing, visiting the wonderful aquarium or riding the cable car to the top of Table Mountain in Cape Town, or just relaxing on a great beach. More adventurous families will have a great time slithering through the Cango Caves near Oudtshoorn or hiking in the Drakensberg.

Facilities such as baby-changing rooms in big stores are scarce. Short-term daycare is becoming more common, and some of the more expensive hotels can arrange childcare.

For tips on keeping children (and parents) happy on the road, see Lonely Planet' *Travel with Children* by Maureen Wheeler

DANGERS & ANNOYANCES

Apart from the high crime rate in South Africa, this is a safe region to visit.

Animals

Bilharzia isn't the only danger you'll face in the water – crocodiles and hippos can be deadly. Be careful near any lowveld stream. If you meet a hippo (most likely on or near the KwaZulu-Natal north coast) do not approach it and be prepared to get away or up a tree very fast. Baboons are also potentially very dangerous – their canine teeth can be larger than those of a lion. A large male baboon can kill a Rottweiler.

You are very unlikely to encounter lions rhinos or elephants when you are walking but take care to heed the warnings not to leave your vehicle in wildlife reserves and national parks. Be careful of elephants in reserves, as they can attack cars if they feel their young are threatened.

Snakes Venomous snakes are a potential problem. To minimise your chances of being bitten, always wear boots, socks and long trousers when walking through undergrowth. Don't put your hands into holes and crevices, and be careful when collecting firewood.

Snake bites do not cause instantaneous death and antivenenes are usually available. Keep the victim calm and still, wrap the bitten limb tightly, as you would for a sprained ankle, attach a splint to immobilise it, then seek medical help. Don't waste time or risk your life trying to catch a live snake. Tourniquets and sucking out the poison are now comprehensively discredited as first-aid methods.

Although reaching medical assistance is of paramount importance, weigh up the dangers of moving the victim. Physical exertion will increase the rate at which the poison travels through the bloodstream, so if at all possible, bring medical assistance to the victim.

Ticks These are present in many areas and it's easy for them to attach to you as you brush past bushes. An insect repellent may keep them away.

If you get bitten, press down around the tick's head with tweezers, grab the head and gently pull upwards. Avoid pulling the rear of the body as this may squeeze the tick's gut contents through the attached mouth parts into the skin, increasing the risk of infection and disease. Smearing chemicals on the tick will not make it let go and is not recommended.

You should always check your body and clothes if you have been walking through a tick-infested area (practically any scrubland, even in city limits, eg, Table Mountain in Cape Town), as they can cause skin infections and other more serious diseases. Apparently ticks like to congregate under camel thorn trees.

Crime
South Africans are obsessed with not becoming victims of crime. This has always been a violent country and the police force has never been in a position to enforce the laws efficiently. The big difference since the 1994 elections is that the white community is suffering from the crime that has long plagued other communities.

The vast majority of South Africans are just as worried about crime as you are, and not surprisingly this worry can cause paranoia. The situation isn't helped by the government's refusal to publish crime statistics.

In the correspondence Lonely Planet has received over the years, letters from travellers saying how surprisingly safe they found South Africa have outnumbered those warning of crime. The four authors of this book encountered no problems themselves with crime while travelling around South Africa and, outside the major cities, generally felt safe.

This said, a Lonely Planet author on holidays at the same time was mugged in broad daylight in Cape Town, and various stories of attacks – some very serious – were recounted to us. You only have to read the headlines in the daily papers to realise that, in certain quarters, South Africa is a very violent country.

The important thing is to keep crime in perspective. Your risk of being a crime victim is probably higher here than in your own country (as is your risk of being injured in a car accident) but try to realistically assess the risks. For example, many foreign visitors stay in the Transkei area of Eastern Cape for weeks without problems, although many white South Africans would not dream of even driving through here and will advise you against it.

On the other hand, the risk of being mugged if you take a stroll around downtown Jo'burg at night is unacceptably high. When in Jo'burg and, to a lesser extent, Cape Town take precautions such as not carrying all your money and documents around with you (see the boxed text 'Survival Tactics').

The big danger during a mugging or a carjacking (again more of a risk in Jo'burg than elsewhere) is that your assailants will assume that you are armed and that you will kill them if you get a chance. Stay calm and don't scare them into shooting you first.

Taxi wars between rival minibus taxi companies have been known to lead to massacres. Once again, it's a matter of knowing the current situation and avoiding being in the wrong place at the wrong time. There are very, very few wrong places and times.

Most blacks aren't racist but if your skin happens to be white, it usually doesn't hurt to make it clear that you are not South African. If your skin is some other shade, there's little risk of major problems from white racists, although there's still an almost

Survival Tactics

Overall, South Africa isn't particularly dangerous, especially compared with some other African countries – or even North America. However, in the cities you should be cautious. Johannesburg is the mugging capital of Southern Africa and some of the crime there is violent. The following are some simple rules that should help keep you out of trouble in big cities:

- Never carry anything you can't afford to lose; in particular, don't flash around a camera.
- Never look as though you might be carrying valuables (wearing an expensive-looking T-shirt makes you look just as rich as wearing jewellery or a suit does).
- Avoid groups of young men; trust older mixed-sex groups.
- Always have some money to give if you are mugged.
- Don't resist muggers.
- Listen to local advice on unsafe areas.
- Avoid deserted areas (such as the downtown area in large cities on weekends) even in daylight.

Unfortunately, the most effective tactics are the most difficult for newcomers to use:

- Don't look apprehensive or lost.
- Don't assume that everyone is out to get you.
- Make friends!

unconscious racism and ignorance about other cultures, which can be infuriating. Whatever your ethnicity, avoid political arguments with drunks.

Police and immigration officials have a bad record of illegally detaining and physically abusing people they think are illegal immigrants from other African countries. You definitely don't want go to jail in South Africa. Conditions have always been harsh but now they are appalling. Funding has been cut back while the prison population has grown.

Road Hazards
For details on dangers encountered on South Africa's roads, see Hazards under Car & Motorcycle in the Getting Around chapter.

EMERGENCIES
Telephone numbers for emergency services include:

Police	☎ 10111
Ambulance	☎ 10117

LEGAL MATTERS
Drugs
Dagga or *zol* (marijuana) was an important commodity in the Xhosa's trade with the San. Today it is illegal but widely available. There are heavy penalties for use and possession but many people still use the drug – often quite openly, as you'll discover in some of the backpacker hostels and bars you may frequent. The legal system does not distinguish between soft and hard drugs.

Ecstasy is just as much part of rave and clubbing culture in South Africa as it is elsewhere. South Africa is also reputed to be the world's major market for the barbiturate Mandrax, which is now banned in many countries (including South Africa) because of its devastating effects. Drugs such as cocaine and heroin are becoming widely available and their use accounts for much property crime.

BUSINESS HOURS
Banking hours vary but are from 9am to 3.30pm Monday to Friday. Many branches

also open from 8.30am to 11am Saturday. Post offices are usually open from 8.30am to 4.30pm Monday to Friday and 8am to noon Saturday. Both banks and post offices close for lunch in smaller towns.

Most shops are open 8.30am to 5pm Monday to Friday and on Saturday morning. Bars usually close around 11pm except in the major cities. Outside the cities it's difficult to get a drink without a meal on Sunday during the day.

PUBLIC HOLIDAYS

Public holidays underwent a dramatic shake-up after the 1994 elections. For example, the Day of the Vow, which celebrated the massacre of Zulus, has become the Day of Reconciliation. The officially ignored but widely observed Soweto Day, marking the student uprisings that eventually led to liberation, is now celebrated as Youth Day. Human Rights Day is held on the anniversary of the Sharpeville massacre.

Public holidays and dates are:

New Year's Day	1 January
Good Friday	March or April
Easter Sunday	March or April
Easter Monday	March or April
Human Rights Day	21 March
Family Day	17 April
Constitution or Freedom Day	27 April
Workers' Day	1 May
Youth Day	16 June
Women's Day	9 August
Heritage Day	24 September
Day of Reconciliation	16 December
Christmas Day	25 December
Boxing Day (Day of Goodwill)	26 December

ACTIVITIES

South Africa has plenty of activities to keep the most demanding of visitors occupied – everything from ostrich riding to the world's highest bungee jump.

The best way to find out about reliable operators is to ask other travellers. Hostels are a good source of information, too, but remember they often have arrangements with particular companies so you can't count on getting unbiased advice. It's some-

times possible to book the activities and tours of larger companies through a travel agency in your home country.

Many smaller outfits offer day trips and these can be excellent. If you're in, say, Durban and want to visit the reserves farther north, it makes sense to travel to a hostel near the reserve and take a day trip from there, rather than sign up for a longer trip from Durban.

Air Sports

Flying, hang-gliding, paragliding (see the boxed text 'Paragliding'), ballooning and parachuting are popular activities. The flying conditions are often superb and the prices, on an international scale, are cheap. Cape Town's Table Mountain must be one of the most beautiful hang-gliding sites but there are numerous other possibilities, particularly in the KwaZulu-Natal Drakensberg. For information on balloon flights check with the **Aero Club of South Africa** (☎ *011-805 0366*).

Bird-Watching

South Africa is a paradise for bird-watchers, and there are bird-watching clubs in the major cities. The regional variation is huge, so keen bird-watchers should aim to cover a range of habitats – Kruger National Park is particularly renowned. Even those with a passing interest will find that binoculars and a field guide are worthwhile investments.

Canoeing & Rafting

South Africa is a dry country with few major rivers. This limits canoeing and rafting options but there are some interesting possibilities. Rafting and canoeing trips on the Orange River in the far north-west, where it forms the border with Namibia, have become very popular. The rapids are not demanding; the main attraction is that you float through a beautiful desert wilderness. The Tugela River (KwaZulu-Natal) offers more challenging rafting, although it is highly variable depending on the rainfall. It is at its best from late December to mid-March.

One of the biggest operators is **Felix Unite** (*in Cape Town* ☎ *021-683 6433*), with offices in Jo'burg and Cape Town.

Diving

The KwaZulu-Natal north coast, particularly around Sodwana Bay, offers excellent warm-water diving and some good reefs. In addition, most resort towns along Western Cape's Garden Route have diving schools. To check an operator's credentials contact **South African Underwater Union** (☎ *021-930 6549*) in Cape Town.

Shark-diving at Gansbaai near Hermanus is also popular. This involves being lowered in a cage and seeing sharks close up. Some operators allow snorkellers in the cage, too, if you're not a qualified diver.

Fishing & Hunting

Sea fishing is a popular activity and there is a wide range of species in the warm and cold currents that flow past the east and west coasts respectively. River fishing, especially for introduced trout, is popular in parks and reserves, with some good highland streams in Drakensberg. You usually need a licence; these are generally available for a few rand at the park office. In some places equipment is available for hire.

Hunting is a bit of a misnomer. It is generally conducted as part of the annual cull in private game reserves and the animals don't stand much of a chance. The other version of hunting involves rich tourists paying enormous fees to shoot just about anything they want in private reserves. We find it pretty distasteful that someone would spend US$20,000 to shoot a lion to death, regardless of whether the lion was baited or tracked.

Hiking

Pack your boots because there's an awful lot of South Africa that's perfect for hiking. There's an excellent system of hiking trails (see following list of South Africa's top hiking trails for recommendations), usually with accommodation, which are popular; many must be booked well in advance.

Most trails are administered by the National Parks Board or the various Forest Region authorities, although KZN Wildlife controls most trails in KwaZulu-Natal.

Guided walks in national parks featuring dangerous animals, accompanied by armed

---

Paragliding

South Africa is one of the world's top destinations for paragliding. The flying is awesome year-round but the strongest thermals are from November to April. For experienced pilots, airspace restrictions are minimal and the potential for long-distance cross-country flying is tremendous.

Your own transport is essential to escape the strong winds in Cape Town and reach the best sheltered sites in Porterville (a ridge site), in Hermanus (a coastal site) and at Sir Lowry's Pass (a ridge site), all in Western Cape. When conditions permit, it's possible to fly from Table Mountain, Lion's Head and Signal Hill and land on the beach at Clifton or Camps Bay. Soaring along the Twelve Apostles as the tablecloth cloud forms around you is a near-biblical experience.

South African Hang Gliding and Paragliding Association (☎ *011-805 5429*, ⓦ *www.paragliding.co.za*) can provide names of operators, and plenty of schools offer courses for beginners. In Cape Town, contact **Paragliding Cape Town** (☎ *082-727 6584*) or **Ferdinand's Tours & Adventures** (☎ *021-465 8550*). A tandem flight will cost around R550.

Hugh Burnaby-Atkins

---

rangers, are available (for details, see Kruger National Park in the Mpumalanga chapter and Hluhluwe-Umfolozi Park in the KwaZulu-Natal chapter).

For details of hiking clubs contact **Hiking Federation of Southern Africa** (☎ *011-968 1202*, ⓔ *info@outdoorworld.co.za*).

The following list summarises South Africa's top hiking trails (for details, see the relevant chapters):

Western Cape
Outeniqua Pass Up to eight days in indigenous forest near Knysna.

Eastern Cape
Wild Coast Three five-day sections along the Transkei coast.

Otter Trail Five days on the coast along the Garden Route (nearly always booked out).

Tsitsikamma Trail Five-day hike running inland parallel to the Otter Trail, but hiked in the opposite direction (rarely booked out).
Amatola Up to six days in the former Ciskei Homelands.

KwaZulu-Natal
Giant's Cup Up to five days in the southern Drakensberg. Also wilderness trails and guided walks in Hluhluwe-Umfolozi, Mkuzi and Lake St Lucia parks and reserves.

Mpumalanga
Blyde River Canyon Trail Up to 2½ days in the Blyde River Canyon area.
Kruger National Park Wilderness trails and guided walks.

Free State
Rhebok Hiking Trail Two days in Golden Gate Highlands National Park.

Northern Province
Soutpansberg Up to two days in the Soutpansberg Range.
Mabudashango Four days in the former Venda Homelands.

Horse Riding
Many places, including some national parks, offer horse riding. There are overnight and longer trails. And don't forget ostrich riding in Oudtshoorn.

Mountain Biking
South Africans have taken to mountain biking in a big way. Some reserves and parks are building trails and several operators organise trips. Paul Leger's *Guide to Mountain Bike Trails in the Western Cape* is a useful book.

Rock Climbing
There are some challenging climbs, especially in the KwaZulu-Natal Drakensberg. For addresses of regional clubs, contact the Mountain Club of South Africa (*MCSA; 7 Hatfield St, Gardens, Cape Town 8001, www.mcsa.org.za*). The club's Web site has links to clubs all over South Africa and a guide to a stack of climbs.

Surfing
South Africa has some of the best and least-crowded surfing in the world. Most surfers will have heard of Jeffrey's Bay but there are myriad alternatives, particularly along the east and south coasts. The best time of the year for surfing in KwaZulu-Natal and the south coast is autumn and early winter (April to July).

Boards and surfing gear can be bought in most of the big coastal cities. New boards sell for around R1600; second-hand boards for R800 to R900. A Rip Curl 'steamer' sells for about R900. If you plan to surf Jeffrey's Bay, you'll need a decent-sized board – it's a very fast wave.

For more information see the boxed texts 'Surfing along the Garden Route' in the Western Cape chapter and 'Surfing in Eastern Cape' in the Eastern Cape chapter. Also check out the Web site of South Africa's biggest surf magazine, *Zig Zag* (W www.wavescapes.co.za).

Wildlife Safaris
In addition to the country's well-organised national parks and reserves, there are a large number of privately owned game reserves and farms where tours are conducted in open vehicles, on horseback or on foot.

Many companies arrange coach tour safaris but these tend to be expensive. It would be cheaper (and probably more fun) to hire a car. Several adventure-travel outfits aimed at backpackers offer safaris. Ask around at hostels, and try to get feedback from someone who has actually been on a tour.

COURSES
Language
For intense cerebral activity and possibly the most rewarding people-friendly activity you can do, contact the **TALK project** (*☎/fax 011-487 1950, 18a Gill St, Observatory, Johannesburg 2198,* W *www.avpsa.com/TALK .htm*). TALK stands for Transfer of African Language Knowledge, and began as a project helping people learn South African indigenous languages. Its method is to pair a student with a mother-tongue speaker, and the two are encouraged to participate in everyday activities together. Most of the fee goes to the mother-tongue speaker. This is a great way to learn not just a language but a culture as well.

TALK also arranges 'immersion visits', where you spend time living in a community while learning the language (or just experiencing the culture – it's up to you). This can be anything from a weekend in Soweto to a month or longer in rural KwaZulu-Natal. Costs vary widely but include a contribution to the family with which you're staying, a fee for the TALK helper, and food and transport (which might involve hiring a car if you're going to a remote rural area). Two weeks in a remote village might cost about R6000 all up.

TALK can organise just about anything for small groups, including meals with African families and visits to townships, with the emphasis on people-to-people contact.

WORK

The best time to look for work is from October to November, before the high season starts and before university students begin holidays. Because of high unemployment and fears about illegal immigration from the rest of Africa, there are tough penalties for employers taking on foreigners without work permits. So far this doesn't seem to have stopped foreigners getting jobs in restaurants or bars in tourist areas, but this might change. Don't expect decent pay – around R12 per hour plus tips (which can be good) is usual.

In Western Cape, hostels might know of fruit-picking work, especially in the Ceres, Citrusdal and Piketberg areas. The pay is negligible but you'll get free accommodation. It's uncommon for travellers to do this, so don't count on it.

ACCOMMODATION

Most places, including caravan parks, have seasonal rates. High season usually means summer school holidays, especially between Christmas and the end of January, and over the Easter break. Prices can double and there might be a minimum stay of one week. The other school holidays are often classified as high season as well, but some places classify them as mid-season and charge a little less at these times.

Other than at hostels and self-catering cottages (usually on farms), both of which have become boom industries, there's a scarcity of

Accommodation Prices

There's one annoying thing to watch out for in accommodation advertising. You might see a hotel boasting that rooms cost R190. This usually means R190 *per person* in a twin or double room. A single room might cost R290. When we quote the cost of a double room in this book we give the full price, not the per-person price.

Most rooms come with a private bathroom; if this isn't the case and there are shared bathrooms we list a price for rooms 'with shared bathroom'. Also note that many places automatically include breakfast in the tariff; if this is the case we quote prices for B&B. If dinner is also part of the package, we quote prices for DB&B, and if all meals are thrown in as standard, the price quoted is for full board.

budget accommodation. However, if you're prepared to camp or pay a little more for a B&B, accommodation is plentiful and generally good. Given the quality of their breakfasts and facilities, some B&Bs are much better value than staying in a private room at a hostel. The gap is being filled, to a certain extent, by the Formule 1 chain of basic hotels (see Hotel Chains under Hotels later in this chapter).

The mid-range is where you'll find really good value accommodation, with the best bargains in B&Bs and guesthouses as well as accommodation in parks and reserves.

There are some simply outstanding places to stay if you're prepared to pay for them. These include private game reserves, top-quality guesthouses and lodges, and the odd superb hotel. There are also many not-so-superb offerings which can be expensive disappointments, so be selective.

Camping

Camping and caravans (that's trailers to North Americans) are very popular and most towns have a cheap municipal caravan park or resort close to the centre of town. These can be very basic but are often both pleasant and good value. The National Parks Board and the provincial authorities operate quality camping grounds. Chains such as **Aventura** (W *www.aventura.co.za*) have elaborate resorts, with guards on the gate, swimming pools, restaurants and sometimes on-site supermarkets. Chalets and cottages are often available at camp sites.

Depending on the level of facilities, camp sites (without electricity) range in price from about R40 to R60 (cheaper in parks and reserves). In summer at beach resorts you may have to pay R100 or more for sites as they are geared to large tents and family holidays. You might be able to negotiate a lower rate for a two-person tent but don't count on it. There's a good chance that a popular resort town will have a backpacker hostel, where you can pitch your tent for about R35.

Many places ban nonporous groundsheets. Most small tents have these sewn in. This is to stop the grass being killed by tents pitched for weeks at a time, so if you're only staying a night or two you might convince the manager that your tent won't do any harm. It's probably best just to avoid the subject. Some caravan parks don't allow tents at all. Often, this is due to bad experiences with drunken locals. If you make it clear that you're a clean-living foreigner, you might get a site.

In some rural areas of the former Homelands (where there are few official camp sites) you can still free-camp (ie, camp anywhere, *not* camp for free). *Always* ask permission from the nearest village or home before setting up (permission given by children doesn't count). The person you ask might have to seek permission from someone else, so be patient. This is not just good manners; you risk robbery or worse if you ignore local sensibilities. Once you have permission you are, to some extent, the guest of the local community. Find the most important person you can but don't go stomping into a village demanding to see the chief. There's a good chance that a community willing to let you camp will offer you a hut for the night.

Cottages, Huts & Rondavels

The cheapest self-catering accommodation is usually in farm cottages, which can be excellent value. You might find something for about R100 a double, although most start at around R150. They are usually comfortable but in some you'll have to do without electricity and you might even have to pump water. Small-town information centres are the best places to find out about inexpensive farm cottages, and in a small community there's a chance that you'll get a ride to the cottage if you don't have transport.

Self-catering cottages are often available in caravan parks and resorts, both municipal and private. The National Parks Board has excellent-value, fully equipped cottages. Most of these cottages are aimed at family groups, so they can be a little expensive for one or two people, starting at around R220 for one or two people, plus R60 for each additional person. Most parks also have other accommodation with shared bathrooms and kitchens from around R100 a double.

To confuse things, cottages are also called chalets, cabins and rondavels. At the top end, a comfortable cottage will come with aircon, bedding and a fully equipped kitchen. At the bottom end, a rondavel might simply have a couple of bunks, with mattresses but no bedding, a table and chairs, and a basin – rudimentary but quite adequate if you are travelling with a sleeping bag and basic cooking equipment.

Hostels

The past few years have resulted in an explosion in the number of backpacker hostels, making South Africa one of the most backpacker-friendly countries in the world. However, the hostels are clustered in popular areas such as Cape Town and along the Garden Route, so there are still large areas of the country where camping is the only option for shoestringers. Nearly all hostels are of a high standard and a dorm bed costs around R50 a night. Many hostels also offer private rooms, which cost from about R140 a double. Some will let doubles as singles for a little less.

The international YHA organisation is represented (it's called Hostelling International here). However, almost all HI hostels are just privately owned hostels which pay a fee to use the HI logo. There's no noticeable difference between HI hostels and any others. For more information, contact the **HI head office** (☎ *021-424 2511, fax 424 4119, 73 St Georges Mall, Cape Town,* **W** *www .hisa.org.za*).

B&Bs & Guesthouses

There is an enormous number of B&Bs and guesthouses (the distinction between them is pretty vague) in South Africa, and it's a rare town that doesn't have at least one. Some of the cheapest places aren't much to write home about, but on the whole the standard is extremely high.

If you're travelling on the sort of budget that would allow you to stay in B&Bs in the UK or motels in Australia or the USA, you will be pleasantly surprised by the standards and prices of B&B places here. Unlike British B&Bs, many South African establishments offer much more than someone's spare room, and unlike motels they are individual and often luxurious. Antique furniture, a private veranda, big gardens and a pool are common. Many have separate guest entrances and private bathrooms.

Breakfasts are enormous and usually excellent. Many hosts offer regional specialities and traditional dishes, giving you an insight into South African food that you don't get in restaurants.

Many regions have B&B organisations that take bookings (ask at local tourist offices). For information on consistently excellent places to stay covering a wide range of budgets, consult the various booklets produced by the **Portfolio Collection** (☎ *011-880 3414, fax 788 4802, Box 52350, Saxonwold, Johannesburg 2132,* **W** *www .portfoliocollection.com*).

Hotels

Before the boom in B&B accommodation, almost every town in the country had at least one hotel offering reasonable accommodation and meals. Now, many of the cheaper places have found that they can't compete and have either lifted their standards and prices or have stopped offering accommodation altogether. This is a pity, as some old country-town pubs were basic but pleasant places with real atmosphere.

If you can find one, the average two-star country-town hotel charges from around R150/200 a single/double, often including breakfast. There might be cheaper rooms with shared bathrooms (maybe R100 per person) but this isn't usual. In areas of tourist interest, prices are usually higher. It's rare to find a hotel which is not clean and comfortable, and the bar is always a good place to meet locals. Most rooms have TV and direct-dial phones. Larger towns have more-expensive hotels as well.

In the former Homelands the hotel situation is a bit different. There is usually a top-end Sun Hotel with an attached casino but the smaller pubs are usually just drinking places.

Hotel Chains   The chain **Formule 1** (☎ *011-807 0750, fax 807 3888,* **W** *www.hotelform ule1.co.za*) offers basic, clean and secure accommodation from R127 for a room that sleeps up to three people. At its 'hotels' all rooms have private bathroom (these rooms cost R159 a night) and there's a continental breakfast available for R9; the cheaper rooms are at the Formule Inn, where all rooms have shared bathrooms and no breakfast. All rooms are pretty small, with a bunk combining a double at the base and a single on top, which makes them fine for a couple or a family of three. Some are scruffy and a bit depressing. There are Formule 1 hotels in most major cities and towns including three in Cape Town and nine in Jo'burg.

City Lodge (☎ *011-884 0660,* **W** *www .citylodge.co.za*) is a group with several levels of purpose-built hotels. Road Lodges are very slightly superior to Formule 1 hotels and cost a little more. Town Lodges cost around R260 a double, City Lodges cost about R360 a double, and Courtyard Hotels cost from R500 a double.

The **Holiday Inn** (☎ *011-482 3500,* **W** *www .basshotels.com/holiday-inn*) chain includes Holiday Inn Express Hotels with 'no-frills' rooms for about R250, and Holiday Inn Garden Court Hotels, which are (usually) modern, reliably comfortable but with low service levels. Singles/doubles cost around R300/450, although there are often specials deals. There are a few Holiday Inns and Holiday Inn Crowne Plazas that offer higher levels of service, and charge from around R500/600, with large weekend discounts.

The Southern Sun group is associated with Holiday Inn and has more-expensive hotels.

Protea (☎ *0800 11 9000 toll free,* W *www.proteahotels.com*) is another large chain of mid-range to top-end hotels. Rates vary quite a lot but the average prices are R300/400 for singles/doubles. Most Protea places are pre-existing hotels that have decided to join the chain, so standards can be a bit inconsistent. If you're planning on staying at a lot of these hotels then check out the Prokard Club, membership of which gives you a discount of at least 20% on all Protea hotel rates.

Sun International (☎ *011-780 7800,* W *www.sun-international.co.za*) is a chain of tourist hotels, invariably with casinos attached and almost all of which are in the former Homelands. They are a hangover from the apartheid era, when gambling was illegal in South Africa but legal in the Homelands. Standards and prices vary a little but are never less than high. Because they are resort-style hotels, their rates aren't geared to overnight stays – a two-night midweek package can cost as little as R600/850, although the same deal at the Palace of the Lost City in Sun City will cost you over R2500.

FOOD

Once, eating out in South Africa was a matter of choosing a cut of steak and, if it was a fancy restaurant, whether you wanted a baked potato or chips. Thanks to the enormous influx of foreign visitors since 1994, the food situation is improving dramatically. There are still plenty of towns where steak and chips (and veg if you insist) are all that's on offer, but in the cities and tourist areas the choice is rapidly expanding.

Unfortunately there are still some hangovers from the old days. Dishes are often 'South Africanised', with far fewer spices and much more sugar or fat than most of us are used to. For example, spaghetti marinara is likely to come smothered in a 'rich, creamy sauce' a couple of centimetres thick and utterly bland. If you're travelling here for a while and eating in restaurants, you'll come to dread the words 'rich and creamy'.

Part of the reason for the blandness is that although many restaurants and cafes have opened, the food is still prepared the way it is in the family home – by poorly paid, untrained kitchen staff. Whites grew up eating this sort of food, so it's fine by them, and they are, after all, the main customers.

Prices are remarkably consistent. In pubs and steakhouses, steak or fish dishes will cost between R40 and R60.

Most restaurants are licensed but some allow you to bring your own wine for little or no corkage charge, especially in the Cape. This works out cheaply, especially if you've done the rounds of a few vineyards. Call ahead to check the restaurant's policy.

There is a small but increasing number of restaurants serving African dishes, most of which don't originate in South Africa. The staple for most blacks is a rice or mealie (maize) meal, often served with a fatty stew. Although it isn't especially appetising, it's cheap. Servings of rice and stew are sold around minibus taxi ranks.

Traditional Afrikaans cuisine shows its Voortrekker heritage in foods such as biltong, the delicious dried meat, and rusks typical of those needed for the long journeys into the hinterland. *Boerewors* (spicy sausage) is the traditional sausage; even committed carnivores can find it unappetising. It may be that what you're eating isn't boerewors but *braaiwors* (barbecue sausage), an inferior grade. Real boerewors must be 90% meat, of which 30% can be fat. You can imagine what goes into unregulated braaiwors!

Cape Malay cuisine (see the boxed text) is available at specialist restaurants across the country, but particularly in Western Cape. Down the Western Cape coast there's also been a miniboom in outdoor restaurants, typically beside the beach, serving all-you-can-eat fish braais (barbecues). Whether you eat at these or not, failing to attend a braai in South Africa would be like failing to eat pasta in Italy.

One recent international success story is that of Nandos, a fast-food chain offering

Cape Malay Cuisine

Although some will undoubtedly find it overly stodgy and sweet, the unique Cape Malay cuisine (along with its close cousin Afrikaner cuisine) is well worth trying. This intriguing mix of Malay and Dutch styles originated in the earliest days of European settlement and marries pungent spices with local produce.

The most common Cape Malay dish you'll come across is *bobotie*, a kind of shepherd's pie made with light curried mince topped with savoury egg custard, and usually served on a bed of turmeric-flavoured rice with a side dab of chutney. There are a variety of *bredies* (pot stews of meat or fish, and vegetables); one unusual example is *waterblommetjie bredie*, a mutton dish with faintly peppery water-hyacinth flowers and white wine. Plenty of recipes make use of game; some include venison, which will be some type of buck.

For dessert there's *malva* pudding, a delicious sponge traditionally made with apricot jam and vinegar, and the very similar brandy pudding (note that true Cape cuisine – which is strongly associated with the Muslim community – contains no alcohol).

spicy, Portuguese-style chicken. Nandos made its name not only through cheap tasty food, but also through in-your-face advertising; one of its billboards on the way to Kruger National Park apparently read: 'Don't poach animals. Grill them'.

DRINKS
Beer

Draught beers are uncommon, and when you find them they are served in large (500ml) or small (250ml) glasses. Usually you will be sold lager-style beer in cans or *dumpies* (small bottles) for around R8. Be warned that in the bar (as opposed to the ladies' bar), beer is usually served in a 750ml bottle, sometimes called a *long tom*. Castle and Black Label are probably the most popular brands but Amstel and Carlsberg are also good. In the Cape provinces, look out for Mitchell's and Birkenhead's beers, which come from small breweries. Windhoek beer, brewed in Namibia, is popular because it is made with strictly natural ingredients. The alcohol content of beer is around 5%, about the same as Australian beer but stronger than UK or US beer. Even Castle Lite has 4% alcohol.

Wine

Wine was first made in South Africa in 1659. It is now an enormous industry, employing around 30,000 people in Western Cape. The wine is of a high standard and very reasonably priced. If you buy direct from a vineyard, you can get bottles for as little as R15, but in a bottle store R30 and up is a more realistic price. Of course, you can pay a lot more and, as always, there is a pretty close correlation between quality and price. Most restaurants have long wine lists and stock a few varieties in *dinkies* (250ml bottles), which is very handy if you want to try a few wines or are eating alone.

There are over 2500 South African wines on the market. No wine may use any estate, variety, vintage or origin declaration on its label without being certified and carrying a certification sticker to that effect. No South African sparkling wine may be called champagne, although a number of producers use chardonnay and pinot noir blends and the *méthode champenoise* (traditional method of making champagne). A few low-alcohol wines are available, and they aren't bad.

For more on wine see the special section 'Cape Wineries'.

ENTERTAINMENT

The low-class 'jazz halls' of the Coloured people's quarters in Durban, with their night-long orgies of drinking, gambling, indecent dancing and immorality, illustrate the depths of degradation to which the Natives, and in this case Asiatics of both sexes, fall when left to their own devices.

South Africa, A Planned Tour
by AW Wells, 1939

Although apartheid put a damper on this sort of behaviour, most travellers will be happy to know that, in the cities at least, the bad old days of unbridled hedonism are back in fashion. Clubbing is a major preoccupation of the young, and in Cape Town, for example, you can take your pick from scores of events on the weekends.

In Cape Town, Durban, Jo'burg and Pretoria you can find most forms of entertainment associated with big, Westernised cities, such as multiplex cinemas, theatres and live music. The quality is often high even if the range is sometimes a bit limited. There are entertainment listings (which include the small but healthy 'alternative' scene) in the newspaper the *Daily Mail & Guardian* and the monthly magazine *SA Citylife*.

Visiting a township shebeen (a previously illegal bar) is probably the most interesting entertainment around, and some have good music and dancing. However, it's unwise to enter a large township at night (or even during the day) without a trustworthy guide – even if your skin colour happens to be black. There are tours that visit shebeens, although you're going to have a better experience if you can arrange to go with someone who actually lives in the township, rather than turn up in a minibus with a whole lot of other tourists.

Outside the big cities and tourist areas, nightlife comes down to bars, the occasional cinema, and the odd casino in the former Homelands.

Pubs

Surprisingly, there are few Western-style pubs in South Africa. Jo'burg, Durban and Cape Town have a wide range of drinking places, and Kimberley is perhaps worth visiting for its atmospheric old pubs alone, but in smaller towns the situation is dire. Most towns have at least one hotel. Franchised bars, such as O'Hagans and Castle Corner, are appearing in larger towns, and while they are reasonable places, they aren't exactly steeped in atmosphere.

In the bad old days most South African pubs had a *kroeg* (bar) where the white men would drink, a ladies' bar and lounge where white couples would drink, and a hole in the wall where bottles would be sold to the blacks and coloureds. Since the collapse of apartheid, hotels are obliged to serve everyone everywhere but unofficial segregation is often the norm.

The men in the ladies' bars are very often embittered travelling salesmen, travel writers and drunks, who study the bottom of their glasses as if they were looking into a crystal ball. In general the bar, with its cheerful and gregarious black clientele, will be far more congenial for travellers, once they have established their bona fides.

SPECTATOR SPORTS

Sport is a very important part of life in South Africa, and is always an easy topic of conversation. Soccer (football) is the country's most popular sport, and is avidly supported by the black community. Rugby, the game of choice of Afrikaners, is still largely the preserve of whites, although efforts are being made by the sporting codes to popularise both games across the colour barriers.

Apart from other popular sports, such as horse-racing, tennis and athletics, there are are a couple of traditional games you might catch, including the Afrikaner game jukskei, where an object is thrown over a fixed distance at a stake driven into the ground. Kroonstad (in Free State) is the centre of national competition. Stick-fighting (like Little John and Robin Hood with their quarterstaffs) is a traditional game for men and boys in Zulu and other indigenous communities.

After Cape Town's failed bid for the 2004 Olympics, it came as a bitter blow for South Africa to narrowly miss out on the chance to host the 2006 soccer World Cup. In 2003, though, the cricket World Cup is scheduled to be played in the country.

Cricket

Fans of cricket tend to be English-speaking South Africans but for a while after South Africa's return to international sport in the 1992 World Cup, cricket occupied centre stage. The game was the first of the 'whites-only' sports to wholeheartedly adopt a nonracial attitude, and development programs in the townships are beginning to pay dividends. The national team, the Proteas, now includes several black and coloured players. The sport suffered a setback in 2000, however, when Hansie Cronje, the youngest captain in South Africa's cricketing history, admitted taking bribes of over US$100,000 to rig matches.

Golf

As elsewhere, golf is a predominantly white sport in South Africa. The international profile of South African golf has been kept up by champions such as Gary Player and Ernie Els. In June 2000, 32-year-old South African Retief Goosen won the prestigious US Open in Okalahoma, after a thrilling play-off against Mark Brooks. The country has several excellent golf courses (Fancourt Country Club Estate, for example, in George on the Garden Route was designed by Gary Player and has 36 holes) and some visitors organise their vacations entirely around golf.

Rugby

Although the 1995 World Cup, hosted and won by South Africa, saw the entire population go rugby mad, Rugby (Union, not League) is traditionally the Afrikaners' sport, Since then, cross-race support for the game has waned somewhat in the face of efforts to make the ethnic composition of teams more representative of society.

The most popular games to watch are those of the Super 12 tournament, in which four teams each from South Africa, Australia and New Zealand compete between late February and the end of May. If you're in town when one of these is on it's worth getting a ticket, as it would be for any international match.

Soccer

Soccer is supported by over 50% of the country (as opposed to 10% support for rugby). The national team is known as Bafana Bafana (literally 'boys boys', meaning 'our lads') and major teams in the local competition include the Kaiser Chiefs and the Orlando Pirates (known as Bucs, as in Buccaneers), both from the Jo'burg area. It was these two teams that were playing when 43 fans died in a crush at Jo'burg's Ellis Park stadium in April 2001.

Professional games are played between August and May, with teams competing in the Premier Soccer League and the knock-out Rothman's Cup.

SHOPPING

You'll find department stores and shopping malls in major cities and larger towns. Most towns have at least a well-stocked supermarket. Note that *kafee* (Afrikaans for cafe) traditionally means a small mixed business such as a milk bar or a small supermarket.

Fresh produce is often sold from roadside farm stalls; these can be simple shelters or elaborate buildings.

Most Western consumer goods are available, although in remote areas the range will be limited. African handicrafts are sold everywhere, ranging from items obviously made for the tourist market to genuine artefacts sold at very high prices. Most carvings of animals and people are not traditional, although some are still very nice. Township-produced crafts, such as wire-work, make great gifts, are inexpensive and light to carry.

For suggestions on other items to look out for, see the boxed text 'Crafts of the Region' in the Facts about South Africa chapter.

PEOPLES OF THE REGION

One of the most fascinating aspects of South Africa is that it is home to so many different peoples and cultures, from the ancient San and Khoikhoi to the Indians, Jews, Portuguese and many other recent immigrants who have added to the nation's ethnic kaleidoscope. The following is an overview of the history and cultures of the original peoples of the region, the San and Khoikhoi, the main Bantu-speaking tribes, the Basotho, Ndebele, Swazi, Tswana, Venda, Xhosa and Zulu, and the original European settlers and their slaves, who today make up the Afrikaner and the Cape coloured communities.

The First Peoples

San & Khoikhoi

The nomadic San (also known as Bushmen) have possibly lived in Southern Africa since around 100,000 BC. Culturally and physically, they developed differently from the Negroid peoples of Africa.

It is likely that among these widely dispersed people of such antiquity there were several distinct San cultures. Evidence does, however, suggest a widespread belief in a 'trickster' god who was not always beneficent, and that there was a spiritual relationship with the land.

Although San technology was simple, it was well adapted to the African environment. The San hunted with bows and poisoned arrows, and their tracking and hunting abilities were exceptional. You could say they were the first backpackers, transportability of their belongings and homes being a priority. They were also model conservationists who knew that to survive they had to preserve their habitat.

The San's principal cultural legacy is their extraordinary rock art. The rocks and caves of South Africa were their canvas, and the whole country is studded with examples of their rock painting. For natural detail, purity of line and an almost eerie sense of movement, the paintings, some of which date back 28,000 years, cannot be surpassed (see Visual Arts under Art in the Facts about South Africa chapter for more details).

Due to introduced diseases, loss of land and colonial genocide, the San have virtually disappeared – less than 10,000 now exist, mainly in Botswana and Northern Cape, with very few of them leading a traditional lifestyle.

There have been some recent successes for the remaining San people, though. In Northern Cape, 55,000 hectares of land was handed back to one surviving San group that had been forced out of the former Kalahari Gemsbok National Park during the apartheid years. The last speakers of one of the surviving San languages were among those accepting the land. There are also plans for a San cultural centre in Rietfontein in the far north-west of Northern Cape province.

Like the San, the Khoikhoi (Hottentot) and their culture have been subsumed into the Christianised and Westernised coloured population of the Cape provinces.

Inset: Zulu adornment (Photo by Mitch Reardon)

It is generally believed the Khoikhoi developed out of San groups living in the region of present-day Botswana. In addition to hunting and gathering food, they were pastoralists, raising cattle and oxen. The Khoikhoi migrated south, reaching present-day Cape of Good Hope about 2000 years ago. Because of the close relationship between the San and the Khoikhoi peoples, who intermarried and coexisted, both are often referred to as Khoisan peoples.

There are a number of physical similarities between the two groups. Both are characterised by almost honey-coloured skin; buttocks that can store reserves of fat (most other peoples store fat on the hips and stomach); and hair that forms tight curls. Also, both the San and Khoikhoi languages feature the suction stops (clicks) now common in other Southern African languages.

The seminomadic Khoikhoi lived in easily transportable huts, which were made with saplings covered with woven mats. The Nama, one of the main existing tribes, still build these characteristic huts (these days using hessian) around Steinkopf in Namaqualand on the north-west coast, and are still small-scale pastoralists. Another group, the Griqua, settled around Kokstad in KwaZulu-Natal.

Dotted around the Northern and Western Cape provinces are small Moravian mission stations where the Khoikhoi sought some kind of refuge from European invaders. Many of these places are still functioning as mission stations today, including Mamre, Witwater, Genadendal, Onseepkans, Elim, Pella and Wuppertal. The people speak a form of Afrikaans, and the church is a feature of their communal life.

Bantu-Speaking Peoples

The Bantu languages are a group of languages belonging to the Benue-Congo branch of the Niger-Congo family of languages. These languages are spoken from the equator to the Cape of Good Hope.

Thought to have migrated down the east coast, reaching present-day KwaZulu-Natal by AD 500, the Bantu-speaking tribes were the first rivals to the Khoisan. These tribes not only had domestic animals, they farmed crops (particularly maize), were metal workers and potters, and lived in settled villages.

By AD 500, Sotho-Tswana peoples (Tswana, Pedi, Basotho) had settled extensively on the highveld and the Nguni peoples (Zulu, Xhosa, Swazi and Ndebele) had moved down the east coast. The Venda, Lemba and Shangaan-Tsonga peoples remained in the north of the country.

Left: The San's principal cultural legacy is their extraordinary rock art. (Illustration by Sarah Jolly)

It seems that the first settlements were limited to areas receiving more than 600mm of rain annually, but between the 12th and 15th centuries AD they expanded onto the highveld of present-day Northern Province, Gauteng, Free State and Lesotho. There were no known Bantu settlements west of Great Fish River, or in territory that receives less than 200mm of rain annually, where crops could not be grown.

Although the Bantu migration must have made an impact on the eastern Khoisan it seems that the two groups either integrated or found a way to coexist. There was intermarriage, and the Xhosa and Zulu languages of the Bantu adopted the clicks characteristic of Khoisan languages. Khoisan artefacts are commonly found at the sites of Bantu settlements. Curiously, only one Bantu tribe adopted the use of bows and arrows, the most important Khoisan weapon.

The Bantu were Iron-Age peoples; the smelting techniques of some groups were not surpassed in Europe until the Industrial Revolution. Gold, copper and tin were also mined, and shafts 25m deep have been discovered. These were the people who, in Zimbabwe, found every known gold deposit except one.

Little is known about the history of these peoples before the twin disasters of European invasion and the *difaqane* or forced migration (see History in the Facts about South Africa chapter). Around this time, several of the peoples that have been more politically important in modern times – the Basotho, the Swazi and the Zulu – became prominent.

Today, the most numerous groups are the Basotho, Swazi, Tswana, Xhosa and Zulu. The Lobedu, Ndebele and Venda peoples are fewer in number, but have maintained very distinct cultures. Most of these groups were named by Europeans who wanted a term to describe a 'nation' of independent tribes who happened to be culturally and linguistically similar. Within the major groupings there are numerous smaller groups who consider themselves to be separate peoples. The main exceptions are the culturally homogeneous Basotho, Swazi and Zulu peoples, all of whom were led by strong leaders in the 19th century.

Although 'Bantu' is an accepted linguistic term, during the apartheid era it became a derogatory term for a black South African.

Basotho

History The Basotho (southern Sotho), who are sometimes just called Sotho, live in and around Lesotho and the Free State. See the History section in the Lesotho chapter for the history of the Sotho peoples.

Lesotho was never part of South Africa, so the traditional owners of the land were never forced off it. Its rugged terrain means that there are still isolated villages where life continues much as it always has. Also, Lesotho has very little industry, so most people still work the land.

Society & Culture Traditional culture in Lesotho consists largely of customs, rites and superstitions. The milestones of birth, puberty, marriage and death are associated with ceremonies. Cattle also play an important role, both as sacrificial animals and as a symbol of wealth and worth, as do the cultivation of crops and the vagaries of the weather.

Much of the folklore puts common sense into practice: Toasting fresh rather than stale bread is bad (because it causes rheumatism); when working at straining beer, take an occasional drink (or your hands will swell); a spider in a hut should not be molested (it's the strength of the family); a howling dog must be silenced immediately (or it will bring evil).

Music and dance play their part in both ceremonial occasions and everyday life. There are various kinds of musical instruments, including the *lekolulo*, a flute-like instrument played by herd boys; the *thomo*, a stringed instrument played by women; and the *setolo-tolo*, a stringed instrument played with the mouth by men.

Traditional medicine mixes rites and customs, with sangomas (healers) developing their own charms and rituals.

The Basotho are traditionally buried in a sitting position, facing the rising sun and ready to leap up when called.

The Basotho believe in a masculine supreme being but place a great deal of emphasis on *balimo* (ancestors), who act as intermediaries between the people and the capricious forces of nature and the spirit world.

Evil is a constant danger, caused by *boloi* (witchcraft; witches can be either male or female) and *thkolosi* (small, maliciously playful beings, similar to the Xhosa's *tokoloshe*). An *ngaka* is a learned man, a combination of sorcerer and doctor, who can combat these forces.

Much of the traditional culture is associated with avoiding misfortune and reflects the grim realities of life in a marginal agricultural region.

Tswana

History By the 19th century, the Tswana, also called Batswana, dominated much of present-day Northern Province, North-West Province, Northern Cape and large parts of Botswana. All hell broke loose in the terrible years of the difaqane. Although the Tswana did not come up directly against Shaka and his Zulu armies, they were ravaged by the Ndebele led by Mzilikazi.

Such was the devastation that when the first whites crossed the Vaal River in the 1830s, they believed the land was largely uninhabited. However, as the Boers moved further north, the Tswana rallied and fought back, sometimes with the help of white mercenaries. The Tswana also petitioned the British for protection. Eventually, in 1885, the British responded to the Boer expansion by establishing the British Protectorate of Bechuanaland (now Botswana), with Mafeking (now Mafikeng) as the capital.

The Transvaal Tswana were left to the tender mercies of the new Union of South Africa when it was created in 1910 after the Boer War. Many were forced to seek work in the new mines and industries that sprang up around Johannesburg. From the time the National Party came to power in 1948, however, the idea of creating black Homelands (based on existing black reserves) was pursued enthusiastically. Although the move was resisted by many black activists and leaders, Bophuthatswana (known as 'Bop') finally accepted 'independence' in 1977.

Bop was one of the most depressing and least coherent of the Homelands. Its territory was made up of seven enclaves. Six of these were scattered in an arc running from north of Pretoria to the west, with one of the main chunks bordering Botswana. The most isolated chunk, Thaba 'Nchu, lay on the highveld within the then Orange Free State just to the east of Bloemfontein.

Society & Culture The peoples of the highveld often built their houses and animal pens from stone and, in places, lived in large communities of up to 15,000 people that can only be described as towns. Not surprisingly, a sophisticated political structure developed. In parts of the Transvaal, some communities specialised in mining and metal production.

The Tswana formed clans within a larger tribal grouping, as did the rest of the Bantu-speaking peoples. This was a dynamic situation, with people entering or leaving clans and tribal groups, and the groups themselves consolidating or fragmenting. Their oral tradition describes dynastic struggles, often with competing sons splitting clans on the death of their father, the old chief. This segmentation often occurred peacefully, partly because there was sufficient land available for groups of people to move on to fresh pastures.

The various groups each had (and continue to have) totem animals, which they must not kill.

Ndebele

History The Ndebele are thought to be partly descended from the members of a renegade Zulu regiment who fled their homeland during the chaos of the difaqane and combined with a much older Nguni

Right: The Ndebele often decorate their houses with striking painted designs. (Illustration by Sarah Jolly)

group of settlers. In the 1820s they were a much feared fighting force whose expansion was only held in check by the Basotho. However, the arrival of the Voortrekkers in 1836 with their guns and horses spelled disaster, and their leader Mzilikazi was eventually forced to withdraw to the area that is modern-day Zimbabwe.

Meanwhile, the Ndebele peoples who remained in the Transvaal came under the heel of their new Boer masters. The former Homeland of KwaNdebele, which was the last to be formed, in 1981, was placed in a typically arbitrary and impoverished location in the north-western corner of what is now Mpumalanga.

Society & Culture Although the Ndebele aren't very numerous, their strikingly painted houses and the elaborate costume and decoration worn by Ndebele women assure them attention. Ndebele beadwork is dazzling; Ndebele women may load on as much as 25kg of beads and jewellery. Some parts of the costume are so elaborate that they cannot be removed without being destroyed, and the masses of copper rings worn on the ankles and neck are there for life.

Most of the Ndebele house painters learn their craft in childhood, under the guidance of parents, by painting toy houses with a mixture of ash and water. Nowadays the geometric paintings are usually done using whitewash and commercial PVA paint. The front of the building and sides of the courtyard usually match. The painting may be done for a special occasion such as *ukwendisa amasokana* (the return of male initiates). The designs of some Ndebele women painters, such as Francine Ndimande, are now exhibited worldwide.

Swazi

History The forebears of the Swazi peoples were an Nguni clan living on the coast of modern Mozambique, and even today their most important ritual involves the waters of the Indian Ocean. A few Swazis live in South Africa, but most are found in the independent Kingdom of Swaziland.

Like the Basotho people, the Swazis live in a country that never suffered from apartheid, so traditional structures are still in place. See the Facts about Swaziland section in the Swaziland chapter for more information about the history of the Swazi people.

Society & Culture In the rich and vigorous culture of the Swazi people, significant power is vested in the monarchy, both the king (Ngwenyama, the Lion) and his mother (Ndlovukazi, the She-Elephant). The kingdom is highly conservative, and in many ways illiberal, but it works and has popular support.

The identity of the Swazi nation is partly maintained by a tradition of age-related royal military regiments. These regiments provided the military clout to hold off invaders during the difaqane and have helped to minimise the potentially divisive differences between clans, while emphasising loyalty to the king and nation. Annual rituals such as the important Incwala or 'first fruits' ceremony and Umhlanga (Reed)

dance have the same effect of bolstering national identity. (See the Swaziland chapter for more details on these ceremonies.)

Mkhulumnchanti is the name of the Swazis' deity. Respect for both the aged and ancestors plays a large part in the complex structure of traditional Swazi society.

Unlike in many other postcolonial countries, the wearing of traditional clothing is as common among people in the Westernised middle classes as it is among rural labourers. It's not unusual to see a man on his way to work wearing an *amahiya* robe, with a spear in one hand and a briefcase in the other.

Most Swazis rely at least partly on traditional medicine. There are two types of practitioners, the *inyanga* (usually a man) and the sangoma (usually a woman).

Singing is important to Swazis and there are many songs to mark occasions or to pass the time. Some may only be sung at specified times.

Venda

Right: The Umhlanga (Reed) dance reminds the Swazi people of their relationship with the king. (Illustration by Sarah Jolly)

History The Venda people are something of an enigma, as no-one is certain of their origin. Just when they arrived in the Soutpansberg Range in the north-eastern corner of present-day Northern Province, and where they came from, remain matters of dispute among historians.

There are elements of Zimbabwean culture in Venda culture, including stone structures similar in style (if not scale) to the Great Zimbabwe

National Monument. Mining and metal-working, rather than agriculture, have long been important elements in the Venda economy and culture. To add to the confusion, there are the associated Lemba people, who claim to be of Jewish descent (for the fascinating story of the Lemba read Tudor Parfitt's *Journey to the Vanished City*), and who may be related to the Falashas of Ethiopia.

What is known is that in the early 18th century a group of Senzi and Lemba people, led by Chief Dimbanyika, crossed the Limpopo River and located a tributary which they called the Nzhelele (Enterer). They moved up the Nzhelele and into the Soutpansberg Range, calling their new land Venda, believed to mean 'Pleasant Land'.

At Lwandali they set up a *dzata* (chief's kraal). When Dimbanyika died, some of his people moved south down the Nzhelele where they established another dzata. Under the new chief, Thohoyandou, the Venda flourished and their influence was felt widely. When Thohoyandou disappeared mysteriously, this dzata was abandoned and there was a period of unrest as his offspring fought over the succession.

Several invaders then tried to take over the Venda lands. First came the Boers, then the Swazis, the Lobedu and the Tsonga. The Venda, however, managed to avoid being overrun throughout the 19th century, only admitting a few missionaries into their territory. This was partly due to its geographical isolation in the Soutpansberg Range, which made attack difficult, and partly due to the presence of the tsetse fly, which made this area unattractive to graziers.

It was not until 1898 that a Boer army of 4000 men made serious incursions into the Venda region, but the outbreak of the second Anglo-Boer War the following year stopped full annexation. Even under apartheid Venda was allowed partial self-government due to its isolation, and it was granted 'independent' Homeland status in 1979.

Society & Culture Traditional Venda society is matriarchal. Female priests supervise the worship of female ancestors. The *domba* (python dance) is a puberty rite performed by girls, but boys are included in the ceremony. This is unusual in that very few societies allow both sexes to attend puberty rituals.

Before the Venda area acquired 'independent' Homeland status (and a South African–supported dictator), there were about 30 independent chiefdoms; there was no overall leader.

Venda culture is extremely rich and diversified, and a visit to the many arts-and-crafts outlets in this region is always rewarding. About 4000 people are actively engaged in local arts-and-crafts industries, particularly pottery. (If you want to enter village workplaces, you'll need a guide.)

More disturbingly, Venda culture is associated with witchcraft and ritual murder, with body parts being used for muti (traditional medicines). An outbreak of muti murders, often of children, was recorded by journalists in the late 1980s and early 1990s, and was linked to politicians and businessmen wanting to acquire potions to ensure their success.

Xhosa

History The history of the original Xhosa clans can be dated back to the early 17th century, when small communities of Nguni pastoralists were loosely united in kingdoms in what is now Eastern Cape province. The main clan was the Gcaleka (in the former Homeland of Transkei), to which all the other clans, including the Mfengu, Ngquika, Qayl and Tembu (the clan of Nelson Mandela), deferred.

The Xhosa first came into contact with Boers in the 1760s. Both groups were heavily dependent on cattle, and both coveted the grazing land in the area known as the Zuurveld (the coastal strip from Algoa Bay to the Great Kei River). Conflict was inevitable, and the first of nine major frontier wars broke out in 1779. Skirmishing and brigandage (by blacks and whites) was virtually continuous over the next century, by which time the Xhosa had been left virtually landless.

By the beginning of the 19th century, the Xhosa were under pressure in the west from white expansion, and in the east and north from peoples fleeing from the difaqane. After the sixth frontier war (1834–35) the British declared the land between the Great Kei and Keiskamma Rivers the Province of Queen Adelaide, and allowed a limited degree of independence. In 1846, however, white colonialists invaded (the theft of an axe at Fort Beaufort was the flimsy pretext), beginning the seventh frontier war. In its aftermath, British Kaffraria was established, with its capital in King William's Town.

Increasing numbers of Xhosa were influenced by missionaries and drawn into the European cash economy as peasant labourers, but Sandile, the last Rharhabe or Xhosa chief in the Ciskei area, was not part of this shift, and provided a focal point for continued resistance. He mobilised the Xhosa in their last, increasingly desperate, attempts to retain their land until he was killed at the end of the ninth frontier war (1877–78).

The tragic events of the Great Cattle Killing of 1856–57 also contributed to the Xhosa's downfall. A young girl, Nongqawuse, saw visions that the desperate Xhosa chief Sarili and his people believed revealed how they could reconcile themselves with a spirit world that had allowed the theft of their lands. The spirits told Nongqawuse of the need to sacrifice cattle and crops, in return for which the whites would be swept into the sea. The British, of course, made no attempt to stop this senseless slaughter and destruction. As a result it is estimated that a third of the 90,000 Xhosa in the colony of British Kaffraria died of starvation and a further third were forced to emigrate as destitute refugees.

Right: Xhosa women often decorate their faces with white clay and wear large, turbanlike hats. (Illustration by Sarah Jolly)

During apartheid the Homelands of Transkei and Ciskei were

carved from former Xhosa lands. While the 'independent' Ciskei government suppressed the African National Congress (often violently), the Transkei became a base for the most radical of black action groups, the Azanian People's Liberation Army (APLA), whose 'one settler, one bullet' slogan continues to strike fear into the hearts of many white settlers.

Society & Culture Xhosa who maintain a traditional lifestyle are known as 'the red people' because of the red-dyed clothing worn by most adults. Different subgroups wear different costumes, colours and arrangements of beads. The Tembu and Bomvana favour red and orange ochres in the dyeing of their clothing while the Pondo and Mpondomise use a very light blue (nontraditional chemical dyes are now much in use). Beadwork and jewellery are culturally important. The *isi-danga* is a long turquoise necklace which identifies the wearer to their ancestors. The *ngxowa yebokwe* is a goatskin bag carried over the left shoulder on important occasions.

The Xhosa's deity is known variously as umDali, Thixo and Qamata. This deity also figured in the San religion – it's probable that the invading Xhosa adopted it from them. There are numerous minor spirits and there is a rich folklore which persists in rural areas.

A belief in witches (male and female) is strong, and witch burning is not unknown. Most witchcraft is thought to be evil, and the Xhosa's main fear is that they will be possessed by depraved spirits. The main source of evil is the tokoloshe, a mythical man-like creature which lives in water but is also kept by witches. One reason that many Xhosa keep their beds raised high off the ground is to avoid being caught in their sleep by the tiny tokoloshe.

Water is not always seen as containing evil, however. If someone drowns and their body is not recovered, it is assumed, joyously, that they have gone to join 'the people of the sea'. It is also believed that the drowned are reincarnated with special knowledge and understanding.

The *igqirha* (spiritual healer), being able to deal with both the forces of nature and the trouble caused by witches, holds an important place in traditional society. The *ixhwele* (herbalist) performs some magic but is more concerned with health. *Mbongi* are the holders and performers of a group's oral history and are like a cross between a bard and a court jester.

While there is a hierarchy of chiefs, the structure of Xhosa society is much looser than that of the Zulu.

Many people have the top of their left-hand little finger removed during childhood to prevent misfortune. Puberty rituals also figure heavily. Boys must not be seen by women during the three-month initiation period following circumcision; during this time the boys disguise themselves with white clay or in intricate costumes made of dried palm leaves. In the female puberty ritual, a girl is confined in a darkened hut while her friends tour the area singing for gifts.

Marriage customs and rituals are also important. Unmarried girls wear short skirts, which are worn longer as marriage approaches.

Facing page: Zulu danc (Illustration by Jenny Bowman)

Married women wear long skirts and cover their breasts. They often put white clay on their faces and wear large, turban-like cloth hats. Smoking long-stemmed pipes is also popular among married women.

Zulu

History The small Zulu clan became a huge and disruptive force in Southern Africa in the early 19th century under the warrior leader Shaka (see History in the Facts about South Africa chapter for more details). Dingaan, Shaka's half-brother, murderer and successor, continued the reign of terror and murdered the party of Trekboers (Wandering Farmers) lead by Piet Retief. That massacre was avenged at the Battle of Blood River in 1838, when 3000 Zulu were slaughtered.

After the disaster of Blood River, and facing internal dissent and further attacks by the Boers and the British colonists, Dingaan lost support and fled to Swaziland, where he was killed in 1840. His successor, Mpane, has been seen as a puppet ruler installed by the Europeans, but there is evidence that he played the British and Boers off against each other. Nevertheless, during his reign much Zulu land was signed over to European interests, especially to the British who had by this stage established the colony of Natal. Mpane was succeeded by his son Cetshwayo in 1873.

Cetshwayo inherited a reasonably stable kingdom, but pressures from the land-grabbing Boers in Transvaal was growing. While the British colonial government in Natal agreed that Boer encroachment was illegal, it gave little assistance to the Zulu, largely because the British had plans of their own. Their grand imperial scheme was to carve a British wedge into Africa, heading north from Durban, and the Zulu kingdom was directly in the way. Diplomatic chicanery ended with a British ultimatum with which Cetshwayo could not comply, and in January 1879 the British invaded the kingdom, beginning the Anglo-Zulu War.

The Zulus decisively defeated the British at the Battle of Isandlwana but, despite their overwhelming superiority in numbers, they failed to capture the small station at Rorke's Drift. After the battle things went downhill for the Zulus and Cetshwayo was defeated by the British in July at Ulundi.

Cetshwayo was summarily jailed and his power was divided between 13 British-appointed chiefs, many of whom opposed Cetshwayo. In 1882 Cetshwayo travelled to England to plead for his restoration, but the British response was to partition the kingdom according to the pro- and anti-Cetshwayo factions. This led to chaos and bloodshed, and in 1887 the British annexed Zululand. Dinizulu, Cetshwayo's son and the last independent Zulu king, was exiled to the island of St Helena. In 1897 the British handed over Zululand to the colony of Natal.

The current Zulu king is King Goodwill Zwelithini but tussling for power is Chief Mangosouthu Buthelezi, leader of the Inkatha Freedom Party (IFP), great-grandson of Cetshwayo, and home affairs minister in the South African government.

Society & Culture The Zulu traditionally believe that the creator of the world is Unkulunkulu (Old, Old Man), but his daughter Unomkubulwana is more important to everyday life as she controls the rain. Still more important are ancestors, who can make most things go well or badly depending on how assiduously a person has carried out the required sacrifices and observances.

In common with other peoples in the region, the important stages of Zulu life – birth, puberty, marriage, death – are marked by ceremonies. The clothes people wear reflect their status and their age. For example, girls may not wear long skirts until they become engaged. Animal skins are worn to reflect status, with a leopard-skin cloak signifying a chief.

Since Shaka's time, when the Zulu clan became a large and dominant tribe, the *inoksa* (king) has been the leader of all the people. Before Shaka there was a looser organisation of local chiefs and almost self-sufficient family groups.

Dancing and singing are important in Zulu culture, and if you see an IFP demonstration, you'll feel something of the power of massed Zulu singing.

Afrikaans-Speaking Peoples
Afrikaners

The Boers' history of geographical isolation combined with often deliberate cultural seclusion, created a unique people who are often called the 'white tribe of Africa'. (See History in the Facts about South Africa chapter for more details.) The Boers' lifestyle and culture, both real and idealised, have been the dominant factors shaping Afrikaners' view of themselves and their place in Africa.

The ethnic composition of the Afrikaners is difficult to quantify, but it is estimated to be made up of 40% Dutch, 40% German, 7.5% French, 7.5% British and 5% other. Some historians have argued that the '5% other' figure includes a significant proportion of blacks and coloureds.

Afrikaans, the only Germanic language to have evolved outside Europe, is central to the Afrikaner identity, but it has also served to reinforce their isolation from the outside world. The Afrikaners are a religious people and their brand of Christian fundamentalism based on 17th-century Calvinism is still a powerful influence.

Rural South Africa, with the exception of Eastern Cape, KwaZulu-Natal and the former Homelands, is still dominated by Afrikaners, and outsiders are often regarded with a degree of suspicion. Life in the country towns revolves around the Dutch Reformed Churches.

There are a number of influential Afrikaner cultural organisations, including the secret Afrikaner Broederbond, which has dominated National Party politics; the Federasie van Afrikaanse Kultuuvereniginge (FAK), which coordinates cultural events and movements; and the Voortrekkers, an Afrikaner youth organisation based on the scouting movement.

Some Afrikaners still dream of a 'volkstaat' (an independent, racially pure Boer state) where the only citizens would be descendants of the Voortrekkers or those who fought in the Anglo-Boer Wars. The Afrikaner-only town of Orania in Northern Cape is one town that residents hope will be the foundation of such a state.

The urbanised middle class tends to be considerably more moderate. The further the distance between the horrors of the apartheid era and the 'new South Africa', though, seemingly the more room there is for Afrikaners to be proud of their heritage. One expression of this has been the growing success of the Klein Karoo Nasionale Kunstefees (Little Karoo National Arts Festival), an all-Afrikaans art festival which attracts an audience of over 70,000 and embraces a diverse range of drama and music (see the Oudtshoorn section of the Western Cape chapter for more details).

Coloureds

The coloureds, sometimes known as Cape coloureds or Cape Malays, and including Cape Muslims, are South Africans of long standing. Although many were brought to the early Cape Colony as slaves, others were political prisoners and exiles from the Dutch East Indies. Some of the first prisoners on Robben Island were Muslims. People were brought from countries as far away as India and present-day Indonesia, as well as East Africa, but their lingua franca was Malay (at the time an important trading language), which is why they came to be called Cape Malays.

Although Islam could not be practised openly in the colony until 1804, the presence of influential and charismatic political and religious figures among the slaves helped a cohesive community to develop. The Cape's Muslim culture has survived intact over the centuries, and has even resisted some of the worst abuses of apartheid. The strongest evidence of it is in Cape Town's Bo-Kaap district, the circle of some 25 karamats (tombs of Muslim saints) that circle the city and, to a lesser extent, in Simon's Town (see the Cape Town & the Peninsula chapter for more details).

The slaves who moved out with the Dutch to the hinterland – many losing their religion and cultural roots in the process – had a much worse time of it. And yet practically all the coloured population of the Western Cape and Northern Cape provinces today are bound by the unique language, Afrikaans, that began to develop from the interaction between the slaves and the Dutch over three centuries ago. One of the oldest documents in Afrikaans is a Quran transcribed using Arabic script.

The most public secular expression of Cape coloured culture today is the riotous Cape Minstrel Carnival (see the boxed text 'The Cape Minstrel Carnival' in the Cape Town & the Peninsula chapter). At the end of Ramadan you can catch thousands of Muslims praying on Cape Town's Sea Point promenade, where they gather to sight the new moon. More privately, *khalifa* – the ritual piercing of flesh with blades while in a religious trance – is still practised by some.

During apartheid, a sense of community developed among coloureds as a result of whites' refusal to accept them as equals and their own refusal to be grouped socially with blacks.

Getting There & Away

AIR

South Africa – and the region's – main international airport remains Johannesburg International Airport (JIA) but there are an increasing number of international flights to Cape Town and a few to Durban. See the Johannesburg (Jo'burg) section in the Gauteng chapter and the Cape Town & the Peninsula chapter for a list of airlines.

Buying Tickets

Buying a plane ticket – probably the single most expensive item in your budget – can be an intimidating business. There is likely to be a multitude of airlines and travel agencies hoping to separate you from your money, so it's always worth putting aside a few hours to research the current state of the market. The Internet is an increasingly useful resource for doing this.

Start early – some of the cheapest tickets have to be bought months in advance,

---

---

and some popular flights sell out early. Talk to other recent travellers, look at the ads in newspapers and magazines and watch for special offers. Then phone around travel agencies or check on the Internet for bargains. (Airlines can supply information on routes and timetables but are unlikely – except during interairline price wars – to tell you about the cheapest tickets. The exception to this is their Web sites, which can sometimes yield good deals.) Find out the fare, the route, the duration of the journey and any restrictions on the ticket. (See Restrictions in the boxed text 'Air Travel Glossary' in this chapter for more details.)

Use the fares quoted in this book as a guide only. They are approximate and based on the rates advertised by travel agencies at the time of going to press. Also, quoted air fares do not necessarily constitute a recommendation for the carrier.

If you're travelling from the UK or the USA, you'll probably find that the cheapest flights are being advertised by obscure 'bucket shops' (small businesses that sell cheap airline tickets) whose names haven't yet reached the telephone directory. Many such firms are honest and solvent but there are a few rogues who will take your money and disappear, to reopen elsewhere a month or two later under a new name. If you feel suspicious about a firm, don't give them all the money at once – leave a deposit of 20% or so and pay the balance when you get the ticket. Better still, pay by credit card if you can, since most card providers will offer refunds if you can prove you didn't get what you paid for. Similar protection can be obtained by buying a ticket from a bonded agent, such as one covered by the **Air Travel Organiser's Licence** *(ATOL;* **W** *www.atol .org.uk)* scheme in the UK. If the agent insists on cash in advance, go somewhere else. And once you have the ticket, ring the airline to confirm that you are actually booked onto the flight.

You may decide to pay more than the rock-bottom fare by opting for the security of a better-known travel agency, such as STA Travel, which has offices worldwide, Council Travel in the USA or Travel CUTS in Canada. All offer competitive prices to most destinations.

Once you have your ticket, write the number down, together with the flight number and other details, and keep this information somewhere separate. If the ticket is lost or stolen, this information will help you get a replacement.

If you purchase a ticket and later want to make changes to your route or get a refund, you may need to contact the original travel agency. Airlines issue refunds only to the purchaser of a ticket – usually the travel agency who bought the ticket on your behalf. Many travellers change their routes halfway through their trips, so think carefully before you buy a ticket that is not easily refunded.

South Africa Although South Africa isn't exactly a hub of international travel, it's still possible to get some good deals to or from Europe, North America and Australia, especially when you take into account the low value of the rand. The low season for flying out of South Africa is any month without school holidays (ie, February, March, May, July, August, October and November), although currently a lot of cheap fares to Europe are available at other times.

The low season to South Africa from Europe and North America is typically in April and May, while the high season is between July and September. The rest of the year, with the exception of several weeks around Christmas (which is considered high season), falls into the shoulder season category.

There aren't many discount-travel outlets in South Africa but as always it is worth shopping around. The following companies are a good start:

Flight Centre (☎ 021-425 6894) Cape Town. This international agency has several offices around the country and guarantees to beat any genuine quoted current price.

Rennies Travel (☎ 011-407 3211, W www .renniestravel.co.za) This is a comprehensiv network of agencies throughout South Afric and is the agent for Thomas Cook.
STA Travel (☎ 011-447 5414, W www.statrave .co.za) The Arcade, 34 Mutual Gardens, Cn Oxford Rd & Tyrwhitt Ave, Rosebank, Jo'burg (☎ 021-418 6570) 31 Riebeeck St, Cape Town This international organisation, which has of fices throughout the country, has practically taken over the student/budget travel agency business in Southern Africa.

Also check out the travel ads in the *Jo'burg Star* and its sister publication, the *Pretori News*, for deals.

Travellers with Special Needs

If you have special needs of any sort – you've broken a leg, you're vegetarian, travelling i a wheelchair, taking the baby, terrified of fly ing – you should let the airline know as soo as possible so that it can make arrangement accordingly. You should remind the airline when you reconfirm your booking (at least 72 hours before departure) and again when yo check in at the airport. It may also be worth ringing around the airlines before you make your booking to find out how they can handle your particular needs.

Airports and airlines can be surprisingly helpful but they do need advance warning Most international airports will provide es corts from the check-in desk to the plane where needed, and there should also be ramps lifts, and accessible toilets and phones.

Aircraft toilets, on the other hand, may present a problem for those with impaired mobility. Travellers should discuss this with the airline at an early stage and, if neces sary, with their doctor.

Guide dogs for the blind generally have to travel in a specially pressurised baggage compartment with other animals, although smaller guide dogs may be admitted into the cabin with their owner. Guide dogs are sub ject to the same quarantine laws as any other animal (six months in isolation) when enter ing or returning to/from countries currently free of rabies (such as Britain or Australia)

Deaf travellers can ask for airport and in flight announcements to be written down fo them.

Air Travel Glossary

Alliances Many of the world's leading airlines are now intimately involved with each other, sharing everything from reservations systems and check-in to aircraft and frequent-flyer schemes. Opponents say that alliances restrict competition. Whatever the arguments, there is no doubt that big alliances are the way of the future.

Courier Fares Businesses often need to send urgent documents or freight securely and quickly. Courier companies hire people to accompany the package through customs and, in return, offer a discount ticket, which is sometimes a bargain. However, you may have to surrender all your baggage allowance and take only carry-on luggage.

Fares Airlines traditionally offer 1st-class (coded F), business-class (coded J) and economy-class (coded Y) tickets. These days there are so many promotional and discounted fares available that few passengers pay full fare.

Lost Tickets If you lose your airline ticket, an airline will usually treat it like a travellers cheque and, after inquiries, issue you with another one. Legally, however, an airline is entitled to treat it like cash and if you lose it then it's gone forever. Take very good care of your tickets.

Onward Tickets An entry requirement for many countries is that you have a ticket out of the country. If you're unsure of your next move, the easiest solution is to buy the cheapest onward ticket to a neighbouring country or a ticket from a reliable airline that can later be refunded if you do not use it.

Open-Jaw Tickets These are return tickets where you fly out to one place but return from another. If available, this can save you backtracking to your arrival point.

Overbooking Since every flight has some passengers who fail to show up, airlines often book more passengers than they have seats. Usually excess passengers make up for the no-shows, but occasionally somebody gets 'bumped' onto the next available flight. Guess who it is most likely to be? The passengers who check in late. If you do get 'bumped', you are normally offered some form of compensation.

Reconfirmation Some airlines require you to reconfirm your flight at least 72 hours prior to departure. Check your travel documents to see if this is the case.

Restrictions Discounted tickets often have various restrictions on them – such as needing to be paid for in advance and incurring a penalty to be altered or cancelled. Others are restrictions on the minimum and maximum period you must be away.

Round-the-World Tickets These tickets give you a limited period (usually a year) in which to circumnavigate the globe. You can go anywhere the carrying airlines go, as long as you don't backtrack. The number of stopovers or total number of separate flights is decided before you set off and they usually cost a bit more than a basic return flight.

Ticketless Travel Airlines are gradually waking up to the realisation that paper tickets are unnecessary encumbrances. On simple one-way or return trips, reservation details can be held on computer and the passenger merely shows ID to claim their seat.

Transferred Tickets Airline tickets cannot be transferred from one person to another. Travellers sometimes try to sell the return half of their ticket, but officials can ask you to prove that you are the person named on the ticket. On an international flight, tickets are compared with passports.

Children under two years travel for 10% of the standard fare (or for free on some airlines), as long as they don't occupy a seat. They don't get a baggage allowance. 'Skycots' should be provided by the airline if requested in advance; these will take a child weighing up to about 10kg. Children aged between two and 12 years can usually occupy a seat for half to two-thirds of the full fare, and do get a baggage allowance. Prams that fold can often be taken on board as hand luggage.

The disability-friendly Web site **W** www .everybody.co.uk has an airline directory that provides information on the facilities offered by various airlines.

Departure Tax

There's an airport departure tax of R34 for domestic flights, R57 for flights to regional (African) countries and R179 for other international flights. The tax is usually included in the ticket price.

The USA & Canada

The *New York Times*, *Los Angeles Times*, *Chicago Tribune* and *San Francisco Examiner* all produce weekly travel sections in which you'll find any number of travel agency ads.

North America's largest student travel organisation, **Council Travel** (☎ 800-226 8624, **W** *www.counciltravel.com*), and **STA Travel** (☎ 800-781 4040, **W** *www.statravel .com*) have offices in major cities throughout the USA. You may have to produce proof of your student status and in some cases be under 26 years of age to qualify for their discounted fares.

Ticket Planet (**W** *www.ticketplanet.com*) is a leading ticket consolidator in the USA and is recommended.

In Canada, the *Globe & Mail*, *Toronto Star*, *Montreal Gazette* and *Vancouver Sun* carry travel agencies' ads. **Travel CUTS** (☎ 800-667 2887, **W** *www.travelcuts.com*) has offices in all major cities as does **Flight Centre** (**W** *www.flightcentre.com*). The Vancouver-based tour company **Great Expeditions** (☎ 800-663 3364, **W** *www.great expeditions.com*) is also useful.

North America is a relative newcomer to the bucket-shop traditions of Europe and Asia, so ticket availability and the restrictions attached to them need to be weighed against what is offered on the standard Apex (advanced purchase expedition) or full-price economy tickets.

It's often cheaper to fly first to London on an inexpensive airline, then buy a bucket-shop or online ticket from there to Africa. Do some homework before setting off (see The UK later in this chapter).

From the US west coast it should be possible to get some good deals via Asia. Malaysia Airlines flies from Los Angeles to Kuala Lumpur (Malaysia) and from there to Jo'burg and Cape Town. There are no direct flights but they usually have good stopover deals. Malaysia Airlines flies from Cape Town to Buenos Aires, so you could put together a very interesting trip.

South African Airlines (SAA) flies to/from New York and Miami. You should be able to purchase one-way/return tickets from New York for US$1600/2200 and from Los Angeles for US$2000/2200.

From Jo'burg/Cape Town, a cheap one-way fare to Los Angeles costs from around R4800/5000, to New York it costs around R3680/4250 and to Toronto around R4270/4670.

Australia & New Zealand

STA Travel and Flight Centre are major dealers in cheap air fares. **STA Travel** (☎ 03 9349 2411, **W** *www.statravel.com.au, 224 Faraday St, Carlton, Melbourne)* has offices in all major cities, with its main office in Melbourne, and on many university campuses. **Flight Centre** (☎ 131 600 Australia-wide, **W** *www.flightcentre.com.au 82 Elizabeth St, Sydney)* has dozens of offices throughout Australia, with its main office in Sydney. It's also worth checking out the Internet (**W** www.travel.com.au) for competitive fares.

The best publications for finding good deals are the Saturday editions of the *Sydney Morning Herald* and the *Age* in Melbourne.

There are no direct flights from New Zealand. **Flight Centre** (☎ 09-309 6171 *www.flightcentre.com)* and **STA Travel** ☎ 09-309 0458, W *www.statravel.co.nz)* have many branches throughout the country.

There are direct flights from Sydney on Qantas and SAA, and from Perth on SAA, to Jo'burg and Cape Town. Expect to pay around A$2200 for a standard shoulder-season economy fare, but A$1600 for special deals. If you're thinking of including South Africa as a stop on a round-the-world ticket or as a stopover on a return ticket en route to Europe you'll be looking at around A$2300.

Air Mauritius has a few direct flights from Perth to Mauritius, with a stopover, then a direct flight to Jo'burg for around A$1300 return. It has other flights to South Africa via Mauritius, originating in Singapore, Hong Kong and Mumbai (Bombay).

Singapore Airlines and Malaysia Airlines often have the cheapest flights from Australia to Jo'burg and Cape Town. The hassle is that you travel via Singapore or Kuala Lumpur, which adds considerably to the flying time. There are more-or-less direct connections but you may want to take advantage of the airlines' stopover deals for each city.

From Jo'burg/Cape Town, one-way cheapies to Sydney go for as low as R3620/ 3780 on Malaysia Airlines. It's cheaper to fly to Perth R3180/3320. However, you'd spend a lot more than R450 getting from Perth to Sydney (even hitching you'd most likely spend more than that on food), so it's definitely worth spending the extra if you are heading for Australia's east coast.

The UK

The majority of travel agents in Britain are registered with **Association of British Travel Agents** *(ABTA;* W *www.abta.com)*. If you have bought your ticket from an ABTA-registered agency that then goes out of business, ABTA guarantees a refund or will arrange an alternative flight.

Buying your ticket from unregistered bucket shops is riskier but sometimes cheaper. London is the national centre for bucket shops, although all major cities have unregistered agencies as well.

The following companies are considered reliable:

Africa Travel Centre (☎ 020-7387 1211, W www .africatravel.co.uk) 4 Medway Court, 21 Leigh St, London WC1H 9QX. Specialises in Africa, and also has a video library.
STA Travel (☎ 020-7361 6262, W www.sta travel.co.uk) 86 Old Brompton Rd, London SW7 3LQ. The largest worldwide student/ budget travel agency.
Trailfinders (☎ 020-7938 3939, W www.trail finders.com) 194 Kensington High St, London W8 7RG. A complete travel service, including foreign exchange, a bookshop, information centre, visa service and immunisation centre. It also puts out a useful quarterly magazine.
Usit Campus (☎ 0870-240 1010, W www.usit campus.co.uk) 52 Grosvenor Gardens, London SW1W OAG. It also has offices in large YHA adventure shops and at university campuses around the UK.

It's worth checking the weekend broadsheet newspapers for ads. In London, there are also several magazines with lots of information and ads, including the weekly listing magazine *Time Out*, the *Evening Standard* and the free magazine *TNT*, which can be picked up at most London Underground stations and on street corners around Earls Court and Kensington. The latter caters mostly to Australians, New Zealanders and South Africans working in the UK.

In the magazines, you'll find discounted fares to Jo'burg as well as to other parts of Africa. Many of these fares are through Olympic or Turkish Airlines, however, these airlines are no longer more competitive than the major European and African airlines, such as SAA and Virgin.

Fares from the UK are very competitive; it's worth shopping around but you should be able to get a return flight to Jo'burg or Cape Town for anything between £350 and £450. Some airlines (eg, British Airways, KLM–Royal Dutch Airlines, SAA) will allow you to fly into Cape Town and leave from Jo'burg or vice versa (fares for travellers under 26 are around £450).

Although it is a long-haul flight to Southern Africa, it's pretty easy to handle (nothing like flying to Asia or Australia). The flight takes about 13½ hrs but it is overnight and as South Africa is only two hours ahead of GMT/UTC the body clock doesn't get too badly out of whack.

There are also interesting tickets available from the UK that include other ports in Africa, such as Cairo (Egypt), Nairobi (Kenya) and Harare (Zimbabwe). If you have plenty of time up your sleeve, you may find some good-value round-the-world tickets that include Jo'burg. Return tickets to Australia via Jo'burg and Asia are also worth looking at (fares for travellers under 26 are currently £800 to £900).

Cheap one-way fares from Jo'burg/Cape Town to the UK can be as low as R2390/R2730.

Continental Europe

You can fly to South Africa from any European capital, but the major hubs are Paris, Amsterdam and Frankfurt. Specialist travel agencies advertise in newspapers and travel magazines, so check their ads and then start ringing around. You can also check the following recommended agencies:

France

Connect Voyages (☎ 01 42 44 14 00) 14 rue de Vaugirard, 75006 Paris; plus branches across France

Nouvelles Frontières (nationwide ☎ 08 25 00 08 25, in Paris ☎ 01 45 68 70 00, W www .nouvelles-frontieres.fr) 87 blvd de Grenelle, 75015 Paris; with branches across France

OTU Voyages (☎ 01 40 29 12 12, W www.otu .fr) 39 ave Georges-Bernanos, 75005 Paris; also with branches across France (OUT and Connect are student and young person specialists.)

Voyageurs du Monde (☎ 01 42 86 16 00) 55 rue Ste-Anne, 75002 Paris

Germany

STA Travel (☎ 030-311 0950) Goethestrasse 73, 10625 Berlin; plus branches in major cities

Usit Campus (call centre ☎ 01805 788336, in Cologne ☎ 0221 923990, W www.usitcampus .de) 2a Zuelpicher Strasse, 50674 Cologne; plus offices around Germany

Italy

CTS Viaggi (☎ 06-462 0431) 16 Via Genova, Rome; student and youth specialist with branches in major cities

Passagi (☎ 06-474 0923) Stazione Termini FS, Galleria Di Tesla, Rome

The Netherlands

Budget Air (☎ 020-627 1251, W www.nbbs.nl) 34 Rokin, Amsterdam

Holland International (☎ 070-307 6307) Offices in most cities

NBBS Reizen (☎ 020-620 5071, W www.nbbs .nl) 66 Rokin, Amsterdam; plus branches in most cities

Switzerland

Nouvelles Frontières (☎ 022-906 80 80) 10 rue Chante Poulet, Geneva

SSR (☎ 022-818 02 02, W www.ssr.ch) 8 rue de la Rive, Geneva; plus branches throughout the country

Africa

Most regional African airlines fly to/from South Africa. Air Afrique flies to various West African countries; Air Gabon flies to Libreville (Gabon), with connections to West Africa and Europe; and Air Botswana flies to various South African cities. There are plenty of other regional airlines and SAA also has inter-Africa flights. The following are air services and peak-season one-way fares to destinations in the region. Sometimes it will be cheaper for you to buy a return rather than a one-way fare. For more fares from Swaziland and Lesotho see the Getting There & Away sections in those chapters.

Botswana Air Botswana flies between Gaborone and Jo'burg for R430.

Lesotho SAA flies frequently between Moshoeshoe international airport, 18km from Maseru and Jo'burg for R450. There are some deals on return fares (around R540) – ask a travel agent

Mozambique SAA flies between Maputo and Jo'burg for R820 (return R980).

Namibia Comair/British Airways and Air Namibia fly between Windhoek and Jo'burg for R1310 (return R1650) and Cape Town for R1200 (return R1500).

Swaziland Airlink Swaziland operates out of Matsapha international airport, west of Manzini (Schedules and tickets often refer to the airport as 'Manzini'.) Services include Jo'burg for R370.

Zimbabwe Air Zimbabwe flies from Jo'burg to Harare daily for R1870 (return R1770). There are also flights to Bulawayo and Victoria Falls. Comair/British Airways also fly between South

Africa and Victoria Falls for R860 and to Harare – see the Getting Around chapter for phone numbers in various cities.

Middle East

Some travel agencies in Israel (particularly in Tel Aviv) and in Istanbul offer discount travel tickets.

In Tel Aviv, there is the **Israel Student Travel Association** *(ISSTA;* ☎ *03-524 6322, 128 Ben Yehuda St)*, which also has an office in Jerusalem *(*☎ *02-625 2799, 31 HaNevi'im St)*.

In Istanbul there are lots of travel agencies on the northern side of Divan Yolu in Sultanahmet, all of them specialising in budget air tickets. **Orion-Tour** *(*☎ *212-248 8437,* **W** *www.oriontour.com)* is highly recommended.

The area around Midan Tahrir in Cairo is teeming with travel agencies but don't expect any amazing deals. One of the best agencies in Cairo is **Egypt Panorama Tours** *(*☎ *02-350 5880,* **e** *ept@intouch.com)* just outside the Al-Ma'adi metro station.

Asia

Bangkok, Singapore and Hong Kong are the best places to shop around for discount tickets. Hong Kong's travel market can be unpredictable, though.

Khao San Rd in Bangkok is the budget travellers headquarters. Bangkok has a number of excellent travel agencies, but there are also some suspect ones; ask the advice of other travellers before handing over your cash. **STA Travel** *(*☎ *02-236 0262, 33 Surawong Rd)* is a good and reliable place to start.

In Singapore, try **STA Travel** *(*☎ *65-737 7188,* **W** *www.statravel.com.sg, 35a Cuppage Road, Cuppage Terrace)*. Chinatown Point shopping centre on New Bridge Rd has a good selection of travel agencies.

Hong Kong has a number of excellent, reliable travel agencies and some not-so-reliable ones. A good way to check on a travel agency is to look it up in the phone book: fly-by-night operators don't usually stay around long enough to get listed. **Phoenix Services** *(*☎ *2722 7378, fax 2369 8884,*

Room B, 6th floor, Milton Mansion, 96 Nathan Rd, Tsimshatsui), is recommended. Other agencies to try are **Shoestring Travel** *(*☎ *2723 2306, Flat A, 4th floor, Alpha House, 27-33 Nathan Rd, Tsimshatsui)*, and **Traveller Services** *(*☎ *2375 2222, Room 1012, Silvercord Tower 1, 30 Canton Rd, Tsimshatsui)*.

In India you can get cheap tickets in both Mumbai and Kolkata (Calcutta), but the real wheeling and dealing goes on in Delhi – there are a number of bucket shops around Connaught Place. One such place is **STIC Travels** *(*☎ *011-332 0239, 1st floor, West Wing, Chandralok Building, 36 Janpath, New Delhi)*, an agent of STA Travel.

Air India, Cathay Pacific, Malaysia Airlines, Singapore Airlines, Thai Airways and other Asian airlines now fly to South Africa (most to Jo'burg).

From Jo'burg/Cape Town to Kuala Lumpur or Singapore costs about R3010/3170; a cheap one-way fare to Mumbai costs from R3860/4615.

South America

SAA and Varig link Jo'burg and Cape Town with Rio de Janeiro and Sao Paulo. Currently, Malaysia Airlines offers good deals on flights to Buenos Aires: A one-way ticket from Jo'burg/Cape Town is around R2335/2260.

LAND

If you're planning an overland trip through Africa you should consider getting a copy of Lonely Planet's *Africa on a shoestring*.

With the exception of the Jordan or Israel-Egypt connection, all overland travel to Africa has to be done through Europe and involves a ferry crossing.

In the past, you had a choice of two routes to South Africa: through the Sahara from Morocco via West Africa and Central Africa, or up the Nile from Egypt to Uganda or Kenya and then through Tanzania. Due to civil wars these routes are effectively closed.

If you take the Sahara route through North and West Africa, your options are currently limited to starting in Morocco and Mauritania, then into Senegal and the rest of West Africa as the routes through Algeria into Mali and Niger are blocked due to political unrest. There's more unrest – to say the least – in Congo (Zaïre), so a flight will be necessary from Accra (Ghana), Lagos (Nigeria) or Yaoundé (Cameroon) to Nairobi (Kenya).

The route from Egypt is notoriously difficult due to the fraught conditions between Sudan and Ethiopia. However, we have had reports from travellers who have managed to cross the Sudan/Ethiopian border at Metema. If your starting point in Africa is Egypt, you could take a flight from Cairo – or at best from Khartoum – to Kampala (Uganda) or Nairobi. Alternatively, fly to Ethiopia and travel south to Kenya from there.

From Nairobi, there are several ways to reach Zimbabwe or Botswana, the most direct entry points to South Africa. The most popular route seems to be the Tazara railway between Dar es Salaam in Tanzania (accessible by bus or plane from Nairobi) and Kapiri Mposhi in Zambia, from where it's possible to pick up another train or a bus on to Lusaka and Livingstone (both also in Zambia). It's extremely inexpensive for the distance travelled, but be prepared for a slow pace and uncomfortable conditions.

Another option takes you across Tanzania to Kigoma on Lake Tanganyika, then by steamer to Mpulungu (Zambia) and overland to Lusaka. It's also possible to enter Zambia at Nakonde or Malawi between Mbeya and Karonga. There's no public transport along the latter route.

Once you're in Zambia, it's fairly straightforward entering either Zimbabwe at Chirundu, Kariba or Victoria Falls, or Botswana at Kazungula. There are good connections from Botswana and Zimbabwe to Jo'burg (see Border Crossings following).

Border Crossings

For details of getting into and out of Lesotho and Swaziland please see the Getting There & Away sections in those chapters.

Botswana Most border posts between Botswana and South Africa are open between 7am or 8am and 4pm. The main border posts are at Ramatlhabama, north of Mafikeng, which is open from 6am to 8pm; Schilpadshek, north-west of Zeerust, which is open from 6am to 10pm; and Tlokweng Gate/Kapfontein, north of Zeerust, which is open from 6am to 10pm.

Intercape Mainliner (☎ 011-333 2312) has a bus service between Jo'burg and Gaborone (R110). Minibus taxis run from Mafikeng (North-West Province) to Gaborone for about R35. Mafikeng is accessible from Jo'burg on City Link buses (R73).

At the time of writing, the *Bulawayo* train that runs between Bulawayo and Jo'burg via Gaborone and Mafikeng, had been suspended. If you're keen on train travel, you can travel the Botswana leg of the journey between Francistown, near the border with Zimbabwe, and Lobatse, near the border with South Africa, via Gaborone.

Mozambique Buses from Jo'burg to Maputo via Nelspruit are run three times a week for about R190 by **Panthera Azul** (☎ 011-33 7409, 887 0383). Intercape Mainliner has a daily service on this route for R185, while **Translux** (☎ 011-774 3333) and **Greyhound** (☎ 012-323 1154) offer a cheaper service for R175. The trip takes about seven hours.

The 'name train' *Komati* runs between Jo'burg and Maputo via Pretoria and Komatipoort (see the Getting Around chapter for details). The *Trans Lubombo*, which runs between Durban and Maputo (Mozambique) via Swaziland, offers a rather haphazard service and was not running at the time of research.

Namibia Four times a week, **Intercape Mainliner** (☎ 021-386 4400) buses run between Cape Town and Windhoek via Upington for R380. See the Cape Town & the Peninsula chapter for details. You can travel between Jo'burg and Windhoek with Intercape Mainliner for R380 but you will have to stay overnight in Upington.

You can't cross the border between Namibia and South Africa at Kgalagadi Transfrontier Park. The nearest alternative is to cross south of the park at Rietfontein border post (open 8am to 4.30pm). The main border post west of Upington is at Nakop (open 24 hours), and on the west coast it's at Vioolsdrif (open 7am to 7pm). Note that visas are *not* available at any of these border posts.

Zimbabwe The only border post between Zimbabwe and South Africa is at Beitbridge on the Limpopo River (open from 5.30am to 10.30pm). There's a lot of smuggling, so searches are thorough. Messina is the closest South African town to the border (15km) and this is where you can change money.

There is a vehicle toll (R130 one way) at Beitbridge for taking your car across the border. Check with your hire-car company whether your car is permitted to cross into Zimbabwe. South Africans need a visa (free) to get into Zimbabwe but can obtain it at the border. Most other nationalities including Commonwealth and US passport holders require visas, which cost about US$60 at the border, payable in US dollars only.

Beware of touts on the Zimbabwe side trying to 'help' you through Zimbabwe immigration and customs. They also try to flog free government forms needed for immigration. If you're gullible enough to listen to these guys, they will ask a ridiculous fee for their services after you've completed formalities. Ignore them completely.

Translux runs between Jo'burg and Harare (R270, 17 hours); some services run via Bulawayo (R220, 14½ hours). There are several other operators – ask around at Jo'burg's Park Station for current deals. See Jo'burg in the Gauteng chapter and Messina in the Northern Province chapter for more transport information on this route, including minibus taxis and train travel.

If you're continuing to Zambia or Malawi **Linking Africa** (☎ 011-331 4412) runs coaches from Jo'burg to Lusaka (R400, 22 hours) via Chirundu or Livingstone at 10am Tuesday to Saturday; and to Blantyre in Malawi (R480, 32½ hours) via Tete at 9am on Thursday and Friday. **Trans Zambezi Express** (☎ 011-333 7447) runs to the same destinations for the same prices. Translux

also goes to these destinations with two services a week to Lusaka (R430) and four services a week to Blantyre (R475). Intercape also goes to Lusaka (R400).

Car & Motorcycle

Drivers of cars and riders of motorcycles will need the vehicle's registration papers, liability insurance and an international driving permit in addition to their home-country licence. Beware: There are two kinds of international permits, one of which is needed mostly for former British colonies. You may also need a *carnet de passage en douane*, which is effectively a passport for the vehicle and acts as a temporary waiver of import duty. The carnet may also need to specify any expensive spare parts that you're planning to carry with you, such as a gearbox. This is necessary when travelling in many countries in Africa and is designed to prevent car-import rackets. Contact your local automobile association for details about all documentation.

Liability insurance is not available in advance for many out-of-the-way countries, but it has to be bought when crossing the border. The cost and quality of such local insurance varies wildly, and you will find in some countries that you are effectively travelling uninsured.

Anyone planning to take their own vehicle needs to check in advance the likely availability of spares parts and petrol. Unleaded petrol is not on sale worldwide, and neither is every little part for your car.

If you're driving a car rented in South Africa you might not be allowed to take it across some international borders, and even if you are, you should get a form from the rental company saying that you do have permission. This is to cover you in case of insurance complications and also so you won't be accused of stealing the car in the other country.

SEA

South Africa is an important stop on world shipping routes. Cape Town is a major port of call for cruise ships, and many stop at Durban as well.

Freighter

There might be regional freight services where a quiet chat with an officer can get you on board but for long-distance travel you are limited to container vessels.

Many container lines do take a limited number of passengers, and while the voyage will be considerably more expensive than flying, the per-day cost can be reasonable. Accommodation can be anything from the owner's suite to a bunk in a self-contained cabin. Passengers generally eat with the officers, and the food is usually good.

The best source of information about routes and the shipping lines plying them is the *OAG Cruise & Ferry Guide*, published quarterly by the Reed Travel Group in the UK. Your travel agent might have a copy.

A few companies take bookings for freighters. Given the complex nature of freight routes (delays and diversions are common) it might be best to deal with one of these. They include the following:

Freighter World Cruises Inc (☎ 626-449 3106, fax 449 9573) 180 South Lake Ave, Suite 335, Pasadena CA 91101, USA
Strand Cruise & Travel Centre (☎ 020-7836 6363, fax 497 0078) Charing Cross Shopping Centre Concourse, London WC2N 4HZ, UK
Sydney International Travel Centre (☎ 02-9299 8000, fax 9299 1337) Level 8, 75 King St, Sydney 2000, Australia (Note, at the time of research no freighter companies were taking passengers between South Africa and Australia.)

South Africa's **Safmarine** *(☎ 021-408 6911, fax 408 6660, W www.safmarine.co.uk)* actively seeks passengers for its container ships, which sail to many of the world's major ports. Fares are relatively high (eg, from US$2200/3000 for singles/doubles between Cape Town and the UK, and more in high season or with a better cabin) but the company states that costs are definitely negotiable. Also, fares *from* South Africa seem to be lower than fares *to* South Africa.

ORGANISED TOURS

Although the days of travelling overland from Cairo to the Cape are over for the time being, quite a few overland-tour operators have taken up the trans-Sahara route through Morocco and West Africa across towards Central Africa, then flying over the Democratic Republic of Congo to East Africa and on to Zimbabwe, Botswana and South Africa. These trips are very popular but aren't for everyone. They are designed primarily for first-time travellers who feel uncomfortable striking out on their own or for those who prefer guaranteed social interaction to the uncertainties of the road.

If you have the slightest inclination towards independence or would feel confined travelling with the same group of 25 or so people for most of the trip (quite a few normally drop out along the way), think twice before booking something like this. One reader, having read this warning, was still bewitched by the colour brochures – her overland tour by truck was hell! So think twice and close your eyes!

If you'd like more information or a list of agents selling overland tour packages in your home country, contact one of the following Africa overland operators, all of which are based in the UK (Exodus also has offices in Australia, New Zealand, the USA and Canada):

Dragoman (☎ 01728-861133, fax 861127, W www.dragoman.co.uk) Camp Green, Kenton Rd, Debenham, Suffolk IP14 6LA
Exodus Expeditions (☎ 020-8675 5550, fax 8673 0779, W www.exodustravels.co.uk) 9 Weir Rd, London SW12 0LT
Guerba Expeditions (☎ 01373-826611, fax 858351, W www.guerba.co.uk) Wessex House, 40 Station Rd, Westbury, Wiltshire, BA13 3JN
Kumuka Expeditions (☎ 020-7937 8855, W www.kumuka.co.uk) 40 Earls Court Rd, London W8 6EJ
Top Deck (☎ 020-244 8641, fax 7373 6201) The Adventure Centre, 131–135 Earls Court Rd, London SW5 9RH

Overland truck journeys from South Africa to other African countries are also possible. Most are round trips and some get very good reviews while others don't. Many hotels will book you on a truck trip but there are some cowboys out there, so deal with hostel-based agency that's been in business a while, such as the Africa Travel Centre at The Backpack hostel in Cape Town.

Companies to look out for include:

African Routes (☎ 031-569 3911, fax 569 3908, ⓔ aroutes@iafrica.com) PO Box 1835, Durban 4000

Drifters (☎ 011-888 1160, fax 888 1020, Ⓦ www.drifters.co.za) PO Box 48434, Roosevelt Park, Jo'burg 2129

Nomad (☎ 021-559 4133, fax 559 4134, Ⓦ www.nomadtours.co.za) 186 Vryburger Ave, Bothasig, Cape Town 7441

Which Way Adventures (☎ 021-845 7400, fax 845 7401, ⓔ whichway@iafrica.com) PO Box 2600, Somerset West 7129

Getting Around

South Africa is geared towards travel by car, with some very good highways but limited and expensive mainstream public transport. If you want to cover a lot of country in a limited time, hiring or buying a car is recommended. If you don't have much money but have time to spare, you might organise lifts with fellow travellers, or if you don't mind a modicum of discomfort there's the extensive network of minibus taxis, cheap buses and economy-class train seats.

AIR

South African Airways *(SAA;* ☒ *www.flysaa .com/800.html)* is the main domestic carrier, as well as the international flag carrier. Its subsidiaries, SA Airlink and SA Express, also service domestic routes. There are plenty of daily flights to most destinations.

Fares aren't cheap; if you plan to take some flights, check with a travel agent before you leave home for special deals on Apex tickets. If you book and pay 21 days in advance there's a 50% discount on the regular fare; for 10 days in advance there's a 30% discount.

The baggage allowance is 40/30/20kg in 1st/business/economy class and excess baggage is charged at R17 per kilogram.

SAA flights can be booked at travel agencies or by phoning the following local booking offices:

Bloemfontein	☎ 051-430 1111
Cape Town	☎ 021-936 1111
Durban	☎ 031-250 1111
East London	☎ 043-706 0203
Johannesburg	☎ 011-978 1111
Port Elizabeth	☎ 041-507 1111
Pretoria	☎ 012-323 0707

Comair *(*☒ *www.britishairways.com)* is an airline operating in conjunction with British Airways. Comair destinations in South Africa include Cape Town, Durban, Johannesburg (Jo'burg) and Port Elizabeth. Book at a travel agency or at one of Comair's offices:

Cape Town	☎ 021-936 9000
Durban	☎ 031-450 7000
Jo'burg	☎ 011-921 0222
Port Elizabeth	☎ 041-508 8000

Nationwide *(*☒ *www.nationwideair.co.za*) is a domestic airline operating in conjunction with Sabena. Nationwide destinations include Bloemfontein, Cape Town, Durban, George and Jo'burg. Book at a travel agency or at one of Nationwide's offices:

Cape Town	☎ 021-936 2050
Durban	☎ 031-450 2087
Jo'burg	☎ 011-390 1660

There are also several smaller airlines, such as **National Airlines** *(*☎ *021-934 0530)*, which flies between Cape Town, Alexander Bay, tiny Kleinsee (Northern Cape) and Springbok; and **Civair** *(*☎ *021-934 4488* ☒ *www.civair.co.za)*, which operates services between Cape Town, Plettenberg Bay and Port Elizabeth.

BUS

Translux, part of the semiprivatised government transport service called Autonet, runs most long-distance buses. The other main national operator is Greyhound, which covers quite a lot of the country, with similar fares to Translux. Mainly in the western half of the country, Intercape Mainliner has useful services at fares that are a little lower than those of Translux.

With the exception of City to City (a poor relation of Translux) and local-area services competing with minibus taxis, bus travel isn't cheap. Return fares are roughly double the one-way fares, with small discounts available sometimes. Both Translux and Greyhound offer customer-loyalty schemes – worth investigating if you're planning on using the services frequently to get around. Also inquire about travel passes (see Translux Routes & Fares and Greyhound later in this chapter for details). You usually can't book

110

eat to a nearby town with the three major bus companies. Prices for short sectors are exorbitant anyway so you're better off looking for local bus or a minibus taxi.

Many travel agents, including **Computicket** (**W** *www.computicket.co.za*), take bus bookings.

Translux

Translux runs express services on the main routes. Tickets must be booked 24 hours in advance. You can get on without a booking if there's a spare seat but you won't know that until the bus arrives – if there isn't a seat it may be a couple of days' wait for the next bus.

You can make bookings with Computicket, many travel agencies and some train stations. There are also reservation offices around the country, including:

Bloemfontein	☎ 051-408 4888
Cape Town	☎ 021-449 3333
Durban	☎ 031-308 8111
East London	☎ 043-700 1999
Jo'burg	☎ 011-774 3333
Port Elizabeth	☎ 041-392 1333
Pretoria	☎ 012-334 8000

Translux offices might have details of the few remaining City to City services (which are cheaper than Translux), but they won't tell you about them unless you ask.

Translux Routes & Fares The fares quoted below are for the main services running during peak season. There are small discounts for return fares, and also for fares from 16 January to 30 March, 18 April to 22 June, 16 July to 28 September and from 8 October to 5 December. The frequency of services is also subject to change.

Translux has plans to introduce a 'go-as-you-please' pass, which will probably offer a similar deal to Greyhound's travel pass – see Greyhound later in this chapter.

Note that services running south from Jo'burg originate in Pretoria, and those running north from Jo'burg run through Pretoria. The trip between the cities takes about 45 minutes and long-distance fares to/from Jo'burg and Pretoria are usually the same.

Unfortunately, nearly all long-distance services run through the night, so you miss out on the scenery.

Cape Town–Durban via Bloemfontein Daily service, 22 hours. Stops (with fares from Cape Town/Durban) include Paarl (R85/375), Beaufort West (R220/310), Bloemfontein (R300/160), Bethlehem (R365/155), Pietermaritzburg (R385/160), Durban (R395).

Cape Town–Durban via Port Elizabeth Daily service, 26 hours (overnight). Stops (with fares from Cape Town/Durban) include Stellenbosch (R85/395), Swellendam (R95/350), George (R130/315), Knysna (R145/295), Plettenberg Bay (R155/290), Port Elizabeth (R190/255), Grahamstown (R205/230), East London (R240/160), Umtata (R320/155), Durban (R395).

Cape Town–East London Daily service, 15½ hours (overnight). Stops (with fares from Cape Town/East London) include Beaufort West (R220/190), Graaff-Reinet (R220/170), Cradock (R220/140), Queenstown (R220/75), King William's Town (R225/75), East London (R240).

Cape Town–Port Elizabeth via Coastal Route Daily service, 11 hours. This service has good scenery. Stops (with fares from Cape Town/Port Elizabeth) include Swellendam (R95/165), Mossel Bay (R115/125), George (R130/115), Knysna (R145/85), Plettenberg Bay (R155/85), Storms River (R175/85), Port Elizabeth (R190).

Jo'burg–Cape Town via Bloemfontein Daily service, 19 hours (overnight). Stops (with fares from Jo'burg/Cape Town) include Bloemfontein (R200/300), Beaufort West (R290/220), Worcester (R365/95), Cape Town (R410).

Jo'burg–Cape Town via Kimberley Daily services, 18½ hours (overnight). Stops (with fares from Jo'burg/Cape Town) include Kimberley (R160/275), Beaufort West (R240/215), Worcester (R360/100), Cape Town (R375).

Jo'burg–Durban Several daily services, eight or nine hours (day and overnight). Stops (with fares from Jo'burg/Durban) include Harrismith (R125/125), Pietermaritzburg (R155/55), Durban (R170).

Jo'burg–East London Daily service, 14 hours (overnight). Stops (with fares from Jo'burg/East London) include Bloemfontein (R200/220), Queenstown (R225/75), King William's Town (R285/75), East London (R285).

Jo'burg–Knysna via Kimberley or Bloemfontein Daily service, 17½ hours (overnight). Stops (with fares from Jo'burg/Knysna) include Bloemfontein (R200/280), Kimberley (R160/280),

Beaufort West (R300/190), Oudtshoorn (R345/85), Mossel Bay (R345/85), George (R345/85), Knysna (R345).

Jo'burg–Port Elizabeth via Cradock or Graaff-Reinet Daily service, 15 hours (overnight). Stops (with fares from Jo'burg/Port Elizabeth) include Bloemfontein (R200/220), Cradock (R265/180), Graaff-Reinet (R265/180), Port Elizabeth (R295).

Jo'burg-Umtata Four services a week, 13½ hours (overnight). Stops (with fares from Jo'burg/Umtata) include Pietermaritzburg (R160/165), Kokstad (R200/100), Umtata (R220).

Jo'burg-Messina (en route to Beitbridge/Bulawayo/Harare in Zimbabwe or Lusaka in Zambia) Daily service, 7½ hours. Stops (with fares from Jo'burg) include Pietersburg (R115), Louis Trichardt (R130) and Messina (R140).

Jo'burg-Nelspruit (en route to Maputo in Mozambique) Daily service, five hours (R120).

Greyhound

Offering services on similar routes to Translux and at much the same prices, **Greyhound** (W www.greyhound.co.za) sometimes has special deals available. One of Greyhound's Jo'burg-to-Durban services runs through Zululand to Richards Bay, then down the coast to Durban, which is handy.

Also worth considering are Greyhound's travel passes, which offer a varying number of days' unlimited travel in South Africa within a particular time period. The current costs are R950 for seven days' travel within

30 days; R1895 for 15 days' travel within 30 days; and R2890 for 30 days' trave within 60 days.

Book through a travel agency or any the following Greyhound offices:

Bloemfontein	☎ 051-447 1558
Cape Town	☎ 021-418 4310
Durban	☎ 031-309 7830
East London	☎ 043-743 9284
Nelspruit	☎ 013-753 2100
Port Elizabeth	☎ 041-363 4555

Intercape Mainliner

The third major bus company is **Intercap Mainliner** (W www.intercape.co.za), and usually charges less than Translux an Greyhound. Most of their services are the western half of the country but there a a few other interesting routes. See the Ge ting There & Away sections in the region chapters for more information.

Services from Jo'burg include: Upingto (R230), Cape Town (R410), Nelspruit (R120 Port Elizabeth (R295) and the Garden Rout

Services from Cape Town include Du ban (R385), Port Elizabeth (R195), Citru dal (R120), Clanwilliam (R130), Calvin (R170) and Upington (R195). It also has service to Windhoek, Namibia (R380).

Reservations must be made 72 hours advance. You can make bookings wi Computicket, at some travel agencies or the following Intercape offices:

Bloemfontein	☎ 051-447 1575
Cape Town	☎ 021-386 4400 (24 h
Port Elizabeth	☎ 041-586 0055
Pretoria	☎ 012-654 4114
Upington	☎ 054-332 6091

City to City

City to City has taken over the old Transta services that once carried people from t Homelands, Lesotho and Swaziland to a from the big cities where they were gue workers under the apartheid regime. The services are cheap and still serve blacks p dominantly, thus going to many off-th beaten-track places, including townshi and mining towns.

City to City offices are few and can difficult to find. Buses often stop at tra

---

What's *this* place?

You might still encounter apartheid-era problems of navigation in South Africa. Most maps didn't (and many still don't) show black townships or 'locations'. That isn't so much of a problem when these areas are on the outskirts of a town, but in many cases, especially in the minor apartheid-era Homelands such as Lebowa or KaNgwane (which themselves didn't make it onto many maps), you can be driving along and come to a large town that just isn't on the map. People naturally give directions involving these major but invisible towns, and if you're using the local transport system you may have a hard time working out just where the bus or minibus taxi is going.

PAUL KENNEDY

ck your board for a 'surfari' of a lifetime – South Africa has some of the best surfing in the world.

PAUL KENNEDY

adrenaline rush like no other – many visitors enjoy the abseiling opportunities in South Africa.

SIMON RICHMOND

ountain biking is a great way to admire the countryside. Try the trails in Western Cape.

SIMON RICHMOND

Kicking back at Camps Bay beach, Cape Town

SIMON RICHMOND

What a view! Cape Town from Lion's Head

LUKE HUNTER

You can't park here! Giraffes check out a vehicle in the Ithala Game Reserve, KwaZulu-Natal.

stations (ask about the 'railways bus'), so you can try asking there. A black employee is more likely to be of help than a white one. Also, some booking offices might be more familiar with the name Transtate than City to City. The bottom line is that it's worth using City to City but it's difficult to find current and reliable information about it.

Many services originate in Jo'burg at the Park Station Transit Centre. There are booking counters and a **Jo'burg information desk** (☎ 337 6650) in the station. Services from Jo'burg include:

Eastern Cape
Pietermaritzburg (R85), Kokstad (R100) and Lusikisiki (R105); daily
Pietermaritzburg (R85), Kokstad (R100) and Umtata (R110); 6pm daily

KwaZulu-Natal
Emanguse (R75); 8am Tuesday and 7pm Friday
Mtubatuba (R75); 8am Tuesday and 7pm Friday
Nongoma (R75) via Ulundi; 8am Tuesday and 7pm Friday

Northern Province
Nelspruit (R60), Hazyview (R65) and Acornhoek (R70); 8am daily
Giyani (R70) via Pietersburg; daily
Messina/Beitbridge (Zimbabwe; R90) and Bulawayo (R150); daily

Mpumalanga and Swaziland
Hlathikulu (R65) via Piet Retief; 8am Monday, Wednesday, Friday
Manzini (R65) via Mbabane and Ermelo; 8am Monday, Wednesday, Friday

Baz Bus
An alternative to the major bus lines, the **Baz Bus** (☎ 021-439 2323, fax 439 2343, W www bazbus.com) is good, if pricey. While it's aimed at backpackers, its routes, organisation and service levels make it very useful for travellers on any budget.

The Baz Bus offers a door-to-door service with hop-on, hop-off fares between Cape Town and Jo'burg via the Northern Drakensberg, Durban and the Garden Route. It also does a very useful loop from Durban up through Zululand and Swaziland and back to Jo'burg, passing close by Kruger National Park. This loop runs through what is arguably the most interesting part of the region and which no other mainstream transport option covers.

The major routes and one-way fares from Cape Town are:

Durban via Garden Route (R930)
Jo'burg via Northern Drakensberg (R1100)
Jo'burg via Swaziland (R1350)

As you can see, these fares are significantly higher than for similar services offered by the big-three bus companies (although you should factor in being taken door to door at most places). You can buy sector tickets, but these will also work out more expensive, so it's important you weigh up how important the flexibility of a hop-on, hop-off fare is to you. For example, if your itinerary is just Cape Town-Knysna-Durban you'd probably be better off travelling with one of the big three.

The Baz Bus drops off and picks up at many hostels along the way, and has transfer arrangements with some hostels in less accessible places, such as Coffee Bay and Port St Johns in the Transkei. Most hostels take Baz Bus bookings.

MINIBUS TAXI

Off the train and main bus routes and if you don't have a car, the only way to get between most places is to take a minibus taxi. Minibus taxis are also a very handy way to get around central Cape Town (see the Cape Town & the Peninsula chapter for details).

If you've come overland through Africa you're in for a pleasant surprise. Minibus taxis here are less crowded and in better condition than in other countries, although most don't carry luggage on the roof, so stowing backpacks can be a hassle. From Jo'burg to Cape Town you'll pay slightly more for a minibus taxi (R240) than you'd pay for an economy-class train ticket.

As well as the usual 'leave-when-full' minibus taxis, there is a small but increasing number of door-to-door services that you can book. These tend to run on the longer routes, and, while they cost a little more, they are convenient.

Minibus taxis tend to run short routes – generally only to neighbouring towns – although you'll nearly always find one running to a distant big city. Because many of the minibus taxi services shuttle people between the location or township where they live and the town where they work (often a long way apart), and because townships and locations are still rarely named on maps, finding out where a taxi is going can be a problem. There's always a chance that you'll end up on the 'wrong' side of a big town.

Which brings us to the question of safety. Away from the big cities robbery on minibus taxis is not much of a problem. There have been isolated outbreaks of 'taxi wars' between rival companies, and crowded taxis have been machine-gunned. However, given the overall number of taxis, the incidence of such attacks is very low. Read the newspapers and ask around for advice on areas to avoid. The biggest risk when using minibus taxis is bad driving and poorly maintained vehicles. This is more of a concern on long trips, when the driver will become very tired.

TRAIN

Spoornet, the company that runs South Africa's railway system, has regular passenger services on 'name trains'. These are a good way to get between major cities, and economy class (the old 3rd class) is very affordable. Another advantage of name trains

---

Minibus Taxi Etiquette

• People with a lot of luggage should sit in the first row behind the driver.

• Pay the fare with coins, not notes. Pass money forward (your fare and those of the people around you) when the taxi is full. Give it to one of the front-seat passengers, not the driver. If you're sitting in the front seat you might have to collect the fares and provide change.

• If you sit on the folding seat by the door it's your job to open and close the door when other people get out. You'll have to get out of the taxi each time.

• Say 'Thank you, driver!' when you want to get out, not 'Stop!'

---

is that, unlike the long-distance buses, fares on short sectors are not inflated.

On overnight journeys the 1st- and 2nd-class fares include a sleeping berth, but there's a charge of R20 for bedding hire. You can also hire a private compartment (sleeping four in 1st class and six in 2nd class) or a coupe (sleeping two in 1st class and three in 2nd class). This is a good way of travelling more securely. Meals are available in the dining car, or can be enjoyed in the comfort of your compartment.

Tickets must be booked at least 24 hours in advance (you can book up to three months in advance). Most stations accept bookings, or you can call the **Main Line Passenger Services Call Centre** (☎ 0860 008 888). Key stations include:

Bloemfontein	☎ 051-408 2941
Cape Town	☎ 021-449 3871
Durban	☎ 031-308 8118
East London	☎ 043-700 2719
Jo'burg	☎ 011-773 2944
Kimberley	☎ 053-838 2631
Nelspruit	☎ 013-752 9257
Port Elizabeth	☎ 041-507 2400
Pretoria	☎ 012-334 8470

Name Trains

Return fares are double the one-way fares (given here in 1st/2nd/economy class). On the Trans Karoo service between Pretoria and Cape Town there is also a new Premier class, which provides a bit more comfort and style than 1st class. For further details contact **Spoornet** (W www.spoornet.co.za). Name trains include:

Algoa
Jo'burg–Port Elizabeth Daily, 19 hours. Departs both Jo'burg and Port Elizabeth at 2.30pm. Stops include Kroonstad, Bloemfontein and Cradock. 1st-/2nd-/economy-class fares are R315/215/135.

Amatola
Jo'burg–East London Daily, 20¼ hours. Departs Jo'burg at 12.45pm, departs East London at noon. Stops include Kroonstad, Bloemfontein and Queenstown. 1st-/2nd-/economy-class fares are R295/200/125.

Blue Train
Cape Town–Jo'burg/Pretoria See following section.

Bosvelder
Jo'burg-Messina Daily, 15¼ hours. Departs Jo'burg at 7pm, departs Messina at 4.30pm. Stops include Pretoria, Pietersburg and Louis Trichardt. 1st-/2nd-/economy-class fares are R185/125/75.

Diamond Express
Pretoria/Jo'burg-Bloemfontein Daily Sunday to Friday, 15 hours. Departs Pretoria at 5.35pm, departs Bloemfontein at 5pm. Stops include Jo'burg and Kimberley. 1st-/2nd-/economy-class fares are R195/135/80.

Komati
Jo'burg-Komatipoort Daily, 12 hours. Departs Jo'burg at 6.10pm, departs Komatipoort at 6.07pm. Stops include Pretoria, Middelburg and Nelspruit. 1st-/2nd-/economy-class fares are R160/110/65. A shuttle (train) bus runs from Komatipoort to Maputo (Mozambique) daily.

Southern Cross
Cape Town–Outdshoorn 14½ hours. Departs Cape Town at 6.15pm Friday, departs Outdshoorn at 5.40pm Sunday. Stops include Worcester. 1st-/2nd-/economy-class fares are R185/125/75

Trans Karoo
Pretoria/Jo'burg–Cape Town Daily, 27 hours. Departs Cape Town at 9.20am, departs Pretoria at 10.10am. Stops include Kimberley and Beaufort West. 1st-/2nd-/economy-class fares are R450/305/190.

Trans Natal
Jo'burg–Durban Daily, 13½ hours. Departs both Jo'burg and Durban at 6.30pm. Stops include Newcastle, Ladysmith, Estcourt and Pietermaritzburg. 1st-/2nd-/economy-class fares are R215/145/90.

Trans Oranje
Cape Town–Durban 30½ hours. Departs Cape Town at 6.50pm Monday, departs Durban at 5.30pm Wednesday. Stops include Wellington, Beaufort West, Kimberley, Bloemfontein, Kroonstad, Bethlehem, Ladysmith and Pietermaritzburg. 1st-/2nd-/economy-class fares are R560/380/235.

Blue Train Some people come to South Africa just to ride on the famous *Blue Train* (**W** www.bluetrain.co.za). The original train ran between Pretoria/Jo'burg and Cape Town, offering 25 hours of luxury. Even more-luxurious trains have replaced the original train, and more routes have been added. If you can't afford to take a whole trip, consider taking just a section.

Some travel agents, both in South Africa and in other countries, take bookings for the *Blue Train*. It's worth inquiring about special packages, including one-way flights from Jo'burg to Cape Town and a night's accommodation. Direct bookings can be made in Cape Town (☎ 021-449 2672, fax 449 3338) and Pretoria (☎ 012-334 8459, fax 334 8464).

Low-season fares apply between 1 May and 31 August. There are two types of fares: regular de luxe and luxury, for the more spacious suites. The one-way de luxe fares given here are for high season and are likely to rise:

Cape Town–Jo'burg/Pretoria 27 hours. Departs Cape Town at 11am Monday, Wednesday and Friday, departs Pretoria at 8.50am on the same days. Single/double suites start at R7600/10,800.

Cape Town–Port Elizabeth 40 hours, one journey a month along the Garden Route. Single/double suites start at R10,300/13,700.

Pretoria-Hoedspruit 16 hours, one journey a month, with connections to Olifants River Game Reserve bordering Kruger National Park. Single/double suites start at R5100/6700

Pretoria–Victoria Falls (Zimbabwe) 48 hours, one journey a month. Single/double suites start at R8025/10,700.

Metro Trains

There are Metro services in Jo'burg, Cape Town and Pretoria. See the Getting There & Away and Getting Around sections in the Gauteng and Cape Town & the Peninsula chapters for more information. Always check the safety situation before using Metro services, as robbery is a problem.

Other Trains

There are a few **steam-train** trips on offer, (and longer steam-train tours; see Organised Tours later in this chapter). They include the *Spier Train* day trips from Cape Town, the *Apple Express* from Port Elizabeth, the *Outeniqua Choo-Tjoe* between Knysna and George, and the *Banana Express* along the KwaZulu-Natal south coast from Port Shepstone. See the Cape Town & the Peninsula, Eastern Cape, Western Cape and KwaZulu-Natal chapters, respectively, for more details.

There are a couple of more upmarket train options. See *Rovos Rail*, the *Shongololo Express* and other trains under Organised Tours later in this chapter.

CAR & MOTORCYCLE

South Africa is a good country to drive in. Most major roads are excellent and carry relatively little traffic, and off the main routes there are interesting back roads to explore.

The country is crossed by many national routes (eg, N1); on some sections a toll is payable. The toll is based on distance and varies considerably, from about R5 to nearly R30. There's always plenty of warning that you're about to enter a toll section, and there's always an alternative route. Toll roads are indicated by a black 'T' in a yellow circle. The turn-off for the alternative route is indicated by a black 'A' in a yellow circle. Be prepared for inadequate signposting on alternative routes. Most signs will direct you to small towns or just give route numbers, not the direction of the next big city.

Most roads are numbered (eg, R44). Signposts show these numbers, and when you ask directions most people will refer to these numbers rather than destinations, so it pays to have a good road map (such as Lonely Planet's *Southern Africa Road Atlas*). The Automobile Association (AA) has free city and regional guides.

Petrol stations are often open 24 hours a day. At the time of writing, petrol cost around R3.30 per litre, depending on the octane level, but prices are constantly rising. Not all petrol stations accept credit cards and of those that do some will charge a fee, typically 10%. An attendant will always fill up your tank for you, clean your windows and ask if the oil or water needs checking – you should tip them 10% for their service.

Road Rules & Etiquette

You can use your driving licence from your home country if it carries your photo, otherwise you're supposed to have an international driving permit, obtainable from a motoring organisation in your home country.

South Africans drive on the left-hand side of the road, as in the UK, Japan and Australia.

On freeways, faster drivers will expect you to move into the emergency lane to let them pass. If you do, they will probably say 'Thank you' by flashing their hazard lights; you may (if you want to adopt US levels of politeness) indicate, 'You're welcome' by flashing your high-beam lights.

There are a few local variations on road rules. The main one is the 'four-way stop' (crossroad), which can occur even on major roads. If you're used to a system where drivers on major roads always have priority over drivers on smaller roads you'll definitely need to stay alert. When you arrive at a four-way stop, you must stop. If there are other vehicles at the intersection, those that arrive before you get to cross ahead of you. Before you proceed, make sure that it *is* a four-way stop – if so, you can safely cross ahead of approaching cars. If you've mistaken an ordinary stop sign for a four-way stop, the approaching cars won't be slowing down!

In many places, particularly in rural areas, you'll see hitchhikers (predominantly black and coloured people). Use your judgment as to whether to pick up at all or who to pick up (a group of young men in the city might not be a wise idea), but giving lifts is a great way to meet locals and have conversations that you'd otherwise never have.

Speed Limits The speed limit is 100km/h (roughly 60m/h) on open roads, and 120km/h on most major highways. Some dangerous sections of rural roads have a limit of less than 100km/h, while the usual limit in towns is 60km/h.

If you stick to the highway speed limit you'll feel lonely – most traffic travels either much faster or much slower.

Hazards

South Africa has a horrific road-accident record. Hundreds of people die whenever there's a long weekend, and the annual death toll is pushing 10,000 a year. A further 150,000 people are injured on the roads annually – appalling figures given that the vast majority of people don't own cars. The most dangerous stretch of road in the country is the N1 between Cape Town and Beaufort West.

Deaths are evenly divided between drivers, passengers and pedestrians, which suggests that multiple-fatality minibus taxi accidents aren't the only thing you need to worry about.

Other Drivers Drivers of cars coming up behind you will expect you to move into the emergency lane to let them pass. However, there might be animals, pedestrians or a slow-moving vehicle already in the emergency lane. Don't move over unless it's safe.

It is possible for an overtaking car to rely on *oncoming* traffic to move into the emergency lane! This is sheer lunacy and you must remain constantly alert. When two cars travelling in opposite directions decide that they will overtake despite oncoming traffic, things get really hairy, especially if the protagonists are travelling at the usual 150km/h.

Drivers on little-used rural roads often speed and they often assume that there is no other traffic. Be careful of oncoming cars at blind corners on these roads.

A couple of provinces introduced alcohol breath-testing in 1999, but given the lack of police resources and the high blood-alcohol level permitted (over 0.08%) drunk drivers remain a danger.

Road Conditions In the former Homelands, beware of dangerous potholes, washed-out roads, unannounced hairpin bends and the like.

You don't have to get very far away from the big cities to find yourself on dirt roads. Most are regularly graded and reasonably smooth, and it's often possible to travel at high speed on them. Don't! If you're cruising along a dirt road at 100km/h and you come to a corner, you won't go around the corner, you'll sail off into the veld. If you put on the brakes to slow down you'll probably spin or roll. If you swerve sharply to avoid a pothole you'll go into an exciting four-wheel drift then find out what happens when your car meets a telephone pole. Worst of all, if another car approaches and you have to move to the edge of the road, you may lose control and collide head-on.

On dirt roads that are dry, flat, straight, traffic-free and wide enough to allow for

unexpected slewing as you hit potholes and drifted sand, you could, with practice, drive at about 80km/h. Otherwise, treat dirt like you would ice.

Animals & Pedestrians In rural areas, watch out for animals and pedestrians on the roads. Standard advice is that if you hit an animal in an area in which you're uncertain of your safety, it's best to continue to the nearest police station and report it there.

Weather Thick fog can slow you to a crawl during the rainy season. This is particularly a problem in steamy KwaZulu-Natal, where it can be a clear day on the coast while up in the hills visibility is down to a few metres. Hailstorms on the lowveld can damage your car.

Carjacking In Jo'burg, and to a lesser extent in the other big cities, carjacking is a problem. People have been killed for their cars. Stay alert and keep windows wound up and doors locked at night. If you are carjacked, make it clear that it's a rental car and you don't give a damn about losing it.

Rental – Car
The major international car-rental companies, such as **Avis** (☎ 0800-021 111), **Budget** (☎ 0800-016 622) and **Hertz** (☎ 0800-021 515) are represented in the region. They have offices or agents across the country. Rates are high but if you book and prepay through your agent at home they will be significantly lower (but still higher than the cheaper companies in South Africa).

Local companies tend to come and go. Currently, larger companies include **Imperial** (☎ 0800-131 000) and **Tempest** (☎ 0800-031 666). Both have agents in the cities and a few other places.

A step down from these are the smaller and cheaper outfits. There seems to be a constant supply of new companies that burst onto the scene with dramatically reduced rates, then they either fold or hike up their prices. This may be good news for visitors. Still further down the scale are outfits in the big cities renting older cars. These can be good value for getting around a local area but are not usually good for longer trips.

Rates If you hire a category B car (usually a smallish Japanese car such as a Toyota Corolla with a 1.6L motor, manual transmission and air-con) for five days, with at least 200 free kilometres per day and collision and theft insurance, you'll pay in the region of R300 per day with the larger companies and from about R250 with the smaller companies. Many hostels can arrange better deals from around R200 per day or less.

You may be charged extra if you nominate more than one driver. If a non-nominated driver has an accident, you aren't covered by insurance.

Choosing a Deal South Africa is a big country but unless you are a travel writer on a tight schedule, you probably don't need to pay higher rates for unlimited kilometres. For meandering around, 400km a day should be more than enough, and if you plan to stop for a day here and there 200km a day might be sufficient.

However, if you're renting with an international company and you book through the branch in your home country, you'll probably get unlimited kilometres at no extra cost. At peak times in South Africa (mainly summer), even your local branch might tell you that unlimited-kilometre deals aren't available. Your travel agent might be able to get around this, though.

One-way rentals are usually possible with larger companies if you are driving between major cities. This may not be the case with the smaller companies. There's also likely to be a drop-off charge with some companies.

When you're getting quotes make sure that they include VAT (value-added tax), as that 14% slug makes a big difference.

Choose a car powerful enough to do the job. The smallest cars are OK for one person but with any more they'll be straining on the hills, which even on major highways are steep. Really steep hills may also make automatics unpleasant to drive.

Read the contract carefully before you sign. Hail damage is a distinct and costly

Hire-Car Check List

One reader sent us this list of things to watch out for when hiring a car (which is particularly useful if you opt for a cheaper deal where the car maintenance might not be so stringent):

- Check the tyres to see if they have sufficient tread.
- Ask when the car was last serviced.
- Check the oil and water before you go and get the petrol station attendants to check them regularly for you while on the road.
- Check the spare tyre and whether there's a jack.
- Check the wipers and windscreen washer water.
- Ask how the car alarm works.
- As you drive away, put the brakes on full to see if the car keeps in a straight line; faulty brakes could be lethal in wet weather.
- Check the insurance details and make sure you know what is and isn't covered.
- If a car is delivered to you with a full tank of petrol, make sure it's full when returned.

Jonathan Sibtain

possibility, so see if it's covered. Many contracts used to stipulate that you couldn't enter townships – that may have changed but check. If you plan to visit another country (eg, Swaziland), make sure that the rental agreement permits this, and make sure you get the standard letter from the rental company granting this permission.

Insurance Excess One problem with nearly all car-rental deals is the 'excess', the amount that you are liable for before the insurance pays the rest. Even with a small car you can be liable for up to R5000, although there's usually the choice of lowering or cancelling the excess for a higher insurance premium. Visitors with little experience of driving on dirt roads have a high accident rate on the region's roads, so excess could be an important consideration. A few companies offer 100% damage and theft insurance at a higher rate.

Camper Vans A way to combine and cut your accommodation and transport costs is to hire a camper van. Note that one-way rentals may not be possible or may attract big fees.

One company with a range of deals is **African Leisure Travel** (☎ 011-792 1884, fax 792 1867, **W** www.africanleisure.co.za, 2 Sambreelboom Ave, Randparkridge, Randburg, Gauteng). It has been in business for quite a while and its rates are good. As well as Toyota Land Cruiser campers they have cheaper 'bakkie' campers, which sleep two in the back of a canopied pick-up. These vehicles include all the necessary camping gear.

Rental – Motorcycle

Renting a motorcycle isn't cheap but the idea of riding around South Africa is an attractive idea. See the Getting There & Away section in the Cape Town & the Peninsula chapter for more information. Mopeds and scooters are available for hire in some tourist areas.

Purchase

Buying your own car is one way around the high cost of transport – if you can sell it again for a good price.

Although you might get a better deal in Jo'burg, Cape Town is by far a nicer place to spend the week or two that it will inevitably take to buy a car. Prices do tend to be a bit higher in Cape Town, so it's not a bad place to sell but as the market is smaller you might wait longer.

Cars that have spent their lives around Cape Town are more likely to be rusty than those kept inland but as one dealer told us, 'What's wrong with rust? It just means that the car is cheaper'.

The main congregation of used-car dealers is on Voortrekker Rd between Maitland and Belleville Sts. Voortrekker Rd is the R102, which runs west from Woodstock, south of, and pretty much parallel to, the N1.

Some dealers, such as John Wayne at **Wayne Motors** (☎ 021-465 2222, **W** www wancars@mweb.co.za, 21 Roeland St, City Bowl), might agree to a buy-back deal. He'll guarantee a buy-back price but he reckons that you'd have a fair chance of selling the car privately for more than that. He doesn't deal in rock-bottom cars, though.

There are also Jo'burg dealers offering buy-back deals. The better Jo'burg hostels can advise and explain how best to draw up a contract that will hold when the time comes to sell back.

Dealers have to make a profit, however, so you will pay less if you buy privately. The weekly classified-ads paper, *Cape Ads* (**W** www.capeads.com) is the best place to look. Other useful Web sites include **W** www.autotrader.co.za and **W** junkmail .co.za, both of which advertise thousands of cars around the country.

No matter who you're buying a car from, make sure that the details correspond accurately with the ownership (registration) papers, that there is a current licence disk on the windscreen and that the vehicle has been checked by the police clearance department (in Cape Town ☎ 021-945 389). Check the owner's name against their identity document, and check the car's engine and chassis numbers. Consider getting the car tested by the **AA** (in Cape Town ☎ 021-462 4462). A full test can cost up to R300; less detailed tests are around R100.

Cheap cars will often be sold without a roadworthy certificate. This certificate is required when you register the change-of-ownership form and pay tax for a licence disk. A roadworthy used to be difficult to get but some private garages are now allowed to issue them, and some will overlook minor faults. A roadworthy costs R135.

Unfortunately, there seem to be very few quality used cars at low prices; a good car will cost about R25,000. You will be lucky to find a decent vehicle for much less than R13,000 (anything under R8000 is a definite gamble).

If you're thinking of getting a 4WD for a trans-Africa trip then Series 1, 2 and 3 Land Rovers will cost anything in the region of R15,000 to R30,000, depending on the condition. A recommended contact in Cape Town is Graham Duncan Smith (☎ 021-797 3048) who's a Land Rover expert and has helped people buy these 4WD in the past;

he charges a R80 consultation fee and R150 per hour for engineering work.

To register your car, present yourself along with the roadworthy, a current licence, an accurate ownership certificate, a completed change-of-ownership form (signed by the seller), a clear photocopy of your ID (passport) along with the original, and your money to the **City Treasurer's Department, Motor Vehicle Registration Division** (☎ 021-400 2385; open 8am to 2pm Mon-Fri) in the Civic Centre, Cash Hall, on the foreshore in Cape Town. Call ahead to check how much cash you'll need, but it will be under R300. It also distributes blank change-of-ownership forms.

Insurance for third-party damage and damage to or loss of your vehicle is a very good idea, as repairs are horrendously expensive. It's easy enough to take out a year's insurance, but if you want to buy insurance by the month it is surprisingly difficult to find an insurance company to take your money when you don't have a permanent address and/or a local bank account. Try the AA; you might be able to negotiate paying for a year's worth of insurance with a pro-rata refund when you sell the car, but get an agreement in writing, not just a vague promise. In Cape Town one recommended insurance agency is **First Bowring** (☎ 021-425 1460).

Membership of the AA is recommended. It has an efficient vehicle-breakdown service and a good supply of maps and information. (It's important to get the window stickers they give you for breakdown service.) The initial joining fee is waived for members of many foreign motoring associations, so bring your membership details.

BICYCLE

Cycling is a cheap, convenient, healthy, environmentally sound and, above all, fun way of travelling. One note of caution: Before you leave home, go over your bike with a fine-toothed comb and fill your repair kit with every imaginable spare. As with cars and motorbikes, you won't necessarily be able to buy that crucial gizmo for your machine when it breaks down in the back of beyond as the sun sets.

South Africa is a good country in which to cycle, with a wide variety of terrain and climate, plenty of camping places and many good roads, most of which don't carry a lot of traffic. Most of the national routes are too busy for comfort, although there are quieter sections in northern KwaZulu-Natal and the Cape provinces.

Keep in mind that parts of South Africa are very hilly and even on main roads gradients can be steep.

Much of the country (except for Western Cape and the west coast) gets most of its rain in summer, in the form of violent thunderstorms. When it isn't raining it can be hot, especially on the lowveld where extreme heat and humidity make things pretty unpleasant in summer. See Climate in the Facts about South Africa chapter for more details.

Distances between major towns can be long but, except in isolated areas such as the Karoo or Northern Province, you're rarely very far from a village or a farmhouse.

If you decide to give up riding and take public transport you may have to arrange expensive transport for your bicycle with a carrier company, as train lines are few and far between and buses aren't keen on bikes in their luggage holds. Minibus taxis don't carry luggage on the roof.

Theft is a problem so bring a good lock. When you stop overnight, bring the bicycle inside your accommodation (preferably inside your room) and chain it to something solid.

Where you go depends on how long you have, how fit you are and what you want to do. There are a few places where meandering between small towns is possible, although these tend to be hilly areas, such as in southern Free State. Cycling through the Transkei area of Eastern Cape (a mountain bike would be best here) would be a good adventure and the northern lowveld offers endless empty plains. The Winelands of Western Cape is another excellent biking area.

There is a boom in mountain biking – usually with support vehicles, braais (barbecues) and beer – so mountain bikes are sold everywhere. See Activities in the Facts for the Visitor chapter for more details. Away from the big cities you might have trouble finding specialised parts for touring bikes. It's a good idea to establish a relationship with a good bike shop in a city before you head off into the veld, in case you need something couriered to you.

It's possible to bring your own bicycle into South Africa by plane. Check with the airline well in advance – some just want you to cover the chain, remove the pedals and turn the handlebars sideways; others require the bike to be completely dismantled and stored in a box. Cardboard bike boxes are available for a small charge or are often free from bike shops. Your bike is probably safer if it's *not* in a box, as it will likely be stowed upright or on top of the other luggage. These days cargo holds are pressurised, so it isn't necessary to let down your tyres. (This is a good thing, as some baggage handlers have been known to have a ride on transported bicycles, which can cause rim damage on flat tyres.)

HITCHING

Hitching is never entirely safe in any country, and it's not a form of travel we recommend. People who decide to hitch should understand that they are taking a small but potentially serious risk. The risk is higher in and around cities – catch public transport well beyond the city limits before you start to hitch. Hitching is safer if you travel in pairs and let someone know where you are going.

That said, hitching is sometimes the only way to get to smaller towns, and even if you're travelling between larger towns the choice is sometimes to wait a day or two for a bus, organise a lift with a fellow traveller or hitch. Out on the side of the road, make it obvious that you're a clean-cut foreign visitor. You may have to wait a while for a lift, especially on major roads, but when you get one there's a good chance that you'll be offered other hospitality.

It helps to carry a sign stating your destination. Instead of writing the whole word, use an abbreviation that will be meaningful to drivers. The old yellow numberplates carried a two- or three-letter code showing

fairly precisely where the car was registered. For example, 'ND' meant Durban; 'BN', Bloemfontein; and 'CAW', George ('cold and wet' was how people remembered that one). The new numberplates are province-based and don't use the city code (motorists in Western Cape are strongly resisting 'WC') but most people remember the old system. Ask someone the code for the city or area you're heading for, and write that on a piece of cardboard.

BOAT

Surprisingly, given South Africa's long coastline, there are few opportunities to travel by boat. You can take a ship between Cape Town and Durban (from US$310/420 for singles/doubles) and Port Elizabeth and Durban (from US$160/210). Contact South Africa's **Safmarine** (☎ *021-408 6911, fax 408 6660,* W *www.safmarine.co.uk*).

LOCAL TRANSPORT

Getting around in towns isn't easy, and many of the towns sprawl for a long way.

The big cities and some of the larger towns have bus systems. Services usually stop running early in the evening and there aren't many buses on weekends. Many towns, even some quite large ones, only have shared taxis. If there is a taxi service, chances are you'll have to telephone for it. You can sometimes make use of minibus taxis but they tend not to run through the areas where there are hotels. Often you'll end up walking.

In Durban and a few other places you'll find the mainstay of South-East Asian public transport, the *tuk-tuk* (motorised tricycle). Tuk-tuks run mainly in downtown and tourist areas.

ORGANISED TOURS

There is a multitude of tours available, with backpackers (and less formal visitors in general) increasingly well catered for. For information on safari-style tours, adventure holidays and the unique TALK project, see both Activities and Courses in the Facts for the Visitor chapter. Also ask for information at the various backpacker hostels around the country.

African Routes (☎ 031-569 3911, e arroutes@iafrica.com, W www.african routes.co.za) offers a whirlwind trip for those wanting to glimpse the region. The safari includes pick-up from Jo'burg, a trip to the Klein Drakensberg in Mpumalanga, Kruger National Park (two days), Swaziland and the Drakensberg in KwaZulu-Natal (two days) and then drop-off in Durban. The cost is R2150 for seven days, all inclusive; tours leave Jo'burg every Monday.

Bus

The major coach-tour operators are *Springbok-Atlas* (☎ 021-460 4700, W www .springbokatlas.com) and *Connex* (☎ 011-884 8110, fax 884 3007). Each has a wide range of fairly expensive tours covering popular routes, as well as day tours. The clientele tends to be older tourists.

Among the choices for backpackers, *Encompass Africa* (☎ 082-650 9448) offers a four-day camping tour (R1250) of the West Coast, including stops at Paternoster, Aurora and the Cederberg, with lots of guided walks and other activities.

Bok Bus (☎ 082-320 1979) offers a five-day tour (R2250) along the Garden Route, starting and finishing in Cape Town. The price includes all accommodation, two meals a day and fees for most attractions and activities. The itinerary takes in a wildlife lodge, Oudtshoorn's Cango Ostrich Farm, the *Outeniqua Choo-Tjoe* steam train and the bungee jump at Bloukrantz (the world's highest).

Train

Mike & Rachel Barry (☎/fax 023-230 0665, e uzahamba@telekomsa.net) organise an interesting range of one- and two-day package trips by train from Cape Town to Tulbagh, the Klein Cederberg Nature Reserve and Matjiesfontein. Prices range from R150 for a day trip to Tulbagh to R700 for the two-night trip combining Tulbagh and

the Klein Cederberg Nature Reserve. Bookings can be made at Computicket in Cape Town.

Union Ltd Steam Rail Tours (☎ 021-44 4391, fax 449 4395, W www.steamsa.co.za) a division of Spoornet, runs restored steam trains. The *Union Limited* was the pre-*Blue Train*, king of the line in South Africa, running to Cape Town with passengers who were meeting liners to Europe. The train was luxurious in its time and has been meticulously restored. Passengers now have more room than they once did, as two people now share a four-berth compartment and singles get a two-berth compartment.

The six-day Golden Thread tour on the *Union Limited* runs from Cape Town along the coast to Oudtshoorn and back again, which is a leisurely trip travelling through some very scenic country. It costs R4900/9800 for singles/doubles (not bad value), or R19,600 for two people in a de luxe suite including meals and a few side trips. Union also runs six- and 15-day 'steam safaris' from about R9000 per person.

Rovos Rail (☎ 012-323 6052, fax 32 0843, W www.rovos.co.za) rivals the *Blue Train* as the most luxurious and expensive service in Africa. Regular trips include Pretoria–Cape Town over two nights/three days (as opposed to the *Blue Train*'s one night/two days), with stops at Matjiesfontein and Kimberley; Pretoria–Kruger National Park; Cape Town–George; and longer trips from Pretoria to Victoria Falls (Zimbabwe) and Dar es Salaam (Tanzania).

A safari by train is also what the *Shongololo Express* (☎ 011-468 2824, fax 011-486 2909, W www.shongo.co.za) package tours are about. Not quite as luxurious as the other classic trains (but still quite acceptable), the concept is to travel by night on this sleeper train and then disembark for a day's sightseeing – a bit like a cruise, but on land. There are several options, including trips from South Africa to Namibia, Zimbabwe, Botswana and Zambia.

Cape Town & the Peninsula

☎ 021 • postcode 8001 • pop 3.1 million

Back in 1580, long before travel writers' hyperbole devalued the language, Francis Drake described the Cape of Good Hope as: 'The most stately thing, and the fairest Cape we saw in the whole circumference of the earth'. The world is a more familiar place today than in Drake's time, but his estimation of the surrounding geography of Cape Town remains true. Whichever way you look at it, Cape Town, or Kaapstad, occupies one of the world's most stunning locations.

Few other cities can boast of a 1073m-tall mountain slap-bang in their centre. The plateau of Table Mountain and its attendant peaks – Devil's Peak and Lion's Head – are the city's most enduring image, making it inaccurate to liken Cape Town (as it often is) to coastal conurbations such as Sydney and San Francisco. As beautiful as the surrounding beaches and vineyards can be, it's this rugged wilderness, coated in a unique flora, that is the focus of everyone's attention.

More than matching the visual drama of its location has been Cape Town's tumultuous history over the past 350 years. It adds a potent kick to an already heady brew. Walk through the lovely Company's Gardens and you are literally walking through that history: past the vegetable gardens planted by the city's founder Jan van Riebeeck; the graceful Cape Dutch architecture of the 18th-century Tuynhuis; the awful reality of the old Slave Lodge; the staunch majesty of St George's Cathedral, focus of Archbishop Desmond Tutu's struggle against the madness of apartheid; and the Houses of Parliament, where Nelson Mandela was proclaimed the nation's first democratically elected president. It's soul-stirring stuff.

What's more, the old 'Tavern of the Seas' is a master of showing visitors a good time. The trendy mix of hostelries along Long and Kloof Sts and at the bustling Waterfront matches up favourably to that in any other cosmopolitan city. There's a lively cultural scene, particularly when it comes to music,

Highlights

- Sail to Robben Island, a UN World Heritage site, to see where the country's future leaders were incarcerated.

- Take a township tour or, better still, stop over at one of the Cape Flats B&Bs.

- Hike up Table Mountain (or take the cable car, if you must) for an unforgettable view.

- Muse at the sunset from the top of Lion's Head.

- Hit the beaches, and soak up a range of postcard-perfect vistas.

- Enjoy Cape Town's music, from the marimba of the shebeens to popular classics in the beautiful Kirstenbosch Botanical Gardens.

- Paddle with the penguins at Boulders Beach near Simon's Town.

- Brave a dip in the shark tank at Cape Town's aquarium.

WESTERN CAPE

Cape Town & the Peninsula p128

Cape Town pp130-1
City Bowl pp138-9
Waterfront, Green Point
& Waterkant p141
Sea Point p144
Tamboerskloof, Gardens
& Oranjezicht p155

False
Bay

Simon's Town p147

SOUTH
ATLANTIC
OCEAN

which seems to pervade every corner of the city. The locals are generally open-minded and the mood is relaxed.

Capital of Western Cape province and the parliamentary capital of the republic, Cape Town works as a city in a way that so few on the African continent do. Sadly, though, the scars of the republic's terrible history still run deep. Apartheid allowed whites to reserve some of the world's most spectacular real estate, and the contrast between Third-world Crossroads and First-world Clifton remains – black and white.

And yet you simply must spend some time in the ever-growing Cape Flats townships to truly understand this city and to glimpse its future. Not everything you see will appal you. On the contrary, it's arguable that a stronger sense of optimism and pride are found in the shacks of Khayelitsha than in the mansions of Tamboerskloof. The fate of the city's large coloured community, summed up so movingly in the District Six Museum, is equally fascinating and essential for putting Cape Town fully into context.

Give yourself at least a week to explore all Cape Town offers. You may well find – like many before you – that a week is far too short.

HISTORY

For the earliest history of the Cape, up until the arrival of the Dutch East India Company (Vereenigde Oost-Indische Compagnie; VOC), see History in the Facts about South Africa chapter.

In 1660, in a gesture that takes on an awful symbolism, the leader of the initial VOC expedition, Jan van Riebeeck, planted a bitter-almond hedge to separate the Khoisan tribes and the Europeans. It extended around the western foot of Table Mountain down to Table Bay – sections can still be seen in Kirstenbosch Botanical Gardens. In another move that would have consequences for centuries ahead, Van Riebeeck then proceeded to import slaves from Madagascar, India, Ceylon, Malaya and Indonesia, to deal with the colony's chronic labour shortage.

The population of whites did not reach 1000 until 1745, but small numbers of free (meaning non-VOC) burghers had begun to drift away from the close grip of the company, and into other areas of Africa, decimating the Khoisan as they went. The survivors were left with no option but to work for Europeans in a form of bondage little different from slavery.

There was a shortage of women in the colony, so the Europeans exploited the female slaves and Khoisan survivors for both labour and sex. In time, the slaves also intermixed with the Khoikhoi. The offspring of these unions formed the basis of sections of today's coloured population.

The VOC maintained almost complete control but the town was thriving, providing a comfortable European lifestyle to a growing number of artisans and entrepreneurs who serviced the ships and crews. Kaapstad, as the Cape settlement became known, gained a wider reputation as the 'Tavern of the Seas', a riotous port used by every sailor travelling between Europe and the East.

British Invasion & Colonisation

Dutch power was fading by the end of the 18th century, and in response to the Napoleonic Wars, the British decided to secure the Cape. In 1806 at Bloubergstrand, 25km north of Cape Town, the British defeated the Dutch, and the colony was ceded to the Crown on 13 August 1814.

The slave trade was abolished in 1808, and all slaves were emancipated in 1833. Such moves contributed to Afrikaners' dissatisfaction and were a catalyst for the Great Trek of 1834–40 (see The Great Trek in the Facts about South Africa chapter).

At the same time that these apparently liberal reforms were introduced, however, the British introduced new laws that laid the basis for an exploitative labour system different from slavery. Thousands of dispossessed blacks sought work in the colony, but it was made a crime to be in the colony without a pass, and without work. It was also a crime to leave your job.

In 1854 a representative parliament was formed in Cape Town, but much to the dismay of the Dutch and English farmers to the north and east, the British government and Cape liberals insisted on a multiracial constituency (albeit with financial qualifications that excluded the vast majority of blacks and coloureds).

The discovery and exploitation of diamonds and gold in the centre of South Africa in the 1870s and '80s led to rapid changes. Cape Town was soon no longer the single dominant metropolis in the country, but as a major port it too was a beneficiary of the mineral wealth that laid the foundations for an industrial society. The same wealth led to imperialist dreams of grandeur on the part of Cecil John Rhodes (premier of the Cape Colony in 1890), who had made his millions at the head of De Beers Consolidated Mines.

In 1860, construction of the Alfred Basin in the docks commenced, finally making the port storm-proof. In 1869, however, the Suez Canal was opened, and Cape Town's role as the 'Tavern of the Seas' began to wane. Today, the massive supertankers that are too big to use the Suez are also too big to enter Table Bay, so they are serviced by helicopter.

Cape Town avoided any direct role in the 1899–1902 Anglo-Boer War but it did play a key role in landing and supplying the half a million imperial and colonial troops who fought on the British side.

Bubonic plague in 1901 gave the government an excuse to introduce racial segregation: Africans were moved to two locations, one near the docks and the other at Ndabeni on the western flank of Table Mountain. This was the start of what later would develop into the townships of the Cape Flats.

After the war, the British made some efforts towards reconciliation, and moves towards the union of the separate South African provinces were instituted. The question of who would be allowed to vote was solved by allowing the provinces to retain their existing systems: Blacks and coloureds retained a limited franchise in the Cape (although only whites could become members of the national parliament, and eligible blacks and coloureds constituted only around 7% of the electorate) but did not have the vote in other provinces.

The issue of which city should become the capital was solved by the unwieldy compromise of making Cape Town the seat of the legislature, Pretoria the administrative capital and Bloemfontein the judicial capital.

Apartheid & the Townships

In 1948 the National Party stood for election on its policy of apartheid and narrowly won. In a series of bitter court and constitutional battles, the right of the coloureds to vote in the Cape was removed and the insane apparatus of apartheid was erected.

Since the coloureds had no Homeland, the western half of the Cape Province was declared a 'coloured preference area', which meant no black person could be employed unless it could be proved there was no suitable coloured person for the job. No new black housing was built. As a result, illegal squatter camps mushroomed on the sandy plains to the east of Cape Town. In response, government bulldozers flattened the shanties, and their occupants were dragged away and dumped in their Homelands. Within weeks, the shanties would rise again.

In 1960 the African National Congress (ANC) and the Pan African Congress (PAC) organised marches against the hated pass laws, which required blacks and coloureds to carry passbooks authorising them to be in a particular area. At Langa and Nyanga on the Cape Flats, police killed five protesters. In response to the crisis, a warrant for the arrest of Nelson Mandela and other ANC leaders was issued. In mid-1963 Mandela was captured and sentenced to life imprisonment. Like many black leaders before him, he was imprisoned on Robben Island, in the middle of Table Bay.

The government tried for decades to eradicate squatter towns, such as Crossroads, which were focal points for black resistance to the apartheid regime. In its last attempt between May and June 1986, an estimated 70,000 people were driven from their homes and hundreds were killed. Even this brutal attack was unsuccessful in eradicating the towns, and the government accepted the inevitable and began to upgrade conditions. Vast townships have sprung up across the

Cape Flats, and are now home to possibly two million or more people – no-one really knows.

District Six Under apartheid Cape Town's coloured communities had no more of an easy time of it than the blacks. District Six, immediately east of the city centre, was the suburb that, more than any other, gave Cape Town its cosmopolitan atmosphere and life. It was primarily a poor, overcrowded coloured ghetto but people of every race lived there. The streets were alive with people, from children to traders, buskers to petty criminals. Jazz was its life blood, and the district was home to many musicians, including the internationally known pianist Dollar Brand (now called Abdullah Ibrahim). Being so close to the centre, it infected the whole city with its vitality.

This state of affairs naturally did not appeal to the National Party government so, in 1966, District Six was classified as a white area. Its 50,000 people, some of whose families had been there for five generations, were gradually evicted, and dumped in bleak and soulless townships like Athlone, Mitchell's Plain and Atlantis. Friends, neighbours, even relations were separated. Bulldozers moved in and the multiracial heart was ripped out of the city, while in the townships, depressed and dispirited youths increasingly joined gangs and turned to crime.

Today District Six largely remains an open wasteland, a depressing monument to the cruelty and stupidity of the government. A ray of hope, though, came on 27 November 2000 when President Thabo Mbeki signed a document handing back the confiscated land to the former residents of District Six. Although it would be impossible for all the 8000 or so forcibly removed families to return (new constructions such as the Cape Technikon college now occupy part of the area), some do plan to reclaim their property and live again in a rejuvenated District Six.

The Bo-Kaap The history of the Bo-Kaap, the largely Cape Muslim area on the north-eastern edge of Signal Hill, provides an interesting contrast to that of District Six. Home to Cape Town's first mosque (the Auwal Mosque on Dorp St dates back to 1798), the district was once known as the Malay Quarter because it was where many of the imported slaves from the start of the Cape colony lived with their masters.

In 1952 the entire Bo-Kaap region was declared a coloured area under the terms of the Group Area Act. There were forced removals, but the community, more homogenous than that of District Six, banded together to successfully fight for and keep ownership of their homes, many of which were declared national monuments in the 1960s (so at least they were saved from the bulldozers). Today, though, the area's Muslim character is noticeably diminishing as economic realities take hold. Defunct mosques on Long St indicate how far Bo-Kaap once extended into the city, and on its northwestern flank, the trendy Waterkant district increasingly encroaches as yuppies snap up the characterful houses.

Cape Town Today

During the 1990s drugs became such a problem in the Cape area that communities, and in particular the coloured community, began to take matters into their own hands. In 1995, People against Gangsterism and Drugs (Pagad) was formed but the movement quickly turned sour in 1996 with the horrific (and televised) death of gangster Rashaad Staggie. A lynch mob burned and then repeatedly shot the dying gangster, and Pagad was labelled as a group of violent vigilantes by both white and black politicians.

Pagad members are mainly coloured Muslims living in the bleak townships of Mitchell's Plain. The group sees itself as defending the coloured community from the crooked cops and drug lords who allow gangs to control the coloured townships.

But this is South Africa and nothing is as simple as it seems. The gangs in the coloured townships grew out of a desperate need for the coloured community to organise itself against criminals from the neighbouring black townships. Gang members saw themselves as upright citizens defending their community. Many blacks bitterly resented the coloureds because they received 'favoured' treatment from the apartheid government and because blacks perceived the coloureds as not being active in the fight against apartheid.

To further complicate the issue, Pagad is in danger of being hijacked by an Islamic fundamentalist group. The battles between Pagad and the gangsters continue; a series of bombings of Cape Town police stations in 1999 and a bomb at the Waterfront have been blamed on the group. The trial of five Pagad members for the murder of Staggie only began, after much legal wrangling, in May 2001.

Suspicion and mistrust between the black and coloured communities remains one of the more heartbreaking legacies of apartheid. In an effort to work towards what former Archbishop Desmond Tutu called the Rainbow Nation, the local media launched a 'One City, Many Cultures' program in 1999. It's proved popular. The process of integration and mutual acceptance and understanding is being further helped along by the restructuring of Cape Town's local government to create six councils each covering a broad range of communities, rich and poor, black, white and coloured.

ORIENTATION

Cape Town's commercial centre – known as the City Bowl – lies to the north of Table Mountain and east of Signal Hill. The old inner-city suburbs of Tamboerskloof, Gardens and Oranjezicht are all within walking distance of it. On the other side of Signal Hill, Green Point and Sea Point are other densely populated seaside suburbs.

The city sprawls quite a distance to the north-east (this is where you'll find the beachside district of Bloubergstrand and the enormous Canal Walk shopping mall, but little else of interest to visitors). To the south, skirting the eastern flank of the mountains and running down to Muizenberg at False Bay, are a string of salubrious suburbs including Observatory, Newlands and Constantia.

On the Atlantic coast, exclusive Clifton and Camps Bay are accessible by coastal road from Sea Point or through Kloof Nek, the pass between Table Mountain and Lion's Head. Camps Bay is a 10-minute drive from the city centre and can easily be reached by public transport, but as you go further south, the communities of Llandudno, Hout Bay and Noordhoek are better explored with your own car or bike. The False Bay towns from Muizenberg to Simon's Town can all be reached by rail.

Stretching along the N2 south-east of Table Mountain, the vast black townships of the Cape Flats are also accessible by rail, but this is not how you'd want to get there (unless you have a burning desire to be mugged).

The spectacular Cape of Good Hope (which is not Africa's southernmost point) is 70km south of the city centre by road. Its extraordinary indigenous flora is protected within the Cape of Good Hope Nature Reserve.

Maps

Lonely Planet's sturdy *Cape Town City Map* includes detailed transport information and a walking tour. Cape Town Tourism produces a free map which will serve most short-term visitors' needs.

Map Studio (☎ 462 4360, *Struik House, 80 McKenzie Rd, Gardens; open 8.30am-4.30pm Mon-Fri*) sells Michelin maps and government topographic maps, which are excellent for hiking. If you're staying for more than a week or so, and have a car, consider buying Map Studio's *Cape Town street directory*.

INFORMATION
Tourist Offices

Cape Town Tourism (☎ 426 4260, *fax 426 4266, Cnr Castle & Burg Sts, City Bowl,* Ⓦ *www.cape-town.org; open 8am-5pm Mon-Fri, 8.30am-1pm Sat, 9am-1pm Sun*) is a very impressive and busy facility. Here you'll find advisers who can book accommodation, tours and hire cars (with member organisations and companies only). Western Cape Tourism has a desk here, and you can

CAPE TOWN & THE PENINSULA

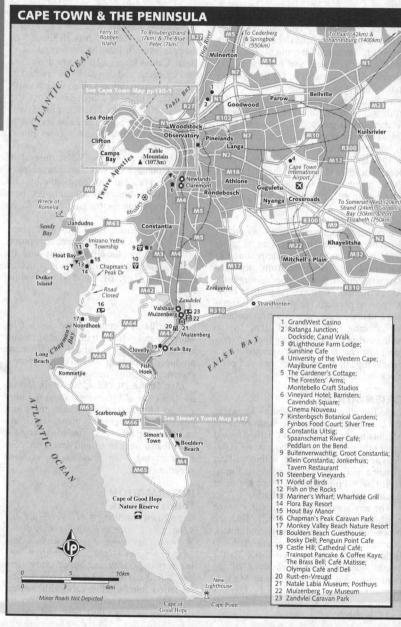

CAPE TOWN & THE PENINSULA

1 GrandWest Casino
2 Ratanga Junction;
   Dockside; Canal Walk
3 @Lighthouse Farm Lodge;
   Sunshine Cafe
4 University of the Western Cape;
   Mayibune Centre
5 The Gardener's Cottage;
   The Foresters' Arms;
   Montebello Craft Studios
6 Vineyard Hotel; Barristers;
   Cavendish Square;
   Cinema Nouveau
7 Kirstenbosch Botanical Gardens;
   Fynbos Food Court; Silver Tree
8 Constantia Uitsig;
   Spaanschemat River Café;
   Peddlars on the Bend
9 Buitenverwachtig; Groot Constantia;
   Klein Constantia; Jonkerhuis;
   Tavern Restaurant
10 Steenberg Vineyards
11 World of Birds
12 Fish on the Rocks
13 Mariner's Wharf; Wharfside Grill
14 Flora Bay Resort
15 Hout Bay Manor
16 Chapman's Peak Caravan Park
17 Monkey Valley Beach Nature Resort
18 Boulders Beach Guesthouse;
   Bosky Dell; Penguin Point Cafe
19 Castle Hill; Cathedral Café;
   Trainspot Pancake & Coffee Kaya;
   The Brass Bell; Café Matisse;
   Olympia Café and Deli
20 Rust-en-Vreugd
21 Natale Labia Museum; Posthuys
22 Muizenberg Toy Museum
23 Zandvlei Caravan Park

0   5   10km
0   6mi
Minor Roads Not Depicted

also get bookings and advice for **Cape Nature Conservation** (☎ 426 0723, Ⓦ www.capenature.org.za) parks and the national parks and reserves. There's also a booking desk for the Baz Bus, an adviser for safari and overland tours, a travel clinic, an Internet cafe, a craft shop and a foreign-exchange booth.

At the Waterfront, **Cape Metropolitan Tourism** (☎ 418 2369, Ⓦ www.waterfront.co.za; open 9am-5pm Mon-Fri Mar-Nov, 9am-6pm Sat & Sun Mar-Nov, 9am-6pm daily Dec-Feb) has a good visitor centre. It can assist with information for other parts of the city (and Western Cape) as well as the facilities close by. It also has a desk at the **airport** (open 7am-5pm daily).

Visa Extensions
For visa extensions, contact the **Department of Home Affairs** (☎ 462 4970, 56 Barrack St, City Bowl).

Money
Money can be changed at most commercial banks; they're open 9am to 3.30pm Monday to Friday, and many also open on Saturday morning.

In addition to its office in the City Bowl, **American Express** (AmEx; ☎ 408 9700, Thibault Square) also has offices at the Waterfront (☎ 419 3917, Outside the arcade at the Victoria & Alfred Hotel; open 10am-5pm daily), and at Cape Town Tourism (see Tourist Offices earlier).

Rennies Travel, the local agent for Thomas Cook, has foreign-exchange offices (some of which have been renamed Thomas Cook offices). For more details, see Travel Agencies later.

There are ATMs all over town – but please read the boxed text 'Beating the ATM Scams' in the Facts for the Visitor chapter before using them.

You can change money at the airport, although the rates aren't as good as you'll get in town.

Post
There is a poste restante counter upstairs at the **main post office** (Cnr Darling & Par-liament Sts, City Bowl; open 8am-4.30pm Mon-Fri, 8am-noon Sat). Identification is (theoretically) required if you're collecting mail.

Telephone
At phone boxes a phonecard is useful (you can buy them at Cape Town Tourism, newsagents and general stores). There are also plenty of privately run public phone businesses, where you can make calls (and usually send faxes) without coins. Check their rates first; they are much more expensive than normal public phones.

If you're looking for a quiet public phone in the city centre, there's one in the foyer of the Cultural History Museum at the Slave Lodge, and a couple at Cape Town Tourism.

At the Waterfront, the **Telekom office** (☎ 419 3944; open 9am-9pm daily) has private phone booths and Internet facilities. It's a good place to make an international or long-distance call.

You can rent cellphones from the Vodacom and MTM desks at the airport, but it'll be cheaper if you wait until you're in town. **Cellurent** (☎ 418 5656, Ⓔ service@cellurent.co.za) charges from R5 a day for a phone plus R3.50 optional insurance. Call rates start at R2.18 a minute. Cellurent delivers phones to wherever you are in the city and will pick up from you before you leave.

Email & Internet Access
You should have no problem finding somewhere to access the Internet, Cape Town being one of the most wired cities in Africa. All the hostels have Internet facilities and in the city there are several handy Internet cafes, including one at **Cape Town Tourism**, charging R10 for the first 15 minutes and R5 per five minutes thereafter.

If you're looking for a quiet and cheap place to surf head to the National Library of South Africa (see Libraries & Archives following) or to its annexe the **Centre for the Book** (62 Queen Victoria St, City Bowl), which charges R10 per 30 minutes.

Internet cafes line Long St in the City Bowl and Main Rd at Sea Point, while at the Waterfront, apart from the Telekom office,

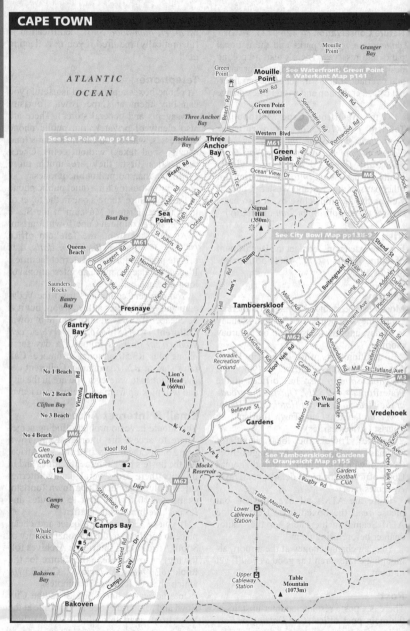

CAPE TOWN

ATLANTIC
OCEAN

Mouille
Point

*Granger
Bay*

Green
Point

**Mouille
Point**

See Waterfront, Green Point
& Waterkant Map p141

Bay Rd

Beach Rd

F Somerberg Rd

Portswood Rd

Green Point
Common

*Three Anchor
Bay*

Western Blvd

M61

**Green
Point**

M6

Dock Rd

See Sea Point Map p144

*Rocklands
Bay*

**Three
Anchor
Bay**

Ocean View Dr

York Rd

Main Rd

Strand St

Somerset St

Beach Rd

Glengariff Tce

Boat Bay

**Sea
Point**

High Level Rd

Ocean View Dr

*Signal
Hill
(350m)*

See City Bowl Map pp138-9

Strand St

M6

St Johns Rd

Buitengracht St

Wale St

Long St

Adderley St

Darling

Queens
Beach

M61

Regent Rd

Kloof Rd

Normandie Ave

Rump

Lion's

Milner Rd

Plein St

Roeland St

*Saunders
Rocks*

Queens Rd

Ocean View Dr

Hill

Government Ave

Buitenkant St

Jutland Ave

*Bantry
Bay*

Fresnaye

Signal

Tamboerskloof

Burnside Rd

M62

Kloof Nek Rd

Camp St

Annandale

Mill St

M3

**Bantry
Bay**

St Michaels Rd

No 1 Beach

Victoria Rd

*Conradie
Recreation
Ground*

Kloof St

Camp St

Molteno Rd

De Waal
Park

Upper Orange St

Vredehoek

No 2 Beach

Clifton

*Lion's
Head
(669m)*

Bellevue St

Gardens

Highlands Ave

Exner Ave

Clifton Bay

No 3 Beach

Kloof

Nek

See Tamboerskloof, Gardens
& Oranjezicht Map p155

Deer Park Dr

No 4 Beach

M6

Kloof Rd

*Glen
Country
Club*

📍1 🏠

📍2

*Mocke
Reservoir*

M62

*Gardens
Football
Club*

Rugby Rd

*Camps
Bay*

Strathmore Rd

Diep

Table Mountain Rd

▼3

Camps Bay

Woodford Rd

Camps Bay Dr

Lower
Cableway
Station

Whale
Rocks

📍4

📍5
📍6

*Bakoven
Bay*

Camps

*Upper
Cableway
Station*

**Table
Mountain
(1073m)**

Bakoven

CAPE TOWN

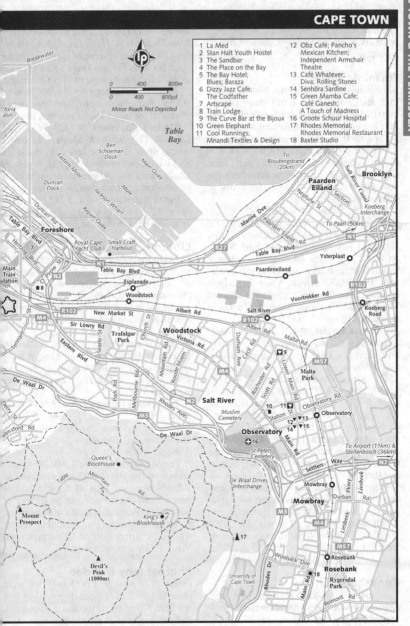

1 La Med
2 Stan Halt Youth Hostel
3 The Sandbar
4 The Place on the Bay
5 The Bay Hotel;
Blues; Baraza
6 Dizzy Jazz Cafe;
The Codfather
7 Artscape
8 Train Lodge
9 The Curve Bar at the Bijoux
10 Green Elephant
11 Cool Runnings;
Mnandi Textiles & Design

12 Obz Café; Pancho's
Mexican Kitchen;
Independent Armchair
Theatre
13 Café Whatever;
Diva; Rolling Stones
14 Senhôra Sardine
15 Green Mamba Cafe;
Café Ganesh;
A Touch of Madness
16 Groote Schuur Hospital
17 Rhodes Memorial;
Rhodes Memorial Restaurant
18 Baxter Studio

there's also **Odyssey Internet** (☎ 418 7289, *Victoria Wharf shopping mall, Waterfront; open 10am-midnight daily)*, above Cinema Nouveau.

Travel Agencies

Most hotels and hostels offer tour bookings (although not always a full range of options). Many have good deals on car hire and they are usually better informed about budget options than mainstream travel agencies.

For international travel, **STA Travel** (☎ 418 6570, 31 Riebeeck St, City Bowl), part of the worldwide chain, offers some good fares. So does **Flight Centre** (☎ 461 8658, Gardens Centre, Mill St, Gardens).

Rennies Travel (☎ 423 7154, 101 St George's Mall, City Bowl; ☎ 439 7529, 182 Main Rd, Sea Point; open Mon-Fri, Sat morning) has agencies throughout South Africa. It's the agent for Thomas Cook and handles international and domestic bookings. It will also arrange visas for neighbouring countries for a moderate charge. The branch at the Waterfront (☎ 418 3744) is open daily.

The **Visa Service** (☎ 421 7826, 9th floor, Strand Towers, 66 Strand St, City Bowl) also arranges visas for countries outside South Africa.

The **Africa Travel Centre** (☎ 423 5555, fax 423 0065, The Backpack hostel, 74 New Church St, ⓦ www.backpackers.co.za) books all sorts of travel and activities, including day trips, hire cars and extended truck tours of Africa. The rates are good. As the centre has been in business for some time, it has vetted many of the operators – and there are some cowboys out there.

Other hostels with reputable travel agencies are Ashanti Lodge and Aardvark Backpackers (see Places to Stay – Budget).

Adventure Village (☎ 424 1580, 229B Long St, City Bowl) is a handy one-stop shop for a host of activities and overland trips.

Bookshops

The main mass-market bookshop and newsagent is CNA, with numerous shops around the city.

Exclusive Books (☎ 419 0905, Victoria Wharf, Waterfront; open 9am-10.30pm Mon-Thurs, 9am-11pm Fri & Sat, 10am-9pm Sun) has an excellent range including some books in French. There's also a branch at the Cavendish Square mall in Claremont.

Travellers Bookshop (☎ 425 6880, Victoria Wharf, Waterfront; open 9am-9pm daily) stocks all the travel books you may need.

Clarke's Bookshop (☎ 423 5739, 211 Long St, City Bowl, ⓦ www.clarkesbooks .co.za; open 9am-5pm Mon-Fri, 9am-1pm Sat) has an unsurpassed range of books on South Africa and the continent, and a great second-hand and antiquarian section.

Ulrich Naumann's (☎ 423 7832, Burg St; open 8.30am-5.30pm Mon-Fri, 8.30am-1pm Sat) has German-language books.

Libraries & Archives

The **National Library of South Africa** (☎ 424 6320, Company's Gardens, Government Ave, City Bowl; open 9am-5pm Mon-Fri) is the national reference library (there's no lending of books). There's an Internet cafe, a small bookshop and an exhibition space on the 2nd floor.

There is a reference library at the **British Council** (☎ 462 3921, 21 St John's St, ⓦ www .britishcouncil.org/southafrica; open 9am-4.30pm Mon, Tues & Thur, 9am-1pm Wed, 9am-4pm Fri).

The **Alliance Française** (☎ 423 5699, ⓔ afducap@iafrica.com, 155 Loop St, City Bowl; library open 2am-6pm Mon-Thur, 10am-2pm Fri, 10am-1pm Sat) also has a reference library.

The **Mayibune Centre** (☎ 959 2954, University of the Western Cape, Modderdam Rd, Modderdam), east of the city centre near the airport, houses a large archive of materials concerned with the history of the anti-apartheid struggle, including letters written by former Robben Island prisoners. Visits are by appointment only.

Photography & Video

Prolab (177 Bree St, City Bowl) is a good place to buy film (especially pro film) that has been stored correctly, and it does quick and competent slide processing.

For regular film you'll find camera shops and fast developers all over the city. Try various outlets at the Waterfront, or **Shap's Cameraland** (*☎ 423 4150, Camera House, 68 Long St, City Bowl; open 8am-8.30pm Mon-Fri, 8am-1pm Sat)*.

Laundry

Laundrettes are scattered throughout the city, although most hostels and many hotels have either a laundry on the premises or a laundry service. To have a medium-size bag of laundry washed, dried and folded costs around R20.

Left Luggage

There's a left-luggage facility next to Platform 24 in the main train station; it's open from 6am to around 2pm daily.

Medical Services

Medical services are of a high standard. In an emergency, you can go directly to the casualty department of **Groote Schuur Hospital** (*☎ 404 9111, Main Rd, Observatory)*. As every local will proudly tell you while driving past on the N2, this is where in 1967 Dr Christiaan Barnard made the first successful heart transplant.

In the City Bowl, the best private hospital is **City Park Hospital** (*☎ 480 6271, 181 Longmarket St, reception on the 8th floor)*.

Contact the **police** (*☎ 10111)* to get directions to the nearest hospital. Many doctors will make house calls; they're listed under Medical in the phone book, and hotels and most other places to stay can arrange a visit.

If you need a late-night pharmacy, try the **Glengariff Pharmacy** (*☎ 434 1685, Cnr Main Rd & Glengariff Tce, Sea Point; open until 11pm daily)*. There's also the **Lite Kem Pharmacy** (*Darling St between Plein & Parliament Sts; open until 11pm daily)*.

For vaccinations, go to the **British Airways Travel Clinic** (*☎ 419 3172, fax 419 3389, Room 314, Fountain Medical Centre, Adderley St, City Bowl; open 8am-5pm Mon-Fri, 9am-1pm Sat)*.

The **SAA Netcare Travel Clinic** (*☎ 423 1401)* is in the Cape Town Tourism office.

Emergency

The phone numbers for emergency services are:

Ambulance	☎ 10177
Automobile Association (AA) emergency rescue	☎ 080 003 3007
AA sales	☎ 086 111 1994
Fire brigade	☎ 535 1100
Lifeline	☎ 461 1111
Police	☎ 10111
Rape Crisis Centre	☎ 447 9762
Tourist police	☎ 418 2853

Dangers & Annoyances

Despite an increase in street crime in recent years, Cape Town remains one of the most relaxed cities in Africa, which can instil a false sense of security. People who have travelled overland from Cairo without a single mishap or theft have been known to be cleaned out in Cape Town – generally when doing something stupid like leaving their gear on a beach while they go swimming.

Paranoia is not required but common sense is. There is tremendous poverty on the peninsula and the 'informal redistribution of wealth' is reasonably common. The townships on the Cape Flats have an appalling crime rate and unless you have a trustworthy guide or are on a tour they are off-limits.

Also take care when driving along the N2 near the airport; reports of rocks being thrown off the cross bridges on to passing cars, so that they'll be forced to stop (and then robbed), are fairly constant. Whatever happens, if at all possible, *never* stop on this stretch of highway.

The rest of Cape Town is reasonably safe. Care should be taken in Sea Point and quiet areas of the city centre at night, and walking to or from the Waterfront is not recommended, day or night. As always, listen to local advice. There is safety in numbers.

Swimming at all the Cape beaches is potentially hazardous, especially for those inexperienced in surf. Check for warning signs about rips and rocks and only swim in patrolled areas.

The mountains in the middle of the city are no less dangerous just because they are in the city. Weather conditions can change rapidly, so warm clothing, water and a good map and compass are always necessary.

Another hazard of the mountains is ticks, which can get onto you when you brush past vegetation (see Health in the Facts for the Visitor chapter).

MUSEUMS & GALLERIES

One thing that Cape Town isn't short of is museums and galleries, with over 15 in the City Bowl area alone. Many, including the South African Museum and the Michealis Collection, are banded together as the **Iziko Museums of Cape Town** (W www.museums .org.za/iziko).

The following museums are listed in order of, in our opinion, the most interesting to see on a short visit to Cape Town. For other recommendations see the Southern Suburbs and False Bay sections of this chapter and the 'Cape Town Architecture' special section.

District Six Museum

If you see only one museum in Cape Town make it this one; note that almost all township tours stop here first to explain the history of the pass laws. The museum (☎ 461 8745, 25A Buitenkant St; admission by donation; open 9am-4pm Mon-Sat) is as much for the people of the now-vanished District Six as it is about them. The displays are moving and poignant: a floor covered with a large-scale map of District Six, ex-residents having labelled where their demolished homes and features of their neighbourhood were; reconstructions of home interiors; fading photographs and recordings. Most memorable of all are the staff, practically all displaced residents, each with a heartbreaking story to tell. By appointment it's also possible to arrange **walking tours** of the old District Six for R20.

South African Museum & Planetarium

The South African Museum (☎ 424 3330, 25 Queen Victoria St; adult/child R8/free, Wed free; open 10am-5pm daily), at the mountain end of the Company's Gardens, is the oldest museum in South Africa and beginning to show its age. This said, there are plans to upgrade it, and the building contains a truly fascinating collection of objects, starting with a fossilised human footprint believed to be 117,000 years old! Next comes the Linton Panel, one of the most amazing examples of San rock art you'll see anywhere. Most of the startlingly lifelike displays of San (made in 1911 from casts of living people, some of whom died in the process) have now been removed.

Other displays to look out for include the terracotta Lydenburg Heads, the earliest known examples of African sculpture (AD 500–700); the Whale Well hung with giant skeletons of these mammals and sometimes used as a venue for concerts; a stuffed quagga foal (the very exhibit that provided the DNA to start the rebreeding of the thought-to-be-extinct quagga); the fascinating Wonders of Nature Gallery; and the 2m-wide nest of the sociable weaver bird, a veritable avian apartment block.

Attached to the museum is a planetarium (☎ 424 3330; adult/child R10/5, evening shows adult R12). If you want to unravel the mysteries of the southern hemisphere's night sky, shows are given on Tuesday (2pm and 8pm including a 3D star show), Thursday (2pm) and Saturday (2.30pm). There are more frequent shows in school holidays.

South African National Gallery

This exquisite gallery (☎ 465 1628, Government Ave; adult/child R5/free, admission free Sun; open 10am-5pm Tues-Sun) in the Company's Gardens always has some very interesting exhibitions as well as permanent displays. Check out the portrait of Desmond Tutu, the remarkable carved teak door in the courtyard, and a dinosaur sculpture made from wire. There's a good shop with some interesting books and a pleasant cafe.

South African Jewish Museum

One of the newest of the city's museums is the imaginative South African Jewish Museum (☎ 445 1546, 88 Hatfield St, W www .sajewishmuseum.co.za; adult/child R20/ 10; open 10am-5pm Sun-Thur, 10am-2pm

Fri). Entry is through the beautifully re-stored old synagogue (1862), from where a wooden gangplank leads to state-of-the-art galleries with displays on the vibrant history of the nation's Jewish community, which today numbers around 90,000. Downstairs you'll find a partial recreation of a Lithuanian *shtetl* (village); many of South Africa's Jews fled this part of Eastern Europe during the pogroms and persecution of the late 19th and early 20th centuries.

Across from the main complex, don't miss the **Cape Town Holocaust Centre** *(☎ 462 5553; admission free; open 10am-5pm Sun-Thur, 10am-1pm Fri)*. This admirable museum is small, but packs a lot in with a considerable emotional punch. The history of anti-Semitism is set in a South African context with parallels drawn to the local struggle for freedom. Stop to watch the video tales of Holocaust survivors at the end.

It's possible to visit the beautifully decorated Baroque **Great Synagogue** *(guided tours 10am-2pm Mon-Thur, 10am-4pm Sun)*. The Gardens Shul, as it was known, was consecrated the same year that Cape Town had its first Jewish mayor, Hyman Liberman.

Bo-Kaap Museum
The small but interesting Bo-Kaap Museum *(☎ 424 3846, 71 Wale St; adult/child R5/2; open 9.30am-4.30pm Mon-Sat)* gives an insight into the lifestyle of a prosperous 19th-century Cape Muslim family and a somewhat idealised view of Islamic practice in Cape Town. The house itself, built in 1763, is the oldest in the area.

Slave Lodge & Cultural History Museum
The rather muddled Cultural History Museum *(☎ 461 8280, 49 Adderley St; adult/child R7/2; open 9.30am-4.30pm daily)* occupies the former Slave Lodge of the VOC and contains displays on that period as well as bits and pieces from ancient Egypt, Greece and Rome and the Far East. It's likely that it will be curated again in the near future, and hopefully it will become a more consistent collection.

Islamic Cape Town

Many Muslim Bo-Kaap residents are descendants of the slaves brought to Cape Town by the Vereenigde Oost-Indische Compagnie (VOC) from the Indian subcontinent and Indonesia (hence the term Cape Malays, although few actually hailed from what is today called Malaysia).

The VOC also used Cape Town as a place of exile for Islamic leaders, such as Tuan Guru from Tidore, who arrived in 1780. During his 13 years on Robben Island he accurately copied the Quran from memory and later helped establish the Auwal Mosque, the city's first, in 1794.

Tuan Guru is buried in Bo-Kaap's Tana Baru cemetery, one of the oldest in South Africa, at the western end of Longmarket St, City Bowl. Within the cemetery (which has fallen into disrepair and is subject to a local preservation campaign) his grave is one of the 20 or so *karamats* – tombs of Muslim saints – encircling Cape Town and visited by the faithful on a mini-pilgrimage. Other karamats are found on Robben Island (that of Sayed Abdurahman Matura), at the gate to the Klein Constantia wine estate (Adbumaah Shah), and by the Eerste River in Macassar (Sheik Yussof, the most significant Muslim leader of his time).

A sizable Muslim community also lived in Simon's Town before the Group Area Act evictions of the late 1960s. Their history can be traced in the Heritage Museum in Simon's Town (see Simon's Town later in this chapter).

Michealis Collection
Donated by Sir Max Michealis in 1914, this art collection *(☎ 424 6367, Greenmarket Square; adult/child R3/free; open 10am-5pm)* is in the Old Townhouse, which used to be the city hall. The Dutch and Flemish paintings and etchings from the 16th and 17th centuries (including works by Rembrandt, Frans Hals and Anthony van Dyck) suit the somewhat gloomy atmosphere. Nip upstairs for views from the balcony overlooking the square, or come for lunch or a drink in the relaxed Ivy Garden Restaurant (see Restaurants under Places to Eat later in this chapter).

Rust-en-Vreugd

This delightful 18th-century mansion *(☎ 465 3628, 78 Buitenkant St; admission by donation; open 8.30am-4.30pm Mon-Sat)* was once the home of the state prosecutor. It now houses part of the William Fehr collection of paintings and furniture (the major part is in the Castle of Good Hope). Paintings by John Thomas Baines show early scenes from colonial Cape Town, while the sketches of Alys Fane Trotter are some of the best you'll see of Cape Dutch architecture. There's also a pleasant garden.

HOUSES OF PARLIAMENT

Visiting the Houses of Parliament *(☎ 403 2537, Entrance on Plein St; admission free; tours by appointment Mon-Fri)* is one of the most fascinating things you can do in Cape Town. If parliament is sitting, fix your tour for the afternoon so you can see the politicians in action. Opened in 1885 and enlarged several times since, this is where British prime minister Harold Macmillan made his famous 'Wind of Change' speech in 1960. The articulate tour guides will proudly fill you in on the mechanisms and political make-up of their new democracy. You must present your passport to gain entry.

CASTLE OF GOOD HOPE

Built to defend Cape Town, the stone-walled Castle of Good Hope *(☎ 469 1084, Entrance on Buitenkant St; adult/child R15/6.50 Mon-Sat, R8/4 Sun; open 9am-4pm daily; tours 11am, noon & 2pm Mon-Sat)* has never seen action in all its 350 years, unless you count the more recent stormings by hordes of school kids and tourists.

It's worth coming for one of the tours (the noon tour on weekdays coincides with the changing of the guard since the castle is still the headquarters for the Western Cape military command), although you can quite easily find your own way around. A key ceremony is held at 10am weekdays.

There are extensive displays of militaria and some interesting ones on the castle's archaeology and the reconstruction of the so-called Dolphin Pool. The highlight is the bulk of the **William Feur Collection** *(open 9.30am-4pm daily)* including some fabulous bits of Cape Dutch furniture such as a table seating 100 and more paintings by John Thomas Baines.

Also within the castle grounds is *Wine Concepts*, a noted wine store, a cafe and a good restaurant, De Waterblommetjie (see City Bowl under Restaurants in Places to Eat later).

SIGNAL HILL

Signal Hill separates Sea Point from the City Bowl. There are magnificent views from the 350m-high summit, especially at night. Head up Kloof Nek Rd from the city and take the first turn-off to the right at the top of the hill. At this intersection you also turn off for Clifton (also to the right) and the lower cableway station (left).

At noon, daily except Sunday, a cannon known as the **Noon Gun** is fired from the lower slopes of Signal Hill. You can hear it all over town. Traditionally this allowed the burghers in the town below to check their watches. It's a stiff walk up here through Bo-Kaap – take Longmarket St and keep going until it ends. The *Noon Gun Tearoom & Restaurant* (see City Bowl under Restaurants in Places to Eat later) is a good place to catch your breath.

LONG ST BATHS

The Long St Baths *(☎ 400 3302, Cnr Long & Buitensingel Sts)* are something of an anachronism, but they have been restored, they're heated and they're very popular. At the **Turkish baths** *(admission R40; open to men 9am-7pm Tues, Wed & Fri, 9am-noon Sun; open to women 9am-7pm Mon, Thur & Sat)* a massage costs R30, and a massage with bath costs R55. The Turkish baths are segregated, unlike the **heated swimming pool** *(admission R6; open 7am-7pm Mon-Sat, 8am-7pm Sun)*.

TABLE MOUNTAIN
Cable Car

The cable car *(☎ 424 8181, [W] www.table mountain.co.za, adult single/return R40/75, child single/return R28/40; open 7.30am-9pm)* on Table Mountain is such an obvious and popular attraction you might have difficulty convincing yourself that it's worth the trouble and expense. It is. The views on the way up and from the top of Table Mountain are phenomenal, and there are some good easy walks on the summit.

There's a small self-service restaurant and shop at the top, where you can also post letters and send faxes. Ride 'n' Dine tickets cover a return trip on the cable car plus breakfast (R100), lunch (R120) or dinner (R120). For an adrenaline rush like no other consider doing the abseil (see Activities later in this chapter).

The cable cars don't operate when it's dangerously windy, and there's obviously not much point going up if you are simply going to be wrapped in the cloud known as 'the tablecloth'. Call in advance to see if they're operating. Weather conditions permitting, they operate every 10 minutes in high season and every 20 minutes in low season. The last car down the mountain leaves at 10pm (these times can change, so check). The best visibility and conditions are likely to be first thing in the morning or in the evening.

To get here from central Cape Town by car take Kloof Nek Rd and turn off to the left (signposted). If you don't have your own transport, Rikkis will come up here for R10; a regular taxi will cost around R45.

It's also possible to ascend (and descend) the mountain from the Kirstenbosch Botanical Gardens side (see Kirstenbosch Botanical Gardens later in this chapter) or the City Bowl side.

Climbing Table Mountain

Climbing Table Mountain looks deceptively easy. Over 300 routes up and down the mountain have been identified, perhaps giving you a clue as to how easy it is to get lost. Lives are lost from time to time, so make sure you're properly equipped with warm and waterproof clothing, sufficient water and some food before setting off.

Bear in mind that the mountain is over 1000m high and conditions can become treacherous quickly. Thick mists can make the paths invisible, and you'll just have to

Table Mountain Weather Lore

As if Table Mountain is not spectacular enough in itself, for much of the summer it is capped by a seemingly motionless cloud that drapes itself neatly across the summit. The cloud is known as the tablecloth. An Afrikaner legend explains this phenomena by telling of an old burgher, who was fond of his pipe, attempting to outsmoke the devil in a competition.

Meteorologists have come up with a more prosaic explanation. The south-easterly wind (the Cape Doctor) picks up moisture as it crosses the Agulhas current and False Bay. When it hits Table Mountain it rises, and as it reaches cooler air around 900m above sea level it condenses into thick white clouds. As the clouds pour over the plateau and down into the City Bowl they once more dissolve in the warmer air at around 900m.

Table Mountain just happens to be at the perfect height and place, and the tablecloth is a dynamic and hypnotic sight.

Many people use the mountain as a weather forecaster, and it's apparently quite accurate. Some things to watch for:

• If there is heavy cloud on Lion's Head, rain is coming.

• If the tablecloth shrouds the mountain, the Cape Doctor is coming.

• If there is no cloud around the upper cableway station (visible from all over town), there is no wind on Clifton Beach.

wait until they lift. You should always tell someone where you are going and you should never walk alone; check with Cape Town Tourism if you want a guide. Climbing the mountain is such a popular pastime that there's a good chance you'll meet someone who will invite you along.

None of the routes is easy but the Platteklip Gorge walk on the City Bowl side is at least straightforward. Unless you're fit, try walking down before you attempt the walk up. It took us about 2½ hours from the upper cableway station to the lower, taking it fairly easy. A better walk is the one called Indian Windows that starts from directly

CITY BOWL

PLACES TO STAY
5 Days Inn
8 St Paul's B&B
   Guest House
11 The Backpack;
   Africa Travel Centre
12 Zebra Crossing
16 Overseas Visitors' Club
17 Travellers Inn
29 Long St Backpackers
41 Cape Heritage Hotel;
   Heritage Square; Africa
   Cafe; Pa Na Na Souk Bar
54 Metropole Hotel
71 Tudor Hotel
97 The Townhouse
99 Parliament Hotel

PLACES TO EAT
2 Biesmiellah
9 Priscilla's
10 Gorgeous
13 Rozenhof
17 Lola's
18 Diablo Bar Tapas;
   Jo'burg
20 Mexican Kitchen
22 Mama Africa
23 Mr Pickwick's
26 Sooz Baguette Bar
31 Kennedy's
37 Long St Cafe
37 Gardens Restaurant
63 Le Petit Paris
64 Primi Piatti
69 Cycles; Shell House;
   Holiday Inn
73 Mesopotamia
76 Café Mozart
78 Bukhara
79 Shambala
81 Five Flies
87 Off Moroka
   Café Africaine
103 De Waterblommetjie
104 D6 Snack Bar

ENTERTAINMENT
21 The Lounge
25 Rhythm Divine
35 Rhodes House
61 The Square All Bar None
62 The Fez
66 The Jet Lounge;
   The Baseline
68 The Purple Turtle
75 Coffee Lounge
80 169 on Long

MUSEUMS & GALLERIES
4 Bo-Kaap Museum
43 Gold of Africa Museum;
   Lutheran Church
52 Koopmans de Wet House
55 South African Missionary
   Meeting House Museum
70 Old Townhouse;
   Michaelis Collection,
   Ivy Garden Restaurant
85 Slave Lodge & Cultural
   History Museum
102 District Six Museum

CONSULATES
27 Ireland
34 Germany
42 Netherlands
45 Australia
46 USA
51 Botswana; UK
56 Mozambique
60 Canada

OTHER
1 Tana Baru Cemetery
3 Atlas Trading Company
6 Auwal Mosque
7 Prolab
14 Downhill Adventures
15 Long St Baths
24 Alliance Française
28 Clarke's Bookshop
30 Adventure Village
33 Morris's
36 Centre for the Book
38 Cecil John Rhodes Statue
39 City Park Hospital
40 St Stephen's Church
44 STA Travel
47 Van Riebeeck Statues
48 Bus Termini & Booking
   Offices of Translux,
   Greyhound &
   Intercape Mainliner
49 British Airways
   Travel Clinic
50 American Express
53 Cape Town Tourism
57 Surf Centre
58 Ulrich Naumann's
59 Rennies Travel;
   Thomas Cook
65 Shap's Cameraland
67 Pan African Market;
   Pan African Kitchen
72 African Image
74 The African Music Store

77 Metropolitan Gallery
82 Tuynhuis
83 National Library of
   South Africa
84 St George's Cathedral
86 Groote Kerk
88 Standard Bank
89 Golden Acre
   Shopping Centre;
   Computicket
90 Main Post Office
91 Mutual Building
92 Wellington Fruit
   Growers
93 Lite Kem Pharmacy
94 Golden Acre
   Bus Terminal
95 Bus Information Kiosk
96 Cape Union Mart
98 Entrance to Houses
   of Parliament
100 Department of
   Home Affairs
101 Police

Waterkant

Bo-Kaap
(Cape Muslim
Quarter)

To
Camps Bay
(3km)

Delville
Wood
Memorial

South African
Museum
& Planetarium

CITY BOWL

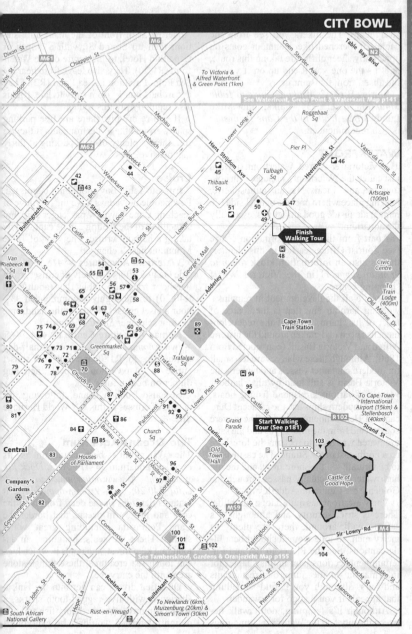

To Victoria &
Alfred Waterfront
& Green Point (1km)

See Waterfront, Green Point & Waterkant Map p141

Roggebaai
Sq

Pier Pl

Table Bay Blvd

N2

Coen Steytler Ave

Tulbagh
Sq

Thibault
Sq

Finish
Walking Tour

Civic
Centre

To
Artscape
(100m)

To
Train
Lodge
(400m)

Cape Town
Train Station

Central

Van
Riebeeck
Sq

Greenmarket
Sq

Trafalgar
Sq

To Cape Town
International
Airport (15km) &
Stellenbosch
(40km)

Grand
Parade

Start Walking
Tour (See p181)

Houses
of Parliament

Company's
Gardens

Church
Sq

Old Town
Hall

Castle of
Good Hope

Sir Lowry Rd

M4

See Tamberskloof, Gardens & Oranjezicht Map p155

South African
National Gallery

To Newlands (6km),
Muizenburg (20km) &
Simon's Town (30km)

Rust-en-Vreugd

behind the lower cableway station and heads straight up. The hikers you see from the cable car, perched like mountain goats on apparently sheer cliffs, are taking this route, and it's the one you'll end up on if you do the abseil from the summit.

Shirley Brossy's *Walking Guide to Table Mountain* details 34 walks, and Mike Lundy's *Best Walks in the Cape Peninsula* is also recommended.

WATERFRONT

The Victoria & Alfred Waterfront (always just called the Waterfront), popular with both tourists and locals, is an atmospheric, buzzing place where pockets of dockside life remain alongside good attractions, especially the aquarium.

Apart from the main information centre (see Tourist Offices earlier in this chapter) there's also an **information kiosk** *(open to 9pm in summer)* in the Victoria Wharf shopping centre.

Despite all the development, it remains a working harbour and that is the source of most of its charm. Most of the redevelopment has been undertaken around the historic Alfred and Victoria Basins (constructed from 1860). Although these wharves are too small for modern container vessels and tankers, the Victoria Basin is still used by tugs, harbour vessels of various kinds, and fishing boats.

Large modern ships use the adjacent Duncan and Ben Schoeman docks. These were constructed from the mid-1930s and the sand excavated was used to reclaim the foreshore area north-east of the Strand. The castle used to be virtually on the shore front, and the old high water line actually passes through the Golden Acre Centre on Adderley St.

The Waterfront has quite a lot of nightlife. There is strict security, and although it is safe to walk around, there are plenty of merry men, so lone women should be a little cautious. See the Places to Eat and Entertainment sections later in this chapter for information on the numerous restaurants and bars, although you'll find something that appeals if you just go for a wander.

Although it's tempting, don't walk between the city and the Waterfront; muggings

do happen here. Shuttle buses run from Adderley St in front of the main train station, then up Strand St, with a stop near Cape Sun Hotel, to the centre of the Waterfront (R1.20). They also leave from near the Sea Point Pavillion in Sea Point (R2). They depart half-hourly from early to late. Rikkis also regularly ply this route.

If you're driving, there are free parking spaces around the Waterfront, and if they're full, there's plenty of paid parking at fairly inexpensive rates.

Cruises

A trip into Table Bay should not be missed. Few people nowadays have the privilege of reaching Cape Town by passenger ship, but something of the feeling can be captured by taking a harbour cruise. The view of Table Mountain hasn't changed.

Waterfront Adventures *(☎ 418 5806)* beside Quay 5 offers a variety of cruises, from one-hour trips into Table Bay (adult/child R40/20) to the highly recommended 1½-hour sunset cruises (R90) on the handsome 58-foot schooner *Spirit of Victoria*.

Nomad Adventure Centre *(☎ 426 5445, W www.nomadtours.co.za)* offers half-day sailing trips for R180, and four-hour sunset cruises down to Clifton and back, including dinner on board, for R235.

See also Robben Island, following, for details of cruises to this UN World Heritage Site.

Two Oceans Aquarium

The Waterfront's best attraction is its excellent aquarium *(☎ 418 3823, Dock Rd, Waterfront, W www.aquarium.co.za; adult/child R40/20; open 9.30am-6pm daily)*. It features denizens of the deep from both the cold and the warm oceans that border the Cape Peninsula, including great white sharks. There are seals, penguins, an astounding kelp forest, and pools in which kids can touch sea creatures; these things alone are worth the entry fee.

Qualified divers can get into the tank – sharing it with five ragged-tooth sharks, a 150kg stingray, other predatory fish and two delightful turtles wouldn't be everyone's

WATERFRONT, GREEN POINT & WATERKANT

PLACES TO STAY
14 Victoria & Alfred Hotel
19 Portswood Square Hotel;
   The Commodore
22 Breakwater Lodge
23 Dungarvin House
24 Check Inn
29 Claridges B&B Hotel
30 The Hip Hop
31 The Big Blue
32 St John's Waterfront Lodge
33 Victoria Junction
35 City Lodge
36 The Cullinan
37 Holiday Inn
46 The Lodge
47 De Waterkant Lodge
   & Cottages
48 Harbour View Cottages

PLACES TO EAT
1 Mugg & Bean; Zerban's
5 Caffé San Marco; Ari's Souvlaki;
   Musselcracker Restaurant
10 Quay 4

12 Den Anker
20 Cape Grace Hotel;
   Quay West; Bascule Bar
26 Gionvanni's Deli World
27 Mario's
28 0932; News Café;
   Buena Vista Social Café
34 Beluga
38 Anapurna; Col' Cacchio
40 Vasco da Gama Tavern
41 Anatoli
45 Robert's Café & Cigar Bar
49 Noon Gun Tearoom
   & Restaurant

ENTERTAINMENT
6 The Sports Cafe
13 Green Dolphin
17 Ferryman's Freehouse
18 IMAX Theatre
39 Fireman's Arms
42 55
43 Chilli 'n' Lime; Bronx; Angels;
   Detour; On Broadway
44 Cafe Manhattan

OTHER
2 Exclusive Books
3 Rennies Travel;
   Thomas Cook;
   Information Kiosk;
   Computicket
4 Travellers Bookshop;
   Cinema Nouveau;
   Odyssey Internet;
   Nu Metro Cineplex
7 Waterfront Adventures
8 Old Departure
   Point for Robben
   Island Tours
9 Telekom Office
11 Future Departure
   Point for Robben
   Island Tours
15 American Express
16 Visitor Centre;
   Vaughan Johnson's
   Wine & Cigar Shop
21 Two Oceans
   Aquarium
25 Post Office

0   200   400m
0   200   400yd

Mouille
Point

To Sea Point

ATLANTIC OCEAN

Table
Bay

*Granger
Bay*

Table Bay

Quay 7

Metropolitan
Golf Course

Green
Point
Common

Fritz Sonnenberg Rd

Beach Rd

East Pier Rd

Victoria
Wharf

Quay 6

Victoria
Basin

Vlei Rd

Green
Point

Fort Wynyard Rd

Portswood Rd

Quay 5
Quay 4

Green
Point
Stadium

Bill Peters Drv

Green Point
Track

Dock Rd

Alfred
Basin

South Arm

South Arm

Western Blvd

Main Rd

Dysart Rd

York

Cavalcade Rd

Vesperdene Rd

Braemar Rd

Main Rd

Hillside Tce

Western Blvd

Dock Rd

**Victoria & Alfred
Waterfront**

Fish Market Rd

West Quay

Duncan
Dock

Wigtown Rd

High Level Rd

Boundary Rd

Ocean View Dr

Old Muslim
Cemetery

Ebenezer Rd

Prestwich St

Somerset Rd

Port Rd

Western Blvd

Dock Rd

Duncan Rd

Foreshore

Merriman Rd

Waterkant St

Loader St

Strand St

Waterkant

Napier St

Alfred St

Table Bay Blvd

N2

To
Paarl

To Signal Hill

Noon
Gun

Longmarket
St

Dixon

Chiappini St

Medcalf St

M6

N2

Coen Steytler Ave

Lower Long St

To
City Bowl

Ella St

M61

idea of fun, but for experienced divers (certificate required) this is a great way to get really close to the ocean action. The cost is R325 including hire of diving gear.

Get your hand stamped on entrance and you can return again any time during the same day for free.

ROBBEN ISLAND

Proclaimed a UN World Heritage site in 1999, Robben Island is unmissable. Most likely you will have to endure crowds and being hustled around on a guided tour that at 2½ hours is woefully too short – such is the price of the island's infamy. It's likely to be truly swamped in the future as the island's tourist infrastructure is developed to include accommodation and better roads. Still you must go to see this shrine to struggle.

Used as a prison from the early days of the VOC right up until the first years of majority rule, Robben Island's most famous involuntary resident was Nelson Mandela. You will learn much of what happened to Mandela and other inmates since one will be leading your tour. The guides are happy to answer any questions you may have, and although some understandably remain bitter, as a whole this is the best demonstration of reconciliation you could hope to see in Cape Town.

Booking a **tour** (☎ 419 1300, W www .robben-island.org.za, adult/child R100/50; hourly ferries 8am-3pm daily, sunset tours at 5pm & 6pm in summer) is essential as they are extremely popular; otherwise be prepared for a long wait. At the time of research boats were departing from Jetty 1 at the Waterfront's Quay 5, but in the future there will be a new departure point from beside the clock tower on Fish Quay.

The tour entails being guided through the old prison, and includes a 45-minute bus ride around the island with commentary on the various places of note, such as the prison house of PAC leader Robert Sobuke, the lime quarry where Mandela and many others slaved, and the church used during the island's stint as a leper colony. There will be a little time for you to wander around on your own; you could check out the penguin colony near the landing jetty (see the boxed text 'Saving the African Penguin' in the Facts about South Africa chapter).

All tours have a set departure and return time, but when you book, consider asking to extend your time on the island so you can see **Cell Stories**, a most remarkable exhibition in the prison's A Section and not on the regular tour. Here in each of 40 isolation cells is an artefact and story from a former political prisoner: chess pieces drawn on scraps of paper; a Christmas card from a forgotten wife; an intricately patterned belt made from fishing nets and old shoe leather; a soccer trophy. It's all unbelievably moving.

KIRSTENBOSCH BOTANICAL GARDENS

These gardens (☎ 762 9120, W www.nb .ac.za, Rhodes Dr, Bishopscourt; adult/ child R15/10; open 8am-7pm Sept-Mar 8am-6pm Apr-Aug) are among the most beautiful in the world. They have an incomparable site on the eastern side of Table Mountain, overlooking False Bay and the Cape Flats. The 36-hectare landscaped section seems to merge almost imperceptibly with the 492 hectares of *fynbos* (fine bush cloaking the mountain slopes (see the boxed text 'The Cape Floral Kingdom' in the Facts about South Africa chapter).

The main entrance at the Newlands end of the gardens is where you'll find plenty of parking, the information centre, an excellent souvenir shop and the **conservatory** (open 9am-5pm daily). Further along Rhodes Dr is the Ryecroft Gate entrance, the first you'll come to if you approach the gardens from Constantia. There's a good restaurant and cafe (see Kirstenbosch Botanical Gardens under Places to Eat later in this chapter). Call to find out about guided walks, or hire the My Guide electronic gizmo (R30) to receive recorded information about the various plants you'll pass on the three signposted circular walks.

Apart from a portion of that famous hedge planted by Van Riebeeck, the gardens are devoted almost exclusively to indigenous plants. About 9000 of Southern Africa's 22,000 plant species are growing here. You'll find a fragrance garden that has been elevated so you can more easily sample the scents of the plants; a Braille Trail; a kopje (hill) that has been planted with pelargoniums; a sculpture garden; and a section for plants used for *muti* (medicine) by sangomas (traditional African healers). There is always something flowering but the gardens are at their best between mid-August and mid-October.

The **Sunday afternoon concerts** *(R25 including entry to the gardens)* from December to March are a Cape Town institution.

Rikkis run out here for R50 if you don't have your own transport. Alternatively, walk down from the top of Table Mountain. This could be done in three hours by someone of moderate fitness, but make sure you have a nap and are prepared for a sudden change in weather. The trails are well marked, and steep in places, but the way to the gardens from the cableway and vice versa is not signposted.

RHODES MEMORIAL

Kirstenbosch was created in 1895 by Cecil Rhodes (see the boxed text 'Cecil Rhodes' in the Northern Cape chapter) when he purchased the eastern slopes of Table Mountain. Part of the Rhodes property is the current grounds of the University of Cape Town closer to the city along Rhodes Dr, and it's along here that you'll find the turn-off to the grandiose Rhodes Memorial, commanding a magnificent view. There's a very pleasant cafe here, the Rhodes Memorial Restaurant (see Southern Suburbs under Places to Eat later in this chapter).

CONSTANTIA

South of Kirstenbosch is lush Constantia, the oldest of South Africa's wine-growing regions. The original estate established by Simon van der Stel in 1685 was called **Groot Constantia** *(☎ 794 5128, Groot Constantia Rd, High Constantia; open 10am-5pm daily, longer in summer)*. Although a bit of a tourist trap, it's among the grandest vineyards and homesteads in the Cape, and is a superb example of Cape Dutch architecture, embodying the gracious lifestyle the wealthy Dutch created in their adopted country.

The beautifully restored homestead is now a **museum** *(adult/child R8/2)* and appropriately furnished; beneath the main building take a look at the tiny slave quarters. The Cloete Cellar, the estate's original wine cellar, now houses old carriages and a display of storage vessels. Tours of the modern cellar run at least twice daily at 11am and 3pm; you need to book.

In the 18th century, Constantia wines were exported around the world and were highly acclaimed. Fine wines are still produced and for R12 you can taste five from the list. Tastings are available from 10am to 4.30pm daily – and you get to keep the glass. Concerts are occasionally held in the Bertrams Cellar tasting room. Avoid visiting on a weekend as it can get very crowded.

The original Groot Constantia estate was divided up after Van der Stel's death in 1712, so today you can also visit **Buitenverwachting** *(☎ 794 5190)*, and **Klein Constantia** *(☎ 794 5188)*. Two more wineries, **Constantia Uitsig** *(☎ 794 1810,* W *www.constantiauitsig.co.za)* and **Steenberg Vineyards** *(☎ 713 2211)*, both with luxury accommodation and restaurants (see Constantia under Places to Eat later), complete the Constantia wine route.

A delightful way to visit is to take Downhill Adventures' cycling tour (see Cycling later in this chapter).

ATLANTIC COAST

The Atlantic coast of the Cape Peninsula has some of the most spectacular coastal scenery in the world. The beaches include the trendiest on the Cape, with the emphasis on sunbaking. Although it is possible to find shelter from the summer south-easterlies, the water comes straight from the Antarctic and swimming is nothing if not exhilarating.

Minibus taxis regularly run along Main Rd to the end of Regent Rd in Sea Point. Golden Arrow buses follow the same route on to Victoria Rd and down to Hout Bay. After that, you're on your own. Hitching is reasonably good. If you plan to drive down to Clifton and Camps Bay in summer be prepared to search a while for a parking space, especially at the weekend.

Bloubergstrand

Bloubergstrand, 25km to the north of Cape Town on Table Bay, was the site of the 1806 battle that resulted in the second British occupation of the Cape. Bloubergstrand is also the area with the most dramatic (and surely the most photographed) view of Table Mountain – you know, the one with wildflowers and sand dunes in the foreground, surf, and, across the bay, the cloud-capped mountain ramparts looming large over the city.

This is a boom area for antiseptic new suburbs but the village of Bloubergstrand itself is attractive enough with a good pub (see Bars & Pubs later in this chapter), picnic areas, and some long, uncrowded, windy stretches of sand. This is windsurfer territory but there's also some surfing, best with a moderate north-easterly wind, a small swell and incoming tide.

You'll need a car to get here. Take the R27 north from the N1.

Sea Point

Separated from the City Bowl by Signal Hill, densely populated Sea Point is a bustling residential suburb with numerous multistorey apartment buildings fringing the coast. Main and Regent Rds are lined with restaurants, cafes and shops. The coast itself is rocky, and swimming is dangerous. However, there are two tidal swimming pools, and plenty of bronzed bodies take advantage of the sun.

The **Sea Point Pavillion** *(Beach Rd at the end of Clarens St; adult/child R6/3; open 7am-6.45pm Oct-Apr, 8.30am-5pm May-Sept)* is a huge outdoor pool complex, which gets very busy on hot summer days. The pools are always at least 10°C warmer than the ocean.

Clifton

A suburb along from Sea Point are the four linked beaches at Clifton accessible by steps from Victoria Rd. They may be the trendiest

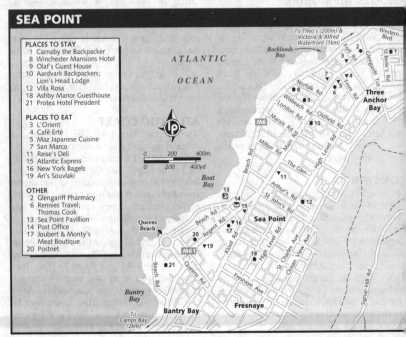

SEA POINT

PLACES TO STAY
1 Carnaby the Backpacker
8 Winchester Mansions Hotel
9 Olaf's Guest House
10 Aardvark Backpackers;
    Lion's Head Lodge
12 Villa Rosa
18 Ashby Manor Guesthouse
21 Protea Hotel President

PLACES TO EAT
3 L'Orient
4 Café Erté
5 Maz Japanese Cuisine
7 San Marco
11 Reise's Deli
15 Atlantic Express
16 New York Bagels
19 Ari's Souvlaki

OTHER
2 Glengariff Pharmacy
6 Rennies Travel;
   Thomas Cook
13 Sea Point Pavillion
14 Post Office
17 Joubert & Monty's
    Meat Boutique
20 Postnet

ATLANTIC

OCEAN

To Theo's (200m) &
Victoria & Alfred
Waterfront (1km)

Rocklands
Bay

Three
Anchor
Bay

0   200   400m
0   200   400yd

Boat
Bay

Queens
Beach

Sea Point

Bantry
Bay

To
Camps Bay
(2km)

Bantry Bay

Fresnaye

irstenbosch Botanical Gardens

aily market, Church St

Trash 'n' treasure: a market in front of the Old Town Hall

ape Town: Few cities can boast of a 1073m-tall mountain slap-bang in their centre.

Market, Grand Parade

Climbing Table Mountain isn't easy. Take the cable car instead!

Fancy a trip to Cape Point?

The bustling and cosmopolitan Waterfront in Cape Town

beaches on the Cape, almost always sheltered from the wind, but the water is still cold. If you care about these things, No 1 and 2 beaches are for models and confirmed narcissists, No 3 is the gay beach, and No 4 for families. Although vendors hawk drinks and ice creams along the beach, there are no shops down here, so bring your own food if you're out for a day of sunbaking.

Camps Bay

With the spectacular Twelve Apostles of Table Mountain as a backdrop and soft, white sand, this is one of the most beautiful beaches in the world. That it is within 15 minutes of the city centre also makes it popular, particularly on weekends. The beach is often windy and again the water is decidedly on the cool side. There are no lifesavers and the surf is strong, so take care if you swim.

Accommodation possibilities here are generally upmarket and you'll have to tough it out for a restaurant or cafe table with a view along Victoria Rd, particularly at the height of summer. The atmosphere though is seductive and you should aim to see the sunset from here at least once during your stay.

Llandudno & Sandy Bay

Although only 18km away, Llandudno seems completely removed from Cape Town, let alone Africa. It's a small, exclusive seaside village clinging to steep slopes above a sheltered beach. It has no shops. The remains of the tanker *Romelia*, wrecked in 1977, lie off Sunset Rocks. There's surfing on the beach breaks, best at high tide with a small swell and a south-easterly wind.

You'll need to head to Llandudno if you want to get to Sandy Bay, Cape Town's nudist beach and gay stamping ground. This said, it is a particularly beautiful stretch of sand and there's no pressure to take your clothes off if you don't want to.

Like many such beaches, it has no direct access roads. From the M6, turn towards Llandudno, keep to the left at forks, and head towards the sea until you reach the Sunset Rocks parking area. The beach is roughly a 15-minute walk to the south. Waves here are best at low tide with a south-easterly wind.

Finding a Windless Beach

As a resident of Cape Town and as a surfer, I realise how difficult it must be to deal with the excessive winds we get down here. Here are some tips on avoiding the wind, which even many Capetonians may not know:

- It's possible to get away from almost any wind if you know where to go. The weather bureau does not give accurate indicators of wind direction or speed, even though its forecasts are the city's main source of weather information.

- If the wind is a northerly or north-easterly (mainly from April to September), head to the Bloubergstrand area. This is away from the cloud and rain that is experienced closer to Table Mountain. The beaches are also more pleasant here because the wind is offshore and cooling, rather than chilly.

- During the westerlies (from November to April), go to the coastal area between Muizenberg and Simon's Town. The mountains by the coast shield this region from the worst of the wind.

- If the wind is a southerly or south-westerly (throughout the summer), head for Llandudno and Sandy Bay. Sandy Bay in particular is shielded by the Sentinel (the tall mountain to the south), and can be gloriously warm when everywhere else is miserable. The city centre and the Waterfront are also wind-free during the southerlies and south-westerlies.

- The most famous wind, the Cape Doctor, gets lifted by Table Mountain, so beaches on the western seaboard such as Camps Bay and Llandudno are protected.

- Surprisingly, Kalk Bay is protected from the Cape Doctor. A 'bubble' seems to form against the mountain and creates an area of calm, while just down the road in Fish Hoek, the wind howls onshore.

- The general rule is to look for the most expensive neighbourhoods, as they are located where the least wind is experienced.

Red Ceglowski

Hout Bay

Hout Bay nestles behind the almost vertical Sentinel and the steep slopes of Chapman's Peak. Inland from the stretch of white sand, there's a fast-growing satellite town that still manages to retain something of its village atmosphere. There's also the township of Imizano Yethu, also known as Mandela Park, in which it's possible to do walking tours (see Organised Tours later in this chapter).

Although increasingly given over to tourism, the harbour still functions and the southern arm of the bay is an important fishing port and processing centre for snoek and crayfish. From here **Nauticat Charters** (☎ 790 7278) runs daily cruises, including one-hour trips (adult/child R35/15) to Duiker Island, also known as Seal Island because of its colony of Cape fur seals, and sunset trips (R75) which include snoek and champagne.

Hout Bay is the start of the truncated (for the time being) **Chapman's Peak Drive**, one of the most beautiful and spectacular stretches of coastal road in the world. Dangerous rock slides have closed the road about 2km in, but coming up here is still worthwhile for the views back across the bay. Perched on a rock in the bay near the Hout Bay end of the drive is a bronze leopard. It has been sitting there since 1963 and is a reminder of the wildlife that once roamed the area's forests (which have also largely vanished).

For information on the relatively low-key local attractions, such as the history museum and the World of Birds aviary, go to the main **information centre** (☎ 790 3270, St Andrew's Rd; open 9am-5.30pm Mon-Fri, 9am-1pm Sat).

Also useful is the **Accommodation Cafe** (☎ 790 0198, Candlewood Centre, Victoria Ave; open 7am-7pm daily), where you can get information and make accommodation bookings for the area.

For information on accommodation and dining possibilities in Hout Bay, see Places to Stay as well as Places to Eat later in this chapter.

Noordhoek & Kommetjie

In the shadow of Chapman's Peak, Noordhoek has a 5km stretch of magnificent beach, favoured by surfers, walkers and horse riders. It tends to be windy and dangerous for swimmers. The Hoek, as it is known to surfers, is an excellent right beach

break at the northern end that can hold large waves (only at low tide) and is best with a south-easterly wind. There's a caravan park here (see Places to Stay – Budget later) and a tiny rustic shopping and dining complex.

Kommetjie (known as 'Kom') is an equally small, quiet and isolated crayfishing village, with precious few tourist facilities. It is, however, the focal point for surfing on the Cape, offering an assortment of reefs that hold a very big swell. Outer Kommetjie is a left point out from the lighthouse. Inner Kommetjie is a more protected, smaller left with lots of kelp (only at high tide). They both work best with a south-easterly or south-westerly wind.

Since the closure of Chapman's Peak Dr the best way to the small beachside communities of Noordhoek and Kommetjie, some 30km south of the city centre, is via the False Bay communities of Fish Hoek and Simon's Town.

FALSE BAY

The beaches on False Bay, to the south-east of the city, are not quite as scenically spectacular (nor as competitively trendy) as those on the Atlantic side, but the water is often 5°C or more warmer, and can reach 20°C in summer. This makes swimming far more pleasant. Suburban development along the coast is more intense, presumably because of the train line, which runs all the way through to Simon's Town, the most interesting single destination besides the Cape of Good Hope Nature Reserve.

The train is the best way to get here (see Getting Around later), the line hugging the coast from Muizenberg to the terminus at Simon's Town offers super views. It's reasonably safe if you travel first class and during the peak times. Also consider hopping off at the fishing village of Kalk Bay, a delightful destination in its own right.

During October and November, False Bay is a favoured haunt of whales and their calves; southern right whales, humpback whales and bryde (pronounced breedah) whales are the most commonly sighted. They often come quite close to the shore.

For more details on the False Bay towns, see Places to Stay and Places to Eat later in this chapter.

Muizenberg & St James

There's a very pleasant coastal walk from the handsome station in down-at-heel Muizenberg to the more upmarket suburb of St James. At both communities' beaches you'll see the much photographed, colourfully painted Victorian bathing huts.

To see Cape Town's best collection of antique playthings, visit the **Muizenberg Toy Museum** (☎ 788 1569, 8 Beach Rd, Muizenberg; adult/child R5/3; open 10am-4pm Tues-Sun).

Also worth a look is the **Natale Labia Museum** (☎ 788 4106, 192 Main Rd, Muizenberg; adult/child R3/free; open 10am-5pm Tues-Sun), a charming Venetian-style mansion and a satellite of the South African National Gallery with a lovely cafe.

Kalk Bay

Kalk Bay (Kalkbaai), named after the kilns that in the 17th century produced lime from seashells for painting buildings, is a busy fishing harbour with a lively daily market.

The swimming here is good, and to the north of the harbour, there's an excellent left reef break (best with a west to north-westerly wind).

With plenty of dining options and a row of quirky antique and craft shops, this is a charming pit stop en route to Simon's Town, or a lazy-day destination in its own right.

Simon's Town

Most people come to Simon's Town just to see the penguins at Boulders Beach. Linger and you'll discover an attractive, historic town that's the nation's third oldest European settlement.

Simon's Town (Simonstad), named after governor Simon van der Stel, was the VOC's winter anchorage from 1741 and became a naval base for the British in 1814. It has remained one ever since, the frigates now joined by pleasure boats that depart for spectacular trips to Cape Point. St George's St, the main thoroughfare, is lined with preserved Victorian buildings and there's an intriguing Muslim side to the town that is slowly being revived.

Lots of information (including walking tours) is available and accommodation

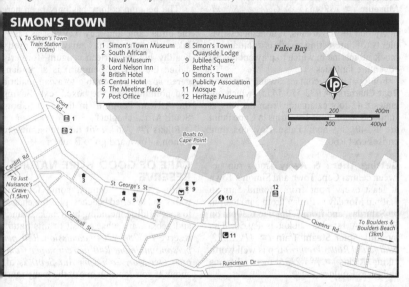

SIMON'S TOWN

1 Simon's Town Museum
2 South African Naval Museum
3 Lord Nelson Inn
4 British Hotel
5 Central Hotel
6 The Meeting Place
7 Post Office
8 Simon's Town Quayside Lodge
9 Jubilee Square; Bertha's
10 Simon's Town Publicity Association
11 Mosque
12 Heritage Museum

False Bay

To Simon's Town Train Station (100m)

Court Rd

Cardiff Rd

To Just Nuisance's Grave (1.5km)

St George's St

Cornwall St

Boats to Cape Point

Runciman Dr

Queens Rd

To Boulders & Boulders Beach (3km)

0   200   400m
0   200   400yd

bookings can be made at the helpful **Simon's Town Publicity Association** (☎ *786 2436, 111 St George's St; open 9.30am-5pm daily)*, next to Jubilee Square marina development.

Things to See & Do The **Heritage Museum** (☎ *786 2302, Almay House, King George Way)*, just east of the publicity association, is the town's most interesting museum. It includes displays on the Muslim coloured community of over 7000 people forcibly removed during the apartheid era, and is enthusiastically curated by Zainab Davidson, whose family was kicked out in 1975. Nearby Alfred Lane leads to the handsome mosque and school, built in 1926.

About 600m south of the train station is the rambling **Simon's Town Museum** (☎ *786 3046, St George's St; adult/child R5/2; open 9am-4pm Mon-Fri, 10am-4pm Sat, 11am-4pm Sun)*. Based in the old governor's residency (1777), its extensive exhibits trace the history of the town and port, and include a display on Just Nuisance, the Great Dane that was adopted as a navy mascot in WWII, and whose grave above the town makes for an healthy walk.

Next door is the **South African Naval Museum** (☎ *787 4635, St George's St; admission free; open 10am-4pm daily)*. Definitely one for naval nuts, it nonetheless has plenty of interesting exhibits including a mock submarine in which to play out boyish adventure fantasies.

For boat trips contact **Sweet Sunshine Boat Charters** (☎ *082-575 5655)*, which operates a 42-foot catamaran from the jetty at Jubilee Square. Four-hour trips to Cape Point are R140; 1½-hour False Bay coastline cruises cost R60.

Getting There & Away Trains run between central Cape Town and Simon's Town at least every hour from around 5am to 7.30pm Monday to Friday, from 5am to 6pm on Saturday, and from 7.30am to 6.30pm on Sunday. A 1st-class ticket is R9.50. The monthly **Spier Steam Train** (☎ *419 5222, adult/child R60/30 return)* trip is well worth taking. **Rikkis** (☎ *786 2136)* meet all trains and go to Boulders.

Boulders

As the name suggests, Boulders, about 3km from Simon's Town, is an area with a number of large boulders and small sandy coves. Within the area is Boulders Beach. The sea is calm and shallow in the coves, so Boulders is popular with families and it can get extremely crowded, especially on holidays and weekends.

Boulders Beach is part of the **Cape Peninsula National Park** (☎ *786 2329,* W *www.cpnp.co.za; open 8am-6.30pm daily)*. The beach is home to a colony of 3000 African penguins. Delightful as they are, the penguins are also pretty stinky, which may put you off spending too long paddling with them. Admission to the penguin colony costs R10/5 for adults/children.

There are two entrances to the penguins' protected area. The first, as you come along Queens Rd (the continuation of St George's St) from Simon's Town, is at the end of Seaforth Rd; the second is at Bellevue Rd, where you'll also find accommodation and places to eat. You can observe the penguins from the boardwalk at Foxy Beach, but at Boulders Beach you can get in the water with them.

The penguin colony has only been here since the mid-1980s; nobody knows why the birds came and they may just as easily take off again. They may look pretty healthy, but the African penguin (formerly called the jackass penguin) is an endangered species susceptible to avian malaria and pollution (see the boxed text 'Saving the African Penguin' in the Facts about South Africa chapter).

Rikkis (☎ *786 2136)* meet all trains to Simon's Town and go to Boulders.

CAPE OF GOOD HOPE NATURE RESERVE

Truly awesome scenery, some fantastic walks and deserted beaches, plus the chance to spot wildlife including bonteboks, elands and zebras, are what a visit to this nature reserve (☎ *780 9204; admission R20 per person, minimum R40 per car; open 7am-6pm Oct-Mar, 7am-5pm Apr-Sept)* is all about. If you come on one of the many tours hat whip into the reserve, now part of the Cape Peninsula National Park, pause at the tourist centre, walk to Cape Point and back, and then zip out again, you'll not even have seen the half of it. If possible, hire a car and take your time to explore the reserve the way it should be: on foot.

If the weather is good – and even if it isn't – you can easily spend at least a day here. It's particularly beautiful in spring, when the wildflowers are in bloom. There are a number of picnic spots as well as the not-overly-expensive *Two Oceans Restaurant* at Cape Point, generally packed with the tour-bus crowds.

It's not a difficult walk, but if you're feeling lazy a **funicular railway** *(adult/child return R22/8, one way R15/6)* runs up from beside the restaurant to the souvenir kiosk next to the old lighthouse (1860). The old lighthouse was often obscured by mist and fog, so a new lighthouse was built at Dias Point in 1919, reached by a thrilling walkway along the rocks; if the winds are howling (they often are), the old lighthouse is likely to be as far as you'll feel safe in going.

Pick up a map at the entrance gate if you intend to go walking, but bear in mind that there is minimal shade in the park and that the weather can change quickly. Also be very careful around the baboons; do not attempt to feed them since they have been known to storm cars for food.

The only public transport to the Cape is with Rikkis (see Getting Around later in this chapter), which run from Simon's Town (accessible by train) and cost R70 per hour.

Numerous tours include Cape Point on their itineraries; both Day Trippers and Downhill Adventures are recommended because they offer the chance to cycle within the park (see Organised Tours later in this chapter). Much better, though, is to hire a car for the day, which will allow you explore the rest of the peninsula.

CAPE FLATS

For most Capetonians, home is in one of the townships sprawling across the shifting sands of the Cape Flats. These are rife with crime and poverty, their dusty, litter-strewn

The Townships

Cape Town's townships have played a major role in the struggle against apartheid (see Apartheid & the Townships under History earlier in this chapter). Langa, meaning 'sun', was established in 1927 and is South Africa's oldest planned township. The type of dormitory accommodation that would become common for migrant labourers was first built here.

Until the pass laws were abolished, such hostels were for men only. They lived in basic units, each accommodating 16 men, who shared one shower, one toilet and one small kitchen. Tiny bedrooms each housed up to three men. After the pass laws were abolished, most men brought their families to live with them (earlier, those who didn't have a job outside the Homelands were not allowed to leave). So each unit became home to up to 16 families, each room sleeping up to three families.

It's no wonder that people moved out and built shacks, joining the hundreds of thousands of others who had come without work and set up home in communities such as Nyanga (literally, 'the moon'), the second formal township that sprouted the famous shanty town of Crossroads, now a township in its own right. Guguletu (Our Pride) was set up in 1962, while Khayelitsha (New Home) has boomed from a squatter settlement that was home to those cleared out of Crossroads into the republic's third-largest township with a possible population of 1.8 million.

While the infrastructure has certainly improved since 1994, with the rows of concrete reconstruction and development project (RDP) houses being the most visible example, vast squatter camps, with a communal standpipe for water and a toilet shared among scores of people in the best of circumstances, still remain and are expanding all the time.

streets are alive with people and wandering livestock. Most white locals, and many coloureds too, wouldn't dream of visiting here and will advise you not to. Don't listen.

If you've toured any other Third World hellhole, what you'll see here will come as little surprise. What is shocking is that it can exist in close proximity to such wealth and apparent indifference, and that the vast majority of residents should show visitors such courtesy and friendliness.

Taking a tour – the only way of safely travelling here besides making friends with and being accompanied by a resident – is one of the most illuminating and life-affirming things you can do while in Cape Town. Most half-day itineraries are similar. After starting in the Bo-Kaap for a brief discussion of Cape Town's colonial history, you'll move on to the District Six Museum, then be driven to the Cape Flats to visit all or some of the following townships: Langa, Guguletu, Crossroads and Khayelitsha. Tour guides are generally flexible in where they go, and respond to the wishes of the group. The following are possible stops (for detailed information on companies that offer tours, see Organised Tours later in this chapter).

In Langa, the **Guga S'Thebe arts and cultural centre** (☎ 082-746 0246) is an arts centre brilliantly decorated with ceramic murals.

In Guguletu, the **Sivuyile Tourism Centre** (☎ 637 8449, W www.sivuyile.co.za; open 8am-5pm Mon-Fri, 8am-2pm Sat, 9am-1pm Sun) has a photographic display on the townships, artists at work and a good gift shop. It's inside the local technical college, where you'll also find the creative Uncedo Pottery Project.

The **Philani Nutrition Centre** (☎ 387 5124, W philani.snowball.co.za) has its printing project in Crossroads. This community-based health and nutrition organisation has been going since 1980 and is now running six projects the townships, including a weaving factory in Khayelitsha's Site C. Women are taught how to feed their families adequately on a low budget, and the creche and various projects enable them to earn an income through weaving rugs and wall hangings, making paper, printing and other crafts. Philani goods are available around the Cape.

In Khayelitsha on Monday and Thursday, there's a **craft market** at St Michael's Church (for details call Matanzima on ☎ 361 2904). **Rosies Soup Kitchen** (☎ 448 0903) is run by a wonderful woman who

serves some 600 meals a day to the poor at 60 cents a plate. Golden is a talented blok who together with his family makes beautiful flowers from scrap tins.

If you want to climb what locals refer to as Khayelitsha's Table Mountain then head to the **Tygerberg Tourism Facility**. An impressive wooden staircase leads to the top of this sand hill, which is the highest point in the townships, and provides a sweeping view of the surroundings, particularly at sunset.

CYCLING

A variety of cycling trips and adventures is available from **Downhill Adventures** (☎ 42. 0388, W www.downhilladventures.co.za Orange St, Gardens, close to the City Bowl) Try a thrilling mountain-bike ride down from the lower cable car station on Table Mountain (R200), or ride through the Winelands and the Cape of Good Hope Nature Reserve (R295).

Day Trippers (☎/fax 531 3274, W www .daytrippers.co.za) also runs trips that include cycling.

The **Cape Argus cycle tour** (W www.cycl tour.co.za) around the peninsula is held in the second week of March and is the largest bicycle race in the world, with over 30,000 entries.

If you just want to hire a bicycle, contact Downhill Adventures or **Le Africa Express** (☎ 439 0901, 16A Main Rd, Three Anchor Bay).

DIVING

Cape Town offers a number of excellent shore and boat dives. Corals, kelp beds wrecks, caves and drop-offs, seals and a wide variety of fish are some of the attractions. The best time is from June to November as the water on the False Bay side is warmer then and the visibility is greater.

Table Bay Diving (☎ 419 8822, Waterfront Adventures, Waterfront) is a PADI approved dive school with a solid reputation. A boat dive costs R130, a shore dive R60 and an open-water dive course R1350 Equipment hire is also available.

For information on diving with sharks, see under Waterfront earlier in this chapter.

Cape Town Adrenaline

Cape Town offers a raft of activities that together constitute an outdoor-thrill-seeker's charter. With Table Mountain on hand, obviously walking and rock climbing are popular, but the city also has a growing reputation for its range of adventure sports.

If it's adventure you're after, you won't have to look far in Cape Town for some operator who'll be quick to take your money. Among the most heart-pumping activities we've come across are the following:

Abseiling off Table Mountain

Don't even think of tackling this unless you've got a head (and a stomach) for heights, but otherwise we guarantee this 112m shimmy down a rope – the world's highest abseil – will give you a huge adrenaline rush. Take your time because the views are breathtaking. Contact **Abseil Africa** (☎ 424 1580, Adventure Village, 229B Long St, City Bowl).

Kloofing in Kamikaze Canyon

This is just one of the kloofs (cliffs or gorges) near Cape Town in which you can go kloofing (called canyoning elsewhere). This sport, which entails climbing, hiking, swimming and jumping, is great fun, but can be dangerous (so check out operators' credentials carefully before signing up). A couple of long-running operators are **Adventure Village** and **Day Trippers** (☎/fax 531 3274, W www.daytrippers.co.za). On the Adventure Village tour the high jumps into pools are optional, but on the Day Trippers tour there's one 15m jump you cannot avoid. The cost for a day trip is around R400.

Gliding down to La Med

On a day when the winds are not too strong, look up while you're lounging at Camps Bay beach or having a beer at La Med at the Glen Country Club in Clifton, and you might see a paraglider heading towards you. Launch sites on Table Mountain, Lion's Head and Signal Hill are popular and it's possible for the total novice to arrange a tandem flight. For more information, see the boxed text 'Paragliding' in the Facts for the Visitor chapter.

Skydiving over Table Bay

Given the shaky rand, this is one of the cheapest places for you to learn to skydive or do a tandem dive. The view over Table Bay and the peninsula alone makes it worth it. Adventure Village can put you in contact with reliable operators. **Delta 200 Flying School** (☎ 082-800 6290) is based in Melkboshstrand, around 20km north of the city centre. All up a dive will cost around R800.

SURFING & SAND-BOARDING

The Cape Peninsula has fantastic surfing possibilities – from gentle shore breaks ideal for beginners to 3m-plus monsters for experts only. There are breaks that work on virtually any combination of wind, tide and swell direction (see the boxed text 'Finding a Windless Beach' earlier in this chapter).

In general, the best surf is along the Atlantic side, and there is a string of breaks from Bloubergstrand through to the Cape of Good Hope. Most of these breaks work best in south-easterly conditions. The water can be freezing (as low as 8°C) so a steamer wetsuit and booties are required.

On False Bay head to Muizenberg and Kalk Bay. The waves here tend to be less demanding in terms of size and temperature (up to 20°C), and work best in north-westerlies. There's a daily surf report on Radio Good Hope at 7.15am.

Downhill Adventures runs a surf school with introductory courses for R395; you're guaranteed to be standing on the board within a day. If getting wet isn't your style, try the sand-boarding trip (R395) on the dunes north of Cape Town. See Organised Tours later for contact details.

Surf Centre (☎ 423 7853, 45 Castle St, City Bowl) has a good stock of wetsuits and second-hand boards for sale or rental. So does **Extreme Sports Shack** (☎ 426 0294, e extremesports@worldonline.co.za, 220 Long St, City Bowl).

WALKING

Apart from walks on Table Mountain (see Table Mountain earlier in this chapter), there are some other fantastic walks around the peninsula, including one to the peak of Lion's Head (start from the road at the top of Kloof Nek; it involves a little climbing but there are chains on the rocks) and others in the Cape of Good Hope Nature Reserve.

It is important to be properly equipped with warm clothing, a map and a compass. There are numerous books and maps that give details, including Mike Lundy's *Best Walks in the Cape Peninsula*.

Cape Union Mart (see Shopping later in this chapter) has a hiking club that runs a weekly schedule of walks around the peninsula; inquire at any of its stores. Serious climbers can contact the **Mountain Club of South Africa** (☎ 465 3412, 97 Hatfield St, Gardens, W www.mcsa.org.za).

Guided city walks are offered; Cape Town Tourism has details. For a walking route around the City Bowl, see the special section 'Cape Town Architecture'.

ORGANISED TOURS

The boom in backpacker accommodation has led to a boom in backpacker-oriented activities. There are some excellent choices.

Day Trippers (☎/fax 531 3274, W www .daytrippers.co.za) gets excellent feedback from travellers. Mountain bikes are taken along on most of its trips, so you can do some riding if you want to. Most tours cost around R195 and include Cape Point, the Winelands and, in season, whale-watching (an extra R250).

Downhill Adventures (☎ 422 0388, Orange St, Gardens, W www.downhill adventures.co.za) is also a good company and runs a wide range of adventure trips.

For a quick orientation on a fine day, you can't beat a tour with **Cape Town Explorer** (☎ 426 4260). This open-top double-decker bus tour runs regularly on a circular route from the Waterfront via Cape Town Tourism and Camps Bay. A full trip (you can hop on and off) costs R60 and takes two hours.

Other major tour companies include **Springbok Atlas Tours** (☎ 417 6545) and **Hylton Ross** (☎ 511 1784, W www.hylton ross.co.za). Cape Town Tourism can fill you in on the myriad other options.

Township Tours

Lots of operators offer township tours. The half-day tours are sufficient since the full-day tours tack on a trip to Robben Island that is best done separately and for which you don't need a guide. You might want to ask a prospective tour operator how much of what you spend actually goes to help people in the townships, since not all tours are run by Cape Flats residents. Bookings for most can be made directly or via Cape Town Tourism.

Grassroute Tours (☎ 706 1006) Tour R195. These tours are highly recommended. The guide Arlene is very enthusiastic and knowledgeable, and tours drop by Vicky's B&B for a chat with this Khayelitsha legend (see Khayelitsha under Places to Stay – Mid-Range later). The company also runs an unusual trip (R300) exploring the culture of the Cape fishermen on board one of their boats.

Sam's Cultural Tours (☎/fax 423 5417 082-970 0564), with the ebullient and informed Sam Ntimba, who also works for Day Trippers on its township tours, offers a half-day trip that includes visits to a dormitory and shebeen in Langa and to a creche project in Khayelitsha (R170). A two-hour tour on Sunday to see a gospel choir in a Baptist church in Langa is R100.

Our Pride Tours (☎/fax 423 2971 e ourpride@mweb.co.za) Township Music Tour R260. These excellent tours run on Wednesday and Friday nights; other cultural tours are available.

Roots Africa Tours (☎ 988 7848) offer a full day in the townships for R240 excluding the traditional African lunch.

Legend Tourism Services (☎ 697 4056, Ⓦ www.legendtourism.co.za) is a major operator. The half-day Walk to Freedom Tour (R210) includes a walk around Langa.

Green Turtle Tours & Safaris (☎ 082 558 2963, 882 7884, Ⓔ grturtle@mweb .co.za) is a good, if rather earnest, operator offering half-day walking tours that are an eye-opening and relaxed alternative to the largely bus-based tours of the Cape Flats. Tours of the Hout Bay township of Imizano Yethu, also known as Mandela Park, are available. Green Turtle also offers a full-day Cape Peninsula Wildlife Tour including the viewing of hippos, flamingos, penguins and bonteboks, and tailor-made itineraries.

Cultural Tours

Bo-Kaap Community Guided Tours (☎ 422 1554) offers good history-based walking tours (R60) of the Bo-Kaap district, for those interested in a Cape Muslim and coloured experience.

Tana Baru Cultural Tours (☎ 424 0719) focuses on the people of the area and includes tea at the guide's home (R70). This company can also arrange B&B accommodation in the Bo-Kaap for R200 per person.

Andrew Bank's Slave Tour (☎ 447 8467, Ⓔ abank@uwc.ac.za) is a highly interesting walking tour of the City Bowl, past locations associated with Cape Town's formative period of slavery. The tour, with history lecturer Andrew Bank, takes around two hours and costs R75 per person.

Air Tours

Spectacular air tours from the Waterfront include those offered by *Civair Helicopters* (☎ 419 5182, Ⓔ civair@mweb.co.za) and *The Seaplane Company* (☎ 0800 006 878, Ⓦ www.seaplane.co.za). There are various deals but you can expect to pay at least R320 for a flight over the peninsula with guaranteed amazing views.

SPECIAL EVENTS

Whichever month you're in Cape Town you can be sure that there'll be some special event in the offing. The year-long party kicks off in style with the **Cape Minstrel**

The Cape Minstrel Carnival

Cape Town's longest-running annual street party is the Cape Minstrel Carnival, held 1 and 2 January and the following two Saturdays. It was first officially documented in 1907, but dates back to the early 1800s when slaves enjoyed a day of freedom over the New-Year period. The carnival was inspired by visiting American minstrels of the time, hence the face make-up and colourful costumes that are all part of the ribald song and dance parades.

The highlight is the parade, which is traditionally held on 2 January and known as *tweede nuwe jaar*; it runs through the city towards Green Point stadium. Around 13,000 revellers organised into separate troupes participate in the parade, and each competes to win trophies in various categories over the course of the carnival, including best dressed, most flamboyant, best band and best singer.

Carnival (see the boxed text, above) and a **Jazzathon** at the Waterfront (held in early January).

In early February the **J&B Met**, held at Kenilworth Racecourse, is the city's top horse-racing event, the equivalent of Australia's Melbourne Cup or the UK's Grand National (with the fashion stakes to match). March sees the running of the **Cape Argus cycle tour** (see Cycling earlier) and the **North Sea Jazz Festival**. And so it goes with various marathons, sporting fixtures, film, performing arts and food festivals, ending up in December with a fabulous costume party put on by **Mother City Queer Projects** (Ⓦ www.mcqp.co.za). Contact Cape Town Tourism for a full list of events.

PLACES TO STAY

There's somewhere in Cape Town to suit practically everyone's budget. If there's somewhere you particularly want to stay it pays to plan ahead, especially during school holidays from mid-December to the end of January and at Easter – prices can double and many places are fully booked.

Think about what part of the city you might want to stay in. If you aim to hit the beaches, then suburbs along the Atlantic or False Bay coasts will make better sense than, say, Gardens or the City Bowl. If you want easy access to nightlife, then any-where within walking distance of Long St should be fine. If you have a car, then any-where's fine, but remember to inquire about the parking options when you make a booking.

Rates at many places fluctuate according to demand, and it's always worthwhile asking about special deals. For longer stays rates are definitely negotiable.

Accommodation Agencies

Cape Town Tourism (see Tourist Offices earlier in this chapter) runs an accommoda-tion booking service; it sometimes has special deals. Like any agency it'll only recommend its members but we found it to be generally reliable.

The organisation *Bed 'n' Breakfast* (☎ 683 3505, fax 683 5159, W www.bnb.co.za) has a number of members around the Cape Peninsula. Most rooms are in luxurious suburban houses (often with swimming pools); self-catering flats and cottages are also available. Advance bookings are pre-ferred (at least a day or so) and most houses are difficult to get to without private trans-port. Prices start at around R100/150 per person in the low/high seasons. You can pay a lot more than this.

For guesthouses check with the *Guest House Association* (☎ 762 0880, fax 797 3115). For self-catering places, try the *Accommodation Shop* (☎ 439 1234, fax 434 2238, W www.accommodationshop.co .za); *Cape Holiday Homes* (☎ 419 0430, fax 422 0306, e info@capehomes.co.za); or *A-Z Accommodations* (☎ 551 2785, W www.a-zholidayhomes.co.za).

PLACES TO STAY – BUDGET
Camping

Several central hostels have tent space, including *Ashanti Lodge*, *The Hip Hop* and *@Lighthouse Farm Lodge* (see Hostels under Places to Stay – Budget following for contact details). For Cape Town's caravan parks a car is virtually a prerequisite.

Zandvlei Caravan Park (☎ 788 5215, fa 788 5250, The Row, Muizenberg) Camp site. R50-90 depending on season, chalets from R200. On the edge of Zandvlei lagoon and within walking distance of Valsbaai station on the Simon's Town line, and the beach From the station walk east along Alberty Rd, cross the bridge, turn left then left again onto The Row.

Chapman's Peak Caravan Park (☎/fa 789 1225, Noordhoek Main Rd, Noordhoek Camp sites from R66. Handy for Atlanti surf beaches, but a longer journey to and from the city now that Chapman's Peak D is closed.

Hostels

The boom in hostels in Cape Town that bega in the mid-1990s is continuing unabated Competition is fierce and many places offe a raft of inducements including free airpor pick-ups and free meals. It's impossible for us to list all the options, so what follows is a selection of the best places we've com across plus a few others for specific reasons

Unless otherwise indicated, you can as sume that the hostels mentioned here have private rooms (usually with shared bath rooms) as well as dorm beds (for whic you'll be paying around R55), but you can' assume that any will be vacant when yo arrive. Book ahead.

City Bowl *The Backpack* (☎ 423 4530, fa 423 0065, W www.backpackers.co.za, 7-New Church St) Dorm beds from R120/160. Grand daddy of the non–Hostelling Internationa hostels in Cape Town, still among the bes (and one of the cleanest), and constantl making improvements. The Africa Trave Centre here is one of the most clued up (se Travel Agencies earlier in this chapter).

Zebra Crossing (☎/fax 422 1265, e zebr crossing@intekom.co.za, 82 New Church St Dorm beds R40, singles/doubles R100/150 Smaller, quieter, more personal – and slightly cheaper – than most. There's a pian to tinkle on and a peaceful atmosphere.

Long St Backpackers (☎ 423 0615, fa 423 1842, e longstpb@mweb.co.za, 20

ong St) Dorm beds R45, singles/doubles
70/120. First of the Long St hostels and
till standing out from the pack. In a block
f 14 small flats, with four beds and a bath-
oom in each, arranged around a leafy, quiet
ourtyard.

Overseas Visitors' Club (☎ 424 6800, fax
23 4870, 230 Long St, W www.ovc.co.za)
Dorm beds R50. Only dorms are available
n this nice old building, with high-quality
acilities and a pub-like bar. This place is
nissing that rowdy backpacker atmosphere,
vhich could be a bonus; there is a 10%
iscount for HI members.

Train Lodge (☎ 418 4890, fax 418 5848,
W www.trainlodge.co.za, Old Marine Dr)
Dorm beds/singles/doubles all R50. When
busy this novel idea for a hostel (the rooms
are in stationary trains) charges more for singles and doubles – otherwise it's a bargain,
although you could end up spending more
on taxis to get safely back to this deserted
part of town late at night.

Gardens & Oranjezicht *Oak Lodge*
(☎ 465 6182, fax 465 6308, 21 Breda St,
Gardens) Dorm beds R55, doubles R160-
180. A hippy air still pervades this one-time

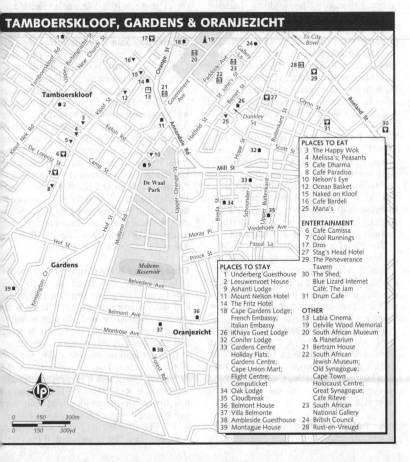

TAMBOERSKLOOF, GARDENS & ORANJEZICHT

PLACES TO EAT
3 The Happy Wok
4 Melissa's; Peasants
5 Cafe Dharma
8 Café Paradiso
10 Nelson's Eye
12 Ocean Basket
15 Naked on Kloof
16 Cafe Bardeli
25 Maria's

ENTERTAINMENT
6 Cafe Camissa
7 Cool Runnings
17 Dros
27 Stag's Head Hotel
29 The Perseverance
   Tavern
30 The Shed;
   Blue Lizard Internet
   Café; The Jam
31 Drum Cafe

PLACES TO STAY
1 Underberg Guesthouse
2 Leeuwenvoet House
9 Ashanti Lodge
11 Mount Nelson Hotel
14 The Fritz Hotel
18 Cape Gardens Lodge;
   French Embassy;
   Italian Embassy
26 iKhaya Guest Lodge
32 Conifer Lodge
33 Gardens Centre
   Holiday Flats;
   Gardens Centre;
   Cape Union Mart;
   Flight Centre;
   Computicket
34 Oak Lodge
35 Cloudbreak
36 Belmont House
37 Villa Belmonte
38 Ambleside Guesthouse
39 Montague House

OTHER
13 Labia Cinema
19 Delville Wood Memorial
20 South African Museum
   & Planetarium
21 Bertram House
22 South African
   Jewish Museum;
   Old Synagogue;
   Cape Town
   Holocaust Centre;
   Great Synagogue;
   Cafe Riteve
23 South African
   National Gallery
24 British Council
28 Rust-en-Vreugd

0 150 300m
0 150 300yd

commune, now the most chilled hostel in Cape Town. It's taken over nearly all the flats in the attached block, which represent a great long-term accommodation option with their own kitchens and bathrooms (in low season you could stay here for R1000 a week).

Ashanti Lodge (☎ 423 8721, fax 423 8790, W www.ashanti.co.za, 11 Hof St, Gardens) Camping R40 per person, dorm beds R55, doubles R140, doubles B&B from R180. Book well ahead to get into this super-popular party hostel in a big and brightly painted old house. For something quieter opt for the excellent B&B rooms in a separate national monument house down the road. There is a 10% discount for HI members.

Cloudbreak (☎ 461 6892, fax 461 1458, e cloudbrk@gem.co.za, 219 Upper Buitenkant St, Oranjezicht) Dorm beds R50, singles/doubles R130/150. This is a friendly little place with a student vibe and is popular with surfers. It's recently taken over another house nearby *(18 Vredehoek Ave)* and has garage space for four vehicles.

Green Point *St John's Waterfront Lodge (☎ 439 1404, fax 439 1424, W www.nis.za/stjohns, 6 Braemar Rd)* Dorm beds R60, doubles R150/180 with shared/private bathroom. Close to the Waterfront and not too far from the city, this often recommended hostel is a large, relaxed and friendly place with very good facilities, including a large garden and two pools.

The Hip Hop (☎ 439 2104, fax 439 8688, e hiphop@cis.co.za, 11 Vesperdene Rd) Camping R30 per person, dorm beds R50, doubles R140. There are mainly dorm beds on offer at this nicely decorated old house with a garden and a larger pool than most. There's a free beer on check-in.

The Big Blue (☎ 439 0807, fax 439 8068, e big.blue@mweb.co.za, 7 Vesperdene Rd) Dorm beds R40, doubles R120/140 with shared/private bathroom. The dorm beds are a bit cramped but this relatively new kid on the block makes all the right moves otherwise.

Sea Point *Carnaby the Backpacker (☎ 439 7410, fax 439 1222, W www.carnaby* backpacker.co.za, 219 Main Rd, Three Anchor Bay)* Dorm beds R55, singles/ doubles from R125/175. This is a rambling old hotel that has been converted into a rather funky backpackers hostel. It has one of the better pools and a happening bar, and most rooms have their own bathroom and TV.

Aardvark Backpackers (☎ 434 4172, fax 439 3813, e aardbp@mweb.co.za, 31 Main Rd, Sea Point) Dorm beds R60, doubles R222.20. In a wing of the good Lions Head Lodge (see Self-Catering later in this section) and sharing its facilities, this hostel has dorms in converted flats. There's a useful travel centre. A 10% discount is available for HI members.

Camps Bay *Stan Halt Youth Hostel (☎/fax 438 9037, e stanh@new.co.za, The Glen, Camps Bay)* Dorm beds R40 for HI members, R45 for nonmembers. This place has only dorms; they are in the one-time stables of the Round House hunting lodge, which is a national monument. At the time of research there was a question mark hanging over its future; its closure would be a great shame since it's in a serene location, surrounded by trees, with sea views to die for. Unless you have transport it's a steep 15-minute walk to the nearest shops and restaurants in Camps Bay, but still worth considering as a place to kick back. If you're coming by public transport, the easiest way is to take a minibus taxi to the top of Kloof Nek, then walk down Kloof Rd towards Camps Bay.

Observatory & Pinelands These suburbs favourites with students at the nearby university, are a long way from the city centre and the Waterfront – by Cape Town standards, anyway. That said, the area is only a few minutes from the city by car or train and has good nightlife and places to eat.

Green Elephant (☎ 448 6359, fax 448 0510, e greenelephant@iafrica.com, 5 Milton Rd) Dorm beds R55, Singles/doubles/triples B&B R150/180/195. In the heart of this student neighbourhood, and split over two houses, this place is spacious and quiet with a tree-climbing dog for entertainment. A simple breakfast is included in the rates.

@Lighthouse Farm Lodge (*☎/fax 447 9177,* e *msm@mweb.co.za, Violet Bldg, Oude Molen Village, Alexandria Rd, Mowbray*) Camping R15 per person, dorm beds R30, doubles R110. An old hospital set in spacious grounds partly turned into one of the city's more original and most relaxing locations for a hostel. This is the nicer of the two hostels on the grounds. There's also horse riding (R40 per hour), with a trail running up to the Rhodes Memorial, an organic permaculture farm, and the *Sunshine Cafe*, which has live jazz on Friday and Saturday nights. A dubious-sounding African village is planned, as are a pool and a vegetarian restaurant. It's best if you have your own transport, but otherwise it's within walking distance of Pinelands train station, and there's good security around the complex.

Guesthouses

City Bowl *St Paul's B&B Guest House* (*☎ 423 4429, fax 423 1580, 182 Bree St*) Singles/doubles with shared bathroom B&B R120/200. One of the best budget places with neat rooms and a quiet courtyard – and Long St is a trice away.

Travellers Inn (*☎ 424 9272, fax 424 9278, 208 Long St*) Singles/doubles B&B from R90/120. In one of the old wrought-iron decorated buildings, this inn has character, but the front rooms can suffer from street noise. Breakfast is a make-it-yourself affair.

Gardens & Oranjezicht *Conifer Lodge* (*☎ 465 6052, fax 465 6051, 6 Scott St, Gardens*) Doubles B&B R170-200. Nice if small rooms, in a good location within walking distance of the Company's Gardens.

Ambleside Guesthouse (*☎ 465 2503, fax 465 3814, 11 Forest Rd, Oranjezicht*) Singles/doubles B&B from R150/240. It's not as flash as some of its neighbours, but has a kitchen for self-catering and pleasant, clean rooms. The owner offers guided walks on the mountain for around R150.

Hotels

Check Inn (*☎ 439 4444, 155 Main Rd, Green Point*) Singles/doubles/triples R170. This budget hotel in the Formule 1 mode

offers air-con rooms, a double bed with a single bunk bed above, and a private shower. Its location, midway between Green Point and Sea Point, is in its favour.

PLACES TO STAY – MID-RANGE
B&Bs & Guesthouses

There are many mid-range B&Bs and guesthouses – the following is just a sample.

Oranjezicht *Belmont House* (*☎ 461 5417, fax 461 6642,* e *capeguest@mweb.co.za, 10 Belmont Ave*) Doubles B&B from R130. The rooms in this smart guesthouse are small, but nicely decorated. There's a kitchen so it's possible to self-cater too.

Green Point & Waterkant *The Lodge* (*☎/fax 421 1106, 49 Napier St, Waterkant*) Doubles B&B from R200. A bargain given how ritzy this area has become, this is a great guesthouse run by a friendly British guy; it's handy for clubbing. Prices rise in high season.

Dungarvin House, (*☎/fax 434 0677,* e *kom@mweb.co.za, 163 Main Rd, Green Point*) Singles/doubles B&B from R160/220 low season to R330/480 high season. Elegant and child-friendly B&B in a restored Victorian mansion.

Sea Point *Ashby Manor Guesthouse* (*☎ 434 1879, fax 439 3572, 242 High Level Rd*) Singles/doubles from R170/200, more in high season. Rambling old Victorian house on the slopes of Signal Hill. All rooms have fridge and hand basin and there's a kitchen.

Villa Rosa (*☎ 434 2768, fax 434 3526,* w *www.villa-rosa.com, 277 High Level Rd*) Singles/doubles from R215/310. Tastefully decorated rooms with huge bathrooms and some with fireplaces, in a nice old house.

Olaf's Guest House, (*☎ 439 8943, 24 Wisbeach Rd*) Singles/doubles B&B R460/ 610. Gorgeous place, with eight individually decorated rooms and a plunge pool in the front garden. German is spoken here.

False Bay *Castle Hill,* (*☎ 788 2554, fax 788 3843,* e *theinn@mweb.co.za, 37 Gatesville Rd, Kalk Bay*) Singles/doubles

B&B from R230/350. Charming rooms are available in this renovated Edwardian home; some overlook the bay and all are decorated with art by local painters.

Boulders Beach Guesthouse (☎ *786 1758, fax 786 1825,* e *boulders@iafrica .com, 4 Boulders Place, Boulders Beach)* Singles/doubles B&B from R270/450, self-catering units R650. Close by the penguin colony, this smart guesthouse also has a range of good-sized self-catering units and a pleasant *cafe* with an outdoor deck.

Bosky Dell (☎ *786 3906, fax 786 1830,* e *bosky@new.co.za, 5 Grant Ave, Boulders Beach)* B&B from R200 per person. On offer here are pretty whitewashed cottages with lovely views across the beach.

Khayelitsha Of the four B&Bs listed here, only Vicky's is in an original shack; the other three are in brick buildings in the more developed parts of the township.

Kopanong (☎/*fax 361 2084,* e *kopa nong@xsinet.co.za, Site C-329 Velani Crescent, Khayelitsha)* Singles/doubles B&B R190/300. The most upmarket option, Kopanong is run by a registered guide and development worker. Two stylishly decorated rooms, one with private bathroom, are available. A three-course dinner is R70.

Majoro's B&B (☎ *361 3412, fax 364 9660, 072-170 6175, 69 Helena Crescent, Graceland, Khayelitsha)* B&B R150 per person. Run by the friendly Maria Maile, this B&B in a quiet part of Khayelitsha has a homely feel. Dinner, available on request, costs R30 to R60 and there's safe parking should you choose to drive here.

Malebo's (☎ *361 2391, 083-475 1125, 18 Mississippi Way, Graceland, Khayelitsha)* B&B R150 per person. Lydia Masoleng is the proprietor of this modern, spacious home with three rooms for guests. The welcome is warm and dinner is available for R50.

Vicky's (☎ *387 4422,* W *www.enkosi.com, Site C-685A, Khayelitsha)* DB&B R150 per person. The dynamic Vicky Ntozini deserves all the rave reviews we've received about her. To call her delightful B&B (designed by her resourceful husband Piksteel) a shack is a grave disservice – especially since Vicky and

Piksteel have probably now added their dreamed-for second storey. Apart from Vicky's bountiful hospitality, there's the added bonus of Cape Town's other *Waterfront*, a long-running and lively shebeen, right across the road.

Hotels

City Bowl ***Tudor Hotel*** (☎ *424 1335, fax 423 1198,* e *tudorhotel@iafrica.com, Greenmarket Square)* Singles/doubles B&B from R195/295. Cosy little hotel with a central location. It could do with renovation but it's OK. Parking is available nearby (at a price).

Metropole Hotel (☎ *423 6363, fax 423 6370, 38 Long St)* Dorm beds R70, singles/doubles from R130/170. Attractive old-style hotel, with a wood-panelled interior, antique elevator, and a few six-bed dorms. Prices are reasonable considering the degree of comfort offered, but the more expensive rooms have rather cheesy decor.

Parliament Hotel (☎ *461 6710, fax 461 6740,* e *reservations@parliamenthotel.co .za, 9 Barrack St)* Singles/doubles B&B R220/280. One of the best inexpensive central hotels, with spotless rooms and a cafe.

The Townhouse, (☎ *465 7050, fax 465 3891,* e *hotel@townhouse.co.za, 60 Corporation St)* Singles/doubles R369/562. Great service and high standards are on offer at this often recommended four-star hotel. The rates rise only slightly in summer. Ask for a room with a view of the mountain.

Days Inn (☎ *422 0030, fax 422 0090,* e *ctydays@new.co.za, 101 Buitengracht St)* Singles/doubles both R395. Not much chop from the outside, but inside the stylishly decorated rooms are fair value. It has a steakhouse on site and underground parking.

Gardens ***Cape Gardens Lodge*** (☎ *432 1260, fax 423 2088,* e *info@capegardens lodge.com, 88 Queen Victoria St)* Singles/doubles/triples B&B from R270/360/450. Great location next to the Company's Gardens for this good mid-market hotel. Rooms with views of Table Mountain are dearer.

iKhaya Guest Lodge (☎ *461 8880, fax 461 8889,* W *www.ikhayalodge.co.za,*

Dunkley Square) Singles/doubles B&B from R395/590, self-catering R630/840. Bags of African style at this excellent option in the heart of the trendy media district. The luxury lofts are worth checking out, especially for the views across to Lion's Head.

The Fritz Hotel (☎ 480 9000, fax 480 9090, W www.fritzhotel.co.za, 1 Faure St) Singles/doubles B&B R350/400. The rooms look as though they've been art-directed with their tasteful mix of Art Deco, 1950s and modern furnishings. No wonder it's a favourite with media types doing business in the area.

Waterfront & Green Point *City Lodge (☎ 419 9450, fax 419 0460,* e *clva.resv@ citylodge.co.za, Cnr Dock Rd & Alfred St)* Singles/doubles R398/560, Fri-Sun rate for doubles R398. A chain hotel offering one of the area's better deals.

Victoria Junction (☎ 419 8800, fax 419 8200, e *vicjunct@icon.co.za, Cnr Somerset St & Ebenezer Rd, Green Point)* Singles/ doubles R450/550. Arty loft-style boutique hotel that's part of the Protea chain. It's popular so book ahead.

Breakwater Lodge (☎ 406 1911, fax 406 1070, e *brkwater@fortesking-hotel.co.za, Portswood Rd, Waterfront)* Singles/doubles from R210/250. Professional operation in a restored jail right next to the Waterfront. The rooms aren't bad but the cheapest ones are small and have a shower rather than a bath.

Claridges B&B Hotel (☎ 434 1171, fax 434 6650, e *cheerin@new.co.za, 47 Main Rd, Green Point)* Singles/doubles B&B R130/200. Great location for this old-fashioned but quite acceptable hotel, which is even cheaper for long stays. The staff are friendly, there's a small pool, the rooms have TVs and big bathrooms (but no phones) and there's a huge buffet breakfast.

Sea Point *Winchester Mansions Hotel (☎ 434 2351, fax 434 0215,* W *www.win chester.co.za, 221 Beach Rd)* Singles/ doubles from R490/630 low season, R710/ 925 high season. Cape Dutch–style beauty on the seafront. You'll pay more for the sea views, but the courtyard with a fountain is

lovely too; come here for Sunday brunch with live jazz from 11am to 2pm (R85).

Atlantic Coast South *Hout Bay Manor (☎ 790 0116, fax 790 0118,* W *www.hout baymanor.co.za, Baviaanskloof Rd, Hout Bay)* Singles/doubles from R395/590. The original building at this small luxury hotel dates from 1871 and has recently been renovated. Rooms are a good size and attractively furnished.

Monkey Valley Beach Nature Resort (☎ 789 1391, fax 789 1143, Mountain Rd, Noordhoek) Singles/doubles B&B from R270/540. Imaginatively designed small resort with the rustic cabins shaded by a milk-wood forest. Offers plenty of activities, but with Noordhoek's splendid beach moments away you might not need other distractions.

Simon's Town *Lord Nelson Inn (☎ 786 1386, fax 786 1009, 58 St George's St)* Singles/doubles B&B from R240/310. Above a small, old-fashioned pub, this is a pleasant, refurbished place, with plain but smart rooms. Some overlook the sea (which is largely obscured by a shed in the naval dockyards) but suffer traffic noise.

Simon's Town Quayside Lodge (☎ 786 3838, fax 786 2241, e *info@quayside.co .za, Off Jubilee Square, St George's St)* Singles/doubles B&B from R450/615. The more expensive rooms here face the water, but all the rooms are quite pleasant and comfortable.

Self-Catering Accommodation

For agencies specialising in rental houses and flats, see Accommodation Agencies under Places to Stay earlier in this chapter.

Gardens *Gardens Centre Holiday Flats (☎ 461 8000, fax 461 5588, Mill St)* 2-person apartments from R240. Modern, well-furnished single-bedroom flats above the Gardens Centre shopping mall. The views are good. Rates vary according to the season, but include free undercover parking.

Waterkant *Harbour View Cottages, (☎ 422 2721, fax 426 5088,* e *reservations@*

hvc.co.za, **W** www.villageandlife.com) Singles/ doubles B&B from R290/380, 2-person flats from R550. The hotel has a plunge pool and rooms have glossy-magazine-style furnishings. Check with Cape Town Tourism for deals. If you want breakfast then it's taken at the nearby Village Cafe.

Sea Point *Lions Head Lodge* (☎ 434 4163, **e** lionhead@cis.co.za, 319 Main Rd) Doubles from R280, 2-person flats from R310. The rates at this good budget hotel fall if you stay longer than one night. It has a reasonable-sized pool and a bar, and does three-course Sunday lunches for R30.

Camps Bay *The Place on the Bay* (☎ 438 7060, fax 438 2504, **W** www.theplaceon thebay.co.za, Cnr Fairways & Victoria Rds) Singles/doubles from R330/550. These are smart, modern self-catering flats but the rates can soar in peak season.

Fairways Singles/doubles from R195/ 385. This classy hotel in the Victorian mould is run by the same management that runs the nearby Place on the Bay.

Atlantic Coast South *Flora Bay Resort* (☎/fax 790 1650, Chapman's Peak Dr, Hout Bay) 2-person flats from R300. There are 27 different self-catering units, all sea-facing, at this complex, which has its own beach.

Simon's Town *British Hotel* (☎/fax 786 2214, **e** british-hotel@iafrica.com, 90 St George's St) Flats for 2/3/4 people from R200/450/500. Huge rooms and amazingly spacious bathrooms are on offer at these grand self-catering apartments, which are clustered around a delightful courtyard.

Central Hotel (☎/fax 786 3775, **e** central hotel@intekom.co.za, 96 St George's St) Singles/doubles R175/250. B&B is available at this characterful renovated hotel, but the top-notch flats are self-catering. It has a three-bed cottage nearby for rent too.

PLACES TO STAY – TOP END
Guesthouses
Gardens & Oranjezicht *Underberg Guesthouse* (☎ 426 2262, fax 424 4059, **W** www.underbergguesthouse.co.za, Cnr Carsten St & Tamboerskloof Rd, Gardens) Singles/doubles B&B from R230/350. This is unmissable pink Victorian mansion, which is a bit twee but very well run.

Leeuwenvoet House (☎ 424 1133, fax 424 0495, **W** www.leeuwenvoet.co.za, 93 New Church St, Gardens) Singles/doubles B&B from R285/330. Pronounced 'Loo-en-foot', this is one of the most stylish of the area's upmarket B&Bs. It has luxuriously decorated rooms.

Villa Belmonte (☎ 462 1576, fax 462 1579, **W** www.villabelmontehotel.co.za, 33 Belmont Ave, Oranjezicht) Singles/doubles B&B R670/890. Ornate and luxurious Italianate villa with huge pool and excellent facilities.

Montague House, (☎ 424 7337, fax 426 0423, **e** montague@mweb.co.za, 18 Leeuwenhof Rd, Higgovale) Singles/doubles B&B from R650/850. Shakespeare's plays are the inspiration for the room design at this delightful boutique guesthouse on the lower slopes of Table Mountain in Gardens.

Waterkant *De Waterkant Lodge & Cottages* (☎/fax 419 1097, **W** www.dewater kant.co.za, 20 Loader St) B&B from R700 per person. Choose either the beautifully restored lodge with its magnificent rooftop views, or one of the exemplary self-catering cottages, each individually decorated with top-quality art and antiques.

Hotels
City Bowl *Cape Heritage Hotel* (☎ 424 4646, fax 424 4949, **W** www.capeheritage .co.za, 90 Bree St) Singles/doubles from R570/780. Delightful five-star boutique hotel – part of the Heritage Square redevelopment – where each room is individually decorated in elegant style. A favourite with politicians when they visit town.

The Cullinan (☎ 418 6920, fax 418 3559, **e** intmktg@southernsun.com, 1 Cullinan St, east of Waterkant) Singles/doubles R555/ 800. A reasonable deal, if you can stand the Greek-temple-on-steroids architecture. The rooms are less OTT and the views are impressive.

Holiday Inn (☎ 409 4000, fax 409 4444, e intmktg@southernsun.com, 1 Lower Buitengragt, east of Waterkant) Singles/doubles from R538/800. The grandest of Cape Town's several Holiday Inns, this place has fine, brightly decorated rooms, but public areas with all the ambience of a shopping mall.

Gardens *Mount Nelson Hotel* (☎ 483 1000, fax 423 1060, W www.mountnelson hotel.orient-express.com, 76 Orange St) Doubles from R2640. Staying here it's easy to imagine the sun has yet to set on the British empire. Surrounded by seven acres of grounds and dating from 1899, the 'Nellie' is a short walk from the city through the Company's Gardens. The rooms are on the chintzy side but full of character, and even if you don't stay, you should drop by for afternoon tea or a meal.

Waterfront & Green Point *Cape Grace Hotel* (☎ 410 7100, 419 7622, W www.cape grace.com, West Quay, Waterfront) Doubles B&B from R1990. More like an exclusive and very pleasant club than a hotel. There's understated luxury in most rooms (go for the ones facing Table Mountain), and kids under 12 get to stay for free.

Victoria & Alfred Hotel (☎ 419 6677, fax 419 8955, e res@v-and-a.co.za, Waterfront) Singles/doubles from R925/R1440. Smart place with the cheaper rooms facing the Waterfront rather than the mountain. No gym or pool but guests can use the facilities of the nearby Virgin Active gym in Green Point.

Portswood Square Hotel (☎ 418 3281, fax 419 7570, Portswood Rd, Waterfront) Singles/doubles R915/1160. On the Green Point side of the Waterfront, this is the slightly cheaper sibling of *The Commodore* next door. Like its neighbour it has a pleasing nautical theme; you can use all the facilities of both hotels whichever one you stay at.

Sea Point *Protea Hotel President* (☎ 434 8111, fax 434 9991, e sales@president .co.za, Alexandra Rd, Bantry Bay) Doubles from R805 including breakfast. Fine upper-range hotel with brightly decorated rooms, and lovely sea views from the pool and dining area.

Camps Bay *The Bay Hotel* (☎ 438 4444, fax 438 4455, W www.halcyonhotels.co.za, Victoria Rd) Singles/doubles from R670/920 up to a minimum of R1410 in high season. This hang-out for the well-heeled is just a stone's throw from the beach. Sea-view rooms, all very comfy, naturally attract a price premium.

Southern Suburbs *Vineyard Hotel* (☎ 683 3044, fax 683 3365, W www.vineyard.co.za, Colinton Rd, Newlands) Singles/doubles from R595/835. This is a fine choice, which is handy for both Kirstenbosch Gardens and the cricket. The facilities and rooms are excellent for the price. It's worth visiting for tea in the lounge and a stroll in the lovely gardens.

Constantia Uitsig (☎ 794 6500, fax 794 7605, W www.constantiauitsig.co.za, Spaanschemat River Rd, Constantia) Singles/doubles from R920/1320. Take your pick from two of Cape Town's top restaurants when dining on this wine estate. The accommodation is suitably exclusive and salubrious.

PLACES TO EAT

Cape Town's dining scene on the whole is impressive. There's a good variety of cuisines on offer (everything from Turkish to Japanese), and the quality of the ingredients is high, with the locally grown fruit, vegetables and seafood all being particularly fine. You shouldn't miss the opportunity to sample some traditional Cape Malay food and there are some good African restaurants in Cape Town, too.

Lovers of fast food and the like will not be disappointed. Among the plentiful local chains are *Steers* for burgers, *Spur* for steaks, and *Nandos*, purveyors of spicy Portuguese-style chicken.

Most restaurants are licensed but some allow you to bring your own wine for little or no corkage charge. Call ahead to check the restaurant's policy.

You'll find many restaurants along Long St and its upper extension Kloof St, at the Waterfront, on Main Rd from Green Point to Sea Point, and along Lower Main Rd in Observatory. For meals with sea views, Camps Bay, Hout Bay, Kalk Bay and Simon's Town are the go. The Heritage Square development in the City Bowl is one of the current trendy spots, sporting no fewer than five fancy restaurants, as is the Waterkant gay district.

Several bars and pubs serve good food too; see Entertainment later in this chapter.

Cape Town is a picnicker's and self-caterer's paradise. Among the great spots to plan an alfresco meal are the Atlantic beaches (particularly Clifton and Camps Bay towards sunset), Lion's Head, Table Mountain, and Kirstenbosch Botanical Gardens.

For provisions, check the large and cheap **Pick 'n' Pay** supermarkets first; there are branches at the Waterfront, Gardens Centre, Sea Point and Camps Bay. Some branches of **Woolworths** also sell a good but pricey range of high-quality foods. You'll find them at the Waterfront, on Adderley St in the City Bowl and at the Cavendish Square mall in Claremont.

For specialist products check out the excellent delis, such as **Gionvanni's Deli World** in Green Point, **Melissa's** in Gardens, **Atlas Trading Company** in the Bo-Kaap district, and **Wellington Fruit Growers** in the City Bowl (see the reviews following for details).

City Bowl
Self-Catering *Atlas Trading Company* (☎ 423 4361, 94 Wale St, Bo-Kaap) Open 8am-5.15pm Mon-Thur, 8am-12.15pm & 2pm-5.15pm Fri, 8.30am-1pm Sat. Atlas provides the Cape Muslim community with over 100 different herbs and spices. It's a wonderfully atmospheric place and the proprietors will happily share some local recipes with you.

Wellington Fruit Growers (☎ 461 7160, 96 Darling St) Open 8am-5pm Mon-Fri, 8am-1pm Sat. A Cape Town institution, this long, narrow shop sells a huge range of nuts, dried and glace fruit, deli items, tinned foods and *lots* of lollies (sweets or candy).

Morris's (265 Long St) This is one of the best places for biltong and *boerewors* (spicy sausage).

Cafes & Snack Bars You'll have no problem finding takeaway food or a cheap cafe in the city centre on weekdays during business hours, but this is generally not the best area to be wandering around late at night or at the weekend (particularly Sunday), when it's practically deserted.

There are several reliable cafes around Greenmarket Square, which are great for people-watching. Check out *Le Petit Paris (36 Shortmarket St)* or *Cycles* on the terrace outside the Holiday Inn Greenmarket Square, which are good for a beer. The *Ivy Garden Restaurant* (see Restaurants following) serves snacks and drinks in front of the Old Town House.

Café Mozart (☎ 424 3774, 37 Church St) Open Mon-Fri 7am-3pm, Sat 8am-1pm. This deservedly popular cafe has tables spilling out onto the street and fine bistro-style food.

Gardens Restaurant (☎ 423 2919, Company's Gardens) Mains around R30. Open 8am-5pm daily. Licensed and with a large menu, this cafe and restaurant, with outdoor tables shaded by the trees, does everything from breakfast (R20 to R27) to *bobotie* (a traditional Cape Malay dish with curried mince, egg custard and rice).

Off Moroka Café Africaine (☎ 422 1129, 120 Adderley St) Breakfast from R14, lunch R25-30. Open 6.30am-9pm Mon-Thur, 6.30am-midnight Fri, 8.30am-midnight Sat. Pleasant and gay-friendly place to sample some fairly genuine African food and listen to tapes of African music. It's decorated with the work (for sale) of local artists.

D6 Snack Bar (☎ 082-970 7217, 104-6 Darling St) Mains R20. Open 10am-9pm Mon-Fri, noon-9pm Sat. This small cafe, bar and takeaway is on the fringes of the old District Six. It does a Friday night special of Afrikaner food for R20 including a free beer.

Long St has a plethora of options. One of the cheapest sit-down lunch-time feeds (around R16) can be had at the *Pan African*

Kitchen in the Pan African Market (for details see Shopping later in this chapter), where the balcony cafe provides a bird's-eye view of the passing parade. Also check out the following Long St places.

Shambala (☎ 426 5452, 134 Long St) Mains R25. Open 9am-9pm Mon-Fri, 9am-4pm Sat. Blissed-out holistic cafe and shop serving a mean range of smoothies and delicious vegetarian food.

Sooz Baguette Bar (☎ 423 3246, 150 Long St) Sandwiches from R15. Open 7.30am-4.30pm Mon-Fri. Make up your own sandwich from a wide range of ingredients or go for soup or one of the hot pies.

Mr Pickwick's (☎ 424 2696, 158 Long St) Mains around R20. Open 8am-1am Mon-Thur, 8am-4am Fri & Sat. Licensed, deli-style cafe that stays open very late for good snacks and meals. Try the foot-long rolls. The place to recuperate after a night out clubbing.

Diablo Bar Tapas (☎ 426 5484, 224B Long St) Mains from R10. Open 11am-midnight Mon-Sat, 5pm-11pm Sun. Offers a good range of reasonably authentic tapas and a relaxed atmosphere.

Lola's (☎ 423 0885, 228 Long St) Open 8am-midnight daily. Funky vegetarian cafe serving interesting food, with street tables and a gay-friendly vibe.

Long St Cafe (☎ 424 2464, 255 Long St) Mains around R30. Open 9.30am-1am Mon-Sat, 5pm-1am Sun. Spacious, appealing cafe and bar with big windows to catch all the street action.

Restaurants *Bukhara* (☎ 424 0000, 33 Church St) Mains around R40. Open noon-3pm Mon-Sat, 6.30pm-11pm daily. This Indian restaurant is everyone's favourite. It has spicy, tasty food in a stylish setting.

Primi Piatti (☎ 424 7466, 52 Shortmarket St) Mains R35. Open 7am-11pm daily. Hyperactive modern Italian cafe serving up yummy pizzas and enormous salads. It has branches at the Waterfront and on Victoria Rd, Camps Bay.

Ivy Garden Restaurant (☎ 423 2360, Old Town House, Greenmarket Square) Mains R40. Open 10am-5pm Mon-Fri, 10am-4pm Sat. Delightful courtyard restaurant serving a range of snacks and full meals including a platter of four Cape specialties for R60. The brandy pudding (R17) is truly wicked.

Five Flies (☎ 424 4442, 14-16 Keerom St) Two courses R77.50, 3 courses R95.70. Open noon-3pm Mon-Fri, 7pm-11pm Mon-Sat. Inventive contemporary cooking at this atmospheric fine restaurant in the restored old Dutch Club building dating from 1752.

Biesmiellah (☎ 423 0850, Wale St) Mains R40. Open noon-11pm Mon-Sat. Authentic Cape Malay and Indian food at this Bo-Kaap institution. It's all halal and no alcohol is served.

Noon Gun Tearoom & Restaurant (☎ 424 0529, 273 Longmarket St, Signal Hill) Mains R45. Open 10am-10pm Mon-Sat. After witnessing the noon blast of the cannon, slip into this pretty place with a great view; it serves Cape Malay dishes such as bobotie and can get busy with tour groups.

Africa Café (☎ 422 0221, 108 Shortmarket St) Meals R95. Open 6.30pm-11pm Mon-Sat. Our favourite of the Heritage Square restaurants. Fantastic decor and the best place in Cape Town to sample a range of African food. No fewer than 15 different dishes make up the pan-continental feast and you can have much as you like of each.

Mesopotamia (☎ 424 4664, Cnr Long & Church Sts) Mains R40-50. Open 7pm-11pm Mon-Sat. Kurdish restaurant dabbling in all things Ottoman, with *kilims* (carpets) on the walls, floor cushions around low copper salver tables. Serves excellent *meze* (snacks) and has belly dancing Friday and Saturday from around 9pm.

Mama Africa (☎ 426 1017, 178 Long St) Mains R40-60. The buzzing atmosphere, fuelled by the swinging African bands playing nightly, outpaces the variable food, which includes a tourist-pleasing range of game and African dishes. Bookings are essential at weekends unless you want to perch at the bar.

Mexican Kitchen (☎ 423 1541, 13 Bloem St) Buffet lunch R27.50, dinner R38.50. Open 10am-11pm daily. Offers authentic Mexican dishes and a relaxed vibe. The daily buffet is great value.

Kennedy's (☎ *424 1212, 251 Long St)* Mains R60-70. Open noon-3pm Mon-Fri, 7pm-11pm Mon-Sat. This stylish restaurant, with a hint of 1930s glamour, serves some interesting dishes using local produce such as springbok, ostrich and crocodile. There's a cigar lounge and bar and good live jazz music from around 9.30pm nightly.

Anapurna (☎ *418 9020, 1st floor, Seeff House, 42 Hans Strijdom Ave)* Mains R40-60. Open 12.30pm-3pm & 6pm-10.30pm Sun-Fri, 6pm-10.30pm Sat. Excellent North Indian cuisine served in a handsome airy setting.

Col' Cacchio (☎ *419 4848, Seeff House, 42 Hans Strijdom Ave)* Mains R35. Open noon-2.30pm & 6.30pm-11pm Mon-Fri, 6.30pm-11pm Sat & Sun. Poor service, but great pizzas with delicious toppings.

De Waterblommetjie (☎ *461 4895, Castle of Good Hope)* Mains R50. Open 7pm-11pm Tues-Sun. Sophisticated restaurant beside the castle walls; it specialises in modern South African cuisine.

Gardens
Cafes & Snack Bars Gardens Centre has a good range of cafes. For sheer indulgence drop by the *Mount Nelson Hotel* (see Hotels under Places to Stay – Top End earlier) for a delicious afternoon tea, which costs R65 and is served from 2.30pm to 5.30pm daily.

Naked on Kloof (☎ *424 4748, 51 Kloof St)* Mains R20. Open 9am-11pm daily. Bright and breezy deli-cafe specialising in fab wraps (flat bread rolled around a variety of fillings) and freshly squeezed fruit juices.

Cafe Bardeli (☎ *423 4444, Longklook Studios, Darter St)* Mains R20-30. Open 9am-1am Mon-Sat. Not quite as trendy as it once was, but still a reliable place to be seen with the beautiful people and eat decently too. The kitchen closes at midnight.

Melissa's (☎ *424 5540, 94 Kloof St)* Buffet R55 per kilogram. Open 7.30am-8pm Mon-Fri, 8am-8pm Sat & Sun. Getting a seat at this super-popular deli can be tricky so perhaps plan a takeaway. It's a serve-yourself buffet with prices worked out on weight; we defy you to resist the tempting cakes.

Restaurants *Maria's* (☎ *461 8887, 3 Barnet St)* Mains R40. Open 11.30am-11pm Mon-Fri, 5.30pm-11pm Sat & Sun. Small friendly taverna facing Dunkley Square offering a decent range of Greek dishes.

Café Riteve (☎ *465 1594, 88 Hatfield St)* Mains R25. Open 9.30am-5pm Mon-Wed, 9.30am-10pm Thur & Sun, 9.30am-3pm Fri. Everything from kosher bagels to crumbed hake is on offer at this contemporary bistro in the grounds of the South African Jewish Museum. It has live music, plays and comedy shows regularly in the evenings, starting at R55 for a meal and show.

Nelson's Eye (☎ *423 2601, 9 Hof St)* Mains around R80. Open 11.30am-2pm Mon-Fri, 6.30pm-10.30pm daily. Darkly atmospheric steakhouse, serving prime meat with some delicious sauces. It may not be the cheapest but it's among the best.

Rozenhof (☎ *424 1968, 18 Kloof St)* Mains R50. One of the area's longest running restaurants. Dishes such as cheese souffle and crispy roast duck have become legendary.

Heading uphill, the seafood chain restaurant *Ocean Basket* (☎ *422 0322, Kloof St)* and the pizzeria *Peasants* (☎ *424 3445, 9 Kloof St)* are reliable and inexpensive.

The Happy Wok (☎ *424 2423, 62A Kloof St)* Mains R30. Open 5.30pm-10.30pm daily. Serving cheap Pan-Asian food. If it's made in a wok (and sometimes if it isn't, as with the Japanese dishes), then you can get it here.

Cafe Dharma (☎ *422 0909, 68 Kloof St)* Mains R60. Open 7pm-1.30am Mon-Sat. The Café del Mar set comes to Cape Town at this so-stylish-it-hurts restaurant and DJ bar. The food, by the way, is fusion.

Café Paradiso (☎ *423 8653, 110 Kloof St)* Mains R30-40. Open 10am-midnight Mon-Fri, 9am-midnight Sat & Sun. Fashionable but informal upmarket cafe, serving the standard range of Mediterranean-inspired dishes.

Waterfront
Despite the Waterfront's convenience and lively atmosphere – especially on balmy nights – the restaurants and cafes here fare rather poorly in comparison with their more

interesting, and generally lower priced, brethren in town. This is just as you'd expect for what is in essence a giant tourist trap.

This said, with scores of options catering to all budgets, there are some decent places here. The Waterfront information centre has a sizable booklet listing them all. As well as the national and international franchises, such as *St Elmo's* (pizza and pasta), *Spur* (mainly steaks), and the ubiquitous *Hard Rock Cafe*, there are some local spin-offs including *Caffé San Marco* (☎ 418 5434, *Victoria Wharf*) and the Greek takeaway *Ari's Souvlaki* (☎ 418 5544, *Victoria Wharf*), both siblings of the Sea Point institutions.

For drinks and snacks other favourite cafes are *Mugg & Bean* (☎ 419 6451) and *Zerban's* (☎ 425 3431), both on the ground floor of the Victoria Wharf mall. For cheap fish and chips, head to the *Fisherman's Choice* takeaway facing Quay Four; there are tables here but everyone has to queue up to be served.

Den Anker (☎ 419 0249, *Pierhead*) Mains R45-65. Open 11am-11pm daily. Charming setting and a great range of authentic Belgian beers with which to wash down a menu heavy on mussels and other seafood.

Musselcracker Restaurant (☎ 419 4300, *Upper level, Victoria Wharf*) Open 12.30pm-2.30pm & 6.30pm-11pm daily. Buffet lunch R75, dinner R95. This blow-out seafood buffet packs them in nightly. Booking advised.

Quay 4 (☎ 419 2000, *Quay Four, Pierhead*) Mains R30-40. Open noon-10.30pm daily, closed for lunch Sat. Right by the water, this pricey seafood brasserie is unbelievably popular, which means you could wait a while for your food.

Quay West (☎ 418 0520, *Cape Grace Hotel, West Quay*) Mains R60-70. Can't afford to stay at one of Cape Town's most exclusive hotels? So come for its buffet breakfast (R69) or for a dinner of delights such as Cape Malay crayfish.

For other Waterfront dining options see *Ferryman's Freehouse* and *The Sports Cafe* under Bars & Pubs, and *Green Dolphin* under Live Music, all under Entertainment later in this chapter.

Waterkant & Green Point

While the main restaurant strips of Waterkant and Green Point are safe, the stretch of Main Rd linking them is where prostitutes ply their trade; you might feel more comfortable catching a cab or minibus taxi for the short distance between the two areas.

Anatoli (☎ 419 2501, *24 Napier St*) Cold meze from R10.50, hot meze from R12.50. Open Tues-Sun. Anatoli has been here since pop fell off the bus and with good reason: its delicious meze brought round on enormous wooden trays makes a great meal.

Vasco da Gama Tavern (☎ 425 2157, *3 Alfred St*) Mains R25. Open 11.30am-8pm Mon-Sat. Munch on excellent seafood, including Mozambique prawns and Portuguese sardines, while old blokes argue the toss at the other end of the laminated bar. Last food orders are at 8pm.

Beluga (☎ 418 2948, *The Foundry, Prestwich St*) Mains R40-50. Chic warehouse where the smart set dines. There's beluga caviar on the menu for R400, but there are plenty of cheaper dishes and a pleasant cafe too.

0932 (☎ 439 6306, *79 Main Rd*) Mains R50. Open noon-11.30pm Mon-Thur, noon-midnight Fri-Sat, noon-10.30pm Sun. A bit pretentious, but this Belgian beer restaurant is a cool place to hang out and the two-course deal from noon to 7pm for R50 isn't bad.

News Cafe (☎ 434 6196, *83 Main Rd*) Mains R20-40. Open 7.30am-2pm Mon-Fri, 9am-2am Sat & Sun. At the other end of the revamped Exhibition Building from 0932, this buzzy cafe-bar is good for a substantial snack or bistro-type meal.

Mario's (☎ 439 6644, *89 Main Rd*) Mains R30-40. Open noon-2.30pm Tues-Fri & Sun, 6.45pm-10.30pm Tues-Sun. Long-established Italian, where customer praise is scribbled all over the walls. Perfect pasta and an extensive list of daily specials.

Gionvanni's Deli World (☎ 434 6983, *103 Main Rd*) Open 8.30am-9pm daily. Not as big as rivals, but bursting with energy and flavoursome products. Gionvanni's will make up any sandwich you fancy from the provisions. If you can't wait to eat, there's a small cafe.

Sea Point

For self-caterers, one of the best places for biltong and boerewors is *Joubert & Monty's Meat Boutique* (53 Regent Rd).

Reise's Deli (☎ 434 3465, 267 Main Rd) Mains R15-30. Open 8.30am-7pm daily. Kerb-side tables and good snacks from the authentic deli (although we found the gefilte fish not as good as grandma makes).

Atlantic Express (☎ 439 3038, 1B Regent Rd) Mains R18-28. Open 8am-midnight daily. Not quite an alternative to the *Blue Train*, but this cafe in a converted Pullman train carriage serves some good light meals including Cape Malay dishes.

New York Bagels (☎ 439 7523, 51 Regent Rd) Mains R10-20. Open 7am-11pm daily. As well as the deli there's the airy multilevel cafe where you wander around various stalls to choose a mix 'n' match meal of, say, hot beef on rye followed by a spicy stir-fry. It serves alcohol, too.

Theo's (☎ 439 3494, 163 Beach Rd, Mouille Point) Mains R50. Open noon-2.30pm Sun-Fri, 6pm-10.30pm daily. Award-winning steakhouse where the meat is matured on the premises. It also does good seafood, and it's not too expensive. There's a branch on Victoria Rd in Camps Bay.

Maz Japanese Cuisine (☎ 439 1806, Adelphi Centre, 127 Main Rd) Mains R30-40. Open 10.30am-9.30pm Mon-Sat. Tiny and reasonably priced sushi bar which is generally packed (you may have to get takeaway).

San Marco (☎ 434 1469, 92 Main Rd) Mains R40-60. Open noon-2.30pm Sun only, 6pm-10.30pm Wed-Mon. Venerable institution, serving great pasta and other Italian dishes. Try the amazing ostrich *carpaccio* (raw ostrich meat). The *gelateria* (open 10am-11.30pm) in front of the restaurant has delicious takeaway *gelato* (ice cream).

Ari's Souvlaki (☎ 439 6683, 83A Regent Rd) Mains R20. Open 10am-midnight daily. Meze, shwarma and felafel (R15) are on offer at this Greek long-runner. It's nothing fancy but it's honest.

Camps Bay

Because Camps Bay is one of the hot spots for sundowners (drinks at sunset) you'd be well advised to book ahead for anywhere with a view. If you haven't booked, a stroll along the beach, followed by a beer and dinner at one of the pavement tables fronting Victoria Rd, is a genuine pleasure.

The Sandbar (☎ 438 8336, 31 Victoria Rd) Mains R22-30. Open 10am-9.30pm daily. Good sandwiches and light meals are the deal at this laid-back cafe with street tables.

Blues (☎ 438 2040, The Promenade, Victoria Rd) Mains from R40. Open noon-midnight daily. Casual dining in the 'Californian tradition', which means the menu has something to please practically everyone. Book well ahead for a window seat.

Dizzy Jazz Cafe (☎ 438 2686, 41 The Drive) Mains R50-60. Cover charge R10-20 at night. Open noon-3pm & 6pm-1am daily. Dizzy's specialises in seafood platters, but many people come here for the live music, which ranges from jazz to country and blues.

The Codfather (☎ 438 0782, 37 The Drive) Mains R40. Open noon-3pm & 6pm-11pm Mon-Fri, noon-midnight Sat. Set back from the main drag but still with a decent beach view is this sophisticated seafood restaurant with a conveyor-belt sushi bar (plates from R6 to R20).

Hout Bay

Hout Bay's attractive harbour is where you'll find several takeaway fish and chipperies, including *Fish on the Rocks*, in a great spot right at the end of Hout Bay Harbour Rd. It's open from 10.30am to 8.15pm daily.

Mariner's Wharf (☎ 790 1100, Hout Bay Harbour) Mains R50. Open 9am-10pm daily. Harbourside complex with several options: in the upmarket *Wharfside Grill* the waiters are dressed as sailors to match the sea-salt decor; the cheaper deal is at the takeaway downstairs.

Observatory

For around 200m along Lower Main Rd in Observatory it's wall-to-wall restaurants, cafes and bars. Observatory station (on the Simon's Town line) is a short walk away although trains stop early evening, when either your own transport or a taxi will be the only way of getting here.

There's little to choose between the following casual places with menus slanted towards the tastes and budgets (mains all around R20 to R30) of the resident student population.

Obz Café (115 Lower Main Rd) is a trendy long-runner; *Café Whatever* (☎ 448 9129, *90 Lower Main Rd)* is a more laid-back bistro; the new *Green Mamba Cafe* (☎ 447 2165, 64 Lower Main Rd) offers up African food; and *Café Ganesh* (☎ 448 3435, 38B *Trill Rd)* is a classic funky student hang-out, dishing out the likes of felafel, roti and curries.

More restaurant options include the cheerful *Pancho's Mexican Kitchen* (☎ 447 4854, 127 Lower Main Rd)*; *Senhôra Sardine* (☎ 448 1979, Cnr Trill & Lower Main Rds)*, serving Portuguese dishes in an appealingly rustic setting; and *Diva* (☎ 448 0282, 88 Lower Main Rd)*, a highly rated Italian with faded Venetian-style decor.

Southern Suburbs

Rhodes Memorial Restaurant (☎ 689 9151, *Groote Schuur Estate, Rondebosch)* Snacks from R15. Open 9am-5pm daily. Fantastic spot, on the side of Devil's Peak and right behind the memorial, for afternoon tea – the scones are huge.

The Gardener's Cottage (☎ 689 3158, 31 *Newlands Ave, Newlands)* Mains R20. Open 8am-4.30pm Tues-Fri, 8.30am-4.30pm Sat & Sun. Cute cafe and tea garden in the grounds of the Montebello craft studios (see Shopping later in this chapter).

The swank shopping mall Cavendish Square at Claremont has a several good cafes and a food court on the upper level, where the most interesting option is *Mango's Grill & Bar* (☎ 674 1350), serving some African and Caribbean dishes.

Kirstenbosch Botanical Gardens

Kirstenbosch has a couple of dining options in case you forgot that picnic basket.

Fynbos Food Court Buffet breakfast R30, lunch R45. Open 9am-5pm daily. This self-service restaurant offers light meals and takeaways, including beer and wine, in a pleasant setting.

Silver Tree (☎ 762 9585) Mains around R55. Open 11.30am-3pm & 6.30pm-10pm daily. This is *the* a la carte restaurant, with crisp white tablecloths. Call about the monthly food-and-wine evenings.

Constantia

Wine-tasting and dining around Constantia is an exceedingly civilised way to spend a day. For details of the wineries, see Constantia earlier in this chapter.

Jonkershuis (☎ 794 4255, Groot Constantia)* Mains R40. Open 9am-11pm Tues-Sat, 9am-5pm Sun & Mon. Specialises in traditional Cape dishes such as bobotie and *bredies* (a traditional Cape Malay stew). Pity the poor waiters who have to dress up in 17th-century slave costumes. The estate also offers the *Tavern Restaurant* (☎ 794 1144) serving continental food.

Spaanschemat River Café (☎ 794 3010, *Spaanschemat River Rd)* Mains R35-50. Open 8am-4pm daily. At the entrance to the Constantia Uitsig estate, this relaxed restaurant is good value and serves huge portions; the club sandwiches are the business and the deserts divine.

Peddlars on the Bend (☎ 794 7747, *Spaanschemat River Rd)* Mains R35. Open noon-11pm daily. If you don't fancy all that highfalutin wine-estate fodder, the hearty dishes such as chicken-and-leek pie and *eisbein* (pork knuckle) served at this large and lively pub should suit you fine.

Kalk Bay

Kalk Bay's Main Rd runneth over with cafes; good ones include the reliable *Cathedral Café (64 Main Rd)* and *Trainspot Pancake & Coffee Kaya*, a funky alfresco joint next to the station.

The Brass Bell (☎ 788 5455) There are several options at this Cape Town institution between the train station and the sea. The formal restaurant serves everything from breakfast to dinner; there's an oriental-food section; an alfresco pizzeria and, of course, the bar. Fish braais are held on the terrace on Sunday from 6.30pm.

Café Matisse (☎ 788 1123, 76 Main Rd) Mains R25-30. Open 8.30am-11pm daily. Eclectic decor and candles at night enhance the atmosphere at this bistro, which serves pizzas and a good meze plate.

Olympia Café and Deli (☎ 788 6396, 134 Main Rd) Mains R20. Open 7am-6pm Tues & Wed, 7am-9pm Thur-Sat, 7am-2pm Sun. Local artists display their work at this relaxed, rustic cafe, which is renowned for its breakfasts and pastries.

Simon's Town

Apart from the cluster of places near the marina, don't forget the *Penguin Point Cafe* further south at Boulders Beach.

Bertha's (☎ 786 2138, 1 Wharf Rd) Mains R35. Open 8am-10pm daily. Right by the harbour, Bertha's serves a variety of dishes. Service is friendly and the mood relaxed.

The Meeting Place (☎ 786 1986, 98 St George's St) Mains R20-25. Open 9am-6pm Sun-Wed, 9am-9pm Thur-Sat. Trendy deli-cafe that's a foodies' delight. The balcony overlooks the street and harbour.

Cape Flats

You need to be on a tour or with a private guide to visit these places.

Gugu le Afrika (☎ 364 3395, 8 Lwandle Rd, Khayelitsha) Mains around R15. Open Mon-Fri 8.30am-4.30pm. Gugu is a catering training centre but still a professional operation, with a full menu of very reasonably priced Western and African dishes. Check out the fabric-printing and design workshop next door.

Lelapa (49 Harlem Ave, Langa) is a restaurant used on the Township Music Tour run by Our Pride Tours (see Township Tours earlier in this chapter). The host, Sheila, is well travelled and a great cook.

Masande Restaurant (☎ 371 7173) is a restaurant in the same Crossroads complex as the Philani Flagship Printing Project. The name means 'let us prosper'. You can try traditional dishes such as *samp* (a mix of maize and beans) with stew, *pap* (maize porridge) and tripe, and *umvubo* (sour milk and mealie meal), as well as *umnqombothi* (rough-and-ready home-brewed beer).

GAY & LESBIAN VENUES

Cape Town is in the business of establishing itself as the gay capital of Africa. The focus of the action is the Waterkant district but there's also a gay flavour to Sea Point and the upper end of Long St. Check out the *Pink Map* available from Cape Town Tourism and most of the venues listed below. Both *Cape Review* and *SA Citylife* include gay listings.

Mother City Queer Projects (see Special Events earlier in this chapter) runs a massive costume party held every year in mid-December. Out in Africa, the gay and lesbian film festival, hits town in Feb.

Cafe Manhattan (☎ 421 6666, 74 Waterkant St, Waterkant) is a convivial, long-running bar and restaurant (call to ask about 'girls only' nights, which were being trialled at the time of research).

Robert's Café & Cigar Bar (☎ 425 2478, 72 Waterkant St, Waterkant) definitely has better food than at the neighbouring Cafe Manhattan.

Gorgeous (☎ 424 4554, 210 Loop St, City Bowl) is a restaurant with a rather fab design and ambitious cooking.

Priscilla's (☎ 422 2378, 196 Loop St, City Bowl) is near Gorgeous and is a gay bar and restaurant with straight decor and a friendly vibe.

Cafe Camissa (☎ 424 2289, 80 Kloof St, Gardens) is up the hill from Priscilla's and is a groovy cafe-bar with live world music on Wednesday and Sunday (R10).

L'Orient (☎ 439 6572, 50 Main Rd, Sea Point) Mains R35-60. Open 6.30pm-10.30pm Mon-Sat. L'Orient serves Malaysian and Indonesian dishes. Try the spicy prawn soup for flavours you might have been missing in South Africa.

Café Erté (☎ 434 6624, 265A Main Rd, Sea Point) Snacks R25. Open daily 11am-4am. This is a vibey Internet cafe and chilled hang-out for the late-night clubbing set.

Bronx (☎ 419 9219, Cnr Somerset & Napier Sts, Waterkant) is the city's premier gay bar – a lively place that has them dancing until dawn (and singing karaoke on Monday). The main bar is on the corner, while from the courtyard you can also enter two other dance spaces, *Angels* and *Detour*.

On Broadway (☎ *418 8338,* **W** *www.on broadway.co.za, 21 Somerset St, Waterkant)* is a cabaret supper venue popular with all Capetonians, so book ahead. The dynamic drag duo Mince are lip-sync specialists and on Monday Pieter-Dirk Uys (whose Evita Bezuidenhout character is a national icon; see also under Darling in the Western Cape chapter) takes to the stage.

55 (☎ *425 2739, Cnr Somerset & Napier Sts, Waterkant)* Admission R10 after 11pm. Diagonally opposite Bronx, this was the hot dance spot at the time of research.

ENTERTAINMENT

The old 'Tavern of the Seas' is still a dab hand at beguiling rands from locals and visiting foreigners alike. The city has such a good atmosphere (especially in summer) that many people put in some very long nights drifting from bar to club to bar to club.

It's not all about drinking and dancing. Cape Town has a good range of cinemas and theatres, while musical performances span the gamut from classical to rock bands via jazz and marimba. Free live music is a feature of the Waterfront, in particular.

Bars and clubs where all races happily rub shoulders are few and far between; practically the only way you're going to safely explore the nightlife of the Cape Flats, for example, is on a tour such as that offered by Our Pride Tours (see Organised Tours earlier in this chapter).

For listings, see the weekly arts guide in the *Mail & Guardian*, the nightly entertainment section in the *Cape Argus*, and the monthly magazines *Cape Review* and *SA Citylife*.

You can book seats for practically anything with **Computicket** (☎ *918 8910,* **W** *www computicket.com).* There are outlets in the Golden Acre Centre, in the Gardens Centre and at the Waterfront.

Bars & Pubs

Wednesday, Friday and Saturday are the biggest nights in the bars and clubs. The upper (south-western) ends of Long and Kloof Sts and the gay Waterkant district are incredibly lively all night long on summer

weekends, as is the Waterfront. Try not to miss out on a night at the Drum Cafe (see Live Music following), a great place for a drink even if you choose not to dive into a session of drumming.

Several other good watering holes, such as *Mama Africa* and *Kennedy's* on Long St, and *The Brass Bell* in Kalk Bay, are listed under Places to Eat earlier.

City Bowl & Gardens *The Square All Bar None* (☎ *082-416 4106, 36 Shortmarket St, City Bowl)* is a pavement cafe and modern bar and dance venue just off Greenmarket Square, playing a range of music, including 1970s to 1990s retro tracks on Thursday.

Pa Na Na Souk Bar (☎ *423 4889, Heritage Square, 100 Shortmarket St, City Bowl)* is a luxurious bar with balconies overlooking Heritage Square's restored courtyard.

The Purple Turtle (☎ *423 6194, Cnr Long & Shortmarket St, City Bowl)* is Grunge and Goth central. Dress in black and wear purple make-up to feel at home.

Jo'burg (☎ *422 0241, 218 Long St, City Bowl)* is the coolest hang-out on Long St by far, with occasional live music. Check out the groovy Boogie Lights, Perspex light sculptures that decorate the walls.

Stag's Head Hotel (☎ *465 4918, 71 Hope St, Gardens)* is a popular and very grungy pub. The ground-floor bar is home to a motley assortment of locals while the lounge bar (in the rear) has a younger crowd. The real action happens upstairs, with plenty of pool tables, pinball machines and loud music (sometimes live).

Cecil Rhodes called *The Perseverance Tavern* (☎ *461 2440, 83 Buitenkant St, Gardens)* his local. The flickering candles in the dim interior still give it plenty of atmosphere and the simple meals (mains around R30) ain't too bad.

Dros (☎ *423 6800, 22 Kloof St, Gardens)* Open 9am-2am daily. An unfortunate choice of name for this otherwise quite acceptable chain pub-restaurant (the letters in the name actually stand for AWOL – absent without leave – in Afrikaans).

The Shed (☎ *461 5892, 43-45 De Villiers St, Gardens),* a happening bar and pool hall that packs an interesting crowd, is part of the complex of venues on the edge of District Six. Next door are the laid-back *Blue Lizard Internet Café* and *The Jam*, a club that also has live music.

Waterfront, Green Point & Waterkant

Bascule Bar, at the Cape Grace Hotel, is a particularly sophisticated option that specialises in whisky. Feeling flush? Then go for the 50-year-old Glenfiddich, a mere R15,200 a tot.

Fireman's Arms (☎ 419 1513, 25 Mechau St) is one of the few old pubs left in town and is a great place to come watch a rugby match on the big-screen TV, grab some seriously tasty pizza, a cheap bar meal or just down a pint or two.

Ferryman's Freehouse (☎ 419 7748, East Pier Rd, Waterfront) adjoins Mitchell's Waterfront Brewery and is a relaxed pub-restaurant serving a variety of freshly brewed beers and good-value meals (around R30 for a meal).

The Sports Cafe (☎ 419 5558, Upper level, Victoria Wharf) offers all the sports action on big-screen TVs and a chance to catch overseas games on live satellite broadcasts. Plenty of burgers and snacky options to go with the amber nectar.

Chilli 'n' Lime (☎ 498 4668, 23 Somerset St, Waterkant), a lively, mainly straight bar and club in the heart of the gay district, has a range of events.

Buena Vista Social Café (☎ 433 0610, Exhibition Bldg, 81 Main Rd, Green Point) is above the buzzy *News Cafe* (see Waterkant & Green Point under Places to Eat earlier in this chapter) and takes its inspiration from the famous Cuban music CD. A tapas menu supplements the mix of cigars, Bacardis and Cokes, and beautiful people.

Clifton & Camps Bay

La Med (☎ 438 5600, Glen Country Club, Clifton) is one of the choice places to be at sunset, although essentially it's just a bar with lots of outdoor tables and a good view. Food is of the steak roll (R30) variety. The entrance, along Victoria Rd on the way from Camps Bay to Clifton, is easily passed.

Baraza (☎ 438 1758, Victoria Rd, Camp, Bay) is a wine and cocktail bar with a kille view; you may have to kill to be able to ad mire it from a hotly contested cane chair.

Observatory

They've dumped sand out side *Cool Runnings* (☎ 448 7656, 96 Station St), a chain reggae bar, to create that beach side feel, carried through in the island-hu decor. A fun hang-out, with a branch o Kloof St in Gardens (minus the beach).

Rolling Stones (☎ 448 9461, 94 Lowe Main Rd) Open noon-3am daily. Otherwise known as Stones, this giant pool bar has long balcony, a great spot from which to ob serve the comings and goings of Lower Mai Rd. There's also a branch at 166A Long S

You can hardly swing a cat at *A Touch o Madness* (☎ 448 2266, 42 Trill Rd), a wack ily decorated bar-bistro, which still manage to have plenty of cosy corners.

The Curve Bar at the Bijoux (☎ 448 0183 178 Lower Main Rd) is at the dodgy end o Observatory, but is safe enough to venture t when there's a club night on (for which you'l pay around R20 admission). Cool industria decor in an old converted cinema space.

Southern Suburbs

The Foresters' Arm (☎ 689 5949, 52 Newlands Ave, Newlands Mains R30. Open Mon-Sat 10am-11pm Sun 9am-4pm. Big mock-Tudor pub, com monly known as 'Forrie's', with a convivia atmosphere and good pub meals.

Barristers (☎ 674 1792, Cnr Kildare Rd o Main St, Newlands) Mains around R40. Th long-time favourite of Newlands' rugge buggers has had an upgrade and now offer a more sophisticated atmosphere for dinin, as well as drinking.

Bloubergstrand

The Blue Peter (☎ 55 1956, Popham St) Mains R25. Open 10am 11pm daily. The thing to do here is grab beer, order a pizza and plonk yourself o the grass outside to enjoy the classic vie of Table Mountain and Robben Island.

Clubs

Keep your ear to the ground for specia events, such as the *Vortex trance partie*

(☎ 794 4032). The main backpacker hostels should know when these monthly out-of-town overnight raves are happening and can often arrange transport.

At clubs, expect to pay a cover charge of between R10 and R30 depending on the night and the event. Most places don't get going until after 11pm. Long St is the epicentre of the city's club scene.

City Bowl *The Jet Lounge (☎ 424 8831, 74 Long St)* is a slick venue offering house, funk and disco beats. There's *The Baseline* preclub bar downstairs.

Rhythm Divine (☎ 0861-400500, 156 Long St) is a happening venue with plenty of different parties to attend and two sizable dance floors and a pool room.

169 on Long (☎ 426 1107, 169 Long St) Open 6pm-late Fri & Sat only. One of the few Long St venues where whites are in the minority. The funky music, often live r'n'b, is probably what accounts for it.

Drum-and-bass or jungle music provide the background for cool drinks on the long iron-lace balcony at *The Lounge (☎ 424 7636, 194 Long St)*.

Old-time artist Tretchikoff features big in *Coffee Lounge (☎ 424 6784, 76 Church St)*, a funky four-storey club and bar that serves up an eclectic range of events.

The Fez (☎ 423 1456, 38 Hout St) is a city-centre hot spot, with queues out the door at the weekends (although given Capetonians' fickle nature it could well have gone off the boil by now).

Rhodes House (☎ 424 8844, 60 Queen Victoria St) Admission R50. Party with the glam set at this imaginative and beautiful venue. Wildly expensive but worth it.

Athlone *Club Galaxy (☎ 637 9132, College Rd, Ryelands Estate, Athlone)* Open 9pm-3am Thur-Sat. A younger crowd haunts this long-time Cape Flats favourite where you can get down to r'n'b and live bands. Women get in free on Thursday until 11pm.

Milnerton Women get in free on Wednesday before 11pm at *Dockside (☎ 552 2030, Century City, Century City Blvd)*, a mega

club beside the Canal Walk mall. International DJs occasionally grace the decks but they'd have to be pretty special to tempt you out here otherwise.

Live Music

At times it seems as if Cape Town is pounding to a perpetual beat. The opportunities to catch musical performances are wide and varied, spanning everything from a cappella buskers at the Waterfront to jazz brunches at Winchester Mansions Hotel in Sea Point (see Hotels under Places to Stay – Mid-Range, earlier in this chapter) and thumping African funk at Mama Africa (see City Bowl under Places to Eat earlier in this chapter).

Drum Cafe (☎ 461 1305, W www.drum cafe.co.za, 32 Glynn St, Gardens) Admission R30, drum hire R20. Every Monday, Wednesday, Friday and Saturday from 9pm there are drumming workshops and live bands or both at this funky hang-out; Wednesday's facilitated drum circle is a blast. See the Web site for details of events, lessons and kids' workshops.

Green Dolphin (☎ 421 7471, Alfred Mall, Waterfront) Cover charge R20. Open noon-midnight daily. This upmarket jazz venue serves decent food and has live bands every evening. The nearby *Quay 4* (see Waterfront under Places to Eat) also sometimes has local bands and musos performing.

Other jazz venues listed under Places to Eat include *Kennedy's* on Long St in the City Bowl, and *Dizzy Jazz Cafe* in Camps Bay. There's good live world music at *Cafe Camissa* in Gardens (see Gay & Lesbian venues earlier). *The Jam* is where top SA bands belt out their stuff, and *The Purple Turtle* is worth checking out for its alternative music gigs (see Bars & Pubs for both of these).

Artscape (☎ 421 7695, W www.artscape .co.za, 1-10 DF Malan St, Foreshore) is the home of the Cape Philharmonic, and here you can catch regular classical concerts as well as ballet, opera and theatre. Every March the Cape Phil performs a proms program in the Old Town Hall. Note that walking around the complex at night is not recommended and you'll need to book ahead for a taxi given that there are none on the streets.

Cinemas

See the local press for a full rundown of cinemas and the films they are showing.

Labia (☎ 424 5927, 68 Orange St, Gardens) Admission R15/18 day/evening shows. This is the best cinema for 'mainstream alternative' films. It is named after the old Italian ambassador and local philanthropist Count Labia.

IMAX Theatre (☎ 419 7365, Waterfront) Adults/children R34/20; shows 10am-9pm daily. For huge-screen entertainment.

Tickets at the following venues are R25, half-price on Tuesday. It pays to book in advance, especially for the Waterfront cinemas, which are very popular.

For commercial films, try the *Nu-Metro cineplexes* (teleticket ☎ 086-110 0220) at the Waterfront and Canal Walk shopping centres. Canal Walk is 5km north of the city centre.

Cinema Nouveau (Cavendish Square ☎ 683 4063, Waterfront ☎ 425 8222) shows a slightly classier range of movies.

Theatre & Comedy

Major productions are staged at *Artscape* (see Live Music earlier). *On Broadway* (see Gay & Lesbian Venues earlier) has great cabaret shows.

Gauloises Warehouse (☎ 421 0777, 6 Dixon St, Waterkant) is neighbour to On Broadway and specialises in cutting-edge and local theatre – this is where *Shopping and Fucking*, the hit London play, had its Cape Town premiere.

Baxter Studio (☎ 685 7880, Main Rd, Rondebosch) offers a really wide range of theatre including kids' shows and Zulu dance spectaculars.

Independent Armchair Theatre (☎ 447 1514, 135 Lower Main Rd, Observatory) is the Sunday night home for the Cape Comedy Collective, a witty bunch of comediennes who do the rounds of other venues including the GrandWest Casino and Galaxy night club. This venue has an eclectic range of other events including Japanese animated movies on Monday nights.

Other Amusements

Ratanga Junction (☎ 550 8504, Century City, Milnerton) Adult/child R69/39 including rides, admission only R29. Open 10am-5pm Sun-Tues & Thur & Fri, 10am-6pm Sat. Big amusement park with an African theme, next to the enormous Canal Walk shopping centre, around 5km north of the city centre along the N1. For a 90-second adrenaline rush the 100km/h Cobra is recommended. You'll need a car to get out here, as you will also for the nearby casino

GrandWest Casino (☎ 505 7174, W www.grandwest.co.za, Old Goodwood show grounds, Milnerton). Apparently this over blown Disneyland of gambling was inspired by Cape Town's architectural heritage, the old post office serving as the model for the facade. It took US$20 million in revenue in its first three months, making it a huge success (or a huge tragedy for the thousands of impoverished gamblers and their families). Still, you might want to come here for it state-of-the-art cinema complex, food court Olympic sized ice rink, kids' theme park and music shows.

SHOPPING

You'll find most things you need at shops in the city centre and the Waterfront but if you hunger for a suburban mall, try the stylish mall *Cavendish Square*, off Protea Rd in Claremont, or *Canal Walk*, the largest mall on the continent, about 5km north of the city centre. The *Gardens Centre* on Mill St is another handy central shopping complex

There are craft and souvenir markets in the City Bowl's Greenmarket Square (Monday to Saturday); beside the train station (Monday to Saturday); and outside Green Point Stadium (every Sunday). The market at Grand Parade near the Castle of Good Hope in City Bowl (Wednesday and Saturday) doesn't sell much of interest to visitors but is much livelier than the others, with people scrambling for bargains, mainly clothing.

Crafts & Souvenirs

There are craft shops all over town but few of the traditional African items come from the Cape Town area itself. Local township produced items, such as toys made from recycled tin cans and wire sculptures, make great gifts.

Along St George's Mall you'll find some very good (as well as some very ordinary) art by township artists. Some of the artists are quite well known but prefer to sell direct to the public rather than pay commission to a gallery. You can pay over R200 for a print but some are worth it.

Khayelitsha Craft Market Mon & Thur. This is a great place to look for interesting souvenirs, and you can be sure that your money goes to the people who need it most (see Cape Flats earlier in this chapter).

Montebello (☎ 685 6445, 31 Newlands Ave, Newlands) Open 9am-5pm daily. Development project aimed at promoting good local design and creating jobs in the craft industry. On weekdays you can visit the artists' studios. There's an outlet in the city beneath Cape Town Tourism.

Pan African Market (76 Long St, City Bowl) Open 9.30am-5pm Mon-Fri, 9.30am-4.30pm Sat & Sun. A microcosm of the continent with a bewildering range of crafts and art packed into its three floors.

The African Music Store (☎ 426 0857, 90A Long St, City Bowl) Open 9am-5pm Mon-Fri, 9am-2pm Sat. The knowledgeable staff here can advise you on the big selection of local music.

African Image (☎ 423 8385, Cnr Church & Burg Sts, City Bowl) Open 9am-5pm Mon-Fri, 9am-1pm Sat. Fab range of new and old craft and artefacts at reasonable prices. There's a branch at the Waterfront too.

Mnandi Textiles & Design (☎ 447 6814, 90 Station St, Observatory) Open 9am-4.30pm Mon-Fri, 9am-1pm Sat. Sells cloth and clothing printed with everything from ANC election posters to animals and traditional African patterns.

Antiques & Art

Cape Town has troves of antiques and collectibles for sale, often at reasonable prices. The City Bowl, Church St and Long St in particular are worth a browse. There's a small market daily along the pedestrianised section of Church St between Long and Burg Sts, and this is where you'll also find several interesting commercial galleries.

Long St is a bibliophile's heaven with many good second-hand and antiquarian bookshops. See Bookshops under Information earlier in this chapter for details of *Clarke's*, which is one of the best.

Metropolitan Gallery (☎ 424 7436, 35 Church St, City Bowl) Open 10am-5pm Mon-Fri, 10am-1pm Sat. Exhibition space for the nonprofit Association for Visual Arts (AVA); it shows some very interesting work by local artists.

Everard Read (☎ 418 4527, 3 Portswood Rd, Waterfront) Open 9am-6pm Mon-Sat. The top gallery for contemporary South African art.

Other

Cape Union Mart has several branches including the Waterfront (☎ 419 0019, Shop 142), City Bowl (☎ 464 5800, Cnr Mostert & Corporation Sts) and in the Gardens (☎ 461 9678, Gardens Centre).

Cape wines are of an extremely high standard and very cheap by international standards. It is worth considering having a few cases shipped home, although you will almost certainly have to pay duty. All wineries can arrange shipping

Vaughan Johnson's Wine & Cigar Shop (☎ 419 2121, e vjohnson@mweb.co.za, Dock Rd, Waterfront) can arrange shipping of wine too. It stocks practically every wine you could wish to buy (plus a few more) and is open, unlike practically all other wine sellers, on Sunday. For detailed information on wine, see the special section 'Cape Wineries'.

GETTING THERE & AWAY
Air
Cape Town international airport (☎ 937 1200) is served by direct flights from many countries, although several will touch down first in Jo'burg before flying on here.

For domestic services the one-way fares quoted here are full economy but discounts are available (see the Getting Around chapter). South African Airways (SAA) flies between Cape Town and major centres, including Port Elizabeth (R570), Upington (R992), Durban (R1174), Kimberley (R992), Jo'burg (R1083) and East London (R1106).

Comair (☎ 936 9000) operates in conjunction with British Airways. **National Airlines** (☎ 936 2050) has flights every weekday to Springbok and Alexander Bay (both R1482).

International airlines with offices in Cape Town include:

Air Mauritius (☎ 421 6294, fax 421 7371) 11th floor, Strand Towers, 66 Strand St, City Bowl
Air Namibia (☎ 936 2755, fax 936 2760) Cape Town international airport
British Airways (☎ 934 0292, fax 934 0959) Cape Town international airport
KLM (☎ 0806-247747, fax 670 2501) Slade House, Boundary Terraces, 1 Mariendahl Lane, Newlands
Lufthansa (☎ 415 3888, fax 415 3636) 9th floor, Picbel Arcade, 58 Strand St, City Bowl
Malaysia Airlines (☎ 419 8010, fax 419 7017) 8th floor, Safmarine House, 22 Riebeeck St
SAA (☎ 936 1111, fax 936 2308) Cape Town international airport
Singapore Airlines (☎ 674 0601, fax 674 0710) 3rd floor, Sanclaire, 21 Dreyer St, Claremont
Swissair (☎ 434 8101, fax 934 8106) Cape Town international airport
Virgin Atlantic (☎ 683 2221, fax 683 3359) Claremont

Bus

The three major bus lines all operate out of Cape Town. Their booking offices and main arrival and departure points are at the Meriman Square end of Cape Town train station (City Bowl), and their details are as follows:

Greyhound (☎ 418 4310) Open 7am to 7pm daily.
Intercape Mainliner (☎ 386 4400) Open 6am to 8pm daily.
Translux (☎ 449 3333) Open 7am to 7pm daily. Phone bookings are taken 8am to 5pm Monday to Friday and 8am to noon Saturday.

These days there's little to choose between their prices but check with each before making a booking since the comapnies' services and routes are similar. For more information on bus routes and fares, and on the Baz Bus, see the Getting Around chapter.

Train

All trains leave from the main Cape Tow train station. It can take a long time to ge to the front of the queue at the **booking office** (☎ 449 3871; open 7.30am-3.55pm Mon-Fri, 7.30am-10.30am Sat).

There's a left-luggage facility next t Platform 24 but it closes at 2pm after th last arrival from Jo'burg.

For detailed information about trai routes and fares to/from Jo'burg, see th Getting Around chapter.

Minibus Taxi

Long-distance minibus taxis cover most c the country with an informal network c routes. Used predominantly by blacks an some adventurous whites, mainly foreig backpackers keen to meet locals, they're cheap (although not quite as cheap as the once were) and generally efficient way c getting around. The driving can occasional be hair-raising but it is mostly OK, esp cially compared with that of similar tran port in other African countries. As th minibus taxis' clientele is largely blac they'll often travel via townships and wi usually depart very early in the morning c in the early evening to cater to the needs c commuting workers and shoppers.

In Cape Town, most minibus taxis sta picking up passengers in distant township especially Langa and Nyanga, and perha make a trip into the main train station if the need more people, so your choices can I limited. The townships are not great plac to be wandering around in the early hours the morning carrying a pack, so *do not* into them without good local knowledge; it preferable to go with a reliable local guid

Langa is currently relatively safe (hov ever, these things can change) and lon distance taxis leave from the Langa shoppi centre early in the morning. A local-ar minibus taxi from the main train station Langa costs about R3. A taxi to Jo'burg cos about R240 (compared with R370 on Inte cape) and departs at around 7am. The trip long, uncomfortable and potentially dange ous because of driver fatigue. Between a fe people, hiring a car would be cheaper.

Car & Motorcycle

Major international companies such as **Avis** (☎ 0800 021111, 123 Strand St, City Bowl) and **Budget** (☎ 0800 016622, 120 Strand St, City Bowl) are represented.

The larger local companies, such as **Imperial** (☎ 0800 131000, Cnr Loop & Strand Sts, City Bowl) and **Tempest** (☎ 0800 031666, Cnr Buitengracht & Wale Sts, City Bowl), offer service comparable to the major companies at slightly lower rates.

Smaller, cheaper companies come and go. You'll find plenty of brochures for them at Cape Town Tourism and all the hostels – the deals may look tempting (R99 a day is a typical one that is seldom, if ever, available) so read the small print, and see Car & Motorcycle in the Getting Around chapter for more information. If all you're looking for is a wreck in which to tootle around the city, contact Christine at **Milnerton Car Hire** (☎ 082-892 9959) and you might get a deal for around R75 a day.

Le Cap Motorcycle Hire (☎ 423 0823, www.lecapmotorcyclehire.co.za, 3 Carisbrook St; open 8.30am-5pm Mon-Fri, 9am-pm Sat) rents motorcycles (from R200 a day) and scooters (from R125 a day) and also runs longer tours.

Harley-Davidson Cape Town (☎ 424 990, e hdcape@mweb.co.za, 45 Buitengracht St; open 9am-5pm Mon-Sat) rents a Harley 1340cc Big Twins or an MG-B convertible sports car for R912 per 24 hours.

Hitching

Lonely Planet does not recommend hitching, which always involves a potentially serious risk. We include the following information for travellers who will hitch despite our warnings.

If you want to hitch long distances, either start in the city centre, or catch public transport to one of the outlying towns such as Paarl for Jo'burg, Somerset West for the Garden Route and Durban, and Malmsbury or Citrusdal for regions in the north. Do not hitch anywhere near the Cape Flats, where safety is a real issue.

In the city centre, make a sign and start on the foreshore near the entry to the Waterfront, where the N1 (to Jo'burg), the N7 (to Windhoek), and the N2 (to the Garden Route) all converge.

Hostel notice boards often have offers of lifts and share-rental arrangements.

GETTING AROUND
To/From the Airport

Several companies offer a shuttle service between the airport and the city and some hostels will pick you up for free if you have a booking. **Backpacker Bus** (☎ 082-809 9185, e bpackbus@mweb.co.za) picks up from hostels and hotels in the city and does airport transfers for R70 per person.

Nonshared taxis are expensive; expect to pay nearly R150.

Bus

Cape Town's Golden Arrow public bus network is reliable if run down. Most services stop running early in the evening. Buses are most useful for getting along the Atlantic coast from the city centre to Hout Bay (trains service the suburbs to the east of Table Mountain). When travelling short distances, people wait at the bus stop and take either a bus or a minibus taxi, whichever arrives first.

The main bus station, the Golden Acre terminal, is on Grand Parade. Here there's also a helpful **bus information kiosk** (☎ 0801-212111, 461 4365; open 8am-5.30pm Mon-Fri, 8am-1.30pm Sat).

Destinations and off-peak fares (applicable from 8am to 4pm) from the city include the Waterfront (R1.90), Sea Point and Kloof Nek (R2.30), Camps Bay (R2.80) and Hout Bay (R5.20). Peak fares are about 30% higher. If you're using a particular bus regularly, it's worth buying 'clipcards', which give you 10 trips at a discount price.

Train

Metro commuter trains are a handy way to get around, although services have been cut back and there are few (or no) trains after 6pm Monday to Friday and after noon on Saturday. The **Metro information office** (☎ 449 4045; open 6am-6pm Mon-Fri, 6.30am-5pm Sat & Sun) is in the main train station next to ticket offices 7 and 8.

Metro trains have 1st- and economy-class carriages only. The difference in price and comfort is negligible, although you'll most likely find the 1st-class compartments to be on the whole safer.

The most important line for visitors is the Simon's Town line, which runs through Observatory and then around the back of Table Mountain through upper-income white suburbs such as Rosebank, down to Muizenberg and along the False Bay coast. On some of these trains you'll find *Biggsy's*, a restaurant carriage and rolling wine bar. There's a small extra charge to use it.

Metro trains run some way out of Cape Town, to Strand on the eastern side of False Bay, and into the Winelands to Stellenbosch and Paarl. They are the cheapest and easiest means of transport to these areas, although they can be a bit rough (where possible, avoid travelling after dark and on weekends).

Some destinations and economy/1st-class fares include Observatory (R3.80/4.50), Muizenberg (R4.50/7.50), Paarl (R5.50/9.50) and Stellenbosch (R5.50/9.50).

The **Spier steam train** (☎ 419 5222) runs occasional trips to the Spier wine estate, Simon's Town and Darling.

Minibus Taxi

Minibus taxis cover most of the city with an informal network of routes and are a cheap way of getting around. Useful routes are from Adderley St (opposite the Golden Acre Centre) to Sea Point along Main Rd (R2.50) and up Long St to Kloof Nek (R2).

The main stop is on the upper deck of the main train station, accessible from a walkway in the Golden Acre Centre or from stairways on Strand St. It's well organised, and finding the right stop is easy. Anywhere else, you just hail minibus taxis from the side of the road. There's no way of telling which route a taxi will be taking except by asking the driver.

Taxi

As always, nonshared taxis are expensive (about R10 per kilometre) but worth con-

sidering late at night or if you are in a group. There is a taxi stop at the Adderley St end of the Grand Parade in the city, or call **Marine Taxi** (☎ 434 0434) or **Unicab Taxis** (☎ 44 4402). There are often taxis outside the Cape Sun Hotel on Strand St and at Waterfront. For a cheaper alternative, take a Rikki.

Rikki

Rikkis (☎ 423 4888, *in Simon's Town* ☎ 78 2136; *operating 7am-7pm Mon-Fri, 7am-2pm Sat*) are tiny open vans providing Asian-style transport in the City Bowl and nearby areas for low prices. They can be hailed on the street or booked, and travel as far afield as Camps Bay and Observatory. A single-person trip from the main train station to Tamboerskloof costs R10; to Camps Bay is about R20. A Rikki from the City Bowl to Kirstenbosch Botanical Gardens costs R5 for the first four people and R10 for each extra person. Rikkis also operates out of Simon's Town.

Although cheap and fun, Rikkis may not be the quickest way to get around, as there is usually a certain amount of meandering as other passengers are dropped off, and they can be notoriously slow to turn up to a booking.

Bicycle & Scooter

The Cape Peninsula is a great place to explore by bicycle but there are hills, and distances can be deceptively large – it's nearly 70km from the centre to Cape Point. Unfortunately you aren't supposed to take bicycles on suburban trains.

For bicycle hire close to the City Bowl contact **Downhill Adventures** (☎ 422 038, **W** *www.downhilladventures.co.za, Orange St, Gardens*).

Le Africa Express (☎ 439 0901, *16A Main Rd, Three Anchor Bay*) has scooter hire from R150 per day, bike hire for R50.

Le Cap Motor Cycle Hire (see Car & Motorcycle earlier) hires scooters cheaply. they've none in, try **African Buzz** (☎ 4. 0052, *202 Long St, City Bowl*), which charges R160 per day.

CAPE TOWN ARCHITECTURE

From the venerable 17th-century Castle of Good Hope to the late-20th-century redevelopment of the Victoria & Alfred Waterfront, Cape Town's wealth of interesting architecture is one of its most attractive features. Although the city has been extensively developed, much that would have been destroyed elsewhere has been preserved, and a walking tour of Cape Town's City Bowl is a great way to get a feel for the different periods of history through which the city has developed.

Dutch Colonial Architecture

Built between 1666 and 1679, the **Castle of Good Hope** is frequently cited as South Africa's oldest surviving colonial structure. This pentagonal fort has been changed over the centuries. The entrance used to be on what is now Strand St, facing directly onto the sea, which once lapped at the walls (land reclamation has since pushed the water a good kilometre away).

Jan van Riebeeck's vegetable garden, forerunner of the **Company's Gardens**, actually predates the castle by 14 years. The first incarnation of the **Slave Lodge** at the gardens' northern end was built in 1660 as a single-storey building to house up to 500 wretched souls. This building would be substantially changed under later British administrations.

Out at Muizenberg on False Bay is the thatched and white-washed **Posthuys** cottage, which dates from 1673. The building's rustic style is still echoed along the Western Cape coast, particularly in fishing villages such as Arniston and Paternoster (see the Western Cape chapter).

Similarly, the more ornate style of Cape Dutch architecture started in Cape Town and spread out around the colony. Governor Simon van Der Stel built his quintessential manor house, **Groot Constantia**, in 1692, thus establishing the prototype for other glorious estates to follow in the Winelands further inland. **Vergelegen** (1699), near Somerset West, **Boschendal** (1685), between Franschhoek and Stellenbosch, and a whole road of reconstructed beauties in Tulbagh are all worth seeing. (For details, see the Western Cape chapter and the special section 'Cape Wineries'.)

In the city centre, the best place to get an idea of what Cape Town looked like during the 18th century is to take a stroll through the Bo-Kaap. Blot out the more modern pastel paint jobs and you'll notice flat roofs instead of gables and a lack of shutters on the outside of the windows: These features are the result of building regulations instituted by the Dutch East India Company (Vereenigde Oostindische Compagnie; VOC) in the wake of fires that swept the city.

On Strand St, the fancy facade of the late-18th-century **Koopmans de Wet House** is attributed to Louis Thibault, who, as the VOC's lieutenant of engineers, was responsible for the design of most of Cape Town's public buildings in this period. Thibault also had a hand in the handsome **Rust-en-Vreugd** (1778), famous for its delicately carved

set: The Old Town Hall in Cape Town, built in 1905, is a mix of Italian Renaissance and British colonial architecture. (Photo by Richard l'Anson)

177

rococo fanlight above the main door and its double balconies and portico.

Bordering the Company's Gardens is the lovely **Tuynhuis** (1700), where you can see the VOC monogram on the building's pediment. Now the official residence of the republic's president (thus off limits to visitors), the building was altered during the British administration of the 19th century.

British Colonial Architecture

British governor Lord Charles Somerset made the biggest impact on the architectural look of Cape Town during his 1814–26 tenure. (It was Somerset who ordered the restyling of the Tuynhuis to bring it into line with Regency tastes for verandas and front gardens.)

Built around 1840, the two-storey brick **Bertram House** at the top of Government Ave is an example of late Georgian style.

As the British Empire reached its zenith in the late 19th century, Cape Town boomed and a whole slew of monumental buildings were erected. Walk down Adderley St and through the Company's Gardens and you'll pass the **Standard Bank** (1880) with its soaring columns, pediment and dome, the small Byzantine-influenced **Old Synagogue** dating from 1862 (the neighbouring and much more baroque Great Synagogue with its twin towers dates from 1905) and the **Houses of Parliament** (1884), outside which stands a marble statue (1890) of Queen Victoria herself.

Long St is where you can see Victorian Cape Town at its most appealing, with the wrought-iron balconies and varying facades of shops and buildings such as the Long St Baths, while in the salubrious suburbs of Tamboerskloof and Orangezicht on the slopes of Table Mountain many mansions of that era still survive.

Left: Parliament
(Photo by
Simon Richmond)

Cecil John Rhodes, prime minister of the Cape from 1890 to 1896, commissioned a young English architect, Herbert Baker, to build his home, **Groote Schuur** (1898), in Rondebosch, thus kicking off the style known as Cape Dutch Revival. Baker also designed **Rust-en-Vrede** (1902), Rhodes' thatched cottage by the sea in Muizenberg, just in time for the mining magnate to die in it. (For more information on the architect, see the boxed text 'Sir Herbert Baker' in the Gauteng chapter.)

As the Victorian era came to a close, Cape Town's grandest public building, the **Old Town Hall** (1905), rose on the southern side of Grand Parade; it was from the balcony here that Nelson Mandela made has first public address as a free man in 1990.

Twentieth-Century Architecture

Edwardian Cape Town is best represented by the **Centre for the Book**, which opened in 1913 as the headquarters of the now defunct University of Good Hope. More recently it has become an annexe of the National Library, and gained some notoriety as the venue for the inquiry into cricket match-fixing in 2000.

Fine examples of Art-Deco architecture can be seen around **Greenmarket Square** (Shell House, now the Holiday Inn, dates from 1929) and along St George's Mall. Opposite the main post office, on Darling St, is the handsome **Mutual Building** (1940), the continent's first skyscraper, decorated with friezes and frescoes, all with South African themes.

There was little architectural development in Cape Town during the apartheid era. Examples of rationalist architecture include Artscape (the Nico performing arts centre) and the adjoining Civic Centre on the foreshore, which display the obsession with concrete that was typical of international modernism (we would call it concrete brutalism at its worst).

Right: Greenmarket square and surrounding city architecture. When the country's economy boomed in the 1960s, many different styles of architecture appeared across Cape Town's skyline. (Photo by Richard I'Anson)

The less said about the total lack of planning or official architectural concern for the townships probably the better, although it is worth mentioning the tremendous ingenuity and resilience that residents showed in creating livable homes from scrap. A visit to the townships today reveals colourfully painted shacks and murals, homes and churches made from shipping crates, and more recent imaginative structures such as the **Guga S'Thebe arts and cultural centre** in Langa.

For the vast majority of visitors, though, contemporary Capetonian architecture is summed up in the redevelopment of the **V&A Waterfront**. Say what you like about this (and many people do), in comparison with the florid bombast of the more recent Grand West Casino and the gargantuan Canal Walk shopping mall in the northern suburb of Milnerton, the V&A Waterfront increasingly looks a model of restraint and thoughtful integration of the old and the new.

Cape Dutch Style

Drive around South Africa for just a short time and you'll realise how pervasive the Cape Dutch style of architecture is. The style began to emerge in the late 17th century. Thanks to Britain's wars with France, the British turned to the Cape for wine, so the burghers prospered and, during the 18th and 19th centuries, were able to build many of the impressive estates that can be seen today. The building materials were brick and plenty of plaster and wood (often teak), and reeds were used to thatch the roof.

The main features of a Cape Dutch manor are the *stoep* (a raised platform, the equivalent of a veranda) with seats at each end, the large central hall running the length of the house, and the main rooms symmetrically arranged on either side of the hall. Above the front entrance is the gable, the most obvious feature, and there are usually less elaborate gables at each end. The house is covered by a steep, thatched roof and is invariably painted white.

The front gable, which extends up above the roof line and almost always contains a dormer window, shows the influence of 18th-century Dutch styles. The large ground-floor windows have solid shutters. The graceful plaster scrolls of the gable are sometimes reflected in the curved moulding above the front door (above which is a fanlight, sometimes with elaborate woodwork). Sometimes the doorway shows neoclassical features such as Doric pilasters or a simple pediment.

Inside, the rooms are large and simply decorated. The main hall is often divided by a louvred wooden screen, which is thought to have derived from similar screens the Dutch would have seen in the East Indies. Above the ceilings many houses had a *brandsolder*, a layer of clay or brick to protect the house if the thatching caught fire. The roof space was used for storage, if at all.

For more information there are several books available, the most useful of which is Phillida Brooke Simons' *Cape Dutch Houses & Other Old Favourites*.

City Bowl Walking Tour

The following walk around the City Bowl could take the best part of a day, depending on the stops you make, although it is only about 6km long. For information on the many museums and galleries you will pass, see Museums & Galleries in the Cape Town & the Peninsula chapter.

Start

Castle of Good Hope ●

The **Castle of Good Hope** is an appropriate place to start. Immediately to the west is Grand Parade, the former military parade and public execution ground, which is now home to a lively market every Wednesday and Saturday. Jan van Riebeeck's original mud-walled fort was here too, and you can see its position outlined in red at the Plein St end of the Parade.

Old Town Hall ●

The impressive **Old Town Hall** on the southern side of the parade has been superseded by the hideous Civic Centre towards the foreshore.

District Six Museum ●

Walk up Buitenkant St towards the **District Six Museum**, turn right onto Albertus St and right again at Corporation St to reach Mostert St and its continuation Spin St. Here, on the traffic island beside pretty Church Square, look down to see the circular plaque marking the tree from where slaves were once sold.

Groote Kerk ●

In front of you is the **Groote Kerk** *(entry free; open 10am-2pm daily)*, the mother church for the Dutch Reformed Church (Nederduitse Gereformeerde Kerk, or NG Kerk). The first church on the site was built in 1704; only parts of this remain, most of the current building dating from 1841. A number of early notables have tombs inside and the mammoth organ and ornate Burmese teak pulpit are well worth seeing.

Slave Lodge ●

Adjacent to the Groote Kerk is the **Slave Lodge**, which was once a brothel and now houses the Cultural History Museum. Opposite at the end of Wale St is **St George's Cathedral**, designed by Herbert Baker in 1897. This was Archbishop Desmond Tutu's cathedral (lunch-time concerts are held here from 1pm to 1.50pm).

t George's Cathedral ●

Turn right into the pedestrianised St George's St, then second left onto Longmarket St, and you'll emerge on cobbled **Greenmarket Square**, created as a farmers' market in the early 18th century. The **Old Town House** (1761) has a balcony overlooking the bustling square, now filled Monday to Saturday with a colourful crafts and souvenir market. Also note the fine Art-Deco architecture of the building opposite, on the Shortmarket St side of the square.

Greenmarket Square ●

Old Town House ●

At the Old Town House turn left onto Burg St and then right into Church St, which is lined with good art and antique shops. The pedestrian section has a flea market specialising in antiques and bric-a-brac. At the junction with Long St turn right, and pause at the **South African Missionary Meeting House Museum** (☎ 423 6755, 40 Long St; admission free; open 9am-4pm Mon-Fri), also known as the Sendinggestig Museum, built in 1802. Its interior is plain but quite handsome, the focus, as always, being the wooden pulpit.

South African Missionary Meeting House Museum

At the junction with Strand St turn right, to view **Koopmans de Wet House** (☎ 4245 2473, 35 Strand St; adult/child R5/2; open 9.30am-4.30pm Tues-Sat), a classic example of a Cape Dutch townhouse and

Koopmans de Wet House ●

furnished with 18th- and early-19th-century antiques. It's an atmospheric place with ancient vines growing in the courtyard and floorboards that squeak just as they probably did during the times of Marie Koopmans de Wet, the socialite owner after whom the house is named.

Head north-west along Strand St towards Buitengracht St, passing on the right-hand side the magnificent old **Lutheran Church** *(98 Strand St; admission free; open 10am-2pm Mon-Fri)*. Converted from a barn in 1780, it also has a striking pulpit, perhaps the best created by the master German sculptor Anton Anreith, whose work can also be seen in Groote Kerk and at Groot Constantia. The next-door parsonage Martin Melck Huis is now the **Gold of Africa Museum** *(☎ 423 7083, 96 Strand St; adult/child R5/2; open 9am-5pm Mon-Sat)*, a new museum.

● Lutheran Church

● Gold of Africa Museum

Turn left on Buitengracht St and walk to Van Riebeeck Square. On the Bree St side of this parking lot is **St Stephen's Church** (1799), originally the African Theatre and later a school for freed slaves before it became a church in 1839. Immediately behind you is **Heritage Square**, a beautiful collection of Cape Georgian and Victorian buildings saved from the wrecking ball in 1996 and since transformed into the city's trendiest enclave of restaurants, bars, shops and an excellent hotel (see Cape Heritage Hotel under Places to Stay – Top End in the Cape Town & the Peninsula chapter) as well as an operational blacksmith's.

● St Stephen's Church

● Heritage Square

Cross Buitengracht St and head uphill along Longmarket St to enter the heart of the preserved Cape Muslim Quarter, better known as the **Bo-Kaap**. The steep streets (some of which are still cobbled) are lined with 18th-century flat-roofed houses and with mosques. Residents of the area are still predominantly Muslim. The Bo-Kaap is well worth exploring in its own right (although take care to do it in daytime since the narrow deserted streets are not safe at night). Chiappini and Rose Sts contain the prettiest houses, many of which have been spruced up with pastel paint. (If you've got the legs for it, hike all the way up Longmarket St to witness the firing of the Noon Gun on Signal Hill.) There's the interesting **Bo-Kaap Museum** on Wale St and the **Auwal Mosque**, the oldest in Cape Town, on Dorp St. One of the best ways to see Bo-Kaap is on a guided tour (see Organised Tours in the Cape Town & the Peninsula chapter). Listen out while you're walking for the fish horn tooted by the mobile fishmonger doing the rounds.

● Bo-Kaap

● Auwal Mosque

From the Bo-Kaap Museum, head south-east down Wale St, cross Buitengracht St again and return to the upper end of Long St. Turn right and follow Long St until it joins with Orange St. The **Long St Baths** are on the corner. Turn left into Orange St, and left again into Grey's Pass, which takes you past the excellent **South African Museum**.

● Long St Baths

● South African Museum

From here, you enter the top end of the **Company's Gardens**. An exceedingly pleasant place to stroll or relax, the surviving six hectares of Van Riebeeck's original 18-hectare vegetable garden originally provided fresh produce for the VOC's ships. As sources of supply were diversified, the garden was gradually changed to a superb pleasure garden, with a fine collection of botanical species from South Africa and the rest of the world.

● Company's Gardens

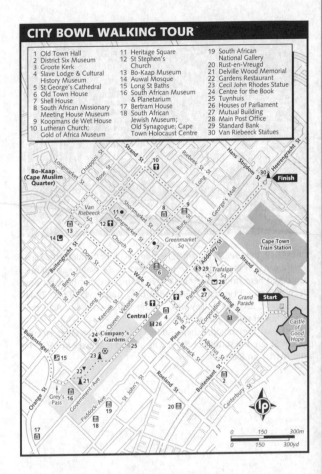

CITY BOWL WALKING TOUR

1 Old Town Hall
2 District Six Museum
3 Groote Kerk
4 Slave Lodge & Cultural History Museum
5 St George's Cathedral
6 Old Town House
7 Shell House
8 South African Missionary Meeting House Museum
9 Koopmans de Wet House
10 Lutheran Church; Gold of Africa Museum

11 Heritage Square
12 St Stephen's Church
13 Bo-Kaap Museum
14 Auwal Mosque
15 Long St Baths
16 South African Museum & Planetarium
17 Bertram House
18 South African Jewish Museum; Old Synagogue; Cape Town Holocaust Centre

19 South African National Gallery
20 Rust-en-Vreugd
21 Delville Wood Memorial
22 Gardens Restaurant
23 Cecil John Rhodes Statue
24 Centre for the Book
25 Tuynhuis
26 Houses of Parliament
27 Mutual Building
28 Main Post Office
29 Standard Bank
30 Van Riebeeck Statues

Among the museums and grand buildings that surround the gardens is **Bertram House** (☎ 424 9381, Cnr Orange St & Government Ave; adult/child R5/2; open 9.30am-4.30pm Tues-Sat). A couple of other things to keep an eye out for are statues designed by Herbert Baker, including the **Delville Wood Memorial** (honouring South African soldiers who fell during WWI), and the statue of **Cecil John Rhodes**, hand held high and pointing north in his vainglorious imperialist dream of an empire from the Cape to Cairo. There's also the Gardens Restaurant if you fancy a reviving cuppa or something more substantial.

Exit the gardens along Government Ave (where you're likely to spot scurrying squirrels) onto Adderley St, which was named after a British parliamentarian and historically regarded as Cape Town's main street.

- Bertram House
- Delville Wood Memorial
- Cecil John Rhodes

Until 1849, the street was named Heerengracht, or Gentlemen's Canal, after a canal of the same name in Amsterdam. (A waterway did once run down here from Government Ave to the sea, but it's long since been built over.) Heading towards the train station you'll pass Trafalgar Square, a covered alley next to the hideous Golden Acre mall, where flower sellers gather.

Just past the station, where Adderley St again becomes Heerengracht St, are the statues of those who started it all back in 1652, Jan and Maria van Riebeeck.

Finish

Above: City architecture of Cape Town and the statue of Batholomeu Dias, Portuguese explorer (Photo by Richard I'Anson)

Western Cape

Many of the attractions of Western Cape, covering the south-western corner of the country, are well known, such as Cape Town (covered in the Cape Town & the Peninsula chapter), the Winelands and the Garden Route. But there's much more on offer, in particular the great diversity of landscape from the rugged West Coast and inland Cederberg Wilderness Area (where you might find San rock art) to the wide-open spaces of the desert Karoo. You could easily spend a month touring the province and still find things to see and do.

Before the whites arrived the area was populated by Khoisan peoples; very few have survived, and their traditional cultures and languages have been almost completely lost. There are lots of 'coloured' people, though, with diverse origins; most lead Westernised lifestyles, are overwhelmingly Christian and speak Afrikaans. In the last couple of centuries, many blacks (in particular Xhosa people from Eastern Cape) have gravitated to this area in search of work. For more information on all these people, see the special section 'Peoples of the Region'.

Winelands

The Boland (meaning 'Upland'), as the wine-producing country around Stellenbosch is known, is the most beautiful of South Africa's several wine-producing areas. The vineyards form a patchwork in the fertile valleys. Dramatic ranges, including the Franschhoek, Wemmershoek and Slanghoek Mountains, shoot up to over 1500m. The Franschhoek and Bainskloof Passes that cross them are among the most spectacular in the country.

With its striking scenery and long history of white settlement, there's a distinctly European feel to the Boland. Stellenbosch is the area's most interesting and lively town, Franschhoek has the most spectacular location and best dining options and Paarl is a

Highlights

- Enjoy Franschhoek, a culinary highlight.
- Sample the wines at the lush green vineyards around Franschhoek, Paarl and Stellenbosch.
- Watch wildlife up close at Monkeyland.
- Hike the Boesmanskloof Trail from McGregor to Greyton.
- Take your chances shark-diving out of Gansbaai.
- Search for San rock art in the Cederberg area.
- Drive through the Swartberg Pass from Oudtshoorn to Prince Albert, best of all the remarkable 19th-century mountain passes.
- Bungee jump along the Garden Route, an adrenaline-junkie's dream destination.
- Enjoy scenery to soothe the soul along Western Cape's southern coast – a wonderful area to spot whales.

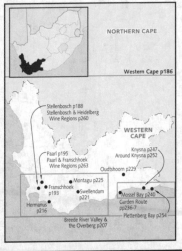

NORTHERN CAPE

Western Cape p186

Stellenbosch p188
Stellenbosch & Heidelberg
Wine Regions p260

WESTERN CAPE

Knysna p247
Around Knysna p252

Paarl p195
Paarl & Franschhoek
Wine Regions p263

Oudtshoorn p229

Montagu p225

Franschhoek
p193

Swellendam
p221

Mossel Bay p240

Garden Route
pp236-7

Hermanus
p216

Breede River Valley &
the Overberg p207

Plettenberg Bay p254

WESTERN CAPE

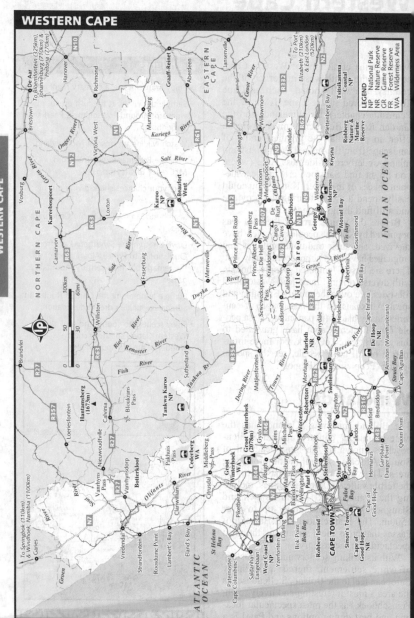

LEGEND
NP National Park
NR Nature Reserve
GR Game Reserve
FR Forest Reserve
WA Wilderness Area

busy commercial centre with plenty to see. All three towns are historically important and attractive, and promote routes around the surrounding wineries.

It is possible to see Stellenbosch and Paarl on day trips from Cape Town. Both are accessible by train, but Stellenbosch is the easiest to get around if you don't have a car. To do justice to the region and to visit the many wineries, you'll need wheels – bicycle wheels will do.

Many of the wineries also offer accommodation and dining, see the special section 'Cape Wineries' for more information.

STELLENBOSCH

☎ 021 • postcode 7600 • pop 184,000

Established on the banks of the Eerste River by Governor van der Stel in 1679, Stellenbosch is the second-oldest town (after Cape Town) in South Africa, and one of the best preserved. The town is full of architectural gems (Cape Dutch, Georgian and Victorian) and is shaded by enormous oak trees. There are several interesting museums, not least the Village Museum, spread across four buildings representing different periods in the town's history.

The Afrikaans-language University of Stellenbosch, established in 1918, continues to play an important role in Afrikaner politics and culture. There are over 17,000 students, which means that during term time, the town's nightlife can get wild – visit in February during the Venster Versiering festival and you'll see what we mean!

Orientation & Information

The train station is a short walk west of the centre. The train line effectively forms the western boundary of the town and the Eerste River the southern. Dorp St, which runs roughly parallel to the river, is the old town's main street and is lined with fine old buildings. The commercial centre lies between Dorp St and the university to the east of the Braak, the old town square.

The staff are extremely helpful at the **Stellenbosch Publicity Association** (☎ 883 3584, W www.istellenbosch.org.za, 36 Market St; open 8am-6pm Mon-Fri, 9am-5pm Sat,

9.30am-4.30pm Sun). Pick up the excellent free brochure *Discover Stellenbosch on Foot*, with a walking-tour map and information on many of the historic buildings (also available in French and German). Another excellent free brochure is *Stellenbosch and its Wine Route*, which gives information about opening times and tastings at many nearby wineries. You'll also find an Internet cafe here.

Guided walks leave from the publicity association at 10am and 3pm. They cost R30 per person (minimum three people).

There's a Rennies Travel/Thomas Cook foreign exchange office on Bird St, a block from Dorp St.

The Bookshop (☎ 886 9277) and **Ex Libris** (☎ 886 6871), both on Andringa St, are good bookshops.

Village Museum

The Village Museum (☎ 887 2902, 18 Ryneveld St; adult/child R10/5; open 9.30am-5pm Mon-Sat, 2pm-5pm Sun) is a group of carefully restored and period-furnished houses dating from 1709 to 1850. The main entrance, on Ryneveld St, leads into the oldest of the buildings, the Schreuderhuis. The whole block, bounded by Ryneveld, Plein, Drostdy and Kerk Sts, is occupied by the museum and includes most of the buildings and some charming gardens. **Grosvenor House** is on the other side of Drostdy St.

Toy & Miniature Museum

Behind the publicity association, in another historic building, is the Toy & Miniature Museum (☎ 887 2937, Cnr Market & Herte Sts; adult/child R5/1; open 9.30am-5pm Mon-Sat, 2pm-5pm Sun, closed Sun May-Aug). This museum is a delightful surprise. Many of the miniatures are amazingly detailed; the highlights are a model railway set and houses made entirely of icing sugar – get the guide to point out some of the best pieces.

The Braak

At the north end of the Braak (Town Square), an open stretch of grass, you'll find the neo-Gothic **St Mary's on the Braak Church**, completed in 1852. To the west is the **VOC**

STELLENBOSCH

PLACES TO STAY
8 Hillbillies Haven
29 Backpackers Inn
31 D'Ouwe Werf
37 Stellenbosch Hotel;
     Jan Cats Brasserie
39 De Oude Meul
40 De Goue Druif
41 Stumble Inn

PLACES TO EAT
2 Studentesentrum &
    Brollocks
3 The Workshop
4 Fusion Café

19 Decameron Italian
     Restaurant
27 Mugg & Bean
28 Wijnhuis
32 Spice Cafe
35 Java Cafe
36 De Soete Inval
38 Coastal Catch
44 The Blue Orange
48 De Oewer
49 De Volkskombuis

OTHER
1 Hospital
5 Bohemia

6 Minibus Taxis
7 Caltex Petrol Station
9 Simonsberg Cheese Factory
10 Bergkelder
11 Tollies; Fandangos
12 Club Btease Fever
13 Dros
14 The Terrace
15 Fick House (Burgerhuis)
16 St Mary's on the
     Braak Church
17 Shopping Mall
18 Botanical Gardens
20 Post Office
21 VOC Kruithuis

22 Van der Bijlhuis
23 Toy & Miniature Museum
24 Stellenbosch Publicity
     Association
25 Minibus Taxis
26 Rennies Travel/Thomas Cook
30 The Bookshop & Ex Libris
33 Village Museum
34 Grosvenor House
42 De Akker & The Hidden Cellar
43 Oom Samie se Winkel
45 BP Petrol Station
     & 24-Hour Shop
46 De Kelder
47 Rembrandt van Rijn Art Gallery

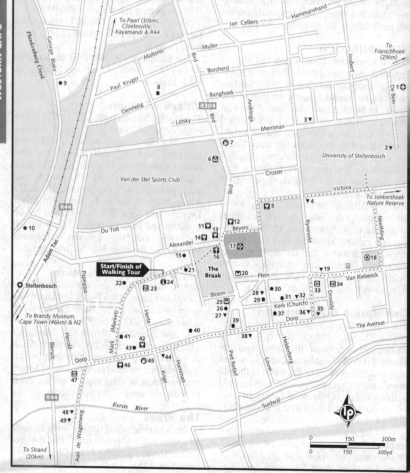

Stellenbosch Walking Tour

Start at the publicity association on Market St and head north-west to the **Braak**, the old town square, where you'll find several old buildings, including the **VOC Kruithuis**, an 18th-century powder magazine.

Cross the Braak and turn left (north) up Bird St, right onto Beyers St, left onto Andringa St and right onto Victoria St. Follow Victoria St and you'll come to the **University of Stellenbosch**. This pretty campus is crammed full of Cape Dutch–style buildings, not surprising for the country's (and thus the world's) leading Afrikaans university.

Find your way back to Victoria St and head west until you come to Neethling St. Turn right, walk past the **Botanical Gardens** to the junction with Van Riebeeck St and turn right again (some of the fine old homes around here offer accommodation) to Ryneveld St, on the edge of the town centre. Turn left down Ryneveld St to visit the **Village Museum**.

Follow Ryneveld St south to Dorp St, one of Stellenbosch's oldest and most impressive streets, where you'll turn right. Continue down Dorp to the **Rembrandt van Rijn Art Gallery** (outside of which you'll see a giant wine press) and turn left to cross the Eerste River; the willow tree–shaded De Oewer (see Places to Eat) is a good spot to revive.

Retrace your steps across the bridge back to Dorp St and follow it back to Market St to return to where you started. On the way you'll pass the elegant 18th-century **Van der Bijlhuis**, now occupied by an architect's office.

Kruithuis *(Powder House; admission free; open 9.30am-1pm Mon-Fri)*, which was built in 1777 to store the town's weapons and gunpowder and now housing a small military museum. On the north-western corner is **Fick House**, also known as the Burgerhuis, a fine example of Cape Dutch–style from the late 18th century. Most of this building is now occupied by Historical Homes of South Africa, established to preserve important architecture.

Rembrandt van Rijn Art Gallery
This small gallery *(☎ 886 4340, Dorp St; admission free; open 9am-12.45pm & 2pm-5pm Mon-Fri, 10am-1pm & 2pm-5pm Sat)* has some fine examples of 20th-century South African art, including paintings by Irma Stern and the incredibly lifelike sculptures of Anton van Wouw; even if the art doesn't interest you, it's worth visiting to see the house, which was built in 1783.

Activities
There are lots of **walks** in the Stellenbosch area – ask the publicity association about permits and maps of the Vineyard Hiking Trails.

Jonkershoek *(☎ 889 1568; admission R10 per car, R5 for walkers & cyclists)* is a small nature reserve within a timber plantation that offers walking and biking trails.

Organised Tours
Easy Rider Wine Tours (☎ 886 4651) is a long-established company offering good value (R180 including lunch) for a full day covering five wineries: Eikendal, Boschendal, Franschhoek Vineyards, Fairview and Ruitersvlei (the last two on the Paarl wine route).

Bergkelder (☎ 809 8492, George Blake St) Open 8am-5pm Mon-Fri, 9am-1pm Sat. If you don't have time to shuttle around Stellenbosch's many wineries, or want an introduction to what's on offer, drop by here. A slide show, cellar tour and tastings of up to 12 wines costs R10. You pour your own tastings, so take it easy or it might be your last stop for the day! The Bergkelder is a short walk from the train station; tours are at 10am, 10.30am (in German) and 3pm.

Special Events
The **Oude Libertas Amphitheatre** *(☎ 918 8950, [W] www.oudelibertas.co.za)* and the

Spier wine estate both hold performing arts festivals between January and March.

The **Van der Stel Festival** at the end of September and early October combines with the festivals of music and arts and the festival of food and wine.

Places to Stay

Hostels *Stumble Inn* (☎/fax 887 4049, **W** *www.jump.to/stumble, 12 Market St*) Camping R30 per person, dorm beds R50, doubles R150. In two old houses, one with a small pool, the other with a pleasant garden, this place has a lively atmosphere. The owners are travellers themselves and are a good source of information. They also run the Easy Rider Wine Tours (see Organised Tours earlier) and rent bicycles for R50 per day.

Hillbillies Haven (☎/fax 887 9905, 24 Dennesig St) Dorm beds R55, singles/doubles R75/R90. There is less of a backpacker scene here; it's more a family home in a quiet area, within easy walking distance of the town centre. The rooms are clean and reasonably spacious.

Backpackers Inn (☎ 887 2020, fax 887 2010, **e** bacpac1@global.co.za, 1st floor De Wett Centre, Entrance just off Church St) Dorm beds R50, singles/doubles R120/160. This rather plain hostel is in a central location. It's been taken over by the folks from Stumble Inn, so expect some upgrading.

B&Bs, Guesthouses & Hotels The publicity association produces a booklet listing the many B&Bs. Prices start at around R90 per person near the town centre, R70 in suburban areas and R110 on nearby farms (less for self-catering cottages). You might have to press them to tell you about the very cheapest places.

Also see the special section 'Cape Wineries' for details of the luxurious *Lanzerac* hotel and *Spier* wine estate.

Wilfra Court (☎/fax 889 6091, 16 Hine St, Cloetsville) Singles/doubles B&B R110/ 220. Readers have recommended this place, which is a fair way from the town centre, but friendly. Interestingly, it's run by the local mayor and his wife, who are a coloured couple. They only have two rooms,

so book ahead and get them to give you directions.

De Oude Meul (☎ 887 7085, fax 883 9549, **W** www.deoudemeul.snowball.co.za, 10a Mill St) Singles/doubles B&B R175/ 225. Above an antiques shop in the centre of town, the accommodation here is very reasonable for the price (which is lower in winter). Some rooms have balconies.

De Goue Druif (☎ 883 3555, 110 Dorp St) Singles/doubles B&B from R200/360. The rooms in this rambling old Cape Dutch home are comfortable and individually decorated.

Stellenbosch Hotel (☎ 887 3644, fax 887 3673, **W** www.stellenbosch.co.za/hotel, Cnr Dorp & Andringa Sts) Singles/doubles R340/490. This is a rather idiosyncratic but comfortable country hotel. Some rooms have four-poster beds. A section dating from 1743 houses the *Jan Cats Brasserie*, which is an OK place to drink but not to eat.

D'Ouwe Werf (☎ 887 4608, fax 887 4646, **W** www.ouwewerf.com, 30 Church St) Singles/ doubles B&B from R570/840. This is an appealing, old-style hotel (dating back to 1802), with a pool and a good restaurant. It's worth dropping by their shady courtyard for lunch. The more expensive luxury rooms are furnished with antiques.

Places to Eat

There's no shortage of places to eat and drink, and several of the nearby vineyards have restaurants as well (see the special section 'Cape Wineries').

Cafes & Snack Bars For a range of reasonably cheap snacks and meals check out the *Studentesentrum* (student centre) at the university (see the boxed text 'Stellenbosch Walking Tour' for directions).

Coastal Catch (☎ 887 9550, 137 Dorp St) Mains R20-25. Open 11am-9pm daily. Come here for high-quality fish and chips. It's mainly takeaway, but there are a few tables if you want to eat here.

Mugg & Bean (☎ 883 2972, Muel St) Open 7am-11pm daily. This reputable chain cafe is a good choice for breakfast with bagels, huge muffins, and self-service bottomless cups of coffee for R5.50.

The Blue Orange (☎ 887 2052, 77-9 Dorp St) Open 8am-5pm Mon-Sat, 9am-5pm Sun. This is a pleasant cafe with attached farm shop, which serves hearty breakfasts. Its shaded stoop is a good spot to relax.

Java Cafe (☎ 887 6261, 2C Ryneveld St) Open 8.30am-11pm daily. Surprisingly high-quality food is available at this simple Internet cafe, which charges R10 per half-hour. It has a quiet courtyard, too.

Spice Cafe (☎ 883 8480, 34 Church St) Mains around R22. Open 9am-5pm Mon-Fri, 9am-2pm Sat, 10pm-2am Sun. They do a self-serve buffet for R35 and gourmet sandwiches at this brightly painted house with a courtyard shaded by a peppercorn tree.

Restaurants *The Workshop* (☎ 887 9985, 34 Merriman St) Mains R40. Open 10.30am-1.30am Mon-Sat. The roomy bistro/restaurant serving good-value fusion-cuisine dishes is upstairs; there is a buzzy bar downstairs. This place is popular with students from the nearby university.

De Soete Inval (☎ 886 4842, 5 Ryneveld St) Mains R30-40. Open 9am-10pm daily. Known primarily for its choice of 30 different pancakes, this cheerful place also does a fine Indonesian *rystafel* (rice with many dishes) with six dishes for R50 or a half portion for R35.

Wijnhuis (☎ 887 7196, Andringa St) Mains R40-50. Open 10am-late daily. This is a stylish option, with indoor and outdoor dining areas, an extensive menu and an even longer wine list. Few wines are by the glass, but they do tastings of six wines for R15.

De Volkskombuis (☎ 887 2121, Aan de Wagenweg) Mains R50. Open noon-2.30pm daily, 7pm-9pm Mon-Sat. This place specialises in traditional Cape Malay cuisine and is favoured by locals, not just tourists. The building was designed by Sir Herbert Baker (see the boxed text 'Sir Herbert Baker' in the Gauteng chapter) and the terrace looks across fields to Stellenbosch Mountain. The Cape country sampler (four traditional specialities) costs R45. Booking is advisable.

De Oewer (☎ 886 5431, Aan de Wagenweg) Mains R30. Open noon-3pm daily, 7pm-10pm Mon-Sat. Next to De Volkskom-buis, this restaurant has an open-air section shaded by willow trees beside the river. Their light-meal menu is typified by dishes like haloumi cheese salad with figs (R18).

Decameron Italian Restaurant (☎ 883 3331, 50 Plein St) Mains R40-50. Open 10am-midnight daily. This is considered the town's best Italian restaurant. It's good for a quick pizza (from R30) or a full meal, and has outdoor seating for those balmy evenings.

Fusion Café (☎ 883 8593, 3 Victoria Rd) Mains R25-60. Open 9am-3.30pm & 6pm-late Mon-Sat. This funky joint with a cooler-than-thou vibe serves everything from a full breakfast (R27) to duck breast with gooseberry chutney or springbok done Thai style.

Entertainment

Stellenbosch has a lively nightlife, geared towards the interests of the university students. It's generally safe to walk around the centre at night, so a pub crawl could certainly be on the cards (if you're staying at the Stumble Inn one will probably be organised for you). All the places listed are open daily until very late.

Dros, *The Terrace* and *Tollies*, clustered together in the complex just off Bird St and north of the Braak, are among the liveliest bars; you can eat at them all, but that's not what most patrons have in mind. If you're looking for a slightly more sophisticated option try *Fandangos*, which is a cocktail bar and Internet cafe in the same complex.

Bohemia (☎ 882 8375, Cnr Andringa & Victoria Sts) This place has live music and the novelty of hubble bubble pipes with a range of different tobaccos to choose from.

De Kelder (☎ 883 3797, 63 Dorp St) This reasonably pleasant restaurant, bar and beer garden is popular with German backpackers.

De Akker (☎ 883 3512, 90 Dorp St) This is a classic student drinking hole, with pub meals from under R20. Upstairs is *The Hidden Cellar*, where bands occasionally play.

At the time of research, *Club 8tease Fever* (Bird St), which is upstairs in the shopping centre opposite Dros, was the dance club of choice. *Brollocks* in the Studentesentrum is notorious for its wet T-shirt antics.

WESTERN CAPE

Shopping

Simonsberg cheese factory (☎ 809 1017, 9 Stoffel Smit St) Open 9am-5pm Mon-Fri, 9am-12.30pm Fri. The free tastings here are very popular with hungry backpackers and it sells inexpensive cheese.

Oom Samie se Winkel (Uncle Sammy's Shop; ☎ 887 0797, 84 Dorp St) Open 9am-5pm daily. This is a tourist trap but it's still worth visiting for the amazing range of goods – from high kitsch to genuine antiques and everything else in between.

Getting There & Away

Bus The only buses running to Cape Town are the long-distance services, which charge high prices for this short sector and do not take bookings.

Train Metro trains run the 46km between Cape Town and Stellenbosch (R9.50/5.50 1st class/economy, about one hour). Note there are no 2nd-class tickets. For inquiries, call **Stellenbosch station** (☎ 808 1111). To be safe, travel in the middle of the day and not at weekends.

Minibus Taxi A minibus taxi to Paarl is about R10 but you'll probably have to change taxis en route.

Getting Around

With largely flat countryside (unless you try to cross Franschhoek Pass), this is good cycling territory. Bicycles can be hired from the Stumble Inn and Hillbillies Haven. Mopeds are available from **Moto** (☎ 887 9965, 42 Ryneveld St) for R170 a day.

Tazzi's (☎ 887 2203) runs its tiny vans here, like Rikki's in Cape Town, and R5 (sharing) will get you just about anywhere in town.

FRANSCHHOEK
☎ 021 • postcode 7690

The toughest decision you'll face in Franschhoek is where to eat. This booming village, nestling in one of the loveliest settings in the Cape, has so many fine restaurants and wineries that you could find yourself lingering here longer than expected – not a bad thing, since Franschhoek is a good base from which to visit both Stellenbosch and Paarl as long as you have transport.

Wining and dining aside, there's an interesting museum commemorating the two hundred French Huguenots who settled in the region in the 17th century, some decent walks in the surrounding mountains and plenty of galleries and designer shops to mop up any spare cash.

Orientation & Information

The town is clustered around Huguenot St. At the southern end it reaches a T-junction at Huguenot Memorial Park. Continue east for the spectacular Franschhoek Pass.

Franschhoek Vallée Tourisme (☎ 876 3603, W www.franschhoek.org.za; open 8.30am-6pm Mon-Fri, 9am-5pm Sat, 10am-5pm Sun Sept-Mar) is in a small building on the main street. The staff can provide a map of the area's scenic walks and issues permits (R10) for walks in nearby forestry areas as well as book accommodation. Call ahead for opening hours in other months.

Internet access is available at the **Stationery Shop** (Bordeaux St; R10 per half-hour; open 9am-5pm daily).

Huguenot Memorial Museum

This engrossing museum (☎ 876 2532, Malherbe St; adult/child R4/1; open 9am-5pm Mon-Sat, 2pm-5pm Sun) celebrates South Africa's Huguenots (see Europeans at the Cape under History in the Facts about South Africa chapter) and houses the genealogical records of their descendants, as well as some hefty Cape Dutch furniture. Some of the names of the original settlers, such as Malan, de Villiers, Malherbe and Roux, are among the most famous Afrikaner dynasties in the country. Behind the main complex is a pleasant cafe, in front is the **Huguenot Monument** (adult/child R3/1; open 9am-5pm daily) and across the road is the annexe, with displays on the Anglo-Boer War and natural history, plus a souvenir shop.

Places to Stay

The cheapest B&Bs cost around R150 for a double, but prices drop if you stay out of

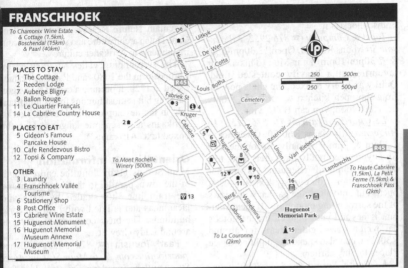

FRANSCHHOEK

To Chamonix Wine Estate
& Cottage (1.5km),
Boschendal (15km)
& Paarl (40km)

0   250   500m
0   250   500yd

PLACES TO STAY
1 The Cottage
2 Reeden Lodge
7 Auberge Bligny
9 Ballon Rouge
11 Le Quartier Français
14 La Cabrière Country House

PLACES TO EAT
5 Gideon's Famous
   Pancake House
10 Cafe Rendezvous Bistro
12 Topsi & Company

OTHER
3 Laundry
4 Franschhoek Vallée
   Tourisme
6 Stationery Shop
8 Post Office
13 Cabrière Wine Estate
15 Huguenot Monument
16 Huguenot Memorial
   Museum Annexe
17 Huguenot Memorial
   Museum

To Mont Rochelle
Winery (500m)

To Haute Cabrière
(1.5km), La Petit
Ferme (1.5km) &
Franschhoek Pass
(2km)

Huguenot
Memorial Park

To La Couronne
(2km)

WESTERN CAPE

town. Also see the special section 'Cape
Wineries' for more details of wineries with
accommodation.

The Cottage (☎ *876 2392,* **e** *thecottage@
sholtz.wcape.school.za, 55 Huguenot St*)
Singles/doubles B&B R150/260. This is
just one cottage sleeping two, or four at a
pinch, but it's a beauty. It's private, quiet,
and is a few minutes' walk from the village
centre – very good value.

Ballon Rouge (☎ *876 2651, fax 876
3743,* **e** *info@ballon-rouge.co.za, 7 Reservoir St East*) Singles/doubles B&B R230/
360. All the quality rooms at this small hotel
open on to the stoop and there's a restaurant
and pool.

Auberge Bligny (☎ *876 3767, 28 Van
Wyk St*) Singles/doubles B&B R290/390.
Once a Victorian homestead, this centrally
located guesthouse has seven pleasant,
comfortable rooms and a small pool.

Reeden Lodge (☎/*fax 876 3174,* **e** *ree
den@telekomsa.net, end of Fabriek St*) Self-
catering cottages from R125 per person. This
farm, about 10 minutes' walk from town,
sleeps from two to six people in well-equipped
cottages. It's good if you've got kids – there
are sheep, a tree house and lots of space.

La Cabrière Country House (☎ *876
4780, fax 876 3852,* **w** *www.lacabriere
.co.za, Middagkrans Rd*) Doubles B&B
R750. La Cabrière is a refreshing break
from all that Cape Dutch architecture. This
is modern boutique guesthouse that has
only four sumptuously decorated rooms and
very personal service.

Le Quartier Français (☎ *876 2151, fax
876 3105, 16 Huguenot Rd*) Doubles from
R1210, DB&B R1800. This is one of the
best places to stay in the Winelands. Set
around a leafy courtyard and pool, guest
rooms are very large with fireplaces, huge
beds and stylish decor. There is also a good
restaurant here (see Places to Eat following).

Places to Eat
Franschhoek is so small that it's easy to
stroll around and see what appeals. Some of
the wineries have cafes, restaurants or offer
picnic baskets; Cabrière Estate's *Haute
Cabrière* cellar restaurant is recommended
(see the special section 'Cape Wineries').

Good cheaper places along Huguenot St
include ***Gideon's Famous Pancake House***
at No 50 and ***Cafe Rendezvous Bistro*** in the
Oude Stallen Centre at No 19, but if ever

there was a place to splash out on a meal, Franschhoek is it.

Topsi & Company (☎ *876 2952, 7 Reservoir St*) Mains R50-60. Open 12.30pm-3pm & 7.30pm-10pm Thur-Mon. This is our favourite, in a heavily contested field. Quirky and very relaxed, the chefs pop out from the open kitchen to serve the totally delicious food; you can BYO wine.

Le Quartier Français (☎ *876 2151, 16 Huguenot Rd*) Mains R60-70. Open noon-2.30pm & 7pm-9pm daily. Recommended for anyone who really likes their food, this highly acclaimed restaurant is neither pompous nor ridiculously expensive. It opens out onto a cottage garden with views of the surrounding mountains. If the restaurant is beyond your budget, try the hotel's bar which does lighter meals for around R30. You can also spend the night here (see Places to Stay earlier).

La Petite Ferme (☎ *876 3016, Franschhoek Pass Rd*) Open noon-4pm daily. Come for the romantic views, the boutique wines and the smoked, de-boned salmon trout, the delicately flavoured signature dish. A shorter menu is available from 3pm to 4pm. If you feel like staying, there are also a few double suites for R750 with breakfast. Booking is absolutely essential.

Getting There & Away
The best way to reach Franschhoek is in your own vehicle. If taking a shared taxi from either Stellenbosch or Paarl, you'll have to change along the way – ask the driver when you get in.

PAARL
☎ 021 • postcode 7646 • pop 154,000

Less touristy and more spread out than Stellenbosch, Paarl is a large commercial centre, surrounded by mountains and vineyards, on the banks of the Berg River. There are vineyards and wineries within the sprawling town limits including the huge Kooperatieve Wijnbouwers Vereeniging, better known as the KWV (see the special section 'Cape Wineries').

Paarl is not really a town to tour on foot, but there is still quite a lot to see and do.

There are some great walks in the Paarl Mountain Nature Reserve, some excellent Cape Dutch architecture and some significant monuments to Afrikaner culture.

The surrounding valley was settled by Europeans in the 1680s and Paarl was established in 1720. It became a centre for wagon building but is most famous for its important role in the development and recognition of Afrikaans as a separate language (see the boxed text 'Afrikaans').

Orientation & Information
Main St runs 11km along the entire length of the town, parallel to the Berg River and the train line. It's shaded by oaks and jacarandas and is lined with many historic buildings. The busy commercial centre is around Lady Grey St.

Paarl Tourism (☎ *872 3829,* W *www .paarlonline.com, 216 Main St, Cnr Auret St; open 9am-5pm Mon-Fri, 9am-1pm Sat, 10am-1pm Sun*) has an excellent supply of information on the whole region. The staff are particularly helpful for arranging accommodation at the many guesthouses that have sprung up around Paarl.

Paarl Museum
Apart from the local wineries, the most interesting place to visit is the Paarl Museum (☎ *863 2537, 303 Main St; adult/child R5/free; open 10am-5pm Mon-Fri*). Housed in the Old Parsonage (Oude Pastorie) built in 1714, this collection of Cape Dutch antiques and relics of Huguenot and early Afrikaner culture is fascinating. There's a bookcase modelled on King Solomon's temple and display sections on the 'road to reconciliation' and the old mosques of the local Muslim community.

Paarl Mountain Nature Reserve
The three giant granite domes that dominate this popular reserve and loom over the town on its western side apparently glisten like pearls if they are caught by the sun after a fall of rain – hence 'Paarl'. The reserve has mountain *fynbos* (literally 'fine bush', primarily proteas, heaths and ericas) and a particularly large number of proteas. There's a

cultivated wildflower garden in the middle that's a nice spot for a picnic, and numerous walks with excellent views over the valley.

Access is from the 11km-long Jan Phillips Dr, which skirts the eastern edge of the reserve. The picnic ground is about 4km from Main St. A map showing walking trails is available from Paarl Tourism.

While up this way you could also visit the **Taal Monument** *(adult/child R5/2; open 9am-5pm daily)*. This is the giant needle-like edifice that commemorates the Afrikaans language. On a clear day there are stunning views from here as far as Cape Town.

Afrikaans Language Museum

This museum *(☎ 8721 3441, Pastorie Ave; adult/child R2/1; open 9am-1pm & 2pm-5pm Mon-Fri)* is of marginal interest. The birth of Afrikaans is chronicled in the former home of Gideon Malherbe, the meeting place for the Association of True Afrikaners and the birthplace of the first Afrikaans newspaper. The house has been painstakingly restored.

Places to Stay

See the special section 'Cape Wineries' for details of great-value accommodation at the *Laborie* winery.

Berg River Resort (☎ 863 1650, fax 863 2583, 5km from Paarl on the N45 towards Franschhoek) Camping for up to 6 from R60, double chalets from R200. Beside the Berg River, this attractive municipal camping ground has a swimming pool, canoes, trampolines and a cafe.

Amber Guest Farm (☎/fax 862 0982, e amberg@mweb.co.za, On R101 along Du Toits Kloof Pass) Dorm beds R45, singles/doubles B&B from R200/300, self-catering cottages from R240. These well-equipped cottages and farmhouse with a pool command a spectacular view. The amiable hosts also run the Swiss-style *Amber Country Kitchen*, serving Swiss specialities and with great views across the valley. They will plan a hiking trail around the farm and pick you up in town for a small fee.

The Manyano Centre (☎ 872 2537, fax 872 2568, e manyanocentre@cci.org.za, Sanddrift St) Dorm beds R35. This is an

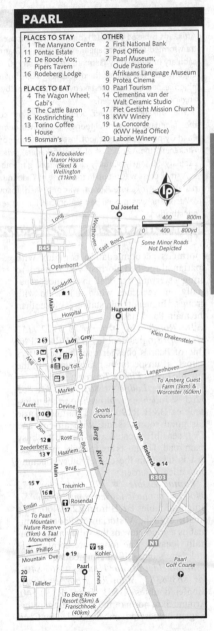

PAARL

PLACES TO STAY	OTHER
1 The Manyano Centre	2 First National Bank
11 Pontac Estate	3 Post Office
12 De Roode Vos;	7 Paarl Museum;
Pipers Tavern	Oude Pastorie
16 Rodeberg Lodge	8 Afrikaans Language Museum
	9 Protea Cinema
PLACES TO EAT	10 Paarl Tourism
4 The Wagon Wheel;	14 Clementina van der
Gabi's	Walt Ceramic Studio
5 The Cattle Baron	17 Piet Gesticht Mission Church
6 Kostinrichting	18 KWV Winery
13 Torino Coffee	19 La Concorde
House	(KWV Head Office)
15 Bosman's	20 Laborie Winery

WESTERN CAPE

Afrikaans

Afrikaans is based on Dutch, but in Africa, exposed to the diverse cultures of the Cape, it has been transformed into an independent language. Grammatical forms have been simplified and the vocabulary influenced by German, French, Portuguese, Malaysian, indigenous African languages and English. Dutch remained the official language, however, and Afrikaans was given little formal recognition, especially after the takeover of the Cape by the English in 1806, when a deliberate policy of anglicisation was pursued.

The Afrikaners, however, deeply resented the colonial approach of the British and began to see their language as a central foundation of their own culture. In 1875 Arnoldus Pannevis, a teacher at Paarl Gymnasium High School, inspired a number of Paarl citizens to form the Genootskap van Regte Afrikaners (the Association of True Afrikaners), who developed and formalised the grammar and vocabulary. Strangely, virtually all the founding members were descended from the French Huguenots.

A small press was set up in the house of Gideon Malherbe and the first issue of an Afrikaans newspaper, *Die Afrikaanse Patriot*, was published, followed by many books.

Afrikaans was proclaimed an official language in 1925, and is still protected under the new constitution.

enormous accommodation complex with spartan three-bed dorms; you'll need to bring a sleeping bag. Call in advance, especially on weekends when it fills up with groups. Huguenot train station is closer than the main Paarl station.

De Roode Vos (☎/fax 872 5912, 152 Main St) Singles/doubles B&B R120/190. One of Paarl's cheaper guesthouses offers homely if unspectacular lodgings, with the reliable bistro *Pipers Tavern* next door.

Rodeberg Lodge (☎ 863 3202, fax 863 3203, e rodeberg@ctm-web.co.za). Singles/doubles B&B R190/300. This guesthouse has good rooms (some with air-con and TV), sensibly located away from the busy main road. The hosts are friendly and breakfast is taken in the conservatory, opening onto a leafy garden.

Pontac Estate (☎ 872 0445, fax 872 0460, e pontac@iafrica.com, 16 Zion St) Singles/doubles B&B from R275/400. This small, stylish, Victorian-era hotel commands a good view of the valley and is centrally located. The rooms are comfortable and there's one self-catering cottage.

Mooikelder Manor House (☎ 863 8491, fax 863 8361, Main Rd, Noorder Paarl) Singles/doubles B&B from R330/540. Around 5km north of the town centre is this elegant homestead, once occupied by Cecil Rhodes. The management is outgoing and the facilities excellent.

Places to Eat

Several of the local vineyards have restaurants or do picnic lunches and they are among the best places to eat. In town, steak is the dominant cuisine.

The Wagon Wheel (☎ 872 5265, 57 Lady Grey St) Mains R50. Open noon-2pm Tues-Fri & 6pm-late Tues-Sat. More than your average steak joint, this cosy wood-panelled restaurant has won many awards and packs them in nightly. Next door they've added on *Gabi's* (open evenings only), a continental-style cafe-bar.

The Cattle Baron (☎ 872 2000, 3 Gymnasium St) Mains R60. Open noon-3.30pm Mon-Fri & Sun, 5.30pm-11.30pm daily. This branch of the upmarket steakhouse chain has a lively atmosphere and a reasonable selection of local wines.

Kostinrichting (☎ 871 1353, 19 Pastorie Ave) Mains R30. Open 8am-4pm Mon-Fri, 8am-1pm Sat. This cafe, in a Victorian-era building that once was a school, is pleasant and is good for a snack or light meal. It has an attached crafts shop.

Torino Coffee House (☎ 872 5967, 130 Main St) Breakfast from R17.50, sandwiches R20. Open 9am-5.30pm Tues-Sun

This cafe is in an elegant restored building with a courtyard out back. There's a very tempting chocolate shop next door.

Bosman's (☎ *863 2727, The Grande Roche, Plantasie St*) Mains R100, 4-course set menu R218. Open 7pm-9pm daily. Outrageously expensive (for South Africa) but undoubtedly classy, this restaurant has chandeliers inside, flickering candles outside and a wine list that runs to over 50 pages!

Shopping
Clementina van der Walt Ceramic Studio (☎ *872 7514*, W *www.clementina.co.za, Parys Farm on Jan van Riebeeck Dr, R301*) Open 9am-5pm Mon-Fri, 9am-4pm Sat, 10am-4pm Sun. This is the showroom and production site for one of South Africa's most appealing and colourful ranges of pottery. The adjoining *A.R.T. Gallery* displays arts and crafts from all over Africa.

Getting There & Away
Several bus services go through Paarl, so it is easy to build it into your itinerary. The bus segment between Paarl and Cape Town is R85, so consider taking the cheaper train to Paarl and then linking up with the buses.

Bus Paarl is a stop on the Translux services between Cape Town and Jo'burg (R390 from Paarl), Durban (R375), Port Elizabeth (R180, via the Mountain Route) and East London (R220; R185 via Graaff-Reinet). Greyhound and Intercape also run to these places at similar prices.

Train Metro trains run roughly every hour between Cape Town and Paarl (R6/12 economy/1st class, 1¼ hours) Monday to Friday. Note there is no 2nd class. The services are less common on weekends. Take care to travel on trains during the busy part of the day, as robberies have been reported.

You can travel by train from Paarl to Stellenbosch: take a Cape Town–bound train and change at Muldersvlei.

Getting Around
If you don't have your own transport your only option for getting around Paarl, apart

from walking, is to call a taxi: try **Paarl Radio Taxis** (☎ *872 5671*).

AROUND PAARL
Wellington
Just 13km from Paarl is Wellington, a sedate and quite pretty little town. Between the two towns is the large **Mbekweni** township, created in 1945 but with little infrastructure to match its half-century history.

The landowner whose property was used by the railway stipulated that all trains must stop in Wellington. This includes the *Blue Train* and it also included King George VI's train in 1947.

The **Tourism Bureau** (☎ *021-873 4604*, W *www.visitwellington.com, 104 Main St*) is next to the Andrew Murray Church. The friendly staff can provide a brochure and map of the wineries in the Wellington area, which are less touristy than Paarl's. A popular one is **Hildenbrand Wine & Olive Estate** (☎/fax *021-873 4115*, W *www.wine-estate-hildenbrand.co.za; tasting R5; sales 9am-5pm daily*) This place also has a restaurant and good accommodation with singles/doubles B&B for R210/340.

Bakkies B&B (☎/fax *021-873 5161*, e *info@bakkiesbb.co.za, Bainskloof Rd*) Singles/doubles R90/160. You can get well-equipped rooms at this lodge just above the Oasis cafe on the Bainskloof Rd. The rates include a permit to hike the Patatskloof Trail (see Bainskloof Pass following).

Bainskloof Pass
This is one of the country's great mountain passes, with a superb caravan park halfway along. Andrew Bain developed the road through the pass between 1848 and 1852. Other than having its surface tarred, the road has not been altered since, and it is now a national monument. It's a magical drive, which would be even better to experience on bicycle.

The R301 runs from Wellington across Bainskloof to meet another road running south to Worcester and north to Ceres.

Tweede Tol Caravan Park & Camp Site (☎ *021-945 4570*) Camping R46 for up to 6 people, plus R5 per vehicle. Gates open

WESTERN CAPE

7.30am-6pm mid-Sept–end May. This camping ground, in a wonderful spot at the head of the pass, is surrounded by magnificent fynbos. There are swimming holes on the Witrivier.

There are several nearby walks including the five-hour **Bobbejaans River Walk** to a waterfall. This walk actually starts back at Eerste Tol and you need to buy a permit (R29), which is available from the Cape Nature Conservation desk at Cape Town Tourism (see Information in the Cape Town & the Peninsula chapter for details).

The Patatskloof Trail is a long day-walk that begins and ends at the *Oasis Tea Room*, which is open from 8.30am to 6pm Thursday to Sunday, on the road leading up to the pass from Wellington. You can make it an overnight walk by arranging to stay in a cave on the trail; call (☎ 021-873 4231) for details.

West Coast & Swartland

Although popular with Capetonians seeking a quick break, few overseas visitors head north of Cape Town up the West Coast and through the area known as the Swartland (Black Land). Those who do are likely to find the rugged, desolate Cederberg Wilderness Area and the West Coast National Park more appealing than the lacklustre resort and fishing towns of Langebaan and Saldanha.

The prettiest coastal village to aim for is Paternoster. Inland, the country town of Darling, home of a South African entertainment icon Tannie Evita Bezuidenhout, is worth a stop. Surfers will have good reason to seek the waves around Eland's Bay.

The unstable dunes of the western coastal strip have been transformed into productive country by the planting of Australian Port Jackson wattle, with its very distinctive golden flowers. But the wattle now poses a major threat to the fynbos (see the boxed text 'The Cape Floral Kingdom' in the Facts about South Africa chapter). Fynbos is one of the region's major attractions, especially in late winter and early spring when wildflowers

carpet the remaining dunes (especially in the West Coast National Park).

The Swartland, both sides of the N7 and east to the foot of the mountains, is a rich agricultural area of rolling plains. It's believed that the area's name derives from the dark foliage of the distinctive *renosterbus* scrub that covered the plains. Combined with the winter rainfall, the rich soil enables farmers to produce over 20% of South Africa's wheat, as well as high-quality wine.

Before white settlement, the plains were occupied by the Khoikhoi Griqua people while the mountains were the province of the San. Piketberg is named after the guards (pickets) who were stationed here in the 1670s to protect the Cape Town settlers from Khoisan attacks.

Most public transport through this area travels from Cape Town north along the N7, either going all the way to Springbok and Namibia or leaving the N7 and heading through Calvinia to Upington. Getting to the coastal towns west of the N7 isn't easy if you don't have a car.

DARLING

Some 70km north of Cape Town is the quiet country town of Darling, recently catapulted to fame by the presence of Tannie Evita Bezuidenhout, the alter ego of actor and satirist Pieter-Dirk Uys.

Things to See & Do

At **Evita se Perron** *(Evita's Platform;* ☎ *022-492 2851,* ⓦ *www.evita.co.za; tickets R65)* there are shows featuring satirist Pieter-Dirk Uys' cast of characters. These run weekly on Friday, Saturday and Sunday; you can also catch him at Cape Town's *On Broadway* every Monday (see Gay & Lesbian Venue in the Cape Town & the Peninsula chapter). Although the shows include a fair smattering of Afrikaans, there's much for English-speaking audiences to enjoy, and they are often hilarious and thought-provoking. The splendidly kitsch theatre-restaurant, in a converted station building next to the railway, is worth a visit in its own right.

Across the road from the theatre is a reasonable **craft market** *(open 10am-4pm)*

Thur-Sun). The typically cluttered **museum** *(☎ 022-492 3361, Cnr Pastorie & Hill Sts; admission free; open 10am-1pm & 2pm-4pm daily)* is worth a browse, and doubles as the town's tourist information centre.

While in the area you could also visit the poor Moravian mission village of **Marme**, 20km south of Darling, or the coastal resort of **Yzerfontein** 15km west. This holiday village has some dramatic views over a rugged, rocky coastline, and a left point for surfers that works on south-easterly winds and moderate south-westerly swells.

Places to Stay & Eat

Darling is so close to Cape Town that there's no pressing need to stay overnight, although there are some very nice guesthouses.

Darling Guest House (☎ 022-492 3062, 22 Pastorie St) Singles/doubles B&B R175/270. This is an elegant and imaginatively decorated place.

Parrot's Guest House (☎ 022-492 3430, 19 Long St) Singles/doubles B&B from R180/300. The upmarket choice, this place has a lovely garden, a pool and a good cafe.

Through the Looking Glass (☎ 022-492 2858, 19 Main Rd; open 9.30am-4.30pm Mon-Fri, 10am-3pm Sat) This is an arty cafe with an Internet connection.

You can also eat at *Evita se Perron*; at show times they do traditional Afrikaans food like chicken pie and *bobotie* (curried mince with a topping of savoury egg custard, usually served on turmeric-flavoured rice) for around R40.

Getting There & Away

To get to Darling, drive up the R27 from Cape Town and look for the signs. It's worth inquiring about the occasional Saturday excursions to Darling on the **Spier Train** *(☎ 021-419 5222)*. The 2½-hour trip includes a picnic lunch and admission to the show at Evita se Perron.

WEST COAST NATIONAL PARK

The West Coast National Park *(☎ 022-772 2144; admission R9-18; open 7am-7pm daily)* covers around 18,000 hectares. It runs north from Yzerfontein along the coast

to just short of Langebaan, surrounding the clear, blue waters of the Langebaan Lagoon. It's made up of a peculiar mix of semi-independent zones, some of which are only leased by the national park authorities.

The park protects wetlands of international significance and important seabird breeding colonies. In summer it plays host to enormous numbers of migratory wading birds. The most numerically dominant species is the delicate-looking curlew sandpiper, which migrates north from the sub-Antarctic in huge flocks. Flamingos, Cape gannets, crowned cormorants, numerous gull species and African black oystercatchers are also among the hordes. The offshore islands are home to colonies of jackass penguins.

The vegetation is predominantly made up of stunted bushes, sedges and many flowering annuals and succulents. There are some coastal fynbos in the east, and the park is famous for its wildflower display, which is usually between August and October. Several game species can be seen in the part of the park known as the Postberg section, which is open from August to September. Game species include a variety of small antelope, wildebeest, bontebok and eland.

The park is only about 120km from Cape Town, so it could easily be visited on a day trip if you have transport. The roads in the park are dirt and can be quite heavily corrugated. The park, which is clearly signposted, begins 7km south of Langebaan. The return trip from Langebaan to the northern end of the Postberg section is more than 80km; allow yourself plenty of time.

LANGEBAAN

Langebaan has been discovered by developers, so although it does have an unusual and rather beautiful location, it is just about spoilt. In its favour, it overlooks the Langebaan Lagoon, which has excellent sailing and windsurfing.

The **tourist information centre** *(☎ 022-772 1515, W www.langebaaninfo.com, End of Hoof St; open 9am-5pm Mon-Fri, 9am-12.30pm Sat, 9am-noon Sun)* is in the same building as the West Coast National Park office.

WESTERN CAPE

WESTERN CAPE

Places to Stay & Eat

None of the three *caravan parks* run by the local municipality allows tents. This is to avoid rowdy parties of locals, so if you don't look like trouble you might be able to persuade the manager to let you camp.

Oliphantskop Farm Inn (☎/fax 022-772 2326) Dorm beds R65, singles/doubles B&B R109/218, self-catering cottage for 4 R220. Around 3km from town, across the road from the Mykonos resort complex, this friendly and attractive place offers backpacker rates for accommodation and has a reputation for good food.

Windstone Backpackers (☎ 022-766 1645, fax 766 1038, W www.windstone .co.za, Route 45) Camp sites R35 per person, dorm beds R55, doubles R160-180. Near Langeenheid train station but a long way from Langebaan and the sea, the facilities in this place are quite good (including an indoor pool). It's also a dog and cat boarding kennel and an equestrian centre.

The Farmhouse (☎ 022-772 2062, fax 722 1980, W www.thefarmhouselangebaan .co.za, 5 Egret St) Singles/doubles B&B from R400/540. Langebaan's best hotel has a good location overlooking the bay, comfortable rooms and a classy restaurant.

Die Strandloper (☎ 022-772 2490) All-you-can-eat deal R95. Open for lunch Wed, Sat & Sun, dinner Wed-Sat. This is a rustic open-air seafood restaurant and bar on the beach, outside of the town on the way to the Mykonos resort. Call ahead to check it's open. Very similar is *Boesmanland Farm Kitchen* (☎ 022-772 1564) in the Mykonos resort, where you'll also find *Bouzouki*, a Greek restaurant by the marina.

Getting There & Away

You might be able to get to Langebaan on the West Coast Shuttle (☎ 083-556 1777), which operates a pricey minibus service (R60 one way) from Cape Town to the Mykonos resort and casino. There's also the seaplane from Cape Town's Waterfront to the casino (see Air Tours in the Cape Town & the Peninsula chapter for details). Otherwise no public transport runs to Langebaan.

SALDANHA

Saldanha, at the northern end of the same lagoon as Langebaan, is dominated by an enormous iron-ore pier, navy yards and fish-processing factories. Despite this, the town's bays are pleasant and, because they are sheltered, much warmer than the ocean. Hoedjies Bay, near the town centre, is the most popular for swimming.

The main road into town is Saldanha Rd and Main (Hoof) Rd runs from the shopping centre up to the headland, along the back bay.

The helpful **information centre** (☎ 022 714 2088, W www.capewestcoast.org, Van Riebeeck St; open 8.30am-4.30pm Mon-Fri 9am-noon Sat) is uphill from Saldanha Rd.

Boat trips (☎ 022-714 4235, W www.sai boats.co.za; from R50, minimum 3 people, on the harbour and to offshore islands run from The Slipway restaurant (see Places to Stay & Eat following). There's an R2 charge to enter the harbour area.

Places to Stay & Eat

Strandloper Guesthouse (☎ 022-714 3099 fax 714 4930, W www.strandloper.co.za, 5 Beach Rd) Singles/doubles B&B R225/320 self-catering from R250 for 2 people. Not much to look at from the outside, but very pleasant inside. All the neat and tidy rooms have sea views.

Saldanha Bay Protea Hotel (☎ 022-714 1264, fax 714 4093, 51B Main Rd, Singles/doubles R395/460. Overlooking the bay, this acceptable mid-range chain hotel is much better value at the weekends when the rates drop to R165 per person.

The Slipway (☎ 022-714 4235) Mains around R30. Open 9am-5.30pm daily Feb-Nov, 8am-11pm daily Dec-Jan. In the docks, right on the waterfront, this is an atmospheric place for a lazy meal.

Meresteijn (☎ 022-714 3345, Main Rd Mains from R20. Open 9am-10pm Sun-Thur, 9am-11pm Fri & Sat. A pub, restaurant and bistro serving seafood, pasta and pizza this place has good views across the bay.

Getting There & Away

There's at least one bus a day to Cape Town (about R25) from the corner of Main and

Saldanha Rds. Local taxis (ask near the Spar supermarket) run north to Vredenburg (R5), where you can pick up taxis to Paternoster. It's difficult to make connections with taxis heading further up the coast because most run direct from Cape Town along the N7.

PATERNOSTER

The sleepy fishing village of Paternoster is 15km from the missable inland town of Vredenburg. It's an attractive, low-key kind of place with a clutch of simple white-washed homes where the local fishing families live – and which are suddenly becoming highly desirable as holiday houses for wealthy Capetonians.

The surrounding countryside is attractive, the rolling hills scattered with strange granite outcrops. The **Columbine Nature Reserve**, 3km past the town, protects 263 hectares of coastal fynbos around Cape Columbine. There's a small, basic *camping & caravan park (Tietiesbaai; ☎ 022-752 2718)* with sites at around R20. Further north along the coast is the similar village of **St Helena Bay**, with a lovely sheltered stretch of water, but no real beach.

Places to Stay & Eat

Ahoy! Guesthouse (☎/fax 022-752 2725) Singles/doubles B&B from R160/250, self-catering cottage sleeping 6 from R400. Around the corner from the general store, this is the nicest accommodation in Paternoster, offering comfortably furnished rooms and a cottage.

Paternoster Hotel (☎/fax 022-752 2703, e paternosterhotel@webnet.co.za) Singles/doubles B&B from R130/260. This rough-edged, quirky country hotel, virtually on the beachfront, is a popular venue for people interested in fishing. Its fish and crayfish *braais* (barbecues) are famous. We warn you, the bar is a feminist's nightmare.

Voorstrandt Restaurant (☎ 022-752 2038, Strandloperweg) Mains R35-50. Open 10am-10pm daily. You can hop from this designer red-and-green painted beach shack right onto the sand. Specialising in seafood, this is also an excellent spot to watch the sunset over a beer.

ELAND'S BAY

Surfers and bird-spotters alike will love Eland's Bay. Mountains run down into the sea and the large lagoon is favoured by all sorts of interesting waterbirds, including flamingos (although they are nomadic and don't hang around). The town itself, though, is ugly.

Accommodation boils down to the basic *municipal caravan park*, which has camp sites at R52. The camp sites are right by the beach, so it's pretty exposed to the wind.

Sandveld Country Cottages (☎ 022-962 1609, e cwykeham@mweb.co.za, Route 366) Camping R40 per person, cottages R80 per person. Although it's 35km from Eland's Bay (and 42km from Piketberg), this farm with self-catering cottages and camp sites is the best place to stay in the area.

Getting There & Away

If you're driving south, it's worth taking the dirt road that runs along the northern bank of the wide and reedy estuary. You can cross over at the hamlet of Rodelinghuys and head south through nice country to the village of Aurora or keep going to join the N7 at Piketberg.

Coming down the dirt road from Lambert's Bay, the turn-off to Eland's Bay takes you onto another dirt road but this has a toll of R15. If you don't want to pay this, head down the toll road a short way and there's a map showing the longer but free route.

Goofy-Footer

Eland's Bay is a goofy-footer's (surfing with the right foot at the front of the board) paradise, with extremely fast left-point waves working at a range of swell sizes. The bay can hold a very big wave. The main left-point break is virtually in front of the hotel, towards the crayfish factory – it breaks along a rocky shelf in thick kelp, after south-westerly winds on a low and incoming tide. There's a right-beach break and more lefts on Baboon Point, along the gravel road past the crayfish factory.

LAMBERT'S BAY

Lambert's Bay is an unattractive fishing town on a bleak stretch of the West Coast. Dominated by fish-processing factories, its major attraction is a rookery of gannets and a classic seaside braai restaurant. The Crayfish Festival on the first weekend of November is apparently quite lively.

The **information centre** (☎ *027-432 1000; open 9am-1pm & 2pm-5pm Mon-Fri, 9am-1pm Sat*) is next to the small and missable **Sandveld Museum** *(admission R2)* on Church St.

Despite the overwhelming pong, birdlovers may be tempted to walk out onto a breakwater to the gannet rookery. Here thousands of aggressive birds mill around making a racket and snapping at each other. They lay eggs between September and November, and the chicks hatch 40 days later.

From July to January you might also spot some humpback whales off the coast, and dolphins are common throughout the year. For boat trips contact **Lamberts Bay Boat Charter** (☎ *027-432 1927*).

Places to Stay & Eat

Lambert's Bay Caravan Park (☎ *027-432 2238, Off Korporasie St)* Camp sites from R50. This place offers basic facilities north of town beside the beach.

Raston Gasthaus (☎ *027-432 2431, fax 432 2422, 24 Kiedeman St)* Singles/doubles B&B R260/400. This guesthouse is smart, if a bit over-the-top in its decor, which includes murals and a small pool.

Lambert Bay Hotel (☎ *027-432 1126, fax 432 1036, Voortrekker St)* Singles/doubles B&B from R250/390. Friendly and comfortable, this is the town's only hotel. It has a pool and is very close to the fish processing factory.

Lambert Bay's two open-air restaurants, which you must book in advance (they'll only open if there are sufficient reservations), offer similar bust-a-gut buffets. To take full advantage, set aside at least three hours to work your way through the fish, seafood stews, salads, homemade bread and jams.

Muisbosskerm (☎ *027-432 1017)* Meals R90, R115 including crayfish. This is the original open-air seafood restaurant, 5km south of town along the dirt road towards Eland's Bay, and it's right beside the sea. Bring your own drinks and be prepared to eat with your fingers or use a mussel shell as an impromptu spoon.

Bosduifklip (☎ *027-432 2735)* Meal R80. The cheaper and slightly more formal of the open-air restaurants is 4km before Lambert's Bay just off the main road.

OLIFANTS RIVER VALLEY

The scenery changes dramatically at the Piekenaarskloof Pass; coming north on the N7 you suddenly overlook the intensively cultivated Olifants River Valley. The elephants that explorer Jan Danckaert came upon in 1660, and which gave their name to the area, are long gone.

Today the river provides irrigation for hectares of grapevines and orange trees which are beautifully maintained by a huge labour force. The comfortable bungalows of the white farmers are surrounded by green and leafy gardens, masking them from the shanties.

On the valley floor are some acclaimed wineries and coops, which specialise in white wine – you can get details of a wine route at tourist information centres. The eastern side is largely bounded by the spectacular Cederberg Range, which is protected by the extensive Cederberg Wilderness Area. Citrusdal and Clanwilliam, to the south-west and north-west of the wilderness area, are the two main towns in the region.

As an alternative to the N7, there's a spectacular partly tarred road (R303) between Citrusdal and Ceres, a great drive through the Cederberg Wilderness Area from Citrusdal to Clanwilliam, and another memorable route (R364) running between Clanwilliam and Calvinia (in Northern Cape to the north-east).

CEDERBERG WILDERNESS AREA

The Cederberg is a rugged, mountainous area of valleys and peaks extending roughly north-south for 100km, between Citrusdal and Vanrhynsdorp. A good proportion is protected by the 71,000 hectare Cederberg Wilderness Area, which is administered by

Cape Nature Conservation. The highest peaks are Sneeuberg (2027m) and Tafelberg (1969m), and the area is famous for its weathered sandstone formations, which sometimes take bizarre shapes. San paintings can be found on the rocks and in some of the area's caves.

The area is also famous for its plant life, which is predominantly mountain fynbos. Spring is the best time to see the wildflowers, although there's plenty of interest at other times of the year. The vegetation varies with altitude but includes the Clanwilliam cedar (which gives the region its name) and the rare snowball protea. The Clanwilliam cedar survives only in relatively small numbers, growing between 1000m and 1500m, and the snowball protea (now limited to isolated pockets) grows only above the snow line.

There are small populations of baboons, rheboks, klipspringers and grysboks; and predators such as caracals, Cape foxes, honey badgers and the rarely seen leopard.

Orientation & Information

The Cederberg is divided into three excellent hiking areas of around 24,000 hectares. Each area has a network of trails. However, this is a genuine wilderness area with a genuine wilderness ethos. You are *encouraged* to leave the trails, and little information is available on suggested routes. It's up to you to survive on your own. Similarly, you probably won't be given directions to the area's rock art. Work out for yourself where the Khoisan were likely to have lived.

There is a buffer zone of conserved land between the wilderness area and the farmland, and here more intrusive activities such as mountain biking are allowed.

There's no real season for walking; from May to the end of September expect rain and possibly snow. From December to April there's likely to be very little water.

A permit is required if you want to walk, and the number of visitors per hiking area is limited to 50 people. The maximum group size is 12 and, for safety, the minimum is three adults. Maps (R14) are available at the Algeria Camping Ground and

the office of the **Chief Nature Conservator** (☎ 027-482 2812, Private Bag X6, Citrusdal 7340).

To be certain you'll get a permit, apply well in advance. Outside school holidays and weekends you may be able to get one on the spot, but you should definitely phone before arriving to make sure. Permits must be booked through the Chief Nature Conservator or through the **Cape Nature Conservation office** (☎ 021-426 0723) in Cape Town. Bookings open on 1 February for the March to June period, 1 June for July to October, and 1 October for November to February. The cost is R12 per person per day, plus the R5 park admission charge.

The entrance to the Algeria Camping Ground closes at 4.30pm (9pm on Friday). You won't be allowed in if you arrive late. If you need to collect your permit (if you haven't already organised it in Cape Town or had it posted to you), this can only be done during office hours, so if you're arriving on Friday evening, you'll need to make arrangements.

Places to Stay

Algeria Camping Ground (☎ 027-482 2812) Camp sites from R46 for 6 people. Entrance closes 4.30pm Sat-Thur, 9pm Fri. These are exceptional grounds in a beautiful, shaded site alongside the Rondegat River, which is the headwaters of the Olifants River. There are swimming holes and lovely spots to picnic beside the river. Day visitors (not allowed during peak periods) are charged R12.

Kliphuis State Forest camping ground (☎ 027-482 2812) Camp sites from R46. Nestling in the forest, near the Pakhuis Pass on Route 364, about 15km north-east of Clanwilliam, this is another excellent camping ground. Surrounded by rock walls and cut by a fresh mountain stream, facilities are fairly spartan but there are toilets, showers and water.

You'll need to book either of these camp sites in the same way that you book hiking. There are basic *huts* for hikers in the wilderness area and a couple of better-equipped *cottages*.

WESTERN CAPE

See both Citrusdal and Clanwilliam later for places to stay outside the Cederberg Wilderness Area.

Getting There & Away

The Cederberg Range is about 200km from Cape Town, accessible from Citrusdal, Clanwilliam and the N7.

There are several roads into Algeria Camping Ground, and they all offer magnificent views. It takes about 45 minutes to get from Clanwilliam by car, much longer if you give in to normal human emotion and stop every now and again. Algeria is not signposted from Clanwilliam, but you just follow the road above the dam to the south. Algeria *is* signposted from the N7 and it's only 20 minutes from the main road; there's an amazing collection of plants, including proteas, along the side of the road.

There are some dusty but interesting back roads that run south-east through the hamlet of Cederberg (where you can buy fuel and stay in huts for about R100) and on to Ceres. There's a good but tough walk from the farm up to the Wolfsberg Crack, a well-known rock formation. Allow at least seven hours for the return trip.

Public transport into Algeria is non-existent; walking from Citrusdal, the nearest town will take about two days.

Inquire with **Ferdinands Tours & Adventures** (☎ *021-465 8550*, **W** *www.ferdinandstours.co.za*) about its two-day weekend trips from Cape Town to the Cederberg for around R650.

CITRUSDAL

☎ 022 • postcode 7340

The small town of Citrusdal is a good base for exploring the Cederberg – both the wilderness area and the equally interesting surrounding mountains. August to September is wildflower season, and the displays can be spectacular. This is also one of the best times for hiking.

The **tourism bureau** (☎ *921 3210, 39 Voortrekker St; open 8am-5pm Mon-Fri, 8am-1pm Sat*) can help you find accommodation in the area and provide information on the local mountain biking and hiking trails.

If the tourism bureau is closed head over to **Craig Royston** (☎ *921 2963, Modderfontein Farm; open 8am-5pm daily)*, the large, old farm building, 2km out of Citrusdal off the N7. It houses a cafe (meals are R25), a shop and a small museum – the old shop is where the farm workers still buy their supplies. It hasn't been renovated to within an inch of its life, and is a welcome relief after all those squeaky clean tourist ventures. There are excellent light meals and you can sample (and buy) local wines. It's also a good place to come for information, and they hold monthly cabaret evenings in Afrikaans.

For guided hikes in the Cederberg area contact Reinhardt Slabber at Gekko Backpackers Lodge (see Places to Stay & Eat following).

Places to Stay & Eat

Drop Zone (☎ *921 3747, fax 921 3467 Voortrekker St)* Dorm beds R50. Accommodation in simple dorm rooms above this African-style cafe on the main road includes a light breakfast. The shower is made from an old oil drum.

Gekko Backpackers Lodge (☎ *921 3353* **W** *home.mweb.co.za/vi/vism, 17.5km from Citrusdal on the N7 towards Clanwilliam)* Dorm beds R50, cottage from R200 per night for 2 people. This is fine backpacker accommodation on a farm with a river pool and San rock art trails within its extensive grounds. Hiking packages are available.

Cederberg Lodge (☎ *921 2221, fax 921 2704,* **W** *www.cedarberglodge.co.za, Voortrekker St)* Singles/doubles from R115/150. This reasonable hotel is not far from the tourism bureau. All rooms have air-con, TV and en suite bathrooms and there's a sizable pool and restaurant.

Staalwater (☎ *921 3337)* Cottage R80 per person. This self-catering cottage sleeping six is in a serene location 12km from town, on the road to The Baths.

The Baths (☎ *921 3609, fax 921 3988* **e** *baths@kingsley.co.za)* Camp sites R30 per person, doubles R120, chalets from R180. About 18km from Citrusdal, this health spa with two outdoor pools in a pretty wooded gorge, is a good place to relax for a ew days. Accommodation options range rom camp sites and fairly inexpensive partments to chalets (all of which cost more n weekends). If you call ahead, they will ick you up from the bus stop on the highvay. The baths are open to day visitors luring the week for R15/7.50 per adult/child.

Tree Tops (☎ *921 3626, PO Box 8, Citusdal)* Chalets R90 per person. In a poplar orest by the Olifants River, 12km further n from The Baths, the wooden chalets here re on stilts. It's a great place, but you'll eed to bring everything with you and book vell ahead.

Patrick's Restaurant (☎ *921 3062, 77 'oortrekker St)* Mains R40-50. Open noon-.30pm Tues-Fri, 7pm-11pm Mon-Thur, pm-midnight Fri & Sat. This is the best, nd practically the only, place for dinner in own. It does good steaks and, for some eason, pizza with banana topping.

Uitspan Cafe (☎ *921 3273, 39 Voortrekker '*) Mains R30. Open 8am-5pm Mon-Fri, am-1pm Sat. This bright cafe next to the ourism bureau does sandwiches, salads nd cakes.

Getting There & Away

ntercape buses stop at the petrol station on e N7 highway outside town; from Cape own the fare is R120. Minibus taxis to 'ape Town and Clanwilliam stop at the altex petrol station in town.

There's an excellent scenic road (R303) ver Middelburg Pass into the Koue (Cold) okkeveld and a beautiful valley on the ther side, which is only topped by the ydo Pass and the view over the Ceres Val-y (see Ceres later in this chapter). The ack road into the wilderness area is also xcellent.

CLANWILLIAM

☎ 027 • postcode 8135 • pop 29,000

lanwilliam is a popular weekend resort. he attractions are the compact town itself vhich has some nice examples of Cape utch architecture and a pleasant main reet), its proximity to the Cederberg and e Clanwilliam Dam, which attracts hordes f noisy water-skiers. The Ramskop Nature

Rooibos Tea

Rooibos, literally 'red bush', is a red-coloured tea with a distinctive aroma. It's made from the leaves of the *Aspalathus linearis* plant, grown in the Cederberg region of Western Cape.

Malay slaves first discovered that the plant could be used to make a beverage, although it was not until the 20th century that a Russian immigrant, Benjamin Ginsberg, introduced it to the wider community, and it didn't become a cash crop until the 1930s. Despite this, some brands feature trek wagons and other icons of old Afrikanerdom.

The drink contains no caffeine and much less tannin than normal tea. This is probably its major health benefit, although it's claimed to have others, due to minute amounts of minerals such as iron, copper and magnesium. It's also a great thirst quencher, drunk straight, or with lemon or milk.

Tours of one of the main packing plants, **Rooibos Ltd** (☎ *482 2155)*, just outside Clanwilliam, are available at 10am, 11.30am, 2pm and 3.30pm Monday to Friday.

Reserve and a short walking trail are near the dam. There are some adventurous dirt roads into the Cederberg and a great drive over the Pakhuis Pass to Calvinia (see Around Calvinia in the Northern Cape chapter).

The **information centre** (☎ *482 2024; open 8.30am-5pm Mon-Sat, 8.30am-12.30pm Sat)* is at the top end of the main street, across from the old tronk (jail in Afrikaans).

While up here, if you have the time, travel out to **Wuppertal** (☎ *482 3410 for inquiries)*. This Moravian mission station, 74km southeast of Clanwilliam, dates back to 1830 and is reached along a gravel road. The original church and the workshops – where handmade leather shoes (called *velskoene*) are still made – are worth seeing.

Places to Stay & Eat

If you're camping, the best spot to stay near Clanwilliam is **Kliphuis State Forest camping ground**, about 30 minutes away just before the Pakhuis Pass on the R364 (see Places to Stay under Cederberg Wilderness Area earlier).

Clanwilliam Dam Municipal Caravan Park & Chalets (☎ 482 2133, fax 482 1933) Camp sites from R42 for 4 people, chalets R307 for up to 6 people. Overlooking the water-skiing action, these grounds are on the other side of the dam from the N7. Travellers arriving here after weeks in Namibia will be pleased to pitch their tents on lush, grassy sites. The chalets are very nice but you need to book ahead for school holidays and weekends.

Strassberger's Hotel Clanwilliam (☎ 482 1101, fax 482 2678, e strassberger@lando .co.za, Main St) Singles/doubles B&B R190/340 (R280/500 in flower season), annexe R125/250. This is comfortable and popular country pub, which has been well renovated and has a pool. The rooms in the annexe (in a delicensed pub nearby) are quite acceptable.

Saint du Barrys (☎/fax 482 1537, e stdu barrys@clanwilliam.co.za, 13 Augsburg Dr) Singles/doubles B&B R250/380. Saint du Barrys is a pleasant guesthouse in a thatched-roof house with decent-sized rooms.

Bushman's Kloof (☎ 482 2627, fax 482 1011, W www.bushmanskloof.co.za) Singles/ doubles full board R1250/1900. This is an upmarket private reserve, 34km east of Clanwilliam along the Pakhuis Pass, known for its excellent San rock-art sites and extensive animal and birdlife. If you've got the cash, they can also arrange fly-in safaris from Cape Town.

Reinhold's (☎ 482 2678, Main St) Mains R40. Open 7pm-9.30pm Tues-Sat. Reinhold's is an a la carte restaurant, run by the Strassberger's Hotel Clanwilliam. If it's closed, the hotel does a set dinner menu for R75.

Oliphants Huis (☎ 482 2301, Main St) This pub-restaurant, in a big house with a shady garden, is a nice place for a drink on a hot night.

Getting There & Away
All the buses that go through Citrusdal also go through Clanwilliam. It's about 45 min-

utes between the two towns, and the far from Cape Town is R130. Minibus taxi running between Springbok (R80) and Cap Town (R70) go through Clanwilliam stopping at the post office.

NORTH OF CLANWILLIAM
The dull archetypal country town of **Van rhynsdorp** lies in the shadow of the distinc tive Matzikamaberg Mountain in th desolate Knersvlakte, the valley of the So (Salt) River. Like much of the West Coas the surrounding countryside can explod into colour after decent rains.

For information about the area, vis Vanrhynsdorp's **tourist information offic** (☎ 027-219 1552, Van Riebeeck St; ope 8am-1pm & 2pm-4.30pm Mon-Fri).

The area around **Unionskraal**, about 10k to the south-east, is particularly renowne for flowers, and there are some interestin drives and walks around the plateau of th Matzikamaberg and Gifberg Ranges.

There is a stunning road trip betwee Vanrhynsdorp and Calvinia (see Arour Calvinia in the Northern Cape chapter fo more information).

Breede River Valley

This region lies to the north-east of th Winelands on the western fringes of th Little Karoo. The Breede River Valle dominates, but it is mountainous count and includes some smaller valleys. The va ley floors are intensively cultivated wi orchards, vineyards and wheat.

Europeans had settled most of the valle by the beginning of the 18th century, but t area did not really take off until passes we pushed through the mountains in the 19 century. The headwaters of the Breede Riv (sometimes called the Breë), in the beautif mountain-locked Ceres basin, escape v Mitchell's Pass and flow south-east f 310km before meeting the Indian Ocean Whitesands. Many tributaries join th Breede, and by the time it reaches Roberts it has been transformed from a rushi mountain stream to a substantial river.

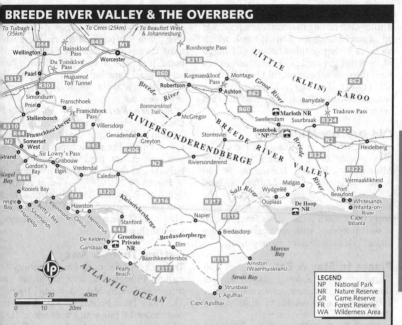

BREEDE RIVER VALLEY & THE OVERBERG

LEGEND
NP   National Park
NR   Nature Reserve
GR   Game Reserve
FR   Forest Reserve
WA   Wilderness Area

WESTERN CAPE

Many travellers are likely to come through the region because it is bisected by the N2 between Cape Town and the north-east. Since the opening of the 4km Huguenot Toll Tunnel east of Paarl, towns like Robertson and Montagu are more quickly accessible from Cape Town (around a two-hour drive), though using the tunnel means missing the wonderful views from the Du Toitskloof Pass.

TULBAGH

☎ 023 • postcode 6820 • pop 31,000

Overshadowed by the dramatic Witsenberg range, Tulbagh is one of the most complete examples of an 18th- and 19th-century Cape Dutch village in South Africa. Many of the buildings were substantially rebuilt after an earthquake in 1969, but it doesn't feel in the least bit fake because of the painstaking restoration.

Although most of Tulbagh's surviving buildings date from the first half of the 19th century, the Tulbagh Valley was first settled in 1699. The village began to take shape after the construction of a church in 1743. It was here, on the outer rim of the settled European areas, that early Boer families would bring their children out of the wilderness to be baptised.

There are several wineries to visit in the area, plus hiking opportunities in the mountains.

Orientation & Information

Church St, the famous street in which every building has been declared a national monument, runs parallel to the town's main thoroughfare, Van der Stel St.

A visitor's first port of call should probably be the **tourist information centre** (*☎ 230 1348, W www.tulbagh.com, 14 Church St*).

Oude Kerk Volksmuseum

The Old Church Folk Museum (*☎ 230 1041, Church St; adult/child R5/2; open 9am-5pm*

Mon-Fri, 9am-4pm Sat, 11am-4pm Sun) is a mildly interesting museum complex made up of three buildings. Start at No 4, which includes a photographic history of Church St, covering the earthquake and reconstruction; then visit the beautiful Oude Kerk itself (1743); then at No 22, you'll find a reconstructed town dwelling from the 18th century.

Old Drostdy Museum
A sweet surprise is available in the atmospheric wine cellar of the Old Drostdy Museum *(☎ 230 0203, Van der Stel St; admission free; open 10am-12.30pm & 2pm-4.50pm Mon-Sat, 2.30pm-4.50pm Sun)*. The former official government residence, 3km north of the town centre, dates from 1806. It is well furnished with appropriate antiques and an odd collection of gramophones.

Places to Stay & Eat
There are more accommodation options than those listed here, particularly some cottages on farms outside town; inquire at the tourist information centre.

Kliprivier Park Resort (☎/fax 230 0506, Van der Stel St) Camp sites from R70, chalet doubles from R180. This is quite a pleasant resort on the edge of town, 1km north of the centre, offering reasonable chalets and caravan sites.

Oude Kerk Kombuis (☎ 230 0428, 14 Church St) Singles/doubles B&B R100/200 with shared bathroom. The best-value option along Church St has only a couple of pleasant rooms so it's best to book ahead.

The Wagon Shed (☎ 230 0107, 16 Church St) Singles/doubles B&B R150/270. There's a plunge pool and an interesting gallery attached to this guesthouse, which has a more contemporary style than some of the other twee Cape Dutch homes.

De Oude Herberg (☎/fax 230 0260, 6 Church St) Singles/doubles B&B R200/350. A guesthouse since 1885 (although not continuously), this is a very friendly and pleasant place. It has a plunge pool and its restaurant, open from 9am to 3.30pm and 7.30pm to 10.30pm, is open to nonguests; booking ahead for dinner is essential.

Paddagang Restaurant (☎ 230 0242, 2 Church St) Mains R50. Open 7.45am-5p daily, 7pm-9.15pm Wed & Fri. The town most famous restaurant, in a beautiful o homestead with a vine-shaded courtyar serves snacks and light meals. A full brea fast is R29; at night one of their big stea is the best bet.

Reader's Restaurant (☎ 230 0087, Church St) Mains R35-40. Open 12.30pm 2.30pm & 7pm-10pm Wed-Mon. This is good choice. The menu changes daily, b you can expect food as varied as be teriyaki and the Cape Malay dish, boboti

Forties (☎ 230 0567, 40 Church St) Ope 7pm-late Wed-Sun. The bar at this live pub retains authentic earthquake damag They might have a braai going on the stoc some nights.

Getting There & Away
Train One of the most interesting ways visiting Tulbagh is to take one of the tra trips organised by Mike & Rachel Barry The Duck Pond holiday chalets. A day tr costs around R150, with a train ride as far Wolseley. See Train under Organised Tours the South Africa Getting Around chapter f more details.

Minibus Taxi Most taxis leave from th 'location', on the hill just outside town b you might find one at Tulbagh Toyota (th Shell petrol station) on the main street.

Car & Motorcycle Keep going along V der Stel St past the Old Drostdy Museum a you'll come to a dead end at the head of t valley (overlooked by the rugged mountai of the Groot Winterhoek Wilderness Are To get back to the R44 (running betwe Ceres and Piketberg, which is on the N7) in the opposite direction down Van der S St. Halfway up the hill leading away from t town, turn right. There's a small, faded si to Kaapstad (Cape Town) and Gouda.

CERES
☎ 023 • postcode 6835 • pop 52,000
Sometimes referred to as the Switzerland South Africa, Ceres has a superb location

he western side of a green and fertile bowl that is ringed by the rugged Skurweberg Range. The passes into the valley are particularly spectacular, but as attractive as the town is there's not a huge amount to linger here for.

Ceres is the most important deciduous fruit- and juice-producing district in South Africa, and seems remarkably prosperous in comparison with many regional towns. The surrounding countryside is densely populated and intensively farmed. The Ceres fruit juice that's been saving you from a diet of sugary drinks all over South Africa is packed here.

The valley has a very high rainfall, mostly between June and September, and four well-defined seasons. It can get very cold in winter, with temperatures dropping below zero (snow on the mountains) and hot in summer (36°C). It is most beautiful in spring and particularly in autumn, when the fruit trees change colour.

Orientation & Information

Coming off Mitchell's Pass (see Around Ceres later) you'll enter the town along the central Voortrekker St. The friendly **tourism bureau** (☎ 316 1051, W www.ceres.org.za/ourism, Cnr Owen & Voortrekker Sts; open Mon-Fri 8am-5pm, Sat 9am-noon) is in the library. It has information on accommodation, tours and activities in the area.

Things to See & Do

Ceres was once a famous centre for making horse-drawn vehicles. Consequently, the **Togryers' Museum** (Transport Riders' Museum; ☎ 312 2045 8 Oranje St; adult/child R3/1; open 9am-1pm Mon-Fri, 9am-noon Sat) has an interesting collection of buggies, wagons and carriages. Oranje St is one street north of and parallel to Voortrekker St.

The **Ceres Fruit Juice Factory** (☎ 316 9100; admission free; open Thur only) and the **Ceres Fruit Growers' Factory** (☎ 316 9400; admission free; open Tues & Thur only) both offer tours. Bookings are essential.

There are several private wildlife and nature reserves within a day's drive of Ceres, including **Klein Cedarberg** (☎/fax 317 0784, e kcedar@informage.co.za), **Inverdoorn**

(☎ 316 1264, fax 312 2187, W www.inverdoorn.com) and **Sadawa** (☎ 312 2512, fax 312 2483, e sadawa@iafrica.com). Day visits are possible but must be booked ahead. For full board and activities at these reserves you're looking at around R500 to R700 per person.

Places to Stay & Eat

The tourism bureau will help you find B&Bs and self-catering cottages, starting at R120 per person.

Pine Forest Resort (☎ 316 1878, fax 312 2070, Carson St) Caravan sites from R50, chalets from R110. Pine Forest Resort is about 1km from the town centre and is signposted from Voortrekker St. The facilities here are good but camping in tents is not allowed; rates rise at the weekend and from September to April.

Die Herberg Guesthouse (☎/fax 312 2325, 125 Voortrekker St) Singles/doubles B&B with shared bathroom from R100/200. More expensive rooms with en suite facilities are available at this reasonably comfortable, slightly old-fashioned place. They also have a cafe serving sandwiches and budget meals.

Belmont Hotel (☎/fax 312 1150, e belmont@intekom.co.za, Porter St) Bungalows from R155/290, doubles from R250/400. This large, old-fashioned hotel offers various standards of accommodation, and a range of dining options, including a pizzeria. The Saturday lunch buffet (R65, 1pm to 3pm) is very popular.

Getting There & Around

Kruger bus service (☎ 316 5901) runs basic daily buses to Cape Town; call for departure times and fares.

Long-distance minibus taxis leave from opposite the John Steyne library. **Peres & Sons** (☎ 316 5730) runs one of the services.

To get around the area contact **Nico Dempers** (☎ 12 1209), a registered guide who can organise transport and tours.

AROUND CERES
Middelburg & Gydo Passes

The Middelburg and Gydo Passes should not be missed if you're in the vicinity of Ceres.

Coming from Citrusdal you almost immediately hit a very bumpy dirt road that takes you up into the Cederberg. Middelburg is an impressive pass but the really good views are on the Ceres side when you come out into a narrow valley completely walled by raw, rock hills with rich mineral colouring.

In stark contrast to the hills, the floor of the valley is irrigated, so it is usually emerald green, and there is a patchwork of orchards. The reds, ochres and purples of the rocky mountains, the blue of the sky, the blossom of the orchards, fresh green pastures, wildflowers, dams and wading birds combine to create a beautiful sight.

About 20km from Ceres you hit a sealed road. Coming south you feel as if you've lost altitude, so when you come out on the 1000m Gydo Pass overlooking the Ceres Valley, the world seems to drop away at your feet.

Mitchell's Pass

The Breede River, forcing its way between the mountains surrounding Ceres, provided the key to the development of the valley. Originally, the settlers dismantled their wagons and carried them over the mountain, but in 1765 a local farmer built a track along the river.

In 1846 the remarkable Andrew Bain began construction of a proper road. It was completed in 1848 and became the main route onto the South African plateau to the north, remaining so until the Hex River Pass was opened in 1875. Mitchell's Pass cut the travel time to Beaufort West from three weeks to one week. The pass has recently been rebuilt to highway standards, but you can still enjoy the views and appreciate what a remarkable engineer Bain was.

On the Ceres side of the pass is *The Toll House* (☎ *316 1571*), where tolls were once collected; it's now a coffee shop and restaurant open daily, with braais every second Saturday.

WORCESTER

☎ 023 • postcode 6850 • pop 134,000

A service centre for the rich farmland of the Breede River Valley, Worcester is a large and fairly nondescript place that needn't detain you longer than it takes to visit its farm museum and botanic gardens.

Most of the town lies to the south of the N1. There are some impressive old buildings near and around the edge of Church Square (off High St). The **tourism bureau** (☎ *348 2795, 23 Baring St; open 8am-4.30pm Mon-Fri, 8.30am-12.30pm Sat*) is on the east side of Church Square.

Kleinplasie Farm Museum

This excellent farm museum (☎ *342 2225 adult/child R12/5; open 9am-4.30pm Mon-Sat, 10.30am-4.30pm Sun*) is 1km from the town centre on the road to Robertson. It's one of the best in South Africa. It takes you from a Trekboers' hut, to a complete, functioning 18th-century farm complex.

It's a 'live' museum, meaning there are people wandering around in period clothes and rolling tobacco, making soap, operating a smithy, milling wheat, spinning wool and so on. It's best to visit in the morning when you can see activities like bread-baking. The place is fascinating and can easily absorb a couple of hours. A miniature train runs around the complex, leaving hourly.

At the museum shop you can sample and buy various flavours of the 60-proof *witblits* (white lightning), a traditional Boer spirit distilled from fruit. To get the full taste, first inhale then sip and roll the liquor around your mouth before swallowing and exhaling. Next door is the Kleinplasse Winery where you can sample less potent libations.

Beck House

Just off the town square, next to the tourism bureau, Beck House (☎ *342 2225, Baring St; adult/child R1/0.50; open 8am-4.30pm Mon-Fri*) is a charming 1841 house furnished in late Victorian style. The outbuildings, including a stable, a bath house and a herb garden, are particularly interesting.

Karoo National Botanic Garden

This is an outstanding garden (☎ *347 0785 adult/child R9/5; open 8am-4pm daily*). The botanic garden includes 140 hectares of semidesert vegetation – with Karoo and fynbos elements – and 10 hectares of landscaped arden, where many of the plants have been abelled. If your interest has been piqued, his is an ideal opportunity to identify some f the extraordinary indigenous plants. The ardens are about 1km north of the N1 and .5km from the centre of town.

There is something to see at any time of he year; bulb plants flower in autumn, the loes flower in winter and the annuals lower in spring. There's also a collection of veird stone plants and other succulents.

KWV Cellar

'his cellar and brandy distillery (☎ 342 '255, Cnr Church & Smith Sts; tours R13; pen 8am-4.30pm Mon-Fri) isn't as famous s the one in Paarl, but it is the largest of its ind in the world under one roof. Hour-long ours in English are held at 2pm.

Places to Stay & Eat

Burger Caravan Park (☎ 348 2765, fax 47 3671, De la Bat Rd) Camp sites R45. 'his pretty ordinary place is close to the N1 nd next to the town's swimming pool.

Wykeham Lodge B&B (☎ 347 3467, fax 47 6776, e wykehamlodge@telkomsa.net, 68 Church St) Singles/doubles B&B R190/ 00. This fine guesthouse is in a thatched-oof building dating from 1835. Rooms with vooden beams and floors face on to a quiet ourtyard and there's also a large garden.

Kleinplasie Country Chalets (☎ 347 '091) Doubles R200. These four-person halets are convenient for the Kleinplasie 'arm Museum, which is next door.

Nekkies (☎ 343 2909, fax 343 2911, 4.5km rom Worcester at the Brandvlei Dam) Chalets from R235. These are smart wooden halets with good facilities, overlooking the am. Bikes are available for hire.

Kleinplasie Restaurant (☎ 347 5118) Mains R35. Open 9am-4.30pm Mon-Sat, 0.30am-4.30pm Sun. Also next to the Kleinplasie Farm Museum, this place offers raditional Cape Malay/Afrikaner dishes uch as bobotie and chicken pie; outdoor eating is available.

St Gerans (☎ 342 2800, 48 Church St) Mains around R35. Open noon-3pm & pm-10pm Mon-Sat. This popular steak house in the town centre also does some seafood and chicken dishes.

Getting There & Away

Bus All Translux, Greyhound and Intercape buses stop at the Shell Ultracity petrol station. Worcester is on several of their routes, the cheapest fare from Cape Town being Translux at R95.

Train The daily Trans Karoo between Cape Town and Jo'burg stops in Worcester; the Southern Cross between Cape Town and Oudtshoorn stops at Worcester on Friday evening when heading east, early Monday morning when heading west. The extremely circuitous Trans Oranje to Durban also stops there. For bookings, call (☎ 348 2203).

Minibus Taxi There are several rival long-distance taxi companies in town and they use different stops. One company, **WUTA Taxis**, stops near the corner of Tulbagh and Barry Sts, near the entrance to the train station. A daily taxi to the Belleville area of Cape Town (R30) leaves sometime after 6am and there are less regular but probably daily taxis to Robertson (R15) and to Ashton (R18), the town at the bottom of the pass that runs up to Montagu. Other places to find taxis are near the corner of Grey and Durban Sts.

ROBERTSON

☎ 023 • postcode 6705 • pop 35,000

At the centre for one of the largest wine-growing areas in the country, and also famous for its horse studs, Robertson is clearly a prosperous town. It's a pretty dull one too, and there's little reason to overnight here with McGregor and Montagu both a short drive away.

The helpful **tourism bureau** (☎ 626 4437, w www.robertson.org.za, Cnr Piet Retief & Swellendam Sts; open 9am-1pm & 2pm-5pm Mon-Fri) is opposite the Dutch Reformed church.

The **museum** (☎ 626 3681, 50 Paul Kruger St; admission free; open 9am-noon Mon-Sat), a few blocks north-east of the church, has a notable collection of lace. Tea is occasionally served in the garden.

WESTERN CAPE

If you're up here to explore the countryside, it's worth inquiring with the tourism bureau about the Dassieshoek and Avangieskop two-day **hiking trails** that take you into the mountains above Robertson.

See Robertson in the special section 'Cape Wineries' for details on some **wineries** in the area.

Places to Stay & Eat

The information centre can tell you about B&Bs and self-catering farm cottages starting at around R70 per person.

Silwerstrand Resort (☎ 626 3321, fax 626 3259, 3km from Worcester off R60) Camp sites from R45, rondavels from R60. This large complex on the banks of the Breede River isn't convenient unless you have transport. It gets pretty hectic during high season when prices increase.

Grand Hotel (☎ 626 3272, fax 626 1158, 68 Barry St) Singles/doubles B&B R195/310. The rooms, a couple with balconies, are of better quality than the foyer would suggest. It also runs the adjacent *Travel Lodge* which has singles/doubles for R130/240 including breakfast. Guests are free to use the Grand Hotel's facilities, including the reasonably priced *Simone's Grill Room & Restaurant* and pool.

Amathunzi (☎ 626 1802, fax 626 1974, W www.amathunzi.co.za) Full board R720. Roughly 26km southwest of Robertson, and well off the beaten track, you'll find this 3500 hectare game lodge with upmarket accommodation for 10 guests in thatched-roof cottages. Given that the price includes all meals, a game drive and a guided walk it's good value. Expect to see antelopes, zebras, wildebeests and, if you're very lucky, mountain leopards.

Branewynsdraai (☎ 626 3202, 1 Kromhout St) Mains R50. Open noon-3pm & 6pm-9pm Mon-Sat. Near the Shell petrol station on Voortrekker St, this pleasant restaurant specialises in local dishes and wines.

Getting There & Away

Bus Translux Mountain Route buses to Port Elizabeth (via Oudtshoorn and Knysna) stop at the train station. Fares from Robertson include: Oudtshoorn (R115), Knysna (R145) Cape Town (R95) and Port Elizabeth (R170)

Train The weekly *Southern Cross* between Cape Town and Oudtshoorn stops here.

Minibus Taxi Taxis running between Cape Town (R40) and Oudtshoorn (R110) stop at the Shell petrol station on the corner of Voortrekker and John Sts. These taxis also run through Montagu (R20). A taxi to McGregor costs R7 but is infrequent.

McGREGOR
☎ 023 • postcode 6780

The tranquil village of McGregor feels like it belongs to another century – the mid-19th century to be precise, from when most of the buildings along its one major thoroughfare Voortrekker St, date. The thatched-roof cottages, many turned into B&Bs and self catering units, are surrounded by orchards vegetable gardens and vineyards; there are some 30 wineries within half an hour's drive. Unsurprisingly, McGregor has become a place of retreat, and, with the magnificent Riviersonderend Mountains on its doorstep, base for hiking. It is one end of the highly recommended Boesmanskloof Trail to Greyton (see Boesmanskloof Trail later).

The **tourism bureau** (☎ 625 1954; open 9am-5pm Mon-Fri, 10am-1pm Sat) is about halfway along Voortrekker St (there are no street numbers). **Villagers Coffee Shop** *(Voortrekker St)* rents bicycles for R15 per hour or R45 per day.

Vrolijkheid Nature Reserve (see Boesmanskloof Trail following for contact details), between Robertson and McGregor has an 18km circular walking trail and bird hides with about 150 species to see. At the south end of Voortrekker St you'll also find the **Krans Nature Reserve** with more walks the tourism bureau can provide details.

Boesmanskloof Trail

The best reason for coming to McGregor is to hike the Boesmanskloof Trail to Greyton, roughly 14km through the spectacular fynbos-clad Riviersonderend Mountains. The trail actually starts at Die Galg, about

15km south of McGregor; you'll need your own transport to get here or can arrange with the folks at Whipstock Farm (see previous) for a transfer. The car park at Die Galg is safe enough to leave your car and there's basic dorm accommodation at the trail head; contact the Vrolijkheid Nature Reserve (see following) for details.

If you don't fancy the full hike, it's quite possible to do a six-hour round trip to the lovely Oak Falls, roughly 6km from Die Galg, where you can cool off with a swim in the tannin-stained waters. To hike the whole trail takes four to six hours, making an overnight stay in Greyton the preferred option; many people then hike back to Die Galg. It's slightly easier walking from McGregor to Greyton than in the opposite direction, and you'll notice that the start of the trail marks the end of a long-abandoned project to construct a pass across the range.

Permits cost R13, plus R20 for each day of walking, and are issued by the **Vrolijkheid Nature Reserve** (☎ *625 1621, fax 625 1674, Private Bag X614, Robertson*). It's best to book in advance, especially for the weekends and during the holidays, since only 50 people a day are allowed on the trail. The office is on the road from Robertson to McGregor. Alternatively, permits are also available from **Greyton Municipal Offices** (☎ *028-254 9620*).

Places to Stay & Eat

The tourism bureau has a full list of the accommodation around the village (including B&Bs from R100 per person per night) but doesn't take bookings.

McGregor Camp Ground (☎ *625 1754, Church St*) is not a camp site but a dorm building that you can hire out for a minimum of R240 – which might work out if there's a crowd of you.

Temenos Country Retreat (☎ *625 1871,* e *temenos@lando.co.za, Bree St*) Singles/doubles R180/250. These unique cottages set in spacious gardens are open to all (except children under 12), not just those on retreat. It's a peaceful place, with a decent lap pool, nooks for contemplation and a coffee shop.

McGregor B&B (☎/*fax 625 1656, Voortrekker St*) Doubles B&B from R250. There's one slightly more expensive self-catering unit at this pleasant B&B with large gardens, a small pool and tiny 'Irish' pub.

Old Mill Lodge (☎ *625 1841, fax 625 1941,* W *www.mcgregor.org.za, Smit St*) Singles/doubles DB&B from R285/470. A clutch of modern cottages, tastefully decorated, surround the old mill and its outhouses at the south end of the village. It's in a beautiful spot, and if you feel active there's a swimming pool and nearby fishing. This is the only place in McGregor open to nonguests for dinner (R77 for three courses) so it's fortunate that the food is excellent.

McGregor Country Cottages (☎ *625 1816, fax 625 1840,* e *mcgregorcottages@ mcgregor.org.au, Voortrekker St*) Double cottages from R250. This complex of seven pretty cottages is beside an apricot orchard at the north end of the village. The cottages, three of which are wheelchair accessible, are fully equipped and great value.

Whipstock Farm (☎/*fax 625 1733,* e *whip stock@netactive.co.za*) Singles/doubles DB&B R170/340. Serenely located and tastefully decorated accommodation is available here in a variety of buildings, some historic. There is also fine food and friendly hosts who'll organise transfers to and from the Boesmanskloof Trail. Whipstock is 7km from McGregor on a dirt road towards the mountains.

Villagers Coffee Shop (☎ *625 1915, Voortrekker St*) Mains R20. Open 9.30am-5pm Mon-Fri, 9.30am-1pm Sat. This is a convivial country store that offers light meals and a refreshing range of home-made fruit juices.

GREYTON

☎ 028 • postcode 7233

Although officially part of the Overberg region, we've included Greyton and the neighbouring village of Genadendal here because of their link to McGregor along the Boesmanskloof Trail.

Much more twee and polished than McGregor, even locals admit that the white-washed, thatched-roof cottages of Greyton are a bit artificial. As pleasant as the village is, it needs to be seen in conjunction with the old Moravian Mission of Genadendal, with its well-preserved historic buildings that couldn't be more authentic.

Greyton comes into its own is as a base for **hiking** in the Riviersonderend Mountains which rise up in Gothic majesty immediately to the village's north. Apart from the Boesmanskloof Trail there are several shorter walks, as well as the two-day **Genadendal Trail** for the serious hiker. This is a 25.3km circular route that begins and ends at Genadendal's Moravian Church; for more details pick up the Cape Nature Conservation leaflet.

The **tourist information office** (☎ *254 9414; open 10am-noon & 2.30pm-4.30pm Mon-Sat)* is on the village's main road.

Genadendal Mission Station

Some 3km west of Greyton is Genadendal, the oldest mission station in South Africa, founded in 1738 and for a brief time the largest settlement in the colony after Cape Town. Entering the village from the R406, head down Main Rd until you arrive at the cluster of national monuments around Church Square.

The Moravian Church is a handsome, simply decorated building; opposite you'll find the **tourist information centre** (☎ *251 8291; open 8.30am-5pm Mon-Fri, 10am-1pm Sat).* There's a cafe here selling home-made bread and souvenirs including pottery.

The village's fascinating history is documented in the excellent **Mission Museum** (☎ *251 8582; adult/child R7/2; open 9am-1pm & 2pm-5pm Mon-Thur, 9am-3.30pm Fri, 9am-1pm Sat),* which is based in what was South Africa's first teacher training college. Elsewhere in this historic precinct is one of the oldest printing presses in the country, still in operation, and a water mill.

Places to Stay & Eat

For its size, Greyton has a wide range of accommodation and places to eat.

Toad Hall (☎ *083-425 2472, Main Rd)* Singles/doubles R90/180. Greyton's cheapest option has large rooms, named after

characters from *The Wind in the Willows* with attached bathrooms.

High Hopes B&B (☎/fax 254 9898, 8? Main Rd) Doubles B&B from R330. This is not the cheapest place to stay but it's certainly one of the nicest. It has tastefully furnished rooms, lovely gardens and a well stocked library. Singles are negotiable and afternoon tea is thrown in for all guests Convenient for hikers, it's the closest B&F to the start of the Boesmanskloof Trail.

Guinea Fowl (☎ 254 9550, fax 254 9653 **W** longreyton.co.za, Cnr DS Botha & Oa? Sts) Singles/doubles B&B R165/330. Com fortable and quiet, this guesthouse has ? pool for summer, log fire for winter and good breakfasts year-round.

Posthaus Guesthouse (☎ 254 9995, fa 254 9920, Main Rd) Doubles B&B from R400. Based around a pretty garden, the gimmick here is to name the rooms afte Beatrix Potter characters (we told you Greyton was a twee place). Their English style pub *The Ball & Bass* is a cosy plac? for a drink or meal.

Greyton Lodge (☎ 254 9876, fax 25? 9672, **e** greytonlodge@kingsley.co.za, 4 Main Rd) Singles/doubles B&B R315/550 A pair of stocks and rampant lion statue flank the entrance to this upmarket hotel i the old police station. There's a pool and ? reasonably priced but unadventurous *bistr?* which is open from 7pm to 9pm daily.

The Oak & Vigne Cafe (☎ 254 9037, D Botha St) Mains R20. Open 8am-6pm Mon Sat, 8am-5pm Sun. Evidence of the creepin? 'yuppification' of Greyton is this trendy deli art gallery-cafe, which is a fine place to gra? a snack, chill out and watch the world go by

Rosie's Restaurant (☎ 254 9640, 2 Hig? St) Mains R35. Open 6.30pm-late Tues Sun. The house specialities are wood-fired oven pizzas (which are delicious and huge and steaks.

Getting There & Away

If you're not hiking in from McGregor, th only way to Greyton is by your own trans port. From Cape Town follow the N2 to jus before Caledon and then take the R406 From Robertson take the R317 south to th

N2 at Stormsvlei then head west to Riviersonderend to connect with the R406.

The Overberg

The Overberg, which literally means 'Over the Mountains', is the region south and west of the Franschhoek Range, and south of the Wemmershoek and Riviersonderend Ranges, which form a natural barrier with the Breede River Valley.

Coming from Cape Town, the R44 from Strand, towards Hermanus around Cape Hangklip, is a thrilling coastal drive, in the same class as the now curtailed Chapman's Peak Dr. The first major stop is Hermanus, a popular seaside resort. In spring, it's famous for the whales that frequent its shores (although it's so famous now that you might choose to do your whale-watching at a less crowded location along the coast).

If you're looking for somewhere quiet to hang out both the miraculously undeveloped fishing village of Arniston and the De Hoop Nature Reserve will fit the bill. The best all-round base for the area is Swellendam, a historic and attractive town beneath the impressive Langeberg Mountains.

This region's wealth of fynbos is unmatched; most species flower somewhere in the period between autumn and spring. The climate basically follows the same pattern as Cape Town – a temperate Mediterranean climate with relatively mild winters and warm summers. Rain falls throughout the year but peaks in August, and it can be very windy any time.

KOGEL BAY

The best bit of the drive along the R44 from Cape Town is between Gordon's Bay and Kleinmond. There's not much reason to stop – other than to admire the views – but the small, isolated beach at Kogel Bay is appealing (despite being exposed to south-westerly winds and being unsafe for swimming) and it does have a place to stay.

Kogel Bay Pleasure Resort (☎ 024-856 1286, fax 856 4741) Camping R45. Don't be misled by the grand name; this is a basic camping ground, but in a fine position and with reasonable facilities. Bring all your own food.

BETTY'S BAY

The next place worth a pause is Betty's Bay, a small, scattered holiday village just to the east of Cape Hangklip. Here you'll find the **Harold Porter National Botanical Gardens** *(☎ 028-272 9311; adult/child R5/free; open 8am-4.30pm Mon-Fri, 8am-5pm Sat & Sun)*, which protect some of the surrounding fynbos, and are definitely worth visiting. There are paths exploring the area and, at the entrance, tearooms and a formal garden where you can picnic. A colony of African penguins can also be found at Stony Point.

KLEINMOND

Although it is not a particularly attractive town, Kleinmond is close to a wild and beautiful beach, has good walking and reliable swells for surfers. If you choose to linger, there are a few places to stay.

Palmiet Caravan Park (☎ 028-271 4050) Camping R34.50/60.75 low/high season. Beside the beach on the western side of town, Palmiet is the most attractive camping option.

Roots Rock Backpackers (☎/fax 028-271 5139, e kaybee90@hotmail.com, Harbour Rd) Dorm beds R45, doubles R140. This small, rustic place facing the sea is close to a cluster of shops and cafes.

The Beach House (☎ 028-271 3130, fax 271 4022, w www.relais.co.za, Sandown Bay) Singles/doubles B&B from R415/640. This is an upmarket choice, overlooking the town's best beach, and has prettily decorated rooms in pastel shades.

HERMANUS

☎ 028 • postcode 7200 • pop 31,000
Within day-tripping distance of Cape Town (122km), Hermanus was originally a fishing village and still retains vestiges of its heritage, including a small museum at the old harbour. It's best known now as a place to view whales (see the boxed text 'Watching the Whales' later in this chapter).

WESTERN CAPE

There are some great beaches, most west of the town centre. Rocky hills, vaguely reminiscent of Scotland, surround the town, and there are good walks and a nature reserve, protecting some of the prolific fynbos. The pleasant town centre, easily negotiated on foot and east of the new harbour, is well endowed with restaurants and shops.

Be warned: Hermanus is packed during the school holidays in December and January.

Information

Hermanus Tourism (☎ *312 2629*, **W** *www .hermanus.co.za, Old Station Bldg, Mitchell St; open 9am-5pm Mon-Sat)* is helpful. This place has a large supply of information about the area including walks and drives in the surrounding hills; staff can also arrange short tours of the local Zwelihle township.

There's a small market daily at Lemms Corner, in the Market Square off Main Rd; on Saturday there's a craft market held there, too.

Hermanus Internet & Information Café *(Waterkant Bldg, Main Rd; R10 for 15 minutes)* offers reliable and speedy Internet connections.

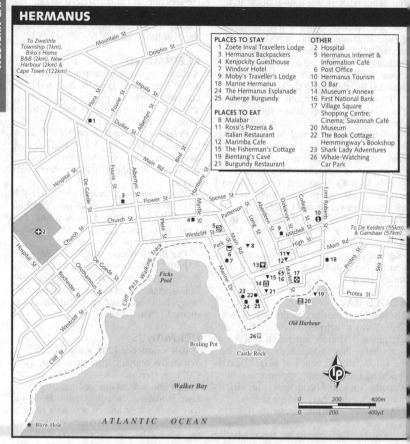

HERMANUS

PLACES TO STAY
1 Zoete Inval Travellers Lodge
3 Hermanus Backpackers
4 Kenjockity Guesthouse
7 Windsor Hotel
9 Moby's Traveller's Lodge
18 Marine Hermanus
24 The Hermanus Esplanade
25 Auberge Burgundy

PLACES TO EAT
8 Malabar
11 Rossi's Pizzeria & Italian Restaurant
12 Marimba Cafe
15 The Fisherman's Cottage
19 Bientang's Cave
21 Burgundy Restaurant

OTHER
2 Hospital
5 Hermanus Internet & Information Café
6 Post Office
10 Hermanus Tourism
13 O Bar
14 Museum's Annexe
16 First National Bank
17 Village Square Shopping Centre; Cinema; Savannah Café
20 Museum
22 The Book Cottage; Hemmingway's Bookshop
23 Shark Lady Adventures
26 Whale-Watching Car Park

To Zwelihle Township (1km), Biko's Home B&B (2km), New Harbour (2km) & Cape Town (122km)

Mountain St
Dolphin St
Impala St
Flora St
Fourie St
Alberyn St
Dulker St
Main Rd
Hospital St
De Goede
Fourie St
Alberyn St
Flower St
Spence St
Patterson St
Church St
Plein St
Westcliff St
Myrtle St
Park St
Main Rd
High St
Aberdeen St
Long St
Drickeuys St
College St
Mitchell St
Lord Roberts St
Marine Dr
Market St
Protea St
Sea St
Protea St

To De Kelders (55km), & Gansbaai (57km)

Hospital St
Church St
De Goede St
Orothamnus St
Rochester St
Westcliff St
Cliff St
Cliff Path Walking Track

Ficks Pool

Old Harbour

Boiling Pot
Castle Rock

Walker Bay

ATLANTIC OCEAN

Blow Hole

0   200   400m
0   200   400yd

Watching the Whales

Between June and November, southern right whales *(Eubalaena australis)* come to Walker Bay to calve. There can be up to 70 whales in the bay at once. South Africa was a whaling nation until 1976 – this species was hunted to the verge of extinction but its numbers are now recovering. Humpback whales *(Megaptera novaeangliae)* are also sometimes seen.

Whales often come very close to shore and there are some excellent vantage points from the cliff paths that run from one end of Hermanus to the other. The best places are Castle Rock, Kraal Rock and Sievers Point. There's a telescope on the cliff top above the old harbour.

It's only recently that the people of Hermanus bothered to tell the outside world that the whales were regular visitors. They took them for granted. Now, however, the tourism potential has been recognised and just about every business in town has adopted a whale logo. There's a whale-spotters hotline (☎ 0800 22 8222) and a whale crier, who walks around town blowing on a kelp horn and carrying a blackboard that shows where whales have been recently sighted. A Whale Festival is held in late September or early October.

Despite all this hoopla, boat-viewing of whales is strictly regulated. No boat-viewing is allowed in the bay and jet skis are banned. There are only two boat-viewing operators licensed to operate in the seas outside the bay: **Southern Right Charters** (☎ 082-353 0550) and **Hawston Fishers** (☎ 082-396 8931). They charge around R250 for a one- to two-hour trip.

Although Hermanus is the best-known whale-watching site, whales can be seen all the way from False Bay (Cape Town) to Plettenberg Bay and beyond. The west coast also gets its share. Check out **W** www.cape-whaleroute .co.za for more information.

The Book Cottage (☎ 313 0834, 10 Harbour Rd) sells travel guides and other new books. Hemmingway's Bookshop (☎ 312 2739, 4 Main Rd) has an extensive collection of second-hand volumes.

Old Harbour

The old harbour clings to the cliffs in front of the town centre; here you'll find a small and generally uninteresting **museum** (☎ 312 1475; adult/child R2/1; open 9am-1pm & 2pm-5pm Mon-Sat, noon-4pm Sun) and a display of old fishing boats. The museum's annexe, in the old schoolhouse on the market square, displays some evocative old photographs of the town and its fishermen.

Shark-Diving

Although all the boats depart from Gansbaai (see Around Hermanus later in this section), some 35km along the coast, cage diving to view great white sharks is heavily promoted

in Hermanus (especially at backpacker hostels), and several operators are based here. There's no doubting the activity's popularity, but it doesn't come without controversy. Operators use bait to attract the sharks to the cage, which means that these killer fish are being trained to associate humans with food. It's not a pleasant scenario, especially if you're a surfer, several of whom have been attacked by sharks in the past.

With most of the operators you must have an internationally recognised diving qualification to take part, although some allow snorkellers into the cage. One experienced operator worth contacting is **Brian McFarlane** (☎ 312 2766, **W** www.hermanusinfo.co .za/greatwhite; 6-hr trips around R600). Another good choice is **Shark Lady Adventures** (☎/fax 313 1415, **W** www.shark lady.net, 61 Marine Dr, trips around R700). The shark lady herself, Kim Maclean, has been running trips for 10 years.

Places to Stay
There's been an explosion of places to stay in Hermanus over the last few years, but in the holiday season the town can still be busting at the seams, so take care to book ahead. Hermanus Tourism will help you and there are agencies such as **Whale Route Accommodation** (☎ 316 1682) and the **Hermanus Accommodation Centre** (☎ 313 0004), which let houses and book other accommodation.

Hostels Budget travellers have a good selection of hostels in town.

Zoete Inval Travellers Lodge (☎/fax 312 1242, e zoetein@hermanus.co.za, 23 Main Rd) Dorm beds R45, singles/doubles R120/150. More a guesthouse than a backpacker hostel, this is one of the friendliest places we've come across, with good amenities and nicely furnished rooms.

Hermanus Backpackers (☎ 312 4293, fax 313 2727, e moobag@mweb.co.za, 26 Flower St) Dorm beds B&B R50, singles/doubles B&B R85/140. This is a smashing place with clued-up staff, great decor and facilities, including a bar and small pool.

Moby's Traveller's Lodge (☎ 313 2361, fax 312 3519, e moby@hermanus.co.za) Dorm beds B&B R50, singles/doubles B&B 125/150. We visited the day Moby's had moved into new premises, but this converted hotel, with a pool, bar and central location, looks like it might shape up to be a popular place.

Shark Lady Adventures (see Shark-Diving earlier for contact details) R100 per person. Though not exactly a hostel, good shared accommodation is offered here.

B&Bs, Guesthouses & Self-Catering
Kenjockity Guesthouse (☎/fax 312 1772, e kenjock@hermanus.co.za, 15 Church St) Singles/doubles with shared bathroom R125/ 250. This guesthouse, the first in Hermanus, has a nice atmosphere and fair-sized rooms. More expensive rooms with en-suite bathrooms are available. You'll pay more in December, but discounts are sometimes available at other times.

Biko's Home B&B (☎ 312 2776, e princessbiko@wam.co.za, 106 Zwelihle) Singles/ doubles B&B R100/200. Run by Princess Biko, this cosy B&B will give you an in sight into township life and hospitality Princess only has two rooms but will make you feel at home and will cook dinner for an extra R50.

Hermanus Esplanade (☎ 312 3610, fax 313 1125, e clarkbro@hermanus.co.za, 6 Marine Dr) Apartments from R250. Some of these standard self-catering apartment overlook the sea; their lowest rates actually cover the whale-watching season from May to October.

Auberge Burgundy (☎ 313 1202, fax 31 1204, e auberge@hermanus.co.za, 16 Harbour Rd) Doubles B&B from R640. This is a wonderful place, built in the style of Provençal villa, with fine facilities and personal touch. If there are six of you, consider splashing out on the penthouse (R1450). The owners also run the excellent *Burgundy Restaurant*, which is located across the road.

Hotels There are a couple of good choices of hotels in Hermanus.

Windsor Hotel (☎ 312 3727, fax 312 218 w www.windsor-hotel.com, 49 Marine Dr Singles/doubles B&B from R250/350 low season, R350/450 high season. Naturally you'll want one of the more expensive sea facing rooms at this characterful old hotel with a new wing; from some rooms you might even be able to see whales without even leaving your bed.

The Marine Hermanus (☎ 313 1000, fax 313 0160, w www.marine-hermanus.co.za Marine Dr) Doubles from R1195. This superbly renovated hotel is the last word in comfort and has an ideal sea-facing spot and a couple of good restaurants. Check about marginally cheaper mid-week and weekend deals.

Places to Eat
There's no shortage of places to eat in Hermanus with new places opening all the time.

Burgundy Restaurant (☎ 312 2800, Marine Dr) Mains around R50. Open 10am-4.30pm daily, 7pm-9.30pm Mon-Sat. Book ing is essential at the Burgundy, one of the most acclaimed and popular restaurants in the province. It's in a pair of cottages, which are the oldest buildings in town (1875), with a garden and sea views.

The Fisherman's Cottage (☎ *312 3642, Lemms Corner)* Mains R30. Open noon-3pm & 6.30pm-10pm Tues-Sun. Good cheap seafood is on offer at this cute restaurant in a whitewashed cottage draped with fishing nets.

Marimba Cafe (☎ *312 2148, 108D Main Rd)* Mains R35. Open 7pm-10pm daily. The lively atmosphere matches the eclectic menu at this restaurant where you can eat traditional African dishes.

Malabar *(Shop 3, Long St Arcade)* Mains R35. Open 6.30pm-late daily. Curries are the go at this cosy spot.

Rossi's Pizzeria & Italian Restaurant (☎ *312 2848, 10 High St)* Mains around R30. Open 6.30pm-late daily. This long-running operation has a pleasant and relaxed atmosphere.

Savannah Café (☎ *312 4259, Village Theatre, Marine Dr)* Mains around R20. Open 9am-5pm Mon-Fri, 8am-8pm Sat & Sun. A good place for lunch or a snack, the Savannah overlooks the beach and is convenient for the cinema next door.

Bientang's Cave (☎ *312 3454, Marine Dr)* Mains R40. Open 11am-5pm daily. Beside the water, between the museum and the Marine Hermanus, this really *is* a seaside cave, containing a good but pricey restaurant. Apart from fish there's also pizza on offer.

Entertainment
O Bar *(121 Main Rd)* Admission R10 Fri & Sat. This stylish DJ bar is *the* late-night place to party on the weekends. At other times there's an open fire and pool tables.

Getting There & Away
There are no regular bus services to Hermanus from Cape Town, although you'll find plenty of tours – see Organised Tours in the Cape Town & the Peninsula chapter for details. You might find a minibus taxi running to Belleville (Cape Town), but not daily – inquire at the tourism bureau.

AROUND HERMANUS
There are several walks and drives in the hills behind the town – the publicity office has maps. The 1400 hectare **Fernkloof Nature Reserve** is worth visiting, particularly if you are interested in fynbos.

If you want to see whales in a much less commercialised environment head south from Hermanus to the sleepy village of **De Kelders**. Next along is **Gansbaai**, an unprepossessing fishing town that is riding the wave of interest in shark-diving (see Shark-Diving under Hermanus earlier). If this is not your bag, then the nearby **Dyer Island**, where the sharks hang out, also hosts colonies of African penguins and seals; regular boat trips are available.

Grootboss Private Nature Reserve (☎ *028-384 0381, fax 384 0552,* **e** *grootbos@ hermanus.co.za)* Singles/doubles DB&B R1700/2200. This beautifully designed and award-winning property, covering 1000 hectares, is the best place to stay in the area. The rates cover all activities such as guided nature walks, horse riding and mountain biking.

On the unsealed inland route between Gansbaai and Cape Agulhas is **Elim**, a picturesque but poor Moravian mission village founded in 1824.

CAPE AGULHAS
Welcome to the southernmost point of Africa. On a stormy day the low, shattered rocks and crashing seas can be atmospheric. Otherwise, Cape Agulhas isn't especially impressive and there's little reason to linger longer than it takes to peek at the nearby **lighthouse** (☎ *028-435 6222; adult/child R5/2; open 9am-4.15pm Mon-Sat, 9am-2pm Sun)*, built in 1848 and the second oldest in South Africa. If you're peckish, the *tearoom* (☎ *028-435 7506)* here isn't bad, serving reasonably priced meals and snacks.

Rolling wheat and sheep country surround the region's largest town **Bredasdorp** through which you'll have to pass to reach the Cape by tarred road. Here you'll find the friendly **Suidpunt Tourism Bureau** (☎ *028-424 2584,* **w** *www.suidpunttourism.co.za, Dowling Bldg, Dr Jansen St)*.

ARNISTON

Arniston is a charming, undeveloped village in a dramatic, windswept setting, named after the vessel wrecked off its treacherous coast in 1815, with the loss of 344 lives. Its Afrikaans name, Waenhuiskrans, means 'Wagon-house Cliff', after the enormous cavern eroded into the cliffs around 1km south from the village.

John Midgely at Southwinds (see Places to Stay & Eat following) runs a 4WD eco-trip (R50, two hours) to see both the scant remains of the *Arniston* (practically covered by sand) and the cave. Apart from walking the dunes, this trip is a fine way to get a feel for this rugged coast washed by a beguilingly brilliant blue ocean.

Apart from this, Arniston's main draw is the rustic fishing community of **Kassiesbaai**, which was established in 1820 and is notable for its whitewashed thatch cottages. Although the cottages are very photogenic, it is evident that their inhabitants are very poor.

Places to Stay & Eat

South of Africa Backpackers' Resort (☎ 028-445 9240, fax 445 9254, W *www.south ofafrica.co.za)* Singles/doubles/triples B&B R95/150/180. Signposted off the R316, 2km outside of Arniston, this place is part of the *Die Herberg* resort, which means it shares all the amenities, including gym, large pool, sauna and two full-size billiard tables. The neighbouring military test site gives a clue as to why such a salubrious hotel was built here and it's possible you'll still rub shoulders with soldiers over the full buffet breakfast.

Arniston Seaside Cottages (☎ 028-445 9772, fax 445 9125, W *www.arniston-online .co.za)* Singles/doubles R225/300. Located in the village, most of these well-equipped self-catering cottages are thatched and some have sea views.

Southwinds (☎/fax 028-445 9303, e *south winds@kingsley.co.za, First Ave)* Singles/doubles B&B R220/350. You'll enjoy a friendly welcome at this B&B, a short stroll from the beach. It has comfortable and nicely furnished rooms.

Arniston Hotel (☎ 028-445 9000, fax 445 9633, W *www.arnistonhotel.co.za)* Singles/doubles B&B from R425/650. This luxury hotel faces the sea. Upgrades of some rooms are planned as is a change of location for its fine *restaurant* to a pair of new cottages to be built behind the hotel. Light meals (R13.50-30) are served during the day in the classy ocean-view bar.

Die Waenhuis (☎ 028-445 9797, Dupreez St) Mains from R40. Arniston's only other dining option serves a good range of dishes, and is tucked behind the Arniston Centre general store.

DE HOOP NATURE RESERVE

Covering 36,000 hectares, plus 5km out to sea is **De Hoop Nature Reserve** (☎ 028-542 1126, e *dehoopinfo@sdm.dorea.co.za; admission R6; open 7am-6pm daily)*. This is one of Cape Nature Conservation's best reserves, including a scenic coastline with stretches of beach, dunes and rocky cliffs, plus a freshwater lake and Potberg Mountain. Accommodation is available in cottages for four from R180 or camping for R46.

Visitors come here to see both mountain and lowveld fynbos and a diverse cross section of coastal ecosystems. Fauna includes the Cape mountain zebra, bontebok and a wealth of birdlife. The coast is an important breeding area for the southern right whale.

Hikers can tackle beach walks, an 8km trail along the cliffs of the De Hoop Vlei (Lake) and day trails of various lengths of Potberg Mountain. There's an overnight mountain bike trail, for which bookings should be made in advance, and good snorkelling along the coast. Because the reserve is east of Cape Agulhas, the water is reasonably warm.

The reserve is about 260km from Cape Town, and the final 50km from either Bredasdorp or Swellendam is along gravel roads. The only access to the reserve is via Wydgeleë on the Bredasdorp to Malgas road. At Malgas a manually operated pont (river ferry) on the Breede River still operates (between dawn and dusk). The village of **Ouplaas**, 15km away, is the nearest place to buy fuel and supplies.

SWELLENDAM

☎ 028 • postcode 6740 • pop 33,200

As well as being a historic and attractive town, dotted with old oaks and surrounded by rolling wheat country and mountains, Swellendam makes a great base for exploring the Overberg and the Little Karoo. It's a handy stop between Cape Town and the Garden Route, and even if you don't have wheels there's the chance to walk in indigenous forest quite close to town.

The town backs up against a spectacular ridge, part of the 1600m Langeberg Range. The distinctive square-topped outcrop is known locally as 12-o'clock Rock because the noonday sun is very close to the rock, making it impossible for anyone in town to see what is going on up there. You can walk up and back in a day. A permit costs R12 and is obtainable either from the Nature Conservation Department (see Activities later) or Swellendam Backpackers (see Places to Stay later).

History

Swellendam dates from 1746 and is the third-oldest magisterial district in South Africa. The expansion by independent farmers and traders beyond the Cape Peninsula meant that by the 1740s they had drifted too far beyond the Dutch East India Company's (VOC's) authorities at Stellenbosch to be controlled.

As a result, Swellendam was established as the seat of a landdrost, an official representative of the colony's governor whose duties combined those of local administrator, tax collector and magistrate. The residency of a landdrost was known as a *drostdy* and included his office and court-room as well as his family's living quarters. The Swellendam Drostdy is now the centrepiece for a fine museum complex.

Official vandalism has ensured that Swellendam, pretty as it is, has not remained a perfect jewel. In 1974 the main road was widened, resulting in the loss of many old oaks and older buildings.

WESTERN CAPE

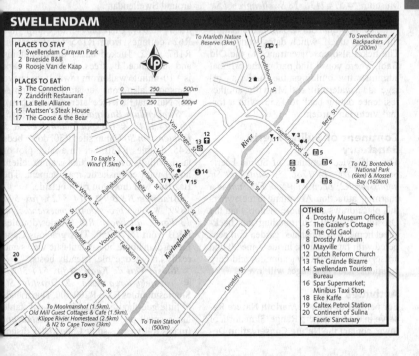

SWELLENDAM

PLACES TO STAY
1 Swellendam Caravan Park
2 Braeside B&B
9 Roosje Van de Kaap

PLACES TO EAT
3 The Connection
7 Zanddrift Restaurant
11 La Belle Alliance
15 Mattsen's Steak House
17 The Goose & the Bear

To Marloth Nature Reserve (3km)
To Swellendam Backpackers (200m)
To Eagle's Wind (1.5km)
To N2, Bontebok National Park (6km) & Mossel Bay (160km)
To Moolmanshof (1.5km), Old Mill Guest Cottages & Cafe (1.5km), Klippe Rivier Homestead (2.5km) & N2 to Cape Town (3km)
To Train Station (500m)

OTHER
4 Drostdy Museum Offices
5 The Gaoler's Cottage
6 The Old Gaol
8 Drostdy Museum
10 Mayville
12 Dutch Reform Church
13 The Grande Bizarre
14 Swellendam Tourism Bureau
16 Spar Supermarket; Minibus Taxi Stop
18 Eike Kaffe
19 Caltex Petrol Station
20 Continent of Sulina Faerie Sanctuary

Information

The **tourism bureau** (☎/fax 514 2770, Voortrek St; open 9am-5pm Mon-Fri & 9am-12.30pm Sat) is in the old mission, or Oefeninghuis, on the main street. Note the twin clocks, one of which is permanently set at 12.15pm. This was the time for the daily service; the illiterate townspeople only had to match the working clock with the painted one to know when their presence was required.

If you're interested in architecture or history, pick up a copy of the *Swellendam Treasures* brochure (R5), which details scores of interesting buildings around town. Also inquire at the bureau about guided walks.

The cheapest Internet connection in town is at a cafe and art/antique gallery, **The Grande Bizarre** (17 Voortrek St; R15 per half-hour).

Drostdy Museum

The centrepiece of the excellent Drostdy Museum (☎ 514 1138, 18 Swellengrebel St; adult/child R10/1; open 9am-4.45pm Mon-Fri, 10am-3.45pm Sat & Sun) is the beautiful drostdy itself, which dates from 1746. The ticket also covers entrance to the **Old Gaol**, where you'll find part of the original administrative buildings; the Gaoler's Cottage and a watermill; and Mayville, another residence dating back to 1853, with a formal Victorian garden.

Continent of Sulina Faerie Sanctuary

The self-styled Continent of Sulina Faerie Sanctuary (☎ 514 1786, 37 Buitekant St; admission R2; open 9am-5pm Fri-Sun) is a charming attraction. According to the owners this place draws even more visitors than the Drostdy Museum. Surrounding this backstreet home is an enchanted garden trail peppered with fairy statues; inside some 20 odd artists display their tiny sculptures and fairy creations. Kids of all ages will love it.

Activities

For permits to walk in **Marloth Nature Reserve** in the Langeberg Range, 3km north of town, contact the **Nature Conservation De-**partment (☎ 514 1410) at the entrance to the reserve, during business hours. There are day, overnight and week-long hikes and also accommodation.

Two Feathers Horse Trails (☎ 082-494 8279, e mwleepip@iafrica.com) offers one-hour horse rides for R85 and caters for inexperienced as well as experienced riders (but doesn't offer hard hats). Overnight rides can be arranged too.

Swellendam Outdoor Adventures (☎ 514 2648), based at Swellendam Backpackers, offers day trips to places like Cape Agulhas and De Hoop Nature Reserve (both R150), and activities from canoeing to gliding. They, and guesthouses in town, can also arrange for sunset cruises on a double-decker wooden raft on the lake near the Buffeljachts Dam in the Langeberg Mountains. The cost is R60.

Places to Stay

The best places to stay in town are the many excellent B&Bs and guesthouses in and around Swellendam.

Swellendam Caravan Park (☎ 514 2705, fax 514 2694, Glen Barry Rd) Camp sites R62, cottages from R155 for 1 person, R167 for 2. Tucked under the mountains and surrounded by trees, this caravan park is a 10-minute walk from town. If you have transport, also consider staying at Bontebok National Park (see later in this section).

Swellendam Backpackers (☎ 514 2648, fax 514 1249, e backpack@dorea.co.za, 5 Lichtenstein St) Camp sites R30, dorm beds R45, doubles R130. Set on a huge plot of land, with its own river, this is an excellent hostel with enthusiastic management. The Baz Bus will drop you right outside.

Braeside B&B (☎ 514 3325, fax 514 1899, W www.braeside4u.homestead.com, 13 Van Oudtshoorn Rd) Singles/doubles B&B from R175/250. This gracious Cape Edwardian home boasts fantastic views and really knowledgeable, friendly hosts.

Roosje Van de Kaap (☎/fax 514 3001, e roosje@dorea.co.za, 5 Drostdy St) Singles/doubles B&B R200/300. This friendly little guesthouse in a converted old stable has a small pool. The excellent *restaurant* (mains R40) serves some Cape Malay dishes and wood-fired-oven pizzas; it's open to the public but booking is essential.

Moolmanshof (☎ 514 3258, fax 514 384, 217 Voortrek St) Singles/doubles B&B from R250/320. Moolmanshof is a gem, around 2km from the town centre. The house, dating from 1798 and furnished with period furniture, is set in lovely gardens.

Old Mill Guest Cottages (☎ 514 2790, fax 514 1292, W *www.oldmill.co.za, 241 Voortrek St)* Doubles B&B R200/260 low/high season. This tiny but cute cottage behind the antiques/craft shop has a pleasant cafe of he same name.

Eagle's Wind (☎/fax 514 3797, e *mwleeip@iafrica.com)* Full board R225 per person. Tired of all that Cape Dutch architecture? Then this encampment of Native American tepees (cone-shaped tents), each sleeping two on twin futons, could be your thing. In a stunning setting 2km north-west of the centre down a dirt road from the golf course, it's part of a holistic centre that also offers workshops and other activities.

Klippe Rivier Homestead (☎ 514 3341, fax 514 3337, e *krh@sdm.dorea.co.za)* Doubles B&B R900. Three kilometres south-west of town, this luxurious homestead (dating from 1820) has six beautifully decorated guest suites. Its top-notch three-course dinner (R120) is available to non-guests if the place isn't not full, but you'll need to book.

Places to Eat

As well as the Klippe Rivier Homestead, the Old Mill Guest Cottages and Roosje van de Kaap (see Places to Stay earlier) the following are recommended.

Mattsen's Steak House (☎ 514 2715, 44 Voortrek St) Mains R35-50. Open 11am-3pm daily, 6pm-late Mon-Sat. Popular for its steaks, seafood and pizzas, Mattsen's also offers meals and snacks during the day.

The Goose & the Bear (☎ 514 3101, 35 Voortrek St) Mains R25. Open 11.30am-2am Mon-Sat, 7pm-midnight Sun. Standard pub meals and the occasional braai are available at this convivial bar.

Zanddrift Restaurant (☎ 514 1789, 132 Swellengrebel St) Mains R45. Open 8.30am-

4.30pm daily. Breakfast (available all day) at the Zanddrift is a must, consisting of a huge platter of omelette, ham, cheese, pâté, fruit and so on. Other dishes depend on what's available that day. The restaurant is across the road from the museum and is in a building that dates from 1757.

La Belle Alliance (☎ 514 2252, 1 Swellengrebel St) Mains R35. Open 8am-5pm daily. This appealing tearoom is in an old masonic lodge with shaded outdoor tables beside the Koringlands River. It's a good spot for an inexpensive snack.

The Connection (☎ 514 1988, 10-12 Swellengrebel St) Mains R50. Open 10am-10pm Thur-Tues. With a new location, this highly recommended restaurant offers similar home-cooked favourites to Zanddrift.

Getting There & Away

Bus All three major bus companies plus the Baz Bus pass through Swellendam on their runs between Cape Town and Port Elizabeth. **Eike Kaffe** *(108 Voortrek)* is the Intercape agent; Greyhound and Translux tickets can only be booked in Cape Town (see Getting There & Away in the Cape Town & the Peninsula chapter).

Train The weekly *Southern Cross* that runs between Cape Town and Oudtshoorn stops here.

Minibus Taxi For information on minibus taxis check at the stop behind the Spar supermarket on Voortrek St. The daily service to Cape Town is about R90, and to Mossel Bay R70.

BONTEBOK NATIONAL PARK

Some 6km south of Swellendam is Bontebok National Park *(☎ 028-514 2735; adult/child R8/4)*. This small chunk of land has been set aside to ensure the preservation of the endangered bontebok, an unusually marked antelope that once roamed the region in large numbers.

As a national park, Bontebok doesn't offer much competition to Kruger et al but as a nice place to relax it's hard to beat. The park falls within the coastal fynbos area and

is on the banks of the Breede River, where swimming is possible. It boasts nearly 500 grasses and other plant species; in the late winter and early spring, the *veld* (grassland) is covered with flowers. In addition to the bontebok, there is the rhebok, grysbok, duiker, red hartebeest and mountain zebra. Birdlife is abundant.

Accommodation can be booked through the National Parks Board (☎ 012-343 1991) Camping costs R65 for two, and six-berth 'chalavans' cost R150 for two people, plus R20 per extra person.

The Little Karoo

The Little (or Klein) Karoo is a region bordered in the south by the Outeniqua and Langeberg Ranges, and in the north by the Swartberg Range about 60km away. It runs east from Montagu for about 300km to Uniondale, and is more fertile and better watered than the harsher Great Karoo to the north.

More people are discovering this region through the promotion of Route 62, a hinterland drive between Cape Town and the Garden Route. Progressing from the Breede River Valley through such interesting places as the hot-spring town of Montagu and the ostrich-breeding centre of Oudtshoorn, not to mention lovely scenery, Route 62 is well worth considering as an alternative to the N2 highway. To get to the coast there are spectacular kloofs and passes that cut through the mountains.

MONTAGU
☎ 023 • postcode 6720 • pop 24,000

Founded in 1851, Montagu is the first town up the pass from the Breede River Valley – once you pop through the Kogmanskloof Pass near Robertson you are suddenly in a very different world. It's a good place to go if you want to escape the 21st century and get a brief taste of the Little Karoo.

The town is populated by artists and other escapees, and there's a peaceful old-world atmosphere. There are some 24 restored national monuments, but what is increasingly attracting more people is Montagu's splendid range of adventure sports activities, including mountain biking, hiking and world-class rock climbing.

Access to the town required numerous crossings of the river until 1877, when master engineer Thomas Bain (son of Andrew) completed the small tunnel that is still in use today. The British added a fort on top in 1899.

Orientation & Information

The town is small, so it's easy to get around on foot. The **tourism bureau** (☎ 614 2471, 24 Bath St; open 8.45am-4.45pm Mon-Fri, 9am-5pm Sat, 9.30am-12.30pm & 2pm-5pm Sun) is particularly helpful and can provide information on accommodation (including a good range of B&Bs and self-catering cottages), hikes and other activities.

Internet access is available at **Printmor** (70 Bath St; R10 per half-hour; open 9am-4pm Mon-Fri & 9am-1pm Sat).

Montagu Museum & Joubert House

The Montagu Museum (☎ 614 1950, 41 Long St; adult/child R2/1; open 9am-1pm & 2pm-5pm Mon-Fri, 10.30am-12.30pm Sat & Sun) is in the old mission church and includes interesting displays and some good examples of antique furniture.

Joubert House (☎ 614 1774, 25 Long St; adult/child R2/1), a short walk away, has the same opening hours as the museum. It's the oldest house in Montagu (built in 1853) and is restored to its Victorian finery.

Hot Springs & Lover's Lane Trail

Water from the hot mineral springs (☎ 614 1150, Avalon Springs Hotel; adult/child R20/12.50 Mon-Fri, R22.50/15 Sat & Sun; open 8am-11pm daily) finds its way into the concrete pools at the hotel, about 3km from town. Heated to 43°C, radioactive and renowned for their healing properties, the pools are a lively place at weekends, when many local families come for a soak.

A great way to get here is to hike along the 2.2km Lover's Lane Trail, a gentle trail which starts at the car park at the end of Barry St; pick up the *Hiking Trails* leaflet

MONTAGU

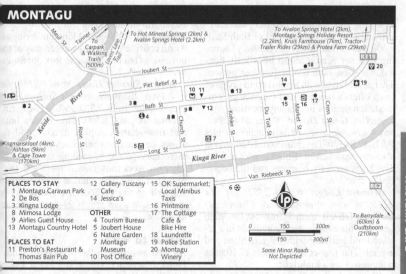

To Hot Mineral Springs (2km) &
Avalon Springs Hotel (2.2km)

To Avalon Springs Hotel (2km),
Montagu Springs Holiday Resort
(2.2km), Kruis Farmhouse (7km), Tractor-
Trailer Rides (29km) & Protea Farm (29km)

To
Carpark
& Walking
Trails
(500m)

To
Kogmanskloof (4km),
Ashton (9km)
& Cape Town
(170km)

Joubert St
Piet Retief St
Bath St
Long St
Kinga River
Van Riebeeck St

Meul St
Tanner St
Lovery Lane
River
Keisie
Rose St
Barry St
Church St
Kohler St
Du Toit St
Market St
Cross St

To Barrydale
(60km) &
Oudtshoorn
(210km)

Some Minor Roads
Not Depicted

0   150   300m
0   150   300yd

PLACES TO STAY	12 Gallery Tuscany	15 OK Supermarket;
1 Montagu Caravan Park	Cafe	Local Minibus
2 De Bos	14 Jessica's	Taxis
3 Kingna Lodge		16 Printmore
8 Mimosa Lodge	**OTHER**	17 The Cottage
9 Airlies Guest House	4 Tourism Bureau	Cafe &
13 Montagu Country Hotel	5 Joubert House	Bike Hire
	6 Nature Garden	18 Laundrette
PLACES TO EAT	7 Montagu	19 Police Station
11 Preston's Restaurant &	Museum	20 Montagu
Thomas Bain Pub	10 Post Office	Winery

from the tourism bureau. The route leads past Montagu's top **rock-climbing** spots. For guidance on climbing and hiking in the area contact **Montagu Rock Adventures** (☎ 626 3083, e *humanvalues@xsinet.co.za*).

Bloupunt & Kogmanskloof Trails

The tourist bureau handles bookings for overnight cabins near the start of the Bloupunt and Kogmanskloof Trails. The huts are fairly basic (wood stoves, showers and toilet facilities) but they are cheap (R40 per person). There are also several camp sites at R20 per person. For both the hikes there's a charge of R5/3 per adult/child.

The **Bloupunt Trail** is 15.6km long and can be walked in six to eight hours; it traverses ravines and mountain streams, and climbs to 1000m. The flora includes proteas, ericas, aloes, gladioli and watsonias. The **Kogmanskloof Trail** is 12.1km and can be completed in four to six hours; it's not as steep as the Bloupunt Trail. Both trails start from the car park at the end of Tanner St.

Mountain Biking

Biking is a great way to see the surrounding countryside. To rent a mountain bike, call

Ron Brunings (☎/fax 614 1932; R55 per day) or visit him at *The Cottage Cafe & Bike Hire* (78 Bath St). Ron also runs **Dusty Sprocket Trails** (e *brunings@lando .co.za*), offering 10 guided mountain-bike trails in the area for all levels of skill; trails range from 12km to 43km.

Tractor-trailer Rides

Niel Burger (☎/fax 614 2471; adult/child R30/15), owner of the Protea Farm (see Places to Stay following), takes fun tractor-trailer rides to the top of the Langeberg Range, from where you can look way down into the Breede River Valley. Even locals enjoy the three-hour trip, so it must be something special. It usually operates on Wednesday at 10am and Saturday at 10am and 2pm. You can have a delicious lunch of *potjiekos* (traditional pot stew) with homemade bread for R40/10 per adult/child. Niel also has an overnight cabin with 20 beds; you'll need transport to get to the farm.

Places to Stay

In Town *Montagu Caravan Park* (☎ 082-920 7863, fax 614 3034, Bath St) Camping from R20 for up to three people, R15 per extra person; wooden cabins singles/doubles R50/ 70. This standard camping and caravan site is at the far west end of Bath St.

De Bos (*☎/fax 614 2532, Bath St*) Camping R25 per person, dorm beds R40, bungalows & en-suite rooms R55 per person. This guest farm (with a pool) on the edge of town offers a range of self-catering accommodation options in a lovely location.

Airlies Guest House (*☎/fax 614 2943,* W *www.beststay.co.za/airlies*) Singles/doubles B&B R150/300. The characterful Airlies is in a roomy thatched-roof house, with a pool. The hosts are very obliging and the breakfast is excellent.

Mimosa Lodge (*☎ 614 2351, fax 614 2418,* W *www.mimosa.co.za, Church St*) Doubles DB&B from R580/750 low/high season. This excellent guesthouse is in a restored old building with large gardens and a pool. The five-course dinners (R105 for nonguests) are a highlight.

Kingna Lodge (*☎ 614 1066, fax 614 2405,* e *kingna@lando.co.za, 11 Bath St*) Singles/doubles B&B from R360/570. Victoriana runs riot at this elegant guesthouse where the five-course dinners (R120) draw rave reviews.

Montagu Country Hotel (*☎ 614 3125, fax 614 1905,* W *www.montagucountryhotel .co.za, 27 Bath St*) Singles/doubles from R225/380 low season, R335/530 high season. This pleasant hotel with reasonably decorated rooms offers all the usual facilities, and has a pool, smart restaurant and bar.

Out of Town If none of the options in Montagu take your fancy, you can head out of town.

Kruis (*☎ 614 2205, 7km from Montagu*) Doubles in flat R150, 6-person farmhouse R250. Apart from the flat and farmhouse there's also a cabin without electricity sleeping two for R100.

Protea Farm (*☎ 614 2471, 29km from Montagu*) Cottages from R160 for 2. If you stay more than one night the price drops to R140 at these cottages situated right at the top of the Langeberg Range. Owner Niel Burger also runs tractor-trailer rides up the mountain (see earlier).

Montagu Springs Holiday Resort (*☎ 61 1050, Warmbronne Hot Springs*) 4-perso chalets from R220-320. Montagu Springs i worth considering if you want to stay at th hot springs but don't want to fork out for th nearby hotel.

Avalon Springs Hotel (*☎ 614 1150, fa 614 1906, Warmbronne Hot Springs*) Sin gles/doubles from R325/550, self-caterin apartments from R300. This luxury hote and time-share complex draws good re views, despite its rather kitsch decor and it mercenary policy of jacking up prices b 25% on weekends (when there's a two night minimum stay) and at holiday times As well as the outdoor hot spring pools massages, a gym and a 24-hour cafe ar available.

Places to Eat

As well as meals in the Montagu Countr Hotel, Mimosa Lodge and Kingna Lodge (for these last two you must book in ac vance), there are a few other options.

Gallery Tuscany Cafe (*☎ 614 2850, 4 Bath St*) Mains R20. Open 10am-4pm Mor Fri, 9am-noon Sat. A relaxing spot fc breakfast or a sandwich, this cafe also ha an attached gallery and a bookshop.

Jessica's (*☎ 614 1805, 47 Bath St*) Mair R35-55. Open 6.30pm-10pm daily. Jes sica's serves up inventive bistro dishe such as butternut-squash gnocchi, in a cos atmosphere.

Preston's Restaurant (*☎ 614 3013, I Bath St*) Mains R35-60. Open 10.30an 2.30pm & 5.30pm-11.30pm daily. Part c the Thomas Bain pub, this restaurant ha light lunches for around R25 and a pleasa courtyard.

Getting There & Away

Translux buses stop at Ashton, 9km fro Montagu on its run between Cape Tow (R95) and Port Elizabeth (R170). Munn Coaches (*☎ 637 1850*) runs six times week between Cape Town and Montagu f about R45.

Minibus taxis running between Cap Town and Oudtshoorn stop near the poli station.

MONTAGU TO OUDTSHOORN

From Montagu, the R62 runs through the upper end of the Little Karoo, passing through some lovely scenery.

Barrydale is an attractive, small town in a verdant valley. For details of several guesthouses contact **Barrydale Tourism Bureau** (☎/fax 028-572 1572; open 9.30am-4.30pm Mon-Fri).

There are also some good places to stop and get a bite.

The Country Pumpkin (☎ 028-572 1019) Mains R30. Open 7am-7pm Mon-Sat, 7am-5pm Sun. On the R62 as you pull into town, this popular cafe and farm stall is an ideal pit stop.

Also consider *Ronnie's Sex Shop* (☎ 028-572 1153), around 20km from Barrydale along the R62 towards Ladysmith. Don't be fooled by the name – see the boxed text How Sex Sells'.

From Barrydale the R62 continues east to Calitzdorp and Oudtshoorn, while the R324 heads south through the spectacular **Tradouw Pass**. The road then branches to run east to Heidelberg or west down a very pretty valley to Swellendam, passing on the way **Suurbraak** – a bucolic English mission village notable as one of the few places in South Africa where whites were required to move out when the Group Areas Act was being enforced.

How Sex Sells

When Frank Ronald Price bought an isolated farmers cottage along the R62 in the late 1980s he struggled along selling farm produce to passers-by. But business really took off when his mates decided to play a practical joke by sneaking out one night and adding the word 'sex' to the sign that said Ronnie's Shop. Now just about everyone does a double take when they drive by and, like as not, pull in to find just your regular rural pub, serving meals (mains around R35) and offering Internet access – albeit one whose walls are plastered with graffiti from its adoring fans.

If you're heading for Oudtshoorn and have time to spare, leave the main road (which mainly follows the drier valley floor) at Calitzdorp and take the unsealed road to **Kraaldorings**, running along the northern side of the range, through some rugged but pretty country. This route loops back to the R62 or heads off to **Cango Caves** (see later).

The Retreat at Groenfontein (☎/fax 044-213 3880) Singles/doubles B&B R180/360, plus R80 for dinner. Along the road to Kraaldorings, this delightful restored Victorian mansion with trimmed gardens comes as something of a surprise amid such an elemental landscape. Lovely hosts make this an ideal bolthole or base for hiking in the Swartberg Mountains.

Calitzdorp

This small town doesn't look very interesting from the R62, which runs through the centre, but it's worth pausing briefly to explore the more attractive back streets. There's a small **museum** (Cnr Van Riebeck & Geyser Sts; admission free; open 9am-noon & 2pm-5pm Mon-Fri, 9am-noon Sat) and the sandstone **Dutch Reformed church** which is a national monument.

The **information centre** (☎ 044-213 3312, Cnr Voortrek & Barry Sts) is open the same hours as the museum, except between May and September when it opens at 10am. It can provide details on accommodation and the local wineries, which are famous for their ports and fortified wines.

Of the five wineries you can visit, **Die Krans** (☎ 044-213 3314; free tastings 8am-5pm Mon-Fri, 9am-1pm Sat) is reckoned to be the best. Cellar tours are available if you book ahead. There's also a port festival held in July.

Heading south-east for around 50km, along the old road to Oudtshoorn, you'll reach **Gamka Nature Reserve** (☎/fax 044-213 3367, e gamkanr@mweb.co.za). There are several day trails plus a two-day walk here and opportunities to spot quite a few animals including the rare Cape mountain zebra, steenbok and duiker. Accommodation in huts costs R50 per person.

Back in town, there are a few options catering to visitors.

Die Dorphuis (☎/fax 044-213 3453, **e** dorphuis@mweb.co.za, 4 Van Riebeeck St) Singles/doubles B&B from R125/250. Facing Calitzdorp's Dutch Reformed church this guesthouse offers a couple of rooms, one of which is self-catering and has a small pool. There's also a **cafe-restaurant** (mains R15-35), serving snacks and traditional meals such as eisbein (a pork dish).

Ebenhart's Restaurant (☎ 044-213 3598, 13 Voortrek St) Mains R35. Open 9am-5pm Mon-Sat. Snacks and more substantial dishes are available to eat in a shaded garden in Ebenhart's. It also sells hand-carved pipes made by South Africa's only pipe maker.

OUDTSHOORN
☎ 044 • postcode 6620 • pop 79,000

They're ostrich crazy in Oudtshoorn – the sedate tourist capital of the Little Karoo – and for good reason. The surrounding farmlands are thick with these birds which have been bred hereabouts since the 1870s. At the turn of the 20th century such fortunes were to be made from the fashion for ostrich feathers that Oudtshoorn grew rich and the so-called 'feather barons' built the grand houses that lend the town its distinct atmosphere today.

Although ostrich feathers have since fallen out of fashion, Oudtshoorn still turns a pretty penny from breeding the birds for meat and leather. The ostriches also pay their way with the tourists – so you can buy ostrich eggs, feathers and biltong (dried meat) all over town, not to mention ride the birds at several show farms.

This sort of entertainment palls quickly, but luckily Oudtshoorn is also well situated as a base for exploring the different environments of the Little Karoo, the Garden Route (it's just 55km to George along the N12) and the Great Karoo. The nearby Swartberg and Seweweekspoort Passes – two of South Africa's scenic highlights – are geological, floral and engineering masterpieces.

Orientation & Information
Since all the main attractions are beyond easy walking distance from town your own transport, or a willingness to take a tour, or hitch, is virtually essential. The main commercial street is High (Hoog) St, to the east of Baron van Rheede St.

Next to the CP Nel Museum is the helpful **Oudtshoorn Tourism Bureau** (☎ 27 2532, **W** www.oudtshoorn.com, Baron van Rheede St; open 8am-6pm Mon-Sat, 10am-6pm Sun). Ask here about the numerous B&Bs in town and about tours of the local sights.

CP Nel Museum & Le Roux Townhouse
The large and interesting CP Nel Museum (☎ 272 7306, 3 Baron van Rheede St; adult/child R8/2; open 9am-5pm Mon-Sa year-round & 2pm-5pm Sun Sept-Apr) is in a striking sandstone building, completed in 1906 at the height of the ostrich feather fever. Unsurprisingly there are extensive displays about ostriches, as well as on the history of the Karoo. The museum also features some impressive reconstructed Victorian shops and the interior of an 1890 synagogue transferred here when its original home was demolished.

Included in the ticket price is admission to the Le Roux Townhouse (☎ 272 3676 Cnr Loop & High Sts; open 9am-1pm & 2pm-5pm Mon-Fri). This place is decorated in authentic period furniture and is as good an example of a 'feather palace' as you're likely to see.

Cango Wildlife Ranch & Cheetahland
At roughly 3km north of the town centre this place (☎ 272 5593; admission R32 open 8am-5pm daily) is one of the few attractions that is feasible to visit on foot. You'll pay an extra R30 if you want to pat a cheetah (the money goes to the Cheetah Conservation Foundation). Other big cats here include lions, pumas and Bengal white tigers, and there are also crocodiles, alligators and other wild animals.

Ostrich Farms
There are four ostrich show farms, each open daily and offering a guided tour of 4

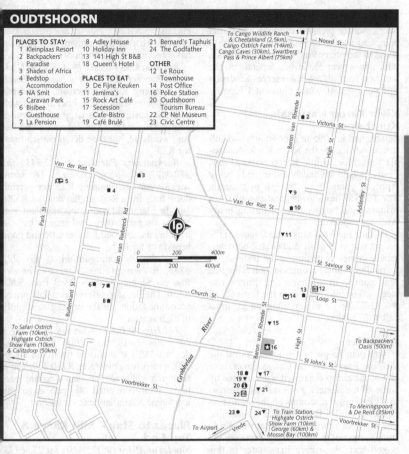

OUDTSHOORN

PLACES TO STAY
1 Kleinplaas Resort
2 Backpackers' Paradise
3 Shades of Africa
4 Bedstop Accommodation
5 NA Smit Caravan Park
6 Bisibee Guesthouse
7 La Pension
8 Adley House
10 Holiday Inn
13 141 High St B&B
18 Queen's Hotel

PLACES TO EAT
9 De Fijne Keuken
11 Jemima's
15 Rock Art Café
17 Secession Cafe-Bistro
19 Café Brulé
21 Bernard's Taphuis
24 The Godfather

OTHER
12 Le Roux Townhouse
14 Post Office
16 Police Station
20 Oudtshoorn Tourism Bureau
22 CP Nel Museum
23 Civic Centre

WESTERN CAPE

minutes to one hour. There's little to choose between them, but some people find the **Cango Ostrich Farm** (☎ 272 4623, W www.cangoostrich.co.za; adult/child R25/10; open 7.30am-5pm daily) to be the least commercial; it's 14km from Oudtshoorn en route to the Cango Caves. Others say that **Highgate Ostrich Show Farm** (☎ 272 7115, W www.highgate.co.za, adult/child R25/10; open 8am-5pm daily) is the best. Call for details, especially if you are interested in activities such as ostrich racing. It's 10km from Oudtshoorn en route to Mossel Bay.

Cango Caves

Named after the Khoisan word for 'a wet place', the Cango Caves are heavily commercialised but impressive caves (☎ 272 7410; open 9am-4pm daily). There's a choice of tours on offer, costing R16.50/9 (half-hour), R33/18 (one hour) and R44/28 (1½ hours) per adult/child. The half-hour tour gives you just a glimpse – it's better to choose a longer tour. The longest tour is the most fun, but involves crawling through tight and damp places so is not recommended for the claustrophobic or unfit. The caves are 30km from Oudtshoorn.

If you continue on past the Cango Mountain Resort (a pleasant camping and chalet complex) up the dirt road for 8km, you'll come to the pretty **Rust en Vrede Waterfall**, which runs year-round but depends on the weather. The falls are in a **reserve** *(admission R10 per vehicle)*, which closes at 4.30pm.

Klein Karoo Nasionale Kunstefees

Established in 1995 to support arts and culture in Afrikaans, the Klein Karoo Nasionale Kunstefees (Little Karoo National Arts Festival), held in Oudtshoorn around March/April, is going from strength to strength. The festival has shown great potential for bridging the huge gulfs separating many Afrikaans speakers.

Despite the Afrikaans theme, some of the program is in English, and Oudtshoorn definitely comes alive during the festival. Be warned that most accommodation is booked out months in advance and prices rise steeply. For information on the festival call ☎ 272 7771; for accommodation inquiries call ☎ 272 0000.

Activities

If you plan to go to an ostrich farm, the Wildlife Ranch and the Cango Caves, take one of the cheap organised tours offered by some of the hostels. For minibus transport to all three plus discounts on the admission tickets it's R30. Better still is to combine this trip with a thrilling **mountain-bike ride** from the top of the Swartberg Pass (see the boxed text 'Swartberg Pass' later in this chapter) – you'll be driven up and then cycle back to town (R80). Be warned, it isn't all downhill and it's a long ride, but there are shorter cycling options available.

Places to Stay – Budget

NA Smit Caravan Park (☎ 272 2446, fax 279 1915, Park St) Camp sites from R48, 4-person vans from R55, rondavels from R120. The cheaper of the town's two caravan parks is set in neat, spacious grounds, west of the centre. Prices rise in holiday seasons.

Kleinplaas Resort (☎ 272 5811, fax 279 2019, e kleinpls@mweb.co.za, 171 Baron

van Rheede St) Camping R75 per site, 4-bed chalets from R240. Fancier and pricier, this caravan park on the northern side of town has a restaurant and big pool.

Backpackers' Oasis (☎/fax 279 1163, e backpackeroasis@yahoo.com, 3 Church St) Camping R30 per person, dorm beds R40, doubles from R120. Friendly and well run, this hostel is in a large house with a good-sized yard and a decent pool. Breakfast isn't available, but they do an ostrich braai for R30.

Backpackers' Paradise (☎ 272 3436, fax 272 0877, e jubilee@pixie.co.za, 148 Baron van Rheede St) Camping R25 per person, dorm beds from R40, singles/doubles R120 140. In a large old house, this excellent hostel has a separate dorm bed annexe, bar, ostrich braais, attached Internet cafe and good breakfasts for R15.

Bedstop Accommodation (☎/fax 272 4746, e bedstop@mail.com, 69 Van der Riet St) Singles/doubles B&B from R80 R130. The Bedstop offers reasonably priced accommodation but the prices rise slightly in high season.

141 High St B&B (☎/fax 279 1751, e grs 74@xsinet.co.za, 141 High St) Singles doubles B&B with shared bathroom R120 200, with private bathroom R130/220. You'll find great-value rooms – and a central location – at this converted 1881 parsonage with handsome Australian teak verandas.

Places to Stay – Mid-Range & Top End

Shades of Africa (☎ 272 6430, fax 272 6333, e shades@pixie.co.za, 238 Jan van Riebeeck Rd) Singles/doubles B&B R250/400. Colourful touches make this contemporary-styled guesthouse, with a small pool, a charming place to stay.

La Pension (☎/fax 279 2445, w www.lapension.co.za, 169 Church St) Doubles B&B from R320. A reliable choice with a decent range of rooms, La Pension includes some self-catering units, plus a good-sized pool, sauna and a large garden.

Bisibee Guesthouse (☎ 272 4784, fax 279 2373, e bisibee@hotmail.com, 171 Church St) Doubles B&B from R300. One of the first guesthouses in town, this is an immaculate but somewhat old-fashioned place.

Adley House (☎ 272 4533, fax 272 4554, W www.adleyhouse.co.za, 209 Jan van Riebeeck Rd) Doubles B&B from R380. Rooms in the 1905 'Feather Palace' have bags of charm, the separate add-on ones less so. There's a couple of pools and smart outdoor braai and bar area.

Holiday Inn (☎ 272 2201, fax 272 3003, Cnr Baron van Rheede & Van der Riet Sts) Singles/doubles R339/538. Despite big bland rooms with all the usual comforts, this place is worth checking because there are frequently special deals.

Queen's Hotel (☎ 272 2101, fax 272 2104, Baron van Rheede St) Singles/doubles with breakfast R438/595. This attractive old-style country hotel, with spacious, understated rooms, is in a convenient location.

Places to Eat

As you'd expect, most places serve ostrich in one form or another. Clustered near the tourist bureau on Baron van Rheede St you'll find a range of cheap options including *Secession Cafe-Bistro* and *Bernard's Taphuis* (both ☎ 272 3208) and *Café Brulé* (☎ 279 2412). All of these places have a European flair and are pleasant spots for a snack or drink.

Rock Art Café (☎ 279 1927, 62 Baron van Rheede St) Mains R20-50. Open 11am-2am Mon-Sat, 6pm-2am Sun. A wide range of simple dishes is served at this often busy bar which has live music on Friday or Saturday.

De Fijne Keuken (☎ 272 6403, 114 Baron van Rheede St) Mains R35. Open noon-10pm Mon-Sat, 6pm-9pm Sun. De Fijne is highly recommended for its varied menu and good food.

The Godfather (☎ 272 5404, 61 Voortrekker St) Mains R20-30. Open 6pm-11pm daily Sept-Apr, closed Sun May-Aug. This convivial bar-restaurant serves all the usual Italian dishes and specialises in ostrich and venison. There's a good selection of board games to while away the evening, and live music on Saturday nights.

Jemima's (☎ 272 0808, 94 Baron van Rheede St) Mains R50. Open 10am-3pm &

6.30pm-10pm Tue-Sat, noon-2pm Sun. There's fine, reasonably priced dining at Jemima's, with delightful small touches such as home-baked warm bread rolls served with an aubergine paste and the complimentary brownie with the bill. The Saturday lunch buffet represents excellent value at R55.

Getting There & Around

In high season, the daily Intercape bus service between Plettenberg Bay and Jo'burg stops in Oudtshoorn. Otherwise, on Translux's daily service from Cape Town to Port Elizabeth you'll need to transfer to a smaller bus at Mossel Bay.

The Baz Bus stops at George, from where you can arrange a transfer to Oudtshoorn with the Backpackers' Paradise (see Places to Stay earlier). One way is R25.

Every Saturday the *Southern Cross* train leaves for Cape Town at 5pm.

Taxis aren't easy to find – try Union St near the Spar supermarket or check with the tourism bureau.

UNIONDALE

Some 100km east of Oudtshoorn, Uniondale is a quiet small town, overlooked by an old fort and surrounded by a striking landscape of flat-topped kopje (little hills) and wheat fields. It's linked to Knysna on the Garden Route by the impressive Prince Alfred's Pass (see Around Knysna later in this chapter).

There's no great reason to linger, other than for a breather on the way to or from the coast. The **information centre** (☎ 044-752 1266) can tell you about B&Bs. A nice one, that also serves meals and snacks in its pleasant garden is *The Cottages* (☎ 044-752 1554, Voortrekker St), which has self-catering accommodation at R85 per person and B&B at R110 per person.

The Karoo

The vast and arid Karoo, covering almost one-third of South Africa's total area, is demarcated in the south and west by the coastal mountain ranges, and to the east and

WESTERN CAPE

north by the mighty Orange River. Although some of the Karoo is in Western Cape, it doesn't respect provincial boundaries and sprawls into Eastern and Northern Cape as well. The section of the Karoo around the lovely town of Graaff-Reinet is possibly the most interesting (see The Karoo in the Eastern Cape chapter).

The population is sparse; off the main highways you can drive for hours without seeing another car. It is certainly not an untouched wilderness – the San and Khoikhoi who roamed the region and hunted vast herds of antelope have gone, and have been replaced by farmers and sheep. Despite this, the Karoo feels untouched. There are very few obvious signs of human occupation, apart from the roads snaking over the plains.

Although the main Karoo towns are all linked by public transport, it is best to have a vehicle. There's nothing like stopping in the middle of nowhere, listening to the silence and wandering off the road into the veld. The road network is excellent; even the unsealed roads are of a high standard.

PRINCE ALBERT
☎ 023 • postcode 6930 • pop 10,000

To many urban South Africans, Prince Albert – a charming village dating back to 1762 and dozing at the foot of the Swartberg Pass – represents an idyllic life in the Karoo. If you have your own transport, you can easily visit on a day trip from Oudtshoorn or even from the coast. Alternatively, stay in Prince Albert and make a day trip to Oudtshoorn via the spectacular Swartberg Pass and Meiringspoort, or – if the weather isn't too hot – consider going on a hike.

Despite being surrounded by very harsh country, the town is green and fertile (producing peaches, apricots, grapes and olives), thanks to the run-off from the mountain springs. A system of original water channels runs through town and most houses have a sluice gate, which they are entitled to open for a set period each week. Arriving here after a long, hot drive through the Karoo is wonderful – just seeing trees again is refreshing.

Apart from some good examples of Cape Dutch, Victorian and Karoo architecture, the town's only standard attraction is the **Fransie**

Flat, Hot & Boring?

For some people the Karoo means nothing more than flat, hot roads and a long, boring trip between Jo'burg and Cape Town. For others, however, the Karoo is one of the most exhilarating regions in South Africa.

As for being flat, some parts are. But others are mountainous, and you are rarely out of sight of a spectacular range – some topping 2000m – hovering on the horizon and changing colour depending on the time of day. They form fantastic shapes, although many take the classic Karoo form: dolerite-capped kopjes, which are flat-topped and sheer-sided. There are a number of spectacular mountain passes, particularly around Oudtshoorn.

Although there are some interesting old towns, richly endowed with distinctive architecture (especially Graaff-Reinet), many places are isolated backwaters, service centres for the surrounding countryside. Still they often have a quiet charm.

The seemingly inhospitable environment also produces fascinating flora of two main sorts: succulents and woody shrubs. The drier the country (the further west you go) the more weird-looking succulents there are, including mesembryanthemums, euphorbias and aloes, among others. The woody shrubs need somewhat easier conditions and include pentzias, daisies and saltbushes.

The average summer temperature is 33°C but it can go a lot higher. The moment the sun sets, however, the temperature plummets. In winter, frosts are common, although daytime temperatures average a pleasant 18°C. Rain is distributed fairly evenly over the year, the main falls occurring in March and April. The best time to visit is spring or autumn, when the weather is fine and temperatures during the day are in the mid-20°C.

Cape gannets, Lambert's Bay

Wildflowers in bloom

Rain clouds over Karoo National Park, Western Cape

Extraordinary indigenous flora is protected within the Cape of Good Hope Nature Reserve.

The hills of Kleinmond are covered with *fynbos* (fine bush), primarily proteas, heaths and ericas.

A pod of Cape fur seals admire the sunset.

African penguins at Boulders Beach

Camps Bay, with the spectacular Twelve Apostles as a backdrop, is just 15 minutes from Cape Town

Pienaar Museum (☎ 541 1172, 42 Church St; adult/child R5/free; open 9am-12.30pm & 2pm-5pm Mon-Fri, 9am-12.30pm Sat). It's marginally more interesting than most country town museums.

Places to Stay & Eat

The publicity association (☎/fax 541 1366, 42 Kerk St), next to the museum, has a full list of local accommodation and takes bookings. Prices start as low as R30 per person for basic self-catering cottages. The village's only hotel, *The Swartberg Country Lodge* (☎ 541 1332, Church St), was closed for renovation following a fire when we visited.

Dennehof Karoo Guesthouse (☎ 541 1227, fax 541 1158, W www.home.intekom com/dennehof) Self-catering R100-135 per person, B&B from R160 per person. On the southern (Swartberg Pass) edge of town, Dennehof may occupy the town's oldest house (1835) but the rooms have contemporary style. For backpackers there's a R95 per person room-only deal. The owners also have the nearby *Olive House*, a gorgeous self-catering cottage with its own little vineyard and exceptional views.

Onse Rus (☎ 541 1380, fax 541 1064, 47 Church St) Singles/doubles B&B R170/300. Onse Rus is a very appealing place with a thatched roof and friendly hosts. Lunches (R25) are also served on its grassy and shaded front garden.

Prince Albert of Saxe-Coburg Lodge (☎/fax 541 1267, W www.saxecoburg.co.za, 60 Church St) Singles/doubles B&B R170/260. The owners of this homely place (with a small pool) are a great source of information and offer guided hikes in the area, including a three-day trip to Die Hell (see Around Prince Albert later).

De Bergkant Lodge (☎/fax 541 1088, e bergkant@iafrica.com) Doubles B&B from R500. Prince Albert's fanciest guesthouse has antique decorated rooms, with underfoot heating and air-conditioning as well as bathrooms with twin showers. An old fire truck is used for sundowner drives.

Karoo Kombuis (☎ 541 1110, 18 Deurdrift St) Mains R35. Open 7pm-9pm Mon-Sat. As good a reason to come to Prince Albert as any, this excellent restaurant serves traditional home-cooked dishes with panache, including a complimentary sherry on arrival, and the possibility of some fun and games afterwards!

Sampie se Plaasstal (Church St) is a simple but good farm-produce stall selling a range of snacks and refreshing home-made ginger beer.

Getting There & Away

Most people visit by driving over one of the area's passes from Oudtshoorn, or from the N1 between Cape Town and Jo'burg. However, if you've come for hiking there's no reason not to take a train, which is cheaper than the buses. Most places to stay will pick you up from the train station, where you can also ask the long-distance buses to drop you.

Bus The nearest Intercape, Translux and Greyhound stop (on the run between Cape

---

Swartberg Pass

Built by the brilliant engineer Thomas Bain, between 1881 and 1888, the Swartberg Pass is arguably the most spectacular in the country. It's 24km long and reaches nearly 1600m in height.

Proteas, watsonias and other fynbos are prolific. After the summit (Die Top) – where there are incredible views over the bleak Karoo and, on the other side, the greenery of the Little Karoo – the road meanders down into a fantastic geology of twisted sedimentary layers. The best picnic sites are on the northern side; the gorge narrows and in spring is full of pelargoniums. There are some quiet spots where you can sunbathe or swim.

Don't be put off by the warning signs at each end of the pass. It's a fairly easy drive as long as you take it very slowly. The road is narrow, there are very long drops and many of the corners are blind.

The hostels in Oudtshoorn will drive you and a bicycle to the top and you can ride back down. This is a huge buzz (although take along plenty of water) but the real beauty of the pass is deeper in, towards Prince Albert.

WESTERN CAPE

Town and Jo'burg/Pretoria) is at Laingsburg, 120km or so away, but you can arrange to be dropped at Prince Albert Road, the railway halt.

Train The nearest train station is Prince Albert Road, 45km north-west of Prince Albert. The daily *Trans Karoo* between Cape Town and Jo'burg stops here. For R90 per person the ***Prince Albert of Saxe-Coburg Lodge*** will not only pick you up but also take you via the Swartberg Pass to Oudtshoorn to connect with the weekly Saturday overnight train service back to Cape Town.

Minibus Taxi If you need a taxi to Oudtshoorn or anywhere else hereabouts, contact **Christe Joorste** (☎ 541 1534).

AROUND PRINCE ALBERT
Die Hell
In a narrow valley in the Swartberg Range is Die Hell, or Gamkaskloof. The first citizens of Die Hell were early Trekboers, who developed their own dialect. There was no road into Die Hell until the 1960s and the few goods that the self-sufficient community needed were carried by donkey from Prince Albert. Maybe it's a coincidence but within 30 years of the roads being built all the farmers had left. Now the area is part of a nature reserve where there is a camping ground.

The dirt road to Die Hell turns off the Swartberg Pass road about 20km from Prince Albert and extends for another 60km or so before hitting a dead end. Allow yourself the best part of a day to explore (or try hiking from Prince Albert), or you can camp here at Elandspad. There are also houses starting at R150 a doubles.

Other Attractions
Prince Albert is a good base for both seeing the Karoo and hiking on the more than 100km of trails in the **Swartberg Nature Reserve**. Overnight walks have to be booked through **Cape Nature Conservation** (☎ 044-279 1739, *Queen's Mall, Baron van Rheede St, Oudtshoorn*). For guides, contact the Prince Albert of Saxe-Coburg Lodge (see Places to Stay under Prince Albert earlier).

There's a good drive east to **Klaarstroom**, a tiny dorp (small town) along the foot of the mountains. The road runs along a valley overwhelmed by the Groot Swartberg Range which is cut by more dramatic gullies, clefts and waterfalls. On the R329 between Prince Albert (40km) and Klaarstroom (10km) **Remhoogte Hiking Trail** can be walked in about five hours but there is a camping place on the trail.

Meiringspoort, south of Klaarstroom, on the N12 route between Beaufort West and Oudtshoorn, is an extraordinary place, following a river that cuts right through the Swartberg Range. It's not quite in the same class as Swartberg Pass, partly because it's a main road and partly because it's not as deep or as narrow.

On the road up to Prince Albert Road station and at the station itself keep an eye out for the work of local celebrity **Outa Lappies**, a septuagenarian artist and philosopher who makes 'something out of nothing'. His old homestead is on the R407, while his new cottage is opposite the station – it's the one with the tin toy windmills on the fence and a front yard full of junk creations.

BEAUFORT WEST
☎ 023 • postcode 6970 • pop 35,000
Established in 1818, Beaufort West is not only the oldest town in the Karoo, but also the largest. In summer it becomes a sluice gate for the torrent of South Africans heading for the coast. Accommodation is booked out and prices rise.

The town is not completely lacking in appeal and is a gateway for the nearby Karoo National Park (see later). But most people will be happy to snatch a cold drink, some petrol and perhaps a sleep.

Tourist information (☎ 415 1488, Cnr Donkin & Church Sts; open 8am-4pm Mon-Fri) is on the main street in the old town hall opposite the church with the tall white spire. Next door is the **museum** (☎ 415 2308, Donkin St; adult/child R5/1; open 8.30am-4.45pm Mon-Fri, 9am-noon Sat), which has displays on local-lad-made-good Dr Christiaan Barnard, who performed the world's first human heart transplant.

Places to Stay & Eat

If you have tents and transport, go to the Karoo National Park. If not, there are plenty of options in town.

Donkin House (☎/fax 414 4287, 14 Donkin St) Singles/doubles with shared bathroom from R90/100, with own bathroom R150. Motel-style accommodation is on offer at this reasonable budget place at the northern end of the main road.

Formule 1 (☎ 415 2421, 144 Donkin St) Singles/doubles/triples all R165. If all you need is a clean bed for the night this sterile chain hotel will do.

Karoo Lodge (☎/fax 414 3877, 94 Donkin St) Singles/doubles R60/120. There are slightly cheaper rooms with shared bathrooms in this old-fashioned hotel with a touch of character. It also has a *restaurant* serving standard meals for around R30 a main.

Oasis Hotel (☎/fax 414 3221, 66 Donkin St) Singles/doubles R146/242. The Oasis is another relic from the past, albeit in reasonable shape with friendly staff and large rooms.

Ye Olde Thatch (☎/fax 414 2209, 155 Donkin St) Singles/doubles R130/220. There are only four rooms at this small guesthouse and restaurant at the southern end of town, but they're nicely decorated and all have en suites. The *restaurant* serves Karoo specialities at around R35 a main and is open from 6.30pm daily.

Matoppo Inn (☎ 415 1055, fax 415 1080, 7 Bird St) Singles/doubles from R240/390. If you plan to splurge on accommodation this is your place. It's in the town's old drostdy, built in 1834, and set back from the northern end of Donkin St. The rooms have high ceilings and are spacious, the more expensive are decorated with antique furniture. There's also a big garden and pool. Breakfast costs R35 and the four-course dinner R75.

Mac Young's (☎ 414 4068, 171 Donkin St) Mains from R40. Open 6.30am-10pm daily. Internet access is also available at this restaurant, by the Caltex petrol station at the southern end of Donkin St. The Scottish theme is played up to the hilt.

Getting There & Away

Bus Beaufort West is a junction for many bus services. Most buses stop on Donkin St outside the Oasis Hotel. The hotel is the Translux agent. The following services all stop at Beaufort West.

Jo'burg–Cape Town Intercape, Translux and Greyhound stop here on their daily service between Jo'burg/Pretoria and Cape Town. All companies run via Bloemfontein, but Translux and Intercape also have service running via Kimberley. Translux fares from Beaufort West include: Bloemfontein (R195), Kimberley (R175), Paarl (R200), Cape Town (R220) and Jo'burg (R290).

Jo'burg–Garden Route Greyhound and Translux run between Jo'burg and Knysna. Greyhound runs via Bloemfontein and Translux alternates between Bloemfontein and Kimberley. From Beaufort West, Translux goes to Oudtshoorn (R65) and to Mossel Bay, George and Knysna (R180). Intercape runs twice a week between Plettenberg Bay and Jo'burg via Bloemfontein.

Cape Town–Eastern Cape Translux runs between Cape Town and East London five times a week. Stops and fares from Beaufort West include: Graaff-Reinet (R100), Cradock (R120), Queenstown (R155), King William's Town (R180) and East London (R190). Most days there's also a Translux service between Cape Town and Durban (R310 from Beaufort West) that runs a roundabout route through Bloemfontein and the Free State highlands.

Train The *Trans Karoo* stops at the station on Church St on its daily journey between Cape Town and Jo'burg.

Minibus Taxi Most taxis stop at the BP petrol station at the southern end of Donkin St, not far from the caravan park. Destinations include Oudtshoorn (R70) and Cape Town (R80).

KAROO NATIONAL PARK

Just 5km to the north of Beaufort West, the Karoo National Park was proclaimed in 1979 and covers 33,000 hectares of impressive Karoo landscapes and representative flora. The plains carry a variety of short shrubs, with well-wooded dry watercourses and mountain grasslands at higher elevations.

The park has 61 species of mammal, the most common of which are dassies (agile, rodent-like mammals, also called hyraxes) and bat-eared foxes. The antelope population is small but some species have been reintroduced and their numbers are growing. These include springbok, kudu, gemsbok, reedbuck, red hartebeest and rhebok. Mountain zebra have also been reintroduced, as has the odd black rhino. There are a great many reptiles and birds.

The entrance gates are open 5am to 10pm and the main reception desk is open 7.30am to 8pm. Day visitors are charged R20 per vehicle. Facilities include a shop and restaurant. There are two short nature trails and an 11km day walk. There are also vehicle routes and day or overnight 4WD guided trails.

Bookings for accommodation (including camp sites) should be made in advance through the **National Parks Board** (☎ 012-343 1991). The cottages and bungalows are of a high standard – fully equipped and air-conditioned. A bungalow (sleeps three) costs R300 a double, a cottage (sleeps six) costs R550 for four people. There's also a pleasant caravan park that charges R44 a double.

MATJIESFONTEIN

One of the most fascinating places in the Karoo, Matjiesfontein (pronounced 'mikeysfontein') is a small railway siding around a grand hotel that has remained virtually unchanged for one hundred years. If you're passing this way, you should certainly pause to look around, or better still stay overnight

The developer of the hotel and surrounding hamlet was one Jimmy Logan, a Scot whose rise through Cape society was so swift that by the age of 36 he not only was a member of parliament, but also ran every railway refreshment room between the Cape and Bulawayo (Zimbabwe). Matjiesfontein was his home base, and the hotel and other accommodation, together with the climate (the crisp air is likened to dry champagne), attracted wealthy people as a health resort.

As well as the attractive old buildings, including a church, courthouse and post office/general store, there's a fascinating **museum** (admission R3; open 8am-5pm Tues, Thur, Sat & Sun, 8.30am-5.30pm Mon, Wed & Fri) in the train station that's a right old jumble sale, containing everything from trophy heads to a collection of commodes

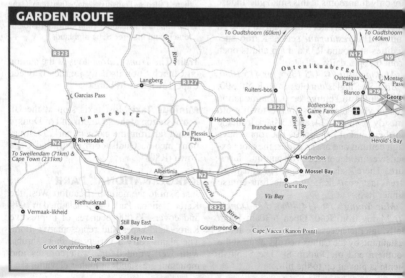

If you decide to stay there are a few choices.

The Lord Milner Hotel (☎ *023-551 3011, fax 551 3020,* W *www.matjiesfontein .com*) Singles/doubles B&B from R240/ 380, six-person cottage R400. You'll enjoy bags of old world charm at this classic period piece, with a range of comfortable rooms and atmospheric reception areas. Get the staff to show you the swimming pool in the gardens at the back. Surprisingly, meals in the hotel's dining room, with waitresses in lace bobble caps, are reasonably priced (mains R40) and there is silver service to boot. It's open 7pm-9pm daily.

The Losieshuis Singles/doubles R170/ 260. The owners of The Lord Milner also run The Losieshuis, which is excellent value accommodation in converted cottages next to the hotel.

For a snack try the **Coffee Shop**, which is open 9am-5pm daily, and for a drink, nip into **The Laird's Arms**, an authentic Victorian boozer.

Getting There & Away

Matjiesfontein is just off the N1, 240km from Cape Town and 198km from Beaufort West. A night in the hotel would be worth a stopover on the *Trans Karoo* train trip between Jo'burg and Cape Town, although 24 hours here might be a bit long unless you have a good book. Alternatively, take the train from Cape Town (arriving at 2.46pm), stay the night and catch the 8.25am train back again next day; it's a 5½ hour trip. The *Blue Train* also pauses here for an hour, with travellers being given a tour of town on the double-decker London bus that stands outside the station.

Garden Route

The much-hyped Garden Route encompasses a verdant and highly attractive stretch of coastline from Still Bay in the west to just beyond Plettenberg Bay in the east. Its main attractions are the beaches, the forests with some excellent walks and a wide range of activities from diving and sailing to bungee jumping and quadbiking.

Backpackers are well catered for, with plenty of hostels in hot competition to make sure you have a good time and stay as long as possible. The hostels also make it feasible

WESTERN CAPE

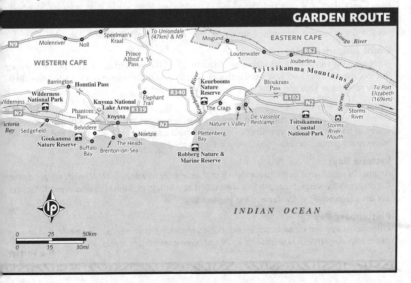

GARDEN ROUTE

INDIAN OCEAN

for those on a budget to stay during the peak summer season, when prices at other places soar. Still, you'd be advised to book ahead whether you're staying in a hostel or an up-market hotel. If you're looking for a base, the best bet is Knysna, closely followed by Plettenberg Bay.

The narrow coastal plain is mostly bordered by extensive lagoons that run behind a barrier of sand dunes and superb white beaches. Inland, the Outeniqua and Tsitsikamma Ranges, which are between 1000m and 1700m high and crossed by some spectacular road passes, split the coast from the semidesert Karoo.

The Garden Route has some of the most significant tracts of indigenous forest in the country including giant yellowwood trees and many wildflowers. The forests are still harvested commercially and there

are also large eucalypt and pine plantations. The climate is mild and noticeably wetter than elsewhere; the highest chance of rainfall and grey days is from August to October.

If you plan to do any walking, it's worth while buying a copy of *On Foot in the Garden Route* by Judith Hopley, sold in some of the information centres along the route.

Although the Garden Route is unquestionably beautiful, it is also quite heavily (and sometimes tackily) developed. Prices jump by at least 30% from late January to May and more than doubles over national December, January and Easter holidays when the crowds here can become ridiculous. Remember, if you leave South Africa without having seen the Garden Route it isn't a disaster; if you leave having seen only the Garden Route, it might be.

Surfing Along the Garden Route

Travelling down from Cape Town, the water gets a lot warmer. A spring suit or baggies in summer and autumn, and a full suit in winter is all you need. Tidal variations and changing wind directions are extremely important when it comes to the quality of the waves you'll find. The following are some recommended breaks.

Still Bay Point

Long right point break, best at pushing tide, you can make waves from all the way outside to the inside. It's a long wave with sections and lots of cutting back into the juice. Does not hold a big swell, 4-6 foot is good, otherwise a strong rip. S/W wind is perfect offshore.

Groot Jongensfontein

Right breaking waves wrap into this small beautiful bay, 11km west of Still Bay. Playful fun wave, 3-5 foot. Needs a medium S/W swell with a rare north wind. Early mornings are a good time. Best at low to medium high tide.

Mossel Bay Peninsula

Offers no less than five excellent and consistent quality reef and point breaks with many secretive waves to be found in the area. Check with locals about conditions and you could end up surfing waves many people, including South Africans, can only dream of!

Victoria Bay

Another beautiful small bay with fun right hand break; early mornings or N/W winds are good, also OK on light S/W winds, holds 2-8 foot waves. Best at lowish to medium high tide. When flat, check out the beach breaks of Wilderness and Herold's Bay.

Plettenberg Bay

Offers some rare and classic beach breaks, but is very fickle and inconsistent. Combine east or west swells with rare N/W or N winds and you'll surf some classic beach breaks

Nic Vorster

TRAVELLING THE ROUTE

As always your own transport will give you the greatest flexibility. If you don't want to drive the whole way, consider taking a bus to Knysna (the three major bus lines run at least daily from Cape Town to Port Elizabeth via the main Garden Route towns) and then hiring a car for a few days.

On Greyhound, Intercape and Translux you can't book short sector trips between the Garden Route towns, and the tickets are expensive anyway. If you plan to explore the area by bus you'd be better off with the hop-on, hop-off pass offered by the Baz Bus. Otherwise, taking minibus taxis is easy enough.

The steam train between George and Knysna stopping at Wilderness (see the boxed text 'Outeniqua Choo-Tjoe & Power Van' later) is popular and recommended.

Between them the three main bus companies also run daily services between Jo'burg/Pretoria and the Garden Route. Greyhound and Translux run to Knysna, and Intercape goes further to Plettenberg Bay. From the Garden Route, fares to Pretoria are the same as fares to Jo'burg; add an hour of travelling time.

From Port Elizabeth (see the Eastern Cape chapter) you can connect with buses to East London, Umtata and Durban.

MOSSEL BAY

☎ 044 • postcode 6500 • pop 59,000

Once one of the jewels of the Garden Route, Mossel Bay (Mosselbaai) is now marred by industrial sprawl, in particular the gas/petrol conversion refinery on its outskirts. Despite this, the town centre has some attractive historic and sandstone buildings, the only north-facing beach in the country and some top surf spots (see the boxed text 'Surfing Along the Garden Route'). This is not a party town, though, and is practically dead during the weekends and in low season.

The first European to visit the bay was the Portuguese explorer Bartholomeu Dias in 1488, and he was followed by Vasco da Gama in 1497. From then on, many ships stopped to take on fresh water, and to barter for provisions with the Gouriqua Khoikhoi who lived in the region. A large milkwood tree beside the spring was used as a postal collection point – expeditions heading east would leave mail to be picked up by ships returning home. The spring and the tree still exist, and you can post letters (they receive a special postmark) from a letterbox on the site.

European farmers established themselves in the area in the second half of the 18th century. In 1786 the VOC constructed a granary (not far from the post office tree and now part of the museum complex) and Mossel Bay developed as a port.

Orientation & Information

The town lies on the northern slopes of Cape St Blaize. The museum complex, which overlooks the bay, is the best place to start your exploration. Nearby is the **tourism bureau** (☎ 691 2202, Market St; open 8am-6pm Mon-Fri, 9am-1pm Sat & Sun). If it's shut try the private **Tourism Information Centre** (☎ 690 8388) nearby, next to the Old Post Office Tree Manor.

Internet access is available at **PostNet** (☎ 690 7779, Bland St; R15 per half-hour; open 8.15am-5pm Mon-Fri & 8.30am-12.30pm Sat).

Bartholomeu Dias Museum Complex

The highlight of the Bartholomeu Dias Museum Complex (☎ 691 1067, Market St; admission to the complex R5; maritime & shell museums open 9am-5pm Mon-Fri, 9am-4pm Sat & Sun; history museum open 9am-5pm Mon-Fri, 9am-1pm Sat) is the replica of the vessel that Dias used on his 1488 voyage of discovery. This caravel is incredibly small, and seeing it brings home the extraordinary skill and courage of the early explorers. The replica was built in Portugal and sailed to Mossel Bay in 1988 to commemorate the 500th anniversary of Dias' trip.

In addition to the maritime museum, the complex includes the spring where Dias watered the postal tree, the 1786 VOC **granary**, a **shell museum** (with some interesting aquarium tanks) and a local **history museum**.

WESTERN CAPE

Activities

There are regular **boat trips** on the *Romonza* (☎ 690 3101) and *The Seven Seas* (☎ 691 3371) to Seal Island from the harbour behind the train station. The trips last one hour and cost around R35. In late winter and spring it's not unusual to see whales on the trip.

Mossel Bay Divers (☎ 691 1441, *Santos Protea Hotel*) rents out snorkel gear and body-boards as well as offering PADI/NAUI courses. **Shark Africa** (☎/fax 691 3796, e *sharkafrica@mweb.com*) organises cage dives and snorkelling to view great white sharks for R600 – you get R300 back if you don't spot sharks.

Kiwi Extreme (☎ 691 2202) offers bridge jumping and bungee jumping at Gouritz Bridge 35km from Mossel Bay. The cost is around R150; the hostels can arrange transfers.

Check with **Real Cape Adventures** (☎ 082-556 2520, W *www.seakayak.co.za*) about sea kayaking here and at other locations on the Garden Route.

Surfing trips are run by **Friends Surfing Adventures** (☎ 698 1269, e *friendz@mweb .co.za*) for US$120 per day for one person,

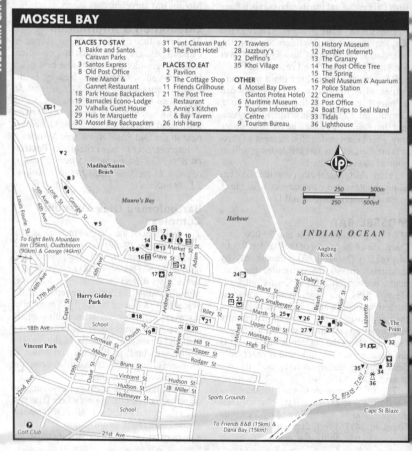

MOSSEL BAY

PLACES TO STAY
1 Bakke and Santos Caravan Parks
3 Santos Express
8 Old Post Office Tree Manor & Gannet Restaurant
18 Park House Backpackers
19 Barnacles Econo-Lodge
20 Valhalla Guest House
29 Huis te Marquette
30 Mossel Bay Backpackers
31 Punt Caravan Park
34 The Point Hotel

PLACES TO EAT
2 Pavilion
5 The Cottage Shop
11 Friends Grillhouse
21 The Post Tree Restaurant
25 Annie's Kitchen & Bay Tavern
26 Irish Harp
27 Trawlers
28 Jazzbury's
32 Delfino's
35 Khoi Village

OTHER
4 Mossel Bay Divers (Santos Protea Hotel)
6 Maritime Museum
7 Tourism Information Centre
9 Tourism Bureau
10 History Museum
12 PostNet (Internet)
13 The Granary
14 The Post Office Tree
15 The Spring
16 Shell Museum & Aquarium
17 Police Station
22 Cinema
23 Post Office
24 Boat Trips to Seal Island
33 Tidals
36 Lighthouse

US$75 per person for two to four people, and US$65 for five or six. The service includes airport pick-ups (Cape Town or George), transport, most accommodation, breakfast and dinner.

Hikers should tackle the magnificent **St Blaze Trail**, running for 15km from The Point to Dana Bay (Danabaai) along the cliff tops. A round trip takes at least eight hours.

Places to Stay

Mossel Bay has lots of affordable accommodation, including some good backpackers and B&Bs; the tourism bureau can suggest alternatives and make bookings if the places following are full.

Caravan Parks There are three municipal parks with the same contact details and prices.

Bakke, Santos and *Punt* (☎ *691 2915, fax 691 1251*) Camp sites from R55, 1-bedroom chalets from R160. There are two adjacent municipal caravan parks, *Bakke* and *Santos*, on pretty Madiba Beach (the bay beach) and also *Punt* on The Point, a little further from the town centre but close to the surf. Prices rise in the high season.

Hostels Mossel Bay has a good selection of backpacker accommodation to choose from.

Park House Backpackers (☎ *691 1937, fax 691 3815,* e *meyer@law.co.za, 118 Montagu St*) Dorm beds R50, doubles R140. The most elegant of Mossel Bay's backpacker options is based in a 130-year-old stone mansion and is smartly decorated. The dorm, in a separate barn-like building at the back, is spacious and clean.

Barnacles Econo-Lodge (☎/*fax 690 4584,* e *bismos@mweb.co.za, 112 High St*) Dorm beds R50, singles R100, doubles R130-180. Barnacles is another very appealing, colourful place, with great views from its roof deck and a friendly vibe. It also has a bar and does budget meals.

Mossel Bay Backpackers (☎/*fax 691 3182,* e *marquette@pixie.co.za, 1 Marsh St*) Dorm beds R50, doubles R140. Close by the beach at The Point and the bars on March St, this long-established place is reliable and

well run. It offers a pool and bar; there are bicycles and boogie boards for rent.

Santos Express (☎/*fax 691 1995, Santos Beach*) Dorm beds R45, singles/doubles B&B R80/120. The position of this converted train, right beside the beach, can't be beaten, even if the compartments are a bit cramped. For dorm beds you'll need your own bedding. There's also a bar-restaurant and beer garden.

B&Bs, Guesthouses & Hotels *Valhalla Guest House* (☎ *691 1075, fax 690 7977,* e *cranbar@yebo.co.za, 86 Montagu St*) Singles/doubles B&B from R100/240. Self-catering units are also available at this convivial guesthouse. Breakfast is taken on the balcony, which has a sweeping view of the bay.

Old Post Office Tree Manor (☎ *691 3738, fax 691 3104,* w *www.oldposttree .co.za, Market St*) Singles/doubles B&B R295/550. More like a hotel than a guesthouse, the Old Post Office has nicely furnished characterful rooms. Also check out the bright and informal *Gannet Restaurant* (mains are R50, and it's open 7pm-11pm daily) and sea-facing *Blue Oyster Bar*.

Huis te Marquette (☎/*fax 691 3182,* e *marquette@pixie.co.za, 1 Marsh St*) Singles/doubles B&B from R250/450. This classy, long-running guesthouse, near The Point, has its more expensive rooms facing onto the pool.

The Point Hotel (☎ *691 3512, fax 691 3513,* w *www.pointhotel.co.za, The Point*) Singles/doubles R385/495. This hotel is an eyesore but in a spectacular location, right above the wave-pounded rocks at The Point. All the spacious rooms have a balcony and ocean views.

Other There are also a couple of good options outside Mossel Bay itself.

Friends B&B (☎/*fax 698 1269,* w *www .friendzsurf.com, 35 Erica St, Dana Bay*) Singles/doubles B&B R150/235. Super-friendly accommodation is provided by cool surfer dudes Nic and Heidi in a residential suburb 5km south-west of Mossel Bay by road (15km along the coastal track). They

WESTERN CAPE

also run surfing safaris along the Garden Route (see Friends Surfing Adventures under Activities earlier) and the new *Friends Grillhouse* takeaway food outlet in Mossel Bay's Bay View shopping centre, opposite the tourism bureau.

Eight Bells Mountain Inn (☎ 631 0000, fax 631 0004, **W** www.eightbells.co.za) Singles/doubles B&B from R365/550. On the R328, 35km north of Mossel Bay, this upmarket country inn is in a very pleasant spot and has good facilities, rooms and service.

Places to Eat

There are plenty of pubs serving food and within walking distance of each other along Marsh St, including *Irish Harp* (☎ 691 2252); *Trawlers* (☎ 691 3073); and *Annie's Kitchen* (☎ 690 3708) at the *Bay Tavern*. Also check out *Tidals* (☎ 691 3777), right on the rocks at The Point.

The Post Tree Restaurant (☎ 691 1177, Cnr Riley & Powrie Sts) Mains from R50. Open noon-2.30pm Mon-Fri, 6.30pm-10.30pm daily. The Post Tree gives friendly service and a good range of dishes including interesting salads and pastas. Eat either indoors or in the candle-lit courtyard.

Pavilion (☎ 690 4567, Madiba Beach) Mains R25-40. Open noon-5pm daily. In a 19th-century bathing pavilion (hence the name), the Pavilion is a fine choice for lunch beside the beach.

The Cottage Shop (☎ 691 2607, Munro Bay) Mains R20. Open 9am-6pm Mon-Sat. Overlooking the water, this is a pleasant spot for an afternoon tea of scones and cream (R10.50).

Jazzbury's (☎ 691 1923, 11 Marsh St) Mains from R50. Open 6pm-11pm Mon-Sat. Come to Jazzbury's to try some traditional African dishes, such as mopani worms and Cape Malay food, as well as the more usual ostrich, beef and seafood creations.

Delfino's (☎ 690 5247, The Point) Mains from R25. Open 7.30am-11.30pm. This eatery is the perfect spot for breakfast by the beach (R21.50), a lazy lunch or a pizza and beer at sunset.

Khoi Village (☎ 690 4940, The Point) Set meal R40. Open 7pm-11pm daily. Be-side the lighthouse, this rather dubious recreation of a Khoi encampment does a good-value buffet of traditional grub. It's also possible to stay overnight here in very basic grass huts.

Getting There & Away

Bus Mossel Bay is off the highway, so long-distance buses don't come into town; they drop you at the Voorbaai Shell petrol station, 7km away. The hostels can usually collect you if you give notice and the Baz Bus will drop you in town.

Greyhound, Intercape and Translux stop here on their Cape Town to Port Elizabeth services. Translux fares from Mossel Bay include: Knysna (R75, you can't book this sector), Plettenberg Bay (R130), Cape Town (R115) and Port Elizabeth (R125).

Translux stops in Mossel Bay on its route between Knysna and Jo'burg via either Bloemfontein or Kimberley. Fares from Mossel Bay include: Kimberley (R260) and Jo'burg (R310). A similar service is offered by Greyhound at similar prices. Intercape runs between Plettenberg Bay and Jo'burg via the Garden Route.

AROUND MOSSEL BAY
Botlierskop Game Farm

The Botlierskop Game Farm (☎/fax 696 6055, Little Brak River) is around 20km east of Mossel Bay along the N2 (take the Little Brak River turn-off and follow the signs towards Sorgfontein). It offers a chance to view a vast range of wildlife, including lions, rhinos, buffalo, giraffe and blue wildebeest, in excellent conditions. This a place where animals are bred for sale to other parks and although they are free to roam in 1500 hectares the chances of spotting most breeds, including the very rare black impala and sable antelope, are high. The four lions – hand-reared, thus incapable of looking after themselves in the wild – are kept in a separate sanctuary. Three-hour game drives (R150 per person) are run either early morning or late in the afternoon; you must book ahead. The owners have plans to open a restaurant here serving traditional South African dishes.

GEORGE

☎ 044 • postcode 6529 • pop 140,000

George, the largest town on the Garden Route, was founded in 1811. It has some attractive old buildings, including the tiny St Mark's Cathedral and the more imposing Dutch Reformed Mother Church. But it's 8km from the coast and, for most people, who come only to ride on the steam train service (see the boxed text 'Outeniqua Choo-Tjoe & Power Van'), there's no great reason to stay.

Orientation & Information

The N2 enters this sprawling town from the south on York St, which is a long, four-lane avenue, terminating at a T-junction with Courtenay St – head west for Oudtshoorn, east for Wilderness. The main commercial area is on the eastern side of York St around Hibernia and Market Sts.

The **tourism bureau** (☎ 801 9295/6, **w** www.georgetourism.co.za, 124 York St; open 8am-4.30pm Mon-Fri, 9am-1pm Sat) has a lot of information and maps and also has an accommodation booking service.

George Museum

This museum (☎ 873 5343, Junction of York & Courtney Sts; adult/child R5/1; open 9am-4.30pm Mon-Fri) occupies the site of George's old drostdy first built in 1813, but reconstructed after a fire 13 years later. The displays, which include ones on the local timber industry and some antique musical instruments, don't amount to much.

Steam Train Museum

The starting point and terminus for journeys on the *Outeniqua Choo-Tjoe* steam train is the Steam Train Museum (☎ 801 8295, Just off Courtenay St; adult/child R5/2; open 7.30am-6pm Mon-Sat) but it's worth visiting in its own right, especially if you're interested in trains. Some 11 locomotives and 15 carriages, as well as many detailed models, have found a retirement home here; some have been better cared for than others, but you can climb into most, including a carriage used by the British royal family in the 1940s. The building uses old carriages to house a collection of vintage cars and a cafe. This museum is around 1km east of George Museum.

Places to Stay

George Tourist Resort (☎ 874 5205, fax 874 4255, York St) Camping R60 for up to 4 people. This large, flash caravan park on the edge of town has a restaurant, indoor heated pool, gym and mini golf course.

George Backpackers (☎ 874 7807, fax 874 6054, 29 York St) Camp sites R25, dorm beds R45, singles/doubles R80/120. Though a bit closer into the town centre than the caravan park, this place is nothing to write home about. You'd do better inquiring with the tourism bureau about local B&Bs, starting at around R85 per person.

Outeniqua Choo-Tjoe & Power Van

The reason most people come to George is to take the *Outeniqua Choo-Tjoe (in George* ☎ 801 8288, in Knysna ☎ 382 1361; one way/return to Krysna R45/55). This steam train, in operation since 1928, chugs at a leisurely pace along the coast and through the country. Two trains run daily, departing from George at 9.30am and 2pm and leaving Knysna at 9.45am and 2.15pm. Reservations are recommended. You can also pick up the service in Wilderness.

The return trip from George is 7½ hours, so if you have to return to collect your car, consider taking the 9.30am train to Sedgefield (arriving 10.53am), then hopping across the platform onto the waiting train from Knysna (departing 10.58am) to return to George at 12.30pm. You'll still see some beautiful scenery on this section.

As well as the steam train there's the Outeniqua Power Van, a rail trolley that runs several interesting excursions around George and also sometimes does the George-Knysna run. You have to book (☎ 801 8239).

WESTERN CAPE

Protea Foresters Hotel (☎ 874 4488, fax 874 4428, e foresters@pixie.co.za, 123 York St) Singles/doubles R335/445. This functional, mid-range option is opposite the tourism bureau, and has frequent special deals for R250 a room.

Fancourt Hotel (☎ 804 0000, fax 804 0700, w www.fancourt.com, Montagu St, Blanco) Doubles from R1000. This is the area's most luxurious place, about 10km from the town centre, and has no less than three 18-hole golf courses (two designed by Gary Player) and a range of accommodation options, all very expensive.

Places to Eat

Keg & Loerie (☎ 873 3482, 127 York St) Mains R30. Open noon-3pm daily, 6pm-10.30pm Mon-Thur, 6pm-11.30pm Fri & Sat, 6pm-9.30pm Sun. A friendly traditional pub, opposite the tourism bureau, Keg & Loerie has a good range of inexpensive tasty dishes including home-made pies and wraps.

Reel n' Rustic (☎ 884 0707, Courtenay St) Mains R50. Open for lunch & dinner daily. Specialising in Creole and Cajun steaks and seafood, this is one of the best restaurants hereabouts, with another popular branch in nearby Wilderness. Booking at weekends is advised.

The Copper Pot (☎ 870 7378, 12 Montagu St, Blanco) Mains R50. Open 7pm-10pm Mon-Sat. A George institution, this formal restaurant has an eclectic menu, ranging from curries to paella.

The King Fisher (☎ 873 3127, 1 Courtenay St) Mains R40. Open for lunch & dinner daily. On the way to the Steam Train Museum, The King Fisher serves good value seafood and pizzas.

Leila's Arms (☎ 870 0292, Witfontein Rd) Set menu R65. Open noon-3pm, 7pm-10pm Wed & Fri. This organic restaurant is 8km west of the town centre in Blanco. Booking is essential.

Entertainment

The liveliest spot at the weekend is the rave club at *Carousel* in the shopping centre on Courtenay St, 500m east of the George Museum.

Getting There & Around

South African Airways (SAA) flies to George airport (☎ 876 9310), which is about 15km south of town.

Most buses stop in St Mark's Square, behind the Geronimo Spur steakhouse on the main street. Greyhound, Intercape and Translux services stop here on their way from Cape Town to Port Elizabeth and on their runs between Jo'burg and the Garden Route. Translux fares from George include Knysna (R75), Mossel Bay (R65), Plettenberg Bay (R75), Port Elizabeth (R115), Cape Town (R130), Kimberley (R260) and Jo'burg (R320).

The Baz Bus drops off in town and you can call the hostels in Oudtshoorn for shuttle services there.

The weekly *Southern Cross* train between Cape Town and Oudtshoorn stops here.

The minibus taxi stop is on Cradock St.

AROUND GEORGE
Montagu & Outeniqua Passes

One interesting drive from George is out on the Montagu Pass and back on the Outeniqua Pass (from Oudtshoorn). The Montagu Pass is a quiet dirt road that winds its way through the mountains; it was opened in 1847 and is now a national monument. Take a picnic, because there are some great picnic sites and beautiful fynbos to admire along the way. The views from the Outeniqua Pass are actually more spectacular than from the Montagu, but it's a main road, so it's a lot more difficult to stop when you want to.

Seven Passes Road

The Seven Passes Road to Knysna used to be the main road link, and it is easy to imagine how difficult and dangerous it must have been for the pioneers and their ox-wagons. The road is still unsurfaced for quite a way and, thanks to the timber trucks, some parts are rough, so the trip will take two hours. It's a pleasant enough route but most of the countryside is now dominated by pine, gum trees and Port Jackson wattle, leaving only small patches of fynbos – if you want spectacular views, stick to the N2.

Herold's Bay

Some 30km southwest of George is the sleepy village of Herold's Bay, with one small shop, a good beach and a beautiful stretch of coast. The town gets very crowded in high season and on summer weekends but it's quiet at any other time.

Herold's Bay Caravan Park (☎ 044-801 9268, fax 873 3776) Camp sites R40. This caravan park boasts a terrific spot close to the beach; prices go up in high season.

The Loft at Dutton Cove (☎ 044-851 0155, fax 851 0041) Singles/doubles B&B R210/360. The Loft offers upmarket accommodation and great views over the bay.

Victoria Bay

Victoria Bay is tiny and picturesque, and sits at the foot of steep cliffs, around 20km south of George. It's a popular surf spot (see the boxed text 'Surfing Along the Garden Route' earlier). There's a *caravan park* (☎/fax 044-889 0081) with sites for R66/ 114 low/high season.

Sea Breeze Holiday Cottages (☎ 044- 889 0098, fax 889 0104, e seabreeze@ pixie.co.za) Self-catering cottages from R140/370 low/high season.

WILDERNESS

This beautiful stretch of coast, with rolling breakers, miles of white sand, sheltered lagoons and lush mountain hinterland has made Wilderness very popular – so much so that its name is now far from apt. Holiday homes, resorts and hotels sprinkle the hills and crowd the beach. The N2 and the George-Knysna train line parallel the coast but everything is quite widely scattered, making life very difficult if you don't have a vehicle.

The **Wilderness Tourism Bureau** (☎ 044- 877 0045; open 8am-6pm Mon-Fri, 9am- 1pm & 3pm-5pm Sat in high season) is on Leila's Lane as you pull off the N2 into the village. It makes accommodation bookings (from R95 per person B&B) and takes reservations for the *Outeniqua Choo-Tjoe* steam train – the most pleasant way to get here (although all the major bus companies run past, too).

Eden Adventures (☎ 044-877 0179) rents out canoes (R80 per day) and mountain bikes (R60 per day) as well as organising tours of the area including abseiling and kloofing (adventure activities in ravines).

Places to Stay & Eat

The Beach House (☎ 044-877 0605, fax 382 5799, e williamhoon@hotmail.com, Western Rd) Camp sites R35, dorm beds R55, singles/doubles R130/150. Keep an eye out for the turn-off for this appealing hostel before you drive past Wilderness on the N2. There's a spectacular beach view and the house and grounds are pretty nice too.

Fairy Knowe Backpackers (☎/fax 044- 877 1285, e fairybp@mweb.co.za, Dumbleton Rd) Camping R30 per person, dorm beds R50, singles/doubles R130/140. Set in spacious, leafy grounds overlooking the Touws River, this 1874 farmhouse was the first in the area; it has yellowwood floors and some original fittings. The bar and cafe are in another pretty little building some distance away, so boozers won't keep you awake. It's a great place to relax, but numbers are limited so book ahead. The Baz Bus comes to the door and the steam train stops just along the lane. If you're driving, head into Wilderness town and follow the main road for 2km to the Fairy Knowe turn-off.

Pirate's Creek (☎ 044-877 1101, fax 877 0367, w www.piratescreek.co.za, on N2 around 1km after Wilderness turn-off) Camping adult/child from R40/20, self-catering chalets from R295 for two. The wooden chalets at this mini-resort are attractive and well equipped. Other features include a nine-hole golf course, free canoes and a riverside restaurant. Prices rise sharply in high season.

Palms Wilderness Guest House (☎ 044-877 1420, fax 877 1422, w www.palms-wilderness .com) Singles/doubles B&B R450/700. Opposite the inferior Wilderness Resort, this is the fanciest place to stay. The elegantly decorated rooms in whitewashed thatched-roof cottages make it worth the money and its *restaurant* (open daily for light lunches and from 7pm to 10.30pm Monday to Saturday for dinner) comes highly recommended.

WESTERN CAPE

WESTERN CAPE

Wilderness Holiday Inn Garden Court *(☎ 044-877 1104, fax 877 1134)* Singles/doubles R379/588. Big, generic rooms, a pool and 'traditional' Irish pub feature at this chain hotel between the N2 and the beach, about 2km east of Wilderness. Discounted room rates are often on offer from Friday to Saturday.

Reel 'n Rustic's Wilderness Grille *(☎ 044-877 0808)* Open 8.30am-10pm daily. This popular grill in the heart of the village is a good place for seafood and steaks.

WILDERNESS NATIONAL PARK

Wilderness National Park *(☎ 044-877 1197; day visitors R20 per vehicle; reception office open daily 8am-5pm Jan-Nov, 8am-7pm Dec)* encompasses the area from Wilderness and the Touws River in the west to Sedgefield and the Goukamma Nature Reserve in the east. The southern boundary is the ocean and the northern boundary is the Outeniqua Range. It covers a unique system of lakes, rivers, wetlands and estuaries that are vital for the survival of many species.

There are three types of lake in the park: drowned river valleys (eg, Swartvlei); drowned low-lying areas among the dune system (eg, Langvlei); and drowned basins that have been formed by wind action (eg, Rondevlei). The rich birdlife includes the beautiful Knysna lourie and many species of kingfisher.

There are several nature trails taking in the lakes, the beach and the indigenous forest. The **Kingfisher Trail** is a day walk that traverses the region and includes a boardwalk across the intertidal zone of the Touws River. The lakes offer anglers, canoeists, windsurfers and sailors an ideal venue. Pedal boats and canoes can be hired at Ebb & Flow South camp, where there is also a small shop.

There are two similar camps in the park to stay in. ***Ebb & Flow North*** and ***Ebb & Flow South*** *(Bookings National Parks Board ☎ 012-343 1991, or direct with park Dec-Jan)* have camp sites R65 for two people, plus R16 for each additional person. Ebb & Flow South has a range of accommodation including four-bed huts with shared bathrooms for R150 a double and huts with bathrooms for R200 a double; cabins and cottages are also available. Ebb & Flow North has only huts, which cost a little less than those at the southern camp.

The park is signposted from the N2. It's possible to walk there from Wilderness.

BUFFALO BAY

Buffalo Bay (Buffelsbaai) is a small holiday village built on a point 17km west of Knysna – a gorgeous beach runs all the way to Brenton-on-Sea. It's 7km from the N2 along the Goukamma Valley.

There's a ***shop and cafe*** *(☎ 044-385 0038)* open from 8am to 6pm daily. Inquire here about local B&Bs.

Caravan Park *(☎/fax 044-383 0045)* From R65. This great park is right beside an excellent right reef break (southerly swell, south-westerly winds).

Wild Side Backpackers *(☎ 044-383 0609, fax 382 5799)* Dorm beds R50, doubles R140. Owned by the same people as Highfield Backpackers in Knysna, this fab hostel has an authentic beach shack atmosphere and plenty of activities. Staff will pick you up from Knysna and offer shuttles into town twice a day.

The **Goukamma Nature Reserve** *(☎ 044-383 0042; admission R12)*, accessible from the Buffalo Bay road, protects 14km of rocky coastline, sandstone cliffs, dunes covered with coastal fynbos and forest, and Groenvlei, a large freshwater lake. There are some small antelopes and much birdlife; 150 species including the Knysna lourie have been recorded.

Most of the reserve is accessible only by foot. There's an 8km circular trail and a 14km trail. A suspension bridge over the Goukamma River takes hikers to the start of the trail. Camping costs R46, and rondavels are R230 for up to four people. The camping ground and rondavels are on the western side of the park and are often full; book on the number given earlier.

KNYSNA

☎ 044 • postcode 6570 • pop 62,000

Perched on the edge of a serene lagoon and surrounded by forests, Knysna (pronounced

KNYSNA

PLACES TO STAY
1 Peregrin Backpackers Lodge
2 Knysna Backpackers
3 Highfield Backpackers
6 Royal Hotel
22 Wayside Inn
25 Inyathi Guest Lodges
27 Yellowwood Lodge
28 Mike's Guest House
29 Overlander's Lodge
30 Knysna Log Inn
31 The Caboose
39 Protea Hotel
   Knysna Quays

PLACES TO EAT
12 Coffee Connection
13 Ocean Basket
14 De Oude Fabriek
21 Changes
26 La Loerie
32 Mackintosh's of
   Knysna Country Store
36 The Oystercatcher
42 34° South

OTHER
4 Knysna Cycleworks
5 Post Office
7 Engen Petrol Station
8 Metamorphosis
9 Zanzibar
10 Tin Roof Blues
11 Woodmill Lane
   Shopping Centre
15 The Forestry Department
16 Bloch's Supermarket;
   Minibus Taxi Rank
17 ABSA Bureau de Change
18 First National Bank
19 Knysna Tourism
20 Harry B's
23 Knysna Movie House
24 Pledge Square;
   Knysna Book Exchange
33 Al's
34 Knysna Fine Art Gallery
35 The Travel Clinic
37 Departure point for
   MV John Benn;
   Knysna Waterfront Ferries
38 Tait Marine;
   Blue Sky Adventures
40 Bush Pig
41 African Attitude; Stones

To Knysna Caravan Park (150m);
Mitchell's Brewery (1km) &
Plettenberg Bay (30km)

To Wilderness (40km)
& George (67km)

To Thesen's
Island (300m)

WESTERN CAPE

'nie-snah') is one of the jewels of the Garden Route. It began as a timber port and ship-building centre, thanks to the lagoon and the rich indigenous forests of the area. Continuing the legacy of the timber industry are a number of excellent woodwork and furniture shops and a thriving artistic community.

With its sylvan setting, good places to stay, eat and drink, and wide range of activities, Knysna has plenty going for it. There's an arts festival in late September and early October, while in May the town goes gay with the **Pink Loerie Festival** (W www.gaymay.co.za). In the holiday season, though, the sheer numbers of visitors threaten to overwhelm it and driving through the town can be hell.

Orientation & Information
Almost everything of importance is on Main Rd, although the Waterfront development is beginning to take off along with the controversial redevelopment of Thesen's Island as a residential area.

Knysna Tourism (☎ 382 5510, W www .knysna-info.co.za, 40 Main Rd; open 8.30am-5pm daily in summer, 8.30am-5pm Mon-Sat at other times) has a good range of information on the region and an accommodation booking service. You can't miss the office – there's an enormous elephant skeleton out the front.

The Travel Clinic (☎ 382 6366, Quayside Office Park, Cnr Hedge & Gordon Sts) is a good spot to get vaccinations if you're planning further travels.

Internet access is available at the hostels and at the Waterfront in the Bush Pig outlet (see Shopping later).

The **Knysna Book Exchange** (☎ 382 2059, Pledge Square) sells a good range of second-hand books.

Knysna Lagoon
Although regulated by the National Parks Board, Knysna Lagoon, covering 13 sq km, is not a national park or wilderness area. Much is still privately owned, and the lagoon

is used by industry and for recreation. The town's famous oysters are bred here – you can find out more about this at the Knynsa Oyster Company (see Places to Eat later) on Thesen's Island.

The protected area starts just to the east of Buffalo Bay and follows the coastline to the mouth of the Noetzie River. The lagoon opens up between two sandstone cliffs, known as The Heads – once proclaimed by the British Royal Navy the most dangerous harbour entrance in the world. There are good views from a lookout on the eastern head, and a nature trail on the western head.

The best way to appreciate the lagoon is to take a cruise. The MV *John Benn* (☎ 382 1697, W *www.featherbed.co.za/cruises.htm*) has cruises for R40. It also offers the recommended Featherbed cruise (R55, four hours), which departs at 10am year-round (and at other times, too, in summer) and runs across to the other side of the lagoon to the privately owned **Featherbed Nature Reserve** where you'll be driven around.

Knysna Waterfront Ferries (☎ 382 5520, W *www.knysnaferries.co.za*) also runs oyster-and-champagne sunset cruises on the lagoon in a 40-foot catamaran for R150, regular trips for R50 and a trip up the Knysna River for R30. Bookings for any of these cruises and for the MV *John Benn* are advised and can be made at the Waterfront.

Mitchell's Brewery

A nice alternative to all that wine tasting is to drop by **Mitchell's Brewery** (☎ 382 4685, *Arend St; tastings R10; tours 10.30am Mon-Fri)*. The beers, which include a draught lager, a bitter, a stout and an ale can be found all over Western Cape. Tastings are available during the brewery's weekday opening hours.

Witlokasia

Follow Gray St uphill and eventually you'll leave town and emerge on the wooded slopes of the hills behind. On top is the sprawling township of Witlokasia, best visited on an excellent tour run by **Eco Afrika Tours** (☎ 082-925 0716, W *ecoafrika.ukweb .nu)*. The two-hour tour (R160) is led by a local guide and takes you into a pre-school and high school with a chance to talk to the students and teachers, plus a visit to a tribal witch doctor and a shebeen.

Hiking & Mountain Biking

The **Forestry Department** (☎ 382 5466, *Main Rd; open 7.30am-1pm & 1.45pm-4pm Mon-Fri)* has an office upstairs in the same shopping centre as Wimpy. This is where you book walking trails, and collect maps and information. Overnight hikes cost R15 per day including the use of trail huts.

The **Outeniqua Trail** is popular and takes a week to walk, although you can also do two- or three-day sections. Other trails through the forest include the three **Elephant Trails** and the superb but tough **Harkerville Trail**.

Bicycles aren't allowed on the walking trails but several bicycle trails have been developed. The forestry department has a map. In low season you can use the hiking huts.

Inquire at Knysna Tourism whether Judith Hopley is leading any walks; her book *On Foot in the Garden Route* is an excellent guide to the region's hikes. Also check here about mountain biking trips.

Other Activities

There are plenty of other activities on offer in the area; start by making inquiries at the **Adventure Centre** (☎ 384 0831, e *adven ture@cyberperk.co.za)*, which has a desk in Knysna Tourism's office. Among the possibilities are abseiling at The Heads (R200), horse riding (R65 for one hour) and scuba diving (R60 for a shore entry dive, R100 for a boat dive; rental gear is R150).

Tait Marine (☎ 382 4460, *6 Long St)* rents out motorboats, canoes and dinghies. **Blue Sky Adventures** (☎ 343 1757) runs guided canoe tours upriver for R100 per hour.

The closest beaches are at Buffalo Bay and Brenton-on-Sea. A surf shop called **Nirvana** (☎ 382 6316, *41 Main Rd)* rents out boards (R60 a day) and wet suits (R15 a day).

Half-day quadbiking trips in the Knysna forests are available with **SEAL Adventures** (☎ 381 0068) for R250.

Places to Stay

Low-season competition between the several backpackers and many guesthouses in town keeps prices down, but in high season expect steep price hikes (except at the backpackers) and book ahead. If you're stuck, the accommodation booking service next to Knysna Tourism can also help find a relatively inexpensive B&B. Also see Buffalo Bay (earlier) and the Around Knysna (later) for other options.

Caravan Parks *Knysna Caravan Park* (☎ 382 2011, *Main Rd*) Camp sites from R30 per person. This quiet and leafy spot has the closest sites to the centre of town.

Woodbourne Resort (☎/fax 384 0316, e *woodb.kny@pixie.co.za, George Rex Dr*) Camp sites from R40, plus R20 per person; 2-/3-bed chalets from R200. This attractive resort has a restaurant at the nearby stables. Prices go through the roof here from mid-December to mid-January.

Hostels *Highfield Backpackers* (☎ 382 6266, *fax 382 5799*, e *highfield@hotmail .com, 2 Graham St*) Dorm beds R50, singles/doubles R120/140. A pleasant, well-run hostel, Highfield has a pool, bar and large number of private rooms, so it feels more like a guesthouse.

Peregrin Backpackers Lodge (☎/fax 382 3747, e *peregrin@cyberperk.co.za, 16 High St*) Dorm beds R55, singles/doubles from R90/120. A good range of rooms are on offer at this fun place in a rambling old house with a view of the lagoon. Rates include a light breakfast.

Overlander's Lodge (☎/fax 382 5920, e *overlanders@cyberperk.co.za, 11 Nelson St*) Camping R40, dorm beds R55, doubles R140. Claiming to be Knysna's party hostel, the Lodge is a bit scruffier than the others, but it throws in some free meals, and also runs Knysna's Adventure Centre, which offers some interesting-looking hiking and canoeing trips.

Knysna Backpackers (☎/fax 382 2554, e *knybpack@netactive.co.za, 42 Queen St*) Dorm beds R55, doubles R140. You'll find mainly dorm beds at this large and spruce

Victorian house on the hill a few blocks up from the main street. It tends to be quieter and more relaxing than other places. Rates include a light DIY breakfast.

B&Bs & Guesthouses *Mike's Guest House* (☎/fax 382 1728, e *dolphins@mweb .co.za, 67 Main Rd*) Singles/doubles B&B from R130/190. Tidy en-suite rooms and some self-catering units make up this guesthouse on the main road.

Inyathi Guest Lodges (☎/fax 382 7768, W *www.inyathi-sa.com, 52 Main Rd*) Singles/doubles B&B from R200/300. This is the most imaginatively designed guesthouse in Knysna with a real African flair that avoids the kitsch.

Yellowwood Lodge (☎ 382 5906, *fax 382 4230*, W *www.yellowwoodlodge.co.za, 18 Handel St*) Singles/doubles B&B from R200/360. A traditional and sumptuously decorated guesthouse, Yellowwood boasts a lovely garden setting and views of the lagoon.

Hotels *Royal Hotel* (☎ 382 1144, *fax 382 2686, 24 Queen St*) Dorm beds R55, singles/doubles B&B R115/190. Although it might not be the smartest place in town, this great-value option has lots of style, with its stripped pine floors and piano in the parlour.

Wayside Inn (☎/fax 382 6011, W *www .waysideinn.co.za*) Singles/doubles B&B from R250/300. Intimate and well managed, the Wayside Inn has nicely decorated rooms and is in a handy location.

The Caboose (☎ 382 5850, *fax 382 5224*, e *knysna@caboose.co.za, Cnr Gray & Trotter Sts*) Singles/doubles/triples B&B R109/148/167, regular singles/doubles (Train Suites) B&B R199/229. Perhaps The Caboose takes its train theme a little too seriously, as the rooms are about the same size as sleeping compartments: *tiny*. Still, the budget accommodation is good quality and there are plenty of spacious public areas.

Knysna Log Inn (☎ 382 5835, *fax 382 5830*, e *log-inn@mweb.co.za, 16 Gray St*) Singles/doubles B&B from R365/470. The Knysna Log Inn is said to be the largest log structure in the southern hemisphere. The rooms are comfortable enough, and there's

WESTERN CAPE

a pool, but the whole place resembles a Disneyland exhibit a little too much.

Protea Hotel Knysna Quays (☎ 382 5005, fax 382 5006, e knysnaq@mweb.co .za, Waterfront Dr) Doubles B&B from R680. Rooms are tastefully decorated at this stylish new hotel, which is a better option than the other Protea on Main Rd. You'll pay R200 extra for the lagoon-facing rooms.

Other *The Phantom Forest* (☎ 386 0046, fax 387 1944, W www.phantomforest.com, 6km west of Knysna, along the Phantom Pass road) Singles/doubles DB&B R1450/ 1850. This 137-hectare private eco-reserve overlooks the lagoon and comprises 10 cleverly designed and elegantly decorated tree houses. Various activities, including conducted nature walks, are available. If nothing else, visit for dinner (R145 for a five-course Pan-African meal) served from 6.30pm to 8.30pm daily; booking is essential.

Lightley's Holiday Houseboats (☎ 386 0007, fax 386 0018, e sandpoint@pixie .co.za) 4- to 6-berth fully equipped houseboats from R400 per day. These houseboats are on the western side of the bridge over the Knysna River. You can navigate up to 20km upriver from The Heads, but you have to pay extra for fuel. Rates vary radically depending on the boat and the season.

Places to Eat

There are plenty of good snack and coffee places along Main Rd, including the excellent *Coffee Connection*, serving 36 types of coffee, and the cheap chain seafood restaurant *Ocean Basket* (☎ 382 1010). Also see *Harry B's* under Entertainment following.

La Loerie (☎ 382 1616, 57 Main Rd) Mains R40-50. Open 6.30pm-10pm Mon-Sat. Booking is essential at this deservedly popular but small place with a French flavour to its menu.

Changes (☎ 382 0456, Pledge Square) Mains R25-35. Open 7pm-10pm Mon-Sat. This gay-friendly restaurant is popular all round for its consistently good food and relaxed atmosphere.

De Oude Fabriek (☎ 382 5723, Cnr Main Rd & Gray Sts) Mains around R50.

This restaurant is a convivial spot to sample some interesting South African dishes at reasonable prices.

Down at the Waterfront several places vie for attention.

34° South (☎ 382 7268) Mains R30. Open 9am-5.30pm daily. One of the best, this is a very tempting deli with some outdoor tables; go for a platter and choose from their vast range of salads and seafood pâtés.

The Oystercatcher (☎ 382 9995, Knysna Quays) Open daily 11am-9pm. The Oystercatcher is a relaxed place serving four sizes of farmed oyster, and other seafood dishes, in a great waterside setting.

Knysna Oyster Company (☎ 382 6941, W www.oysters.co.za, Thesen's Island) Mains from R20. Open 9am-6pm daily, but call first to check. This company grows its own oysters out in the lagoon; you can take a tour of the processing plant and have a tasting of a cultivated and wild oyster for R15 at their restaurant afterwards.

Paquita's (☎ 384 0408, The Heads) Mains R35-40. Open noon-10pm daily. Seafood, steaks, pizza and pasta are available at this ideally located restaurant and bar next to The Heads. Bookings are advised and the car park will be packed in summer.

East Head Caffé (☎ 384 0933, The Heads) Mains R25. Open 7am-7pm daily. The East Head is a lovely spot to head for breakfast, lunch or coffee, with an outdoor deck overlooking the lagoon and ocean.

Mackintosh's of Knysna Country Store (☎ 382 6607, Thesen House, 6 Long St) Located in a historic building, this is an excellent place to stock up on organic produce and supplies for picnics.

Entertainment

Starting off from Long St and heading west along Main Rd there are several bars worth a visit.

Zanzibar (☎ 382 0386) has a relaxed vibe, a balcony area and a theatre where shows are held occasionally. This is the most sophisticated of Knysna's watering holes.

Tin Roof Blues (☎ 382 6870) is across the road from Zanzibar and is a reliable old trouper, where there's often live music.

Harry B's (☎ 382 5065, 42 Main Rd) is Knysna's first residence (1863) and now houses a good restaurant and bar.

Al's (☎ 382 6305, Queen St) is a dance club and live music venue – strictly a late-night affair. You'll know Al's is in business when you see the laser beam lighting up the sky.

Down at the Waterfront, there's a branch of the ever-reliable pool bar *Stones*.

If you're craving the silver screen, *Knysna Movie House* (☎ 382 7812, 50 Main Rd) is a movie house that has daily shows on two screens.

Shopping

At the Waterfront there's a daily craft market as well as several interesting gift shops, the best of which is *African Attitude* (☎ 382 1650), stocking some colourful works from around the continent.

Metamorphosis (☎ 382 5889, 12 Main Rd). This shop has a great range of interesting souvenirs made from recycled materials.

Bush Pig (☎ 388 4807) Open 10am-4pm Mon-Fri. Brilliantly inventive print designs on fabric and paper are available at Bush Pig. Although there's an outlet at the Waterfront, it's well worth driving over to its design and printing studio: Take the Rheenendal turn-off 2.5km west of the Knysna bridge and drive on for 7km.

Getting There & Away

Bus The major bus companies stop at the Engen petrol station; Baz Bus will take you where you want. For travel between nearby towns on the Garden Route, you're better off looking for a minibus taxi (see following) than travelling with the major bus lines, which are very expensive on short sectors.

Greyhound, Intercape and Translux stop here on their Cape Town to Port Elizabeth services. Translux fares from Knysna include: George (R75), Mossel Bay (R75), Port Elizabeth (R85) and Cape Town (R145). All three companies also run from Knysna to Jo'burg/Pretoria.

Train The historic *Outeniqua Choo-Tjoe* steam train runs between Knysna and George daily except Saturday and public

holidays. See the boxed text 'Outeniqua Choo-Tjoe & Power Van' earlier for details.

Minibus Taxi The main minibus taxi stop is behind Bloch's supermarket off Main Rd. Taxis to Plettenberg Bay cost R9. Taxis depart for Cape Town in the morning from about 7.30am (R90).

Car & Motorcycle If you're heading to Oudtshoorn, consider going via Prince Alfred's Pass and Uniondale. The road is dirt and quite steep in places but if you take it easy it's OK.

Getting Around

In Knysna there's a **Hertz Rent-a-Car** (☎ 876 9999). Even if you have a car, the summer traffic jams on the main street (much worse than anything you'll find in Cape Town) will make you look for alternative transport.

Knysna Cycleworks (☎ 382 5153, 3A Church St) is one of several places selling and renting good bicycles. You can also rent bicycles at **Olde's Pub & Grill** (☎ 382 0354, 14 Gray St).

AROUND KNYSNA
Prince Alfred's Pass

The Knysna-Avontour road climbs through the Outeniqua Range via the beautiful Prince Alfred's Pass, regarded by some as even better than the superb Swartberg Pass. Needless to say it was built by a Bain, in this case Thomas, in the 1860s. Be warned that the road is a bit rough and it's slow going.

Outside Knysna, the road passes through pine and eucalypt plantations and indigenous forest (the home of Knysna's elephants). There are few really steep sections but the pass does reach a height of over 1000m, and there are magnificent views to the north before the road winds into the Langkloof Valley.

Belvidere & Brenton-on-Sea

There's a slightly creepy feel to immaculate Belvidere, around 10km west of Knysna on the road to Brenton-on-Sea. Still, it's worth a quick look for the beautiful Norman-style church built in the 1850s for a homesick Englishman, Thomas Duthie.

Belvidere Manor (☎ *044-387 1055, 387 1059,* Ⓦ *www.belvidere.co.za, Duthie Dr)* Doubles B&B R880. This 150-year-old house was also built by Duthie, and has been turned into the reception building for a group of surrounding luxury guest cottages.

Another 10km further, the fynbos-covered hills drop to Brenton-on-Sea overlooking a magnificent 8km beach, stretching from the western head of Knysna Lagoon to Buffalo Bay. There's a small store where you can get some food; otherwise, bring your own or eat at the hotel.

Brenton-on-Sea Hotel (☎ *044-381 0081, fax 381 0026,* Ⓦ *www.brentononsea.co.za)* Singles/doubles B&B from R200/350, self-catering chalets sleeping 6 from R600. This upmarket complex has a fantastic location and a range of comfortable rooms and self-catering chalets overlooking the sea. The rates vary widely depending on the season.

Knysna to Plettenberg Bay

Not to be outdone by Captain Duthie at Belvidere, another romantic English family built holiday homes in a mock castle–style at **Noetzie**, reached by a turn off along the N2, 10km east of Knysna. The homes are still privately owned, and are not as bad as you might imagine. Noetzie has a lovely surf beach (spacious but dangerous) and a sheltered lagoon running through a forested gorge. It's a steep trail between the car park and the beach.

Knysna Castles (☎ *044-375 0100, fax 384 0963,* Ⓦ *www.knysnacastles.com)* 4-bedroom home from R450 per person. If you're looking for a romantic getaway, renting one of these cosily decorated Noetzie castles right beside the beach might be just the ticket.

It's extremely unlikely that you will see the last remaining wild elephants that live in Knysna's forests, but you are sure to see them at **Knysna Elephant Park** (☎ *044-532 7732,*

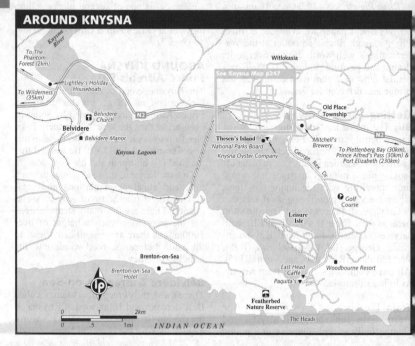

AROUND KNYSNA

To The Phantom Forest (2km)

Knysna River

To Wilderness (35km)

Lightley's Holiday Houseboats

Witlokasia

See Knysna Map p247

N2

Belvidere Church

Belvidere

Belvidere Manor

Old Place Township

N2

Knysna Lagoon

Thesen's Island

National Parks Board

Knysna Oyster Company

Mitchell's Brewery

To Plettenberg Bay (30km), Prince Alfred's Pass (30km) & Port Elizabeth (230km)

George Rex Dr

Golf Course

Leisure Isle

Brenton-on-Sea

Brenton-on-Sea Hotel

East Head Caffe

Woodbourne Resort

Paquita's

Featherbed Nature Reserve

The Heads

INDIAN OCEAN

0   1   2km

0   .5   1mi

W *www.knysna.co.za/elephant, 22km east of Knysna on the N2; admission R50; open 8.30am-5pm daily).* Here small groups of visitors go on walking tours with the three elephants and a baby. It really is a delightful experience.

There are some good places to stay off the N2, many in or near forest.

Harkerville Forest Lodge & Backpackers (☎ 532 7777, fax 532 7881, e *bacpac@ mweb.co.za)* Camping R30, dorm beds R45, 2-bed tree house R90. This clean friendly place, halfway between Knysna and Plettenberg Bay, is at the head of the Perdekop Trail. There's a large purpose-built backpacker section, a self-contained flat, plenty of room to pitch a tent and even a secluded tree house. Free pick-ups from Knysna or Plett and horse riding is available.

PLETTENBERG BAY

☎ 044 • postcode 6600 • pop 54,000

Plettenberg Bay, or 'Plett' as it's often known, is a resort town, with a rare combination of mountains, white sand and crystal-blue water. It's a trendy and popular destination (the town's population doubles during the summer holiday season), so things tend to be upmarket. However, there are hostels, the locals are very friendly, and if you want to be close to the beach, it's a better place to stay than Knysna. The scenery to the east in particular is superb, with some of the best coast and indigenous forest in South Africa. The dramatic Robberg Peninsula is also a great place to go hiking.

Orientation & Information

Plettenberg Bay is large and sprawling. The town centre is on a high promontory overlooking the Keurbooms River lagoon and Beacon Island.

The **tourism bureau** *(☎ 533 4065,* W *www .plettenbergbay.co.za, 1 Victoria Cottage, Kloof St; open 8.30am-5pm daily in summer, 8.30am-5pm Mon-Fri & 9am-1pm Sat at other times)* has a great deal of useful information, ranging from accommodation to a craft trail and walks in the surrounding hills and reserves.

Activities

Apart from lounging on the beaches or hiking on the Robberg Peninsula (see Robberg Nature & Marine Reserve under Around Plettenberg Bay later) there's a lot to do in Plett; check with the Albergo (see Places to Stay later) as they can organise most things, often at a discount.

For information on the surrounding nature reserves and walks through them, contact **Cape Nature Conservation** *(☎ 533 2125, 7 Zenon St).* Ask about canoeing on the Keurbooms River. There's an overnight canoe trail and they rent out canoes (R25 per hour). The Albergo also runs canoe trips up the Keurbooms River for R70. Mountain bike trails are being developed in the area and **Outeniqua Biking Trails** *(☎ 532 7644)* offers two-day rides.

A couple of places offer diving: **Diving International** *(☎ 533 0381)* and **Beyond the Beach** *(☎ 533 1158).* Boat trips to view dolphins and whales in season are available with **Ocean Adventures** *(☎ 533 5083,* W *www .oceanadventures.co.za)* and **MTN Centre for Dolphin Studies** *(☎/fax 533 6185,* W *www.dolphinstudies.co.za).*

Equitrailing *(☎ 533 0599)* offers horse riding. **Dolphin Adventures** *(☎ 083-590 3405)* has sea kayaking. And for that ultimate thrill, there's always the world's highest commercial bungee jump at the Bloukrans River Bridge, 45km east of Plett on the N2 (see Activities under Storms River in the Eastern Cape chapter).

Places to Stay

There is a great deal of holiday accommodation in town and nearby – in low season there are bargains. The tourism bureau has a full list and can tell you about the many camping options, all out of town. If you want to rent a house or an apartment, contact an agent such as *The Accommodation Bureau (☎ 533 2101, 7 Gibb St).* In low season you might get an apartment for two for R150 or less.

Hostels & B&Bs If it's budget accommodation you're after, there are several good places to choose from.

Albergo (☎ *533 4434, fax 533 2149,* Ⓦ *www.albergo.co.za, 8 Church St*) Camping R35 per person, dorm beds R45, doubles R120-140. Well run and friendly, Albergo encourages activities in town and in the area and claims it can organise anything.

Northando Backpackers & Deios B&B (☎/*fax 533 0220,* Ⓔ *mwdeois@mweb.co.za, 3 Wilder St*) Dorm beds R50, doubles with shared bathroom from R145, with private bathroom R165, B&B R125 per person. Spotless and spacious, this YHA-affiliated hostel and B&B has a homely feel.

Hup 'n' Down (☎ *533 1317, 1 Park Lane*) Dorm beds R50, doubles R120. A new place with a thrown-together feel, Hup 'n' Down is worth a look if other places are full.

Hotels Options range from the plain to the luxurious.

Bayview Hotel (☎ *533 1961, fax 533 2059, Cnr Main & Gibb Sts*) Doubles from R300. Right in the town centre, this is a small, serviceable and modern place with a range of rather plain rooms.

Weldon Kaya (☎ *533 2437, fax 533 4364*) Doubles B&B R190-225. Very funky accommodation can be found at this idealised version of a tribal village, with rooms in huts made of clay and straw. There are four wheelchair-friendly units, a poo and traditional music every Saturday nigh in their ***restaurant***, which serves Africar dishes. It's off the N2 at the corner o Piesang Valley Rd.

Periwinkle Guest Lodge (☎/*fax 533 1345,* Ⓦ *www.periwinkle.co.za, 75 Beachy Head Dr*) Doubles B&B R800. This bright colourful guesthouse offers individually decorated rooms, all with great views.

Beacon Island Resort (☎ *533 1120, fax 533 3880,* Ⓔ *reservations@beaconisland .co.za, Beacon Island*) Doubles B&B R1386 The views from inside this multi-storey hotel on Beacon Island (linked to the main land by a causeway) are much better than

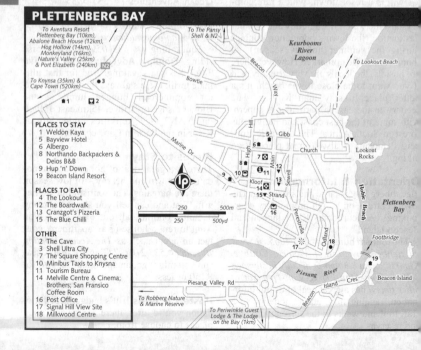

PLETTENBERG BAY

PLACES TO STAY
1 Weldon Kaya
5 Bayview Hotel
6 Albergo
8 Northando Backpackers & Deios B&B
9 Hup 'n' Down
19 Beacon Island Resort

PLACES TO EAT
4 The Lookout
12 The Boardwalk
13 Cranzgot's Pizzeria
15 The Blue Chilli

OTHER
2 The Cave
3 Shell Ultra City
7 The Square Shopping Centre
10 Minibus Taxis to Knysna
11 Tourism Bureau
14 Melville Centre & Cinema; Brothers; San Fransico Coffee Room
16 Post Office
17 Signal Hill View Site
18 Milkwood Centre

hose of its ugly exterior. The rooms are suitably well equipped for the price.

The Lodge on the Bay (☎ 533 4724, fax 533 2681, W www.thelodge.co.za, 77 Beachy Head Dr) Singles/doubles B&B from R750-1450, depending on the size of room. The highly sophisticated Lodge has just six rooms and very personal service. It's worth splashing out on.

Out of Town See Around Knysna earlier for places to stay between Knysna and Plettenberg Bay. East of Plett, towards Tsitsikamma Coastal National Park, there are many more places to stay.

Aventura Resort Plettenberg Bay (☎ 535 0309, fax 535 9912, Off N2 10km east of Plett) Camping from R109 for 2, chalets from R302 for 2. Prices shoot up in high season at this resort, which has timber chalets and a choice of camp sites – the one beside the river is the more expensive. There's also a pool, tennis courts and a shopping kiosk.

Abalone Beach House (☎/fax 535 9602, e beachhouse@global.co.za, 50 Ifafi Properties, Keurboomstrand) Dorm beds R50, doubles R140. It's literally a hop to the beach from this great hostel run by friendly people. And what a beach! Surf and boogie boards can be hired (R10).

Hog Hollow (☎/fax 534 8879, W www .hog-hollow.com, 18km east of Plett along the N2) Singles/doubles B&B from R740/990. Hog Hollow provides delightful accommodation in African art–decorated units, which are around an old farmhouse overlooking the forest. It's possible to walk to Monkeyland (see later) from here. A four-course dinner costs R135.

Places to Eat
The Lookout (Lookout Rocks) Mains around R30. Open 10am-10pm daily low season, 9am-midnight high season. With a deck overlooking the beach, this is a great place for a simple meal and perhaps views of dolphins surfing the waves.

Brothers (☎ 533 5056, Melville Centre, Main St) Mains R25-50. Open 8.30am-3pm & 6.30pm-10.30pm Tues-Sun, daily in high season. This is a popular, relaxed cafe-

restaurant serving everything from bagels and pitta bread to steaks. Also check out the *San Francisco Coffee Room* downstairs.

The Boardwalk (☎ 533 1420, 6 Yellowwoods Bldg, Main St) Mains R30-45. Open 9am-10pm daily. A hang-out for local surfies and visitors, this pleasant cafe offers plenty of snacks and meals at reasonable prices.

Cranzgot's Pizzeria (☎ 533 1660, 9 Main St) Mains R25-46. Open 10am-10.30pm daily. This perennial Plett favourite serves mouthwatering pizzas, pastas and chargrilled steaks. You might have to wait for a table in the evenings, but there is also a bar.

The Blue Chilli (☎ 533 5104, 1st floor, One Plett Centre, Marine Dr) Open 6pm-10pm daily. This is a lively Mexican restaurant and bar that comes highly recommended by locals.

The Pansy Shell (☎ 533 5080, Beacon Way) Mains R50. Open 7pm-10.30pm Mon-Sat. Just off the N2, this formal restaurant doesn't look like much, but gets rave reviews for its steaks and seafood.

Entertainment
The Cave (☎ 533 2118, Old Arches Hotel on Marine Dr near junction with N2), open Friday and Saturday in the low season, nightly high season, is the hip club of the moment.

Getting There & Away
Civair flies four times a week between Plettenberg Bay and Cape Town and twice a week between Plett and Port Elizabeth (see Air in the Getting Around chapter for contact details).

All the major buses stop at the Shell Ultra City on the N2; the Baz Bus will come into town. Translux fares from Plett include: George (R75), Port Elizabeth (R85), Mossel Bay (R115) and Cape Town (R155). Intercape also runs to Jo'burg (R350) via Oudtshoorn (R115), Graaff-Reinet (R200) and Bloemfontein (R270).

If you're heading to Knysna you're better off taking a minibus taxi – services leave from the corner of Kloof and High Sts. Most other long-distance taxis stop at the Shell Ultra City on the highway. Taxis to Knysna cost around R8.

AROUND PLETTENBERG BAY
Robberg Nature & Marine Reserve

This reserve (☎ 533 2125, 9km south-east of Plettenberg Bay; admission R15; open 7am-5pm daily Feb-Nov, 7am-8pm daily Dec-Jan) protects a 4km-long peninsula with a rugged coastline of cliffs and rocks. There's a great circular walk approximately 11km long, with rich intertidal marine life and coastal-dune fynbos. The peninsula acts as a sort of marine speed bump to larger sea life, with mammals and fish spending time here before moving on. To get here head along Robberg Rd, off Piesang Valley Rd, until you see the signs.

Keurbooms Nature Reserve

This reserve, 7km north-east of Plett, covers a hilly plateau with steep cliffs and banks above the Keurbooms River. There is a short, one-hour hiking trail along the river banks. A canoe trail goes further up the river to an overnight hut (R52 per person) that sleeps 12 people. The reserve is open 6am to 6pm, but visitors must get a permit from Cape Nature Conservation in Plett (see Activities under Plettenberg Bay earlier).

Keurbooms River Ferries (☎ 532 7876) has cruises up the river for R65, departing from near the eastern side of the N2 bridge at 11am, 2pm and around 5pm for sunset.

Monkeyland

One of the best attractions in this area is Monkeyland (☎ 534 8906, W www.monkeyland .co.za, 16km east of Plett off the N2; adult/child R60/30; open 8am-6pm daily). Home to over 200 primates from 14 different species, this 12-hectare sanctuary helps rehabilitate the wild monkeys that have been in zoos or private homes. The walking safari through a dense forest and across a 120m-long rope bridge is a brilliant way to find out about these creatures. There are plans to build the largest aviary in the southern hemisphere here, too.

Other Attractions

The best-known reserve near Plettenberg Bay is the **Tsitsikamma National Park**, which is in Eastern Cape (see that chapter for information).

The road east of Plett is brilliant. Don't take the toll road but turn off to Nature's Valley and the **Bloukrans Pass**. It's a beautiful drive across a plain with plenty of surviving fynbos, forests dominated by the Outeniqua yellowwood, and a road plunging in and out of deep gorges that have been cut by rivers running out to sea.

CAPE WINERIES

It was Stellenbosch that first promoted a wine route for people to follow in the 1970s, an idea that has since been enthusiastically taken up by 13 other parts of the country. Stellenbosch's wine route remains the largest, covering some 80 wineries; if you lump in the nearby areas of Franschhoek, Helderberg and Paarl, you're looking at over 160 wineries within a day's drive of Cape Town.

Several wineries are capitalising on the industry's popularity by opening restaurants, accommodation (much of it luxurious) and other attractions. The following selection includes some of the more notable wineries that include such features, as well as vineyards that are renown for their fine wines. For more information, the wine taster's bible is *John Platter's South African Wine Guide*.

History

Today, praise be the Lord, wine was pressed for the first time from Cape grapes.

Jan van Riebeeck, 2 February 1659

Although the founder of the Cape Colony had planted vines and made wine himself, it was not until the arrival of Governor Simon van der Stel in 1679 that wine making began in earnest. Van der Stel created Groot Constantia (see Constantia in the Cape Town & the Peninsula chapter for details), the superb estate on the flanks of Table Mountain, and passed on his wine-making skills to the burghers settling around Stellenbosch.

Between 1688 and 1690, some 200 Huguenots arrived in the country. They were granted land in the region, particularly around Franschhoek (French Corner), and although only a few of the Huguenots had direct wine-making experience, they gave the infant industry fresh impetus.

For a long time, Cape wines were not in great demand (with the exception of those produced at Groot Constantia), and most grapes from the area were used for making brandy. But the industry received a boost in the early 19th century when war between Britain and France meant there was a need for more South African wines to be imported into the UK.

Apartheid-era sanctions and the power of the Kooperatieve Wijnbouwers Vereeniging (KWV), the cooperative formed in 1918 to control minimum prices, production areas and quota limits, hampered the industry. However, since 1992, KWV, now a private company, has relinquished some of its influence.

Many new and progressive wine makers are leading South Africa's re-emergence onto the world export market. New wine-producing areas are being established away from the hotter inland areas, in particular in the cooler coastal areas east of Cape Town around Mossel Bay, Walker Bay and Elgin.

Inset: Grapes ripe for the picking (Photo by Olivier Cirendini)

CAPE WINERIES

Wines

The most common variety of white wine is chenin blanc. In the last decade or so more fashionable varieties such as chardonnay and sauvignon blanc have been planted on a wide scale. Other widely planted white varieties include colombard, semillon, crouchen blanc (known as Cape riesling) and various sweet muscats. Table whites, especially chardonnay, once tended to be heavily oaked and high in alcohol; now lighter, more fruity whites are in the ascendancy.

Older, more robust red varieties such as shiraz, cabernet sauvignon and the Cape's own pinotage (a cross between pinot noir and hermitage or shiraz, which produces a very bold wine) are being challenged by lighter blends of cabernet sauvignon, merlot, shiraz and cabernet franc, in keeping with a style similar to Bordeaux wines. The reds attracting the highest prices are cabernet sauvignon and the Bordeaux-style blends.

The inland wine region of Worcester is the national leader for fortified wines, including port, brandy and South Africa's own *hanepoot* (honey pot), a dessert wine made from the muscat of Alexandria grape variety to produce a strong, sweet and suitably high-alcohol tipple for the domestic market.

In Worcester you'll also find the KWV Brandy Cellar, the largest brandy cellar in the world and the final stop on the Brandy Route running from **Van Ryn Brandy Cellar** (☎ 021-881 3875), at Vlottenburg, 8km southwest of Stellenbosch. For more information contact the **South African Brandy Foundation** (☎ 021-886 6381, Ⓦ www.sabrandy.co.za).

Workers' Wines

One scandalous aspect of the Winelands was the infamous 'tot' system, whereby the wages of labourers – mainly poor coloureds – were partly paid in wine. Such practices still go on, causing disastrous social and physical results.

Balancing this is a hopeful recent development – the emergence of workers' cooperative wineries. Fair Valley, one of the first such empowerment initiatives, is a 17-hectare farm next to Fairview (see Paarl under Wineries later). It's still developing its own vineyards, but has already produced three seasons of chenin blanc (sold through the UK wine-shop chain OddBins) made with grapes from Fairview.

Up the road, north of Paarl, is **Nelson's Creek** (☎ 021-863 8453), where the owner has donated part of the estate to his workers to produce their own wines. Under the label New Beginnings, these wines – a classic dry red, a rosé and a dry white – are being sold in the UK, the Netherlands and Japan. And at the **Backsberg Estate** (☎ 021-875 5141) in Paarl, the Freedom Road wine (a sauvignon blanc) helps fund a workers' housing project.

Other workers' empowerment wines to look out for include those from **Thandi** (☎ 021-859 0605), from the Elgin area (available at Tescos in the UK), and **Tukulu** (☎ 021-808 7911), from the Darling area. Tukulu is a highly successful operation run by Carmen Stevens, a coloured woman, and is getting rave reviews for its pinotage and its chenin blanc.

Wineries
Stellenbosch

For details on the many other wineries in this area, contact the **Wine Route Office** (☎ 021-886 4310) or the **Stellenbosch Publicity Association** (☎ 021-883 3584). See also the Stellenbosch section of the Western Cape chapter.

Hartenberg Estate (☎ 021-882 2541, ℮ hartenberg@cyber trade.co.za, tastings free; open 9am-5pm Mon-Fri, 9am-3pm Sat) was founded in 1692. Thanks to a favourable microclimate, this estate produces many award-winning wines, notably its cabernet sauvignon, merlot and shiraz. Lunch is available from noon to 2pm (bookings essential). The estate is off Bottelary Rd, 10km north-west of Stellenbosch.

Morgenhof (☎ 021-889 5510, ⓦ www.morgenhof.com; tastings R10; open 9am-6pm Mon-Fri & 10am-5pm Sat & Sun Nov-April, 9am-4.30pm Mon-Fri & 10am-3pm Sat & Sun May-Oct) is an old estate on the slopes of Simonsberg that has fine architecture. Light lunches are available and there's a coffee shop also serving breakfast from 9am to noon daily. It's on the R44 towards Paarl.

Delaire (☎ 021-885 1756, ℮ delaire@iafrica.com; tastings R10; open 10am-5pm Mon-Sat, 10am-4pm Sun) on the Helshoogte Pass is a small, friendly winery with great views. There's wheelchair access to the restaurant and picnics are available in season (bookings essential). Delaire is on the R310 towards Franschhoek.

Lanzerac (☎ 021-887 1132, fax 887 2310, ℮ info@lanzerac.co.za, Jonkershoek Valley; tastings R15; open 10am-4pm Mon-Fri, 10am-2pm Sat) produces a very good merlot and quaffable cabernet sauvignon and chardonnay. The winery has Stellenbosch's most luxurious hotel, which includes a 300-year-old manor house and several pools and restaurants. Singles/doubles including breakfast start at R850/1240 in the low season and R1475/1990 in the high season.

Blaauklippen (☎ 021-880 0133, ℮ mail@blaauklippen.com; tastings R10; open 9am-4.45pm Mon-Fri, 9am-4pm Sat) is a rustic 300-year-old estate which has several fine Cape Dutch buildings. Cellar tours are by appointment only, and lunch is available (call for times, as they change according to the season). It's on the R44 towards Somerset West.

Spier (☎ 021-809 1100, fax 809 1134, ⓦ www.spier.co.za; tastings R12; open 9am-5pm daily) has something for everyone. This mega-estate offers steam-train trips from Cape Town (call ☎ 021-419 5222 for information), horse riding, performing arts centres and beautifully restored Cape Dutch buildings. The only aspect we're unsure about is the cheetah park, where listless animals pose for photos with the tourists. Its wines are nothing to shout about, but in the tasting you can try lots of other vineyards' wines. Check out the annual arts festival that runs from January to March – it's as good a reason as any for coming here. There's a good Cape Malay–style hotel, The Village at Spier, where doubles cost from R950, and there's a wide range of dining options. The estate is off the R310 towards Cape Town.

STELLENBOSCH & HELDERBERG WINE REGIONS

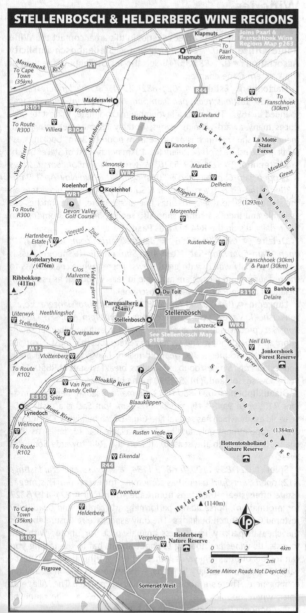

Joins Paarl &
Franschhoek Wine
Regions Map p263

Klapmuts

To
Paarl
(6km)

Klapmuts

Mosselbank River

To Cape
Town
(35km)

N1

R44

Backsberg

To
Franschhoek
(30km)

Muldersvlei

Koelenhof

R101

Elsenburg

Lievland

Villiera

R304

Skurweberg

La Motte
State
Forest

Kanonkop

Swart River

Simonsig

WR2

Muratie

Meulstroom

Groot

Koelenhof

Koelenhof

WR1

Delheim

Klippies River

Simonsberg

(1293m)

To Route
R300

Devon Valley
Golf Course

Morgenhof

Hartenberg
Estate

Vineyard Trail

Rustenberg

To
Franschhoek (30km)
& Paarl (30km)

Bottelaryberg
(476m)

Clos
Malverne

Ribbokkop
(411m)

Valckenberg River

Du Toit

Banhoek

R310

Delaire

Paregaaiberg
(254m)

Stellenbosch

Uiterwyk

Neethlingshof

See Stellenbosch Map
p188

Lanzerac

WR4

Stellenbosch

Overgaauw

Kloof

Neil Ellis

Jonkershoek
Forest Reserve

M12

Vlottenberg

Jonkershoek River

To Route
R102

Blouklip River

Stellenbosch berge

Van Ryn
Brandy Cellar

R310

Spier

Blaauklippen

Lynedoch

Bonte River

Welmoed

Rusten Vrede

To Route
R102

(1384m)

Eikendal

Hottentotsholland
Nature Reserve

R44

Avontuur

Helderberg

To Cape
Town
(35km)

Helderberg

(1140m)

Helderberg
Nature Reserve

R102

Vergelegen

0   2   4km
0   1   2mi

Firgrove

N2

Somerset West

Some Minor Roads Not Depicted

Helderberg

This area around Somerset West, 20km south of Stellenbosch, has some 20 wineries, including Vergelegen, arguably the most beautiful estate in the Cape.

Vergelegen (☎ 021-847 1334, W www.vergelegen.co.za, Lourensford Rd, Somerset West; admission R10; tastings R5 Mon-Sat May-Oct; open 9.30am-4pm daily) is a lovely estate where vines were first planted by Simon van der Stel's son Willem in 1700 – it's well worth a visit, although you have to pay an entrance fee. The buildings and elegant grounds have ravishing mountain views and a 'stately home' feel to them. On the dining front you can choose from the casual Rose Terrace overlooking the Rose Garden, the upmarket Lady Phillips Restaurant, or a picnic hamper (R140 for two people) – bookings are essential for the last two options.

Franschhoek

Many of Franschhoek's wineries are within walking distance of the town centre, but to reach Boschendal you'll need transport. Call **Vignerons de Franschhoek** (☎ 021-876 3062) for information on other wineries in the area.

Boschendal (☎ 021-870 4210, W www.boschendal.com, Pniel Rd) is tucked beneath some awesome mountains, and is the classic Winelands estate, with great architecture, food and wine. Note the Taphuis wine-tasting area (where tastings cost R6) is at the opposite end of the estate from the Groote Drakenstein manor house (admission is R6) and restaurants. The blow-out buffet lunch (R125) in the main restaurant is mainly a group affair; far nicer, especially in fine weather, is Le Café (open from 10am to 5pm daily), where you can have a snack or something more substantial. Also very popular are 'Le Pique Nique' hampers (R62.50 per person, minimum two people) served under parasols on the lawn from mid-October to the end of April (bookings are essential – call ☎ 870 4274). Boschendal is on the R310 towards Stellenbosch.

Chamonix (☎ 021-876 2498, fax 876 3237, W www.chamonix.co.za, Uitkyk St; tastings R10; open 9.30am-4.30pm daily) has cellar tours at 11am and 2pm by appointment. The tasting room is in a converted blacksmith's; there's also a range of schnapps and mineral water to try. You can stay at the good-value, self-catering cottages, which are in the midst of the vineyards (four-bed cottages cost from R120 per person). The pretty La Maison de Chamonix restaurant (open from 12.30pm to 3pm daily and 6.30pm to 9pm Friday) has a reasonably priced lunch menu, with mains R30 to R60.

Cabrière Estate (☎ 021-876 2630, W www.cabriere.co.za, Berg St; tastings R15/20 without/with cellar tour at 11am & 3pm Mon-Fri, 11am Sat; sales 9.30am-4.30pm Mon-Fri, 11am-2pm Sat) offers tastings that include sparkling wines and one of the vineyard's excellent range of white, red and dessert wines and brandies. At the Saturday session, stand by for the proprietor's party trick of slicing open a bottle of bubbly with a sabre. An ideal way to sample the wines is to dine at the separate Haute Cabrière Cellar restaurant (☎ 876 3688) on Fran-schhoek Pass Rd, which is open from noon to 3pm daily and 7pm to 9pm Wednesday to Monday. This dramatic dining space in a cellar cut into the mountain side has an intriguing menu with mains from R60 to R80.

La Couronne (☎ 021-876 2770, fax 876 3788, **W** www.lacouron nehotel.co.za, Robertsvlei Rd; tastings R5; open 10am-4pm Tues-Sun) is a boutique hotel, restaurant and winery offering gilt-edged luxury and magnificent views across the valley. The Ménage à Trois Bordeaux blend gets high marks. Doubles including breakfast at the winery cost from R1300. The restaurant, open from noon to 2.30pm and 7pm to 9.30pm daily, has mains for R60.

Mont Rochelle (☎ 021-876 3000, **e** montrochelle@wine.co.za; tastings R5; open 11am-5pm Mon-Sat, 11am-1pm Sun) has cellar tours at 11am, 12.30pm and 3pm Monday to Friday. This is another vineyard in a beautiful location offering great wines and good-value picnic baskets (R40 per person, minimum two people) or soup and bread by a roaring fire in winter.

For details about a horseback tour of this and other nearby estates contact **Mont Rochelle Equestrian Centre** (☎ 083-300 4368, fax 021-876 2363); the cost is R70 per hour.

Paarl

For information about other wineries in the area, contact **Paarl Vintners** (☎ 021-872 3841). See also under Workers' Wines for details of wineries run by local workers' cooperatives.

KWV (☎ 021-807 3007, **W** www.kwv.co.za, Kohler St; tastings R10; open 9am-4pm Mon-Sat) is no longer the all-controlling body it used to be, but remains one of the best known of the country's winer-ies since its products are mostly sold overseas. Some KWV port and sherry is available inside South Africa, and their fortified wines, in par-ticular, are among the world's best. The firm's impressive offices are at La Concorde on Paarl's Main St, but the cellar tours are at their complex near the railway line. Call for times of cellar tours (R20). It's well worth taking the tour (available in English, German and French as well as Afrikaans) if only to see the enormous Cathedral Cellar built in 1930.

Laborie (☎ 021-807 3390, **W** www.kwv-international.com, Taille-fert St; tastings R7; open 9am-5pm daily Oct-Apr, 9am-5pm Mon-Sat May-Sept) is KWV's attractive showcase vineyard, just off Main Rd. There's a 3.5km hiking trail through the vineyards. The new guest-house (☎ 807 3271) has singles/doubles including breakfast for R250/500 and the restaurant (☎ 807 3095), open from noon to 2pm daily and 6.30pm to 9pm Tuesday to Saturday, has mains from R35 to R50. Both are in old Cape Dutch buildings, and are excellent value con-sidering the quality. Picnic baskets are available for a bargain at R60 for two.

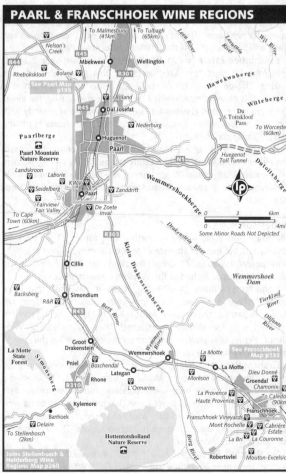

PAARL & FRANSCHHOEK WINE REGIONS

Nederburg Wines (☎ *021-862 3104*, W *www.nederburg.co.za; tastings free; open 8.30am-5pm Mon-Fri, 9am-1pm Sat*) has cellar tours in English, German, French and Spanish for R12.50 (bookings essential). This is a big but professional and welcoming operation; the vast range of wines here are among the most widely available across the country. The picnic lunches cost R55 per person(December to March only, bookings essential) and are very popular. Nederburg is off the N1, 7km east of Paarl.

Fairview (☎ *021-863 2450*, e *fairback@iafrica.com; tastings R10; open 8.30am-5pm Mon-Fri, 8.30am-1pm Sat*) is a small and deservedly popular winery. Peacocks and a goat in a tower (apparently goats love to climb) greet you at the entrance to this winery. The tasting is great value – it covers over 20 wines *and* a wide range of sheep's, goat's and cow's milk cheeses. It's off the R101, 5km south of Paarl.

Landskroon Estate *(☎ 021-863 1039; tastings free; open 8.30am-5pm Mon-Fri, 9am-1pm Sat)* represents nine generations of wine making. The de Villiers family continues to perfect its wine-making skills on this pleasant estate with a nice terrace overlooking the vines. There are some good cheeses for sale, which will go very nicely with their celebrated cabernet sauvignon and port. The estate is off the R101, 6km south of Paarl.

Just 13km from Paarl is Wellington, which is less touristy than Paarl. The **Hildenbrand Wine & Olive Estate** *(☎/fax 021-873 4115, ☒ www .wine-estate-hildenbrand.co.za; tastings R5; sales 9am-5pm daily)* in Wellington has a restaurant and good singles/doubles B&B for R210/340.

Robertson

The Robertson Wine Valley is worth a visit for its 27 wineries, its scenery and the general absence of tourist coaches. Staying the night in the peaceful village of McGregor is a good way to end a day's tasting (see the McGregor section in the Western Cape chapter).

Robertson Winery *(☎ 023-626 3059, ☒ www.robertsonwine .co.za; tastings free; open 8am-5pm Mon-Thurs, 8am-4.30pm Fri, 9am-1pm Sat)* has the region's oldest cellar (but is in a boring modern building), with a small museum attached. The sauvignon blanc, Wide River cabernet sauvignon reserve and semisweet wines are the ones to go for. The entrance is on Voortrekker St.

Graham Beck *(☎ 023-626 1214, ☒ www.grahambeckwines.co.za; tastings free; open 9am-5pm Mon-Fri, 10am-3pm Sat)* is based in a striking orange aircraft hangar–like building. This winery comes as a breath of fresh air after all those Cape Dutch estates – as do its eminently drinkable products. Its fizzy wines give French champagne a run for its money and the muscatel is heaven in a glass. The winery is off the R60 towards Worcester.

De Wetshof Estate *(☎ 023-615 1853, ☒ www.dewetshof.co.za; tastings free; open 8.30am-4.30pm Mon-Fri, 9.30am-12.30pm Sat)* produces some of the best chardonnay in the country as well as an award-winning botrytis dessert wine.

Organised Tours

Plenty of companies offer day trips to the Winelands from Cape Town, but unless you're tight for time, it's better (and possibly cheaper) to stay overnight in, say, Stellenbosch and take a tour from there.

Ferdinand's Tours & Adventures *(☎ 465 8550, ☒ www.ferdinands tours.co.za)* is a popular backpacker option, but is not the tour for those who are seriously into their wines. The tour takes in at least four

winery in Franschhoek village

RICHARD I'ANSON

RICHARD I'ANSON

ape Dutch architecture

Vineyards in the wine-growing area of Franschhoek

RICHARD I'ANSON

SIMON RICHMOND

e elegant Vergelegen Wine Estate, where vines were first planted in 1700

MANFRED GOTTSCHALK

Dutch flavour: ornate Dutch Colonial architecture

RICHARD I'ANSON

Vineyards stretching down to Groot Constantia

RICHARD I'ANSON

The Groot Constantia homestead, a superb estate on the flank of Table Mountain

wineries and includes lunch for R200. Things can get pretty raucous: '...a merry rockin' time. Hell, we danced our way back to Cape Town', said one enthusiastic patron.

Day Trippers (☎/fax 531 3274, **W** www.daytrippers.co.za) is another option.

Mother City Tours (☎ 448 3917, **W** www.mctours.co.za) offers a reasonably priced package (R200) including a cellar tour at KWV in Paarl, and cheese and wine tasting at Fairview.

Eastern Cape

Eastern Cape is a diverse and largely undeveloped province. It includes the former Homelands of Ciskei and the Transkei, so most of its population is Xhosa.

Eastern Cape played a pivotal role in the fight against apartheid. Several important figures in the freedom struggle hailed from this region, including President Thabo Mbeki, ex-president Nelson Mandela, Steve Biko, Robert Sobukwe, Chris Hani and Oliver Tambo.

Eastern Cape's long coastline extends from Tsitsikamma National Park, Cape St Francis and Jeffrey's Bay (famous for their surf) in the west, through Port Elizabeth and the Sunshine Coast to the Shipwreck Coast of former Ciskei. Beyond East London it takes in the spectacular subtropical Wild Coast of the Transkei.

Inland, the rolling green hills around Grahamstown are known as Settler Country, after the British migrants who settled the area in the early 19th century. This was the 'border' between expansionist Boer farmers and the Rharhabe or Ciskei Xhosa. Beyond Settler Country are the highlands that lead up into the foothills of the main South African plateau and Lesotho.

Further north, on the plateau, is the Karoo, a vast semidesert, as well as the intriguing old towns of Cradock and Graaff-Reinet.

The rainfall and climate reflect the geographic variation, with around 700mm of rain (mostly in summer) and a moderate climate on the coast; heavy rainfall of over 1000mm (including snow in winter) in the mountains; and low rainfall of around 450mm on the fringes of the Karoo.

Eastern Cape is the meeting point of four different types of flora: the subtropical forests found in sheltered valleys; the *fynbos* (literally 'fine bush', primarily proteas, heaths and ericas) on the coastal plains; the eastern grasslands at higher altitudes; and the succulent thorny scrub of the river valleys.

Highlights

- Sign up for the five-day Otter Trail hike through the Tsitsikamma National Park.
- Marvel at a herd of elephants taking a refreshing mud bath at Addo Elephant National Park.
- Catch some fine breaks at the surfers' mecca of Jeffrey's Bay.
- Take respite from the hot and empty Karoo in beautiful old oasis towns such as Graaff-Reinet.
- Start the day watching the sun rise over the Valley of Desolation in the Karoo Nature Reserve.
- Hike the Transkei's superb Wild Coast trails.

Western Region

The western region includes the Sunshine Coast, which is a stretch of coastline running from Nature's Valley to Port Alfred. Further inland is Grahamstown, at the heart of Settler Country. Also in this region are the Addo

EASTERN CAPE

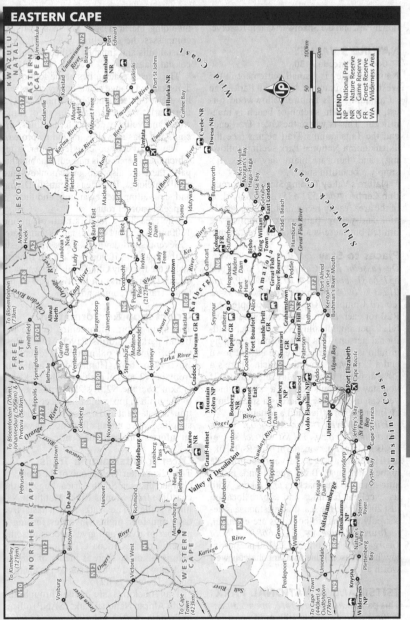

LEGEND
NP National Park
NR Nature Reserve
GR Game Reserve
FR Forest Reserve
WA Wilderness Area

Elephant National Park, the Zuurberg National Park and the Shamwari Game Reserve.

NATURE'S VALLEY
☎ 044 • postcode 7130

Nature's Valley is a small settlement in the west of Tsitsikamma National Park. The surrounding hills feature yellowwood forest, and the 5km stretch of beach is magnificent. This is where the Otter Trail ends and the Tsitsikamma Trail begins (see the Tsitsikamma National Park section following), and there are many day walks. It's simply a beautiful spot.

Nature's Valley Trading Store & Information Centre (☎/fax 531 635) is the only shop in the area, easily recognisable by its gaudy pink-and-yellow paintwork. Supplies are limited but there is an attached restaurant.

Places to Stay

De Vasselot Rest Camp (☎ 531 6700, fax 531 6881, bookings ☎ 012-343 1991, fax 012-343 0905, e reservations@parks-sa .co.za) Camping R65 for 1-2 people plus R20 for each additional person, forest huts R120 per double plus R25 for each additional person. This national park camping ground is on the river's edge east of town and a 2km walk from the beach. There's a 20% discount between May and August. If you stay in the huts you get a canoe, which you can use for free. There is a small shop, an information office and a restaurant.

Hikers Haven (☎/fax 531 6805, e pat bond@mweb.co.za, 411 St Patrick's Ave) B&B R110 per person, dorm beds R49. Hikers Haven is a large and very comfortable home catering to B&B guests and, in the attic dorm, to backpackers and hikers. With its excellent facilities and superb location just 200m from the sea, this guesthouse is deservedly popular, so bookings are essential.

Tourist Lodge (☎ 531 6681, 218 St Georges Ave) Bed only R135/150 per person low/high season. This pleasant chalet is well worth a look.

TSITSIKAMMA NATIONAL PARK

This park *(adult/child R14/7; open 5.30am-9.30pm daily)* protects 100km of coast between Plettenberg Bay and Humansdorp, including the area 5km out to sea. It encompasses the shoreline, steep cliffs and coastal hills and finishes at the edge of the coastal plateau.

The coastal plateau lies at the foot of the Tsitsikamma Range and is cut by rivers that have carved deep and abrupt ravines. The flora varies from evergreen forests of stinkwood and yellowwood to ferns, lilies, orchids and coastal fynbos, including proteas.

The elusive Cape clawless otter, after which the Otter Trail is named, inhabits this park; there are also baboons, monkeys and small antelopes. Birdlife is plentiful. Diving and snorkelling are rewarding, and there is a special snorkel route.

The area has a high rainfall of around 1200mm a year but the climate is temperate.

Several short day walks give you a taste of the coastline if you don't have time to tackle the five-day Otter Trail. The waterfall circuit (four hours) on the first part of the Otter Trail is recommended.

Orientation & Information

The main information centre for the national park is Storms River Mouth Rest Camp, which is 68km from Plettenberg Bay, 99km from Humansdorp and 8km from the N2 coastal highway. The park gate is 6km from the N2. It's 2km from the gate to the main camp, which has accommodation, a restaurant and a shop selling drinks, supplies, souvenirs and firewood, as well as an information/reception centre.

Otter & Tsitsikamma Trails

The 42km Otter Trail is one of the most acclaimed hikes in South Africa, hugging the coastline from Storms River Mouth to Nature's Valley. The walk, which lasts five days and four nights, involves fording a number of rivers and gives access to some superb stretches of coast. The longest day's hike is 14km, so there is plenty of time to walk slowly and swim or snorkel in the tidal pools. The cost is R275.

Trail bookings are made through the **South African National Parks** (SANP) offices in Pretoria (☎ 012-343 1991, fax 343 0905, e *reservations@parks-sa.co.za*, w *www .parks-sa.co.za, 643 Leyds St, Muckleneuk)*. Unfortunately, the trail is usually booked up one year ahead. Some travellers have been lucky enough to arrive and find that a booking has been cancelled but this is rare.

Accommodation is in six-bed *rest huts* with mattresses but without bedding, cooking utensils or running water. Camping is not allowed.

The 64km Tsitsikamma Trail runs parallel to the Otter Trail but takes you inland through the forests. As it begins at Nature's Valley and ends at Storms River Mouth (travelling in the opposite direction to the Otter Trail), you could combine the two. This hike also lasts five days and four nights.

Unlike the Otter Trail, there is little difficulty getting a booking, and midweek you may have the trail to yourself, except during school holidays. Accommodation is in *huts*. Book both the trail and accommodation through the **Forestry Department** (☎ *012-481 3615)* in Pretoria or contact De Vasselot camping ground near Nature's Valley for information.

Places to Stay & Eat

Storms River Mouth Rest Camp (bookings ☎ 012-343 1991, fax 012-343 0905, e re servations@parks-sa.co.za) Camping R65 for 1-2 people plus R20 for each additional person, 2-bed forest huts R120, 2-bed/4-bed log cabins R290/540, 4-bed 'Oceanettes' R540. This camp offers different types of cottages; all except the forest huts are equipped with kitchens (including utensils), bedding and bathrooms. The forest huts have communal facilities. All accommodation except the forest huts is discounted by 20% between May and August. Bookings are made through the SANP offices in Pretoria.

Storms River Restaurant at the reception complex has great views over the coast and reasonable prices.

Getting There & Away

There is no public transport to the Storms River Mouth Rest Camp, which is an 8km walk from the N2. Buses run along the N2 (see Getting There & Away in the Cape

Town & the Peninsula chapter and in the Port Elizabeth section later in this chapter for details). The **Baz Bus** (☎ *021-439 2323)* stops at Nature's Valley (see the Getting Around chapter earlier in this book for more information on the Baz Bus).

STORMS RIVER
☎ 042 • postcode 6308

There can be some confusion between Storms River and Storms River Mouth in Tsitsikamma National Park. From the N2 the Storms River signpost points to the village that lies outside the national park. Despite what some maps show, the turn-off is 4km east of the turn-off to the national park. The turn-off to the park is signed as Storms River Mouth.

Storms River is a tiny and scattered hamlet with tree-shaded lanes, a couple of places to stay and an outdoor centre. **Tsitsikamma Tourism Information Office** (☎ *281 1561, fax 281 1563)* at the Petro Port petrol station on the N2 provides information.

East of the village on the N2 is the **Big Tree**, a huge, 36m-high *outeniqua* (yellowwood), and a forest with many fine examples of candlewood, stinkwood and assegai. An interpretative **trail** (entry R3), with signs in English and Afrikaans, describes the trees in this forest, one of the best preserved in South Africa.

Activities

The world's highest **bungee jump** (☎ *281 1463; R500)*, at 216m, is at the Bloukrans River Bridge, 21km west of Storms River. You can have one hell of an adrenaline rush, but don't be fooled – this may be the highest jump but it is not the longest. You don't fall anywhere near the 216m. Still, it's a daunting view from the bridge.

Storms River Adventures (☎ *281 1836, fax 281 1609,* e *adventure@gardenroute.co .za,* w *www.stormsriver.com, Darnell St, Storms River)*, offers black-water tubing (R325). The four- to five-hour trip, down Storms River, includes professional guides, lunch, permits and use of a wetsuit. Other heart-pumping activities on offer include abseiling (R120) and snorkelling (R140).

For the less adventurous, the company also books some more relaxing ventures. These include cruises up the Storms River Gorge to the first set of rapids on the Spirit of Tsitsikamma (R35 per person). The trip is relatively short (30 minutes) but the rock overhangs are impressive. There is also a tractor/trailer drive called the Woodcutter's Journey, which follows an elephant trail through indigenous forest to the old Storms River Pass (R65 or R105 with lunch or supper).

Many **walking trails**, including the Plaatbos Forest Trail (four options) and the Ratel Trail (4.2km), start at the Big Tree. You can hire **mountain bikes** (R80 per day) at the Storms River Adventures centre and then attempt the 22km Storms River Cycle Route; a round trip should take three to four hours. The **Robbehoek Biking Trail** (☎ 281 1816) has chalets for both hikers and bikers.

Places to Stay & Eat

Storms River Rainbow Lodge (☎/fax 281 1530, e rainbowl@lantic.net, 72 Darnell St) Dorm beds R50, doubles without/with bathroom R130/150. The Rainbow is a comfortable lodge with a range of accommodation and nice gardens at the back. Breakfast is available for R20.

The Old Village Inn (☎ 281 1711, fax 281 1669, e info@village-inn.co.za, w www.village-inn.co.za) Doubles B&B from R175. While not especially fancy, this hotel has a certain old-world charm after the tour buses depart.

Ploughman's Rest (☎/fax 281 1726, 31 Formosa St) B&B R105-135 per person. This friendly B&B is just off the eastern side of the road before you enter Storms River.

Armagh Country Guest House (☎ 541 1512, fax 541 1510, e armagh@mweb.co.za, w www.thearmagh.com) B&B R125-195 per person. This homely guesthouse, while a little more expensive than Ploughman's Rest, is the perfect place to relax for a few days. Its restaurant serves good meals.

Tsitsikamma Lodge (☎ 750 3802, fax 750 3702, e info@tsitsikamma.com, w www.tsitsikamma.com) Garden cabins R295, deluxe suites R395 per person. This lodge,

8km east of Storms River, is a group of upmarket log cabins. Aimed at love-struck honeymooners, the lodge tempts guests to undertake its tacky 'striptease river trail'.

Getting There & Away

The Baz Bus stops at Storms River.

HUMANSDORP
☎ 042 • postcode 6300

Humansdorp is an uninspiring town 87km south-west of Port Elizabeth. While there is little of interest for travellers, it is the gateway to the coastal resorts of Cape St Francis and St Francis Bay.

However, this may change with the opening of the new **Kouga Cultural Centre** (Cnr Voortrekker & Main Sts) at the town's main entrance. The centre, with its impressive domed roof, has been developed to promote cultural tourism within the region. It will also be a major stop for the *Apple Express* tourist train from Port Elizabeth (see Steam Train under Port Elizabeth later in this chapter for details about the train).

Information is available from the **Humansdorp Publicity Association** (☎ 295 1361, fax 291 0567, 24 Du Plessis St); there is a possibility that the association's office may relocate to the new cultural centre.

There are a number of pleasant B&Bs in Humansdorp; expect to pay around R120 per person. Contact the publicity association for details. There's only one hotel here.

Palm Inn Hotel (☎/fax 295 1233, 16 Alexander St) Singles/doubles B&B R125/224. Humansdorp's only hotel offers your standard B&B with few surprises.

Greyhound stops daily at the Total petrol station en route to Port Elizabeth. The Baz Bus stops at the Boskloof Centre.

CAPE ST FRANCIS
☎ 042

Cape St Francis, 22km south of Humansdorp, is a worthwhile destination and not only when the surf's up at Seal Point break. The area was occupied more than 10,000 years ago by Khoikhoi and San, and there are still many middens (mounds of refuse marking early settlements) in the area.

Surfing in Eastern Cape

Eastern Cape's coast is one of the greatest and most consistent surfing regions in the world. Head the Kombi anywhere between Jeffrey's Bay and Port Edward for excellent, uncrowded surf, and meet some of the friendliest locals. They include Wendy Botha (world women's surf champion), Brad Bricknell, Royden Bryson (current South African junior champion), Greg Emslie (South African 'top 44' star) and Dave Malherbe.

Jeffrey's Bay is world famous and those with the slightest interest in the motion of the waves will have heard of Supertubes. In July it hosts the Billabong Pro and in August the Pro Junior competition – partying, bands and a few hangovers are commonplace.

Also consider nearby Cape St Francis, seen in the movie *Endless Summer*, and the more consistent Seal Point. Jeffrey's Bay, also known as 'J Bay', is a surfie town and a great place to buy cheap surf clothing and order surfboards. Remember it can get crowded on good swells; be patient, and at all times respect the locals and afford them some space. Keep your eye on the low-pressure systems – anything below 970 millibars and you will be in heaven.

Heading north, Port Elizabeth is at its best with an unusual easterly swell or a big south swell and a south-westerly wind. With the right conditions, excellent waves can be found, particularly at The Fence, a hollow wedging left on the south side of the harbour wall.

Rock on to Port Alfred where there are excellent right-handers from the eastern pier of this sleepy fishing town. Travelling through the former Ciskei on the way to East London there are some remote secret spots, but don't expect the locals to reveal them. Go out and explore.

Then on to East London, home of the legendary Nahoon Reef, a world-class right-hander known to be one of the most consistent waves in the country. This thick juicy wave rises from deep water and thumps down on a boulder reef. If you find yourself stuck in the bowl, this wave will rattle your bones. Due to the abundance of swell and the huge variety of excellent breaks in the area, which work in variety of conditions, East London is a great place to hang out. Nahoon Beach and The Corner are the nursery for East London grommets and ideal for debutantes wanting to learn to surf. Buccaneers pub, next to the Sugarshack, is the meeting place for those in the know. Buy these guys a beer and they will let you in on Graveyards, Yellow Sands and Igoda.

Further north is Wacky Point, a great barrelling right-hander on a big swell. Then finally there's the Transkei's Wild Coast, an essential stop for any traveller visiting the continent. It boasts some of the most spectacular coastline you will ever see and point breaks reputed to be as good as Supertubes, some known and many others as yet unnamed and yet to be surfed.

Chester Mackley & David Malherbe

EASTERN CAPE

There is heaps to do at Cape St Francis. You can walk to the lighthouse, built in 1878 and the tallest masonry tower on the South African coast, or enjoy a late afternoon drink at Sunset Rocks. You can also walk or drive (4WD only) through the Cape St Francis Nature Reserve via Shark Point; examine coastal fynbos amid the dune ridges in the Irma Booysen Flora Reserve or peer out to sea in search of the southern right whale (June to November).

St Francis Bay is a small resort village 10km north of Cape St Francis. Bounded to the north by the Kromme River, the resort has been partially constructed around a network of artificial canals.

In the past we have been pretty harsh on St Francis Bay and we're not changing our opinion for this edition. Quite simply, it's a bleak place that is as artificial as the canals it's built around. Every house has a security warning plastered over it and few are occupied full time. That said, not all our readers agree:

We would have missed out on St Francis Bay if we had taken heed of your 'upper middle-class ghetto' warning. We found it intriguing, the people welcoming and the accommodation affordable.

R & P Booth

Places to Stay & Eat

Full Stop Lodge & Seal Point Backpackers (☎ 298 0128, 📧 sealsbackpackers@web online.co.za, 🌐 www.seals.co.za, Da Gama Rd) Dorm beds R50, doubles R160, self-catering units R240 for 2 people plus R60 for each extra person. This well-located lodge is just 200m from the legendary Seal Point. Dorms are clean, and the spacious self-catering units are good value. Downstairs you'll find the lively *Full Stop Pub*. The nature reserve, with its 3km of beachfront, is nearby.

Stoney Boma's Bushcamp 6-bed chalet R80 per person. Stoney Boma's Bushcamp, located in an idyllic bird sanctuary, is the perfect getaway from the Garden Route glitz. Bookings can be arranged through Seal Point Backpackers. The price includes the return river boat trip.

Cape St Francis Resort (☎ 298 0054, fax 298 0157, 📧 seals@iafrica.com, 🌐 www .capestfrancis.co.za) Camping R70 for 2 people, small cottages R280 for 2 people plus R70 for each extra person, large cottages R300 for 2 people plus R75 for each extra person. This resort has all the facilities you need: swimming pool, restaurant, a good bar and proximity to a beach.

JEFFREY'S BAY

☎ 042 • postcode 6330

Surfing is the reason to come to J Bay, as it is usually called. Few would disagree that the waves at Jeffrey's Bay are the best in Southern Africa and among the best in the world. Ex-world champion Shaun Tomson has claimed that Supertubes is the most perfect wave in the world. It can be more than a three-minute ride from Boneyards to the end. Development is raging at a furious pace, but so far the local board-waxing vibe has been retained.

There is windsurfing and great bird-watching at Kabeljous Beach. You could go walking in the Seekoei and Noorsekloof Nature Reserves or watch dolphins cavorting in the waves along most beaches. And there are always shells for beachcombers to discover.

Information

Jeffrey's Bay Tourism (☎ 293 2588, fax 293 2227, 📧 jbay@ilink.co.za, Da Gama Rd; open 8.30am-5pm Mon-Fri, 9am-noon Sat) is friendly and helpful.

The **Network Internet Cafe** (☎ 293 3239, 🌐 www.lantic.co.za, Opposite the shell museum; open 9am-5pm Mon-Fri, 9am-3pm Sat) charges R20 per hour. **Cafe Dulce Internet** is near the Spar supermarket.

Aloe Afrika Tours & Trails (☎/fax 296 2974, 📧 aloe@agnet.co.za) offers tours to surfing spots, horse trails (R80 for two hours including beach riding), cycling trips and sand boarding (half-day R80) or you can get a taste for the 'real Africa' with their Simphiwe's Choice tour (R150). On the day tour Simphiwe (pronounced sim-pee-we) invites you to experience traditional village life through his eyes. You'll find the office in the blue bus on Da Gama Rd.

Shell Museum

More than 400 types of seashells are found around Jeffrey's Bay. The **shell museum** (☎ 293 1111, ext 286, Drommedaris St; admission by donation; open 9am-4pm Mon-Sat, 9am-noon Sun), next to the information office, started with the collection of one woman and has been augmented with 350 deep-water and rare shells.

Places to Stay – Budget

Jeffrey's Bay Caravan Park (☎ 200 2241, fax 293 1114) Camping R47/75 for 2 people low/high season. This park is exposed but it is strategically located beside the sea, off Da Gama Rd, midway between the town centre and the surf. There are three other caravan parks nearby.

Island Vibe (☎ 293 1625, fax 293 3469, 📧 ivibe@lantic.co.za, 10 Dageraad St) Camping R25, dorm beds R40, doubles R140. Island Vibe sits above Kitchen Windows – you could literally fall into the surf! It is a bit out of town (follow the signs) but it epitomises Jeffrey's Bay and the attendant raft of surfies attests to its prime location.

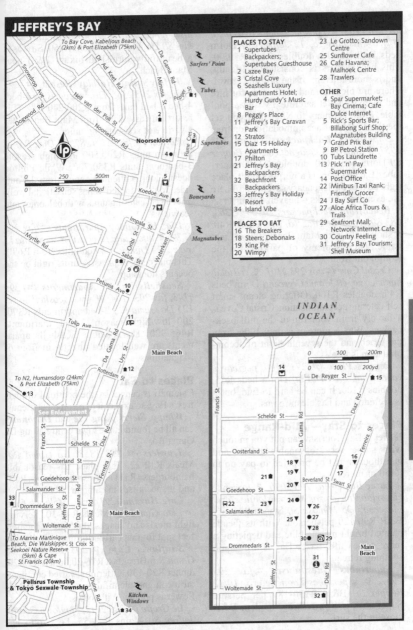

JEFFREY'S BAY

PLACES TO STAY
1 Supertubes Backpackers; Supertubes Guesthouse
2 Lazee Bay
3 Cristal Cove
6 Seashells Luxury Apartments Hotel; Hurdy Gurdy's Music Bar
8 Peggy's Place
11 Jeffrey's Bay Caravan Park
12 Stratos
15 Diaz 15 Holiday Apartments
17 Philton
21 Jeffrey's Bay Backpackers
32 Beachfront Backpackers
33 Jeffrey's Bay Holiday Resort
34 Island Vibe

PLACES TO EAT
16 The Breakers
18 Steers; Debonairs
19 King Pie
20 Wimpy

23 Le Grotto; Sandown Centre
25 Sunflower Cafe
26 Cafe Havana; Malhoek Centre
28 Trawlers

OTHER
4 Spar Supermarket; Bay Cinema; Cafe Dulce Internet
5 Rick's Sports Bar; Billabong Surf Shop; Magnatubes Building
7 Grand Prix Bar
9 BP Petrol Station
10 Tubs Laundrette
13 Pick 'n' Pay Supermarket
14 Post Office
22 Minibus Taxi Rank; Friendly Grocer
24 J Bay Surf Co
27 Aloe Africa Tours & Trails
29 Seafront Mall; Network Internet Cafe
30 Country Feeling
31 Jeffrey's Bay Tourism; Shell Museum

EASTERN CAPE

Jeffrey's Bay Backpackers (☎ 293 1379, fax 296 1763, e backpac@netactive.co.za, W www.hisa.org.za, 12 Jeffrey St) Dorm beds R40, singles/doubles from R50/90. This backpackers is consistently friendly and is more tolerant of the nonsurf crowd. There are bicycles and surfboards for hire and there's M-Net satellite TV and a pool table. From February to November you get the third night of accommodation for free.

Supertubes Backpackers (☎/fax 293 2957, e supertubes@agnet.co.za, 6 Pepper St) Dorm beds R40, doubles R140. Supertubes Backpackers is a purpose-built place right next to the legendary surf break. There are even board racks – heaven for surfers.

Beachfront Backpackers (☎ 293 3363, 082-892 1689, 36 Diaz Rd) Dorm beds R40. A short walk from Main Beach, this is great value. There's plenty of parking for the Kombi out front.

Cristal Cove (☎/fax 293 2101, e cristal@ lantic.co.za, 49 Flame Crescent) Dorm beds R45, doubles R100. Offering clean, smart self-catering accommodation, Cristal Cove is a far cry from your run-of-the-mill backpackers. What's more, it is only 100m from the beach and the seventh night of accommodation is free!

Peggy's Place (☎ 293 2160, pegjbay@ yahoo.com, 8A Oribi St) Dorm beds R35, doubles R100. It can be hard to find, but it is secluded and has clean rooms.

Places to Stay – Mid-Range

Jeffrey's Bay Tourism can put you in touch with some very reasonable B&Bs and guesthouses, but be prepared to pay up to R150 or more.

Lazee Bay (☎/fax 296 2090, e lazeebay @worldonline.co.za, W www.lantic.co.za/ ~lazeebay, 25 Mimosa St) Standard/luxury B&B R90/120 per person. With its facade painted bright marine blue and depicting a maze of sea life, Lazee Bay is a tranquil, soothing retreat.

Supertubes Guesthouse (☎/fax 293 2957, e supertubes@agnet.co.za, 10/12 Pepper St) B&B R150-180 per person. Supertubes is a refreshing, modern B&B close to the surf.

Stratos (☎ 293 1116, fax 293 3072, e stra tos@agnet.co.za, W www.stratos-za.com, 11 Uys St) Doubles B&B from R450. Stratos is a beautifully furnished luxury B&B near Main Beach.

Jeffrey's Bay Holiday Resort (☎ 293 1330, fax 293 2365, Drommedaris St) 2-bed/ 4-bed/6-bed units from R200/240/280. This resort, an easy walk from Main Beach, has a variety of self-catering units.

Philton (☎/fax 293 1287, 25 Diaz Rd) 2-bedroom units R200/500 low/high season, 3-bedroom units R350/700. While Philton doesn't look particularly good from the outside, don't be fooled. It has sensational well-priced self-catering units with balconies and sea views.

Diaz 15 Holiday Apartments (☎/fax 293 1779, e info@diaz15.co.za, W www.diaz15 .co.za, 15 Diaz Rd) 4-bed units from R690. This place has impressive units right on the ocean's doorstep.

Seashells Luxury Apartments (☎ 293 1143, fax 293 1104, W www.seashell.co.za, 125 Da Gama Rd) 2-bed apartments R390/ 200 low/high season, 3-bed apartments R465/900. The spacious Seashells apartments are well located directly in front of Magnatubes.

Places to Eat

Calamari is caught by the boatload off Jeffrey's Bay, so expect it to be on most menus.

Wimpy, *Steers*, *King Pie* and *Debonairs* can all be found in the town centre along Da Gama Rd.

Trawlers (☎ 293 1353, Da Gama Rd) Meals R12-22. This place has reasonable hamburgers (R11) and fish and chips (R13) and it specialises in calamari (R22).

Cafe Havana (293 1510, Malhoek Centre, Da Gama Rd) Meals R15-30. Serving light meals and snacks, this cafe is the perfect spot for that early-morning caffeine fix.

Sunflower Cafe (☎ 293 1682, 20 Da Gama Rd) Breakfast R16-20, lunch R15-20, dinner R20-130. Offering a varied continental menu and plentiful veg meals, the Sunflower is popular with locals.

Le Grotto (☎ 293 2612, Sandown Centre, Jeffrey St) Mains R14-55. Le Grotto has good seafood and meat dishes, but avoid the veg meals!

The Breakers (☎/fax 293 1975, Ferreira St) Mains R35-70. Overlooking the ocean, this is an excellent place for a bit of a splurge. Other than pasta, the menu is mainly seafood (R55 and over).

Tapas Lapa Seaside (☎ 292 0119) Mains R18-60. Tapas is on the seashore, and the sand on its floor is blown across from the beach. Meals range from calamari on rice (R30) to a veritable seafood feast (R60).

Die Walskipper (☎ 292 0005) Mains R30-95. This another alfresco eatery just metres from the lapping sea at the Marina Martinique beach. It specialises in seafood and all types of barbecued meat.

Entertainment

Rick's Sports Bar (☎ 082-564 9379, Magnatubes Building, Da Gama Rd) Open 10am-late daily. This long-preferred drinking spot for the local surfers now has a new young manager who is making some changes.

Diagonally opposite each other on Da Gama Rd are *Hurdy Gurdy's Music Bar* and the *Grand Prix Bar*.

In nearby Pellsrus and Tokyo Sexwale townships there are *shebeens* (drinking establishments) where you can meet local blacks and coloureds while listening to kwaito (South African pop music) and jazz.

Bay Cinema, near the Spar supermarket, screens current movies.

Shopping

Country Feeling (☎ 293 1210) runs most of the surf shops in town and has a clothing factory. *J Bay Surf Co (☎ 293 1900, Cnr Da Gama Rd & Goedehoop St)* sells new boards for R950 to R2000. There's a fairly limited stock of second-hand boards for R500 to R1000. *Billabong Surf Shop (☎ 296 1797, Da Gama Rd)* hires boards for R15 per hour and wetsuits for R10 an hour. They also offer surfing lessons for R50 per hour with a wetsuit and a surfboard included.

Getting There & Away

The Baz Bus stops daily at hostels in both directions. A fare from Jeffrey's Bay to

Cape Town costs R405; Port Elizabeth to Jeffrey's Bay costs R70. **Shekinah Tours** *(☎ 292 0282)* operates a daily service to Port Elizabeth (R30) and Humansdorp (R10). **Sunshine Express** *(☎ 293 2221)* runs between Port Elizabeth and Jeffrey's Bay (R65).

Minibus taxis depart from the Friendly Grocer; it's R6 to Humansdorp and R20 to Port Elizabeth.

PORT ELIZABETH

☎ 041 • postcode 6000

Port Elizabeth is 1115km from Johannesburg (Jo'burg), 785km from Cape Town and 310km from East London. It's a major transport hub. The city centre is on steep hills overlooking Algoa Bay and there are some pleasant beaches and parks virtually in the centre of town. The city, now part of the new Nelson Mandela Metropole, also has some interesting historical architecture. Unfortunately, the 20th century has been unkind to Port Elizabeth. What must once have been a fine example of a Victorian/Edwardian port city has become a victim of neglect.

Port Elizabeth (commonly known as 'PE') bills itself as the 'Friendly City'. Remarkably, given the hype, Port Elizabeth is a genuinely friendly place.

There are enormous townships around Port Elizabeth and its sister city Uitenhage, and the problems associated with a high unemployment rate, poverty and violence are prevalent here. It was here in Port Elizabeth's Sanlam Centre that Steve Biko, a well-known leader of the Black Consciousness Movement, was held captive for 26 days and tortured (see also the boxed text 'Steve Biko' in the King William's Town section later in this chapter).

Orientation

The train station is just to the north-west of the Campanile, an unmistakable bell tower (admission by donation), now isolated from the city by the ghastly freeway.

Information

Tourist Offices Well-organised **Tourism Port Elizabeth** *(☎ 585 8884,* e *information@ tourismpe.co.za,* w *www.ibhayi.com, Donkin*

EASTERN CAPE

Reserve; open 8am-4.30pm Mon-Fri, 9.30am-3.30pm Sat & Sun) has an excellent supply of information and maps, including the *Donkin Heritage Trail (R18)*, which details a walk around the city's historic buildings. The information office is in the lighthouse building in Donkin Reserve.

Money You'll need to go to Summerstrand for **AmEx** (☎ *583 2025, The Boardwalk, Marine Dr, Summerstrand; open 10am-noon Mon-Fri, 10am-2pm Sat & Sun)*. **Rennies Foreign Exchange** (☎ *363 1185, The Bridge Shopping Centre)* is a long way from the town centre.

Email & Internet Access Cyber Diner II Internet Cafe (☎ *583 6076,* e *cyberjt@ mweb.co.za, The Boardwalk, Marine Dr, Summerstrand; open 10am-midnight Sun-Thur, 10am-2am Fri & Sat)* charges R20 for 30 minutes.

Dangers & Annoyances The city centre, especially the main street (Govan Mbeki St) has been more heavily policed in recent years, resulting in a noticeable reduction in crimes such as bag snatching. Still, many businesses have moved out to the wealthy white western suburbs and are difficult to access if you don't have a car. The industrial areas and the city centre can be dangerous at night and should be avoided. The city's main beachfront, however, is considered one of the safest in the country.

Steam Train
The *Apple Express* tourist steam train (☎ *507 2333, fax 507 3233, Humewood Rd Station, Humewood; adult/child R60/25; every weekend in high season)* runs a day trip to Thornhill and back, with a two-hour stop for a braai (barbecue). It crosses over the highest narrow-gauge bridge in the world.

Donkin Reserve
The Donkin Reserve is immediately behind the town centre and has good views over the bay. It's a handy point for getting your bearings. The pyramid on the reserve is a memorial to Elizabeth Donkin, the wife of Sir Rufane Donkin, after whom the city is named. The pyramid has two plaques. The first one is in memory of '…one of the most perfect human beings who has given her name to the town below' and the second one

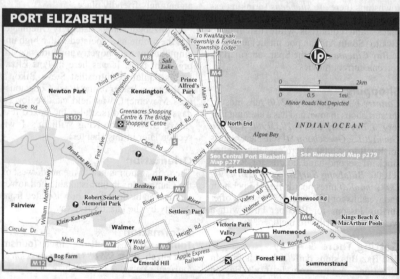

PORT ELIZABETH

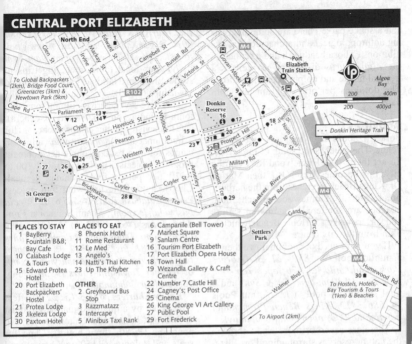

CENTRAL PORT ELIZABETH

PLACES TO STAY	PLACES TO EAT	6 Campanile (Bell Tower)
1 BayBerry	8 Phoenix Hotel	7 Market Square
Fountain B&B;	11 Rome Restaurant	9 Sanlam Centre
Bay Cafe	12 Le Med	16 Tourism Port Elizabeth
10 Calabash Lodge	13 Angelo's	17 Port Elizabeth Opera House
& Tours	14 Natti's Thai Kitchen	18 Town Hall
15 Edward Protea	23 Up The Khyber	19 Wezandla Gallery & Craft
Hotel		Centre
20 Port Elizabeth	**OTHER**	22 Number 7 Castle Hill
Backpackers'	2 Greyhound Bus	24 Cagney's; Post Office
Hostel	Stop	25 Cinema
21 Protea Lodge	3 Razzmatazz	26 King George VI Art Gallery
28 Jikeleza Lodge	4 Intercape	27 Public Pool
30 Paxton Hotel	5 Minibus Taxi Rank	29 Fort Frederick

refers to '…the husband whose heart is still wrung by undiminished grief'. The lighthouse beside the pyramid houses the information office. Also on the reserve is the **Port Elizabeth Opera House**, the oldest opera house in the country. The reserve is flanked by some fine Victorian architecture: a row of terraces on the northern side and the Edward Protea Hotel on the western side.

Settlers' Park & Fort Frederick

Settlers' Park, virtually in the centre of the city, includes 54 hectares of cultivated and natural gardens in the valley of the Baakens River. The main emphasis is on native plants and flowers, so it's also a good place for birdlife. The main entrance is on How St (off Park Dr, which circles St Georges Park and its sporting fields) – there's a great view from the car park.

Fort Frederick *(Belmont Terrace; admission free; open 8am-4.30pm daily)*, overlooking the Baakens River, was built in 1799 to defend the original harbour in the river mouth. A shot has never been fired from here in anger.

Jewish Pioneers' Memorial Museum

This museum *(☎ 373 5197, Raleigh St; admission free; open 10am-noon Sun)* features an intriguing collection of memorabilia detailing Jewish history in Port Elizabeth. Its displays include ceremonial items, photographs and a Jewish ex-servicemen's memorial. The museum is housed in the original synagogue used by the city's Jewish community between 1912 and 1954.

Bayworld

One of the best and largest museum complexes in the country, Bayworld *(☎ 586 1051, W www.bayworld.co.za, Beach Rd; museum adult/child R10/5, snake park & tropical house R10/5, oceanarium R17/9; open 9am-1pm & 2pm-4.30pm daily)* incorporates the Port Elizabeth Museum, an oceanarium and a snake park. There are some interesting anthropological and archaeological exhibitions (Xhosa beadwork and a replica of the *Algoasaurus* dinosaur), as well as a tropical house and dolphin demonstrations. The dolphins perform at 11am and 3pm daily.

Activities

Port Elizabeth is a major water sports venue. The beaches are south of the centre. To get there, take Humewood Rd from the city; this becomes Beach Rd, then Marine Dr. Kings Beach stretches from the harbour breakwater to Humewood Beach; both beaches are sheltered. Catamaran sailors and surfers make for Hobie Beach, which is 5km from the city centre.

If you're in need of cooling down there's a public **pool** (☎ 585 7751, *St Georges Park; adult/child R3/1.70; open 7am-7pm Mon-Fri, 10.30am-6pm Sat & Sun*) and a tidal swimming pool at **MacArthur Pools** (☎ 586 3412, *Kings Beach Promenade; adult/child R4/3; open 10am-6pm daily*).

There are seven or more walks through the nature reserves surrounding Port Elizabeth for which you can get guides. Contact Dr Paul Martin at **Bird & Eco-Tours** (☎ 466 5698, fax 466 1815, e *apmartin@global .co.za, PO Box 61029 Bluewater Bay, Port Elizabeth*). He provides a variety of informative bird-watching and natural history tours, including transport to/from the walking trails. Prices start at R90.

Good diving sites around Port Elizabeth include some wrecks and the St Croix Islands, a marine reserve. Contact either **Ocean Divers International** (☎ 583 1790, e *mario@odipe.co.za,* **w** *www.odipe.co.za, The Boardwalk, Marine Dr, Summerstrand*) or **Pro Dive** (☎ 583 5316, e *dive@ prodive .co.za,* **w** *www.prodive.co.za, Marine Dr, Summerstrand*); both of these offer PADI and NAUI diving courses, starting at around R799.

Boogie boards are sold and hired out for R50 plus deposit by the **Surf Centre** (☎ 585 6027, *Opposite MacAuthur Pools on Marine Dr, Humewood*).

Organised Tours

Bay Tourism & Tours (☎ 585 5427, fax 584 0016, e *gary@baytours.co.za,* **w** *www.bay tours.co.za, Humewood; open 9am-5pm daily*) runs local tours, including trips to Addo Elephant National Park (R250) and townships (R180).

There are several cross-cultural township tours including one to Walmer (Gqebera). The tours visit squatter camps, shebeens (for a traditional meal), *abakhwetha* (initiation camps for boys) and resource development program projects. The cost is from R100 to R120 per person and includes a meal. Choose any of the following tour guides: Paul at *Calabash Tours* (☎ 585 6162, e *cala bash@iafrica.com*); Xhanti Singapi at *Fundani Tours* (☎/fax 463 1471, *cultours@ iafrica.com*); Tshokwana at *Pembury Tours* (☎ 581 2581, fax 581 2332, e *info@pem burytours.com,* **w** *www.pemburytours.com*); or *Walmer Township Tours* (☎ 581 7085, *gqeberatours@hotmail.com*).

Raggy Charters (☎ 073-152 2277) offers cruises led by a qualified marine biologist to St Croix, Jahleel and Benton Islands. See penguins (R280, three hours), Cape fur seals and dolphins (R150, two hours), and whales (R280, three hours).

Places to Stay – Budget

Port Elizabeth Backpackers' Hostel (☎ 586 0697, fax 585 2032, e *pebakpak@global .co.za, 7 Prospect Hill*) Dorm beds R50, doubles R130. This friendly, well-run hostel is in a 100-year-old building within walking distance of the city and places to eat and drink up on the headland. Email facilities are available and manager Ian organises transport to the Owl House in Nieu Bethesda (see under The Karoo later in this chapter).

Jikeleza Lodge (☎ 586 3721, fax 585 6686, e *winteam@hinet.co.za, 44 Cuyler St*) Dorm beds R45, doubles R120. Jikeleza Lodge is small and clean and the owners are a veritable mine of information – ask about local township tours. It runs a courtesy bus to the beach.

Kings Beach Backpackers (☎ 585 8113, fax 585 1693, e *kingsb@agnet.co.za, 41 Windermere Rd, Humewood*) Camping R25.

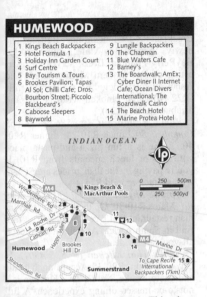

HUMEWOOD

1 Kings Beach Backpackers	9 Lungile Backpackers
2 Hotel Formula 1	10 The Chapman
3 Holiday Inn Garden Court	11 Blue Waters Cafe
4 Surf Centre	12 Barney's
5 Bay Tourism & Tours	13 The Boardwalk; AmEx;
6 Brookes Pavilion; Tapas	Cyber Diner II Internet
Al Sol; Chilli Cafe; Dros;	Cafe; Ocean Divers
Bourbon Street; Piccolo	International; The
Blackbeard's	Boardwalk Casino
7 Caboose Sleepers	14 The Beach Hotel
8 Bayworld	15 Marine Protea Hotel

INDIAN OCEAN

Kings Beach &
MacArthur Pools

Windermere Rd

Marshall Rd

La Roche Dr

Cathcart Rd

Happy Valley

Humewood   Brookes
            Hill Dr

Strandfontein Rd

Marine Dr

Summerstrand

To Cape Recife
International
Backpackers (7km)

0   250   500m
0   250   500yd

dorm beds R45, doubles R110. This place epitomises what we mean by 'backpackers': adequate digs in friendly surroundings.

Lungile Backpackers (☎ 582 2042, fax 582 2083, e lungile@netactive.co.za, 12 La Roche Dr, Humewood) Camping R30, dorm beds R50. On the beachfront, this backpackers is excellent value. There is a swimming pool and a large entertaining area that rocks most nights.

Cape Recife International Backpackers (☎ 583 4004, fax 583 3839, e plodge@ iafrica.com) Camping R30, dorm beds R45, doubles R135. For the perfect getaway you can't beat this place. It has an idyllic beach location, 7km from the city, and is surrounded by the Cape Recife Nature Reserve. The hostel has an information centre for travellers and offers a variety of adventure activities, including sea kayaking and mountain biking.

Places to Stay – Mid-Range

B&Bs & Guesthouses Tourism Port Elizabeth assists with B&B bookings; most places charge between R100 and R150 per person.

Calabash Lodge & Tours (☎ 585 6162, e calabash@iafrica.com, W www.axxess

.web.za/calabash, 2 Dollery St, Central) Singles/twins without bathroom R130/180, singles/doubles with bathroom R150/220. The recently expanded Calabash Lodge is by far the best-value B&B in town. Its clean, spacious rooms have a distinct African feel and attention to detail is shown in the little things such as soaps and shampoos. Its Real City (R180) and Shebeen (R180) township tours reveal another side of Port Elizabeth (see Organised Tours earlier in this section for more details).

BayBerry Fountain B&B (☎ 585 1558, fax 585 1559, e bayberry@mail.co.za, 7 Lutman St) Singles/doubles B&B R200/ 220. The upmarket BayBerry Fountain is another good centrally located B&B.

Fundani Township Lodge (☎ 463 1471, 69 Theko St, KwaMagxaki) Singles/doubles with bathroom R90/130. The Fundani Township Lodge offers you the rare opportunity to stay in and experience life in a township, although you get a rose-coloured view. It is great value and the price includes township walks, shebeen visits, good old-fashioned conversations and Ubuntu (fellow felling; kindness).

Caboose Sleepers (☎ 586 0088, fax 586 0087, e pe@caboose.co.za, W www.ca boose.co.za, Brookes Hill Dr, Humewood) Singles/doubles/triples R109/148/167. This a good-value place modelled on a sleeper train. Its only drawback (but the reason for its economy) is the claustrophobic little rooms with plastic shower and toilet cubicles.

Hotels Port Elizabeth has a good range of hotels, most lining the beachfront, that will suit all budgets.

Hotel Formula 1 (☎ 585 6380, fax 585 6383, Cnr La Roche Dr & Beach Rd) 1-3 person room R155. Hotel Formula 1 is has small, clean, simple rooms. Breakfast is available for R10.

The Chapman (☎ 585 0300, fax 585 0305, e chapmail@iafrica.com, W www.chapman .co.za, 1 Lady Bea Crescent, Brookes Hill, Summerstrand) Singles/doubles R299/370. The family-run Chapman, overlooking the sea south of the city centre, is a superb choice. Breakfast is available for R28.

EASTERN CAPE

Edward Protea Hotel (☎ 586 2056, fax 586 4925, e edward@cyberhost.co.za, *Belmont Terrace*) Singles/doubles R325/410. The Edward Protea Hotel, in the heart of the city, is a gracious, old-style Edwardian hotel with comfortable rooms. It's a superior member of the Protea chain. Breakfast is available for R45.

Paxton Hotel (☎ 585 9655, e paxton@iafrica.com, *Carnarvon Place, Humerail*) Singles/doubles R335/410. The Paxton is a fairly upmarket, if a little impersonal, hotel.

Holiday Inn Garden Court (☎ 582 3720, fax 585 5754, *La Roche Dr, Kings Beach*) Singles/doubles R399/488. As would be expected from the Holiday Inn chain, rooms here are modern, clean and on the expensive side. Breakfast is available for R46.

The Beach Hotel (☎ 583 2161, e reservations@pehotels.co.za, *Marine Dr, Summerstrand*). The classy Beach Hotel is well positioned opposite Hobie Beach and next to The Boardwalk. Special weekend rates are available and breakfast costs R30.

Marine Protea Hotel (☎ 583 2101, fax 583 2076, e pehotels@mweb.co.za, *Marine Dr, Summerstrand*) Singles/doubles R585/720. The Marine Protea is possibly the best – and therefore the most expensive – hotel in Port Elizabeth. Breakfast here costs R50.

Places to Eat

There are cheap places and takeaways at *Bridge Food Court* at Greenacres shopping centre and *Brookes Pavilion* in Humewood. During the day there is plenty of street food in central Port Elizabeth.

If you haven't yet experienced the full splendour of a South African breakfast, head along to the *Edward Protea Hotel* where a stupendous spread in a dignified room will set you back R45. Nonguests are welcome.

Phoenix Hotel (☎ 586 3553, 5 Chapel St) Mains R10-23. The Phoenix Hotel is an entertainment institution with live music and the best value pub meals in Port Elizabeth.

Angelo's (☎ 585 2929, Parliament St) Mains R10-20. Angelo's is a small, casual restaurant with a cheap and flavoursome menu. It's popular, so you might have to wait for a table.

Bay Cafe (☎ 585 1558, Lutman St) Breakfast R8-19, lunch/dinner R10-23. The newly opened Bay Cafe, adjoining the BayBerry Fountain B&B, serves an interesting mix of modern Mediterranean and Asian cuisines including California rolls (R22.50), Thai chicken wrap (R18) and arrabiata pasta (R20).

Rome Restaurant (☎ 586 2731, 63 Campbell St) Lunch R10-24, dinner R20-40. Rome is a fun pizza-and-pasta place with lots of lunch specials from R10. If you're paying by the dish, prices aren't bad, with pasta at around R25.

Up The Khyber (☎ 582 2200, 2 Western Rd) Mains R10-30. Up the Khyber is an Indian restaurant that's vegan-friendly, a rare find in South Africa. Ask about its special all-you-can-eat deals.

Natti's Thai Kitchen (☎ 585 4301, 21 Clyde St) Mains R20-35. According to locals and visitors alike, Natti's Thai Kitchen is a not-to-be-missed dining experience. A full meal with curries and side dishes costs from R25 to R55.

Le Med (☎ 585 0321, 66A Parliament St) Breakfast R10-19, mains R19-42. Le Med is a top-notch Mediterranean restaurant with a cruising bar at the back.

Blue Waters Cafe (☎ 583 4110, Marine Dr, Summerstrand) Mains R25-50. Blue Waters Cafe is a bright, lively cafe/restaurant on The Boardwalk overlooking the ocean.

Piccolo Blackbeard's (☎ 586 3588, Brookes Pavilion) Mains R30-50. For sumptuous seafood platters (R50 plus), look no further than Piccolo Blackbeard's, a relaxed seafood bistro in Brookes Pavilion on the main beachfront.

Wild Boar (☎ 581 1523, 3rd Ave, Walmer) Mains R30-45. Just 300m from the airport, the Wild Boar has been recommended for its interesting, well-priced cuisine which includes crocodile, ostrich, kudu (antelope) and wild boar, either as steaks or *potjie kos* (meat and vegetables cooked in a special three-legged cast-iron pot over an open fire).

Entertainment

For some reason, Wednesday seems to be the biggest night in the pubs and clubs,

EASTERN CAPE

although Friday and Saturday are popular as well.

Phoenix Hotel (☎ 586 3553, 5 Chapel St) This is a grungy and occasionally rough little pub with live music on some nights.

Razzmatazz (☎ 082 576 1811, 3 Grace St) This black club features live jazz and well-known musicians from Jo'burg and Cape Town. Be careful in this area at night.

Cagney's (☎ 585 2422, Kine Park Centre, Rink St) Cagney's is a dark pub 'n' grill with a relaxing cocktail lounge that attracts an older crowd.

There are a number of restaurant-cum-nightclubs at Brookes Pavilion.

Tapas Al Sol (☎ 586 2159, Brookes Pavilion, Humewood) As the name suggests, this is a tapas bar; live bands play most nights and the Sunday afternoon deck party is legendary.

Chilli Cafe (☎ 584 0011, Brookes Pavilion, Humewood) This friendly Mexican restaurant turns into a hip, hot and happening party venue after dark. Eat quickly or you'll be in for a night of tequila slamming or even the odd cheesy wet T-shirt contest.

Dros (☎ 585 1021, Brookes Pavilion, Humewood) Part of the fast-growing South African chain, Dros is a favourite spot to quaff down a beer while watching the rugby.

Bourbon Street (☎ 082-389 9998, Brookes Pavilion, Humewood) Open 9am-late Thur, Fri & Sat. At the time of writing the newly opened Bourbon Street was *the* night spot in PE, playing a great mix of dance and rock music.

The Boardwalk Casino (☎ 507 7777, The Boardwalk, Marine Parade) Open 24 hours. Admission R20. The Boardwalk Casino is a little further down opposite Hobie Beach; there is an obligatory gun check at the entry.

Barney's (☎ 503 4500, The Boardwalk, Marine Parade) Barney's is an old-fashioned English-style pub 'n' grill. Test your drinking skills with the Fireman's Bucket (R30) – a silver bucket containing six local brews.

Fundani Tours (☎ 463 1471, @ cultours@iafrica.com) Fundani Tours operates night-time Lesbi-Gay tours for R350 per person. Alternatively, contact the *Lesbi-Gay Social Club (☎/fax 585 8409, @ gaype@bigfoot.com, W www.bigfoot.com/~gaype)* for an up-to-date list of popular night venues.

Shopping

Wezandla Gallery & Craft Centre (☎ 585 1655, 27 Baakens St) Open 9am-5pm Mon-Fri, 9am-1pm Sat. This brightly coloured centre has a good selection of African art and craft.

Getting There & Away

Air BA Comair (☎ 508 8099) has daily flights between Jo'burg and Port Elizabeth for R1024. SA Airlink (☎ 507 1111) flies daily from Port Elizabeth to Jo'burg (R718), Bloemfontein (R832), East London (R479) and Cape Town (R707).

Bus Greyhound (☎ 585 8648) buses depart from 6 Nile St, near the Health & Racquet Club at Greenacres shopping centre, and from 107 Govan Mbeki St, Central; reservations can also be made at Computicket at Greenacres shopping centre (☎ 374 4550). Translux (☎ 507 1333) has an office in Greenacres shopping centre on Ring Rd. Intercape (☎ 586 0055) only accepts telephone bookings; buses depart from the corner of Fleming and North Union St (behind the old post office).

To Cape Town Translux has a daily bus to and from Cape Town (R190) via the Garden Route. There is an additional service on Monday, Wednesday, Friday and Saturday in both directions. Translux also runs buses to Cape Town (R190) on what it calls the 'Mountain Route'. On Tuesday, Thursday and Sunday a bus follows the Garden Route to Oudtshoorn then runs via Montagu, Paarl and Stellenbosch. The bus returns from Cape Town on Monday, Wednesday and Friday.

Intercape also has two daily Garden Route services linking Cape Town and Port Elizabeth (R195). They do not go via Oudtshoorn.

Greyhound's daily Durban–Cape Town service stops in Port Elizabeth; it's R190 to Cape Town.

EASTERN CAPE

The Baz Bus runs daily from Cape Town to Port Elizabeth (R470).

To Johannesburg Greyhound has nightly buses from Port Elizabeth to Jo'burg (R295, 16 hours) via East London. Translux has Tuesday, Wednesday, Thursday, Friday and Sunday services from Port Elizabeth to Jo'burg via Bloemfontein and Graaff-Reinet (R295, 11 hours). There is also Monday and Saturday services via Cradock (R260, 14½ hours). During the busy season, Intercape has daily services from Port Elizabeth to Jo'burg direct (R260), and via Cradock (R250).

To Durban & East London Translux runs to Durban daily (R255) via Grahamstown (R80), East London (R100), Umtata (R175) and Port Shepstone (R250). Greyhound runs to Durban daily (R255). Intercape runs between Port Elizabeth and East London daily (R105).

The Baz Bus runs Monday, Tuesday, Wednesday, Friday and Saturday from Port Elizabeth to Durban, and returns on Monday, Tuesday, Thursday, Friday and Sunday; it's R380 hop-on, hop-off, or R240 direct.

Train The *Algoa* runs to Jo'burg via Bloemfontein; fares are R215/315 in 2nd/1st class.

The *Southern Cross* runs between Port Elizabeth and Cape Town; fares are R215/305 in 2nd/1st class.

For fare and schedule inquiries, contact **Spoornet** (☎ 507 3176).

Car All the big car-rental operators have offices in Port Elizabeth or at the airport, including **Avis** (☎ 581 1306), **Budget** (☎ 581 4242) and **Imperial** (☎ 581 1268). Also try **Economic Car Hire** (☎ 581 5826, 104 Heugh Rd, Walmer).

Minibus Taxi Norwich (☎ 585 7253) does long-distance runs, including a daily service to Cape Town (R140, nine hours). Taxis depart from under the freeway near the bell tower; there's an office in a small shed.

J-Bay Sunshine Express (☎ 581 3790) taxis run between Jeffrey's Bay, Port Elizabeth and other coastal areas.

Most taxis leave from the large townships surrounding Port Elizabeth and can be difficult to find. The taxi rank on Strand St, a few blocks north of the bell tower services the local area.

Getting Around

There's no public transport to the airport. A taxi costs R20 to R30. Taxis and hire cars are available at the airport. For taxis call **Super Cab** (☎ 457 5590) or **Hurter's Radio Cabs** (☎ 585 5500).

For information about bus services, contact **Algoa Bus Company** (☎ 404 1200), which runs scheduled central city services. To get to the Humewood beachfront from the city catch the bus marked 'UPE', and to get to Greenacres shopping centre catch the 'Greenacres' bus.

ADDO ELEPHANT NATIONAL PARK
☎ 042 • postcode 6105

This national park (☎ 223 0556; adult/child R12/6; open 7am-7pm daily) is 72km north of Port Elizabeth, near the Zuurberg Range in the Sundays River Valley. The park protects the remnants of the huge elephant herds that once roamed the Eastern Cape.

Unfortunately, when farmers started to develop the area at the beginning of the 20th century, they found themselves in conflict with the elephants. A man named Major Pretorius was commissioned to deal with the 'menace', and until he was stopped by a public outcry, he seemed likely to succeed. It was thanks to two local landowners who allowed the elephants to stay on their land that any survived. When Addo was proclaimed a national park in 1931, there were only 11 elephants left.

The South African government is working on plans to turn Addo into a 'superpark' covering approximately 340 sq km. The Greater Addo Park will stretch from Donaldson Dam along the Zuurberg Range to the coast, engulfing the Zuurberg National Park and the coastal Woody Cape Reserve, and stretching dozens of kilometres into the sea. When complete the park will be big enough to support an elephant population of 2500.

Today, there are more than 326 elephants in the park and you'd be unlucky not to see some.

Information

The park's dirt roads can become impassable in the wet, so the park is closed if there has been heavy rain – if in doubt call ahead. A well-stocked shop is open 8am to 7pm daily.

It's best to arrive at the park by mid-morning and to stake out one of the waterholes where the elephants tend to gather during the heat of the day. There are about 45km of roads, so it pays to take advice from a ranger on where to go.

Places to Stay & Eat

Camp site (bookings ☎ 012-343 1991, fax 343 0905, ⓔ reservations@parks-sa.co.za, ⓦ www.parks-sa.co.za) Camping R36 for 2 people plus R11 for additional person, 4-bed forest hut R154 for 2 people, 6-bed cottages R550 including breakfast, 2-bed bungalows R220, 5-bed chalets R300 for 2 people, rondavels (no kitchen) R220 for 2 people plus R66/33 per extra adult/child. The camping area is small but pleasant; there is a communal kitchen and bedding is supplied in all huts.

Meals are also available at the park's *restaurant* which is presided over by the stuffed head of the legendary bull, Hapoor.

Schotia (☎ 235 1436, fax 235 1368, ⓔ schotia@intekom.co.za) DB&B R400 per person. Schotia is a private game reserve near Addo and some 60km from Port Elizabeth. Accommodation is available in the park in either the six-bed Orlando Lodge or a two-bed cottage. The price includes a wildlife drive.

Getting There & Away

It's an interesting drive from Port Elizabeth to Addo, although you'll pass some very depressing townships and industrial developments in the immediate vicinity of Port Elizabeth. The park is signposted from the N2. Alternatively, you can travel via Uitenhage on the R75; there are attractive citrus farms along the banks of the Sundays River from Kirkwood to Uitenhage.

ZUURBERG NATIONAL PARK
☎ 042

This national park (☎ 233 0581), which covers both Zuurberg Mountain and the Sundays River Valley, was created in 1994. The entrance is 34km from Addo village at the top of Zuurberg Pass on the R335.

The park has become a popular destination for keen walkers, equestrians and 4WD drivers. The four-hour Doringnek and one-hour Cycad **hiking trails** are open during the day (R12/6 for adults/children). **Horse riding** is R70/90/120 for one/three/five hours; one- or two-night trails are also possible. Rides can be booked through the Zuurberg Mountain Inn & Backpackers. A series of **4WD trails** leads to two accommodation places, *Kabouga Guest House* and *Mvubu Camp*.

Zuurberg Mountain Inn & Backpackers (☎ 233 0583, fax 233 0070, ⓔ zuurberg@ ilink.co.za) Dorm beds R60, doubles B&B R220-380. This place is outside the park on the R335, an unsealed road that runs from Addo to Somerset East. The inn, built in 1861, is an elegant old gem. Drinking sundowners on the veranda is unforgettable. The backpackers is attached to the inn and bedding is provided. Mountain bikes are also available for rent.

SHAMWARI GAME RESERVE
☎ 042

This private reserve (☎ 203 1111, fax 235 1224, ⓔ shamwaribooking@global.co.za, ⓦ www.shamwari.com), 30km east of Addo Elephant National Park, is dedicated to restocking large tracts of land with animals that were once common in the region. The Big Five animals (black rhino, Cape buffalo, elephant, leopard and lion) are present but the lions are essentially caged in an enclosure.

There are a number of accommodation options on the reserve, all with similar prices and the prices are comparable. Expect to pay R2025/2700 for singles/doubles DB&B in low season or R3750/5000 in high season. Try *Eagles Cragg Lodge*, a refurbished 1820s settlers lodge, or *Long Lee Manor*, a fully restored Edwardian mansion.

KENTON-ON-SEA & BUSHMAN'S RIVER MOUTH
☎ 046 • postcode 6191

Kenton-on-Sea, near Bushman's River Mouth (Boesmanriviermond), is an expensive resort on a beautiful bit of coast for those after a quiet holiday in unspoilt surroundings.

If you are driving from Port Elizabeth, turn off the N2 to the R72 as soon as you can. There are attractive rolling hills and a 'dunefield' (also known as a dune sea) around Alexandria, and scenic forest that runs for 10km along the coast.

The **Kenton/Bushman's Publicity Association** (☎ 648 2418, fax 648 2118, e mc nulty@xsinet.co.za) provides information on activities and accommodation. There is a 4km hiking trail from the river mouth to Kwaaihoek, where Bartholomeu Dias erected a cross in 1488.

Bushman's Caravan Park (☎ 648 1227, fax 648 2113) Camping R50/100 low/high season plus R10 per person. This caravan park is an attractive sheltered place where foreigners are warmly welcomed.

There is a daily minibus taxi service from Port Alfred (R10).

PORT ALFRED
☎ 046 • postcode 6170

Port Alfred is a pleasant seaside town that is being developed into an upmarket holiday resort. Some people would argue that it has already been spoilt but many visitors will find it a bustling, enjoyable place to stay for a night or longer.

Often called 'The Kowie', after the river around which the town developed, Port Alfred is in fact the town's third name. Originally known as Port Kowie, the town was renamed Port Frances in 1825 after the wife of the commandant of the frontier. Then, in 1860, the town was renamed Port Alfred, in honour of Queen Victoria's second son, who was scheduled to visit the town. His trip was cancelled at the last moment – the offer of an elephant hunt proved far more enticing.

Information
Tourism Port Alfred (☎ 624 1235, e pa tourism@intekom.co.za; open 8.30am-5pm

Mon-Fri, 8.30am-1pm Sat), near the municipal offices on the western bank of the Kowie River, has brochures detailing accommodation, walks and canoe trails.

Homenet (☎ 624 5222, e homenetpa@ imaginet.co.za, 65 Campbell St) has Internet access for R7 for 15 minutes.

Activities
Three Sisters Horse Trails (☎ 675 1269, e janwebb@telkomsa.net; 1-hour trails/ 90-minute trails R50/70, 1-day trails for experienced riders R450) offers daily horse rides on the beach and through bushland.

For **surfers**, there are good right- and left-hand breaks at the river mouth; for golfers, there's the beautiful **golf course**, one of the four 'Royals' in South Africa. There's also a pleasant 8km **hiking trail** through the Kowie Nature Reserve. For the fit there are **mountain-bike trails** (☎ 624 1469) and **dune skiing** on inexpensive sand boards (a piece of plywood with rope) available from D&A Timbers on Main St for R20.

The two-day **Kowie Canoe Trail** (☎ 624 2230; R80 per person) is a fairly easy 21km canoe trip upriver from Port Alfred, with an overnight stay in a hut at Horseshoe Bend Nature Reserve.

Both introductory and advanced diving courses are offered by **Keryn's Dive School** (☎ 624 4432, e keryn@compushop.co.za; advanced diver courses R650, resort course R250, introductory scuba R80). Diving is between May and August as the water temperature in winter (18° to 24°C) is actually higher than in summer (12° to 18°C). Visibility is not outstanding but there are plenty of big fish, sponges and soft corals. Locals claim the reef here is South Africa's most colourful.

Places to Stay
Willows Caravan Park (☎/fax 624 5201, Off the R72) Camping R35/70 low/high season plus R15/20 per person. Next to the river, the Willows has powered camp sites.

Medolino Caravan Park (☎ 624 1651, fax 624 2514, w www.caravanparks.co.za/ medolino, 23 Stewart Rd) Camping R35/75 low/high season plus R30 per person, 2-bed

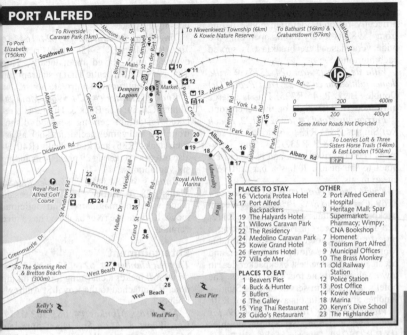

PORT ALFRED

To Port Elizabeth (150km)

To Riverside Caravan Park (1km)

To Nkwenkwezi Township (6km) & Kowie Nature Reserve

To Bathurst (16km) & Grahamstown (57km)

Southwell Rd

Mentone Rd
Masonic St
Campbell St
Biscay Rd
Main St
Van der Riet St
Alfred Rd
Bathurst St

Atherstone Rd
George St
Dempers Lagoon
Kowie River
Market
Pascoe Cres
Alfred Rd
Ferndale Rd
York La
York St
Park Ave

Dickinson Rd
Wesley Hill
Beach Rd
Albany Rd
Park Rd
Halstead St

Royal Port Alfred Golf Course
Princes Ave
St Andrews Rd
Muller Dr
Grand St
Royal Alfred Marina
Admiralty Rd
Sports Rd
Way
Albany Rd

R72

To Loeries Loft & Three Sisters Horse Trails (14km) & East London (150km)

Some Minor Roads Not Depicted

0   200   400m
0   200   400yd

Greenmantle Dr

To The Spinning Reel & Bretton Beach (300m)

West Beach Dr

West Beach

Kelly's Beach

West Pier

East Pier

PLACES TO STAY	OTHER
16 Victoria Protea Hotel	2 Port Alfred General Hospital
17 Port Alfred Backpackers	3 Heritage Mall; Spar Supermarket; Pharmacy; Wimpy; CNA Bookshop
19 The Halyards Hotel	
21 Willows Caravan Park	
22 The Residency	7 Homenet
24 Medolino Caravan Park	8 Tourism Port Alfred
25 Kowie Grand Hotel	9 Municipal Offices
26 Ferrymans Hotel	10 The Brass Monkey
27 Villa de Mer	11 Old Railway Station
	12 Police Station
PLACES TO EAT	13 Post Office
1 Beavers Pies	14 Kowie Museum
4 Buck & Hunter	18 Marina
5 Butlers	20 Keryn's Dive School
6 The Galley	23 The Highlander
15 Ying Thai Restaurant	
28 Guido's Restaurant	

chalet R245/345, 4-bed chalet R325/425. This park, in town off Princes Ave, is near both Kowie River and Kelly's Beach.

Riverside Caravan Park (☎ 624 2230, fax 624 2702, Mentone Rd) Chalets from R200 for 2 people. Riverside is also on the western side of the river but it's some way north of the town centre and more than an easy walk from the beach. It's a pleasant spot, although it gets crowded in high season.

Loeries Loft (☎ 675 1269, e janwebb@ elkomsa.net) R50 per person. Loeries Loft, 14km east of Port Alfred on the Three Sisters Horse Trails farm, is a very rustic tree house perched in the branches of a magnificent yellowwood tree beside the Riet River. This tranquil retreat is only for the adventurous; the loft is a 1½-hour hike from the main farmhouse (a map is supplied) and you must carry all your own supplies.

Port Alfred Backpackers (☎ 624 4011, fax 624 2397, e backpack@border.co.za, 29 Sports Rd) Dorm beds R40, doubles R60, 3-bed flat R60 per person. In recent years this hostel has improved considerably; excess bunk beds have been removed from rooms, creating more space, and it has been given an overall facelift, creating a cheery, relaxing atmosphere. Take the first left turn off the R72 as you approach the marina and follow the resort security fence; the hostel is on your left.

The tourist information centre lists Port Alfred's numerous B&Bs.

The Spinning Reel (☎ 624 4281, fax 624 4062, e spinreel@imaginet.co.za, Freshwater Rd) Doubles B&B R240, cottages R115/250 low/high season for 2 people, R205/430 for 6 people. On the beach, 4km from town, the rooms at this B&B have fantastic sea views. Its comfortable self-contained cottages are set amid the dunes, each with their own private beach access.

The Residency (☎/fax 624 5382, e the residency@cybertrade.co.za, 11 Vroom Rd) B&B R135/225 per person low/high season.

The Residency is a gracious B&B in a magnificently restored Victorian house dating from 1898. Its lovely rooms open out onto wide verandas where breakfast is served each morning.

Villa de Mer (☎/fax 624 2315, e *villa demer@intekom.co.za, 22 West Beach Dr*) Doubles B&B R145-R225. This is a large ultra-modern B&B right on the beachfront.

Ferrymans Hotel (☎/fax 624 1122, *Beach Rd*) Singles B&B R137/162 low/ high season, doubles B&B R232/273. The Ferrymans is on the river bank and is the closest hotel to the beach. It has a bar and very cheap meals.

Kowie Grand Hotel (☎ 624 1150, fax 624 3769, *Cnr Grand St & Princes Ave*) Bed in backpackers cottages R30, doubles R112/125 low/high season. Although looking a little tired, this hotel still has comfortable rooms with great views of the river and ocean and offers the best backpacker deal in town – cheap, private four-bed cottages. The hotel's dining room serves famous Sunday lunches and breakfast is available for R30.

Victoria Protea Hotel (☎ 624 4709, fax 624 1134, 7 *Albany St*) Singles/doubles B&B R225/380. This run-of-the-mill Protea hotel, on the east bank of the Kowie, offers special rates out of season.

The Halyards Hotel (☎ 624 2410, fax 624 2466, e *ramch@intekom.co.za, Royal Alfred Marina, Albany Rd*) Singles/doubles R255/390, B&B R295/470, DB&B R350/598. This comfy waterfront hotel with attractive Cape Cod–style architecture has large well-equipped rooms overlooking the harbour.

Places to Eat
Beavers Pies (☎ 624 2760, *Southwell Rd*) Beavers is an excellent 24-hour takeaway which serves cheap, mouthwatering pies from R4.

The Galley (☎ 624 9062, 33 *Van der Riet St*) Mains R15-40. The Galley is a small, friendly restaurant on the river bank which serves mostly seafood dishes.

Guido's Restaurant (☎ 624 5264 *West Beach Dr*) Mains R16-33. Guido's is a trendy pizza-and-pasta restaurant, on the beach. It's got ambience and is good for a late-night tipple.

Ying Thai Restaurant (☎ 624 1647, 6 *York Rd*) Mains R15-45. Open Fri & Sat evenings only. Raved about locally, Ying Thai is a cosy, authentic Thai restaurant run from the front room of a private house.

Buck & Hunter (☎ 624 5960, *Main St*) Mains R20-50. The Buck & Hunter is a relaxed restaurant serving seafood dishes from R35 and game specialities such as ostrich steaks (R36) and kudu steaks (R40). It also offers a staggering 29 pizzas – including six veg options.

Butler's (☎ 624 3464, 25 *Van der Riet St*) Mains R28-76. Butler's is a very pleasant place with an imaginative and delicious menu. It's near the river bank and has a nice veranda.

Entertainment
The Highlander (☎ 624 1379, 19 *St Andrews Rd*) makes a charming local drinking hole. It's attached to the Royal St Andrews Lodge.

The Brass Monkey (☎ 083-502 5539, *Cnr Wharf & Main Sts*) Open 5pm-late Mon-Fri, 5pm-3am Wed, Sat & Sun. The Brass Monkey is the best late-night venue in town with a disco, bar and a pool table.

Getting There & Away
The Baz Bus stops at Port Alfred on its run from Port Elizabeth to Durban (R470) on Monday, Tuesday, Wednesday, Friday and Saturday.

The minibus taxi rank is on Biscay Rd outside the Heritage Mall. There are daily services to Port Elizabeth (R40), Grahamstown (R20) and East London (R40). Local daily services include Bathurst (R7) and Kenton-on-Sea (R10).

GRAHAMSTOWN
☎ 046 • postcode 6140
Grahamstown is the capital of Settler Country (see the boxed text 'There Will Always Be an England...'). It still feels like a strange English transplant, and this is emphasised by the lack of neon signs and billboards. The town has some fine churches

and 19th-century buildings. There are 40 churches that each manage to draw a healthy congregation.

Information

Tourism Grahamstown (☎ 622 3241, fax 622 3266, e info@grahamstown.co.za, w www.grahamstown.co.za, 63 High St; open 8.30am-5pm Mon-Fri, 8.30am-noon Sat) is efficient and friendly. It has a useful magazine, *What's On*, and brochure, *Where to Stay in and Around Grahamstown* (R6). Another good guide available here is *Grahamstown: The Untold Story* (R15). Tourism Grahamstown is in a small building next to the Standard Bank on Church Square. It is an agent for Translux buses.

GBS Travel (☎ 622 2235, e marianl.gbs travel@galileosa.co.za, Upper Grove Mall, Cnr African & Allen Sts) handles bookings for all local travel; it is also the agent for most car rental companies and cashes travellers cheques (no commission charged). **Nexus Computers** (☎ 636 1141, 127 High

St) acts as an Internet cafe; access costs R10 for 20 minutes.

Museums

The **Albany Museum** (☎ 622 2312) has four components. The most interesting is the wonderfully eccentric **Observatory Museum** (Bathurst St; adult/child R8/5; open 9.30am-1pm & 2pm-5pm Mon-Fri), which is highly recommended. Originally a private house, it includes the only camera obscura in the southern hemisphere – a complicated series of lenses, a bit like a periscope. The camera obscura functions only in clear weather.

The **Natural Science Museum** (Somerset St; adult/child R8/5; open 9.30am-1pm & 2pm-5pm Mon-Fri, 9.30am-1pm Sat) depicts early human history and has some interesting artefacts including a Xhosa hut. The **History Museum** (Somerset St, adult/child R8/5; open 9.30am-1pm & 2pm-5pm Mon-Fri, 9.30am-1pm Sat) details the history and art of the peoples of the Eastern Cape, which includes the Xhosa and the

There Will Always Be an England...

In 1820, English settlers, duped by their government into believing they were going to a peaceful land of plenty, arrived at Algoa Bay. In reality, they were arriving in a heavily contested border region, where Boers on one side of the Great Fish River and Xhosa on the other battled interminably over the country known as the Zuurveld.

The Zuurveld was suitable for cattle grazing, and the Boers and the Xhosa constantly rustled each other's herds. Grahamstown was at the centre of the maelstrom. In 1819, in the Fifth Frontier War, 9000 Xhosa under the leader Makana attacked Grahamstown and very nearly defeated the garrison. The story goes that Makana would have succeeded had he not observed the Xhosa war code and given free passage to a woman who carried a hidden keg of gunpowder to the defenders.

The only government-sponsored migration in South Africa's history was intended to create a buffer of market gardeners between the cattle-farming Boers and Xhosa, but the Zuurveld was completely unsuitable for intensive cultivation. It was not long before the thousand immigrant families found farming untenable. The odds were stacked against them: Inexperience, hostile neighbours, labour shortages, floods, droughts and crop diseases all played a role. By 1823, nearly half the settlers had retreated to the townships to pursue trades and businesses they had followed in England.

As a result, Grahamstown developed into a trading and manufacturing centre. Most of the trade was between whites and blacks. Axes, knives and blankets were exchanged for ivory and skins. Travelling merchants, using Grahamstown as their base, ventured further and further afield. Tradespeople among the settlers produced metal implements, wagons and clothes.

Port Elizabeth and Port Alfred developed to service what had quickly become the second-largest city in the Cape Colony. The Sixth Frontier War (1834–35) sent even more refugees into Grahamstown, and the surrounding countryside was almost totally abandoned.

1820 settlers. The art exhibitions in its gallery change regularly.

Fort Selwyn (☎ *622 2397; adult/child R8/5; admission by appointment*), a military museum on Gunfire Hill, is the fourth component of the Albany Museum.

The first coelacanth ever caught is exhibited in the **JLB Smith Institute of Ichthyology** (☎ *636 1002, Prince Alfred St, Rhodes University; admission free; open 8.30am-1pm & 2-5pm Mon-Fri*) – until 1938 this primitive fish was thought to have been extinct. Also on campus is the interesting **International Library of African Music** (see the boxed text for more details).

Settlers' Cottages

Have a wander around Grahamstown and you'll see early settler history come to life. The city's tree-lined streets are home to a number of quaint, beautifully restored settlers' cottages dating from the 1820s. Near the intersection of Cross and Bartholomew Sts you'll find the greatest concentration and best examples of these charming cottages.

Dakawa Art & Craft Project

This project (☎ *622 9303, 6-11 Froude St open 8.30am-4.30pm Mon-Fri*) originated in the African National Congress (ANC) refugee camp in Dakawa, Tanzania, and moved to Grahamstown in 1991, when the ban on the ANC was lifted. Dakawa offers locals training in weaving, graphic art and textile printing and a sales outlet for their work.

Township Tours

There are plenty of opportunities to meet local Xhosa in the townships. The **Masithandane Association** (☎ *622 5944*) sells products made from discarded plastic bags and organises traditional evening meals with Xhosa families. **Umthathi** (☎ *622 505.. ask for Fiona, ☎ *622 9720 ask for Marthie*) also organises traditional Xhosa meals at its

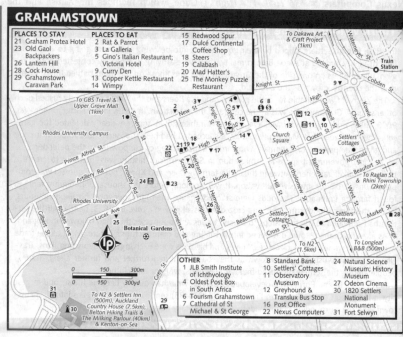

GRAHAMSTOWN

PLACES TO STAY	PLACES TO EAT	
21 Graham Protea Hotel	2 Rat & Parrot	15 Redwood Spur
23 Old Gaol	3 La Galleria	17 Dulcé Continental
Backpackers	5 Gino's Italian Restaurant;	Coffee Shop
26 Lantern Hill	Victoria Hotel	18 Steers
28 Cock House	9 Curry Den	19 Calabash
29 Grahamstown	13 Copper Kettle Restaurant	20 Mad Hatter's
Caravan Park	14 Wimpy	25 The Monkey Puzzle
		Restaurant

To Dakawa Art & Craft Project (1km)

Train Station

OTHER		
1 JLB Smith Institute	8 Standard Bank	24 Natural Science
of Ichthyology	10 Settlers' Cottages	Museum; History
4 Oldest Post Box	11 Observatory	Museum
in South Africa	Museum	27 Odeon Cinema
6 Tourism Grahamstown	12 Greyhound &	30 1820 Settlers
7 Cathedral of St	Translux Bus Stop	National
Michael & St George	16 Post Office	Monument
	22 Nexus Computers	31 Fort Selwyn

International Library of African Music

The International Library of African Music (ILAM; ☎ 603 8557, ⓦ archive.ilam.ru.ac.za, Prince Alfred St, Rhodes University; open 8.30am-12.45pm & 2pm-5pm Mon-Fri; admission by appointment only) is a treasure-trove of instruments and recordings; it alone is a good reason to visit Grahamstown. There is enough material here to create another 100 inspirational albums in the style of Paul Simon's Graceland.

The ILAM collection was initially the work of Hugh Tracey, who first started writing down the words of songs from Rhodesia in the 1920s. The collections were moved to Grahamstown in 1978, and Hugh's son Andrew has enthusiastically taken over his father's quest.

You can examine one of the 200 or so instruments, listen to field recordings and then try and emulate what you have heard. This could be on diverse instruments such as *nyanga* pipes from Mozambique, a kora (stringed instrument) from West Africa, wrist bells, a Ugandan *amadinda* (xylophone), a horizontal bow harp, antelope horns or a *kalimba* (thumb piano).

garden project (one of 65 set up since 1993) in Rhini, a township at the far eastern end of Raglan St (a continuation of Beaufort St).

Special Events

Grahamstown hosts the very successful **National Arts Festival** (based at the 1820 Settlers National Monument) and an associated Fringe Festival. The Fringe alone has more than 200 events. The festival runs for nine days, beginning in mid-June; accommodation can be booked out a year in advance. For more information, contact the **Grahamstown Foundation** (☎ 622 4341, fax 622 7082, ⓔ sbaf@foundation.co.za, ⓦ www.sbfest.co.za).

The **Sasol Scifest** (☎ 603 1106, fax 603 143, ⓔ scifest@foundation.intekom.com, ⓦ www.scifest.org.za), held in March/April, is a feast of interactive science for the layperson.

Places to Stay

Grahamstown Caravan Park (☎ 603 6072, fax 622 9488, Grey St) Camp sites R35, 4-bed rondavels R90, 5-bed chalets R180. The park is a pleasant spot, although it's a bit of a walk from the town centre. Bedding is not supplied for the rondavels.

Old Gaol Backpackers (☎ 636 1001, Somerset St) Dorm beds R35, doubles R50. Despite its ominous name, the Old Gaol backpackers, opposite the Albany Museum, is not a place for itinerant convicts to gather. Built in 1824, the former jail – now a national monument – offers good, cheap accommodation.

There are more than 40 B&Bs and 20 or so farmstays in the area; book with Tourism Grahamstown and expect to pay R100/200 and up for singles/doubles at both types of accommodation.

Lantern Hill (☎/fax 622 8782, ⓔ lanternhill@imaginet.co.za, ⓦ www.imaginet.co.za/lanternhill, 2 Thompson St) Singles/doubles B&B from R140/240. The charming Lantern Hill is on a quiet street close to Rhodes University. Hosts Ursula and John Case speak German.

Longleaf B&B (☎ 622 6163, ⓦ www.imaginet.co.za/longleaf, 9 Mount St) Singles/doubles B&B R100/200. This beautiful B&B is in a historic house with a large, pleasant garden.

Auckland Country House (☎ 622 2401, fax 622 5682, ⓔ info@aucklands.co.za, ⓦ www.aucklands.co.za) Singles/doubles B&B from R300/500. Auckland Country House, 8km west of Grahamstown on the N2, is an upmarket B&B in a renovated 1800s homestead set on 272 hectares of indigenous bushland.

Graham Protea Hotel (☎ 622 2324, fax 622 2424, ⓔ grahotel@intekom.co.za, 123 High St) Singles/doubles B&B R299/359. This hotel is a characterless building but it is comfortable and well located.

Cock House (☎ *636 1287*, **e** *cockhouse@ imaginet.co.za*, **w** *www.imaginet.co.za/cock house, 10 Market St*) Singles/doubles B&B from R270/400. The Cock House, an 1820s national monument, is by far the best place to stay in town if you can afford it. And you'll be in good company, claim hosts Belinda and Peter Tudge, who add that former president Nelson Mandela always stays at their place when he is in town. The impeccable guest rooms merit that special-occasion visit, and the meals are exceptional.

There are also some accommodation options out of town.

Belton Hiking Trails & The Milking Parlour (☎/*fax 622 8395*) Farmhouse bed R40, cottage bed from R100. At Belton Hiking Trails, 40km from Grahamstown on the road between Salem and Kenton-on-Sea, accommodation is in a converted old farmhouse that sleeps 35 people. Next door is the Milking Parlour, a fully equipped cottage, that accommodates up to six guests. The main attractions are the walking trails (from 2.5km to 17km) in the Bushman's River Valley.

Settlers Inn (☎ *622 7313*, fax 622 4951, **e** *settlersinn@intekom.co.za*, **w** *www .settlersinn.co.za*) Singles/doubles B&B R250/360. Settlers Inn offers B&B accommodation in private garden chalets. It has a pub and restaurant and there are scenic nature trails right on its doorstep. To get there, follow the signposts from the N2 towards Port Elizabeth.

Places to Eat

There are plenty of cafes and takeaway places on High St, including *Steers* and *Wimpy*.

Curry Den (☎ *636 1261, 3 High St*) With meals between R6-15, this is the best-value takeaway in town, with generous helpings of mutton and beef curries from R9.

Mad Hatter's (*118 High St*) Mains R19-30. Mad Hatter's, as the name suggests, serves mostly teas, coffees, scones and muffins from its 'Tea Party Menu' as well as light meals of sandwiches and salads.

Dulcé Continental Coffee Shop (*112 High St*) Breakfast R15-30, meals R20-25.

Dulcé is a busy modern coffee shop serving big breakfasts and good strong coffee.

Redwood Spur (☎ *622 2629, 97 High St*) Mains R30-35. This chain restaurant delivers no surprises with its standard Tex-Mex menu.

Copper Kettle Restaurant (☎ *622 4358 7 Bathurst St*) Breakfast R19-32, mains R15-42. While not boasting an overly stimulating menu, the Copper Kettle serves good, well-portioned meals.

The Monkey Puzzle Restaurant (☎ *62. 5318, Botanical Gardens*) Mains R20-50. The Monkey Puzzle, in the grounds of Rhodes University, is a good choice for old fashioned 'farmer's food'.

La Galleria (☎ *622 3455, 13 New St*) Mains R20-45. Bookings are essential at this smart, authentic Italian restaurant.

Calabash (☎ *622 2324, 123 High St*) Mains R22-70. Calabash offers a true African dining experience with a menu devoted to traditional South African fare such as delicious Xhosa hotpots. The blackboard out the front lists the daily specials.

Gino's Italian Restaurant (☎ *622 7208, New St, entrance via Hill St*) is in the Victoria Hotel and is popular for pizza, pasta, steak and burgers. The hotel's pub adjoining the restaurant is extremely popular with Rhodes students. As they say, 'All Rhodes lead to the Vic'.

Rat & Parrot (☎ *622 5002, 59 New St*) is a pseudo-British pub and another popular student haunt, serving traditional pub fare.

Getting There & Away

Bus The Bee Bus (☎ *082-651 6646*) runs to Port Elizabeth, Port Alfred and Kenton-on-Sea from Sunday to Friday, and **Mini Lux** (☎ *043-741 3107*) runs from Grahamstown to East London and Port Elizabeth from Sunday to Friday.

Translux (☎ *622 3241*) buses stop at the corner of Bathurst and High Sts on the daily run between Port Elizabeth (R80) and Durban (R230) via East London and Umtata.

Greyhound buses also stop at the corner of Bathurst and High Sts on their run from Durban to Port Elizabeth; the fare to Port Elizabeth is R70 and to Durban R205.

Minibus Taxi You'll find taxis on Raglan St but most leave from Rhini township. Destinations include Fort Beaufort (R19), King William's Town (R29), Port Elizabeth (R29) and East London (R31).

BATHURST
☎ 046 • postcode 6166

On the road between Port Alfred and Grahamstown, this scattered village with its trees, lanes and hedges is a pleasant place for a break. The town was founded in 1820 and South Africa's oldest Anglican church was built here. Information and maps are available from the Bathurst Arms opposite the Pig & Whistle Hotel.

Near the turn-off to Bathurst is **Summerhill Farm** (☎ 625 0833, fax 625 0621, Off the R67; tours adult/child R20/15; open 8am-4pm Mon-Fri), which has the dubious honour of being home to the world's Biggest Pineapple – a rip-off of the Big Pineapple on the Sunshine Coast in Queensland, Australia. Standing 16.7m high, it is a mere 70cm taller than the original. There's also a reconstructed Xhosa village where you can buy handicrafts; meals are available from its restaurant.

Round Hill Nature Reserve (☎ 625 0631) is east of Bathurst at Trappes Valley. The small endangered oribi, a springbok-like antelope, breeds here.

Pig & Whistle Hotel (☎ 625 0673, Kowie Rd) Doubles B&B R250/280 low/high season. The Pig & Whistle could be in England, which is not at all surprising considering it was built in 1831 and is in the centre of Settler Country. It's a popular stopping point on the Port Alfred–Grahamstown road for good-value pub lunches. With its good selection of wines and local brews, every hour is happy hour. Bookings are essential for Sunday lunch.

The Karoo

The Karoo, a vast semidesert on the great South African plateau, is demarcated in the south and west by the coastal mountain ranges and to the east and north by the mighty Orange River. Though it's a dry, hot and inhospitable region, the sense of space is intriguing. The Karoo's south-eastern extension is in Eastern Cape and includes quintessential Karoo towns, Mountain Zebra National Park and the weird Owl House in Nieu Bethesda.

See also the Karoo section in the Western Cape chapter for more information about other parts of the Karoo.

MIDDELBURG
☎ 049 • postcode 5900

Middelburg is a nondescript town nestled on a plain just north of the Sneeuberg Range. Nearby is the spectacular Lootsberg Pass. The **Middelburg-Karoo Publicity Association** (☎/fax 842 2188, 8 Meintjies St; open 8am-4.30pm Mon-Fri) is a helpful source of information. The **Cultural History Museum** (☎ 842 1104, extension 204, Cnr Bennie & Du Plessis Sts; admission R2; open 8am-1pm, 2pm-4.30pm Mon-Fri) has memorabilia of the well-known playwright Athol Fugard, who once lived in the town.

Karoo Country Inn (☎ 842 1126, fax 842 1681, e kci@yebo.co.za, Cnr Meintjies & Loop Sts) Doubles B&B from R190. The Karoo Country Inn, overlooking the pleasant town square, has the best value accommodation in town.

Intercape buses stop in Middelburg en route to Johannesburg/Pretoria (R250) via Graaff-Reinet (R100). Translux buses also stop here.

CRADOCK
☎ 048 • postcode 5880

Cradock, on the banks of the Great Fish River, is 240km north of Port Elizabeth and was established as a military outpost in 1813. It is now a busy agricultural and commercial centre for the rich farming district along the river banks.

Cradock has retained some interesting old buildings and there is a distinct Karoo atmosphere, created largely by some shady trees, the river and a superb church built in 1867 and modelled on St Martin-in-the-Fields, London.

Information is available from the **Cradock Publicity Association** (☎ 881 2383, fax 881

EASTERN CAPE

1421, W *www.cradock.co.za*) in the town hall building. Internet access (R10 per half-hour) is available at **Eceisis Computer Store** (☎/fax 881 5103, e *lcoetzer@worldonline .co.za, Spar shopping centre)*, opposite the information office.

Numerous vendors on the roads leading in and out of the town sell wire-and-bottlecap model windmills, the windmill being the symbol of the Karoo. These working models can be beautifully crafted. You should be able to buy a good one for between R10 and R30.

Things to See

Olive Schreiner House (☎ 881 5251, 9 *Cross St; admission by donation; open 8am-12.45pm & 2pm-4.30pm Mon-Fri)* is a good example of a typical Karoo house. The novelist Olive Schreiner lived here as a girl, and Cradock is the centre of the area where she taught, wrote and spent part of her married life. Schreiner is best remembered for her provocative novel *Story of an African Farm* (written under the pseudonym Ralph Iron), which advocated views considered radical even by today's standards. Her **grave** is on the summit of Buffelskop, 24km

south of Cradock on the Mortimer road (the R390).

The **Great Fish River Museum** (☎ 88 4509, Hoog St; admission by donation open 8am-1pm & 2pm-4pm Mon-Fri, 8am-noon Sat) was originally the parsonage of the Dutch Reformed Church. The house was built in 1825 and the displays depict pioneer life in the 19th century.

Places to Stay

Cradock Spa (☎ 881 2709, fax 881 1421 Marlow Rd/N10) Camping R30/40 low high season plus R10/11 per person, 2-bed chalets R124/152, 4-bed chalets R173/207 Cradock Spa, 4km from town, has a natural sulphur spring-water pool but otherwise it's a sterile place surrounded by a huge barbed wire fence. Its brick chalets are virtual ovens in summer; thankfully the pools are close at hand. Admission to the pools and picnic area for nonguests is R10.

Heritage House B&B (☎/fax 881 3210 45 Bree St) B&B R120 per person. The homely Heritage House offers comfortable rooms and good old-fashioned country hospitality. Its gardens are home to a growing brood of quacking ducks.

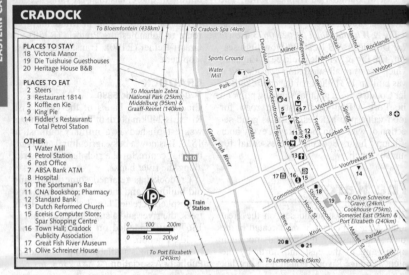

CRADOCK

PLACES TO STAY
18 Victoria Manor
19 Die Tuishuise Guesthouses
20 Heritage House B&B

PLACES TO EAT
2 Steers
3 Restaurant 1814
5 Koffie en Kie
9 King Pie
14 Fiddler's Restaurant;
    Total Petrol Station

OTHER
1 Water Mill
4 Petrol Station
6 Post Office
7 ABSA Bank ATM
8 Hospital
10 The Sportsman's Bar
11 CNA Bookshop; Pharmacy
12 Standard Bank
13 Dutch Reformed Church
15 Eceisis Computer Store;
    Spar Shopping Centre
16 Town Hall; Cradock
    Publicity Association
17 Great Fish River Museum
21 Olive Schreiner House

To Bloemfontein (438km)
To Cradock Spa (4km)
Sports Ground
Water Mill
Park
To Mountain Zebra National Park (25km), Middelburg (95km) & Graaff-Reinet (140km)
Great Fish River
N10
Train Station
To Port Elizabeth (240km)
To Lemoenhoek (5km)
Deurslaan
Milner
Kallegaweg
Hospital
Albert
Naested
Rocklands
Webber
Stockenstroom
Skeeren
Dundas
Victoria
Frere
Spring
Durban St.
Addley St.
Voortrekker St.
Commissioner
Stockenstroom
Hoog St.
Bree St.
Krus
Market St.
Parade
Regent
To Olive Schreiner Grave (24km), Cookhouse (75km), Somerset East (95km) & Port Elizabeth (240km)
0 100 200m
0 100 200yd

Victoria Manor (☎ 881 1650, Cnr Market & Voortrekker Sts) Rooms R130 per person. The Victoria Manor is a pleasant, big, old country pub. Breakfast is available for R30.

Die Tuishuise Guesthouses (☎ 881 1322, fax 881 5388, e tuishuise@east cape.net, 36 Market St) B&B R185 per person. It is almost worth making a special trip to Cradock to spend a night here. This is a unique concept in tourist accommodation – in one of Cradock's old streets, 18 cottages have been beautifully restored and are rented nightly. You have your own quaint and enchanting cottage, with a lounge, fireplace, kitchen and garden. Staying in one of these cottages is like stepping back in time.

Places to Eat & Drink

You can get your fast-food fix at *Steers* on Stockenstroom St or *King Pie* in Adderley St.

Koffie en Kie (☎ 881 3779) Breakfast R25, light meals R15-20. Koffie en Kie serves delicious breakfasts and is the only place that has half-decent coffee in town.

Restaurant 1814 (☎ 881 5390, 66 Stockenstroom St) Breakfast R14-16, mains R15-30. Restaurant 1814 is good for breakfasts and lunches, with a menu dedicated to burgers, pies and curries.

Fiddler's Restaurant (☎ 881 1497, Voortrekker St) Breakfast R15-23, mains R24-40. Adjoining the Total petrol station – not an overly salubrious location – Fiddler's serves excellent pizzas, steak and seafood dishes.

The Sportsman's Bar (☎ 881 2431, Cnr Stockenstroom & Durban Sts) is a great place to drink up the local atmosphere. It's near the CNA bookshop.

Getting There & Away

Translux stops here on the run between Cape Town (R230) and East London (R150) via Beaufort West, Graaff-Reinet (R95) and King William's Town (R135). Intercape has daily services from Port Elizabeth to Jo'burg via Cradock in high season.

The *Algoa* train between Port Elizabeth and Jo'burg stops here.

Most minibus taxis leave from the nearby township; ask at the petrol stations in town.

MOUNTAIN ZEBRA NATIONAL PARK

This national park *(adult/child R10/5; open 7am-7pm 1 Oct-30 Apr, 7.30am-6pm daily 1 May-30 Sept)*, 26km west of Cradock, is on the northern slopes of the Bankberg Range (2000m) and has superb views over the Karoo. The small park (7000 hectares) protects one of the rarest animals in the world: the mountain zebra *(Equus zebra)*.

The mountain zebra is distinguished from other zebra species by its small stature, reddish-brown nose, and dewlap (a loose fold of skin hanging beneath the throat). It has no shadow stripes, a white stomach and a distinctive gridiron pattern on the rump, with stripes continuing down the legs.

Mountain zebras were probably never numerous but by the 1960s there were fewer than 50 of them. The minimum number necessary to guarantee their survival is thought to be 500. There are now more than 200 zebras in this national park and another 200 or more resettled in other parks and reserves around the Cape provinces.

The park has superb mountain scenery and unique vegetation. Thick patches of sweet thorn and wild olive are interspersed with grasslands and succulents. The park also supports many antelope species. The largest predator is the caracal, and there are several species of small cats, genets, bat-eared foxes and black-backed jackals. Some 200 bird species have been recorded.

Information

The entrance gate is well signposted off the R61. It's quite feasible to get a taste of the park in a half-day excursion from Cradock. There's a shop and restaurant in the main camp. Visitors must drive themselves through the reserve.

Places to Stay & Eat

Park accommodation (bookings ☎ 012-343 1991, fax 012-343 0905, e reservations@ parks-sa.co.za, w www.parks-sa.co.za) Camping R40 a double plus R11 for each additional person, 4-bed cottages R270 for 1-2 people plus R66/33 per extra adult/child, 6-bed farmhouse R475 for up to 4

EASTERN CAPE

people plus R66/33 per extra adult/child. The most interesting place to stay in the park is at Doornhoek, a restored historic farmhouse, built in 1836 and hidden in a secluded valley. Alternatively, there are comfortable, fully equipped four-bed cottages and a pleasant camping area. There is a 20% discount available from early June to the end of September, excluding school holidays.

SOMERSET EAST
☎ 042 • postcode 5850

This attractive old town at the foot of the Bosberg Range (1600m) is sometimes referred to as the 'oasis of the Karoo', since it receives a soaking 600mm of rainfall annually (thanks to the mountains). After the dry country to the north and south, the rich forest on the mountain slopes is a surprise. The area was first settled in the 1770s and a village was established in 1835.

The **museum** and **information bureau** (☎ 243 1448, Beaufort St; open 8am-1pm & 2pm-5pm Mon-Fri) are in a classic Georgian building at the top end of Beaufort St. Both stock useful leaflets, including A Stroll Through Old Somerset East.

Caravan park (☎ 243 1376, Bosberg Nature Reserve) Camp sites R30. The park is 3km from town past the golf course, tucked into a valley surrounded by the Bosberg Nature Reserve.

Nearby is **Besterhoek Chalets** (☎ 243 1333) which offers handy accommodation for hikers.

BOSBERG NATURE RESERVE

This reserve covers 2000 hectares of diverse habitats: mountain fynbos on rocky parts of the plateau; thickly wooded ravines with stinkwood and yellowwood; a dense grassland on the highest parts; and Karoo shrubs and grasses on the lower areas.

Several walks are possible, including the circular 15km-long **Bosberg Hiking Trail** (R35 per person), which has a 10-bed rest hut with toilet facilities. Hikers must register, and those planning to stay overnight must book in advance. For inquiries and bookings, contact the information bureau in Somerset East (see that section for more

details). The entrance to the reserve is 33km from Somerset East, along Auret Dr

GRAAFF-REINET
☎ 049 • postcode 6280

Graaff-Reinet is the quintessential Karoo town – it is often referred to, justifiably, as the 'gem of the Karoo'. If you visit only one inland town in Eastern Cape, make it this one.

It's the fourth-oldest European town in South Africa, and it has a superb architectural heritage that, fortunately, has been recognised and restored. More than 220 buildings (mostly private dwellings) have been declared national monuments. These dwellings range from Cape Dutch houses with their distinctive gables, to classic flat-roofed Karoo cottages and ornate Victorian villas. The excellent Karoo Nature Reserve is within walking distance of town.

History

In 1786 a landdrost (an official whose duties combined those of local administrator, tax collector and magistrate) was despatched to establish order in the lawless Cape interior. When not fighting among themselves, the Boers were in constant conflict with the Khoisan in the Sneeuberg and the Xhosa to the east around the Great Fish River.

The official didn't have much success; in 1795 the citizens of Graaff-Reinet drove out the landdrost and established a short-lived independent republic. The British re-established limited control during their first occupation (1795–1803) but the expansionist Boers continued to cause trouble. On top of this, on two occasions, the Khoisan and Xhosa joined forces to fight the Europeans.

Between 1824 and 1840, the Boers' continuing dissatisfaction with Cape Town control led to the Great Trek, and Graaff-Reinet became an important stepping stone for Voortrekkers heading north. It continued to be an important commercial and trading centre, linking the Karoo with the south.

Orientation & Information

Graaff-Reinet is built in a cleft in the magnificent Sneeuberg Range on a bend of the

Sundays River. The centre of town is easy to get around on foot.

The helpful **Graaff-Reinet Publicity Association** (☎ 892 4248, [W] *www.graaffreinet .co.za, Church St, open 8am-1pm & 2pm-5pm Mon-Fri, 9am-noon Sat & Sun*) has an abundance of maps and information about the town and about farms that offer B&B. If you are interested in architecture, *Graaff-Reinet: National Monuments & Places of Interest* (R5) is a must. The association sells a combined pass (R10) that gives access to three of the town's four museums, but it is not valid on Sunday.

Iets Anders (see Places to Eat later in this section) has a small Internet cafe attached to its restaurant.

Karoo Connections (☎ 892 3978, fax 891 061, [e] *karooconnections@intekom.co.za*) operates tours to the Valley of Desolation at sunset (R75, sundowners on request – the preferred drop is gin and tonic), Nieu Bethesda (R150) and the Karoo Nature Re-serve (R75). For something a little different, go along on one of its Graaff-Reinet Club tours (R20). This one-time 'men's only' club, the second oldest in South Africa, of-fers a fascinating insight into days long gone. But be warned – its walls and halls are adorned with numerous hunting trophies including a giant pair of elephant feet that, unbelievably, someone saw fit to turn into wine coolers!

Museums

Reinet House (☎ 892 3801, *Murray St; adult/child R5/1; open 9am-12.30pm & 2pm-5pm Mon-Fri, 9am-noon Sat & Sun*), built between 1806 and 1812, is a beautiful example of Cape Dutch architecture. It is furnished with a collection of 18th- and 19th-century furniture. The cobblestoned rear courtyard and garden has one of the largest grapevines in the world.

The **Old Residency** (☎ 892 3801, *Parsonage St; adult/child R3/1; open 9am-12.30pm*

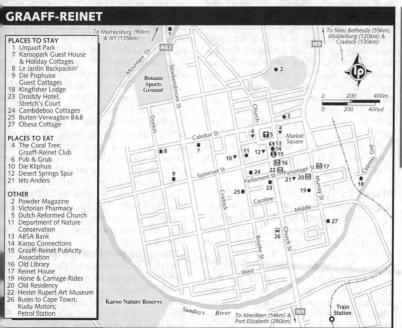

GRAAFF-REINET

PLACES TO STAY
1 Urquart Park
7 Karoopark Guest House & Holiday Cottages
8 Le Jardin Backpackin'
9 Die Pophuise Guest Cottages
18 Kingfisher Lodge
23 Drostdy Hotel; Stretch's Court
24 Cambdeboo Cottages
25 Buiten Verwagten B&B
27 Obesa Cottage

PLACES TO EAT
4 The Coral Tree; Graaff-Reinet Club
6 Pub & Grub
10 Die Kliphuis
12 Desert Springs Spur
21 Iets Anders

OTHER
2 Powder Magazine
3 Victorian Pharmacy
5 Dutch Reformed Church
11 Department of Nature Conservation
13 ABSA Bank
14 Karoo Connections
15 Graaff-Reinet Publicity Association
16 Old Library
17 Reinet House
19 Horse & Carriage Rides
20 Old Residency
22 Hester Rupert Art Museum
26 Buses to Cape Town; Kudu Motors; Petrol Station

To Murraysburg (90km) & N1 (135km)

To Nieu Bethesda (55km), Middelburg (120km) & Cradock (130km)

Botanic Sports Ground

Market Square

Caledon St

Somerset St

Parliament St

Parsonage St

Caroline

Middle

West

Karoo Nature Reserve

Sundays River To Aberdeen (54km) & Port Elizabeth (290km)

Train Station

EASTERN CAPE

& 2pm-5pm Mon-Fri, 9am-noon Sat) is another well-preserved 19th-century house, now displaying a large collection of firearms.

The **Old Library** (☎ 892 3801, Cnr Church & Somerset Sts; adult/child R4/1; open 9am-12.30pm & 2pm-5pm Mon-Fri, 9am-noon Sat & Sun) houses a collection of photos and clothing from the 19th century, a collection of fossils from the Karoo (including some nasty-looking skulls of 'mammal-like, flesh-eating reptiles' of 230 million years ago) and a photographic collection of more than 25 of the most significant bushman paintings in Southern Africa.

The **Hester Rupert Art Museum** (☎ 892 2121, Church St; open 10am-noon, 3pm-5pm & 10am-noon Sat & Sun) was originally a Dutch Reformed Mission church, consecrated in 1821. It now houses an exhibition of contemporary South African art.

Drostdy & Stretch's Court

The residence of a landdrost was known as a *drostdy* and included his office and courtroom as well as his family's living quarters. The Graaff-Reinet drostdy on Church St was built in 1806. It has been beautifully restored and is now the focus of a unique hotel complex (see Places to Stay, following). The reception and the hotel restaurant are in the drostdy, while guests stay in restored mid-19th-century cottages, originally built for freed slaves along Stretch's Court. Have a look at the old slave bell, which was restored and then, in an awful piece of irony, unveiled by former prime minister BJ Vorster, one of the arch criminals of apartheid.

Places to Stay

Urquart Park (☎/fax 892 2136, Stockenstroom St/R63) Camp sites R40/50 low/high season plus R2 per person, double rondavels from R60/80, double bungalows from R100/120, chalets from R130/150 for 2 people plus R10 for each extra person. Situated to the north of town near the Van Ryneveld Dam, Urquart isn't a particularly attractive caravan park and camping ground. There are, however, some very excellent chalets.

Le Jardin Backpackin' (☎ 892 3326 892 5890, 103 Caledon St) Beds R60 pe person. The homely Le Jardin Backpackin is Graaff-Reinet's best-value budget option offering clean, comfortable accommodation. Hosts Terrance and Nita Gush, both wells of information, are refreshingly and genuinely hospitable.

Karoopark Guest House & Holiday Cot tages (☎ 892 2557, fax 892 5730, e info@ karoopark.co.za, 81 Caledon St) Singles doubles from R130/250, cottages R210 double plus R15 for each extra person. Ka roopark has pleasant self-contained cottage as well as comfortable – if a little fussy rooms in its guesthouse. Breakfast is avail able for R30.

Cambdeboo Cottages (☎ 892 3180, fa 891 0919, e sunnykaroo@worldonlin .co.za, 16 Parliament St) Cottages R190 double plus R45 for each extra person. Th modest but charming Cambdeboo Cottage are restored Karoo cottages, featuring *rietda* (reed ceilings) and lovely yellowwood floors All are national monuments. Linen is sup plied and the cottages are fully equippec There's a coffee shop that serves breakfa and light meals, a pool and a braai area.

Drostdy Hotel (☎ 892 2161, fax 89 4582, e drostdy@intekom.co.za, w ww .come2.co.za/drostdy, 30 Church St) Single doubles from R300/390, luxury suite R640. The Drostdy Hotel is simply ou standing. The main part of the hotel is in beautifully restored drostdy. If you wer ever going to splurge, this would be th time. Booking ahead is recommendec Breakfast is available for R43.

Kingfisher Lodge (☎/fax 892 2657, 3 Cypress Grove) Singles R170-250, dou bles R200-400. The upmarket Kingfishe Lodge is in a historic home in a quiet se ting and has its own wine cellar. Breakfa is available for R20.

There are plenty of B&Bs and gues houses in Graaff-Reinet – the publicity as sociation can provide you with a list.

Die Pophuise Guest Cottages (☎/fax 89 0404, diepophuise@eastcape.net, 104 Son erset St) B&B from R150 per person. D Pophuise Guest Cottages is another grou of lovely restored Karoo cottages each with their own private garden or courtyard.

Buiten Verwagten B&B (☎ *892 4504, fax 892 5780,* e *hvj@eastcape.net, 58 Bourke St)* Singles/doubles B&B from R120/220. This is a delightful B&B with nicely furnished rooms.

Obesa Cottage (☎/*fax 892 3143,* e *cj bouwer@acc.co.za,* w *www.obesa.co.za, 49 Murray St)* Singles/doubles B&B R150/240. This peaceful B&B gained its name from the *Euphorbia obesa*, a rare and protected species of succulent found in the Karoo. In its garden centre you'll find a marvellous collection of cacti.

Places to Eat

Desert Springs Spur (☎ *892 3202, 22B Church St)* Mains R30-35. This lively chain restaurant has a good salad bar as well as great Spur steaks and Mexican dishes.

Die Kliphuis (☎ *892 2345, 46 Bourke St)* Breakfast R11-20, mains R18-45. Long known for its tasty breakfasts and lunches, Die Kliphuis is now open for dinner.

Pub & Grub (☎ *892 2464, Cnr Church & Muller Sts)* Mains R15-40. This place, opposite the Dutch Reformed Church, serves the usual pub fare; a filling serve of steak and chips costs R25.

Drostdy Hotel (☎ *892 2161, 30 Church St)* Buffet lunch R43, dinner R73. There are a couple of eating options at the Drostdy Hotel. Stoep Stories, a pleasant outdoor area under an old vine, serves light meals. The hotel's 18th-century dining room, which is lit by candelabra, has a superb atmosphere and is not to be missed. You can also order a la carte. An after-dinner drink in the pleasant bar, or in the garden on a hot night, is a delight.

The Coral Tree (☎ *892 5947, 3 Church St)* Mains R20-35. This new cafe-restaurant specialises in traditional Karoo meals and is highly recommended. Menu items include kudu steak (R35), ostrich burgers (R25) and a great veg platter (R30).

Iets Anders (☎ *892 5062, 3 Parsonage St)* Mains R8-28. Iets Anders is a small cafe-cum-restaurant serving delicious cakes, burgers and sandwiches as well as more substantial South African dishes such as *bobotie* (delicately flavoured mincemeat curry with a topping of beaten egg baked to a crust) served with rice and salad (R28).

Getting There & Away

Bus The publicity association office acts as the Translux agent. Translux stops here on the run from Cape Town (R220) to East London (R170), via Paarl (R200) and Cradock (R95). Buses to Cape Town depart from Kudu Motors on Church St.

Intercape's Plettenberg Bay–Jo'burg/Pretoria service passes through Graaff-Reinet daily (R265 to Jo'burg, R200 to Plettenberg Bay).

Minibus Taxi Taxis leave from Market Square. Major destinations are Port Elizabeth, Cape Town and Jo'burg. For more information call **J Kane** (☎ *892 4390*).

AROUND GRAAFF-REINET
Karoo Nature Reserve

This reserve, which virtually surrounds Graaff-Reinet, protects 16,000 hectares of mountainous veld typical of the Karoo. The flora is extraordinary, with the weird Karoo succulents well represented. There's also wildlife, interesting birdlife, spectacular rock formations and great views overlooking the town and the plains. It's a lot more interesting for visitors than some of the other more desiccated bits of the Karoo.

The reserve is subdivided into three main sections: the wildlife-viewing area to the north of the dam; the western section with the Valley of Desolation; and the eastern section with the overnight hiking trail.

In the **wildlife-viewing area** *(admission free; open 7am-dusk daily)* there are buffaloes, elands, kudus, hartebeests, wildebeests, springboks and smaller mammals. Visitors must stay in their vehicles.

The **Valley of Desolation** *(admission free; open 24 hours daily)* can be reached by car on a steep but sealed road. There are outstanding views over the town and the rugged valley. It's the sort of place that makes you wish you were an eagle. There's a 1.5km circuit walk.

EASTERN CAPE

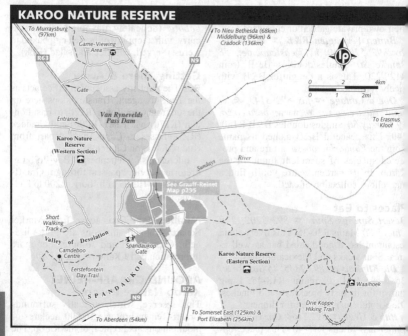

KAROO NATURE RESERVE

The **Eerstefontein Day Trail** is also in the western section and can be reached from Mountain Dr. There are three trail options: 5km, 11km and 14km long. The information office supplies a map. Wildebeests, kudus, springboks and smaller antelope species can be seen in this section. Free permits are available from a self-help permit box at the Spandaukop gate.

The **Drie Koppe Hiking Trail** (R15 per person plus R2 admission) is in the mountains of the reserve's eastern section. Plenty of wildlife, including mountain zebras, can be seen. There is a *waaihoek* (overnight hut) that can accommodate 10 people in bunks. The starting point is on Lootsfontein Rd. To get to the trail, you must get a key from the Department of Nature Conservation office in the Petrus de Klerk building, Bourke St, Graaff-Reinet. Bookings and inquiries should be directed to the Officer in Charge, Karoo Nature Reserve (☎ 892 3453), upstairs in the Provincial Adminis-

tration building on Bourke St in Graaff Reinet.

Farm Trails

Farmers of the Cambdeboo region have developed walks and activities on their beautiful properties. *Rheboksberg (☎ 89 8004)* Bed only/B&B R65/85 per person. The friendly Rheboksberg farm, 24km north-west of Graaff-Reinet, is highly recommended. Dinner is available for an extra R35.

Van Der Waltshoek (☎ 845 9007) B&B/DB&B R120/160 per person. Some 46km north-west of Graaff-Reinet, Van der Waltshoek is a historical farm that is typical of this type of accommodation.

Nieu Bethesda & Around
☎ 049 • postcode 6286

The tiny, isolated village of Nieu Bethesda is home to the extraordinary **Owl House** (☎ 841 1603; adult/child R9/6; open 9am

5pm Mon-Sun). It was the home, studio and life's work of artist Helen Martins (1898–1976). She used mainly concrete and glass for her creations – eerie sculptures of figures, camels and owls. Whether it's a monument to madness or a testament to the human spirit is difficult to say, although there is no shortage of art critics offering fashionable theories.

Whichever is the case, the idea of a lone woman creating such weird things in this tiny village in the middle of the Karoo is mind-boggling. It even serves to shake the standard view of apartheid-era South Africa as a drab and conformist society.

Even without the Owl House, Nieu Bethesda is worth a look to get an idea of life in rural hamlets. The pretty village has dirt roads, a shop or two, a pleasant tearoom and the Zen-inspired garden of **Rusty Metal Place**. It is advisable to stock up on supplies before you arrive if you plan on self-catering.

Nieu Bethesda is 55km from Graaff-Reinet. The drive here is very scenic with the **Compassberg Range** (2502m) dominating the region as you approach; there are several turn-offs from the N9 between Graaff-Reinet and Middelburg. Petrol is not available in Nieu Bethesda.

The **Accommodation Booking Agency** (☎ *841 1760)*, based at the Ibis Art Centre on the main road, arranges accommodation in guesthouses in and around Nieu Bethesda.

Owl House Backpackers (☎ *841 1642, fax 841 1657,* e *owlhouse@global.co.za, Martin St)* Camping R30, dorm beds R50, doubles R120-140. Owl House Backpackers is a tranquil eco-friendly place run by very trusting people. The day we visited there was not a soul in sight, but fortunately the door was open and a kindly sign advised us to 'make ourselves at home'. It organises all sorts of activities and hires bikes (half day/full day R50/30) – or so another sign informed us. It occasionally does an evening meal if there are enough guests.

Stokkiesdraai Guesthouse (☎/fax *841 1658, Murray St)* Singles/doubles R80/200. The Stokkiesdraai Guesthouse has ingeniously converted old horse stables into

modest but comfortable guest cottages. It also serves great budget Karoo breakfasts (R15) and dinners (R25).

Village Inn Coffee Shop (☎ *841 1635)* Breakfast R12-18, light snacks R8-14. This small coffee shop is OK for light lunches and a quick coffee.

Waenhuis Pub 'n Grub (☎ *841 1748)* Meals R15-30. The Waenhuis – literally 'Wagon House' – is a quiet pub with a limited menu including bobotie for R20.

Valley Guest House (☎/fax *841 1400)* Bed only R80 per person. Valley Guest House, 35km from Nieu Bethesda and a perfect base for the Compassberg ascent, is a comfortable four-bedroom farmhouse. It is fully equipped, although hot water is by means of a wood-fired 'donkey' or old-style geyser.

The stages on the **Compassberg hiking trail** are as follows: 16km from Klipkoppie Stop Cottage on the first day, with an ascent of Compassberg (strenuous) and an overnight stay in The Barn; 14km to the farmhouse at the Valley Guest House on the second day; and 8km back to Klipkoppie Stop Cottage on the third day.

The Amatola

The stretch of coast and hinterland known as Amatola (from Xhosa for 'Calves') extends from the Great Fish River to the Great Kei River on the coast, and inland as far as Cradock and Queenstown. It includes the vibrant surf-side city of East London; the Amathole mountain retreats of Hogsback and Katberg with their testing hiking trails; and the provincial capital Bisho. Much of it was the former Xhosa Homeland of Ciskei.

SHIPWRECK COAST

The coast between the Great Fish River and East London is also known as the Shipwreck Coast, as it is the graveyard for many ships. The coast is still largely unspoilt. There are a couple of resort towns and the inevitable casino-hotel, but it's easy to get away from it all here.

Shipwreck Hiking Trail

The 64km Shipwreck Hiking Trail *(R20 per person per night)* leads from the Great Fish River to the Ncera River but it is possible to do any section as there are several easy entry and exit points. This is one of the few walking areas in South Africa where hikers can set their own pace and camp more or less where they choose. They are rewarded with wild, unspoilt sections of surf beach, rich coastal vegetation and beautiful estuaries.

The climate is generally mild, although it can rain at any time of the year. The walking is relatively easy, but there are no facilities so hikers must carry water, tents and cooking equipment. Water is available only at the holiday resorts. Hikers can camp on the beach but not on private property. Driftwood fires are permitted, providing they are on sand away from vegetation.

It's 11.5km from the Great Fish River (easily accessible from Port Alfred) to Mpekweni; 11km from Mpekweni to Bira River (where the coastal road bends inland); 20km from Bira River to Hamburg (a small village); 6km from Hamburg to Kiwane Resort; 15.5km from Kiwane to the Ncera River; and another 29km to East London. The trail must be booked through the **Keiskamma Ecotourism Network** *(☎/fax 043-642 2571)* in King William's Town.

Jaynee Levy, in *Complete Guide to Walks & Trails in Southern Africa*, recommends the sections from the Great Fish River to Bira River and from Hamburg to Kiwane Resort.

Great Fish River to Mpekweni
☎ 046 • postcode 5883

This is still a wild area with remote beaches and a rugged hinterland to explore.

Mpekweni Sun (☎ 676 1026, fax 676 1040, W *www.suninternational.co.za)* Singles/doubles B&B from R406. Mpekweni Sun is on the R72, 11.5km east of the Great Fish River beside the sea; there's a restaurant, several bars and a pool. In addition to a surf beach, there's a protected lagoon.

Fish River Sun Hotel (☎ 676 1101, fax 676 1115, W *www.suninternational.co.za)*

Singles/doubles from R380. This newly reopened Sun hotel on the R72 has large rooms equipped with all mod cons. For golf lovers there's an 18-hole course (R175). Golf clubs/carts can be hired for R80/120.

Intercape buses running between Port Elizabeth and East London stop here.

Hamburg
☎ 040 • postcode 5641

The small village of Hamburg, on the wide river flats at the mouth of the Keiskamma River, is near some of the best coast in South Africa. The river flats are home to many birds, especially migrating waders in summer. They also offer good fishing. The name Hamburg is derived from a village established by soldiers of the British German Legion in 1857.

Oyster Lodge (☎/fax 678 1020, e *oyster lodge@yahoo.com,* W *www.oysterlodge .ismad.com, 279 Main Rd)* Camping R25, bed in 4-bed dorm R60/80 low/high season. From the outside the excellent Oyster Lodge is not much to look at, but don't be put off – inside it's spacious, clean and welcoming. There is a big garden and braai area and a large deck out the back overlooking the river. Meals are available.

Hamburg Hotel (☎/fax 678 1061, Main Rd) B&B R80/120 per person low/high season. The Hamburg Hotel is a comfy family-run hotel.

There's a daily minibus taxi to/from East London, about 100km to the east. Fortunately, the Baz Bus picks up and drops off here.

EASTERN CAPE GAME RESERVES
☎ 040

There are three main game reserves administered by the **Eastern Cape Tourism Board** *(ECTB; ☎ 635 2115, fax 636 4019,* e *info@ ectourism.org.za,* W *www.ectourism.co.za PO Box 186, Bisho; admission to all reserves R10/5 adults/children)*. All reserves organise wildlife viewing.

Tsolwana Game Reserve *(☎ 842 2026, fax 645 2115)* is 57km south-west of Queenstown. It protects some rugged Karoo landscape south of the spectacular Tafelberg

(1965m) and adjoining the Swart Kei River. The reserve's rolling plains are interspersed with valleys, cliffs, waterfalls, caves and gullies.

There is a diverse range of animals including large herds of antelope, rhino, giraffe and mountain zebra. The largest four-legged predator is the Cape lynx.

The park is managed in conjunction with the local Tsolwana people, who benefit directly from the jobs and revenue produced.

Double Drift Game Reserve (☎ 653 8010, fax 635 2115), between Fort Beaufort and Alice, has been combined with the Sam Knott Nature Reserve and the Andries Vosloo Kudu Reserve to form the **Great Fish River Reserve**. There is much large wildlife to be seen in this area of thick bushveld, which is sandwiched between the Great Fish and Keiskamma Rivers. The Double Drift Foot Safari (36km) follows the Great Fish River.

To the north of Fort Beaufort is the compact but interesting **Mpofu Game Reserve** (☎ 864 9450, 635 2115) where you are likely to see *mpofu* (eland), a large antelope. The grassland and valley bushveld make the region ideal for wildlife viewing. The three-day Katberg Trail starts here (see Katberg Area under Amatola & Katberg Mountains later in this chapter).

Book trails with the **Keiskamma Ecotourism Network** (☎/fax 043-642 2571) in King William's Town.

Places to Stay

Tsolwana Game Reserve has three comfortable *lodges* (R280 for up to 4 people, plus R50 per additional person) in old farmhouses, each with a lounge, dining room, three bedrooms (each with two beds) and two bathrooms. There are also two trail huts here, *Phumlani* and *Fundani*; book them with ECTB.

Double Drift Game Reserve also has three comfortable lodges: *Double Drift* (R160 a quad), *Mbabala* (R280 a quad) and *Mvubu* (R180 a double).

Mpofu Game Reserve has two lodges: *Ntloni* and *Mpofu* (both are R280 for up to four, R50 for each extra person).

KING WILLIAM'S TOWN
☎ 043 • postcode 5600

Established by the London Missionary Society in 1826, King William's Town (known as 'KWT') became an important military base in the interminable struggle with the Xhosa. After the Seventh Frontier War (1846–47), the British crown colony of British Kaffraria was established in 1853 with King William's Town as its capital.

Although the nominal capital of the former Homeland of Ciskei was Bisho (now the Eastern Cape provincial capital), King William's Town remains the real commercial and shopping centre for the region. Though there are several interesting buildings dating from the mid-19th century, such as British Kaffrarian Savings Bank, as well as a good museum, there is no pressing reason to stay in King William's Town.

The **library** (☎ 642 3450, fax 642 3677, Ayliff St) has some tourist information (although not much) and Eastern Cape tourism brochures.

Hiking trails must be booked through the **Keiskamma Ecotourism Network** (☎/fax 642 2571, 9 Chamberlain St).

Things to See

The collection of the **Amathole Museum** (☎ 642 4506, Alexandra Rd; open 9am-1pm & 1.45pm-4.30pm Mon-Fri, 10am-12.30pm Sat) was begun by the local naturalists' society in 1884, and consequently has a large natural history section. Pride of place is given to the stuffed corpse of Huberta, the hippo that became famous between 1928 and 1931 when she wandered down the coast from St Lucia in Natal – more than 1000km away – to the vicinity of King William's Town, where she was unfortunately shot by hunters.

The most interesting displays, however, are in its **Xhosa Gallery** in the old post office building. The gallery has some excellent material on the cultural history of the Xhosa nation, including all the tribes. One highlight is the fantastic wire cars made by local craftspeople.

Political activist Steve Biko, who died in police custody, is buried nearby (see the boxed text).

Steve Biko

Steven Bantu Biko (1946–77), known as Steve Biko, is buried in the Ginsberg cemetery just outside King William's Town. Biko was the best known of the leaders of the Black Consciousness Movement that grew out of student protest in the 1970s.

This former medical student from the University of Natal became more and more outspoken, and was eventually put under house arrest and was banned by the government from speaking in public. In 1977, he was detained in Port Elizabeth for 26 days under the Terrorism Act. He died in police custody after a series of brutal assaults.

Biko's life is portrayed in the movie *Cry Freedom*. Some observers believe that Biko's callous killing was an important contributing factor in the downfall of apartheid.

To reach Biko's grave follow Cathcart St south of the town and turn left down a dirt track that is signposted to the cemetery.

Places to Stay & Eat

There are a few hotels but the best options are in East London.

The Grosvenor Lodge (☎ 604 7200, fax 604 7205, 48 Taylor St) Singles/doubles R275/350, suites R285/360. Formerly the Grosvenor Hotel, this small lodge has well-priced rooms and is centrally located.

The information office can provide a list of local B&Bs and guesthouses.

Grosvenor Guest Lodge (☎ 604 7200, fax 604 7205, 10 Bryson St) Singles/doubles B&B R200/255. This appealing B&B is in a restored farmhouse in a quiet area of town.

Dreamers Guest House (☎ 642 3012, e dreamers@imaginet.co.za, W www.imaginet.co.za, 29 Gordon St) Singles/doubles B&B R170/280. Dreamers Guest House is a friendly B&B in a charming Victorian house. All rooms have private bathrooms, and email facilities are available.

Takeaways in town include ***Steers***, ***Nando's***, ***KFC*** and ***Wimpy***.

Kings Head (☎ 604 7200, 48 Taylor St) Mains R27-40. This cosy bar-restaurant adjoins the Grosvenor Lodge.

Getting There & Away

Greyhound buses run daily between Cape Town (R205) and East London (R95). Buses arrive at and depart from the Engen One petrol station on Cathcart St.

Greyhound also runs daily between Jo'burg/Pretoria (R250) and East London (R85) via Bloemfontein (R205).

BISHO

☎ 040 • postcode 5605

Bisho, once capital of Ciskei, is now the administrative capital of Eastern Cape. It was originally the black 'location' for nearby King William's Town. The centre of Bisho does have some shops but it was built to house Ciskei's bureaucrats and politicians, so there is a compact bunch of suitably grandiose and ugly public buildings, which are now in the service of the new provincial bureaucracy.

Curiosity might inspire a visit but the only practical reason would be to visit the **Eastern Cape Tourism Board** (☎ 635 2115, fax 636 4019, e info@ectourism.org.za, W www.ectourism.co.za, *Opposite the post office*), which has brochures and also handles bookings for hiking trails.

Amatola Sun (☎ 639 1111, W www.suninternational.co.za) Singles/doubles R630/860. At the time of writing, the Amatola Sun, part of the Sun chain, was closed for renovations.

Regular minibuses run from the King William's Town train station to Bisho.

AMATOLA & KATBERG MOUNTAINS

The area north and west of King William's Town is partly degraded grazing land and partly rugged mountains with remnant indigenous forest. There are some good walks. When the mists are down on the Amatola Mountains, the forests take on an eerie silence.

The easiest way into this area is via King William's Town or Queenstown. City to City daily buses stop in Katberg, Seymour and Alice on the Jo'burg–King William's Town run. There are occasional minibus taxis.

EASTERN CAPE

Amatola Trail

The 105km, six-day Amatola Trail *(R150 per person)* begins at the Maden Dam, 23km north of King William's Town, and ends at the Tyumie River near Hogsback. Accommodation is in huts.

The Amatola Trail ranks as one of South Africa's top mountain walks but it is pretty tough and should only be attempted if you are reasonably experienced and fit. Walkers are rewarded with great views, although about a third of the walk goes through dense forest and numerous streams with waterfalls and swimming holes.

The Pirie-Evelyn Walk and Zingcuka Loop trails both incorporate parts of the Amatola Trail. The trails must be booked with the **Keiskamma Ecotourism Network** *(☎/fax 043-642 2571)* in King William's Town.

Alice & Fort Hare
☎ 040

Alice was established as a missionary and military centre in 1847. It's now a busy little town, near the University of Fort Hare. The university was established in 1916 as the South African Native College and has played an important role in the development of Southern Africa. Former students include Oliver Tambo, Nelson Mandela, Robert Mugabe (Zimbabwe's prime minister) and Kenneth Kaunda (former president of Zambia).

Within the university, the **FS Malan Museum** *(☎ 602 2239; admission free; open 8am-1pm & 2pm-4.30pm Mon-Fri)* has displays of traditional costumes, charms and medicines. Parts of the original Fort Hare are also preserved in the grounds.

Frequent minibus taxis run from King William's Town to the main gates of the university and to Alice; they cost R7. From Alice to Fort Beaufort is R6. A taxi to Hogsback will cost R15 but you'll probably have to change taxis en route.

Fort Beaufort
☎ 046 • postcode 5720

In 1846 a relative of Sandile, leader of the Rharhabe or Ciskei Xhosa, stole an axe from a shop in Fort Beaufort. In a rather disproportionate retaliation, a mixed force of regular soldiers and volunteers invaded the semi-independent Xhosa province of Queen Adelaide, beginning the Seventh Frontier War or the War of the Axe (1846–47). Today, Fort Beaufort is a small, attractive and quiet town with interesting historical relics. The prominent building up on the hill is the **Martello Tower**, built more than 200 years ago for defensive purposes.

The **Historical Museum** *(☎/fax 645 1555, 44 Durban St; adult/child R2/0.50; open 8.20am-5pm Mon-Fri, 8.20am-12.45pm Sat)* is in the old officers' mess and contains a large collection of firearms, curios and paintings. There is a small craft shop behind the museum. The local publicity association is based here.

Savoy Hotel *(☎ 645 1146, fax 645 2082, 53 Durban St)* Singles/doubles B&B R175/265. The uninspiring Savoy Hotel, opposite the museum, is the best hotel in town. Its a la carte restaurant is open daily.

Town Lodge *(☎/fax 645 1598, 114 Campbell St)* Bed only/B&B R80/100 per person. The Town Lodge, formerly Uncle Mike's Guest House, has simple rooms.

De Villa Guest House *(☎/fax 645 4071, 13 Henrietta St)* Singles/doubles B&B R100/180. This appealing B&B is not far from the town centre.

Hogsback
☎ 045 • postcode 5721

Hogsback is a magical resort high in the beautiful Amatola Mountains, about 100km north-west of Bisho. The small village has a sprinkling of holiday homes and old-style mountain guesthouses. It is here that Tolkien is said to have been inspired to write *The Hobbit*.

The steepest slopes around Katberg and Hogsback are still covered in beautiful indigenous rainforest; yellowwood, assegai and tree fuchsia are all present. There are also, sadly, extensive pine plantations on land that was once indigenous forest. The peaks of the hills are high and bare, reminiscent of a hog's back, hence the town's unusual name.

There are some great walks and drives in the area. Some of the best roads are unsealed, so check locally before trying anything ambitious, and definitely think twice if it has been snowing (it snows a couple of times each winter). This is a summer rainfall area, and thunderstorms and mists are common. Bring money, as there is no bank in Hogsback.

The hogs made of mud that you'll see being sold along the road (R5 to R10) are not fired; when they get wet they make a hell of a mess.

The information office on the main road is only open from 11am to noon Monday to Friday; during peak season it's open longer hours.

Places to Stay & Eat There are a few mountain guesthouses in Hogsback and only a handful of places to eat. Your best bet is a meal in one of the many hotel restaurants, where set menus range from R42 to R65.

Away with the Fairies (☎ 962 1031, fax 722 8240, ☜ sugarsk@iafrica.com, Hydrangea Lane) Camping R30, dorm beds R50, doubles R120. Away with the Fairies is a magical mountain getaway with a magnificent view of Hogsback Ridge. Dan, your host, is happy to introduce you to the pathways and forests, and to make sure you relax at the end of the day – either in front of a log fire or out enjoying a sundowner or two in the tree house. There are traditional Xhosa meals, mountain bikes for hire (R50), maps, and whatever else you need (except TV). New additions include a bar and a water-tank pool.

The Edge (☎/fax 962 1159, ☜ theedge@execunet.co.za, Bluff End) Camping R30, hikers huts singles/doubles/triples R70/100/135. This delightful haven is right on the mountain's edge. Run by a friendly gay couple, it is a collection of stunningly decorated self-catering cottages and a large well-maintained camp site with the cleanest ablutions you're likely to find in all of Africa! Follow the signs from the main road (look for the pink triangle).

Hogsback Mountain Lodge (☎/fax 962 1005, ☜ arminel@webmail.co.za, Main Rd) 6-bed cottages R50/60 per person low/high season, B&B from R120/150 per person,

DB&B from R150/180 per person. Also known as the Arminel Mountain Lodge, this lodge has pleasant cottages, a swimming pool and a huge, beautiful garden.

Hogsback Inn (☎ 962 1006, 962 1015, ☜ hogsbackinn@xsinet.co.za, Main Rd) DB&B R180/275 per person low/high season. The Hogsback Inn is an amiable place with a large garden, log fires and a pool.

Hogsbreath (☎ 082-6247910, Main Rd) Meals R10-35. At the time of writing Hogsbreath provided the only nonhotel meals in Hogsback.

Tolkien's Tipple Open Dec-Jan. This small but excellent watering hole down by the river is a good place to stop for a drink or two after a hike.

Getting There & Away There is no public transport to Hogsback, however, it is possible to catch one of the shuttles that runs from the Sugarshack Backpackers in East London to Away with the Fairies on Monday, Thursday and Saturday (R40 one way).

Katberg Area
☎ 040

Katberg, 110km north-west of Bisho, is a small town at the foot of a wooded range. The surrounding area is still much as it was when it was Ciskei: overworked and underfunded.

It's an interesting drive from Katberg to Hogsback, 27km to the east. There are some great views around the Katberg Pass. The road over the pass is unsealed and although it is in a reasonable condition, check locally before tackling it after a lot of rain or snow.

The 50km, three-day **Katberg Trail** (bookings ☎/fax 043-642 2571; R30 per person per night) begins in Mpofu Game Reserve and ends at the Katberg Forest Station, just below the Katberg Pass. Accommodation in timber cabins is provided. It's a hike of medium difficulty and you cover a reasonable distance.

Protea Hotel Katberg (☎ 653 1010, fax 864 1014) Singles/doubles from R305/440. About 8km from Katberg, this Protea hotel is nothing short of luxurious. There are lots of pleasant walks in the vicinity and the hotel offers horse riding, swimming, squash and tennis. Its restaurant is open for lunch and dinner.

EAST LONDON

☎ 043 • postcode 5200 • pop 750,000

This bustling port has a good surf beach and a spectacular bay that curves around to huge sand hills. The port, on the Buffalo River, is the country's largest river port. After being hit hard by recession, East London (known universally as 'EL') is regaining its family holiday atmosphere.

If it is the quintessential beach/surfer lifestyle you are after, East London is definitely the right place to gravitate to – it's perfect for making contacts before heading to Jeffrey's Bay.

Orientation

The main street in the centre is Oxford St, with the city centre extending from about Argyle St south to Fleet St. Fleet St runs east, and eventually, after a few corners and name changes, meets the Esplanade.

Orient Beach, which is east of the river mouth, is popular with families and has a tidal pool. Eastern Beach is the long main beach fronting the Esplanade but Nahoon Beach on the northern headland is better, with great surf, especially at Nahoon Reef.

The massive and sprawling township of Mdantsane, 15km from town, was established in 1962 to house East London's blacks. It's now the largest town in the area, with a population estimated to be in excess of 400,000. It's the second-largest township in South Africa after Soweto.

Information

Tourist Offices The helpful **Tourism East London** (☎ 722 6015, fax 743 5091, W www .eastlondontourism.co.za, 35 Argyle St; open 8.30am-4.30pm Mon-Fri, 9am-noon Sat) is behind the city hall. **Wild Coast Holiday Reservations** (☎ 743 6181, 743 6188), next door, books accommodation in the Transkei.

Money There is a branch of the First National Bank on the corner of Oxford and Union Sts, and several ATMs nearby. For your safety, only use ATMs during the day; better still use one of the ATMs in the Vincent Park shopping centre.

Post & Communications You can make international calls at the **Telkom office** (Gladstone St; open 8am-4pm Mon-Thur, 8am-3.30pm Fri, 8am-11.30am Sat).

For Internet access, the **Cyber Lounge** (☎ 083-375 9040, 58 Beach Rd, Nahoon) charges R20 per half-hour. You could also try the **Milky Lane Cyberstation** (King's Entertainment Centre).

Gay & Lesbian Travellers The Gay Social Society can be contacted at PO Box 709, East London.

Things to See & Do

The exhibits at the **East London Museum** (☎ 743 0689, Upper Oxford St; admission R5; open 9.30am-5pm Mon-Fri, 2pm-5pm Sat, 11am-4pm Sun) include the world's only dodo egg, a model of a coelacanth and Xhosa displays.

The **Ann Bryant Art Gallery** (☎ 722 4044, St Marks Rd; admission free; open 9.30am-5pm Mon-Fri, 9.30am-noon Sat), south of the museum, is in an old mansion featuring a mixture of Cape Dutch and Victorian styles.

Gately House (☎ 722 2141, 1 Park Gates Rd; admission by donation; open 10am-1pm & 2pm-5pm Tues-Thurs, 10am-1pm Fri, 3pm-5pm Sat & Sun) was the residence of the first mayor of East London, John Gately, and is furnished in period style. It's near the entrance to Queen's Park.

If you have children there is a small **zoo** (☎ 722 1171; adult/child R8/5; open 9am-5pm Mon-Sun) at Queen's Park and a small **aquarium** (☎ 705 2637, Esplanade; adult/child R10/5; open 9am-5pm Mon-Sun) on the beachfront. Otherwise try the **Water World Fun Park** (☎ 748 4265; admission R20; open summer only) in West Bank (near the Race Track) where the kids can ride endlessly on the supertube and speed slides.

Get information about **diving** clubs at **Pollock's Sport & Surf** (☎ 726 8486, Bell St, Vincent Park). For **fishing** charters, contact **Mr MacArthur** (☎ 735 2604).

EAST LONDON

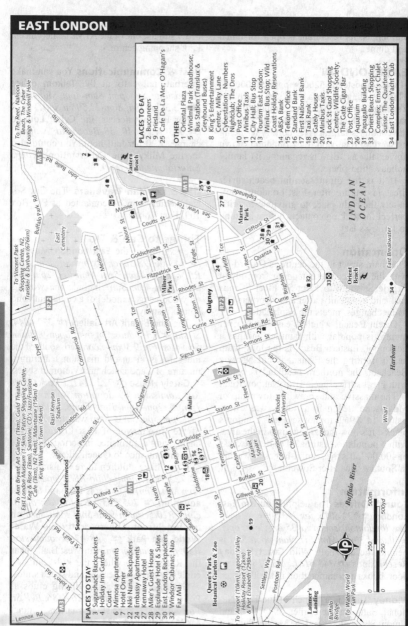

PLACES TO EAT
1 Oriental Plaza
2 Buccaneers
9 Friesland
25 Cafe De La Mer; O'Hagan's

OTHER
1 Oriental Plaza
5 Windmill Park Roadhouse; Bus Station (Translux & Greyhound Buses)
8 King's Entertainment Centre; Milky Lane Cyberstation; Numbers Nightclub; The Dros
10 Post Office
11 Minibus Taxis
12 City Hall; Bus Stop
13 Tourism East London; Minibus Bus Stop; Wild Coast Holiday Reservations
14 ABSA Bank
15 Telkom Office
16 Standard Bank
17 First National Bank
18 Taxi Rank
19 Gately House
20 Minibus Taxis
21 Lock St Gaol Shopping Centre; Wildlife Society; The Gate Cigar Bar
23 Post Office
26 Aquarium
31 Papagallo Building
33 Orient Beach Shopping Complex; Ernst's Chalet Suisse; The Quarterdeck
34 East London Yacht Club

PLACES TO STAY
3 Sugarshack Backpackers
4 Holiday Inn Garden Court
6 Mimosa Apartments
7 Hotel Osner
22 Niki Nana Backpackers
24 Embassy Apartments
27 Kennaway Hotel
28 Mike's Guest House
29 Esplanade Hotel & Suites
30 East London Backpackers
32 Windsor Cabanas; Nato Faz Mal

Amanzi River Adventures (☎/fax 048-
?81 2976, e aman@intekom.co.za) oper-
tes **rafting** trips on the Great Fish, Little
'ish and Tsomo Rivers.

If there are enough people, you can hire
he yacht *Miscky* for a sunset **cruise** (☎ 735
'232; R50).

Not far up the Nahoon River, in Dorch-
ster Heights, is Windmill Hole, a great
wimming spot; park in Snowy Waters Rd,
hen walk along the river bank for about 20
ninutes.

The best **surfing** is near Bats Cave, to-
vards the southern end of Nahoon Beach.

Organised Tours
Various half-day tours of the city and the sur-
ounding area cost around R35 per person;
ontact the tourist office or *Amatola Tours*
☎ 743 0472, fax 722 6914, 20 Currie St,
Quigney).

Tours to the townships of Mdantsane and
welitsha and to Bisho and King William's
'own are operated by *African Magic* (☎ 745
428, e travel@africamagic.co.za) and Am-
tola Tours. There are also full-day tours
o Qunu in the Transkei, where Nelson
Mandela spent his childhood.

Places to Stay – Budget
Niki Nana Backpackers (☎ 722 8509, e niki
ana@nfb.co.za, 4 Hillview Rd) Dorm beds
?40. Niki Nana Backpackers, easily recog-
isable by its striking zebra-striped facade,
s a small but comfortable backpackers with
private garden and a large swimming
ool.

Sugarshack Backpackers (☎/fax 722
240, e sugarsk@iafrica.com, Eastern Es-
Janade, Eastern Beach) Dorm beds R45,
oubles R110. With the beach just metres
way and its distinct surfer feel, it is no
vonder the surf is always up at Sugarshack
backpackers. There are plenty of activities
indulge in from its wild 'Sugar Rush'
ay trips to 'hanging ten' down at the beach
oards and lessons are free). Then as the
un goes down you can party at the Shack's
ar or wander next door to Buccaneers,
vhich rocks until dawn. This is a place to
ut loose, not to sleep!

East London Backpackers (☎ 722 2748,
e kaybeach@iafrica.com, w www.london
backpackers.active3.com, 11 Quanza St)
Dorm beds R45, doubles without/with
bathroom R120/140. This well-maintained
place will delight discerning backpackers.
Dorms are spacious and clean and there is
an excellent terraced braai area and a
plunge pool.

Mike's Guest House (☎ 743 3647, fax 743
0308, e mikes@his.co.za, 22 Clifford St)
Bed only R60 per person, singles/doubles
R130/180. Near the beachfront, this is
another good budget option.

Lagoon Valley Holiday Resort (☎ 736
9785, fax 736 9753, e lagoonv@lagoon
valley.co.za, w www.lagoonvalley.co.za)
Caravan sites R20/65 low/high season, cottages R130/180. About 12km south-west of
town, just off Marine Dr, is the picturesque
Lagoon Valley Holiday Resort. It's a great
place for bird-watching; more than 150
species have been spotted here.

Places to Stay – Mid-Range
Esplanade Hotel & Suites (☎ 722 2518,
fax 722 3679, e esphotel@iafrica.com,
Clifford St) Singles/doubles B&B R195/
230, single/double suites R210/250. The recently refurbished Esplanade Hotel, near
the beach, has well-appointed rooms, most
of which have sea views.

Holiday Inn Garden Court (☎ 722 7260,
fax 743 7360, e gceastlondon@southern
sun.com, Cnr John Bailie Rd & Moore St)
Singles/doubles R394. Rooms at this Holiday Inn have sweeping sea views but are
otherwise typical of this genre. Breakfast is
available for R46.

Osner Resorts (☎ 743 3433, e osaccom@
iafrica.com), which runs the following
places to stay, has a virtual monopoly of the
hotels and apartments in East London; all
the quoted prices include breakfast.

Embassy Apartments (☎ 743 0182, Fitzpatrick St) Singles/doubles R120/170.
Recommended by readers, Embassy Apartments has good rooms and is the cheapest
of the group.

Kennaway Hotel (☎ 722 5531, fax 743
3433, Esplanade) Singles/doubles R140/189.

The Kennaway Hotel, close to the beach, has charming colonial-style rooms.

Mimosa Apartments *(☎ 743 3433, Marine Terrace)* Singles/doubles R140/170. Mimosa's self-contained units are good value and are often booked out.

The Reef *(☎ 735 1620, Nahoon)* Singles/doubles R165/195. The Reef, near the river in Nahoon, is slightly more expensive. It has bright, comfortable rooms.

Windsor Cabanas *(☎ 743 2225, Currie St)* Singles/doubles cabanas R320/365, basic rooms R185/235. Windsor Cabanas is fairly upmarket. Basic rooms in the courtyard are slightly cheaper (as they are cramped).

Hotel Osner *(☎/fax 743 3433, Court Cres)* Singles/doubles R250, family rooms R290. The Hotel Osner, near Eastern Beach, has breezy rooms that are ideal for families.

Places to Eat

Restaurants Most of the beachfront hotels have restaurants. You can also try the following mid-range places.

Buccaneers *(☎ 743 5171, Esplanade)* Lunch R15-35, dinner R21-29. Next to Sugarshack Backpackers, Buccaneers serves a hearty T-bone steak with vegetables and chips for around R20 and has pizzas from R11.

O'Hagans *(☎ 743 8713, Aquarium Complex, Esplanade)* Mains R14-45. O'Hagans, a popular pub 'n' grill, is good for steaks, burgers, chicken and salads. It offers plenty of seafood too.

Keg & Rose *(☎ 726 6164, Patcyn Centre, Frere Rd, Vincent)* Mains R22-45. The ever-popular Keg & Rose is a good spot for both meals and after-work drinks.

Santorini *(☎ 726 3730, 6A Balfour Rd, Vincent)* Mains R25-50. Santorini's delicious Greek menu will leave your mouth watering for more.

Nao Faz Mal *(☎ 743 2225)* Buffet dinner R65. The excellent Nao Faz Mal, near Windsor Cabanas, is the best splurge in town. Its authentic Mozambique-Portuguese buffet includes *peri-peri* chicken (chicken in a spicy sauce) and marinated Portuguese steak.

Ernst's Chalet Suisse Mains R30-175. The recently renovated Ernst's Chalet Suisse, at the Orient Beach shopping complex,

is an upmarket place specialising i seafood dishes such as *sole pascal* (par fried fish topped with lobster-flavoure sabayon and green peppercorns) for R5(

The Quarterdeck *(☎ 722 1840)*, with i good old-fashioned pub meals, is next doo

Cafes & Fast Food For a good-valu breakfast (R20), try the ***coffee shop*** at th front of Mimosa Apartments. For chea cafes, try along College St near the minibu taxi rank.

Fast-food options include ***Friesland*** o the corner of Goldschmidt and Tennyso Sts and ***Steers*** with its four locations: o Oxford St in the centre of town, on De ereaux Ave in the Vincent Park shoppin centre, in the Papagallo building on th waterfront and in Nahoon.

Windmill Park Roadhouse *(☎ 722 290: Moore St)* Meals under R20. Windmill Par Roadhouse, at the bus station, is a takeawa with a difference; the staff come to your ca to ask you for your order.

Cafe De La Mer *(☎ 743 0491, Aquariu Complex, Esplanade)* Mains R15-21. Th cafe has great views and good prices.

Entertainment

Bars & Discos East Londoners know ho to enjoy themselves and there is no shortag of party venues in town. Many restauran have live entertainment on Friday or Satu day nights.

Buccaneers *(☎ 743 5171, Esplanade)* without doubt the top venue in East Lor don, with a happy hour on Wednesday fror 7pm to 9pm and live bands on Wednesda Friday and Saturday.

Numbers Nightclub *(☎ 743 9274, King Entertainment Centre, Esplanade)*, not f from Hotel Osner, is a popular nightclu where you can dance the night away to retr disco hits.

O'Hagans *(☎ 743 8713, Aquarium Con plex, Esplanade)* is good on Friday nig and is the perfect place for a beer on a sunn afternoon.

The Dros *(☎ 743 3157, King's Enter tainment Centre, Esplanade)* is a tradition Afrikaner haunt.

CD's Jazz/Fusion Cafe (☎ 726 3766, 10 Balfour Rd, Vincent) should not be missed by jazz enthusiasts. There is live jazz every Friday and Saturday night.

The Gate Cigar Bar (Lock St Gaol Shopping Centre) is a popular gay bar with live music most Friday nights and dancing on Saturday night.

Cinemas & Theatres The *Vincent Park Cinemas* (☎ 726 8122) play all the latest flicks. To get to the Vincent Park shopping centre, (where the cinemas are) first follow Fitzpatrick St to the Northeast Expressway, take the Pearce/Gleneagles Sts exit west, and then turn right at Chamberlain St and left into Devereaux Ave.

Guild Theatre (☎ 743 0704, Dawson Rd) is in Selborne and a very busy place in high season, hosting everything from ballet to beauty contests.

Arts Theatre (☎ 722 6957, Paterson St, Arcadia) shows musicals that are even enjoyed by surfers.

Getting There & Away
Air The airport is 10km from the centre. SAA (☎ 704 1111) has daily flights to Port Elizabeth (R455/260 full/Apex fare) and to Durban (R875). There are also periodic flights to Jo'burg (R950/540 full/Apex fare), Cape Town (R992) and George (R700/390 full/Apex fare).

Bus Translux and Greyhound stop at the Windmill Park Roadhouse on Moore St; Intercape buses stop at the main train station, on Station St, and at the airport.

Translux (☎ 700 1999) has daily buses to Umtata (R90), Port Elizabeth (R100), Durban (R160), Graaff-Reinet (R170), Cape Town (R240) and Jo'burg/Pretoria (R285).

Greyhound has a daily bus between Durban (R155) and Cape Town (R240) via Port Elizabeth (R100).

Intercape (☎ 722 2254) has daily buses from East London to Butterworth (R75), Umtata (R95), Durban (R155), and Cape Town (R240). Minilux (☎ 741 3107) runs to Port Elizabeth (R90); it departs from Tourism East London (35 Argyle St).

The Baz Bus runs from Port Elizabeth to Durban via East London Monday, Tuesday, Wednesday Friday and Saturday. It runs in the other direction Monday, Tuesday, Thursday, Friday and Sunday. It picks up from hostels.

Train The *Amatola* (☎ 744 2719) from East London to Jo'burg departs daily, arriving in Jo'burg the following day. It goes via Bloemfontein, where there is a connecting service to Cape Town (see under Train in the Getting Around chapter for more details).

Minibus Taxi On the corner of Buffalo and Argyle Sts are long-distance minibus taxis to destinations north of East London; nearby on the corner of Caxton and Gillwell Sts are minibus taxis for King William's Town, Bisho and the local area. Destinations include King William's Town (R12), Butterworth (R30), Umtata (R60), Port Elizabeth (R67), Jo'burg (R160) and Cape Town (R180).

Getting Around
Most city buses stop at the city hall on Oxford St. For information on bus times and routes, contact **Amatola Regional Services** (☎ 722 1251). One of the most useful bus routes is the Beach route, which runs down Oxford St, east along Fleet, Longfellow and Moore Sts, then back along The Esplanade to Currie St and to the city.

There's a **taxi rank** (☎ 722 7901) on the corner of Oxford and Union Sts.

EAST LONDON TO THE KEI RIVER
There are many resorts on the coast north of East London including two good backpackers in Cintsa. The East Coast Resorts turn-off from the N2 will get you to most of them. The excellent Strandloper Hiking Trail is the best introduction to this beautiful coastline.

Gonubie
☎ 043 • postcode 5256
The first series of beaches to the north is centred on Gonubie. There is a small nature reserve here where 130 species of birds, mostly waterfowl, have been recorded.

EASTERN CAPE

Gonubie Caravan Park (☎ 705 9748, fax 740 5937) 4-bed cottages R120/190 low/high season, 4-bed chalets R180/380. This well-maintained caravan park offers good budget accommodation.

Gonubie Backpackers (☎ 740 0275, fax 726 7761, e *gonubiebp@webmail.co.za,* w *www.geocities.com/gonubiebp, 16 Hart St)* Camping R35, dorm beds R55, doubles R110. With an emphasis on relaxation, Gonubie Backpackers makes a good stopover before or after hiking the Strandloper Trail. For those who wish to test their artistic talent there is an art studio equipped with a pottery wheel and paints.

Blue Waters Lodge (☎/fax 740 2019, e *bwlodge@iafrica.com)* Singles B&B R119/207 low/high season, doubles B&B R179/334. Blue Waters Lodge is a friendly family-run place only 50m from the sea. It is reached from the N2 – follow the signs to Gonubie, then turn off before the municipal offices and follow 7th St to the end.

Strandloper Hiking Trail

The 60km, five-day Strandloper Hiking Trail *(bookings Strandloper Ecotourism Board ☎ 841 1888)* runs between Kei Mouth and Gonubie. The Strandlopers (Beach Walkers) were a Khoisan tribe who lived on the coast but disappeared as a distinct group after white settlement. To walk the trail costs R37/45 per day unguided/guided. You'll need a copy of the tide tables, as there are several estuaries to cross and it's dangerous to do so when the tide is flowing out. The *Daily Dispatch* newspaper has the monthly tide tables. The trail is usually walked from Kei Mouth to Gonubie.

Weekend packages can be booked through **Wild Coast Holiday Reservations** *(☎ 743 6181, fax 743 6188,* e *meross@iafrica .com)* in East London.

There are four *overnight huts* (Pumphouse, Double Mouth, Cape Henderson Log Cabin and Beacon Valley Environment Centre), and the cost of staying in these is included in the booking fee. The Pumphouse has a tidal swimming pool in front and is underneath the Kei Mouth lighthouse. Camping on the beach is prohibited,

but the coast is littered with resorts, most of which have camp sites.

Cintsa
☎ 043 • postcode 5275

Thirty-eight kilometres from East London, this is one of the best spots on the South African coast and a great place to hang out for a few days (or weeks).

The **Marijuana Trail** *(☎ 734 3590, fax 734 3990,* e *info@marijuana-trail.com,* w *ww .marijuana-trail.com)*, based at Moonshine Bay (see Places to Stay & Eat, following) offers interesting 4WD adventures into the heart of the Transkei that take in rough coastal roads and scenery few travellers get to see. What is unique about the Marijuana Trail's concept is that it has divided the coast between Cintsa and Port St Johns into seven separate zones, allowing travellers to hop on and hop off along the way. Each zone costs R150. (The name is a little misleading, as drugs are not permitted or sold on the trips.)

Buccaneer's Backpackers also offers an incredible Transkei 4WD day trip (R185), as well as tours to Cintsa township and Bulugha Farm School.

Places to Stay & Eat Cintsa offers a couple of good accommodation options, and a great place to eat.

Buccaneer's Backpackers (☎ 743 3012, fax 734 3749, e *cintsabp@iafrica.com, Cintsa West)* Camping R30, dorm beds R50, doubles R120. Most travellers will have undoubtedly heard of Buccaneer's Backpackers long before they before they make it to Cintsa. Many consider it to be the best hostel in South Africa. You can use the canoes, surfboards and paddle skis for water play on the Cintsa River for free. There is also a pool, volleyball court, bar, poolside cafe, climbing wall, daily organised activities (including shebeen visits and drinking sundowners on the dunes) and its infamous free booze cruises. On Sunday morning, the hosts cook a big breakfast for the guests and serve it in the dining room (free). To get to Buccaneer's, follow the Cintsa West turn-off for about 200m until you reach the entrance; the main buildings are a further 2km along the dirt road.

Moonshine Bay (☎ *734 3590,* e *moonshine_sa@hotmail.com)* Camping R25, dorm beds R45, doubles R110. This is a good clean place that boasts a huge entertainment area, a terrace upstairs, tennis and squash courts, a large swimming pool and comfortable African-theme rooms. Breakfast is free. While it lacks the party atmosphere of Buccaneer's, it rates highly with Lonely Planet's readers, who sing its praises. Moonshine Bay also offers horse riding (R50) and is the base for the Marijuana Trail. To get here, follow the directions for Buccaneer's but continue on past the Buccaneer's entrance until the end of the sealed road.

Michaela's (☎ *738 5139, Steenbras Dr, East Cintsa)* Mains R38-52, buffet (Sun only) R75. Perched high up on the hillside and with sweeping ocean views, Michaela's offers a truly superb dining experience. Wooden stairs lead diners up through a mini-rainforest to the restaurant; for the less fit there is always the lift.

Getting There & Away To reach Cintsa from East London take Exit 26 (East Coast Resorts) on the N2. Double back under the freeway, follow the road for 1km to the Cintsa East turn-off, and then follow this road for another 16km to the Cintsa West turn-off.

Haga-Haga & Kei Mouth
☎ 043

The next concentration of beaches is around Haga-Haga, a small seaside village about 72km north of East London (30km of this is on gravel after you turn off the N2). The northern tip of **Cape Henderson Nature Reserve** adjoins Haga-Haga. This is a scenic reserve with sandy stretches of beach, rugged coastline and coastal forest.

North of Haga-Haga, and reached by turning off the N2 onto the R349, are Morgan's Bay (85km from East London) and Kei Mouth, where there is a vehicle ferry. Kei Mouth is the last resort before the Wild Coast. Most visitors are attracted to this area by the fishing and beachcombing.

Haga-Haga Resort (☎/fax *841 1670,* e *haga@intekom.co.za)* DB&B from R160 per person. The comfortable rooms at this resort all face the sea.

Morgan Bay Hotel (☎ *841 1062, fax 841 1130,* e *mb.hotel@mweb.co.za)* DB&B from R190/220 per person low/high season. Morgan Bay Hotel is quite pricey, but meals in its restaurant are good value.

Kei Mouth Backpackers & Surfaris (☎ *841 1238)* Dorm beds R35, doubles R90. While its location is beautiful – close to the legendary Wacky Point surf break and one of the great dividing lines of South African history, the Kei River, once the natural boundary between the Ciskei and Transkei – Kei Mouth Backpackers is looking a little tired and could do with a little TLC. Pick-up from the Baz Bus on the N2 is free.

Kei Mouth Beach Hotel (☎ *841 1017, fax 841 1212,* e *beachhotel@keimouth.co.za)* DB&B R225/395 per person low/high season. This hotel has plenty of pleasant rooms with sea views.

North-Eastern Highlands

This area is surrounded on three sides by the former Transkei and has a short border (but no crossing point) with Lesotho. It's high country, in the southern tail of the main Drakensberg range, and is a bleak but atmospheric place. Winter brings snowfalls, and even in summer Barkly and Naudesnek Passes can be cold – watch out for ice if you're driving.

While this part of the Drakensberg range isn't as spectacular as that in KwaZulu-Natal, there are no crowds or resorts and there are good walking trails near Rhodes, Lady Grey, Elliot, Barkly East and Maclear. Many San rock-painting sites can be visited.

There isn't much public transport in this area; even minibus taxis are scarce.

BARKLY EAST
☎ 045 • postcode 9787
On the R58, this town, with its scenic and mountainous location, bills itself as the

EASTERN CAPE

'Switzerland of South Africa'. The **Barkly East & Rhodes Tourism Association** (☎ 083-733 8683, fax 971 0720, e elizcou@hotmail.com, 14 Molteno St), in the Magic Moments shop, also doubles as an Internet cafe.

The **trout fishing** near Barkly East is reputedly some of the best in the country. Keen anglers should contact the **Wild Trout Association** (e dave@wildtrout.co.za, w www.wildtrout.co.za).

Ben Macdhui Caravan Park (☎ 971 0123, Victoria Park) Camping sites R40 for 2 people. This caravan park has clean ablution facilities and pleasant sites.

Old Mill Inn (☎ 971 0277, fax 971 0972, Cnr White & De Smidt Sts) Singles/doubles from R120/200. The Old Mill Inn is good value and is a pleasant place to relax.

RHODES & TIFFINDELL
☎ 045 • postcode 5582

It can get cold up here! Rhodes, halfway between Maclear and Barkly East on the R396, is a picturesque village with some quaint old buildings. The large pine trees in the town were a gift from Cecil Rhodes.

Tiffindell (2800m) is the skiing centre of South Africa; with its snow-making facilities, a season of 100 or so days is guaranteed. Tiffindell is in an area of breathtaking mountain scenery. Nearby is Ben Macdhui (3001m), the highest mountain peak in the Cape, where the slopes are virtually vertical; fortunately there are ski lifts to get you up to the top.

The **Ben Macdhui Hiking Trail** (☎ 971 0446) is not too steep for the Drakensberg range, but parts of the route run over rough terrain; there's one overnight hut.

Rhodes Hotel (☎ 04542 ext 21) is a charming establishment that looks very much as it would have when it operated as the Horseshoe Hotel a century ago. Most rooms have fireplaces and are decorated with antique furnishings. Mountain-biking and horse-riding trips are also available.

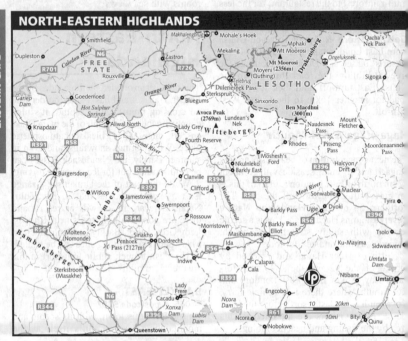

NORTH-EASTERN HIGHLANDS

Tiffindell Ski Resort (☎ 011-787 9090, 886 9443, e tiffindell@global.co.za, w www .snow.co.za) Private chalets DB&B R450-850 winter, R200-225 summer. The resort's winter package price includes ski-lift charges, equipment hire and emergency medical facilities. Summer activities include mountain biking, horse riding, grass skiing and rock climbing.

Walkerbouts Country Retreat (☎ 974 9290, fax 974 9306, e dave@lesoff.co.za, w www.junex.co.za/walkerbouts/) Singles R165-195. Walkerbouts is a spacious guesthouse overlooking Rhodes. Your host Dave is a wealth of information on the best fishing spots in the area.

ELLIOT
☎ 045 • postcode 5460

Nestled in a particularly scenic region south-east of Barkly East, Elliot is the centre of a very interesting area. The Xhosa name for the town is Ecowa, which refers to the mushrooms that grow here in summer.

Local attractions are the **Gatberg**, a peak that seems to have a hole bored through it; the lofty **Kransies**, from where you can sometimes see the sea some 80km away; and the **Baster Footpath**, a historic stock route.

On Denorbin farm, near Barkly Pass between Barkly East and Elliot, are some well-preserved examples of **San paintings**. At 82m in length, this is the longest 'gallery' of San rock paintings in South Africa.

Near Elliot are the **Ecowa Circular Hiking Trails**. For information, contact the **Elliot municipality** *(☎ 931 1011, fax 931 1361, Maclear Rd).*

Merino Hotel (☎ 931 1137, 21 Maclear Rd) Singles/doubles DB&B R156/276. The Merino, Elliot's only hotel, offers average rooms and prices.

Rose Garden (☎ 931 1158, 13 Dampier St) Bed only R90, B&B/DB&B R120/160 per person. The Rose Garden provides a more comfortable and homely alternative.

Mountain Shadows (☎ 931 2233, fax 931 1139, e jacquies@isat.co.za) Singles/doubles DB&B R220/350. The poorly signposted Mountain Shadows, 20km north of town on the R58, is a tranquil retreat.

LADY GREY
☎ 051 • postcode 9755

The countryside around Lady Grey, some 50km east of Aliwal North, is quite beautiful and has the Witteberge as an impressive backdrop. Founded in 1861, the town was named after the wife of a Cape governor, Sir George Grey. The 157km zigzag railway line that runs from Aliwal North to Barkly East passes through town.

The **Lady Grey Tourism Association** *(☎ 603 0176, fax 603 1114, e margot@eci .co.za, 24 David Ross St)* has plenty of information on the region.

Mountain View Country Inn (☎ 603 0421, fax 603 0114, 36 Botha St) Singles B&B/DB&B R180/210, doubles R300/399. This small country inn is the perfect place to bed down for the night; its Sportsman's Bar serves delicious pub lunches. The inn also offers a self-catering option (R60 per person) in either the town's original old goal or the old post office.

City to City buses leave Jo'burg travelling to Lady Grey (R80) on Monday, Wednesday and Friday at 8am; there is also a Friday service at 7pm.

MACLEAR
☎ 045 • postcode 5470

This is a trading town on the R396. Northwest of the town, just before Naudesnek (the highest pass in South Africa at 2620m), are some exposed fossilised dinosaur footprints believed to be 200 million years old. Rock shelters not far from the town have some well-preserved examples of San paintings. The streams around town are great for trout fishing. The **Maclear Publicity Association** *(☎ 932 1025, fax 932 1003)* provides information.

Royal Hotel (☎ 932 1176, fax 932 1003, Van Reibeeck St) Bed only/B&B R160/170. Not all rooms at the Royal Hotel have bathrooms.

ALIWAL NORTH
☎ 051 • postcode 5530

On the Orange River, the border between Eastern Cape and the Free State, is Aliwal North, popular for its mineral baths and hot springs. There's a big **spa complex** *(admission R10; open 7am-10pm Mon-Sun)* a few kilometres from the old town centre; contact the **North-East Cape Tourism Association** *(☎ 633 3567, fax 633 3569, ⓔ ectban@intekom.co.za, ⓦ www.ectourism.co.za)* for information.

At the southern end of town is a **Boer Concentration Camp Memorial** dedicated to the 700-plus Afrikaners including children, who died in the British-run camp.

Places to Stay & Eat

There are plenty of places to stay near the spa.

Aliwal North Spa Resort (☎ 633 2951, fax 633 3008, De Wet Dr) Camp sites R38 plus R11 per person. The resort has plenty of space to pitch your tent.

Thatcher's Spa (☎ 634 2189, fax 576 4261, 14 Dan Pienaar Ave) Doubles from R275. Thatcher's Spa is very conveniently located near the Spa Resort.

Riverside Lodge (☎ 633 3282, fax 633 3754) Singles/doubles B&B from R205/285. Located on the banks of the Orange River the lodge has spacious rooms, with heavy wooden furniture.

Pink Lady steakhouse at Thatcher's Spa is a popular spot with local diners. At the Riverside Lodge's *Pub & Grill* you can enjoy a beer while you watch the sun set over the river.

Getting There & Away

A daily City to City bus stops here on the Jo'burg-Idutywa (via Queenstown) run.

Translux, Greyhound and Intercape services stop at Nobby's Restaurant (on the N6 near the junction with the R58).

The nearest passenger train station is at Burgersdorp, 60km south-west on the Jo'burg–East London *(Amatola)* line.

The minibus taxi rank is on Grey St, near the corner of Somerset St.

QUEENSTOWN

☎ 045 • postcode 6320

This town was established in 1847 and laid out in the shape of a hexagon for defence purposes. This pattern enabled defenders to shoot down the streets from a central point. Fortunately, such defence of the town has never been necessary.

The **Queenstown Publicity Association** *(☎/fax 839 2265, Cathcart Rd)* office is in the Pick 'n' Pay complex.

There are some fine buildings in town including the 1882 town hall with its impressive clock tower, and the Old Market building in the Hexagon. Queens College well over 100 years old and one of the many fine schools in the town, produces good cricketers – Tony Greig and Daryl Cullinan studied here.

There is good fishing in nearby dams. The Bongolo Dam, about 5km from town on the Lady Frere road, is good for black bass and blue gill and the Xonxa Dam, in the Transkei, is best for eels and carp.

Places to Stay & Eat

Alisa Cottage (☎/fax 839 2761, 37 Haig St) Singles/doubles B&B R120/190. The best place to stay in town is the excellent Alisa Cottage. You'll undoubtedly feel at home in its comfy well-decorated rooms.

Hexagon Guest House (☎ 838 4036, fax 838 1428, 7 Longview Crescent and 3 Buxton St) Singles/doubles B&B R220/310. Both residences are in quiet streets and offer pleasant rooms.

There isn't a great choice of places to eat.

Buffalo Springs Spur (125 Cathcart Rd) Steak eaters will appreciate Buffalo Springs Spur.

Rock's Pub & Grill (☎ 083-693 2447, Cathcart Rd) Meals R20-30. This fun pub and grill is in the Pick 'n' Pay complex.

Getting There & Away

Queenstown is well served by City to City buses, with daily services to Jo'burg/Pretoria (R100). Another daily City to City bus run from Jo'burg to Idutywa via Queenstown (R90).

Intercape buses pass through on the daily Port Elizabeth to Jo'burg and East London to Jo'burg runs. Translux runs daily from Cape Town to East London via Queenstown, and from East London to Jo'burg and Pretoria.

Greyhound passes through Queenstown on the Jo'burg/Pretoria–Port Elizabeth run (Port Elizabeth R160, Jo'burg R205). All buses stop at the Shell Ultra City petrol station on Cathcart St. Greyhound buses also run from Queenstown to Aliwal North (R130).

From the minibus taxi rank (cnr Victoria & Komani Sts) you can travel to Cathcart (R10), Stutterheim (R15), King William's Town (R35) and East London (R72).

The Transkei

With its natural boundaries, the Great Kei River and the Drakensberg, the Transkei was a logical division of the country, unlike most of the Homelands. The northern pocket of Eastern Cape, along the Umzimkulu River, is surrounded by KwaZulu-Natal.

The Transkei's major attraction is its coastline, where you'll find superb warm-water surf beaches and lush subtropical veg-

Warning

Although many of the roads within the former Homeland of Transkei are of a reasonable standard, there is a real risk of children and livestock straying onto them. Exercise extra care when driving here.

etation. There is a good range of accommodation and there are some excellent hiking trails. Away from the coast, the hills are dotted with villages. If you plan to hike around inland Transkei, remember that traditional life continues in the rural areas. Always ask permission before camping but never approach a chief's house without an invitation.

Summers on the coast are hot and humid. Inland, summers can be hot but many areas have winter frosts. Most rain falls in March, and spring also sees heavy rains. Unsealed roads can be impassable after rain, especially in the coastal areas which have clay soil.

THE TRANSKEI

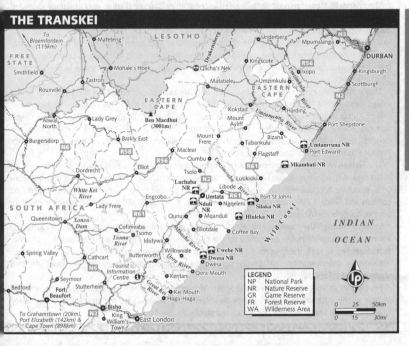

EASTERN CAPE

WESTERN & SOUTHERN TRANSKEI

The best-known part of the Transkei is the Wild Coast. However, there are many other interesting places. The south-west part of the Transkei is a fascinating region of rolling hills and picturesque Xhosa villages.

The numerous dams at the top of the Great Kei River, on the White Kei and Tsomo Rivers, attract anglers in search of eels and other fish. The villages in this region consist of scattered, brightly coloured houses pic-turesquely set in front of dramatic mountain backdrops. It's a magical place where the pace of life has changed little in centuries.

On the N2, just north of the Great Kei, is **Butterworth**, the oldest town in the region; it was established around a Wesleyan mission in 1827.

The town of **Idutywa** gets its name from a tributary of the Mbashe River. North-east of the town are the **Colleywobbles**, unusual rock formations studding the cliffs overlooking the Mbashe. It is extremely beautiful

The Nelson Mandela Museum

The new Nelson Mandela Museum (☎ 532 5110, e mandelamusem@intekom.co.za; open 9am-4pm Mon-Fri, 9am-12.30pm Sat), located in the heart of the Transkei, is a fitting dedication to the man who has been described as one of the world's greatest statesmen. Ten years to the day after his release from prison in February 1990, Nelson Mandela officially opened the museum that honours his lifelong fight for freedom.

The museum has three components: the Mandela Museum in Umtata; a cultural centre and a youth centre in the village of Qunu; and a memorial near the remains of his family homestead in Mveso.

The **Mandela Museum** in Umtata, housed in the former Bhunga (Parliament) building, is divided into three separate sections. In the first hall the numerous honours bestowed upon Mandela are displayed, including the Nobel Peace Prize he won jointly with FW De Klerk. From here you continue to a second hall that contains just some of the thousands of gifts given to the former president, ranging from school children's artwork to expensive presents from world leaders and celebrities. In the third hall is an impressive multimedia exhibition that encapsulates Mandela's role in the liberation of South Africa.

Thirty-one kilometres away, in Qunu you'll find the second component of the museum. At the village's entrance is the **Jonopo Traditional Village** (☎ 083-768 9904). This village combines an excellent Xhosa culture and craft centre, a restaurant and a market. The second feature of this development is the **Nelson Mandela Youth Heritage Centre**, a few hundred metres from the ex-president's **country residence**. Interestingly, Mandela modelled this residence on the Victor Verster Prison where he spent his last days in jail.

The **Nelson Mandela Monument**, the final component of the museum, is well off the beaten track in the unassuming small village of Mveso where he was born. The monument itself is a simple concrete structure adorned with photographs of Mandela. To get there, turn off the N2 between East London and Umtata (the turn-off is signposted) onto a dirt track and head southwards for half an hour or so down to Mveso.

Walking through the museum and retracing the ex-president's childhood steps through Qunu and Mveso it is impossible not to be moved by the plight of not only Mandela himself but that of a nation struggling to walk the long road to freedom. In the face of unimaginable hardships, it was their unrelenting determination that finally secured equality and democracy for all South Africans regardless of colour.

For his part in the reconciliation of the South African nation, Nelson Mandela will be remembered as one of the 20th century's greatest heroes. (For more information, see the boxed text 'Nelson Mandela' in the Facts about South Africa chapter.)

around here. South African president Thabo Mbeki comes from Willowvale, east of here.

An icon in this part of the country is the childhood home of Nelson Mandela. The first president of free South Africa was born in the village of **Mveso** on the Mbashe River but he spent most of his childhood at **Qunu**, 31km south of Umtata. A new **museum** that incorporates both these areas has been built to commemorate the man who became the symbol of freedom and reconciliation for the new South Africa (see the boxed text 'The Nelson Mandela Museum').

UMTATA
☎ 047 • postcode 5100

Umtata, the main town in the Transkei, was founded in 1871, when Europeans settled on the Umtata River at the request of the Thembu tribe to act as a buffer against Pondo raiders. Today, Umtata is a crowded town that some consider dangerous. Umtata bears little resemblance to the rural town it

was before the creation of Transkei, but unless you prefer neat kerbing to vitality, the change is for the better. It's a bustling place that is wonderfully free of racism.

Orientation & Information
Most of the hotels and services are within the grid of the small original town. There is an **Eastern Cape Tourism office** (☎ 531 5290/2, e ectbwc@icon.co.za, 64 Owen St) and there is also an **information caravan** at the Shell Ultra City petrol station, 4km from town.

Book the Wild Coast hiking trails and accommodation at the **Department of Nature Conservation** (☎ 531 2711). Excellent books available include *Birds of the Transkei* (R10) and *A Guide to the Coast & Nature Reserves of the Transkei* (R10).

The queues at the Standard and First National Banks are interminable; even so, do your banking here before heading to the Wild Coast.

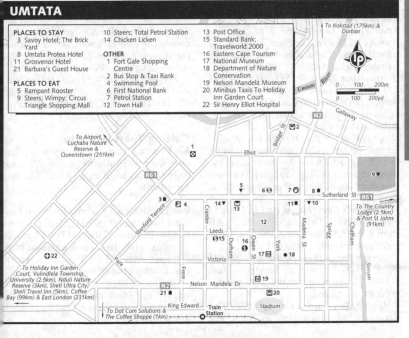

UMTATA

PLACES TO STAY
3 Savoy Hotel; The Brick Yard
8 Umtata Protea Hotel
11 Grosvenor Hotel
21 Barbara's Guest House

PLACES TO EAT
5 Rampant Rooster
9 Steers; Wimpy; Circus Triangle Shopping Mall

10 Steers; Total Petrol Station
14 Chicken Licken

OTHER
1 Fort Gale Shopping Centre
2 Bus Stop & Taxi Rank
4 Swimming Pool
6 First National Bank
7 Petrol Station
12 Town Hall

13 Post Office
15 Standard Bank; Travelworld 2000
16 Eastern Cape Tourism
17 National Museum
18 Department of Nature Conservation
19 Nelson Mandela Museum
20 Minibus Taxis To Holiday Inn Garden Court
22 Sir Henry Elliot Hospital

↑ To Kokstad (175km) & Durban

EASTERN CAPE

To Airport, Luchaba Nature Reserve & Queenstown (251km)

To The Country Lodge (2.5km) & Port St Johns (91km)

To Holiday Inn Garden Court, Vulindlela Township, University (2.5km), Nduli Nature Reserve (3km), Shell Ultra City; Shell Travel Inn (5km), Coffee Bay (99km) & East London (231km)

To Dot Com Solutions & The Coffee Shoppe (1km)

Train Station

Dot Com Solutions (☎ *532 2572, Southerwood Shopping Centre, Errol Spring Rd*) is a modern, well-organised Internet cafe; access costs R20 per half hour.

Travelworld 2000 (☎*/fax 531 2011, Leeds St*) advises about the chaotic state of transport in and out of Umtata.

Things to See

The highlight of the trip to Umtata is the new **Nelson Mandela Museum** dedicated to the former president (see the boxed text 'The Nelson Mandela Museum' for more details).

The **National Museum** (☎ *531 2427; admission by donation; open 8am-4.30pm Mon-Thurs, 8am-4pm Fri*), opposite the tourist office, displays traditional costumes and beadwork.

Nduli, in a valley 3km south of Umtata, and Luchaba, on the Umtata Dam and next to the water-sports area, are nature reserves with grassland and open water. There are zebra, wildebeest and antelope species as well as many wetland birds.

Places to Stay

Shell Travel Inn (☎ *537 0761*) Singles/doubles R229/299. The Shell Travel Inn is a fortified motel behind the Shell Ultra City. Its rates are laughable.

Grosvenor Hotel (☎ *531 2118, fax 531 2119, Cnr Sutherland & Madeira Sts*) Singles/doubles R100/120. The old Grosvenor Hotel exudes a colonial mustiness. Breakfast is available for R15.

Savoy Hotel (☎*/fax 531 0791, Cnr Stanford Terrace & Sutherland Sts*) Singles/doubles from R169/195. Out on the Queenstown bypass, the Savoy is a big airy hotel. The more luxurious rooms are in 'The Courtyard' at the rear.

Barbara's Guest House (☎ *531 1751, 55 Nelson Mandela Dr*) Singles/doubles B&B from R230/320. This guest house offers an oasis of calm amid Umtata's bustle.

Umtata Protea Hotel (☎ *531 0721, fax 531 0083, 36 Sutherland St*) Singles/doubles R340/420. The rooms at this well-guarded hotel are overpriced.

Holiday Inn Garden Court (☎ *537 0181, fax 537 0191*) Singles/doubles R369. The

Holiday Inn, south of town on the N2, has quality rooms. Breakfast is available for R46. A local minibus taxi departing from Nelson Mandela Dr stops at the Holiday Inn.

The Country Lodge (☎ *532 5730, fax 531 1683*) Singles/doubles R145/250. Just 2.5km out of town on the Port St Johns road, this lodge is a breath of fresh air. Breakfast is available for R30.

Places to Eat

Fast-food outlets are well represented in Umtata. Noisy, crowded **Wimpy** can be found in the Munitata building, on the corner of Sutherland and Owen Sts; at the new Circus Triangle shopping mall on the Port St Johns road; and by the Holiday Inn Garden Court.

For chicken fanciers, **Chicken Licken** and **Rampant Rooster** are found at the western end of Sutherland St.

There are also two **Steers**, one next to the Total petrol station opposite Grosvenor Hotel, and the other in the Circus Triangle.

The Coffee Shoppe (☎ *531 4972, Southerwood Shopping Centre, Errol Springs Rd*) Snacks R10-20. The Coffee Shoppe, next door to Dot Com Solutions, serves delicious creamy cappuccinos (R8) and a limited variety of light snacks.

The Brick Yard (☎ *531 0188, Cnr Stanford Terrace & Sutherland Sts*) Pizzas R22-42. The Brick Yard, adjoining the Savoy Hotel, is pure pizza heaven.

Getting There & Away

Air Umtata's Mantanzima airport is 17km from the city. **SA Airlink** (☎ *536 0024*) has daily services to Jo'burg (R1220/912 full Apex fare).

Bus Translux's daily service from Port Elizabeth to Durban stops in Umtata. Fares are R155 to Durban and R175 to Port Elizabeth. Translux also has an Umtata-Jo'burg-Pretoria service (R220). The daily service to East London costs R90.

Greyhound has a daily service from Durban to Cape Town and vice versa (Durban to Umtata is R150 and Umtata to Cape Town is R310.)

Intercape also runs a daily service to Durban (R145) and to Port Elizabeth (R150); from there it is another R150 to Cape Town.

The Grandliner (☎ 532 5138) is a private bus service running daily from Umtata to East London (R90). The bus departs from outside the Wimpy near the Holiday Inn.

The Baz Bus passes through Umtata on its Port Elizabeth–Durban run Monday, Tuesday, Wednesday, Friday and Saturday; it runs in the other direction Monday, Tuesday, Thursday, Friday and Sunday.

Translux, Greyhound and the Baz Bus stop at the Shell Ultra City, which is the pick-up point for backpackers heading to the coast. Coastal hostel owners literally beat each other up to get business.

Minibus Taxi Minibus taxis depart from the main bus stop and taxi rank near Bridge St. Destinations include Port St Johns (R20), Coffee Bay (R20), Butterworth (R25), Kokstad (R45) and East London (R60).

THE WILD COAST
The Transkei coast is notoriously dangerous for ships. Shipwrecked sailors were the first Europeans to visit this part of the world and few were rescued or managed to make the harrowing journey to Cape Town or Lourenço Marques (now Maputo, Mozambique). One party did struggle through to Cape Town to organise a rescue ship, but when it arrived most of the women had disappeared or were living with the Xhosa and didn't want to be rescued (see the boxed text 'Wild Coast Shipwrecks').

About 40,000 hectares of indigenous forest survives along the coast. While there is plenty of birdlife (and butterflies galore), the numbers of animals are dwindling.

Wild Coast Hiking Trail
Though there is a hiking trail running the length of the Transkei coast, only one section – from Port St Johns to Coffee Bay – maintains trail huts. From the Umtamvuna

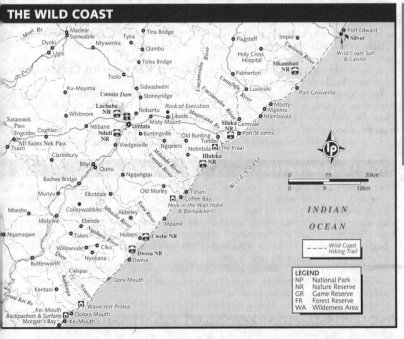

THE WILD COAST

EASTERN CAPE

Warning

Many rivers cut across the Wild Coast trail and crossing them presents the main difficulty for hikers. There are ferries at a few of the larger rivers, but some rivers require wading or swimming. It's important that you know what the tide is doing before you cross – about 30 minutes after low tide is the safest time. You'll need a plastic bag to protect your pack. Never try to cross a river while wearing your pack, and wear shoes as protection against stone fish or stingrays. It's usually easier to cross a little upstream from the mouth, where you're less likely to encounter the sharks that sometimes enter the estuaries.

River (the northern point) to Port St Johns and from Coffee Bay to Kei Mouth (the southern point) tents are required. Walking fees are currently only payable for the five-day Coffee Bay Trail running from Port St Johns to Coffee Bay (R45).

A walk along even just a part of the trail is an unforgettable experience – you'll see bottlenose dolphins frolicking out at sea, meet the locals who welcome you into their villages as you wait for ferries, and experience the hauntingly quiet starry nights. To walk the whole trail takes about two weeks; most people only do a section.

Three major sections of the trail are described in *Exploring Southern Africa on Foot: The Guide to Hiking Trails,* available from most bookshops in larger cities. These sections are Coffee Bay to Mbashe River

(44km, four days), Port St Johns to Coffee Bay (60km, five days) and Umtamvuna River to Port St Johns (100km, six to 11 days).

The walking isn't especially difficult, but some planning is required as you have to take all your own supplies. Water is available at trail huts or camp sites (about 12km apart) and from the streams and rivers, but it must be purified. (See Health in the Facts for the Visitor chapter for information about water purification.)

As well as trail huts between Coffee Bay and Port St Johns, there are 15 camping areas along the coast, where you can camp for up to 31 days. (Note that Mbotyi camping area has closed.) There are from eight to 40 sites available at these places. Most have basic facilities; sites cost R30. Although the sites are on the hiking trail, most can also be reached by car (you'll need a 4WD to get to some). The trail also passes near backpacker hostels, hotels and resorts scattered along the coast.

The trails must be booked at the **Department of Nature Conservation** (☎ 047-531 2711) in Umtata, and must be walked from north to south. Good maps of the trail sections are available from the department for R1.50 each.

Great Kei River to Coffee Bay
☎ 047

Port St Johns and Coffee Bay are the only towns on the Wild Coast but there are a number of hotels and resorts along the stretch from the Great Kei River to Coffee Bay; check with **Wild Coast Holiday Reservations**

Wild Coast Shipwrecks

Famous Wild Coast shipwrecks include the *São João* (St John), which was wrecked in a storm in June 1552. After a harrowing journey, only eight of the original 440 survivors (more than 100 people drowned) made it to Ilha de Moçambique (Mozambique Island) 1600km away. Two years later the *São Bento* was wrecked near the mouth of the Umtata River; one of the survivors had been on the *São João* and, faced with the prospect of another epic attempt to survive, died in despair. The *Santo Alberto* sank near the Hole in the Wall in 1593 while heading for Portugal, supposedly with a huge cargo of gold from the New World.

The Indiaman *Grosvenor*, which sank in August 1782 on the way home from India, is another reputed treasure ship. There's even a legend that Persia's Peacock Throne was on board. Only 18 survivors made it to the Dutch settlement at the Cape.

One of the most recent sinkings was the cruise liner *Oceanos* in 1991.

...uth Africa is blessed with idyllic beaches and surf as if sent from heaven.

...tsikamma National Park in Eastern Cape protects 100km of spectacular coast.

...ly morning at the magical Second Beach, Eastern Cape

Grahamstown, the heart of Eastern Cape's Settler Country

The City Hall, East London

Victorian style, East London

Big, bigger, biggest

The Transkei is a fascinating region of rolling hills and Xhosa villages

(☎ 043-743 6181) in East London. Most are family-oriented places charging from R150 to R200 per person, with prices rising dramatically around Christmas; prices include meals.

There are a few places north of the mouth of the Great Kei.

Seagulls Beach Hotel (☎/fax 498 0044) DB&B R195/300 per person low/high season. The hotel is reached by crossing the Kei on a punt (R30 for a car); there is a restaurant that features seafood braais, and a beach bar.

Trennery's Hotel (☎ 498 0044, fax 498 0011) DB&B from R200 per person. Trennery's is a 20-minute drive north of Seagulls. It has thatched bungalows, and on Saturday night the restaurant features a seafood extravaganza.

Wavecrest Protea (☎/fax 498 3273, e wavecrest@pixie.co.za, w www.wavecrest.co.za) This is near the mouth of the Nxaxo River. It's reached from Butterworth via Kentani; turn left at Kentani.

The following collection of places, at the mouth of the Qora River, is reached from the N2 by turning off at Idutywa and taking the road via Willowvale.

Mazeppa Bay Inn (☎ 490 0033, fax 498 0034, w www.wildcoast.co.za/mazeppa) DB&B from R220 per person. The comfortable Mazeppa Bay Inn is on the southern side of the river.

Kob Inn (☎/fax 499 0011, e koninn@ bigfoot.com) DB&B from R225 per person. Knob Inn is an hour's walk north of Mazeppa Bay. It can be reached by car from Idutywa via Willowvale. It is not unusual for this hotel to provide fresh oysters and mussels as bar snacks.

The Haven (☎ 576 0006, fax 576 0008) DB&B from R180 per person. The Haven is near Cwebe Nature Reserve, close to the mouth of the Mbashe River. Coming from the south, you can reach The Haven via Elliotdale (Xhora); turn off at the village of Qunu, 31km south of Umtata. It is about 70km from Qunu to the hotel and the road is unsealed from Elliotdale. If you're coming from the north, turn off at Viedgesville, 20km south of Umtata.

Dwesa & Cwebe Nature Reserves

These adjoining reserves take in about 6000 hectares of coastal land. Both have tracts of forest as well as good beaches, and there are hiking trails. The reserves are separated by the Mbashe River.

Dwesa Nature Reserve, one of the most beautiful reserves in South Africa, is bounded by the Mbashe River in the north and the Nqabara River in the south. In the estuaries of both rivers there are mangrove communities. Crocodiles have been reintroduced to the Kobole River, although they are rarely sighted. You may see the herd of eland come down to the beach near the Kobole estuary in the late afternoon.

For Dwesa, turn off the N2 at Idutywa (about 40km north of Butterworth) on the road to Willowvale (Gatyana). Continue until you come to a fork with another sign to Willowvale – take the other, unmarked direction. After heavy rain this is no place for 2WD cars.

In Cwebe Nature Reserve you can walk to the Mbanyana Falls or to the lagoon where, if you are lucky, you may see a Cape clawless otter in the late afternoon. On the southern edge of the reserve near the Mbashe is a small cluster of white mangroves where crabs and mudskippers are found near the stems.

To get to Cwebe, take the Elliotdale (Xhora) turn-off from the N2 (about 40km south-west of Umtata). The reserve is 65km further on; the road to The Haven hotel is signposted.

There is self-catering accommodation at Dwesa, and there are *camp sites* at Cwebe and Dwesa. Sites cost about R20 and *chalets* around R40 per person, although during peak times you might have to take the whole chalet for R160. Book sites at the **Nature Conservation office** (☎ 043-742 0340) in East London.

Coffee Bay

☎ 047

Coffee Bay is just a tiny hamlet, but it is growing in popularity with travellers. No one is sure of how it got its name, but there is a theory that a ship wrecked here in 1863 deposited its cargo of coffee beans on the beach. Its Xhosa name, Tshontini, refers to a dense wood nearby.

Three rivers flow into the sea near here: the Henga (Place of the Whale), Mapuzi (Place of Pumpkins) and the Bomvu (Red Clay). The scenery is dramatic, with cliffs behind and a kilometre-long beach in front. While you are here, the coastal walk to the **Hole in the Wall** is worth doing. The Hole in the Wall is a rock formation featuring an impressive natural hole that has been carved through the cliffs by the pounding of the ocean.

The rustic **golf course** has great views but with cliffs close by, your slice could be costly.

Places to Stay & Eat Competition is fierce for backpacker bucks in Coffee Bay.

Bomvu Backpackers (previously Wood-house Backpackers, ☎/fax 575 2029, e bom vu@intekom.co.za) Camping R25, dorm beds R45, doubles R90-120. Not only the name has changed at Bomvu Backpackers. The original manager has taken over the reigns again and has been busily renovating the hostel. Once complete, Bomvu will boast a yoga school, surf shop and an Internet cafe. For now it remains an attractive hostel with a large garden area in the front and a great bar/restaurant out the back. Breakfast is available for R15. Bomvu runs a shuttle service to Umtata (R35) and at Easter, it hosts a music festival by the river.

The Coffee Shack (☎ 575 2048, e coffee shack@wildcoast.com) Camping R25, dorm beds R50, doubles R120-150. The Coffee Shack, while lacking home comforts, is a genuine and unaffected mecca for fun-loving travellers. There is a good common room, kitchen and bar, and a well-used braai area outside. And there aren't too many places in the world where you'll get free surfing lessons from a bona fide surfing champion – hostel owner David Malherbe. The Coffee Shack is across from Bomvu.

Ocean View Hotel (☎ 575 2005, fax 575 9001) DB&B from R210 per person. Ocean View offers good bungalow-style accommodation. There is a restaurant in the hotel and seafood snacks are served in the bar.

Hole in the Wall (☎ 575 2002, e hole itwh@iafrica.com) DB&B from R200 per person. This hotel, south of Coffee Bay, has pleasant rooms and self-catering cottages. The landmark after which the hotel is named is a 2km walk away.

Hole in the Wall Backpackers (☎ 083-317 8786, fax 047-575 0010) Camping R30, dorm beds from R40, doubles R120. Within the Hole in the Wall hotel complex is a new backpackers place that's being raved about. Facilities include use of the hotel's swimming pool and volleyball court, and horse riding is available (R25 per hour).

You can buy mussels, crayfish and other *seafood* from locals and there's a well-stocked *grocery store*. The backpacker hostels organise visits to a local *Xhosa restaurant* where kids sing while you enjoy a hearty traditional three-course meal which is good value at R30.

Getting There & Away Take the sealed road that leaves the N2 at Viedgesville. When you reach Coffee Bay, continue past the derelict Lagoon Hotel, cross the river and you will come to the backpackers' enclave. A minibus taxi from Umtata to Coffee Bay costs R17 and takes one hour. People from the backpacker hostels meet the Baz Bus at the Shell Ultra City, 4km south of Umtata.

The signposted turn-off to the Hole in the Wall is about 30km before Coffee Bay. There is also a direct unsealed road from Coffee Bay to the landmark (about 8km).

Coffee Bay to Port St Johns

The Kraal (☎ 683 2384, fax 683 2098 thekraal@hotmail.com) Camping R35, dorm beds R50. The Kraal at Mpande Sinangwana is a fantastic, eco-friendly place halfway between Port St Johns and Coffee Bay (via the coastal walk). There is no electricity, no TV and no telephones, just peace – it truly is one of the most idyllic spots on the coast. Nearby villagers look upon it as an extension of their community and come to sell fish and vegetables; visitors are welcome to go with them to their shebeens. Plan to stay a few days, as there is much to absorb your attention.

From Umtata it is 70km to Tombo Stores, where you turn south (from Port St Johns it's 20km). It is a 30- to 40-minute drive on a rough road from the turn-off to Mpande. Dillon does daily pick-ups from Umtata – if you book to stay at The Kraal, make sure you show up for the lift as he will have driven some distance to collect you.

Hluleka Nature Reserve Midway between Coffee Bay and Port St Johns is Hluleka Nature Reserve, which combines sea, lagoons and forest. The coast is rocky, although there is a quiet lagoon flanked by a large salt marsh. As in Mkambati Nature Reserve, further north, there is a diverse range of flora.

Self-catering chalets (☎ 047-531 2711) cost around R40 per person.

To get to the reserve, take the road from Umtata to Port St Johns and turn off to the right at Libode, about 30km from Umtata. The reserve is about 90km further on. The road isn't good but cars can usually handle it.

Silaka Nature Reserve This small coastal reserve, 6.5km south of Port St Johns, runs from Second Beach to Sugarloaf Rock. Birdwatchers will be delighted by the species found in the forest next to the Gxwaleni River.

By the shoreline are many interesting tidal rock pools. Near the estuary, where the Gxwaleni flows into the sea, aloes grow down almost to the water. Clawless otters are often seen on the beach and whitebreasted cormorants *(Phalacrocorax carbo)* clamber up onto Bird Island. It's a magical place (see the boxed text 'Bird-Watching on the Wild Coast' later in this chapter for more information).

Accommodation in four-bed park *rondavels* (☎ 047-564 1177) is a good option at R200. The only drawback here is the isolation, although that will suit some.

Port St Johns
☎ 047 • postcode 5120

The deliciously traditional Port St Johns (also known as 'PSJ') is a magnet for hippies both young and old. This idyllic little town

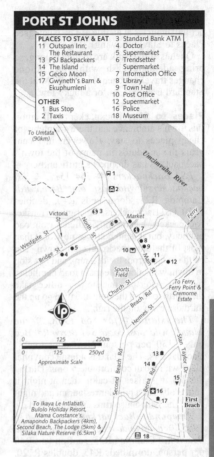

PORT ST JOHNS

PLACES TO STAY & EAT		3	Standard Bank ATM
11	Outspan Inn;	4	Doctor
	The Restaurant	5	Supermarket
13	PSJ Backpackers	6	Trendsetter
14	The Island		Supermarket
15	Gecko Moon	7	Information Office
17	Gwyneth's Barn &	8	Library
	Ekuphumleni	9	Town Hall
		10	Post Office
OTHER		12	Supermarket
1	Bus Stop	16	Police
2	Taxis	18	Museum

on the coast at the mouth of the Umzimvubu River has tropical vegetation, dramatic cliffs, great beaches, a relaxed atmosphere and no traffic lights. It is about as close as you'll come to the new rural South Africa, with a dominant black population in town.

The town is named after the *São João*, a ship wrecked here in 1552 (see the boxed text 'Wild Coast Shipwrecks' earlier in this chapter).

The **information office** (☎/fax 564 1206, e tourismpsj@wildcoast.co.za, w www .ruraltourism.org.za/portstjohns), currently on Main St, is planning to relocate to the entrance of the town. Internet access (R20 per half-hour) is available at The Island (see Places to Stay, following).

Queues at the bank are tediously long, so bring adequate cash with you; no-one changes travellers cheques. The ATM at the Standard Bank works for a lucky few.

Places to Stay Backpackers will enjoy this town's ambience and there are plenty of cheap places to stay. However, in recent years the standards in many of the town's backpackers have dropped significantly.

PSJ Backpackers (☎ 564 1517, e psj backpackers@wildcoast.com, Berea Rd) Camping R25, dorm beds R40, doubles R110. PSJ Backpackers, the original Transkei backpackers, has recently suffered from bad publicity, but it is no better or no worse than most of the other backpackers in town. You be the judge. From the taxi rank and bus stop in town, walk along the main road parallel to the river. After passing the post office, take the fourth road on the right and then go up the third driveway on the right.

The Island (☎/fax 564 1958, e the island@wildcoast.co.za, 341 Berea Rd) Bed only R130 per person. Next door to PSJ Backpackers, The Island is a large convivial place with clean comfortable rooms. During the day it is a sea of calm, then at night it comes alive as a popular restaurant and night spot. The Island also runs an Internet cafe.

Amapondo Backpackers (☎ 082-630 7905, e amapondo@hotmail.com, Second Beach Rd) Camping R25, rooftop tent R40 per person, dorm beds R45, doubles R120. Amapondo, at Second Beach, advertises itself as the 'home of Pondo fever' (ie, the reluctance of visitors to depart this lovely region!). With its long veranda, cheap meals and nightly fires, it has nearly all the ingredients to achieve that state.

Ikaya Le Intlabati (☎/fax 564 1266) Singles R60, doubles R100-140. Ikaya Le Intlabati (Xhosa for 'House on the Beach') is a tranquil place right on Second Beach's doorstep. Accommodation is offered in private rooms or in shared cottages. From PSJ take the road to Second Beach until it ends, then follow the signs.

Gwyneth's Barn & Ekuphumleni (☎/fax 564 1506) 2-bed to 4-bed cottage R250/300 low/high season. The best find on our trip to PSJ this time was Gwyneth's Barn & Ekuphumleni. Ekuphumleni (meaning 'Place to Rest') is an adorable group of wooden self-catering cottages set among indigenous bushland. A raised walkway connects the cottages to a shared braai area, kitchenette and a dreamy outdoor shower. Each cottage has scented candles and fluffy towels and the kitchenette is stocked with real wine glasses, a picnic basket and even a coffee plunger. Accommodation is also available in the main house, Gwyneth's Barn, on the adjoining property. To get there follow the signs from Main St.

Outspan Inn (☎ 564 1345, fax 564 1057, e outspan@wildcoast.co.za, Main St) Singles/doubles B&B R179/325, 4-bed self-catering unit R300. The Outspan Inn offers comfortable well-furnished rooms and has a restaurant that serves excellent a la carte meals (see Places to Eat, following).

Ferry Point (☎/fax 564 1197) Camping R30, dorm beds R60, 5-bed chalets R250. The roomy chalets at Ferry Point, on the north bank of the Umzimvubu River, are cheap and spacious but a little on the musty side – open the windows and let some fresh air in.

Cremorne Estate (☎ 564 113, e info@ cremorne.co.za, w www.cremorne.co.za) Doubles B&B R294, 4-bed units R460. Discerning travellers should head straight for the Cremorne Estate, also on the north bank of the river, which has clean and comfy rooms. There is a cosy pub and scenic bushwalks. Follow the signs from Pondoland Bridge.

Bulolo Holiday Resort (☎ 564 1245, fax 641 124, Second Beach Rd) Camp sites R30 plus R5 per person, 4-bed chalet R152/170 low/high season, 6-bed chalet R228/270. At Second Beach, this resort offers reasonably priced accommodation.

The Lodge (☎/fax 564 1171, Second Beach Rd) Singles/doubles B&B R180/240. The Lodge, also at Second Beach, is a simple place with tidy rooms superbly situated on the lagoon with views across to a dramatic surf beach. There can't be many places in the world with a better location.

Places to Eat Let's face it, you came to Port St Johns for the solitude, not the food.

The Island (☎ 564 1958, 341 Berea Rd) Mains R15-35. Open noon-midnight Thur-Mon, 6pm-midnight Wed. The Island, set at the top of a hill in a large house, is a laid-back restaurant and night spot. Its menu is small but varied, and vegetarians are well catered for.

The Restaurant (☎ 564 1057, Main St) Breakfast R15-25, mains R19-35. The Restaurant, at the Outspan Inn, serves good hearty breakfasts and scrumptious evening meals.

Gecko Moon (☎/fax 564 1221, Stan Taylor Dr) Mains R27-42. Gecko Moon's menu focuses mostly on tasty Italian-style pizzas and pasta.

Otherwise, do what the locals do – buy cheap mussels, crayfish and fish and cook your own meal.

Getting There & Away Most backpacker places in Port St Johns will pick you up from the Shell Ultra City 4km south of Umtata. If you organise a lift with a particular backpacker place, make sure you honour that arrangement as they drive a long way to pick you up. For bus services, see under Getting There & Away in the Umtata section earlier in this chapter.

If you decide to get a minibus taxi to Port St Johns, you will have to get off the bus in Umtata, not at the Shell Ultra City. There are regular taxis to Port St Johns (R20).

If you're driving from Durban, take the N2 to Port Shepstone, continue along the coast to Port Edward, and then take the R61 to Port St Johns. There is a good sealed road to

Bird-Watching on the Wild Coast

The Wild Coast is a great place to take *Newman's Birds of Southern Africa* and a pair of high-powered binoculars.

In **Mkambati Nature Reserve**, the strelitzias in the grasslands are a fertile watching ground for Gurney's sugarbird (*Promerops gurneyi*) and the lesser double-collared sunbird (*Nectarinia chalybea*). The forests are alive with birds: the trumpeter hornbill (*Bycanistes bucinator*), rameron pigeon (*Columba arquatrix*), forest weaver (*Ploceus bicolor*) and noisy Cape parrot (*Poicephalus robustus*) can all be spotted.

The lagoon at **Hluleka Nature Reserve** is a great spot to see the African jacana (*Actophilornis africanus*) tiptoeing across the waterlilies. Near the rivers of the reserve you'll see plenty of kingfishers: the pied (*Ceryle rudis*), pygmy (*Ispidina picta*), brown-hooded (*Halcyon albiventris*), half-collared (*Alcedo semitorquata*) and giant (*Ceryle maxima*) kingfishers all frequent these areas. The forests are full of robins such as the Cape (*Cossypha caffra*), starred (*Pogonocichla stellata*), chorister (*Cossypha dichroa*) and brown (*Erythropygia signata*).

In the forest clearings of **Cwebe Nature Reserve**, look for the black-headed oriole (*Oriolus larvatus*), the black saw-wing swallow (*Psalidoprocne holomelas*) and the crowned hornbill (*Tockus abboterminatus*). In the reeds by the lagoon, spectacled (*Ploceus ocularis*), thickbilled (*Amblyospiza albifrons*) and yellow (*Ploceus subaureus*) weavers build nests. Water dikkop (*Burhinus vermiculatus*) inhabit the white mangroves.

The many estuaries of **Dwesa Nature Reserve** are good places to look for the shy, furtive African finfoot (*Podica senegalensis*) and the rare white-backed night heron (*Gorsachius leuconotus*). By the sea there are African black oystercatchers (*Haematopus ostralegus*), at their northern limit, and the curious turnstone (*Arenaria interpres*). Occasionally, jackal buzzards (*Buteo rufofuscus*) can be seen soaring in the thermals above Kolobe Point. The forests are particularly rich in species such as Narina trogons (*Apaloderma narina*), green twinspots (*Mandingoa nitidula*) and Knysna woodpeckers (*Campethera notata*).

Lusikisiki and then 17km of dirt road; watch out for maniacal drivers on blind corners. The very scenic road (part of the R61) from Umtata to Port St Johns is sealed, and police speed traps enforce the low speed limit.

The ferry (R1.50) is the fastest way to get across the Umzimvubu River to Agate Terrace, even though there is a bridge 4km upstream.

Port St Johns to Umtamvuna River

The 8000-hectare **Mkambati Nature Reserve** *(admission R5)* includes the Msikaba and Mtentu River Gorges and features some great scenery. The reserve takes its name from the *mkambati*, or Pondo coconut palm *(Jubaeopsis caffra)*. This is the only place in the world where it is found. In the grassland you can see patches of the banana-like *Strelitzia nicolai*. Orchids abound in the rocky recesses of gorges; proteas, tree ferns and date palms are found on the river banks.

You can take canoes (R10 an hour) up the Msikaba River, which is navigable upstream for 2km. There are also walking trails. A shop sells basic food. *Self-catering chalets (☎ 047-531 2711)* are around R40 per person.

You get there from Flagstaff, which is 65km south of the N2. Take the turn-off to Holy Cross Hospital, just north of Flagstaff. There are also buses running from Port St Johns to Msikaba, on the southern edge of the reserve.

NORTHERN TRANSKEI

Sizable towns such as Qumbu, Mount Frere (Kwabhaca) and Mount Ayliff (Maxesibeni) are on the N2 between Umtata and Kokstad, in KwaZulu-Natal. Other large towns in the north are Bizana and Lusikisiki, both in the north-east and not far from the coast. North of the Kokstad corridor is the isolated tract of Eastern Cape, with Umzimkulu as it main centre.

The **Ntsikeni Nature Reserve** is in the piece of Eastern Cape cut off from the main body of the province by the Kokstad corridor. It's a wetlands reserve, with several species of crane and many other birds. Keen bird-watchers may see the rare wattled crane *(Grus carunculatus)*.

The **Umtamvuna Nature Reserve** is being developed as a twin to the one across the Umtamvuna Gorge in KwaZulu-Natal. Umtamvuna is rich in flora; the prehistoric looking Eastern Cape cycad *(Encephalartos altensteinii)* grows on the cliffs.

Amadiba Adventures *(☎ 031-791 0178, fax 305 6456, e cropeddy@iafrica.com)*, a local tourism community initiative, ha started six-day **horse trails** in the officially closed northern section of the Wild Coast Trail, between the Mzamba and Mtentu Rivers; accommodation is in camps a Kwanyana and Mtentu. Trails can be organised to continue further south but tent are necessary. The cost for everything i R250 per person per day, or R1500 for the six-day trail.

Wild Coast Sun Casino & Country Club (☎ 039-305 9111, fax 039-305 2778 Singles/doubles R728/844. This glitzy over the-top hotel is near the KwaZulu-Natal border and south of Port Edward. It's reached from the Kokstad region via Bizana on the R61. If coming from Durban, turn off the N2 at Port Shepstone and follow the R61 (there are numerous signs along the way).

Northern Cape

Northern Cape is by far the largest of South Africa's provinces, although it is the least populated. The mighty Orange River is a lifeline that runs through country that becomes desert-like on the fringes of the Kalahari in the north and in the Karoo in the south. The Orange River and its tributary, the Vaal River, combine to create the longest and largest river in South Africa but its flow can vary significantly depending on the rainfall on the highveld.

The Orange River flows west to form the border between South Africa and Namibia; this area of Northern Cape is spectacularly harsh country and includes the isolated and magnificent Richtersveld National Park. South of here is Namaqualand, famous for its extraordinary spring flowers. Northern Cape's coast is singularly bleak, with cold seas breaking onto a near-desert coast. To the south, the coast becomes more attractive and offers good surfing.

The indigenous population is varied, and includes the San, who can still be seen around the Kalahari (small numbers of San continue to lead semitraditional lifestyles in isolated parts of neighbouring Botswana); the Tswana; and some Khoikhoi groups.

Diamantveld & Upper Karoo

Kimberley, capital of Northern Cape, is the main centre of the *diamantveld* (diamond fields). The north-south N12, an alternative route between Johannesburg (Jo'burg) and Cape Town, passes through Kimberley and crosses the east-west N10 at Britstown in the Upper Karoo.

Kimberley is a captivating place and the surrounding area is rich in Anglo-Boer War history. The Upper Karoo has few assets; it's probably the least enticing part of the expansive Karoo (see also the Karoo sections in the Eastern Cape and Western Cape chapters).

- Admire Namaqualand in spring, when this otherwise remote, sparsely populated area has an astounding display of wildflowers.
- Spot a cheetah at Kgalagadi Transfrontier Park, a remote and pristine haven for wildlife, one of the greatest national parks in the country.
- Pub-crawl the many atmospheric old bars in the diamond town of Kimberley, also home of the mighty De Beers Consolidated Mines.
- Paraglide with raptors in the skies above Kuruman.
- Hike the barren trails in Richtersveld National Park, a stunning mountainous desert.
- Revel in the red and white sands and bleached grasses of the Kalahari, which form a semidesert area of epic grandeur teeming with wildlife.

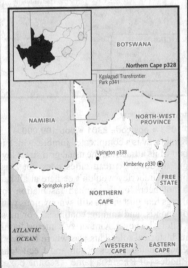

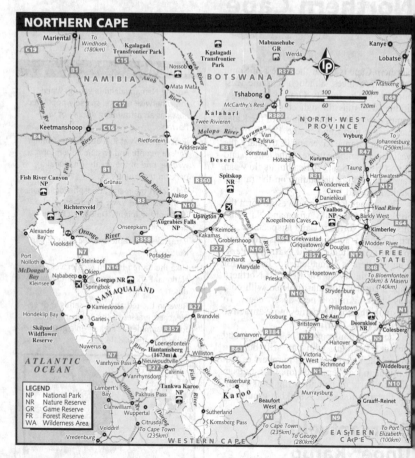

NORTHERN CAPE

KIMBERLEY
☎ 053 • postcode 8301 • pop 109,000

Kimberley is a complicated jumble, which is part of its attraction; the usual grid street layout of South African cities does not exist here. Kimberley wouldn't be here at all had it not been for the human fascination for things that glitter. It is still synonymous with diamonds, and mining continues. For most visitors, however, Kimberley's interest lies in its historical role: This was where De Beers Consolidated Mines began and Cecil John Rhodes (of Rhodesia fame – see the boxed text 'Cecil Rhodes' later in this section) and

Ernest Oppenheimer (mining magnate and mayor of Kimberley) made their fortunes.

After a trip across the Karoo the relatively bright lights of Kimberley are a welcome sight. The Big Hole is amazing, there are some excellent galleries in town, Galeshewe township is inextricably linked with the history of the struggle against apartheid, and the silence of the Karoo will be forgotten amid the din of Kimberley's many busy pubs.

History
Diamonds were discovered in the Kimberley region in 1869, and by 1872 there were

Cecil Rhodes

Cecil John Rhodes (1853–1906), the sickly son of an English parson, was sent to South Africa in 1870 to improve his health. By 1887 he had founded the De Beers Company and could afford to buy Barney Barnato's Kimberley Mine for UK£5 million. By 1891, De Beers owned 90% of the world's diamonds and Rhodes also had a stake in the fabulous reef of gold discovered on the Witwatersrand (near Jo'burg).

Rhodes was not satisfied with merely acquiring personal wealth and power. He believed in the concept of the empire and dreamed of 'painting the map red', and building a railway from the Cape to Cairo which would run through British territory all the way. The times were right for such dreams and Rhodes was a favourite of Queen Victoria as well as voters (both Boer and British) in the Cape. In 1890 he was elected prime minister of the Cape Colony.

Rhodes was successful in establishing British control in Bechuanaland (later Botswana) and the area that was to become Rhodesia (later Zimbabwe), but the gold mines there proved to be less productive than those on the Witwatersrand.

The Transvaal Republic in general, and Paul Kruger in particular, had been causing Rhodes difficulty for some time. It irked Rhodes that Kruger's republic of pastoralists should be sitting on the richest reef of gold in the world, and the republic was also directly in the path of British expansion.

The miners on the Witwatersrand were mainly non-Boers, who were denied any say in the politics of the republic. This caused increasing resentment, and in late 1895 Captain Leander Jameson led an expedition into the Witwatersrand with the intention of sparking an uprising among the foreigners.

The Jameson raid was a fiasco. All the participants were either killed or captured and Jameson was jailed. The British government was extremely embarrassed when it became apparent that Rhodes had prior knowledge of the raid and probably encouraged it. He was forced to resign as prime minister and the British government took control of Rhodesia and Bechuanaland, his personal fiefdoms.

Rhodes' health deteriorated after these disasters. His empire-building days were over but one more stock episode from the Victorian omnibus awaited: where an honourable chap becomes entangled in the schemes of a glamorous and ruthless woman. In Rhodes' case it was the 'Princess' Randziwill (she was later jailed for her swindles).

After his death in 1906, Rhodes' reputation was largely rehabilitated by his will, which devoted most of his fortune to the Rhodes Scholarship, which still sends winners from the Commonwealth and other countries to study at Oxford University.

an estimated 50,000 miners in the vicinity. It was thought that the diamonds lay at a depth of 15m to 18m, which allowed virtually anyone with a shovel to get at them. In 1871 diamonds were discovered at a small hill that came to be known as Colesberg Koppie (later Kimberley), and the excavation of the mine known as the Big Hole commenced. A number of problems faced the diggers, not the least of which was how to allow each miner access to their claims (which measured about 7m by 9m). These small claims were even further subdivided, and eventually there were 1600 claims and

over 30,000 men toiling in an area measuring roughly 200m by 300m.

The miners soon found that the diamonds continued as they dug further and further down. And as they did so, the difficulties of managing the mine, which was rapidly resembling an insane anthill, increased. The ever growing crater was soon crisscrossed by an elaborate spider web of ropes and pulleys, which were used to haul out the gravel. This kind of chaos couldn't continue indefinitely and to make things worse, diamond prices dropped because of overproduction.

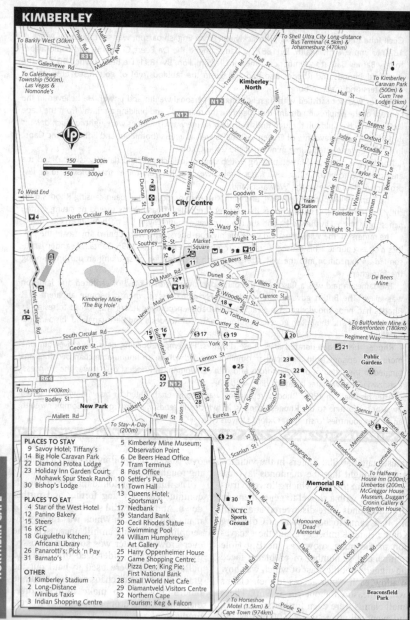

KIMBERLEY

PLACES TO STAY
9 Savoy Hotel; Tiffany's
14 Big Hole Caravan Park
22 Diamond Protea Lodge
23 Holiday Inn Garden Court;
   Mohawk Spur Steak Ranch
30 Bishop's Lodge

PLACES TO EAT
4 Star of the West Hotel
12 Panino Bakery
15 Steers
16 KFC
18 Gugulethu Kitchen;
   Africana Library
26 Panarotti's; Pick 'n Pay
31 Barnato's

OTHER
1 Kimberley Stadium
2 Long-Distance
   Minibus Taxis
3 Indian Shopping Centre

5 Kimberley Mine Museum;
   Observation Point
6 De Beers Head Office
7 Tram Terminus
8 Post Office
10 Settler's Pub
11 Town Hall
13 Queens Hotel;
   Sportsman's
17 Nedbank
19 Standard Bank
20 Cecil Rhodes Statue
21 Swimming Pool
24 William Humphreys
   Art Gallery
25 Harry Oppenheimer House
27 Game Shopping Centre;
   Pizza Den; King Pie;
   First National Bank
28 Small World Net Cafe
29 Diamantveld Visitors Centre
32 Northern Cape
   Tourism; Keg & Falcon

NORTHERN CAPE

In 1871 Cecil John Rhodes, the 19-year-old, tubercular son of an English parson, arrived at the diamond fields; by the mid-1870s he had gained control of the De Beers mine, and from this base he bought every claim and mine he could lay his hands on. A little over 20 years after the first discovery, virtually the entire diamond industry was owned by one company, which was in turn controlled by the powerful Rhodes, by then the richest man in Africa.

Orientation

The town centre is a tangle of streets, a legacy of the not-so-distant days when Kimberley was a rowdy shantytown, sprawling across flat and open veld. If you're trying to find the train station, look for the red-and-white communications tower. The tourist tram, which departs from the town hall, is a good means of getting your bearings.

The satellite township of Galeshewe is north-west of the city centre.

Information

The well-organised **Diamantveld Visitors Centre** (☎ 832 7298, e tourism@kbymun .org.za; open 8am-5pm Mon-Fri, 8am-noon Sat) is south of the city centre near the corner of Bultfontein and Lyndhurst Rds. It has brochures and good maps of Kimberley and Northern Cape.

There is a branch of **Northern Cape Tourism** (☎ 833 1434, 187 Du Toitspan Rd).

Small World Net Cafe (☎ 831 3484, 42 Sidney St) charges R30 per hour for Internet access.

Kimberley Mine Museum

On the western side of the Big Hole you'll find the excellent open-air museum (☎ 833 1557, West Circular Rd; adult/child R15/10; open 8am-6pm daily). Some 48 original or facsimile buildings are grouped together to form a reconstruction of Kimberley in the 1880s complete with streets, miners cottages, shops, auction rooms, a tavern and so on. De Beers Hall has a collection of diamonds and there are demonstration models of diamond-recovery technology. There is also a dramatic view over the Big Hole.

One of the old businesses still in operation is the skittle alley, which offers vastly trickier amusement than tenpin bowling. You get six balls for R5.

There's a cafe offering a full breakfast for R25 and burgers from R13.

The Big Hole

The Big Hole is the largest hole in the world dug entirely by manual labour. It is 800m deep and water now fills it to within 150m of the surface, which still leaves an impressive void. Don't forget, however, that there is over four times as much hole below the water's surface.

The Kimberley Mine, which took over after open-cast mining could no longer continue, went to a depth of around 1100m. It closed in 1914. Altogether, 14.5 million carats of diamonds are believed to have been removed from under Colesberg Koppie. In other words, 28 million tonnes of earth and rock were removed for just three tonnes of diamonds. For the best view of the Big Hole, you need to enter via the museum (and pay the museum's admission fee).

Anglo-Boer War Battlefields

At the beginning of the 1899–1902 war against the British, the Boers, after swift early victories, got bogged down in lengthy sieges at Ladysmith in Natal (now KwaZulu-Natal), Mafeking (now Mafikeng) in North-West Province and Kimberley in Northern Cape. The siege of Kimberley lasted for 124 days before the town was relieved by the British army of Lords Roberts and Kitchener on 15 February 1900.

The **Honoured Dead Memorial** to those who lost their lives in the siege is at the intersection of Memorial and Dalham Rds, 6km south of the city centre. The large gun is **Long Cecil**, built and used in Kimberley during the siege.

Several major battles were fought in the vicinity of Kimberley, both during the siege and after. The most important was Magersfontein on 11 Dec 1899, when the famous Highland Brigade was decimated by entrenched Boers. Other important battles include Graspan, Modder River, Paardeberg and Sunnyside. For tours of the **Magersfontein battlefield** *(admission R5)* contact ☎ 832 7298. All these battlefields are south and east of Kimberley. The Diamantveld Visitors Centre has details on the Diamond Fields N12 Battlefields Route.

Just off Egerton Rd you'll find **McGregor Museum** *(☎ 842 0099, Atlas St; admission R8; open 9am-5pm Mon-Sat, 2pm-5pm Sun)*, which has information about the 1899–1902 Anglo-Boer War; Rhodes sat out the siege in two downstairs rooms of this building.

Galleries

South-east of the city centre in the suburb of Belgravia is **Duggan Cronin Gallery** *(☎ 842 0099, Egerton Rd; admission by donation; open 10am-5pm Mon-Sat, 2pm-5pm Sun)*. This museum features a unique collection of photographs of black tribes taken in the 1920s and 1930s before many aspects of traditional tribal life were lost.

To experience one of the finest galleries in South Africa visit **William Humphreys Art Gallery** *(☎ 831 1724; admission R2; open 10am-5pm Mon-Sat, 2pm-5pm Sun)*. In addition to Dutch, Flemish, English and French works, it includes an excellent collection of contemporary works by black artists.

The **Africana Library** *(Du Toitspan Rd; admission free; open Mon-Fri)* covers the first period of contact between the Tswana and the missionaries. Included in the collection is missionary Robert Moffat's copy of his translation of the Old Testament into Tswana.

Galeshewe

The satellite township of Galeshewe rates with Soweto as an important source of activists in the struggle against apartheid. Galeshewe is home to the house and grave of Sol Plaatje, a founding member of the African National Congress (ANC), noted journalist and first black South African to have a novel published in English. It's also the home of Robert Sobukwe, founder and first president of the then Pan African Congress (PAC). Galeshewe was where the Self Help Scheme was implemented by Helen Joseph, former secretary of the Federation of South African Women and an organiser of the 1956 mass demonstration in Pretoria against the extension of passes.

It is possible to do a tour of Galeshewe (see Organised Tours, following) and this may well be one of the highlights of your stay in South Africa. Unlike Soweto, tours of this township are not common. You can tailor an itinerary to suit your interests and some of the notable things to see are places associated with Robert Sobukwe and Sol Plaatje. However, it is the opportunity to see how the majority of South Africans live, and how the ANC's commitment to provide housing for people living in abject poverty is progressing, that makes a tour so absorbing. Much new housing has been provided, but the reality is that there are too many people and too little money.

The spirit of the people in Galeshewe is undeniable and you'll be met with a smile and a handshake from adults and laughter and waving from kids. Make an effort to visit a primary school, where you'll see kids booting around a football, or trying to play cricket in the dust; the lack of facilities makes it a far cry from the cities and towns. Montshiwa Primary School is a good place to start; the principal is very knowledgeable about the area.

Organised Tours

The Diamantveld Visitor's Centre has a list of registered tour guides in Kimberley.

De Beers Tours (☎ 842 1321) Tours R10. 9am & 11am Mon-Fri. Groups visit the diamond treatment and recovery plants at Bultfontein Mine east of the centre on the city's outskirts. Tours depart from the visitors centre at the mine gate.

Underground Tours (☎ 842 1321) Tours R70. 9.30am Mon, 8am Tues-Fri. You can't wear contact lenses because of the pressure at the depths you'll descend to and you have to be over 16 to go on one of these 3½-hour tours.

Fikile (Michael) Bili (☎ 083-692 6058, 083-279 3399) is a Satour-registered guide operating tours into Galeshewe. He is very familiar with the history of the area, and the horrors of the apartheid era are brought to life with his vivid descriptions. He is also passionate about improving conditions in the township. These tours are highly recommended, cost R150 per person, and run for about three hours. You need to contact Fikile directly as the tourist office know more about the Anglo-Boer Battlefields than the nearby township. There will be a guesthouse opening in the township in the near future and it's worth asking Fikile about this if you're interested.

Places to Stay – Budget

Big Hole Caravan Park (☎ 830 6322, West Circular Rd) Camp sites R20 plus R10 per person. This is an attractive park with good grassed areas for camping and a few trees. There is also a pool. The mine museum and Big Hole are a short walk away.

Kimberley Caravan Park (☎ 082-442 5097, Hull St) Camp sites R15 plus R6 per person. Kimberley Caravan Park is 2.5km east of town. It's shadier, friendly and secure; braai (barbecue) use costs R10.

Stay-A-Day (☎ 832 7239, 72 Lawson St) Dorm beds R35, doubles without/with bathroom R110/130, 2-person self-contained flat R160 plus R25 for an extra person. South of the city, this is without a doubt the best value, central budget accommodation in Kimberley. Rooms are immaculate and come with TV and tea- and coffee-making facilities. Formerly an orphanage, the proceeds go towards the existing children's home near the property.

Gum Tree Lodge (☎ 832 8577, fax 831 5409, Cnr Hull St & Bloemfontein Rd) Singles/twins R70/120. Once a jail, the lodge is now a large and pleasant place to stay, with shady lawns and a pool. Accommodation is in fairly basic flats with a stove and fridge. It's about 3km east of the town centre.

Places to Stay – Mid-Range & Top End

The Diamantveld visitors centre has details of B&Bs, which all charge from about R100 per person.

Edgerton House (☎ 831 1150, 5 Edgerton Rd) Rooms from R275 per person.

Edgerton is a charming guesthouse that is on the expensive side, but is recommended. It has the honour of having had Nelson Mandela stay on more than one occasion in the 'presidential' suite (R520 per person).

Halfway House Inn (☎ 831 6324, 229 Du Toitspan Rd) Singles/doubles B&B R120/160. There's a drive-in bar here, which is probably not a particularly big selling point if you're staying. It's a pleasant old-style pub, however, with a friendly atmosphere. Rhodes, afraid to dismount from his horse and reveal his true height, invented the concept of the ride-in bar.

Bishop's Lodge (☎ 831 7876, fax 831 7479, ⓔ bishops@global.co.za, Bishop St) Twin room R199, 2-person self-contained flat R290. Bishop's is new, modern and spotless inside. The flats have TV and air-con, and there is secure parking.

Horseshoe Motel (☎ 832 5267, fax 831 1142, Memorial Rd) Singles/doubles B&B R175/240. Rooms at the Horseshoe have TV, air-con, bathroom and phone; it's a pity the motel is a bit of a way south of the centre. There's also a swimming pool.

Holiday Inn Garden Court (☎ 833 1751, fax 832 1814, 120 Du Toitspan Rd) has weekend specials from R329. This large hotel delivers high standards at a reasonable price and is an option for a splurge. Children stay free.

Diamond Protea Lodge (☎ 831 1281, fax 831 1284, ⓔ dplkim@global.co.za, 124 Du Toitspan Rd) Singles/doubles R325/350 Mon-Fri, R250/270 Sat & Sun. This Protea has larger then usual rooms and is in hot competition with the Holiday Inn next door.

Savoy Hotel (☎ 832 6211, 15 Old De Beers Rd) Singles/doubles R219/279 Mon-Fri, R159/209 Sat & Sun. This gracious and old-fashioned hotel is excellent value.

Places to Eat

Fast-food places include **Nando's** (Jones St); **Panarotti's** in the Pick 'n' Pay Centre; **Steers** and **KFC** (Cnr George/York St & Bultfontein Rd); and **Pizza Den** and **King Pie** in the Game Shopping Centre. For top-notch bakery treats, try **Panino Bakery** (Cnr Jones St & Old Main Rd).

NORTHERN CAPE

For traditional African food, seek out *Las Vegas* (☎ 871 1690, 953 Ottoskpje St) and *Nomonde's* (☎ 871 1243) in Galeshewe.

Gugulethu Kitchen (☎ 831 5856) Meals R12.50. This is a good eatery in town for cheap African food, including traditional dishes such as *drero*, a thick stew.

Umbertos (☎ 832 5741, 229 Du Toitspan Rd) Starters R18-27, pizzas R30-40, seafood R40-70. Open until late. Next to Halfway House Inn, Umbertos is a relaxed place with superb Italian food. They serve snacks, pasta and more substantial meals. The seafood platter (R70) is excellent. Occasionally, Umberto himself gets up and gives an impromptu opera solo.

Star of the West Hotel (☎ 832 6463, North Circular Rd) Starters R15-17, mains under R30. This place is old and atmospheric, it was reputedly built from timber salvaged off a wrecked yacht on the west coast. You can get here on the tourist tram. A ploughman's platter is R29.

Tiffany's (☎ 832 6211, Old De Beers Rd) Starters R10-20, mains R30-45. In the Savoy Hotel, Tiffany's is a lovely old-style restaurant with good service. The calamari and chicken curry in cashew-nut sauce (R28) is excellent. There is an old leather and wood bar adjoining Tiffany's, which is good for a quiet drink before dinner.

Barnato's (☎ 833 4110, 6 Dalham Rd) Mains R45-80. Open lunch & dinner Mon-Fri, dinner only Sat, lunch only Sun. This is one of the poshest places in this rough-and-tumble town; the food is excellent and the place is deservedly popular.

Keg & Falcon (☎ 833 2075, 187 Du Toitspan Rd) Starters R10-20, mains R25-45. The Keg serves traditional pub fare a notch higher in quality than most of the other 'chain' pubs in the country. The gourmet sandwiches are good.

Entertainment

Kimberley is one of the few towns in the country with a range of decent pubs, some of which have been pubs from the times that diamonds were the lifeblood of the town.

Halfway House Inn (☎ 831 6324, 229 Du Toitspan Rd), also known as The Half, has live music on Friday and Saturday nights in the pleasant rooftop beer garden.

Settler's Pub (Old De Beers Rd) is next to the Savoy Hotel and is dingy but is a good spot to shoot some stick.

Queens Hotel (☎ 831 3704, 12 Stockdale St) is a large pub in the centre of town that gets busy on weekends and has gambling.

Sportsman's (☎ 831 3704) is within the Queens Hotel, and has a techno-pop vibe, not a bad place to console yourself after blowing all your rands on the tables next door.

Star of the West Hotel (☎ 832 6463, North Circular Rd) often has live bands in the big beer garden. There are pool tables and a cocktail bar upstairs.

Keg & Falcon (☎ 833 2075, 187 Du Toitspan Rd) is entertainment for the older crowd – you have to be over 23 to get in and the dress code is smart casual.

Getting There & Away

Air SA Express has regular direct services from Jo'burg (R913 seven-day advance purchase). **SA Airlink** (☎ 838 3337) has a direct service to Cape Town (R1210).

Bus Translux stops in Kimberley daily on the run between Jo'burg/Pretoria (R168, seven hours from Kimberley) and Cape Town (R300, 10 hours from Kimberley).

Intercape also stops in Kimberley on Monday, Tuesday, Thursday and Saturday on the way to Jo'burg/Pretoria and on Wednesday, Friday and Sunday on the way to Cape Town.

Many services make the seven-hour trip to/from Jo'burg. The cheapest is Greyhound's daily service (R130). Buses can be booked at **Tickets for Africa** (☎ 832 6043) at the Diamantveld Visitors Centre. Greyhound, Intercape and Translux stop at the Shell Ultra City long-distance bus terminal on the N12.

Train For information on trains call Spoornet (☎ 838 2111, W www.spoornet.co.za). The *Trans Karoo* runs daily between Cape Town and Jo'burg/Pretoria via Kimberley; the *Diamond Express* runs overnight between Jo'burg/Pretoria and Bloemfontein via Kimberley; and the *Trans Oranje* between Cape Town and Durban (one service weekly in each direction) takes a slow and circuitous route via Kimberley.

Minibus Taxi The main minibus taxi area is around the Indian shopping centre on Duncan St in the city centre (where there's a produce market and takeaways). You'll find long-distance taxis here, a short walk from the regular taxis, near Crossley St.

Destinations and fares from Kimberley include Bloemfontein (R42), Kuruman (R70), Jo'burg (R85), Upington (R80) and Cape Town (R130).

Getting Around

Kimberley has one surviving antique tram that runs between the town hall and the mine museum. On weekdays it departs from the terminus near the town hall at 15 minutes past the hour. A one-way/return trip is R4/8.

A minibus taxi around town costs about R1.30. For a private taxi from the pubs, try **AA Taxi** (*☎ 861 4015*) or **Rikki's Taxi** (*☎ 083-342 2533*).

VAALBOS NATIONAL PARK

This national park (*☎ 053-561 0088*), 61km north-west of Kimberley on the R31 and proclaimed in 1986, is divided into two by a belt of private land. It is the only park in the country where three distinct ecosystems are present: Karoo, *grassveld* (grasslands) and Kalahari. Unfortunately, Vaalbos looks as though it will be the first South African national park to be de-proclaimed (in favour of diamond mining leases). Local groups, having learnt of the threat, are protesting. As this book went to press, the future of the park was still uncertain.

DE AAR

☎ 053 • postcode 7000

De Aar is a major service centre for the Karoo but its claim to fame is as a railway junction – it's one of the busiest in South Africa. De Aar is too big to be called a one-horse town – maybe it's a two-horse town. The author Olive Schreiner (who wrote *Women and Labour*) lived here from 1907 to 1913. There is so little to see or do here that an overnight stay can be unnerving.

Van Der Merwe Municipal Caravan Park (*☎ 631 0927, Cilliers St*) Camp sites R35. It's a minuscule park, but doesn't get crowded very often anyway.

De Aar Hotel (*☎ 631 2181, Friedlander St*) Singles/doubles R100/170. Rooms here have air-con, but the place has a depressing atmosphere.

As well as the reasonable *dining room* at De Aar Hotel, there's a *restaurant (Cnr Grundlingh & Vanzyl Sts)* in historic Olive Schreiner House.

Trains that pass through here are the *Trans Karoo* and the *Blue Train* (Jo'burg/Pretoria –Cape Town), and the *Trans Oranje* (Durban–Bloemfontein–Kimberley–Cape Town).

BRITSTOWN

☎ 053 • postcode 8782

Britstown in the Upper Karoo is at the crossroads of the N10 and the N12. It's the centre of a prosperous sheep-grazing area and is a pleasant enough little town.

Transkaroo Country Lodge (*☎ 672 0027, fax 672 0363*) Singles from R145, doubles R120-230. This long-established guesthouse runs activities such as bird-watching trips, and excursions to San rock art sites.

COLESBERG

☎ 051 • postcode 9795

As well as being a major stopover on the N1 between Cape Town and Bloemfontein, Colesberg is an attractive place. A classic Karoo town, it was founded in 1829 and many old buildings have survived, including a beautiful Dutch Reformed church (1866). There are also shops with verandas that front onto the main street, and attractive old houses and cottages on the side streets.

Colesberg's friendly **information centre** (*☎ 753 0678*, **e** *belinda@mjvn.co.za, Murray St; open 8am-4.30pm Mon-Fri*) is in the museum.

Places to Stay & Eat

Most of the places to stay are found along Kerk St.

Colesberg Backpackers (*☎ 753 0582, 39 Kerk St*) Camping R25, dorm beds/doubles

R40/100. This is a good stopover if you're making the long journey by car between Cape Town and Jo'burg.

Sunset Chalets (☎ 082-493 8814, 14 Torenberg St) Self-contained chalets R70 per person. Conveniently situated on the right when you first come into town from the N1, Sunset has strictly nonsmoking chalets that have everything except a TV.

The Light House (☎ 753 0043, 40A Kerk St) Singles/doubles R110/190. A comfortable and homely guesthouse, it's sparkling clean and the best place to stay in town.

Colesberg Lodge (☎ 753 0734, fax 753 0667, Church St) Standard/with bathroom/ luxury rooms R168/186/265. This place is central, good value and has a pool, bar and restaurant. The luxury rooms have TV and air-con.

The information centre lists many other places, which range from ordinary B&Bs to the restored **Karoo Tuishuis** (☎ 753 0582), once the town cottages of wealthy Karoo farmers.

Bordeaux Coffee Shop & Restaurant (☎ 753 1582, 7A Church St) Lunches R15-22. The shady garden here makes it a pleasant spot for lunch or coffee.

Getting There & Away

Translux and Intercape both pass through Colesberg on their Jo'burg to Cape Town run and stop at the Shell Ultra to the north of town on the N1. There are daily Intercape services to Bloemfontein (R90) and Cape Town (R280).

AROUND COLESBERG

North of Colesberg and just off the R369 you'll find **Doornkloof Nature Reserve** (☎ 753 1315, e janniedoornkr@hotmail .com; adult/child R5/3; open 8am-6pm daily). Both here and on the shores of Vanderkloof Dam, it's possible to see mountain reedbucks, duikers, kudus and steenboks (and if you're very lucky: aardvarks, aardwolfs and bat-eared foxes).

There is an overnight *hut* which costs R88 for up to four people, but you'll need your own bedding, food and cooking utensils. Very basic *camp sites* are R35 per night.

The Kalahari

The magnificent Kalahari has two distinct parts – the arid, semidesert and desert regions on its periphery and the 'green' Kalahari, the irrigated, fertile region along the banks of the Orange River.

Most visitors to South Africa miss the Kalahari. However, if you allow a few extra days for the drive from Jo'burg to Cape Town, you can see Augrabies Falls, the shifting red and white Kalahari sands, frontier towns with evocative names, unforgettable sunsets and large expanses punctuated by prehistoric vegetation. A visit to the remote Kgalagadi Transfrontier Park entails a substantial commitment of time and energy but you'll be well rewarded.

KURUMAN
☎ 053 • postcode 8460

This town feels as if it sits at the edge of wild and interesting country – as indeed it does. Kuruman derives from a San word but the area was also settled by the Batlhaping, a Batswana tribe, around the time the first whites appeared in the area (around 1800).

West of Kuruman there's a long, empty stretch of road to Upington, and a landscape of low, sandy ranges.

The main through-road is simply called Main Rd; most businesses are concentrated around the intersection of this and Voortrekker/Tsening Sts. Adjacent to the Eye of Kuruman is a useful **tourist office** (☎ 712 1095; Main Rd; open 8am-4.30pm Mon-Fri, 8am-12.30pm Sat).

Things to See & Do

The **Raptor Rehabilitation Centre** (☎ 712 0620, Tsening Rd; open 8am-4.30pm Mon-Fri) provides a map of the best routes to follow in search of birds of prey. The skies now have to be shared with a recent influx of human soarers. Kuruman has become world renowned as a **paragliding** centre, with several height and distance records being achieved here. For more information contact ☎ 712 1471.

The **Eye of Kuruman** (Main Rd; adult/ child R1/0.50) is an amazing natural spring that produces 18 to 20 million litres of water per day, every day. It has never faltered. The surrounding area has been developed into a pleasant enough picnic spot, and is a good place to break your journey – note the masked weaverbirds and their nests over the pond.

Places to Stay & Eat

Kuruman Caravan Park (☎ *712 1479, Voortrekker St)* Camp sites R50, double/triple chalets R165/200. A pleasant spot to break your journey, the chalets are well-equipped and comfortable. There are some shady camp sites and it's all a short walk from the centre of town.

Riverfield Guesthouse (☎ *712 0003, 12 Seodin Rd)* Singles/doubles B&B R180/280. Riverfield is run by the ebullient Alfie. The bar here is a great meeting place, the rooms are good value (especially the cosy rondavel) and the breakfast is mighty.

Eldorado Motel (☎ *712 2191, Main St)* Singles/doubles B&B R210/325, double suites from R396. This place is probably the best of the town's hotels/motels, if you like your facilities modern. It's cheaper on weekends.

De Oude Drostdy (☎ *712 0620)* Snacks from R7. Next to the Eye, this is a good choice for coffee and a snack.

Over-de-Voor (☎ *712 3224, Hoof St)* Meals from R20. Over-de-Voor, which serves 'Kalahari cuisine', is the town's best place – it serves meat plus meat.

Tavern Bar (☎ *712 1148)*, a bar in the Grand Hotel, is a fiercely conservative Afrikaner bastion. The ennui here can be cut with a knife – though it does have a *boerewors* (spicy sausage) collection as a centrepiece!

Getting There & Away

Kuruman is a stop on Intercape's Jo'burg-Upington service – for more details, see Getting There & Away under Upington later in this chapter. From Kuruman it costs R100 to Upington and R160 to Jo'burg.

The taxi rank is next to the Shop Rite supermarket on Voortrekker St (if coming from Jo'burg, turn right at the traffic lights).

Very few taxis run west from Kuruman. Destinations include Vryburg (R30), Kimberley (R55) and Mafikeng (R85).

AROUND KURUMAN
Moffat Mission

This mission (☎ *053-732 1352; adult/child R5/2; open 8am-5pm Mon-Sat, 3pm-5pm Sun)* was the first white settlement in the area. It was established by the London Missionary Society in 1816 to work with the local Batlhaping people. The mission site, 4km from the Eye of Kuruman on the road to Hotazel, was chosen at a cultivable part of the valley.

It was named after Robert and Mary Moffat, two Scots who worked at the mission from 1817 to 1870. They converted the Batswana to Christianity, started a school and translated the Bible into Tswana. The mission became a famous staging point for explorers and missionaries heading further into Africa. The Moffats' daughter, Mary, married David Livingstone in the mission church, which is a stone and thatch building with 800 seats.

The mission is a quiet and atmospheric spot, with stone and thatch buildings shaded by large trees; a perfect escape from the desert heat. Self-catering *accommodation* is available.

The mission is along the R31 to Hotazel, about 4km from the N14.

HOTAZEL TO VAN ZYLSRUS
☎ 053 • postcode 8490/8467

The most interesting thing about Hotazel is its name. Say it quickly: 'hot as hell'.

Van Zylsrus is a dusty little frontier town, one of the most isolated in South Africa. There's a stop sign, a petrol station, post office and pub – all the necessities of life!

About halfway between Hotazel and Van Zylsrus near Sonstraal is *Tswalu Private Desert Reserve* (☎ *781 9211, fax 781 9316)* which has singles/doubles for R4650/6200 full board. South Africa's largest private game reserve is something special, offering the chance to spot rare animals such as black rhino, sable and roan in a stunningly beautiful landscape. The staff are very experienced

NORTHERN CAPE

and it's possible to tailor a safari to your own interests. As you'd expect for the price, accommodation and rations are top notch.

UPINGTON
☎ 054 • postcode 8801

Upington is on the banks of the Orange River and is the principal commercial town in the far north. It's an orderly, prosperous place that is full of supermarkets and chain stores. It is generally very friendly, although street kids can be a nuisance.

The surrounding area is intensively cultivated thanks to the limitless sunlight and irrigation water. Cotton, wheat, grapes and fruit are all produced. It's a good place to stock up on supplies for a visit to Kgalagadi Transfrontier Park.

Information
The helpful **tourist office** (☎ *332 6046,* **e** *greenkal@mweb.co.za*) is in the Kalahari Oranje Museum.

The **First National Bank** is on the northwestern corner of Schröder and Hill Sts; the **Standard Bank** is on the corner of Hill and Scott Sts.

To traverse the distance home in seconds you can get wired at the **Internet cafe** in the Pool & Games Hall at the Pick 'n Pay Centre (R20 per hour).

Organised Tours
To see another side of Upington, have a great night out and perhaps gain some insight into the plight of the local black population, do a *Township Tavern Tour* (☎ *332 6064*). Tours depart from the tourist office on Monday, Wednesday and Thursday evenings (R85 per person). You can visit local taverns, have some traditional African food and indulge in a chinwag with the locals.

Places to Stay
Spitskop Nature Reserve (see Around Upington later in this chapter) is a good alternative accommodation option, which is close to town.

Eiland Holiday Resort (☎/*fax 334 0286*) Camp sites R40, single/double rondavels R100/144, 4-bed huts from R195, 3-bed units from R195. There's a range of huts and bungalows here, all varying in price depending on their age and facilities. The resort is a fair walk from town, on the eastern bank of the Orange River.

Yebo Guesthouse & Backpackers (☎ *331 2496, fax 332 1336, 21 Morant St*) Dorm beds R50, singles/doubles R85/170. Yebo is just north of the sports stadium. It's a pleasant stopover with a swimming pool, kitchen and tidy rooms.

River City Inn (☎ *331 1971, Cnr Park & Scott Sts*) Doubles R186. We get many readers' letters praising this inn. It's great value

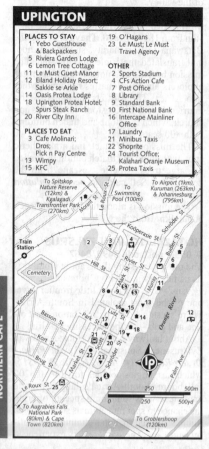

UPINGTON

PLACES TO STAY
1 Yebo Guesthouse & Backpackers
5 Riviera Garden Lodge
6 Lemon Tree Cottage
11 Le Must Guest Manor
12 Eiland Holiday Resort; Sakkie se Arkie
14 Oasis Protea Lodge
18 Upington Protea Hotel; Spurs Steak Ranch
20 River City Inn

PLACES TO EAT
3 Cafe Molinari; Dros; Pick n Pay Centre
13 Wimpy
15 KFC

19 O'Hagans
23 Le Must; Le Must Travel Agency

OTHER
2 Sports Stadium
4 CFs Action Cafe
7 Post Office
8 Library
9 Standard Bank
10 First National Bank
16 Intercape Mainliner Office
17 Laundry
21 Minibus Taxis
22 Shoprite
24 Tourist Office; Kalahari Oranje Museum
25 Protea Taxis

To Spitskop Nature Reserve (12km) & Kgalagadi Transfrontier Park (270km)

To Swimming Pool (100m)

To Airport (1km), Kuruman (263km) & Johannesburg (795km)

Train Station

Cemetery

Koöperasie St
Schröder St
Rivier St
Hill St
Le Roux St
Morant St
Butler St
Mark St
Murray St
Keimoes St
Basson St
Park St
Lutz St
Kort St
Market St
Scott St
Schröder St
Brug St
Palm Ave
Orange River

Le Roux St

To Augrabies Falls National Park (80km) & Cape Town (820km)

To Groblershoop (120km)

0   250   500m
0   250   500yd

NORTHERN CAPE

and the generous-sized rooms have TV, telephone and air-con. Breakfast is R35.

Budler St has some gorgeous guesthouses with grassed areas overlooking the river.

Riviera Garden Lodge (☎ 332 6554, 16 Budler St) Singles/doubles B&B R185/295. This excellent lodge has beautifully appointed rooms separate from the main house.

Lemon Tree Cottage (☎ 332 1255, 14 Budler St) Singles/doubles from R120/220. Next door to Riviera, this cottage is friendly and offers high-class accommodation with a simple touch.

There are two Protea hotels opposite each other on the corner of Lutz and Schröder Sts; they both offer weekend specials.

Upington Protea Hotel (☎ 337 8400, fax 337 8499, 24 Schröder St) Doubles with/without river view from R295/345. This is the older Protea, though rooms have all mod cons.

Oasis Protea Lodge (☎ 337 8500) Doubles around R299. This lodge is pleasant and a little characterless, as is the nature of this hotel chain; however, of the two Proteas, it's definitely friendlier.

Le Must Guest Manor (☎ 332 3971, fax 332 7830, e lemusttravel@galileosa.co.za, 12 Murray Ave) Singles/doubles from R295/385. This place near the waterfront is the creation of the superb chef at the eponymous restaurant. Most rooms have M-Net, air-con and heating.

Places to Eat

There are takeaways arrayed along the main road, Schröder St. At the corner of Lutz St there is a *KFC*; a little further north you will find a *Wimpy* (great for kids).

Cafe Molinari (☎ 331 2928, Pick 'n Pay Centre) Breakfast R10-24. Open 8am. Not a bad place for breakfast (pancakes R9) before driving to Kgalagadi Transfrontier Park.

Spurs Steak Ranch (☎ 331 1240, 24 Schröder St) Mains from R30. Under the Upington Protea Hotel, Spurs has the usual grills, to keep the carnivore happy, as well as salads for herbivores.

Le Must (☎ 332 3971, 11 Schröder St) Starters R20-26, mains R50. This restaurant is attached to Le Must Travel Agency next door. The food is excellent, and of far better quality than you usually find in a country town. The Cape Malayan pot-fried lamb flavoured with tamarind strongly reasserts the restaurant's name.

O'Hagans (☎ 331 2005, 20 Schröder St) Starters R12-25, mains R25-50. O'Hagans has the best food of the 'chain' pubs. The menu here is very good, and the portions are generous, especially the seafood. For the adventurous, try the *potjiekos* (ostrich neck or oxtail served with rice and veg) for R25.

Sakkie se Arkie (☎ 082-564 5447) is a barbecue boat that leaves from Eiland Holiday Resort for sundowner cruises (R20) – a pleasant way to start the evening.

Entertainment

CFs Action Cafe (☎ 332 1414, 65 Market St) is for a younger, mixed crowd; there's a dance floor and pool tables.

O'Hagans (☎ 331 2005, 20 Schröder St) has a beer garden, which generally entertains an Afrikaner horde. They have a good range of beers and a few decent wines.

Dros (☎ 331 3331, Pick 'n' Pay Centre) is similar to O'Hagans, but lacks the quality meals.

Getting There & Away

Air SA Airlink flies to/from Jo'burg (R1027, seven-day advance purchase) daily and to/from Cape Town (R1016) Sunday to Friday. Upington hotels usually provide a free taxi from the airport.

Bus Two Intercape services run through Upington and provide good links to the rest of the country; for tickets go to the **Intercape Mainliner office** (☎ 332 6091, Lutz St). Buses depart Jo'burg for Upington (R215, nine hours) and Pretoria daily except Wednesday. Buses to Jo'burg/Pretoria via Kuruman and Potchefstroom depart Upington on the same days.

These services connect with buses to/from Windhoek (Namibia). The overnight journey between Upington and Windhoek costs R250 and takes 10 hours.

Intercape also has buses to/from Cape Town (R195, 10½ hours) via Calvinia (R120 from Upington) and Clanwilliam (R160 from Upington). Heading south, buses depart Upington on Tuesday, Thursday, Friday and Sunday; heading north, buses depart Cape Town on Sunday, Monday, Wednesday and Friday.

Greyhound has a daily service to Jo'burg (R225) departing Upington at 7am.

Minibus Taxi You'll find taxis near the Checkers supermarket near the corner of Market and Basson Sts. Not all long-distance taxis leave from here but it's a good place to start asking. Fares from Upington include Kimberley (R90), Jo'burg (R120), Cape Town (R120) and Windhoek (R160).

VIP Taxis (☎ 027-712 2006 in Port Nolloth) operates a weekday taxi service from Port Nolloth to Upington, via Springbok. It picks up at Masonic Hotel in Springbok at 3pm and departs Upington the following morning at 7am. It costs R65 from Upington to Springbok.

Car Rental If you want to see Kgalagadi Transfrontier Park and are short of time, it makes sense to fly to Upington and hire a car. There's an agent for **Avis** (☎ 332 4746) at Upington airport. **Tempest** (☎ 337, 8560, toll free ☎ 0800-031 666) is a good, cheap local car-rental company. The Oasis Protea Lodge rents 4WDs from around R500 per day, with unlimited kilometres; also try **Upington 4X4 Hire** (☎ 337 5200).

AROUND UPINGTON

Around 13km north of Upington you'll find the small **Spitskop Nature Reserve** (☎ 054-332 1336, e teuns@intekom.co.za; adult/child R12/6). The reserve has gemsboks, springboks, wildebeests, bonteboks, zebras, elands and other smaller animals. It is the unusual species that make this place so interesting. Most intriguing are the black springbok (there are six), whose colour results from genetic mutations that are seldom seen. The all 'black' zebra you see dominating a group of female zebra is a runt of a pony who decided to take over the herd – just look at the intensity on his face when he rounds up one of the females who breaks

away. The camels are remnants of those that the German cameleers left in the region after skirmishes during WWI.

There are short hiking trails and a 4WD trail for those city slickers who put the Land Cruiser through its paces once a year. You can view wildlife through a telescope from the top of the prominent Spitskop.

Accommodation options include camping (adult/child R20/10), a 4-bed chalet (R70 per person) and, most fascinating of all, a rustic, isolated 'veld hut' (R50 per person) in the middle of the reserve (bring your own bedding).

WITSAND NATURE RESERVE

Approximately 200km east of Upington (or 200km south-west of Kuruman) you'll find this reserve (☎ 053-313 1062; adult/child R10/5), which is based on a 9km wide by 2km long by 100m high white sand dune. This extensive dune system, surrounded by typical red Kalahari sands, is famous for its 'roaring sands'. When the wind blows, a bass, organ-like sound is produced; walking on the sands produces a muted groan.

You can walk anywhere in the park but 4WDs are restricted to the roads.

There's a delightful *bush camp* with two swimming pools and 10 thatch-roofed, open plan, tastefully decorated, self-catering chalets (R150 per person) with bathrooms. Camping (R60) is also an option.

KGALAGADI TRANSFRONTIER PARK

This park (☎ 054-561 0021; R25/12 adult/child per day, vehicle R5) was proclaimed in April 1999 and is the result of a merger between the former Kalahari-Gemsbok National Park in South Africa and the Mabuasehube-Gemsbok National Park in Botswana. Covering an area about twice the size of Kruger, Kgalagadi is not as famous as many other African parks but it is, nonetheless, one of the greatest.

The accessible section of the park lies in the triangular segment of South African territory between Namibia and Botswana. This region covers 9591 sq km. The protected area continues on the Botswana side of the border (there are no fences) for a further 28,400 sq km. South Africa's side of the park was proclaimed in 1931 and Botswana's in 1938. Kgalagadi is one of the largest protected wilderness areas in Africa, allowing the unhindered migration of antelopes, which are forced to travel great distances in times of drought to reach water and food.

Although the countryside is described as semidesert (with around 200mm of rain a year) it is richer than it appears and supports large populations of birds, reptiles, rodents, small mammals and antelopes. These in turn support a large population of predators. Most of the animals are remarkably tolerant of cars. This allows you to get extraordinarily close to animals that are otherwise wild – it's as if you are invisible.

The landscape is hauntingly beautiful. The Nossob and Aoub Rivers (usually dry) run through the park and meet each other a few kilometres north of the entrance, at Twee Rivieren. Much of the wildlife is concentrated in these river beds, so they are easy to spot. The only significant human interference in the park's ecology are the windmills and water holes.

In the south of the park, the Nossob river bed is between 100m and 500m wide, with grey camel thorn trees growing between the limestone banks. In the north the river bed opens up to more than a kilometre wide, and becomes sandy. The bed of the Aoub is narrower and deeper. Between the two rivers, the Kalahari dunes are characteristically red due to iron oxide. In other areas the sand varies from pink and yellowish to grey.

Orientation & Information

Visitors are restricted to four gravel/sand roads – one running up the bed of the Nossob River, one running up the bed of the Aoub River (there are also some small loop roads), and the two linking these. Visitors must remain in their cars, except at a small number of designated picnic spots.

The only negative thing to say about the park is that while the river beds are the best places to view wildlife, it can become almost claustrophobic being stuck in a car and enclosed by the river banks.

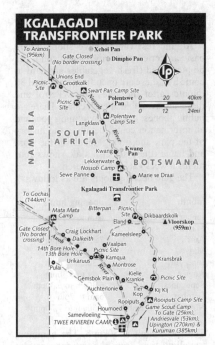

The opportunities to really get a feel for the empty expanses of the Kalahari are limited; the exceptions are the roads linking the rivers, and they should not be missed. During the infrequent rains, flash floods often wreak havoc on some of the roads, which can be closed for weeks.

More looping roads are needed to take you into the veld and walks need to be organised. A few dead-end roads with viewing points have been added.

The best time to visit is in June and July when the days are coolest (below freezing at night) and the animals have been drawn to the bores along the dry river beds. August is windy and, for some reason, is a favourite time for tour buses. September to October is the wet season and if it does rain, many of the animals scatter out across the plain to take advantage of the fresh pastures. November is quiet, and daily temperatures start to rise. Despite the fact that temperatures frequently reach 45°C in December and January, the chalets in the park are fully booked during the school holidays.

All the rest camps have shops where basic groceries, soft drinks and alcohol can be purchased (fresh vegetables are hard to come by); these are open from 7am until 30 minutes after the gates close. Petrol and diesel are available at each camp. There are public phones, a pub, a swimming pool and an information centre detailing the history of the park and giving details of the flora and fauna (there are also slide shows four nights a week) at Twee Rivieren.

The gate opening hours are as follows:

month	opening hours
January–February	6am to 7.30pm
March	6.30am to 7pm
April	7am to 6.30pm
May	7am to 6pm
June–July	7.30am to 6pm
August	7am to 6.30pm
September	6.30am to 6.30pm
October	6am to 7pm
November–December	5.30am to 7.30pm

The speed limit is 50km/h. The minimum travelling time from the entrance gate at Twee Rivieren to Nossob is 3½ hours and to Mata Mata it's 2½ hours. Allow plenty of time to get to the camps as no driving is permitted after dark.

If you want to venture into the Botswana side of the park, this is only possible via a 4WD trail. You need to make arrangements with the **Botswana Department of Wildlife & National Parks** (☎ 09-267 580774) in Gaborone.

Staff at park headquarters in Twee Rivieren organise sundowner night drives for R60 per person, giving you the chance to spot some of the park's nocturnal species.

Flora

Only hardy plants survive the periodic droughts that afflict the Kalahari. Many have adapted so that they germinate and produce seed within four weeks of a shower of rain.

The river beds have the widest variety of flora. The Nossob River is dominated by camel thorn trees *(Acacia erioloba)* in the

north and grey camel thorn trees *(Acacia haematoxylon)* in the south. Sociable weaverbirds favour the camel thorns for their huge nests, and all sorts of creatures feed off the foliage and seeds.

Various grasses and woody shrubs survive on the dunes. There are occasional shepherd's trees *(Boscia albitrunca)*, which have white bark and a dense thicket of short low branches where many animals take refuge in the heat of the day. The driedoring shrub *(Rhigozum trichotomum)*, with fine leaves and forked branches, is the most common shrub in the park.

Many of the animals depend on plants as their source of moisture. In particular, the tsamma *(Citrillus lanatus)*, a creeper with melon-like fruit, is an important source of water. There are several prickly cucumbers that are important for the survival of animals, especially the gemsbok.

Fauna

Finding fauna requires luck, patience and a little intelligence. There is no guarantee that you will see one of the big predators but you are more likely to here than in many other places. Most of the region's wildlife, with the exception of elephants, rhinos and zebras, are found in the park.

There are 19 species of predator here, including the dark-maned Kalahari lion, cheetah, leopard, wild dog, spotted hyena, black-backed jackal, bat-eared fox, Cape fox, honey badger and meerkat. The most numerous antelope is the springbok but there are also large numbers of gemsbok, eland, red hartebeest and blue wildebeest.

Spend an hour or so in the morning and the afternoon by a water hole. Watch for signs of agitation among herds of antelope – they don't automatically flee at the sight of a predator but wait until the predator commits itself to a charge before they run. Be sure to keep an eye on the top of the ridges overlooking the river beds, especially near herds of grazers, as these are good places to spot predators surveying their next meal. The lions like to walk along the side of the road because the soft dust is kind to their paws. Look for recent prints, as the lion may have moved off the road at the sound of your vehicle. Binoculars are essential (see Wildlife Viewing in the Kruger National Park chapter for more tips).

Birds Some 215 species of bird have been recorded here. Sighting birds of prey is a real treat and they are incredibly numerous; the Mata Mata road is especially good. Perhaps the most dramatic are impressive species such as the bateleur eagle, martial eagle, red-necked falcon, pygmy falcon, pale chanting goshawk and tawny eagle.

Two common birds are the secretary bird, seen strutting self-importantly over the clay pans, and the kori bustard, the largest flying bird in Southern Africa.

Perhaps the most distinctive sight are the huge thatched nests of the sociable weaverbird. The birds live in many-chambered nests that can last for more than a century and are inhabited by as many as 200 birds at a time. They weave twigs and straw together in the crowns of acacias, on quiver trees and atop telephone poles.

Organised Tours

Theuns Botha (☎ 054-332 1336, e *teuns@ intekom.co.za*) operates Spitskop Safaris and runs informal, flexible tours to Kgalagadi Transfrontier Park and Augrabies Falls National Parks.

Kalahari Tours & Travel (☎ 332 7885, fax 338 0375, e *dantes@kalahari-tours.co.za, PO Box 113, Upington*) has a good reputation and has been recommended by readers.

Places to Stay & Eat

There is accommodation both inside and outside the park. The park's only restaurant is at Twee Rivieren.

Inside the Park There are rest camps at Twee Rivieren, Mata Mata and Nossob. Some facilities at Mata Mata and Nossob are being upgraded, so tariffs could rise again soon. Camp sites are usually available but booking is advised for huts/chalets from June to September, and during holiday periods. Book with the **National Parks Board** (☎ 343 9770, W *www.parks-sa.co.za,*

643 Leyds St, Muckleneuk, Pretoria) or **Cape Nature Conservation** (☎ *426 0723,* W *www.capenature.org.za*) in Cape Town.

All rest camps have *camp sites* without electricity and with shared ablution facilities. Sites cost R65 for two people plus R20 per extra person.

All camps also have a range of huts, bungalows and cottages equipped with bedding, towels, cooking and eating utensils. At *Twee Rivieren*, four-bed bungalows with kitchen and bathroom cost R250 for 2 people plus R70 per extra person; four-bed cottages are R420. All the bungalows and cottages have air-con.

At *Mata Mata*, three-bed huts with shared facilities cost R165 and six-bed cottages with kitchen are R300 for up to four people plus R70/35 per extra adult/child.

At *Nossob*, three-bed huts with shared facilities are R165 while three-bed huts with private facilities are R250 (two people). Cottages (for up to four people) cost R300.

Lapa Restaurant Starters R15-32, mains R40-55. Open 7.30am-9am & 6.30pm-9pm. This pleasant place overlooking the camp in Twee Rivieren offers surprisingly reasonable value. Seafood dishes are around R48. There's also a snack bar selling burgers and other takeaways. If you're coming for dinner, let them know by 6pm.

Outside the Park *Motel Molopo* (☎ *054-511 0088, 083-695 7865,* e *molopo@inte kom.co.za*) Camp sites R40 plus R25 per vehicle, single/double chalets R345/490. Motel Molopo is in the hamlet of Andriesvale, about 60km south of the park's gate. It's a comfortable, attractive spot with a pool and thatched chalets, camp sites and a restaurant. If you're aiming for the park but arrive late, this motel could save your bacon.

There are a number of other places, mainly farms, offering accommodation between Upington and Kgalagadi Transfrontier Park. *Rooipan* (☎ *054-902,* ask for *912411*) Rooms R100 per person, cottage DB&B R200 per person. This friendly stopover has a resident 'guard' kori bustard and a pool to provide relief from the heat. It's situated 120km from Upington. Turn off the R360 at the Koopan Suid turn-off on the left (coming from Upington); Rooipan is 2km further on.

Kalahari Sands (☎ *054-511 0021*) Rooms R100 per person, self-catering chalet sleeping four R350. This spacious guesthouse in Ashkam, 60km south of Twee Rivieren, has great braai areas and lots of grass.

Loch Broom Guest Farm (☎ *054-902 916620, 082-824 4954*) Camping R40 per person, tented camp R100 per person, DB&B R225 per person. Don't be put off by the trophy heads hanging from the living room walls of this working cattle, sheep and game farm. It's 110km east of the Kgalagadi Transfrontier Park on the R31, on the way to Van Zylsrus. The welcome is warm, there's a pet cheetah to meet and even if you don't stop overnight you can drop by for a cuppa or to have lunch and go on a wildlife viewing drive (R80).

Getting There & Away

It's a solid five- or six-hour drive from Kuruman to Twee Rivieren (385km). The drive from Upington to Twee Rivieren gate is 250km, made up of about 190km on bitumen and 60km on dirt roads (the bitumen is gradually being extended).

Be very careful driving on the dirt roads as we've had several letters from travellers who wrecked their cars on this trip. If you stop, don't pull too far off the road or you might become bogged in the sand. Beware of patches of deep sand and loose gravel, which makes corners treacherous. Petrol is not available between Upington and Twee Rivieren, so start out with a full tank.

It's important to carry water, as you may have to wait a while for help if you break down. When the temperature is over 40°C you can quickly become dehydrated.

UPINGTON TO SPRINGBOK
Keimos & Kakamas

The road west from Upington follows the course of the Orange River and passes through oases of vineyards (still irrigated with the aid of wooden water wheels) and the pleasant little towns of Keimos and Kakamas. The turn-off to Augrabies Falls National Park is at Kakamas.

The Orange River Wine Cellars Cooperative has a number of **wine-tasting** venues. These are at Groblershoop (☎ 054-741 0001), south-east of Upington on the N10; Keimos (☎ 054-461 1006); and Kakamas (☎ 054-431 0830). Wine-tasting here is a much less pretentious affair than is the case in Western Cape.

Harvest Moon Guesthouse (☎ *054-461 1401, 23 Main St, Keimos*) Singles/doubles B&B R100/180. This friendly place has a few rooms with shared bathroom; you can book the whole place to yourself if they're not busy. Coming from Upington, turn left at the only traffic lights in town; Harvest Moon is 400m down the road.

Kalahari Gateway Hotel (☎ *054-431 0838*) Singles/doubles R180/229. This place in Kakamas is under new management; they had major renovations planned when we passed through, they also provide tourist information about the area.

Augrabies Falls National Park

For much more than just an impressive waterfall visit this national park (☎ *054-452 9200; adult/child R12/6*). Certainly the falls can be spectacular (particularly if they are carrying a lot of water) but the most interesting facet of the park is the fascinating desert/riverine ecosystems on either side of the river.

The name of the falls derives from the Namaqua word for 'Place of Great Noise'. The Orange River meanders across the plain from the east but following an uplift in the land around 500 million years ago it began to wear a deep ravine into the underlying granite. The ravine is 18km long and has several impressive cataracts. The main falls drop 56m, while the Bridal Veil Falls on the northern side drop 75m.

The park has a harsh climate, with an average rainfall of only 107mm and daytime summer temperatures that often reach 40°C. The flora includes kokerboom aloes, the Namaqua fig, several varieties of thorn trees and succulents. The park has 47 species of mammal (most of which are small) including klipspringer and other antelope species, rock dassie and ground squirrel.

The area across the Orange River was once a sanctuary for black rhino and tours were operated there from Augrabies. Sadly the highly endangered rhino have been driven out by the brainless tour operators running 4WD trails.

Orientation & Information There are three-hour nature walks and some interesting drives. Allow yourself a minimum of an hour to look at the falls, at least two hours to explore the park and an hour or so in the pleasant open-air cafe that overlooks the ravine.

Maps and information are available from the main complex; there's also a well-stocked shop (but it has few hiking supplies). It is necessary to book night wildlife drives (R50) in advance.

Activities The three-hour **Dassie Trail** is well worth doing, particularly if your time is short. It involves clambering over rocks through some magical landscape – if you haven't seen any of the cute little dassies yet, this is your big chance.

The popular three-day, 40km **Klipspringer Hiking Trail** *(R70 per person)* runs along the southern bank of the Orange River. Two nights are spent in huts built from local stone (these can sleep 12 people). Camping is not allowed. Hikers must supply their own sleeping bags and food. Advance booking is advised; the walk costs R70 per person. The trail is closed from mid-October to the end of March because of the heat. The **Gariep 3-in-1 Route** *(adults/children R120/60)* includes canoeing, walking and mountain biking; book at the main complex.

The **Kalahari Adventure Centre** *(☎ 054-451 0177,* [e] *info@kalahari.co.za)* runs canoeing and rafting on the Orange River. Their very popular 'Augrabies Rush' rafts an exciting grade 2 to 3, 8km section of the river and the pull-out point is only 300m above the falls; it costs R225 per person. The Onseepkans Gorge trip is a two-day adventure on some of the river's best white water in two-person inflatables (R895). The four-night Augrabies Canoe Trail covers 60km of the river and is well worth the R1450 cost, which includes all meals.

Places to Stay & Eat At the *camping ground*, sites cost R44 for two people plus R11 for each extra person. There is also a camp kitchen.

Self-contained accommodation includes four-person *cottages* for R420 and *chalets* from R270 a double, plus R66/33 per extra adult/child. Many of the cottages and chalets have outstanding views and are within earshot of the falls. Book with the National Parks Board in Pretoria or Cape Town.

There's a *cafeteria* where you can buy sandwiches and cold drinks, and a *restaurant* with meals such as fillet steak or chicken for R40. Cold water is free from the dispenser – you'll probably drink it dry if you are here in summer.

The friendly *Kalahari Adventure Centre Backpackers* has camp sites for R20 per person and dorm beds/doubles for R60/150. Breakfast costs R20, main meals R30.

Getting There & Away Private transport is recommended. The park is 38km northwest of Kakamas and 120km from Upington. The Kalahari Adventure Centre will pick up from Upington (and other towns in the area). The shuttle fare is R150 per person (minimum of four).

Pofadder & Pella Mission Station
☎ 054 • postcode 8890

Apart from Pofadder's evocative name (which is not only the name of a snake and a short, fat sausage but also the name of a local chief), there's really not much to Pofadder. The town is something of a byword for an archetypal little place in the middle of nowhere.

Pofadder Overnight Flats (☎ 933 0039) R75 per person. This place will do if you need to stay overnight.

Pella is a small mission surrounded by extensive groves of date palms. It was started in 1812 by the London Missionary Society, abandoned after the murder of the missionary, and re-founded by French Roman Catholics in 1882. The extraordinary church was built by an untrained French missionary, who was armed only with an encyclopaedia.

Namakwa 4X4 Route

The Namakwa 4X4 Route is over 610km long and traverses some of South Africa's most remote and rugged territory east and south of Richtersveld. The route has been divided into two parts: Pella Mission Station to Vioolsdrif (R150 per vehicle, 328km) and Vioolsdrif to Alexander Bay (R150, 284km). At the end of the journey, drivers have the option of visiting Richtersveld National Park. Vehicle permits (R28) are obtained from the Tourism Information Office (☎ 027-712 2011) in Springbok. You can hire 4WDs in Upington or Springbok for about R500 per day, with unlimited kilometres.

An incredible diversity of succulent plants can be seen along the way, many of which are unique to the region. The terrain varies as much as the plant types – it can be mountainous, green along the river beds or just miles of sandy dunes.

Klein Pella Guest House (☎ 054-971 0008) B&B R155 per person, rondavels R85 per person. This is the only accommodation at the mission.

Namaqualand

Namaqualand is an ill-defined region in the north-western corner of Northern Cape, north of Vanrhynsdorp (in Western Cape) and west of Pofadder. It is a rugged, mountainous plateau that overlooks a narrow, sandy coastal plain and the bleak beaches of the west coast. In the east it runs into the dry central plains that are known as Bushmanland. It has a noticeable 'frontier atmosphere' due largely to its bleak and beautiful landscape, and the presence of diamond miners.

The cold Benguela current runs up the west coast and creates a barren desert-like environment. However, this apparently inhospitable environment produces one of the world's natural wonders. After decent winter rains there is an extraordinary explosion of spring flowers that cover the boulder-strewn mountains and plains with a multi-coloured carpet. Namaqualand's flora is characterised by a phenomenal variety of daisies but there are also mesembryanthemums, gladioli, aloes, euphorbias, violets, pelargoniums and many other species.

The area is sparsely populated, mainly by Afrikaans-speaking sheep farmers, and in the north-west by the Namaqua, a Khoikhoi tribe. The Namaqua were famous for their metalworking skills, particularly in the copper that occurs in the region. Not surprisingly, this attracted the attention of Dutch explorers, who came into contact with the tribe in 1661. Because of the region's isolation, however, the Namaqualand copper rush did not properly begin until the 1850s. The first commercial mine (now a national monument) was established just outside Springbok in 1852, and there are still a number of working mines including one at Nababeep.

Namaqualand is also an important source for alluvial diamonds. In 1925 a young soldier, Jack Carstens, found a glittering stone near Port Nolloth. Prospectors converged on the area, and it soon became clear that an enormously rich source of diamonds had been discovered. All the major west-coast alluvial fields are now classified as prohibited areas and are closed to the general public. Diamonds are only bought and sold by licensed traders.

You may meet locals who offer to sell you cheap diamonds – not only is this highly illegal, you may end up with a fake. For more information, see the boxed text 'Illegal Diamond Mining' later in this chapter.

SPRINGBOK
☎ 027 • postcode 8240

Springbok, which considers itself the capital of Namaqualand, lies in a valley among harsh, rocky hills that explode with colour in flower season. The first European-run copper mine, the Blue Mine, was established on the town's outskirts in 1852. From a rough-and-tumble frontier town, Springbok has been transformed into a busy service centre for the copper and diamond mines in the region.

The town is quite spread-out but most places are within walking distance of the small kopje in the elbow of the main street's right-angled bend. The kopje is covered with the strange local flora.

In the old church next to the post office you'll find the friendly, well-run **Tourism Information Office** (☎ 712 2011, ⓔ namak waland@intekom.co.za; open 7.30am-4.15pm Mon-Fri year-round, 8am-1pm Sat & Sun flower season only).

Springbok Lodge & Restaurant (☎ 027-712 1321, ⓔ sbklogde@intekom.co.za) just off Voortrekker St and near the kopje, also provides tourist information about the area.

Melkboschkuil Travel Shop (☎ 718 1600, 75 Voortrekker St) has Internet facilities for R8 per 15 minutes.

In the 1920s, Springbok had a large population of Jews who traded in the region. Most have moved away and their synagogue (built in 1929) has been converted into a small but good **museum** (☎ 712 2011; admission free; open 9am-4pm Mon-Fri).

Places to Stay

During flower season accommodation in Springbok can fill up. The tourist office can tell you about private, overflow accommodation. There is a big difference between low prices (given here) and flower season prices.

Springbok Caravan Park (☎ 718 1584, Gamoep Rd) Camp sites R50, self-catering flat for 2 people R135. At 2km out of town, it's a long walk, though occasional buses do run past. Bring your own bedding for the flat.

Namastat (☎ 712 2435 for bookings, fax 712 1926) Dorm beds R35, chalets R60 per person, 2-bed Nama huts R50 per person. This interesting place is 2km south of the centre on the Cape Town road. Accommodation is in traditional woven Nama 'mat' huts, similar in shape to Zulu 'beehive' huts (matjieshuis in Afrikaans). Prices can be considerably less if you have your own bedding and sleep on the ground.

Springbok Lodge 51-62 (☎ 712 1321, fax 712 2718, Voortrekker St) Singles/doubles R90/180, self-catering flats R240. These old houses have been steadily upgraded over the years; the cottages range in size from the small Matchbox to the sizable Die Gewelhuis and Die Ark.

Annie's Cottage (☎ 712 1451, 4 King St) B&B R150 per person. North of the centre, Annie's Cottage is very friendly and a popular stopover for overlanders on their way to Namibia.

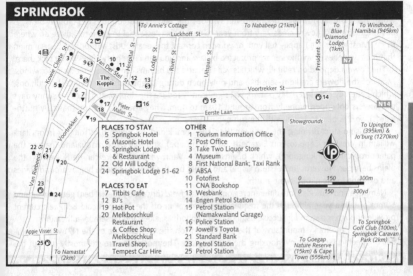

SPRINGBOK

PLACES TO STAY
5 Springbok Hotel
6 Masonic Hotel
18 Springbok Lodge
   & Restaurant
22 Old Mill Lodge
24 Springbok Lodge 51-62

PLACES TO EAT
7 Titbits Cafe
12 BJ's
19 Hot Pot
20 Melkboschkuil
   Restaurant
   & Coffee Shop;
   Melkboschkuil
   Travel Shop;
   Tempest Car Hire

OTHER
1 Tourism Information Office
2 Post Office
3 Take Two Liquor Store
4 Museum
8 First National Bank; Taxi Rank
9 ABSA
10 Fotofirst
11 CNA Bookshop
13 Wesbank
14 Engen Petrol Station
15 Petrol Station
   (Namakwaland Garage)
16 Police Station
17 Jowell's Toyota
21 Standard Bank
23 Petrol Station
25 Petrol Station

NORTHERN CAPE

Old Mill Lodge (☎ 718 1705, 69 Van Riebeeck St) Rooms R180/230. Old Mill Lodge is an upmarket guesthouse under the lee of a huge basalt outcrop, so the neighbours aren't a problem. Breakfast is R20 extra.

Blue Diamond Lodge (☎ 718 2624, 19 Union St) B&B R150 per person. North of the centre, this is an attractive place with neat units set around a swimming pool, a resident macaw and a trail up the mountain behind the lodge with good views.

Springbok Hotel (☎ 712 1161, fax 712 1932, 87 Van Riebeeck St) Singles/doubles R75/170. This old-style hotel is a bit dowdy, but terrific value. Rooms have TV, air-con and telephones. Breakfast is R30.

Masonic Hotel (☎ 712 1505, fax 712 1730, 2 Van Riebeeck St) Singles/doubles R132/242. This fine Art-Deco edifice has been upgraded and there is a great balcony. Buffet breakfasts cost R30.

Places to Eat

For takeaways, there is the friendly *Titbits Cafe* (☎ 718 1455) near the kopje.

Melkboschkuil Restaurant & Coffee Shop (☎ 718 1789) Breakfast R13-38, lunch R20-24, mains R30-50. This place, at the travel shop of the same name, is by far the best restaurant in town. They do specialities such as ostrich fillet with honey mustard sauce and Springbok pie. The pitta sandwiches make a great lunch.

Springbok Lodge & Restaurant (☎ 027-712 1321, e sbklogde@intekom.co.za) Starters R12-15, mains R25-50. Open until 10pm. It's rare to find such a pleasant place in a small South African town. The menu is large and includes grills, breakfast, pizzas,

Wildflowers of Namaqualand

Although the wildflowers of Western Cape are spectacular, they are overshadowed by the brilliance of Namaqualand's floral displays. Generally, Namaqualand's flowers bloom a couple of weeks earlier than those further south, so it makes sense to begin your flower viewing in the north.

The optimum time to visit varies from year to year but you have the best chance of catching the flowers at their peak between mid-August and mid-September (sometimes the season can begin early in August and extend to mid-October). Unfortunately for overseas visitors with fixed itineraries, there can be no guarantee that you will be in the right place at the right time. A visit may be worth the gamble, however, because even without the flowers the countryside, though bleak, is beautiful. The best flower areas vary from year to year, so it is essential to get local advice on where to go. Most locals will happily tell you, or you can contact the local tourist authorities. Bear in mind that most varieties of wildflower are protected by law and you can incur heavy fines if you pick them.

The flowers depend on rainfall, which is variable, and the blooms can shrivel quickly in hot winds. Many of the flowers are light-sensitive and only open during bright sunshine. Overcast conditions, which generally only last a day or two, will significantly reduce the display, and even on sunny days the flowers only open properly from around 10am to 4pm. They also face the sun (basically northwards), so it is best to travel with the sun behind you.

There is no strict dividing line between the Cape floral kingdom (which runs roughly from Clanwilliam in Western Cape to Port Elizabeth in Eastern Cape), and that of Namaqualand (part of the palaeotropical floral kingdom), which begins north of Vanrhynsdorp. There can be flowers on the plains between Nuwerus (in Western Cape) and Garies but the major spectacle begins around Garies and extends to Steinkopf in the north.

Namaqualand is divided into different regions. The *sandveld* (dry, sandy coastal belt) gets only around 50mm of rain a year, although the frequent fogs that roll in off the Atlantic's cold Benguela current provide enough moisture for succulents, including euphorbias, aloes and mesembryanthemums.

Inland are the rocky mountains of the escarpment (on the western side of the N7) with a number of spectacular passes overlooking the coastal plain. The mountains are still mostly dry but the

snacks and salads. It's just off Voortrekker St, near the kopje.

Hot Pot (☎ 718 1475, Voortrekker St) Meals R25-40. Hot Pot offers similar food to Springbok Lodge & Restaurant but with a smaller menu. The best thing here is the balcony eating area overlooking the main street.

BJ's (☎ 718 2270) Meals R20-55. Open noon-3pm & 7pm-late Mon-Fri, 7pm-late Sat. Several readers have recommended BJ's, which is a fully licensed steakhouse with an extensive menu.

Getting There & Away

Air There are flights from Cape Town to Springbok (R950, seven-day advance purchase) on Monday to Friday with **National Airlines** *(in Cape Town ☎ 021-936 2050, in Springbok ☎ 712 2061)*. Flights continue on to Alexander Bay, near Richtersveld National Park.

Bus Intercape's Cape Town–Windhoek (Namibia; 1469km) service runs through Springbok, picking up opposite the main Springbok Lodge near the kopje. Buses leave for Cape Town (R240) on Monday, Tuesday, Thursday and Saturday at 4.45am. Buses leave for Windhoek (R230) on Tuesday, Thursday, Friday and Sunday at 7.45pm. Book at the Melkboschkuil Travel Shop.

Minibus Taxi To Cape Town, **Van Wyk's Busdiens** *(☎ 713 8559)* run a daily door-to-door taxi (R100). You'll find ordinary minibus taxis to Cape Town (also R100) at the Caltex petrol station near the traffic lights on Voortrekker St, or at the taxi rank at the rear of First National Bank near the kopje.

Wildflowers of Namaqualand

rainfall increases to around 100mm, which is sufficient for wheat farming. The fallow fields are prime habitats for flowering annuals such as daisies, oxalis and gazanias. The hills around Springbok and Nababeep have more rain (around 150mm) and a particularly rich variety of flowers.

Trees are scarce, although visitors will certainly see the characteristic kokerboom, or quiver tree *(Aloe dichotoma)*, an aloe that can grow to a height of 4m, on the hills. The tree stores water in its trunk and is known as the quiver tree because the Khoisan used its branches as quivers. The quiver tree has large yellow blooms in June or July. In the north you'll see 'halfmens', or elephant trunk *(Pachypodium namaquanum)*, weird tree-like succulents with a long, inelegant trunk topped by a small 'face' of foliage. They always look to the north; according to legend, they are the transformed bodies of Khoikhoi people who were driven south during a war. It is said that those who turned to look towards their lost lands were transformed into trees.

Getting There & Away

There are generally good flowers east of the N7 between Garies and Springbok. Even if there are no flowers, there are spectacular roads to Hondeklip Bay from Kamieskroon, Springbok and Garies. Other reliable flower-viewing routes are between Springbok and Port Nolloth, and through Kamiesberg, which is south-east of Kamieskroon in the direction of Garies. The Goegap Nature Reserve, east of Springbok, and the hills around Nababeep are also good.

Springbok is 555km from Cape Town (six to seven hours), 395km from Upington and 1270km from Jo'burg, so just getting there is a reasonable undertaking; it's possible to fly to Springbok. You need to spend a minimum of two or three days here to do justice to the area.

During flower season there are plenty of sightseeing tours of the area (departing from Cape Town). Kamieskroon Hotel & Caravan Park (see under Kamieskroon later in this chapter) organises a number of week-long photographic workshops between August and September, each hosted by well-known photographers. The courses are expensive but well patronised; they cost R3900/7000 including single/double accommodation and all meals.

VIP Taxis (☎ 712 2006, ☎ 027-851 8780, in Port Nolloth) operate a taxi from Port Nolloth to Upington Monday to Friday. It picks up at the Masonic Hotel in Springbok at 3pm, departing Upington the following morning at 7am and reaching Springbok at about 11am. The Upington-Springbok leg costs about R65.

Car Rental Ask at the main Springbok Lodge, the tourism information office or the Melkboschkuil Travel Shop about car hire from local garages such as Jowell's Toyota or Tempest Car Hire. A 2WD hire car costs from around R76 per day, plus R1.50 per kilometre.

AROUND SPRINGBOK
Nababeep
☎ 027 • postcode 8265
Nababeep is the site of a large copper mine, and the surrounding hills have spectacular blooms in flower season. For those interested in mining, a visit to the **Nababeep Mine Museum** (☎ 713 8121; admission free) is worthwhile.

Nababeep Hotel (☎ 713 8151) has singles/doubles for R65/120. Breakfast is R31.50, while main meals cost R65. Prices go up considerably here in flower season.

Goegap Nature Reserve
Don't miss this semidesert nature reserve (☎ 027-712 1880; admission R5; open 7.45am-4.15pm daily). The name of this reserve is derived from 'go-harp', which means 'water hole' in Nama. It is famous for its extraordinary display of spring flowers and a nursery of 200 amazing Karoo and Namaqualand succulents at the **Hester Malan Wildflower Garden**.

There are a couple of driving routes around the reserve but you'll see more on one of the circular walks (4km, 5.5km and 7km). There are two incredible **mountain-biking** routes (14km and 20km), which are particularly memorable during flower season; bring your own bikes. There's a permit fee of R12/27 per person for half/full day. The **horse trails** are for riders with their own horses.

PORT NOLLOTH
☎ 027 • postcode 8280
Port Nolloth is a sandy and exposed little place but it has a certain fascination. It was originally developed as the shipping point for the region's copper but it is now dependent on the small fishing boats that catch diamonds and crayfish. The boats are fitted with pumps, and divers vacuum up the diamond-bearing gravel found on the ocean floor. The town has attracted a multicultural group of fortune-seekers and they give the town a frontier vitality, reminiscent of a pirate haunt on the Spanish Main.

The **information centre** (☎ 851 8229) is in the town hall, just off the main road into town. There's a branch of First National Bank, a petrol station, a pharmacy and a few shops.

Places to Stay
The Bedrock (☎ 851 8865, e bedrock@ icon.co.za) Doubles R150, 2-bed self-catering cottages R170, 7-bed house R300. This is a guesthouse in one of the old wooden cottages

Illegal Diamond Buying

In South Africa it is illegal to sell diamonds to any person or company other than the De Beers Consolidated Mines Company. The diamond mines are thus hives of security. The independent divers who work Port Nolloth and other submarine diamond fields on the west coast, however, have more opportunity to get away with extracting diamonds from their catch and selling them on the black market. Diamond diving is hard work and it isn't lucrative – the divers can only work about 10 days a month because of the weather.

Illegal diamond buying (known as IDB) is a subcurrent of life in this area and chances are that a few of your fellow patrons in a diamond town bar are undercover members of the police IDB branch. You may meet locals who offer to sell you cheap diamonds – don't do it! Not only is this highly illegal, you are also likely to end up with what is known as a *slenter*, or fake diamond. These are cut from lead crystal and only an expert can pick them.

lining the seafront. As well as being a friendly and comfortable place to stay, with big rooms and sea views, it's a social must, as it's owned by a local personality, Grazia de Beer, known as Mama. Turn right onto the beachfront road as you come into town and The Bedrock is the second building along. Mama also owns a couple of nearby houses, so a range of accommodation options is available.

McDougall's Bay Chalets & Caravan Park (☎ 851 8657) Camp sites R68, 6-bed chalets R216.50. This place is acceptable but don't expect five-star comforts (bring your own towels and dishcloths). The park is 4km south of Port Nolloth by road, less on foot if you can find a path through the shantytown.

Places to Eat
For freshly baked bread, go to the *Welcome Bakery*; for fast food and chicken, head to *Southern Fried* in the main street.

The Crow's Nest Mains R12-25. This place is attached to The Bedrock, and serves seafood, meat, pasta dishes and pizza.

Captain Pete's Tavern Mains R25-40. This place across from the Scotia Inn Hotel is owned by a diamond diver who struck it rich.

Getting There & Away
There is little public transport, and hitching from the N7 turn-off at Steinkopf would be slow. **VIP Taxis** (☎ 851 8780) operate a taxi from Port Nolloth to Upington, via Springbok, Monday to Friday.

It's a great drive from Springbok (145km), with bare mountains looming to the north and the exhilarating drop down to the coastal plain through the Aninaus Pass. As you drive along the coastal flats you'll notice that all the land is fenced. This isn't to keep stock in – it's to keep poachers and others out of the diamond leases.

ALEXANDER BAY
☎ 027 • postcode 8290
Alexander Bay is a government-controlled diamond mine on the southern bank of the mouth of the Orange River (Namibia is on the north). It's the archetypal, remote seaside community. The road from Port Nolloth is open to the public but the Namibian border is closed. Restrictions on access are beginning to lift and the town is looking at its tourism potential. There are *mine tours* (☎ 831 1330; 8am Thur, book one day in advance) and a **museum**.

Bird-watchers come here looking for Barlow's lark, which is found nowhere else in the world.

Brandkaros (☎ 831 1856, fax 831 1390) Camp sites R50, double self-catering rondavels R150. Brandkaros is a citrus farm by the river, about 30km north-east of Alexander Bay. It has a great swimming pool. The farm is en route to Richtersveld National Park and is a good base from which to tour this area.

VIOOLSDRIF
☎ 027
This town is at the border post with Namibia on the N7, 677km north of Cape Town. The short drive from Steinkopf, with its views of the Orange River carving its way through desolate mountains, is spectacular. The border is open from 7am to 7pm; visas are available in Cape Town (R138) but not at the border.

Peace of Paradise (☎ 761 8968) Camp sites R20, plus R40 per person. This camping ground is 22km from the border (west of the border post) on the banks of the Orange River. It has hot showers, clean toilets and electricity, as well as canoes for hire. There are San engravings 100m from the camp.

RICHTERSVELD NATIONAL PARK
This enormous (185,000 hectares) national park (☎ 027-831 1506, PO Box 406, Alexander Bay 8290; adult/child R30/20, fishing permit R12) is in the northern loop of the Orange River, north-west of Vioolsdrif and the N7. The park is the property of the local Nama people who continue to lead a semi-traditional, seminomadic pastoral existence; hopefully they will benefit from increased job opportunities from tourism and the rent paid by the park authorities.

NORTHERN CAPE

The area is a mountainous desert, a spectacular wilderness with jagged rocky peaks, grotesque rock formations, deep ravines and gorges. The hiking possibilities, though demanding, are excellent. Despite its apparent barrenness, the region has a prolific variety of succulents – 30% of South Africa's known succulent species grow here.

At present, most of the park is virtually inaccessible without a properly equipped expedition and local guides. The southern section is accessible by high clearance 2WD vehicles (such as a *bakkie*) but it would be worth checking this before going in. A good companion is *Tracks and Trails of the Richtersveld* by Heinz Reck.

Fill up your tank at Alexander Bay before entering the park; fuel emergencies are only dealt with at Sendelingsdrift.

Hiking Trails
Three hiking trails have been established in the park. The **Ventersvalle Trail** (42km, four days) takes in the mountainous south-west wilderness; the **Lelieshoek-Oemsberg Trail** (23km, three days) takes in a huge amphitheatre and waterfall; and the **Kodaspiek Trail** (15km, two days) allows the average walker to view stunning mountain desert scenery. Accommodation is in matjieshuis and there are field toilets.

In early 2001 all hiking trails were being upgraded. You need a guide for all the trails. It costs about R20 per person per night and R200 per day for a guide. Contact **Sandra** (☎ 027-831 1175, e sandrat@parks-sa .co.za) for more information and to make bookings.

Organised Tours
Marius Opperman (☎ 027-851 8041, 083-314 3351) operates the 'Richtersveld Experience' from Port Nolloth. Tours are R540 for each person, per day (minimum of four people). You'll need your own bedding and you should book in advance from July to September as they get very busy.

Rey van Rensburg (☎ 027-718 1905) is a Springbok photographer who also runs tours. The 'Richtersveld Challenge' operates between April and October. Rey is enthusiastic, experienced and very knowledgeable about the area. A five-day vehicle tour costs around R2750 per person. You'll need at least eight people and your own bedding; book two or so months in advance.

Places to Stay & Eat
There is *guesthouse* accommodation at Sendelingsdrift on the western edge of the park.

Camping at the designated *camp sites* is R65 for two people. *Arieb Guest Cottage* in the park costs R550 for four people and an additional R70/35 per extra adult/child. This accommodation must be booked through the National Parks Board in Pretoria.

Within Richtersveld is *Eksteenfontein* (☎ 027-851 8775), a community guesthouse hosted by Nama people. Rooms are R60 per person. Traditional meals (R25) are prepared here for tourists.

HONDEKLIP BAY
☎ 027 • postcode 8222
In most ways Hondeklip Bay is just a smaller, less interesting version of Port Nolloth. It's a small, dusty little town on a bleak stretch of the coastal plain.

Die Honnehok Chalets (☎ 652 3041) is a good option for those without camping equipment. Chalets cost R150.

Having said that, the local dirt roads are spectacular. After climbing through rocky hills, you drop onto the desert-like coastal plain, which is dotted with enormous diamond mines. The flora is fascinating – make sure you take time to walk around, even if it's just off the side of the road. It is possible to get permission to drive through the sandveld on the private coastal road connecting Kleinzee and Hondeklip Bay; contact Springbok Lodge & Restaurant (☎ 027-712 1321) in Springbok. A 2WD is OK for this area.

KAMIESKROON
☎ 027 • postcode 8241
Kamieskroon, which means 'Jumble' or 'Huddles Together' in Nama, is an ordinary little town perched high in the mountains and surrounded by boulder-strewn hills. The *kroon* (crown) is an unmistakable

Native springboks grace the plains of Kgalagadi Transfrontier Park in Northern Cape.

ABWP

n spring, African daisies grow wild in in Northern Cape's Goegap Nature Reserve.

ROB DRUMMOND

.ook – some tourists! Take a safari tour in KwaZulu-Natal and give the animals something to look at.

LUKE HUNTER

Celebrating in style: Major festivals pay tribute to the rich culture of the Zulu people.

300m peak, which looms over the town. *Lita Cole* (☎ *672 1762*) is a registered Sa-tour guide who offers guided walks through some beautiful areas around here.

For information, contact the **Kamieskroon & Sandveld Tourism Forum** (☎ *672 1710; open in flower season*). Outside the flower season the post office dishes out limited tourist information.

Kamieskroon is a great spot to get away from it all and is an ideal base for exploring the area.

Places to Stay

Kamieskroom Bed & Breakfast (☎ *672 1652, Charlotta St*) B&B R130 per person. This is a relaxing little oasis, which makes a good base and has all the creature comforts.

Pedroskloof (☎ *672 1666*) B&B R90 per person. Pedroskloof is a good farmstay and is worth trying if you have a car, ask for directions at the tourist office.

Kamieskroon Hotel & Caravan Park (☎ *672 1614, fax 672 1675,* e *kamieshotel@kingsley.co.za*) Camp sites R35, singles/doubles R125/200, B&B R160/210. This very civilised hideaway is deservedly popular, especially from July to September (when bookings are essential and prices rise).

Getting There & Away

Both **Van Wyk's Busdiens** (☎ *713 8559*) and **Intercape** run buses along the N7. Kamieskroon is an hour south of Springbok.

AROUND KAMIESKROON
Skilpad Wildflower Reserve

About 18km north-west of Kamieskroon is this reserve (☎ *672 1614; admission R12*), which was established by the World Wide Fund for Nature (WWF) to increase world awareness of the floral heritage and biodiversity of Namaqualand. The shrubland and old wheat fields burst into flower (Namaqualand daisies) in spring, often surpassing all other areas in the region.

Garies

☎ 027 • postcode 8220

Just off the main road, Garies (named after a species of local grass, 'th'aries') does not have the same appeal as Kamieskroon, al-though there are some nice old homes and buildings lining the main street.

The **municipal office** (☎ *652 1014*) has an information desk but despite the sign, they're not much help with travel queries.

Garies Municipal Caravan Park (☎ *652 1014*) Camp sites R40. This place near the sports ground would be OK if there was anything in the way of shade.

Sophia's Guesthouse (☎/*fax 652 1069, 33 Main Rd*) Rooms with/without bathroom from R160/120. Rooms here are tidy, and the whole place looks like a boarding school. Breakfast is R25.

Hantam Karoo

Hantam (meaning 'Where Red Bulbs Grow' in Khoisan) is a basin-shaped area of vast semidesert plains and is one of the largest geographical regions in South Africa. In early spring, rain transforms the landscape into a burst of colourful wildflowers. Outside spring, tourists leave the sleepy little dorps (villages) to themselves; the only sound you may hear at this time is the clatter of donkey carts. The expanses are wide open and the starry skies stretch to eternity.

CALVINIA

☎ 027 • postcode 8190

Calvinia, an attractive town surrounded by 'Wild West' country, is the main centre of the Hantam Karoo. A ridge of the Hantamsberg Range dominates the town, which is it-self over 1000m above sea level. As the church clock quietly tolls the hours it's easy to imagine that decades, if not centuries, have slipped away. The nearby township is very friendly, with several convivial eateries and shebeens (bars).

The **information office** (☎ *341 1712; open 8am-1pm & 2pm-5pm Mon-Fri, 8am-noon Sat*) which adjoins the museum is very well organised. They provide a walking-tour map of town. Farmstays and B&Bs are plentiful, and the information office will help you arrange accommodation; bookings are advisable in flower season.

NORTHERN CAPE

Calvinia Museum

For a small country town, this museum (☎ 341 1712; admission R2) is of a surprisingly high standard and is definitely worth visiting. The main building was a synagogue – it's incongruous but not unusual to find disused Jewish buildings in tiny, remote South African towns. The museum concentrates on the white settlement of the region, including sheep and farming activities, and there are some wonderful oddities such as a four-legged ostrich chick (a fake used by a travelling con artist), and a room devoted to the lives of a local set of quadruplets.

Places to Stay & Eat

Calvinia Caravan Park (☎ 341 2931) Camp sites R50. Undistinguished but close to the centre of town, the caravan park is flat and ordinary. Unfortunately, this may be all you get during the Meat Festival in August.

The restored historic buildings, which now operate as guesthouses, are good places to stay.

Die Tiushuis & **Die Dorphuis** (☎/fax 341 1606) B&B standard/luxury rooms R135/160 per person. These are wonderful old places furnished with antiques.

Traut Ties

The barman at Holden's Commercial Hotel is an engaging, somewhat eccentric old character by the name of Cecil Traut. His claim to fame (of which he has a modicum) is his collection of ties from around the country and the world – his business card reads 'Tycoon of Calvinia: World Famous Tie Collector'. He has more than 2400 ties, which cover several walls of the bar, and he will be only too happy to show them to you.

Cecil also collects the signatures of famous people, usually as replied-to mail. Elizabeth Taylor is one of his favourites. A model of the Titanic – another Traut masterpiece – takes pride of place amid the ties.

And in case you're wondering, Cecil has worked behind bars for a long time and pours a good beer.

Die Hantamhuis (☎ 341 1606, Hoop St) Breakfast R25, mains R85. This is the oldest building in town and is now a cafe. Bookings can be made here for Tiushuis and Dorphuis; Die Hantamhuis is where you'll have breakfast if you stay at one of them. It also offers a traditional three course evening meal.

The information office can suggest other B&Bs; the list of the guesthouse owners reads like a local Afrikaner social register.

Pionierslot (☎ 341 1263, 35 Water St) B&B R120 per person. One of the nicest B&Bs in town, the owners here are hospitable without being overwhelming.

Hantam Hotel (☎ 341 1512, fax 341 2462, Kerk St) Singles/doubles R110/180. This place is plain but comfortable and as clean as a whistle. The hotel's steakhouse, the **Busibee**, has braaied lamb as a perennial feature. Breakfast is R27.50, mains are R50.

Holden's Commercial Hotel (☎ 341 1020, Water St) Singles/doubles from R80/160. This hotel is of a pretty high standard but hideously ugly, which is a shame considering it was a beautiful old building before 'modernisation'.

Die Blou Nartjie Restaurant (☎ 341 1484, Pionierslot) Starters R15-18, mains R25-65. Open 10am-2.30pm & 7pm-late Mon-Fri, 10am-6.30pm Sat. The range of dishes at this excellent restaurant is limited but very good quality for such a small town. We love an open kitchen! Traditional bobotie (curried mincemeat topped with beaten egg, and served with turmeric rice and chutney) is R35.

Cobusegat (☎ 341 2326) Self-catering cave R60 per person. This is the most interesting of the farmstay B&Bs, and the area boasts glacier scrapings from the last ice age. It's 116km south of Calvinia on the R355.

Getting There & Away

Intercape's Cape Town–Upington service goes through Calvinia, departing Calvinia for Upington (R120, 3¾ hours) on Monday, Wednesday, Friday and Sunday; and for Cape Town (R170, 5¾ hours) on Tuesday, Thursday, Friday and Sunday. Book at the travel agency (☎ 344 1373) incongruously situated in the *slaghuis* (butchers); buses stop at the *trokkie* (truck) stop on the western side of town.

Go to the trokkie stop for minibus taxis as well. It's R85 to either Cape Town or Upington but they don't run every day. If you have no luck here, try the Total petrol station on the eastern (Upington) side of town.

AROUND CALVINIA
Calvinia to Clanwilliam
The R364 between Clanwilliam and Calvinia is a superb road through unspoilt, empty countryside and several magnificent passes. There are excellent displays of wildflowers in early spring. There's a great view from the top of **Botterkloof Pass**, and a couple of nice flat rocks overlooking the gorge that are perfect for a picnic. Sit and dream what this country must have been like 300 years ago, before the wildlife was shot out of existence.

You hit irrigation country around Doringbos and start to get dramatic views of the Cederberg Range. The **Pakhuis Pass** takes you through an amazing jumble of multicoloured rocks. There's an excellent *camping ground* on the Clanwilliam side of the pass. Allow at least two hours for the journey – more if you have a picnic or are tempted by the side road to **Wuppertal**. This is an old Rhenish mission station, little changed since it was established in 1830. It has whitewashed, thatched cottages, as well as cypresses and donkeys.

Calvinia to Vanrhynsdorp
☎ 027
There is a stunning road between Calvinia and Vanrhynsdorp, with magnificent views over the Knersvlakte Plain from **Vanrhyns Pass**. In spring there can be a dramatic contrast between the green and fertile wheat fields, the flowers at the top of the pass and the desert far below.

Just before the pass on the Calvinia side but off the main road, is the small town of Nieuwoudtville, which has a handsome church and a couple of nearby reserves.

The small **Nieuwoudtville Wildflower Reserve** (*☎ 218 1336*), just to the north of the R27 and clearly signposted, has a fantastic range of flowers, including gladioli and other bulbs.

Theresa Rabe's (*☎ 218 1139*) 2-bed self-catering flats R80 per person. This friendly place is a good, cheap overnight stop.

Die Smidswinkel (*☎ 281 1535*) Meals R30-50. Come here for good, traditional Karoo fare (lamb and veg).

The 5000-hectare **Oorlogskloof Nature Reserve** (*☎ 218 1159*) runs along the eastern bank of the Oorlogskloof River and overlooks the plains. The terrain is rugged; there's rich birdlife and flora and a superb waterfall. There are hiking trails ranging from day hikes to three-night hikes. Permits for hiking can be obtained from Die Smidswinkel in Nieuwoudtville. All visits must be arranged in advance as there's no public access road.

Fraserburg & Sutherland
☎ 023 • postcode 6960/6920
Fraserburg is about 210km south-east of Calvinia in a little visited part of the country. Some 5km out of Fraserburg is the **Gansfontein Palaeosurface**; about 190 million years ago a large five-toed quadruped mammal lumbered across a muddy plain leaving several tracks that are still visible today. Get information from the **Old Rectory** (*☎ 741 1012*).

Sutherland is 165km south-east of Calvinia on the R354; it too receives few visitors (apart from astronomers). At an altitude of 1600m, high up in the Roggeveld Plateau, the night skies are particularly clear, making it an ideal location for the huge telescopes of the South African Astronomical Observatory.

Tourist information is available from the **Town Clerk** (*☎ 571 1020, Piet Retief St*).

KwaZulu-Natal

Despite being a relatively small province, KwaZulu-Natal manages to cram in most of the things that visitors come to South Africa to see, plus a few things that they may not expect.

There's the spectacular Drakensberg range in the south-west of the province, a long coast of subtropical surf beaches, remote lowveld savanna in the far north, and historic battlefields of the Anglo-Boer and Anglo-Zulu Wars. In the middle of it all is Zululand, the Zulu heartland. KwaZulu-Natal Wildlife (KZN Wildlife, the successor to KwaZulu-Natal Nature Conservation, one of the continent's leading conservation bodies) has many excellent parks that offer opportunities to see the best-known Southern African animals. Another attraction is Durban, a subtropical east-coast city with surf on the doorstep and a distinctly Indian vibe.

KwaZulu-Natal, with 8,726,300 people, has the largest population of any of South Africa's provinces.

History

Just before the 1994 elections, Natal Province was renamed KwaZulu-Natal, in belated recognition of the fact that the Zulu heartland of KwaZulu comprises a large part of the province.

Natal was named by Vasco da Gama, the Portuguese explorer, who sighted the coast on Christmas Day 1497 and named it for the natal day of Jesus. It was not until 1843 that Natal was proclaimed a British colony, and in 1845 it was made part of Cape Colony. In 1856, when it had a European population of less than 5000, Natal was again made a separate colony.

The introduction of Indian indentured labour in the 1860s and the consequent development of commercial agriculture (mainly sugar) boosted development, and from 1895, when train lines linked Durban's port (dredged to accommodate big ships) with the booming Witwatersrand, the colony thrived.

Highlights

- Take in the fresh mountain air and the magnificent scenery of the Drakensberg, the awesome basalt escarpment that splits South Africa from Lesotho.

- Eat well and dance up a storm at the many restaurants and clubs in Durban.

- Have a beer at Stan's Pub, the infamous drinking hole of Michael Caine and the cast of *Zulu*.

- Learn more than you ever wanted to know about what lurks beneath the sea, at the Natal Sharks Board at Umhlanga Rocks.

- Watch hippos frolic as you cruise the Greater St Lucia Wetland Park aboard the *Santa Lucia*.

- Photograph the last wild elephants in the region at Tembe Elephant Park on the Mozambique border.

- Tour the Battlefields Route in the Thukela region.

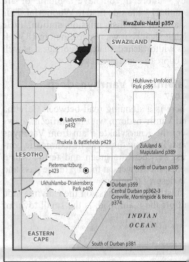

KWAZULU-NATAL

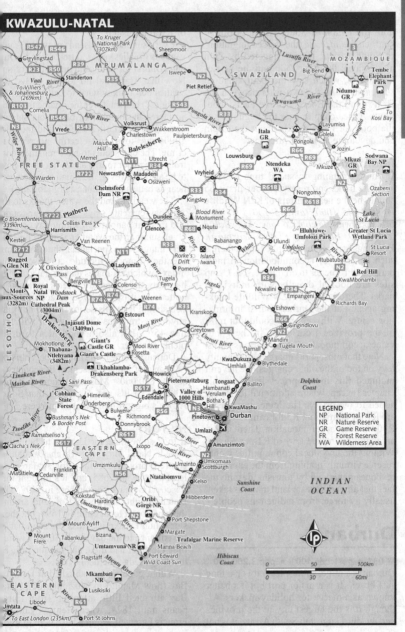

LEGEND

NP	National Park
NR	Nature Reserve
GR	Game Reserve
FR	Forest Reserve
WA	Wilderness Area

KWAZULU-NATAL

The recorded history of the province up until the Union of South Africa is full of conflict: the *mfeqane* (the 'forced migration' of South African tribes, triggered by Zulu aggression); the Boer-Zulu and the Anglo-Zulu Wars, which saw the Zulu kingdom subjugated; and the two wars between the British and the Boers. See the Facts about South Africa chapter near the beginning of the book for more details about the origin and development of the mfeqane.

Information

If you're planning to spend time in KZN Wildlife parks and reserves, your first stop should be the headquarters of **KZN Wildlife** (☎ *033-845 1000, fax 845 1001,* e *book ings@kznwildlife.com,* w *www.kznwildlife .com, PO Box 662, Pietermaritzburg).* Bookings can be made by phone, but there's such an array of accommodation in most parks that it's better to do it in person. Camp sites are booked directly with individual parks. There is also a KZN Wildlife booking agency at the Durban tourist information centre. With a car you could tour most of the province from bases in the good-value accommodation at the various parks.

Note that most parks charge a community levy on top of the other charges. We haven't included this in the prices listed in this chapter (except where additional levies are added to the price). The levies per person are R1 for admission, R5 for camp sites and R10 for other accommodation. There is also an additional rescue levy of R1 per person. Without the levy, local communities would receive virtually nothing from the enormous revenues generated by tourism, despite the fact that all parks are on land that was taken, usually by force, from indigenous people.

Durban

☎ 031 • postcode 4001 • pop 3,200,000

Durban is a large, subtropical city on a long surf beach. It is a major port but it's better known as a mecca for holiday-makers. Although it is the largest city in the province and the third largest in South Africa, it is not the capital – Pietermaritzburg is the capital of KwaZulu-Natal.

Every summer, thousands of white Transvaalians (Vaalies) used to trek down to Durban (Durbs) for sun, sand and a hint of sin. Now that Transvaal no longer exists, the Vaalies don't know what to call themselves (Gauties?) but whatever their name they, and an increasing number of black tourists, are again pouring in after a fall-off in the mid 1990s due to a post-election increase in crime. The city seems to have regained control of the major tourist areas, but it still pays to be alert. However, the situation is nowhere near as bad as in Johannesburg (Jo'burg).

The weather (and the water, thanks to the Agulhas current) stays warm year-round and there are about 230 sunny days a year. Over summer the weather is quite hot and very humid, with spectacular thunderstorms. Weather reports include a 'discomfort index', which estimates that on days of high humidity the temperature feels up to 10°C hotter than it is. Until you've acclimatised you should take this seriously and not plan anything strenuous on a day that will feel like 45°C. It's also a good idea to drink plenty of water.

Durban is home to the largest concentration of people of Indian descent in the country about 800,000. Muslims number about 200,000, so it's not surprising that South Africa's biggest mosque is found here.

HISTORY

It took some time for Durban to be established. Natal Bay, on which Durban is centred, provided refuge for seafarers at least as early as 1685, and it's thought that Vasco da Gama anchored here in 1497. The Dutch bought a large area of land around the bay from a local chief in 1690, but their ships didn't make it across the sand bar at the entrance to the bay until 1705, by which time the chief had died, and his son refused to acknowledge the deal.

With a good port established at Delagoa Bay (now Maputo in Mozambique), Natal Bay attracted little attention from Europeans until 1824, when Henry Fynn and Francis Farewell set up a base here to trade

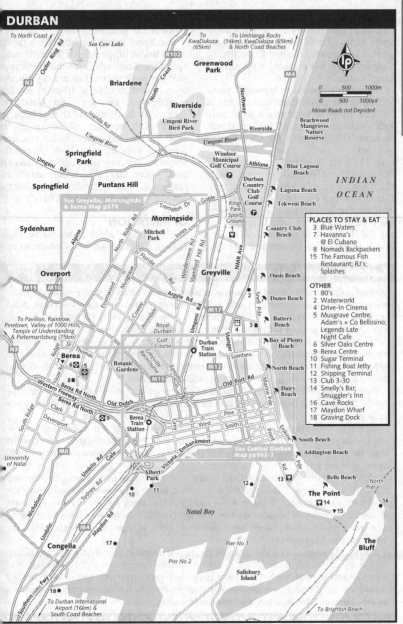

DURBAN

KWAZULU-NATAL

To North Coast

Sea Cow Lake

To KwaDukuza (65km)

To Umhlanga Rocks (14km), KwaDukuza (65km) & North Coast Beaches

R102

Greenwood Park

M4

N2

Outer Ring Rd

Inanda Rd

North Coast

Briardene

Riverside

Umgeni River Bird Park

Northway

Riverside

Beachwood Mangroves Nature Reserve

Umgeni River

Umgeni River

0   500   1000m
0   500   1000yd

Minor Roads not Depicted

Springfield Park

Umgeni Rd

Windsor Municipal Golf Course

Athlone

Blue Lagoon Beach

INDIAN OCEAN

Springfield

Puntans Hill

Durban Country Club Golf Course

Laguna Beach

See Greyville, Morningside & Berea Map p374

Trematon Dr

Goble

Kings Park Sports Ground

Tekweni Beach

Sydenham

Alpine

North Ridge Rd

Morningside

Mitchell Park

Innes

Stamford Hill Rd

Windermere Rd

Country Club Beach

PLACES TO STAY & EAT
3 Blue Waters
7 Havanna's @ El Cubano
8 Nomads Backpackers
15 The Famous Fish Restaurant; RJ's; Splashes

1

Overport

M15 M10

Florida

Musgrave

Esenwood

Cowey

Avondale

Argyle Rd

Umgeni Rd

Greyville

M17

NMR Ave

Oasis Beach

2

Snell Pde

Dunes Beach

To Pavilion, Rainbow, Pinetown, Valley of 1000 Hills, Temple of Understanding & Pietermaritzburg (75km)

N3

Ridge Rd

St Thomas

Berea

6 5

Royal Durban Golf Course

Greyville Racecourse

Umgeni Rd

Epsom

Durban Train Station

3

Stanger

Battery Beach

Bay of Plenty Beach

Somtseu

M12

North Beach

8

Berea Rd North

Western Freeway

Berea Rd North

Old Dutch

Botanic Gardens

M15

Grey

Old Fort Rd

Marine Pde

Dairy Beach

Clark

Davenport

9

Berea Train Station

West

Smith

Pine

Point Rd

South Beach

South Ridge

M8

Umbilo Rd

Gale

Victoria Embankment

See Central Durban Map pp362-3

Addington Beach

University of Natal

Nicholson

Sydney Rd

Albert Park

11

12

13

Erskine

Pde

Bells Beach

North Pier

OTHER
1 80's
2 Waterworld
4 Drive-In Cinema
5 Musgrave Centre; Adam's + Co Bellissino; Legends Late Night Cafe
6 Silver Oaks Centre
9 Berea Centre
10 Sugar Terminal
11 Fishing Boat Jetty
12 Shipping Terminal
13 Club 3-30
14 Smelly's Bar; Smuggler's Inn
16 Cave Rocks
17 Maydon Wharf
18 Graving Dock

10

M4

Maydon Rd

Congella

17

Natal Bay

The Point

14

15

16

The Bluff

Southern Fwy

18

Pier No 1

Pier No 2

Salisbury Island

To Durban International Airport (16km) & South Coast Beaches

To Brighton Beach

for ivory with the Zulu. Shaka, a powerful Zulu chief (see History in the Facts about South Africa chapter for more information) granted land around the bay to the trading company and it was accepted in the name of King George IV.

The settlement was slow to prosper, partly because of the chaos Shaka was causing in the area. By 1835 there was a small town with a mission station, and that year it took the name D'Urban, after the Cape Colony governor.

In 1837 the Voortrekkers crossed the Drakensberg and founded Pietermaritzburg, 80km north-west of Durban. The next year, after Durban was evacuated during a raid by the Zulu, the Boers claimed control. It was reoccupied by a British force later that year, but the Boers stuck by their claim. The British sent troops to Durban to secure their claim, but were defeated by the Boers at the Battle of Congella in 1842.

The Boers retained control for a month until a British frigate arrived (fetched by teenager Dick King, who rode the 1000km of wild country between Durban and Grahamstown in Eastern Cape in 10 days) and dislodged them. The next year Natal was annexed by the British and Durban began its growth as an important colonial port city. In 1860 the first indentured Indian labourers arrived to work the cane fields. Despite the iniquitous system – slave labour by another name – many free Indian settlers arrived, including, in 1893, Mohandas Gandhi (see the boxed text 'Gandhi in South Africa').

ORIENTATION

Marine Parade, which fronts the beach, is Durban's focal point. Many places to stay

Gandhi in South Africa

Mohandas Karamchand Gandhi was born in October 1869 in Porbandar, by the sea on the Kathiawar Peninsula in Gujarat in western India. In 1888 he sailed for England to study law; he was called to the bar in June 1891 and immediately returned to India. He practised law in India for two years and, unimpressed with the petty politics of Porbandar, left for South Africa in 1893.

Gandhi was soon embroiled in the politics of South Africa and became a victim of the widespread prejudice against his people. He was ejected from a train in Pietermaritzburg, and when he returned to South Africa after fetching his family he was beaten up at the docks by an angry mob. He founded the Natal Indian Congress in 1894 to fight for Indian emancipation.

During the Anglo-Boer War Gandhi raised a volunteer corps of stretcher-bearers to assist the British. Gandhi and his bearers distinguished themselves on the battlefield, including at the bloody battle of Spioenkop, braving enemy fire to bring wounded to the base hospital.

Inspired by the writings of British essayist John Ruskin, he purchased a farm, Phoenix, just outside Durban in 1903. He transferred the printing presses and office of the magazine *Indian Opinion* there. He and his followers, known as satyagrahas, lived a self-sufficient lifestyle and embraced self-denial, truth and love.

In 1907 the Asiatic Registration Act was passed to prevent Indians from entering the Transvaal. It's hardly surprising that Gandhi saw this as an affront, and his law offices in Durban became the headquarters for opposition to the repressive law. Opposition slowly evolved into mass resistance. Thousands of indentured labourers went on strike and Gandhi's followers were thrown into already overflowing prisons (Gandhi himself joined them on occasion), as negotiations between General Jan Smuts and Gandhi dragged on.

In June 1914 Smuts and Gandhi agreed on the terms of the Indian Relief Bill and a victory of sorts (with many conditions) was won for the Indian community. Gandhi, happy that this struggle was over, sailed for England in July 1914, never to return. Gandhi's commune, part of what the Zulu called Bhambayi (Bombay), was destroyed by squatters from the surrounding Inanda township in violent clashes in 1985. Hopefully it will rise from the ashes.

and eat are on the parade and in the streets behind it, as are many of the entertainment venues.

West St starts as a mall, but further west it becomes one of central Durban's main streets. The city hall and the centre of town are about 1km west of the beach, straddling West and Smith Sts.

On the western side of the city centre, around Grey and Victoria Sts, is the Indian area. There's a bustle and vibrancy present here that is missing from most commercial districts in South Africa.

Near the Indian area, especially around Berea train station, thousands of Zulu squatters have set up camp to make an extraordinarily jumbled 'township' right on the city centre's doorstep. Most of these people are near-destitute and live in appalling conditions, so conspicuously wealthy tourists are an obvious target.

The suburb of Berea (pronounced b-**ree**-a) is further inland, on a ridge overlooking the city centre. The ridge marks the beginning of the wealthy suburbs. Wild elephants roamed the Berea Ridge well into the 1850s.

The increasingly popular areas of Greyville and Morningside, around Florida and Windermere Rds, have many restaurants and clubs.

The Umgeni River marks the northern boundary of the city, although the suburbs have sprawled over the river all the way up the coast to Umhlanga Rocks, a big resort and retirement town. Inland from Umhlanga Rocks is Phoenix, an Indian residential area named after Gandhi's commune.

On the city's western fringe is Pinetown, a vast collection of dormitory suburbs. A fair proportion of Durban's mainly black population lives in townships surrounding the city. These include Richmond Farm, KwaMashu, Lindelani, Ntuzuma and the Greater Inanda area.

INFORMATION
Tourist Offices
The main tourist information centre is in the old train station and is known as **Tourist Junction** (☎ 304 4934, 304 6196, e funinsun@ africa.com, w www.durban.org.za, Cnr Pine

& Gardiner Sts; open 8am-5pm Mon-Fri, 9am-2pm Sat). There are various booking agencies in the complex, including one which takes reservations for both KZN Wildlife and the **National Parks Board** (☎ 304 4934). There is a second **tourist information office** (☎ 332 2595, North Beach) near Joe Kool's, and tourist information is also available at the airport.

Pick up a copy of the What's On in Durban pamphlet at Tourist Junction. The monthly Durban for All Seasons is available from most hotels. There is also information in the KwaZulu-Natal Experience magazine. The **municipal library** (☎ 300 6911) in the Natal Science Museum produces a full listing of clubs and societies.

Money
Rennies Travel (☎ 305 5722, 2nd floor, 333 Smith St; open 8.30am-4.30pm Mon-Fri, 8.30am-11.30am Sat), the agent for Thomas Cook, has several branches around town. **American Express** (☎ 301 5541, Denor House, Smith St; open 8am-5pm Mon-Fri, 8.30am-11am Sat) is opposite Rennies Travel.

You'll find plenty of other banks around the city and in the suburbs. Some larger branches are open on Saturday morning.

Post & Communications
Poste restante is at the main post office. From the entrance foyer, go through the doors on the right and ask at the desk immediately inside. The post office keeps letters for a month.

International phone calls can be made from **Cash Call Telkom** (1st floor, 320 West St; open 8am-9.50pm Mon-Sat closed for lunch, 6-9pm Sun).

AV-8 Computer & Cyber Studios (☎ 313 2001, e jerry@av-8.com, 200A Florida Rd, Morningside; Internet access R0.33 per minute) is a 24-hour Internet cafe. It's a pleasant place and the staff here are very helpful.

In the city try the **Internet Café** (☎ 305 6998, fax 301 3044, The Workshop, Aliwal St; Internet access R10/20 per half-hour/ hour).

Bookshops

Adam's & Co (☎ *304 8571,* **e** *adams.west@ saol.com, 341 West St*) is a good bookshop (there is a second outlet at the Musgrave Centre in Berea). On the 1st floor of the city store there are textbooks, including some dictionaries and phrasebooks in the many South African languages.

Laundry

One of several central laundrettes is on Palmer St, near Gillespie St. A bag of washing (you drop it off and it's returned to you washed, dried and folded) costs about R15.

Medical Services

The **medical centre** (☎ *304 9767, Cnr Smith & Broad Sts; consultation R80; doctors available 8.30am-8pm daily; pharmacy open 7.30am-10pm daily*) in the city offers medical, dental and optometry services. For those who are travelling into malarial areas a trip to the **Travel Doctor** (☎ *360 1122, fax 360 1121,* **e** *travelc@icc.co.za, International Convention Centre, 45 Ordnance Rd; open 8am-4pm Mon-Fri, 8am-noon Sat*) might be in order.

Emergency

The phone numbers for emergency services are:

Ambulance	☎ 10177
Fire	☎ 361 0000
Police	☎ 10111

Worryingly, there's another number (☎ 1022) you should ring 'in case of difficulty with emergency calls'.

Dangers & Annoyances

Many areas are potentially dangerous at night, notably the Indian area and nearby squatter camps and parts of Point Rd. At night central Durban takes on the feel of a ghetto as people head to the restaurants in places such as Morningside or to the big hotels and clubs along the beachfront.

In the past the crowded beachfront Promenade has been a happy hunting ground for pickpockets, and violent robberies have

CENTRAL DURBAN

PLACES TO STAY
27 Banana Backpackers
28 Tudor House Hotel
33 Albany Hotel
35 Royal Hotel; Ulundi; Royal Carvery; Royal Grill
46 Road Lodge
48 Durban Hilton International; Rivets
50 City Lodge
57 Holiday Inn Garden Court – North Beach
58 Holiday Inn – Elangeni; Daruma; Jewel of India
60 The Palace Hotel
61 Parade Hotel; The Big Blue
63 Holiday Inn Garden Court – Marine Parade; Saagris
64 Edward Protea Hotel
66 The Balmoral
73 Palm Beach; London Town Pub
75 Tropicana
76 Holiday Inn Garden Court – South Beach
77 Four Seasons
79 Impala Holiday Flats

PLACES TO EAT
3 Victory Lounge
25 Roma Revolving Restaurant; Oriental Palace; John Ross House
32 Fiddler's
40 The Garden Bistro
62 Joe Kool's; Tourist Information Office; Ocean Sports Centre Time-warp Surf Museum
68 Thatcher's
74 Golden Chopsticks

OTHER
1 Bus Depot
2 Minibus Taxis
4 Juma Mosque
5 Madrassa Arcade

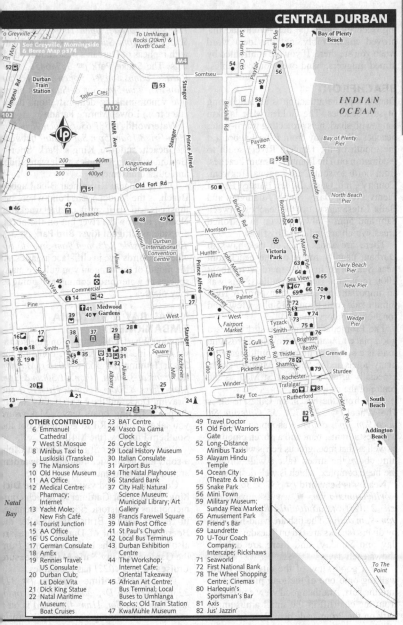

CENTRAL DURBAN

KWAZULU-NATAL

OTHER (CONTINUED)
6 Emmanuel
   Cathedral
7 West St Mosque
8 Minibus Taxi to
   Lusikisiki (Transkei)
9 The Mansions
10 Old House Museum
11 AA Office
12 Medical Centre;
   Pharmacy;
   Internet
13 Yacht Mole;
   New Fish Café
14 Tourist Junction
15 AA Office
16 US Consulate
17 German Consulate
18 AmEx
19 Rennies Travel;
   US Consulate
20 Durban Club;
   La Dolce Vita
21 Dick King Statue
22 Natal Maritime
   Museum;
   Boat Cruises

23 BAT Centre
24 Vasco Da Gama
   Clock
26 Cycle Logic
29 Local History Museum
30 Italian Consulate
31 Airport Bus
34 The Natal Playhouse
36 Standard Bank
37 City Hall; Natural
   Science Museum;
   Municipal Library; Art
   Gallery
38 Francis Farewell Square
39 Main Post Office
41 St Paul's Church
42 Local Bus Terminus
43 Durban Exhibition
   Centre
44 The Workshop;
   Internet Cafe;
   Oriental Takeaway
45 African Art Centre;
   Bus Terminal; Local
   Buses to Umhlanga
   Rocks; Old Train Station
47 KwaMuhle Museum

49 Travel Doctor
51 Old Fort; Warriors
   Gate
52 Long-Distance
   Minibus Taxis
53 Alayam Hindu
   Temple
54 Ocean City
   (Theatre & Ice Rink)
55 Snake Park
56 Mini Town
59 Military Museum;
   Sunday Flea Market
65 Amusement Park
67 Friend's Bar
69 Laundrette
70 U-Tour Coach
   Company;
   Intercape; Rickshaws
71 Seaworld
72 First National Bank
78 The Wheel Shopping
   Centre; Cinemas
80 Harlequin's
   Sportsman's Bar
81 Axis
82 Jus' Jazzin'

KWAZULU-NATAL

occurred here at night. At the time of writing, security along the beachfront had improved considerably; get the local word when you are there. If you are confronted by armed muggers, hand over your valuables!

BEACHFRONT

Durban's prime attraction is its long string of surf beaches. The Golden Mile is 6km long, with shark nets protecting warm-water beaches all the way from Blue Lagoon (at the mouth of the Umgeni River) south to Addington on The Point. The main beaches, from north to south, are Laguna, Tekweni, Country Club, Oasis, Dunes, Battery, Bay of Plenty, North, Dairy, South, Addington and Bells. Lifesavers patrol the beaches between 8am and 5pm – always swim in patrolled areas, which are indicated by flags.

There are about a dozen rickshaws in Durban, usually found on the beachfront near Seaworld. In 1904 there were about 2000 registered rickshaw pullers; this was an important means of transport. A five-minute ride costs about R15 plus a few rand for the mandatory photo.

The Promenade fronts the surf and is a good place to watch the crowds. Across the road is a screen of high-rise buildings with many hotels and restaurants. Marine Parade, especially around the West St Mall, is the centre of the action.

Back from the beach, on Gillespie St, is **The Wheel** (☎ 332 4324, 55 Gillespie St; open 9am-9pm daily), a shopping complex with restaurants, bars and a dozen cinemas, as well as that incongruous Ferris wheel spinning above the street. Take a walk through the huge complex, which is well designed.

Nearby is **Seaworld** (☎ 337 3536, e sea world@dbn.lia.net, w www.seaworld.org.za, 2 West St; adult/child R35/20; open 9am-9pm daily). The fish are hand-fed daily by divers (sharks are fed on Tuesday, Thursday and Sunday) and there are dolphin shows each day.

For a good view of the city, it's worth walking onto one of the long piers that jut into the surf. Another good view can be had from the chairlift in the small **amusement park** on the Promenade near West St.

Further north is **Mini Town** (☎ 337 7892, 114 Snell Parade; open 10am-5pm Tues-Sat, 10am-4pm Sun), a tacky model city with replicas of Durban's best-known buildings. The **Snake Park** (☎ 337 6456, Snell Parade; admission R15; open 9am-4.30pm Mon-Fri, 9am-5pm Sat & Sun) has about five venom-milking demonstrations daily; enter from Lower Marine Parade.

Waterworld (☎ 337 6336; open 9am-5pm Mon-Fri, 8.15am-5pm Sat & Sun) between the beach and the King's Park Sport's Ground is a large complex with waterslides and other amusements.

On the Umgeni River, near Blue Lagoon Beach, is the Model Yacht Pond where enthusiasts sail their craft on the weekend. Nearby, also on the river but on the northern side, is **Umgeni River Bird Park** (☎ 579 4600, Riverside Rd; open 9am-5pm daily), where the birds live in cliff-face aviaries. At the mouth of the Umgeni you will see many species of water birds coming and going as they please.

NATAL BAY & VICTORIA EMBANKMENT

Maydon Wharf, which runs along the south-western side of the harbour, contains the **Sugar Terminal** (☎ 365 8100, 51 Maydon Rd; tours at 8.30am, 10am, 11.30am & 2pm Mon-Thurs, 8.30am, 10am & 11am Fri), the Graving Dock and the Fishing Jetty, where deep-sea fishing boats leave. Make sure you take Maydon Rd to get there, not the Southern Freeway (the M4).

West of Gardiner St is the Durban Club, a solid jumble of Victorian and Edwardian architectural elements.

Continue east and you come to the **Dick King Statue**, near Gardiner St, which commemorates the historic ride of this teenager in 1842 to fetch a British frigate after the Boers took control of Durban. There are also boat tours of the harbour running from the Gardiner St jetty. **Sarie Marais Pleasure Cruises** (☎ 305 4022) has timetables.

The **Natal Maritime Museum** (☎ 31 2230, Maritime Dr; admission R3; open 8am-4pm Mon-Sat, 11am-4pm Sun) is on a service road running parallel to Victoria

Embankment – enter on the corner of Fenton St and Victoria Embankment. It has two tugboats and the minesweeper SAS *Durban*. You can clamber all over the boats.

Further along Maritime Dr is the **BAT Centre** (☎ *332 0451,* [e] *bat@dbn.lia.net, 45 Marine Place; shops open 10am-4.30pm daily*). This arts centre has studios for a wide range of arts, and there's a shop where you can buy out-of-the-ordinary souvenirs. There are a couple of bars that are pleasant places for a drink on a hot afternoon or evening. Check the newspapers for other events here.

The **Vasco da Gama Clock**, a florid Victorian monument on the Embankment east of Aliwal St, was presented by the Portuguese government in 1897, the 400th anniversary of Vasco da Gama's sighting of Natal.

Durban's **harbour** is the busiest in Africa (and the ninth busiest in the world) and much of the activity centres on the Shipping Terminal near Stanger St, where there are public viewing areas. You can also see the activity on the water from the ferry that runs across the harbour mouth from North Pier on The Point to South Pier on The Bluff.

Down at the southern end of the beachfront, The Point is an old area on a spit of land between the harbour and the ocean. At the very end of The Point you can watch ships coming through the narrow heads into the harbour. The dense indigenous forest on The Bluff, across the narrow channel (which is the harbour mouth), is in stark contrast to the sprawling city. There's a weekend market at The Point, and a bar and restaurant or two, which are popular on weekends. Point Rd, leading down to The Point, runs through a very run-down area and is definitely unsafe at night.

CITY CENTRE

The impressive **city hall** (☎ *311 1111*), built in 1910 in modern renaissance style, is worth a look inside and out. In front of the hall is Francis Farewell Square, where Fynn and Farewell made their camp in 1824, which features several statues and memorials to historical figures.

In the city hall building is the **Natural Science Museum** (☎ *311 2256; Smith St;* *open 8.30am-4pm Mon-Sat, 11am-4pm Sun*). Check out the cockroach display, the reconstructed dodo and the life-sized dinosaur model. There are sometimes free films here – some dull, some very good.

Upstairs is the **Art Gallery** (☎ *300 6234, open 8.30am-4pm Mon-Sat, 11am-4pm Sun*) which houses a good collection of contemporary South African works, especially Zulu arts and crafts. In particular, look out for the collection of baskets from Hlabisa, finely woven from a variety of grasses and incorporating striking natural colours.

The **municipal library** (☎ *300 6268; open 9am-5.30pm Mon-Fri, 8.30am-2.30pm Sat*) is also in this complex.

The **Local History Museum** (*Aliwal St; admission free*) is in the 1863 courthouse behind the city hall. It has interesting displays on colonial life as well as a useful bookshop.

Across West St, on the corner of Gardiner St, is the main post office, which predates the city hall. On the eastern side of the main post office is **Church Square**, with its old vicarage and the 1909 **St Paul's Church** at the rear on Pine St. Near Church Square is **Medwood Gardens** which has an outdoor cafe, the Garden Bistro.

The **old train station**, on the corner of Soldiers Way (the continuation of Gardiner St) and Pine St, was built in 1894 and gives an idea of Durban's size and importance at the end of the 19th century. The building currently houses Tourist Junction, the tourist information centre. You'll also find the **African Art Centre** (*open 8.30am-5pm Mon-Fri, 9am-1pm Sat*) here. It is not a curio shop, but a nonprofit gallery with work by rural craftspeople and artists. It also sells some 'authentic' pieces which are usually old and were made for traditional use. Local dealers and galleries often snap these up.

The Workshop (☎ *304 9894, 99 Aliwal St; open 8am-5pm Mon-Fri, 9am-5pm Sat, 10am-5pm Sun*) is a shopping centre which was another railway building (a train shed, hence the huge doors) which became redundant when the new station opened.

Across from The Workshop is the **Durban Exhibition Centre** (*DEC;* ☎ *360 1000,*

Aliwal St), which hosts the Durban Military Tattoo each year in July. On Sunday a flea market is held in the DEC's South Plaza.

From The Workshop, walk north across some vacant land to Ordnance Rd, where you'll find the excellent **KwaMuhle Museum** *(☎ 311 2223, 130 Ordnance Rd; open 8.30am-4pm Mon-Sat, 11am-4pm Sun)* in the former Bantu Administration building. The museum has a permanent display (with good oral history tapes) on the 'Durban System' by which whites subjugated blacks, and temporary exhibitions relating to Zulu culture and contemporary issues.

Old Fort, north of the centre on Old Fort Rd, is where the British were besieged by the Boers in 1842. Just east is **Warriors Gate** *(☎ 307 3337, Old Fort Rd; open 11am-3pm Tues-Fri, 10am-noon Sat, 11am-3pm Sun)* which is the general headquarters of MOTH (Memorable Order of Tin Hats), a former servicepersons' club. There's a small collection of militaria here.

In the south-west of town, the **Old House Museum** *(☎ 311 2229, 31 St Andrews St; open 8.30am-4pm Mon-Sat, 11am-4pm Sun)* is the restored home of Natal's first prime minister.

INDIAN AREA

The **Victoria St Market** *(☎ 306 4021, Victoria St; open 9am-4.30pm Mon-Fri, 8am-3pm Sat, 10am-2pm Sun)* is at the western end of Victoria St and has replaced the old Indian Market which burned down in 1973. It is the main tourist attraction of the area and is worth wandering around, but a walk through the nearby bustling streets is equally interesting. Just be on the lookout for pickpockets.

Grey St, between Victoria and West Sts, is the main shopping area. Prices are low and you can bargain. Most Muslim shops close between noon and 2pm on Friday.

The big **Juma Mosque** *(☎ 306 0026, Cnr Queen & Grey Sts; open to visitors 9am-4pm Mon-Fri, 9am-11am Sat)* is the largest in the southern hemisphere; call ahead for a guided tour. Madrassa Arcade runs between the mosque and the Catholic Emmanuel Cathedral, exemplifying a commercial ecumenism.

Hindu & Muslim Festivals

The annual Kavadi Festival, held twice a year (January to February and April to May) is the major Hindu festival. It honours the god Muruga, who heals and dispels misfortune and, as a sign of devotion, much self-inflicted pain accompanies the ceremony.

In April or May, an 18-day festival is held to honour the goddess Draupadi that culminates in firewalking. For 10 days during July and August the Mariamman, or Porridge Festival, is celebrated.

Other festivals include the three-day Diwali, the Festival of Lights, celebrated in November; and the colourful five-day Hare Krishna festival Ratha Yatra, Festival of Chariots, celebrated in December.

Each year there's the Muslim observance of the death of the Prophet's grandson, which culminates in a parade down Centenary Rd.

On West St, near the corner of Grey St, is the less flamboyant West St Mosque. Further west along West St, opposite the cemetery, is The Mansions, a big Edwardian building, all verandas and wrought iron.

West of Berea train station is a bustling fruit and vegetable market, now the centre of the maelstrom of a squatter settlement; it's interesting to visit, but don't take valuables.

Alayam Hindu Temple *(Somtseu Rd; open to visitors 7am-6pm daily)* is the oldest and biggest in South Africa. It's away from the main Indian area, on Somtseu Rd, which runs between Stanger St and NMR Ave.

CAMPBELL COLLECTIONS

The Campbell Collections *(☎ 207 3432, 220 Marriott Rd; open by appointment only)*, in Berea on the corner of Marriott and Essenwood Rds, are worth seeing. Muckleneuk, a superb house designed by Sir Herbert Baker, holds the documents and artefacts collected by Dr Killie Campbell and her father Sir Marshall Campbell (KwaMashu township is named after him) which are extremely important records of early Natal and Zulu culture. Thanks to a grant from the Mellon Foundation in the USA, a catalogue of the entire collection is available on the Internet; researchers can order CD-ROMS.

Killie Campbell began collecting works by black artists 60 years before the Durban Gallery did, and she was the first patron of Barbara Tyrrell. Barbara Tyrrell trained as a fashion illustrator in Europe in the 1930s, but on returning home to South Africa she decided that recording the traditional costumes of the indigenous peoples was more important than illustrating catalogues of the latest Paris couture. Her paintings convey the clothing and decoration, and also give real grace to the people wearing them. You can buy cards of her work or a portfolio of limited edition prints (R400) at the Campbell Collections shop. Ms Tyrrell is still painting and there are sometimes originals for sale.

The house itself is worth seeing; it contains some wonderful old Cape Dutch furniture.

MITCHELL PARK
This park (☎ 312 2318, 10 Ferndale Rd, open 7.30am-4pm Mon-Fri) has a small zoo, with a few animals, and an outdoor restaurant. King's House, on the edge of the park, was the Natal governor's residence and is now the Durban home of the South African president.

BOTANIC GARDENS
The 20-hectare Botanic Gardens (☎ 201 1303, Botanical Gardens Rd; open 7.30am-4.45pm daily; Orchid House open 9.30am-12.30pm & 2pm-4.45pm daily) is west of Greyville Racecourse. One of the rarest cycads, Encephalartos woodii, can be seen here, as well as many species of bromeliad. There is also a picturesque tea garden.

TEMPLE OF UNDERSTANDING
The Temple of Understanding (☎ 403 3328, Bhaktieedanta Sami Rd; open 9am-4pm daily), the biggest Hare Krishna temple in the southern hemisphere, is just outside Durban. It's an unusual building, and now houses a vegetarian restaurant. Follow the N3 towards Pietermaritzburg and then branch off to the N2 south. Take the Chatsworth turn-off and turn right towards the centre of Chatsworth.

CANOEING
Durban, the canoeing centre of South Africa, caters for all types of canoeing: marathon, slalom, white-water, canoe polo and sea kayaking.

Each year the popular Dusi Marathon starts 80km inland at Pietermaritzburg and ends at the mouth of the Umgeni River.

CYCLING
Durban is a good city for cycling, particularly in the flatter areas near the beach. You can rent bicycles on South Beach and North Beach (near the Holiday Inn hotels). Tekweni Backpackers (see Places to Stay – Budget later in this section) can organise various cycling tours.

Cyclist's eyes will light up when they enter Cycle Logic (☎ 332 29550, Cnr Cato & Timber Sts). It's a good bicycle shop with professional service, and also sells used parts at reasonable prices.

DIVING
Simply Scuba (☎/fax 309 2982, Marriott Rd, Berea) offers PADI or NAUI courses, equipment hire and sales. Other schools include Underwater World (☎ 332 7690, 251 Point Rd). Check the Yellow Pages telephone directory under Clubs – Cultural, Social & Hobby for the contact number of the Durban Undersea Club. The club is a good source of information and also rents equipment. There are diving schools and hire places in many of the major towns along the KwaZulu-Natal coast.

GOLF
KwaZulu-Natal is a great place to vent your frustration on the small white ball. The area to the south of Durban is known as the Golf Coast. Pick up the free Golf: Southern Natal from Tourist Junction for contact numbers.

HIKING
Local hiking clubs include the Durban Ramblers and the Mountain Backpackers Club. Their contact numbers depend on the office-holders, so try the phone book.

The Ramblers take things more easily and concentrate on the social and aesthetic pleasures of hiking. The Mountain Backpackers are more likely to be seen sweating it out on a high traverse of the Drakensberg. The club welcomes visitors, including novices. Members of the Natal section of the **Mountain Club of SA** *(PO Box 4535, Durban)* are the spider-like forms you will see scaling the sides of the Monk's Cowl in the central Drakensberg.

HORSE RACING

Horse racing, which is very popular in Durban, is held throughout the year at Greyville Racecourse near the Botanic Gardens, and at Clairwood Park Turf Club near the freeway south of the city. South Africa's main racing event is the Rothman's July, held on the first Saturday of July at Greyville. It's worth driving along DLI Ave, which cuts across Greyville, for its banks of carefully tended tropical flowers.

SAILING

Durban is an excellent place to learn to sail. Travellers have recommended the **Ocean Sailing Academy** *(☎ 301 5726, e academy@ oceansailing.co.za, W www.oceansailing.co .za, 38 Fenton Rd)*. It offers five-day courses for yacht hands (R2000) and skippers (R2400). If you take both courses you'll pay R4000.

SURFING

If you're a surfer and you're in Durban then you've cruised to the right place. There are a multitude of good beaches with any number of breaks (see the boxed text 'The KwaZulu-Natal Surf Scene' for more information). *Zigzag* magazine has surfing information crammed between glossy ads; it comes out every two months.

WHITE-WATER RAFTING

The mighty Tugela River (uThukela in Zulu, meaning 'the Startling One') is the scene of most of the rafting in KwaZulu-Natal. When the water level is high, usually from November to April, you can ride through sections of the river known locally as Horrible Horace, the Rollercoaster, Four-Man Hole and the Tugela Ravine. Rafting operators include **Tugela River Adventures** *(☎ 035-834 9188)* and **Umko Whitewater Rafting** *(☎ 039 834 0029, W www.dlangala .co.za)*.

ORGANISED TOURS

Perhaps the best way to experience Durban is in the company of someone who knows what they are looking at. The Tourist Junction (see Tourist Offices under Information earlier) runs walking tours of the city at 9.30am Monday to Friday for three hours; it costs R25.

Most hostels arrange backpacker-oriented tours and activities in the Durban area and around KwaZulu-Natal. By far the largest range is offered by *Tekweni Eco-Tours* *(☎ 303 1199)*, based at Tekweni Backpackers (see Places to Stay – Budget later in this section) in Durban.

There are a couple of tours that get you out of the white cocoon. *Umkhumbane Tours* *(☎ 309 7058)* has a good tour for R120 per person (minimum four people) which includes visiting a township and meeting people involved in various traditional activities.

Contact Tekweni Eco-Tours to organise a trip to the small, friendly village of isiThumba in the Valley of 1000 Hills, staying at Jabu's Place. An overnight stay costs R300 per person which includes transport.

The *Coloured Experience (☎/fax 468 8609)* has been highly recommended by readers. The four-hour tour costs R240.

The tour operator and guide leads you on a powerful journey through the coloured townships and her own personal journey of seeing her home bulldozed under the Group Areas Act and being moved with her family and many others to an unfinished house in an instant township beside industrial tracts. You end up at her family's home for a lunch of *bunny chow* (a traditional snack). Not your usual tourist gloss, but it is an experience that you will remember.

Jim Gaskell

PLACES TO STAY – BUDGET

There are plenty of budget options in the area, but not many are centrally located.

Durban Caravan Park (☎ 467 8865, 55 Greys Inn Rd) Camp sites for 2 people R75.

The Durban Caravan Park is a long way from town. To get there from Durban, take the Brighton Beach exit from the N2 and head south-east on Edwin Swales VC Dr, which meets Bluff Rd, near the intersection of Greys Inn Rd.

Hostels

Durban doesn't have the range of hostels you'll find in Cape Town or even Jo'burg, but there are some good ones here, and more are opening all the time. Most are some way west and north-west of the city

centre in the wealthier suburbs. Many will, however, collect you from the airport or train station, and they usually arrange trips to the beach and other places of interest.

Banana Backpackers (☎ *368 4062, fax 368 5783,* e *aroutes@iafrica.com, 61 Pine St)* Dorm beds R50, singles/doubles R70/110. The Banana Backpackers, in the city centre 1km from the beach, is a big place that gets both good and bad feedback (loud music late at night and overcrowded rooms seem to be the main problem). The location is excellent for both the beach and the city

The KwaZulu-Natal Surf Scene

Durban and the KwaZulu-Natal coast has a surf culture, quality and history to match anywhere in the world. It is the home of true legends such as Shaun Tomson, Frankie Oberholzer (also known as The Search) and up-and-comers such as Simon Nicolson, David Weare and, more recently, Shaun Gossman.

Durban itself has a range of quality breaks, given the right swell, all best when the sou'wester blows. South Beach and Addington are normally the best beginner spots, but with the right swell they can throw some gaping barrels. Dairy Pier has the best left-hander of the lot while New Pier, North Beach, Bay of Plenty and Snake Park can be long and hollow, often with great right-handers breaking off the piers. If town starts getting a little too crowded, then head for the northern town beaches, Battery and Tekweni, which can produce quality waves with fewer people in the water.

In July, North Beach is the home of the Mr Price Pro (formerly the Gunston 500), the feature event of the Ocean Africa Festival. Ocean Africa is a unique extravaganza encompassing every beach activity possible, including night surfing, beauty contests, fashion shows, beer tents, bands and stands selling everything imaginable. The turnout is usually huge and the action on the beach rivals that in the water. Joe Kool's, right on North Beach is the most popular after-surfing *jol* (good time).

Don't forget to stop in at the **Time-warp Surf Museum** (☎ *368 5842, Ocean Sports Centre; open 10am-4pm daily)* behind New Pier; they have some fantastic surf memorabilia. Try coaxing legend Baron Stander with a cold beer and he may share a lifetime of incredible and outrageous stories about South African surfing, and may even be persuaded to spill the beans on a few secret spots.

The Bluff, just south of Durban, has some good spots, with the infamous Cave Rock being its showpiece. Often compared with Hawaii's Backdoor, The Rock is for experienced surfers only.

The KwaZulu-Natal coast really comes into its own on the north and south coasts, which offer a selection of world-class point breaks and the chance to get away from the city crowds. The coast is best in winter, from April to August, before about 10am or 11am, when you're basically guaranteed a north-west land breeze. When solid groundswells roll in from the south you are assured solid waves. On the north coast the best-known spots are Westbrook (arguably the hollowest wave around), Ballito Bay and Zinkwazi Beach. The south coast offers Greenpoint, Scottburgh, Happy Wanderers, St Michaels and The Spot (all right-handers). Each produces incredibly rideable 1m to 2.5m-plus grinders over rock and sand bottom, with the occasional ride that is a couple of hundred metres. Plenty of barrels are around, but check with locals to be safe. Lucien Beach near Margate is the place to check when the north-easterly is blowing. Further south are more right-hand points along the Transkei Wild Coast (see the Eastern Cape chapter), with plenty of quality waves between.

Patrick Moroney & David Malherbe

centre, although there's usually a fair bit of traffic noise.

Brown Sugar (☎ 209 8528, e brown sugar2000@hotmail.com, Kinnord House, 6 Kinnord Place, 607 Essenwood Rd, Essenwood) Camping R30, dorm beds R40, doubles with/without bathroom R150/120, all prices include breakfast. The very laidback Brown Sugar is in a large colonial house in Essenwood. The century-old house, built by the founder of Rennies Shipping, has commanding views of the city. There's a great swimming pool out the back and plenty of space to camp.

Nomads Backpackers (☎ 202 9709, e no madsbps@netralink.com, W www.zing.co .za/nomads, 70 Essenwood Rd, Berea) Dorm beds R50, doubles R130. Nomads Backpackers is run by a friendly expat couple who are a wealth of information about the area. It's close to the Musgrave Rd shopping centre and there are plenty of restaurants in the area.

Tekweni Backpackers (☎ 303 1433, fax 303 4369, e tekweni@global.co.za, W www .tekweniecotours.co.za, 167 Ninth Ave, Morningside) Dorm beds from R50, doubles from R120. This large hostel, which occupies three houses, is a manageable distance north of the centre, and is very popular. Tekweni Eco-Tours booking office is based here. To get here take a Mitchell Park Circle or Musgrave Rd Circle Mynah bus to the corner of Florida Rd and Ninth Ave.

Traveller's International Lodge (☎/fax 303 1064, e travelers-lodge@saol.com, 743 Currie Rd, Morningside) Dorm beds R50, doubles R140. This homely lodge has reasonable prices and is a little quieter than your run-of-the-mill backpackers. Follow the directions given for Tekweni Backpackers to get here.

Hippo Hide Lodge & Backpackers (☎/fax 207 4366, e michelle@hippohide .co.za, W www.hippohide.co.za, 2 Jesmond Rd, Berea) Dorm beds R65, doubles with/ without bathroom R160/130. Travellers have raved about Hippo Hide and it is easy to see why. It's a relaxed, friendly place with good clean rooms, great views, a large garden and a cooling rock pool.

Hotels & Apartments

The streets near the beach, especially Gillespie St, are the place to look for cheaper hotels and apartments. Be warned that as more and more expensive accommodation opens in this area, standards at the cheaper places are slipping, so check the room before handing over your cash.

Palm Beach (☎ 337 3451, fax 301 6622, Cnr Gillespie & Tyzack Sts) Doubles B&B R120/140 low/high season. Although not overly appealing, the Palm Beach Hotel is cheap. Rumour has it that new management has taken over and major renovations are planned.

Four Seasons (☎ 337 3381, fax 337 3380, 81 Gillespie St) Singles/doubles R120/170. The once-grand Four Seasons is looking a little tired; still, the rooms are reasonable. Around Christmas it is packed and no singles are available.

Parade Hotel (☎ 337 4565, 332 0251, W www.paradehotel.co.za, 191 Marine Parade) Singles/doubles R152/243. The Parade Hotel is an old but comfortable place. At these prices it's definitely worth a look.

Impala Holiday Flats (☎ 332 3232, fax 337 3192, 40 Gillespie St) Apartments for 1-2 people R150/190 low/high season. This place, with its tidy spacious flats, is another option worth trying.

Hotel California (☎ 303 1146, fax 312 4355, Florida Rd, Morningside) Singles R145/165 low/high season, doubles R190/ 210. Hotel California offers good, wellpriced accommodation in the heart of Morningside. The downside is that its bar is a popular nightspot and can be a little rowdy.

PLACES TO STAY – MID-RANGE

Most of the mid-range and top-end places are listed in the *KwaZulu-Natal Accommodation Guide*, available for R4 from Tourist Junction. There's an **accommodation booking desk** (☎ 304 3868) in the complex, and staff should be able to find you a B&B starting at R150/200 a single/double. Check out its excellent Web site, Book-A-Bed-Ahead (W www.bookabedahead.co.za).

Road Lodge (☎ 304 8202, fax 304 8265, e rldurb@citylodge.co.za, 189 Old Fort

Rd) Rooms (up to 3 people) R187. This place is formulaic and impersonal but modern and spotless. It has small rooms with powerful air-con, TV and phone (local calls only, but they're free). Things would be pretty cramped with two people, let alone three. Breakfast is R19.

Albany Hotel *(☎ 304 4381, fax 307 1411,* **e** *albany@iafrica.com,* **w** *www.albanyhotel .co.za, 225 Smith St)* Singles/doubles B&B R167/260. The Albany Hotel is well located, across from the city hall and next to the Natal Playhouse theatre. It's also close to the Royal Hotel, and the money you save on staying here could be well spent at a few of the Royal Hotel's restaurants. This was probably a very good hotel in the 1950s, and while it hasn't had much done to it lately, it's still in quite good condition and is clean and secure.

Tudor House Hotel *(☎ 337 7328, fax 337 7060, 197 West St)* Singles B&B R180/200 low/high season, doubles B&B R320/320. This place, a few blocks from the beach, is good value. It's basically a pub with accommodation, but for that sort of thing it's quite good. All rooms have air-con, phone and TV.

The Palace Hotel *(☎ 332 8351, fax 332 8307, 221 Marine Parade)* 2-bed apartments R295/385 low/high season, 4-bed apartments R460/585, 6-bed apartments R960/ 1230. The Palace, opposite the beachfront, has old-fashioned but reasonable quality self-catering apartments.

Blue Waters *(☎ 332 4272, fax 337 5817,* **e** *bwhotel@dorea.co.za, 175 Snell Parade)* Singles/doubles R250/380. Blue Waters is a classic hotel on the northern end of the beachfront, away from the crowded Promenade.

City Lodge *(☎ 332 1447, fax 332 1483,* **e** *cldurb.resv@citylodge.co.za,* **w** *www .citylodge.co.za, Cnr Brickhill & Old Fort Rd)* Singles/doubles R255/450. The City Lodge is a big, motel-like place with luxurious rooms and secure parking. Breakfast is R30-38 per person.

Tropicana *(☎ 368 1511, fax 332 6890,* **e** *tropican@iafrica.com, 85 Marine Parade)* Singles B&B 299/350 low/high season, doubles B&B R398/499. The bright and breezy Tropicana has spacious rooms, all with air-con and TV.

PLACES TO STAY – TOP END

Many top-end places line the beachfront.

The Holiday Inn chain is well represented in Durban, with four hotels along the beachfront. Confusingly, three are called the Holiday Inn Garden Court – it is not unheard of for guests to find they have arrived at the wrong one! Their prices vary marginally and all offer discounts and deals in low season.

Holiday Inn Garden Court – South Beach *(☎ 337 2231, fax 337 4640,* **e** *gcsouth beach@southernsun.com, 73 Marine Parade)* has standard rooms from R329; ***Holiday Inn Garden Court – Marine Parade*** *(☎ 337 3341, fax 337 5929,* **e** *gcmarine parade@southernsun.com, 167 Marine Parade)* has singles/doubles from R429/ 518; ***Holiday Inn – Elangeni*** *(☎ 362 1300, fax 332 5527, 63 Snell Parade)*, previously known as Holiday Inn Crown Plaza, has standard rooms from R495; and ***Holiday Inn Garden Court – North Beach*** *(☎ 332 7361, fax 337 4058,* **e** *northres@southern sun.com, 83/91 Snell Parade)* has standard rooms from R379.

The Balmoral *(☎ 368 5940, fax 368 5955,* **w** *www.raya-hotels.com, 125 Marine Parade)* Singles/doubles B&B R350/465. The Balmoral is a large, stately hotel overlooking the beachfront. Its renovated rooms are clean and spacious with a rather regal air.

Edward Protea Hotel *(☎ 337 3681, fax 332 1692,* **e** *hoteled@worldonline.co.za, 146 Marine Parade)* Singles/doubles B&B R550/650. This hotel is one of the Protea chain's more upmarket hotels. Each of its comfortable rooms has air-con, TV and a private balcony.

Royal Hotel *(☎ 304 0331, fax 304 5055,* **w** *www.theroyal.co.za, 267 Smith St)* Singles/ doubles B&B from R595/700. The Royal Hotel, near the city hall, has long established its reputation as Durban's swankiest hotel. From the doorman in top hat and tails to the fine restaurants and lavish rooms, not a beat is missed.

Durban Hilton International *(☎ 336 8100, fax 336 8200,* **e** *dbnhilton@icon.co.za,* **w** *www.hilton.com, 12 Walnut St)* Rooms standard/with sea view B&B R675/725. The Hilton's high season is different from most other hotels – it runs from March to June and September to October. With well-furnished modern rooms, this place is attempting to wrest top-hotel status from the venerable Royal Hotel.

PLACES TO EAT

Most of Durban's many hotels have restaurants or dining rooms, ranging from one-star pubs where you can get bar meals to classy a la carte places. Several of the beachfront hotels have terraces, which are nice places to cool off and have a drink or a meal, and down on the sand there are several cafes.

Beach Area

There's a *Steers (Cnr Point Rd & West St)* steakhouse which is open 24 hours.

Joe Kool's (☎ 332 9697, Lower Marine Parade, North Beach) Mains R21-52. Joe Kool's is a popular nightspot. Its restaurant is promoted as the 'world's worst restaurant' – a statement that is not too far from the truth – but it does serve a great Sunday morning 'recovery' breakfast for R18.

Golden Chopsticks (☎ 332 8970, Belmont Arcade, Cnr West St & Marine Parade) Mains R30-75, set menus R38-45. Golden Chopsticks is a large authentic Cantonese restaurant with good-value set menus.

Thatcher's (☎ 337 4311, Cnr Gillespie & Sea View Sts) Mains R28-96. Thatcher's, located in a block of apartments, is a sedate place with surprisingly inexpensive dishes.

Along the beachfront, the Holiday Inn – Elangeni (see Places to Stay – Top End earlier) corners a large section of Durban's dining market. *Daruma* is an expensive sushi bar (mains R55 to R125) where you can feast on Japanese delicacies prepared for you before your eyes by quick-handed, theatrical chefs. The upmarket *Jewel of India* is a good Indian restaurant with an excellent selection of veg dishes. Mains cost from R25 to R55.

Saagris (☎ 332 7922) Mains R25-55. Saagris, in the Holiday Inn Garden Court – Marine Parade, specialises in delicious seafood curries as well as dishes from the tandoori oven.

At the end of The Point, with great views of the harbour mouth, are a number of trendy eating places.

The Famous Fish Restaurant (☎ 368 1060, The Point) Mains R35-95. The Famous Fish Restaurant has lost some of its gloss with locals but is still recommended by readers. Bookings are essential.

RJ's (☎ 332 7353, The Point) Mains R20-55. This version of the popular steakhouse chain serves up no surprises but does have excellent views of the harbour.

Splashes (☎ 332 7351, Kings Battery, The Point) Mains R20-60. This relatively new restaurant has a great relaxed feel; both indoor and outdoor tables are available. As its name suggests, it has a mostly seafood menu.

City Area

Takeaway places around the city have good Indian snacks including *bunny chow,* a half or quarter loaf of bread hollowed out and filled with beans, traditionally, or curry stew. It's cheap and filling.

You'll find small Indian places on Grey St, such as *Victory Lounge*, upstairs from a good pastry shop on the corner of Grey and Victoria Sts, and the Gujarati-style *Patel's Vegetarian*. These are cheap, but the food, while OK for fuel, isn't *haute cuisine*.

On the ground floor of The Workshop is the *Oriental Takeaway*. The food is OK and inexpensive (meals cost from R4 to R35), although on a hot, humid day you feel you could be in South India. Up on the terrace level is the air-con restaurant, with good food, good service and a pleasant atmosphere.

The Garden Bistro (☎ 304 1461, Medwood Gardens, 232A West St) Breakfast R9-22, mains R14-30. The Garden Bistro, in Medwood Gardens near the main post office, is inexpensive, outdoors and a great place to read your snail mail. Breakfast is served all day and Hostelling International card holders get a 10% discount.

Fiddler's (☎ 306 7796, 58 Albany Grove) Mains R12-45. Fiddler's serves decent pub lunches. Staples such as bangers and mash costs R14 and burgers are R20.

Roma Revolving Restaurant (☎ 332 3337, 32nd floor, John Ross House, Victoria

Embankment) Mains R30-55. Open noon-2.30pm, 6pm-10.30pm Mon-Sat. The view from this restaurant is amazing and the Italian food isn't horrifyingly expensive. There's parking in adjacent Mills Lane.

Oriental Palace *(☎ 368 3751, John Ross House, Victoria Embankment)* Mains R25-55. The Oriental Palace is a good but not too expensive Indian restaurant.

La Dolce Vita *(☎ 301 8161, Durban Club, Victoria Embankment)* Mains R40-70. La Dolce Vita, one of Durban's oldest restaurants, is worth visiting for its superb location, but the food is pretty good too. You'd be lucky to get away with spending less than R100 here.

New Fish Café *(☎ 305 5062, Yacht Mole)* Mains R48-75. The New Fish Café is a trendy, modern restaurant on the waterfront. Its friendly and attentive staff and scrumptious seafood menu assures its popularity.

The Royal Hotel (see Places to Stay – Top End earlier) has a number of restaurants. *Ulundi* is the place to sample a Bombay fish curry or a lamb dish, and has mains from R47 to R62. *Royal Carvery* has a set menu (starting with sherry) for both lunch and dinner; the buffet costs R89. *Royal Grill* is a little more adventurous and more expensive. You can dine a la carte, with mains from R56 to R125, or have a six-course set menu starting at about R150.

Greyville & Morningside

There are plenty of places to eat and drink in the Greyville and Morningside area.

Loafers Bakery *(☎ 232 1000, 514 Windermere Rd)* Breakfast R14-26, meals R10-29. Loafers Bakery has a takeaway counter serving filling pastries and sweet buns as well as a sit-down cafe, which is great for greasy breakfasts and light meals.

Bean Bag Bohemia *(☎ 309 6019, 18 Windermere Rd)* Mains R24-48. This place is a cafe and bar serving excellent food in a light, healthy style with a spicy Mediterranean flavour. Baguettes with tasty fillings start at around R24, with larger meals such as Moroccan lamb tangine costing around R48. It's near the Florida Rd junction – look for the BBB sign.

El Turko *(☎ 312 7893, 413 Windermere Rd)* Mains R20-53. El Turko is a bright, fun Mediterranean restaurant that offers dolmades, dips and pitta.

El Bandido *(☎ 303 3826, Windermere Rd)* Mains R20-53. This cheap and cheery Mexican restaurant is next door to El Turko.

Christina's *(☎ 303 2111, 134 Florida Rd)* Mains R20-55. Christina's, near the corner of Eighth St, is attached to a local cooking school. It serves gourmet a la carte dishes such as roast duck for around R40 as well as a choice of set menus. The school's students help prepare and serve the meals.

Baanthai *(☎ 303 3467, 138 Florida Rd)* Mains R20-55. Baanthai is a reasonably authentic Thai place.

A Gruta *(☎ 312 8675, 200C Florida Rd)* Mains R25-60. A Gruta is a good Portuguese restaurant that's not too pricey.

Berea

There are plenty of stylish (or wannabe stylish) restaurants in the area.

Mimmo's *(☎ 201 4482, The Silver Oaks Centre, 30 Silverton Rd)* Mains R14-35. Mimmo's has very cheap pizzas and pastas. Takeaway is also available, and every Tuesday night is 'Ladies Nite' when all 'Ladies' dine for half-price.

Bellissimo *(☎ 201 4768, Musgrave Centre, Musgrave Rd)* Mains R23-50. Bellissimo is an Italian restaurant with a lively menu of pastas, pizzas and seafood, including dishes such as polenta with eggplant for R23; it serves a good selection of veg dishes.

Mykonos *(☎ 202 5636, 156 Essenwood Rd)* Lunch/dinner buffet R45/60. The ever-popular Mykonos serves delicious all-you-can-eat Greek buffets.

Havana's @ El Cubano *(☎ 202 9198, Silvervause Centre, Cnr Silverton & Vause Rds)* Mains R25-60. Havana's @ El Cubano is a stylish, modern restaurant with an appealing menu featuring zesty dishes such as triple chilli steak bruschetta.

ENTERTAINMENT

Durban is a fun city with a vibrant cultural scene and heaps of nightlife. Many events are booked with **Computicket** *(☎ 304 2753)*.

Pubs & Clubs

The Wheel shopping centre (☎ 332 4324, 55 Gillespie St) has several bars and is a good place to begin your night out.

Friend's Bar (☎ 368 7233, 130 Gillespie St) Open 24 hours. Friend's Bar (also known as 'Buddies') is a relaxing spot, if a little rough around the edges. The owner, an ex-boilermaker, can often be found at the bar.

Harlequin's Sportsman's Bar (☎ 337 6882, Rutherford Rd) Open 10.30am-late daily. Harlequin's is a lively pub off Gillespie St. It has live bands on Thursday night.

Club 3-30 (☎ 337 7172, 330 Point Rd) Open 10pm-late Fri & Sat. Club 3-30 is *the* place for Durban groovers. It's basically a crowded dance club that masquerades as an 'alternative' club on Friday night. This place plays all types of dance music – techno, hip-hop, acid house, garage.

Smelly's Bar (*Smuggler's Inn, 124 Point Rd*) Live bands from 9pm Sat. Smelly's Bar is further down Point Rd from Club 3-30, in the run-down Smuggler's Inn, an old Durban landmark. It's a great rock'n'roll venue with a good (if at times a little scary) atmosphere.

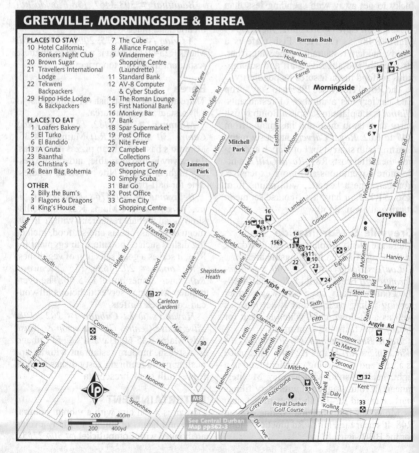

GREYVILLE, MORNINGSIDE & BEREA

PLACES TO STAY
10   Hotel California;
     Bonkers Night Club
20   Brown Sugar
21   Travellers International
     Lodge
22   Tekweni
     Backpackers
29   Hippo Hide Lodge
     & Backpackers

PLACES TO EAT
1   Loafers Bakery
5   El Turko
6   El Bandido
13   A Gruta
23   Baanthai
24   Christina's
26   Bean Bag Bohemia

OTHER
2   Billy the Bum's
3   Flagons & Dragons
4   King's House
7   The Cube
8   Alliance Française
9   Windermere
     Shopping Centre
     (Laundrette)
11   Standard Bank
12   AV-8 Computer
     & Cyber Studios
14   The Roman Lounge
15   First National Bank
16   Monkey Bar
17   Bank
18   Spar Supermarket
19   Post Office
25   Nite Fever
27   Campbell
     Collections
28   Overport City
     Shopping Centre
30   Simply Scuba
31   Bar Go
32   Post Office
33   Game City
     Shopping Centre

Joe Kool's (☎ 332 9697, Lower Marine Parade, North Beach) Open 10am-late daily. Joe Kool's is one of Durban's oldest and hippest nightspots (especially on Sunday nights). There's an admission charge of R10 most Thursday, Friday, Saturday and Sunday nights.

80's (☎ 303 7775, Collegians Complex, Walter Gilbert Rd) Admission R10. Open 8pm-late Tues, Fri & Sat. Next to the sports ground, 80's attracts an older crowd. As the name suggests, plenty of hits from the 1980s are played along with a sprinkling of modern favourites.

There's plenty on offer at the *BAT Centre* (☎ 332 0451, 45 Marine Place, Victoria Embankment), on the harbour, from local bands and DJs on Friday and Saturday nights to its drum circle on Tuesday evenings; it's also a nice place for a drink.

Fiddler's (☎ 306 7796, 58 Albany Grove) Open 11.30am-late daily. Fiddler's is a cosy little late-night pub right in the centre of Durban.

Crash! (☎ 304 6524, Durban Station, NMR Ave) Open until late Wed, Fri & Sat. On the main concourse at Durban station, Crash! is a huge and trendy club with three dance floors and a cigar bar.

Monkey Bar (☎ 312 9436, 258 Florida Rd, Morningside) Open 10.30am-late daily. The Monkey Bar is a hip bar that dares you to 'come and get funky at the monkey'.

Billy the Bum's (☎ 303 1988, 504 Windermere Rd, Morningside) Open noon-late Mon-Sat. Billy the Bum's is an upmarket cocktail bar boasting the best mixes and mixers in town.

Flagons & Dragons (☎ 303 8621, Windermere Rd, Morningside) Open 11am-late Mon-Sat. This small, cosy sports bar, across from Billy the Bum's, runs a comedy night on Wednesday, karaoke on Friday and has a pool table and dartboard.

Bar Go (☎ 309 6066, 15 Mitchell Crescent, Greyville) Admission from R15. Open 4pm-1am Tues, Wed & Thurs, noon-late Fri & Sat. Overlooking the Greyville Racecourse, Bar Go offers everything from house music to extreme parties, live bands and a cocktail bar.

Nite Fever (☎ 309 8422, Argyle Rd, Greyville) Cover charge R10. Open until late Thurs, Fri & Sat. Nite Fever is packed with party-loving Durbanites most weekends. It's hard to miss – look for the large purple neon sign emulating John Travolta's famous *Saturday Night Fever* pose.

Legends Late Night Café (☎ 201 0733, W www.legendscafe.co.za, Musgrave Centre) Open noon-3pm, 6pm-3am daily. A hot spot in the Musgrave Centre, Legends Late Night Café is a chic cocktail bar with a fun atmosphere and delicious food.

News Café (☎ 201 5241, Silver Oaks Centre, Silverton Rd) Open 7.30am-late Mon-Fri, 9am-late Sat & Sun. Another popular cocktail bar which plays 'cool' jazz on Sunday afternoons.

Gay Venues

Axis (☎ 332 2603, Cnr Gillespie & Rutherford Sts) is a popular gay nightclub catering to both men and women. It plays a good range of dance, house and garage music.

The Roman Lounge (☎ 303 9023, 202 Florida Rd, Morningside) is a good place to hook up; this place caters to both men and women.

Strictly Ballroom (☎ 304 5552, Victoria Embankment) is a friendly gay club playing lively Latin-American music.

Club 3-30 (see Pubs & Clubs, earlier) is a hot spot for the local gay scene on Saturday night.

Jazz

The jazz scene in Durban deserves a special mention. There is a real blend of styles using American jazz rhythms as a base. Imagine the effect a sprinkling of Indian classical, indigenous South African and township jazz influences has on the sound.

BAT Centre (☎ 332 0451, 45 Marine Place, Victoria Embankment) often plays host to performances by the best jazz musicians in the country.

Jus' Jazzin' (☎ 368 7727, Shearer Rd) Open 9pm-midnight Thurs-Sat. Jus' Jazzin' is one of Durban's most popular jazz venues.

Rivets (☎ 336 8204, 12 Walnut St) Open 7.45pm-11pm Thurs. On Thursday night

Rivets, at the Durban Hilton International, turns into a smooth jazz club with a range of performances from up-and-comers to genre veterans.

Rainbow (23 Stanfield La, Pinetown) Admission around R25. The Rainbow is a monthly Sunday jazz venue that attracting top musicians. According to reports, the African Jazz Pioneers, Ladysmith Black Mambazo and Sakhile (with jazz-fusion king Sipho Gumede) have been spied here.

The *Centre for Jazz & Popular Music* (☎ 260 3385, *University of Natal, Berea*) hosts various jazz musicians as well as other interesting events throughout the year. Contact the university for details.

Classical Music & Theatre
Natal Playhouse (☎ 369 9444, ℮ *playco@ mweb.co.za*, ₩ *www.playhousecompany .com, Smith St)*, opposite the city hall, has dance, drama and music most nights. It's built in two old movie theatres, and there are some restaurants in the complex.

KwaZulu-Natal Philharmonic Orchestra (☎ 369 9438, ℮ *knzpo@kznpo.co.za*, ₩ *www .kznpo.co.za)* has an interesting spring concert program with weekly performances in the city hall. It also plays in the Botanic Gardens some Sundays.

The University of Natal's Music Department has free lunch-time concerts on Monday (Howard College), as well as concerts on many evenings. On Wednesday at 1 pm, go to the city hall steps and listen to a variety of musicians and exceptional gospel choirs.

Cinemas
The Wheel shopping centre houses a cinema complex, as does The Workshop, the Sanlam Centre in Pinetown, The Pavilion in Westville and the Musgrave Centre. Some complexes show Indian movies as well as the normal fare, and seeing a 'Bollywood' extravaganza in Durban is a lot more comfortable than seeing it in India. The BAT Centre also shows the occasional film. For any movie bookings, call ☎ 304 5560.

The University of Natal hosts the International Film Festival in September; the Elizabeth Sneddon Theatre is the main venue.

SPECTATOR SPORTS
Several different types of football are played in KwaZulu-Natal, but the most popular is soccer. Professional teams such as AmaZulu and Manning Rangers play in town, and international teams also visit.

Natal has always been a strong rugby province. The 60,000-seat *King's Park Sport's Ground* (☎ 308 8400, *Jackson Dr)* is home to the Natal Sharks.

Durban's large Indian population is one reason for the popularity of cricket. *Kingsmead Cricket Ground* (☎ 332 9703, *2 Kingsmead Close)* hosts the international matches.

SHOPPING
The shops in the city centre and the shopping centres in the nearby suburbs (especially the Musgrave Centre in Berea) will cater to most of your needs, but if you want to see where the wealthy minority hides from the poor majority in a glitzy local version of the American dream, drop into the enormous *Pavilion* (☎ 265 0558, *Westville)*, which is open from 9am to 6pm Monday to Thursday, 8am to 6pm Friday, 8am-5pm Saturday and 10am-5pm Sunday. It's on the city's outskirts but is a quick drive from the centre on the N3 towards Pietermaritzburg. On Wednesday and Saturday there's a **bus service** (☎ 265 0558) from the city (R3 one way).

GETTING THERE & AWAY
Air
Durban International Airport is off the N2, about 16km south of the city. The **South African Airways** (*SAA;* ☎ 250 1111/3 for *domestic/international reservations)* office has moved to the airport.

SAA flies to Jo'burg (R740), Port Elizabeth (R830), East London (R820), Cape Town (R1391) and George (R1471). **Sun Air** (☎ 469 3444) flies to Jo'burg (R690) and Cape Town (R1117), and Comair and **British Airways** (☎ 303 5885) fly to Jo'burg (R690). SA Airlink (book through SAA) flies to various destinations, including Nelspruit (R980) and Bloemfontein (R950). These fares are the full economy one-way fares – with advance purchase deals the fare you pay will probably be much less.

A proposal has been put forward for a new airport, King Shaka International, to be built north of the city on a site in La Mercy. Although the government has agreed in principle to the proposal, financial concerns have stalled negotiations. Should the proposal be approved the new airport will open in 2006.

Bus

Most long-distance buses leave from the rear of Durban train station. If you're going to the station by car, enter from NMR Ave, not Umgeni Rd. **Translux** (☎ 308 8111) is here, and the **Greyhound** (☎ 309 7830) office is nearby. **Intercape** (☎ 307 2115) has an office at the beachfront, near Seaworld.

The Margate Mini Coach leaves from the rear of the station.

Don't forget the Baz Bus (see under Bus in the Getting Around chapter), with its services to Cape Town and Jo'burg, some via northern KwaZulu-Natal.

Bloemfontein Daily Translux and Greyhound services stop in Bloemfontein (R160), where you can pick up buses to many other destinations.

Cape Town Translux has a daily service to Cape Town (R370) via Bloemfontein. There's a daily service to Port Elizabeth (R235) that connects with a service to Cape Town via the Garden Route. Greyhound runs to Cape Town (R395), via either Bloemfontein or the Garden Route, daily.

Drakensberg & Sani Pass Three times a week the Sani Pass Couriers (☎ 033-701 1017, e sani passcarriers@wandata.com) picks up at hostels and runs via Pietermaritzburg to Underberg, Himeville and Sani Lodge.

Illovo & Amanzimtoti Enbee runs commuter buses to Illovo and Amanzimtoti from the Dick King Statue (on Victoria Embankment) weekday afternoons and at 1.30pm Saturday.

Margate & Port Edward The Margate Mini Coach (☎ 312 1406) runs between Margate and Durban daily for R50 (same-day return R70) – advance booking is advisable. The same people run the Flutter Bus, a cheap gamblers' service to the Wild Coast Sun Casino (just over the border in Eastern Cape, near Port Edward). The return fare is just R35. You have to book and if there are fewer than six passengers they don't go.

Jo'burg & Pretoria The Translux express to Jo'burg and Pretoria (R150) via the N3 runs at least daily, taking eight hours. There's another daily service stopping at more places and taking an hour longer. Greyhound has similar services (R170). Greyhound also has a daily service running via Empangeni (R80), Melmoth (R95) and Vryheid (R140); the fare to Jo'burg and Pretoria is the same as on the N3 services, but the trip is several hours longer.

Pietermaritzburg Cheetah Coaches runs to Pietermaritzburg (R35) at 10.30am and 4.45pm Monday to Thursday, 4.15pm and 6.30pm Friday, 10.45am and 2.45pm Saturday and 4.45pm Sunday. The bus leaves from Aliwal St outside the Local History Museum.

Richards Bay Richards Bay Interport (☎ 0351-91791) runs north to Mandini, Gingindlovu, Mtunzini, Empangeni and Richards Bay daily. The three-hour trip to Richards Bay costs R60. The bus departs from outside St Paul's Church on Pine St. One of Greyhound's Jo'burg buses also runs this route.

Umhlanga Rocks The Umhlanga Express (☎ 268 0651) bus leaves from a number of points in Durban including Pine St near the corner of Dick King St (outside Kay Makan Electronics) and the rear entrance of the Holiday Inn – Elangeni, near the beachfront. The one-way fare is R15.

Umtata & Port Elizabeth Translux has a daily service to Port Elizabeth from Durban; stops include Kokstad (R95), Umtata (R135), East London (R165), Grahamstown (R200) and Port Elizabeth (R210). One of Greyhound's daily Cape Town services also runs this route.

Maputo (Mozambique) Intercape runs buses daily to Jo'burg (R165) from where you can catch a connecting bus to Maputo in Mozambique (R180). Book at Intercape's office at the beachfront.

Train

The **Durban train station** (☎ 361 7609, 086-000 8888, Umgeni Rd) is huge. The daily *Trans Natal* (Durban-Jo'burg via Kimberley and Bloemfontein) and the weekly *Trans Oranje* (Durban–Cape Town) run from Durban. Some fares for economy/2nd/1st class are: Bethlehem R65/110/150; Bloemfontein R100/160/245; Cape Town R235/290/560; and Jo'burg R90/145/215.

There are also commuter trains running down the coast as far south as Kelso and north to KwaDukuza (Stanger). The service once ran south as far as Port Shepstone, and might do so again (call the train station for information). You can catch southbound

KWAZULU-NATAL

commuter trains at Berea train station as well as at Durban station. Note that even hardy travellers report feeling unsafe on these trains.

Minibus Taxi

Some long-distance minibus taxis leave from stops in the streets opposite the Umgeni Rd entrance to the train station. To Jo'burg it costs R80, and to the Swaziland border it costs about R70. Other taxis, running mainly to the south coast and the Transkei region of Eastern Cape, leave from around the Berea train station.

Car

The major car-rental companies have offices here and all have toll-free phone numbers, including **Avis** (☎ *0860 021 111*), **Budget** (☎ *0860 016 622*) and **Imperial** (☎ *0860 131 000*). Several smaller companies, often with lower rates, also have offices here, including **Tempest** (☎ *0860 031 666*). There are also some small local companies offering good deals, but you usually have to return the car to the Durban office.

Hitching

Although we don't recommend it, if you do choose to hitch, and are heading south, hitch from the M4 interchange near Albert Park. The N2 north starts at the top end of Stanger St.

GETTING AROUND
To/From the Airport

A bus (☎ *211 1333*) runs to the airport from near the corner of Aliwal and Smith Sts for R20. Some hostels can get discounts and pick-ups for backpackers on the return trip. By taxi, the same trip should cost about R80, although you may be offered a 'special' price of R200!

Bus

The main bus terminal and information centre is on Commercial Rd across from The Workshop.

The **Durban Rickshaw Bus** (☎ *202 1660*), an open-topped double-decker, runs along the beach between The Point to the south

and Blue Lagoon Beach to the north six times a day. The fare is adult/child R10/5.

The Mynah service of small, fairly frequent buses covers most of the central and beachfront areas. The disadvantage is that the service stops early in the evening on most routes. Trips cost around R4 and you get a slight discount if you pre-buy 10 tickets. Routes are as follows:

North Beach This service runs from Sandown Rd, which meets Snell Parade near Battery Beach, down Playfair Rd, Boscombe Terrace and Sea View St, to join Smith St. It then runs up Smith to Russell St and St Andrews St and returns down West St.

South Beach This service runs from Bell St north up Gillespie/Prince St, up Smith St to Russell St and St Andrews St, and back along West St.

Musgrave Rd Circle From the terminus near The Workshop, this service runs north along Smith St, up Berea Rd past the Berea Centre, east along Musgrave Rd to Mitchell Park, and returns down Florida Rd, Kent Rd, Umgeni Rd (passing the train station) and Soldiers Way. Some buses (Musgrave Rd Circle via Market) take a loop past Berea train station and through the Indian area on Russell and Leopold Sts and Market Rd.

Mitchell Park Circle This route is the same as the Musgrave Rd route but runs anticlockwise, using West St rather than Smith St, and Field St rather than Soldiers Way.

The Ridge/Vause This service runs up Smith St to Berea Rd, north along Ridge Rd to Earl Haig Rd and Valley Rd, and then back along Vause Rd, Berea Rd and West St. Some buses (the Ridge via Market) make a detour along Russell St, Leopold St and Market Rd.

Tollgate This is the same as the previous route but runs only as far as Entabeni Hospital on Ridge Rd.

Botanic Gardens This route goes up Smith St and Berea Rd, then past the Botanic Gardens on Botanic Gardens Rd and Cowey Rd, down Clarence Rd and back to the city on First Ave and Soldiers Way. It runs clockwise and anticlockwise (using West St rather than Smith St).

Kensington/Mathias Rd This route goes north along Soldiers Way, First Ave and Windermere Rd. From Kensington it heads west into Trematon Dr and runs to North Ridge Rd and returns from there (this is the service to take to get to the Morningside restaurants). The St Mathias route keeps going north on Goodwin Dr and returns from Salisbury Rd. Both routes run past the train station.

As well as the Mynah bus services there are slower and less frequent full-size buses, which also depart from the station across from The Workshop. They run more routes and travel further from the city centre than Mynah.

Taxi
A taxi between the beach and the train station costs about R20. **Bunny Cabs** (☎ 332 1795) runs 24 hours. Other taxi companies include **Eagle** (☎ 368 1706) and **Aussies** (☎ 309 7888).

Tuk-Tuk
Asian-style three-wheelers (tuk-tuks) congregate on the beachfront near Palmer St. Over short distances their fares are lower than taxis, but for anything more than 1km or so the fares are comparable. Tuk-tuks run only to the city centre and beachfront areas.

West of Durban

PINETOWN
☎ 031
Pinetown, a centre of light industry, is the third-biggest population centre in KwaZulu-Natal and the second-largest industrial area. There are areas of this city that possess a certain charm, including Paradise Valley and Marianhill Nature Reserves and the Japanese Gardens in Sarnia. A visit to Pinetown will give you a taste of modern South African suburbia, and is an indication of the massive task of integration that is yet to be undertaken.

SHONGWENI RESOURCE RESERVE
☎ 031
About halfway between Durban and Pietermaritzburg, off the N3, the Shongweni Resource Reserve (☎ 769 1238, fax 769 1125) protects a river valley and grassland, and has quite a few animals and birds. Horse riding and canoeing are available, but you must book ahead. No accommodation is available.

VALLEY OF 1000 HILLS
☎ 031
The Valley of 1000 Hills runs from the ocean at Durban to Nagle Dam, east of Pietermaritzburg. The rolling hills and traditional Zulu villages are the main reason visitors drive through here, usually on the R103 which begins in Hillcrest, off the M13 freeway. You can also get to Hillcrest from the N3 between Durban and Pietermaritzburg. If you want to see more of the valley you'll have to head north from this road, which just skirts the southern edge.

For information, contact **Thousand Hills Tourism** (☎/fax 777 1874, e thtouris@iafrica.com, Old Main Rd, Botha's Hill; open 8.30am-4.30pm daily).

There's a reptile park and a traditional Zulu village complete with touristy cultural displays at the **PheZulu Safari Park** (☎ 777 1000, fax 777 1405, e crocodile@dbn.lia.net, Old Main Rd; shows 10am, 11.30am, 1.30pm & 3.30pm daily).

Places to Stay & Eat
The Valley Trust (☎ 777 1955, 777 1114, e vtrust@wn.ace.org, W www.thevalleytrust.org.za, Off Old Main Rd, Nyuswa) Dorm beds R45. Accommodation is in various sized rooms at the trust's centre in Nyuswa. The trust is involved in Zulu community development projects and offers guests a tour (R15). From The Workshop bus stop in Durban, take a bus to Old Main Rd, Pinetown, and from Pinetown take a bus to Nyuswa.

Queensburgh Caravan Resort (☎ 464 5800, fax 445 800, Haslam Rd, Northdene) Camp sites R35/55 low/high season plus R15 per person & 14% VAT. The resort is in Northdene, about 12km west of Durban city centre. It's in a nice spot by a creek with a nature reserve on the other side. To get there, take the M7 west from Durban and exit at Bellville Rd/Old Main Rd/M5. Continue west on the M5 for some way and just after the civic centre turn right onto St Augine Rd then right onto Haslam Rd and follow it to the end.

Tekweni Backpackers in Durban (see Places to Stay – Budget under Durban earlier in this chapter) can arrange accommodation at *Jabus' Place* in a village called isiThumba. The experience costs R300 per person including transport, all meals, accommodation and a Zulu guide for two days.

Rob Roy (☎ *777 1305, fax 777 1364,* ✉ *robroy@dbn.lia.net, Rob Roy Crescent, Botha's Hill)* Deluxe suite singles/doubles R365/500, balcony rooms R380/520. This amazing hotel in Botha's Hill is eerily reminiscent of the Lookover Hotel in Stanley Kubrick's film *The Shining.*

Chantecler (☎ *765 2613, fax 765 6101, 76 Clement Stott Rd, Botha's Hill)* Singles/doubles B&B R285/385. This hotel in Botha's Hill is an old-style place with somewhat lower prices than the Rob Roy.

Many Durbanites visit the hills for the food. The Chantecler and Rob Roy have restaurants, and the Chantecler has music on Sunday afternoon. Several old train stations in the area, such as Botha's Hill and Kloof, have been renovated into English-style pubs and tea gardens.

The Pot & Kettle (☎ *777 1312,* ✉ *kettle@ 1000hills.co.za, Old Main Rd, Botha's Hill)* Mains R12-32. The Pot & Kettle is a casual restaurant with a delightful outdoor terrace overlooking the valley. On Saturday a buffet meal is available (R6 per 100g) and on Sunday there's a carvery meal.

Karibu Bush Pub (☎ *765 4846, 6 Clement Stott Rd, Botha's Hill)* Mains R17-28. Open 8am-late Tues-Sun. The Karibu Bush Pub has only a limited menu but its secluded leafy setting makes it an ideal place to relax over a drink.

South of Durban

There are some good beaches on the south coast, the strip between Durban and Port Edward, just across the Umtamvuna River from the Transkei region of Eastern Cape. There are also shoulder-to-shoulder resorts for much of the 150km, and in summer there isn't a lot of room to move.

The south coast begins at Amanzimtoti, a huge resort and residential area not far from Durban international airport. Further south

the major centres are Umkomaas, Scottburgh, Park Rynie and Hibberdene. This area is called the Sunshine Coast. A large built-up area begins just after Hibberdene, centring on Port Shepstone and Margate, about 10km south. This region, the Hibiscus Coast, continues almost unbroken to Marina Beach near the Trafalgar Marine Reserve. Port Edward is the last centre before Transkei and the Umtamvuna River.

Getting There & Away
SA Airlink (book through SAA) flies daily between Margate and Jo'burg for R913.

The **Margate Mini Coach** (☎ *031-312 1406)* runs from Durban down to Margate (R50), with some services running down to the Wild Coast Sun Casino, just over the border in Eastern Cape.

Commuter trains run from Durban down the coast as far as Kelso, on the northern edge of Pennington. The line on to Port Shepstone may be reopened. The security situation on these trains is not good.

The freeway system down the coast should soon reach all the way to Port Edward, but there's no reason not to use the old coast road – on which you don't pay tolls. Now that most traffic uses the freeway, the coast road is quite a good run, although weekends in summer are very busy. The N2 (which is currently signposted as both the freeway and the coast road) runs down to Port Shepstone, where it heads west.

SUNSHINE COAST
The Sunshine Coast stretches about 60km from Amanzimtoti to Mtwalume. All the beaches are easily accessible from the N2 but the area suffers from its proximity to Durban – Amanzimtoti is almost in the shadow of the southern industrial areas.

Amanzimtoti & Kingsburgh
☎ 031
Called 'Toti' for short, Amanzimtoti (Sweet Waters) is a high-rise jungle of apartment blocks. Warner Beach is at the southern end of Amanzimtoti, and while it's still a built-up area, the atmosphere is more relaxed. From here Amanzimtoti merges into Kingsburgh

to the south. Beaches nearby are Winkle-spruit, Illovo and Karridene.

The helpful **Amanzimtoti Information Office** (☎ *903 7498, fax 903 7493, e apa@ csurf.co.za, 95-97 Beach Rd; open 8am-12.30pm & 1-4pm daily*) is not far from the Inyoni Rocks.

The tiny **Ilanda Wilds Nature Reserve** is on the Manzimtoti River and many birds live in the forest. Even smaller is **Umdoni Bird Sanctuary** (*admission free; feeding times 7am & 3pm*), off Umdoni Rd. More than 150 species of birds have been spotted here. The **Umbogovango Nature Reserve**, near the corner of Umdoni Rd and Blaze Way, has been established in an industrial area to conserve bird and tree species.

Places to Stay & Eat There are many caravan parks in the area, although they fill up in January and prices are high. There are also plenty of B&Bs, flats and holiday homes – visit the Amanzimtoti Information Office for details.

Ocean Call Caravan Park (☎ *916 2644, e oceancall@caravanparks.co.za, w www .caravanparks.co.za/oceancall*) Sites R45/ 52 per person low/high season with bath-room, R35/44 per person without bath-room. Ocean Call Caravan Park, 1.5km from Winklespruit train station, is relatively inexpensive.

Angle Rock Backpackers (☎ *916 7007, fax 904 3812, e anglerock@mweb.co.za, w www.anglerock.co.za, 5 Ellcock Rd, Warner Beach*) Dorm beds R50, doubles R130-140. Angle Rock Backpackers is right by the beach and offers free surfing lessons. The facilities are good. Management does free pick-ups from Durban.

Illovo Beach Resort (☎ *916 3472, fax 916 6595, 17 Elizabeth Ave, Illovo Beach, e illovo@netactive.co.za*) Self-catering chalets R200/390 low/high season, cabins R100/150, doubles B&B R320/360. Illovo Beach Resort has a restaurant and an on-site swimming pool.

Villa Spa (☎ *916 4939, fax 916 4455, e info@villaspa.co.za, w www.villaspa.co .za, Illovo Beach*) is a shady resort with clean, comfortable chalets.

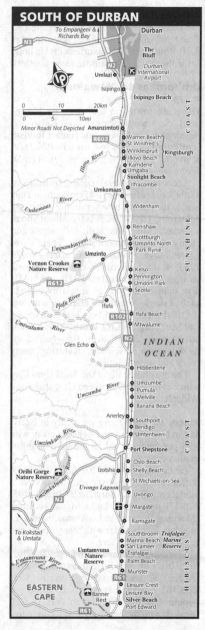

SOUTH OF DURBAN

KWAZULU-NATAL

Protea Hotel Karridene (☎ 903 3355, fax 916 7237, **W** www.protea-hotels.co.za, Old Coast Rd, Illovo Beach) Singles/doubles B&B R600/690. This luxurious Protea hotel is for those who like a little more comfort.

Umkomaas to Mtwalume
☎ 039

The main towns on this strip are Umkomaas, Scottburgh, Park Rynie, Kelso and Pennington. For information contact **Tourism Scottburgh** (☎ 976 1364, fax 039-978 3114, **e** publicity@scottburgh.co.za, 136 Scott St, Scottburgh).

According to several readers, Umkomaas, a small, peaceful village 45km south of Durban, is the perfect base for diving – they are not wrong. Off its beach is the **Aliwal Shoal**, a fantastic dive site, with soft corals and plenty of ragged-mouth sharks. There's also a wreck dive. **Aliwal Dive Charters** (☎ 973 2233, **e** adc@sco.eastcoast.co.za, **W** www.aliwalshoal.co.za) offers PADI and NAUI dive courses as well as speciality courses such as shark-, wreck and orientation diving.

Off the coast road between Umkomaas and Scottburgh is **Croc World** (☎ 976 1103; adult/child R20/10; open 8am-4pm daily, feeding time 3pm Sun), featuring many crocs and other reptiles.

The are craft stalls at the Shell Ultra City which is on the N2 between Umgababa and Widenham.

Places to Stay There are plenty of B&Bs and in low season you might get away with R75 per person – ask at the various information centres.

La La Manzi (☎ 973 0161, fax 973 0633, **e** lala@sco.eastcoast.co.za, **W** www.lalamanzi.co.za) Bed only/B&B/DB&B R95/120/170 per person. La La Manzi, meaning 'Sleeping Waters', in Umkomas, is recommended. It is popular with many divers and has a great atmosphere.

Scottburgh Caravan Park (☎ 976 0291, fax 976 2148, **e** caravanpark@scottburgh.co.za, **W** www.scottburgh.co.za) Sites R33/161 low/high season plus R9.60 per person. Scottburgh Caravan Park is well located, with the beach right at its doorstep.

Blue Marlin (☎ 978 3361, fax 976 0971, **e** info@bluemarlin.co.za, **W** www.bluemarlin.co.za, 180 Scott St, Scottburgh) Bed only/B&B R150/165 per person. The Blue Marlin is a colourful hotel with cheerful airy rooms.

Happy Wanderers (☎ 975 1104, fax 975 1467, **e** happywanderers@scottburgh.co.za, **W** www.caraville.co.za/happywanderers) Sites from R55/160 low/high season, chalets from R150/340. Happy Wanderers is a resort on the beach about 2km from Kelso station. The resort has a restaurant and pub and offers plenty of activities, from fishing and scuba diving to day trips to Oribi Gorge.

Vernon Crookes Nature Reserve

Inland from Park Rynie, off the R612 past Umzinto, this reserve (☎ 033-845 1000; admission R7 per person) has a few game animals and some indigenous forest. If you walk through the reserve, beware of ticks.

KZN Wildlife Accommodation offers two-bed huts for R70 per person. Unlike most KZN wildlife reserves, you can book locally between 8am and 7pm.

HIBISCUS COAST
☎ 039

This section of the south coast includes the seaside towns of Hibberdene, Port Shepstone, Shelly Beach, St Michaels-on-Sea, Uvongo, Margate, Ramsgate and Marina Beach.

Port Shepstone is an unattractive industrial centre and Margate is a large, tizzy resort town which compares itself to the English seaside town of Margate. Enough said. Near Port Edward the rugged coastal bush grows almost to the water's edge. Port Edward adjoins the Transkei region of Eastern Cape and the Wild Coast is to the south. Just south of town, opposite the entrance to the Wild Coast Sun Casino & Country Club, is the interesting Mzamba Village market where a range of Xhosa crafts is sold.

You can get information about the Hibiscus Coast from **Tourism Margate** (☎ 312 2322, fax 312 1886, **e** tmargate@iafrica.com, Panorama Parade, Main Beach, Margate).

Banana Express

This steam train *(☎ 682 4821)* departs from Port Shepstone at 10am on Saturday for the six-hour trip to Paddock Station (R80). There are 1½-hour excursions to Izotsha at 11am on Thursday, some Sundays and a few Tuesdays (R24/36 in 2nd/1st class).

Oribi Gorge Nature Reserve

This reserve *(admission R7 per person)* is inland from Port Shepstone, off the N2. The spectacular gorge, on the Umzimkulwana River, is one of the highlights of the south coast. Apart from the scenery, there are many animals and birds, and a mountain bike trail.

Oribi Gorge Hotel (☎/fax 687 0253, e oribigorge@worldonline.co.za) is a large archaic establishment near the viewing site overlooking the gorge; it charges an extortionate R9 per person to view the gorge from the lookout. It's 11km off the N2 along the Oribi Flats Rd.

KZN Wildlife Accommodation (☎ 033-845 1000) Camping R15 plus R5 community levy per person, huts R80/160 singles/doubles, 7-bed chalet R85 per person (minimum R340). Additional queries about the camp site should be directed to the Camp Manager (☎ 679 1644).

Trafalgar Marine Reserve

This reserve protects ancient fossil beds but most visitors are attracted by the excellent surfing and sailboarding it offers. When there's a westerly wind, Trafalgar Point is the best place for sailboarding on the south coast.

Umtamvuna Nature Reserve

On a gorge on the Umtamvuna River, which forms part of the border with Eastern Cape, this reserve is densely forested, with wildflowers in spring. There are quite a number of animals and birds, including peregrine falcons. This reserve has a twin across the Umtamvuna Gorge in Eastern Cape (see under Northern Transkei in the Eastern Cape chapter.)

Beware of bilharzia in the river. There is no accommodation here. To get to the reserve, head to Banner Rest, a small town south-west of Port Edward, and drive north towards Izingolweni for a few kilometres.

Places to Stay

In Margate there are many hotels, resorts and self-catering apartments. It is a good idea to book ahead; contact **Tourism Margate** *(☎ 312 2322, fax 312 1886, e tmargate@iafrica.com, Panorama Parade, Main Beach, Margate)* for details.

Caravan Parks There are a few caravan parks to chose from in the area.

Villa Siesta (☎ 681 3343, fax 681 2105) Camp sites R50/140 low/high season, 4-bed chalets R120/270. Villa Siesta in Anerley is a relatively inexpensive option.

De Wet (☎ 312 1022, fax 312 2212, St Andrews Ave, Margate) Camp sites R50/180 plus R5/10 per person low/high season. De Wet has only a few camp sites so it would pay to call ahead.

Margate Caravan Park (☎/fax 312 0852) Camping R20/60 low/high season. This caravan park is a large, clean park opposite the police station, between the R620 and Valley Rd, in Margate.

Hostels There are several good hostels along this stretch of coast.

The Mantis & Moon Backpacker Lodge (☎ 684 6256, 7/178 Station Rd, Umzumbe) Camping R35, dorm beds R50. New on the backpacking scene, The Mantis & Moon Backpacker Lodge has been given the thumbs up by our readers:

The Mantis & Moon was absolutely one of the best places I have stayed in. It was special because the owner was one of the few hostel owners I met who didn't seem to be continually in search of money. Surfboards are free and the accommodation is amazing for the price, as are the meals.

Dan Knowles

The Spot Backpackers (☎ 695 1318, fax 695 0439, e spotbackpackers@netactive .co.za, Ambleside Rd, Umtentweni) Camping R30, dorm beds R45, doubles R110. The Spot Backpackers is another well-regarded place. From its spot right on the beach you can fill your days with swimming, surfing and scuba diving or you can just relax and soak up the sun.

Margate Backpackers *(☎/fax 312 2176,* e *ulrika@venturenet.co.za, 14 Collis Rd, Margate)* Camping R30, dorm beds R50, doubles R140. The homely Margate Backpackers is a quiet retreat compared with your average overcrowded and noisy hostel. Rooms are clean and meals are available for around R25.

Hotels, Apartments & B&Bs There are plenty of hotels, apartments and B&Bs along this stretch of the coast.

Hibberdene Beach Hotel *(☎/fax 699 2146, 653 Barracuda Blvd, Hibberdene)* Singles B&B R95/120 low/high season, doubles B&B R140/240. The Hibberdene Beach Hotel is a nice place with simple well-furnished rooms.

Pumula Beach Hotel *(☎ 684 6717, fax 684 6303,* e *pumula@mweb.co.za, 67 Steve Pitts Rd, Umzumbe)* B&B/DB&B R225/ 250 per person. Pumula Beach Hotel, a little place on the beach south of Hibberdene, has cheaper weekend packages and big discounts for five nights or longer.

Sunlawns Hotel *(☎/fax 312 1078, Uplands Rd, Margate)* B&B R125/150 per person low/high season, DB&B 140/175 per person. This long established hotel has delightful old English charm. There is a 'Ladies Lounge' and pub as well as a good-sized pool.

Nellelani Holiday Flats *(☎ 312 1022, fax 317 2212, Forest Rd, Margate)* 4-bed apartments R140/400 low/high season. Nellelani Holiday Flats has comfortable apartments right on the beachfront. Each apartment has a small balcony and braai (barbecue) area.

Kapenta Bay Resort *(☎ 682 5528, fax 682 4530,* e *hotel@kapentabay.co.za)* Self-catering suites (maximum 6 people) R545/ 645 low/high season, singles/doubles B&B R460/500. A large and modern place, Kapenta Bay Resort, which is located off Panorama Parade in Port Shepstone, overlooks the ocean.

Neptune's Corner *(☎ 684 6266, Second Ave, Pumula)* 4-bed chalets R120/300 low/ high season. Neptune's Corner has pleasant

chalets that offer a very affordable alternative to camping. There is a colour TV in each chalet and a laundry service is also available.

Gracelands *(☎ 083-758 0713, 082-803 5269, 7 Owen Ellis Dr, Port Edward)* 6-bed chalets R75 per person. Gracelands is a quiet place, five minutes from the beach. There is a bar and restaurant here.

PORT EDWARD TO THE N2

The R61, which runs a short way south from Port Edward to the Wild Coast Sun Casino & Country Club then heads northwest to meet the N2 about 12km east of Kokstad, runs through the Xhosa villages of eastern Transkei, beginning in pleasant rolling country then, after Bizana, rising into the foothills. Coming from Port Edward, when you arrive at a T-intersection in a bustling little trading town, turn left. Further on, the R61 splits, with the left-hand road going to Lusikisiki (and on to Port St Johns) and the right to the N2 and Kokstad.

The road is in good condition but it is narrow and the usual warnings about watching out for pedestrians and animals on the roads of the old Homelands apply.

There are local buses and minibus taxis running between villages along this route but few run long distances, so there's a chance that the trip (about 120km between Port Edward and Kokstad) would take more than a day. There is no formal accommodation available along the way. However, it's worth asking around at the craft stalls near the Wild Coast Sun (across the provincial border from Port Edward) as people there might know of something.

The more usual route from Port Edward to the N2 heads north from the highway.

North of Durban

The stretch of coast from Umhlanga Rocks north to Tugela Mouth is less developed than the coast south of Durban, and the beaches are better. With lots of time-share apartments and retirement villages, things aren't very lively.

Before swimming at the beaches on the north coast you might want to check the status of the shark netting. Some towns have removed the netting because it was killing too many sharks – sharks 'drown' if they can't keep water flowing through their gills.

Other than some commuter services between Durban and Umhlanga Rocks there is very little public transport along the coast. There are, however, commuter trains and plenty of buses and minibus taxis between Durban and KwaDukuza and other inland towns.

UMHLANGA ROCKS
☎ 031 • postcode 4320

This big resort town is about 14km north of Durban. Umhlanga means 'Place of Reeds' (the 'h' is pronounced something like a 'sh', so it's beautifully onomatopoeic).

On the mall, near the intersection of Lagoon Dr and Lighthouse St (the continuation of the road in from the main Durban road), you'll find **Sugar Coast Tourism** (*☎ 561 4257, fax 561 1397, e info@sugarcoast.co.za; open 8.30am-4.30pm Mon-Fri*). If you can't find out what you need to know here, try **Infonet Cafe** (*☎ 561 1397; Internet access R15/30 per half-hour/hour; open 8am-10pm daily*), an Internet cafe which doubles as an information office.

Natal Sharks Board

The Natal Sharks Board (*☎ 561 1001, Umhlanga Rocks Dr; audiovisual adult/child R6/4, audiovisual & dissection adult/child R12/7; open 8am-4pm Mon-Fri*) is a research institute dedicated to studying sharks, specifically in relation to their danger to humans. With the great white shark, a big shark with a fearsome (but perhaps undeserved) reputation for attacks on humans, frequenting the KwaZulu-Natal coast, this is more than an academic interest.

There're audiovisual presentations at noon, 1pm and 3pm Monday to Thursday, and audiovisual presentations and dissection of a shark at 9am and 2pm Tuesday to Thursday. The presentation and dissection is also held at 2pm on the first Sunday of the month. The squeamish should avoid the dissection.

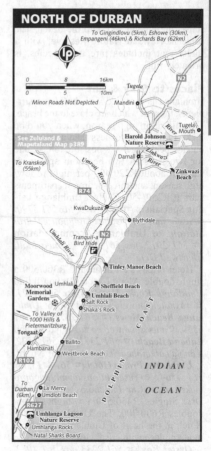

You can go along in the boat with Sharks Board personnel when they 'service' (ie, collect trapped sharks from) the shark nets that protect Durban's beach front. The two-hour trip departs early in the morning.

The Sharks Board is about 2km out of town, up the steep Umhlanga Rocks Dr (the M12 leading to the N3).

Umhlanga Lagoon Nature Reserve

This reserve *(admission free)* is on a river mouth just north of the town. Despite its small size (26 hectares) there are many bird species. The trails lead through dune forest, across the lagoon and onto the beach. The adjacent **Hawaan Nature Reserve**, with a forest that includes rare tree species, is privately run.

Places to Stay & Eat

Umhlanga is crowded with *holiday apartments*, most of which are close to the beach. They fill up in high season, when you'd be lucky to rent one for less than a week, but outside peak times it's possible to take one for two days. A two-bedroom apartment starts at about R220/400 per night in low/high season, and three-bedroom apartments start at R250/450. Contact **Umhlanga Letting Specialists** (☎ 561 5893, fax 561 5790, e uls@saol.com, Caltex Lighthouse Petrol Station) or **Umhlanga Accommodation** (☎ 561 2012, fax 561 3957, Protea Mall, Chartwell Dr).

Hotel prices start at around R300/500 a single/double. Along Lagoon Dr you'll find *Umhlanga Rocks Hotel* (☎/fax 561 1321, e roxhotel@mweb.co.za) at No 6; *Umhlanga Beach Mews* (☎ 561 2371, fax 561 6359, e mews@mweb.co.za) at No 10; and *Cabana Beach* (☎ 561 2371, fax 561 3522, jeanb@cabanabeach.co.za) also at No 10.

Umhlanga Protea Hotel (☎ 561 4413, fax 561 4564, e reservations@umhlangapro teakzn.co.za, Cnr Lighthouse & Chartwell Drs) Singles R450/550 low/high season, doubles R600/700. The Umhlanga Protea Hotel, in the heart of Umhlanga, is a large modern place with crisp, clean rooms.

Oyster Box (☎ 561 2233, fax 561 4072, 2 Lighthouse Rd) Singles B&B R460/500 low/high season, doubles B&B R700/760. The three-star Oyster Box is a charming old-fashioned hotel. The hotel's seafood restaurant is raved about locally.

Beverley Hills Sun Intercontinental (☎ 561 221, fax 561 3711, Lighthouse Rd) Singles/doubles B&B R1150/1600. The plush Beverley Hills Sun Intercontinental, overlooking the beach, is undoubtably Umhlanga's ultimate splurge. Its rooms are first class and are equipped with all mod cons. The hotel's restaurant is also worth a look.

Getting There & Away

A commuter bus runs from the publicity kiosk in Umhlanga to Durban, seven times a day, for R15.

DOLPHIN COAST
☎ 032

The Dolphin Coast starts at Umdloti Beach and stretches north to the Tugela River. It includes the areas of Tongaat, Ballito, Shaka's Rock, Umhlali, Salt Rock, Blythdale, Kwa-Dukuza, Zwinkazi Beach and Tugela Mouth. The coast gets its name from the pods of bottlenose dolphins that frolic offshore.

The **Dolphin Coast Publicity Association** (☎/fax 946 1997, e info@thedolphincoast .co.za, W www.dolphincoast.co.za, Ballito Dr) is near the BP petrol station, just where you leave the N2 to enter Ballito. It books B&Bs and lists other accommodation.

Tongaat

A big, sedate sugar town with some fine old buildings, Tongaat is on the train line running north from Durban. With a large Indian population, Tongaat is home to a handful of temples including the small but fascinating **Shri Jagganath Puri Temple**.

Ballito to Sheffield Beach

Ballito, Shaka's Rock, Umhlali, Salt Rock and Sheffield Beach form a continuous settled strip, although the density of settlement is nothing like that on the south coast. They are connected by the old coast road, so you don't have to jump back and forth on the N2 to travel between them.

Much of the accommodation is in apartments, and in high season most are let by the week. Rental agencies in Ballito include **Ballito Flat Letting** (☎ 946 2141, fax 946 3489, e ballito@saol.com, 21 Sandra Rd)

Dolphin Holiday Resort (☎ 946 2187, fax 946 3490) Camp sites R72/207 for 2 people low/high season, 2-bed cottages R184/392. This resort in Ballito has a minimum of a two-night stay.

Salt Rock Hotel (☎ 525 5025, fax 525 5071, W www.saltrockbeach.co.za, Basil Hulett Dr, Salt Rock) Standard room from R230/365 in low/high season, apartment from R250/385. This hotel offers resort-style accommodation.

KwaDukuza
☎ 032 • postcode 4450

Shaka founded the original settlement here as his capital and called it KwaDukuza. The settlement was later abandoned until 1872 when the site was surveyed for the town of Stanger – a name which it retained for over a century. However, following the 1994 elections, the city's original name was restored in honour of the great king.

Today KwaDukuza (still commonly referred to as Stanger) is an industrial town with no accommodation and it's altogether on the wrong side of the tracks. The town has a gritty, run-down feel. As the biggest service centre on this section of coast, however, it has a lively atmosphere after all those pristine coastal villages basking in their exclusivity.

The **Dukuza Interpretive Centre** (5 King Shaka St; admission free; open 8am-4pm Mon-Fri, 9am-4pm Sat & Sun) features various displays on Shaka. For more details about the interpretive centre, contact the **KwaDukuza municipality** (☎ 551 3091).

Tranquil-a Bird Hide (☎ 437 2222) is south of KwaDukuza at the Sappi Paper Mill; there's no admission fee. Newman (of the bird-book fame) saw 48 species here in less than two hours. You have to collect a key from the mill security; visits are restricted to two hours.

Blythedale
☎ 032 • postcode 4450

Blythedale is a quiet seaside village with a sandy beach and decidedly noisy surf.

La Mouette Caravan Park (☎ 551 2547, fax 552 1430, ⓔ lamouete@iafrica.com, 1 Umvoti Dr) Camp sites from R75/110 for 2 people low/high season. Sites here are fairly expensive.

Mini Villas (☎ 551 1277, fax 552 1628, Umvoti Dr) 2-/6-bed villas R163/310 low season, R220/350 high season. Mini Villas offers excellent value-for-money accommodation. During school holidays there's a minimum stay of a week.

Zinkwazi Caraville Resort (☎ 485 3344, fax 485 3340, ⓔ zinkwazi@caraville.co .za, Zinkwazi Beach) Camping R57/125 per person low/high season, singles B&B R220/300, doubles B&B R290/400. The Zinkwazi Caraville Resort is a large and modern place north of Blythedale.

Occasional minibus taxis run between Blythedale and KwaDukuza, 7km away.

Tugela Mouth

The Tugela River, once an important tribal boundary, enters the sea at Tugela Mouth to end its journey from Mont-aux-Sources in the Drakensberg. Several major battles took place near the river mouth, notably the Battle of Ndondasuka in which Cetshwayo defeated his brother, Mbuyasi, and many thousands were killed.

Shaka Sites

In July 1825 Shaka established KwaDukuza as his royal settlement. The settlement of 2000 beehive huts was intended as a halfway station between Zululand and the settlers of Port Natal (present-day Durban). Throughout present-day KwaDukuza there are reminders of the town's regal past.

In the centre of town, near the old police station, is the site of Shaka's royal residence. In front of the municipal offices in Roodt St is an old *mkuhla* (Natal mahogany) tree, reputedly the site of Shaka's indabas (meetings to discuss important matters). A large fig tree stood in the Nyakambi kraal at the opposite end of KwaDukuza, marking the spot where, in September 1828, Shaka was murdered by his half-brothers Dingaan and Umhlanga.

On Couper St are the Shaka Memorial Gardens where you can see the memorial stone erected in 1932 over Shaka's burial chamber, originally a grain pit.

Other sites in town associated with Shaka are the Mavivane Execution Cliff, north of the R74 at the end of Lindley St, and the Mbozambo Valley (now the site of the Shakaville township). Known as his 'playground', the valley is said to be where Shaka bathed and relaxed.

Harold Johnson Nature Reserve (☎ *486 1574; admission R5 per person*) is on the southern bank of the Tugela, east of the highway. There's a crocodile dam – feeding time is at 2pm on Saturday (summer only). Nearby are the ruins of Fort Pearson, a small British fort from the Anglo-Zulu War of 1879, and the Ultimatum Tree, where, in 1878, the British presented their demands to Cetshwayo's representatives.

KZN Wildlife Accommodation (☎ *486 1574*) has camping within the reserve for R24 per person

Zululand & Maputaland

For many travellers in South Africa, Zululand is the first and often the only taste they get of the real Africa. It is a region dominated by one tribal group, the Zulu, with their customs, traditions and culture. The name Zulu (Heaven) comes from an early chief; his descendants were abakwaZulu, or 'people of Zulu'.

Zululand covers a large part of central KwaZulu-Natal and extends in a rough triangle from the mouth of the Tugela River to Kosi Bay on the border of Mozambique, across to Vryheid in the west. North of the Tugela you'll find the Zulu capital, Ulundi, the large port of Richards Bay, the large Hluhluwe-Umfolozi Park and many traditional Zulu villages. Northern Zululand is not as diverse as the coastal region. It does, however, encompass two spectacular natural areas, Ithala Game Reserve and the Ntendeka Wilderness Area. The main towns are Louwsburg, Nongoma, Vryheid and Paulpietersburg.

The area east of the N2 and north of the Mtubatuba–St Lucia road is known as Ma-

Warning
There is malaria in Zululand and other places in the north of KwaZulu-Natal; there is bilharzia in some waterways and dams.

putaland. Maputaland is one of the wildest and most fascinating regions of South Africa and an absolute must for nature lovers. It takes its name from the Maputo River which splits into the Usutu and Pongola Rivers on the border of Mozambique and South Africa. Much of Zululand is a mass of attractive rolling hills.

Maputaland is sparsely settled and much of it is protected in parks and reserves. It encompasses three huge lakes, including the significant St Lucia Wetland Park; the last wild elephants in the country in Tembe Elephant Park; coral reefs; and many wildlife reserves where you can see the Big Five.

The climate becomes steadily hotter as you go north and, thanks to the warm Indian Ocean, summers are steamy and almost tropical. The humid coastal air causes frequent dense mists on the inland hills, reducing visibility to a few metres. Be careful of pedestrians and animals suddenly appearing around a corner. In the sugar areas, slow-moving vehicles are common.

Although few white South Africans live in the region, there are several major holiday centres, especially in the St Lucia area. Sea-fishing is a major attraction in Maputaland and the coral reefs are popular with divers – as well as with sharks. You'd be unwise to dive without first consulting locals.

There is a good network of minibus taxis and local bus companies covering this area. However, timetables and routes are vague, so be prepared for delays and hassles. But then, this is Africa.

The Baz Bus (see under Bus in the Getting Around chapter near the beginning of this book) also runs up the coast on the run between Durban and Jo'burg via Swaziland.

GINGINDLOVU
☎ 035 • postcode 3800
After you cross the Tugela River, the first town of any size is Gingindlovu (meaning 'Swallower of the Elephant'), at the junction of the R66 to Eshowe and the N2 north. It was once one of Cetshwayo's strongholds. Two battles of the Anglo-Zulu War of 1879 were fought in the vicinity, and the town itself was razed.

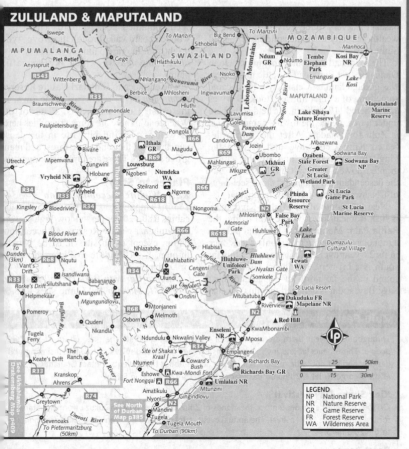

ZULULAND & MAPUTALAND

Mine Own Country House (☎ *337 1262, fax 337 1025*) Doubles B&B from R590. This grandiose homestead, on a sugar plantation 4km north of Gingindlovu off the R102, harks back to days long gone. It's definitely a tempting splurge.

Inyezane (☎ *082-704 4766, **e** inyezane@ iphone.co.za*) Camping R30, dorm beds R40, doubles R120. Inyezane is a great hostel on an old plantation near Gingindlovu, off the D134. There are craft workshops and plenty of other events such as Zulu music, sessions with a private sangoma (witch doctor or herbalist), battlefield walks and sessions

about medicinal plants. And of course there's the famous mud bath. It's quirky, a little rough around the edges, and great fun.

The Interport bus between Durban and Richards Bay stops in Gingindlovu, from where it's 3km to Inyezane. Call ahead and they'll pick you up. Otherwise, take the R66 heading towards Eshowe; after you pass Gingindlovu, turn left onto the D134.

MTUNZINI
☎ 035 • postcode 3867

If you want to stay on the coast while you explore this part of KwaZulu-Natal, the

KWAZULU-NATAL

small town of Mtunzini makes for a good base. It's a very quiet, very lush pocket of wealth, in many ways the epitome of the old South Africa.

The town had a colourful beginning. John Dunn, the first European to settle in the area, was granted land by Cetshwayo. He became something of a chief himself, took 49 wives and fathered 117 children. He held court here under a tree, hence the town's name (*mtunzi* is Zulu for 'shade'). After the British defeated King Cetshwayo and divided the kingdom, Dunn was one of the chiefs granted power. It wasn't until recently that the descendants of Dunn and the descendants of Cetshwayo were formally reconciled.

Near the mouth of the Mlalazi River there is lush tropical forest where you'll find the **Raffia Palm Monument**. The raffia palm is a monocarp, meaning that it only seeds once in its 25-year cycle, and its presence this far south is a mystery. Its closest relatives are found in the far north of Tongaland, near Kosi Bay, and it is believed that this unusual grove was planted in around 1910 from seeds obtained near Maputo. There is a wooden boardwalk through the grove – you might spot the rare palmnut vulture (*Gypohierax angolensis*), which favours raffia palms.

The entrance to **Umlalazi Nature Reserve** (*admission R7*) is 1.5km east of the town, on the coast. Umlalazi means 'Place of the Whetstone'. There are some crocodiles here as well as plentiful bird life in the dense vegetation of the sand-dune forest and mangrove swamp. There are three walking trails.

Places to Stay

KZN Wildlife Accommodation (☎ 34(1836) Camping R30 per person, 5-bed log cabins R80/120 per person low/high season. At Umlalazi Nature Reserve all accommodation except camp sites must be booked through KZN Wildlife in Pietermaritzburg or Durban.

Xaxaza Caravan Park (☎ 340 1843, fax 340 1181, Mimosa Dr) Camp sites R35/6(

Zulu Festivals

Throughout the year there are a few major festivals that celebrate the rich culture of the Zulu people. These peaceful and joyous occasions involve colourful displays of traditional singing and dancing and are not to be missed. For further details about these festivals contact Graham Chennels at the **George Hotel & Zululand Backpackers** (☎ 035-474 4919) in Eshowe.

King Shaka Day Festival
On the last Saturday in September, thousands of Zulus converge on KwaDukuza (formerly Stanger) for the King Shaka Day Festival. The annual event, attended by the current Zulu king, pays homage to the Zulu hero.

Reed Dance
Every year thousands of young bare-breasted Zulu 'maidens' gather before their king, honouring the ancient tradition of the Reed Dance. In days long gone, the king would select a new bride from the mass of beautiful young maidens presented before him. The dance takes place the Saturday before the King Shaka Day Festival at King Nyonkeni's Palace which lies between Nongoma and Ulundi.

Shembe Festival
During the month of October, over 30,000 Zulus gather at Judea, 15km east of Eshowe, for the annual Shembe Festival. This eye-opening festival celebrates the Shembe, the Church of the Holy Nazareth Baptists – an unofficial religion that somehow manages to combine Zulu traditions with Christianity. Presiding over the festivities is the church's saviour, Prophet Mbusi Vimbeni Shembe. Throughout the festival the emphasis is on celebration, with much dancing and singing and the blowing of the horns of Jericho.

per person low/high season. The Xaxaza Caravan Park has decent-sized sites but is a long walk from the beach.

Trade Winds Country Inn (☎ *340 1411, Hutchinson Rd*) Singles/doubles B&B R225/345. The old Trade Winds Hotel, thanks to a change of management, has had a minor face-lift along with a minor name change.

Mtunzini Chalets (☎ *340 1953, fax 340 1955*) 6-bed chalets from R116/122 per person low/high season (minimum charge R235/295). The spacious chalets are in a densely forested nature reserve by the sea. This is a very attractive place with good facilities including a pool, a bar and private beach access. During school holidays it fills up, but at other times it's a tranquil escape from the outside world.

RICHARDS BAY
☎ 035 • postcode 3900

The port at Richards Bay is second to Durban's in size, but it handles more cargo than any other in the province. The town feels as though it was meticulously planned for a boom that hasn't quite happened yet. It's spread out, with tourist-oriented facilities a long way from what passes for the centre. Unless you have business here, there is not much for visitors to do.

For information on the region, try the **Richards Bay Publicity Association** (☎ *788 0039, fax 788 0040,* **e** *rbtour@uthunglu.co za, Newart Rd, Tuzi Gazi Waterfront*).

Imvubu Log Cabins (☎ *753 4122, fax 735 4120,* **e** *imvubu@iafrica.com, Krewelk Rd*) Camping R70/110 for 2 people low/high season, dorm beds R50, 6-bed chalets R460. If you do find yourself stuck in Richards Bay, your best option is Imvubu Log Cabins. The leafy resort, right on the beach, offers a variety of well-priced accommodation. Its log cabins (chalets) are spacious, spotlessly clean and even air-conditioned.

EMPANGENI
☎ 035 • postcode 3880

Empangeni (pronounced m'pan-**gay**-nee) started out as a sugar town, but the huge eucalypt plantations nearby are rivalling the cane in their importance to the town's economy. It's a jumping-off point for the coast and the inland areas of Zululand.

The **Empangeni Tourist Information Office** (☎ *792 1283, fax 792 5196,* **e** *empangeni@intekom.co.za, Turnbull St; open 7.30am-4pm Tues-Fri, 8am-noon Sat*) can be found at the Local History Museum which is housed in the old town hall, dating from 1916; admission to the museum costs R1. Adjacent to the museum is the new **Empangeni Arts & Crafts Centre** (☎ *772 7622,* **e** *artcraft@freemail.absa.co.za, Turnbull St; open 9am-4pm Mon-Fri, 9am-2pm Sat*).

Places to Stay & Eat
Imperial Hotel (☎ *792 1522, 52 Maxwell St*) Singles R145/190 without/with bathroom, doubles R200/250 without/with bathroom. This decidedly shabby hotel has OK rooms.

Harbour Lights (☎ *796 6239,* **e** *zebra@harbourlights.co.za,* **w** *www.harbourlights.co.za*) Backpacker accommodation R70 per person, self-catering units R120 per person. Harbour Lights is an unappealing but affordable caravan park off the N3 between Empangeni and Richards Bay. Breakfast costs R20.

Protea Hotel (☎ *772 3322, fax 772 3617, 64 Turnbull St*) Singles/doubles R325/395. Also still known locally by its previous name, De Schoon Hof Lodge, the Protea Hotel has large comfy rooms. The Protea's restaurant, *De Hof Cellar*, serves the best meals in town. Breakfast costs R37.

Apart from the Protea's restaurant, your choices are limited to *Spur* and *Wimpy*.

ENSELENI NATURE RESERVE
The small Enseleni Nature Reserve *(open 8am-5pm daily)*, 13km north-east of Empangeni on the N2, is on a bend in the Nseleni River. As well as game species and zebras there are also hippos and crocodiles in the river. There are several walks (the longest is a 5km swamp trail) but no accommodation.

ESHOWE
☎ 035 • postcode 3815

This town, on the R66, is inland in the misty Zululand hills. The name Eshowe is said to be the sound the wind makes when passing through the trees. Eshowe was Cetshwayo's stronghold before he moved to Ondini, and like Ondini, Eshowe was destroyed during the Anglo-Zulu War. The British occupied the site and built Fort Nongqai in 1883, establishing Eshowe as the administrative centre of their newly captured territory.

For information on the area, visit **Eshowe Tourism** (☎ 474 1141, fax 474 4733, e esh owe@uthungulu.co.za, Hutchinson Rd).

Things to See & Do

If you arrive on a day of thick mist, seeing *anything* might be a problem. In the three-turreted Fort Nongqai, made of mud and brick, is the **Zululand Historical Museum** (☎ 474 7141; adult/child R10/2; open 7am-4pm Mon-Fri, 9am-4pm Sat & Sun). The fort has only three towers because, according to rumour, it collapsed while it was being built and builders couldn't salvage enough bricks to complete the fourth tower. In the museum is a copy of *The Sausage Wrap*, an early news-sheet. It contains a quite funny parody of Henry Rider Haggard.

The shop here sells souvenirs, crafts and some interesting books, including *Fearful Hard Times* (R275), a fairly gung ho account of the 1879 siege and relief of British forces in Eshowe, and *The Destruction of the Zulu Kingdom*, the story of the aftermath of the Anglo-Zulu War (R80).

From the museum you can walk to **Mpushini Falls** (40 minutes return) – don't swim in or drink the water as there is a risk of bilharzia.

Vukani Museum (☎ 474 5274, Osborn St; open 9am-1pm Mon-Fri) has an interesting collection of Zulu crafts.

Dlinza Forest Reserve is a 200-hectare strand of forest; on a misty day this is an eerie place. The birdlife is rich and there are some walking trails, some of which are believed to have been made by British soldiers stationed here after the Anglo-Zulu War. In mid-2001 the 100m-long **Dlinza Forest Aerial Boardwalk** opened. The walkway, which ranges from 10m to 20m in height, was jointly funded by the World Wide Fund for Nature (WWF) and Sappi to promote the conservation of indigenous forests.

Bird-watchers should look for crowned eagles *(Stephanoaetus coronatus)*, green coucals *(Ceuthmochares aereus)*, Narina trogons *(Apaloderma narina)* and Delegorgue's pigeon *(Columba delegorguei)*.

Places to Stay & Eat

Eshowe Caravan Park (☎ 474 1141, Saunders St) Camp sites R30 (minimum 5 people). The park is some way from the town centre, but is close to Dlinza Forest. Follow Osborn Rd west, continue along Main Rd as it doglegs, and turn right onto Saunders St. The park is on your left after a couple of blocks.

George Hotel & Zululand Backpackers (☎ 474 4919, fax 474 2894, e channels@ iafrica.com, W www.zululand.co.za/eshowe, 38 Main St) Camping R40, dorm beds R60, backpacker singles/doubles R75/160, hotel singles/doubles B&B R195/295. We consistently receive good feedback from travellers who have frequented the George Hotel (the backpacker rooms are in a separate wing of the hotel). The rooms are good (breakfast is R15) and the owner has developed a great range of activities (101 in all), from rock sliding to 'real life' cultural Zulu experiences such as attending a traditional wedding or overnighting in a local village. The hotel even has its own micro brewery. Check it out!

Getting There & Away

Minibus taxis leave from the Kwik Spar car park on the main street. The fare to Empangeni is R16 and to Melmoth (the best place to catch taxis deeper into Zululand) it is R9.

Washesha Buses (☎ 477 4504) runs several services in the area including a scenic but rough run on dirt roads through forest areas to Nkandla for about R20. There's no accommodation at Nkandla, but you can get a taxi from there to Melmoth, where there's a hotel. A bus from Eshowe to Empangeni costs around R17. Washesha, meaning 'Hurry' in Zulu, is pretty reliable but on dirt roads rain can strand the buses. For more information ask at the office, behind KFC on the main street.

AROUND ESHOWE

Entumeni Nature Reserve *(admission free)* is larger than Dlinza, and preserves indigenous mist-belt forest. It's 16km west of town, off the road to Ntumeni and Nkandla.

On the south-eastern side of Eshowe, off the R66, **Ocean View Game Park** *(open 7am-5pm daily)* has many birds as well as some other animals.

If you head east from Eshowe on the Gezinsela road for a few kilometres you'll come to Imbombotyana (Signal Hill to the British in the Anglo-Zulu War). From here there are good views, sometimes all the way to the coast.

NKWALINI VALLEY

Shaka's kraal (fortified village), KwaBulawayo, once loomed over this beautiful valley but today the valley is regimented into citrus orchards and cane fields rather than impi (Bantu warriors). From Eshowe head north for 6km on the R66 and turn off to the right onto the R230 (a dirt road that will eventually get you to the R34 and Empangeni) and keep going for about 20km.

Across the road from the KwaBulawayo marker is **Coward's Bush**, now just another marker, where warriors who returned from battle without their spears or who had received wounds in the back were executed.

Further west, a few kilometres before the R230 meets the R66, the **Mandwe Cross** was erected in the 1930s, against the wishes of the Zulu. There are excellent views from the hill.

KwaBhekithunga

Previously a tourist trap, KwaBhekithunga *(Stewart's Farm; ☎ 460 0644, fax 460 0876, ⒠ kwabhenki@netactive.co.za, ⓦ www .zamazama.com/kwabheki)* has now been taken over by a local Zulu family and is operated as a craft and cultural centre, with the proceeds going to support a health clinic. The craft shop is open daily (closed for lunch) and a tour of the kraal, with dancing and also traditional meals, is by appointment only.

Accommodation is available from R75 per person at *The Rest Camp*; breakfast costs R25. Contact the centre for details.

Take the R34, which runs east to Empangeni from the R66 near Nkwalini village, which is about 20km north of Eshowe on the R66. Turn off the R34 onto a dirt road about 6km east of the intersection with the R66. From there it's 5km on a dirt road, the last section of which is very difficult when wet.

Shakaland

Created as a set for the telemovie *Shaka Zulu* and managed by the Protea chain, complete with have-a-nice-day reception staff, Shakaland *(☎ 460 0912, fax 460 0824, ⒠ res@shakaland.com, ⓦ www.shakaland .com; admission R137, displays 11am & 12.30pm)* isn't exactly a genuine Zulu village. The Nandi Experience (Nandi was Shaka's mother) is a display of Zulu culture and customs (including lunch). The 'experience' costs R715/1178 for DB&B.

Shakaland is at Norman Hurst Farm, Nkwalini, a few kilometres off the R66 and 14km north of Eshowe.

MELMOTH

☎ 035 ● postcode 3835

Named after the first resident commissioner of Zululand, Melmoth is a small town dozing in the hills, on the point of going to seed.

Melmoth Inn (☎ 450 2074, Victoria St), in the centre of town, is an inexpensive option. Singles/doubles cost R145/195 without bathroom, R185/225 with bathroom.

ULUNDI

☎ 035 ● postcode 3838

The town of Ulundi was the capital of the KwaZulu Homeland. The town is fairly new, but this area has been the stronghold of many Zulu kings, and several are buried in the nearby Valley of the Kings. Although small, Ulundi is spread out, with residential areas dotted around the neighbouring countryside. The town itself offers little to see but there are important historical sites in the area.

For information visit the **Ulundi Information Bureau** *(☎ 870 0501, fax 870 0598, ⒠ ceogc@mweb.co.za, Princess Magogo St)*.

The former KwaZulu Legislative Assembly is just north of the train line, and has some interesting tapestries and a statue of

Shaka. The building isn't always open to visitors.

Opposite the Legislative Assembly is the site of King Mpande's *iKhanda* (palace), kwaNodwengu. Mpande won control from Dingaan after the disaster at Blood River. He seized power with assistance from the Boers but Zululand declined during his reign. The king's grave and a small museum are there.

Close to Ulundi is Fort Nolela, near the drift on the White Umfolozi River where the British camped before attacking Ondini in 1879, and KwaGqokli, where Shaka celebrated victory over the Ndwandwe in 1818. Another place of great significance to the Zulu is **eMakhosini**, Valley of the Kings. The great *makhosi* (chiefs) Nkhosinkulu, Senzangakhona (father of Shaka, Dingaan and Mpande) and Dinizulu are buried here.

Ulundi Holiday Inn Garden Court (☎ 870 1012, fax 870 1220, ℮ higculundi@southern sun.com, Princess Magogo St) is a large, modern hotel that looks out of place in this small dusty town. Singles/doubles cost R419/518; breakfast is R46.

The minibus taxi park is opposite the Holiday Inn. The fare to Vryheid is R15, Eshowe is R20 and to Jo'burg about R65.

ONDINI

Ondini (High Place) was established as Cetshwayo's capital in 1873 but was razed by British troops after the Battle of Ulundi (July 1879), the final engagement of the 1879 Anglo-Zulu War.

It took the British nearly six months to defeat the Zulu army, but the Battle of Ulundi went the way of most of the campaign, with 10 to 15 times more Zulus killed than British. Part of the reason for the British victory at Ulundi was that they adopted the Boer laager tactic, with troops forming a hollow square to protect the cavalry, which attacked only after the Zulu army had spent itself trying to penetrate the walls.

The royal kraal section of the Ondini site is still being rebuilt but you can see where archaeological digs have uncovered the floors of identifiable buildings. The floors, of mud and cow dung, were preserved by the heat of the fires which destroyed the huts above them. The huge area is enclosed in a defensive perimeter of gnarled branches, some of which act as fencing for a herd of white Nguni cattle, prized by Zulu kings.

Also at Ondini is the **KwaZulu Cultural-Historical Museum** (☎ 870 2050; admission R8; open 8am-4pm Mon-Fri, 9am-4pm Sat & Sun) with good exhibits on Zulu history and culture and an excellent audiovisual show. It also has one of the country's best collections of beadwork on display. You can buy souvenirs, including some interesting books.

Accommodation is available in traditional *umuzi* or 'beehive' **huts** (☎ 870 2050) for R160 per person for DB&B, or R115 without dinner. Unless you've made other arrangements you must be there by 6pm.

To get to Ondini, take the Cultural Museum turn-off from the highway just south of Ulundi and keep going for about 5km on a dirt road. Minibus taxis occasionally pass Ondini. This road continues on to Hluhluwe-Umfolozi Park, but several foreigners have been attacked near the park entrance in recent years.

MGUNGUNDLOVU

This was Dingaan's capital from 1829 to 1839, and it's here that Piet Retief and the other Voortrekkers were killed by their host in 1838, the event that precipitated the Boer-Zulu War. (There are several variations of the spelling of Mgungundlovu, including Ungungundhlovu.) The area is being restored and there's a small **museum** (open 8am-5pm daily) and a monument to the Voortrekkers nearby. In 1990 excavations revealed the site of Dingaan's *ndlunkulu* (great hut).

The site is 5km off the R34, running between Melmoth and Vryheid. Turn off to the left (west) about 5km north-east of the intersection with the R66 to Ulundi.

BABANANGO
☎ 035 • postcode 3850

This village is on the R66 between Melmoth and Dundee. Babanango (literally, 'Father, there it is') is near interesting battlefields. An essential stop is Stan's Pub, at the Babanango Hotel, a favourite drinking hole of Michael Caine during the filming of *Zulu*.

Babanango Hotel (☎ *835 0029, 16 Justice St*) Singles/doubles B&B R150/250. Sadly, Stan, the original owner of the hotel, passed away and this infamous hotel has fallen into ruin. However, new management has taken over and hopes are high that the hotel will be restored to its former glory. The hotel is near the police station and the town's main crossroads, it still remains a little rough around the edges but exudes atmosphere.

Halls Habitat (☎ *835 0035, fax 835 0173, Lot 6 Wilson St*) Singles/doubles B&B R330/600. Halls Habitat is a pleasant place with a large tranquil garden and first-class restaurant.

Babanango Valley Lodge (☎ *835 0062, fax 835 0160*, e *bvlodge@mweb.co.za*) DB&B R590 per person. The Babanango Lodge is an excellent place on historic Goudhoek Farm, in the beautiful Nsubeni Valley. Management organises outstanding tours of nearby battlefields for R250 per person. This sylvan valley is quite isolated, off the R66 about halfway between Melmoth and Dundee. Turn north off the R66 about 4km west of Babanango and continue on (veer left at the fork) for about 12km – you are on the right track if you head down a very steep hill.

HLUHLUWE-UMFOLOZI PARK
☎ 035

This park (☎ *562 0289; admission R10 per person plus R35 per vehicle; open 5am-7pm daily Nov-Feb, 6am-6pm daily Mar-Oct*) is best visited in winter as the animals can range widely without congregating at water sources, although the lush vegetation sometimes makes viewing difficult. However, summer visits can also be very rewarding, especially at Umfolozi where there is more open savanna country.

The two reserves of Hluhluwe and Umfolozi were first proclaimed in 1895 and today they are among the best in South Africa. They are not adjoined to one another, but a linking Corridor Reserve (established

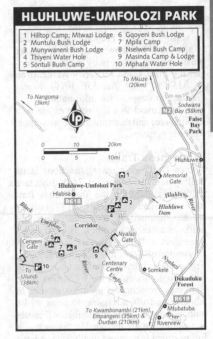

HLUHLUWE-UMFOLOZI PARK

1 Hilltop Camp; Mtwazi Lodge
2 Muntulu Bush Lodge
3 Munywaneni Bush Lodge
4 Thiyeni Water Hole
5 Sontuli Bush Camp
6 Gqoyeni Bush Lodge
7 Mpila Camp
8 Nselweni Bush Camp
9 Masinda Camp & Lodge
10 Mphafa Water Hole

in 1989) between them allows animals to move freely from one park to the other. The three reserves, now combined into one park, have a total area of 96,000 hectares.

The park has lions, elephants, rhinos (black and white), giraffes and birds. The land is quite hilly except on the river flats: the White Umfolozi River flows through Umfolozi, and the Black Umfolozi forms the northern border of the park; the Hluhluwe River bisects Hluhluwe, and the dam on it attracts wildlife.

New to the park is Centenary Centre, a wildlife-holding centre with an attached museum and information centre in the eastern section of Umfolozi. The centre, which incorporates rhino bomas (enclosures) and antelope pens, was established to allow visitors to view animals in transit to their new homes.

The wildlife drives here are very popular. Unlike some other tours you aren't sweltering in Kombis but sitting in open Land Rovers.

Schoolchildren in the Hluhluwe-Umfolozi area put on regular Zulu cultural shows in the various schools. They are aimed squarely at tourists but they are not slick and are great fun; admission is by donation. Contact the **Mtubatuba Publicity Association** (☎ *035-550 0781, fax 550 4019,* e *mtubatuba@uthungulu)* for information.

Bear in mind that the reserves are in a malarial area and there are lots of mosquitos, so come prepared.

Wilderness Trails

One of Umfolozi's main attractions is its trail system, in a special 24,000-hectare wilderness area. On the **Traditional Trail** (three days and four nights; R1370) hikers are accompanied by an armed ranger and donkeys to carry supplies. Hikers spend three days walking in the reserve covering an average of 12km to 15km each day. The first and last nights are spent at a base camp, with two nights out in the wilderness area. Bookings are accepted up to six months in advance and it's advisable to book early, with alternative dates if possible. All meals and equipment are included in the cost, and full payment is required in advance. A variation on this is the **Primitive Trail** (four nights; R1500), on which you provide everything except food and carry it all yourself. Taking the Primitive Trail might be more fun as you get to participate more (for example, hikers must sit up in 1½-hour watches during the night).

There is also the **Weekend Trail** (32km, two nights; R740) and the **Bushveld Trail** (two nights; R920). The Bushveld Trail runs from mid-December to mid-February only.

However, there is a hitch – both walks require a party of eight, which must be pre-arranged (the KZN Wildlife doesn't make up groups). The trails operate all year but in the hottest months (from December to February) the routes are modified and there's some transport.

Organised Tours

Several tours include Hluhluwe-Umfolozi. One inexpensive option is the three-day trip with *Tekweni Eco-Tours* (☎ *031-303* *1199, fax 303 4369,* e *tekweni@global.co* *.za,* w *www.tekweniecotours.co.za)*, which also takes in the Greater St Lucia Wetland Park. However, unless you are watching every rand, you're better off hiring a car and travelling at your own pace through the park.

Places to Stay & Eat

Book accommodation through **KZN Wildlife** (☎ *033-845 1000, fax 033-845 1001)* in Pietermaritzburg or at the Tourist Junction in Durban.

Hilltop Camp (☎ *562 0255, fax 562 0113)* Self-catering 2-bed chalets from R275 per person (minimum R410), 2-bed rondavels without bathroom R145 per person (minimum R215), 2-bed chalets without kitchen R275 per person (minimum R410). Hilltop Camp, in Hluhluwe, at the top of a forested ridge, has stupendous views over the Hluhluwe section of the park and Zululand. It is a great place to stay. The Mpunyane Restaurant here serves game dishes at reasonable prices. The camp also offers wildlife drives (R80), guided walks (R50) and boat cruises (R50). However, there are drawbacks to the good views and facilities at Hilltop: it's the most popular destination for tour buses and is generally quite busy. If you want peace and quiet and can't afford to stay at a bush lodge, try one of the accommodation centres in Umfolozi, which are smaller.

If you're after a bush lodge, try *Muntulu Bush Lodge*, perched high above the Hluhluwe River, or *Munywaneni Bush Lodge*, which is secluded and self-contained. Both have eight-bed bush lodges for R300 per person (minimum R1500). There's also a nine-bed lodge at *Mtwazi Lodge* for R275 per person (minimum R1100).

The two main accommodation centres in Umfolozi are *Mpila Camp* in the centre of the reserve and *Masinda Camp & Lodge* near the Centenary Centre. Both have four-bed huts for R100 per person (minimum R200). Mpila camp also has 'safari camp' accommodation starting at R145/160 per person low/high season. There are also eight-bed bush camps available at *Sontuli Bush Camp* and *Nselweni Bush Camp* for R200 per person, minimum R800 (which includes your own ranger and cook); and eight-bed bush lodges at *Gqoyeni Bush Camp* and *Hlathikulu* (minimum R1240).

Getting There & Away
The main entrance, Memorial Gate, is about 15km west of the N2, about 50km north of Mtubatuba. Alternatively, just after Mtubatuba, turn left off the N2 onto the R618 to Nongoma, entering the reserve through the Nyalazi Gate.

Umfolozi also has a gate on the western side, Cengeni Gate, accessible by rough roads from Ulundi (but note that there have been a few attacks on foreigners along this road in recent years). Petrol is available at Mpila Camp in Umfolozi and at Hilltop Camp in Hluhluwe.

KWAMBONAMBI
☎ 035 • postcode 3915
KwaMbonambi (often called Kwambo) is a tiny but lush and beautiful town off the N2, about 30km north of Empangeni and the same distance south of Mtubatuba. However, there's no real reason to stop here except that there's an excellent hostel, the Cockoos Nest, making it an ideal base for backpackers exploring St Lucia, Hluhluwe-Umfolozi and other attractions in northern Zululand and Maputaland.

Some believe that KwaMbonambi means 'Place of the Gathering of Kings', while others believe it means 'Place of the Blacksmith', as Shaka's spears were made here.

Cuckoos Nest (☎ 580 1001/2, fax 580 1002, e cuckoos@mweb.co.za, 28 Albizia St) Camping R30, dorm beds R45, doubles R110, tepee R110, tree house R120, including breakfast. This is a cheerful, carefree hostel, which has few rules and lots of activities. Meals are available. Management offers trips to Hluhluwe-Umfolozi Park and Sodwana Bay, or excursions (sometimes free) to a secluded stretch of beach where camping is available.

MTUBATUBA & AROUND
☎ 035 • postcode 3935
The name Mtubatuba comes from a local chief, Mthubuthubu, meaning 'He who was Pummelled Out', referring to his difficult birth.

This is a trading town that is busy on weekends. The main reason to visit is that buses and minibus taxis run through here on the way south to Durban, north to Pongola (via Hluhluwe and Mkuze) and west into Zululand. Coming from those destinations, Mtubatuba is the stop for St Lucia (St Lucia Resort is 25km east; R5 by minibus taxi).

On the southern side of Mtubatuba is Riverview, a poor but neat town with a sugar mill.

Dukuduku Forest Reserve (including Mihobi Nature Reserve), on the R620 between Mtubatuba and St Lucia, is one of the largest remaining coastal forests in KwaZulu-Natal. It is home to many varieties of butterflies as well as other insects, birds and animals. There are walking trails and a nice picnic spot. Camping is not permitted.

Places to Stay & Eat
Hotel Paradiso Guesthouse (☎ 550 0153, fax 550 1499, Club Rd, Mtubatuba) Singles/doubles B&B R110/180. Although a little shabby, Hotel Paradiso is a friendly place with reasonable rooms. Its small Italian restaurant Forza Italia is popular with locals.

Wendy's B&B Country Lodge (☎ 550 0407, fax 550 1527, e wendybnb@iafrica .co.za, w www.wendybnb.co.za, 3 Riverview Rd, Riverview) B&B R165-225 per person. Wendy's is a charming family-run place in a secure residential area of Riverview. It has a verdant tropical garden with a swimming pool and a guest's bar stocked with plenty of gin and tonic.

DUMAZULU CULTURAL VILLAGE
North of Mtubatuba, Dumazulu Cultural Village (☎ 035-562 2260; admission R70; shows at 8.15am, 11am & 3.15pm daily), east of the N2, is probably the best of the 'Zulu experience' villages. Lunch and dinner are available.

Dumazulu Lodge (☎ 031-337 4222, e lodges@goodersons.co.za, w www.good ersonleisure.com) is a comfortable lodge in the village which has singles/doubles for R600/900 DB&B.

HLUHLUWE

☎ 035 • postcode 3960

Hluhluwe village (roughly pronounced 'shloo-shloo-wee') is located to the north-east of Hluhluwe-Umfolozi Park.

There is as good a selection of Zulu baskets, beadwork and other handicrafts as you will see anywhere at **Ilala Weavers** (☎ *562 0630*, @ *ilala@iafrica.com*, W *www.zulu land.com; open 8am-5pm Mon-Fri, 9am-4pm Sat & Sat)*. It is quite a centre, with a gallery, museum and restaurant.

Places to Stay

Apart from the places mentioned here, there's a guesthouse or two in town, and plenty of other accommodation in the area. On the road in from the N2, 4km before town, there's a signboard showing the location of accommodation in the area.

Isinkwe Backpackers Lodge (☎/fax 562 2258, @ *isinkwe@saol.com)* Camping R35, dorm beds R50, doubles R120. Isinkwe is arguably one of the best backpacker hostels in South Africa. It's next to Dumazulu Cultural Village, 1km off the N2 south of Hluhluwe (take the Bushlands exit). The hostel is on a big, beautiful patch of virgin bush and has small but comfortable cabins, 'rustic' huts, tents and a dorm, all in a pleasant garden. There's a kitchen and bar area. Good meals are available.

Hluhluwe Inn Hotel (☎ *562 0251, fax 562 0254, 104 Bush Rd)* Singles B&B/DB&B R260/340, doubles B&B/DB&B R480/640. Prices here are quite high, and it's often booked out by tour groups. Some evenings performances of Zulu dancing are put on.

Warning

! ● This is a malarial area, and there are lots of mosquitoes. Ticks and leeches can be a problem. Also be aware of crocs and hippos: both can be deadly. Be careful at night, as this is when hippos roam. In more remote areas hippos might be encountered on shore during the day – maintain your distance and retreat quietly. Sharks sometimes venture up the estuary near St Lucia Resort.

Bonamanzi Game Ranch (☎ *562 0181, fax 562 0143*, @ *bonamanzi@hit.co.za)* 4-bed rustic tree house R87/108 per person low/high season, 2-bed luxury tree house R288/360 low/high season. Bonamanzi Game Ranch, a private wildlife reserve, is 5.5km south of Hluhluwe village. There is a number of self-catering accommodation options. Book in advance.

GREATER ST LUCIA WETLAND PARK

☎ 035 • postcode 3936

One of the world's great ecotourist destinations, Greater St Lucia Wetland Park stretches for 80km from Sodwana Bay, in the north of Maputaland, to Mapelane, at the southern end of Lake St Lucia. The park's value as an international conservation site was recognised in 1999 when it was formally granted Unesco World Heritage status.

The park protects five interconnected ecosystems: marine (coral reefs and beaches); shore (the barrier between lake and sea); Mkuze reed and sedge swamps; the lake (the largest estuary in Africa); and western shores (fossil corals, sand forest, bushveld and grasslands).

Lake St Lucia, its surrounds and the nearby ocean beaches are popular holiday destinations, and the area is made up of a number of parks and reserves, including St Lucia Park, St Lucia Game Reserve, False Bay Park, Tewati Wilderness Area, Mfabeni Section, Ozabeni Section, Sodwana Bay National Park, Mapelane Nature Reserve and the St Lucia and Maputaland Marine Reserves. To the south is Mhlatuze State Forest.

The main population centres in the area are Mtubatuba and St Lucia Resort.

Thirty elephants, acquired from Hluhluwe-Umfolozi Park and Tembe Elephant Park, were released into this World Heritage site in mid-2001.

All the parks and reserves are administered by KZN Wildlife, but there is private accommodation in the town of St Lucia Resort, which is a sizable holiday village.

Remember that all accommodation other than camping run by KZN Wildlife must be booked in Pietermaritzburg or at Durban's Tourist Junction.

Hiking Trails

The main trails are the guided **St Lucia Wilderness Trail** (four days; R1300 per person), and the self-guided **Mziki Trail** (40km, three days; R35/45 per person per night low/high season) and **Emoyeni Trail** (65km, five days; R25/33 per person per night low/high season), all in the Cape Vidal area. There are also day walks, detailed in KZN Wildlife literature available at the office at St Lucia Resort.

Organised Tours

Leisure Eco-Tours (☎ 590 1143), based at the tourist information office on McKenzie St in St Lucia Resort, can organise just about anything in the area, including night drives for R110. BiB's International Backpackers in St Lucia Resort offers similar tours.

One of the highlights of a trip to the Greater St Lucia Wetland Park is the **boat trip** on the *Santa Lucia*. It leaves from St Lucia Resort, from the wharf on the western side of the bridge on the Mtubatuba road, at 8am, 10.30am and 2.30pm daily, and there are sunset cruises at 4.05pm Friday and Saturday (adult/child R55/35). The number of trips each day changes seasonally. The slow-moving launch is a great platform from which to photograph and observe. The sparse commentary allows you to get on with watching.

St Lucia Resort

☎ 035 • postcode 3936

This is the main centre for the area, with KZN Wildlife offices, shops, boat hire and other services, as well as a lot of private accommodation. In high season it's a very busy place. Despite the numbers of humans, animals from the nearby national park wander close to the residential areas. Hippos and even leopards have been seen.

As well as **KZN Wildlife** *(☎ 590 1340, fax 590 1343, Pelican Rd)*, there's the official **St Lucia Tourism & Information Centre** *(☎ 590 1075, fax 590 1467, e leisure@futurenet .co.za, Cnr McKenzie St & Katonkel Rd)*. You can book tours and accommodation here.

BiB's International Backpackers operates an **Internet cafe** *(Internet access R30 per hour; open 7am-10pm daily)*.

There are two ATMs in town: at First National Bank, next to the Dolphin supermarket, and at Standard Bank.

About 2km north of St Lucia, on the road to Cape Vidal, is the **Crocodile Centre** *(☎ 590 1386, fax 590 1355, e croc-centre@kznnca .org.za; adult/child R15/10; open 8.30am-5pm Mon-Fri, 9am-4pm Sat & Sun, feeding time 3pm Sat)*, where there are pools of crocodiles as well as displays on the ecosystems in the region. After you've looked at the first set of enclosures, be sure to follow the path labelled 'Juvenile Crocodiles'. This leads to smaller pools swarming with young crocs of several species, as well as some 'Golden Oldies'.

Places to Stay There is also a huge range of private accommodation, mainly in holiday apartments. You can make bookings at the St Lucia Tourism & Information Centre.

KZN Wildlife Accommodation (bookings ☎ 590 1340) Camping R25/45 per person low/high season, powered sites (Sugarloaf) R30/50 per person low/high season. There are KZN Wildlife camping grounds at Sugarloaf, Eden Park and Iphiva. At the time of writing there was speculation that the Iphiva camp site might close.

BiB's International Backpackers (☎ 590 1056, 590 1360, e info@bibs.co.za, 310 McKenzie St) Camping R30, dorm beds R50, doubles without/with air-con R120/ R130, 2-person chalets R130. BiB's International Backpackers is a huge barn converted into backpacker and guesthouse accommodation. It has an Internet cafe and organises heaps of activities, including snorkelling at Cape Vidal and hippo tours on the estuary.

African Tale Backpackers (☎/fax 550 4300, e africantale@hotmail.com, 3 Main Rd) Camping R30, dorm beds R45, doubles (beehive huts) R110. African Tale, on the road between Mtubatuba and St Lucia, is a great place to hang out for a day or two. Management offers free shuttles into St Lucia, Internet access and various trips and activities.

St Lucia Wilds (☎/fax 590 1033, e *stlucia wilds@netactive.co.za, McKenzie St)* 5- or 6-bed chalet R45 (older chalets) to R85 (new chalets) per person. St Lucia Wilds is one of the real bargains in town. To get there, head all the way down the main street and instead of following the road around to the left to the KZN Wildlife office, keep going straight on down the small road. St Lucia Wilds is at the end of this road.

Places to Eat Cheap eats include *Wimpy* and the nearby *Mighty Bite*, both of which are on McKenzie St.

St Pizza (☎ 590 1048, McKenzie St) Mains R27-44, pizzas R14-33. St Pizza serves pizzas and seafood on its large shaded terrace. If you have developed a taste for South African meats try the biltong pizza (R24/29 small/large).

Alfredo's Italian Restaurant (☎ 590 1150, McKenzie St) Mains R27-45. Alfredo's is a relatively inexpensive Italian restaurant serving a mixed menu of pastas, fish dishes and grills.

The Quarterdeck (☎ 590 1116, McKenzie St) Mains R25-75. The pricey Quarterdeck specialises in seafood. According to the menu, 'one very hungry man ate a prawn combo, then had a double seafood platter, ate it all and loved every morsel'.

The Zulu & I (☎ 590 1144, e *thezulu@ stlucia.co.za,* w *wetlands.co.za/thezulu, Crocodile Centre)* Mains R30-45. The Zulu & I, overlooking a murky crocodile pit at the Crocodile Centre, is for those who are a little more adventurous. Its menu naturally specialises in crocodile dishes and there is Zulu cultural dancing from 7pm Monday to Saturday.

St Lucia Game Park

This game park *(admission R10)*, which takes in the water body of the lake and a ribbon of land around it, the islands and Mapelane Nature Reserve, was declared in

1897, making it the oldest reserve in South Africa.

Lake St Lucia is in fact a large and meandering estuary (Africa's largest) with a narrow sea entrance, and its depth and salinity alter depending on seasonal and ecological factors. It is mainly shallow and the warm water is crowded with fish, which in turn attract huge numbers of water birds. There are lots of pelicans and flamingos in the area, and fish eagles breed around here. Frogs make a veritable din during the summer mating season. However, the Lake St Lucia area is best known as a crocodile and hippo reserve.

The 38km, three-day **Mziki Trail** (R40 including accommodation) is in the Mfabeni section of St Lucia (formerly the Eastern Shores State Forest). Admission to Mfabeni is R8 per person plus R35 per vehicle. The base camp for this trail is Mt Tabor, inland just north of Mission Rocks and accessible from the road running between St Lucia and Cape Vidal. Mt Tabor was a base for submarine-spotting Catalina flying boats during WWII, and the wreckage of one of the planes can be seen in the lake south-west of the camp.

The Mziki is actually three easy trails. Day one (10km) is a walk south through dune forest and along the coastline; day two (10km) is a walk west through indigenous forest to the freshwater Mfazana Pan, along the shore of Lake St Lucia, then east over Mt Tabor; and day three (18km) is a walk that descends into Bokkie Valley (named after the *mziki* or reedbuck there) and returns through dune forest and along some pristine coastline. The trail is part of a system that will eventually link St Lucia with Cape Vidal.

Places to Stay As well as the accommodation at St Lucia Resort, there is also the KZN Wildlife–administered accommodation, *Fanies Island (☎ 550 1631)*, where camping costs R25/35 in low/high season and huts are R60/105 per person. Fanies Island is by the lake, 11km north of Charters Creek. You can't swim there because of the crocodiles.

Charters Creek has two-bed chalets starting at around R135/180 per person in low/high season, seven-bed cottages for R100 per person (minimum R400), four-bed huts for around R60/105 per person in low/high season. Charters Creek is a place to stay on the western shore of Lake St Lucia's southern arm, and is accessible from a turn-off from the N2, about 20km to the north of Mtubatuba.

False Bay Park

This park *(admission R8)* runs along the western shore of Lake St Lucia. As well as the lake's hippos and crocs, the park has several antelope species and other animals, including zebras and wart hogs. The park boasts prolific bird life and a great variety of vegetation. There are three hiking trails through the park averaging around 8km each; contact Dugandlovu camp for details.

In the northern part of False Bay is the **Mpophomeni Trail**, which is divided into two routes that are both suitable for families; the longer 10km section takes about four to five hours, the shorter 7km section, takes three hours.

Dugandlovu (☎ *562 0425)* Camping around R20/30 per person low/high season, rustic 4-bed huts starting at R75 per person (minimum R150). The Dugandlovu camp site is on the Dugandlovu Trail, about 9km from the entrance gate; you can drive to the camp site.

The main road into the park runs from Hluhluwe village, off the N2. Hluhluwe village is also the nearest place to buy fuel and other supplies.

Tewati Wilderness Area & Cape Vidal

The Tewati Wilderness Area *(☎ 590 9012, fax 590 9007; admission R8 per person plus R35 per vehicle; open 5am-7pm daily Oct-Mar, 6am-6pm daily Apr-Sept)* takes in the land between the lake and the ocean, north of Cape Vidal. Some of the forested sand dunes are 150m high.

The **Cape Vidal office** *(☎ 590 9012, fax 590 9007)* is the starting place for the four-night St Lucia Wilderness Trail, a guided hike costing R1200 per person, including all equipment and meals (book with KZN Wildlife in Pietermaritzburg). Walks are only possible from April to the end of September. The minimum number of people is four. There is a lot of wading involved, so bring spare shoes.

Bhangazi (☎ *035-590 1404)* Camping R40/45 per person low/high season (minimum R80/180 low/high season), log cabins starting at R145 per person (minimum R435), dormitory beds in cabins starting at R60 per person (minimum R5300), 8-bed bush lodge R200 (minimum R800). This place is located within the Tewati Wilderness Area.

From St Lucia head north up past the Crocodile Centre and through the entrance gates. Cape Vidal is approximately 30km further on.

St Lucia & Maputaland Marine Reserves

When combined, these reserves cover the coastal strip and three nautical miles out to sea, running from Cape Vidal right up to Mozambique. The reserves include the world's most southerly coral reefs, in particular those around Sodwana Bay (which is a national park), and nesting sites of leatherback and loggerhead turtles.

Mapelane Nature Reserve

South across the estuary from St Lucia Resort, this popular fishing spot *(admission R8)* will probably become the major visitors centre for Mhlatuze State Forest when that area is developed for recreational use. The dense bush around the camp is flanked by a giant dune, the Mjakaja.

KZN Wildlife Accommodation (☎ *590 1407)* includes camping for R38/40 per person in low/high season and five-bed cabins for R100/130 per person (minimum R390 in high season).

Although Mapelane is across the estuary from St Lucia Resort, travel between St Lucia Resort and Mapelane is circuitous unless you have a boat. Mapelane is reached by 40km of sandy and sometimes tricky road from KwaMbonambi, off the N2 south

KWAZULU-NATAL

of Mtubatuba. Follow the KwaMbonambi Lighthouse sign.

SODWANA BAY
☎ 035

When travellers debate the best spots in South Africa, Sodwana Bay is invariably mentioned. Its appeal lies in its isolation, the accessibility of the world's most southerly coral reef, walking trails, fishing and magic coastal scenery.

The small **Sodwana Bay National Park** *(☎ 571 0051, fax 571 0115; admission R7 per person)* is on the coast, east of Mkuze. There are some animals, and the dunes, swamps and offshore coral reefs are worth visiting, but the area is very congested during holidays and it becomes noisy and crowded. Over Christmas there are turtle-viewing tours. The park office is open 8am to 12.30pm and 2pm to 4pm daily. You can hire small safety deposit boxes at the park office; this is a good idea, as there have been reports of theft from parked cars.

For a more peaceful look at a similar ecosystem, head south to the adjoining Sodwana State Forest, now called **Ozabeni**

(☎/fax 571 0011; admission R7 per person plus R15 per vehicle), which runs all the way down to Lake St Lucia. Bird-watchers will go wild, as over 330 species have been recorded. North of the lake is a prohibited area. Camp sites are available.

Places to Stay & Eat

KZN Wildlife Accommodation (bookings ☎ 571 0051/2/3/4) Camping R33 per person (minimum R66/132 low/high season), 5-bed cabins R130 per person (minimum R390). You need to make reservations early. There is a shop in the resort and fuel is available.

Sodwana Bay Lodge (☎ 571 0095, fax 571 0144, ⓔ sodwana@mweb.co.za, ⓦ www .sodwanadivelodge.co.za) Singles DB&B R475/585 low/high season, doubles DB&B R840/950, 6-/8-bed self-catering units R650/800. Sodwana Bay Lodge, on the main road, is a big private resort offering comfortable accommodation and a good restaurant.

Coral Divers (☎ 571 0290, fax 571 0042, ⓔ coraldivers@mweb.co.za, Sodwana Bay National Park) Safari tents R80, budget cabins R120, standard cabins R140, cabins

---

Marine Turtles

Five species of turtle occur off the South African coast but only two actually nest on the coast: the leatherback turtle *(Dermochelys coriacea)* and the loggerhead turtle *(Caretta caretta)*. The nesting areas of the leatherback extend from the St Lucia mouth north into Mozambique, but the loggerhead only nests in the Maputaland Marine Reserve.

Both species nest at night in summer. The female moves above the high-tide mark, finds a suitable site and lays her eggs. The loggerheads' breeding area is more varied as they clamber over rocks in the intertidal zone; leatherbacks will only nest on sandy beaches.

The hatchlings scramble out of the nest at night, about 70 days later, and make a dash for the sea. Only one or two of each thousand hatchlings will survive until maturity. The females return 12 to 15 years later to the very same beach to nest.

KZN Wildlife has night turtle tours in December and January. They cost R70/35 for an adult/child in a park vehicle; R35/17.50 in private vehicle. Children younger than five aren't allowed on the tours.

SARAH JOLLY

with private bathroom R210 (all prices per person). Coral Divers offers good backpacker rates; however, as the site is within the KZN Wildlife park you pay an extra charge for entry – even more than you pay for staying in KZN Wildlife's accommodation. Breakfast is R28, dinner R46.

Both Coral Divers and the lodge offer dive packages and instruction (see the boxed text for more details).

Getting There & Away

There are two road routes from the N2. The northern route leaves the highway about 8km north of Mkuze and runs up into the Lebombo Mountains to the small town of **Jozini**. After Jozini it's a dirt road running through flat country. The southern route leaves the N2 north of the turn-off for Hluhluwe village. In recent years work has begun on a sealed road on the southern route. Although work is continuing, at the time of writing the sealed road ran from Hluhluwe village for about 40km. Both routes converge at the village of Mbazwana, from where it's about 20km of sealed road to the park.

A conventional car will have no trouble on either route but you'll need to take it easy on the northern route because the road is quite sandy in places, and there are lots of people and animals on it.

Minibus taxis run from the N2 up to Jozini. From there to Sodwana Bay you shouldn't have trouble finding transport (taxis) as it's a fairly densely populated region. There are far fewer taxis on the southern route but there is a fair amount of tourist traffic, so hitching should be easy.

TONGALAND
☎ 035

The area of Maputaland on the Mozambique border was once known as Tongaland, as it was settled by the Tonga people of Mozambique. It's a distinct ecological region and the only part of South Africa east of the Lebombo range. The southern tail of the region, known as the Ubombo, peters out near the Phinda Resource Reserve. The soil of this flat, hot region is sandy and the rivers

---

Snorkelling & Diving

The coastline near Sodwana Bay, which includes the southernmost coral reefs in Africa, is a diver's paradise. Schools of fish glide through the beautiful coral, turtles swim by, and moray eels peer inquisitively from rock crevices. Predominantly soft coral over hard, the reef has one of the world's highest recorded numbers of tropical fish species. All of these wonders can be seen using scuba or snorkelling equipment, and excellent visibility and warm winter waters allow for diving year-round.

Popular snorkelling spots are Cape Vidal, Two-Mile Reef off Sodwana Bay, Mabibi, and the Kosi Mouth with its famous 'aquarium', so named because of the diversity of fish. Scuba divers should head for Tenedos Shoal, between the Mlalazi River and Port Durnford, and Five-Mile, Seven-Mile and Nine-Mile Reefs. Courses are held at Two-Mile Reef.

Sodwana Bay Lodge (☎ 035-571 0117, fax 571 0055, e sblsc@icon.co.za, w www.sodwanadiving.co.za) specialises in PADI diving packages. **Coral Divers** (☎ 035-571 0290, fax 571 0042, e coraldivers@mweb.co.za) also offers PADI courses. Both offer equipment hire.

---

harbour crocodiles and hippos. Inland there are forests of huge figs, especially along the Pongola River, and nearer the coast, palms grow among the saltpans and thornveld.

There has been little development here and there are some good wildlife reserves. One of the most common creatures is the mosquito and malaria is a risk, so take precautions.

Mkuze
☎ 035 • postcode 3965

Mkuze, a small town on the N2 and the Mkuze River, is west of a pass over the Lebombo range. The road through the pass is one route to Sodwana Bay. **Ghost Mountain**, south of the town, was an important burial place for the Ndwandwe tribe and has a reputation for eerie occurrences, usually confined to strange lights and noises. Occasionally human bones are found near Ghost Mountain which date from a big battle between rival Zulu factions in 1884.

Ghost Mountain Inn (☎/fax 573 1025, ⓔ ghostinn@iafrica.com, ⓦ www.ghost mountaininn.co.za) Singles/doubles B&B R355/590. This upmarket inn, at the foot of the infamous Ghost Mountain, is a nice place with welcoming rooms. It offers bargain weekend specials and organises wildlife drives to Mkhuzi Game Reserve.

Mkhuzi Game Reserve

Established in 1912, Mkhuzi Game Reserve *(admission R8 per person plus R35 per vehicle)*, covering some 36,000 hectares, lacks lions and elephants but just about every other sought-after animal is represented, as well as over 400 species of birds, including the rare Pel's fishing owl *(Scotopelia peli)*.

Better still, this KZN Wildlife reserve has hides at pans and water holes which offer some of the best wildlife viewing in the country. The walk to Nsumu Pan features two bird-watching hides, and there are six wildlife-viewing hides, the most notable being Bube and Masinga. Morning is the best time.

Nestled below the Ubombo range, the country is partly dense thornveld, partly open savanna, and gets very hot in summer; winters are generally mild.

Night game drives (R70) are available. Fuel is sold at the main gate.

KZN Wildlife Accommodation (☎ 573 0003) Camping R30 per person (minimum R60/120 low/high season), 3-bed rest huts R85/110 per person (minimum R85/220), 2-bed safari camps R135/145 per person (minimum R203/217), 3-bed chalets & cottages from R120/145 per person (minimum R120/310). The camp site also has larger chalets and cottages, as well as a two-bed bush lodge (minimum R300/800 low/high season) and two-bed tented bush lodges in summer (minimum R240/640).

From the north you can get there from Mkuze town; from the south, turn off the N2 around 35km north of Hluhluwe village.

Phinda Resource Reserve

This 17,000-hectare reserve, to the north-west of Lake St Lucia, is very much an 'ecotourism' showpiece. It was set up by the Conservation Corporation, a private reserves chain.

There are nine different ecosystems in the park. They include hilly terrain, sand forest, riverine woodland, natural pans and savanna grasslands. This diversity attracts a great variety of birdlife (more than 360 species) and promotes a diverse range of plant life. There are about 10,000 animals, many reintroduced, including nyala and the rare suni antelope *(Neotragus moschatus)*. Lion and cheetah kills can occasionally be spotted and leopards are now seen during wildlife drives. In addition to the wildlife drives there are also accompanied walks, canoeing and river-boat cruises.

The only problem with Phinda is that all the 'eco' features don't come cheap: low-season doubles start at R4500 for full board, including activities. Bookings can be made through **Conservation Corporation Africa** *(☎ 011-809 4300, fax 809 4400, ⓔ book ings@ccafrica.com, ⓦ www.ccafrica.com)*.

Zulu Nyala Lodge (☎ 562 0177, ⓔ zulu res@zulu.co.za) Singles/doubles DB&B from R940/1530. Zulu Nyala Lodge, not far from Phinda Resource Reserve, also has a reserve and offers several of the Big Five (but not lion), walks, horse riding, game drives and a cruise. The all-inclusive rates are much cheaper than those at Phinda.

To get to either place, take the Southern Maputaland turn-off from the N2 and follow the signs.

Ndumo Game Reserve

This reserve *(admission R8 per person plus R35 per vehicle)* is beside the Mozambique border and close to the Swaziland border, about 100km north of Mkuze. On some 10,000 hectares, there are black and white rhinos, hippos, crocodiles and antelope species but it is the birdlife on the Pongola and Usutu Rivers and their flood plains and pans that attracts visitors. It's known as a 'mini Okavango'.

Guided walks (R30), for wildlife viewing and bird-watching, and vehicle tours (R70) are available. This is the southernmost limit of the range of many bird species and the reserve is a favourite of bird-watchers, with more than 400 species recorded. Watch for the southern banded snake eagle *(Circaetus fasciolatus)*, yellow-spotted nicator *(Nicator gularis)* and the green-capped eremomela *(Eremomela scotops)*.

Fuel and limited supplies are usually available 2km outside the park gate.

KZN Wildlife Accommodation (☎ 033-845 1000) includes camping for R15/25 per person in low/high season (minimum R30/50) and two-bed rest huts for R200/260.

Tembe Elephant Park

South Africa's last free-ranging elephants are protected in the sandveld (dry, sandy belt) forests of Tembe Elephant Park *(admission R8 per person plus R35 per vehicle)* on the Mozambique border. There are now about 140 elephants in the area, many of them the last remnants of elephant herds from the Maputo Elephant Reserve, saved from Mozambique's civil war. There are also white rhinos and leopards.

Although this is a KZN Wildlife park, the accommodation is privately run.

Tembe Lodge (☎ 031-202 9090, fax 202 8026, ℮ tembesafari@mweb.co.za, ☒ www .tembe.co.za) Semiluxury suites from R745, luxury suites from R1045. At the Tembe Lodge, accommodation is in secluded safari tents built on wooden platforms. In the centre of the camp there is a large dining area, a shaded pool and braai facilities. The prices include meals and activities.

There's a sealed road all the way to Tembe, but only 4WD vehicles are allowed to drive through the park.

COASTAL FOREST RESERVE
☎ 033

This reserve stretches from Mozambique in the north to Sodwana Bay in the south, and includes Lake Sibaya, Kosi Bay, Bhanga Nek, Black Rock, Rocktail Bay, Manzeng-wenya, Mabibi and Nine-Mile Beach. The reserve is administered by KZN Wildlife.

Lake Sibaya Nature Reserve

This reserve *(admission R8 per person plus R15 per vehicle)* protects the largest freshwater lake in South Africa, and covers between 60 and 70 sq km, depending on the water level. It lies very close to the coast, and between the eastern shore and the sea is a range of sand dunes up to 165m high. There are hippos, some crocs and a large range of birdlife (more than 280 species have been recorded). The lake is popular for fishing; you can hire boats (complete with skipper) for fishing trips.

Baya Camp (☎ 845 1000) 2-/4-bed rest hut R85 per person (minimum R128/255 high season). Administered by KZN Wildlife, the Baya Camp is located on the southern side of the lake. You must bring your own food but there are cooks to prepare it if you want.

The main route to the reserve is via the village of Mbazwana, south of the lake, either from Mkuze or from Mhlosinga, off the N2 north of Hluhluwe village.

Kosi Bay Nature Reserve

Like Sodwana, Kosi Bay Nature Reserve *(admission R8 per person plus R15 per car)* is another place listed by travellers as among the 10 best South African destinations, although you may need a 4WD to get there. On the coast near the Mozambique border, this remote reserve encompasses fig and raffia palm forests, mangrove swamps, sand dunes and freshwater lakes. The 'bay' is in fact a string of four lakes: Nhlange, Mpungwini, Sifungwe and Amanzimnyama. There are pristine beaches that are usually deserted, and a coral reef with great snorkelling.

There are antelope species in the drier country and hippos, Zambezi sharks and some crocs in the lake system. More than 250 bird species have been identified there, including the rare palmnut vulture. The research station at the reserve studies the local population of leatherback turtles; during the nesting season there are turtle-viewing tours. Canoes are also available for hire.

The **Kosi Bay Trail** (44km, 4 days; R250 self-catered) is a guided hike around the Kosi estuarine system, stopping each night in remote camps which focus on different aspects of the reserve. This trail includes a walk to the Kosi Mouth.

Visitor numbers to the reserve are limited.

KZN Wildlife Accommodation (bookings ☎ 845 1000) Camping R45 per person (minimum R90/180 low/high season), lodges from R150 per person (minimum R225 high season).

Rocktail Bay Lodge (bookings ☎ 011-884 1458, fax 883 6255) Singles/doubles R1445/1950. The privately run Rocktail Bay Lodge is an exclusive coastal camp. The lodge was built so that it blends into the coastal forest canopy; large trees provide shade, and beds are at canopy level.

On the road to the reserve is a small settlement where you can buy supplies and fuel.

Getting There & Away To get to Kosi Bay, take the Jozini turn-off from the N2 and head towards Ndumo Game Reserve but turn hard right (east) just before Ndumo village. Most of the road is sealed but you could still encounter deep sand – you may need a 4WD.

NTENDEKA WILDERNESS AREA

This is a truly beautiful and tranquil area of grassland and indigenous coastal and inland tropical forest, with some dramatic dolerite and sandstone cliffs (Ntendeka means 'Place of Precipitous Heights'). More than 180 species of trees, 60 species of ferns and 190 species of birds have been recorded. The rare Ngoye red squirrel is found in the forest and unusual birds such as the blue swallow *(Hirundo atrocaerulea)* and cuckoo hawk *(Aviceda cuculoides)* can also be spotted. The wilderness area is bordered by **Ngome State Forest**, a good example of inland tropical forest.

This is an important region in Zulu history as Cetshwayo was once holed up here; his rock-shelter refuge is in the north-eastern corner of the park. Another famous figure to hide out here was Mzilikazi, one of Shaka's disloyal generals. Mzilikazi was eventually chased north, where his descendants established the Ndebele tribe in the Pretoria area and the Matabele in present-day Zimbabwe.

There are walking trails but it is not possible to drive through the wilderness area.

There's a *camp site* with ablution facilities on the north-eastern edge of the park; this is the only place in the wilderness where you can camp. Call ☎ 035 867 1883 or visit the Ngome Forest Station, south of the R618 just past the south-eastern corner of the wilderness area, to see if permits are still necessary.

The nearest big town is Nongoma (which is an important trading town but has no facilities for visitors), along 50km of unsealed road. Nongoma is about 60km north-east of Ulundi. Alternatively, get to Ntendeka by travelling east from Vryheid on the R618 for about 70km, or south from Pongola on the R66, then north-west on the R618.

VRYHEID
☎ 034 • postcode 3100

Vryheid (Liberty) is the largest town in northern Zululand. Today Vryheid is an agricultural and coal-mining centre but in 1884 it was the capital of the Nieuwe Republiek, which was absorbed into the Zuid-Afrikaansche Republiek (ZAR; South African Republic) four years later. After the Anglo-Boer War, the area was transferred to Natal. There are Anglo-Boer War sites and several people offer guided tours of the battlefields; contact the information centre for details.

Vryheid Tourism *(☎ 982 2133, fax 982 3498, @ information@vhd.dorea.co.za, Cnr Market & High Sts)* can provide information on the surrounding areas.

There are three museums in town. The **Nieuwe Republiek Museum** *(Landdrost St; open 7.30am-4pm Mon-Fri, by appointment Sat & Sun)*, in the Old Raadsaal building, is devoted to the short-lived Nieuwe Republiek. South of the main street, Kerk St, is the **Lucas Meijer Museum** *(☎ 982 2133, Cnr Landdrost & Mark Sts; open 7.30am-4pm Mon-Fri, by appointment Sat & Sun)*. This small local history museum is in the old Lucas Meijer House (Meijer was the only president of the Nieuwe Republiek). The third **museum** is in the old Carnegie library.

Just north of town, the **Vryheid Nature Reserve** has zebra and antelope species and there's a bird hide next to a saltpan.

Places to Stay

Vryheid Lodge (*☎ 981 5201, fax 981 5467, 200 Kerk St*) Singles/doubles R130/190. In town, the Vryheid Lodge is an inexpensive option.

Stilwater Protea Hotel (*☎ 981 6181, fax 980 8846, Dundee Rd*) Singles/doubles B&B R254/320. This slightly dowdy hotel is 6km out on the Dundee road.

Shonalanga Lodge (*☎/fax 982 2086, 136 Kerk St*) Singles/doubles B&B R210/280. The Shonalanga Lodge is a modern motel-style place with good units.

Oxford Lodge (*☎ 980 9280, fax 981 5673, Cnr Kerk & Deputasie Sts*) Singles/doubles R240/320. The comfy Oxford Lodge is in a large old house.

Villa Prince Imperial (*☎/fax 983 2610, e princeimperial@intekom.co.za, 201 Deputasie St*) Standard singles/doubles B&B R265/440, luxury rooms B&B R310/530. The Villa Prince, at the base of Lancaster Hill, is Vryheid's most upmarket hotel. Its stylish rooms all have TV, tea and coffee facilities and even a hair dryer. Evening meals are available.

Getting There & Away

The well-organised minibus taxi park is near the train station. Drop into the taxi association office for information. Vryheid is the centre for minibus taxis in this part of KwaZulu-Natal. Fares from Vryheid include: Nongoma R15, Ulundi R15, Dundee R16, Pongola R20, Eshowe R25, Durban (via Melmoth) R45 and Jo'burg R55.

ITHALA GAME RESERVE

KZN Wildlife's Ithala Game Reserve (*admission R7 per person plus R30 per vehicle*) has all the trappings of a private game reserve but much lower prices. It also doesn't get the crowds that flock into Hluhluwe-Umfolozi, as it's slightly off the main routes.

Most of the 30,000 hectares is taken up by the steep valleys of six rivers (tributaries of the Pongola), with some open grassland on the heights, rugged outcrops and about 25% bushveld.

Animals, mostly reintroduced, include black and white rhinos, elephants, tsessebes

(the only herd in KwaZulu-Natal), nyalas, hyenas, buffaloes, baboons, leopards and cheetahs. There are more than 75 mammal species in the park, plus crocodiles and 100 or so other species of amphibians and reptiles, and 20 species of indigenous fish. The diverse habitats support more than 320 species of bird, including the endangered southern bald ibis *(Geronticus calvus)*.

Places to Stay

Ntshondwe (*bookings ☎ 033-845 1000*) 2-bed units (with communal kitchen) R180/196 per person low/high season, chalets from R200/225 per person. Ntshondwe is the main centre, with superb views of the reserve below. Facilities include a restaurant, shop and swimming pool.

KZN Wildlife also has three **bush camps** that offer privacy and proximity to wildlife but without the luxuries of the main camp.

At **Thalu**, the smallest and cheapest of the bush camps, there are 4-bed bush camps for R160 per person (minimum R320). There are also a few basic camp sites available for R16 per person.

Getting There & Away

Ithala is reached from Louwsburg, about 55km north-east of Vryheid on the R69, and about the same distance south-west of Pongola via the R66 and the R69. Louwsburg is much smaller than many maps indicate.

PONGOLA

☎ 034 • postcode 3170

Pongola is a small town in a sugar-growing district near the Mpumalanga border, not far from Swaziland. There's an ATM and petrol is available 24 hours.

Pongola Caravan Park (*☎ 413 1789, fax 413 2505, 219 Lucas Meyer St*) Camping R70 for 2 people, 5-bed chalets R140 per person. This park is off the N2 on the western outskirts of town.

Pongola Country Lodge (*☎ 413 1352, fax 413 1353, e pongolacountrylodge@intekom.co.za, w home.intekom.com/pclodge, 14 Jan Mielie St*) Singles/doubles from R240/290, breakfast R35, dinner R65. In the centre of town, the old Pongola Hotel has been extensively upgraded and has reopened as the Pongola Country Lodge. It is now a modern hotel with well-appointed rooms.

Riverview Backpackers (☎ 413 1713, fax 413 2100, ⓔ casamia@iphone.co.za) Camping R20, dorm beds R60, doubles R160. Riverview Backpackers, on an old sugar farm south of Pongola, is a rustic place with a lush garden. To get there follow the N2 south, then turn right before the biltong stall and follow this for about 1km, turn left, then right, then follow the signs.

South-east of Pongola (you'll see it from the N2, which is the western border) is the **Pongolapoort Biosphere Reserve**, a lovely area backed by the Lebombo range and encompassing a large lake. There are no roads in the reserve.

PAULPIETERSBURG
☎ 034 • postcode 3180

This town is a centre for timber and agricultural production, and gets its name from Paul Kruger and Pieter Joubert. The **Paulpietersburg Publicity Association** *(☎ 995 1650, fax 995 1255, 10 Hoog St)* has information on the town and the surrounding area. Outside town is the **Natal Spa** *(☎ 995 0300, ⓔ natalspa@bigfoot.com, ⓦ www .users.lantic.net/natalspa)*, where you can lie back in the warm or cold mineral pools.

Paulpietersburg has many descendants of the original German settlers from the Hermannsburg Missionary Society established in 1848. The main German towns the settlers came from are Gluckstadt, Braunschweig and Luneberg.

Ukhahlamba-Drakensberg Park

The awe-inspiring Drakensberg range is a mountainous basalt escarpment forming the border between KwaZulu-Natal and Lesotho, and continuing a little way into the Free State. In late 2000 the Drakensberg was formally granted World Heritage status and renamed the Ukhahlamba-Drakensberg Park.

Drakensberg means 'Dragon Mountains'; the Zulu named it Quathlamba, meaning 'Battlement of Spears'. The Zulu word is a more accurate description of the sheer and jagged escarpment but the Afrikaans name captures something of the Drakensberg's otherworldly atmosphere. People have lived here for thousands of years – this is evident by the many San rock-art sites – yet many of its peaks were first climbed a little over 50 years ago (for more details, see the boxed text 'Taming the Dragons').

The San, already under pressure from the tribes who had moved into the Drakensberg foothills, were finally destroyed with the coming of white settlers. Some moved into Lesotho where they were absorbed into the Basotho population but many were killed or simply starved when their hunting grounds were occupied by others. Khoisan cattle raids annoyed the white settlers to the extent that the settlers forced several black tribes to relocate into the Drakensberg foothills to act as a buffer between the whites and the Khoisan. These early 'Bantu locations' meant that there was little development in the area, which later allowed the creation of a chain of parks and reserves. (Of course, this meant that the 'Bantus' were again forced to move.)

Orientation

The Ukhahlamba-Drakensberg Park is usually divided into three sections, although the distinctions aren't strict. The northern Drakensberg runs from the Golden Gate Highlands National Park in Free State (see that chapter for details) to the Royal Natal National Park. Harrismith and Bergville are sizable towns in this area. There are a number of nature reserves within Ukhahlamba-Drakensberg Park.

The central Drakensberg's main feature is Giant's Castle Game Reserve, the largest reserve in the area. North of Giant's Castle is Cathedral Peak and two wilderness areas. Bergville, Estcourt and Winterton are towns adjacent to the central Drakensberg.

The southern Drakensberg runs down to the Transkei area of Eastern Cape. This area, where the Drakensberg bends around

KWAZULU-NATAL

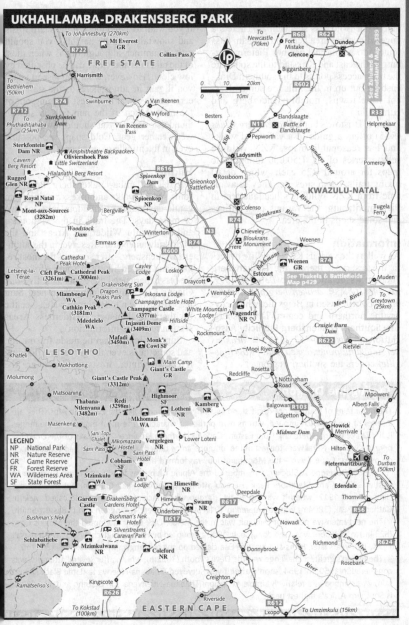

UKHAHLAMBA-DRAKENSBERG PARK

To Johannesburg (270km)

Mt Everest GR

R722

Collins Pass

To Newcastle (70km)

R68 R621

Fort Mistake

Dundee

Glencoe

FREE STATE

Biggarsberg

R602

To Bethlehem (50km)

Harrismith

Van Reenen

Swinburne

R74

R712

To Phuthaditjhaba (25km)

Wyford

Van Reenens Pass

Besters

Klip River

Elandslaagte

Battle of Elandslaagte

N11

Pepworth

R33

Helpmekaar

Sterkfontein Dam

Sterkfontein Dam NR

Amphitheatre Backpackers
Oliviershoek Pass
Little Switzerland

Cavern Berg Resort

Ladysmith

Pomeroy

Hlalanathi Berg Resort

R616

Spioenkop Dam

Spioenkop Battlefield

Rossboom

Tugela River

KWAZULU-NATAL

Rugged Glen NR

Royal Natal NP

Mont-aux-Sources (3282m)

Spioenkop NP

Bergville

Woodstock Dam

Emmaus

Winterton

N3

R600

R74

Colenso

Bloukrans River

Chieveley
Bloukrans Monument

Frere

Weenen

Tugela Ferry

Bushmans River

Weenen GR

R74

Muden

Cathedral Peak Hotel

Cayley Lodge

Loskop

Draycott

Estcourt

Wembezi

See Thukela & Battlefields Map p429

Letseng-la-Terae

Cleft Peak (3261m)

Cathedral Peak (3004m)

Drakensberg Sun
Dragon Peaks Park

Mlambonja WA

Inkosana Lodge

Champagne Castle Hotel

Champagne Castle (3377m)

White Mountain Lodge

Wagendrif NR

Mooi River

To Greytown (25km)

Cathkin Peak (3181m)

Mdedelelo WA

Injasuti Dome (3409m)

Hillside

Rockmount

Mooi River

Cruigie Burn Dam

Mafadi (3450m)

Monk's Cowl SF

R622

Rietvlei

LESOTHO

Khatleli

Mokhotlong

Main Camp
Giant's Castle

Rosetta

Redcliffe

Nottingham Road

Lions River

Molumong

Giant's Castle Peak (3312m)

Giant's Castle GR

Balgowan

R103

Mpolweni

Albert Falls

Matsoaning

Thabana-Ntlenyana (3482m)

Redi (3298m)

Highmoor SF

Lotheni NR

Kamberg NR

Lidgetton

Midmar Dam

Howick
Merrivale

Masenkeng

Mkhomazi WA

Hilton

Sani Top Chalet

Sani Pass

Mkomazana Hostel

Vergelegen NR

Lower Loteni

Pietermaritzburg

To Durban (50km)

LEGEND
NP	National Park
NR	Nature Reserve
GR	Game Reserve
FR	Forest Reserve
WA	Wilderness Area
SF	State Forest

Cobham SF

Sani Pass Hotel

Edendale

Mzimkulu WA

Sani Lodge

Himeville NR

Deepdale

Thornville

Garden Castle

Drakensberg Gardens Hotel

Himeville

Swamp NR

R617

R56

Bushman's Nek

Underberg

Bulwer

Nowadi

Bushman's Nek Hotel

Silverstreams Caravan Park

R617

Umzimkulu River

Richmond

Lovu River

R624

Sehlabathebe NP

Mzimkulwana NR

Coleford NR

Donnybrook

Mkomazi River

Rosebank

Ngoangoana

Kingscote

Creighton

Ramatseliso's

R626

EASTERN CAPE

Riverside

Lxopo

R612

To Umzimkulu (15km)

To Kokstad (100km)

0 5 10 20km
0 5 10mi

See Zululand & Maputaland Map p389

to the south-west, is less developed than the others but is no less spectacular. There's a huge wilderness area here and the Sani Pass route into southern Lesotho. Pietermaritzburg to the east and Kokstad to the south are the main access points to the southern Drakensberg but up in the hills are some pleasant little towns, notably Underberg and Himeville.

David Bristow's book *Drakensberg Walks* (R85) offers a guide to a variety of walks and has reasonable maps. KZN Wildlife sells a series of six 1:50,000 topographic maps for around R25 each, which detail hiking trails, camp sites etc. They're available from KZN Wildlife's headquarters in Pietermaritzburg, the various park offices and some shops in the area.

Information

As well as the various KZN Wildlife offices in the reserves, there's the **Drakensberg Tourism Association** (☎/fax 036-448 1557, fax 448 1088, ℮ *drakensbergtourismass@ mweb.co.za*), based in Bergville, which covers the northern and central Drakensberg. The **Southern Drakensberg Publicity Association** (☎/fax 033-702 1158, ℮ *drakens berginfo@futurenet.org.za, Main Rd, Himeville*) covers the southern region.

Climate

If you want to avoid most of the sharp frosts and snowfalls (on the heights), you should visit in summer, although this is when most of the rain falls and views can be obscured by low cloud. However, what you lose in vistas you'll gain in atmosphere, as the stark and eerie peaks are at their best looming out of the mist. Much of the rain falls in sudden thunderstorms so you should always carry wet-weather gear. Cold snaps are possible even in the middle of summer.

Hiking

The Ukhahlamba-Drakensberg Park has some superb walks and hikes, ranging from gentle day walks to strenuous hikes of two or more days. The trails in the Mkhomazi and Mzimkulu Wilderness Areas and the Mzimkulwana Nature Reserve, in the southern Drakensberg, offer some of the most remote and rugged hiking in South Africa. For the less experienced there's also the five-day Giant's Cup Trail, running from near Sani Pass Hotel down to Bushman's Nek (see the Southern Drakensberg Wilderness Areas section for more information).

Summer hiking can be made frustrating, and sometimes even dangerous, by flooding rivers; in winter, frosts and snow are the

---

Taming the Dragons

The mountains of South Africa don't stand as a single, solid range like the European Alps. They are a series of ranges, each imbued with its own particular character. The most majestic of the ranges is the Drakensberg, stretching from Eastern Cape to Northern Province. The peaks of the Drakensberg in KwaZulu-Natal were the last of the 'dragons' to be tamed, as most activity had concentrated on peaks near Cape Town – the Mountain Club was formed there in 1891.

In 1888, Reverend A Stocker, a member of the Alpine Club, was the first to climb Champagne Castle (3377m) and Sterkhorn Peak. He also attempted Cathkin Peak (3181m) but this was not climbed until 1912, when it was scaled by a group which included a black guide called Melatu. Cathedral Peak (3004m) was conquered in 1917 by two climbers, R Kingdon and D Bassett-Smith.

The next intensive period of climbing was in the 1940s. Dick Barry attempted the Monk's Cowl (3234m) in 1938, but was killed doing so. In 1942 a group led by Hans Wongtschowski scaled its basalt faces. Two years later, Hans and his wife Elsa clawed up the seemingly impregnable Bell (2991m).

The region's greatest challenge was the Devil's Tooth (3022m), which, after several attempts, was conquered in 1950. In 1954, shortly after it was surveyed, Thabana-Ntlenyana (Little Black Mountain) was climbed as a relatively simple excursion. Thabana-Ntlenyana is in Lesotho and, at 3482m, is Southern Africa's highest peak.

main hazards. April and May are the best months for hiking.

Make sure you get the relevant maps (see under Information earlier), which show trails and have essential information for hikers.

Permits are needed on most of the hikes; get them from KZN Wildlife offices at the various trailheads. Trail accommodation is often in huts and caves (meaning that you don't need a tent). In northern Drakensberg accommodation must be booked well in advance, but in southern Drakensberg, this isn't a problem.

Places to Stay

The perfect way to see the Ukhahlamba-Drakensberg Park is to stay at one of KZN Wildlife's excellent reserves. The biggest and most popular are Royal Natal and Giant's Castle but accommodation and camp sites can also be found in the state forests and other reserves. Free camping is allowed in most designated wilderness areas but check in at the National Parks Board or Forestry offices; there's a small fee.

Usually more expensive than the Parks Board's accommodation are the private resorts which dot the foothills near Royal Natal and Giant's Castle.

Getting There & Away

There is little public transport in the northern and central Drakensberg, although there is a lot of tourist traffic. With so many resorts all needing staff there are some minibus taxis. The main jumping-off points are on or near the N3 (for more details, see under Estcourt, Mooi River, Winterton and Bergville later in this chapter). The Baz Bus drops off and picks up at a couple of hostels in the area. Through hostels in Durban you can arrange a lift to the hostels near Sani Pass and Himeville.

Sani Pass is the best-known Drakensberg route into Lesotho. There are other passes over the escarpment but most don't connect with anything in Lesotho larger than a walking track (if that) a long way from anywhere.

Many roads in the Drakensberg area are unsealed and after rain some are impassable but it's usually possible to find an alternative

route. Tourist routes in the northern and central Drakensberg are indicated by brown signs with a lammergeier (bearded vulture) symbol.

ROYAL NATAL NATIONAL PARK
☎ 036

Although it is little over 8000 hectares, Royal Natal National Park (admission R8 per person) has some of the Drakensberg's most dramatic and accessible scenery. The southern boundary of the national park is formed by the Amphitheatre, an 8km stretch of cliff which is spectacular from below and even more so from the top. Here the Tugela Falls drop 850m in five stages (the top one often freezes in winter). Looming up behind is Mont-aux-Sources, so called because the Tugela, Elands and Western Khubedu Rivers rise here; the latter eventually becomes the Orange River and flows all the way to the Atlantic.

Other notable peaks in the area are Devil's Tooth, the Eastern Buttress and the Sentinel. Rugged Glen Nature Reserve adjoins the park on the north-eastern side.

The park's big **visitor centre** is about 1km in from the main gate. There's a bookshop where you can pick up a copy of KZN Wildlife's excellent booklet Royal Natal National Park, which has detailed information including descriptions of walks and a sketch map. Fuel is available in the park.

Flora & Fauna

With plentiful water, a range more than 1500m in altitude and distinct areas such as plateaus, cliffs and valleys, it isn't surprising that the park's flora is extremely varied. Broadly speaking, much of the park is covered in grassland, with protea savanna at lower altitudes. This grassland depends on fire for reproduction and to discourage other vegetation. In areas that escape the park's periodic fires, scrub takes over. At lower levels, but confined to valleys, are small yellowwood forests. At higher altitudes grass yields to heath and scrub.

Royal Natal is not as rich in wildlife as Giant's Castle and other sections of the Drakensberg but there is still quite a lot to be seen. Of the six species of antelope, the most common is the mountain reedbuck. Hyraxes are everywhere, as are hares, and you'll probably meet some baboons. Most other species in the reserve are shy and not often seen. They include otter, jackal and mongoose. More than 200 species of bird have been reported.

Rock Art

There are several San rock art sites, although Royal Natal's are fewer and not as well preserved as those at Giant's Castle; the latter has many more rock shelters and caves and has suffered less from vandalism. The notable sites are Sigubudu Shelter, north of the road just past the main gate; and Cannibal Caves, on Surprise Ridge, outside the park's northern boundary.

Hiking Trails

Except for the **Amphitheatre to Cathedral** (62km, four to five days) and the **Mont-aux-Sources** (20km, 10 hours) hikes, all of the 30-odd walks in Royal Natal are day walks. Only 50 day visitors and 50 overnighters are allowed on Mont-aux-Sources (3282m) each day. The hike to the summit starts from the Mahai camp site, takes you up to Basotho Gate and to Sentinel car park, from where you take the chain ladder up to the summit. However, if you are short of time you can drive to the Sentinel car park on the road from Phuthaditjhaba in QwaQwa (see under QwaQwa Area in the Free State chapter for more details), shortening the hike by five hours.

If you plan to camp on the mountain you should book with the **Free State Agriculture Department** (☎ 058-713 4444, fax 713 4342, *Phuthaditjhaba*). Otherwise there's a basic mountain hut on the escarpment near Tugela Falls. Unlike other KZN Wildlife accommodation you don't need to book (except for registering before walking here) and there's no fee for the hut, but an overnight hiking permit costs R16.

Climbing

As some of the peaks and faces were first climbed by mountaineers just over 50 years

ago, the park is a mecca for climbers. You must apply for a permit from the KZN Wildlife office before you attempt a climb; unless you are experienced, it may not be granted. Take your passport if you plan to venture into Lesotho.

Places to Stay

Tendele (bookings ☎ 033-845 1000) Chalets from R180 per person (minimum R270). Tendele is the main camp in the park and has a variety of accommodation, including more expensive options.

Mahai (☎ 438 6303) Camping R37 per person (R47 with power). Mahai is a large well-established camp site.

Rugged Glen Nature Reserve (☎ 438 6231) This reserve has a smaller camp site on the north-eastern edge of the park. Horse riding is available.

At the time of writing the *Royal Natal National Park Hotel* was closed for renovation and was not expected to reopen until mid-2002.

The following places are all outside the park.

Amphitheatre Backpackers (☎ 036-438 6016, ⓔ amphilbackpackers@worldonline .co.za) Camping R30, dorm beds R45, doubles R130. Amphitheatre Backpackers, off the R74 in the heart of the Pocolane Nature Reserve at Oliviershoek Pass (1780m), has been recommended by readers. The accommodation is basic but the view is unsurpassed. The hostel operates a twice-weekly bus service to Malealea Lodge in Lesotho. The return trip costs R350.

Little Switzerland Hotel (☎ 036-438 6220, fax 438 6222, ⓔ res@lsh.co.za, ⓦ www .lsh.co.za) 4-bed chalets R390 Mon-Fri, R500 per night Sat & Sun, standard singles/doubles R565/800, deluxe (mountain view) rooms R615/860. Little Switzerland is a large place off the R74 near Oliviershoek Pass. The rugged scenery around here is impressive but the escarpment is some way off. Staff will collect you from Swinburne, on the N3 near Harrismith (in the Free State), where Translux buses stop.

Hlalanathi Drakensberg Resort (☎ 036-438 6308, fax 438 6852) Camp site R30 plus R30 per person, 2-bed chalets R240/280 low/high season, 4-bed chalets R400/500. The resort, off the road into Royal Natal from the R74, offers well-priced roomy chalets. It has a good restaurant and pub and there is a small shop at the entrance.

Cavern Berg Resort (☎ *036-438 6270, fax 438 6334,* e *cavern@iafrica.com,* w *www.cavernberg.co.za)* DB&B R310-425 per person. This family-oriented place, 10km north-west of Hlalanathi, offers horse riding and walks.

Orion Mont-aux-Sources Hotel (☎ *036-438 6230, fax 438 6201,* e *reservations mont@orion-hotels.co.za)* Singles/doubles DB&B R436/582 Mon-Fri, R485/646 Sat & Sun. The Orion is a large upmarket hotel not far from Hlalanathi.

Getting There & Away

The only road into Royal Natal runs off the R74, about 30km north-west of Bergville and about 5km from Oliviershoek Pass.

BERGVILLE

☎ 036 • postcode 3350

This small town is a handy jumping-off point for both the northern Drakensberg and the Midlands – if you have a car.

The **Drakensberg Tourism Association** (☎ *448 1557, fax 448 1088,* e *drakensberg tourism@mweb.co.za, Tatham Rd)* has an office here.

On the third Friday of each month there are local cattle sales and the sleepy town takes on an altogether different atmosphere.

In the courthouse grounds is the Upper Tugela Blockhouse, a base built by the British during the Anglo-Boer War.

Places to Stay & Eat

The Drakensberg Inn (☎ *448 2946, fax 448 1298, Cnr South & West Sts)* B&B R150 per person. The Drakensberg Inn (previously Hotel Walter) offers reasonable accommodation in the town centre.

Sanford Park Lodge (☎ *448 1001, fax 448 1047)* Singles/doubles B&B R225/440. The lodge is a few kilometres out of Bergville, off the road to Ladysmith (the R616). It has good rooms in thatched

rondavels or in a big, 150-year-old farmhouse. It's a little too large to feel personal but it's a nice place.

Drakensville Holiday Resort (☎ *438 6287, fax 438 6524,* e *drakensville@dorea .co.za,* w *www.drakensville.co.za)* Camping R30/40 per person low/high season, 6-bed house R300/440. This big resort, just off the Bergville to Harrismith road (the R74), at Jagersrust, has 70 three-bedroom homes. It's a little bleak but it isn't bad value. Bed linen is not provided.

Getting There & Away

None of the long-distance bus lines run very close to Bergville. You'll probably have to get to Ladysmith and take a minibus taxi from there. The Translux service from Durban to Bloemfontein stops at both Montrose (at the Shell Ultra on the N3 near Swinburne) and Ladysmith. Translux's Jo'burg/Pretoria-Umtata and Jo'burg/Pretoria-Durban services also stop at Montrose. A daily Greyhound bus stops at Estcourt, Swinburne (in the Montrose bus service area) and Ladysmith.

The minibus taxi park is behind the Score supermarket. Taxis run into the Royal Natal National Park area for about R10 but few run all the way to the park entrance.

CENTRAL BERG

In some ways the Central Berg is the most attractive part of the range. Some of the most challenging climbs of the Drakensberg, Cathkin Peak (3181m), the Monk's Cowl (3234m) and Champagne Castle (3377m), are found there. The central region also includes the grand Giant's Castle Peak (3312m). Midway between Cathedral and Cathkin Peaks is Ndedema Gorge, where there is some fine San rock art.

The area between Cathedral Peak and Giant's Castle comprises two wilderness areas, Mlambonja and Mdedelelo (together some 35,000 hectares). Both are administered by KZN Wildlife. Grey rheboks, klipspringers and mountain reedbucks occur naturally in the area.

Just off Dragon Peaks road is **Drakensberg Boys' Choir School** (☎ *036-468 1012,* *fax 468 1260,* **e** *marketing@db choir.co.za,* **w** *www.dbchoir.co.za).* There are public performances at 3.30pm on Wednesday during term.

Also not to be missed are the falcon flying demonstrations and informative talks at **Falcon Ridge** (☎ *082-774 6398; admission R20, talks at 11.30am & 2.30pm daily).*

Cathedral Peak
☎ 036

Cathedral Peak (3004m) is between Royal Natal National Park and Giant's Castle, west of Winterton. It's part of a small chain of peaks that jut out east of the main escarpment. The others, which are all challenging for climbers, include the Bell, the Horns, the Pyramid and Needles. Cathedral Peak is a long day's climb (10km, six to seven hours) but other than being physically fit no special ability or equipment is required. The trail begins near the Cathedral Peak Hotel.

The **park office**, where you can book camp sites and overnight hiking (R16), is off the road running west from Winterton, near the hotel; admission to the park is R8 per person.

There's a fee of R35 to drive up Mike's Pass, near Cathedral Peak, where there are good views.

KZN Wildlife Accommodation (☎ *488 1880)* within Cathedral Peak includes camping for R25/30 per person in low/high season, and six-bed huts for R50 per person.

Cathedral Peak Hotel (☎*/fax 488 1888,* **e** *cph@ls.lia.net,* **w** *www.cathedralpeak .co.za)* DB&B R360-935. This hotel, 40km from Winterton, is close to the escarpment, near Cathedral Peak. There are mid-week specials and staff will collect guests from Estcourt.

Monk's Cowl State Forest
☎ 036

Monk's Cowl *(admission R7),* another truly beautiful region of the Drakensberg range, offers superb hiking and rock climbing. Within Monk's Cowl State Forest are the two peaks Monk's Cowl and Champagne Peak.

The **park office** (☎ *468 1103)* is 3km beyond Champagne Castle Hotel, which is at the end of the R600 running south-west from Winterton. The office takes bookings for *camping* (R25/35 low/high season) and overnight hiking (R16 per person).

If you're driving into this area don't get carried away by the good road; there are a couple of very steep sections and a nightmarish hairpin bend with reverse camber and a long drop.

Places to Stay & Eat As well as camping in the state forest there are also some other accommodation options.

Inkosana Lodge (☎*/fax 468 1202,* **e** *inko sana@futurenet.co.za,* **w** *www.inkosana.n .net)* Dorm beds R60, doubles R160, suite R220. The Inkosana Lodge, off the R600, gets good feedback from readers. It is a nice place to stay and a good base for treks – it offers excellent information on hiking. Breakfast is R20.

Dragon Peaks Park (☎ *468 1031, fax 468 1104,* **e** *dragonpeaks@futurenet.co .za)* Camping R40/70 per person low/high season, cottages from R115/160 per person. This park, off the R600, is a Club Caravelle resort with the usual maze of prices and minimum stays depending on seasons and school holidays. In low season, prices are comparable to those at KZN Wildlife facilities. Horse riding is also available.

Champagne Castle Hotel (☎ *468 1063, fax 468 1306,* **e** *champagnecastle@fu turenet.co.za,* **w** *www.champagnecastle.co .za)* Standard rooms R325/410 per person low/high season Mon-Fri, R355/410 Sat & Sun, superior rooms R350/435 per person Mon-Fri, R380/435 Sat & Sun, all meals included. Champagne Castle is one of the best-known resorts, conveniently located in the mountains at the end of the road to Champagne Castle Peak, off the R600. The hotel will collect you from Estcourt (a Greyhound stop) for R70 for the first person, and R30 for each additional person.

Drakensberg Sun (☎ *468 1000, fax 468 1224,* **e** *reservations@draksun.co.za,* Singles/doubles B&B R618/956. The Drakensberg Sun's pricey rooms are typical o this chain; special packages are available. It's off the R600.

WINTERTON
☎ 036 • postcode 3340

This pretty town is the gateway to the central Drakensberg and is not too far from the northern end. There is a great little **museum** on Kerk St which concentrates on the geology, flora and fauna of the Drakensberg; it's a good place to read up before venturing further. There are also a few good places to stay in town.

Bridge Lodge (☎/fax 488 1554, @ bernvar@intekom.co.za, Main Rd) Singles/doubles B&B R150/245. This a friendly hotel and local pub on the main street.

Ntabeni Backpackers (☎ 488 1773/1372) Camping R35, dorm beds R40, huts R50. The Ntabeni Backpackers, 7km from Winterton off the R600, has good accommodation and facilities, but it is popular with local schools. The Baz Bus will stop here.

The Nest (☎ 468 1068, fax 468 1390, @ the nest@futurest.co.za, W www.thenest.co.za) Rondavels from R297/374 per person low/high season, including all meals. The Nest is midway between Winterton and the Berg, off the R600. It's a resort-style hotel with plenty of activities, such as horse riding and tennis, to amuse all.

A minibus taxi to Cathedral Peak costs R8, to Bergville R6 and to Estcourt R8.

GIANT'S CASTLE GAME RESERVE

Giant's Castle Game Reserve *(admission R8 per person)*, covering 34,500 hectares, was established in 1903, mainly to protect the eland. It's in high country; the lowest point is 1300m and the highest tooth of the Drakensberg in the reserve is Injasuti Dome (3409m), also the highest peak in South Africa. With huge forest reserves to the north and south and Lesotho's barren plateau over the escarpment to the west, it's a rugged and remote place, although it attracts plenty of visitors.

Limited supplies (including fuel) are available at Giant's Camp and there's a basic shop near the White Mountain Resort but the nearest shops are in Estcourt, 50km away.

Flora & Fauna

The reserve is mainly grassland, wooded gorges and high basalt cliffs with small forests in the valleys. There's also some protea savanna that has survived the grassfires caused by lightning strikes and, recently, controlled burning. During spring there are many wildflowers.

Because of the harsh conditions many of the reserve's animals lead a precarious existence, and the balance of numbers and available food is delicate – an event such as a hard winter can disturb the equation and threaten a species' existence.

The reserve is home to 12 species of antelope, with relatively large numbers of elands, mountain reedbucks, black wildebeests, red hartebeests, grey rheboks and oribis. The rarest antelope is the klipspringer, which is sometimes spotted on the higher slopes. The rarest species is a small short-tailed rodent called the ice rat, which lives in the boulders near the mountain summits. Altogether there are thought to be about 60 mammal species but some, such as the leopard and aardwolf, have not been positively sighted.

The rare lammergeier, or bearded vulture *(Gypaetus barbatus)*, which is found only in the Drakensberg, nests in the reserve. Because there's a danger that the birds will feed on poisoned carcasses, which some farmers in the area use to kill jackals, the reserve puts out meat on weekend mornings between May and September to encourage the birds to feed in the reserve. The Lammergeier Hide has been built nearby, and it's the best place to see the vultures. The fee for using the hide is R100 per person (minimum R400), and you must book through KZN Wildlife.

The number of other bird species spotted in the reserve is around 200. There are also about 30 reptile species, including the puff adder.

Rock Art

Giant's Castle Game Reserve is rich in San rock art, with at least 50 sites. It is thought that the last San lived here at the beginning of the 20th century.

The two main sites of paintings are **Main Cave** (about 550 paintings) and **Battle Cave**

(750 paintings); admission to both is R15. Main Cave is 2km south of Main Camp (a 30-minute walk) and there's also a display on San life here. The cave is open 9am to 3pm Saturday and Sunday and holidays; Monday to Friday you have to go with a tour which departs from the camp office at 9am and 3pm (R25).

Battle Cave is near Injasuti and must be visited on a tour which leaves the Main Camp daily at 9am (R25). It's an 8km walk each way, and there's a good chance of seeing wildlife en route. Battle Cave was so-named because some of the paintings here record a fight between San groups.

Another site near Giant's Camp is **Bamboo Hollow**, which features two good sites, Steel's Shelter and Willcox's Shelter. Here you can see a figure known as the Moon Goddess. More paintings can be seen near Injasuti at Grindstone Cave and Fergie's Cave (fires are not allowed). Ask the Environmental Officer at Giant's Camp for maps and information about more remote sites.

Hiking

Trails begin at Giant's Camp and lead to Meander Hut (5.5km, two hours), on a cliff above the Meander Valley; Giant's Hut (10.5km, four hours), under Giant's Castle itself; and Bannerman's Hut (11km, 4½ hours), close to the escarpment near Bannerman's Pass.

Hikers can stay at *mountain huts (R48 per person plus R16 trail fee)* for which you'll need sleeping bags and cooking utensils (a gas stove is provided). If you're planning to walk between huts rather than return to Giant's Camp you have to arrange to collect keys. Unless you've booked the entire hut you must share it with other hikers.

There are other trails. The booklet *Giant's Castle Game Reserve* gives details and has a basic map of the trails. Before setting out on a long walk you must fill in the rescue register; those planning to go higher than 2300m must report to the warden.

Don't confuse trails here with the Giant's Cup Trail, further south in the Drakensberg, and covered under Southern Drakensberg Wilderness Areas later in this chapter.

Places to Stay

Within the Reserve There are three main *camping areas*, as well as trail huts and caves for hikers. Note that nowhere in the park are you allowed to cut or even collect firewood; hikers are not allowed to light fires, so you'll need to bring a stove. Litter must be brought back, not burned or buried. There's a small supermarket near Main Camp.

Giant's Camp (bookings ☎ 033-845 1000) Chalets from R210 per person (minimum R315), 6-bed cottage R210 per person (minimum R630). Camping is not permitted.

Injasuti Hutted Camp (☎ 036-431 7848) Camping R28/32 per person low/high season, chalets from R110/120 per person (minimum R220/360). Injasuti is a secluded and pleasant spot on the northern side of the reserve; admission to the camp is R8 per person.

Outside the Reserve There are several places on and near the R600 which runs south-west from Winterton towards Cathkin Peak and Champagne Castle, some of which have been listed under Central Berg earlier in this chapter.

Mount Lebanon Farm (☎/fax 033-263 2214) Camping R60 per person, dorm beds R60 per person, DB&B R135 per person. The farm is on a 200-hectare property on the edge of Giant's Castle Reserve, off Giant's Castle Rd. Phone for directions or a pick-up from Mooi River (R30). The Baz Bus, Greyhound and trains stop at Mooi River.

Drakensberg International Backpackers (☎ 033 263 7241, e wildchild@telkomsa .net, 21 Highmoor Rd) Camping R35, dorm beds R45, twins R110, doubles R120. The backpackers is on Grace Valley Farm. Staff can pick you up from Mooi River.

White Mountain Lodge (☎ 036-353 3437, fax 353 3644, e whitemountain@future net.co.za, w www.caraville.co.za/whitemtn .htm) Powered caravan sites from R50/100 for 2 people low/high season, doubles in self-catering cottages from R160. In high season there's a minimum stay of five days, it's two days at other times. The lodge will collect you from Estcourt (for free) if you arrange it beforehand, and it has a small shop. The Lodge is off the Giant's Castle to Estcourt Rd.

Getting There & Away

Giant's Camp The best way into Giant's Camp is via the dirt road from Mooi River although the last section can be impassable when wet. It's also possible to get there by following the route from Estcourt; however, until the road is sealed don't attempt this in wet weather.

Infrequent minibus taxis run from Estcourt to villages near the main entrance (Kwa-Dlamini, Mahlutshini and KwaMankonjane) but these are still several kilometres from Main Camp.

Minibus taxis pass near here, running between Estcourt and the large village of Malutshini on the Bushmans River where you turn off for Giant's Camp.

Injasuti The Injasuti camp is accessible from the township of Loskop, north-west of Estcourt. Turn south 4km west of Loskop or 6km east of the R600; the road is signposted.

SOUTHERN DRAKENSBERG WILDERNESS AREAS

Four state forests, Highmoor, Mkhomazi, Cobham and Garden Castle, all run south from Giant's Castle to beyond Bushman's Nek, to meet Lesotho's Sehlabathebe National Park at the top of the escarpment. The big Mkhomazi Wilderness Area and the Mzimkulu Wilderness Area are in the state forests.

The wilderness areas are near the escarpment and to the east are Kamberg, Lotheni, Vergelegen and Mzimkulwana Nature Reserves. A spur of Mzimkulwana follows the Mkhomazana River (and the road) down from Sani Pass, separating the two wilderness areas.

The wilderness areas are administered by KZN Wildlife. Admission to each is R10 per person and overnight hiking costs R16.

Kamberg Nature Reserve

South-east of Giant's Castle and a little away from the main escarpment area, this small (2232 hectares) KZN Wildlife reserve *(admission R8 per person, overnight hiking R16)* has a number of antelope species. The country in the Drakensberg foothills is pretty, but it's trout fishing that attracts most visitors. The reserve's office sells fishing permits (R50 per person per day).

The cheapest accommodation is in *rest huts* at R75/90 per person in low/high season (minimum R150/180).

You can get there from Rosetta, off the N3 south of Mooi River, travelling via either Nottingham Road or Redcliffe.

Highmoor State Forest

Part of the Mkhomazi Wilderness Area is in Highmoor. The **park station** *(☎ 033-263 7240)* is off the road from Rosetta to Giant's Castle and Kamberg. Turn off to the south just past the sign to Kamberg, 31km from Rosetta.

Camp sites with limited facilities cost R20, as does overnight hiking.

Lotheni Nature Reserve

In this reserve *(admission R8, overnight hiking R16)* is a **Settlers' Museum** and some very good day walks.

KZN Wildlife Accommodation (bookings ☎ 033-845 1000) includes camping for R28 (minimum R84 in high season) and chalets from R95/120 in low/high season (minimum R240 high season).

The access road runs from the hamlet of Lower Loteni, about 30km north-east of Himeville or 65km south-west of Nottingham Road (off Mooi River). The roads aren't great and heavy rain can close them. They are, however, some of the most scenic in South Africa, with the Drakensberg as a backdrop and many picturesque Zulu villages in the area.

Mkhomazi State Forest

Mkhomazi State Forest forms the southern part of Mkhomazi Wilderness Area, and includes the 1200-hectare **Vergelegen Nature Reserve** *(admission R8 per person)*. There are no established camp sites in the area, but you can *camp* on hikes (R16). The turn-off to the state forest is 44km from Nottingham

Road, off the Lower Loteni to Sani Pass road, at the Mzinga River. From there it's another 2km.

Cobham State Forest

The Mzimkulu Wilderness Area and the Mzimkulwana Nature Reserve are in Cobham State Forest *(admission R8 per person)*. The **park office** (☎ 033-702 0831) is about 15km from Himeville on the D7; it's a good place to get information on the many hiking trails in the area (some with trail huts).

Basic *camp sites* cost R16, as does overnight hiking.

Garden Castle

The **park office** (☎ 033-712 1722) is 3km from the Drakensberg Gardens Hotel, 30km west of Underberg; admission is R10.

You can hike to the top of the escarpment and back in about eight hours if you're physically fit (and well prepared with cold-weather gear); early risers might make it to the top of spectacular Rhino Peak and back in a day.

You can't camp near the office but there's a nearby *hut* (part of the Giant's Cup Trail) which you can use if it isn't fully booked (it often is); it costs R48. You can camp at *Drakensberg Gardens Hotel* (see Places to Stay under Underberg later in the chapter) or walk at least 3km into the state forest and camp in the wilderness, which is allowed and costs R16.

Bushman's Nek
☎ 033

This is a South Africa–Lesotho border post. From here there are hiking trails up into the escarpment, including to Lesotho's Sehlabathebe National Park. You can walk in or hire a horse for about R50. How often do you get to enter a country on horseback?

Bushman's Nek Hotel (☎ 701 1460, 031-562 9505 for bookings) DB&B R120/155 per person low/high season. A few kilometres east of the border post, this hotel is good value.

Silverstreams Caravan Park (☎ 701 1249, 701 1227, ℮ info@silverstreams.co .za, ⊠ www.silverstreams.co.za) Camp sites R60/80 low/high season. The Silverstreams Caravan Park is about as close to the border post as you can get.

Giant's Cup Trail

The Giant's Cup Trail (68km, five days), running from Sani Pass to Bushman's Nek, is one of the great walks of South Africa. Any reasonably fit person can walk it, so it's very popular. Early booking (up to nine months ahead, through KZN Wildlife in Pietermaritzburg) is advisable. Although the walking is relatively easy, the usual precautions for the Drakensberg apply – expect severe cold snaps at any time of the year.

The stages are: day 1 (14km), day 2 (9km), day 3 (12km), day 4 (13km) and day 5 (12km). The highlights include the **Bathplug Cave** with San rock paintings, beautiful **Crane Tarn** and breathtaking mountain scenery on day 4.

Camping is not permitted on this trail; accommodation in *shared huts* costs R40 per person. No firewood is available so you'll need a stove and fuel. *Sani Lodge* (see Places to Stay under Sani Pass, following) is situated at the head of the trail; arrange for the lodge to pick you up from Himeville or Underberg.

SANI PASS
☎ 033

This steep route into Lesotho, the highest pass in South Africa (2865m) and the only road between KwaZulu-Natal and Lesotho, is one of the most scenic parts of the Drakensberg (see also under Sani Pass in the Lesotho chapter). The drive up the pass is magic, with stunning views out across the Umkhomazana River to the north and looming cliffs, almost directly above, to the south. There are hikes in almost every direction and inexpensive horse rides are available.

At the top of the pass, just beyond the Lesotho border crossing, is *Sani Top Chalet* (see Sani Pass in the Lesotho chapter for details). Various operators run 4WD trips up to the chalet – contact the information centres in the nearby towns of Underberg and Himeville.

Occasional minibus taxis bring people from Mokhotlong (Lesotho) to South Africa for shopping; if there's a spare seat going back this would be the cheapest option, and you would get to a town, not just the isolated lodge at the top of the pass. Ask around in Himeville or at the Mkomazana hostel, where the drivers sometimes stay. You need a passport to cross into Lesotho.

Khotso Horse Trails (☎ *701 1502)* offers rides and treks in the area and has been highly recommended by readers.

Places to Stay

There are two budget places at the bottom of the pass and a three-star hotel.

Sani Lodge (☎ *702 0330, fax 702 1401,* e *suchet@futurenet.co.za,* w *www.sani-lodge.co.za)* Camping R25, dorm beds R40, standard/luxury doubles R110/130. The lodge is behind Mokhotlong Transport (also known as Giant's Cup Motors), just before the Sani Pass Hotel and 19km from Underberg. The lodge is run by Russell Suchet, a great source of information and author of *A Backpackers' Guide to Lesotho*. The hostel is a simple but pleasant place, and plenty of activities are run from here. Meals, drinks and even cakes are available.

Mkomazana Backpackers Hostel (☎ *702 0340,* e *sound.advice@pixie.co.za)* Camping R20, dorm beds R35-45, standard/elite doubles R110/150. The hostel is another 5km along the road from the Sani Lodge and is the closest place to the pass. It's much larger than Sani, taking in the buildings of an old farm, and it's a pleasant and relaxed place with a variety of accommodation and plenty of walks in the area. There's also a nearby waterfall with a pool for swimming. There are free pick-ups from Himeville if you get there with Sani Pass Carriers (see Getting There & Away under Underberg, following).

Sani Pass Hotel (☎ *702 1320, fax 702 0220,* e *sanipasshotel@futurenet.co.za,* w *www.sanipasshotel.co.za)* Standard/luxury doubles DB&B R740/840. This expensive three-star hotel, complete with guards and razor-wire fence, is at the bottom of the pass, 14km from Himeville.

UNDERBERG
☎ 033 • postcode 4590

This quiet little town in the foothills of the southern Drakensberg is the centre of a farming community and is increasingly the base for activities in the southern Drakensberg.

The region offers excellent wilderness hiking, and the Underberg Hiking Club is a good source of information. Another source of local knowledge is **Major Adventures & Tourist Information** (☎ *701 1628, fax 702 1035,* e *majoradventures@futurenet.co.za)*, on the main street next to the Underberg Inn.

It's a sign of the number of visitors this area attracts that a village like Underberg has a good bookshop and a well-stocked shop dedicated to trout fishing. Both are in the new shopping centre on the main street. There's also a First National Bank here.

South of Underberg, off the R626 to Kokstad, the KZN Wildlife's **Coleford Nature Reserve** (1272 hectares) has some wildlife but it's more of a recreation spot than a nature reserve. Trout fishing is popular here and you can get a permit and hire equipment in the reserve. You can't camp here but there are inexpensive rustic cabins and chalets.

The **Splashy Fen Festival**, held during the last week in April, is a long-running music festival featuring gentle alternative styles.

Fire Fury

In July 2000 devastating fires swept through southern KwaZulu-Natal, killing a farmer, decimating livestock and causing millions of rands worth of damage. The fire, fanned by gale-force winds of up to 100km/h, quickly spread from the Lesotho border and raged down the Drakensberg slopes through Bushman's Nek, Underberg, Evatt and Kokstad.

In Underberg the blaze caused extensive damage to hotels and guesthouses; the Castle Burn Holiday Resort and the Drakensberg Gardens were the hardest hit.

Although today the towns show little sign of the fire's destruction, the surrounding plantations will be counting the costs for years to come.

It's held 20km from Underberg, on the road to Drakensberg Gardens.

Pick up a copy of the *Sani Saunter* brochure, which has a map of this area showing accommodation options.

Places to Stay & Eat

For information on B&Bs and cottages in the area contact Major Adventures & Tourist Information (see earlier for details).

Underberg Inn (☎ 701 1412, Main Rd) Dorm beds R70, singles/doubles B&B R160/260. The archaic inn, on the main street, has an attached pub and grill, renowned locally for its trout.

Drakensberg Gardens Hotel (☎ 701 1355, fax 701 0020) Singles/doubles B&B R309/458. The Drakensberg Gardens Hotel, west of Underberg on Garden Castle Forest Station Rd, is a fairly impersonal resort-style place. The unsealed 29km road from R617 to Drakensberg Gardens is in good condition but gets slippery after rain, especially the last 6km. There are quite a number of other places to stay along this road.

Eagles' Rock Mountain Retreat (☎/fax 701 1757, e eagles@futurenet.co.za, w www.eaglesrock.co.za) 2-bed cottages from R95/110 per person low/high season, 4-bed cottages R250/300. The excellent-value self-catering cottages at Eagles' Rock are highly recommended. It's 7.7km west of Underberg, off Drakensberg Gardens Rd.

In the new shopping centre is the delicious *Petina's Pancakes*, and on the southern edge of town is the *Bull & Tankard* restaurant. *Mike's Restaurant*, on the northern edge of town, is recommended by locals.

Getting There & Away

Sani Pass Carriers (☎ 701 1017, e sani passcarriers@wandata.com) runs minibuses to Underberg from Kokstad (R75, daily), Pietermaritzburg (R75, daily) and Durban (R120, Monday, Wednesday and Friday). Return fares are slightly cheaper than buying two one-way tickets. Let them know if you want to connect with other buses at Kokstad.

Minibus taxis run to Himeville (R3) and Pietermaritzburg (R20) and you might find one running to the Sani Pass Hotel.

The main routes to Underberg and nearby Himeville are from Pietermaritzburg on the R617 and from Kokstad on the R626 but it's possible to drive here from the northeast via Nottingham Road, south of Mooi River, and Lower Loteni. These last roads are mainly unsealed and can be closed after rain.

HIMEVILLE

☎ 033 • postcode 3256

Not far from Underberg, this town is smaller and more pleasant; it is over 1500m above sea level so winters are coolish.

The **Southern Drakensberg Tourism Association** (☎/fax 702 1158, e sdpa@future net.org.za), on the main street, arranges accommodation and activities. There's a **museum** (open 8.30am-12.30pm daily) on the main street, in a building that was originally a small fort and these days has displays on local history.

KZN Wildlife's **Himeville Nature Reserve** (admission R3 per person), on the northeastern side of town, is popular for trout fishing (you can hire rowing boats) and there are a few antelopes around. On the Pevensey Rd, 14km east of Himeville, is the **Swamp Nature Reserve**, which has the Polela River as 3km of its southern boundary. This is a small wetlands reserve, home to many species of water bird including the rare wattled crane.

Places to Stay & Eat

Check with the Southern Drakensberg Tourism Association for details of other accommodation in the area.

KZN Wildlife Accommodation (bookings ☎ 033-845 1000) Camping R20/30 per person low/high season. The camp site is in the Himeville Nature Reserve not far from town.

Himeville Arms (☎/fax 702 1305, e hime villearms@futurenet.co.za, w himevillehotel .co.za, Main Rd) Dorm beds R50-70, singles/doubles R190/360. This is a friendly hotel in the centre of town.

Robin's Nest (☎ 702 1039, e bather@ icon.co.za, w wheretostay.idws.com/kzn/dr/ 15/robins, 11 Thomas St) Singles/doubles DB&B R230/380. Robin's Nest is a comfy

B&B on a quiet street not far from the centre.

See under Sani Pass earlier in this chapter for information on a couple of hostels near Himeville on the road to Sani Pass.

Getting There & Away

About the only regular transport from Himeville are minibus taxis to Underberg (R3) and twice-daily KZT buses to Pietermaritzburg. The road to Underberg is lined with oak trees, the result of a reconciliation between the two towns after a feud.

See Sani Pass earlier in this chapter for details on transport into Lesotho.

The road from Himeville to Nottingham Road is well worth driving. The distance between the two towns is 92km, with 60km on a dirt road that winds through some spectacular country. The section between Himeville and Lower Loteni is well-gravelled. The section between Lower Loteni and the sealed road that runs to Nottingham Road has at least one hill that looks as if it would give 2WD vehicles problems after heavy rain.

GRIQUALAND EAST

Historically, the Voortrekkers had been moving into the Griqua territory between the Vaal and Orange Rivers, around Philippolis, since the 1820s. The Griqua chief, Adam Kok III, realising that there would soon be no land left, encouraged his people to sell off their remaining titles and move elsewhere.

In 1861, Kok's entire community of 2000, along with about 20,000 cattle, began their epic, two-year journey over the rugged mountains of Lesotho to Nomansland, a region on the far side of the Drakensberg. When they reached the southern slopes of Mt Currie they set up camp. Later, in 1869, they moved to the present site of Kokstad. Nomansland was called Griqualand East after annexation by the Cape in 1874. Kok died the following year when he was thrown from his cart.

Today the main towns in the area are Kokstad, Matatiele and Cedarville. It is a pleasant place to visit and the residents are extremely friendly.

Kokstad

☎ 037 • postcode 4700

Kokstad is named in honour of Adam Kok III. It lies 1280m above sea level in the Umzimhlava River valley, between Mt Currie and the Ngele mountains. Today it's a bustling little place with some solid buildings and excellent transport connections.

The **Kokstad Municipality** (☎ 727 3133, fax 727 3676, 75 Hope St) has information on the area.

The pleasant **East Griqualand Museum** (Main St) has some interesting information on the history of the Griquas, as well as the usual small-town relics.

Places to Stay & Eat Only stay at the municipal *caravan park* (☎ 727 3133), next to the sports ground near the town centre, if you're desperate.

Country Lodge (☎/fax 727 2070, Hope St) Singles/doubles B&B R187/280. Despite its new name, the Country Lodge (previously the Balmoral Hotel) hasn't changed all that much – it's still run-down and overpriced, but the rooms are OK. It's on one of the town's two main roads, so rooms at the front might be noisy.

Mount Currie Inn (☎ 727 2178, fax 727 2196, e mciriaan@venturenet.co.za) Standard singles/doubles R255/335, executive singles/doubles R275/375. This hotel, on the outskirts of town on the main road leading to the N2, is without doubt the best place to stay in Kokstad. There's a petrol station and a Wimpy out the front, which doesn't bode well, but it's actually a very nice hotel with a pleasant bar and the good Tipsy Trout restaurant.

For eating options, there's also a *Spur* steakhouse at the Country Lodge and *Norah's Pie Place* on Barkley St.

Getting There & Away Greyhound and Translux run to Umtata, Durban and Port Elizabeth, both stopping at the Wimpy, a little way from the town centre on the Durban to Umtata road.

The train station is a few blocks west (downhill) from the main street. You can book buses here or through **Keval Travel**

(☎ 727 3124, Main St), which is in the same building as the Kokstad Pharmacy.

The minibus taxi park is between Hope and Main Sts and regular taxis or buses go to Pietermaritzburg, Durban, Mt Frere and Matatiele.

See Underberg earlier for details of Sani Pass Carriers, a company that offers transport options out of Kokstad.

Around Kokstad

A few kilometres north of Kokstad, off the R626 to Franklin, is **Mt Currie Nature Reserve** *(☎/fax 037-727 3844)*. There are walking trails and several antelope species in this grassy, 1800-hectare reserve. A memorial marks the site of Adam Kok's first laager. Open *camp sites* in the reserve cost R25 per person.

There is an isolated chunk of Eastern Cape, north-east of Kokstad, called Umzimkulu (also the name of the main town); the boundaries are subject to a referendum in the future. The R56 road running off the N2, 3km south of Kokstad, runs through this interesting area, en route to Pietermaritzburg. Part of the Transkei Homeland, Umzimkulu is quite densely populated, with many traditional Xhosa houses. The road is in good condition but take it slowly due to wandering people and animals. The distance from the N2 to Pietermaritzburg is only about 200km but it can be a slow trip, as the road climbs many steep hills and descends into just as many valleys. The hills can chew up your petrol and the towns of Umzimkulu and Richmond (near Pietermaritzburg) are the only places to buy fuel.

The Midlands

The Midlands run north-west from Durban to Estcourt, skirting Zululand to the north-east. This is mainly farming country with little to interest visitors. The main town is Pietermaritzburg – KwaZulu-Natal's capital.

West of Pietermaritzburg there is picturesque, hilly country, with horse studs and plenty of European trees. This area was settled mainly by English farmers and looks a little like England's West Country. The various art and pottery galleries here are included in the *Midlands Meander*, available from one of the larger tourist offices.

PIETERMARITZBURG

☎ 033 • postcode 3200

After defeating the Zulu at the decisive Battle of Blood River, the Voortrekkers began to establish their republic of Natal. Pietermaritzburg (usually known as PMB) was named in honour of leader Pieter Mauritz Retief, and was founded in 1838 as the capital (later the 'u' was dropped and, in 1938 it was decreed that Voortrekker leader Gert Maritz be remembered in the title). In 1841 the Boers built their Church of the Vow here to honour the Blood River promise. The British annexed Natal in 1843 but they retained Pietermaritzburg – well positioned, less humid than Durban and already a neat little town – as the capital.

As well as the Afrikaner and British presence there's a large Indian population. Streets around Retief St, such as Church and Longmarket Sts, echo the subcontinent.

Pietermaritzburg rightly bills itself as the heritage city, as it has numerous historic buildings and a British colonial air. Get a copy of the *Mini-Guide* from the Publicity Association, which details the interesting buildings in the centre of town.

Orientation

The central grid of Pietermaritzburg contains most places of interest to travellers and is easy to get around. However, as is becoming common in South Africa, white-run businesses are beginning to flee the city centre. South-east of the centre is the University of Natal.

The northern end of the city, beyond Retief St, is a largely Indian commercial district. It shuts down at night and is the most unsafe part of the city centre. North of here is the Indian residential area of Northdale (with suburbs such as Bombay Heights and Mysore Ridge). To the south-west of the city is Edendale, the black dormitory suburb. To the north-west, on the Old Howick Rd beyond Queen Elizabeth Park, is the

PIETERMARITZBURG

PLACES TO STAY
24 Ngena Backpackers Lodge
26 City Royal Hotel
28 Imperial Protea Hotel
31 Crown Hotel
34 Tudor Inn
35 Sunduzi Backpackers
41 Project Gateway Backpackers' Inn

PLACES TO EAT
10 Da Vinci's Restaurant & Bar
11 Golden Dragon
12 Café Bavaria
22 Upper Crust Patisserie

OTHER
1 Islamia Mosque
2 Hindu Temple
3 Hindu Temple
4 Voortrekker Museum
5 Modern Memorial Church
6 Elephant Pub & Grill
7 Fiasco's Nite Club
8 80's Fever
9 Crowded House
13 Long-Distance Buses; City Buses
14 City Hall
15 Old Colonial Buildings
16 American Express
17 Standard Bank
18 First National Bank
19 Statue of Gandhi
20 Tatham Art Gallery (Old Supreme Court)
21 Publicity Association
23 Natal Provincial Administration Collection
25 McDonald's Plaza; Greyhound Bus Stop
27 Giga Zone
29 Natal Museum
30 AA Office
32 Police Station
33 Main Post Office
36 Bus Station; KZT Buses
37 Minibus Taxis to Underberg
38 Minibus Taxis to Ladysmith
39 Minibus Taxis to Johannesburg
40 Macrorie House Museum

Map labels: To KwaZulu-Natal Wildlife Headquarters, World's View & Hilton Hotel (10km) • To Johannesburg (520km) • Dorpspruit River • To Greytown (73km) • To Durban (80km) • Old Howick Rd • Boom • Retief • East • Victoria • Greyling • Boom • Winston • Berg • Chapel • Commercial Rd • Longmarket • Loop • To Natal Botanic Gardens (1.4km) • Mayor's Walk • Pietermaritz • West • Church • Longmarket • Prince Alfred • Burger • See Enlargement • Havelock • Loop • Burger • Train Station • Pine • To R56, Edendale, Underberg (109km), Himeville (118km) & Sani Pass (130km) • Jan Richter Centre & Ixopo (86km) • Flea Market • To The Lizard's Rock (500m); Café 21 (800m); Scottsville (1.5km) & Msunduzi Caravan Park (2km) • Voortrekker Cemetery • Umsunduzi River • Commercial • 0 250 500m • 0 250 500yd • 0 200m • 0 200yd

---

village of Hilton, a leafy and slightly twee residential area. Hilton is only about 10km from Pietermaritzburg but it's a long way up. If it's rainy in Pietermaritzburg then Hilton will probably be in the clouds.

Information

The **Publicity Association** (☎ 345 1348, fax 394 3535, ℮ ppa@futurenet.org.za, 177 Commercial Rd; open 8am-5pm Mon-Fri, 8am-3pm Sat, 9am-3pm Sun) is extremely helpful.

Rennies Travel (☎ 394 1571, 207 Pietermaritz St) is near the corner of Levy St. For Internet access try **Giga Zone** (☎ 345 1555, fax 342 6695, ℮ zlj@saol.com, Cnr Commercial & Loop Sts; Internet access R20; open 8.30am-5pm Mon-Fri, 8.30am-1pm Sat, 9am-1pm Sun).

KZN Wildlife Headquarters This is the office (☎ 845 1000, fax 845 1001, ℮ bookings@kznwildlife.com, ⓦ www.kznwildlife.com) where you make bookings for most of the accommodation and walks in KwaZulu-Natal parks; it is a long way from the city centre, in Queen Elizabeth Park, a small nature reserve. You can make phone bookings with a credit card but you'll have a long wait – it's better to visit to collect the useful literature and talk with the knowledgeable staff.

To get to the office, head out to the Old Howick Rd (Commercial Rd) and after some kilometres you'll come to a roundabout – don't go straight ahead (to Hilton) but take the road veering to the right. This road has a very small sign directing you to 'QE Park', which is 2km further on. Some minibus taxis running to Hilton pass this roundabout.

Things to See & Do

Two of Pietermaritzburg's best features are its avenues of huge old **jacaranda trees** and the maze of narrow pedestrian **lanes** running off the mall between Church and Longmarket Sts.

There are a number of colonial-era buildings. The massive red-brick **city hall**, on the corner of Church and Commercial Sts, is a good example, as is the **Old Supreme Court** across the road (now the Tatham Art Gallery). The Publicity Association office, itself housed in the old borough police and fire complex (1884), has a walking-tour map.

At the **Macrorie House Museum** (☎ 394 2161, 11 Loop St; adult/child R5/2; open 11am-4pm Mon, 9am-1pm Tues-Fri, by appointment only Sun) are displays of items related to early British settlement. For another view, visit the **Voortrekker Museum** (☎ 394 6834, e voortmus@iafrica.com, Cnr Long-market & Boshoff Sts; adult/child R3/1; open 9am-4pm Mon-Fri, 9am-1pm Sat), near the city hall. The museum is in the Church of the Vow, built in 1841 to fulfil the Voortrekkers' part of the Blood River bargain. Afrikaner icons on display include Retief's prayer book and water bottle, and a replica of a trek wagon. The words of the Vow are in the Modern Memorial Church next door.

The **Natal Museum** (☎ 345 1404, 237 Loop St; adult/child R4/1; open 9am-4pm Mon-Fri, 2pm-5pm Sat) has a range of displays, including African ethnography.

Tatham Art Gallery (☎ 342 1804, fax 394 9831, Commercial Rd; open 10am-6pm Tues-Sun), housed in the old Supreme Court, has a good collection of French and English 19th- and early 20th-century works. Perhaps the best collection of artworks in Pietermaritzburg is the least known: the **Natal Provincial Administration Collection** (☎ 345 3201, 330 Longmarket St; open by appointment only) includes some of the finest examples of indigenous art, including beadwork, pottery and weaving.

Architect Phillip Dudgeon modelled the **Standard Bank**, in the Church St Mall, on the Bank of Ireland in Belfast. It has an unusual set of stained-glass windows depicting the four seasons as one would experience them in the northern hemisphere!

There are two **Hindu temples** at the northern end of Longmarket St. The main **mosque** is nearby, on Church St. Recently a **statue of Gandhi** was erected opposite the old colonial buildings on Church St.

From Pietermaritzburg Station to Mahatma

Anyone who has seen Richard Attenborough's film *Gandhi* will recall the scene when Gandhi is ejected from the train and his suitcases are unceremoniously dumped onto the station platform.

The station was Pietermaritzburg. The 24-year-old Gandhi was on his way to Pretoria in the Transvaal for legal business. He had boarded the train with a 1st-class ticket and duly went to his allocated compartment. A white passenger complained to railway officials, who ordered Gandhi to the baggage car.

When he protested, displaying his 1st-class ticket, they called a police officer, who threw him out. He could have gone to the 3rd-class compartment but he refused. Instead, he meditated in the station's cold waiting room. Some years later, in India, when asked about the most influential experiences in his life, he cited this incident. There is now a plaque at the station.

Natal Botanic Gardens, 2km west of the train station on the continuation of Berg St, has exotic species and a garden of indigenous mist-belt flora.

The **Natal Steam Railway Museum** (☎ 343 1857, Cnr Hilton Ave & Quarry Rd) is in Hilton, and offers occasional steam train excursions.

There's a good view of the city from **World's View**, a lookout on a hill reached from the Old Howick Rd.

Organised Tours

Walking tours of the city centre leave from the Publicity Association. Tours depart at 9.30am daily. They take two hours and cost R70 per person; a minimum of two people is required. There are also a couple of driving tours.

Places to Stay – Budget

Msunduzi Caravan Park (☎ 386 5342, fax 346 2662, 50 Cleland Rd) Camp sites with/without electricity R35/25 plus R12.50 per person. The park is nearly 5km from the train station. Head south-east on Commercial Rd, which becomes Durban Rd after you cross the creek. Go left onto Blackburn Rd across the freeway, then take the first road to the right.

Sunduzi Backpackers (☎ 394 0072, fax 342 2428, e Sunduzi@hotmail.com, 140 Berg St) Camping from R25, dorm beds R45, doubles from R100. The owner of the hostel is a licensed game hunter, so there are a lot of animal skins about the place and photos of hunters gloating over the bodies of big cats. However, it is a comfortable place with a pleasant garden out the back. You can also arrange to stay at the owner's game farm.

Ngena Backpackers Lodge (☎ 345 6237, e ngena@sai.co.za, 293 Burger St) Dorm beds R50, doubles with/without bathroom R160/140. Ngena is more upmarket than your usual run-of-the-mill backpackers. Its sizable rooms are as neat as a pin and it's in a good spot, close to cafes, pubs and restaurants.

Project Gateway Backpackers' Inn (☎ 394 3342, 2 Burger St) Dorm beds R50.

The Comrades Marathon

This is the most famous athletics event in South Africa. The race was conceived to honour the comrades who fought in WWI, and every year since May 1921, runners from throughout the country and all over the world have come to run between Durban and Pietermaritzburg. The race is reversed on alternate years – from Durban to Pietermaritzburg one year and from Pietermaritzburg to Durban the next.

In 1921 the race (89km) was completed by the winner, Bill Rowan, in eight hours and 59 minutes. Today the times are much faster. Women have only officially competed since 1975 but many had completed the distance long before that. The undisputed king of the event was Bruce Fordyce, who won nine times between 1980 and 1990.

This hostel, in a converted old prison, was closed at the time of writing pending changes to windows. It seems they were too small and too high up – but then again it was designed for criminals not backpackers.

Places to Stay – Mid-Range & Top End

There are many B&Bs in the area; pick up a copy of the handy *Pietermaritzburg Accommodation Guide* at the Publicity Association.

Crown Hotel (☎ 394 1601, fax 394 1690, 186 Commercial St) Singles/doubles B&B R150/230. This small creaky hotel is handy for the long-distance bus stop and the town centre.

Tudor Inn (☎ 342 1778, fax 345 1111, 18 Theatre Lane) Doubles B&B from R250. The excellent Tudor Inn has light, airy rooms and is in a handy spot. There's a good cafe on the ground floor.

City Royal Hotel (☎ 394 7072, fax 343 3273, 301 Burger St) Singles/doubles B&B R197/252. While the hotel doesn't look all that impressive from the outside, the stylishly furnished rooms are very good, and it's off the main streets so there's no traffic noise. There's a restaurant and bar, secure parking, and the staff are courteous and helpful.

Imperial Protea Hotel (☎ 342 6551, fax 342 9796, e imperial@iafrica.com, 224 Loop St) Executive singles B&B R350-400, standard doubles B&B R460. The well-located Imperial Protea Hotel has simply furnished clean rooms.

Hilton Hotel (☎ 396 2312, fax 343 3722, 1 Hilton Ave) Budget singles/doubles R230/280, standard rooms R310/370, luxury rooms R400/480. This impressive hotel, high up in the leafy village of Hilton, has large modern rooms.

Places to Eat

Across from the train station and along Church St are a couple of basic cafes selling takeaway food.

Upper Crust Patisserie (☎ 342 7625, 272 Longmarket St) Light meals R12-15. The Upper Crust serves upmarket snacks.

Café Bavaria (☎ 345 1952, Cnr Commercial Rd & Church St) Breakfast R8-23, lunch R12-38. This small cafe in the NSB building is good value.

Da Vinci's Restaurant & Bar (☎ 345 5172, fax 342 7184, e brokie@davincis .co.za, 117 Commercial Rd) Mains R34-42. Da Vinci's is a popular Italian restaurant with cheap filling lunches. Its bar heats up after dark (see Entertainment later).

Golden Dragon (☎ 345 7745, Ground floor, Capital Towers, 121 Commercial Rd) Mains R10-20. The Golden Dragon, in the Karos Capital Towers, is an inexpensive Chinese restaurant and takeaway.

Café 21 (☎ 342 3644, 50 Durban Rd) Lunch R19-25, mains R20-36. Café 21 is a very hip and modern cafe-cum-cocktail bar, which serves breakfast all day and has well-priced lunches.

The Lizard's Rock (☎ 345 7745, Durban Rd) Mains R20-40. The Lizard's Rock is a funky restaurant is south-east of the centre.

Entertainment

Pietermaritzburg has quite a lively nightlife thanks to its large student population, but if you want full-on entertainment catch a bus to Durban.

Da Vinci's Restaurant & Bar (☎ 345 5172, 117 Commercial Rd) Open noon-late daily. Da Vinci's bar is *the* place to head for when the town's nightclubs close.

Elephant Pub & Grill (☎ 345 4380, 80 Commercial Rd) Open 11am-late daily. The Elephant is an atmospheric watering hole.

Crowded House (☎ 345 5977, fax 345 5972, 99 Commercial Rd) Open 8pm-4am Tues-Sat. Crowded House draws in its large student following with specials such as its 'Pigs Night', where for R25 you can down as many drinks as you can stomach for three hours.

Other favourite haunts include *80's Fever*, on Commercial Rd next door to Crowded House; and *Fiasco's Nite Club*, on Berg St opposite the Elephant Pub & Grill. Both are only open Thursday, Friday and Saturday nights.

Getting There & Away

Air SA Airlink (☎ 031-250 1111) flies to Durban (R195) and Jo'burg (R868).

Bus Greyhound stops on Commercial Rd at the McDonald's Plaza, and Translux stops just around the corner from the information office. Translux goes to and from Jo'burg/ Pretoria (R160) via Harrismith (R130), and Bloemfontein (R163) via Bethlehem (R128). Greyhound has several services each day between Durban and Jo'burg/ Pretoria via Ladysmith and Newcastle. The Durban-Kimberley run also stops in Pietermaritzburg. Book Translux and Greyhound at the Publicity Association.

Cheetah Coaches (☎ 342 0266, 206 Longmarket St) runs daily between Durban, Pietermaritzburg and Durban international airport. The fare to Durban is R35.

Sani Pass Carriers (☎ 701 1017) runs up into southern Drakensberg. See Underberg earlier in this chapter for more details.

Train The train station has had its Victorian charms partially restored. Here, you can catch the weekly *Trans Oranje* (Durban-Cape Town) and the daily *Trans Natal* (Durban-Jo'burg) services.

Minibus Taxi Generally minibus taxi ranks are found near the train station. Fares from

Pietermaritzburg include: Durban R14, Estcourt R20, Ladysmith R25, Newcastle R38 and Jo'burg R60. Other taxis depart from Market Square (behind Publicity House) and may run to Umtata and Maseru.

Car & Motorcycle If you're heading north, a nicer route than the N3 is the R103, which runs through picturesque country between Howick and Mooi River. For a long but scenic drive to Durban, head north on the R33 (the continuation of Church St) to Sevenoaks, then cut back to the coast on the R614. Watch out for pedestrians and slow-moving cane trucks on this road.

Avis (☎ 0800 21111), **Budget** (☎ 0800 16622) and **Imperial** (☎ 0800 131 000) have agents here. All phone numbers are toll free.

Hitching In general Lonely Planet does not recommend hitching, but if you are hitching on the N3, get off at Exit 81 (Church St) for the city centre, Exit 76 (northbound) or Exit 74 (southbound) for the municipal caravan park.

Getting Around
The main rank for city-area buses is on the road running behind the Publicity Association on the corner of Longmarket St and Commercial Rd. Services have been greatly reduced lately.

For a taxi, phone **Springbok** (☎ 345 1111), **Junior** (☎ 394 5454) or **Unique** (☎ 391 1238).

AROUND PIETERMARITZBURG
Howick
☎ 033 • postcode 3290

In the town of Howick, about 25km northwest of Pietermaritzburg on the N3, are the popular Howick Falls. Just before the falls there is the small **Howick Museum** *(open 9am-noon, 2pm-3.30pm Tues-Fri, 10am-3pm Sat)*, an unabashedly parochial celebration of the town.

The small (656 hectare) **Umgeni Valley Nature Reserve**, with walks and some more falls, is nearby. This is one of the best conservation education centres in South Africa. More than 200 bird species have been recorded in the confines of the reserve.

Howick has a few choices for visitors wanting to stay overnight.

Eagle's Nest Caravan Park *(☎/fax 330 2797, Morling St)* Camping R35 per person. The park is near the falls on the banks of the Umgeni River.

Howick Falls Hotel *(☎ 330 2809, fax 330 2018, 2 Main St)* Rooms without/with bathroom R75/85 per person. Howick Falls Hotel is an old place with inexpensive rooms. Breakfast is R15.

Harrow Hill Guest Farm *(☎ 330 5033, 8 Karkloof Rd)* Singles/doubles B&B R190/320. This comfy B&B is about 4km from Howick.

Midmar Nature Reserve
This reserve *(☎ 033-330 2067, fax 033-330 5868; admission R5 per person)* is 7km from Howick off the Greytown Rd. Although there are some animals in the reserve, it is mainly a recreation area, and has water sports on the dam. There's accommodation at **Munro Bay**, the cheapest of which is in chalets, and camping at **Dukududku**, **Morgenzon** and **Munro Bay** from R25 to R30 per person.

Albert Falls Resources Reserve
This reserve *(☎ 033-569 1202, fax 033-569 1371)* is 25km from Pietermaritzburg, off the road north to Greytown.

Camp sites at **Notuli** are R25 per person, and there are inexpensive rondavels and

---

End of Freedom

One of the most significant events in South Africa's apartheid history occurred in the KwaZulu-Natal Midlands.

It was just outside Howick that in August 1962 Nelson Mandela's days of freedom ended and his lengthy incarceration began.

Mandela, disguised as a chauffer, had been driving to Johannesburg along the Old Howick road with MK member Cecil Williams when their car was stopped by police.

The actual spot of his arrest on the R103 is now marked by a memorial, which Mandela unveiled himself in 1996.

chalets. Note that there have been outbreaks of bilharzia associated with the dam.

Ecabazini Zulu Cultural Homestead (☎ *033-342 1928)* DB&B R100 per person. Ecabazini has accommodation in traditional huts. You need your own linen and towel. There are traditional meals and cultural displays; however, visits are by prior arrangement only. Book through a backpacker agency such as Tekweni in Durban.

MOOI RIVER
☎ 033 • postcode 3300
Mooi River is a nondescript town but the early Voortrekkers probably had high hopes for it, as *mooi* means 'beautiful'. The Zulu were more matter of fact, calling it Mpofana, 'Place of the Eland'. The surrounding countryside, especially to the west, is worth exploring. It's horse-stud country on rolling land dotted with old European trees.

Mooi River is closer to Giant's Castle than Estcourt and, while there are fewer minibus taxis, the town is right on the N3 so hitching to and from here may be easier.

Riverbank Caravan Park *(☎/fax 263 2144, Greytown Rd)* Camping R25, 2-bed chalets R75 per person. Unfortunately, over the last few years a housing project has been built on the park's doorstep, but it is still a safe and secure place to camp. Breakfast is R20.

Argyle B&B *(☎ 263 1106, Giant's Castle Rd)* B&B R85 per person. The old Argyle Hotel has been turned into a charming and relatively inexpensive B&B.

There are some excellent country guesthouses in the surrounding area – see Nottingham Road & Around, following for details.

Getting There & Away
Greyhound buses running between Durban and Jo'burg/Pretoria stop at the Wimpy, at the big truck stop on the Rosetta road near the N3, 1km from the centre.

The *Trans Oranje* and *Trans Natal* trains stop here. Book tickets at the goods office, across the tracks from the old station.

Minibus taxis aren't frequent and run mainly to nearby villages.

NOTTINGHAM ROAD & AROUND
☎ 033 • postcode 3280
The quaint little town of Nottingham Road was so-named to honour the Nottinghamshire Regiment of the British Army, which was garrisoned here. After the Cape Winelands, this is probably the most gentrified rural area in the country and there are some expensive but excellent guesthouses in the area. Most have extensive gardens.

The Outpost *(☎/fax 263 6836, Old Main Rd)* B&B from R125 per person. The Outpost, 2km from Nottingham Road, is one place that isn't very expensive but it's still good.

Thatchings *(☎ 263 6275, fax 263 6276,* e *thatchings@futurenet.co.za,* w *www .thatchings.co.za)* B&B start at R235 per person. Thatchings is a smart well-equipped guesthouse 3km from town.

Granny Mouse Country House *(☎ 234 4071, fax 234 4429,* e *info@grannymouse .co.za,* w *www.grannymouse.co.za, Old Main Rd)* B&B from R410 per person. The Granny Mouse, near the village of Balgowan, south of Mooi River, is one of the better-known places. It's off the R103, a scenic road running parallel to the N3 between Howick and Mooi River. It also offers mid-week specials.

Penny Lane *(☎ 234 4332, fax 234 4617,* e *pennylane@pixie.co.za,* w *www.penny lane.co.za, Old Main Rd)* Singles/doubles B&B R250/400. Not far from Granny Mouse is the charming Penny Lane B&B. Set on a large estate it offers plenty of activities, including swimming, tennis, horse riding and trout fishing.

Hartford House *(☎ 263 2713, fax 263 2818,* e *info@hartford.co.za,* w *www.hart ford.co.za)* This place, the home of a former Natal prime minister, is one of the country's top luxury lodges.

Thukela

Bird-watchers may be attracted to the St Lucia Wetland Park, walkers and climbers to the Drakensberg and wildlife lovers to Kruger but the historian will be happy in

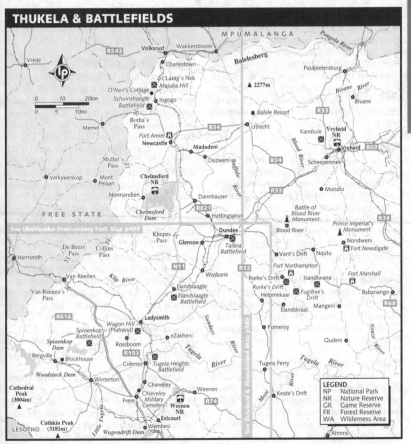

THUKELA & BATTLEFIELDS

Thukela. The Thukela region, at the head-waters of the Tugela River, officially also includes the northern and central Drakens-berg, but these are covered in a separate section earlier in this chapter.

Some of the more important conflicts in South Africa's history took place in the area, including the Siege of Ladysmith, the Battle of Spioenkop, the bloody defeat of the British by the Zulu at Isandlwana, the heroic Defence of Rorke's Drift and the battles of Majuba Hill and Blood River; the region is often described as the Battlefields Route. Get free copies of *Natal Battlefields* *Route*, *Dundee* and *Natal Battlefields Chronicle* from local publicity associations and the Tourist Junction in Durban.

ESTCOURT
☎ 036 • postcode 3310

Estcourt, named after an early sponsor of an immigration scheme to the area, is at the southern edge of Thukela. It's close to the central Drakensberg resorts and Giant's Castle, and is on the Jo'burg/Pretoria to Durban bus route. It also has good train and minibus taxi connections. The black township of Wembesi is about 8km west of Estcourt.

For information, contact **Bushman's River Tourism Association** (*☎/fax 352 6253,* e *br ta@futurest.co.za, Upper Harding St; open 8am-5pm Mon-Fri, 8am-11am Sat*).

Fort Durnford (*admission by donation; open 9am-noon & 1pm-4pm daily*), which is now a museum, was built in 1874 to protect Estcourt from Zulu attack. There are interesting displays and a reconstructed Zulu village in the grounds.

Places to Stay

The tourism association can book you a B&B from around R120 per person.

The inexpensive municipal *caravan park* isn't far from the town centre on Lorne St.

Val-U-Lodge (*☎/fax 352 6760, 86 Harding St*) Doubles R89/69 with/without bathroom. The old Plough Hotel is now the no-frills Val-U-Lodge. Its rooms are OK and *very* cheap. Breakfast is R15.

Getting There & Away

Bus Greyhound buses on the Durban to Kimberley and Durban to Jo'burg/Pretoria routes leave from the information centre, as do Translux buses on the Durban to Jo'burg/Pretoria route.

Train The weekly *Trans Oranje* (Cape Town to Durban) and the daily *Trans Natal* (Jo'burg/Pretoria to Durban) stop here. Book tickets at the goods (freight) depot, not at the train station. The depot is a few blocks southwest of the station, past the Nestlé factory and under the railway overpass.

Minibus Taxi The main minibus taxi rank is at the bottom of Phillips St in the town centre, downhill from the post office. This is one of the better organised taxi parks and the staff at Estcourt Taxi Association office (in the small two-storey building at the back of the park) are friendly and helpful. Fares from Estcourt include: Winterton R8, Ladysmith R14, Pietermaritzburg R20, Durban R30 and Jo'burg R60.

Taxis run to the road leading into Giant's Castle (about R7) but you can arrange for a taxi to take you all the way to the entrance. This costs about R25 and takes a while, as the taxi has to complete its normal route before taking you up to the park. Contact the **taxi office** (*☎ 352 7107, 352 7115*).

AROUND ESTCOURT

There's not much to do or see at **Wagendrift Nature Reserve** (*☎/fax 036-352 5520; admission R7 per person*) but you can swim and fish in the dam, camp for R28 per person or stay in the one four-bed chalet for R50/60 per person in the low/high season. The reserve is 7km south-west of Estcourt on the road to Ntabamhlope. A little further on from the reserve, at the head of the dam, is **Moor Park Nature Reserve**, which overlooks Wagendrift Dam and Bushmens River. There are zebras, wildebeests and antelopes.

Around 25km north-east of Estcourt is the 5000-hectare **Weenen Nature Reserve** (*☎ 036-354 7013; admission R7 per person plus R15 per vehicle*), which has black and white rhinos, buffaloes, giraffes and several antelope species, including the rare roan. There are three good walking trails: Impofu (2km), Beacon View (3km) and Reclamation (2km). *Camp sites* here cost R22 per person, and five-bed cottages are R50/72 per person in low/high season (minimum R100/144). Sometimes there's also Zulu dancing in this area.

Almost at the point where the R103 meets the R74, 16km north of Estcourt, is the site where the young Winston Churchill was captured by the Boers in 1899 when they derailed the armoured train he was travelling in; there is a **plaque** just off the road.

COLENSO

☎ 036 • postcode 3360

Colenso, a small town about 20km south of Ladysmith, was the British base during the Relief of Ladysmith. As well as Spioenkop, there are several other Anglo-Boer War battlefields near here.

There is a museum and some memorial sites relating to the Battle of Colenso (December 1899) – another disaster for the hapless General Buller at the hands of Louis Botha. The **museum** is in the toll house adjacent to the bridge. Keys are available from the police station between 8am and 6pm.

Lord Roberts' only son, Freddy, was among those slaughtered here (with about 1100 other British); he is buried in the **Chieveley Military Cemetery**, south of the town.

Battlefields Lodge (☎ *422 2242, 75 Sir George St)* B&B R100 per person. Battlefields Lodge is a good B&B that has a swimming pool and conference facilities.

The Settlement (☎ *422 2535, fax 422 2536, 23 Club Rd)* Singles/doubles B&B R165/250. This place has a good restaurant and weekend specials are available.

SPIOENKOP NATURE RESERVE
The 6000-hectare Spioenkop Nature Reserve (☎ *036-488 1578, fax 036-488 1065; admission R7 per person)* is based on the Spioenkop Dam on the Tugela River. The reserve is handy for most of the area's battlefield sites and not too far from the Drakensberg for day trips into the range. There are two reserves in the resort; animals include white rhinos, giraffes, zebras and various antelope species. There's a swimming pool and horse riding, and tours of the Spioenkop battlefield are available.

Spioenkop has six-bed chalets for R55/70 per person in the low/high season (minimum R55/280).

iPika has camping for R20/30 per person in the low/high season; four-bed tented bush camps cost R100. Book all accommodation directly through the reserve.

The reserve is just north of Bergville but the entrance is on the eastern side, off the R600, which runs between the N3 and Winterton. If you are coming from the south on the N3 take the turn-off to the R74 to get to Winterton.

LADYSMITH
☎ 036 • postcode 3370
Ladysmith (not to be confused with the town of Ladismith in Western Cape) was named after the wife of Cape governor Sir Harry Smith, but it could well have had a much more colourful name. She wasn't just plain Lady Smith, she was Lady Juana Maria de los Dolores...Smith.

The Battle of Spioenkop

On 23 January 1900 the British, led by General Buller, made a second attempt to relieve Ladysmith, which had been under siege by the Boers since late October 1899. At Trichardt's Drift, 500 Boers prevented 15,000 of his men from crossing the Tugela River, and Buller decided that he needed to take Spioenkop – the flat-topped hill would make a good gun emplacement from which to clear the annoying Boers from their trenches.

During the night, 1700 British troops climbed the hill and chased off the few Boers guarding it. They dug a trench and waited for morning. Meanwhile, the Boer commander, Louis Botha, heard of the raid. He ordered his field guns to be trained onto Spioenkop and positioned some of his men on nearby hills. A further 400 soldiers began to climb Spioenkop as the misty dawn broke.

The British might have beaten off the 400, but the mist finally lifted, and was immediately replaced by a hail of bullets and shells. The British retreated to their trench and by mid-afternoon, continuous shellfire combined with the summer heat caused many to surrender. By now, reinforcements were on hand (summoned, according to some, by the young Winston Churchill) and the Boers could not overrun the trench. A bloody stalemate was developing.

After sunset, the British evacuated the hill; so did the Boers. Both retreats were accomplished so smoothly that neither side was aware that the other had left. That night Spioenkop was held by the dead.

It was not until the next morning that the Boers again climbed up Spioenkop and found that it was theirs. The Boers had killed or wounded 1340 British and taken 1000 prisoners, at a loss of 230 casualties, unusually high for their small army. Gandhi's stretcher-bearer unit performed with distinction at this battle. Buller relieved Ladysmith a month later on 28 February.

The town achieved fame during the 1899–1902 Anglo-Boer War, when it was besieged by Boer forces for 118 days. Apart from the historical aspect – several buildings in the city centre were here during the siege – Ladysmith is a pleasant place to walk around.

You can ask about guided tours of the battlefields at the **information office** (☎/fax 637 2992, ℮ info@ladysmith.co.za, ☒ www .ladysmith.co.za, Murchison St), which is in the Siege Museum.

A handy Internet cafe is **Computer Dimensions** (☎ 631 3804, ℮ dimension@ mweb.co.za, Oval Shopping Centre, Murchison St; Internet access R20 per half-hour).

Things to See & Do

The very good **Siege Museum** (☎ 637 2231; adult/child R2/1; open 9am-4pm Mon-Fri, 9am-1pm Sat), next to the town hall in the Market House (built in 1884), was used to store rations during the siege.

You can also pick up a walking-tour map of Ladysmith there.

There's also the small **Cultural Museum** (25 Keate St; adult/child R2/1; open 9am-4pm Mon-Fri, 9am-1pm Sat), with displays including a room dedicated to the Ladysmith Black Mambazo band.

Outside the town hall are two guns, **Castor** and **Pollux**, used by the British in defence of Ladysmith. Nearby is a replica of **Long Tom**, a Boer gun capable of heaving a shell 10km. Long Tom was put out of action by a British raiding party during the siege but not before it had caused a great deal of damage.

On the corner of King St and Settlers Drive is the police station, which includes the wall with loopholes from the original **Zulu Fort**, built as a refuge from Zulu attack.

Across the river on the southern side of town (there's a footbridge) is a **Sufi mosque**, built by the Muslim community; it's been in Ladysmith almost since the town's inception, and the mosque is worth seeing. There's also a Hindu **Vishnu temple**, and while the building is undistinguished you'll meet some friendly people there. As well as religious statues inside the temple, in the garden is a **statue of Gandhi**. The statue was imported from Mumbai and depicts Gandhi as the Mahatma and not as a stretcher bearer with Buller's forces at Spioenkop, which might have been more appropriate.

South of town, near the junction of the N11 and R103, is an area generally known as **Platrand** (Wagon Hill). There is an unusual monument to the Boers who died attempting to wrest Wagon Hill from the British on 6 January 1900.

Places to Stay

The information office in town has details of farmstays and B&Bs. Prices start at around R160 a double.

The municipal *caravan park* (☎ 637 6804, fax 637 3151) is on the northern side of town; follow Poort Rd over the hill, where it becomes the Harrismith road.

Natalasia Hotel (☎/fax 637 6821, 342 Kandahar Ave) Singles/doubles R100/150. The modern Natalasia Hotel has OK rooms. Breakfast is R15.

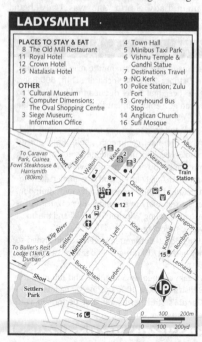

LADYSMITH

PLACES TO STAY & EAT
8 The Old Mill Restaurant
11 Royal Hotel
12 Crown Hotel
15 Natalasia Hotel

OTHER
1 Cultural Museum
2 Computer Dimensions;
   The Oval Shopping Centre
3 Siege Museum;
   Information Office

4 Town Hall
5 Minibus Taxi Park
6 Vishnu Temple &
   Gandhi Statue
7 Destinations Travel
9 NG Kerk
10 Police Station; Zulu
   Fort
13 Greyhound Bus
   Stop
14 Anglican Church
16 Sufi Mosque

To Caravan Park, Guinea Fowl Steakhouse & Harrismith (80km)

To Buller's Rest Lodge (1km) & Durban

Klip River

Settlers Park

Train Station

0   100   200m
0   100   200yd

Buller's Rest Lodge (☎ 631 0310, fax 637 3549, 61 Cove Crescent) Singles/doubles B&B R175/275. On a quiet street not far from the centre, this friendly place has a magnificent deck overlooking Ladysmith.

Near the town hall, on Murchison St (the main street), there are two venerable old hotels. One, the *Crown Hotel (☎ 637 2266, fax 637 6458)* at No 90, has singles/doubles for R297/367, including breakfast; the other, *Royal Hotel (☎/fax 637 2176, ℮ royal@inte kom.co.za, 140 Murchison St)* at No 140, has singles/doubles for R250/440, including breakfast.

Places to Eat
There are several eateries in the big shopping centre off Murchison St. For cheap eats, try the stalls and shops around the minibus taxi park.

The Royal Hotel is home to three of the town's best eateries.

Swainson's Restaurant (☎ 637 2167) Mains R20-40. The restaurant serves the usual steaks and salads, plus some game and seafood.

The Tipsy Trouper Mains R22-39. The Tipsy Trouper is a good pub and grill.

Mario's Mains R19-34. Mario's is an Italian restaurant with lunch specials such as tagliatelle.

The Old Mill Restaurant (☎ 637 4301, Old Mill Centre, Queen St) Mains R15-35. The Old Mill serves inexpensive lunches.

Guinea Fowl Steakhouse (☎ 637 8163, Shop 13, San Marco, Cnr Francis & Harrismith Rds) Mains 20-40. Guinea Fowl is a good steakhouse with a large menu.

Getting There & Away
Bus Translux buses leave from the train station and run to Durban (R80) and Bloemfontein (R140). Greyhound has daily services to Durban (R110) and Jo'burg/Pretoria (R125). Book at the Shell petrol station on the corner of Murchison and King Sts, or at **Destinations Travel** *(☎ 631 0831)*.

There are local companies serving the former QwaQwa Homeland in Free State and the immediate area, some of which will get you fairly close to the Drakensberg.

Train The *Trans Oranje* (Durban to Cape Town) and the daily *Trans Natal* (Durban to Jo'burg/Pretoria) both stop here but at inconvenient times.

Minibus Taxi The main (and surprisingly large) taxi rank is east of the town centre near the corner of Queen and Lyell Sts. Taxis bound for Harrismith and Jo'burg are nearby on Alexandra St. Some destinations are Harrismith (R10), Durban (R30) and Jo'burg (R55).

NEWCASTLE
☎ 034 • postcode 2900
Not surprisingly, Newcastle is a coal-mining and steel-producing town. The white population is 25,000, there are 16,000 Indians in Lennoxton and Lenville, and 250,000 blacks in the nearby townships of Madadeni and Osizweni.

There's an Anglo-Boer War museum in **Fort Amiel** *(open 9am-1pm Tues-Thur, 11am-4pm Fri, 9am-1pm Sat)*, which was established in 1876 when the British anticipated conflict with the Zulu.

The colonial-era **town hall**, on Scott St, is worth a look, and you can get information (including details of local accommodation) from the enthusiastic staff.

The turn-off to **Chelmsford Nature Reserve** *(☎/fax 377 7205; admission R5 per person)* is on the R23 25km south of Newcastle. As well as water sports on the dam there's a game reserve with white rhinos.

Places to Stay & Eat
KZN Wildlife Accommodation (bookings ☎ 033-845 1000) Camping R20 per person, 5-bed chalet R65/75 per person low/high season (minimum R225 high season). KZN Wildlife administers camp sites at Leokop and Sandford.

Majuba Lodge (☎ 315 5011, fax 315 5023, ℮ majuba@newcastle.co.za, Victoria Rd) Chalets from R209 per person. The well-built Majuba Lodge, across from the Holiday Inn, has pleasant chalets and the best restaurant in town.

Holiday Inn Garden Court (☎ 312 8151, fax 312 4142, ℮ amarh@southernsun.com,

Victoria Rd) Standard rooms from R294 per person. This Holiday Inn has a restaurant, bar and a pleasant pool.

There's a ***Spur*** on Voortrekker St and ***Longhorn*** (also for steak) on Allen St. The meals at ***Newcastle Golf Club*** have also been recommended.

Getting There & Away
Greyhound runs daily to Jo'burg (R110) and Durban (R130) from the Shell petrol station on Allen St. Eagle Liner bus service (KwaZulu Transport) operates to Osizweni. Minibus taxis to Jo'burg cost about R40.

The daily *Trans Natal* train runs to Jo'burg and Durban.

Car-rental companies with agents in Newcastle include **Imperial** *(☎ 312 2806)*, based at Newcastle airport; and **Avis** *(☎ 312 1274, Leon Motors, Allen St)*.

HOLKRANS TRAIL
The Holkrans Trail *(☎/fax 034-351 1600)* is 25km south-west of Newcastle just off the Normandien road and in the Drakensberg foothills. The trail (25km, two days) is divided into two stages: an 11.5km walk to the night stop, a *holkrans* (overhang) in the sandstone cliffs, and a 6km walk via a ravine and grassveld back to the start point.

MAJUBA HILL
The first Anglo-Boer War ended abruptly, 40km north of Newcastle, with the British defeat at Majuba Hill in early 1881. The site has been restored and a map is available; there is a small admission fee. The Laing's Nek and Schuinshoogte battlefields are also signposted.

Peace negotiations took place at **O'Neill's Cottage** in the foothills near Majuba. The cottage, used as a hospital during the battle, has been restored and has a photographic display.

UTRECHT
☎ 034 • postcode 2980
Today a quiet little town in prime cattle country, Utrecht was once the capital of one of the original Voortrekker republics, this one measuring just 30km by 65km! The town was the British headquarters during the Anglo-Zulu War, and a number of fine 19th-century buildings remain. There's a

---

The Battle of Majuba Hill

The British annexed the first Zuid-Afrikaansche Republiek (ZAR, South African Republic) of Transvaal on 12 April 1877. After peaceful protest failed, more than 8000 armed Boers met at Paardekraal and pledged to reinstate the ZAR government as from 13 December, using force if necessary. The first shots were fired at Potchefstroom on 16 December and several British garrisons were besieged. The obvious route for British reinforcements sent to relieve the garrisons was from Durban to Transvaal via Newcastle. Piet Joubert moved 2000 mounted troops to the strategic position of Laing's Nek, north of Newcastle, in anticipation of this move.

The British, under Sir George Colley, attacked the Boers on 28 January 1881 at Laing's Nek but had to retreat after an hour. On 8 February a British wagon column was encircled by Boers at Schuinshoogte (Ingogo) and suffered heavy casualties.

On the night of 26 February, Colley and nearly 600 troops climbed Majuba Hill to overlook the Boer positions. The British wore bright uniforms and cumbersome helmets and were armed with Martini Henry rifles (with their sights incorrectly adjusted) – no match for the highly mobile Boers. The British panicked and began to flee. At around 1pm on 27 February, Colley was fatally wounded; in all, 285 British soldiers were killed, wounded or taken prisoner.

When news was received of Colley's death, General Sir Evelyn Wood was sworn in as acting governor of Natal. On 6 March he met the Boer commanders at O'Neill's Cottage, at the base of Majuba, to negotiate peace. The battle and events before and after are described in GA Chadwick's *The First War of Independence in Natal: 1880-1881*.

museum *(open 9am-noon Mon-Fri)* in the old parsonage.

Balele Resort (☎ 331 3041, fax 331 4312) Camp sites R50, 2-bed chalets R136. The resort is 2km north of town on the Wakkerstroom road. You can book here to do the **Balele Waterval Trail** (25km, three days), which passes through the Enhlanzeni Valley in the Langalibalele Range. The trail fee is R20 per person and accommodation costs R50 per person; the first night is in an old farmhouse, and the overnight camp has beehive huts.

DUNDEE
☎ 034 • postcode 3000

Dundee is a large coal-mining town, not especially attractive but perhaps useful as a base for the area's historical sites. It was named by an early settler who came from a village near Dundee in Scotland.

On the Vryheid road, 1.5km out of town, is **Talana Museum** *(☎ 212 2654, e info@ talana.co.za, w www.talana.co.za; adult/ child R8/1; open 8am-4.30pm Mon-Fri, 10am-4.30pm Sat & Sun)*, dedicated to 'small men who had to take root or die, not to the captains and kings who departed'. It's a large place with several old buildings and displays on coal mining and local history, including both the Anglo-Zulu and the Anglo-Boer Wars. Some good pamphlets on the area's history are available.

You can obtain information from **Tourism Dundee** *(☎ 212 2121, fax 218 2837)*, which is by the gardens on Victoria St. It can put you in touch with battlefield guides, who charge between R150 and R300 for a one-day tour.

Starting at Dundee caravan park, the **Mpati Mountain Trail** (18km) leads to the top of Mpati Mountain, where there's an overnight hut. Contact Tourism Dundee for bookings.

To the east of Dundee, 52km away via the R33 and R66, is the fascinating regional centre of **Nqutu**. This is an important trading centre for the surrounding Zulu community and about as close to a buzzing urban black town as you will see. About 30km north of Nqutu, near Nondweni, is the memorial to the Prince Imperial Louis Napoleon, the last of the Bonaparte dynasty, who was killed here on 1 June 1879.

The Battle of Isandlwana

The Battle of Isandlwana was the first major engagement of the 1879 Anglo-Zulu War, precipitated by an ultimatum to Cetshwayo that the British knew he would not and could not meet. The demands included the complete reorganisation of the Zulu political structure and the abolition of the Zulu army.

On 22 January 1879 a soldier from one of the five British forces sent to invade Zululand happened to look over a ridge near Isandlwana Hill. He was surprised to discover 25,000 Zulu warriors sitting in the gully below, silently awaiting the time to attack. This was to have been the following day, the day after the full moon, but on being discovered the impi adopted their battle formation – two enclosing 'horns' on the flanks and the main force in the centre – and attacked the utterly unprepared British camp. By the end of the day almost all of the British were dead, along with many Zulus.

Meanwhile, the small British contingent that had remained at Rorke's Drift (where the army had crossed into Zululand) to guard supplies, heard of the disaster and fortified their camp. They were attacked by about 4000 Zulus but the defenders, numbering fewer than 100 fit soldiers, held on through the night until a relief column arrived. Victoria Crosses were lavished on the defenders – 11 in all – and another couple went to the two officers who died defending the Queen's Colours at Fugitive's Drift, about 10km south of Rorke's Drift.

Many people will know of these battles by the movies made of them: *Zulu Dawn* for Isandlwana and *Zulu* for Rorke's Drift. Perhaps the best account of the Anglo-Zulu War is *The Washing of the Spears* by D Morris, although *The Destruction of the Zulu Kingdom* by Jeff Guy gives a more thorough understanding of the forces at work.

Places to Stay

There are several B&Bs in Dundee and nearby; check with Tourism Dundee.

Dundee Caravan Park (☎ *218 2486, fax 212 3697, Union St*) Camping R30 per person. This park has reasonably sized sites.

Royal Country Inn (☎ *212 2147, fax 218 2146,* e *royal@dundee.kzn.co.za, Victoria St*) Singles/doubles R185/310, backpacker singles/doubles R125/190. The large Royal Country Inn is opposite the town hall. The backpacker rooms are in an older section of the inn.

Battlefields Country Lodge Backpackers (☎ *218 1641, fax 212 3502,* e *stay@ battlefieldslodge.co.za,* W *www.battlefields lodge.co.za)* Camping R25 per tent, dorm beds R50. This lodge, 7km from Dundee on the R33 road to Vryheid, has been recommended by readers. It does pick-ups from Ladysmith (R50).

ISANDLWANA & RORKE'S DRIFT
☎ 034 • postcode 3005

You have probably heard of the Defence of Rorke's Drift but not the Battle of Isandlwana – the former was a British imperial victory of the misty-eyed variety, the latter was a bloody disaster.

Isandlwana should not be missed. At the base of this sphinx-like rock there are graves and memorials to those who fell in battle on 22 January 1879. The Isandlwana museum, with artefacts taken from the battlefield, is in St Vincent's (the bluestone buildings in the nearby village) just outside the site.

At Rorke's Drift, 42km from Dundee, there is a splendid **museum** (☎ *642 1687; adult/child R8/1; open 8am-4pm Mon-Fri, 9am-4pm Sat & Sun)*, a self-guided trail around the battlefield, several **memorials** and the **ELC Zulu Craft Centre** (☎ *642 1627; open 8am-4.30pm Mon-Fri, 10am-3pm Sat & Sun)*. The rugs and tapestries woven and sold here are world-renowned and therefore not cheap.

The Zulu know this site as Shiyane, their name for the hill at the back of the village. The *Rorke's Drift-Shiyane Self-Guided Trail* brochure is helpful for understanding the close nature of the fighting in this battle.

About 10km south of Rorke's Drift is **Fugitive's Drift**. Two British officers were killed here while attempting to prevent the Queen's Colours from falling into Zulu hands.

While you are in this area it is worth taking a side trip to the spectacular **Mangeni Falls**, at the head of a tributary of the Buffalo River. About 35km west of Babanango, at Silutshana, turn south and follow the road to Mangeni. At Mangeni you will probably have to ask the way to the falls as the track is not obvious.

Isandlwana Lodge (☎ *271 8301, fax 271 8306,* e *isand@icon.co.za,* W *www.isandl wana.co.za)* Standard singles R775/1025 low/high season, standard doubles R1450/ 1750, including all meals. All rooms at the luxurious Isandlwana Lodge have spectacular views of the battlefield. Attention to detail is evident throughout this 'African' themed lodge, from its magnificent yet unimposing

The Battle of Blood River

The Battle of Blood River occurred on 16 December 1838 when a small party of Voortrekkers avenged the massacre by the Zulus of Piet Retief's party. The Voortrekkers defeated 12,000 Zulu warriors, killing 3000 while sustaining only a few casualties themselves. This battle is a seminal event in Afrikaner history. The victory came to be seen as the fulfilment of God's side of the bargain and seemed to prove that the Boers had a divine mandate to conquer and 'civilise' Southern Africa, and that they were in fact a chosen people.

However, Afrikaner nationalism and the significance attached to Blood River simultaneously grew in strength and it has been argued (by Leach in *The Afrikaners – Their Last Great Trek* and others) that the importance of Blood River was deliberately heightened and manipulated for political ends. The standard interpretation of the victory meshed with the former apartheid regime's world view: hordes of untrustworthy black savages were beaten by Boers who were on an Old Testament–style mission from God.

exterior to its beautifully decorated rooms. Gourmet meals are served in its elegant dining room where evening meals are sometimes followed by traditional singing performed by the Zulu staff. The lodge's resident historian, Rob Gerrard, runs personal tours of the battlefields from R200 per person.

Getting There & Away

The battle sites are south-east of Dundee. Isandlwana is about 70km from Dundee, off the R66; Rorke's Drift is 42km from Dundee, accessible from the R66 or R33 (the R33 turn-off is 13km south of Dundee). The road to Isandlwana is sealed but the roads to Rorke's Drift and Fugitive's Drift can be dusty and rough.

BLOOD RIVER MONUMENT

The Blood River battle site is marked by a full-scale bronze recreation of the 64-wagon laager. The cairn of stones was built by the Boers after the battle to mark the centre of their laager. The monument and the nearby **Blood River Museum** (*☎/fax 632 1695; admission R10; open 8am-5pm daily*) are 20km south-east of the R33; the turn-off is 27km from Dundee and 45km from Vryheid. There's a small cafe there.

The rationale behind this place is so utterly politically incorrect that it's almost worth a visit for that reason alone. And the village kids, kept out by a high fence, certainly want you to visit so they can sell you handicrafts.

Interestingly, the **Ncome Museum** (*☎ 082-639 6684; admission by donation; open 8am-4.30pm daily*) has opened on the other side of the river. The museum, shaped like the famous Zulu horn battle formation, offers a 'reinterpretation' of the battle and provides a good insight into Zulu culture.

Mpumalanga

Mpumalanga, meaning 'Place of the Rising Sun', was once part of the larger Transvaal province (and was later part of Eastern Transvaal).

There's a lot to do in this often overlooked province. There are some of Southern Africa's best hiking, horse riding and mountain-biking trails in the vicinity of the Klein Drakensberg escarpment; picturesque and historic towns such as Pilgrim's Rest, Sabie, Graskop and Barberton; and the spectacular Blyde River Canyon. For information on the world-famous Kruger National Park, which is bordered by private game reserves, see the Kruger National Park chapter.

Get a copy of *Mpumalanga Tourist & Route Street Atlas* (R50) which has good town maps and accommodation information.

The Eastern Lowveld

To the north the lowveld (low-altitude grassland) is dry and hot, particularly in summer, when there are storms and high humidity. Further south the temperatures moderate and the scrubby terrain gives way to lush subtropical vegetation around Nelspruit and the Crocodile River. South, near Barberton, the dry country resumes with a vengeance – gold prospectors last century dubbed the area the 'Valley of Death'.

NELSPRUIT
☎ 013 • postcode 1201
Nelspruit, in the Crocodile River Valley, is the largest town in Mpumalanga's steamy subtropical lowveld. Once a bit of a sleepy hollow, the provincial capital now has a reasonable selection of accommodation, pubs and restaurants. The town is the centre of an important citrus-fruit region, and is the last major stop before Kruger, making it popular with tourists.

Highlights

- Drive the spectacular route around Blyde River Canyon from Graskop, or just enjoy the awesome view from God's Window, where the canyon floor drops a sheer 1000m.
- Peer over the cliffs of the Klein Drakensberg escarpment.
- Relax at Pilgrim's Rest – once a gold mining town, now a national monument.
- Raft the Blyde and Sabie Rivers in the morning, abseil surrounding cliffs in the afternoon.

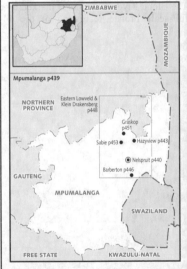

Orientation & Information
The Promenade Centre is a large shopping complex. Greyhound, Translux and Intercape buses stop in front of the Promenade Centre.

As in a lot of South African towns and cities, businesses here are moving into the

MPUMALANGA

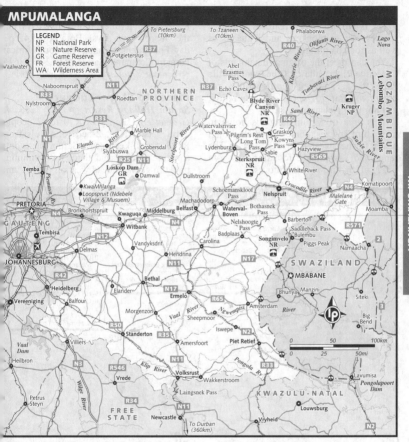

LEGEND

NP	National Park
NR	Nature Reserve
GR	Game Reserve
FR	Forest Reserve
WA	Wilderness Area

suburban shopping malls. The huge River-side Mall is 5km north of town on the White River road.

The helpful **Nelspruit Publicity Association** *(☎ 755 1988, fax 755 1350, Cnr N4 & Nel St; open 8am-4.30pm Mon-Fri, 9am-5pm Sat, 10am-2pm Sun)* has recently been downsized and is located in the municipal buildings.

Other useful places include the **Welcomp Computer Internet Café** *(☎ 741 2303, Son-park Centre; open daily)*, which charges R18 per hour; the Standard and ABSA banks on Brown St; the Nel Forum Medical Centre on the corner of Rothery and Nel Sts; and **Lowveld Promotions** *(☎ 752 5134, ✉ lprom@global.co.za, Sanlam Centre, Louis Trichardt St)*, which can book travel arrangements including buses.

Things to See & Do
The 150-hectare **National Lowveld Botanic Gardens** *(☎ 752 5531; adult/child R5/2; open 8am-6pm daily)* are on the banks of the Crocodile River. Take the R537 from Nelspruit, then the R37 to get here. There are formal gardens, baobabs, and indigenous forest encompassing cycads, ferns and aloes.

The **Sonheuwel Nature Reserve** (☎ 759 9111; admission free) features antelope species, vervet monkeys and leguaans as well as rock paintings.

You can meet the original inhabitants of Crocodile River Valley at **Croc River Reptile Park** (☎ 752 5511, e reptile@pix.co.za; adult/child R30/15; open 9am-5pm daily), just north of Nelspruit.

This area of Mpumalanga is home to many bird species, some of which do not occur further west in South Africa. The renowned **Lawson's Bird Safaris** (☎ 744 9371) offers bird-watching tours.

There are two **hiking trails** in the area, the Kaapschehoop (three, four or five days) and the Uitsoek (two days). Both cost R42 per day. For bookings, contact the **South African Forestry Company** (Safcol; ☎ 012-481 3615 e ecotour@mail.safcol.co.za) in Pretoria.

Places to Stay – Budget

Safubi Holiday Resort (☎ 741 3253, 4. Graniet St) Camp sites R70 for 2 people extra person R10, 2-bed rondavels from R225. A well-kept resort, Safubi backs ontc a nature reserve and there's a swimming pool. To get here head west on the N4, and

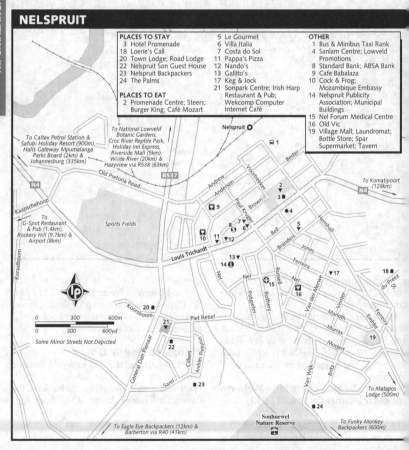

NELSPRUIT

PLACES TO STAY	PLACES TO EAT	OTHER
3 Hotel Promenade	5 Le Gourmet	1 Bus & Minibus Taxi Rank
18 Loerie's Call	6 Villa Italia	4 Sanlam Centre; Lowveld
20 Town Lodge; Road Lodge	7 Costa do Sol	Promotions
22 Nelspruit Son Guest House	11 Pappa's Pizza	8 Standard Bank; ABSA Bank
23 Nelspruit Backpackers	12 Nando's	9 Cafe Babalaza
24 The Palms	13 Gallito's	10 Cock & Frog;
	17 Keg & Jock	Mozambique Embassy
PLACES TO EAT	21 Sonpark Centre; Irish Harp	14 Nelspruit Publicity
2 Promenade Centre; Steers;	Restaurant & Pub;	Association; Municipal
Burger King; Café Mozart	Wekcomp Computer	Buildings
	Internet Café	15 Nel Forum Medical Centre
		16 Old Vic
		19 Village Mall; Laundromat;
		Bottle Store; Spar
		Supermarket; Tavern

To Caltex Petrol Station & Safubi Holiday Resort (900m), Halls Gateway Mpumalanga Parks Board (2km) & Johannesburg (335km)

To National Lowveld Botanic Gardens, Croc River Reptile Park, Holiday Inn Express, Riverside Mall (5km), White River (20km) & Hazyview via R538 (63km)

Nelspruit O

To Komatipoort (128km)

Old Pretoria Road

R537

To G-Spot Restaurant & Pub (1.4km), Rockery Hill (9.7km) & Airport (8km)

Sports Fields

Louis Trichardt

Some Minor Streets Not Depicted

0   300   600m
0   300   600yd

To Eagle Eye Backpackers (12km) & Barberton via R40 (41km)

Sonhuewel Nature Reserve

To Matapos Lodge (500m)

To Funky Monkey Backpackers (600m)

MPUMALANGA

turn left at Graniet St (at the Caltex petrol station). It's 1km further on.

Funky Monkey Backpackers (☎ *083-310 4755, fax 752 5920, 102 Van Wijk St)* Camping R25, dorm beds/doubles R45/110. Funky Monkey is in a spacious house; there's a pool table, a swimming pool and braai (barbecue) facilities. The owners know a lot about the region, and where to find the swinging nightspots in town. Pick-up from the bus terminal is available.

Nelspruit Backpackers (☎ *741 2237,* [e] *nelback@hotmail.com, 9 Andries Pretorius St)* Camping R30, dorm beds/doubles R50/120. Another good option, with a laidback atmosphere, it's equipped with a kitchenette, a bar, a pool and a pool table and backs onto a nature reserve.

Rockery Hill (☎ *741 5011)* Dorm beds R40, cottages R120 for 2 people, each extra person R40 (up to 6 people). This place, 1km out of town, is very rustic. It has no electricity but there is gas hot water. To get here, turn right off Kaapschehoop Rd at the Lughawe turn-off, just past the G-Spot Restaurant & Pub, go past the airport, turn right at the T-junction and it's the first farm on the left.

Nelspruit Son Guest House (☎ *741 2253,* [e] *ghoeks@iafrica.com, 7 De Villiers St)* Dorm beds/doubles R45/150. At the back of the Sonpark Centre, this guesthouse has a range of comfortable, clean accommodation slightly classier than the backpackers; it's less of a party environment.

Eagle Eye Backpackers (☎ *750 1073,* [e] *andre@lowveldinfo.com)* B&B rondavels R70 per person. We've heard good things about this lodging. It's on an organic farm and visitors have the chance to work on the property. To get here take the R40 towards Barberton and after 9km turn right, go for 1.5km, turn left, go a further 1km and it's on your left.

Places to Stay – Mid-Range
For details about the numerous B&Bs in the area contact the Nelspruit information office.

Matapos Lodge (☎ *753 3549,* [e] *matopo@ nweb.co.za, 14 Sheppard Ave)* Doubles

R295. Matapos Lodge, 'for culture-vultures and art-varks', is in a secluded spot.

The Palms (☎*/fax 755 4374, 25 Van Wijk St)* B&B R140 per person. This place has a swimming pool and is under new, friendly management.

Loerie's Call (☎ *752 4844, fax 744 0548,* [e] *info@loeriescall.co.za, 2 du Preez St)* Double R190. A classy, well-presented, popular guesthouse; bookings are advised.

Town Lodge (☎ *741 1444, fax 741 2258, Cnr General Dan Pienaar Rd & Koorsboom St)* Singles/doubles R260/300. Downmarket from the City Lodge, and a little cheaper, it's part of the same 'chain' of hotels. Breakfast is R32.

Road Lodge(☎ *741 1805, fax 741 4850)* Rooms R180. Next door to the Town Lodge, this utilitarian place is devoid of character, but is cheaper again, making it a good-value overnight stop.

Holiday Inn Express (☎ *011-482 3500)* Doubles B&B R299. The inn is near Riverside Mall, on the road to White River. Rooms have TV and telephone and there's a swimming pool.

Hotel Promenade (☎ *753 3000, fax 752 5533,* [e] *hotprom@global.co.za)* Rooms R250. A very pleasant hotel in the old town hall (in the Promenade Centre) in the middle of town. Weekend specials are available.

Places to Eat
In the Promenade Centre, **Steers** and **Burger King** have their usual crop of burgers and ready-to-go meals. **Nando's** and **Pappa's Pizza**, south-west of the centre, are both reliable. **Gallito's**, a Nando's lookalike, is nearby.

Cafe Mozart (☎ *752 2637, Promenade Centre)* Breakfast R21-26. This is a local favourite that offers quality meals. The food is healthier here than in most South African eateries.

The Riverside Mall is a one-stop place where there's plenty of choice. Most chain 'fasties' are represented and there are a number of good coffee houses.

Caffe Rossini (☎ *757 0291, Riverside Mall)* Mug of coffee R8-10, gourmet sandwiches R24-34. This place has great coffees, including a 'choccolaccino' – not for the caffeine purist.

Mediterranean Seafood Restaurant (☎ 757 0170, Riverside Mall) Mains R35-80. A good spot for seafood lovers; the curry is worth trying (R40).

Villa Italia (☎ 752 5780, Cnr Louis Trichardt & Paul Kruger Sts) Starters R20, mains R35-55. Open daily. This place is popular with the young set for delectable pasta.

Costa do Sol (☎ 752 6382, Cnr Louis Trichardt & Paul Kruger Sts) Line fish R39, 12 large prawns R68. Open Mon-Sat. This quaint little Portuguese place is in the same building as Villa Italia.

Irish Harp Restaurant & Pub (☎ 741 3580, Sonpark Centre) Starters R13-18, mains R25-50. Opposite the Town Lodge, this is supposed to be a 'real' Irish pub – where's the Murphys? If you like your food deep-fried you'll enjoy eating here.

Keg & Jock (☎ 755 4969, Ferriera St) Starters R15-25, mains R25-50. Open daily. Some of the best pub meals in town are available here, with a particularly interesting selection of salads.

G-Spot Restaurant & Pub (☎ 083-254 5037, Kaapschehoop Rd) Open from 11am daily. This is *the* place in town for a prawn feast – it is simply superb and no one goes away disappointed. The prices, like the prawns, are seasonal.

Le Gourmet (☎ 755 1941, Branders St) Mains from R40. A French restaurant specialising in game dishes, it's worth splashing out here.

Entertainment
Cafe Babalaza (☎ 083-310 4755, Cnr De Waal & Anderson Sts) is a new place run by the owners of Funky Monkey Backpackers. An African-theme bar, it regularly has local musos blasting out jazz, funk and African fusion.

If you're up for beers, a game of pool and a few laughs, you'll have a good chance of meeting locals and other travellers at the *Old Vic* (☎ 755 3350, Nel St).

A bit further up the road is a new place, the *Cock & Frog* nightclub; it wasn't open when we were in town.

Getting There & Away
Air The airport is 8km south of town or Kaapschehoop Rd. There are daily flights with **SA Airlink** (☎ 741 3536) to Jo'burg (R638, 7-day advance) and Durban (R844). **Mozambique Airlines** (LAM; ☎ 011-622 4889) has flights to Maputo in Mozambique (R820 one way), via Jo'burg.

Bus Intercape runs a daily return service between Jo'burg (and Pretoria) and Maputo (in Mozambique). From Nelspruit, destinations and one-way fares include Maputo (R120) and Jo'burg (R135). From Jo'burg to Maputo costs R185. The bus company **Panthera Azul** (☎ 011-337 7430) stops outside the Promenade Centre on its Jo'burg-Maputo run.

Greyhound (☎ 753 2100) has a daily service to Jo'burg and Pretoria for R120, departing from the Promenade Centre at 8am.

Lux Liner (☎ 0800-003537) runs from Jo'burg airport to Hazyview, via Nelspruit. The fare from Nelspruit to Hazyview is R95.

Train The *Komati* (☎ 011-773 2944) runs between Jo'burg and Komatipoort via Nelspruit daily; you need to carry out immigration formalities at Lebombo and Ressano Garcia (Mozambique) first before catching the connecting shuttle to Maputo. The fare from Jo'burg to Komatipoort is R110/160 in 2nd/1st; Komatipoort to Maputo is R28/35.

Minibus Taxi The large, well-organised local bus and minibus taxi stop is in the car park behind the Nelspruit Plaza, on the corner of Bester and Henshall Sts. Minibus taxi destinations and fares include White River (R5), Barberton (R10), Sabie (R15), Hazyview (R16), Graskop (R35), Komatipoort (R40) and Jo'burg (R75).

The **City Bug** (☎ 741 4114) operates in town; the cost door-to-door is R12.

Car Rental Avis (☎ 741 1087), **Budget** (☎ 741 3871), **Europcar** (☎ 741 3062) and **Imperial** (☎ 741 2834) have offices at the airport. Or try **National Car Rental** (☎ 75. 4335) where a small car will cost R160 pe day for four to six days, including 250km free per day, but excluding insurance.

WHITE RIVER

☎ 013 • postcode 1240

White River (Witrivier) is a little higher and less humid than nearby Nelspruit. It's a green, pleasant little town with a colonial feel. The town is the self-styled 'nut capital of South Africa' and in **Nutcracker Valley**, just south of the town off the R40, you can visit some plantations.

The **tourist office** (☎ 750 1073) is on the R40 at the Casterbridge Centre, on the way to Hazyview.

Hardy Ventures (☎ 751 1693, ⓔ hven ture@iafrica.com) organises rafting trips on the Sabie, Olifants and Blyde Rivers.

Lalela (☎/fax 751 2812, ⓔ hawk@yebo .co.za, SS Ranch, Plaston Rd) Dorms/tepees R40/50, doubles R120. Set on a farm, accommodation here is in Indian 'tepees' or in the farmhouse. There are windsurfers and a sailboat for guests' use. Pick-up from Nelspruit is available and lifts to Swaziland can be organised.

Karula Hotel (☎ 751 2277, fax 750 0413, Old Plaston Rd – Route 538) Singles/doubles B&B from R170/260. Karula is on Route 538, but here the road is more reminiscent of an English country lane than a South African road. The hotel is pleasant enough, has a new luxury wing and is set in spacious grounds.

Bag-dad Cafe (☎ 751 1777) Lunch R20-35, dinner R35-50. This is a delightful bar and restaurant attached to a craft shop. It's on the R40, opposite the tourist information office.

HAZYVIEW

☎ 013 • postcode 1242

Hazyview is a small village with large shopping centres. Kruger Park's Numbi and Paul Kruger gates are nearby (15km and 47km away, respectively). Hazyview is near the junction of the R535 (which runs down the escarpment from Graskop), the R536 from Sabie and the R538 from White River.

The staff at the **Hazyview Tourism Association** (☎ 737 7414, fax 737 7415; open 9am-6pm Mon-Fri, 8.30am-1pm Sat), in the

HAZYVIEW

1 Shangana Cultural Village
2 Thembi
3 Casa do Sol
4 Mpumalanga Lounge
5 Petrol Station
6 Minibus Taxis
7 Hazyview Tourism Association; Haznet Internet Café; Simunye Shopping Centre; Pick 'n Pay
8 Shopping Centre; Police; KFC
9 Shopping Centre; Spar; ABSA Bank; King Pie
10 Hysterical Hornbills
11 Hotel Numbi; Pioneer Grill
12 Rissington Inn
13 Total Petrol Station
14 Thulamela
15 Kanaan
16 Kruger Park Backpackers
17 Big 5 Backpackers

Pick 'n' Pay Centre next to the Simunye Shopping Centre, are very helpful.

You can get wired at Haznet Internet Café in the Pick 'n' Pay Centre (behind Fotofirst). Connections cost R30 per hour.

There are banks, takeaway outlets and supermarkets near the four-way stop.

Shangana Cultural Village

This village (☎ 737 7007, Ⓦ www.shangana .co.za, Graskop Rd) is 5km north of Hazyview. In the shade of chestnut trees, it has been carefully and sympathetically arranged so that visitors can get a feel for Shangana culture. Short educational trips cost R65, midday visits with traditional meal are R115, and the evening program with full dinner costs R160.

At various times of the day visitors can see a vibrant market, farming activity, house building, displays of uniforms and weaponry of the *masocho* (warriors), the relation of customs and history by a sangoma (witch doctor or herbalist), cooking, singing, dancing, and the imbibing of *byala* (traditional beer).

Places to Stay

Big 5 Backpackers (☎ 082-645 8248) Dorm beds R45, rooms R60 per person. This place is 3km up the hill from the junction of the R40 and the R538. Water reservoirs have been converted into bomas (enclosures) where guests can cook or rest; above these is a 'contemplation' area from which you can see distant Kruger. There's also a pool for relief during those lowveld 'scorchers'.

Kruger Park Backpackers (☎ 737 7224, e krugback@mweb.co.za) Camp sites R25, dorm beds R50, Zulu-style huts R60 per person. The hostel is about 2km south of the four-way stop, just past the White River turn-off. It offers loads of activities, including trips to Kruger.

Thika Tika Guest Farm (☎ 737 8108) Dorm beds/doubles R50/160, chalets R110 per person (up to 4 people). Thika has great backpacker accommodation with dorms that have an adjoining lounge. There's a huge outdoor area in front of the property. The double-storey chalets set on a river with private braai areas are well worth the extra rands.

Kanaan (☎/fax 737 7460) Chalets R75 per person. This place has great-value fully self-contained chalets on an attractive property. Each chalets contains two, four or six beds. The place is much cheaper than most in the area, and also has some backpacker rooms (R50). Kanaan is on the R40, close to the junction with Route 538

There are many B&Bs around Hazyview. The tourism association has a full list.

Rissington Inn (☎ 737 7700, fax 737 7112, e rissington@mweb.co.za) Rooms from R195 per person. Rissington has a restaurant, a pool and very comfortable rooms.

Thulamela (☎ 737 7171, e info@thulamela.co.za) Rooms R280 per person. In a bush setting, 13km from Kruger, Thulamela is very reasonable for what you get. There are majestic views and free-roaming wildlife in the area. Unfortunately, no chil-

dren are allowed. To get here, take the turn-off to Umbhaba from the R40.

Hotel Numbi (☎ 737 7301, fax 737 7525, e hotelnumbi@worldonline.co.za) Camp sites R60 for 2 people, single/double bungalows R250/420, B&B R295/470. In spacious grounds with a swimming pool, this place is not far south of the four-way stop.

Casa do Sol (☎ 737 8111, fax 737 8166, e casa_do@soft.co.za, Route 536 to Sabie) Double rooms R880, villas R1060. A Spanish-style villa, this place revels in its sheer luxury. There are some great walks in the nature reserve here.

Places to Eat & Drink

Pioneer Grill (☎ 737 7301) Starters R15-20, mains R25-50. Hotel Numbi's grill has a good selection including roquefort rump. Cheap pub food is available too (potato skins R13).

Thembi (☎ 737 7729) Starters R15-20, mains R40-70. This a la carte restaurant is near the junction of the R535 and the R40. It's a cosy little eatery with a bar. Friday is pub night – no food, just plenty of beer.

Hysterical Hornbills (☎ 737 7404) Starters R15-20, light meals R20, mains R35-60. Open daily. Hornbills is a pub and restaurant serving decent fare. The scrumptious seafood specialities include chilled prawn tails. It also has a couple of good veg dishes.

Mpumalanga Lounge is not for the faint-hearted. You'll enjoy rowdy conversation here with local blacks. It's behind the Pick'n Pay.

Getting There & Away

City to City's daily Jo'burg-Acornhoek bus service (8am) stops at Hazyview; the fare from Jo'burg is R60. The backpacker accommodation places can pick guests up from the Baz Bus in Nelspruit; expect to be charged for the transfer.

Lux Liner (☎ 0800-003537) runs from Jo'burg airport to Hazyview, via Nelspruit The fare from Nelspruit to Hazyview is R95.

A minibus to Nelspruit costs R15; to Sabie it costs R12.

MALELANE
☎ 013 • postcode 1320

Malelane, on the banks of the Crocodile River, is on the border of Kruger National Park. It's a modern town with a distinctive wagon-wheel layout, surrounded by sugarcane fields.

Mthethomusha Game Reserve (☎ 764 114) is jointly administered by the Mphakni tribe and the Conservation Corporation. It adjoins Kruger.

Bongani Lodge (☎ 011-809 4300) DB&B US$115 per person. This exceptional place is the centrepiece of the Mthethomusha Game Reserve. Few places have a better setting and very few can boast such a diversity of wildlife on their doorstep.

River Cottage (☎ 790 0825, fax 790 281) 2-bed cottages without/with breakfast R260/300. Set on the Crocodile River, this is a well-tended place with friendly owners and good views over the river. Your chances of seeing hippos are high here as the owners grow special grass at the river's edge to attract them.

MARLOTH PARK
☎ 013

Marloth Park describes itself as a 'wild township' – it's a rather peculiar place. Wildlife, including zebras, lions, impalas, wildebeests, baboons, warthogs and giraffes, wanders around the streets in between residential homes, which are set in lowveld bush. The road system is mainly gravel, in good condition, and if you drive around the streets you'll probably spot a giraffe munching on a tree in someone's front yard.

Marloth overlooks the Crocodile River between Malelane and Komatipoort and here is a supermarket, a petrol station and pub inside the park.

Marloth Park (☎ 790 4604) Camp sites R70, rondavels R145, 4-bed chalets R175. This place is well presented and an absolute bargain, especially if there's a group of you. It overlooks the river and you've a good chance of seeing hippos and crocodiles. Don't leave any food outside as cheeky vervet monkeys run riot through the place. Rondavels have share kitchen and

braai facilities, while the chalets are larger and self-contained. For both you need a sleeping bag or bedding.

Wildlife Outing Hostel (☎ 790 4891, 083-724 5426) Beds R55 per person. Wildlife Outing is the first house on the left after the entrance gate to Marloth. It's a large house which uses a couple of rooms for guests. You can get a bunk or a double bed. Meals are provided on request and it's possible to book wildlife-viewing drives here. The Baz Bus can drop you on the doorstep.

KOMATIPOORT
☎ 013 • postcode 1340

This border town is at the foot of the Lebombo Mountains, near the confluence of the Komati and Crocodile Rivers. It is only 10km away from the Crocodile Bridge into Kruger. Komatipoort is also close to the Mozambique border and the Mananga border post in the north of Swaziland.

A craft shop called **Duve** (☎ 790 7559, 79 Rissik St) provides tourist information.

Places to Stay & Eat
Komati Lodge (☎ 790 8330, Skool St) Singles/doubles R100/170. The cheapest option in town, it doesn't win any awards for presentation or ambience, but then it probably doesn't want to.

Komati River Chalets (☎ 790 7623) 2-person cottages R260. Not far from the Border Country Inn, this place is good value and very comfortable. Tiger fishing (fishing for tiger fish) is possible in season and there's a pub here.

Border Country Inn (☎ 790 7328, fax 790 7100, N4) Singles/doubles B&B R250/330. This inn is close to both the Mozambique border post and Kruger.

Tambarina Restaurant (☎ 790 7057, Rissik St) Starters R10-15, mains R30-40. Before you cross into Mozambique, have a prawn feast at this friendly place (curry prawns R35).

Getting There & Away
The road journey to Maputo has become much quicker with the extension of the N4. The 'Maputo corridor' running from Jo'burg

to Maputo is now complete. The trip from Komatipoort to Maputo takes about one hour by car.

Minibus taxis leave from Rissik St and regularly do the run between Komatipoort and Maputo for around R45.

BARBERTON

☎ 013 • postcode 1300

Barberton is a quiet but alluring town in harsh but interesting lowveld country 45km south of Nelspruit. It was something of a boom town during gold rushes last century and was home to South Africa's first stock exchange. However, most miners soon moved on to the newly discovered Rand fields near Jo'burg. Today, all working gold mines in the region are over 100 years old.

The big township outside Barberton is **Emjindini**.

The **information centre** (☎ *712 2121,* e *barinfo@netactive.co.za, Market Square, Crown St; open 8am-1pm & 2pm-4.30pm* *Mon-Fri, 8.30am-noon Sat)* is extremely well organised. Ask about day hikes in the area here.

Things to See & Do

There are several restored houses in town. **Belhaven House** *(Lee St; adult/child R8/4 open Mon-Fri)* is a middle-class home built at the turn of the century and is open for inspection. **Stopforth House** *(Bowness St open Mon-Fri)* is a typical middle-class home dating from the diggers' period (the 1890s). A ticket to Belhaven also admits you to Stopforth House. **Fernlea House** *(Lee St open 8.30am-4pm Mon-Fri)* has temporary exhibits.

Barberton has a modern **museum** (☎ *71. 4281, Pilgrim St; admission free; open 9am-4pm daily)*. In between Lee and Judge Sts is an iron and wood blockhouse from the Anglo-Boer War, part of the chain built by the British when the war entered its guerrilla phase.

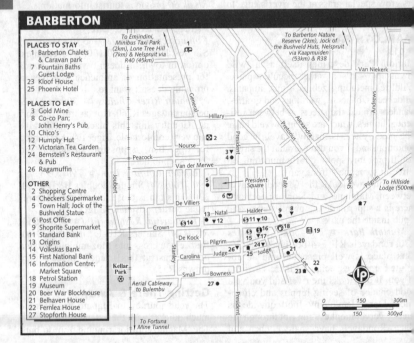

BARBERTON

PLACES TO STAY
1 Barberton Chalets & Caravan park
7 Fountain Baths Guest Lodge
23 Kloof House
25 Phoenix Hotel

PLACES TO EAT
3 Gold Mine
8 Co-co Pan; John Henry's Pub
10 Chico's
12 Humpty Hut
17 Victorian Tea Garden
24 Bernstein's Restaurant & Pub
26 Ragamuffin

OTHER
2 Shopping Centre
4 Checkers Supermarket
5 Town Hall; Jock of the Bushveld Statue
6 Post Office
9 Shoprite Supermarket
11 Standard Bank
13 Origins
14 Volkskas Bank
15 First National Bank
16 Information Centre; Market Square
18 Petrol Station
19 Museum
20 Boer War Blockhouse
21 Belhaven House
22 Fernlea House
27 Stopforth House

To Emjindini, Minibus Taxi Park (2km), Lone Tree Hill (7km) & Nelspruit via R40 (45km)

To Barberton Nature Reserve (2km), Jock of the Bushveld Huts, Nelspruit via Kaapmuiden (53km) & R38

Van Niekerk

Central

Hillary

Pretorius

Alexandra

Andrews

Sheba

Pilgrim

To Hillside Lodge (500m)

Nourse

President

Peacock

Van der Merwe

Tate

President Square

De Villiers

Joubert

Natal

Halder

Crown

De Kock

Pilgrim

Carolina

Judge

Judge

Lee

Stanley

Kellar Park

Small

Bowness

Aerial Cableway to Bulembu

To Fortuna Mine Tunnel

President

0   150   300m
0   150   300yd

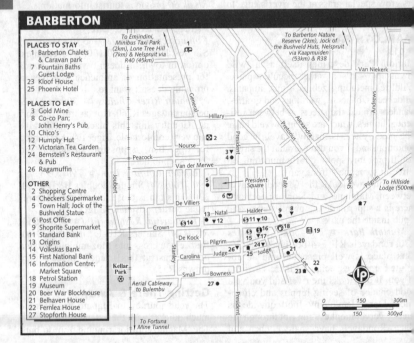

The 20.3km **aerial cableway**, purported to be the longest industrial cableway in the world, brings asbestos down from a mine in Swaziland. Coal is carried in the other direction to provide counterweight.

Origins (☎ *712 5055, General St; tours 9am; R130)* runs a number of tours including a Eureka City Ghost Town tour of the old Barberton gold mines. Lunch is included and the tour takes in some spectacular scenery, as well as giving an insight into the life of early pioneers who mined completely by hand. Origins also has an interesting African arts and crafts store.

Places to Stay

Barberton Chalets & Caravan Park (☎/fax 712 3323, General St) Camp sites R40 for up to 3 people, R10 for each extra person, chalets R200 for 2 people or R370 for 6 people. The caravan park is close to the centre of town and has plenty of shade and grassed areas.

Fountain Baths Guest Lodge (☎ 712 2707, fax 712 3361, 48 Pilgrim St) Self-contained doubles without/with bathroom R170/240. This lodge is at the southern end of the street where it resumes after merging into Sheba Rd (Crown St). Built in 1885, it used to be Barberton's public pool, and is the best value accommodation in town.

Jock of the Bushveld Huts (☎ 712 4002, fax 712 5915, Nelspruit Rd) Single rooms R75, double chalets R250. On a mango farm, Jock is just off the road between Barberton and Nelspruit. It has a pool and offers horse riding. Microlighting (flying in an ultra-light aircraft) costs R100 per 15 minutes.

Kloof House (☎ 712 4268, 1 Kloof St) B&B R130 per person. This place is nestled under the Mkhonjwe Mountains.

Hillside Lodge (☎/fax 712 4466, 62 Pilgrim St) B&B R120 per person. The lodge is a friendly guesthouse with magnificent views, a pool and a lovely garden.

Phoenix Hotel (☎ 712 4211, fax 712 4741, Cnr Pilgrim & President Sts) Singles/doubles B&B R160/280. A clean, old-style country pub, the hotel has a bar, a tea garden and a pleasant dining room.

Places to Eat & Drink

Humpy Hut and *Chico's*, in Crown St, are good takeaway places.

Gold Mine (☎ 712 4373, President St) Bar lunch R25, mains R35-50. Open 6pm-9.30pm Mon & Sat, noon-9.30pm Tues-Fri. Next to Checkers supermarket, this place covers most tastes.

Co-co Pan (☎ 712 2653, Crown St) Starters R10-15, mains R30-45. Opposite the museum, this is a casual place serving a variety of basic dishes, including burgers, salads and seafood. Entry is through a small general shop. *John Henry's Pub* is attached.

Victorian Tea Garden (☎ 712 4985,) Light meals R25. A great spot to relax and watch the passing parade, the Victorian Tea Garden is between Pilgrim and Crown Sts.

Ragamuffin (☎ 712 6735, 18 Pilgrim St) Starters R15-18, mains R30-40. In the historic old Globe Tavern, this is both a tea garden and a boutique shop. The coffee here is good (R6).

Bernstein's Restaurant & Pub (☎ 712 4722, 22 Pilgrim St) Starters R11-16, mains R25-45. Open for lunch & dinner Tues-Sat. Bernstein's is on the first floor of an historic building and has a smallish menu and enthusiastic service. There is also a pub here.

Getting There & Away

The scenic road from Barberton to Swaziland via the Josefdal and Bulembu border posts is unsealed and rough; allow two hours. Don't attempt it in a 2WD in bad weather. There's a check post at the Bulembu mine.

There is a local bus to Nelspruit at 5am, 6.30am and 7am daily for R5.50.

There's a small minibus taxi park by Emjindini, 3km from town on the Nelspruit road, or you can get a taxi in town. The fare to Nelspruit is R10; to Badplaas it is R17.

AROUND BARBERTON
Lone Tree Hill

About 7km from town, Lone Tree Hill is a prime paragliding launch site. Contact **Mpumalanga Paragliding Clubs** (☎ *013-712 3111)*. Advice about keys and access is provided by **Hi Tech Security** (☎ *792 6088)*. A deposit of about R50 is required.

MPUMALANGA

MPUMALANGA

EASTERN LOWVELD & KLEIN DRAKENSBERG

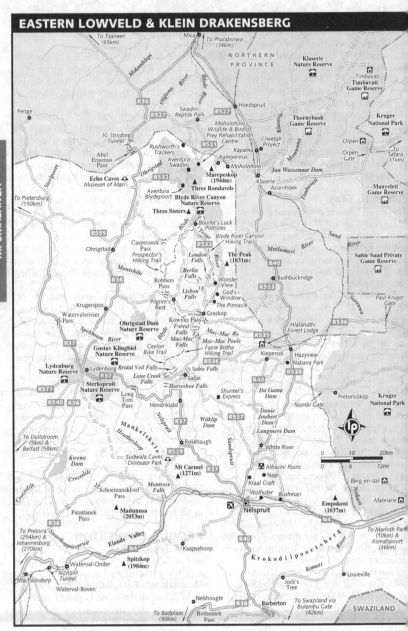

To Tzaneen (65km)

Mica

To Phalaborwa (34km)

NORTHERN PROVINCE

Klaserie Nature Reserve

Timbavati Game Reserve

Kruger National Park

Molomklopi

Oliphants River

Blyde River

R36

R527

Swadini Reptile Park

Hoedspruit

Klaserie

Thornybush Game Reserve

Manwana

Orpen

Orpen Gate

To Satara (31km)

Penge

JG Strijdom Tunnel

Abel Erasmus Pass

R527

R531

Rushworth's Trackers

Moholoholo Wildlife & Bird of Prey Rehabilitation Centre

Cheetah Project

Kapama

Kampersrus

Moholoholo

Jan Wassenaar Dam

Manveleti Game Reserve

Steelpoort

R532

Echo Caves
Museum of Man

Ohrigstad

Aventura Swadini

Marepeskop (1944m)

Three Rondavels

Klaserie

Acornhoek

To Pietersburg (150km)

Aventura Blydeepoort

Blyde River Canyon Nature Reserve

Three Sisters

Bourke's Luck Potholes

Blyde River Canyon Hiking Trail

Sand River

Ohrigstad

R555

Caspersnek Pass
Prospector's Hiking Trail

Mantshibi

London Falls

Berlin Falls

The Peak (1831m)

Mutlumuvi River

R40

Sabie Sand Private Game Reserve

Sareting

Paul Kruger Gate

Bushbuckridge

R36

Robbers Pass

Lisbon Falls

Blyde River

Wonder View

God's Window

The Pinnacle

R533

Krugerspos

Watervalsrivier Pass

Pilgrim's Rest

Graskop

Hlalanathi Forest Lodge

R536

Speekboom River

Ohrigstad Dam Nature Reserve

Kowyns Pass

Blyde

Forest Falls

Mac-Mac Rv

Mac-Mac Pools

Fanie Botha Hiking Trail

R535

Kiepersol

Hazyview

Nabana Park

R37

Gustav Klingbiel Nature Reserve

Ceylon Bike Trail

Mac-Mac Falls

R538

Lydenburg Nature Reserve

Lydenburg

Bridal Veil Falls

Sabie Falls

R536

Sabie

Da Gama Dam

R40

Pretoriuskop

Kruger National Park

R577

Sterkspruit Nature Reserve

Lone Creek Falls

Horseshoe Falls

Shunter's Express

Numbi Gate

R540 R36

Long Tom Pass

Hendriksdal

Danie Joubert Dam

Longmere Dam

Mankelekele

Houtbosloop

Witklip Dam

R37

R537

To Dullstroom (5km) & Belfast (58km)

Kwena Dam

Crocodile

R539

Rosehaugh

White River

Napi

Albasini Ruins

Kraal Craft

Berg-en-dal

Sudwala Caves Dinosaur Park

Mt Carmel (1271m)

R37

Schoemanskloof Pass

Montrose Falls

Wolhuter

Bushman

Empakeni (1037m)

Malelane

To Pretoria (254km) & Johannesburg (270km)

R36

Swartkoppiespruit

Patattanek Pass

Madunusa (2053m)

Elands Valley

N4

Kaapsehoop

Krokodilpoortsberg

Nelspruit

N4

To Marloth Park (10km) & Komatipoort (36km)

Waterval-Onder

NZASM Tunnel

Spitzkop (1984m)

Machadodorp

Waterval-Boven

Jock's Tree

Louieville

To Badplaas (30km)

Nelshoogte

R38

Bothasnek Pass

Barberton

To Swaziland via Bulembu Gate (42km)

SWAZILAND

0 10 20km

0 6 12mi

Songimvelo Game Reserve

This reserve is a spectacular 56,000-hectare area in harsh lowveld country south of Barberton, with some highveld (high-altitude grassland) on the eastern side, which runs along the mountainous Swaziland border. The lack of threatening predators in the reserve means that walking and horse riding are popular activities; there are, however, elephants and white rhinos.

There are still big plans for this wilderness region – we can only hope it is developed sympathetically without the ruination of one of South Africa's most pristine regions.

Komati River Chalets (☎ 013-790 7623, fax 755 3928) Single/double chalets R187.50/260. These chalets are fully self-contained. There is fishing in the Komati River.

BADPLAAS

☎ 017 • postcode 1190

Pleasant sulphur springs and the dramatic Hlumuhlumu Mountains as a backdrop make Badplaas worth a visit.

Aventura Spa Badplaas (☎ 844 1020, fax 844 1445) Camp sites R60, 2-bed units R408, 4-bed units R705. The Aventura has the standard huge fence and lots of playthings inside to amuse guests. It's even more expensive in high season.

Badplaas Valley Inn (☎ 844 1040, fax 844 1496) Singles/doubles B&B R110/192. This inn is cheaper, simpler and quieter than its neighbour. There's a bar, a restaurant and a TV room; it's 300m down the road from Aventura.

Klein Drakensberg

The highveld ends suddenly at this dramatic escarpment, which tumbles down to the eastern lowveld. The Klein Drakensberg (Small Drakensberg), also known as the Transvaal Drakensberg, consists not so much of peaks as of cliffs, and offers stunning views. As it is prime vacation territory there's a lot of accommodation, much of it expensive, that fills up in high season.

Apart from the overpopulated Lebowa Corridor near Acornhoek in the north-east of the province, the population density is low, resulting in little public transport. In towns such as Graskop, Sabie and Lydenburg, you'll need to rely on minibus taxis; to explore the area properly a hire car is the best option.

BLYDE RIVER CANYON NATURE RESERVE

The 26,000-hectare Blyde River Canyon Nature Reserve snakes north almost 60km from Graskop, following the escarpment and meeting the Blyde River as it carves its way down to the lowveld. The Blyde's spectacular canyon, nearly 30km long, is one of South Africa's scenic highlights.

The following route description, from north to south, begins near the Manoutsa Cliffs at the junction of the Tzaneen road (R36) and the R527 (marked on some maps as a continuation of the R531).

Follow the R36 as it turns south and climbs up from the lowveld through the JG Strijdom Tunnel and scenic Abel Erasmus Pass. You'll pass the turn-off to the R532 and come to the village of Mogaba and the road to the **Museum of Man** *(adult/child R5/3; open 8am-5pm daily; half-hour guided tour adult/child R18/12)*, an archaeological site with rock paintings and other finds. Also in the area are the **Echo Caves** where Stone Age relics have been found. The caves get their name from dripstone formations that echo when tapped. The guides might demand a huge tip of anything up to R50, which is not compulsory, regardless of the taunts.

If you return to the R532 junction and proceed east along the R532 you'll come to the Aventura Eco Blydepoort resort. There is a good view of the **Three Rondavels** from a viewpoint a few kilometres past the resort. The Three Rondavels are huge cylinders of rock with hutlike pointed 'roofs' rising out of the far wall of the canyon. There are a number of short walks in the area to points where you can look down to the Blydepoort Dam.

A visit to the **Moholoholo Wildlife and Birds of Prey Rehabilitation Centre** *(☎ 015-795 5236; R40 per person; open 9am-3pm)* will increase your powers of observation in spotting magnificent birds of prey while

MPUMALANGA

you're touring in the area. It's at the beginning of the road to Aventura Swadini.

Bourke's Luck Potholes *(admission R10)*, weird cylindrical holes carved into the rock by whirlpools in the river, can be found at the confluence of the Blyde and Treur Rivers. They are interesting, although perhaps not as great an attraction as they are touted to be. There is a good visitor centre with information on the geology, flora and fauna of the canyon.

The R532 follows the Treur south to its source, and further on is a turn-off to the R534 loop road. This road leads to the spectacular viewpoints of **Wonder View** and **God's Window**, now tightly controlled by the Mpumalanga Parks Board. (You can also take the R532 north from Graskop to get here; it's well signposted.) Once you could park quietly and enjoy the view at the lookouts; now there are entry gates and a battery of souvenir sellers. At God's Window there's a short trail to views of the lowveld, 1000m below.

A few kilometres further on is **The Pinnacle**, an impressive rock formation that juts out from the escarpment; lock up your car here as there have been thefts. The R534 joins the R532 3km north of Graskop.

Hiking Trails

There are several great hiking trails in the area but unfortunately they have been closed as a result of a lack of finance, with the exception of the Blyde River Canyon Hiking Trail and the Belvedere Day Walk. There are plans to reopen some of the other walks so ask at the Graskop information centre or at the visitor centre at Bourke's Luck Potholes.

The 2½-day **Blyde River Canyon Hiking Trail** begins at Paradise Camp and finishes at Bourke's Luck Potholes. The first night is spent at Watervalspruit Hut, while the second night is at Clearstream Hut. The hike costs R30 per night and reservations can be made through the **Mpumalanga Parks Board** *(☎ 013-759 5432, fax 013-755 3928, PO Box 1990, Nelspruit 1200)*.

The **Beleveedere Day Walk** is a trail to the Belvedere hydroelectric power station at Bourke's Luck Potholes. The station was

built in 1911 and was the largest of its kind in the southern hemisphere. The trail is reasonably strenuous and the last departure is at noon. The trail takes about five hours and costs R3.

Places to Stay

There is accommodation in the towns on top of the escarpment, and there are a number of places to stay close to the canyon.

Aventura Eco Blydepoort (☎ 013-769 8055, fax 769 8059) Camp sites R27/32 in low/high season, 2-bed units from R285/340, standard 4-bed units R425/581. This is a large resort with all the usual facilities.

Aventura Eco Swadini (☎ 015-795 5141, fax 795 5178) Camp sites R52/58 in low/high season, 4-bed units 399/604. This place is at the bottom of the escarpment, on the eastern side but still on the Blyde River. It's a spectacular location but the brick units are fairly ordinary. Midweek specials (R275 per unit) make it better value.

The self-catering *Belvedere House* is operated by the Mpumalanga Parks Board (☎ 013-759 5432, fax 013-755 3928, PO Box 1990, Nelspruit 1200). It sleeps nine and costs R540/650 per night on weekdays/weekends.

Rushworth's Trackers (☎ 015-795 5033) Camping R20 per tent, cottages R115 per person, DB&B R250 per cottage. At the bottom of the escarpment to the north of Swadini is this beautifully situated private reserve. It takes in the strikingly different ecosystems of the highveld and the lowveld. It's a great spot for an 'alternative Big Five' – cheap digs, peace, quiet, views and the Narina trogon bird. Trips to study the natural vegetation of the region, which varies from *fynbos* (fine bush) to baobabs, are conducted from Rushworth's Trackers by Tamboti Botanical Trails. We've had varying reports from readers in the last few years about Rushworth, so let us know what you think.

To get to Rushworth's Trackers take the R527 west from Hoedspruit and after about 20km turn south onto the small Driehoek road, just after you cross the Blyde River. After 6.5km you will see their signpost; it's a steep climb up towards the escarpment.

GRASKOP

☎ 013 • postcode 1270

Graskop is on the edge of the Drakensberg escarpment, at the top of Kowyns Pass. Nearby are some spectacular views of the lowveld, almost 1000m below. A walking trail that includes places described in *Jock of the Bushveld* starts at the municipal resort; the resort will provide a map. There are good **mountain-biking trails** in the region; permits are R5.

In the Spar supermarket there is an **information office** (*☎ 767 1833, e wild@iafrica .com, Spar Centre, Pilgrim St*) The Green Castle Backpackers can also offer plenty of tips.

Places to Stay

Graskop Municipal Holiday Resort (*☎ 767 1126*) Camp sites for 2 people R35, plus R10 per extra person, 4-bed bungalows R125. The resort is good value and not too far from the centre of town at the end of Louis Trichardt St.

The Green Castle Backpackers (*☎ 767 1761, e graskop@global.co.za, 69 Eeufees St*) Camp sites for 1/2 people R20/25, dorm beds/doubles R45/120. This backpackers is in a castle-like building across the train line from the town. The owner is enthusiastic

about the surroundings and arranges good trips, which include kloofing (clambering around in ravines), cave-crawling and hiking (from R50).

Panorama Rest Camp (*☎/fax 767 1091*) Camp sites for 2 people R50, chalets for two/five people R140/260. Panorama is about 2km east of town on the road to Kowyns Pass (the R535). It's stunningly situated at the top of a deep gorge: The small pool is right on the edge and has astounding views down to the lowveld.

Summit Lodge (*☎ 767 1058, fax 767 1895*) Dorm beds R50, B&B R120 per person, chalets R275. This place has a range of accommodation including a converted train (now stationary) for backpackers, but it isn't great value. It's 500m down the road towards Pilgrim's Rest and is popular with local motorcycle enthusiasts.

Log Cabin Village (☎ 767 1974, fax 767 1975, Louis Trichardt St) Chalets R200. Close to the pancake eateries (a good or bad thing?), these excellent chalets have TVs and fireplaces.

Mogodi Lodge (☎/fax 767 1110) Singles/ doubles R120/195, chalets R185/295. Above the Graskop Falls and on the opposite side of the gorge from Panorama, Mogodi also has excellent views.

Graskop Hotel (☎/fax 767 1244, ⓔ info@ graskophotel.co.za, Cnr Main & Louis Trichardt Sts) Singles/doubles B&B R195/340. Avoid rooms facing the street, as timber trucks roll by in the night.

Places to Eat & Drink
This town is a gourmet's delight.

Harrie's Pancake Bar (☎ 767 1273, Louis Trichardt St) Savoury pancakes R13-25, sweet pancakes R7-20. This pancake bar is recommended by Jo'burg's Chosen Few motorcycle gang.

Lonely Tree Pancake Cabin (Louis Trichardt St) Breakfast R15-27, pancakes R10-19. Just across the road from Harrie's and a good alternative, it offers a larger range of meals than its neighbour.

Eastern Delights (Main St) Snacks R1-20. Here you'll find basic cheap Indian food such as *bunny chow* (a loaf of bread hollowed out and filled with curry; R10 for a quarter), samosas (R1.50) and biryani.

Notty Pine Restaurant & Bar (☎ 767 1030, Pilgrim St) Dishes R35-50. Open noon-3pm & 6pm-late Sat-Thur, 6pm-late Fri. Notty Pine is known for its excellent trout dishes.

Pubs in town include *Biyafuthi*, a popular shebeen (bar). *House of Beers* is good for its range of amber nectars, and has local favourites such as Forresters from the Cape. *Loco Inn (☎ 767 1961)* is across from the library and well signposted – it's 'your passport to pleasure' (their words, not ours).

As well as pub lunches it has pool tables and a lively bar.

Getting There & Away
At the time of research the Baz Bus no longer serviced this area, so the only public transport option is a minibus taxi. The stand is at the southern end of Main St. Taxis go to Pilgrim's Rest (R7), Sabie (R10), and Hazyview.

SABIE & AROUND
☎ 013 • postcode 1260
The R37 between Sabie and Lydenburg over Long Tom Pass is, like many routes in this area, spectacular. The highest point at the top of the pass is 2150m above sea level, after which the terrain changes from mountainous valleys blanketed in pine forests to velvet hills dotted with rocky outcrops.

Sabie is the largest town in the region but it's still a manageable size. The town is quite prosperous, being a tourist centre and a timber town. Tourists come for the cool climate, the trout fishing and the extensive pine and eucalyptus plantations in the area, but if you prefer your forests wild this might not be such an attraction.

Sondelani Travel & Info (☎ 764 3492), near The Woodsman at the corner of Mac-Mac Rd and the R536, provides information on accommodation and activities.

Play Web Internet Cafe (Sabie Market Square) has email facilities for R8 per half-hour.

There is a **Safcol** office in town, next to the post office, but bookings for the trails must be made through the Pretoria branch. However, it's worth dropping into the office here if you're after any last minute information.

Things to See & Do
There are a number of **waterfalls** in the area. Closest are the Sabie Falls, just beyond town on the R532 (the road to Graskop). South-west of Sabie, off Old Lydenburg Rd, are the 70m Bridal Veil Falls. Also off Old Lydenburg Rd are the 68m Lone Creek Falls (R5 per person); there is wheelchair access to the falls on the right-hand path. Nearby are Horseshoe Falls. Off the R532 to Graskop are the Mac-Mac Falls

R5 per car), named because of the many Scottish names on the area's mining register; and the beautiful Forest Falls, 10km from Graskop.

The **Forestry Museum** *(adult/child R5/3; open 8.30am-4pm Mon-Fri, 10am-3pm Sat)* has displays on local forests, exhibits of match paintings that will 'take your breath away' and an audiovisual presentation. There is wheelchair access.

Horse riding is popular; Sondelani can arrange half-day rides for R150 and two-day rides for R450, taking in falls that can't be reached on foot. Accommodation is in basic huts and the price is all inclusive.

There are two excellent marked **mountain-bike trails** starting at Merry Pebbles (see Places to Stay, following). The Long Tom Trail consists of two sections, one 36km and the other 20km long. The Ceylon Trail is 21km and has a steep section that takes you to the top of Bridal Veil Falls. There is an entrance fee of R30 for each trail. You can hire bicycles from Merry Pebbles for about R50.

Hardy Ventures *(☎ 751 1693)* organises plenty of activities such as white-water rafting on the Blyde and Sabie Rivers. A three-hour ride on the Sabie River costs R175, including lunch. Or you can combine abseiling and rafting on the Blyde River for R380. Overnight trips are also available.

Places to Stay

Sabie Backpackers Lodge (☎ 764 2118) Dorm beds R40, A-frame double huts R100, tree houses R50 per person. The only backpackers in town this place is friendly and, for the adrenaline freaks, can organise tubing, kloofing and bungee jumping.

Merry Pebbles (☎ 764 2266, fax 764 1629, e info@merrypebbles.co.za) Camp sites from R40/60 in low/high season, double/triple rooms from R220/250 in low season, chalets from R500. This place is north of town off Old Lydenburg Rd and has a bar and shop. It's good for families.

Jock of the Bushveld Chalets & Caravan Park (☎ 764 2178, fax 764 3215, e jocksabi@netactive.co.za) Camp site R70 for 2 people, each extra person R15, dorm beds R80, basic chalets from R220 for 2

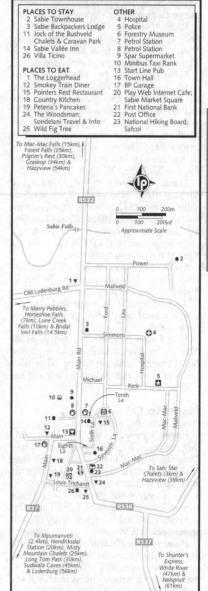

SABIE

PLACES TO STAY
2 Sabie Townhouse
3 Sabie Backpackers Lodge
11 Jock of the Bushveld
   Chalets & Caravan Park
14 Sabie Vallée Inn
26 Villa Ticino

PLACES TO EAT
1 The Loggerhead
12 Smokey Train Diner
15 Pointers Rest Restaurant
18 Country Kitchen
19 Petena's Pancakes
24 The Woodsman;
   Sondelani Travel & Info
25 Wild Fig Tree

OTHER
4 Hospital
5 Police
6 Forestry Museum
7 Petrol Station
8 Petrol Station
9 Spar Supermarket
10 Minibus Taxi Rank
13 Start Line Pub
16 Town Hall
17 BP Garage
20 Play Web Internet Cafe;
   Sabie Market Square
21 First National Bank
22 Post Office
23 National Hiking Board;
   Safcol

MPUMALANGA

people. Handy for the town centre, the sites here are exorbitantly priced, although there is a large range of other accommodation.

Misty Mountain Chalets (☎ *764 3377*) Self-catering cottages from R135 per person. These chalets, 25km from Sabie on the R37, are ideally located for mountain-bikers.

Sabie Vallée Inn (☎ *764 2182, fax 764 1362, Tenth Lane*) DB&B R185 per person, log cabins R280. This place is very central and has lots of accommodation options.

Sabi Star Chalets (☎ *764 3328, fax 764 2686,* W *www.soft.co.za/sabistar*) 2-bed chalets R155/180 in low/high season . The chalets are 3km out of town on the R536; you can book them through the Web site.

Shunter's Express (☎ *764 1777*) Singles/ doubles B&B R300/440. South-east of Sabie on the R537 to White River, accommodation here is in 1930s railway coaches. You can go horse riding for R25 per hour.

There are many B&Bs in the area; inquire at the information office.

Sabie Townhouse (☎ *764 2292, fax 764 1988,* e *sabieth@iafrica.com, Power St*) Rooms from R230 per person, family suites R240 per person. This is a perfect place for a well-earned indulgence. It's popular so book ahead.

Villa Ticino (☎ *764 2598,* e *stay@villa ticino.co.za, Cnr Louis Trichardt & Second Lane*) Rooms R165 per person. This place has been recommended by readers and has a friendly host.

Places to Eat
Pancakes are big in the hills.

Petena's Pancakes (☎ *764 1541, Main Rd*) Pancakes R12-18. Open 9am-5.45pm Tues-Sat, 10am-5.45pm Sun. Petena's does a similar job to Harrie's in Graskop. For the adventurous there's the biltong pancake.

The Loggerhead (☎ *764 3341*) Meals around R40. Just south of Sabie Falls, this is a good steak and fish place. Baby chicken spatchcock is R38

Pointers Rest Restaurant (☎ *764 2630*) Starters R10-16, mains R40. Opposite the Forestry Museum, this place specialises in trout braais (deboned stuffed trout is R42), and also serves filling pastas for R35.

The Woodsman (☎ *764 2204, Cnr R536 & Mac-Mac Rd*) Starters R15-20, mains R35-50. A terrific Greek menu and an outdoor eating area make dining here very pleasant.

Wild Fig Tree (☎ *764 2239, 6 Third Ave*) Starters R15-25, fish dishes R45. Wild Fig Tree has local specialities such as biltong pâté (R15), ostrich fillet (R50) and homemade apple pie (R16). The food here is superb, as is the service – you won't leave disappointed.

Country Kitchen (☎ *764 1901, Main Rd*) Starters R15-30, mains R35-50. Open 11.30am-3pm & 6.30pm-late daily. Country Kitchen also specialises in local cuisine You can dine on creations such as pan-fried julienne of crocodile with squash (R26) and braised oxtail with herbs (R45).

Smokey Train Diner (☎ *764 3445, Main Rd*) Tapas R15-20, mains R38-50. Open daily. At the western end of the road, this place is the ticket for the dedicated Afrikaner diner – the *potjiekos* (stew cooked in a three-legged pot) is flavoured with sentimentality Neil Diamond is usually the background noise. The kitchen closes at 8.45pm.

Start Line Pub (☎ *764 1800, Main St*) is a pub owned by a former SA drag-racing champion, and it's a bikie haven. It's probably the best bet for a night of darts and pool

Getting There & Away
There are daily buses from Jo'burg to Nelspruit, from where you can take minibus taxis to Sabie. The fare from Nelspruit to Sabie is R15; from Hazyview it's R12 Sabie's minibus taxi stop is behind the Spar supermarket on Main Rd and has an office that dispenses timetable information. Most taxis operate only in the local area.

Sondelani will organise lifts to and from towns in the area. To White River or Nelspruit is R50.

PILGRIM'S REST
☎ 013 • postcode 1290

Gold was discovered here in 1873, and for 10 years the area buzzed with diggers working small-scale alluvial claims. When the big operators arrived in the 1880s, Pilgrim's Rest became a company town, and when the gold finally fizzled out in 1972 the town was sold to the government as a ready-made historical village (it's now a national monument). Avoid it on weekends and watch out for car washers charging ridiculous fees.

The **information centre** (☎ *768 1060; open 9am-12.45pm & 1.15pm-4.30pm daily)* is on the main street.

Things to See & Do

A **tractor cart** *(adult/child R6/3)* shuttles between Uptown and Downtown.

There are three **museums** *(☎ 768 1060, total admission R5)*: the Pilgrim's Rest & Sabie News, a printing shop; the House Museum, a restored home; and the Dredzen Shop & House Museum, a general store. Buy tickets at the information centre.

Also worth a visit is historic **Alanglade** *(☎ 768 1060; admission R20; guided tours R20 11am & 2pm Mon-Sat)* a former mine manager's residence furnished with period objects from the 1920s. Admission includes refreshments.

Places to Stay & Eat

Prices given here are low-season prices; they rise substantially in high season.

Pilgrims Rest Caravan Park (☎ 768 1427) Camp sites R50, 2-bed chalets R100. The chalets here are a bargain and the park is well set out.

District Six Miners Cottages (☎ 768 1211) 2-person cottages R140, R20 for each extra person. These restored and refurbished cottages are a cheap option in town. Cottages have private gardens and braai. Bookings can be made only between 8am and 1pm.

Royal Hotel (☎ 768 1100, fax 768 1188, ℮ royal@mweb.co.za) Singles/doubles R335/470. This is the historic centrepiece of Uptown and a fine example of wooden Victorian architecture. The rooms are elegantly furnished in period style and include brass four-poster beds. The adjoining *Church Bar* is a great place to relax.

Crystal Springs Mountain Lodge (☎ 768 5000, fax 768 5024) Rooms R144/210 per person weekdays/weekends, children half price. This lodge near Pilgrim's Rest is superbly situated and has self-catering

chalets. It's a good place for the kids with trampolines and minigolf.

Scott's Cafe (☎ 768 1061, Uptown) Pancakes R16-22, open sandwiches R25-29. This is a rather stuffy eatery, but the food is pretty good.

At *Digger's Den* you can dine on traditional meals including ostrich fillet. Sunday buffet lunch costs R50, a la carte dishes are R30 to R45.

Pilgrim's Pantry (☎ 768 1042, Downtown) Breakfast R15-25, light meals R20. This coffee shop and pancake place is good for brunch.

Get a bottle of wine for lunch at *Edwin Wood's Wine Cellar (☎ 768 1025, Uptown)*.

Getting There & Away

There is little public transport to or from Pilgrim's Rest: The roads are narrow and steep so buses are not inclined to make the trip, and minibus taxis are infrequent because there are few blacks living in the area (R7 to Graskop when available).

LYDENBURG

☎ 013 • postcode 1120

Lydenburg (Town of Suffering) was established by Voortrekkers in 1849 and was once the capital of the Republic of Lydenburg. Today it's a quiet service centre for the farming district.

Lydenburg Tourist Information *(☎ 235 3076, ℮ beehivetourism@intekom.co.za)* is at the southern end of Viljoen St.

The **museum** *(☎ 235 2121, Long Tom Pass Rd; admission free; open 8am-1pm & 2pm-6pm Mon-Fri, 8am-5pm Sat & Sun)* is a few kilometres from town. It has a fascinating collection of animal and human terracotta masks, and the 'Lydenburg Heads', which date from AD 490.

Gustav Klingbiel Nature Reserve *(☎ 235 2121; admission R9 per car)* is next to the museum on the R37. As well as antelopes it contains Iron Age sites and Anglo-Boer War trenches.

Places to Stay & Eat

Uitspan Caravan Park (☎ 235 2914, Viljoen St) Camp sites R42 for two people,

3-bed rondavels R150. This pleasant park is on the road to Jo'burg.

Morgan's Hotel (☎ *235 2165, fax 235 2166, 14 Voortrekker St*) Singles/doubles B&B R100/200. This is a small country hotel, good for an overnight stop.

Long Tom Guest House (☎ *235 2459, fax 235 2749, 33 Sterkspruit St*) Units from R140 per person. Units on this peaceful property have fireplaces and braai facilities and are very comfortable.

Trout Inn Restaurant & Pub (☎ *235 1828, Potgieter Rd*) Trout dishes R40-45. A snug little spot with a good bar, this is probably the best value eating option in town.

Getting There & Away
City to City services stop at Lydenburg (R85) on their Jo'burg-Phalaborwa run.

The minibus taxi stop is in a yard off the main shopping street. Taxis to Sabie are R20. Your own transport is the best bet for touring.

Southern Mpumalanga

PIET RETIEF
☎ 017 • postcode 2380

This solid, medium-sized town has few attractions but it is the largest in the south of Mpumalanga and might be a good stopover on the way to Swaziland or KwaZulu-Natal.

The helpful **tourism association** (☎ *826 5477, De Wet St*) is between Church and Mark Sts.

Places to Stay & Eat
There are plenty of good value guesthouses to choose from in this town.

Lala's Lodge (☎*/fax 826 1838, ☎ 083-302 2466*) Dorm beds/doubles R40/150. Signposted off the N2 towards Ermelo, and only 500m from town, this is a great budget place set on a large grassed property. There's a communal lounge with satellite TV.

Green Door Guest House (☎ *826 3208, fax 826 0126, 1 Mark St*) Singles/doubles B&B R185/250. There are 17 very well-presented rooms here with some interesting African decoration.

LA Guest House (☎*/fax 826 2837, 3 Mark St*) Singles/doubles B&B R160/220. This place has immaculate rooms and a family atmosphere. It's a good place for the kids and has been recommended by readers.

The Green Door Restaurant (☎ *826 3208, Church St*) Starters R18-23, mains R35-50. Open 11am-11pm Mon-Fri, 6pm-11pm Sat. Run by the guesthouse of the same name, this is a friendly place with a large menu. Meals are served with a platter of farm fresh fruits. There is a cosy *bar* here as well, which has a good selection of beers and a weird collection of matches, cigarette lighters, ties and caps!

Getting There & Away
Greyhound stops in town at the Waterside Lodge on Kerk St on its daily Pretoria-Durban run. The fare from Piet Retief to Pretoria is R130; to Durban it's R150.

Minibus taxis stop at the back of Super-Mac on Brand St. From here to the Swaziland border post at Mahamba costs R12.

SOUTH AFRICAN MUSIC

Music in South Africa is inextricably linked to politics and social life. The country's turbulent history has provided for a unique mixture of European and indigenous African influences, resulting in a range of music, arguably unequalled on the African continent.

The banjo and the violin arrived in Southern Africa with Malayan labourers during the 19th century, while the English brought the concertina with them at the beginning of the 20th century. These instruments, along with the guitar, would have a profound influence on the South African traditions of polyphony and vocal harmonies.

Despite these influences, a strong African identity has always been maintained. The music industry in South Africa is the oldest in Africa, and highly developed, with the major international record companies having had a stake since the 1930s (however, musicians were often exploited by the record companies, who paid lowly session fees rather than royalties).

Township music has its roots in the forced dispossession and urbanisation of blacks at the beginning of the 20th century. In the Homelands, music was important as a form of entertainment, as a means of communication, and as an expression of struggle. Township music has come to encompass styles such as marabi, jazz, kwela, mbaqanga, bubblegum, and most recently kwaito. The Zulu a-cappella voices of Ladysmith Black Mambazo are probably the best known to the outside world, but South Africa boasts many other internationally recognised stars operating in a variety of genres, such as jazz trumpeter Hugh Masekela, and 'Mama Africa' herself, Miriam Makeba.

Inset: A busker in St George's Mall, Cape Town (Photo by Richard I'Anson)

ght: Gospel singers on a Cape Town Saturday morning (Photo by Richard I'Anson)

From Marabi to the Manhattan Brothers

From the 1920s, American jazz was to radically transform South African music. Records by Duke Ellington, Count Basie and Louis Armstrong provided the biggest inspiration to 1930s jazz bands such as the Jazz Maniacs and the Merry Blackbirds. As South Africa became increasingly urbanised, Western instruments and jazz were combined with local melodies to create marabi. During the 1940s, tsaba tsaba, a forerunner of kwela and township jive, began to develop in the shebeens of Sophiatown, Johannesburg (Jo'burg).

Brass instruments were rare in comparison with the guitar, and seminal musician Kippie Moeketsi was one of the first to play clarinet, which he learnt from a saxophone tutor. He joined the Harlem Swingsters in 1949, but the 1950 Group Areas Act, which restricted people to living in designated areas, exacerbated the demise of big bands such as this one.

Moeketsi eventually backed the Manhattan Brothers, credited as being South Africa's first 'superstars'; they were influenced by African American vocal quartets such as the Mills Brothers and the Ink Spots. Their voices were accompanied by swinging piano and brass, including, at times, trumpet player Hugh Masekela and pianist Dollar Brand (Abdullah Ibrahim), who got their start accompanying the group. The Manhattan Brothers also recruited female singers, including, in the early 1950s, 21-year-old Miriam Makeba. With her roots in mbube, a church-inspired vocal tradition, she became one of the focal points of the group.

Miriam Makeba & the Rise of Jazz

In 1956 Miriam Makeba formed her own close-harmony female vocal group, the Skylarks, who rarely performed live, being more of a studio entity. In 1957 she joined the African Jazz and Variety Review, mainly playing to a white audience that was largely unaware of the success of the Manhattan Brothers.

Makeba landed a small part in the film *Come Back Africa*, which helped to launch her international career. A few years later she took one of the leading roles in the musical *King Kong*, based on the life of Ezekiel Dlamini, a celebrated African boxer. The Manhattan Brothers, Hugh Masekela and Kippie Moeketsi were also featured and the show became a big hit, touring across Southern Africa. It eventually opened in London's West End in 1961, and although Makeba had left by this time, *King Kong* was the first international exposure for several musicians.

Some musicians, including the Manhattan Brothers, decided to stay in the UK after the show had completed its London run. One of those who returned to South Africa was Kippie Moeketsi. He helped to form

JENNY BOWMAN

the Jazz Epistles, who were to become the definitive township jazz ensemble, featuring Hugh Masekela, Dollar Brand, Jonas Gwangwa on trombone and Makhaya Ntshoko on drums. The Jazz Epistles were the first black South African group to record a full album, even if it was pressed in limited quantities.

As the general political climate worsened, many of the best musicians, including the Jazz Epistles and Miriam Makeba, were forced into exile abroad, which advanced their international careers. Makeba moved to the USA and became a protege of Harry Belafonte. In 1956 she became the first African musician to have a record in the US charts. During the 1960s, she married Masekela; both much later became involved in Paul Simon's controversial *Graceland* tour, during the anti-apartheid cultural boycott of South Africa.

A new generation of jazz musicians emerged in the early 1960s, and included saxophonist Dudu Pukwana and pianist Chris Mc-Gregor and their group the Blue Notes. Eventually the second wave of township jazzers were also forced into exile; some of them were to create a healthy South African jazz scene in London. Only after the end of the cultural boycott did many of the most famous musical exiles, Masekela and Makeba among them, return to perform at home for the first time in a number of years.

JENNY BOWMAN

Kwela, Jive & Mbaqanga

Small boys on the street corners of Soweto had begun to develop their own interpretation of American swing, known as 'kwela', meaning 'get on top' as well as 'jump up'. Kwela combos featured the penny whistle (mainly because it was cheap) plus, usually, banjo, guitar and a one-string bass, and became a common sight in Jo'burg throughout the 1950s and into the 1960s. 'Little' Lemmy Special, Spokes Mashiyane and others became popular throughout South Africa, their fame even spreading to the UK, where kwela gained popularity on the back of the skiffle boom. The biggest hit of all was 'Tom Hark' by Elias and his Zig Zag Flutes, which reached number two and stayed on the British charts for 14 weeks in 1958.

By the beginning of the 1960s saxophones had replaced penny whistles, guitars had become electric and drums and organ had been added to the combo to produce jive, which came in a variety of styles, most notably sax jive. Popular artists included the Soul Brothers, who are still going strong today, and others who would have a lasting effect on South African music: West Nkosi, Boyoyo Boys and guitarist Marks Mankwane.

South African vocal traditions, based on church choirs and doo-wop, developed simultaneously. When combined with sax jive, the result was christened, at first disparagingly, mbaqanga, literally 'dumpling' in Zulu. Alexandra Black Mambazo, forerunners of Ladysmith Black Mambazo, had been founded by Aaron Lerole, who went on to direct Dark City Sisters, the first mbaqanga group. Both of these groups had

Ladysmith Black Mambazo

The 10 men of this a-cappella band from Ladysmith in KwaZulu-Natal have been harmonising together for more than 30 years. In that time they have released over 30 albums, becoming Africa's biggest-selling musical export and cultural ambassadors for South Africa.

In the 1960s Mambazo founder Joseph Shabalala was one of millions of young Zulu men working in South Africa's mines. After days of back-breaking labour these men would spend their rest day singing in the displaced workers' tradition of *isicathamiya*, a soft-shoe shuffle style meant to appease guards and workers alike.

Shabalala recalls days when he was angry, fighting, and stoning cars. He says the sound of voices in harmony made him realise he had another weapon to make people listen. He says he 'dropped the stone' and formed Ladysmith Black Mambazo.

The onstage presence of the band's 10 members and their often humorous shows inspired one reviewer to describe seeing them perform as 'witnessing pure, unadulterated joy'.

The band got their big break in 1986 when they sang with Paul Simon on the hugely popular *Graceland* album. Since then they have scored American Broadway shows; appeared in video clips for Spike Lee and Michael Jackson; featured in an ad for IBM; and appeared on *Sesame Street*.

The band's status as cultural ambassadors for South Africa has been built on such honours as performing for the English monarchy at London's Royal Albert Hall; singing at Mandela and De Klerk's Nobel prize acceptance ceremony, and performing at the official 'reopening ceremony' of the 1996 Atlanta Olympics after it was bombed.

Shabalala is now an associate professor in ethnomusicology at the University of Natal, and his latest and most ambitious dream is the establishment of the Mambazo Foundation for South African Music and Culture.

Check out the band's Web site at **w** www.mambazo.com.

Susan Holtham

featured a young male singer, Simon 'Mahlathini' Nkabinde, who later joined the Mahotella Queens to forge mbaqanga's most celebrated partnership, Mahlathini & The Mahotella Queens.

Mahlathini's deep 'groaning' style of singing became a staple in other groups, but the Queens had the added advantage of being backed and produced by West Nkosi, and featured Marks Mankwane and the superb Makhona Tsothle Band. Their career was revived in the late 1980s by associations with Paul Simon, singing at Mandela's birthday celebrations and being released in Europe on the pioneering Earthworks label. They became regular performers in Europe as well as Japan. Since the death of Mahlathini in 1999, and both Mankwane and Nkosi, the Mahotella Queens have made a comeback with a new album *Sebai Bai*, released in 2001.

JENNY BOWMAN

Neotraditional Styles

While most urban music became pan-tribal, the traditional music of the Zulu, Xhosa and Sotho peoples incorporated Western instruments to produce unique musical styles.

One of the most interesting is the Zulu traditional guitar music, maskanda, which often incorporates other instruments such as the concertina. The vocals are sometimes delivered in a fast rap style. Maskanda had its heyday in the 1970s, but is still popular today as one of the representative musical styles of KwaZulu-Natal. Maskanda's most popular singer of all is Phuzekhemisi, whose hit album *Imbizo* sold over 100,000 copies. A guitarist currently working in a more traditional vein is the excellent Mfiliseni Magubane.

The other style typical of KwaZulu-Natal is the a-cappella vocal style of *isicathamiya*, popularised by Ladysmith Black Mambazo (see the boxed text). Competitions between isicathamiya groups began in the Homelands and continue today. On Saturday nights at community halls in Durban and the townships, it is possible to listen as up to 30 groups come together in friendly competitions.

Bubblegum to Kwaito & Current Trends

Musicians in South Africa, like those in most other countries, have incorporated contemporary Western styles into their music, from 'marabi soul' in the 1970s, through to funk and the pop-influenced bubblegum of the 1980s. Without the rough edges of mbaqanga, bubblegum was aimed squarely at the young, but it still retained an urban edge. The star of this genre is Brenda Fassie, her main rival being Yvonne Chaka Chaka; both have enjoyed pan-African success. Lucky Dube embraced reggae and had several big-selling albums at the start of the 1990s – he took his South African reggae to Europe and America.

The 1994 free elections had a dramatic effect on the music scene. Radio stations proliferated, and international music was released by major companies, now able to set up local offices.

International music now far outsells local music, but a positive result of the influx of imported dance sounds has been the emergence of the hugely popular kwaito, a mix of mbaqanga, jive, hip-hop, house, ragga and other dance styles. Kwaito is the new street music of South Africa, and the first post-apartheid music that youth can call their own. Lyrics are mostly chanted in local languages and street slang. It has its own style of dancing and fashion, and has made live music popular once again, even if its singers are mostly singing over backing tapes.

The king of kwaito is Arthur Mafokate. He is also a producer and works with several younger bands, such as Aba Shante. Other popular artists are Bongo Maffin, Boom Shaka, M'du, Spokes H, Jimmy B, and bubblegum artist Brenda Fassie, whose music now has a strong kwaito flavour.

Other styles of music that have been brought into the post-apartheid era include the maskanda dance of Bhekumuzi Luthuli and

Isu Labasa. Female singer Busi Mhlongo, one of those yet to return from exile, updated maskanda (usually the domain of men) with the help of producer Wil Mowat, with remarkable results on her album *Urban Zulu*.

In 2000 Busi Mhlongo returned to visit KwaZulu-Natal to perform at the Awesome Africa music festival (usually held during September). Featuring top South African musicians, and some from other African countries, with a smattering of international artists often collaborating with local musicians, Awesome Africa is a great place to see South African music in the beautiful setting of the Shongweni Resources Reserve.

If the results of the 2000 Kora All Africa Music Awards (often dubbed 'Africa's Grammy Awards') are anything to go by, South African music is in a very healthy state. South African artists dominated the awards, winning four of the eight pan-African categories, including Lucky Dube for Best African Video, Bongo Maffin for Best African Arrangement, and Miriam Makeba's granddaughter Zenzi took the honours for Most Promising Female Artist. Ladysmith Black Mambazo picked up a special award for contribution to African music.

Black-owned labels are burgeoning in the wake of the popularity of kwaito. Arthur and other producers have spurned the majors (who originally rejected them) to set up their own companies and have released some of South Africa's best-selling records in recent years. With improved local business infrastructure, and producers with their ears to the streets, hopefully local musicians will continue to be influenced rather than dominated by world trends, keeping the sounds and styles positively South African.

SARAH JOLLY

Kruger National Park

Kruger National Park attracts more than 00,000 visitors each year, and deserves its eputation as one of the most famous wildlife arks in the world; it's also one of the biggest nd oldest. Sabie Game Reserve (as Kruger vas originally called) was established by the resident of the Zuid-Afrikaansche Republek (ZAR; South African Republic), Paul ruger, in 1898. Since its establishment the eserve has been much expanded: it now pans nearly two million hectares, which is bout the size of Wales in the UK.

Park authorities claim that Kruger has the reatest variety of animals of any park in frica, with lions, leopards, elephants, Cape uffaloes and black rhinos (the Big Five), as vell as cheetahs, giraffes, hippos and many pecies of antelope and smaller animals. Altogether, the park is home to 147 species of nammals, 507 bird species, 114 reptile species, 49 species of fish and 34 types of amhibians. There are also 336 species of trees.

Unlike some of the parks in East Africa, ruger does not offer a true wilderness xperience (although some would argue hat the walking trails do approach this leal) – The park's infrastructure, which ncludes a network of sealed roads and omfortable camps, is too highly devel-ped. None of this should deter you, how-ver, because Kruger will undoubtedly be highlight of your South African trip. And espite Kruger's popularity, the crowds re by no means intrusive if you avoid veekends and school holidays (numbers re lower north of the Phalaborwa Gate nd on gravel roads) – it's not unusual to ravel for an hour or so without seeing nother vehicle.

The landscape is both beautiful and fasinating, and although you would be lucky to ee all the large predators you will almost ertainly see some of the Big Five as well as n extraordinary variety of smaller mammals nd birds. Since many of the animals are sed to the presence of cars, it is possible to et very close to them.

Highlights

- Get up close and personal with the wildlife on an early morning or afternoon bush walk.
- Explore the relatively untouched eastern boundary of the park, in the foothills of the Lebombo mountains, on a five-day eco-trail.
- Stay in a bushveld camp and wake up to the sounds of a rhino snorting outside your safari tent.
- Spoil yourself in one of the many luxurious private game reserves bordering Kruger.

There are a number of interesting historical sites in Skukuza rest camp, including the Campbell Hut Museum, which sustained water damage in the 2000 floods. It was one of the first restored huts and now houses a collection of furniture and photographs.

Speedy visits aren't recommended; try to spend at least two nights in the park. Find a spot near a water hole and just wait to see what comes by.

ORIENTATION

Kruger stretches almost 350km along the Mozambique border to the east; Northern Province and Mpumalanga are on the western and southern borders respectively. There are large private wildlife reserves adjoining the western boundaries (see Private Wildlife Reserves later in this chapter).

Most of the park consists of flat grass and bush-covered plains (savanna bushveld), sometimes broken by rocky outcrops. The Lebombo mountains mark both the eastern border of the park and South Africa's border with Mozambique. A number of rivers flow across the park from east to west, including the Limpopo, Luvuvhu, Shingwedzi, Letaba, Olifants, Timbavati and Sabie Rivers.

There are eight *heks* ('entrance gates' in Afrikaans): Malelane and Crocodile Bridge

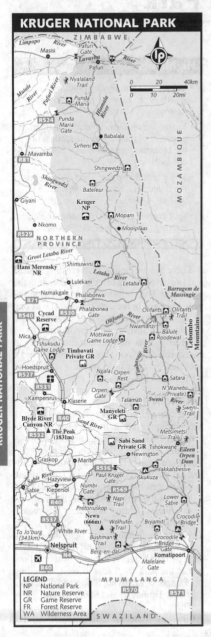

KRUGER NATIONAL PARK

LEGEND
NP National Park
NR Nature Reserve
GR Game Reserve
FR Forest Reserve
WA Wilderness Area

on the southern edge, accessible from the N4 which is the quickest direct route from Johannesburg (Jo'burg); the Numbi and Paul Kruger gates, accessible from Hazyview (turn off the N4 before Nelspruit); Orpen which is convenient if you have been exploring Blyde River; Phalaborwa, accessible from Pietersburg; Punda Maria, accessible from Louis Trichardt; and Pafuri, in the far north, accessible from Thohoyandou in the Venda region.

There are a number of sealed roads, one of which runs the entire spine of the park. The gravel side roads are recommended if you want to get away from the crowds. Altogether, the road network extends for nearly 2000km.

INFORMATION
Bookings
Accommodation can be booked through the head office of the **National Parks Board** (☎ 012-343 1991, fax 343 0905, e reservations@parks-sa.co.za, w www.parks-sa.co.za, PO Box 787, Pretoria 0001). There is also an office at **Cape Town Tourism** (☎ 021-426 4260, fax 426 4266, Cnr Castle & Burg Sts, City Bowl, Cape Town, w www.cape-town.org; open 8am-5pm Mon-Fri, 8.30am-1pm Sat, 9am-1pm Sun). Maps and publications are sold in the larger rest camps. The magazine Timbila (R19.95) has a heavy emphasis on Kruger.

Written applications for rest camps and wilderness trails can be made up to 13 months in advance. Except in the high season (school holidays, Christmas and Easter and weekends, bookings are advisable but not essential.

Entry
Day or overnight entry to the park costs R30/15 for adults/children plus R24 for a car (bicycles, motorcycles and open vehicles must not enter the park). During school holidays you can stay in the park for a maximum of 10 days and at any one rest camp for five days (10 days if you're camping). The park authorities restrict the total number of visitors within the park, so in the high season it pays to arrive early if you don't have a booking.

months	entrance gates open	camps open	gates & camps close
January	5.30am	4.30am	6.30pm
February	5.30am	5.30am	6.30pm
March	5.30am	5.30am	6pm
April	6am	6am	6pm
May	6am	6am	5.30pm
June	6am	6am	5.30pm
July	6am	6am	5.30pm
August	6am	6am	6pm
September	6am	6am	6pm
October	5.30am	5.30am	6pm
November	5.30am	4.30am	6.30pm
December	5.30am	4.30am	6.30pm

It's an offence to arrive late at a camp and you can be fined for doing so (the camps are fenced). With speed limits of 50km/h on sealed roads and 40km/h on dirt roads, it can take a while to travel from camp to camp, especially if you encounter a traffic jam near an interesting animal.

PLANT & ANIMAL DISTRIBUTION

Kruger encompasses a variety of landscapes and ecosystems, with each ecosystem favoured by particular species. Most mammals are distributed throughout the park, but some show a distinct preference for particular regions. The excellent *Find It* booklet, available from the park shops located at some of the bigger camps and at the National Parks office in Pretoria, points out the most likely places to see particular species.

Impalas, buffaloes, Burchell's zebras, blue wildebeests, kudus, waterbucks, baboons, vervet monkeys, cheetahs, leopards and other smaller predators are all widespread. Birdlife is prolific along the rivers and north of the Luvuvhu River.

Rainfall is highest (700mm a year) in the south-western corner between the Olifants and Crocodile Rivers. This area is thickly wooded and has a variety of trees including acacias, bushwillows, sycamore figs and flowering species such as the red-and-orange coral tree. This terrain is particularly favoured by white rhinos and buffaloes, but is less favoured by antelope and, therefore, by predators.

Conservation the Winner

Gaza–Kruger–Gonarezhou Transfrontier Park is certainly a mouthful, but it's also an historic step in Southern African cooperation. The new park will incorporate Kruger National Park, the Gaza Province wildlife area in Mozambique and the Gonarezhou National Park in Zimbabwe (as well as a slice of land linking the Zimbabwean and Mozambique side with Kruger). An agreement to form the park was signed by the respective governments on 21 February 2001 and will constitute one of the biggest conservation areas in the world and the largest wildlife reserve on the African continent; altogether the park will be more than 35,000 sq km, and will have a mammal population in excess of 100,000.

By tearing down the fences that have physically and symbolically divided this massive territory into three autonomous entities, environmentalists hope to re-establish biodiversity and crucial animal migration routes. The park will be one of the only protected areas in Southern Africa that is capable of maintaining a carnivore-prey system.

There is still a lot of work to be done before the park is opened (the target date is 2003) but this is a major coup for conservation.

The eastern section of the park, to the south of the Olifants River on the plains around Satara and south to the Crocodile River, experiences reasonable rainfall (600mm) and has fertile soils. There are expanses of good grazing, with buffalo grass and red grass interspersed with acacia thorn trees (especially knobthorn), leadwood and marula trees. In this region there are large populations of impalas, zebras, wildebeests, giraffes and black rhinos. Predators, particularly lions, prey on impalas, zebras and blue wildebeests.

North of the Olifants River the rainfall drops below 500mm and the veld's dominant tree is mopani. This grows widely in the west, among red bushwillow, but has a tougher time on the basalt plains of the north-east, where it tends to be more stunted. The mopani is a favoured food of elephants, which are most common north of Olifants, and is also eaten by tsessebes, elands, roans and sables.

Perhaps the most interesting area is in the far north around Punda Maria and Pafuri, which has a higher rainfall (around 700mm at Punda Maria) than the mopani country and therefore supports a wider variety of plants (baobabs are particularly noticeable) and animals in higher density. There is woodland, bushveld, grass plains and, between the Luvuvhu and Limpopo Rivers, a tropical riverine forest.

All the rivers have riverine forest along their banks, often with enormous fig trees, which supports populations of bushbuck and nyala. Needless to say, the rivers are where you will find hippos and crocodiles.

WILDLIFE DRIVES

There are morning and night wildlife drives available at all rest camps. The morning drive departs at 5am and the night drive leaves at 5pm. The duration for both is about three hours. At some of the larger camps a late-night drive at 8.30pm is also available. The drives cost R35/70 for children/adults.

These drives are worthwhile as many animals, including lions, leopards and rhinos, are at their most active from first light to around 10am, and then become active again later in the day.

BUSHWALKING

Guided morning and afternoon bush walks have recently been introduced at Kruger. These are a great way to experience the park as they get you out of the car and up close and personal with the animals in their environment. Walking around the bush makes for a completely different wildlife experience from seeing animals through the car window. It's also a good opportunity to learn more about the native flora.

You needn't be concerned about safety because two armed rangers accompany the small walking parties, although they are reluctant to use their firearms except in the most extreme circumstances (which are very rare).

The morning walk is recommended as that is when you'll have a better chance of

seeing wildlife on the move. The walks generally start at 5am, last for three to four hours and cost R140 per person; book in advance as they're very popular.

Walks are offered from the larger rest camps, including Satara, Skukuza, Lower Sabie and Pretoriuskop.

Wilderness Trails

There are seven guided trails offering a chance to walk through the park. Small groups are guided by highly knowledgeable armed guides. The walks are not terribly strenuous, and the itinerary is determined by the interests of the group, the time of year and the disposition of the wildlife.

Most trail walks last two days and three nights. Accommodation is in basic, though comfortable, huts and you don't need to provide food or equipment (bring your own beer and wine if you'd like a drink).

These walks are popular and must be booked well in advance through the National Parks Board in Pretoria or Cape Town. The maximum number of people on any trail is eight and the cost is R1300 per person.

On the **Bushman** trail, near Berg-en-dal in the south-western corner of the park, you can trek to rock paintings as well as see large herds of antelopes, lions and rhinos.

The **Wolhuter** trail, based near the Bushman Trail camp, is also in an area inhabited by lions and rhinos. The name commemorates legendary father and son rangers Harry and Henry Wolhuter. You will find out more about Harry's exploits – he singlehandedly wrestled a lion – if you visit Skukuza Museum, at Skukuza Camp.

The **Napi** trail runs through mixed bushveld midway between Skukuza and Pretoriuskop. There are white and black rhinos, lions, leopards, cheetahs, wild dogs, buffaloes and elephants. The trail is good for seeing the Big Five.

Midway between Lower Sabie and Satara, the **Metsimetsi** trail is in an area containing myriad animals. The terrain consists of undulating savanna, ravines and the rocky gorge of the Nwaswitsonto River.

The **Sweni** trail is near Satara. Many lions are attracted to the herds of wildebeests, zebras and buffaloes here. The region and the prevalent species are reminiscent of the Serengeti National Park in Tanzania.

With a base on the Olifants River, the **Olifants** trail offers the chance to get close to elephants, hippos and crocodiles as well as other animals. Sometimes fish eagles and Pels fishing owls can also be seen.

The **Nyalaland** trail is in the far north of the park near the Luvuvhu River, a region of strikingly diverse ecosystems. It is more memorable for its beauty than for opportunities to witness the Big Five. The birdlife is prolific.

WILDLIFE VIEWING

Wildlife spotting is a game of chance, but you have a better probability in Kruger than any other national park in South Africa. This is not only because of the variety of animals that the park sustains, but also because of the number of animals.

Viewing is best in the winter dry season, when trees lose their leaves and plant growth is sparser, improving visibility. At this time the animals tend to be concentrated around the dwindling water sources. On the other hand, the park is more attractive in summer, with lots of fresh green growth, and this is when most animals bear their young.

It can be difficult to spot animals at any time of the year. It is amazing how often you first notice an animal, stop the car, and only then realise that there are many other animals in the immediate area. Even elephants, which you imagine would be fairly conspicuous, can be very well camouflaged when not in motion.

Rest camps provide maps that have a 'coloured pin system' showing where animals have been spotted in the area that day and on the previous day. This is a good place to start.

Patience and perseverance are vital prerequisites, so drive slowly. The excellent road system means you can get off the main roads quite easily: You don't need a 4WD for most of the secondary gravel roads (although if it has been raining heavily it's worth checking with the rangers at your rest camp for routes that should be avoided).

When you find a decent vantage point, stop the car and scan the surrounding countryside. It is always rewarding to sit still and stake out a water hole. Sunglasses and binoculars are essential; ideally have one set of binoculars per person.

Though different animals display varying behaviour at different times of day (and tend to be more active in the morning and again in the late afternoon and evening), they do not follow rules. A hungry or thirsty animal will eat and drink when it wants to, so there is always something to be seen.

Look out for the big cats enjoying the views and breezes from rocky knolls. Leopards will often rest high off the ground in the branches of trees.

The more you know about the animals (especially their distribution and behaviour) the better your chance of finding them, so

Where Should I Go?

If you're spending time in the south of the park, the road between Lower Sabie and Olifants, via Tshokwane and Satara, is usually fruitful for wildlife spotting and is a very beautiful route. If you're interested in birds you may strike it lucky between Satara and Olifants, where the plains open up and many of the long-legged birds of the grasslands (such as bustards), birds of prey (eagles) and hornbills (the extraordinary ground hornbill) can be found. You'll probably also start to see more rollers and bee-eaters. We were lucky enough to witness the symbiotic relationship between a stately secretary bird stalking around the grassland and brilliantly coloured carmine bee-eaters. (The agile bee-eaters are extraordinary to watch as they hover and dart around, plucking their prey out of midair.)

Around Satara, other very good routes for wildlife are the road to N'Wanetsi and Orpen. There are plenty of grazers (zebras, impalas, kudus and wildebeests) and giraffes around here, which attract predators. Leopards and cheetahs have been spotted along these routes and there have been fairly common lion sightings. There have also been sightings of wild dogs, but these are now quite rare.

it is worth buying detailed books: many are available at the rest camp shops. Two obvious signals to look for are circling vultures and a number of parked cars. Take particular notice of excited motorists waving madly and attempting to flag you down – they've probably just seen something worth a detour.

Warthogs, baboons, zebras, giraffes and many antelope species will happily graze together, so if you see one species, there will often be more close by. The presence of feeding herbivores does not preclude the possibility of a predator in the vicinity. Look carefully, as predators are expert stalkers and may not be obvious. Many animals do, however, seem to know whether a predator is actually hunting; if it isn't they will be quite relaxed in its presence.

Antelopes will be nervous and alert if they are aware of a predator on the hunt, but may not immediately flee. They know they can nearly always outrun a predator if they have a sufficient head start, so they maintain a 'flight distance' between themselves and the threat. If the hunter encroaches, the antelope will move, but will try to keep the hunter in sight. If the hunter charges, the antelope will obviously flee, but may not go far.

Do not drive too close to the animals; the closer you are the more likely you are to disturb their natural behaviour. Sudden movements disturb most animals, so if you do approach, be slow and steady. Avoid frequent stopping and starting of the car engine, but bear in mind that engine vibrations may create a problem with camera shake. There are only a few designated spots where you are permitted to get out of your car.

Other Activities

The **Lebombo Motorized Eco Trail** is a 500km 4WD route along the eastern boundary of the park, departing from Crocodile Bridge. The trail lasts five days and you must provide your own vehicle – you'll be accompanied by a ranger. It costs R3500 per car (maximum of four people per vehicle), and is self-catering.

There are **bird-watching weekends** held annually in the park. The cost includes accommodation in bungalows, wildlife drives and visits to bird-watching sites. On past weekends the black coucal, tree pipit, sooty falcon and European hobby have been identified. Call ☎ 011-472 7203 for more information. Some of the larger camps may also run more informal bird-watching excursions; inquire at your camp's reception.

There is currently a **mountain bike trail** being constructed at Bateleur that should be open in the near future.

PLACES TO STAY & EAT

There are several styles of accommodation in Kruger, all of which are of a high standard; bookings can be made through the **National Parks Board** (☎ 012-343 1991, fax 343 0905, **e** reservations@parks-sa.co.za, **w** www.parks-sa.co.za, PO Box 787, Pretoria 0001).

All huts and cottages are supplied with bedding and towels. Most have fridges and air-con or fans. If a kitchen is not part of the accommodation, visitors must bring their utensils if they want to prepare their meals.

Rest Camps

Most visitors stay in rest camps, which have a wide range of facilities, including braais, and good restaurants with reasonable prices; steak and fish dishes cost around R35. The menus are usually fairly standard, although some do have local game dishes

Accommodation varies but usually comprises huts and bungalows (some of which include shared kitchens and bathrooms) and self-contained cottages.

In addition to huts, bungalows and cottages, some rest camps also have 'sponsored accommodation', which is privately owned and is often better equipped and more comfortable; this should also be booked through the National Parks Board.

Unless otherwise stated, the camps all have electricity, a shop, a restaurant, public telephones, shared cooking facilities (sinks, hotplates and braais) and fuel supplies (petrol and diesel).

All camps are fenced, attractively laid out and immaculately maintained. There are swimming pools at Berg-en-dal, Pretoriuskop (a converted natural rock pool), Mopani and Shingwedzi.

Most accommodation has a minimum charge for two or four people plus R70/35 for each additional adult/child. For those with tents or caravans, camping facilities are available at rest camps (unless indicated otherwise); booking is not generally necessary. The rate for a camp site is R70 for one or two people, and R20 for each extra person (maximum of six).

The huts and bungalows described here have shared kitchen and private bathroom (unless indicated otherwise); the rates quoted are for one to two people.

Berg-en-dal This modern, medium-sized camp near Malelane gate has *bungalows* from R315 and *family cottages*, sleeping up to six people, for R600. It's laid out in natural bush on the banks of Matjulu Spruit, about 5km from a water hole popular with rhinos. There's a visitors centre and, during school holidays, nature trails.

Crocodile Bridge Near the gate of the same name, this small camp is in a great position by the Crocodile River. There are crocodile and hippo pools a few kilometres away, and large numbers of zebras, impalas, buffaloes and wildebeests in the surrounding acacia. *Safari tents* cost R150 and *bungalows* cost R315. There is no restaurant, and diesel fuel is not available.

Pretoriuskop Kruger's oldest camp is near Numbi gate and is in higher country than other places in the park, so it's a little cooler in summer. *Huts* with shared bathroom and without/with kitchen cost R100/150, *bungalows* cost R315 (R345 with kitchen) and *family cottages* that sleep up to four people start at R600. The surrounding country is attractive, with granite outcrops, and is frequented by white rhinos. The large camp has a certain old-style charm and includes a natural rock swimming pool that is popular with kids. There are also two *sponsored cottages* (R1000, one to four people).

Lower Sabie This medium-sized camp, about one hour (35km) from Crocodile Bridge gate, is in a prime wildlife-viewing region. It overlooks a dam on the Sabie River that attracts many animals. Elephants, buffaloes, cheetahs and rhinos are often seen in the surrounding country. *Huts* with shared bathroom cost R80, *bungalows* cost R350 (R400 with kitchen) and *cottages* that sleep up to four people will set you back R600. There are plans to redevelop the facilities at Lower Sabie as many buildings were gutted by a fire a few years ago. The reception operates from a temporary building.

Skukuza On the Sabie River, Skukuza (☎ 013-735 5611) is the main camp in Kruger and has facilities similar to those in a small town. There's an ABSA bank, an Automobile Association (AA) workshop garage, a doctor, a library, the police, a post office and an excellent information centre.

Safari tents for one or two people with shared bathroom cost R150, *bungalows* cost R350 (R375 with kitchen) and *cottages* that sleep up to four people cost R600 (R150 for an extra person). There are also four *sponsored cottages*. There is a huge variety of accommodation and, although the camp is large, it's well laid out and doesn't overwhelm. The camp sites are distinctly average.

Selati Restaurant & Bar is in an old train station at Skukuza. It's open from 3pm to 11pm.

Orpen Near Orpen gate, this is a small, attractive camp with a nearby water hole that attracts wildlife. *Huts* cost R150 and *cottages* that sleep up to four people cost R600. There is no restaurant; cooking facilities are shared and no utensils are provided. Some accommodation doesn't have electricity, so bring a torch (flashlight).

There are basic camp sites available at Maroela, 4km away.

Satara East of Orpen gate, Satara (☎ 013-735 6306) is situated in an area of flat and fertile plains that attracts large numbers of grazing animals and has the highest lion population in the entire park. There are several water holes; you can see one of them from the terrace of the pleasant self-serve restaurant.

Bungalows cost R350 (R375 with kitchen) and *cottages* sleeping up to four people cost R600. Satara is the second-largest camp, and although it is not the most appealing (it's a bit flat for a start), there's a range of facilities. There are also three *sponsored cottages*.

Olifants This camp (☎ 013-735 6606) has a fantastic position on the bluff high above the Olifants River and offers spectacular views. From the camp you can see elephants, hippos and many other animals as they come down to the river 100m below. Much of the camp is terraced and some of the huts are literally on the edge of the cliffs. *Bungalows* cost R315 (R345 with kitchen) and fully equipped *cottages* that accommodate up to four people cost R600. There are no camp sites at Olifants but it is possible to camp at nearby Balule (see Bushveld Camps, following). There are also two sponsored cottages.

There's an interesting information centre that focuses on elephants here.

Letaba About 20km to the north, Letaba (☎ 013-735 6636) has excellent views over a wide bend of the Letaba River. It's an attractive camp with lots of shade, trees and grassy camp sites. There are plenty of animals, especially in winter. *Safari tents* will set you back R150, *huts* cost R150 (with shared bathroom), *bungalows* cost R315 (R350 with kitchen) and *cottages* that sleep up to four people cost R600. There are two *sponsored cottages*. The restaurant overlooks the river.

The museum here focuses on the elephant and includes mounted tusks of the big bulls (Mafunyane, Dzombo, Shingwedzi and Shawu) that have died in the park. There are sections on poaching, the illegal ivory trade, geomorphology and biology; there are also descriptions of elephant habits.

Mopani A superb modern rest camp, Mopani (☎ 013-735 6536) is on the edge of the Pioneer Dam, 45km north of Letaba. Natural materials have been used and all the buildings are thatched. *Bungalows* cost R350, *cottages* that sleep one or two people cost R415 and *cottages* accommodating up to four people cost R600. There's a *sponsored cottage* here, but no camp sites. There are some great spots overlooking the dam.

Shingwedzi The largest camp, Shingwedzi (☎ 013-735 6806/7) is in the northern section of the park. It's an old-style place, with many huts and cottages arranged in circles and shaded by tall mopani trees and palms. *Huts* cost R150, *bungalows* cost R275 (R315 with kitchen) and *cottages* accommodating up to four people cost R400. A restaurant overlooks the Shingwedzi River and there's a swimming pool. There are excellent drives in the vicinity.

Punda Maria The northernmost rest camp, Punda Maria (☎ 013-735 6873) is in sandveld (dry, sandy belt) country by Dimbo mountain. It's a long-established camp with an attractive setting and a wilderness atmosphere. The area's ecology is fascinating and there is a wide range of animals including lions and elephants. *Bungalows* here cost R315 (R320 with kitchen) and *cottages* that sleep up to four people cost R600. It's the perfect place for a night-time braai (come prepared).

Bushveld Camps

Bushveld camps are smaller, more remote clusters of self-catering cottages without shops and restaurants, and tend to get fewer people passing through. Most are reasonably close to a rest camp where supplies can be bought. All bushveld camps have solar power, so electrical appliances other than lights, fans and fridges cannot be used. Bookings are essential. The following is by no means an exhaustive list; prices quoted here are the minimum charges.

At *Balule*, camp sites for one or two people cost R70 (extra person R20), and there are huts for R100. This place is 11km south of Olifants. The only services it offers are hot water and wood stoves. It's quiet and atmospheric, however, and you'll almost certainly hear hippos grunting in the nearby river. Definitely bring a torch.

We've heard great things about *Tamboti*, which has wildlife wandering outside its safari tents (R150); it's situated just 7km north-east of Orpen.

The following places have cottages for up to four people that cost R500 and two-bathroom cottages that sleep six for R900: *Biyamiti* on the southern border of Kruger, between Malelane and Crocodile Bridge gates; *Talamati* on the western border of Kruger, about 30km south of Orpen gate; *Shimuwini* on the Letaba River, 50km north of Phalaborwa gate; and *Sirheni*, about 55km south-east of Punda Maria.

Private Camps

Private camps are not to be confused with the private reserves that border Kruger. Private camps cater for groups, which must book out the entire camp, so there's plenty of privacy. Unless you're in a largish group they are pretty expensive (about R3000 for up to 12 people, plus R70/35 for each additional adult/child). You need to take all your own supplies, except bedding. Bookings are essential (book through the National Parks Board).

GETTING THERE & AROUND

See also the Phalaborwa section in the Northern Province chapter for information about visiting Kruger from Phalaborwa.

Air

SA Airlink flies daily from Jo'burg to Skukuza (R674 for a seven-day, advance-purchase ticket) and Phalaborwa (R731). SA Express flies from Jo'burg to Skukuza daily (R650 one way) and less frequently from Cape Town to Hoedspruit (there's an additional R60 tax if you fly into the East-gate airport at Hoedspruit, as this airport is privately owned).

Bus & Minibus Taxi

For most visitors, Nelspruit is the most convenient large town near Kruger, and is well served by bus and minibus taxi to and from Jo'burg.

Phalaborwa, in the north, is on the edge of Kruger and is served by regular bus ser-

Tuberculosis Threat

Bovine tuberculosis (BTB) is threatening the wildlife in Kruger. Not much is really known about the disease, but in the park the main host appears to be the buffalo; infections have also been found in lions, leopards, cheetahs, kudus and baboons. The disease spreads slowly, and is airborne among buffaloes; lions contract the disease by killing and eating infected animals.

BTB was first diagnosed in 1990, but subsequent studies have led researchers to believe that it came into the park in the 1950s. The disease is widespread in the south of the park. If you wish to make a donation towards research into BTB in Kruger National Park contact **The Animal Tuberculosis Fund** (*The Manager: Scientific Services, Private Bag X402, SKUKUZA 1350, South Africa*). You can contact **e** researchknp@parks-sa.co.za for more information.

vices, both City to City and North Link Tours. From the Venda region in Northern Province, minibus taxis run close to the Punda Maria gate.

Train

The *Komati* runs from Jo'burg to Komatipoort (via Nelspruit), around 12km from Kruger's Crocodile Bridge gate.

Car

Skukuza is 500km from Jo'burg (six hours); Punda Maria is about 620km from Jo'burg (eight hours). Hire cars are available at Skukuza, Nelspruit and Phalaborwa.

Most visitors drive themselves around the park, and this is definitely the best way to experience Kruger. If you're running low on funds, hiring a car between three or four people for a few days is relatively cheap.

Organised Tours

The Mopani Package is a two-night getaway trip that is perfect for those on a tight schedule. It includes return flights between Jo'burg and Phalaborwa, airport transfers, two nights' accommodation, two meals a day and either a bush walk or a wildlife

KRUGER NATIOANL PARK

drive. The cost is R2050 per person. Contact *SA Airlink* (☎ 011-395 3333, e karinegly@ saairlink.co.za) for bookings.

For those with limited funds, a great way to glimpse the park is with *African Routes* (☎ 031-569 3911, e aroutes@iafrica.com, w www.africanroutes.co.za). Its safari also includes the Klein Drakensberg in Mpumalanga, Swaziland and the Drakensberg (see Organised Tours in the Getting Around chapter for more details).

Smaller operators include *Bundu Bus* (☎ 011-693 1808, e frsryan@bundusafaris .co.za), which offers four-day tours (departing Monday and Friday) around Mpumalanga and Kruger Park for about R1400, all inclusive; *Max Maximum Tours* (☎ 011-933 4177), which runs three-day tours for R2500, including B&B; and *Wildlife Safaris* (☎ 011-888 6896, w www.wildlifesaf.co.za), which has four-day panorama tours around the Blyde River and into Kruger for R3170, including DB&B.

Around Kruger National Park

The area just west of Kruger contains a large number of private reserves, most of which share a border with Kruger and thus offer an opportunity to see most of the Big Five. They are often extremely pricey – around R1000 to R2500 per person (all inclusive) is quite common and it can get a lot more expensive. They have an economic stake in their guests getting close to animals so they have good viewing facilities. It is possible to find cheaper and perhaps more enjoyable accommodation in bush camps.

Listed here are some of the reserves and accommodation options. Before deciding which private reserve to visit, it's worth contacting a travel agency to find out about any special deals. **Sondelani Travel & Info** (☎ 013-764 3492) in Sabie; **Nelspruit Information** (☎ 013-755 1988) office in Nelspruit; and **BaPhalaborwa (Community) Tourism Association** (☎ 015-781 6770) in Phalaborwa all handle bookings.

KLASERIE NATURE RESERVE

South of Phalaborwa and east of Hoedspruit, the Klaserie Nature Reserve (☎ 015 793 1718) covers 60,000 hectares and contains a range of animals (including lion and elephants).

For accommodation in the reserve, try *Motswari* and *M'Bali* (☎ 011-463 1990 e martinek@)motswari.co.za, for both) where shared rooms start from R975 pe person.

TIMBAVATI PRIVATE GAME RESERVE

Timbavati (☎/fax 015-793 2394, e warden@ timbavati.co.za; admission R40 per person plus R35 per vehicle), known for its white lion population, has a good reputation. The reserve is jointly owned by a large numbe of people dedicated to conservation.

Most places to stay in the Timbavati area have all-inclusive deals including wildlife drives and bush walks.

Thornybush (☎ 015-793 2771) Full board R2180 per person. Walks and wildlife drives included. This is a luxurious place in its own wildlife reserve on the road into Timbavati. It has four lodges: Jackalberry, Chapungu, n'Kaya and Serondella.

Otter's Den (☎ 015-795 5250) Full board R420 per person. This place is 35km from Hoedspruit; the chalets are out on an island on the Blyde River and are reached by a suspension bridge.

Tanda Tula (☎ 015-793 3191, e cuisine@ iafrica.com) Singles/doubles full board R1690/2900. This place has possibly the most luxurious tented accommodation in the country. The tariff is significantly higher in the high season.

Ngala (☎ 015-793 1555) Full board US$475 per person. Ngala is on the Kruger border and is very luxurious. Its exclusive Safari Suite has a lounge and sun deck overlooking a water hole.

Lerato Game Lodge (☎ 015-793 1350 e leratolodge@mweb.co.za) Self-catering R200 per person, B&B R250 per person Lerato Game Lodge has a range of good value accommodation in tents and chalets It's about 30km from Hoedspruit.

ot the tall, the leggy and the cunning at Kruger National Park: The giraffe is the tallest of all
ammals; when alarmed, impalas can jump 9m in a single bound; the leopard is a solitary, agile animal.

LUKE HUNTER

RICHARD I'ANSON

RICHARD I'ANSON

Kruger National Park spans nearly two million hectares. Park authorities claim that it has the greatest variety of animals of any park in Africa. Add it to your list of must-sees.

Pezulu Tree House Game Lodge (☎ 015-793 2724, ℮ pezlodge@mweb.co.za) Singles/doubles full board R795/1350, self-catering R180/300. This lodge is north of Guernsey Rd and is a good option if you're looking to self-cater.

MANYELETI GAME RESERVE
This reserve is between Kruger's Orpen gate and Sabie Sand Game Reserve. Manyeleti shares a border with Kruger and therefore shares some of its animals, including all of the Big Five. It offers some of the area's least expensive accommodation in the *public camp*. There is also privately run accommodation within Manyeleti.

Honeyguide (☎ 011-880 3912, ℮ ten bomp@global.co.za) Rooms B&B R1200. Developed by the Meeser family, Honeyguide is expensive, but it is an exceptional place.

Khoka Moya (☎ 015-793 1729, 0861-000333, ℮ ceres@threecities.co.za) Singles/doubles full board R927/1232. Khoka Moya means 'Capture the Spirit' and that is exactly what Johnny Meeser, the inspirational founder, ensured guests did. But with Johnny gone, the bush experience has become more of a yuppie retreat. The tariff includes two wildlife drives.

SABI SAND GAME RESERVE
This is a very large private conservation area on the south-western edge of Kruger Park. Within Sabi Sand are a number of private reserves, all sharing the same lowveld country and, now that the fence has come down, Kruger's wealth of birds and animals.

The Sabi Sand Game Reserve consists of two reserves: **Sabi Sabi** (☎ 011-483 3939, ☒ www.sabisabi.com) in the south on the Sabie River, and **Inyati** (☎ 011-880 5907) in the north on the Sand River. While the Big Five are found in both, you have a better chance of seeing lions at Sabi Sabi; Inyati is better for spotting hippos and crocodiles. Accommodation is in luxury *chalets* (Inyati's are much cheaper), and the tariff includes meals, drives and guided walks.

Idube (☎ 011-888 3713, ☒ www.idube.com) is a luxurious place north-west of Sabi

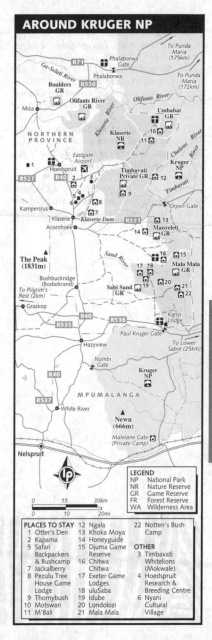

AROUND KRUGER NP

NORTHERN PROVINCE

MPUMALANGA

LEGEND
NP National Park
NR Nature Reserve
GR Game Reserve
FR Forest Reserve
WA Wilderness Area

PLACES TO STAY		
1 Otter's Den	12 Ngala	22 Notten's Bush
2 Kapama	13 Khoka Moya	Camp
5 Safari	14 Honeyguide	
Backpackers	15 Djuma Game	**OTHER**
& Bushcamp	Reserve	3 Timbavati
7 Jackalberry	16 Chitwa	Whitelions
8 Pezulu Tree	Chitwa	(Mokwale)
House Game	17 Exeter Game	4 Hoedspruit
Lodge	Lodges	Research &
9 Thornybush	18 uluSaba	Breeding Centre
10 Motswari	19 Idube	6 Nyani
11 M'Bali	20 Londolozi	Cultural
	21 Mala Mala	Village

Sabi. Other accommodation nearby includes *Djuma Game Reserve* (☎ 013-735 5118, Ⓦ www.djuma.com), *Exeter Game Lodges* (☎ 013-741 3180, Ⓦ www.exeter-lodges .com), *Singita* (☎ 011-234 0990, Ⓦ www .singita.co.za), *Nottens Bush Camp* (☎ 013-735 5105, Ⓦ www.nottens.com) and *Chitwa Chitwa* (☎ 011-883 1354, Ⓔ chitwa@iafrica .com).

The rock lodge at *uluSaba* (☎ 013-735 5460), set in bush south of Inyati, has winter specials, although outside of these, rates start at around R4000 per person.

Londolozi (☎ 011-809 4300, Ⓦ www .ccafrica.com) is operated by CCAfrica Safari Destinations and has a variety of accommodation options ranging from a main camp with luxury chalets to bush camps. To get here take the R536 from Hazyview west towards Kruger gate and Skukuza, and turn to the left after 36km; it's 28km further on.

MALA MALA GAME RESERVE

Mala Mala (☎ 031-765 2900, Ⓦ www.mala mala.com), a world-famous reserve (and rightly so), is geared towards 'safari-suited' foreigners who want to see the Big Five while remaining in a five-star cocoon; its 'jeep jockeys' with radios and all sorts of gizmos make sure they extract the right 'oohs' and 'aahs' out of their patrons when the Big Five are spotted. Head towards Londolozi in Sabi Sand Game Reserve and then follow the signposts.

Northern Province

Northern Province is a combination of high-veld and lowveld. The forested Soutpansberg Range, the lush Letaba Valley with its tropical fruit farms, and the nearby cycad forests surrounding the Rain Queen's home provide some contrast to the bushveld plains.

To the west of the N1 highway is the fascinating Waterberg region; north of the Soutpansberg you're well into tropical, baobab-studded plains; and to the east is the mystical Venda region. As well as Kruger National Park and the private wildlife reserves that border it, there are many other reserves and good hiking trails in the area.

Northern Province can be broken into four distinct geographical areas: Capricorn in the south; Bushveld in the west; Valley of the Olifants in the east; and Soutpansberg in the north. Local tourist offices use these distinctions and can provide a free glossy booklet on each area containing smatterings of useful information.

The N1 highway from Johannesburg (Jo'burg) and Pretoria to the Zimbabwe border neatly divides Northern Province. Along this artery are the main provincial towns. The tropic of Capricorn crosses the N1 35km south of Louis Trichardt.

Warning

Take precautions against malaria and bilharzia while in Northern Province.

Capricorn

At the heart of the southern Capricorn region is Pietersburg, the provincial capital. This area also takes in areas of bushveld around Potgietersrus in the west.

PIETERSBURG-POLOKWANE
☎ 015 • postcode 0699 • pop 140,000
Pietersburg-Polokwane, known locally as Pietersburg, is the provincial capital, and was

Highlights

- Skirt around the sacred sites of the former Homeland of Venda.
- Join a walking safari of the famed historical African Ivory Route.
- Ride horses among wildlife in the Waterberg range.
- Spot the many species of water birds in the Nylsvley (Nyls Valley).
- Learn about indigenous bushcraft and wildlife tracking at the spectacularly situated Ndzalama Wildlife Reserve.

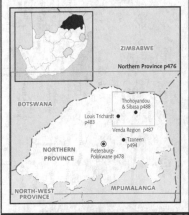

founded in 1886 by a group of Voortrekkers who had been forced to abandon a settlement further north because of malaria and 'hostile natives'. Today, Pietersburg (renamed Pietersburg-Polokwane after the large black community in the vicinity) is a big, sedate place serving agricultural and mining communities. It is pleasant enough, with coral trees and jacarandas lining the broad streets and, reputedly, the lowest crime rate of any South African provincial capital.

Possibly the most efficient tourist office we've come across in South Africa is the

NORTHERN PROVINCE

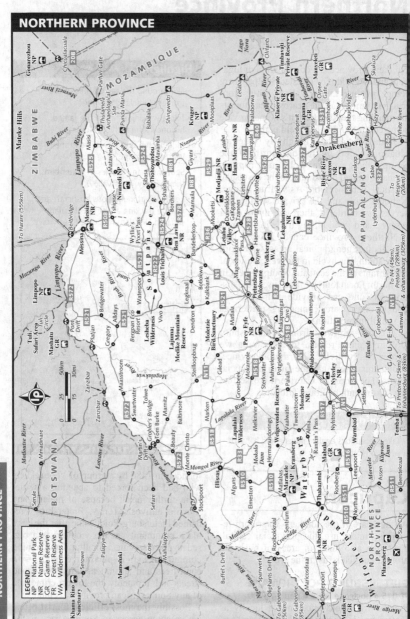

Pietersburg-Polokwane Marketing Company (☎ 290 2010, e elaine.vrensburg@ pietersburg.org.za, Civic Square, Landdros Mare St).

The major banks are all represented, but the best for changing money is **ABSA** (Hans van Rensburg St).

For Internet access, the **TSA Community Internet Cafe** (☎ 297 6207, Landdros Mare St) has the cheapest connections (R25 an hour).

Things to See & Do

If you want to familiarise yourself with the city, the tourist office has a brochure detailing a walk around the central business district.

The **Pietersburg Nature Reserve** (☎ 290 2331; adult/child R8.55/5.70 plus R11.40 per vehicle; open 7am-6.30pm daily) is south of the town centre in Union Park on the road to Silicon. It's very big for a reserve adjacent to a city and is one of the largest of its kind in the country. All of the South African antelopes are represented, and you can see zebras, giraffes and white rhinos from the Rhinoceros Walking Trail.

The **Bakoni Malapa Northern Sotho Open-Air Museum** (☎ 295 2432; adult/ child R3/1.50; open 8.30am-noon Mon, 8.30am-3.30pm Tues-Fri), 9km south-east of Pietersburg on the R37 to Chuniespoort, is devoted to northern Sotho culture and includes an authentic 'living' village. There are archaeological remains and paintings dating back to AD 1000 and there's evidence of Ndebele iron and copper smelting.

Australian visitors may want to take a peek over the fence at the house where anti-hero Harry ('Breaker Morant') Harbord was tried for crimes committed during the Anglo-Boer War. It's at 4 Hans van Rensburg St.

Places to Stay

Accommodation options have improved in recent years, although places are concentrated mainly in the mid-range bracket. Those wanting a bit of luxury will be better off at an upmarket guesthouse.

Union Caravan Park (☎ 295 2011) Camp sites R45.60, 2-bed/4-bed/6-bed chalets R114/182/228. This park is 5km from the town centre past the stadium. If you're walking the trail in the adjacent nature reserve, sites cost only R20.

Northern Star (☎/fax 295 8980, 46 Landdros Mare St) Singles/doubles R130/160. An old, solid hotel, it's the cheapest central option in town; there are also weekend specials. Rooms are pretty basic.

Arnotha's (☎ 291 3390, fax 291 3394, 42 Hans van Rensburg St) Singles/doubles Mon-Fri R159/190. A popular refuge for salespeople, Arnotha's is one of the best places in town in this price range. The old self-catering rooms are huge and there are specials on weekends. B&B is also available.

Travellers Lodge (☎ 291 5511, 43 Bok St) Singles/doubles Mon-Fri R175/195, Sat & Sun R150/175. This place is a similar standard to Arnotha's – the rooms here are fully self-contained.

Vivaldi Guest House (☎ 295 6162, e sa tours@cis.co.za, 2 Voortrekker St) Singles/ doubles R230/296. More expensive, but well worth the extra, Vivaldi is a great place to stay, complete with talking parrot and a macaw. If it's full, the hosts will look for a suitable alternative.

Victoria Place (☎ 295 7599, fax 291 3559, e schofield@lantic.co.za, 32 Burger St) Singles/doubles R275/360. Run more like a hotel than a guesthouse, Victoria Place has good security and is set up for 'the discerning businessman'.

Plumtree Lodge (☎ 295 6153, fax 295 6150, e plumtree@pixie.co.za, 138 Marshall St) Singles/doubles R300/380. This place has spacious rooms and it's very well kept. There's a swimming pool for guests.

Holiday Inn Garden Court (☎ 291 2030, fax 291 3150, Thabo Mbeki St) Doubles B&B R390. Holiday Inn has smallish rooms with all the comforts.

Places to Eat

Grobler St has several fast-food outlets including *Pizza and Pasta Magic*, *KFC*, *Nando's* and *Chicken Licken*. Just about every chain 'fastie' is found in the Savannah Centre on Thabo Mbeki St, about 250m along the Tzaneen road from the city centre.

NORTHERN PROVINCE

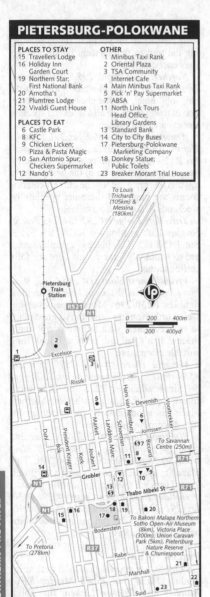

PIETERSBURG-POLOKWANE

PLACES TO STAY
15 Travellers Lodge
16 Holiday Inn
   Garden Court
19 Northern Star;
   First National Bank
20 Arnotha's
21 Plumtree Lodge
22 Vivaldi Guest House

PLACES TO EAT
6 Castle Park
8 KFC
9 Chicken Licken;
   Pizza & Pasta Magic
10 San Antonio Spur;
   Checkers Supermarket
12 Nando's

OTHER
1 Minibus Taxi Rank
2 Oriental Plaza
3 TSA Community
   Internet Cafe
4 Main Minibus Taxi Rank
5 Pick 'n' Pay Supermarket
7 ABSA
11 North Link Tours
   Head Office;
   Library Gardens
13 Standard Bank
14 City to City Buses
17 Pietersburg-Polokwane
   Marketing Company
18 Donkey Statue;
   Public Toilets
23 Breaker Morant Trial House

San Antonio Spur (☎ 295 8146, *Checkers Centre*) Burgers R18-25. The burgers here are huge and there is a reasonable salad bar

Panarotti's (☎ 296 0170, *Savannah Centre*) Pasta dishes R25, pizzas R30. Panarotti's purveys pizza and pasta with panache. It has moved from downtown echoing a retreat to the suburbs that is happening all over the country.

Villa Italia (☎ 296 0857, *Savannah Centre*) Salads R19, pasta dishes R20-32, large pizzas R30-40. This reliable restaurant will make dishes to order. The seafood is particularly good. Try the mussels fettuccine with just a hint of chilli (R48).

There are other restaurants and cafes in the Savannah Centre including *Burgundy* (☎ 296 0963) and *Caffe Rossini* (☎ 296 3827), which serve good coffee (not that indigestible chicory stuff).

Castle Park (☎ 297 3281, *Biccard St*) Pub meals R15-35. Pietersburg used to have very few night venues. Now there is Castle Park (formerly O'Hagan's) for Irish-style boozing and pub meals.

Cock 'n' Bull (☎ 296 0961, *Savannah Centre*) Starters R13-30, mains R30-70. Open daily. With possibly the most interesting menu in town this place offers fresh oysters on Tuesday and Wednesday, a seafood combo (R66) and snails florentine (R32). The food's great, but the menu warns 'patrons disembarking from stage coaches are to be checked for fleas, ticks and other small animals which will find their way to the kitchen'. Leave the stage coach at home.

Getting There & Away

SA Airlink flies daily to/from Jo'burg (R662, seven-day advance purchase).

City to City buses run daily between Jo'burg and Sibasa (R60) and stop at the garage on the corner of Grobler and Dahl Sts. There is also a service from Jo'burg to Messina and Beitbridge (R70).

The Greyhound daily service between Jo'burg and Harare stops at the Shell Ultra on the highway about 10km south of Pietersburg; the fare to and from Jo'burg is R125. A taxi from the Shell Ultra to town is R60; try **City Taxis** (☎ 297 0348).

The Translux daily service on the same route stops outside Big Bite on Grobler St; the fare is R115.

North Link Tours services between Phalaborwa and Jo'burg stop at the Library Gardens on Hans van Rensburg St. Buy tickets at the head office of **North Link Tours** (☎ 291 1867) nearby in the mall; Pietersburg to Phalaborwa is R75.

The *Bosvelder* train (Jo'burg-Beitbridge) stops here; Jo'burg to Pietersburg costs R75/110 in 2nd/1st class.

The main minibus taxi rank is in Kerk St, not far from the Pick 'n' Pay supermarket, and there's another on Excelsior St near the train station; most Jo'burg taxis leave from here. Destinations and fares from Pietersburg include Thohoyandou (R15), Louis Trichardt (R16) and Jo'burg (R75).

POTGIETERSRUS & AROUND
☎ 015 • postcode 0601

This conservative town (they all seem to be up this way), 227km north of Pretoria, was settled early by Voortrekkers, not without resistance from the people already living there. The **Bosveld Publicity Association** (☎ 491 8458) is on the R101 and has plenty of local information.

The **Arend Dieperink Museum** (☎ 491 8458; adult/student/child R3/1/1; open 7.30am-4.30pm Mon-Fri) at the back of the Publicity Association tells the story of the local resistance.

Create a Craft (Cnr De Klerk & Voortrekker Sts) has excellent local crafts at very reasonable prices.

Makapansgat Caves (☎ 491 8458; adult/student R15/10; R180 for a group guide), 23km north-east of town, are a palaeontological site of world significance, and have yielded bones of an early human, *Australopithecus africanus*, radiocarbon dated to be three million years old. The Cave of Hearths records human development from the Early Stone Age through to the Iron Age. Extinct animals found in the cave include a miniature buffalo and a species of hare. You must book at the Arend Dieperink Museum and sign an indemnity form before visiting.

The **Game Breeding Centre** (☎ 491 4314; admission R10; open 8am-4pm Mon-Fri, 8am-6pm Sat & Sun) on the R101 is a breeding centre for the National Zoo in Pretoria and has a wide variety of native and exotic animals. You can drive through the reserve.

The **Percy Fyfe Nature Reserve** (☎ 491 5678; admission R5 plus R7 per vehicle; open 8am-4pm daily), 27km from town, is a breeding centre for species of rare antelopes, and also has other wildlife.

Places to Stay & Eat
There is a *camp site* (☎ 083-340 2861) opposite the entrance to the breeding centre (sites R40).

Lonely Oak Lodge (☎ 491 4560, Hooge St) Singles/doubles R190/250. Rooms here are functional, but comfortable.

Protea Park Hotel (☎ 491 3101, fax 491 6842) Doubles Sat & Sun R225, Mon-Fri R260. Rooms here have air-con. Although this chain suffers from being rather staid, it's probably the most luxurious option in town.

Jaagbaan (☎ 491 7833) B&B R100 per person. Jaagbaan, 8km south of town, is recommended. The owners know how to look after their guests, who are greeted by a pack of yelping sausage dogs on arrival.

There are a number of chain's on the N1 (Voortrekker St) including *Nando's*, *San Domingo Spur*, *Steers* and *Wimpy*.

Westhuis Guesthouse (☎ 491 7602, 82 Rabe St) Meals R30-50. For traditional Afrikaner meals, try this place.

Oaks Pub & Grill (☎ 491 4355, Van Riebeeck St) Starters R18-22, mains R30-45. The food here is very good, especially the seafood.

For African meals, ask about the whereabouts of *Tuku's Place* and *Kgasi Tavern*.

Getting There & Away
Greyhound buses stop at the Wimpy on Voortrekker St on its Jo'burg-Bulawayo run. Jo'burg to Potgietersrus costs R105; Pietersburg to Potgietersrus costs R85.

Translux also stops in town at the Wimpy; its prices are similar.

Pietersburg to Potgietersrus costs about R15 in a minibus taxi.

NORTHERN PROVINCE

Bushveld

The Bushveld region in the south-west is flat, dry and the most typical of South African savanna. It includes a string of towns along the N1, including Naboomspruit and Nylstroom as well as the holiday resort of Warmbad. West of the N1, the bushveld turns into the rolling mountains and scenic valleys of the Waterberg (part of the Bushveld), so named because of the abundance of streams and rivers in the area.

NABOOMSPRUIT & AROUND
☎ 014 • postcode 0560

This town (everyone calls it 'Naboom') is in the centre of a rich agricultural and mining district. There are also many mineral springs in the area. It's a conservative place, but after a few glasses of mampoer (home-distilled brandy) the clothes may well come off, as there is a huge nudist camp nearby.

The helpful **tourist office** (☎ 743 1111) can be found at the corner of Louis Trichardt and Sixth Sts.

The 3000-hectare **Nylsvley Nature Reserve** (☎ 743 1074; admission R7.50 plus R7.50 per car; open 6am-6pm daily) is 20km south of Naboom. It's one of the best places in the country to see birds (see the boxed text 'No Moses but Plenty of Birds'). There's a basic *camp site* (☎ 743 1074). To get to the reserve, head south on the N1 for 13km and turn off to the east on the road to Boekenhout.

There are many resorts around the natural springs close to town that have camp sites; ask at the tourist office for more details.

Naboom Hotel (☎ 743 0321, fax 743 0321, 1 Louis Trichardt St) Singles/doubles R65/200. There's an a la carte restaurant called *Skilpads* here and a pub (meals under R10).

Nylsvley Guest Farm (☎ 082-921 9529) Camp sites R40, chalets R50 per person. This newly opened rustic guest farm has thatched chalets. It's a good place for mountain biking and is close to the Nature Reserve of the same name, off the Nylsvley and Boekenhout turn-off.

Greyhound buses stop in town; the fare to Pietersburg is R85. A minibus taxi to Potgietersrus is about R15.

No Moses but Plenty of Birds

When the Nylsvley (Nyls Valley) floods in summer, a cacophony of sounds emanates from the reeds, but it is no baby crying. This flood plain is rich in a number of diverse species of water birds.

Over 100 different species of water birds have been recorded here and in the adjoining private Mosdene Nature Reserve. This number includes 85 of the 94 species known to breed in South Africa, more than in any other wetland in the republic.

After the rains, the food supply in the vlei (low marshy area) is plentiful and the flocks of birds begin to arrive. Some 17 species of ducks are to be found, including the white-faced whistling duck (Dendrocygna viduata). Up to 17 species of herons begin hunting in the shallow water. They include the great white egret (Egretta alba) and the black egret (Egretta ardesiaca) – over 12,000 birds. Bird-watchers will get the opportunity to see rare species such as the bittern (Botaurus stellaris), the dwarf bittern (Ixobrychus sturmii) and the rufous-bellied heron (Ardeola rufiventris). Apart from water birds, more than 300 other species have been recorded in the valley, making it one of the richest places in Africa to see birds.

NYLSTROOM
☎ 014 • postcode 0510

Nylstroom, a small town in cattle country, was named by Voortrekkers who thought they'd found the source of the Nile. After all, the river here seemed to fit the biblical description of the Nile: It was a river, it was in Africa and it had papyrus reeds growing along the banks.

The **Tourism Association** (☎ 717 5211) provides information at a stand in the library.

Avuxeni Stokkiesdraai Motel & Caravan Park (☎ 717 4005, fax 717 5997) Single/double B&B units R120/240, chalets R170, camp sites for 1/2 people R50/60. This place, 3km north of Nylstroom on the R101 to Naboomspruit, has everything for the weary Voortrekker wishing to rest, water the horses, oil the wagon wheels and play putt-putt.

Shangri-La Country Lodge (☎ 717 5381, fax 717 3188, ⓔ shangrila@chips.co.za) B&B R265 per person. Ten kilometres from the Kranskop tollgate, this lodge has thatched rondavels in a magnificent bush setting – it's perfect for escaping the hustle and bustle of the cities for a few days. It's off the R33 on the Eersbewoond road.

WARMBAD

☎ 014 • postcode 0480

This sleepy little town off the N1, 90km north of Pretoria, has become a popular holiday spot because of its mineral springs.

The **information centre** (☎ 736 3694) is on the corner of Voortrekker and Pretoria Sts. The Computer Shop at the Pick 'n' Pay Centre has email facilities (R30 per hour).

Admission to the **mineral springs** (☎ 736 2200; day visits adult/child R40/25) includes access to all facilities. Children under three are not allowed in the hydro spa.

Places to Stay & Eat

Aventura Spa Warmbaths (☎ 736 2200) Powered camp sites R60, 3-bed chalets R335/480 low/high season, hotel doubles R480/575. This place administers the baths and has plenty to keep the kids happy.

Elephant Springs Hotel (☎ 736 2101, 31 Sutter Rd) Doubles without/with breakfast R380/475. Upmarket with prices reflecting the town's popularity with domestic tourists, it's a two-minute walk from the spa.

There are numerous holiday flats along Moffat St, ranging from R150 to R250 for two people. *Casa Blanca* (☎ 736 2480, 42 Moffat St) and *Dula Monate* (☎ 736 3168, 17 Moffat St) are as good as any.

The Pancake Inn (☎ 736 2787) Breakfasts R16-22, pancakes R8-12. Across from the Aventura Spa, this place has English breakfasts and pancakes.

The Keg (☎ 736 2101) Meals R27-45. In the Elephant Springs Hotel, you'll get high-quality pub meals here.

O'Hagans (☎ 736 5068) Meals R30-50. Near the intersection of the link road to the N1 and the R101, this is an Irish-theme pub with a good selection of beers; it also serves good food.

Getting There & Away

Jo'burg to Warmbad is R90 on Greyhound buses, but only R60 with **North Link Tours** (☎ 015-291 1867). Minibus taxis go to towns in the area including Nylstroom (R15).

THE WATERBERG

The 150km-long Waterberg range stretches from Thabazimbi in the south to the La-palala River in the north-east. It is a wild and inspirational place, with *sourveld* (a type of grassland) and bushveld etched by rivers. An unpleasant feature of the Water-berg, though, is the hunting lodge. Its ad-vertising depicts hunters with high-powered rifles posing with dead zebras, kudus and leopards.

Thabazimbi

☎ 014 • postcode 0380

Thabazimbi (Mountain of Iron) is 129km north of Rustenburg on the R510. Nearby is the imposing Kransberg, the highest peak of the Waterberg.

Ben Alberts Nature Reserve (☎ 777 1670; admission free if overnighting; open 6am-6pm), about 7km south of town, has an abun-dance of wildlife and good wildlife-viewing vantage points. Accommodation in the re-serve is in *chalets* (R150 for two people).

Hotel Kransberg (☎ 777 1586) Singles/doubles B&B R190/280. This comfortable hotel has the *Rhino Restaurant* and *Buffalo Pub* attached.

Marakele National Park

This is a relatively isolated national park (☎ 012-343 1991, emergencies 014-777 1745; adult/child R10/5) in the heart of the Waterberg in spectacular mountain country. Elephants, rhinos and many other large wildlife species, apart from lions, are now resident, with many having been relocated from Kruger National Park. The birdlife is prolific and includes the largest colony of the endangered Cape vulture (Gyps cop-rotheres) in the world. Marakele is now be-ginning to live up to its Tswana name, 'Place of Sanctuary'. It has patches of rare vegetation, including *outeniqua* (yellow-wood), cycads, ferns and cedar. The park has a very 'wild' feel, and offers visitors true adventure.

It can be reached from Thabazimbi by tarred road – in the park itself the roads deteriorate markedly. A 4WD is necessary to reach the safari camp and on surrounding routes. A 4WD with high ground clearance is necessary for reaching the bush camp. It is possible, however, to visit the park on a day trip in a 2WD car.

The booking office (open from 8am) is on the Thabazimbi-Alma road, 3km from where this road intersects with the Matlabas-Rooiberg road; entry is on the left and is signposted (this last 3km is on a limestone road).

There is four-bed tented accommodation in the *safari camp*; tents cost R250. These furnished tents, on the banks of the Matlabas River, have a bathroom, and a kitchen with refrigerator and stove. There are communal barbecue facilities. The camp is not fenced, so keep a look out for wildlife.

The more rustic *bush camp* has A-frame huts which sleep six. Each hut is R450 for six people and an additional R66 for each extra person. There are three huts in all. If you book one hut, you'll probably have the place to yourself.

Vaalwater & Around
Vaalwater, the centre of the Waterberg, is a quiet little town 60km north-west of Nylstroom on the R517.

Lapalala Wilderness
This big private reserve (☎ 082-740 7754) is an area of high ecological value (25,600 hectares). The gates close at 5.30pm from April to August and at 6.30pm from September to March. It has a number of animals, including black rhinos, white rhinos, zebras, blue wildebeests and several species of antelopes, as well as hippos and crocodiles in bilharzia-free rivers. Over 270 species of birds have been recorded.

In 1990, Lapalala became the first private reserve to obtain black rhinos. The history of rhino preservation is told at the **Rhino Museum**, which is housed in the old Melkrivier school adjoining the Waterberg Cultural Museum.

Ask the rangers to point out the unusual termite mounds built under layers in the sandstone. It appears that ants have managed to lift the sandstone slabs and build beneath them, earning them the name 'Arnold Schwarzenegger ants'.

There are many San paintings in the reserve, especially along the Kgogong and Lapalala Rivers. There are also a number of Iron-Age sites.

Small *bush camps* are scattered through the wilderness, with accommodation ranging from R92 to R165 per person, depending on numbers. There are cooking facilities but you must bring all your own supplies. The minimum stay is two nights and there are midweek specials; book in advance as Lapalala is popular.

Lapalala Wilderness is north of Nylstroom, in the heart of the Waterberg. From Nylstroom take the R33 to Vaalwater and from there head in the direction of Melkrivier. Take the turn-off to Melkrivier school 40km from Vaalwater, and continue for 25km to Lapalala.

Activities
There are a number of attractions in the area including horse riding. **Equus Trails** (☎ 011-788 3923, e equus@equus.co.za), within the Touchstone Game Ranch, is south-east of Marken off the R518. It can be reached from Vaalwater or Potgietersrus. The hiking trails here pass through Waterberg bushveld and near the Lapalala River. It's not unusual to encounter rhinos and many other wildlife species. (Accommodation is in overnight *bush camps* and costs R850 per person, all-inclusive.)

Another popular horse-riding location is Triple B Ranch, the country's biggest cattle, crops and game ranch, 28km from Vaalwater. **Horizon Horsetrails** (☎ 014-755 4003, 083-287 2885, e horizonranch@yebo.co.za) operates on the ranch and rides include mustering of cattle. Beginners and experienced riders are catered for. A hippo enclosure has recently been established, and you can explore it on horseback. The cost is US$170 per person, including accommodation, all meals and rides.

Ant's Nest (☎ 014-755 4296, ⓔ iti01824@mweb.co.za, ⓦ www.waterberg.net/antsnest) is a small reserve on Triple B Ranch. Activities include rhino tracking, bush walks and visits to ancient bushman art and archaeological sites.

Places to Stay

Zeederburg Cottage & Backpackers (☎ 083-332 7088) Dorm beds R40, doubles B&B R170. The only backpackers around in this area, friendly Zeederburg is located just off the R33, about 2km past Vaalwater (coming from Nylstroom). It's signposted from the Spa supermarket and the Total garage.

Bosveldrus (☎ 014-755 3696) Camp sites R20 plus R15 per vehicle, 2-person single/double chalets R110/190. This is a great place to stay with very tidy chalets (shared kitchen) and there is plenty of grass for camping.

Waterberg Game Lodge (☎/fax 014-775 3626) B&B R200 per person. This rather expensive hotel is the only source of nightlife in the region.

Soutpansberg

The Soutpansberg region incorporates the most northern part of South Africa, scraping southern Zimbabwe. The rainforest of the Soutpansberg is strikingly lush compared with the hot, dry lowveld to the north. The N1 towns of Louis Trichardt and Messina are here, as is the ancient Venda region to the east.

LOUIS TRICHARDT
☎ 015 • postcode 0920

Louis Trichardt nestles into the southern side of the Soutpansberg Range and is cooler and wetter than the harsh thorn-bush country that suddenly appears north of the range. This is frontier country and Louis Trichardt is a quiet town; everything closes

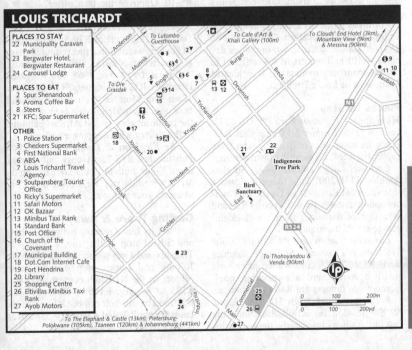

LOUIS TRICHARDT

PLACES TO STAY
22 Municipality Caravan Park
23 Bergwater Hotel; Bergwater Restaurant
24 Carousel Lodge

PLACES TO EAT
2 Spur Shenandoah
5 Aroma Coffee Bar
8 Steers
21 KFC; Spar Supermarket

OTHER
1 Police Station
3 Checkers Supermarket
4 First National Bank
6 ABSA
7 Louis Trichardt Travel Agency
9 Soutpansberg Tourist Office
10 Ricky's Supermarket
11 Safari Motors
12 OK Bazaar
13 Minibus Taxi Rank
14 Standard Bank
15 Post Office
16 Church of the Covenant
17 Municipal Building
18 Dot.Com Internet Cafe
19 Fort Hendrina
20 Library
25 Shopping Centre
26 Eltivillas Minibus Taxi Rank
27 Ayob Motors

To Lutombo Guesthouse
To Cafe d'Art & Khali Gallery (100m)
To Clouds' End Hotel (3km), Mountain View (9km) & Messina (90km)
To Die Grasdak
Indigenous Tree Park
Bird Sanctuary
To Thohoyandou & Venda (90km)
To The Elephant & Castle (13km), Pietersburg-Polokwane (105km), Tzaneen (120km) & Johannesburg (441km)

NORTHERN PROVINCE

down early and the streets are deserted after 7pm. It makes a handy base for visits into the Venda region and the Soutpansberg mountains.

The knowledgeable **Soutpansberg tourist office** (☎ 516 0040, ⓔ info@northnet.co.za) is on the N1 at the northern entrance to town.

There are two ABSA banks in town. Standard Bank is on Krogh St, and First National Bank is on Trichardt St.

Dot.Com Internet Cafe (Joubert St) charges R30 per hour for email.

Things to Do

Face Africa (☎ 516 2076, 082-969 3270) runs informative tours in the Soutpansberg. You can make up your own itinerary according to your interests; a tour of scenic treats such as Lake Funduzi is possible as are arts-and-crafts tours. A day trip costs about R1600 for up to six people.

Saddles (☎ 516 4482, 082-494 1155, ⓔ ingagilf@yebo.co.za) has horse-riding day trips for R180 per person. Both companies will pick you up if you ring ahead.

For hikes in the area, the **Schoemansdal Environmental Education Centre** (☎ 516 4881, ⓔ sdaleec@lantic.net) organises day hikes (R10) and overnight hikes (R30) in the Soutpansberg mountains. It is located 25km west of Louis Trichardt.

Places to Stay

Municipality Caravan Park (☎ 516 0212, fax 516 1195, Grobler St) Camp sites R33. There are camp sites only here, under huge paperbark trees; it's near the town centre.

Carousel Lodge (☎ 516 4482) Singles/doubles R130/200. This lodge is down a side street off Rissik St and is the best budget option in town. Breakfast costs R30 and as a sign of the times there's a 'lock-up' garage for R20 a night.

Lutombo Guesthouse (☎ 516 0850, fax 516 1846, 141 Anderson St) Singles/doubles B&B R150/210. A comfortable place with smallish rooms and a swimming pool. Home-made dinners are R40 (with notice).

Bergwater Hotel (☎/fax 516 0262, Rissik St) Singles/doubles R180/280. While the rest of the town closes early, the bar at this

hotel is probably your best chance of a drink and a game of pool.

Clouds' End Hotel (☎ 517 7021, fax 517 7187) Camp sites R30 for two people, singles/doubles B&B R189/325. This hotel, 3km north of town, offers 'booze and snooze' but it isn't as tacky as it sounds. It's a friendly, solid old place. Watch out for the voracious vervet monkeys!

Mountain View (☎ 517 7031, fax 517 7206, ⓔ mview@zoutpansberg.co.za) Singles/doubles B&B from R180/280. Mountain View is 9km north of town, and as the name suggests it is in a beautiful location. An a la carte dinner costs about R50.

Places to Eat

The dining scene is abysmal. There's **Spur Shenandoah** on Krogh St, **KFC** on Trichardt St, and **Steers** appropriately plonked on Burger St.

Aroma Coffee Bar (☎ 516 1157, Krogh St) Toasted sandwiches R7-14, pancakes R5-10. Opposite the post office, this is a hub for home-decorator enthusiasts.

Bergwater Restaurant (☎ 516 0262) Starters R15-20, mains R30-55. Open daily. In the Bergwater Hotel, this restaurant has a good selection of dishes. Grilled sole is R52.

Cafe d'Art (☎ 516 4068, 129 Krogh St) Breakfast R12-26, burgers R14-22. Open 10am-9pm Mon-Sat. You can have lunch here on the outside grassed area or admire the beautiful pottery and African paintings in the gallery while sipping a coffee.

The Elephant & Castle (☎ 516 5540) Pub lunches R15-25. A cosy pub located about 13km south of Louis Trichardt on the N1, it's worth a stop for a drink and a bite to eat on your way out of town.

Getting There & Away

City to City buses running between Jo'burg and Sibasa stop at the train station. The Translux and Greyhound services between Jo'burg and Harare stop outside Safari Motors on the N1. Both companies charge R135 to Jo'burg, R165 to Bulawayo and R210 to Harare. You can book buses at the **Louis Trichardt Travel Agency** (☎ 516 5042), down an alley off Burger St.

The train station is at the south-western end of Kruger St. The *Bosvelder* stops here (for more information, see the Getting Around chapter).

The minibus taxi rank is in the OK Bazaar supermarket car park off Burger St, a block north-east of Trichardt St. There is another minibus taxi rank in Eltivillas. Destinations and fares from Louis Trichardt include Thohoyandou (R15), Pietersburg (R18), Zimbabwe border (R25), Messina (R20), and Tzaneen (R25).

AROUND LOUIS TRICHARDT
Soutpansberg Hiking Trails

The trail between Hanglip and Entabeni forest stations has closed but there are still good walks in the Soutpansberg range. The two-day 20.5km **Hanglip Trail** includes a climb up a 1719m peak; it begins at Hanglip forest station. Take precautions against malaria, bilharzia and ticks. Overnight accommodation is in huts and there's a trail fee of R35 per person per day, which includes a good walking map. To book the walk, contact **South Africa Forestry Company** *(Safcol; ☎ 012-481 3615)* in Pretoria.

Places to Stay *Medike Mountain Reserve (☎ 015-516 0481)* Camp sites R25 per person, self-contained cottages R100 per person. Keen hikers can stay in the western end of the Soutpansberg at this reserve surrounded by the Sand River Gorge. There are a number of hiking trails where you can see rock paintings. Take the R522 from Louis Trichardt and turn right on a gravel road after 35km (just before the railway crossing). Continue on steeply for 8km, then turn right towards the signposted entrance.

Lajuma Mountain Retreat (☎ 015-593 0352) Self-catering valley lodges R110 per person, hillside lodges R120 per person. The retreat is 7km off the R522 between Louis Trichardt and Vivo on the flanks of Letjuma (Soutpansberg's highest peak). This beautiful region is a hiker's paradise and there are archaeological sites, rare animals and a host of outdoor activities. The hillside lodges are spectacularly situated with great views. Seldom do you come across such good value.

Bergpan Eco Resort (☎ 015-593 0127, fax 593 0087) Self-catering R90 per person. On the northern flank of the Soutpansberg, this resort offers saltpan tours, mountain hiking trails, archaeological sites and bird-watching.

Ben Lavin Nature Reserve

Ben Lavin is a 2500-hectare reserve *(☎ 516 4534, e benlavin@mweb.co.za; admission R30; open 6am-7pm daily)* worth visiting. There are four marked hiking trails, which are all rewarding. The 8km **Tabajwane Trail** is good for wildlife viewing and the **Fountain Trail** follows the Doring River; there are hides at water holes along the way. Mountain-bike trails range in length from 3.7km to 15km. The reserve contains quite a good range of birds (about 240 species have been recorded) and animals, including giraffes, zebras and jackals. The African rock python, the only species of python in this part of Africa, may be spotted in the reserve.

Tent sites cost R35, or you can stay in *luxury tents* for R140, *huts* for R190 a double or the *lodge* for R230 a double. You have to bring your own food.

Take the N1 south from Louis Trichardt for about 3.5km, then take the Fort Edward turn-off to the left. After a short distance, you'll see the entrance gate on your left.

MESSINA
☎ 015 • postcode 0900

The closest town to the Zimbabwe border, Messina is a hot, dusty little town with a frontier feel to it. The town grew around the copper mines which began operating in 1905 and are still functioning today. Away from the mines the town centre is a sleepy place.

The current problems in Zimbabwe have hit Messina hard – the passing tourist trade has been substantially reduced. However, there are moves to promote Messina as a regional centre in its own right, along with nearby tourist attractions such as the Vhembe Dhonge National Park.

Information

The **tourist office** *(☎ 534 3500)* is hidden away in the office of Far North Tours & Safaris. To get there turn off the N1 at the

Messina Hospital, take an immediate right, go past Nando's and the office is through a small car park on your right in a thatched-roof building.

You can change money at the First National Bank, ABSA or the Standard Bank. At First National, which is open from 9am to 3pm Monday to Friday for foreign currency transactions, you can change American Express (AmEx) cheques only. You must have your purchase agreement and commission is 2% or R50, whichever is greater.

An alternative to the banks is **Prestige Bureau** (☎ 082-821 6292; open daily). Its rates are slightly lower than the banks', but so is the commission (1.71% or R34.20, whichever is greater).

If you're bursting to tell the folks at home about your trip to Zim, you can do so via email at the Computer Shop on the N1.

Things to See & Do

Far North Tours & Safaris (☎ 534 3500, e farnorth@lantic.net) offers tours of the area including the Soutpansberg and the Vhembe Dhonge National Park. It also claims to have the cheapest car rental in South Africa. A Toyota Corolla is R95 a day and a Motorhome is R350 a day. You can take the cars into neighbouring countries including Zimbabwe. Far North also arranges transfers from Jo'burg airport.

You'll see some big baobabs on the road south of here, and 5km south of the town just off the N1 is **Messina Nature Reserve** (☎ 534 3235; admission free), which was established to protect the trees. There are animals such as nyalas, kudus, Sharpe's grysboks and over 50 species of reptiles. You can *camp* here in permanent tents, all with reed-enclosed *lapa* areas (a circular building with low walls and a thatched roof, used for cooking, partying etc), or stay in the three-bedroom *guesthouse*. There are picnic facilities and an 8km hiking trail.

Places to Stay

Baobab Caravan Park (☎ 534 3504) Camp sites R25 plus R12 per person, single/double chalets R150/175. Baobab is on the southern outskirts of town, about 1.5km from the town centre. Chalets have a fridge, a TV and air-con.

Impala Lelie Hotel (☎ 534 0127) Single/double rondavels R170/190, luxury rooms R230. Next to the caravan park, this hotel has a pool. The rondavels are spacious.

Limpopo River Lodge (☎/fax 534 0204, National Rd) Singles/doubles R95/115 with shared bathroom, R115/140 with private bathroom. Rooms here are pretty small and have TV and air-con. Not an inspiring place, but it's cheap and central.

Ilala Country Lodge (☎/fax 534 3220, Venetia Mine Rd) Singles/doubles R210/250. This lodge, 8km from Messina, is signposted from the Beitbridge road; accommodation is in grass-roofed stone cottages and there are braais and a pool.

Places to Eat

There are several fried-chicken places in town, including *KFC*, *Chicken Licken* and *Nando's*, near the hospital.

Pot Belly (☎ 534 2314) Breakfasts from R10, starters R7-17, mains R32-50. Opposite KFC on the N1, this restaurant has excellent breakfasts, and is the best eating option in town – if you come here for breakfast you'll probably end up back here for dinner.

Vhembe Dhonge National Park

This national park (☎ 015-534 0102) is not yet open to the public, but keep an eye on developments, as it's part of a very exciting venture. The park will form the core of a new transfrontier park stretching over 4900 sq km into neighbouring Botswana and Zimbabwe.

Greefwald Farm was recently incorporated into the park, marking a significant addition, as the farm, a candidate for listing as a UNESCO World Heritage site, boasts within its boundaries the Iron-Age archaeological sites K-2 and Mapungubwe.

There is still much work to be done before the park opens but it's possible to take limited cultural tours into areas of Vhembe Dhonge – see the Messina section.

NORTHERN PROVINCE

Kremetart a la Carte Restaurant (☎ *534 0127*) Starters R15-22, mains R25-50. Open daily. Next to the Impala Lelie Hotel, this place isn't cheap, but if you've had a few hard weeks on the road it may be worth a splurge.

Getting There & Away

For detailed information on crossing the border into Zimbabwe, see Border Crossings in the Getting There & Away chapter.

Bus Translux buses on the Jo'burg-Harare route stop at the Limpopo River Lodge; the fare from Messina to Jo'burg/Bulawayo/ Harare/Lusaka is R140/155/185/275. City to City buses run the Jo'burg-Harare route daily for R70. Greyhound buses stop at Beitbridge on the other side of the border.

Train The daily *Bosvelder* terminates at Messina; fares to Jo'burg are R125/185 in 2nd/1st class. (See the Getting Around chapter for more details.)

Minibus Taxi If you're coming from Zimbabwe and want to take a minibus taxi further south than Messina, catch one at the border as there are many more there than in Messina; to Jo'burg it's R95. Destinations and fares from Messina include Louis Trichardt (R20) and Pietersburg (R38). Taxis between the border and Messina cost as little as R5 but you might have to pay more.

VENDA REGION

The Venda region, once the homeland of the Venda people under apartheid, is an intriguing place to visit for its culture and scenery. It is likely that you will feel that you are really 'in Africa' here more than in any region in South Africa, with perhaps the exception of parts of the former Transkei.

Several forests and lakes in the region are of great religious significance to the Venda people.

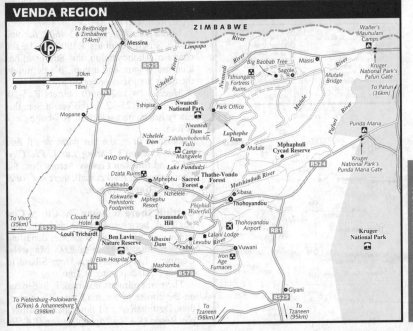

VENDA REGION

NORTHERN PROVINCE

You might want to try local delicacies such as *nziya* (locusts) or *mopani worms* (caterpillars that live on the mopani tree): These are a crunchy snack, often dried on an open fire and added to a thick spicy sauce.

Thohoyandou & Sibasa
☎ 015

Created as the capital of the former Venda Homeland, Thohoyandou has a casino, a large shopping mall, some impressive public buildings and not much else. The huge mall buzzes, however, and is about the closest you will come to a true 'African' city in South Africa – disorganisation, ghetto blasters, street stalls and all. The adjacent town of Sibasa is a few kilometres north. Most public transport leaves from Sibasa.

Several interesting tours are run from the town. A half-day tour of the Venda area costs R150 per person and a full-day tour is R200 (both with a minimum of three people). Longer tours and guided walks are also available. For more information about tours, contact ☎ 962 1500 or ☎ 0721-745 775, or ask at Acacia Park. Not far from Thohoyandou, the Phiphidi Waterfall on the Mutshindudi River is often included in the tours; admission to the falls is R3.

The highlight of the Southern Venda day tour is meeting Noria Mabasa, a woman who sculpts traditional Venda characters in clay and wood (wood was traditionally a 'men only' medium).

Places to Stay & Eat *Acacia Park (☎ 962 3095)* Powered camp sites R35, self-contained double chalets R120. Acacia is looking distinctly run down these days, although we're told renovations are on the way. It's on the R524.

Bougainvillea Lodge (☎ 962 4064, fax 962 3576) Economy singles/doubles B&B R175/210. This lodge is about a kilometre from Thohoyandou, up the hill towards Sibasa. It is friendly, clean and comfortable, but not particularly cheap. Meals (apart from breakfast) are R40.

Venda Sun Hotel (☎ 962 4600, fax 962 4540) Singles/doubles R399/444. In the centre of Thohoyandou, this Sun hotel has a casino, a gym and a pool. It's definitely the most luxurious option in town.

MacRib (☎ 962 4600) Starters R15-20, pasta dishes R25-32. In the Venda Sun, this eatery has a good selection. A T-bone steak is R45.

Close to or in the bus park, you'll find *Nando's*, *Zapa's Eating Land*, *Pie City*, *KFC* and *Chicken Licken*. Across from the Venda open-air market mall, there is *Fish & Chix* and *Super Munch*.

Getting There & Away The City to City bus runs between Pretoria and Thohoyandou and Sibasa via Nzhelele, departing daily at 8am; the fare is R60. Magweba Company has a daily bus from Sibasa to Sagole (R8), departing at 1pm.

The main minibus taxi rank is in Sibasa, on the corner of the road from Thohoyandou. Destinations and fares include Mphephu Resort (R4.50), Mphephu town (R4.50),

THOHOYANDOU & SIBASA

1 Shopping Centre	11 Nando's; Zapa's Eating
2 Minibus Taxi Rank	Land; Pie City; KFC;
3 Buses	Chicken Licken
4 Bougainvillea Lodge	12 Shopping Centre
5 Venda University	13 Venda Open Air Market
6 Standard Bank ATM	Mall; Minibus Taxi Rank
7 Venda Sun Hotel; MacRib	14 Fish & Chix; Super Munch
8 Government Buildings	15 Shell Petrol Station
9 Radio Thohoyandou	16 Total Petrol Station
10 Police Station	17 Acacia Park

Mutale (R5), Sagole (R10), Louis Trichardt (R15) and Jo'burg (R70).

In Thohoyandou, minibus taxis congregate in the car park of the shopping centre near the Venda Sun Hotel. The fare to Sibasa is R2.50.

Nwanedi National Park

The dry northern side of the Soutpansberg provides an extremely scenic backdrop to this park (☎ 015-539 0723; open 6am-6pm daily), although it's a contrast to the Venda's lush landscapes. The vegetation is mainly mopani and mixed woodland. It can be very hot here in summer. The main attraction for most visitors is fishing on the Nwanedi and Luphephe dams and on tributaries of the Nwanedi, which feeds into the Limpopo River. The major walk in the park is to the very scenic **Tshihovhohovho Falls**. You can hire canoes for R45.

The park has *camp sites* for R50 as well as four-person *rondavels* for R180 and *B&B* doubles at R220. Basic supplies are available and there's a fully licensed *restaurant*.

You can reach the park from Thohoyandou, entering at the Nwanedi gate; though the road is scenic there's a good chance of getting lost, and there are several kilometres of bad dirt road. It's simpler to come via Tshipise and enter from the west. Tshipise is the nearest place to buy fuel.

Mphephu & Around
☎ 015

Mphephu was one of the great chiefs of the Venda and ruled from the late-19th century until his death in 1924. He was the son of Makhado, the 'Lion of the North'.

The area around the **Levubu River**, about 48km east of Louis Trichardt, is particularly scenic.

Known for its hot springs, *Mphephu Resort* (☎ 973 0282) is 34km west of Thohoyandou. The resort has 20 chalets that cost from R120. There is a licensed self-service *restaurant* in the complex. A day visit costs R4.

Lalani Lodge (☎ 583 0218) Singles/doubles R175/300. Not far from Thohoyandou, Lalani is a pleasant stop for the night.

Land of Legend

The lakes, rivers, mountains, caves and forests of the Venda form a rich spirit world. Stories of natural and ancestral beings abound. Almost every body of water, whether it be a stream, waterfall or lake, is inhabited by *ditutwane* (water elves or spirits).

Most famous of these is sacred Lake Fundudzi, which can be visited only with the permission of the priestess of the lake. Around the lake there are a number of spirit gardens where spirits tend their crops, large rocks in the shape of drums where spirits meet in celebration and other sacred rocks where the Venda make offerings to allow the spirits to sample recent crops.

Within the Thathe-Vondo Forest, west of Thohoyandou, is the Sacred Forest, where no strangers are permitted to enter. At Lwamondo Hill, south-west of Thohoyandou, the baboons (which once warned the Venda of approaching enemies) are venerated. The nearby forest manifests a plague of snakes if anyone tries to steal firewood without the permission of the priest Tshifhe. If you are observant you may see the furtive ditutwane when you visit Phiphidi Waterfall. These water spirits resemble 'half people' and have only one eye, one leg and one arm.

Herbalists and traditional doctors are very much part of daily life in the Venda. By using an intricately carved *ndilo* (divining bowl), a diviner is able to communicate with spirits and share their wisdom.

Shiluvari Lakeside Lodge (☎ 556 3406) B&B/DB&B R185/245 per person. Close to Albasini Dam, this lodge has thatched chalets. There's also an excellent restaurant, where a sumptuous dinner for two costs R100.

Lake Fundudzi

This lake is a sacred site, as its water is believed to have come from the great sea that covered the earth before land was created. The python god, who holds an important place in the rites of the Venda's matriarchal culture and once required human sacrifice, lives here. The lake is 35km north-west of Thohoyandou, but unfortunately you can't visit it without permission from the lake's priestess, which is unlikely to be granted. You do get a glimpse of the lake if you take a tour from Thohoyandou or Louis Trichardt.

Near the lake is **Thathe-Vondo Forest**, and within that is the Sacred Forest. A spirit lion guards the burial grounds of Venda chiefs in the forest.

Camp Mangwele (☎ 082-768 8801) Camp sites R30 per person. North of Lake Fundudzi is Camp Mangwele, situated within the rugged country of the Soutpansberg, and accessible only by a 4WD with high ground clearance. There are hot showers, braai facilities and firewood, and many activities are within range of the camp: scrambling, rock climbing and mountain biking.

To get to Camp Mangwele, head first to Makhado. Some 2km north-east of Makhado, turn north towards Musekwa. Follow this road for 21.7km, then turn right (east) and follow the road towards Tshixwadza. After 9km there is a signboard indicating Mangwele Pothole; follow this road south for 1km until you reach the camp.

Mabudashango Hiking Trail

The four-day 50km Mabudashango Hiking Trail starts at Mabudashango Hut near the Thathe-Vondo Forest station. Take precautions against ticks, mosquitoes and malaria. Accommodation is in basic trail shelters and in the forester's cottage at the Thathe-Vondo Forest station. You book with the **Department of Tourism** *(☎ 015-962 4724, Private Bag X50008, Thohoyandou, Northern Province)*.

Mutale & Around

☎ 015 • postcode 0956

Near Mutale, north of Thohoyandou, there is a wood-carving workshop where you can see the ceremonial *domba* drums being made. The drums are beaten during the python dance, an integral part of the female fertility ceremony.

Waller's Camps Mavhulani (☎ 963 3802, 083-255 8463) Shared accommodation R100 per person (minimum age 16). On the banks of the Mutale River and only a couple of kilometres from the Kruger National Park's Pafuri gate, Waller's Camps is a great secluded bush camp. Although a fair way away, this is the closest accommodation option in the area.

Vuwani & Mashamba

Just south of Vuwani, you can see the remains of Iron-Age furnaces where the Venda smelted high-grade iron for centuries. Many of their metal-working skills have been lost but they continue to make attractive pottery. Mashamba also has several metal-working foundries.

Valley of the Olifants

The east of Northern Province, formerly known as north-eastern Transvaal, is well worth a visit. The region is culturally very rich, being the traditional home of the Tsonga-Shangaan and Lobedu peoples. It is also popular for a north-south traverse through Kruger National Park or a visit to one of the many private wildlife reserves in the Hoedspruit area. The main town of Tzaneen in the Letaba Valley is pleasant and a good base for trips into the nearby scenic Modjadji and Magoebaskloof regions.

VENDA REGION TO TZANEEN

This area is the former Homeland of the Tsonga-Shangaan (Gazankulu) and is extremely poor. Despite the dust, flies and poor sanitation, kids laugh as they kick a football around on the barren plains. Hopefully these people will be given more of a chance in the future.

Giyani

☎ 015 • postcode 0826

This town, the region's main centre, is north-west of Phalaborwa and has a frontier atmosphere (it has few facilities). It is best reached via the road running north from the R36 at Mooketsi (the R81) or the R81 running south from the intersection with the

R524, 25km north-east of Thohoyandou. On no account try to cut across country from the R81 to the R524; you'll get horribly lost.

Ndzalama Wildlife Reserve

This reserve (☎ 015-307 3065, fax 307 3066, e ndzalama@pixie.co.za), near Letsilele, is quite simply one of the best wildlife reserves and lodges in South Africa, built around stunning rocky kopjes (little hills, usually flat-topped). The reserve is based on a spectacular, phallic rock formation, Ndzalama. The emphasis is not so much on 'must see the Big Five' but rather on the subtle nuances of the bush, from practicalities to legends. You come here to learn about bushcraft, survival, orientation, wildlife tracking and Tsonga-Shangaan culture: starting fire with sticks, *basha* (shelter) construction, medicinal use of plants and recognition of bush foods. Viewing of animals is woven into the experience – the lowly dung beetle is as important as the elephant.

There are two styles of accommodation, both self-catering.

Leopard Rock Bush Camp is based on a kopje shaded by many trees. There are five rondavels (sleeping 12) which have gas facilities, including a fridge and a stove. The cost is R100 per person.

The luxurious *Ndzalama Lodge* has six stone-and-thatch chalets with air-con for R250 per person. A guide is provided for wildlife drives.

To get to the reserve from Tzaneen or Phalaborwa, take the R71. The southern turn-off is 9km north of Gravelotte; turn right and follow the dirt road for 12km to the reserve. The northern turn-off is 28km east of Tzaneen; at this turn-off, go left. After 16km, turn right. The reserve is 4km further on.

Modjadji Nature Reserve

This small reserve (☎ 015-232 5221) of 305 hectares protects forests of the ancient Modjadji cycad. In the summer mists, this place and the surrounding Vulovedu Mountains take on an ethereal atmosphere.

Ravenshill (☎ 015-305 3607, 082-807 8182) Rooms R125 per person. This is a delightful homestead only minutes from the cycads.

Hopefontein Nature Reserve & Tree Houses (☎ 015-305 3607) R125 per person. Below Ravenshill, this place has two camps. *Ficus* has two tree houses built into the branches of wild fig trees and *Schotia* has two raised chalets built around trees.

Take the GaKgapane turn-off from the R36 about 10km north of Duivelskloof; the turn-off to the reserve is a further 18km.

Duivelskloof-GaKgapane
☎ 015 • postcode 0835

This small village is in the wooded hills north of Tzaneen. The name refers to the devilishly hard time the early European settlers had getting their wagons up and down the hills. In 1916 it was to be called Modjadji, after the Rain Queen (see the boxed text), but the white population objected to the name's 'heathen connotations' – they named it after the devil instead! It is now combined with the name of the large black community nearby, GaKgapane. Tourist information is available from the **town hall** (☎ 309 9246).

There are a number of **hiking trails** in the vicinity. The Panorama and Piesangkop trails are accessible to most people. The library provides free walking notes.

Duivelskloof Resort (☎ 309 9651) Camp sites R50, 4-person rondavels R110. To get to the resort turn left after the BP petrol station when driving from Tzaneen.

There are also guest farms and holiday cottages in the area; ask at the town hall for details.

LETABA VALLEY

The Letaba valley is east of Pietersburg-Polokwane, between two chunks of the former Lebowa Homeland. The valley is subtropical and lush, with tea plantations and crops of tropical fruits, while on the hills are forests, mainly of the plantation variety.

At Haenertsburg the road splits, with the R71 reaching Tzaneen via the steep Magoebaskloof Pass, while the R528 runs along the more gentle George's Valley.

NORTHERN PROVINCE

Haenertsburg

☎ 015 • postcode 0730

Haenertsburg, a village established during the 1887 gold rush, is on the escarpment above the Letaba Valley, and is the centre of a forestry and cherry-growing region. The **Cherry Blossom Festival** is held at Cheerio Gardens (R6 admission) in late September or early October.

The helpful **Byadladi Tourism Association** (☎ 276 4972, ⓔ mta@magoebaskloof .com) is situated behind the Atholl Arms on Rissik St.

Hiking trails near Haenertsburg include the one-hour **Lesodi Trail** which passes patches of indigenous forest; the 11km **Louis Chang-uion Trail** which has spectacular views; and the **Bifrost Mountain Trails** which pass waterfalls and ascend to the summit of Iron Crown (2126m).

The upmarket *Glenshiel Country Lodge* (☎ 276 4335) is 2.5km from Haenertsburg on the R71 to Magoebaskloof Pass. It was closed at the time of research but should reopen soon.

The Chalets (☎ 276 4264) Chalets R60-R100 per person. These Swiss-style log cabins, 1km from town on the R71, are great value.

Iron Crown Tavern (☎ 276 4221) Pub meals R8-25. This tavern has home cooking and a good range of beers. It's a nice spot for drinks on a hot day.

Pot 'n' Plow Restaurant (☎ 082-691 5790) Chicken pies R5, trout dishes R24. Open daily. Come here for home-made pies and cakes.

Magoebaskloof Pass

The Magoebaskloof is the escarpment on the edge of the highveld, and the road here drops quickly down to Tzaneen and the lowveld, passing through plantations and large tracts of thick indigenous forest. The Woodbush Forest is the largest indigenous forest in the Transvaal and contains some very tall trees.

The high summer rainfall means there are a number of waterfalls in the area including Debengeni Falls in the De Hoek State Forest. You can swim in the pool at the bottom

---

Modjadji, the Rain Queen

In Africa it is unusual for a woman to be sovereign of a tribe, but the Rain Queen is an exception. The queen resides in the town of GaModjadji in the Bolebodu district near Duivelskloof. Every year, around November, the Queen presides over a festival held to celebrate the coming of the rains. The *indunas* (tribal headmen) select people to dance, to call for rain, and to perform traditional rituals, including male and female initiation ceremonies. After the ceremony, the rain falls. The absence of rain is usually attributed to some event such as the destruction of a sacred place – a situation resolved only with further ritual.

During the rest of the year, the queen performs a number of other functions. She never marries yet still bears children. When she dies, succession normally falls to the eldest of her daughters (the fathers have very insignificant roles). The queen is buried in the evening and only close relatives and indunas are permitted to go to the burial place.

When President Mandela first visited the Rain Queen, he was accompanied by a large entourage. On his second visit to GaModjadji, he substantially reduced the number of hangers-on, at the queen's special request.

Henry Rider Haggard's novel, *She*, is based on the story of the original Modjadji, a 16th-century refugee princess.

In June 2001, the most recent Rain Queen, Modjadji V, died in Pietersburg. However, in an unfortunate turn of events, her heir, Princess Makheala, had died three days earlier. The only matrilineal monarchy on the continent, which has enjoyed an unbroken lineage for the past 200 years, now finds itself in a state of confusion. Attempts to find a successor will be made in late 2001, after a three-month mourning period.

of the falls but be careful, as there have been many deaths here. To get here, turn west off the R71 at Bruphy Sawmills.

Magoebaskloof hiking trails include walks that take up to five days and pass through some beautiful country. The walking can be challenging and you should be fit before setting out.

Two recommended trails are the two-day, 21km **Debengeni Falls Trail** and the three-day, 40km **Dokolewa Waterfall Trail**; both are rated moderately difficult. Overnight stays for the Dokolewa Waterfall Trail are in huts near waterfalls and streams. The trails cost R47 per day. You can make bookings with **Safcol** (☎ 012-481 3615) in Pretoria.

Places to Stay *Magoebaskloof Hotel* (☎ 276 4276, fax 276 4280, R71) Singles/doubles B&B from R350/480. Author John Buchan once lived near this hotel, 25km south of Tzaneen, and his book *Prester John* is set in the area.

Magoebaskloof Lodge (☎ 305 3142, R71) Singles/doubles R190/295. This lodge has self-contained rondavels with private braais on the edge of a wilderness area.

Wolkberg Wilderness Area

South of Tzaneen in the northern tail of the Drakensberg range, this 22,000-hectare wilderness area (☎ 015-295 9713) has hiking trails and, in the valleys to the south and east, strands of indigenous forest. Some animals, including a few shy leopards and hyenas, have returned since the area was shot out by hunters and the *dagga* (marijuana) growers who flourished here until the 1950s. Hikers should be aware of snakes such as black mambas, puff adders and berg adders. Over 150 bird species have been recorded here.

Places to Stay *Coach House* (☎ 015-307 3641) Singles/doubles from R360/780. About 15km south of Tzaneen, near the New Agatha Forest, this is an old refurbished hotel with views and good food. Breakfast (sometimes pan-fried trout) is an extra R80.

Bifrost Mountain Retreat (☎ 011-784 0314) B&B R205 per person. Off the R528

south-east of Haenertsburg, this retreat also has a self-contained lodge. It's a good base for walks to the Wolkberg and the summit of Iron Crown.

TZANEEN & AROUND
☎ 015 • postcode 0850

Tzaneen, the largest town in the Letaba Valley, is a good place to base yourself. Limited information is available from the **Tzaneen Tourism Office** (☎ 307 8055/1294, e alfa@mweb.co.za, 21A Danie Joubert St; open 8am-5pm Mon-Fri, 8am-11am Sat), based in Harvey World Travel.

You can change money at ABSA or the First National Bank in the town centre. There is a telephone bureau in the Oasis Mall. **Speedphone** (Danie Joubert St) in the Tzaneng Mall has Internet connections and charges R30 per hour.

The small **Tzaneen Museum** (☎ 307 8056; admission by donation) has an interesting collection of Tsonga cultural artefacts including a Rain Queen ceremonial drum, and is well worth a visit.

Green Rhino (☎ 307 5979) operates out of the tourist office and offers a number of trips in the area. A three-day trip to Kruger costs about R1600 per person, while half-day/full-day trips around the Letaba Valley are R295/395.

The hillsides behind Tzaneen are a mosaic of tea plantations. Tours of the **Sapekoe Tea Estate** (☎ 307 3120) are good fun; they are conducted at 11am, 1pm and 3pm Tuesday to Saturday. The estate is near the junction of the R36 and the R71.

Places to Stay

Satvik Backpackers Village (☎ 082-853 6645, e satvik@pixie.co.za, George's Valley Rd) Dorm beds/doubles R45/R140, self-contained cottages R250. This is a pleasant rustic farm 3km from Tzaneen. Accommodation is in converted workers' cottages. The braai area on Tzaneen Dam is another plus; the access road is about the only negative. Ask here about local agricultural tours.

Fairview Lodge & Caravan Park (☎ 307 2679, e fairstay@mweb.co.za) Economy/

business-class chalets from R160/200. Fairview is 1km from town and has a good range of chalets with pleasant views.

Arborpark Lodge *(☎/fax 307 1831,* e *arborpark@mweb.co.za, Cnr Soetdoring & Geelhout Sts)* Dorm beds R50, backpacker doubles R190, singles/doubles B&B R225/295. This place is a bit out of the centre, but offers free pick-ups from town. There is a good restaurant here called ***Addison's*** *(☎ 307 6261).*

There are many B&Bs in the area, which cost around R160 per person; inquire at the tourism office.

Places to Eat

The dining scene is fairly ordinary ***Butterfield Bread*** *(Danie Joubert St)* is a good spot for fresh bread and tasties. ***Nando's*** *(Cnr Lannie Ave & Danie Joubert St)* has chicken packs for R60. ***Emerald Creek Spur*** *(Morgan St)* and ***Steers*** serve patrons large steaks (R35) and burgers (R22).

Tino's Pizzeria *(☎ 307 1893, Agatha St)* Pizzas from R25. The pizzas at this long-established pizzeria are pretty good.

Villa Italia *(☎ 307 2795, Danie Joubert St)* Salads R20, standard pizzas R17-30, antipasto around R25. Villa Italia could be

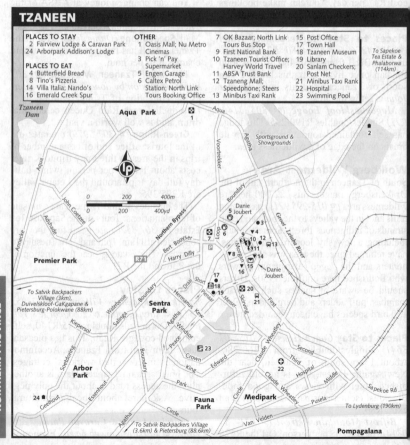

TZANEEN

PLACES TO STAY	OTHER
2 Fairview Lodge & Caravan Park	1 Oasis Mall; Nu Metro Cinemas
24 Arborpark Addison's Lodge	3 Pick 'n' Pay Supermarket
PLACES TO EAT	5 Engen Garage
4 Butterfield Bread	6 Caltex Petrol Station; North Link Tours Booking Office
8 Tino's Pizzeria	
14 Villa Italia; Nando's	
16 Emerald Creek Spur	

OTHER (cont)	
7 OK Bazaar; North Link Tours Bus Stop	15 Post Office
9 First National Bank	17 Town Hall
10 Tzaneen Tourist Office; Harvey World Travel	18 Tzaneen Museum
11 ABSA Trust Bank	19 Library
12 Tzaneng Mall; Speedphone; Steers	20 Sanlam Checkers; Post Net
13 Minibus Taxi Rank	21 Minibus Taxi Rank
	22 Hospital
	23 Swimming Pool

NORTHERN PROVINCE

your best bet for a sit-down meal. It's a reliable Italian eatery with half-price specials on Monday.

Pekoe View Tea House (☎ *305 3241*) Open 10am-5pm daily. Located at Sapekoe Tea Estate, come here for 'cuppas' and cakes after your tour of Sapekoe.

Getting There & Away

North Link Tours buses stop at the rear of the OK Bazaar. They run from Phalaborwa to Jo'burg via Tzaneen (R125), four days a week. You can book tickets at the Star Shop in the Caltex petrol station on Danie Joubert St.

Translux's City to City service runs to Pretoria/Jo'burg for R95/100 every morning. Book tickets at the tourist office.

The minibus taxi rank is behind the OK Bazaar, off Agatha St in the centre of town. Destinations and fares from Tzaneen include Duivelskloof (R5), Haenertsburg (R10), Pietersburg (R17; change at Boyne), Phalaborwa (R18), Louis Trichardt (R20) and Jo'burg (R75).

PHALABORWA

☎ 015 • postcode 1390

Phalaborwa is a clean and planned town. The town has an interesting mix of cultures: Tsonga, Shangaan, Pedi, Sotho, Venda and Afrikaner. The majority of the black population live in the nearby townships of Namakgale, Lulekani, Majeje and Namakushan. Phalaborwa means 'Better than the South', and was so called because Nguni tribes returned here after a foray to the south.

The Phalaborwa gate into Kruger National Park is 3km from town. The amiable **BaPhalaborwa (Community) Tourism Association** (☎ *781 6770; open 6.45am-3pm Mon-Fri, 9am-1pm Sat, lunch time Sun*) is near the gate.

The **Hans Merensky Country Club** (☎ *781 3931*) is an 18-hole championship golf course with a difference: Here you have to hold your shot while wildlife, elephants included, crosses the fairways. Be careful – the wildlife is 'wild'. A round of nine holes costs R80, plus R60 for the caddie.

Copper Mining

Phalaborwa is a copper-mining town. You can tour the current mine (☎ *780 2911*) at 9am on Friday. Foskor's open-cut operation is the biggest excavation in Africa.

Copper and iron have been mined here for at least 1200 years. There are Iron-Age sites at **Sealene** (in present day Phalaborwa) and **Masorini**, just inside the Kruger National Park gate.

Touring Kruger National Park

For people with limited time in South Africa, it is possible to visit Kruger by flying from Jo'burg to Phalaborwa, hiring a car for touring the park and then returning the car at Phalaborwa airport before returning by air to Jo'burg. Some reasonable fly-drive packages are available. Hire cars are available from **Avis** (☎ *781 3169*), **Imperial** (☎ *781 0376*) and **Budget** (☎ *781 5404*).

Jumbo River Safaris (☎ *781 6168*) has wildlife-viewing raft trips down the Olifants River at sunset; the cost is R50 per person. **Microflight Flips** (☎ *781 1520*) flights over private parks adjacent to Kruger offer great wildlife viewing; the cost is R70 for 10 minutes, R150 for 30 minutes. There are also **night drives** (☎ *781 0027*) into Kruger including a braai afterwards for R120 per person.

For more information, see the Kruger National Park chapter.

Places to Stay

Elephant Walk (☎ *781 2758, 082-495 0575, 30 Anna Scheepers Ave*) Camp sites R20 per person, dorm beds/doubles R55/120. This is a great backpacker place, offering a range of accommodation. The friendly owner will pick you up from the tourist centre. She also organises trips to Kruger, the white lions of Timbavati and the Valley of the Olifants.

Self-catering *cottages* near the entrance to Kruger cost R80/50 for adults/children (minimum R250). Contact Elephant Walk for more details.

Allin's Travel Lodge (☎ *781 3805, fax 781 3808*) Singles/doubles R160/220. The rooms at this old-style lodge are large; they have a fridge, a TV and air-con. It's good value.

Daan & Zena's (☎/fax 781 6049, 15 Birkenhead St) Self-catering/B&B doubles R200/240. This excellent B&B advertises itself as 'your friendliest stay in town' – which could just be right. Nothing seems too much trouble for these congenial hosts, who have good tips about the area.

Lantana Lodge (☎ 781 5191, fax 781 5193, Cnr Kiaat & Hall Sts) Camp sites R50, single/double flatlets R195/290. Lantana has a large bar with pool tables, and there's also a swimming pool.

Sefapane Lodge (☎ 781 7041, e reserva tions@sefapane.co.za, Cnr Koper & Essenhout Sts) Singles/doubles from R325/450. Rondavels here are a bit expensive but the lodge runs some good safaris. The name means 'Southern Cross'.

Steyn's Cottage (☎ 781 0836, 67 Bosvlier St) Singles/doubles R280/310. This is another good guesthouse that's a bit more upmarket. Rooms have air-con, TV and telephone.

Impala Protea Inn (☎ 781 3681, fax 781 5234, 52 Essenhout St) Double rooms R250. This small, spick-and-span Protea hotel often seems busy – book ahead.

Places to Eat

The Phalaborwa Mall has the usual food chains: *Steers*, *Panarotti's* and *Wimpy*. There's a *Campico Spur* in the Sanlam Centre.

Casa de Café (☎ 083-627 5977) Sandwiches R18. Open Mon-Sat. Casa has fresh food, free of the dollops of cream and cheese you get at a lot of South African eateries. The coffee here is also good (R6.50).

Yurok Spur (☎ 781 1091) Dishes R20-45. Yurok Spur, in the mall, has a good range of veg and meat dishes as well as Mexican tasties such as enchiladas (R23).

Getting There & Away

Air SA Airlink (☎ 781 5823) flies to and from Jo'burg (R707 one way, seven-day advance purchase).

Bus North Link Tours (☎ 291 1867) has buses on Monday, Friday, Saturday and Sunday to Jo'burg (R145) and other towns on the N1. In Phalaborwa, you can buy tickets from the tourist office, which is where the buses depart.

Translux's City to City service from Jo'burg to Phalaborwa (R105) goes via several towns including Lydenburg. Tickets can be booked through **Turn Key Travel** (☎ 781 7760, e mariak.turnkeytravel@galileosa .co.za) in the mall. There is an administration fee of R10.

Minibus Taxi There aren't many minibus taxis in this area, and even fewer run south to the lowveld between Kruger National Park and the Drakensberg escarpment. Most run to Tzaneen (R18) and south as far as Hoedspruit (R17). The taxi rank is near the corner of Sealene Rd and Mellor Ave, 300m south-west of the town centre.

AROUND PHALABORWA

The following reserves and private lodges are to the east of the R527, on the road between Mica and Hoedspruit. They are much cheaper than other private reserves bordering the south-west of Kruger.

Tintshaba (☎ 015-793 3234) Singles/ doubles R432/R824. There are a number of private lodges near Kruger's Phalaborwa gate, including the beautifully presented Tintshaba. Prices here are reduced in low season.

Matomani Lodge (☎ 015-781 5680) Singles/doubles R120/320. This lodge is 2km from the Paul Kruger gate and is excellent value.

Tulani Safari Lodge (☎ 015-781 5414, e tulani@xsinet.co.za) DB&B R290 per person. Tulani Safari lodge organises tours to Kruger and around the Blyde River Canyon, as well as wildlife drives on its own private reserve.

For information about the area south and east of Phalaborwa, see the Kruger National Park chapter.

HOEDSPRUIT & AROUND
☎ 015 • postcode 1380

Hoedspruit, at the junction of the R527 and the R40, is a good jumping-off point for trips to the northern private reserves that border Kruger.

Information can be obtained from the **Jumbo Junction Visitor Centre** (☎ *793 3000, fax 793 3001*). It's run by McFarlane Safaris, which has tours to Kruger and Mozambique. There are several banks in town including ABSA, First National and Standard.

Just south of Hoedspruit, off the R40, is the 11,000-hectare **Kapama Game Reserve** (☎ *015-793 1038,* e *gentour@iafrica.com*) has *guesthouse* and *camp* accommodation starting at R600 per person, all inclusive.

Off Beat Safaris (☎ *793 2422, 082-494 1735*) in Hoedspruit operates seven- to 21-day trips into Mozambique; the price of R350 per day includes use of a rubber dinghy, spear guns and cooking items; it doesn't include drinks and visas. The company has a *safari camp* 12km north-east of Hoedspruit; the cabins are thatched and elevated.

SA Express flies to and from Jo'burg daily (R650 one way) and less frequently to and from Cape Town. There's a tax of R60 if you fly into the Eastgate airport at Hoedspruit; this is not included in the price of your ticket as this airport is privately owned.

There is a minibus taxi rank near the train station; taxis go to Jo'burg, Phalaborwa (R17) and Pietersburg.

Nyani Cultural Village

For an opportunity to see how traditional Shangaan families live, visit this nontouristy cultural village (☎ *793 3816, Guernsey Rd; admission R45*), home of the descendants of former local chief Kapama. Within the village all of the idiosyncrasies of daily life, customs and architecture are explained. It is like taking a journey back 150 years. This village recreates all aspects of tribal culture, and chief Axon Khosa is happy to explain traditional medicines and aspects of Tsonga life.

The village is on the road heading towards Thornybush Game Reserve, 4km from Route 40, near Klaserie Dam.

Safari Backpackers & Bushcamp (☎ *793 3816, Route 531*) Dorms/doubles R50/150. This bush camp offers a true wildlife-park experience at a backpacker's price. The camp has a swimming pool and braai facilities and organises wildlife drives. This place is just past Nyani Cultural Village, and is run by the same people. Dinner is available for R35.

AFRICAN IVORY ROUTE

The famed African Ivory Route was a route etched out centuries ago by African and Arab traders for moving ivory, ebony and gold as well as that most notorious of trades, the slave trade (mainly labourers from Mozambique destined to slave in the Jo'burg mines).

Today the Ivory Route starts near Orpen in Manyeleti Game Reserve and ends at Atherstone Nature Reserve near Thabazimbi. It includes Vhembe Dhonge National Park near Messina and areas in the fabulously scenic Waterberg.

The 'golden horseshoe' of camps that rings Northern Province includes many camps that lie along the route, and these are the basis of many of the tours operated by *Trans Frontier Safaris* (☎ *015-793 3816, 083-700 7987*), on the R531 at Safari Backpackers & Bushcamp. The company offers a selection of unique experiences in real African wilderness. It provides all the necessary infrastructure and charges R1000 per person per day; trips range in length from one to three weeks.

There are walking safaris from Monday to Friday or shorter trips from Friday to Monday in the Manyeleti and Letaba area, based on a camp in the Letaba Valley. The safaris are tremendous value at R2200 per person for the Monday to Friday trip and R1800 per person for the Friday to Monday trip, all-inclusive. The trips include bushcraft, a night in a Shangaan village, sleeping out in the bushveld and encounters with wildlife.

Gauteng

Gauteng (southern Sotho for 'Place of Gold' and pronounced 'how-teng') is by far South Africa's smallest province (17,010 sq km), but in almost every other way it is the powerhouse that drives all of Southern Africa. It is fuelled by people and money, both of which are in plentiful supply. A look at the statistics is instructive. Gauteng has arguably the largest population of any South African province (if you believe the estimate that three million people did not participate in the last census) at about 11 million people, including more than 40% of South Africa's whites and 70% of the total workforce. It has the highest percentage of urban dwellers (99%) and the lowest level of poverty (17%). Gauteng is responsible for 38% of South Africa's gross domestic product (GDP). To put that into perspective, this one province accounts for more than 20% of the GDP of all Africa!

For all its wealth, Gauteng remains a geographically boring place. There's none of the beauty of the Cape coast here, rather a countryside increasingly crowded by urban sprawl surrounded by fields of *mealies* (maize) and polluted by power stations. However, a rich history (see History in the Johannesburg and Pretoria sections in this chapter) goes some way towards masking the ugly face of contemporary Gauteng.

For most visitors a quick visit to Johannesburg (Jo'burg, as it is always called) and perhaps Pretoria will be enough, but Gauteng is most rewarding to those who stay long enough to find there is more here than just a bad reputation.

Jo'burg lies at the centre of an enormous conurbation, which is rapidly developing into a megalopolis. Diminishing green belts separate it from Pretoria to the north, but in all other directions the sprawl rolls on apace.

The Witwatersrand, which is often shortened to just 'the Rand', literally means 'Ridge of White Waters'. The ridge runs from Randfontein through Jo'burg and then

Highlights

- Hear stories of the struggle on a guided shebeen crawl through Soweto, the most important place you can visit while in Johannesburg (Jo'burg).

- Plot Jo'burg's dynamic growth through the eyes of black and white at the fascinating Museum Africa.

- Take the double-decker bus from Sandton to Soweto; from mansions to matchbox homes.

- Discover distant ancestors and Africa's most dangerous animals in the serenity of the Kromdraai Conservancy.

- Feel the intense symbolism of the Afrikaaners' colossal Voortrekker Monument in Pretoria.

- Party all night long on Burnett St, Pretoria's hippest – and safest – food and bar strip.

- Observe the magnificent king cheetah at the De Wildt Cheetah & Wildlife Centre.

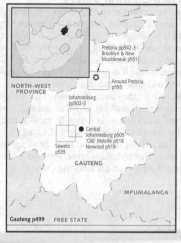

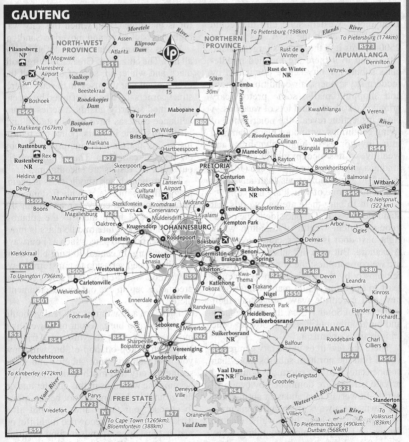

GAUTENG

east beyond Brakpan and Springs. The term is now used to describe most of southern Gauteng, which is heavily developed and urbanised.

Although the ridge is over 1700m above sea level at its highest point, it is not particularly impressive. It's more famous for its underground geology than its above-ground form.

The Vaal Triangle lies to the south of the Rand and is another heavily developed area, occupying the triangle formed by Vanderbijlpark, Vereeniging and Sasolburg (across the border in the Free State).

Johannesburg

☎ 011 • pop 4.9 million • elevation 1766m

Jo'burg (also known as Jozi or eGoli, 'the City of Gold') is a city of astonishing contrasts. Merely 115 years old, it has long been the wealthiest city in Africa and, given that the official figures are ridiculously low, the third-largest on the continent, after Egypt's Cairo and Nigeria's Lagos. Indeed by 2010 it's estimated that Greater Jo'burg will be one of the world's ten biggest cities by population – if you accept that the official population figure of 4.9 million is absurdly low.

On first appearances, Jo'burg is another anonymous, Western-style city that could just as easily be in the USA. It's big – at 2500 sq kms it is the world's largest inland city – and in it there are fortified middle-class suburbs; a city centre dominated by modern skyscrapers, air-conditioned shops and shopping malls; some pretty scary crime; black ghettos and lots of weapons. A close inspection reveals the polarisation of living conditions, with poor blacks jammed into tiny homes in huge townships, and wealthy whites occupying huge houses among a virtual rainforest of green (Jo'burg is said to have more trees than any other city, almost none of which are native).

Within Jo'burg there are two worlds that stand side by side. On one side is the outrageous, opulent wealth of Sandton while right next door is the desperate poverty of Alexandra. But with the shocking contrasts are welcome ironies; the hope of this city is felt mostly by those who seem to have the least to hope for. While many whites seek new and inventive ways of getting their money out of South Africa, the smiling faces and burgeoning businesses in Soweto belie an infectious optimism.

There are few trees in the city centre but you'll find the northern suburbs more than compensate. Here the enormous houses and private gardens are dominated by beautiful purple-flowering jacarandas in spring, and the lawns are always green and manicured. Most properties have high walls, electric fences and large, vicious-sounding dogs. New offices have sprung up in areas such as Parktown (often in old mansions) as many whites rushed to abandon the city centre.

There's no denying crime is a big issue in this city. The pressures associated with a rapid growth in population and a huge shift in social make-up have seen the city develop and maintain a reputation as one of the most dangerous on earth (see the boxed text 'Surviving Johannesburg's Dangers & Annoyances' later in this section). Parts of the city centre and adjoining suburbs such as Hillbrow have become no-go zones; businesses have moved north and even the Johannesburg Stock Exchange, for so long

a potent symbol of the entrepreneurial spirit (or is that greed?) on which this city was built, has packed up and moved to Sandton.

But as grim as it may sound, Jo'burg's not all bad. The citizens of Greater Jo'burg, both black and white, are sick of crime and the ever-present fear it causes. In the city centre, street corners have been occupied by green-uniformed security guards, a series of surveillance cameras have been installed and, for the first time in years, police are returning to foot patrols in a high-profile 'bobby on the beat' campaign. This is no quick fix but so far the results are encouraging.

The growing black middle class is beginning to flex its muscle, moving first into bigger and more expensive areas within the townships and from there to the suburbs. Meanwhile, the white middle class is moving further north to places such as Fourways and Randburg. In central Jo'burg billions of rand have been set aside to transform Newtown into a world-class – and safe – cultural precinct. Keep an eye out for developments there.

There are a few things you really should see while in Jo'burg. A tour of Soweto is a must, as is a visit to Museum Africa in Newtown. A hop-on, hop-off bus will show you both rich and poor suburbs and make seeing the city that much easier. And while heeding the warnings in this chapter and on the ground in Jo'burg, do not be too afraid to choose your target and head out after dark to discover the renowned nightlife; no matter what type of music, food or drink you prefer, you'll find it in Jo'burg.

If your time isn't limited and you consult with the locals before giving in to fear, you'll find Jo'burg a stimulating and interesting place that is definitely worth a visit of a few days. This is the heart of the new South Africa, and this is where change – good and bad – occurs first. Remember, life goes on for its inhabitants – you're here only for a brief moment.

HISTORY

At the beginning of 1886 the undistinguished stretch of the Transvaal highveld that was to become Jo'burg consisted of four sleepy farms: Braamfontein, Doornfontein, Turffontein and Langlaagte. In March of that year, however, an Australian prospector, George Harrison, found traces of gold on Langlaagte. Harrison didn't realise that he had stumbled on the only surface outcrop of the richest gold-bearing reef ever discovered. He sold his claim for £10.

Within a matter of months, thousands of diggers descended on this site. Because the gold was deep – in reef form, not the more easily accessible alluvial form – mining was quickly concentrated in the hands of men who had the capital to finance large underground mines. Mining magnates, who had made their money at the Kimberley diamond field, bought up the small claims and soon came to be known as the Randlords. Cecil Rhodes and Barney Barnato were among them.

By 1889 Jo'burg was the largest town in Southern Africa – a rowdy place full of the inevitable bars and brothels. The multicultural fortune-seekers – blacks and whites – were regarded with deep distrust by the Boers, by the Transvaal government and especially by the president, Paul Kruger. Kruger introduced electoral laws that effectively restricted voting rights to the Boers, and laws aimed at controlling the movement of blacks were passed.

The tensions between the Randlords and uitlanders (outsiders) on one side and the Transvaal government on the other were crucial factors in the events that led to the 1899–1902 Anglo-Boer War. Jo'burg, which already had a population in excess of 100,000, became a ghost town during the war. It recovered quickly when the British took control and massive new mines were developed to the east and west. Although the British entrenched the privileged position of white workers, the miners' unions were growing stronger and peace was not to last.

By 1921 the 21,000 white miners earned almost twice as much as the 180,000 black miners, which suggested an obvious possibility to the mining companies. In 1922 the Chamber of Mines attempted to lower costs by employing blacks in skilled jobs that had previously been reserved for whites. The strike called by the white unionists soon became an open revolt. The Imperial Light Horse was ambushed at Ellis Park and artillery and aircraft were used against the strikers. By the time peace was restored, over 200 people, including 129 soldiers and policemen, had died in the Rand Revolt.

Although gold-mining remained the backbone of the city's economy, manufacturing industries soon began to spring up, gaining fresh impetus during WWII. Under increasing pressure in the countryside, thousands of blacks moved to the city in search of jobs. Racial segregation had become entrenched during the interwar years, and from the 1930s onwards, vast squatter camps had sprung up around Jo'burg.

Under black leadership these camps became well-organised cities, despite their gross overcrowding and negligible services. But in the late 1940s many were destroyed by the authorities, and the people were moved to new suburbs known as the South-Western townships, now shortened to Soweto.

The official development of apartheid during the 1960s did nothing to slow the expansion of the city or the arrival of black squatters. Large-scale violence finally broke out in 1976 when the Soweto Students' Representative Council organised protests against the use of Afrikaans (regarded as the language of the oppressor) in black schools. Police opened fire on a student march and over the next 12 months more than 1000 would die fighting the apartheid system.

The regulations of apartheid were finally abandoned in February 1990 and since the 1994 elections the city has, in theory, been free of discriminatory laws. The black townships have been integrated into the municipal government system; the city centre is vibrant with black hawkers and street stalls; and inner suburbs have become multiracial.

Unfortunately, serious problems remain. Crime is rampant and middle-class whites are retreating to the north where new shopping malls and satellite business centres are mushrooming. It's another world out there in the northern suburbs, practically a volkstaat (an independent, racially pure Boer state) by default.

GAUTENG

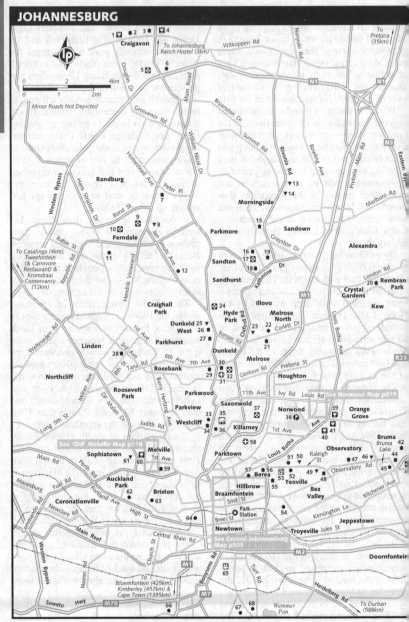

JOHANNESBURG

To Pretoria (35km)

Craigavon
1 2 3 4

To Johannesburg Ranch Hostel (3km)

Witkoppen Rd
Naryuki Rd
N1
N1

5 6

Douglas Dr
Main Road
William Nicol Dr
Bryanston Dr
Summit Rd
Rivonia Rd
Bowling Ave
Pretoria Main Rd
N3
Eastern Bypass

Grosvenor Rd

Minor Roads Not Depicted

0   2   4km
0   1   2mi

Randburg

Homestead Ave
Hans Strijdom Dr
Western Bypass
Rabie St
Republic Rd
Peter Pl
Bond St
7
Jan Smuts Ave
Hendrik Verwoerd

Morningside
13
14

Marlboro Rd

9
10
Ferndale

8

Parkmore

15
Sandown

Grayston Dr

Alexandra

To Casalinga (4km), Tweefontein (& Carnivore Restaurant) & Kromdraai Conservancy (12km)

11

12

Sandton
16 19
17
18
Katherine Dr

Sandhurst

London Rd
20 Rembran Park

Crystal Gardens
Kew

Craighall Park

24
Hyde Park
Oxford Rd
Illovo

Melrose North
Corlett Dr

22
23

Louis Botha Ave
M1
R25

Dunkeld West
25
26
27

Bompas Rd

Dunkeld

21

Linden
1st Ave
3rd Ave
8th St
Tana Rd
28
Weltevreden Rd

Parkhurst

6th Ave 7th Ave

30
Rosebank
29
32
31

Melrose

Pretoria St
Glenhove Rd
Houghton

Northcliff
Milner Ave
Dr Malan Dr
Barry Hertzog Ave

Roosevelt Park

Parkwood

11th Ave
Ivy Rd
Louis Rd
See Norwood Map p519

Long 5th St
Judith Rd

Parkview
Westcliff
33
35
34
36

Saxonwold
37

Killarney
58
1st Ave
Norwood
38
39 Orange Grove
40
41

Bruma
Bruma Lake
42

See 'Old' Melville Map p518

Melville
1st Ave
Sophiatown
60
61
59

Parktown

Louis Botha
51 50
Raleigh St
Observatory
47 46
Observatory Rd
45
44

Main Rd
Perth Rd
Fuel Rd
Auckland Park
62

57
56
53
52
55
Berea
Yeoville
49
48
Bez Valley
Kitchener Ave

Maraisburg
Commando Rd
Coronationville
Newclare Rd
Portland Ave
High St
Brixton
63

Hillbrow
Smit St
Braamfontein

54
Kensington La
Jeppestown

Main Reef

64

Bree St
Park Station
Newtown
Troyeville
Jules St

See Central Johannesburg Map p505

Church St
Central Main Rd
M1
M2
Doornfonte

Western Bypass
Nasrec Rd

Bezuidenhout Rd
65
Turf Rd
Heidelberg Rd

To Bloemfontein (425km), Kimberley (457km) & Cape Town (1395km)

M70
M7
66
67
68
Wemmer Pan
To Durban (588km)

Soweto Hwy

To Dynamite Museum (2km)

To Bob's Bunkhouse (3.5km), Caesars Casino (3.5km), J Duneden Hotel (4km), Airport Backpackers (11km), Johannesburg International Airport (18km), Emerald Guest House (20km) & Madiba Freedom Museum (Kempton Park, 22km)

Sydonia St
Stanhope St
Eastern Bypass

Gold-mining is no longer undertaken in the city area, and the old, pale-yellow mine dumps that created such a surreal landscape on the edge of the city are being reprocessed. Modern recovery methods allow the mining companies to extract as much gold from these waste tailings today as was found in the raw ore 100 years ago. The classic view of Jo'burg – a mine dump in the foreground and skyscrapers in the background – will be retained, however, as some dumps are being preserved as historical monuments.

ORIENTATION
Despite its size, it's not difficult to find your way around Jo'burg. Johannesburg International Airport (JIA) is 25km north-east of the city centre, accessible by freeway. Regular buses connect the airport with the Park Station on the northern edge of the city centre (see Getting There & Away later in this section for more information on JIA and Park Station).

Two major communication towers on the ridges to the north of the city centre make good landmarks. The JG Strijdom (Berea) Tower, just behind Hillbrow, is 269m high and used by the post office. To the west of the city, the South African Broadcasting Commission (SABC) runs the 239m-high Brixton Tower.

The city centre, which is laid out on a straightforward grid, is dominated by office blocks, in particular the 50-storey Carlton Centre on Commissioner St. There's no reason to stay in the city centre; after the shops close, the centre becomes a virtual ghost town and extremely unsafe unless you're in a car. However, redevelopment of the Newtown cultural precinct, at the western edge of the city, is at the core of an effort to clean up downtown Jo'burg (see the boxed text 'A New Town from Newtown' later in this chapter). North of the city centre, a steep ridge runs west-east from Braamfontein across to the dangerous suburb of Hillbrow. To the north-east of the centre is the also dangerous Yeoville.

The northern suburbs are predominantly white middle- and upper-class areas, within an arc formed by the N1 and N3 freeways. These suburbs of big houses, big trees and big fences are where most travellers stay. Sterile shopping malls form the centre of most social life, although there are a few pockets of resistance. The inner-suburban restaurant enclaves of Melville and Norwood make a refreshing change.

The black townships ring the city and are a stark contrast to the northern suburbs. Conditions within them range from reasonable to appalling. Accessibility and convenience were never factors in the planning process, so they are a considerable distance from the city centre and the white suburbs (out of sight and out of mind?). The main township is Soweto (see the special section 'Soweto' in this chapter) but there are also big townships at Tokoza (south of Alberton), Kwa-Thema and Tsakane (south-east and south of Brakpan respectively), Daveyton

---

Photographing Johannesburg

Carrying a camera around Johannesburg (Jo'burg) is as good as wearing a sign saying 'Mug Me'. Even in the relative safety of the northern suburbs you will never see Jo'burgers carrying cameras; to do so is to make yourself an unnecessarily attractive target.

Until recently this has been a problem with no easy answer. Driving around to take pictures, particularly in the city centre, has been one option, but with 3176 carjackings recorded in Jo'burg in 2000 this is also risky, not to mention technically difficult.

The introduction of double-decker tourist buses (see Hop-On, Hop-Off Bus under Getting Around later in this chapter) has been a blessing for all photographers. These buses, especially the open-topped City Slicker bus, provide the perfect platform from which to shoot photos. They're fairly slow moving, take interesting routes, are high enough to see over the walls of the wealthy suburbs and make you remote enough that most people don't even see the camera. But most importantly, they're safe enough that you can wave your SLR camera around as much as you like.

(east of Benoni), Tembisa (to the north-east) and Alexandra (inside the N3 freeway to the north-east of the city centre).

Maps

For maps try the **Map Office** (☎ 339 4941, *Ground floor, Standard House, 40 De Korte St, Braamfontein, postal address: Box 207, Wits 2050, Gauteng; open 7.30am-4pm Mon-Fri*) This place sells government maps for R30 a sheet. Drakensberg maps are available only from the KwaZulu-Natal Parks Board in Durban. Tourist maps are available but they deal with specific areas rather than the city as a whole.

INFORMATION
Tourist Offices

Jo'burg just can't seem to get its act together when it comes to information, and it's difficult to keep up with the various agencies purporting to represent the city. There is an overwhelming number of brochures available at the agencies as well as in hotels and hostels, but the tourist offices can seem more interested in conferences than independent travel and often don't know much about the tours they are advertising.

Gauteng Tourism Authority (☎ 327 2000, **W** www.gauteng.net) is the best bet and has an office in the Rosebank Mall. **Info Africa** (☎ 390 9000) has a desk in the international arrivals hall at JIA and it has brochures and some useful books. **South African Tourism** (☎ 970 1669, **W** www.south africa.net) also has an office in the JIA international arrivals hall.

Ignore the 'glitz' in all the tourism publications – it will only lull you into a false sense of security.

National Parks Board & Hiking Organisations

The National Parks Board doesn't have an office in Jo'burg. The head office is inconveniently located on the southern outskirts of Pretoria (see Information under Pretoria later in this chapter).

The **Hiking Federation of Southern Africa** (☎ 968 1202, **W** www.linx.co.za/trails) has useful information.

On the outskirts of Johannesburg, Soweto, the best known of South Africa's townships, is home to more than 3.5 million people. From the 1950s onwards, Soweto was the centre of resistance to apartheid.

Embrace all things kitsch at the Valley of the Waves, Sun City.

Old and new: Church Square, Pretoria (left) and modern Johannesburg (right)

CENTRAL JOHANNESBURG

PLACES TO STAY
4 Devonshire Hotel
6 Protea Hotel Parktonian
11 Johannesburger Hotel
14 Formule 1 Hotel
   Park Station
21 Mariston Hotel Apartments

PLACES TO EAT
40 Chinese Restaurants
46 Kapitan's
51 Guildhall Bar & Restaurant

OTHER
1 The Heartland;
   Therapy; Fly Bar;
   AKWA Cocktail Lounge
2 The Map Office
3 Braamfontein Centre;
   Swaziland Consulate
5 Stardust Palace

7 Civic Theatre
8 Johannesburg Fort;
   Constitutional Hill
9 Skyline
10 Windybrow Centre for the Arts
12 Taxis to Bulawayo (Zimbabwe)
13 Taxis to Maputo (Mozambique)
15 Taxis to Upington, Kimberley
   & Cape Town
16 City to City Bus Office
17 Taxis to Durban
18 To the North & East Buses
19 Taxis to Pretoria
20 Johannesburg Art Gallery
22 Taxis to Lesotho, Bloemfontein,
   Kroonstad & Ficksburg
23 Taxis to Soweto
24 Shell House
25 St Mary's Anglican Cathedral
26 Taxis to Rosebank & Sandton
27 Car Licensing Department

28 Department of
   Home Affairs
29 Carfax
30 French Institute
   of South Africa;
   National Arts Council
   of South Africa
31 Market Theatre;
   Kippie's Jazz International;
   Gramadoela's; Janco's Bar
32 Museum Africa
33 Market Square Market
34 Workers' Museum
35 Mega Music Warehouse
36 Electric Workshop
37 Horror Cafe
38 SAB World of Beer
39 SA Police Headquarters
41 Law Office of
   Mandela & Tambo
42 Magistrates Court

43 Hindu Temple
44 Kwa Zulu Muti
45 Anglo Gold Building
47 Kohinoor Music Store
48 Zimbabwe High
   Commission
49 Johannesburg Library;
   Library Square
50 Elizabeth Hotel; Press Bar
52 Soweto Art Gallery
53 Rand Club
54 City Hall
55 Rissik St Post Office
   (closed)
56 GPO; Rasta Market
57 Supreme Court
58 Weleda Pharmacy
59 ABSA Bank North Tower;
   Mobile City
60 Top of Africa
61 Metro Bus Terminal

Money

Banks are open 9am to 3.30pm Monday to Friday and 8.30am to 11am Saturday. The foreign exchange counters at the airport are open for two hours before the first flight departs and two hours after the last plane arrives.

ATMs are everywhere but whatever you do, don't use them until you've read the boxed text 'Beating the ATM Scams' in the Facts for the Visitor chapter.

At the airport you'll find an office for **American Express** *(AmEx;* ☎ *390 1233).* It also has offices in the northern suburbs including Sandton (☎ 883 1316, 78A Sandton) and Rosebank (☎ 880 8382, Nedbank Gardens, 33 Báth Ave).

Rennies Travel is the agent for Thomas Cook and advertises a commission-free exchange for all travellers cheques. Its foreign exchange outlets include JIA (☎ 390 1040); Sandton City (☎ 884 4035); and Bedfordview (☎ 616 2077, Shop L20a, Eastgate Mall, Bradford Rd).

The airport offices are open 24 hours.

Post

There is a poste restante service at the main post office *(Jeppe St, between Von Brandis St & Smal St Mall; open 8am-4.30pm Mon, Tues, Thurs & Fri, 8.30am-4.30pm Wed, 8am-noon Sat).* In theory you need some sort of identification, although tellers are not very strict about this. Do be careful about having anything too valuable sent here. Rastafarians congregate at an informal music and herb market outside the post office.

The charming Rissik St post office is opposite the city hall. It has closed for renovation but is worth a look.

Telephone

There are many commercial phone services scattered through the city. The main post office also has an international telephone exchange. Always check rates before calling. Phonecards, purchased at Telkom branches, are the best way to make local and international calls. International calls on coin phones usually cut out, as your money is used faster than you can replace

it. For local directory inquiries call ☎ 1023 for international inquiries call ☎ 0903.

Users of cell phones (mobile phones) will find Vodacom and MTN stores in every mall and at plenty of other places too. Vodacom sell SIM cards for R90 and cards for prepaid services for R29, R55, R110 and R275. Both companies have stores in the international arrivals hall at JIA.

Email & Internet Access

Most hostels and hotels have Internet and email facilities, usually for about R30 an hour. Alternatively, most Jo'burg malls have Internet cafes, but the charges can be exorbitant. For a cheaper option, try the **Milky Way Internet Cafe** *(☎ 487 1340, W www .milkyway.co.za, 2nd floor, Time Square, 3é Raleigh St, Yeoville).* Enter from behind the Time Square Cafe. The service is fast and costs just R10 per hour, with coffee and snacks to graze on as you go.

Travel Agencies

The **SA Students' Travel Service** *(SASTS* W *www.sasts.org.za)* is a national organisation with offices around the country. They offer all the regular facilities plus student and youth cards, special fares and flights. At the University of Witwatersrand there is a branch at the **Student Union Building** *(☎ 71é 3045; open 9am-4pm Mon-Fri).*

Rennies Travel *(☎ 407 3343)* has a large network of agencies. Rennies and **Flight Centre** *(☎ 0860-400 747)* can be found in most shopping malls.

For flight bargains, check the travel lift out in Saturday's *Jo'Burg Star,* or try **Seekers** *(☎ 790 0000,* W *www.travel.co.za).*

Bookshops

The **Exclusive Books** *(☎ 622 4870, Eastgate Mall)* chain is the best in town, with the widest range of local press, travel guides and international newspapers. It has outlets at Hyde Park Mall (☎ 325 4298), Sandton City Mall (☎ 883 1010) and Rosebank Mall (☎ 447 3028). For Exclusive Books' other stores call ☎ 0800-332 550. **Book Dealers of Melville** *(☎ 726 4045, 12 7th St, Melville* has a good antiquarian selection.

Surviving Johannesburg's Dangers & Annoyances

Many people don't have problems walking around Johannesburg (Jo'burg) but there are enough true-life horror stories to make caution essential. South Africa has an appalling tradition of violence and there's a huge gulf between rich and poor. It's a rough city, hence these survival tips – this Lonely Planet guide may be worth buying for the following advice alone!

If your hostel/hotel transport does not arrive at the airport, bus station or train station when expected, catch a legitimate taxi to your intended destination (even pay up to R250, US$31). This small investment may save the contents of your backpack and money belt. Don't become one of the many independent travellers who lose the lot in their first moments in the city – ie, those trying to walk or catch a bus to their accommodation to save money. Never walk out of Park Station with luggage unless you're getting straight into a car.

When you get to your hostel/hotel, immediately store your passport, travellers cheques, plane tickets and spare cash in its safe. It is usually safer here than in the dorms and rooms where interlopers, including fellow travellers, prey.

When you head off for your first meal or pub experience, carry as much money as you are prepared to lose (in your pocket), and more in your socks for the taxi home – maybe they won't find it. Forget carrying cameras and videos, or wearing watches and jewellery (including gold ear studs) or good quality clothes. Wearing a T-shirt, shorts/skirt and sandals should make you reasonably inconspicuous.

Don't head into the centre (near the Carlton Centre or Smal St Mall), Braamfontein, Hillbrow, Berea or even Yeoville to 'discover the real South Africa' until you have well and truly sussed these places out. Avoid the city centre at night and on weekends when the shops close and the crowds thin out. With the exception of some of the busy northern suburbs (eg, Melville, Norwood and Rosebank), you would be crazy to walk around Jo'burg at night. Daylight muggings in the city centre and other inner suburbs, notably Hillbrow (at gunpoint and knifepoint), are not uncommon. Staff at your hostel/hotel will advise on 'no-go' areas – definitely heed their advice!

There are plenty of beggars on the streets – both black and white. Some of them can be very persistent. Consider carrying a rand or two in change in an accessible pocket, so that you can give money to beggars without flashing your wallet or purse around.

Be aware of what's going on around you. Walk on the road side of the footpath and don't hesitate to cross the street to avoid an alleyway or a threatening individual or group. In general, you're safe so long as there are plenty of people around, or you're in a group. Have a healthy respect for your circumstances but don't be overly paranoid – most of the people you meet are genuine and not trying to rip you off. But don't succumb to offers that people are insisting you 'can't refuse'. There are a lot of scumbags out there ready to make you a victim. If the situation looks bleak, run! If the muggers produce a knife or gun, give them all they want. A smile often goes a long way to ameliorate the situation. And if you are mugged, for the sake of your own emotional health, try and accept it as a fact of life in this city.

If you are driving make sure the car doors are locked; when you're at stop lights leave a car's length between you and the vehicle in front so you can drive away if necessary – running a red light is not illegal if you're in reasonable fear of assault. When you park your car, immobilise it or attach a gear-stick lock or a steering-wheel lock (such as a 'Gorilla') – or do all three.

The Jo'burg-Pretoria Metro train is targeted by muggers these days, so don't go to Pretoria this way.

When all else fails, head to Soweto with a black friend to reaffirm that there are heaps of nice South African people out there.

This advice has been comprehensively road tested.

Jeff Williams

There are **CNA bookshops** throughout Jo'burg. They have good South African sections, road atlases, local guidebooks and glossy picture books. Call (☎ 491 7500) for locations.

Universities

The **University of Witwatersrand** (☎ *717 1000, Jan Smuts Ave, Braamfontein)* is more commonly known as Wits (pronounced 'Vits') University. This is the largest English-language university in the country, with over 20,000 students. It's an attractive campus and visitors can visit the Gertrude Posel Gallery (see under Galleries later); Jan Smuts House to see Smuts' study; the Student Union Building for a cheap cafe meal and the Students' Travel Service office.

Cultural Centres

The **National Arts Council of South Africa** (☎ *838 1383,* e *info@nac.org.za, 66 Wolhuter St, Newtown)* shares an office with the French Institute of South Africa. The arts council has a brief to promote, through the arts, the free and creative expression of South Africa's cultures.

Alliance Française (☎ *646 1169, 17 Lower Park Dr, Parkview)* organises a variety of French-language theatre productions and exhibitions by French artists.

Medical Services

Medical services are of a high standard but they are expensive, so make sure you're insured. Doctors are listed under 'Medical' in the phonebook. Doctors will generally arrange for hospitalisation, although in an emergency you can go directly to the casualty department of **Johannesburg General Hospital** (☎ *488 4911, Jubilee Rd, Parktown)*, less than 1km north of Hillbrow. Contact the **Police Flying Squad** (☎ *10111)* to get directions to the nearest hospital.

For a recommended clinic try **Rosebank Clinic** (☎ *328 0500, 14 Sturdee Ave, Rosebank; open 7am-10pm daily)*. There is a **Daelite Pharmacy** (☎ *883 7520, Suite 56, Sandton City; open until 8pm daily)*. If you're after holistic, antimalarial prophylactics try

the **Weleda Pharmacy** (☎ *333 1888, Cn Pritchard & Von Brandis Sts)*.

Emergency

The phone numbers for emergency service are:

AIDS line	☎ 0800-012 322
Ambulance	☎ 10111
Battered Women & Rape Crisis Centre (POWA)	☎ 231 5050, 083-765 1235
Fire brigade	☎ 10111
Lifeline	☎ 728 1347
Police Flying Squad	☎ 10111
St John's Ambulance	☎ 10777

Dangers & Annoyances

Jo'burg's myriad dangers can be very annoying indeed, but before you write off the city completely, it's important to remember that most travellers come and go without incident. The secret to success is simple: seek local advice, listen to it, and then turn up your personal awareness gauge as far as it will go whenever you leave your lodgings.

A couple of important things to remember are that you are really very unlikely to become the victim of a violent crime – even criminals understand that assault and murder attract far more attention from the authorities than robbery alone – and that you are most vulnerable when using an ATM (see the boxed text 'Beating the ATM Scams' in the Facts for the Visitor chapter). Oh, and you know the safes and security boxes in hostel and hotels that you usually ignore, use them. For everything else see the boxed text 'Surviving Johannesburg's Dangers & Annoyances', and when you think of all those stories you've seen or read, remember that the media doesn't usually report good news.

NEWTOWN

The cultural precinct in Newtown is an attempt to rejuvenate Jo'burg's city centre (see the boxed text 'A New Town from Newtown'). The Museum Africa is the main drawcard, and there are theatres, shops, the classy Gramadoela's restaurant (see City Centre under Places to Eat later in his section), live music venues and the SAB World of Beer.

Museum Africa

Founded in the 1930s, this important museum (☎ 833 5624, 121 Bree St; admission adult/child R5/2; open 9am-5pm Tues-Sun) is now housed in the impressive old Bree St fruit market, next to the Market Theatre complex.

The superb exhibition on the Treason Trials (1956–61), which featured most of the important figures in the 'new' South Africa, is a must see for anyone looking for a better understanding of the country's more recent history. The 'Transformations' exhibition details the evolution of Jo'burg and includes a simulated descent into one of the gold mines. The Sophiatown display is outstanding. There's also a large collection of rock art, a geological museum, a display on Gandhi's time in Jo'burg and the Bensusan Museum of Photography, which charts the history of photography and has regular exhibitions by famous South African snappers.

Soweto Art Gallery

In the city centre, not far from Newtown, you'll find this small but significant gallery (☎ 492 1109, Suite 34, 2nd floor, Victory House, Cnr Commissioner & Harrison Sts; open 8am-6pm Mon-Fri, 8am-1pm Sat). This gallery is directed by well-known Sowetan artist Peter Sibeko and is one of the few places contemporary black artists from the townships can exhibit their paintings and sculptures. All works are for sale. There are plans for a gallery space beside the Hector Pieterson memorial in Soweto.

Market Theatre

This theatre complex (see Theatres later in this section), at the western edge of the city centre, is one of the highlights of Jo'burg. Developed in several old, recycled market buildings, the complex is an attractive and enjoyable place to hang around fro a while. With Museum Africa nearby, this corner of Jo'burg could easily absorb most of a day and a fair part of the night – especially on Saturday when the market sets up in nearby Market Square. Janco's Bar is as a good place to meet young black people.

SAB World of Beer

This is a popular, refreshing and, to any beer drinker, ultimately fascinating museum (☎ 836 4900, 15 President St, Newtown;

A New Town from Newtown

Newtown is being hailed as Johannesburg's (Jo'burg's) last hope of salvation. The cultural precinct at the western end of the city centre is about to have a long-overdue (but well worth the wait) R1.2 billion facelift in an effort to draw local and international tourists back to a reinvigorated city centre.

The area was once the home of industry, in the form of the city's first power station, and a variety of market traders. But for years now it has been at the heart of the city's arts community, with the Market Theatre, Museum Africa, Kippies Jazz International, the some-time rave venue the Electric Workshop and several other cultural venues dotted around. The problem is they've been dotted through what is essentially a giant, deserted and wholly uninspiring car park. Add to this its proximity to one of Jo'burg's rougher neighbourhoods and it's no wonder most tourists just aren't coming.

The plan is to renovate and expand the existing buildings, construct market facilities for 800 traders, create a taxi rank for 2800 taxis and build five housing projects. The new Nelson Mandela Bridge, under construction now, would then link the whole shebang with the Civic Theatre in Braamfontein. Another, perhaps even more ambitious, project is to redevelop the old Johannesburg Fort in Hillbrow into Constitutional Hill.

If all goes according to plan, Newtown will indeed become a world-class tourist attraction within the lifetime of this book. Even so, it may be a few years yet before you can walk from Newtown to Hillbrow without taking your life in your hands.

admission R10; open 10am-6pm Tues-Sat). It unlocks the secrets of brewing (malting, mashing, lautering and wort boiling) in South Africa, from the time when the crudely brewed sorghum beer first passed the lips of early Africans. In the Ales Pavilion, the European tradition of brewing ales and lagers is described; sorghum brewing is covered in the *Ukhamba* exhibition and there is a recreation of a 1965 Soweto she-been – all heavenly for appreciators of the amber fluid. The guided tour takes about 90 minutes; entry includes two beers.

Workers' Museum

In the restored Electricity Department's compound you'll find this museum *(☎ 834 2181, 52 Jeppe St, Newtown; admission free; open 9am-5pm Mon-Sat)*. It was built in 1910 for 300-plus municipal workers and has been declared a national monument, but it is not as inspiring as it could be. There is a Workers' Library and resource centre and a display of the living conditions of migrant workers.

Oriental Plaza & Chinatown

A short walk from Newtown, you'll find the Oriental Plaza *(☎ 838 6752, Bree St, Fordsburg; open 8.30am-5pm Mon-Fri, 8.30am-1pm Sat)*. It has over 350 Indian-owned shops. If you have a rough idea of prices and don't mind bargaining, you will make some good purchases. At the least, you'll find cheap, delicious samosas at Just Samoosas.

There was once a vibrant Chinatown, near the SA Police Headquarters on Commissioner St. It has shrunk significantly and a new Chinatown has blossomed almost overnight in Cyrildene, near Bruma Lake (see Other Suburbs under Places to Eat later in this section).

CITY CENTRE

The city centre's appalling reputation for safety means people generally don't go there. As a result, most tourist-oriented businesses have long-since moved on. However, if you're smart and a little bit brave, there are plenty of colonial-era buildings that are worth a look; the presently closed

Rissik St post office being one. Sights aside the thousands of hawkers and the smells o corn and beef being cooked at street-side stalls give the centre an African atmosphere that you won't find in the northern suburb and that alone makes it worth a well planned visit. See the boxed text 'Surviving Johannesburg's Dangers & Annoyances and 'Photographing Johannesburg'.

Johannesburg Art Gallery

On the Klein St side of the Joubert Park i the Johannesburg Art Gallery *(☎ 725 3130 W www.saevents.co.za, Joubert Park; ad mission & parking free; open 10am-5pm Tues-Sun)*. This place has a reputable col lection of European and South African land scape and figurative paintings, and severa exhibitions featuring more adventurou contemporary work and long-overdue retro spectives of black artists. Sadly, it is deserte these days.

Top of Africa

If you do make it into the city centre, one o the best things to do is to take the lift to th Top of Africa *(☎ 331 2629, 50th floor, Carl ton Centre; adult/child R7.50/5; open 9am 7pm daily)*. The view from the observatio deck is great; from the quiet remoteness o this height the sprawling city seems posi tively serene. The entrance is via a specia lift one floor below street level.

Mobile City

One of the few highlights of the city centr is the amazing Mobile City *(ABSA Ban North Tower, 180 Commissioner St; ope 9am-5pm Mon-Fri)*. The interior of th building has been decorated with an eclec tic mix of art from some of South Africa' top contemporary artists, but the highligh is undoubtedly the world's biggest, rotat ing, lifting and falling mobile that domin ates five floors of open space in the Nort Atrium. The aluminium artwork by Pau Cawood, Susan Woolf and Lewis Levin represents Jo'burg old and new, includin the mine shafts, tunnels and skyscrapers The building has a security desk but a polit request should see you in.

SOUTH AFRICAN NATIONAL MUSEUM OF MILITARY HISTORY

Perhaps it's South Africa's fascination with guns, or maybe it's the country's bloody history, but every year this is Jo'burg's most popular museum (☎ 646 5513, 22 Erlswold Way, Saxonwold; adult/child R5/2; open 9am-4.30pm Tues-Sun). If gunpowder is your thing you'll find this museum is actually quite well done. You can see artefacts and implements of destruction from the 1899–1902 Anglo-Boer War through to the Namibian wars. The museum is at the eastern end of the grounds of the Jo'burg Zoo.

MADIBA FREEDOM MUSEUM

East of the city centre you'll find this museum (☎ 970 1355, Erikson Diamond Centre, 20 Monument Rd, Kempton Park; admission free; open 8am-5pm Mon-Fri, 8am-1pm Sat). It's a shrine to Madiba (Nelson Mandela's endeared clan title), which attempts, with some success, to cover the history of the man once known as 'The Black Pimpernel'. It concentrates on Mzabalazo (Long Struggle for Equality), and has many photographs from the time.

There is a neighbouring diamond-cutting display (free).

GERTRUDE POSEL GALLERY

Among the university art galleries you'll find Gertrude Posel Gallery (☎ 717 1365, e gallery@atlas.wits.ac.za, Ground floor, Senate House, University of Witswatersrand; admission free; open 10am-4pm Tues-Fri, closed public holidays). Also housed in the university campus is the Standard Bank Foundation Collection of African tribal art, which includes masks, Ndebele fertility dolls and beadwork.

OTHER MUSEUMS

There are other museums in and around Jo'burg (see also under Newtown earlier). Well worth a look is the **Dynamite Museum** (☎ 606 3206, 2 Main St, Modderfontein; open 10am-2pm Mon & Fri, 2pm-4.30pm Wed), which is a 'blast'. Also worth checking out is the **Bernberg Fashion Museum** (☎ 646 0716, Cnr Duncombe Rd & Jan Smuts Ave, Forest Town; admission free; open 9am-5pm Tues-Sat). On display are a variety of fashions from yesteryear.

At the University of Witwatersrand is the **Planetarium** (☎ 717 1390, Yale Rd; adult/concession R15/8 for hour-long show). It has various programs that have been recommended by travellers. There are 12 museum collections in the university, including collections of African art, anthropology, geology, palaeontology (with some items from Sterkfontein), music and zoology. To visit, call the university and make an appointment.

JOHANNESBURG ZOO

North of the city centre is the zoo (☎ 646 2000, Jan Smuts Ave, Westcliff; adult/child R15/10; open 8.30am-5.30pm daily). It seems rather bizarre going to a zoo in Africa but you can combine a visit to Jo'burg Zoo with the South African National Museum of Military History. The zoo is about 4km north of the city centre; it has a particularly interesting wild-dog enclosure.

There are also night tours three times a week for R50 (no children); book through Computicket (☎ 340 8445).

HILLBROW & BEREA

On the ridge to the north-east of the train station, Hillbrow and adjoining Berea were once the most lively and interesting suburbs in Jo'burg. This is now a densely populated and dangerous area, dominated by towering apartment buildings and residential hotels.

Hillbrow and Berea have disintegrated into lawlessness. There are late-night bars, discos, gay clubs and brothels but little else. A visit to the 'Brow' is undoubtedly exhilarating and adrenaline pumping but danger is omnipresent. Be aware that if you cause trouble in this area, a knife in the ribs will be your probable reward. You should only venture here after you've got your bearings, and stringently observe the recommendations of the boxed texts 'Surviving Johannesburg's Dangers & Annoyances' in this chapter and 'Survival Tactics' in the Facts for the Visitor chapter.

The old **Johannesburg Fort** at the end of Kotze St was built in the 1890s to defend

GAUTENG

and garrison the military forces responsible for keeping the miners under control. It has never seen action and after the 1899–1902 Anglo-Boer War it was converted into a prison. Number Four, as it was known, was where pass-law violators (in apartheid days) were imprisoned – and it's recalled with dread. The area is to be redeveloped as Constitutional Hill, with the fort itself being transformed into the Constitutional Court. There are plans for museums and other attractions but the whole thing remains a fair way from completion.

YEOVILLE

For a long time, **Raleigh/Rockey St** (the name changes midway) in Yeoville was the counter-culture capital of South Africa. Sadly, that has changed somewhat. Drugs and crime have arrived from nearby Hillbrow and a spate of muggings and violent robberies has driven away travellers and the hostels they supported.

However, it's not as bad as Hillbrow and if you're looking for a real African night out this is probably the best place to find it. There are a few restaurants and plenty of bars – though women alone could feel uncomfortable in some of these macho establishments. Its saving grace is the **Tandoor**, which may sound like a curry house but is actually one of Jo'burg's best venues for live kwaito (township dance music) and, partly due to the reputation of its owners, the safest place on Rockey St for men and women alike (see Live Music later under Entertainment).

Raleigh/Rockey St is a short taxi ride north-east of the centre of Jo'burg, or west from Eastgate Mall (R40 maximum either way). It would be foolish to walk there after dark, or at any time if you're carrying valuables.

RANDBURG WATERFRONT

North-west of the centre is the Randburg Waterfront (☎ 789 5052, ⓦ www.rwater front.co.za, Republic Rd, Ferndale; open daily). Inland and bereft of a real waterfront like Cape Town's Victoria & Alfred, the solution in Jo'burg was to toss lots of money at a small pond on the Jukskei River. It was

then surrounded with shops, more than 50 restaurants and pubs, and the **Harbour Flea Market** with over 300 stalls (open Tuesday to Saturday); a musical fountain was then stuck in the centre. The result isn't that bad – a day at the Randburg Waterfront can be a pleasure, especially if you have kids in tow. The impressive Liquid Fireworks display is shown at 7.30pm and 8.30pm nightly.

GOLD REEF CITY

Eight kilometres south of the city, just off the M1 freeway you'll find Gold Reef City (☎ 248 6800, ⓦ www.goldreefcity.co.za; admission R50 or R35 for fewer rides, children under 120cm free; open 9.30am-5pm, Tues-Sun). This place is a tourist trap that can't quite make up its mind whether it's a Disneyland clone or a serious historical reconstruction of old Jo'burg. However, it might help fill a Jo'burg weekend.

It features scary rides, a Victorian fun fair and various reconstructions, including bank, brewery, pub and newspaper office. Visitors can go 220m down a shaft to see a gold mine from the inside (an extra R32), watch a gold pour and see an entertaining program of tribal or 'gumboot' dancing.

There are numerous places to eat and drink, plus Gold Reef City Arts & Crafts Centre and an expensive craft/souvenir shop. There are often special programs on the weekend, sometimes with live music performed in an open-sided amphitheatre, and fireworks. Check the entertainment section in the Jo'burg Star.

Beside the theme park is the new **casino** (☎ 248 5000; open 24 hours). Unfortunately, it's a bit tricky to reach by public transport and a taxi would be expensive, but it's included in most Jo'burg day tours.

Gold Reef City Hotel (☎ 248 5152, fax 248 5400, ⓦ www.threecities.co.za, Cnr Northern Parkway & Data Cres, Ormonde) has secure, luxurious rooms.

GOLF

Golf in Jo'burg has become an expensive proposition. Most courses will only allow you to play if you are a member of a club, making it tough for the part-time hacker.

You can play a round of golf at **Houghton Golf Club** (☎ 728 7337, *Norwood; tees R175 Mon-Fri, R205 Sat & Sun, club/caddy hire R100/100*) if you've got your handicap card.

ORGANISED TOURS

All Jo'burg budget hostels should have information on cheap packages to Kruger National Park and on the best (and cheapest) travel links to Cape Town, Durban, Swaziland, Lesotho, Namibia, Botswana, Zimbabwe and Mozambique.

Tour Companies

There are several companies running tours to various parts of the city.

Max Maximum Tours (☎ 938 8703, 082-770 0247, e *max.maximum@pixie.co.za*) is one of the best and cheapest companies. **Neng Kapa Neng** (☎ 936 9738, 082-649 6368) is also good. They both charge R180 for a half-day city tour, R250 for a half-day Pretoria city tour, and Max charges R240 for its full-day Sun City & Lost City tour. Both pick up from hostels and some major hotels.

Springbok Atlas (☎ 396 1053, W *www .springbokatlas.com*) offers half-day city tours (R260), longer tours that include Gold Reef City (R330) and half-day tours to Pretoria (R300). Springbok Atlas is the largest tour operator in the country; it caters mainly for the high-end hotel market, and its prices reflect this.

For details of the City Slicker and Adventure Bus hop-on, hop-off city tours see under Getting Around later in this section.

Township Tours

All of the companies under Tour Companies previous organise tours to Soweto (see also the special section 'Soweto' in this chapter). **Once More Tours** (☎ 838 2667, *fax 781 1564*) and **Imbizo Tours** (☎ 838 2667, *fax 781 8564*, W *www.imbizo.co.za*) run tours to Alexandra township, the city's oldest and perhaps grimmest township. Sights include the slums along the Jukskei River and Mandela's 'first' house in Jo'burg. Far grittier and less touristy than Soweto, a trip to Alexandra can be fascinating.

Walking Tours

Just the idea of walking Jo'burg would have many locals seeking psychotherapy, but it's actually a great way to see the city.

Walks Tours (☎ 444 1639, 083-269 9769, W *www.walktours.co.za*) Tours R50-100. This company offers regular weekend walking tours around parts of Jo'burg as diverse as the city centre, Sandton, Troyeville, Parktown and Alexandra township. The walks go for between three and six hours and are led by well-informed guides. The only downside is that unless you can get enough people together for a private tour, you might have to wait weeks for the walk you want.

Parktown and Westcliff Heritage Trust (☎ 482 3349) Three-hour tours R150. This company leads several tours of the more salubrious end of town.

SPECIAL EVENTS

The big **Arts Alive Festival** (☎ 838 6407, W *www.artsalive.co.za*) is held in September and October. Since South Africa's liberation, the arts have been going through an exciting time, with an explosion of optimism and mainstream acceptance of long-suppressed talents. A strong element in the festival is the workshops that reveal the continent's rich cultures, denigrated for so long by the Eurocentrism of the apartheid years. The festival is a particularly good time to hear excellent music, on and off the official program.

Other festivals include the **Rand Easter Show** at the National Exhibition Centre in April; **Chinese New Year** at Wemmer Pan south of the centre; the **Jo'burg Jazz Festival** in late September; and the annual **Gay Pride March** held on the last Saturday of September.

PLACES TO STAY

Hotels and hostels are scattered across Jo'burg with the only pattern being a steady drift north. The range of quality is broad, from the bare basics of some hostels to the opulence and complete service of the many five-star hotels. But with the rand so weak, whatever level of comfort you choose you will get amazing value for money compared with Europe or North America.

Yeoville was for years a backpacker favourite but is not any more. All of the hostels have either closed or relocated to safer areas. There is cheap accommodation in the city centre, Hillbrow and Berea, but these areas are not recommended as places to sleep.

If you're looking to party, a bed near Melville or Norwood would be handy if you can find one. Otherwise the Rosebank and, increasingly, Fourways areas have decent after-hours entertainment.

PLACES TO STAY – BUDGET
Camping

Some Jo'burg hostels will allow you to pitch a tent, but it's wise to check before you arrive. If backyards are not to your liking, the best caravan parks that permit camping are in the far south of the province.

Aventura Kareekloof (☎ 016-365 5334, fax 365 5628, 25km from Meyerton) Camp sites R55/66 in low/high season plus R20 per person. Near the Suikerbosrand Nature Reserve, 40km south of Jo'burg, Kareekloof has 240 stands. Look for signs from Meyerton or call for directions before setting off.

Aventura Heidelbergkloof (☎ 016-341 2413, fax 341 6758, R23 near Heidelberg) Camp sites R44/55 in low/high season plus R15 per person. Also adjoining Suikerbosrand, this park has 125 stands.

Hostels

When you arrive in Jo'burg most hostels will pick you up from the airport or Park Station for free. If a car doesn't show up, call the hostel or get a taxi! Nearly all of the hostels are on the route of the Baz Bus (see under Getting There & Away later in this section). Internet and satellite TV facilities are standard and most will organise tours to Soweto, Kruger National Park and elsewhere.

Berea *Johannesburg Central Youth Hostel* (☎ 643 1213, 4 Fife Ave, Berea) Dorm beds R30, doubles R70. This place is in a dodgy part of town and tends to appeal more to African students than backpackers. Be very, very careful about coming and going.

Northern Suburbs *Backpackers Ritz* (☎ 325 7125, fax 325 2521, ℮ ritz@iafrica .com, W www.backpackers-ritz.co.za, 1A North Rd, Dunkeld West) Dorm beds R55, singles/doubles R100/150. There are discounts for HI and VIP members. Just off Jan Smuts Ave, the Ritz is within an easy and safe walk of the Hyde Park Mall, bars and restaurants. Of all the hostels in huge old mansions, this is undoubtedly the most impressive. The historical building offers stunning views across the city and some of the best dorm-room views you could hope to see. It has a pool, a crypt-like bar and a strong emphasis on security. Well worth it.

African Zoo Lodge (☎ 788 5182, fax 788 3292, W www.zoolodge.co.za, 233A Jan Smuts Ave, Parktown North) Dorm beds R50, singles/doubles R100/140. Near to the architecturally rich Parktown, renovations on the house and large back gardens of the lodge were under way at the time of writing, with plans for jungle-style bomas (enclosures) around the two pools. Some of the rooms are a bit dark and pokey but the atmosphere is relaxed. It also runs diving tours to Mozambique. The *Explorers Club* (W www.explor.co.za, 235 Jan Smuts Ave, Parktown North) adjoins the zoo and the two share just about everything, including contact numbers and prices.

Rockey's of Fourways (☎ 465 4219, fax 467 2597, W bacpacrs.www.icon.co.za, 22 Campbell Rd, Fourways) Camp sites R30, dorm beds R55, or R50 if you stay more than one night, singles/doubles from R100/130. Crime has forced Rockey's away from it's long-time home in Yeoville and into the relative tranquillity of Fourways. It's a fair way north of town but makes up for it with a friendly atmosphere and very knowledgeable, obliging hosts. It has a pool and a bar, and it's a 15-minute walk from Fourways Mall and the aptly named Monte Casino. The open spaces will appeal to four-wheel drivers.

Inchanga Ranch (☎ 708 2505, fax 708 1464, W www.ecovisiononline.com, Inchanga Rd, Witkoppen) Camp sites R30 per person, dorm beds R55, doubles in wooden chalets R150-200. Along the road from Rockey's, Inchanga's is in a rural setting and offers basic hostel-style accommodation and more comfortable African-style chalets that sleep up to four. There is also the Pap 'n' Chopsticks restaurant, which serves African fare at reasonable prices.

Gemini Backpackers (☎ 882 6845, 082-574 4270, fax 882 5022, **W** www.gemini backpackers.com, 1 Van Gelder Rd, Crystal Gardens) Camp sites R20, dorm beds R45, doubles R120. This place is big and friendly, and has a gym, pool and tennis court, but it can be difficult to find. It's way out of town near Rembrandt Park, but not far from Sandton.

Pension Idube (☎ 482 4055, 082-682 3799, **e** idube@mail.com, 11 Walton Ave, Auckland Park) Singles/doubles R100/160. The Pension is very close to trendy Melville and only 5km from the city centre. It is secure, has off-road parking, serves inexpensive meals and has a pool and a patio.

Eastern Suburbs *Airport Backpackers* (☎/fax 394 0485, 083-758 4344, **e** air backp@mweb.co.za, 3 Mohawk St, Rhodesfield, Kempton Park) Camp sites R30, dorm beds R55, singles/doubles R110/150, day stay R50, HI discounts. Just 2km from the airport (free pick-ups and drop-offs), this place has a swimming pool and thatched *lapa* (low-walled building for cooking and socialising). It's run by an ex-overland guide who knows his stuff.

Bob's Bunkhouse (☎ 453 2294, fax 453 2238, **e** bobsbunk@netactive.co.za, 40 St Anne Rd, Hurlyvale, Edenvale) Dorm beds R50, doubles R130. You can't help but like this clean and homely place near the airport, and the down-to-earth couple who own it. Less frenetic than some of the bigger hostels, it will appeal to young and old alike.

Eastgate Backpackers (☎ 616 2741, 615 1092, **e** egatebp@netactive.co.za, 41 Hans Pirow Rd, Bruma) Dorm beds R40, singles R100, doubles R120-140, plus R15 breakfast. Walking distance from Bruma Lake and Flea Market World, this clean two-storey mansion has a pool. It attracts a 'vibey' group into music and chilling out.

Africa Centre (☎/fax 894 4897, **W** www .africacentre.co.za, 37 Louw Ave, Lakefield) Camp sites R30, dorm beds R40, singles/doubles R100/150. Another clean and comfortable suburban-house conversion not far from the airport. These guys apply a lot of pressure to first get you to stay and then convince you to buy tours. If you don't like hassle choose somewhere else.

Brown Sugar (☎ 648 7397, **e** brown sugar2000@hotmail.com, 75 Observatory Ave, Observatory) Camp sites R30, dorm beds R40, doubles R100. This big, castle-like, pink mansion was built as a party house by a Mafia drug baron and has clearly seen better days. It's disorganised and short on comfort, but will appeal to smokers or anyone wanting to check out Yeoville nightlife.

Hotels

City Centre & Berea Most of the budget hotels in the city centre, Berea and Hillbrow are run down and depressing. You can't really go out at night on foot and you can get a backpackers double somewhere safer for the same price as a double room here, so there's not much argument for staying. If you do, the following places are the pick of the bunch.

Crest Hotel (☎ 642 7641, fax 642 7640, 7 Abel Rd, Berea) Singles/doubles R90/125. The Crest is comfortable, convenient and well run. Rooms are large, well maintained and have radios and telephones; there's also secure parking.

Mariston Hotel Apartments (☎/fax 725 4130, Cnr Claim & Koch Sts) Rooms from R65/400 daily/weekly. This enormous multistorey hotel between the city centre and Hillbrow was once among the best in town and now charges a fraction of its old rates. Some rooms have cooking facilities. If you're in any doubt about the security of the neighbourhood, check out the 'bouncers' wielding AK-47s at the door.

Formule 1 Hotel Park Station (☎ 720 2111, fax 720 2112, **W** www.southernsun .com, Park Station) Rooms for 1-3 people R127. Basic rooms for a basic price. This hotel is near the north-east corner of the huge Park Station complex and might appeal if you arrive late. It's a short walk from the main bus and train arrivals hall, but be careful when taking this walk or heading anywhere outside the arrivals hall itself.

Northern & Eastern Suburbs The *Formule 1* (☎ 807 0750, e all@formule1 .co.za) chain has many hotels, including at Edenvale (☎ 453 5945, fax 453 3755, 130 Boeing Rd East) and Isando (☎ 392 1453, fax 974 3845, Cnr Herman & Kruin Sts). It charges R155-165 for a room for one to three people, and a basic breakfast is R13. Both hotels listed are close to the airport.

The City Lodge group offers slightly better budget accommodation in its *Road Lodges*. A room for one to three people is R180, with breakfast (R19) an optional extra. For locations, contact the reservation centre (☎ 884 0660, w www.citylodge .co.za).

Ascot Hotel (☎/fax 483 1101, 59 Grant Ave, Norwood) Singles/doubles R120/160. On the corner of Algernon Rd, this place is nothing flash but it is in a great location in the middle of the Norwood strip.

PLACES TO STAY – MID-RANGE
B&Bs & Guesthouses

Portfolio (☎ 880 3414, fax 788 4802, e col lection@iafrica.com, w www.portfoliocol lection.com) is an agency that lists a number of top B&Bs, mainly in the northern suburbs; they're upmarket and reasonably expensive, with singles from R150 to R325 and doubles from R200 to R450.

Emerald Guest House (☎ 393 1390, fax 975 1822, e emerald.g.h@intekom .co.za, 5 Blouborsie St, Van Riebeeck Park, Kempton Park) Singles/doubles R180/ 280. There are surprisingly few independent B&B and guesthouse operations, and this place is a good choice close to the airport; a transfer is included in the room rate.

Cottages Guest House (☎ 487 2829, fax 487 2404, e mckenna@iafrica.co.za, 30 Gill St, Observatory) Singles/doubles from

R275/350. This is a classy place in a good location, with self-catering thatched cottages high on Observatory Hill.

Hotels & Apartments
City Centre Some of the better hotels in this area are good value, as the escalating crime rate has chased away custom.

Devonshire Hotel (☎ 339 5611, fax 403 2494, w www.orion-hotels.com, Cnr Melle & Jorissen Sts) Singles/doubles from R350/ 410 including breakfast. To the west in Braamfontein, this is a comfortable, midsized hotel. It has all mod cons, including undercover parking. It's also close to the Civic Theatre.

Johannesburger Hotel (☎ 725 3753, fax 725 6309, 60 Twist St) Singles/doubles R95/150 including breakfast. This is a large international-style hotel, with undercover parking and with TVs in all rooms. It's near Joubert Park and the prices reflect how bad this neighbourhood has become.

Northern & Eastern Suburbs *Linden Hotel* (☎/fax 782 4905, Cnr 7th St & 4th Ave, Linden) Singles/doubles R280/320 including breakfast. This is an attractive, comfortable, personalised hotel. Unfortunately, it's a long way north-west of the city. It has a restaurant and a ladies' bar.

Duneden Hotel (☎/fax 453 2002, 46 Van Riebeeck Ave, Edenvale) Singles/doubles R305/418. This well-equipped hotel is close to shops and the airport; it's good value.

The hotel group *City Lodge* (w www.city lodge.co.za) also offers good-value midpriced accommodation; singles/doubles cost about R280/310 in Town Lodges and R380/450 in City Lodges, and breakfast is an extra R38. Options include *Town Lodge JIA* (☎ 974 5202, fax 974 5490, Herman Rd, Germiston), off the R24 Barbara Rd exit; *City Lodge Sandton Morningside* (☎ 884 9500, fax 884 9440, Cnr Rivonia & Hill Rds), a jog from the shops; and *City Lodge Randburg* (☎ 706 7800, fax 706 7819, Cnr Main Rd & Peter Place, Bryanston West). Near the airport is *City Lodge JIA* (☎ 392 1750, fax 392 2644, Sandvale Rd, Edenvale).

Holiday Inn Garden Courts (☎ *392 1062, fax 974 8097, 2 Hulley Rd, JIA,* W *www .southernsun.com)* Singles/doubles R382/ 472. There are a few other Holiday Inns scattered around, all of a high standard, including one at Sandton (☎ 884 5660, fax 783 2004, Cnr Katherine St & Rivonia Rd), which has singles/doubles for R409/518 and at Eastgate (☎ 622 0570, fax 622 7994, Ernest Oppenheimer Dr), which has singles/ doubles for R454/558. Most offer cheaper weekend rates.

Holiday Inn Express Eastgate (☎ *622 0060, fax 622 0030,* W *www.southernsun .com, 8 South Blvd, Bruma)* Rooms R299. Almost next door this is a cheaper incarnation of the Holiday Inn, but still comfortable.

Don Suites Apartments at Rosebank (☎ *880 1666, fax 880 3366, 10 Tyrwhitt Ave)* Singles/doubles R530/655 including breakfast. The Don Suites Apartments is the only black-owned hotel chain in the land and it offers excellent rooms. This place is no exception.

PLACES TO STAY – TOP END
Hotels
City Centre *Protea Hotel Parktonian* (☎ *403 5741, 0800 124 567, fax 403 2401,* W *www.proteahotels.com, 120 De Korte St, Braamfontein)* Singles/doubles R495/590. The Parktonian is the best hotel in the central Jo'burg area. Not surprisingly, this place is popular with businesspeople.

Northern & Eastern Suburbs *Westcliff* (☎ *646 2400, fax 646 3500,* W *www.west cliffhotel.orient-express.com, 67 Jan Smuts Ave, Westcliff)* Rooms from R1560. Sprawling down a hill opposite the zoo, the Westcliff is luxurious and well located. The rooms and suites are big, and few expenses have been spared with the decoration. The business facilities are excellent.

Holiday Inn Johannesburg International (☎ *975 1121, fax 975 5846,* W *www.south ernsun.com, Jones Rd, JIA)* Singles/ doubles R690/830. The clean and well-equipped rooms are complimented by efficient service. This hotel is 1km from the airport.

Protea Hotel Wanderers (☎ *770 5500, fax 770 5555,* W *www.proteahotels.com, Cnr Rudd Rd & Corlett Dr)* Singles/doubles R660/ 750. This hotel is across the road from the famous cricket ground and is ideal for cricket lovers. Rooms are often heavily discounted.

Ten Bompas (☎ *325 2442, fax 341 0281,* W *www.tenbompas.com, 10 Bompas Rd, Dunkeld West)* Suites R1200. Just off Jan Smuts Ave, this boutique hotel has 10 mid-sized suites (each by a different designer), a restaurant and one of the biggest wine cellars in the city.

The Grace (☎ *280 7300, fax 280 7333,* W *www.grace.co.za, 54 Bath Ave, Rosebank)* Singles/doubles R1650/1500. Known for its personal service, this imposing place claims a galaxy of stars and caters predominantly for business travellers.

Intercontinental Sandton Sun & Towers (☎ *780 5000, fax 780 5002,* W *www.south ernsun.com, Cnr Fifth & Alice Sts)* Rooms at the Sun from R875; at the Towers R1040-2220. Just across the road from Sandton City and Sandton Square, this place is the pride of the Southern Sun Group. The Sandton Sun caters for the wealthy while the Towers has everything the megarich visitor would expect.

Michelangelo (☎ *282 7000, fax 282 7171,* W *www.michelangelo.co.za, West St, Sandown)* Singles/doubles from R1550/ 1760. Off West St and adjoining Sandton Square, these luxury rooms are among the best in town.

PLACES TO EAT
Jo'burg is stacked with places to eat. There are cuisines of every type available for almost every budget. Unfortunately for visitors, especially those without cars, most of the safe places are scattered around the northern suburbs and they can be difficult to find. The big hotels have restaurants and in shopping centres you'll find franchised steakhouses such as Spur Ranch and Italian places such as Panarotti's.

City Centre & Inner Suburbs
Cafes & Snack Bars There are few decent eateries remaining in the city centre and

even cafes and sandwich shops are at a premium. There's no shortage of takeaways but they are not inspiring – for example, roasted mealies in the husk. For a cheap meal of *mealie pap* (maize stew) and braaied (barbecued) meat, try the stalls on and nearby Diagonal St – just follow your nose. A couple of the chain places – ***Chicken Licken***, ***Wimpy***, ***Nando's***, ***KFC*** and ***McDonald's*** – seem to have a representative at every major road junction or large mall.

Just finding somewhere to sit down in the city centre can be a major problem.

Guildhall Bar & Restaurant (☎ 836 5560, 88 Market St) Pub food from R15. This historic place serves basic lunches from noon to 3pm on the 1st-floor balcony, offering a rare chance to watch street life without worrying about being mugged.

Restaurants ***Kapitan's*** (☎ 834 8048, 11A Kort St) Meals from R25. Don't be put off by the grubby stairwell, Kapitan's (just behind Diagonal St) is a Jo'burg institution. The authentic Indian food has been attracting luminaries for years – Nelson Mandela and Oliver Tambo used to eat here in the 1950s when they had a law office nearby. Vegetable curry is R30, meat curries are R40, chicken vindaloo or biryani is R45.

Gramadoela's (☎ 838 6960, Bree St, Newtown) Meals around R60. Open for lunch & dinner Mon-Sat. In the Market Theatre complex, this is arguably the city's best restaurant, and undoubtedly offers the best value in town. Its interesting decor is matched by equally interesting nouvelle cuisine; the specialities are based on Cape Dutch/Malay and African cuisines. The kudu (R49) is recommended. Past diners include Hillary Clinton, Denzel Washington and Nelson Mandela.

Northern Suburbs

In general, the restaurants in the northern suburbs are of high quality and, relatively speaking, highly priced. There are restaurant/cafe enclaves in Melville, Norwood and Illovo, and there are many restaurants scattered throughout the shopping malls in Rosebank and Sandton.

Melville North-west of Braamfontein, Melville has become the trendiest eating strip in Jo'burg. Restaurants and cafes have sprung up in the area around 7th St, known as 'Old Melville', and around the busier Main Rd about 1km away, known as 'New Melville'.

The best food is in Old Melville, where four of South Africa's top 100 restaurants (according to the CNA restaurant guide) are within a two-minute walk of each other. Most of the cafes have outdoor seating and in the warmer months 7th St takes on a Parisian ambience, with patrons sipping drinks and watching the world go by. Moving from north (4th Ave) to south (1st Ave), the following six places are the pick of the bunch.

Scala Grande (☎ 482 5572, 16 7th St) Mains from R25. Open 11am-late Mon-Fri, from 8.30am-late Sat & Sun. Mediterranean-style food is here served in an open-plan cafe setting. Try the lamb skewers (R42).

Chaplin's (☎ 482 4657, 85 4th Ave) Mains from R50. Open lunch & dinner Mon-Fri, dinner Sat. The international menu at Chaplin's has become the stuff of legend in Jo'burg. Locals rave about the prawn curry and the *créme brûlée* (cream dessert with caramelised sugar). It also caters for vegans.

'OLD' MELVILLE

PLACES TO EAT
1 Scala Grande
3 Koffiehuis
4 The Questionmark Cafe
5 Chaplin's
6 Sahib
7 Sam's Cafe
8 De la Creme Cafe
10 Koala Blu
12 Horatio's
14 Pomegranate
16 Melville's Fish-Monger
17 The Corporation
18 Mozzarella's
19 Full Stop Cafe
20 Nuno's Portuguese

OTHER
2 The Mixer
9 Book Dealers of Melville
11 Ratz Bar
13 ATM; Buzz 9
15 Bassline

Pomegranate (☎ 482 2366, *79 3rd Ave*) Meals from R60. This place is not cheap but is great for something different. The cuisine combines African food with Eastern flair.

Horatio's (☎ 726 2890, *Cnr 7th St & 3rd Ave*) Meals around R80. Open lunch & dinner Mon-Fri, dinner Sat & Sun. This place is more formal than most other Melville restaurants. It's speciality is seafood – very good seafood.

Full Stop Café (☎ 726 3801, *4A 7th St*) Mains R25-40. A pleasant street-side setting and a variety of good food make this one of the most popular places on 7th St.

Nuno's Portuguese (☎ 482 6990, *082 453 0970, 7th St between 1st & 2nd Aves*) Mains R25-35. Open from breakfast until late. Nuno's serves good-value Mediterranean fare in an upbeat, noisy atmosphere.

Other places along 7th St include *The Corporation* (☎ 482 5593) for Belgian food; *Koala Blu* (☎ 482 2477) for Indonesian (no kangaroo) that's well worth the money; *Sahib* (☎ 482 6670) for average Indian; *Melville's Fish-Monger* (☎ 482 4781) for good-value seafood; *The Questionmark Cafe* (☎ 886 8003) for jazz and sandwiches; *Koffiehuis* (☎ 726 4106); and the overpriced *Sam's Café* (☎ 726 8142).

Eateries in New Melville are generally not as good as those around 7th St, but there are still a couple worth trying.

Suan Thai (☎ 482 2182, *11 Main Rd*) Mains from R30. In a casual setting, this place is great value for money. There are good veg dishes, including the green vegetable curry (R30).

Catz Pyjamas (☎ 726 8596, *Cnr Main Rd & 3rd Ave*) Mains from R30. Open 24 hours. The Catz Pyjamas can be a little sterile, but the cheap and agreeable food makes it a good place to start or finish a night out. Try the chilli chicken (R32) and wash it down with the incredible sangria.

Other places along the Main Rd strip include the *Chinese Lantern* (☎ 726 6839), where most dishes are under R20; *Roma* (☎ 726 3404), for pizzas and basic Italian food; and yet more branches of the chain restaurants, *Panarotti's* (☎ 482 5875) for Italian, *Nando's* (☎ 726 6406) for Por-

tuguese chicken, *Ocean Basket* (☎ 726 8672), and the *Big Time Taverna* (☎ 482 3240), a smashing Greek place.

Norwood This enclave of restaurants has grown and matured into a strip to rival that of 7th St. There are more than 20 bars, restaurants and cafes along Grant Ave, most of which are open every day. All the competition means prices are generally very reasonable, with mains from R25-50. The following places are among the best, and run along Grant Ave from north (Ivy Rd) to south (Dorothy Rd).

Moyo (☎ 483 1246/7, *80 Grant Ave*) serves an interesting mix of North African food in a street-side setting and is also a good place for an afternoon drink. Vegetarians will love the African spinach curry with pepper lentils (R35).

The French bistro *Voulez-Vouz* (☎ 728 9888, *Cnr Grant Ave & William Rd*) is one of the more romantic places on Grant Ave.

NORWOOD

PLACES TO STAY & EAT
1 Sizzling Wok
3 Voulez-Vouz
4 Shahi Khana
8 Italian Delicatessen
10 Ascot Hotel
11 Kirin Garden
13 Zest
14 Urban Cafe;
   Brazilian Cafe
15 Benkei
16 Nando's; Debonair's
18 Nick's Original
   Fishmonger
19 Portuga

OTHER
2 Sam's Place; Moyo
5 Spar Supermarket
6 Norwood Pharmacy
7 Sundeck Bar
9 Off Broadway Theatre
12 BP Petrol Station
17 Library

The calamari stuffed with spinach, fetta and rice is recommended.

The paninis at the tiny *Italian Delicatessen* (☎ 483 3673, 64 Grant Ave) are reputed to be the best in Jo'burg, and the pasta's not bad either. You'll need to be early, or very late, to get a seat.

Benkei (☎ 483 3296, 48 Grant Ave) has almost 100 different Japanese dishes to make your choice from, so sushi and noodles are not your only options. We recommend the curried noodles (R37).

Just off Grant Ave, *Zest* (☎ 728 7532, 87 Iris Rd) does a range of healthy meals and some sensational smoothies; the Hangover Helper (R10) is a marvel.

Nick's Original Fishmonger (☎ 728 2257, 38 Grant Ave) is classier than some of its neighbours and serves a huge range of seafood. Assorted sushi is R40 and the stuffed trout (R39) is recommended.

Portuga (☎ 728 0415, 37 Grant Ave) is across the road from Nick's and is another seafood place but with more of a Mozambique flair. The portions are not huge, but the grilled calamari (R26) tastes great.

Grant Ave is also home to the *Sizzling Wok* (☎ 728 8972) and the *Kirin Garden*, both serving cheap Asian dishes. Adjoining and very trendy are *Urban Cafe* and *Brazilian Cafe* (☎ 728 3181). Nearby are *Shahi Khana* (☎ 728 8157), serving Indian, and the usual chain takeaways – *Nando's* for spicy chicken and *Debonair's* for pizza.

Rosebank, Sandton & Nearby Suburbs

The many eating options in these mainly white suburbs are centred around the huge shopping malls that form the core of northern suburbs society. The expensive cafes and restaurants are uniformly slick and are often chain operations; many being devoid of individuality and, in Sandton, completely lacking in atmosphere once the shops have closed.

But for all their formulaic qualities there is some good food to be found. For a dose of fun with your food, head to Rosebank.

Cranks (☎ 880 3442, Shop 52, Rosebank Mall) Mains from R35. Still going after almost 20 years, Cranks was one of the first

Thai/Vietnamese places in Jo'burg. Among the tried-and-tested favourites is fish fillet with lemongrass (R45).

Codes (☎ 447 4509, 1st floor, The Zone, Rosebank Mall) Meals from R20. This cafe is the trendiest place to be seen in Rosebank.

Paros Taverna (☎ 788 4976, Hutton Court, Cnr Jan Smuts Ave & Summit Rd, Hyde Park) Mains from R29. The Paros is another of the irrepressible Greek places that punctuate Jo'burg, emphasising their existence most nights with a cacophony of smashing crockery and the not-so-Greek twirlings of a belly dancer. The food here is pretty good, reasonably priced and comes in huge portions. The huge meze (snack) plate (R75) will fill two people by itself.

The Codfather (☎ 803 2077, Cnr 1st Ave & Rivonia Rd, Morningside) Meals from R40. Near Sandton, The Codfather is the best-value seafood restaurant in Jo'burg. There is a huge selection of fresh fish (flown from the coast daily) that you can have cooked however you like.

El Fuego (☎ 802 6374/5, Pavilion Centre, Cnr Rivonia & Kelvin Rds, Morningside) Mains from R48. Laid out more like a theatre than a restaurant, this intimate Argentinian place is a shrine to beef. Tables are positioned around the lowered, glassed-off kitchen, which is essentially a huge grill. If you are very hungry you might consider the mixed grill Parrillada (R139 for two people).

Wangthai (☎ 784 8484, Upstairs, Sandton Square) Mains from R40. This Thai restaurant seems out of place in its faux-Roman setting, but even sterile Sandton is forgiven when the food arrives.

Randburg Waterfront It's worth considering an expedition to the Randburg Waterfront in the northern suburbs, but there's nothing left at the Bruma Lake Waterfront where the floating victims of a ruthless drug lord once turned diners off their meals. Randburg has something for everyone (but mostly whites), pulsating fountain included.

Babylon Taverna (☎ 789 9812) Meals from R30. This is a good-value Greek place where smashing plates is seen as a right, not a privilege. Try the *kleftiko* 'stolen lamb'

(R35). Other decent places include the **Laughing Buddha** (☎ 789 4567) for a wide selection of delicious Eastern food; and the 24-hour **Cafe Porto** (☎ 787 0925) for light Mediterranean-style meals. There are also a couple of pubs here.

Yeoville

Yeoville is no longer the hip food precinct of Jo'burg. Crime is out of hand and the best places have closed or moved, but there are still a few decent eateries.

Time Square Cafe (☎ 648 6906, 38 Raleigh St) Mains from R15. This cafe has hearty breakfasts and a mix of European and Israeli fare. It's a good place to chat with locals, particularly on a Sunday afternoon.

Thamae Village (☎ 083-522 5759, 26 Kenmere St) Meals R10-15. Open for lunch & dinner. Home-style African dishes such as pap and stew attract plenty of locals. It's cheap and there's not much choice, but this is a great place to meet and speak with locals.

Charros Curry (☎ 487 1068, Time Square) Mains from R25. Open noon-11pm Mon-Sat. This is a good place for authentic Indian food. Vegetarian curries are R25, plus poppadoms, dhal and raita. There is secure parking behind Time Square.

Ba Pita (☎ 487 0505, 5 Rockey St) Pitas from R14. Once the counter-culture headquarters of the street, Ba Pita is but a faded shadow of its former self. Appropriately, the adjoining bar has been renamed Shanty's.

Hard Rock Cafe (☎ 447 2853, Thrupps Centre, 204 Oxford Rd) Open daily until late. The Hard Rock attracts foreign visitors who come to buy a T-shirt (some people collect them!). The food is good and reasonably priced; happy hour is from 5pm to 7pm.

Other Suburbs

Near Bruma Lake is Derrick Ave, Cyrildene, off Observatory Rd, where a new **Chinatown** with more than 10 cheap restaurants has sprung up. Represented are Taiwanese, Korean, Szechwan, Shanghai and Hong Kong styles served in those lifeless places with formica-top tables and plastic chairs; most close their kitchens at about 9.30pm.

Sun Fat (☎ 615 1392, 14 Derrick Ave) Mains from R25. Sure, it doesn't sound appetising, but the honey roast pork in syrup (R30) is a treat.

Casalinga (☎ 957 2612, Muldersdrift Rd, Honeydew) Meals from R60. Open for lunch & dinner Wed-Sat, lunch only Sun. This Italian restaurant, in a rural setting at the Rocky Ridge Driving Range, is a perennial favourite. Bookings are essential.

Carnivore (☎ 957 2099, W www.carni vorerestaurant.co.za, Muldersdrift Estate, 69 Drift Blvd, Muldersdrift) Meals from R100. This is the place to go if you are inclined to eat some of the animals you have seen in South Africa's parks. There is a selection of salads and desserts, potjie (a variety of meat and vegetables stewed in an iron pot), soups, and all-the-meat-you-can-eat carved from Masai tribal sword skewers at your table.

Swiss Inn (☎ 789 3314, 170 Hendrik Verwoerd Dr, Randburg) Open lunch Mon-Fri, dinner only Sat. Looking very Swiss, right down to the clinically clean bathrooms, this place is worth the long drive. Locals rave about the ambience and the international menu.

ENTERTAINMENT

The best entertainment guide is in the weekly *Mail & Guardian*. 'Tonight' in the *Jo'burg Star* is also good. For entertainment bookings by credit card, contact **Computicket** (☎ 340 8445), which they can arrange seats for almost every theatre, cinema and sports venue. For the latest on Jo'burg nightlife check W www.sacitylife.com/nightlife.

Bars, Pubs & Clubs

Jo'burg is renowned as the party capital of Africa and we are inclined to agree. There is a constantly changing mix of bars, pubs and clubs ranging from the outrageous to the downright boring, but whatever you prefer you'll find somewhere to feel comfortable. Jo'burg's traditional drinking haunts are Hillbrow and Yeoville, but these days they're a little too exciting; only the brave or foolish venture there without a well-muscled local for company. Instead, Melville, Norwood and Rosebank have growing scenes and the rest of the northern suburbs is really littered with bars – just ask around.

There's a surprising paucity of mannered bars in the city centre.

Press Bar (☎ *833 3181, Elizabeth Hotel, Cnr Pritchard & Sauer Sts*) may not be entirely mannered, but the Press Bar (opposite the *Jo'burg Star* offices) is everything a journos' bar should be: dark, smoky and serving some of the cheapest beer in town.

Another possibility in the city is the *Guildhall Bar & Restaurant*, Jo'burg's oldest pub (see Places to Eat earlier).

Horror Cafe (☎ *838 6735, 5 Becker St, Newtown*) is right next to the SAB World of Beer on the edge of the Newtown cultural precinct. Someone forgot to tell these guys that orange is the new black, not lime green. Still, this place is worth a visit just to see the kitschest decor in town. Go on a Friday or Saturday night.

Melville has several bars and pubs and 7th St is home to three small and ambient affairs, including the hip *Bassline* (see Live Music following), while the Main Rd area has some bigger theme establishments.

The neighbouring bars *Buzz9* and *Ratz Bar* (☎ *726 2019, 9 7th St, Melville*) are small and seem to be busy no matter what night you are there. Ratz Bar in particular plays good music to a cool crowd.

Cool Runnings (☎ *482 4786, 27A 4th Ave, Melville*) is a chain of Rasta-style bars that has become popular – with good reason. The dreadlocks, cane bomas and reggae music make you feel like you're in the Caribbean, mon, which is a great escape from Jo'burg.

If you're counting your pennies, *Exchange Café* (☎ *482 8384, 23 4th Ave, Melville*), a trendy cigar bar and coffee lounge, is not the place for you.

Punter & Trouserleg (☎ *726 1030, 1st floor, Melville Terrace, Cnr 5th Ave & Main Rd, Melville*) is guaranteed to appeal to youthful backpackers. This place is full of sexy young things partaking in the regular beer and shooter specials and boogieing to commercial music.

In Norwood, Grant Ave is full of licensed cafes and restaurants and has a couple of dedicated bars.

The Lebanese *Sam's Place* (☎ *082-217 7043, 80 Grant Ave*) is the place for you if you fancy puffing on a hubble-bubble pipe while listening to Middle Eastern music.

The roof-top *Sundeck Bar* (☎ *728 2279, 72 Grant Ave*) is the ideal place to sit and watch the Grant Ave action.

East of Norwood in Orange Grove, *206 Live* and *208* (see Live Music following) are both good places for a drink and a dance.

The Radium (☎ *728 3866, 282 Louis Botha Ave, Orange Grove*) is one of the few neighbourhood pubs left in Jo'burg. It's the sort of pub that you might imagine would be ubiquitous in South Africa – masculine but laid-back and dedicated to the thirst of workers. That isn't the case, though, so The Radium is almost unique.

The Randburg Waterfront has plenty of bars and well-oiled restaurants and cafes, where a fertile imagination will allow you temporary respite from the big city.

McGinty's (☎ *789 4572*) is an upbeat beer-drinking place that is among the best and as close to an Irish pub as you'll find around here.

Waterfront Arms (☎ *789 1514*) is a well-positioned joint and a good place to sit and drink beer with classic rock and the odd band in the background. Be careful of the cocktails, they'll blow a hole in your pocket.

Further north, the area around Fourways is gaining recognition as a good place to party.

Boston Tea Party (☎ *658 1830, Glen Narine Centre, Witkoppen Rd, Fourways*) is supposed to be the best of the new breed of dinner-dance venues that are taking the country by storm. As many as 1000 people jam into this upmarket place on Friday and Saturday nights to eat good food and then dance the night away.

O'Hagans (☎ *658 1879*) is in the same centre as Boston Tea Party. This Irish pub serves good food and promises good *craic* (Irish for a 'good time').

Brass Monkey (☎ *465 6163, Pineslopes Centre, Witkoppen Rd, Fourways*) is another popular dinner-dance venue, this one with a decent continental menu. Friday nights are huge with music from rave to classic hits.

GAUTENG

Live Music

Jo'burg is home to a thriving live music scene, and on any given night you can see rock, pop, kwaito, jungle, jazz and hip-hop acts, and all manner of house and techno (see the special section 'South African Music' for more on kwaito and other local sounds). On weekends, the Jo'burgers really come out to play and regularly hold enormous raves. There's little pattern to the spread of venues, but you'd be safe to assume that in most cases the further north you go the tamer they become.

For something a little different, the area around the Newtown cultural precinct is a good place to start (see the boxed text 'A New Town from Newtown', earlier).

Kippie's Jazz International (☎ 833 3316, W www.kippies.co.za, Newtown cultural precinct, Bree St, Newtown) Admission R45. Kippie's is a small but very popular jazz venue, named after the great Kippie 'Morolong' Moeketsi. It's a 'must do' when in Jo'burg as it's one of the best places to see South African jazz talent, which happens to be exceptional.

Mega Music Warehouse (☎ 834 2761, Cnr Gough & Jeppe Sts, Newtown) is a medium-sized venue that is perfect to see African, jazz and rave artists. Sadly, it's only open periodically and bookings are essential.

Carfax (☎ 834 9187, 39 Pim St, Newtown) Admission from R15. Carfax is an eclectic venue that usually features DJs and a variety of multimedia acts. This industrial venue is worth a visit for the artwork alone.

Melville has a couple of live venues and there are suggestions of more soon.

Bassline (☎ 482 6915, 7th St, Melville) Admission from R20. Bassline is a small, hip place where the jazz sometimes has an acid bent. Local and international acts play nightly Tuesday to Sunday.

Roxy Rhythm Bar (☎ 726 1255, 20 Main Rd, Melville) is one of the oldest and best-known venues in Jo'burg for pop and hard rock. It appeals to a younger crowd.

In the city centre there is a constantly changing batch of dance clubs. Check the Mail & Guardian for current favourites. If you do go into the centre after dark we strongly advise you use a taxi, take a local friend and head straight to your venue of choice.

As you'd expect from the gay precinct, Braamfontein has a good house and techno scene (see Gay & Lesbian Venues following for details).

The next three places are in areas where we recommend you take a taxi to and from the venue.

Tandoor (☎ 614 6737, Rockey St, Yeoville) Admission from R20. Near the corner of Bezuidenhout St, this is the only place in Yeoville worth going for live music. It also happens to be one of the best kwaito clubs in Jo'burg. There's usually kwaito or hip-hop on the weekends, and other interesting sounds during the week. Be warned that the venue is just a smoky barn with a concrete floor – pretty depressing unless there's a good crowd. If not, go upstairs to the rooftop bar – it's 'smoking'.

The Spartan interior of **The Abelarde Sanction** (☎ 837 5832, 21 Ripley St, Brixton), on the corner of Fulham St, apparently appeals to northern suburbs hipsters and a hard core of locals. Call to check if there's actually a band playing before you turn up.

Electronic music is the go at **HomeBass** (☎ 837 0256, 106 High St, Brixton), with trance, big beat and drum'n'bass all regular features.

206 Live (☎ 728 5333, 206 Louis Botha Ave, Orange Grove) and next door at 208 are the places for acid jazz; 206 also does funk, hip and trip-hop. Tuesday night is students' night.

Warhol's (☎ 082-369 0483, Cnr 10th St & Louis Botha Ave, Orange Grove) Open from 8pm Fri-Sat. Kwaito, house and pop are the steady, if slightly confusing, diet at Warhol's.

In the northern suburbs the predominantly white crowd exact their own rhythmical isolation at a succession of mainstream venues.

As the name suggests, **Blues Room** (☎ 784 5527/8, W www.bluesroom.co.za, Lower level, Village Walk Shopping Centre, Cnr Rivonia Rd & Maude St, Sandown) is a blues and jazz venue, but it also has the occasional foray into rock.

GAUTENG

Morgan's Cat *(☎ 886 4408, Shop 137, Randburg Waterfront)* When the DJs have stopped, this is a good place to see fresh young acts on a Sunday afternoon, it and attracts a similarly young crowd.

If you're looking to marry into Jo'burg wealth, ***Deniro's*** *(☎ 884 1882, Intercontinental Sandton Sun & Towers, Cnr Fifth & Alice Sts)* is your place. Deniro's draws the trendiest young society types to see (or be seen). Bands perform from Tuesday to Thursday and you can dance to the most expensive DJs on Friday and Saturday nights.

Hurricanes *(Shop L27, Fourways Mall)* Open from 7.30pm Wed-Sat. When you get over the fact that this place is in a shopping mall, it's not too bad. Acts are mainly rock and pop.

See the special section 'Soweto' for venues in the township.

Gay & Lesbian Venues
Jo'burg has a thriving gay scene and, since the liberalisation of the constitution in 1994, has become a centre for gays and lesbians from across Africa. Gays are well organised and increasingly accepted – a far cry from the puritanical attitudes of the past.

The annual Gay Pride March, held on the last weekend of September, is the focal point, but by no means the only organised activity. For information check the local publication *rush*, and the *Pink Map*, both available from the Gauteng Tourism Authority (see under Information earlier in this chapter). Also contact the **Lesbian & Gay Equality Project** *(☎ 487 3810, fax 487 1670, 36 Grafton Rd, Yeoville, postal address: PO Box 27811, Yeoville 2143)*. For other sources of information see Gay & Lesbian Travellers in the Facts for the Visitor chapter.

Gay and lesbian venues open and close with disconcerting regularity in Jo'burg, so it is worth checking before you head out. There are nearly 20 bars and clubs, many now located in an area in Braamfontein known as The Heartland, centred around Henri and Juta Sts, where security is good and people can walk from club to club without fear. The Heartland is mainly gay and is frequented mainly by whites.

Fly Bar *(☎ 083-588 0925, W www.flybar .co.za, Cnr Henri & Juta Sts, Braamfontein)* Open 7 days. This popular gay/bi nightclub is the first stop for many, with patrons moving downstairs to the ***Venom*** dance club.

AKWA Cocktail Lounge *(☎ 837 9139, e hmalan@iafrica.com, 12 Henri St, Braamfontein)* Open from 7pm Wed-Sun. Slightly less frenetic than the adjoining Fly Bar, light meals and cocktails are available in this upmarket cruise bar.

Therapy *(☎ 339 7791, W www.therapy-on-line.co.za, 39a Juta St, Braamfontein)* Open from 10pm Fri-Sat. Two dance floors and a summer balcony–cocktail bar make this a popular house-music club.

Stardust Palace *(☎ 082-495 2585, W www .stardustnightclub.co.za, 61 Jorissen St, Braamfontein)* Open from 9pm Wed & Fri-Sat. Big and bold, many gay Jo'burgers call this their favourite. There are two dance floors, cabaret shows and strippers.

Shaft *(14 Juta St, Braamfontein)* Open from 4pm Mon-Thur, from noon Fri-Sun. A smaller and more chilled-out bar with a pool table and a variety of back-room events.

On the corner of Twist St, ***Skyline*** *(Harrison Reef Hotel, 27 Pretoria St, Hillbrow)* is Jo'burg's oldest gay club and is the place of choice for black gays and lesbians, but welcomes all comers. It was the birthplace of the local Pride movement.

Cinemas
Huge cinema centres can be found across Jo'burg, with almost every shopping centre boasting one. Some that are handy to accommodation centres include the 15-screen *cinema (☎ 784 3133/4, Rivonia Rd, Sandton City, Sandton)*; the slightly unorthodox *Cinema Nouveau (☎ 820 2866, 50 Bath Ave, Rosebank Mall, Rosebank)*; the brand new 12-screen *cinema (☎ 465 6470/1, Cnr Witkoppen Rd & William Nicol Rd, Fourways Mall)*; and if it's a large screen that you're seeking, the latest addition to Jo'burg's entertainment scene is the *Imax Theatre (☎ 325 6182, Jan Smuts Ave, Hyde Park Mall, Hyde Park)*. Check out the Web site W www.themoviesite.co.za for details of what's playing where and when.

Theatres

Market Theatre (☎ 832 1641, W www.mar ket.theatre.co.za) is the most important venue for live theatre. There are three live theatre venues, the Main, Laager and Barney Simon Theatres, as well as galleries, a cafe and the excellent Kippie's Jazz International (see Live Music earlier). There is always some interesting theatre, ranging from sharply critical contemporary plays to musicals and stand-up comedy; check the program in the *Mail & Guardian* entertainment section.

Civic Theatre (☎ 403 3408, W www.show business.co.za, Loveday St, Braamfontein) has a variety of productions in its Main and Tesson Theatres.

Windybrow Centre for the Arts (☎ 720 7009, Cnr Nugget & Pietersen Sts, Hillbrow) This is a testing ground for emerging black playwrights.

Rand Club (☎ 883 5274, Cnr Fox & Loveday Sts, Central Jo'burg) Performances 11.30am Tues-Sat, 7.30pm Fri. This is a great way to get into one of the most famous and exclusive clubs in Africa, with the Timewarp Theatre Company re-enacting the deals and drama of Jo'burg's formative years.

There are other venues that are worth keeping your eye on, including *Agfa Theatre on the Square (☎ 883 8606, Sandton Square)*; the *Alhambra* and *Richard Haines (☎ 402 6174, 109 Sivewright Ave, Doornfontein)*; the *Off Broadway Theatre (☎ 403 1563, W www.artslink.co.za/peoples, Grant Ave, Norwood)*; and *The Mixer (☎ 482 1806/7, 7th St, Melville)*, between 4th and 5th Aves, which is a cafe/theatre specialising in music-oriented productions.

SPECTATOR SPORTS

South Africans love their sport. Their inability to prove themselves the world's best (due to international sanctions) no doubt contributed significantly to the dismantling of apartheid.

Rugby

Jo'burg boasts some excellent venues, the pick of which is *Ellis Park (☎ 402 8644,* *Doornfontein)*, just to the east of the city centre. Ellis Park is the headquarters of rugby union and was the scene of one of the new nation's proudest moments – victory in the 1995 World Cup. Rugby supporters are fanatical, and Ellis Park can hold 70,000 – a Saturday afternoon at the football can be an almost religious experience. The local team in the Super 12 competition is the Cats, and they play between February and June.

Soccer

The Rand Stadium, near Turffontein; FNB Stadium, further east on Baragwanath Rd near Soweto; and, increasingly, Ellis Park are the major venues for soccer, which is the sport black South Africans follow most passionately. The most popular teams are also the greatest rivals: Soweto teams the Orlando Pirates (known as the 'Bucs') and the 'mighty, all conquering' Kaizer Chiefs.

Tragically, it was these teams that were playing at Ellis Park in April 2001 when a crowd crush claimed 47 lives. At the time of writing, measures were being taken to improve crowd flow and security procedures at all soccer venues.

Cricket

The most important cricket venue is *Wanderers Cricket Ground (Corlett Dr, Melrose North)*. Just off the M1 freeway to Pretoria; it's one of the most beautiful cricket grounds in the world, and one of the few where you can watch an international match and braai yourself a steak at the same time. The uninitiated will find the game fairly obscure but if you go to a one-day game with someone who can explain the rules, you'll certainly get plenty of entertainment. Wanderers will host several matches during the World Cup in February 2003.

Other Sports

Kyalami (☎ 466 2440, W www.motorsport .co.za), off the M1 between Jo'burg and Pretoria, is the venue for motor sports.

There are several horse-racing tracks but the best known is *Turffontein Race Course (☎ 681 1500)*, 3km south of the city. There are race meetings most weeks.

GAUTENG

Ellis Park is also home to the South African Open Tennis Tournament; next door are the smooth lines of the Johannesburg Athletics Stadium.

SHOPPING
Malls

Jo'burg prides itself on its shops, and the city's malls are up there with the best. Jammed with Western consumer goods of every description, they're as much a wealthy white habitat as a place to buy goods.

In the city centre, the Smal St Mall is probably the place to start. But if you're a serious buyer head to the Rosebank Mall in Rosebank, which is an interlocking series of malls, with central parking on the corner of Cradock Ave and Baker St, or head to the adjoining and very plush Sandton City and Sandton Square Malls. Other malls worthy of mention include the Randburg Waterfront and Fourways Mall, both well north of the city centre. The Eastgate Mall, off the N12 just east of Bruma Lake, boasts of being Africa's largest and is worth a visit if you're in the east.

Markets

A market is held in Market Square at 9am and 1pm on Saturday, in the car park opposite the Market Theatre. There's a lively, cheerful atmosphere (with buskers), and although most of the stalls sell flea market rubbish, there are reasonable crafts amid the dross.

The Rosebank Mall car park market is great. Open from 9am Sunday on the second-top floor of the mall car park, it boasts one of the widest varieties of African arts and crafts found anywhere. There are a vast array of good quality carvings from as far away as Togo in West Africa, and the rare Lesotho mohair is said to be particularly fine.

Flea Market World (☎ 616 6714, Marcia St, Bruma) Admission R2. Open Tues-Sun. This big, fairly commercial operation is not far from Bruma Lake and Eastgate Mall. On the opposite footpath, near McDonald's, many craft stalls are set up. There is a very wide range of goods, although you'll look hard for high quality.

Arts & Crafts

Far and away the best place to shop for traditional carvings, beadwork, jewellery and fertility dolls is the Rosebank Mall car park market (see Markets previous). However, if you can't make it on a Sunday, Rosebank also has a series of small stands selling crafts just outside the mall.

There are slick and expensive curio stores in all the main hotels, or if you're interested in seeing your hard-earned cash go into the hands of the artist, there are plenty of street vendors who set up on the footpaths around town and sell more basic craft work; bargaining is expected. At Bruma Lake there are craft sellers with a wide range of crafts, but lots of kitsch.

Camping Equipment

There are a number of specialist camping shops selling a wide range of up-to-date equipment. *ME Stores* (☎ 789 1604, Crossroads Shopping Centre, Hill St, Randburg) is the biggest. There's also another store in Craighall (☎ 787 7960, 369 Jan Smuts Ave).

Camping for Africa (☎ 787 3498, Hill St Mall, 698 Oak Ave, Randburg) is another good shop.

Music

You can get most titles in the big malls. *Kohinoor* (☎ 834 1361, 54 Market St) is one of the best sources of ethnic/African music, selling everything from kwaito to jazz.

Traditional Medicines

If you wish to remind yourself that you're still in Africa, visit a muti (traditional medicine) shop. *Kwa Zulu Muti* (☎ 836 4470, 14 Diagonal St, Newtown) is between Market and President Sts and there are others nearby. Muti shops sell herbs and potions prescribed by a sangoma (witch doctor or herbalist). Many problems, from broken hearts to headaches, are treated. Despite being dim, pungent caves full of animal parts, muti shops are definitely businesses.

The muti tradition, which has religious overtones, is regarded with great seriousness by most black South Africans; please respect this.

GAUTENG

GETTING THERE & AWAY
Air
South Africa's major international and domestic airport is JIA (☎ 975 9963, flight inquiries 390 1420). There are direct links with most African and European capitals, North America, Asia and Australia (see the Getting There & Away chapter).

Distances in South Africa are large, so if you're in a hurry some domestic flights are definitely worth considering. For regular flights to national and regional destinations try **SA Airlink** (☎ 961 1700, W www.saairlink.co.za). Services include the following (all are one-way, full economy fares; cheaper fares can be found – particularly on the busier routes – if you hunt around).

destination	one way (R)
Cape Town	1277
Durban	752
East London	1037
Kimberley	969
Manzini, Swaziland	770
Maseru, Lesotho	700
Nelspruit	844
Pietersburg	844
Upington	1334

Smaller airlines reach most places in the country and, as usual, there are significant advance-purchase discounts.

BA Comair (☎ 921 0222, W www.british airways.co.za) is a UK-based company that charges R1277 to Cape Town and R752 to Durban.

Airlines offices in Jo'burg include the following:

Air Afrique (☎ 880 8537) 1st floor, Sanlam Arena, Cradock Ave, Rosebank
Air France (☎ 770 1601) 1st floor, Oxford Manor, 196 Oxford Rd, Illovo
Air Mauritius (☎ 444 4413) Grayston Ridge Office Park, Cnr Grayston Dr & Katherine St, Sandown
Air Namibia (☎ 390 2876) Lower Mezzanine Level South, JIA
Air Zimbabwe (☎ 615 7017) Finance House, Ernest Oppenheimer Dr, Bruma Lake
Alitalia (☎ 721 4500) 1st floor, Oxford Manor, 196 Oxford Rd, Illovo
BA Comair (☎ 921 0222) Cnr Atlas & Marignane Rds, Bonaero Park
British Airways (☎ 441 8600) Grosvenor Corner, 195 Jan Smuts Ave, Rosebank
InterAir (☎ 616 0636) Finance House, Ernest Oppenheimer Drive, Bruma Lake
KLM-Royal Dutch Airlines (☎ 881 9600, W southafrica.klm.com) Sable Place, 1a Stan Rd, off Grayston Dr, Sandton
Lufthansa (☎ 484 4711, W www.lufthansa.co.za) 22 Gerton Rd, Parktown
Qantas Airways (☎ 441 8550) Grosvenor Corner, 195 Jan Smuts Ave, Rosebank
SA Airlink (reservations ☎ 961 1700) SA Airlink Hangar, Bonaero Dr, Bonaero Park
SA Express (☎ 978 5577) Terminal 3, Mezzanine level, JIA
SAA (reservations ☎ 978 1111, JIA international terminal ☎ 978 9033, domestic terminal ☎ 978 3118)
Singapore Airlines (☎ 880 8560) 257 Oxford Rd, Illovo
Varig (☎ 289 8065) Holiday House, 158 Hendrik Verwoerd Dr, Randburg

Bus
The new Park Station is the result of a huge and much needed redevelopment of the 22 city blocks bounded by Wolmarans, Rissik, De Villiers, Hoek, Noord and Wanderers Sts. The centre connects luxury buses to Main Line trains from platform Nos 11 to 19. A Metro concourse was built for Metro trains from platform Nos one to 10, and a road transport interchange is being built over the web of train tracks between the Metro concourse and Wanderers St to deal with about 150 long-distance taxis and 1200 minibus taxis.

A number of international bus services leave Jo'burg for Mozambique, Lesotho, Botswana, Namibia, Swaziland and Zimbabwe. See the Getting There & Away chapter for details.

The main long-distance bus lines (national and international) depart from and arrive at the Park Station transit centre, in the northwest corner of the site. There are booking counters and a **Jo'burg information desk** (☎ 337 6650) in the station. City to City, the inexpensive government bus service, leaves from the centre of Park Station – behind the Formule 1 hotel.

GAUTENG

Baz Bus Backpackers can now be connected to the most popular parts of the region (Swaziland, Durban, Garden Route and Cape Town) by **Baz Bus** (☎ 021-439 2323, W www.bazbus.com). The beauty is that Baz Bus picks up at hostels in Jo'burg and Pretoria, saving you the hassle of going into the city to arrange transport. All hostels have current timetables and prices; there are direct prices, which are considerably less than hop-on, hop-off prices, but still a lot more expensive than the intercity buses.

Baz Bus departs from Jo'burg/Pretoria for Swaziland on Monday, Wednesday and Saturday (returning on Tuesday, Thursday and Saturday). There is a service to Durban via the northern Drakensberg mountains on Wednesday, Friday and Sunday (returning Tuesday, Friday and Sunday).

Other Bus Companies The most comprehensive range of services is provided by the government-owned lines, **Translux** (☎ 774 3333, W www.translux.co.za) and **City to City** (☎ 773 6002, 309 7768).

In general, Translux is slightly cheaper than **Greyhound** (☎ 830 1301, W www.grey hound.co.za), and City to City is the cheapest of all. Another company with a wide coverage is **Intercape** (☎ 012-654 4114, W www .intercape.co.za).

With the exception of City to City buses, which commence in Jo'burg, all services that are not heading north commence in Pretoria at the Pretoria station. The times given here are from Pretoria to the final destination; services from Jo'burg are approximately one hour less in duration.

To Cape Town Translux has at least one bus running daily to Cape Town (R410, 19 hours) via Bloemfontein (R200, six hours). There are five services (daily, except Tuesday and Thursday) to Cape Town (R375, 18 hours) via Kimberley (R160, eight hours).

Greyhound has daily buses to Cape Town (R410, 18 hours) via Bloemfontein (R150, 6 hours) and Kimberley (R155, eight hours).

Intercape has four services a week (Tuesday, Thursday, Friday, Sunday) to Upington (R215, 10½ hours) and on to Cape Town

(R195). You might have to wait to change buses in Upington, but total road travel time from Jo'burg to Cape Town is about 19 hours.

From Upington you can also get an Intercape bus to Windhoek, Namibia (R250, 11 hours), but there isn't a direct connection (allow one hour time difference for daylight saving in summer).

To Durban Greyhound has four daily buses to Durban (R170, 8½ hours); there is also a daily service to Durban (R170, 11 hours) via Empangeni. Translux has at least one bus a day to Durban (R170, eight hours).

Eldo's Coaches (☎ 773 4552) has a daily service to Durban (R150). Several small companies operate a door-to-door service to Durban (R110 to R130); call the **South African Black Taxi Association** (☎ 683 2034).

To Mpumalanga & Kruger National Park The nearest large town to Kruger National Park is Nelspruit; Greyhound runs there daily (R125, 5½ hours). Note that this service starts in Jo'burg and picks up in Pretoria an hour later. Translux runs to Maputo, Mozambique daily (R175, nine hours) and stops in Nelspruit (R120, 4½ hours); this service also starts in Jo'burg and picks up in Pretoria an hour later.

City to City has some slow, cheap services from Jo'burg to Nelspruit (R60, seven hours) that continue on to Hazyview (R65, eight hours) and Acornhoek (R70).

Hazyview is closer to Kruger than Nelspruit and has backpacker hostels that can arrange trips to the park. See To the North (following) for buses to the Phalaborwa Gate.

To the North Several services run north up the N1. For example, Translux has a daily bus to Bulawayo, Zimbabwe, via Beitbridge. The journey times and fares are: Pietersburg (R115, 5½ hours), Louis Trichardt (R125, six hours) and Messina (R140, nine hours). Greyhound has daily services (except Sat) to Harare, Zimbabwe (R265, 16½ hours), and Bulawayo (R220, eight hours) that stop in Pietersburg (R120, four hours).

There are daily City to City services to Sibasa, Venda (R75), Giyani/Malamulele via Pietersburg (R70) and Beitbridge (R90). These services, which wind north through townships and ex-Homelands, also stop in major towns on the N1.

North Link Tours (☎ 015-291 1867) runs buses between Jo'burg and Phalaborwa (R135) via Pretoria, Naboomspruit, Potgietersrus, Pietersburg-Polokwane (R85) and Tzaneen; call for current rates. There is a separate service to Louis Trichardt. Kruger's Phalaborwa gate is farther from Jo'burg than some of the others but you might want to enter the park in the north and work your way south (you can hire cars in Phalaborwa or Hoedspruit).

For more companies going to Zimbabwe and beyond, see the Getting There & Away chapter.

To the South Translux operates a daily service to East London (R285, 11½ hours) via Bloemfontein. There's also a daily service to Bloemfontein (R200, 6¾ hours). Translux also has five services a week (not on Sunday and Tuesday) from Jo'burg to Port Elizabeth via Bloemfontein and Graaff-Reinet (R295, 14½ hours), and a Tuesday and Sunday service via Cradock (R295, 14½ hours).

Intercape has daily services to Port Elizabeth via Cradock (R295, 13½ hours) and on to Plettenberg Bay (R350, 17 hours).

Greyhound has daily buses that travel overnight from Jo'burg to Port Elizabeth (R285, 17 hours) and East London (R260, 13 hours).

Translux runs to Knysna (R345) via Kimberley (Wednesday, Friday and Sunday) or Bloemfontein (Monday, Tuesday, Thursday, Friday), then Oudtshoorn, Mossel Bay and George (all R345 from Jo'burg); the trip takes 17 hours. Intercape also operates to Knysna for the same price.

City to City runs to Umtata (R115), the closest large town to Port St Johns and Coffee Bay, daily at 7pm. There are daily City to City services to Lusikisiki via Pietermaritzburg (R110) and to Idutywa via Queenstown (R115); call for times. Translux and Greyhound both run to Umtata (R220, 12½ hours); Translux runs on Sunday, Tuesday,

Thursday and Friday and Greyhound runs daily except Saturday.

Train

Main Line (☎ 086-000 8888, W www.spoornet.co.za; bookings 7.30am-5pm Mon-Fri, 7.30am-1pm Sat) tickets can be booked at its kiosk on the main concourse at Jo'burg's Park Station. This company operates 'name trains' that are undoubtedly a more agreeable way to travel than the buses, but the privilege will cost you plenty of time. As a general rule, trains take about half as long again as buses. But they cost only marginally more and you have the freedom to move up and down the train; on a long trip this is worth gold. First-class fares are very competitive with Translux and Greyhound buses and 2nd-class fares are less than bus fares.

The various services are:

Algoa This train runs daily between Jo'burg and Port Elizabeth via Bloemfontein and takes 19 hours. Fares for 1st/2nd/economy are R315/215/155.
Amatola This train runs daily between Jo'burg and East London via Bloemfontein and takes 18 hours. Fares for 1st/2nd/economy are R295/200/125.
Blue Train (☎ 773 7631, W www.bluetrain.co.za) This is an extremely luxurious train that travels between Cape Town and Jo'burg. It has individual suites and compartments of varying degrees of comfort and expense. There are departures on Monday, Wednesday and Friday and it is essential to book in advance.
Bosvelder This train runs north from Jo'burg to Messina via Louis Trichardt and takes 14½ hours. Fares for 1st/2nd class are R185/125.
Diamond Express This train runs from Pretoria to Bloemfontein via Kimberley, daily except Sat, and takes 14½ hours. First/2nd-class fares from Jo'burg to Bloemfontein are R195/135.
Komati This train runs eastwards to Komatipoort, on the Mozambique border, via Nelspruit, and takes 12½ hours. It's a daily service (a shuttle service continues on to Maputo. First/2nd-class fares from Jo'burg to Komatipoort are R180/110. To continue on to Maputo, the additional cost is R45/35.
Trans Karoo This train runs daily to Cape Town via Kimberley, De Aar and Worcester, and takes 28 hours. Fares for 1st/2nd class are R450/305. Although it takes an extra nine hours, it is worth considering taking the train rather than the bus.

GAUTENG

Trans Natal This train runs daily between Jo'burg and Durban and takes 13½ hours. Fares for 1st/2nd/economy are R215/145/90. The train fares are competitive but the buses run during the day and only take about seven hours.

Minibus Taxi

The main long-distance taxi ranks are sandwiched between the Park Station and Joubert Park, mainly on Wanderers and King George Sts (they will hopefully soon be in the Park Station Road Transport Interchange). There are set areas for taxis to particular destinations (see the Central Johannesburg map).

Despite the apparent chaos, the ranks are well organised; ask for the queue marshal. You'll find taxis going in the direction of Kimberley, Cape Town and Upington on Wanderers St near Leyds St; Bulawayo taxis at the northern end of King George St; Pretoria taxis on Noord St; Lesotho, Bloemfontein (and other Free State destinations) on Noord St, east of Joubert Park; and Durban taxis near the corner of Wanderers and Noord Sts. Because of the risk of mugging, it isn't a good idea to go searching for a taxi while carrying your luggage. Go down and collect information then return in a taxi, luggage and all. Fares tend to fluctuate in line with petrol prices, but trips from Jo'burg include:

destination	fare (R)
Bulawayo (Zimbabwe)	200
Cape Town	240
Durban	115
Gaborone (Botswana)	85
Harrismith	65
Kimberley	120
Komatipoort	125
Manzini (Swaziland)	90
Maputo (Mozambique)	150
Nelspruit	90
Pietersburg-Polokwane	95
Pretoria	17
Thohoyandou (Venda)	90
Tzaneen	90

As well as these taxis, which only leave when they're full, there are a few door-to-door services you can book through hostels.

Car

All the major rental operators have counters at JIA and at various locations around the city. Operators include the following:

Avis	☎ 0861-021 111
Budget	☎ 0860-016 622
Europcar	☎ 0800-011 344
Hertz	☎ 0800-600 136
Imperial	☎ 0861-131 000
Tempest	☎ 0860-031 666

There is a range of local firms renting cars, usually at similar prices. If you're looking for a long-term rental it's worth ringing around for the best deal. **Swans Rent A Car** (☎ 975 0799, W www.swans.co.za) is probably the best of the few budget alternatives, renting out new cars for R99 a day with 100km free. Ask around the hostels/hotels for other options.

Hitching

We say don't hitch – especially here – but people do. Heading north, a popular place to begin hitching is on the M1 near the Killarney Mall, a couple of kilometres northwest of Yeoville. The N12 running east towards Kruger begins just east of Eastgate Mall. Heading south on the N1 (to Cape Town) you could try hitching on one of the freeway on-ramps.

The hostels always have notice boards where there are details of free or shared-cost lifts. Don't expect hostels to take any responsibility – it is up to you to check out the lift giver and to decide whether or not you wish to travel with that person.

GETTING AROUND
To/From the Airport

Don't be one of those travellers who lose the lot trying to get to their accommodation the cheap way (see the boxed text 'Surviving Johannesburg's Dangers & Annoyances' earlier in the chapter).

The **Magic Bus** (☎ 608 1662) is the main shuttle-bus service between JIA and the northern suburbs. It leaves half-hourly for expensive hotels in Sandton (R75) and hourly for similar establishments in Rosebank (R75) and Randburg (R85). Door-to-door services cost more.

Between 5am and 10pm, buses run every half hour (a quarter to and a quarter past the hour) between JIA and Park Station (R60, about 40 minutes); call **Impala Bus** (☎ 975 0510) for details. The area immediately around Park Station is known for muggings problem so be very careful (see advice under Minibus Taxi). **Airport Link** (☎ 792 2017) and **Welcome Tours** (☎ 442 8905) are other reputable shuttles.

Taxis are expensive at R200 to R300 depending on where you're going. Agree on a price before getting in the cab.

Most hostels will collect you from the airport, and some still 'tout' there.

Hop-On, Hop-Off Bus

It may be the height of optimism, but Jo'burg has two hop-on, hop-off double-decker bus tours. Both the City Slicker and the **Adventure Bus** (☎ 975 9338) began operating in late 2000 and offer similar services using slightly different routes. They are, we think, one of the best ways to see Jo'burg (see the boxed text 'Photographing Johannesburg' earlier in this chapter).

The green, open-topped City Slicker bus picks up from five of Sandton's best hotels, heads to the Randburg Waterfront, Rosebank and the zoo before winding through the mansions of Parktown, Melville's 7th St and the Oriental Plaza on its way to the city centre. City stops include the Newtown cultural precinct and the Carlton Centre. The three-hour route ends in Soweto, via Gold Reef City. The return trip takes the same route. It operates between 9am and 9pm seven days, with one-day (R70), two-day (R120) and three-day (R150) passes available. Buy them on the bus or through **Computicket** (☎ 340 8445).

The red Adventure Bus also starts from Sandton but heads south to Bruma Lake (with an optional side trip to Caesars Casino) before looping into the city centre and back to Sandton via the zoo, Rosebank and the Randburg Waterfront. Tickets are valid for 24 hours and cost R60/40 for adults/children (R100/60 if you include the side trips).

Unfortunately, Jo'burg's tourist market is probably not strong enough to support both buses, but it's anyone's guess which one will fold first.

Local Bus

Metropolitan Bus Services (☎ 403 4300, W www.johannesburg.org.za) runs services covering 108 routes in the Greater Jo'burg area. The main bus terminal is at Gandhi Square (formerly Vanderbijl Square), two blocks west of the Carlton Centre, and fares work on a zone system ranging from zone one (R2) to zone six (R7). Prices could be higher during the evening rush, from 4pm until 5.30pm. Not many buses run later than this. Tickets can be bought from the driver or in books of 10 from kiosks in Gandhi Square, which also have route information. If you are on a bus without a ticket, the damage is R200.

The following routes are useful:

route No	destinations
5	Parktown, Houghton, Rosebank & Illovo
10 & 118	Hillbrow/Berea & Yeoville
22	Yeoville & Bruma Lake
75	Braamfontein, Auckland Park & Melville
80	Rosebank & Dunkeld via Jan Smuts Ave

The buses that run out to Sandton are operated by **Padco** (☎ 474 2634). They leave the city centre from the corner of Kruis and Commissioner Sts. The buses run hourly from 6.30am to 5.15pm, more frequently at peak times; the fare to Sandton is R7.

See under Hop-On, Hop-Off Bus earlier for details of the City Slicker and Adventure Bus tours.

Train

For inquiries about train services call ☎ 773 5878 (☎ 0800 127 070) or visit the helpful information office in the Park Station concourse. There has been a very serious problem with violent crime on the Metro system, mostly on those lines connecting with black townships. The Jo'burg-Pretoria Metro line should also be avoided.

Minibus Taxi

Fares differ depending on routes, but R4 will get you around the inner suburbs and the city centre and R6 will get you almost anywhere. It's easy enough to catch a minibus taxi into the city and, if you're waiting at a bus stop, the chances are a taxi will show up before the bus does. If you do take a minibus taxi into central Jo'burg be sure to get off before it reaches the end of the route – avoid the taxi ranks as they are a mugging zone. Getting a minibus taxi home from the city is a more difficult proposition. Even locals often give up and take the bus.

There's a complex system of hand/finger signals to tell a passing taxi where you want to go (the driver will stop if he/she is going the same way). Just raising your index finger in the air will stop most taxis – but it means 'town'. A down-turned index finger means 'Sandton'. The last three fingers held up is 'Dobsonville, Soweto'.

Taxi

Taxis are an expensive but necessary evil in this city. They all operate meters, which, unfortunately, seem to vary markedly in their assessment, if they work at all. Consequently, it's wise to ask a local the likely price and agree on a fare at the outset. From Park Station to Rosebank should cost between R50 and R70, and significantly more to Sandton. Two reputable firms are **Maxi Taxi** (☎ 648 1212) and **Rose's Radio Taxis** (☎ 403 9625).

AROUND JOHANNESBURG
Western Gauteng

The **Kromdraai Conservancy**, also referred to as the Cradle of Humankind, is one of only three World Heritage sites in South Africa. The heritage listing comes from the palaeontological significance of the area, but fossils are not the only things worth seeing. Plan to spend a day exploring the Kromdraai area as few of the attractions warrant the long drive.

The most famous site is **Sterkfontein** (see the boxed text 'Sterkfontein Caves') and its hominid remains. Not far away is the **Old Kromdraai Gold Mine** (☎ 957 0211, Ibis Ridge Farm, Kromdraai Rd; adult/child R25/10; open 9am-5pm Sat & Sun, Tues-Fri by appointment). This was the first gold mine on the Witwatersrand. Guided tours leave the converted shed every hour.

In the Swartkop Mountains near Wonder Cave is the **Rhino & Lion Nature Reserve** (☎ 957 0109, Kromdraai Rd; adult/child R30/15; open 8am-5pm daily). This place goes from strength to strength and is a good option for those who cannot afford the time to go to Kruger National Park. You can see cheetahs, wild dogs (painted wolves), buffaloes, lions and rhinos close up. There is comfortable *chalet* accommodation (R400 for four people) in a camp within the reserve.

West of the Rhino & Lion Nature Reserve, and just off Kromdraai Rd, is **Wonder Cave** (☎ 957 0106, Wondercave Rd; adult/child R25/15; open 8am-4pm Mon-Fri, 8am-5pm Sat & Sun). With some beautiful formations, Wonder Cave is a good fillip for those that came to Sterkfontein expecting a pristine interior. Wonder Cave is nothing more than a commercial tourist cave, however. Visit Sterkfontein for the prehistory before you come here. Tours run hourly.

Krugersdorp Game Reserve (☎/fax 665 1735; open 8am-5pm daily), a small grassland reserve 7km west of Krugersdorp on the R24 in the direction of Magaliesberg, has four of the Big Five (no elephants).

Ngonyama Lion Lodge (☎ 665 4342, Rustenberg Rd) 2-, 4- & 6-bed lodges from R330. This place within the reserve has camp sites, a restaurant and a shop. Good for those wishing to stay out of town.

Near Lanseria airport is a **Lion Park** (☎ 460 1814, Cnr Hans Strijdom Rd & Old Victoria Rd; admission R70; open 8.30am-5pm Mon-Fri, 8.30am-6pm Sat & Sun). This place, on the R55, is notable for its 'tree-climbing lions', terrible takeaways and 'lekker jol festing' Afrikaners. If you do go, avoid going on Sunday at all costs.

Southern Gauteng

This area, with its cities of Vereeniging, Sebokeng and Vanderbijlpark, is dissected by

GAUTENG

Sterkfontein Caves

There is no doubt that these caves, on Johannesburg's doorstep, are one of the most significant archaeological/palaeontological sites in the world – up there with Olduvai Gorge in Tanzania. The discovery in 1998 of 'Mr Ples', an almost complete 3.5-million-year-old hominid skeleton, has renewed interest in this veritable time capsule.

The caves themselves were formed by the solution of dolomite beneath the water table, a process that began about 2.5 billion years ago. But it is that which was washed in much later (3.5 million years ago) that has spurred latter-day interest: deposits rich with bones.

In August 1936, Dr Robert Broom visited the caves after learning that extinct baboon fossils had been found in the dumps left from crude lime quarrying. A week after arriving in the area he had found the first adult skull of an 'ape-man', believed to be 2.6 to three million years old – he named it *Australopithecus transvaalensis*. In 1947, the cranium of 'Mrs Ples' was blasted out of the debris and almost 10 years later, in 1956, Dr CK Brain discovered much younger stone tools. In 1995, the significance of the articulating foot bones of 'Little Foot' was revealed – their relationship to an ankle bone indicated that this 'ape-man', our ancestor, walked upright. In all, Sterkfontein has so far given up more than 600 hominid fossils, making it the most bountiful site for evidence of Australopithecus.

Sterkfontein is significant as it indicates that erect walking creatures (hominids) roamed and hunted across this landscape more than three million years ago, side by side with several other now-extinct species (eg, giant leaf-eating monkeys, hunting hyena and sabre-toothed cats).

Be warned, the caves limestone interior has been mined out so they are not attractive caves. The pokey Broom Museum contains fossils from some of the more significant finds. Admission to the caves (with a guide) is R20/10 adults/children and one-hour tours start every 30 minutes.

the Vaal River and is very rich in history. The natural barrier of the Vaal River – the *gij!garib* (tawny) to the San, *lekoa* (erratic) to the Sotho, and *vaal* (dirty) to the Afrikaners – has been an important dividing line in southern African history, separating the 'transvaal' from the south.

The Peace of Vereeniging treaty was negotiated near the Vaal, effectively ending the 1899–1902 Anglo-Boer War, and in more recent times southern Gauteng has been an important place in the struggle for freedom.

It was at Sharpeville and Evaton, on 21 March 1960, that black civilians protested against the pass laws by publicly burning their pass books. The police opened fire on the protestors at Sharpeville, killing 69 and wounding about 180; most were shot in the back. Now, 21 March is commemorated in South Africa as Human Rights Day.

In 1984 in Sebokeng, the security forces violently reacted to a black boycott of rent and service tariffs, tearing apart townships

looking for activists. About 95 people were killed. These slaughters galvanised the black population into a more unified force, and ultimately hastened the fall of apartheid.

Suikerbosrand Nature Reserve Named after the sugar bush *Protea caffra*, the Suikerbosrand Nature Reserve *(adult/child R15/7.50; open 6.30am-5.30pm daily Oct-Apr, 7am-5.30pm in winter)* is nestled between the N3 and R59 freeways, and can be reached by either. There are 66km of walking trails and several drives, and accommodation in camps and caravan parks (see Places to Stay – Budget earlier).

For maps and interpretative books try the **visitors centre** (☎ 904 3930).

Inside the reserve is the historic **Diep-kloof Farm**, originally built in 1850 by Voortrekker Gabriel Marais, and renovated in the 1970s after being burnt during the Boer War.

[Continued on page 540]

SOWETO

The idea was simple. Move anyone who wasn't white as far away from the 'chosen race' as possible, but still close enough that they could be used as cheap labour.

Thus was born Soweto (the name is an acronym of South West Townships), the biggest, most political, most violent, most dynamic and easily the best known of South Africa's townships, a term that doesn't seem quite right for such an enormous place. That it's on the outskirts of Johannesburg (Jo'burg) seems appropriate; Soweto has almost as many grating contrasts as does its patronising parent.

Dozens of the shanties and three-room matchbox houses that make up Soweto would fit onto a single stately block in Jo'burg's Westcliff or Parktown, but most white Jo'burgers wouldn't know this. Most whites have never been to Soweto or any of the six other main townships that surround the city; most simply cannot understand why anyone, especially visitors, would want to.

The first impression as one approaches the township is of an enormous, undifferentiated sprawl, punctuated by light towers. Soweto covers about 150 sq km, but when you consider that its population of more than 3.5 million is similar to that of the whole of Ireland you begin to understand the close proximity in which people live.

While many Sowetans live in shanty towns as bad as those of any developing-world slum, some suburbs seem quite ordinary, and not that far removed from the middle-class suburbs of Europe, Australia and North America. Places such as Orlando West (known locally as Beverley Hills), Dube and the Diepkloof Extension are occupied by the wealthy few and can be distinguished by the manicured pavements and gardens surrounding double-storey and brick-veneered homes, often with an expensive German sedan parked in the double garage. Those wealthy enough to own a set of clubs even have the choice of two golf courses, although with cows appearing to be the only greenkeepers around, they're a far cry from the exclusive courses found elsewhere in Jo'burg.

Inset: Wall mural detail (Photo by Richard I'Anson)

Left: Middle-class housing, with low-cost housing in the background (Photo by Richard I'Anson)

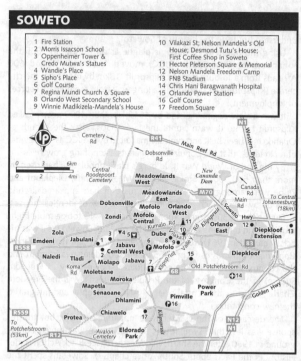

SOWETO

1 Fire Station	10 Vilakazi St; Nelson Mandela's Old
2 Morris Issacson School	House; Desmond Tutu's House;
3 Oppenheimer Tower &	First Coffee Shop in Soweto
Credo Mutwa's Statues	11 Hector Pieterson Square & Memorial
4 Wandie's Place	12 Nelson Mandela Freedom Camp
5 Sipho's Place	13 FNB Stadium
6 Golf Course	14 Chris Hani Baragwanath Hospital
7 Regina Mundi Church & Square	15 Orlando Power Station
8 Orlando West Secondary School	16 Golf Course
9 Winnie Madikizela-Mandela's House	17 Freedom Square

These, however, are the lucky few of Soweto. Just 20m across the road from the modern comforts of the Diepkloof Extension is the Nelson Mandela Freedom Camp – so named because the first shanties went up soon after Mandela (also known as Madiba) was freed in 1990. The camp is home to about 9000 people, who live in about 3500 corrugated-iron shacks and share 90 communal toilets and just five fresh-water taps. There is no electricity. About 40% of Sowetans live like this.

Between these extremes live the rest. Most Sowetans now have electricity and water, and an increasing number now have a phone. The government-funded development at Dobsonville is the latest example of Soweto's ongoing expansion. Thousands of identical three-room homes are being built on tiny blocks. They cost just R16,000 and come with internal plumbing and power. Their occupants have been moved from the shanty towns, and their sense of house pride is obvious in the small rectangles of grass pushing hesitantly out of the red earth. Some of the would-be lawns are surrounded by rusty razor wire, erected to keep children and dogs off, not to shut out the rest of the world, as is the case in much of Jo'burg.

Soweto's role in South Africa's recent history is unrivalled. As African National Congress (ANC) stalwart and long-time Soweto resident

Walter Sisulu once said, 'the history of South Africa cannot be understood outside the history of Soweto'.

Using the outbreak of bubonic plague as an excuse, in 1905 the Johannesburg City Council (JCC) moved 1358 Indians and 600 Africans from a Jo'burg slum to Klipspruit, 18km by road from the city centre (Klipspruit was, and still is, a long way from the primary sources of employment).

It was a slow beginning, and by 1919 less than 4000 people called Klipspruit home. It wasn't until the late 1930s, after the suburb of Orlando had been built and cynically marketed by the JCC as 'Somewhat of a paradise', that the population began its astonishing growth.

By the end of World War II, Jo'burg's black population had risen by more than 500,000. Moroka, Jabavu, Meadowlands, Diepkloof and Dube were among the 21 new suburbs that had appeared around Orlando by 1958, each filled with row upon row of identical houses.

During the 1950s, organisations such as the ANC took a more high-profile role in opposing apartheid and before long Soweto (as it was officially named in 1961) would be recognised as the centre of resistance. Confirmation of this came in 1955 when 3000 delegates from around the country gathered in Kliptown Square (known today as Freedom Square) at the Congress of the People. The result was the Freedom Charter, which is the central pillar of ANC philosophy and integral to the new constitution.

The demands of the charter were not unreasonable, but the response was less than sympathetic and resistance was forced underground in 1960 after the Sharpeville Massacre (see Black Action under History in the Facts about South Africa chapter). Sowetans spent the next 15 years in a state of definite uncertainty – definite they wanted change but uncertain how and when it would come.

While the struggle continued at a slower pace over these years it was not the only change taking place in Soweto. The demographics of the

Right: Smoke and peo on a street lined with squatter housing (Pho by Richard I'Anson)

townships were changing, and as second-generation Sowetans matured so did Soweto style. New forms of music (see the special section 'South African Music') emerged and the youth led the developments of a unique urban culture. Soccer also offered an escape, and massive support for teams such as the Moroka Swallows, the Orlando Pirates and, after they split from the Pirates, the Kaizer Chiefs reflected the development of an urban black identity. The development of this new identity only served to strengthen the desire to be treated as equals. Resistance eventually spilled over on 16 June 1976, when students organised a peaceful protest against the introduction of Afrikaans as a language of instruction in secondary schools. The students marched to the Orlando West Secondary School on Vilikazi St. When they arrived and refused to disburse, police fired tear gas into the crowd.

The chain of events that followed would eventually be seen as the turning point in the whole liberation struggle. In the resulting chaos police opened fire and a 13-year-old boy, Hector Pieterson, was shot dead. The ensuing hours and days saw students fight running battles with the security forces in what would become known as the Soweto Uprising. Dozens of government buildings were torched, but the euphoria of fighting the oppressor was tempered by the frightening human cost. On the first day alone, the official toll put two white policemen and 23 students as dead, but in reality closer to 200 teenage protesters had perished.

Many of the dead were buried as martyrs in Soweto's vast Avalon Cemetery, and the Hector Pieterson Memorial was built to commemorate all those who died in the struggle.

Within days, world opinion had turned irreversibly against the apartheid regime and Soweto became the most potent symbol of resistance to a racist South Africa.

Scenes of burning cars, burning people and mass funerals flowed out of Soweto throughout the 1980s as the death throes of apartheid swept over the country. Mandela was released in 1990 and returned to live in his tiny home in Vilikazi St, just 200m from Archbishop Desmond Tutu. Sowetans now boast of having the only street in the world where two Nobel peace laureates have homes. Tutu still lives in his modest grey-walled home, while Winnie Madikizela-Mandela has converted the house she shared with Mandela into an overpriced, uninspiring museum (R20); don't be tempted by the bottled dirt from 'Nelson's backyard'.

Right: Outlined figures carved in stone: detail from the Hector Pieterson Memorial (Photo by Richard I'Anson)

However, Mandela's release was no panacea. Encouraged by the government, supporters of rival political parties murdered each other by the hundreds in the run up to the 1994 free elections. In the early 1990s, Soweto was one of the most dangerous places on earth.

More recently, however, life has been stable, and since 1994 Sowetans have had ownership rights over their properties.

Visiting Soweto

It may seem grotesque to treat Soweto as another tourist attraction but to really appreciate South Africa you have to visit. At present, the easiest, safest and ultimately the best way to visit is on a tour, so a tour it must be. It's still too risky to drive around by yourself and the township is so poorly signposted that you're almost guaranteed to get lost.

If you're interested in something along the lines of cultural immersion rather than sightseeing contact the TALK project (see Courses in the Facts for the Visitor chapter) for details of its Soweto homestay and tour programs.

There are several Soweto tours. They follow roughly the same route and stop at most of the struggle sites mentioned in this section. Other stops will likely include a squatter camp, migrant hostels, the Regina Mundi Church, Freedom Square, Winnie Madikizela-Mandela's house, the Oppenheimer Tower, FNB Stadium and the huge Chris Hani Baragwanath Hospital. If you want to get off the beaten track, use one of the smaller companies and tell the driver where you'd like to go. As long as all the passengers are keen, drivers are usually fairly obliging. Tours will collect passengers from hostels and hotels. (For other local tours see Organised Tours in the Johannesburg section of the Gauteng chapter.)

The name **Neng Kapa Neng** (☎ 936 9738, 082-649 6368) means 'Any Time, Any Place' and Jabu and Letlela run fairly flexible tours to fit the bill. Jabu is a fount of knowledge on all things Soweto, but does have a tendency to talk too much. Soweto tours are good value at R160 (R250 from Pretoria), while longer tours that include Jo'burg cost R250. Homestays can be arranged.

Max Maximum Tours (☎ 933 8703, 082-770 0247, e *max .maximum@pixie.co.za*) is also recommended. Max is a long-time Soweto resident and a very good guide, although some of his younger guides don't rate so highly. Soweto tours cost R190/100 for adults/children, homestays are R300 and evening shebeen (bar) routes cost R190.

Jimmy's Face to Face Tours (☎ 331 6109, fax 331 5388, W *www .face2face.co.za*) is the oldest and probably the most consistently good company offering Soweto tours. Half-day tours are R190 and night tours are R415, including dinner.

Springbok Atlas (☎ 396 1053 W *www.springbokatlas.com*) is the biggest of these tour companies and it runs the most comfortable, but least personal, tour buses. It picks up from Rosebank, Sandton and city hotels and costs more than the competition.

It is also possible to stay overnight in Soweto. Despite much talk, at the time of writing there were no recognised hostels or guesthouses within the township. There are, however, plenty of families willing to have visitors. Homestays usually involve a walk around the host's suburb, dinner, a drink in a local shebeen and breakfast the next morning. The best, and at the moment the only, way to organise such a trip is through a tour guide or some hotels and hostels.

When you're visiting Soweto, you'll find that you're never more than a short stagger from a drinking establishment, the quality of which varies greatly. In the squatter camps the favourite tonic is the African beer made from maize meal. It comes in 1L plastic bottles for R3, and is definitely an acquired taste. For most Sowetans a trip to the pub involves sitting in a neighbour's front room and being served lager from a cooler.

If you're doing particularly well you might find yourself in one of the more upmarket shebeens, where you could even find Guinness on tap.

Sipho's Place (☎ 082-255 4499, *Dube*) is one such upmarket establishment, where locals swap stories of time spent in the police station across the road.

Once a popular shebeen, ***Wandie's Place*** (☎/fax 982 2796, 🇼 *www .wandiesplace.com, 618 Dube)* has matured into Soweto's best restaurant. The African buffet (R40 all you can eat) is so good that Wandie's now sees as many white patrons as black.

GAUTENG

[Continued from page 533]

Pretoria

☎ 012 • pop 1.8 million

Pretoria (known as 'Tshwane' by the Sotho population, and 'ePitoli' in township-speak) is South Africa's administrative capital and a city with deep roots in the country's Afrikaner-dominated past. It's only some 50km north of Jo'burg but for most of its history the social and cultural gulf has been huge.

All this is changing fast. Suburban sprawl is advancing across the shrinking green belt that separates the cities, and despite all the bitter struggles, all the wars and all the statutes, the uitlanders are now engulfing the old capital of the first Zuid-Afrikaansche Republiek (ZAR; South African Republic).

Nonetheless, Pretoria and Jo'burg remain very different. Pretoria is uncompromisingly 'Boer', owing its existence and growth to the twin Boer dreams of independence from the British and domination of the blacks. The city itself became a powerful metaphor for the apartheid system that was born and administered here, but today evidence of its demise is everywhere. Poor whites, almost exclusively Afrikaners, walk barefoot and dirty through areas of the city from which blacks were once banned. White beggars are commonplace – a situation that would have been almost unimaginable 10 years ago.

Majority rule has brought scores of embassies back to the leafy suburbs of Arcadia and Hatfield, but not everything has changed – the military and educational institutions associated with the capital remain. The universities are huge and tens of thousands of students drive Pretoria's vibrant nightlife.

Greater Pretoria, which has been officially renamed Tshwane, has a population of over 1.8 million. Most blacks living here are Sotho people, about 60% of the whites are Afrikaners.

There are several sites that must be seen. The colossal Voortrekker Monument and the neofascist lines of JG Strijdom Square are

very different but are united in their hardline Afrikaner origins. The Union Buildings are architecturally classic, while the charm of Church Square is best appreciated from the benches of Cafe Riche. Burgers Park, an English garden, is a midcity oasis and a relaxing spot for lunch. After dark, the music and cuisine centres of Hatfield and Brooklyn are buzzing; meanwhile jazz is played in the township shebeens.

Pretoria is quite an attractive city, especially during October and November when the city is dominated by 70,000 flowering jacarandas. There are still a few old houses, incongruous not just for their size when compared with the neighbouring ranks of apartment blocks, but for their lack of high walls and razor wire. This is a far more relaxed place than Jo'burg, but there has been a sharp rise in crime in recent years, with the city centre and Sunnyside copping most of the flak. Most of the city is safe by day but things change fast so take all the usual precautions and a large dose of local advice.

HISTORY

The area around the Apies River was well watered and fertile, so it supported a large population of cattle farmers for hundreds of years. These were Nguni-speaking peoples (from the same origin as the Zulus and Swazis) who came to be known as the Ndebele by the Sotho people of the Transvaal and as the Matabele by the Europeans.

However, the disruption caused by the Zulu wars resulted in massive dislocation. Much of the black population was slaughtered and most of the remaining people fled north into present-day Zimbabwe. In 1841 the first Boers trekked into a temporary vacuum. With no-one around they calmly laid claim to the land that would become their capital, thus beginning the long-held myth that white people arrived in the area first.

By the time the British granted independence to the ZAR in the early 1850s, there were estimated to be 15,000 whites and 100,000 blacks living between the Vaal and Limpopo Rivers. The whites were widely scattered, and in 1853 two farms on the Apies River were bought as the site for the

epublic's capital. The ZAR was a shaky
nstitution. There were ongoing wars with
he black tribes, and violent disputes among
he Boers themselves. Pretoria, which was
amed after Andries Pretorius, the hero of
lood River, was the scene of fighting
uring the Boer civil war of 1863–69.

Pretoria was nothing more than a tiny
ontier village with a grandiose title, but
he servants of the British Empire were
atching it with growing misgivings. They
cted in 1877, annexing the republic. The
oers went to war – Pretoria came under
ege at the beginning of 1881 – and won
ack their independence.

The discovery of gold on the Witwater-
and in the late 1880s revolutionised the
tuation and within 20 years the Boers
ould again be at war with the British. Pret-
ria was abandoned by President Paul
ruger and the Boer forces in June 1900,
ut the war ground on until 31 May 1902,
hen the Peace of Vereeniging was signed
Melrose House.

With the British making efforts towards
conciliation, self-government was again
ranted to the Transvaal in 1906, and
rough an unwieldy compromise Pretoria
as made the administrative capital. The
nion of South Africa came into being in
910 but Pretoria was not to regain its sta-
s as a republic until 1961, when the Re-
ublic of South Africa came into existence
nder the leadership of Dr Verwoerd.

Ironically, the city that for so long was a
yword for white domination is now home
the liberated country's black president.
habo Mbeki has his office in the Union
uildings, while a black mayor and a black-
ominated council hold seat in the less
andiose local government buildings.
ruger and many of his successors must be
rning in their graves.

RIENTATION

ke most people you'll likely arrive in
etoria by road from Jo'burg. You'll know
u're almost there by the enormous Uni-
rsity of South Africa (Unisa) campus,
uth-west of the city centre, looking like a
ounded Battlestar Galactica, stretched

along a hillside to the right. A couple of
kilometres on is the city proper, spreading
west to east below a long kopje (hill), on
the south side of which stand the Union
Buildings.

The backbone of the city grid is Church
St which, at 26km, is claimed to be one of
the longest straight streets in the world.
Church St, runs through Church Square, the
historic centre of the city, and east to Arcadia, home to hotels, embassies and the
Union Buildings. The main nightlife and
restaurant zones are Hatfield and Brooklyn.

INFORMATION
Tourist Offices

An organisation that tends to change name
about once a year is the **Tourist Information
Bureau** (☎ 337 4337, *Old Nederlandsche
Bank Bldg, Church Square*), but the staff
are helpful and there is a wide range of
brochures available, including the excellent
Pretoria Quick Reference Guide and its
associated map. Web sites worth looking at
include Ⓦ www.pretoria.co.za and, for
what's happening around town, Ⓦ www
.pta-online.co.za.

Most hostels and hotels provide similar
information.

National Parks Board

Not far from Unisa is the head office of the
National Parks Board (☎ 343 9770, Ⓦ *www
.parks-sa.co.za, 643 Leyds St, New Muckleneuk*). It only books accommodation and
is loath to provide information.

Visa Extensions

Apply for visa extensions at the **Department
of Home Affairs** (☎ 324 1860, *Sentrakor
Bldg, Pretorius St*).

Money

Most banks are open 9am to 3.30pm Monday to Friday, 8.30am to 11am Saturday;
some exchange foreign currency. The First
National Bank has branches on Church
Square and in Burnett St. ATMs are everywhere, but be sure to read the boxed text
'Beating the ATM Scams' in the Facts for
the Visitor chapter before using them.

GAUTENG

PRETORIA

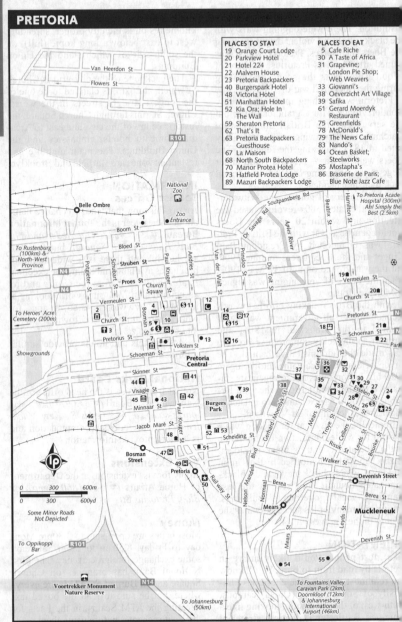

PLACES TO STAY
19 Orange Court Lodge
20 Parkview Hotel
21 Hotel 224
22 Malvern House
23 Pretoria Backpackers
40 Burgerspark Hotel
48 Victoria Hotel
51 Manhattan Hotel
52 Kia Ora; Hole In The Wall
59 Sheraton Pretoria
62 That's It
63 Pretoria Backpackers Guesthouse
67 La Maison
68 North South Backpackers
70 Manor Protea Hotel
73 Hatfield Protea Lodge
89 Mazuri Backpackers Lodge

PLACES TO EAT
5 Cafe Riche
30 A Taste of Africa
31 Grapevine; London Pie Shop; Web Weavers
33 Giovanni's
38 Oeverzicht Art Village
39 Safika
61 Gerard Moerdyk Restaurant
75 Greenfields
78 McDonald's
79 The News Cafe
83 Nando's
84 Ocean Basket; Steelworks
85 Mostapha's
86 Brasserie de Paris; Blue Note Jazz Cafe

PRETORIA

GAUTENG

OTHER
1 Craft Stalls
2 Paul Kruger House; Pass Office
3 Dutch Reformed Church (Paul Kruger's Church)
4 GPO
6 Tourist Information Bureau
7 SA Police Museum
8 Department of Home Affairs
9 Taxi Rank
10 Church Square; Bus Terminus
11 First National Bank
12 Mosque
13 Sanlam Centre; Rennies Travel

14 JG Strijdom Square; Taxi Rank
15 ABSA Bank
16 Tramshed
17 State Theatre Complex
18 Sterland Cinemas
24 Shoprite
25 Police Station
26 ABSA bank
27 Laundry World
28 Duplica Printing
29 Pharmacy
32 Post Office
34 London Tavern
35 Camping & Outdoor Living
36 Sunnypark Mall
37 Voodoo Lounge
41 Science & Technology Museum

42 Transvaal Museum of Anthropology & Geology
43 City Hall
44 Catholic Cathedral of the Sacred Heart
45 African Window
46 Correctional Service Museum
47 Long-distance Minibus Taxis
49 Greyhound, Translux Intercape Terminal
50 Police Station
53 Melrose House
54 UNISA
55 National Parks Board Head Office
57 Pretoria Art Museum
58 Swaziland Embassy
60 Ulysses Tours & Safaris

64 Eastwood Tavern
65 US Embassy
66 Australian Embassy
69 Shell Petrol Station
71 Hatfield Galleries; Odyssey Internet Cafe; Tings an' Times
72 Cool Runnings
74 First National Bank
76 ABSA Bankteller
77 STA Travel
80 Hatfield Square; McGinty's; Drop Zone; Mozarellas
81 Post Office
82 Hatfield Plaza; Pick 'n' Pay
87 Hillcrest Heated Swimming Pool
88 OUT (Gay Community Centre)
90 Magnolia Dell 'Moonlight' Market

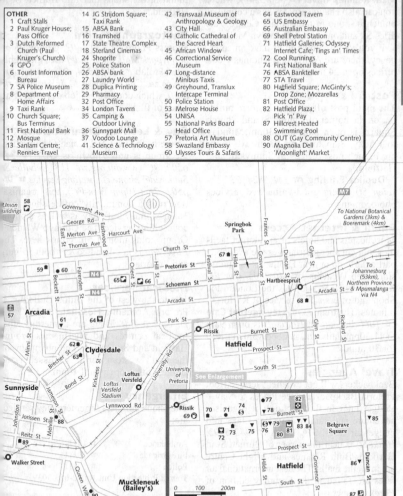

GAUTENG

AmEx (☎ 346 2599) is in the Brooklyn Mall. **Rennies Travel** (☎ 320 2240), where you can also change money, has a couple of branches – one in the Sanlam Centre, Andries St, and one in the Brooklyn Mall.

If you've just flown in or have an emergency, there are AmEx and Thomas Cook offices open 24 hours at JIA.

Post & Fax
The main post office, in a historic building on the corner of Church St and Church Square, is open 8am to 4.30pm Monday to Friday, 8am to noon Saturday. There are branch post offices in Sunnyside and Hatfield.

Duplica Printing (☎ 341 5824, 237 Esselen St) offers good-value fax services photocopying.

Email & Internet Access
Most hostels and hotels offer Internet facilities, but cheaper alternatives are available, particularly on or near Esselen St in Sunnyside. **Web Weavers** (☎ 440 2905, Cnr Esselen & Troye Sts) adjoins the London Pie Shop and offers a fast service at R7 for 30 minutes. The trendy **Odyssey Internet Cafe** (☎ 1066 Burnett St, Hatfield) is open 9am to 11.30pm daily and is good value at R10 for 30 minutes.

Travel Agencies
Backpackers will get excellent service from Pretoria Backpackers (see Places to Stay – Budget later in this section); it organises adventure and student travel and taps into budget air fares. **STA Travel** (☎ 342 5292, Hilda St) is near the corner of Burnett St in Hatfield. Both Rennies and Flight Centre are in all the malls. The best international air fares are found in the Saturday edition of *Pretoria News*.

A gay-friendly agency is **Ulysses Tours & Safaris** (☎ 344 4377, W www.ulysses.co.za, 770 Pretorius St, Arcadia). The agency runs informative half-day city tours for R240.

Bookshops
Sunnypark Mall, Sunnyside, has branches of Exclusive Books and CNA. Most of the books and maps a traveller needs can be found in the shops that line Burnett St in Hatfield.

Photography & Film
Express Photo (☎ 440 1802, Ground floor, Sunnypark Mall, Sunnyside) uses the highly rated **Prolab** (☎ 346 8334, e graphic@pro lab.co.za, Cnr Crown & Main Sts, Waterkloof), which does a good job developing all types of film.

Gay & Lesbian Organisations
Formerly the Gay & Lesbian Organisation the group is now known as **OUT** (☎ 34 6500, W www.out.org.za, 118 Melville St, Sunnyside; phone counselling service ☎ 34 6502, 7pm-10pm Tues-Fri), this organisation runs a community coffee shop from 10am Monday to Friday as well as a phone counselling service. The Uthingo Women's Group holds monthly meetings here. The *Pink Map* is good and covers both Jo'burg and Pretoria.

Medical Services
Just to the west of the Union Buildings is **Pretoria Academic Hospital** (☎ 329 1111, Dr Savage Rd). There are numerous other medical centres and pharmacies around Hatfield and Sunnyside. The pharmacy on the north-western corner of Esselen and Celliers Sts is open until 10pm.

Emergency
The phone numbers for emergency services are:

Ambulance	☎ 10111
Fire Brigade	☎ 10111
Police	☎ 10111
Tourist Protection Unit	☎ 082-653 3039

Dangers & Annoyances
Although Pretoria is certainly safer and more relaxed than Jo'burg, crime rates have been rising steadily in recent years. The city centre and Sunnyside have been worst hit with restaurants and other businesses moving to the safer Hatfield and Brooklyn areas. The square roughly formed by Vermeulen

Du Toit, Boom and Schubert Sts has a bad reputation.

It's important to remember that almost two million people live in Pretoria and live relatively regular lives, so don't be scared into never leaving your lodgings. At the same time, things change quickly in South Africa, and Pretoria is no exception – always seek local advice before venturing into the unknown, and take all the usual precautions (see Dangers & Annoyances in the Facts for the Visitor chapter). During the day you may see members of the Tourist Protection Unit (☎ 082-653 3039) on patrol.

MUSEUMS
African Window
Concentrating on the archaeological and anthropological records of Southern Africa, African Window (☎ 324 6082, Cnr Visagie & Bosman Sts; admission R5; open 8am-4pm daily) is not the most fascinating museum you will ever see, but it does reward the interested visitor. Special emphasis is given to the African tribes of Gauteng.

Paul Kruger House
A short walk west from Church Square, the residence of Paul Kruger has been turned into a museum (☎ 326 9172, 60 Church St; adult/child R10/5; open 8.30am-4pm Mon-Fri, 9am-4pm Sat & Sun). It's interesting, but, partly due to its setting right on a busy street, it's difficult to get a feeling for the man (unlike at Smuts' House Museum, Doornkloof; see Around Pretoria later in this section), despite the fact that he was undoubtedly an extraordinary human being.

There are clues. The house is unpretentious, although there would have been few grander homes when it was built in 1883. Among all sorts of bric-a-brac there's the knife that Kruger used to amputate his thumb after a shooting accident (the thumb isn't on display). The Dutch Reformed Church, where he worshipped and preached, is across the road.

Immediately left of the house is the neo-Georgian **Pass Office** (1932). Hated by blacks for its function of racial classification, the building was nevertheless known to them as GaMothle, the beautiful place, because the friezes and tableaux decorating it represented black African peoples. Sadly it's now falling into disrepair and is not open to the public, but there are interesting explanations of its history outside.

Melrose House
Opposite Burgers Park is Melrose House (☎ 322 2805, 275 Jacob Maré St; admission R3; open 10am-5pm Tues-Sun). This neo-Baroque mansion was built in 1886 for George Heys, and it's a somewhat fanciful cross between English Victorian and Cape Dutch styles.

During the 1899–1902 Anglo-Boer War (sometimes known as the Second War of Independence), Lords Roberts and Kitchener (both British commanders) lived here. On 31 May 1902 the Peace of Vereeniging treaty, which marked the end of the war, was signed in the dining room. The house is a National Monument.

Transvaal Museum of Anthropology & Geology
Opposite City Hall you'll find this museum (☎ 322 7632, Paul Kruger St; adult/child R6/3.50; open 9am-5pm Mon-Sat, 11am-5pm Sun). This place has static displays of animals and birds in glass exhibition cases. The most dramatic exhibit is the enormous skeleton of a whale outside the building. The museum is between Visagie and Minnaar Sts.

Pretoria Art Museum
Off Schoeman St, a kilometre or so east of the city centre, you'll find this museum (☎ 344 1807, Arcadia Park; admission R3; open 10am-5pm Tues & Thurs-Sat, 10am-8pm Wed, 10am-6pm Sun). With displays of South African art from many periods of the country's history, this is a good place to get a feel for the contrasting influences that make up modern South Africa.

Other Museums
There are a couple of other museums worth visiting, such as the **Correctional Service**

Museum (☎ 314 1766, Prison Reserve, Central Prison, Potgieter St; admission free; open 9am-3pm Tues-Fri, closed public holidays). Those keen enough can visit the hands-on **Science & Technology Museum** (☎ 322 6404, 211 Skinner St; admission R5; open 8am-4pm Mon-Fri, 2pm-5pm Sun). Also keep an eye out for the **SA Police Museum** (Cnr Pretorius & Volkstem Sts), which was being renovated at the time of writing.

CHURCH SQUARE

Church Square, the heart of Pretoria, is surrounded by imposing public buildings, including the Ou Raadsaal (Old Government) building on the southern side; the Old Capitol Theatre in the north-west corner; the First National Bank in the north-east; the Palace of Justice on the northern side; the Old Nederlandsche Bank building, which adjoins the Cafe Riche and houses the Tourist Information Bureau (see under Information earlier in this section); and the main post office at the western side. Look for the clock surrounded by nude figures by Anton van Wouw above the Church Square entrance to the post office.

In the centre, the 'Old Lion' (Paul Kruger) looks disapprovingly at office workers lounging on the grass. The bronze figures of Kruger and the sentries, also by Van Wouw, were cast in Italy at the turn of the century but lay in storage until 1954. In the early days, Boers from the surrounding countryside would gather in the square every three months for communion.

HEROES' ACRE

Around 1.5km west of Church Square you'll find this cemetery (Church St; open 8am-6pm). This is the burial place of a number of historical figures, including Andries Pretorius, Paul Kruger and Hendrik Verwoerd. Henry H 'Breaker' Morant, the Australian Boer War antihero executed by the British for war crimes, is also buried here – look for the low sign pointing to the grave stone from one of the north-south avenues. If you miss this you'll never find it.

To get here by bus take the West Park No 2 or Danville service from Church Square.

JG STRIJDOM SQUARE

A striking example of neofascist architecture, the square was until recently dominated by a huge bust of JG Strijdom, the prime minister from 1954 to 1958 and an architect of apartheid, and a group of charging horses (apparently an archetypal heroic and martial image). But in an incredibly ironic twist of fate, in May 2001 Strijdom's head crashed down from its mount and cracked in two - 40 years to the day after South Africa was declared a republic. Exactly what will become of the square remains to be seen, although you can be fairly sure the new government won't be resurrecting Strijdom.

UNION BUILDINGS

The Union Buildings are the headquarters of government, South Africa's equivalent of the Kremlin. The impressive red sandstone structures – with a self-conscious imperial grandeur – are surrounded by expansive gardens and are home to the presidential offices.

The architect was Sir Herbert Baker (see the boxed text 'Sir Herbert Baker'), who was responsible for many of the best public buildings built immediately after the Union of South Africa was formed. If you wish to see more of Baker's work, contact **Baker's Dozen** (☎ 344 3197).

The buildings are quite a long walk from the city centre, alternatively catch just about any bus heading east on Church St and walk up through the gardens.

NATIONAL ZOO

About 1km north of the city centre is the zoological gardens (☎ 328 3265, Cnr Paul Kruger & Boom Sts; adult/child R20/14; open 8am-5.30pm in summer, 8am-5pm in winter). The national zoo is an impressive and a pleasant enough spot to while away an afternoon. There is an aquarium here, as well as a decent cafeteria and some areas of lawn. The highlight is probably a cable car that runs up to the top of a kopje that overlooks the city.

There are regular guided evening trips (R20 per person).

VOORTREKKER MONUMENT

A 'holy ground' for many Afrikaners is the enormous Voortrekker Monument (☎ 326 670, Eufees Rd; adult/child R15/10; open 9am-4.45pm daily). It was built between 1938 and 1949 to commemorate the achievements of the Boers, who trekked north over the coastal mountains of the Cape into the heart of the African veld. In particular, it commemorates the Battle of Blood River, during which on 16 Dec 1838, 470 Boers under the command of Andries Pretorius defeated approximately 12,000 Zulus. Supposedly, three trekkers were wounded and 3000 Zulus were killed.

The trekkers went on to found independent republics that in many ways form the genesis of the modern South African state. In terms of drama, determination, courage, vision and tragedy, their story surpasses the history of European colonists (or invaders if you like) anywhere else in the world. Some Afrikaners go one step further, saying that the trek parallels the biblical Exodus, and that the Battle of Blood River was a miracle that can only be explained by divine intervention, proof that the trekkers were a chosen people.

The monument was built at the time of a great resurgence of Afrikaner nationalism. The scars of their defeat in the 1889–1902 Anglo-Boer War were still fresh and the monument provided an emotional focal point for the Afrikaners' ongoing struggle. The building's inauguration in 1949 was attended by 250,000 people. It remains a powerful symbol of the 'white tribe of Africa' and their historical relationship to South Africa.

The edifice is surrounded by a stone wall carved with 64 wagons in a traditional defensive laager (circle). The building itself is a huge stone cube inspired by the ruins of Great Zimbabwe. Inside, a detailed bas-relief tells the story of the trek and of the Battle of Blood River. On 16 December a shaft of light falls on the words Ons vir jou, Suid Africa (We for thee, South Africa). A staircase and elevator lead you to the roof and a great panoramic view of Pretoria and the Transvaal highveld.

Sir Herbert Baker

The day after a mob of angry rail commuters vented their frustration by burning down Pretoria station in February 2001, the gutted shell of the building seemed destined for demolition. It's a measure of the respect that South Africans have for its architect, Sir Herbert Baker, that by the following day money had been found to rebuild the station and talk of demolition was a distant memory.

Born in Kent in 1862, Baker arrived in South Africa 29 years later to visit his brother and his cousin, the latter an admiral with the Royal Navy based in Cape Town. His timing was perfect and through the well-connected admiral he soon formed a friendship with the colony's richest and most powerful man, Cecil John Rhodes.

This carefully cultivated relationship would be a turning point in Baker's life. Rhodes commissioned Baker to redesign his home, and the young architect took the radical step of using the vernacular Cape gable on a double-storey building. The result was the timeless magnificence that is Groote Schuur in Cape Town – Rhodes was delighted.

Baker was prolific and designed an eclectic mix of homes and public buildings for the colony and its wealthiest citizens, many of whom made their fortune on the Witwatersrand goldfields. His credits include a raft of mansions in Johannesburg's Parktown district, the South African Institute for Medical Research in Braamfontein, St George's Cathedral in Cape Town, the Sunnyside and Arcadia cathedrals in Pretoria and the work for which he is best remembered, the classical lines of the imposing Union Buildings.

Baker left for India in 1913, eventually returning to England where he worked on South Africa House in London's Trafalgar Square. He died in 1946 and is buried in Westminster Cathedral.

In the basement there is an excellent small museum that reconstructs the lives of the trekkers, and a magnificent tapestry that almost eclipses the bas-relief above in its combination of naive artistry and tub-thumping chauvinism.

The monument is 3km south of the city and is clearly signposted from the N1 freeway. It is possible to catch the Voortrekkerhoogte or Valhalla bus from Kruger St near the corner of Church Square. Ask the driver to let you off at the entrance road to the monument, from where it is a 10-minute walk uphill.

ORGANISED TOURS

Backpackers will get super service from *Pretoria Backpackers* (☎ 343 9754, fax 343 3524, e ptaback@netactive.co.za, 34 Bourke St, Sunnyside). It organises four-day drive/five-day walking safaris to Kruger National Park for R980/2200 and local tours to an Ndebele village (R180), Pretoria City (R150) and Cullinan Diamond Mine (R140).

Expeditionary Force (☎ 667 2833, 083-281 2646) conducts specialist history tours.

Part of North South Backpackers is *North South Tours* (☎ 362 0989, w www.northsouth backpackers.com), which specialises in full-day tours to the Kromdraai Conservancy (R240), and organises a scenic Pretoria Sundowners trip on request.

Contact the *Atteridgeville/Saulsville Taverners & Shebeen Association* (☎ 373 0446) for trips into Atteridgeville and other townships to see live jazz on the Jazz Tour Route.

SPECIAL EVENTS

The immensely popular **Pretoria Show** is held during the third week of August at the showgrounds. **Oppikoppi Music Festival** is a Woodstock-type bash where local and international rock bands congregate in a celebration of peace, love and music. It was held twice during 2001, over the Easter weekend, in the more intimate original setting of a farm outside Northam, and in August at Fountains Valley. To check the latest dates, cost (about R150) and line-up check w www.oppikoppi.co.za.

PLACES TO STAY – BUDGET
Caravan Parks & Hostels

Fountains Valley Caravan Park (☎ 440 2121, fax 341 3960, Off the M18) Camp sites R49. This is a good facility with plenty of sites, a pool, a restaurant and tennis courts.

Pretoria Backpackers (☎ 343 9754, fax 343 3524, e ptaback@netactive.co.za, 34 Bourke St, Sunnyside) Camp sites R30, dorm beds R50, singles/doubles R100/140. This hostel is a short walk from Esselen St. It's a great travellers' place run by a registered tour guide who's passionate about Pretoria. Like most Pretoria hostels, pickups from JIA are free; drop offs cost R70. There is also an excellent backpackers travel agency.

North South Backpackers (☎ 362 0989, fax 360 0960, e northsouth@mweb.co.za, 355 Glyn St, Hatfield) Camp sites R30, dorm beds R55, doubles R140. This is a friendly, well-organised and comfortable modified suburban house with a swimming pool, bar, veranda and good travel centre. Its location is ideal, being a short walk from Burnett St.

Kia Ora (☎ 322 4803, fax 322 4816, e kia-ora@vakaneo.co.za, 257 Jacob Maré St) Dorm beds R45, rooms from R110. Kia Ora is next to Melrose House and is the only backpacker accommodation near Pretoria station. Entry is through the genial twilight of the Hole in the Wall pub. The Kia Ora has a great balcony for people watching.

Mazuri Backpackers Lodge (☎/fax 343 7782, e bogbrush@pixie.co.za, 503 Reitz St, Sunnyside) Dorm beds R55, doubles R135. This one-man operation is more of an old-style hostel – big on helpful advice but short on luxury. It's clean and homely and serves decent meals. Ask about trips to Venda.

Ah! Simply the Best (☎ 329 0801, fax 329 3928, w www.backpackerslodge.co.za, 292 Talana Ave, Pierneef Ridge) Dorm beds R45, singles/doubles R70/130. This place is big and well-appointed but is a fair hike north-east of town. In its favour are the African-style bar, cheap Afrikaner dinners and doubles with bathroom. Call for a pick-up.

Hotels & Guesthouses

Pretoria Backpacker's Guesthouse (☎ *083-302 1976, 425 Farenden St, Clydesdale)* Doubles R140. This quieter guesthouse is near the famous Loftus Versfeld rugby stadium. It is clean, stylish, comfortable and grossly underpriced. There is a beauty salon at the guesthouse, which could appeal after weeks on an overland truck.

Parkview Hotel (☎ *325 6787, fax 3256 5201,* e *kolmet@mweb.co.za, 179 Zeederberg St, Arcadia)* Singles/doubles R50/70. Opposite the Union Buildings' gardens, this hotel is Spartan but friendly and clean. Rooms are small but each has a shower. Toilets are shared.

Malvern House (☎ *341 7212, fax 341 4430,* W *www.malvernhouse.co.za, 575 Schoeman St, Arcadia)* Singles/doubles R105/150, with breakfast. This large guesthouse is within walking distance of the city and Sunnyside. It's spotlessly clean and comfortable but bathrooms are shared. There are competitive rates, including two meals, for longer stays.

PLACES TO STAY – MID-RANGE

That's It (☎ *344 3404, fax 343 5270,* e *thatsit@icon.co.za, 5 Brecher St, Clydesdale)* Singles/doubles from R160/ 240, with breakfast. Located near the corner of Farenden St, this is a guesthouse in a leafy suburb, not far from Loftus Versfeld. It's a pleasant house with good-sized rooms, a garden and pool.

Hotel 224 (☎ *440 5281, fax 440 3063,* e *hotel224@satic.co.za, Cnr Schoeman & Leyds Sts, Arcadia)* Doubles from R225. This hotel is looking a little worn but it's still fair value. Breakfast is R35.

Manhattan Hotel (☎ *322 7635, fax 320 0721, Cnr Andries & Scheiding Sts)* Rooms R300, suites R400. More upmarket, this is one of the few black-run hotels in town. It's clean, comfortable and handy to Pretoria Station.

Orange Court Lodge (☎ *326 6346, fax 326 2492,* e *orange@lantic.co.za, 540 Vermeulen St)* 1-bedroom apartment from R400, apartment for 4 people R500. On the corner of Hamilton St, this oasis among concrete blocks is an excellent option. It offers serviced apartments (with one, two or three bedrooms), with phone, TV, kitchen and linen in a historic building.

There is a stack of other B&Bs around town. For details, contact the *Bed & Breakfast Association* (☎ *430 3571)*, *Jacana Country Homes* (☎ *346 3550, fax 346 2499)* or the *Hospitality and Touring Association* (☎ *361 3597)*.

PLACES TO STAY – TOP END

La Maison (☎ *430 4341, fax 342 1531,* W *www.lamaison.co.za, 235 Hilda St, Hatfield)* Singles/doubles R415/660 with breakfast. La Maison has beautiful, rooms in an old Pretoria house surrounded by a leafy garden and with a pool. Alan, the owner, is a cordon bleu chef – a glass of wine in the kitchen as he prepares dinner is a delight. A four-course meal is R115 and can be eaten in a room that is a (tasteful) shrine to the Viennese artist, Gustav Klimt.

Victoria Hotel (☎ *323 6054, fax 324 2426, Cnr Paul Kruger & Scheiding Sts)* Suites R335-825, including breakfast. This is the oldest hotel building in Pretoria that is still used for its original purpose. It was built in 1896 and has a gracious Victorian atmosphere. It's no longer associated with the ultraposh Rovos Rail and as a result all but the Presidential Suite are an affordable R435 a double.

Sheraton Pretoria (☎ *429 9999, 0800 994 274, fax 429 9300,* W *www.sheraton.com, 643 Church St, Arcadia)* Doubles from R565. One of the newest and definitely the best hotel in the city. Britain's Queen Liz opted to stay here rather than the official guest residence.

Burgerspark Hotel (☎ *322 7500, fax 322 9429,* e *hotel@burgerspark.co.za, Cnr Van der Walt & Minaar Sts)* Singles/doubles from R344/428. Opposite the well-manicured Burgers Park, this place is big, efficient and central.

Manor Protea Hotel (☎ *362 7077, fax 362 5646,* e *mphotel@satis.co.za, Cnr Burnett & Festival Sts, Hatfield)* Singles/doubles from R380/440. Up an escalator from Burnett St, this hotel is looking a little battered, but it makes up for this with its position. If it's full ask about the *Hatfield Protea Lodge*, across the street.

PLACES TO EAT
Food in Pretoria is generally of a high standard and prices, especially when compared with those in Jo'burg, are very reasonable. There are a few places in the city centre but most people head to Hatfield, Brooklyn and New Muckleneuk, Arcadia or Sunnyside for meals. Most eateries seem to be concentrated along a few streets, so if there's nothing that appeals to you here, just choose a street and cruise.

City Centre
Cafe Riche (☎ 328 3173, 2 Church St) Light meals from R25. This place is the most chic of the town's cafes, and being right on historic Church Square is in an excellent spot to watch people. Although the meals are exquisite, many customers choose to just sit outside and sip coffee or imported beer.

Safika (☎ 320 0274, 357 Visagie St) Meals R25. Looking more like a cafeteria dining room than a restaurant, Safika serves cheap and tasty food from across Africa. The fish curry is delicious.

Sunnyside & Arcadia
A shadow has fallen across Esselen St, Sunnyside, and it's not the eating experience it once was. As white folk have moved east so too have many of the restaurants they used to patronise. What's left is a depressing field of takeaway chains scattered among the pawn and porn shops, with the odd cafe and restaurant thrown in.

A Taste of Africa (☎ 440 1514, Shop 7, Sunnyside Galleries) Meals from R35. Open for lunch & dinner Mon-Sat. Hiding away behind the palm trees, this place serves an interesting mix of African cuisines from across the continent.

Grapevine (☎ 440 6910, 204 Esselen St) A long-time resident of Esselen St, Grapevine is popular for its coffee and cakes.

Giovanni's (☎ 440 8323, 151 Esselen St) Salads from R16, pizzas & pastas from

R25. Upstairs and diagonally opposite the Sunnypark Mall, Giovanni's is fairly pricey but the food is pretty good.

The Secret Garden (☎ 341 3785, 109 Gerhard Moerdyk St) Meals under R20. Part of the ever-changing Oeverzicht Art Village, this place used to be the Pancake Palace, and, appropriately enough, its speciality is still pancakes. You'll find a cocktail bar out the back.

Scattered through Arcadia, north of Sunnyside, are plenty of more upmarket eateries.

Gerhard Moerdyk Restaurant (☎ 344 4856, 752 Park St) Three courses R120. Open for lunch Mon-Fri, dinner nightly. On the corner of Beckett St, Gerhard Moerdyk serves traditional South African dishes such as *waterblommetjie* (a type of mutton dish), *bobotie* (similar to shepherd's pie) when in season, and oxtail. It's classy – there are no prices on the menu. For menu translations, see the boxed text 'Cape Malay Cuisine' in the Facts for the Visitor chapter.

Hatfield
Hatfield is one of the main beneficiaries of the growing security problem in the centre of Pretoria. However, Burnett St is thriving. It's full of restaurants, cafes and bars and is safe at any hour.

Hatfield Plaza, on the corner of Grosvenor and Burnett Sts, has takeaways such as *Anat* (☎ 362 5874), which does cheap, tasty felafel and shwarma. Across the road is *Nando's* (☎ 362 6616) and on the corner is a big *Ocean Basket* (☎ 362 6626) seafood place, with fish and chips from about R25. For the more adventurous diner, go west to *McDonald's* on the corner of Hilda St.

The News Cafe (☎ 362 7190, Hatfield Square, Burnett St), at the entrance to Hatfield Square, is a popular spot for coffee or cocktails and also does decent light meals. A Thai chicken wrap and chips is R18.

Mozarellas (☎ 362 6464, Shop 34, Hatfield Square) Meals from R30. Open noon-10.30pm Sun-Mon, noon-11.30pm Fri-Sat. One of several restaurants and cafes in the very trendy Hatfield Square, Mozarellas does the full range of Italian food and is recommended by locals.

Greenfields (☎ 362 6095, Cnr Hilda & Burnett Sts) Cafe food from R13. This is a perennial favourite with locals, who spend hours here reading papers and drinking coffee.

Mostapha's (☎ 342 3855, 478 Duncan St) Meals from R25. Mostapha is reputed to have cooked for Moroccan royalty – to taste his food you can believe it. A good night for a good price.

Brasserie de Paris (☎ 362 2247, 525 Duncan St) Mains from R45. A little further up Duncan St, this French restaurant is considered one of the best in Pretoria. It's accordingly expensive.

Brooklyn & New Muckleneuk

As the dining and nightlife has moved eastwards, away from a city centre plagued by crime at night, the area around Middle and Fehrsen Sts has become home to a host of good restaurants. The food is generally better and more expensive than at Hatfield.

Crazy Nut Restaurant & Natural Food Centre (☎ 460 2874, Cnr Dey & Bronkhorst Sts, New Muckleneuk) Buffets from R32.50. Open for breakfast, noon-3pm, 5.30pm-8pm. This is the place for vegetarians. It gets rave reviews for its great-value buffets, healthy breakfasts (R35) and bottomless soups (R18).

Villamoura (☎ 346 1650, 273 Middle St) is a Portuguese/Mozambique restaurant specialising in shellfish. Meat dishes start at R70; prawns at R130. It's an expensive place where diners dress up.

Khum Thai (☎ 012 460 3199, 541 Fehrsen St) Meals from R25. The service here is super-friendly and, for the price, the food is a bargain.

Crawdaddy's (☎ 460 0889, Shop 3, Brooklyn Piazza, Cnr Middle & Dey Sts) Meals from R40. Easily Pretoria's best steakhouse, half-kilo rumps are R45, a kilo of lamb chops goes for R55 and all meals come with salad and chips, rice or a baked potato.

Blue Crane (☎ 460 7615, Melk St, New Muckleneuk) Meals from R40. Open for breakfast, lunch & dinner Tues-Sat, breakfast & lunch only Sun-Mon. The Blue

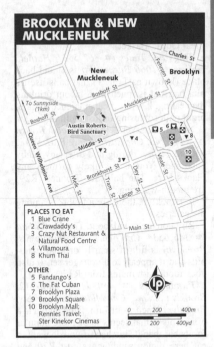

Crane is part of the Austin Roberts Bird Sanctuary – the Roberts of the famous bird books. The restaurant overlooks a lake that is the breeding site for the endangered blue crane, South Africa's national bird. It does Afrikaner *potjie* (a variety of meat and vegetables stewed in an iron pot) meals in season. Otherwise try the mango veal cutlet (R58). The pub is great at sundown. The entrance to the restaurant is off Melk St, which is a right turn off Middle St as you head west.

ENTERTAINMENT
Bars & Clubs

There are several bars and nightspots in trendy Hatfield, catering for all types.

McGinty's (☎ 362 7176, Hatfield Square) Open 11am-late. This is a very popular Irish-style pub.

After the periodic re-branding that seems to befall all nightclubs, the Replay Cafe has returned as *Steelworks* (☎ 362 6623, 1st floor, Cnr Burnett & Grosvenor Sts). It's the last late-night stop on the Hatfield circuit (near Ocean Basket).

Tings an' Times (☎ 362 5537, Hatfield Galleries, 1066 Burnett St) is a laid-back place (known as T 'n' T) that calls itself a pita bar, but is much more about drinking than eating. It offers great ambience for late-night philosophising or just chilling.

Near Loftus Versfeld, **Eastwood Tavern** (☎ 344 0243, Cnr Eastwood & Park Sts) is packed before, during and after any rugby encounter. You're not likely to meet any blacks here. The half-kilo T-bones (R29) are mouth-watering.

In Brooklyn, there are a few bars among the eateries.

Right on the roundabout, **The Fat Cuban** (☎ 346 6534, Cnr Fehrsen & Middle Sts, Brooklyn) is full of smartly dressed trend-oids and it appeals to a younger set. It also does food, with mains from R35.

Fandango's (☎ 460 1124, Shop 12, Brooklyn Square, Cnr Middle & Veale Sts, Brooklyn) Open from 7am. Fandango's is a trendy place that seems to be more popular for its bar than its kitchen. If you do want to eat here, fancy sandwiches cost R20 and pastas R29.

Oppikoppi Bar (☎ 082-499 7668) Open 10am-10pm Mon-Thur, 10am-late Fri-Sat. On Magasyn Hill (opposite the Voortrekker Monument), this is one of the best-located and safest pubs in Pretoria – it's owned and operated by serving police officers. The views over the city are great, particularly at sunset, and a DIY braai costs R30.

Live Music

With so many students calling Pretoria home, you'd expect there to be more quality live music than there is.

Blue Note Jazz Cafe (☎ 362 988, 525 Duncan St, Hatfield) Open Fri-Sat only. The Blue Note, located above the Brasserie de Paris (see Places to Eat earlier in this section), has a great range of black jazz acts.

The successful chain **Cool Runnings** (☎ 362 0100, 1075 Burnett St, Hatfield) is alive and kicking in Pretoria. Specialising in reggae it attracts travellers, students and trendy locals alike.

Once you're through the thorough security check you'll find **Drop Zone** (Upstairs, Hatfield Square) essentially a disco. However; occasional one-man bands enliven proceedings. Drop Zone is the pick-up joint of choice for Pretoria's student population.

These days, most of the live entertainment in Sunnyside involves disrobing. However, there are still a couple of decent places hiding along Esselen St.

Voodoo Lounge (☎ 072-240 1116, 47 Esselen St) is one of the best live music venues in Pretoria, jamming 3000 people into six bars and onto three dance floors. It attracts big-name DJs and mainly black bands.

At **London Tavern** (☎ 341 4182, Cnr Jeppe & Esselen Sts) drink cheap beer and watch members of the one-man-band fraternity ply their trade on Wednesday, Friday and Saturday nights.

The surrounding townships, especially Mamelodi and Atteridgeville have plenty of shebeens; these are best visited with a black friend. It's estimated that Gauteng has over 36,000 shebeens.

Mamelodi's **Mississippi** (☎ 801 1145) shebeen is a lively venue that specialises in jazz and blues. Most shows are held on weekends.

Justice 'JaJa' Seema's (☎ 373 0446, Ramkatsane St, Atteridgeville) still attracts good jazz acts from near and far and is an integral part of the Jazz Tour Route (see Organised Tours earlier in this section).

Theatres

State Theatre (☎ 322 1665, Cnr Prinsloo & Church Sts) was designed by Hans and Roelf Botha, who also dreamt up the JG Strijdom Square. This huge theatre complex hosts quite a range of high-culture productions (including opera, music, ballet and theatre) in its five theatres: the Arena, Studio, Opera, Drama and Momentum. Book tickets at the theatre or through **Computicket** (☎ 328 4040). Check local newspapers for listings.

Cinemas

There are several enormous cinema complexes in Pretoria. The *Pretoria News* lists screenings daily.

Ster Kinekor Cinemas (☎ 346 3435, Brooklyn Mall, Fehrsen St, Brooklyn) is the largest cinema complex offering mainstream releases on 16 screens and independent films on a further four.

Sterland (☎ 341 7568, Cnr Pretorius & Beatrix Sts, Arcadia) has 13 cinemas and possibly the most horrible fluorescent decor in Africa.

South-east of the city, past the N1 Ring Rd, you'll find a drive-in cinema (☎ 348 8766) on the rooftop of Menlyn Park Shopping Centre car park (R40 per car).

SHOPPING
Markets

On Saturday and Sunday a flea market is held in Sunnypark Mall on Esselen St in Sunnyside.

The *Sunday flea market* (☎ 342 3769, Hatfield Plaza car park, Burnett St, Hatfield; open 9am-4.30pm) has all the usual flea market stuff, as well as a few African items you just can't import from China.

Boeremark (*Farmers' market*; Meiring Naude Rd, opposite the CSIR complex) Open 6am-8am Sat. Out of town, east of the centre, this market is the place to find fresh produce and old-style Boers, with traditional food and music.

Arts & Crafts

Magnolia Dell *Moonlight Market* (☎ 811 0552, Magnolia Dell, Queen Wilhelmina Ave, New Muckleneuk) Last Friday evening of the month. If your stay in Pretoria happens to coincide with this market you'll find it a charming event. Stalls sell an array of mostly local crafts with origins in both Africa and Europe.

There are also some interesting craft stalls along Boom St to the west of Paul Kruger St, near the zoo, with particularly good beadwork. Bargain hard.

The best deals are to be found at the Hartbeespoort Dam market on the road to Sun City. It's huge and cheap.

Camping Equipment

There are camping and outdoor stores in each of Pretoria's malls.

Camping & Outdoor Living (☎ 440 1910, 86 Greef St, Sunnyside), near the corner of Kotze, is the place to repair backpacks, zips and tents.

GETTING THERE & AWAY
Bus

Most national and international bus services commence in Pretoria before picking up in Jo'burg, unless the general direction is north. Most buses leave from the Pretoria train station forecourt (building 1928).

Most **Translux** (☎ 315 2333), **Intercape** (☎ 654 4114) and **Greyhound** (☎ 323 1154) services running from Jo'burg to Durban, the south coast and Cape Town originate in Pretoria. Translux and **City to City** (☎ 315 8069) services running north up the N1 also stop here – see Getting There & Away under Jo'burg earlier in this chapter.

Translux, Greyhound and Intercape fares from Pretoria are identical to those from Jo'burg regardless of the one-hour difference in time. If you only want to go between the two cities it will cost R25.

Baz Bus (☎ 021-439 2323) will pick up and drop off at Pretoria hostels.

North Link Tours (☎ 323 0379) runs from the 1928 building, Pretoria train station, north to Pietersburg, Louis Trichardt and Phalaborwa.

Zimbabwe Travel (☎ 543 1236) runs the Zimbus between Jo'burg, Pretoria and Bulawayo for R250, or to Victoria Falls for R450. It picks up at the BP petrol station on the corner of Charles St and Atterbury Rd (south-east of the city centre).

Train

The historic Pretoria train station was burned down by angry commuters in February 2001 and so some services have been moved to the nearby Bosman St station. However, most trains are still coming and going from Pretoria station, including the *Blue Train*. The station is due to be rebuilt but it's anyone's guess when the job will be finished.

Pretoria train station is about a 20-minute walk from the city centre. Buses run along Paul Kruger St to Church Square, the main local bus terminal.

Metro Warnings first: There have been many robberies at gunpoint on the Metro, and we don't recommend travelling between Pretoria and Jo'burg by Metro. A 1st-class train ticket to Jo'burg on the Metro system is R15. The journey takes over an hour. From Monday to Friday, trains run every half hour early in the morning then hourly until 10pm. On weekends, trains run about every 1½ hours.

Main Line For long-distance train services use **Main Line train Main Line** (☎ 334 8470, 086-000 8888, **W** www.spoornet.co.za). This trip between Pretoria and Jo'burg will cost R25/35 in 2nd/1st class and is considered to be safe.

Main Line trains running through Pretoria are the *Trans Karoo* (Pretoria to Kimberley and Cape Town, daily) and the *Komati* (Jo'burg to Komatipoort via Nelspruit, daily). There is also the *Bosvelder*, which runs north via Pietersburg to the Zimbabwe border daily. Fares from Pretoria for 2nd/1st class are R10/15 less or more than from Jo'burg, depending on your direction of travel (see Train under Getting There & Away in the Jo'burg section for the 'name train' services).

Car
The larger local and international companies are represented in Pretoria; see Getting There and Away in the Jo'burg section for the toll-free numbers. For the best value try **Swans Rent a Car** (☎ 082-658 0078, **W** www .swans.co.za); if you book ahead of time this company delivers.

GETTING AROUND
To/From the Airport
Get You There (☎ 346 3175) operates shuttle buses between JIA and Pretoria. The company does not have a set timetable but runs day and night about every hour, charging R85 to/from hostels and hotels. **Pretoria**

Airport Shuttle (☎ 322 0904) leaves from the Protea Hotel (on the corner of Visagie and Van der Walt Sts in central Pretoria) on the hour between 6am and 10pm. It costs R75 (the same if they pick up from a hostel) or R90 to go to/from Hatfield. Most hostels will pick up for free if you call ahead.

Bus & Minibus Taxi
There is an extensive network of local buses. The main bus terminal and the inquiry office (☎ 308 0839) are on the southeastern corner of Church Square. A booklet of timetables and route maps is available from the inquiry office or, for some strange reason, from pharmacies. Fares range from R5 to R7, depending on the distance. Some services, including the No 3 bus to Sunnyside, run until about 10.30pm – unusually late for South Africa. Other handy buses include Nos 5 and 8, which run between Church Square and Brooklyn via Burnett St in Hatfield.

Minibus taxis run just about everywhere and the standard fare is about R4. You won't see many white faces on these buses, but that doesn't mean they're unsafe. Seek local advice before you ride.

Taxi
Taxis are relatively inexpensive – budget on R5 per kilometre. There are ranks on the corner of Church & Van der Walt Sts and on the corner of Pretorius and Paul Kruger Sts. Or you could call **Rixi Taxis** (☎ 0800 325 807).

AROUND PRETORIA
About 50km west of Pretoria you find De Wildt Cheetah Research Centre, which is worth a visit. See the boxed text 'The Fragile Cheetah' in the North-West Province chapter for details.

Smuts' House Museum
General JC Smuts was a brilliant scholar, Boer general, politician and international statesman. He was an architect of the Union of South Africa, and was the country's prime minister from 1919 to 1924 and from 1939 to 1948.

AROUND PRETORIA

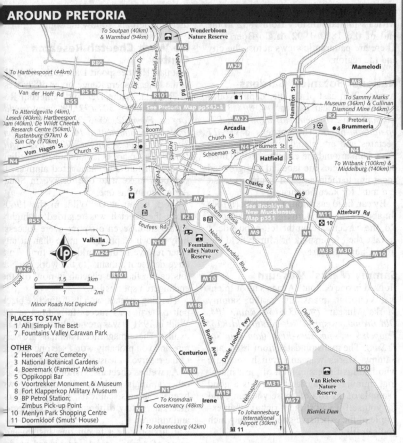

PLACES TO STAY
1 Ah! Simply The Best
7 Fountains Valley Caravan Park

OTHER
2 Heroes' Acre Cemetery
3 National Botanical Gardens
4 Boeremark (Farmers' Market)
5 Oppikoppi Bar
6 Voortrekker Monument & Museum
8 Fort Klapperkop Military Museum
9 BP Petrol Station;
   Zimbus Pick-up Point
10 Menlyn Park Shopping Centre
11 Doornkloof (Smuts' House)

Smuts' home was once known as Doorn-kloof *(☎ 667 1176, Nelmapius Rd, Irene; admission R10, free to garden; open 9.30am-1pm, 1.30pm-4.30pm Mon-Fri, 9.30am-1pm, 1.30pm-5pm Sat & Sun)* and has been turned into an excellent museum. It is well worth visiting if you have private transport and are travelling to or from Pretoria. The wood and iron building was originally a British officers' mess at Middelburg but Smuts bought it and re-erected it on his 1600-hectare property at Irene, 16km south of Pretoria. Surrounded by a wide veranda and shaded by trees, it still has a warm family atmosphere,

and it gives a vivid insight into Smuts' amazing life.

Unfortunately, there is no access by public transport. The house is signposted from both the N14 freeway (R28) and the R21. The most direct route from Pretoria is along Louis Botha Ave to Irene.

Fort Klapperkop Military Museum

The best-preserved of four forts that were built after the Jameson Raid is Fort Klapperkop *(Johann Rissik Dr; admission R5; open 10am-3.30pm)*. This place is 6km south of the city. A shot was never fired from here

GAUTENG

in anger, but it now illustrates South Africa's military history from 1852 to the end of the 1899–1902 Anglo-Boer War. There are panoramic views across the city and the region.

National Botanical Gardens

Around 9km east of the city centre you'll find the botanical gardens (☎ 804 3200, Cussonia Ave, Brummeria; admission R7; open 6am-6pm). The gardens cover 77 hectares and are planted with indigenous flora from around the country. The 20,000-odd plant species are labelled and grouped according to their region of origin, so a visit is a must for keen botanists.

By car, head east along Church St (R104) for about 8km, then turn right into Cussonia Rd; the gardens are on the left-hand side.

Take the Meyerspark or Murrayfield bus from Church Square.

Sammy Marks' Museum

Housed in one of South Africa's most splendid Victorian mansions is the Sammy Marks' Museum (☎ 803 6158, Route 104, Old Bronkhorstspruit Rd; adult/child R13/7; open 9am-4pm Tues-Fri, 10am-4pm Sat & Sun). The mansion dates from 1884, and Sammy Marks was an English magnate who had his fingers in a lot of pies: industrial, mining and agricultural. It is a good example of the sort of house you can build for yourself if you strike it rich (and an example of the expensive goodies with which you can fill it).

Cullinan Diamond Mine

After visiting Sammy Marks' Museum, go north to historic Cullinan, home to Cullinan Diamond Mine (☎ 734 0081, 083-261 3550; R30 guided surface tours 10.30am daily, 2pm Mon-Fri), one of the biggest and most productive diamond-bearing kimberlite pipes in the world. It has produced three of the largest diamonds ever found. The largest, the 3106-carat Cullinan, as it was called, was 11cm by 6cm in rough form and was presented to King Edward VII.

Bookings are recommended for the guided surface tours. To get here, take the N4 east and the Hans Strijdom off-ramp, then turn left and follow the signs.

De Wildt Cheetah Research Centre

Just past Hartbeespoort Dam in the foothills of the Magaliesberg Range, about 50km west of Pretoria, is the De Wildt Cheetah Research Centre (☎ 504 1921, W www.dewildt .org.za, Farm 22, R513 Pretoria North Rd, tours by appointment at 10.30am & 1.30pm Tues, Thur, Sat & Sun for R90 or R130 with lunch). This place is famous for its breeding success of rare and endangered animals. If you only make it to one reserve in South Africa, go to this one.

Work began at De Wildt in the 1960s when the cheetah was regarded as highly endangered. Seven offspring were successfully bred in captivity – more than at any other reserve in the world at the time. To a large degree it's thanks to the work done at this centre that the cheetah is now off the endangered species list.

The king cheetah, with its distinctive black pelt pattern, was successfully bred at De Wildt in 1981; it was previously thought to be extinct. These magnificent animals are very rare and you probably won't see one outside of the reserve, at least not this close up!

As well as cheetahs, visitors can also see other animals such as wild dogs, brown hyenas, servals, caracals, honey badgers, meerkats, a few different antelope species and vultures.

Tours provide a fascinating insight into some of Africa's most endangered predators. In an open truck you'll see cheetahs of different age groups being fed, and learn about their precarious existence in the wild. Bookings are essential and the tours are popular.

To get to De Wildt from Pretoria (via Hartbeespoort Dam) take the R5131 west for 34km – the centre is on the left about half a kilometre off the main road.

Lesedi Cultural Village

For a day out of town and a dose of culture why not check out the Lesedi Cultural Village (☎ 205 1394, 0800-119 000, e marketing@

lesedi.com; on the R512 between Lanseria & Broederstroom; open 11.30am & 4.30pm lunch & dinner), which is very touristy but gets a lot of good reports from readers.

Lesedi means 'Place of Light' and there's plenty of dancing, singing and traditional African meals; Xhosa, Ndebele, Pedi, Zulu and Sotho cultures are all represented.

Lesedi is south-west of Pretoria and north of Lanseria airport. It's a good idea to book if you're going for the full meal and show. Accommodation is also available.

North-West Province

The North-West Province is a region of wide, hot plains. It was once covered entirely in bushveld (open grassland) and thorn trees but it is now an important agricultural region. Diamonds were discovered here in the 1870s and there was an enormous rush to the fields around Lichtenburg. Mining is still important here, and the world's largest platinum mines are near Rustenburg.

As part of the apartheid regime's Homelands policy, the Tswana were relocated to Bophuthatswana (Bop); the North-West Province takes in most of the area once covered by this fragmented creation.

The Voortrekkers fought a hard battle to survive the vicissitudes of nature and the political turmoil of the region. Their descendants are a tough and uncompromising lot – many towns today remain Afrikaner Weerstandsbeweging (AWB; right-wing Afrikaner movement) strongholds.

Although some of the region's towns have interesting histories, today they're generally uninspiring places with little to see and do. The places to head for include Sun City, a fabulous kitsch creation that simply revels in its tackiness and the beautiful and yet under-rated Pilanesberg National Park.

RUSTENBURG
☎ 014 • postcode 0299

Rustenburg is a large and prosperous town (with a distinct Voortrekker feel), founded in 1841, which lies at the western edge of the Magaliesberg Range; Thlabane is the huge black township nearby. Rustenburg is about 115km north-west of Johannesburg (Jo'burg), at the centre of a thriving agricultural region and near two huge platinum mines.

On the way into town, you'll find the well-stocked **information centre** (☎ 597 0904; open 7.30am-5pm Mon-Fri, Sat morning) between Plein and Van Staden Sts. There is also an art gallery here and an arts and crafts shop.

Highlights

- Laze around Sun City, one of apartheid's glittering icons, now enjoyed by all sorts of people in the new South Africa.

- Scale extinct volcanoes and view an impressive array of wildlife in Pilanesberg National Park.

- Gain insight into traditional cultures at Lotlamoreng Dam & Cultural Village.

- View endangered wildlife in the riverine forest of Madikwe Game Reserve.

Things to See & Do

Paul Kruger's farm **Boekenhoutfontein** (☎ 573 3218; admission free; open 8am-5pm Tues-Sat, 3pm-5pm Sun), just to the north of town, is worth visiting. A small section of the farm and several buildings have been preserved. These include a pioneer cottage built in 1841; the house that Kruger built for himself in 1863, which now serves as a coffee shop; and the main family homestead built in 1875, which is a fine example of Colesberg Cape Dutch style. There is also a museum here, which concentrates on the early Boer settlers.

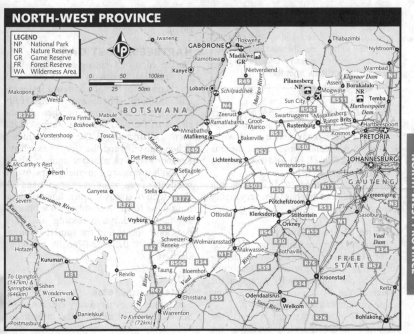

NORTH-WEST PROVINCE

LEGEND
NP National Park
NR Nature Reserve
GR Game Reserve
FR Forest Reserve
WA Wilderness Area

Places to Stay

The information centre has a list of guesthouses and B&Bs in town.

Tom's Lodge (☎ 592 0435, 51 Heystek St) Singles/doubles R125/180. Tom's is a convenient overnight stop, reminiscent of a block of flats. Rooms are compact and tidy.

Traveller's Inn (☎ 592 7658, fax 594 0635, 99 Leyds St) Singles/doubles R125/250, breakfast R25. This guesthouse is quite lively and has a good bar, open every night. There are also lock-up garages for cars.

Cashane Hotel (☎ 592 8541, 66 Steen St) Singles/doubles B&B R180/260, double only R170. A solid place, but a bit rundown, it's probably the cheapest central option.

Joan's B&B (☎ 533 3086, 61 Wildevy Ave, Protea Park) Singles/doubles R120/200. Joan's is a good old-fashioned B&B; the owners serve a hearty breakfast with a smile.

Ananda Country Lodge (☎ 597 3875, fax 597 1639) Singles/doubles R180/310. Ananda is 7km from town and close to a spectacular, looming kloof (ravine). There are braai (barbecue) facilities and there is also a great swimming pool. The comfortable rooms in this thatched hotel are well worth the cost; there are also camping and caravan facilities available.

Bushwillows B&B (☎ 537 2333) Rooms R130 per person. Some 12km from Rustenburg, off the R24, this tranquil B&B is set in natural bush, and the owner (an artist) knows a lot about South African wildlife.

Places to Eat

There are a number of fast-food places that cater to through traffic, including *KFC* and *Nando's* on Van Staden St.

In the Waterfall Mall, off the R30 around 3km south of town, you'll find most of the fast-food chains and a couple of decent restaurants. If you need that caffeine kickstart, *House of Coffee* and *Brazilian* are both here, serving fine coffee, and the former also does good cheap meals.

Warning

Precautions should be taken against malaria during the summer months. Also, as many of the dams and rivers carry bilharzia, don't swim in them or drink from them.

Royal Dutchman (☎ 537 3626) Starters R17-25, mains R35-50. The Royal Dutchman has a great menu and a good wine. Seafood is particularly good here; there is grilled monkfish (R48) and the pickled herring is superb (R19).

Karl's Bauernstube (☎ 537 2128) is a German restaurant that has been very highly recommended.

Getting There & Away

Intercape has a service running from Jo'burg/Pretoria to Gaborone (Botswana) via Rustenburg daily; it also returns from Gaborone daily. The bus stops at the BP garage on the corner of Van Staden and Smit Sts, from where you can catch a taxi into town.

The main minibus taxi rank is west of the corner of Van Staden and Malan Sts, on the Sun City side of town.

THE MAGALIESBERG RANGE

The 120km-long Magaliesberg Range, north of the N4, swings in a half moon from Rustenburg to Hartbeespoort Dam. The region has attractive mountain scenery and some good walks.

At the western end of the Magaliesberg Range is **Rustenburg Nature Reserve** (☎ 533 2050; admission R15; open 8am-4pm daily). The area is dominated by rocky ridges and wooded ravines, and lies to the south of Rustenburg; it is clearly signposted. There is an enormous number of plant species, including quite a few that are both rare and protected. You may see shy predators such as leopards, hyenas, black-backed jackals and small antelopes.

Hunter's Rest Hotel (☎ 537 2140, fax 537 2661) Full board from R345 per person. This is an attractive resort in the Magaliesberg Range, 14km south of Rustenburg. There is a big swimming pool and

extensive sports facilities, including horse riding.

HARTBEESPOORT DAM

On the edge of Gauteng and North-West Province, Hartbeespoort Dam is the watersports resort for Pretoria and, to a lesser extent, Jo'burg. There are several fully fledged holiday towns perched on the slopes of the Magaliesberg Range on the north-eastern side of the dam, including Schoemansville and the trendy, expensive Kosmos. They're pleasant enough places and both towns are extremely attractive to residents of nearby cities over summer. For short-term overseas visitors, however, visiting these towns probably isn't a priority. At the Damdoryn Crossing in Hartbeespoort you'll find the **tourist information office** (☎ 012-253 0266, ⓔ info@infoshop.co.za).

SUN CITY

☎ 014 • postcode 0316

Sun City is the extraordinary creation of Mr Sol Kerzner (Sol means 'sun' in Spanish). This large 'entertainment' complex, based around a couple of big architectural spaces full of slot (poker) machines, is dominated by the kitsch but undeniably imposing Palace of the Lost City.

Sun City has been wholeheartedly embraced by the black population, who flock there on weekends. One of the nicest things you'll see these days in the 'new' South Africa is the mix of people on the beach at the Valley of the Waves. Sol Kerzner no longer runs the place, because he has undertaken a new venture: Atlantis Paradise in the Bahamas. His interests have all been sold off to people such as pop star Michael Jackson – if you're really lucky you may spot the 'single-gloved one' and llama on the beach.

All this extravagance in the middle of one of the poorest corners of the country is, at best, incongruous. Sun City has, nonetheless, been fantastically successful. Losers at the tables can console themselves with the thought that they are helping to pay over 3500 salaries.

Orientation & Information

The car park for day visitors is at the entrance, about 2km from the entertainment centre. An elevated 'sky' train shuttles from the car park to Sun City Cabanas, Sun City Hotel, The Cascades and the entertainment centre.

There's a **welcome centre** (☎ 557 1544; *open 9am-8pm Sun-Thur, 9am-midnight Fri-Sat)* where you can get maps and information at the entrance to the entertainment centre, right next to the bus station.

Admission to Sun City, which is R50, gives you R30 in 'Sunbucks' (one Sunbuck is equal to R15); these are used as currency within the resort for activities or meals. One or two of the attractions have separate entry charges, notably the Valley of the Waves, which costs another R50.

Things to See & Do

The spectacular centrepiece of Sun City is **The Lost City**, an extraordinary piece of kitsch that would be fun if it didn't claim to symbolise African heritage. It has less to do with African heritage than Disneyland Paris, has to do with French heritage. As well as some Disneyesque attractions, there's also the **Valley of the Waves** where there is, not surprisingly, a large-scale wave-making machine – perhaps the best reason for non-gamblers to come here. The kids can enjoy 'tubing' the Lazy River, crossing the Bridge of Time, riding the water slides and, in the summer, Kamp Kwena activities.

In the heart of The Lost City is The Palace of the Lost City, a hotel that could inspire hallucinations – unfortunately you can't wander around much unless you're a guest, and you can't be a guest unless you are wealthy. The lucky get to sip cocktails in the sumptuous Tusk Bar and Lounge.

A round of golf at the superb **Gary Player Country Club** costs about R250 for 18 holes if you're a resident, or R280 for day visitors. A caddy is compulsory and will cost at least R75. Club hire is about R80. Even more expensive is the **Lost City Golf Course**, where golf carts are mandatory. Backpackers who have played the 'Player' course love it, but moan about the big tips that are

expected by caddies inured to more well-heeled visitors.

It is worth taking a tour of the **botanical gardens** of Sun City (R15 or one Sunbuck). The 1½-hour tour focuses on several habitats; a plant and bird species list from the welcome centre is very useful. Near the main entrance is **Kwena Gardens Crocodile Sanctuary** (R25), which is home to over 7000 crocs. **Waterworld**, on the shores of a large artificial lake, has facilities for parasailing (R189), water-skiing, jet-skiing (R110) and windsurfing.

A new attraction at Sun City, and well worth a visit, is the **Birds of Prey Rehabilitation Centre**. It was developed to look after injured birds such as eagles, hawks, owls and falcons. Every day at 10am and 4pm there are sessions with demonstrations of the birds' hunting prowess. A falcon hurtling to earth at 200km an hour from 300 metres is an impressive sight! The sessions are very educational and may well improve your understanding of these majestic birds in the wild, particularly useful if you plan on visiting any national parks. The sessions are free, but a donation of R20 will be gratefully received.

A **balloon flight** is also on offer for those who have won on the tables and can afford R1750 for an hour's flight; contact **Gametrackers Wildlife Adventures** (☎ 557-5830).

Places to Stay & Eat

All these hotels can be contacted or booked through *Sun City* (☎ 557 1000, fax 557 1902) or *Sun International central reservations* (☎ 011-780 7800).

Sun City Cabanas has standard rooms from R890. This is the cheapest alternative; it's laid-back and aimed at family groups. Though it has its own pool and adventure playground, guests can also make use of all the facilities in Sun City Hotel. The pleasant twin rooms are fully equipped with all of life's little luxuries.

Sun City Hotel has standard rooms from R1340. This is the oldest and cheapest of the five-star hotels. It's by no means shabby, however, and cheap is hardly the right word. It's the most lively of the hotels, with gambling facilities on the premises, as well as a number of restaurants, an enormous pool and bar, a disco and nightclubs.

The Cascades has rooms from R1455. The Cascades has been displaced by The Palace of the Lost City as the most luxurious hotel in the complex, although it too is surrounded by elaborate landscaped grounds with swimming pool and waterfalls. Standard rooms are easily described as palatial.

The Palace of the Lost City has standard rooms from R2470 and suites from R3590. The Palace is totally opulent and would overwhelm anyone other than the world's 10 richest people.

All the hotels have a selection of restaurants. *Palm Terrace* in Sun City Cabanas is the cheapest. There are plenty of fast-food *eateries* and a number of reasonably priced *restaurants* representing a variety of cuisines (in the entertainment centre). Expect to pay from R50 to R70 for a basic meal.

The best of the bars in the entertainment complex is *Trader Horn's*, which has a giant video screen.

If these places are too expensive (and you have your own transport), consider staying at Pilanesberg National Park (see following) or make Sun City a day trip only.

Getting There & Away

Air Tiny Pilanesberg airport (☎ 552 1261) once gloried in the name 'Pilanesberg international airport', when it was the home of Bop Air. It's about 9km north-east of the Sun City complex. **SA Airlink** (☎ 011-978 1111, 552 1844) operates daily flights from Jo'burg (R490). **SA Express** (☎ 021-936 1111) has a direct service from Cape Town, which costs R1505 one way.

Bus Sun City Buses (☎ 657 3382) has buses on weekends from the Thlabane Sun hotel (just outside Rustenburg) to Sun City (R30).

Car If you are at a hostel and on a tight budget, get a group together, hire a car and tour both Sun City and Pilanesberg National Park in the same day.

Surprisingly, the Sun City complex is poorly signposted, so navigators will really need to concentrate to not miss it. From Jo'burg it's a two-hour drive. The most straightforward route is via Rustenburg and Boshoek on the R565; a clever navigator could make it shorter via the R556. Both roads run north from the N4.

PILANESBERG NATIONAL PARK

This is a superb national park (☎ 014-555 5351, adult/child R20/10, R15 per vehicle). It lies just north of Sun City, so it is easy to combine a visit to both. It protects over 500 sq km of an unusual complex of extinct volcanoes, and is the fourth-largest national park in South Africa. The countryside is attractive, with rocky outcrops, ridges and craters, and is mostly covered in sparse woodland. There are two vegetation zones, Kalahari *thornveld* (vegetation characterised by thorns) and sour bushveld, and the atmosphere is quintessentially African. Pilanesberg has been described by some as a better wildlife viewing experience than Kruger National Park.

Until the 1970s Pilanesberg was farmed, but was subsequently recognised as an ideal site for a national park, partly because the hills provide a natural barrier to the more densely populated surrounding plains. Today the park is once again home to extensive populations of many of Africa's most impressive animals. There are white and black rhinos, elephants, giraffes, hippos, buffalos, a wide variety of bucks (including sables, elands, kudus and gemsboks), zebras, leopards, lions, jackals, hyenas and even cheetahs (yes, the Big Five are all there). Since early 2000, for the first time in decades, African wild dogs can be seen again in the Pilanesberg National Park. In an on-going effort to reestablish this highly endangered carnivore across South Africa, nine wild dogs were translocated to Pilanesberg after being caught on farmland (where they risked being shot). The region also has a diverse population of birds – over 300 species have been recorded.

There is an excellent 100km network of gravel roads, hides and picnic spots, and some good value accommodation. Since it is no more than 25km from one end of the

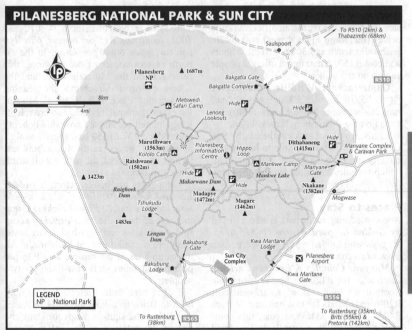

PILANESBERG NATIONAL PARK & SUN CITY

park to the other, it is easy to cover the range of different environments in the park and to see a wide variety of animals. To do any real justice to it, however, you need a full day. On no account miss the viewpoints over the crater from Lenong Lookout.

Orientation & Information
Signposting in this area, even around Sun City and the park itself, is less than terrific. However, you can't really go wrong once you get to Sun City because the Pilanesberg are the only significant hills in the region. Enter from the direction of Sun City using either the Bakubung gate to the west (via R556) or the Manyane gate to the north-east (via the R556 and R510 if you're coming from Pretoria and Jo'burg).

The Pilanesberg Range forms four concentric mountain rings, with Mankwe Lake at the centre of an extinct 1200-million-year-old crater. Information and useful sketch maps are available at the main Manyane

gate, where overnight visitors must enter and report to the reception office. The Manyane gate reception office is open 24 hours.

Gates into the park proper (beyond the Manyane gate) are open from:

months	gates open	gates close
November to February	5.30am	7pm
March to April	6am	6.30pm
May to August	6.30am	6pm
September to October	6am	6.30pm

There is an information centre with an interpretative display and shop in an old magistrates' court in the centre of the park; the shop sells curios, refreshments and a range of basic food items.

Activities
There are now loads of activities in the park available through an information office just

inside the Manyane gate or a booth just outside the Manyane reception office. Wildlife drives (including night drives) cost R120; bushwalks leave at 5.30am, last three hours and cost R150. A maximum of eight people can go on the walks.

Gametrackers Wildlife Adventures (☎ 557 5830; tours at 5.30am, 4pm & 7pm) runs 2½-hour open-vehicle tours (R140) into the adjoining Pilanesberg National Park.

Lastly, if you got lucky at the nearby Sun City casino you will be able to burn a few rand on an early morning balloon flight, which includes breakfast back at the camp and costs R1750.

Places to Stay

Accommodation in the park is administered by *Golden Leopard Resorts* (☎ 555 6135, e goldres@iafrica.com, w www.golden leopard.co.za).

Manyane Complex & Caravan Park has camp sites for R120 for up to four people (more in the high season); safari tents cost R200; and chalets for two people cost from R425. Near the Manyane gate, this complex is excellent, thoughtfully designed and laid out, and has high quality facilities. There's a small pool, a bar, a shop with a reasonable range of food items and a decent restaurant. Although it isn't cheap, it's only about 20km from Sun City and is a lot cheaper than staying there.

Bakgatla Complex has camp sites for R120 and five-bed chalets for R580. This is a smaller camp to the north-west of Manyane gate and has limited facilities. It's probably only a good option if Manyane is full.

Safari camps in the park include *Mankwe Camp*, *Kololo Camp* and *Metswedi Safari Camp*. At the time of research they were all closed and it was unclear if and when they would be reopening. Contact the reception office at the Manyane gate for more information. If they have reopened, they may have cheaper accommodation available.

Time-share resorts in the park include *Kwa Maritane Lodge*, *Bakubung Lodge* and *Tshukudu Lodge*. The future of these resorts was also unclear; inquire about their availability at Manyane gate.

BORAKALALO NATURE RESERVE

This is an excellent reserve (☎ 012-729 1008; admission R15 per person, plus R10 per car; open 6am-7pm daily). In the far north-eastern corner of the province, this reserve is on the Moratele River and the Klipvoor Dam, and lives up to the meaning of its name: 'Place of Relaxation'. Most of the original animal inhabitants were relentlessly hunted out and are now slowly being reintroduced. With 350 bird species as well as leopards, otters, aardwolfs, zebras and jackals now resident, the park is well worth a day trip from Gauteng.

Camp sites are booked through *Golden Leopard Resorts* (☎ 014-555 6135, e gold res@iafrica.com). At *Pitjani Fishing Camp* there are 25 camp sites; at *Moretele* you can find camp sites and four-bed safari tents; and there are safari tents at *Phudufudu*. All the camp sites in the reserve cost R38 per person, and safari tents cost R180 for two people.

To get here from Pretoria and Jo'burg head to Brits, then take the R511 to Assen and follow the signs to Klipvoor Dam; the way to the entrance of Borakalalo Nature Reserve is signposted.

ZEERUST

☎ 018 • postcode 2865

The countryside around Zeerust is rather attractive hilly bushveld which flattens out as you head south-west to Mafikeng. Zeerust's main claim to fame is as a jumping-off point for Gaborone (Botswana), and there are always a lot of people moving through. The town is quite large; there are plenty of shops strung along Church St, including a couple of banks and 24-hour petrol stations.

In the municipal building, just behind Church St, you'll find the **tourist information office** (☎ 642 1081). Inquire here about information on the local Mampoer Route, which refers to a fiery distilled liquor brewed in the region.

Places to Stay

Transvaal Hotel (☎ 642 2003, Church St) Rooms without/with bathroom R90/R110 per person. This is an old-style country hotel that remains pretty much unchanged since the 1920s. The high prices might reflect the hotel's historical interest but otherwise it isn't great value.

Marico Bosveld (☎ 642 3545, 5 President St) Singles/doubles B&B R175/250. If you're looking for a bit more luxury in a central location try this refined B&B.

Abjaterskop Hotel (☎/fax 642 2008) Camp sites R45, singles/doubles self-catering R90/110 (bungalows), single/double R275/375 (hotel room). Around 2km from Zeerust on the N4, the Abjaterskop is a comfortable option in a great setting. There's a swimming pool, and the restaurant serves some excellent meals.

Getting There & Away

Intercape passes through Zeerust on its daily Jo'burg/Pretoria to Gaborone service. The bus stops at the Chicken Licken, in Church St. The fare is R60/90 to Gaborone/Jo'burg.

The minibus taxi rank is on Church St on the Mafikeng side of town.

MADIKWE GAME RESERVE

Along the banks of the Marigo River you'll find Madikwe Game Reserve (☎ 0183672, ask for 2411; admission R20 per person). At 60,000 hectares, this is one of the largest reserves in South Africa, and is composed of bushveld, savanna grassland and riverine forest. It's stocked with about 30 species of wildlife (some 8000 animals) introduced as part of a scheme to relocate endangered species called Operation Phoenix. Black rhinos were introduced in 1996 and all of the Big Five are now present.

Madikwe River Lodge (☎ 014-778 0891, fax 778 0893, e lodge@madikwe.three cities.co.za, R49) Singles/doubles R2250/3300. This lodge is on the Botswana border at the northern end of R49 (reached from the N4 at Zeerust). It is a luxurious resort befitting its high price tag. It offers chalets, a bird-viewing lounge, wildlife drives and a great deal of pampering.

Tau Game Lodge (☎ 011-809 4300, fax 809 4400) Singles/doubles US$413/550. The superb Tau Game Lodge is very expensive,

but the price is all-inclusive. Bookings for the lodge can also be made through the **Conservation Corporation Africa** *(CCAfrica;* W *www.ccafrica.com).*

MAFIKENG
☎ 018 • postcode 2745

Mafikeng and Mmabatho were, up until a few years ago, twin towns about 3km apart; the two towns have been combined and Mmabatho is now part of Mafikeng. Mmabatho was built as the capital of the 'independent' Homeland of Bop, and then became capital of North-West Province after 1994.

There is a reasonable selection of shops and a few interesting historical sites. Mmabatho, developed as Bop's showcase, has a number of suitably grandiose and ugly buildings including a sports stadium and Megacity, a huge American-style shopping mall.

History

Mafeking (as the Europeans called it) was established as the administrative capital of the British Protectorate of Bechuanaland (present-day Botswana). The small frontier town was besieged by Boer forces from October 1899 to May 1900. Led by Colonel Baden-Powell, the siege came to symbolise British courage and steadfastness. In reality, the Boers made only one determined attempt to capture the town and were for the most part content to maintain a civilised siege – there was seldom fighting on Sundays, for instance.

Perhaps the most lasting significance of the Mafeking siege was the role it played in the development of Baden-Powell's ideas. During the siege he created a cadet corps for the town's boys, which was the forerunner to the Boy Scout movement.

Orientation

It's easy to get around Mafikeng on foot. Most shops and banks are around the central local bus station. It's 5km from the centre of Mafikeng to Megacity in Mmabatho; catch one of the many local buses. Megacity is a useful starting point if you are heading further north or west. There are banks, a post office, a number of large, well-stocked department

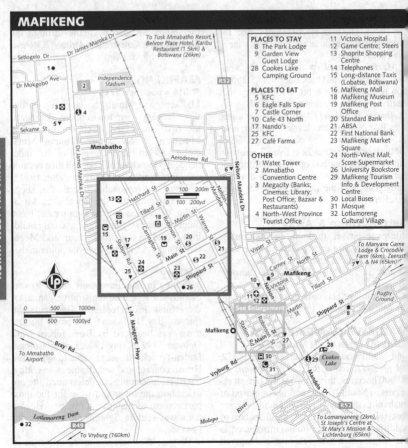

MAFIKENG

PLACES TO STAY
8 The Park Lodge
9 Garden View Guest Lodge
28 Cookes Lake Camping Ground

PLACES TO EAT
5 KFC
6 Eagle Falls Spur
7 Castle Corner
10 Cafe 43 North
17 Nando's
25 KFC
27 Café Farma

OTHER
1 Water Tower
2 Mmabatho Convention Centre
3 Megacity (Banks; Cinemas; Library; Post Office; Bazaar & Restaurants)
4 North-West Province Tourist Office
11 Victoria Hospital
12 Game Centre; Steers
13 Shoprite Shopping Centre
14 Telephones
15 Long-distance Taxis (Lobatse, Botswana)
16 Mafikeng Mall
18 Mafikeng Museum
19 Mafikeng Post Office
20 Standard Bank
21 ABSA
22 First National Bank
23 Mafikeng Market Square
24 North-West Mall; Score Supermarket
26 University Bookstore
29 Mafikeng Tourism Info & Development Centre
30 Local Buses
31 Mosque
32 Lotlamoreng Cultural Village

stores (good for food and camping equipment), numerous smaller shops and several fast-food restaurants.

Information

Tourist Offices Check out the grandiose Mafikeng Tourism Info & Development Centre (☎ 381 3155, Licthenburg Rd; open Mon-Fri, Sat morning). After a long wait, this centre, at the Cookes Lake Camping Ground entrance, is finally open!

Money There are no American Express (AmEx) or Rennies agencies in Mafikeng or Mmabatho, so for changing money around this area, the banks in Mafikeng and Megacity are your only option. Try First National Bank (Robinson St) between Main and Shippard Sts, ABSA (Cnr Warren and Main Sts) and Standard Bank (Cnr Main and Robinson Sts).

Post & Communications The main post office is next to Megacity. There is another post office on Carrington St between Main and Martin Sts.

At the time of research there were no public email facilities.

Medical Services If you need a dentist or a doctor, go to the **Victoria Hospital** (☎ *381 7043, Victoria Rd*).

Emergency In an emergency, you can contact the police on ☎ 10111 and the ambulance on ☎ 392 3333.

Mafikeng Museum

For interesting relics (mainly relating to the famous siege) try the Mafikeng Museum (☎ *381 6102, Martin St; admission free; open 8am-4pm Mon-Fri, 10am-12.30pm Sat*). Among the relics is a menu for a dinner for senior officers given to celebrate the queen's birthday on 24 May 1900 – life may have been tough for some, but the senior officers managed to maintain standards!

Lotlamoreng Dam & Cultural Village

Lotlamoreng Cultural Village (☎ *382 2095; village admission free, Dam admission R5; open 7am-5pm daily*) is the brainchild of Credo Mutwa, a Tswana priest, historian, artist and author. It was formed as a collection of small traditional villages and kraals (fortified villages) on the banks of the Lotlamoreng Dam. The village is still there (and is a photographer's delight), but it is no longer a hive of cultural activity. This is sad, as this region badly needs an infusion of traditional culture. Some visitors come solely to see the curious statuary.

There are a couple of local artists here who look after the place and sell some high quality wonderstone carvings which they make at the village. If you're after a stone carving this is a good place to buy and you'll be directly supporting these local artists.

The complex is 5km west of Mafikeng on the Vryburg road. Right beside the dam here is a dilapidated aviary, as well as a refreshment kiosk, lawns, a bar that is popular on weekends and braais.

Places to Stay

Cookes Lake Camping Ground (☎ *381 5611*) Camp sites R15. Cookes is dusty and unattractive but it would do at a pinch. There are few facilities. You must pay a one-off entry fee to the game reserve of R10 per person plus R5 per car.

St Joseph's Centre (☎ *383 2377*) Dorm beds R50. You can stay here at St Mary's Mission in Lomanyaneng, 2km south of the train station; there are cooking facilities available.

There are a few B&Bs, starting at around R120 per person. Ask at the tourist office for a complete list.

The Park Lodge (☎ *381 6752, 70 Shippard St*) Singles/doubles R150/200. The rooms here are small but uncluttered. The lodge is handy if you're entering town from the north-east.

Garden View Guest Lodge (☎ *381 3110; Cnr North & Havenga Sts*) Singles/doubles with shared bathroom R100/160, suites R180/260, 2-bed flats R280. This is the best that Mafikeng has to offer at a reasonable price. The lodge has secure parking, M-Net TV in all rooms, night security and a very convivial restaurant-bar.

Ferns Country House (☎ *381 5971, fax 381 6764, Cook St*) Singles/doubles B&B R299/349. Ferns is stylish and elegant with ultra-modern furnishings, a beautiful garden and a swimming pool. It's well sign-posted off Shippard St.

Belvoir Place Hotel (☎ *386 2222, fax 386 2100,* e *ihtm@iafrica.co.za, Nelson Mandela Dr*) Singles/doubles B&B R250/345, self-contained rooms R180/210. Next to the Mmabatho Sun Hotel, this is a hotel training school. The self-contained rooms are good value.

Tusk Mmabatho Resort (☎ *389 1111, fax 386 1661,* e *mmabatho@tusk-resorts.co.za, Nelson Mandela Dr*) Singles/doubles R350/440. Mafikeng's luxury option, this opulent resort was formerly a Sun Hotel. There is a pool, two restaurants, five bars, tennis courts, a casino and a cinema.

Places to Eat

Megacity has many takeaway places such as *Wimpy*, *Steers* and an *OK Bazaar* for self-caterers. Opposite Megacity you'll find a *KFC* (*Cnr Main St & Vryburg Rd*).

For poultry lovers ever-reliable *Nando's* is on the corner of Station Rd and Martin St, and around town there are three easily reached branches of *Chicken Licken*.

Eagle Falls Spur (☎ 381 0347, Cnr Nelson Mandela Dr & Aerodrome Rd) Meals R20-45. This steak restaurant has specials such as steak and calamari (surf 'n' turf) for R45 and kids burgers (with free drinks) for R20.

Café Farma (☎ 381 4906, 17 Nelson Mandela Dr) Breakfast R25. In Era's Pharmacy, this is *the* place for breakfast, light meals and cakes.

Cafe 43 North (☎ 381 6463, 43 Nelson Mandela Dr) Lunch R35. In a delightful setting this is an ideal place to relax over lunch and is the closest Mafikeng gets to sophistication.

Karibu Restaurant (☎ 386 2222, Nelson Mandela Dr) Meals R17-25. Open noon-2.30pm & 7pm-10.30pm daily. In the same building as the Belvoir Place Hotel, Karibu does good meals, tasty pastries and occasionally has 'seafood feast' nights with a buffet of ocean delights.

Castle Corner (☎ 381 5358, Cnr Tillard & Gemsbok Sts) Salads R12, mains R30. Castle Corner, formerly O'Hagans, does standard pub meals and offers a fine pint of Kilkenny.

Getting There & Away

Many people come through Mafikeng on their way to/from Botswana. Ramatlhabama, 24km to the north, is the busiest border post and lies on the main route to/from Gaborone (Botswana).

SA Airlink *(☎ 385 1119)* has regular flights to Jo'burg (R525) Sunday to Friday, with connections to other cities.

City Link *(☎ 381 2680)* buses run daily from Megacity to Jo'burg (R75, six hours).

Long-distance minibus taxis leave from the forecourt of the Mafikeng train station. As usual, most leave early in the morning. Fares from Mafikeng include to the Botswana border (R5, running all day); Zeerust (R12); Lobatse (Botswana; R17); Vryburg (R30, very few taxis); Gaborone (R35); and Rustenburg (R30).

The *Bulawayo* train that used to run from Jo'burg/Pretoria via Mafikeng and Gaborone

to Bulawayo (Zimbabwe) had been suspended at the time of research.

Getting Around

Numerous city buses ply the route between Mafikeng (from the corner of Main St and Station Rd) and Megacity for a few rand Buses also run out to Lotlamoreng Dam.

POTCHEFSTROOM
☎ 018 • postcode 2531

Potchefstroom, known locally as Potch, is off the N12 about 115km south-west of Jo'burg. It's a large town, verging on a city that looks rather unappealing from the main road. There are, however, some pleasant leafy suburbs.

It might not look it, but Potchefstroom was the first European town to be established in the former Transvaal, and it remains a staunchly conservative town.

Maps of Potch and the Vredefort Dome trail are available at the **information office** *(☎ 293 1611, Cnr Potgieter & Church Sts)*

Lake Holiday Resort (☎ 299 5473, fax 299 5475) 2-bed rondavels R80, *longdavels* (family houses) R200, camp sites R35 per person for up to 4 people (all prices rise in the high season). The whole of Potch can be found here on a sunny weekend. The sign posting is a bit erratic, but anyone should be able to direct you – it's about 4km from the N12, on the north side of town. Facilities include swimming pools, fair-ground attractions, boats, a cafe and plenty of braais.

Elgro Hotel (☎/fax 297 5411, 60 Wolmarans St) Singles/doubles DB&B R285/395. Elgro Hotel is fairly upmarket and also has a disco.

VRYBURG
☎ 053 • postcode 8601

There's very little here to interest visitors. Readers have been challenged to write about this place in previous editions – no one has written back in eight years! Hope springs eternal – advertising for Stellaland (as the Vryburg region was proclaimed in 1882) describes the place 'as the tourist destination of the 1990s'. Thankfully the 1990s are over!

To delve deeper into the region, contact **Vryburg Tourism** (☎ 927 2222, *Market St*), which is next to Steers.

Intercape also stops here.

International Hotel (☎/*fax 927 2235, 43 Market St*) Singles/doubles R235/335. This is a possibility if you are stuck waiting for something to happen. (The Bullring Pub here may help while away the hours.)

Ngulube Lodge (☎ 927 0700, *fax 927 0808*) Singles/doubles B&B R205/310. This place describes itself as 'new and over-whelming'. Well, it's clean and comfortable, and there are weekend specials.

Free State

The landlocked Free State consists largely of the veld of the Southern African plateau. To the east are highlands with weirdly eroded sandstone hills.

Free State's borders reflect the prominent role it has played in South African history. To the south is the Orange River, which the Voortrekkers crossed to escape from the Cape Colony. The northern border is defined by the Vaal River, which was the next frontier of Boer expansion. To the east, across the Mohokare (Caledon) River, is Lesotho, where mountains and King Moshoeshoe the Great halted the tide of Boer expansion. To the south-east, however, Free State spills across the Mohokare (Caledon) River as the mountains dwindle to grazing land; this area proved harder for Moshoeshoe to defend.

There are important gold mines in and around Welkom and diamonds are also mined in Free State. The western half of the province is bare, rolling grazing country, while the hillier east is a major grain-growing region.

While there are fewer attractions in Free State than in most other provinces, many of the quiet dorps (small villages) and prosperous towns have a Rip van Winkle–air about them, where dreams of an Afrikaner Arcadia linger. However, older dreams of a Sotho land also linger.

Bloemfontein

☎ 051 • postcode 9301

Bloemfontein ('Bloem' as it is usually called) is the provincial capital of Free State and South Africa's judicial capital. It occupies an important place in the country's history. Bloemfontein means 'Fountain of Flowers'; the Tswana name for the area is Mangaung, 'Place of Cheetahs'.

Bloemfontein is one of the more pleasant cities in South Africa and while the influence of its conservative past is evident, there

Highlights

- Spot a rare bearded vulture, black eagle or jackal buzzard in Golden Gate Highlands National Park.
- Soak up dignified Bloemfontein by day, party at its many hot spots by night.
- Take a tour of peaceful Intabazwe township outside Harrismith, one of the best township tours in the country.
- Hike in the foothills of the Maluti Mountains in the QwaQwa Conservation Area.
- Relinquish your Western ideals and take on some traditional culture at the Basotho Cultural Village in the QwaQwa Highlands National Park.
- Hang out in the alternative enclave of Rustler's Valley.

is a vastly improving nightlife scene, it's a relatively safe city to wander around and culturally it provides a fascinating insight into South Africa, past and present. There are pockets of impressive buildings around

FREE STATE

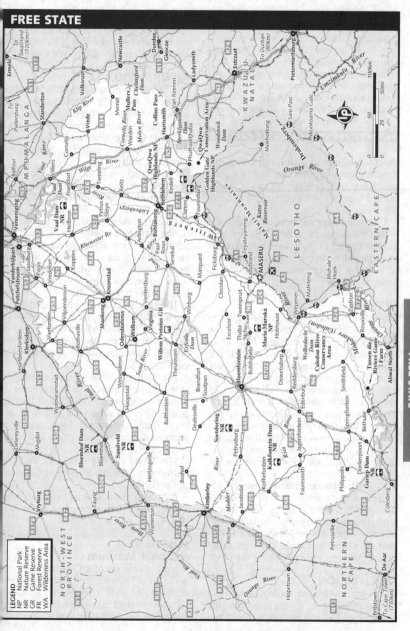

LEGEND
NP National Park
NR Nature Reserve
GR Game Reserve
FR Forest Reserve
WA Wilderness Area

Lord of Bloemfontein

JRR Tolkien, author of *Lord of the Rings*, was born here in 1892. He moved to England when he was four but his memory of the Bloemfontein district as '...hot, dry and barren' might well have influenced his creation of Mordor. We saw some graffiti in a Cape Town pub claiming that Tolkien was 'just another Bloemfontein boy on acid'.

the city, making a stroll down streets such as President Brand worthwhile. At first sight it can seem like another sprawling, modernised town, but it's worth giving this city a few days.

Unusually there are quite a few destitute whites wandering the streets of Bloem, begging and trying to 'keep an eye on cars' for a few rand. It is striking to see the first seeds of a change in economic fortunes in Afrikaner heartland.

HISTORY

Bloemfontein wasn't the first Boer capital in the lands across the Orange River. The Voortrekkers established their first settlement near modern-day Thaba 'Nchu and various embryonic republics came and went, as well as a period of British sovereignty after the Anglo-Boer War. In 1854 the Orange Free State was created, with Bloemfontein as the capital. Bloemfontein was named after a farm built in 1840 by Johannes Brits. By 1854 it was only a small village but it had its own parliament, presiding over the republic's 12,000 widely scattered white citizens.

In 1863 Johannes Brand began his 25-year term as president, and it was during this time that Bloemfontein grew from a struggling frontier town, in constant danger of being wiped out by Moshoeshoe's warriors, to a wealthy capital city with many public buildings and rail links to the coast.

ORIENTATION

There are endless sprawling suburbs in Bloemfontein but the central area is laid out on a grid and is easy to navigate. Hoffman Square is the centre of the downtown area. Mangaung township is south of the city centre. Botshabelo, on the Thaba 'Nchu road, is one of the largest townships in the country.

INFORMATION

The friendly and very helpful **information centre** (☎ 405 8489, e blminfo@iafrica.com, Park Ave) is in the tourist centre, not far from the stadium. You can pick up a walking tour map here and a Bloemfontein Art Route, detailing galleries, museums and handicraft outlets.

For information about national parks and reserves in the area, contact the **Free State Department of Environmental Affairs & Tourism** (☎ 051-405 4062, fax 403 3778, PO Box 264, Bloemfontein 9300).

Transgariep Tourism (☎ 447 1362) has information about most of Free State, and has an office in the information centre. The tourist centre is also where long-distance buses arrive, and there are ticket counters for all major bus companies.

There's a handy ATM at the tourist centre and at the Waterfront; there's an AmEx office in the Mimosa Mall and a branch of ABSA (with bureau de change) in the Pick 'n' Pay Centre opposite the western side of the Mimosa Mall.

The main post office is on Groenendal St, near Hoffman Square. The Internet cafe on Tweedelaan (2nd Ave), attached to Bimbos near Kellner St, stays open late (R16 per hour). Connix Internet at the Waterfront is pretty flash, has fast connections and prices to match (R25 per hour).

STA Travel (☎ 444 6062, e laudep@statravel.co.za) in the Mimosa Mall can organise flights.

A 24-hour pharmacy can be found in the College Square shopping complex on Zastron St, west of King's Park.

MUSEUMS
National Museum

A great re-creation of a 19th-century street is the most interesting display at this museum (☎ 447 9609, Cnr Charles & Aliwal Sts; admission R5; open 8am-5pm Mon-Fri 10am-5pm Sat, 1pm-6pm Sun).

Queens Fort

Now restored as a military museum, Queens Fort (☎ 447 5478, Church St; admission free; open 10am-4pm Mon-Fri, 2pm-4pm Sun) was built in 1848 during the Orange Free State–Basotho wars. The fort is south of the stream near the corner of Goddard St.

National Women's Monument & War Museum

The National Women's Monument, which is outside the military museum to the south of the city centre, commemorates the 26,000 Afrikaner women and children who died in British concentration camps during the 1899–1902 Anglo-Boer War (see the boxed text 'Concentration Camps' for more details). Emily Hobhouse, the British 'turncoat' hero who alerted the world to this infamy, is buried here.

The War Museum (☎ 447 3447, Monument Rd; admission R5; open 8am-4.30pm Mon-Fri, 10am-5pm Sat, 2pm-5pm Sun) is devoted to the Anglo-Boer Wars and has some interesting displays and a great deal of trivia; a sign of how deeply the war still affects the national psyche. There is a very small section explaining the role of blacks in the war. It may have been considered a white man's war, but by the end there were 10,000 blacks employed by the Boers and 100,000 working for the British.

Freshford House Museum

To get an idea of how Bloemfontein burghers lived at the turn of the 19th and 20th centuries, visit Freshford House (☎ 447 0609, 31 Kellner St; admission R3; open 10am-1pm Mon-Fri, 2pm-5pm Sat & Sun), just north-west of the city centre.

National Afrikaans Literature Museum

This museum (☎ 405 4711, President Brand St; admission free; open 7.30am-4pm Mon-Fri, 9am-noon Sat) is in the Old Government building. It houses an Afrikaans research centre and displays on Afrikaans literature.

Old Presidency

Just north of the corner of St Georges and President Brand Sts is this grand Victorian-style building (☎ 448 0949, President Brand St; admission free; open 10am-4pm Tues-Fri, 2pm-4pm Sun). Orange Free State presidents once lived in these spacious chambers, in what must have seemed like extraordinary opulence to the rural citizens. Behind the Old Presidency is a collection of old agricultural machinery.

SAND DU PLESSIS THEATRE

A modern building of interest is the 1985 Sand du Plessis Theatre (☎ 552 4071, Cnr Markgraaff & St Andrews Sts; admission R2;

FREE STATE

Concentration Camps

During the 1899–1902 Anglo-Boer War, the British invented the concentration camp. Guerrilla bands (helped by and including Afrikaner farmers) were harassing the British; in response the British burned the farms of suspected combatants and shipped huge numbers of their women and children off to concentration camps. In the first years of the 20th century, without modern medicines and vaccines and without modern engineering, any large-scale incarceration of people was bound to be disastrous.

By the end of the war, 200,000 Afrikaner women and children had been imprisoned in the camps. More than 26,000 of them, mostly children, had died, accounting for about 70% of total Afrikaner deaths in the war. There were also concentration camps for blacks and of the 80,000 people interned, it is estimated that 14,000 died.

For Afrikaners, the image of a man returning to find his farm destroyed and his children dead remains a powerful one. The loss of political independence and the destruction of family, home and farm left little for the Afrikaners but the Bible, deep bitterness and a determination to survive against any odds.

tours by appointment 2.30pm Wed), which has artworks on display. The local paper lists music, ballet, drama and opera performances held here.

NAVAL HILL

This hill, dominating the town to the northeast, was the site of the British naval gun emplacements during the Anglo-Boer War. On the eastern side of the hill is a large white horse, a landmark for British cavalry during the war; it was laid out by a homesick regiment from Wiltshire.

There are good views from the hill, and on the hilltop is the **Franklin Game Reserve** *(☎ 405 8124; admission free; open 8am-5pm daily)* where you can see antelopes. You can walk in the reserve, although one traveller reports being chased by a wildebeest! To get to the reserve, take bus No 2 to Union Ave and walk from there.

On Union Ave, north of where the road up the hill turns off, is **Orchid House** *(☎ 405 8488; admission free; open 10am-4pm Mon-Fri, 10am-5pm Sat & Sun)* with a large collection of flowers.

BLOEMFONTEIN ZOO

The Bloemfontein zoo *(☎ 405 8498, Kingsway; adult/student R15/6; open 8am-5pm daily Mar-Nov, 8am-6pm daily Dec-Feb)* houses an extensive collection of primates, among many other animals. And yes, there is a 'liger' here – a cross between a lion and a tiger – but these days it's stuffed. The entrance to the zoo is on Henry St.

WATERFRONT

Yes, Bloemfontein has a waterfront, modelled on Cape Town's. You'd think that entrepreneurs could think up something new. Although it's a bit tacky, and it certainly isn't original, Bloem's Waterfront is a lot more pleasant to stroll around than the huge shopping malls that are popping up on the outskirts of so many South African cities. It's outside for starters, set on a small body of water and the atmosphere is relaxed – it's a great place for the kids. For travellers there are plenty of services, including ATMs, an Internet cafe, cheap eats, movie theatres and, most importantly, a good pub (Barney's) to kick back and enjoy a drink.

Alluring Architecture

The most interesting buildings are along President Brand St, where aromatic cypress trees improve the air. These solid buildings demonstrate how comfortable and self-assured burgher life once was, as well as emphasise the hideousness of modern South African architecture.

If you head south down President Brand St from Voortrekker St, the city hall (1934), with its reflecting pool, is on the right. In the next block, on the other side of the road, is the appeal court (1929) in understated neoclassical style. The carvings and panelling inside are worth a look. Opposite the court is the Fourth Raadsaal (1893), which was the parliament house of the Free State republic; its almost light-hearted Renaissance-style architecture blends well with down-to-earth red brick.

On the corner of Elizabeth St is the Waldorf Building (1928), not all that impressive until you remember how few buildings of this vintage survive in South African cities. Opposite is the Old Government Building (1908), which now houses the National Afrikaans Literature Museum. Diagonally opposite, in the block between Maitland and St Andrew Sts, is the Jubileum Building Hall. The pompous and menacing hall was once the headquarters for Orange Free State's Dutch Reformed Church.

Further down, on the corner of Fontein St, are the fire station (1933) and the imposing supreme court (1906).

Just east of President Brand St, on St Georges St is the original parliament house, the oldest building in town, still with its thatched roof and dung floors. It's open 10am to 1pm Monday to Friday, and 2pm to 5pm Saturday and Sunday; admission is R2.50.

PLACES TO STAY

The information centre has an excellent list of accommodation and makes bookings. Note that accommodation can be scarce on cricket and rugby match weekends.

Camping

Neither of the caravan parks is convenient unless you have your own wheels.

Dagbreek Caravan Park (☎ 433 2490, 0 Hillside St) Camp sites R40, 2-bed chalets R175, train coaches R40 per person (for groups of 12 to 48 persons). It's off Andries Pretorius St.

Reyneke Caravan Park (☎ 523 3888, fax 523 3887, Petrusburg Rd) Caravan sites R70, single/double chalets R140/180. Two kilometres out of town, this well-organised park has a swimming pool, trampoline and basketball court. This is a good place for the kids.

Hostels

Naval Hill Backpackers (☎ 447 4413, fax 430 7962, e descover@iafrica.com, Delville St) Camp sites R25, dorm beds R45, doubles R110. This place is just before the entrance to the Franklin Game Reserve. It's in

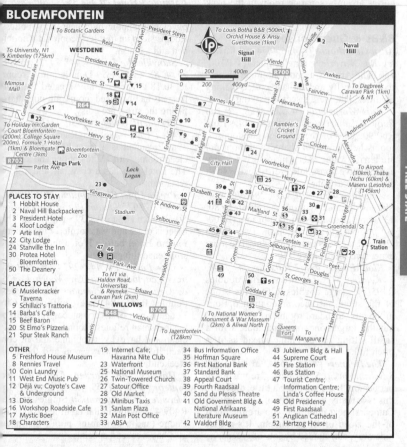

BLOEMFONTEIN

FREE STATE

PLACES TO STAY
1 Hobbit House
2 Naval Hill Backpackers
3 President Hotel
4 Kloof Lodge
7 Arte Inn
22 City Lodge
24 Stanville the Inn
30 Protea Hotel Bloemfontein
50 The Deanery

PLACES TO EAT
6 Musselcracker Taverna
9 Schillaci's Trattoria
14 Barba's Cafe
15 Beef Baron
20 St Elmo's Pizzeria
21 Spur Steak Ranch

OTHER
5 Freshford House Museum
8 Rennies Travel
10 Coin Laundry
11 West End Music Pub
12 Déjà vu; Coyote's Cave & Underground
13 Dros
16 Workshop Roadside Cafe
17 Mystic Boer
18 Characters
19 Internet Cafe; Havanna Nite Club
23 Waterfront
25 National Museum
26 Twin-Towered Church
27 Satour Office
28 Old Market
29 Minibus Taxis
31 Sanlam Plaza
32 Main Post Office
33 ABSA
34 Bus Information Office
35 Hoffman Square
36 First National Bank
37 Standard Bank
38 Appeal Court
39 Fourth Raadsaal
40 Sand du Plessis Theatre
41 Old Government Bldg & National Afrikaans Literature Museum
42 Waldorf Bldg
43 Jubileum Bldg & Hall
44 Supreme Court
45 Fire Station
46 Bus Station
47 Tourist Centre; Information Centre; Linda's Coffee House
48 Old Presidency
49 First Raadsaal
51 Anglican Cathedral
52 Hertzog House

an old water-pumping station (1902) and has inherited an industrial decor that interior designers would kill for. The grounds are large, and despite being fairly close to the centre of town, it feels like you're out in the country. Activities and transport to Lesotho can be arranged here.

Louis Botha B&B (☎ 436 4533, 18 Louis Botha St, Waverley) Dorm beds R65, singles/doubles R80/150. In a private home, the Louis Botha describes itself as 'a B&B for overseas travellers'. Monastic in its sobriety, it's not a place for party animals; however, it is pleasant, clean and friendly. The dorms are in a separate room in the back garden.

B&Bs & Guesthouses

Ansu Guesthouse (☎ 436 4654, 80 Waverley Rd, Waverley) Singles/doubles R100/160. The Ansu is a good suburban choice; rooms have TV and tea- and coffee-making facilities, and there's secure parking.

Huis Margrietjie (☎ 522 4128, 28 Van Rooy St, Universitas) Singles/doubles from R60/90. One of the cheaper guesthouses, rooms here are with shared bathroom but are terrific value. Keep in mind it's a very conservative household – dirty jokes won't endear you to your host!

Arte Inn (☎/fax 430 7667, 28 Kellner St) Singles/doubles without bathroom R80/130, singles/doubles with bathroom (R100/140). Closer to the action on Tweedelaan (2nd Ave), Arte is excellent value. The more expensive rooms have TV.

Kloof Lodge (☎ 447 7603, fax 447 7746, 7 Kellner St) Standard singles/doubles R195/245, large doubles R265. This is one of the stand-out accommodation options in the city. Standard rooms are fairly small but the larger ones are spacious, with a small sitting room. Phone ahead as it is often full.

The Deanery (☎ 447 3684, fax 447 5874, 3 Saltzmann St) Self-catering rooms R120 per person. For something a little different, this is actually the deanery of the Anglican Cathedral next door, and you are the guest of the Dean of Bloemfontein. It's a nice hideaway, surrounded by lots of greenery.

Bloemfontein Club (☎ 430 3247, 8 Elizabeth St) Singles/doubles R140/220. If you can meet the dress code, you can stay here in the city centre.

Hobbit House (☎/fax 447 0663, e hobbit@intekom.co.za, 19 President Steyn Ave, Westdene) Singles/doubles R395/495. Guesthouses don't come much better than the enchanting Hobbit. The owners pride themselves on their faultless service and impeccable facilities. Forget the bill and spoil yourself!

Hotels

Formule 1 Hotel (☎ 444 3523, 200 Zastron St) Rooms R175. West of King's Park; it's a bit claustrophobic but cheap and spotless. Rooms sleep up to three people (in a double bed and a bunk).

Stanville the Inn (☎ 447 7471, fax 447 7514, 85 Zastron St) Double/family room R130/180. The centrally located Stanville has reasonably priced rooms, although those facing the street are noisy.

President Hotel (☎ 430 1111, fax 430 4141, 1 Union Ave) Singles/doubles R355/398. President is a large hotel that offers clean rooms with TV, telephone and air-con. The hotel also has a cosy bar and a good restaurant.

Protea Hotel Bloemfontein (☎ 430 8000, fax 447 7102, Sanlam Plaza, East Burger St) Weekend special R395 per room. This hotel is older and was formerly the Bloemfontein Hotel before Protea took over and smartened things up.

City Lodge (☎ 444 2974, e clbloem .resv@citylodge.co.za, Cnr Voortrekker St & General Dan Pienaar Ave) Singles/doubles R355/384. The comfortable City Lodge is part of a very successful chain of businessman refuges. Rooms are spotlessly clean and have TV, telephone and air-con. Security here is very good and there are weekend specials.

Holiday Inn Garden Court Bloemfontein (☎ 444 1253, fax 444 0671, Cnr Melville Dr & Zastron St) Singles/doubles R409/428. With similar facilities to the City Lodge (and a swimming pool), this place also has weekend specials.

PLACES TO EAT

Linda's Coffee House (☎ 430 6436) Breakfast R15-28, light lunches R22. Near the information desk at the tourist centre, Linda's does good breakfasts (and coffee) for those early bus arrivals.

House of Coffees (☎ 430 1447, Waterfront) Breakfast R10-20, toasted sandwiches R13-17. The food here has a refreshingly healthy bent. Filter coffee is R4.90 (refills R2.50).

Spur Steak Ranch (☎ 448 1493, 208 Zastron St) Meals R18-55. This is a good place to take the kids. As well as steaks and burgers, there are also Mexican dishes.

Beef Baron (☎ 447 4290, 22 2nd Ave, Westdene) Meals R30-50. Perhaps the best of the steak houses, the Baron has carnivore delights such as rump rossini.

St Elmo's Pizzeria (☎ 447 9999, Cnr Zastron & Kellner Sts) Normal/gourmet large pizzas R45/50. St Elmo's does good wood-fired pizzas and on Sunday, and Monday it offers an all-you-can-eat deal for R25.95.

Musselcracker Taverna (☎ 430 6528, Zastron St) Meals R25-100. Open Tues-Sat. A small, airy place overlooking the street, diners at this place are treated to some cracking good seafood, including a mixed platter for R92 and specials such as grilled stuffed squid.

Schillaci's Trattoria (☎ 447 3829, 115 Zastron St) Starters R16-18, mains R26-34. Open 12.30pm-2.30pm & 6.30pm-11.30pm daily. This is a good and very popular Italian restaurant with some shady outdoor tables. Prices are reasonable and there are good midweek specials.

Barba's Cafe (☎ 430 2542, 16 2nd Ave) Starters R20, Greek dishes R30-75. Barba's is recommended by locals and rightly so; it's one of Bloem's hidden secrets. The Greek specialities, including chicken souvlaki (R29), are delicious. It also has a large cocktail list.

Jazz Time Cafe (☎ 430 5727, Waterfront) Mains R20-50. This hip eatery has one of the most interesting menus we've seen in South Africa and servings are huge. Look out for the zippy *zivas* – Yemeni-style layered dough wrapped around a variety of fillings

Township Tours

Bloemfontein is a good place to do a township tour and the information centre can help with bookings. Tours to the local township of Mangaung visit sites of historical interest, including Maphikela House, a national monument building and home of Mr Thomas Maphikela, the first general secretary of the African National Congress (ANC). Even more interesting are the visits to local shebeens (drinking establishments) and restaurants (on request) where you have the opportunity to meet and chat with people you'll never see in an O'Hagans in a South African city.

Tours are informal and usually run for as long as you want. They cost about R150 per person, but it's less for a group or if you have your own transport.

(such as Cajun chicken, fetta and avocado) folded and toasted. The salads here are also very good.

ENTERTAINMENT

As a university town, Bloemfontein has a good range of places to drink, party and, increasingly, listen to live music. The corners of Tweedelaan (2nd Ave) and Kellner, Zastron and Voortrekker Sts get pretty lively and compete for the nightlife scene with the Waterfront. Generally these places are OK for single women, although bear in mind South African cities in general are not great places for single women (see Women Travellers in the Facts for the Visitor chapter for more information).

Mystic Boer (☎ 430 2206, 84 Kellner St) Open late. This is a good place to start and finish the night. It attracts a mixed crowd – ravers, New Agers and long-socked Boer farmers.

Characters (☎ 448 2396, Cnr Tweedelaan & Kellner St) is very modern – it has a ladies night on Tuesday with sit-down meals! There are DJs some nights.

Workshop Roadside Cafe (☎ 447 2761, Cnr Tweedelaan & President Reitz) is a bikies hang-out that is pretty mellow but may get a bit rough later in the evening; the

FREE STATE

wall devoted to Elvis Presley seems a little incongruous.

Don't bother showing up at *Havanna Nite Club (Tweedelaan)* before midnight, then you'll get to see those with a bit of stamina around town. Havanna is next to the Internet cafe.

Dros (☎ 448 7840, 149 Zastron St) is a conservative hang-out with mainly Afrikaner patrons. Stick to the drinks as the food is pretty ordinary.

Déjà Vu (☎ 448 8617, 158 Voortrekker St) is pretty well-established and a good place to start a pub crawl. *Coyote's Cave* (with a good beer garden) and the funky *Underground* are next door.

The Fat Cuban (☎ 444 5912, Bloemgate Centre, Zastron St) Open late. Word on the street is that The Fat Cuban is a good place to chill out and listen to tunes, although it's a little inconvenient, being about 4km west from the city centre.

West End Music Pub (142a Voortrekker St) is a large venue and is a pretty cool place for a game of pool and a quiet drink. The bar area is a very relaxed and friendly spot to hang out.

If you're up for a boogie *Barney's (☎ 430 2600)* at the Waterfront is a good place to carve up the dance floor and show the locals your latest moves. There is live music here on the weekends.

There are *cinemas* in the Mimosa Mall and at the Waterfront.

GETTING THERE & AWAY
Air
Bloemfontein airport is 10km from the city centre and there is no transport to/from the airport, except by private taxi.

SA Airlink *(☎ 433 3225)* and Nationwide connect Bloemfontein with Cape Town, Durban, George, Kimberley, Port Elizabeth, Upington and Johannesburg (Jo'burg). One-way Apex fares to Jo'burg/Cape Town are R680/1030; to Durban it is R890.

Bus
Fares change according to the season, but the following information was relevant at the time of writing. Long-distance buses leave

from the tourist centre. **Translux** *(☎ 408 4888)* runs buses to Durban (R160), Jo'burg/ Pretoria (R200), Port Elizabeth (R200), East London (R205), Knysna (R265) and Cape Town (R300).

Greyhound *(☎ 447 1558)* runs to Durban, Pretoria, Cape Town, Port Elizabeth, Kimberley and Upington. **Intercape Mainliner** *(☎ 447 1575)* runs to Jo'burg (R190) and Cape Town (R300) daily.

Local buses to Thaba 'Nchu leave a long way from the town centre – they leave from along the main road to Thaba 'Nchu just before the corner of Mimosa St. You'll need to either walk or get a taxi.

Minibus Taxi
Most minibus taxis leave from opposite the train station. A minibus taxi to Maseru (Lesotho) costs about R30, to Kimberley it's R40 and to Jo'burg it's R70.

Train
For information/bookings call ☎ 408 4850/ 3. The *Trans Oranje* (Durban–Cape Town), the *Amatola* (Jo'burg–East London) and the *Algoa* (Jo'burg–Port Elizabeth) all stop here. There is also the *Diamond Express* (Bloemfontein-Pretoria via Kimberley). See under Train in the Getting Around chapter for more details.

GETTING AROUND
Bloemfontein has a public bus system called Interstate, but buses are infrequent on many of the routes and services stop early in the evening. The best place for schedules and information is the **Interstate office** *(☎ 448 4951)* in Central Park. There is also an information office in Hoffman Square.

If you're after a private taxi, try **President Taxis** *(☎ 522 3399)* or **Silver Leaf Taxis** *(☎ 430 2005)*.

AROUND BLOEMFONTEIN
Thaba 'Nchu
☎ 051

Thaba 'Nchu (pronounced ta-**baan**-chu, meaning 'Black Mountain') is a small Tswana town to the east of Bloemfontein, he surrounding area was once a small piece f the scattered Bophuthatswana Homeland, nd this too was known as Thaba 'Nchu. As /ith most Homelands, a Sun casino was uilt here.

There's an information office on the main treet, at the other end of town from the upermarkets. There are a few historical uildings and a church designed by the riest-cum-artist Father Claerhout. Look ut for the Aran jerseys (sweaters) that are andcrafted in town.

'laces to Stay *Thaba 'Nchu Hotel (☎ 875 514)* is an inexpensive hotel that is basic ut clean. It was closed at the time of re-earch, but should have reopened by the me you read this. Coming from the main ırn-off to Bloemfontein, continue up the ıain street, turn left onto Market Square nd follow the road around to the right.

Naledi Sun (☎ 875 1060, fax 875 2329, Bridge St) Standard rooms R487. This lace has the usual 'Sun' comforts and is uite pricey, although there are good deals or longer stays.

Thaba 'Nchu Sun (☎ 871 4200, fax 873 161, on the N8) Standard/luxury rooms ₹615/769. This place is about 10km from 'haba 'Nchu and is even more expensive, ut for the high rollers the casino is here.

ietting There & Away There are morn-ıg and evening buses to Thaba 'Nchu Sun om Bloem, departing from the tourist entre on most days. It costs R30, but you eceive an R10 food voucher and an R20 asino voucher.

There are also minibus taxis between loemfontein and Thaba 'Nchu (about R7) nd from Thaba 'Nchu to Ladybrand around R16). A minibus taxi from Thaba Nchu town to the casino costs R5 but it's impler to take the free shuttle that operates etween the Naledi and Thaba 'Nchu Sun otels.

Maria Moroka National Park
his beautiful park *(☎ 873 2427; admis-ion R5)* centres on a natural amphitheatre ormed by the Thaba 'Nchu hills and in-

cludes the Groothoek Dam. It has a large variety of wildlife, including zebras, elands, blesboks, springboks and red hartebeests.

There are two relatively short hiking trails. The **Volstruis Hiking Trail** takes about one to two hours to walk; it passes through a wooded ravine and winds by an old kraal (fortified village) and the Groothoek Dam. The **Eland Hiking Trail** takes about four to five hours. It too passes through the ravine and by the kraal but the stiff climb up to a viewpoint adds to its difficulty.

There are 2-bed *chalets* for R160.

To get to the park from Thaba 'Nchu you'll need a car.

Northern Free State & Goldfields

Gold was discovered in Free State in April 1938 and a rush started immediately. Now the Free State goldfields produce more than a third of the country's output. The extraction of gold is centred on three towns: Welkom, Virginia and Odendaalsrus.

Much of the region is given over to intensive farming, mainly maize. Kroonstad is the largest town between Jo'burg and Bloemfontein. The other towns are sleepy, pleasant places and if a farm holiday is your bag you have come to the right place.

WINBURG
☎ 051 • postcode 9420
It's difficult to imagine that this sleepy little town, founded in 1842, was the first capital of a Boer republic in present-day Free State. It's a forceful reminder of just how the Boer republics really began at a grass-roots level. It was in the dining room of Ford's Hotel (now a large shop on the town square) that the leaders of five Voortrekker groups finally agreed to form a government under the leadership of Piet Retief.

Tourist information is available at the **library** *(☎ 881 0003; open Mon-Fri)*, in the town square.

The **church** on the Winburg town square was used as a hospital and school during the

FREE STATE

1899–1902 Anglo-Boer War. There are some old photos of the town here.

The **Voortrekker Monument**, about 3km from town, comprises five columns symbolising the five trek parties led by Louis Trichardt, Hendrik Potgieter, Gert Maritz, Piet Retief and Pieter Uys, all of whom created the republic. You'll probably have noticed that just about every town in the Free State has variations of these as street names!

Places to Stay & Eat

Winburg Guesthouse (☎ 881 0233, fax 881 0234) Singles/doubles R140/190. The only decent option in town, this guesthouse is across the square from the Winburg Hotel (now closed). There is secure parking and the small, tidy rooms come with TV and telephone. The attached restaurant and bar are probably your best eating and drinking options.

Getting There & Away

City to City buses between Welkom and Thaba 'Nchu, Maseru and Ficksburg stop here. Other buses running along the N1 stop out on the highway, from where you can walk into town, hail down a minibus taxi or catch a private taxi.

There are a few minibus taxis running to the Goldfields area and some heading towards Bloemfontein. Ask at the petrol station on the northern edge of town.

AROUND WINBURG

Off the N1, about 20km north of Winburg and 70km south of Kroonstad, is the **Willem Pretorius Game Reserve** *(☎ 057- 65 4003; admission R20; open 7am-6.30pm daily)*. Animals in the game reserve include giraffes, white rhinos, buffaloes and various species of antelope. Fishing is popular here (you need to get a Free State angling licence from the resort) and there are hiking trails.

Aventura's Aldam Resort (☎ 057-65 2200, fax 652 0014) Camping from R50 (2 people), 2-bed chalets from R215, 4-bed units from R277. A range of accommodation is available here, much of which has magnificent views over Allemanskraal Dam. Rates increase on weekends and in high season.

WELKOM
☎ 057 • postcode 9459

This modern town is at the centre of the Goldfields area. It's something of a show piece, as it was completely planned – there

Free State Battlefields

The most significant of the Voortrekker battlefields is Vegkop, south of Heilbron, the scene of a bloody battle between Hendrik Potgieter and the Ndebele army of Mzilikazi in 1836. When confronted by the Ndebele, who employed Zulu-style fighting methods, about 50 Voortrekkers formed their wagons into a laager (defensive circular formation) and held off the attackers.

There are at least 20 major battlefields and sites from the 1899–1902 Anglo-Boer War in and around Free State.

There were a number of battles around Bloemfontein and the most significant site is Sannapos, east towards Thaba 'Nchu, where Free Staters inflicted heavy losses on the British on 31 March 1900. Bloemfontein had been captured by the British 18 days earlier and the Boers were withdrawing eastwards. Two other significant battles took place at this time: Mostertshoek on 4 April, and Jammerberg Drift, five days later.

In May 1900 the battles raged near the Sand River, which flows through the Goldfields region. During a battle at Biddulphsberg, between Winburg and Bethlehem, the veld caught fire and many British soldiers died in the flames. On 31 July 1900, at Surrender Hill near Fouriesburg, a major Boer force led by General Prinsloo surrendered to the British.

The war ended with the signing of the Peace of Vereeniging in May 1902.

re no traffic lights (known locally as ro-
bots), which is touted as proof of a masterpiece of town planning. However, this just
means that it's sprawling, soulless and hell
to get around if you don't have your own
transport.

Information

The information centre (☎ 352 9244; open
8am-4.30pm Mon-Fri) is in the clock tower
at the civic centre on Stateway, the main
street. The staff are friendly but they don't
have much information. Travel Experience
(☎ 353 3041, e fly.travexp@galileosa.co
za, Shop 11, Sanlam Plaza, Stateway) is a
good source of tourist information. It can
also assist with travel arrangements.

Not far from Stateway is Mooi St, which
encloses most of the central shopping area
in its horseshoe curve. The First National
Bank is on Elizabeth St, the Standard Bank
is on Tulbagh St and the main post office is
on Bok St.

Things to See & Do

Tours of the mines in Welkom and those
in the nearby town of Virginia can be
arranged but you'll need to contact the
Welkom information centre in advance.

The area's huge mine-evaporation pans
are home to a wide variety of birdlife, including the greater flamingo (Phoenicopterus
ruber), the lesser flamingo (Phoenicopterus
minor) and the grey-headed gull (Larus cir-
rocephalus). More than 200 species of bird
have been seen around the city, including
90% of all waterfowl species found in South
Africa.

Try Flamingo Pan off the R30 just west
of the town, or Witpan at Oppenheimer
Park, about 4km south-east of the town
centre on the continuation of Stateway. Two
other bird-watching spots are Theronia and
Flamingo Lakes.

Places to Stay & Eat

Hotel 147 (☎ 352 5381, Stateway) Singles/
doubles R90/130. It isn't the best hotel but
it's bearable. Room rates are also available
by the hour (R40), making us wonder about
the usual clientele.

Stanville the Inn (☎ 353 2452, 180 Tempest Rd) Double/family rooms R120/180.
The Stanville is compact, and has spick-
and-span budget accommodation; there is
secure parking.

Welkom Inn (☎ 357 3361, fax 352 1458,
e w-inn@global.co.za) Singles/doubles
R265/285. This place is three-star rated and
is a few blocks east of the centre. Neat
rooms have TV, air-con and telephone.

If you're after some genuine South
African hospitality contact the **Guest House
Association** (☎ 353 3041) for a listing of
guesthouses in the area, or pick up a copy
from Travel Experience.

Giovanni's Pizzaghetti (☎ 353 2290, 15
Mooi St) Pasta and pizza from R22. It also
offers steak and seafood. Giovanni's is
found on the innermost curve of the central
area. It feels a little more human than the
usual franchised places.

Saddles Steak Ranch (☎ 353 4248, Stateway) Steaks R40. Opposite the Sanlam
Plaza, Saddles has decent steaks. If you're
thirsty, the **Keg & Mustang** is next door.

Getting There & Away

Being a mining town, Welkom is a major
depot for City to City buses, with a few services to Jo'burg/Pretoria and more south to
the QwaQwa region, Lesotho and the
Transkei.

Several Intercape services stop in town
on their way to destinations including
Bloemfontein (R95), Jo'burg (R190) and
Knysna (R285). Greyhound buses stop at
the Orange Hotel on Stateway, on the way
to Cape Town (R310). Book for either bus
line at Travel Experience in Sanlam Plaza.

The minibus taxis in the supermarket car
park in town are mainly for the local area
but you may find long-distance taxis here in
the early morning. A minibus taxi to Jo'burg
costs about R45. The long, uncomfortable
ride to Cape Town costs about R100.

KROONSTAD
☎ 056 • postcode 9499

Kroonstad, on the N1, is a typical large
rural Free State town. The town dates back
to 1855, and the Voortrekker Sarel Celliers

was one of the first settlers here. Kroon may have been named after the Voortrekker's horse, Kroon.

Tourist information can be obtained from the local library (☎ 216 9911; open Mon-Fri).

Things to See & Do

The old market building opposite the pretty magistrate's building, on the corner of Mark and Murray Sts, is a national monument. Upstairs in the library there's the small Sarel Celliers Museum (☎ 216 9911; open Mon-Fri).

You can see the Celliers statue in the grounds of the impressive NG Moederkerk (Mother Church) on Cross St. Celliers is standing on a gun carriage making the Blood River vow. His farm, Doornkloof, is 45km out of town and can be visited by appointment – ask at the library.

Kroon Park (admission R15) offers swimming and other water activities (see Places to Stay & Eat, following for more details).

The national tournament of Jukskei (an Afrikaner game in which clubs are tossed at a peg) is held annually in Kroonstad.

The 4000-hectare Koppies Dam Nature Reserve (☎ 05672 ask for 2521; open 7am-9pm daily) north-east of Kroonstad, is on the Rhenoster River. It is home to various wildlife and water birds but fishing is the main pursuit.

Places to Stay & Eat

Kroon Park (☎ 213 1942, fax 213 1941) Camp sites R23/29/35 low/mid/high season plus R15 for each extra person, 2-bed chalets R184/230/253. This is more like a resort than a municipal park, with a couple of swimming pools and good facilities. There are some beautiful camping spots on the river's edge. It's across the river and further south down Cross St and is very popular with families – book ahead.

Kroon Lodge (☎ 212 2942, Louw St) Singles/doubles R150/200. This place isn't particularly savoury, but may be your cheapest option. It has live music on weekends.

Arcadia Guesthouse (☎ 212 8280) Singles/doubles R200/280. This guesthouse is on a large shady property; the lovely rooms here

make it one of the best places to stay in Kroonstad. It's extremely well signposted from most arteries into town.

Angelo's Trattoria (☎ 213 2833, 38 Rei St) Seafood dishes R45, pasta R35. Open daily. This restaurant is great for Italian delights as well as seafood dishes.

Cats & Whiskers (☎ 212 8470, 44 Bran St) Light lunches R16-30. A cool eatery near the town centre, it does coffee-shop snacks and pub grub. It's fully licensed.

Getting There & Away

The City to City bus service between Welkom and Jo'burg stops at the Welkom train station.

There are three Translux services (between Jo'burg/Pretoria and either East London, Port Elizabeth or Knysna) that stop out on the highway at the Shell Ultra City, as does Greyhound's Jo'burg/Pretoria to Port Elizabeth service.

The Amatola (Jo'burg–East London) and Algoa (Jo'burg–Port Elizabeth) trains stop here. See under Train in the Getting Around chapter for more details.

The minibus taxi rank is opposite the train station. Most minibus taxis go to relatively nearby towns only, although there are occasional services to Jo'burg – get there early in the morning.

CANNA CIRCLE

This region takes its name from the annual cultivation of masses of colourful canna plants. These are in bloom from the end of December to April, and each of the towns within the Circle cultivates plants of a different colour.

If you are travelling between Jo'burg and Free State's Eastern Highlands, it is easy to deviate to several of these pleasant towns. Reitz is at the junction of the R57 and R26, Heilbron is on the junction of the R57 and R34, Frankfort is near the junction of the R26 and R34, and Vrede is on the R34 east of the N3.

Frankfort Lodge (☎ 058-813 1080, fax 813 3519, 55A Brand St, Frankfort) Singles/doubles B&B R135/200. Frankfort Lodge is a comfortable place to stay.

Eastern Highlands

This is the most beautiful part of Free State, stretching from Zastron in the south to Harrismith in the north, following the Lesotho border. Roughly, it is the area that fringes the R26 and the R49 east of Bethlehem to Harrismith. In addition to being a tremendously scenic area, it is also archaeologically and historically important. The drives alone, past sandstone monoliths that tower above rolling fields, are reason enough to visit.

HARRISMITH
☎ 058 • postcode 9880

Harrismith is a quiet rural centre, well situated for exploring the northern Drakensberg, the QwaQwa area and Golden Gate Highlands National Park. It probably has the best facilities for travellers in the area.

The **information centre** (☎ 622 3525, e alisono@internext.co.za; open Mon-Fri

& Sat morning) is in the town hall. An excellent source of information in town is Barno Jackson at **Maluti Destinations** (☎ 622 2579, barno@malutidestinations.co.za), next to the Spur restaurant on the N5. He's making a real effort to make Harrismith the centre of tourism in the area and can help with excursions to nearby attractions.

There's an **Internet cafe** (49 Stuart St; open Mon-Sat) opposite the post office. Connections cost R15 per hour.

Things To See & Do
The extensive **botanic gardens** (☎ 623 1078; admission R5; open 7am-7pm daily Sept-May, 7.30am-7pm daily June-Aug), about 5km south of town at the foot of the Platberg, has many plant species from the Drakensberg. There's an information centre and a British blockhouse from the Anglo-Boer War. Next door, the **Platberg Nature Reserve** (☎ 623 1078, admission R25 for vehicle & driver plus R10 for each extra

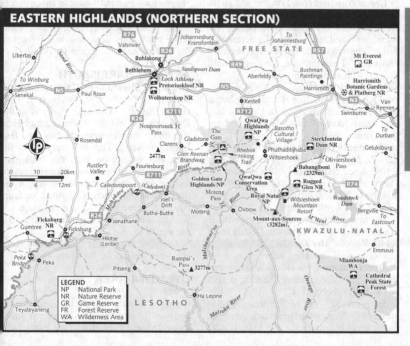

EASTERN HIGHLANDS (NORTHERN SECTION)

FREE STATE

LEGEND
NP	National Park
NR	Nature Reserve
GR	Game Reserve
FR	Forest Reserve
WA	Wilderness Area

person; open 7am-7pm daily) has a fair amount of wildlife, including wildebeests and ostriches.

The information centre arranges tours of **Intabazwe**, a township on a hill outside town, for R80 and can arrange half-board accommodation in the township (see Places to Stay & Eat, following). It's great to see a small, conservative town promoting this sort of thing, and the peaceful township is small enough for visitors to get a good feel for township life. Unusually for Free State, both Zulu and Sotho people live here.

Places to Stay & Eat

Harrismith International Backpackers (☎ 623 0272, 083-412 6728, 44 Piet Retief St) Camping R25, dorm beds R50, singles R65. There's a garden and braai (barbecue) facilities in this home-turned-backpackers. The staff can do pick-ups from Swinburne (R25), if you're coming from KwaZulu-Natal.

Grand National Hotel (☎/fax 622 1060, Cnr Warden & Boshoff Sts) Singles/doubles from R100/180. The old-style Grand National was built in 1896 and is crammed full of character. The outside has recently had a coat of paint; inside, the rooms could also do with some attention.

Harrismith Inn (☎ 622 1011, N5) Singles/doubles R189/219. This is a modern hotel, next to Spur and similar to a Holiday Inn. The rooms have TV and telephone and are good value.

Harrismith Country Lodge (☎ 622 2151, fax 622 2152, McKechnie St) 2-bed chalets R169, 4-bed chalets R219. The former Sir Harry Motel is getting a major overhaul, and the brand new facilities look as if they will be well worth the rand.

The information centre can arrange B&B accommodation in Intabazwe; DB&B costs R140. We saw *Mrs Gambu's B&B*, which is a large, well-furnished house.

Model Bakery Cafe (Warden St) is central and good for takeaway snacks; it also has a small supermarket.

Spur (☎ 623 1319) Burgers R19-25, steaks R40. Next to the Harrismith Inn, Spur has a great playroom for the kids. It also

does Mexican dishes, such as *eeta fajita* which is recommended.

Getting There & Away

Translux runs to Durban (R150), Bloemfontein (R145), Jo'burg (R150) and Cape Town (R355), stopping at the Harrismith Country Lodge on McKechnie St.

If you are interested in travelling to Lesotho, there is a bus that leaves from Amphitheatre Backpackers, just across in KwaZulu-Natal, on Monday to Friday. The trip, via a few South African towns along the Lesotho boarder, costs R220/350 one-way/return and it drops you off at Malealea Lodge in Maleala. Contact Maluti Destinations in Harrismith for information and possibly a transfer to the backpackers.

The Baz Bus may also stop here on its Jo'burg to Durban run if you give enough notice.

For minibus taxis, take a bus to Phuthaditjhaba (see QwaQwa Area later in this chapter) where you'll have a much larger choice of routes and more frequent taxis.

The *Trans Oranje* (Durban–Cape Town) name train stops here. See under Train in the Getting Around chapter for details.

AROUND HARRISMITH

The small **Sterkfontein Dam Nature Reserve** *(☎ 058-622 3520; admission R20 per vehicle; open 7.30am-4pm daily)* is in the Drakensberg foothills, 23km south of Harrismith on the Oliviershoek Pass road into KwaZulu-Natal. This is a very beautiful area, and looking out over this expansive dam with rugged peaks as a backdrop is like gazing across an inland sea. At one of the many viewpoints there's a vulture 'restaurant', but there's no set day or time for feeding. Sunset cruises on the dam's lake are available.

Camping is possible for R30, and there are *4-bed chalets* for R170 per night.

QWAQWA AREA
☎ 058

QwaQwa (master the 'click' pronunciation and you'll win friends) was once a small and extremely poor Homeland east of the

Golden Gate Highlands National Park. QwaQwa (meaning 'Whiter than White'), was named after the sandstone hill that dominates the area.

QwaQwa was created in the early 1980s as a Homeland for southern Sotho people. The dumping of 200,000 people on a tiny patch of agriculturally unviable land, remote from employment centres, was one of the more obscene acts of apartheid. Today, this area is one of the best spots to visit in Free State, now that the 'free' part of that appellation has been realised.

Phuthaditjhaba, adjacent to the town of Witsieshoek and about 50km south-west of Harrismith, was the 'capital' of QwaQwa. There is a **tourist information centre** (☎ 713 0012, fax 713 4342; open Mon-Sat) here, and a few craft shops.

QwaQwa Highlands National Park

This 22,000-hectare park (☎ 713 5301, fax 713 5302) adjoins the eastern side of Golden Gate Highlands National Park and shares the scenery. The **Avondrus Trail** (also known as the Spelonken Trail) is a 27km, two-day (one or two nights) hike. A maximum of 15 people are allowed on the trail and it costs R30 per person for accommodation in *basic huts*. No camping is allowed.

Basotho Cultural Village Within the park, under the lee of Vulture Mountain, you'll find the small but interesting Basotho Cultural Village (☎ 721 0300, ⓔ basotho@ lorea.co.za; tours R15; open daily). A tour is the only way to see the village. There's a curio shop and tearoom, which is pleasant and inexpensive. Try the home-made ginger beer. A guided hiking trail (two hours, R20 per person) explores medicinal and other plants, and a rock-art site.

You can stay in *rondavels* for R120 a double plus R10 for each additional adult. Bring your own food or order it when you book (bookings are essential).

This is a pleasant, friendly place, with a lot of good information on traditional culture but it's a little idealised. To see how most Sotho live in South Africa, take a

township tour in nearby Harrismith (see that section earlier in this chapter).

QwaQwa Conservation Area

The conservation area covers 30,000 hectares in the foothills of both the Maluti Mountains and the Drakensberg. The usual warnings about sudden changes of temperature in the mountains apply, with storms and mists possible in summer and snow in winter.

There are some animals and rare birds, such as the Cape vulture, but the main reason to visit is for the great hiking trails. Even if you don't want to hike, it's well worth making the drive up to the Sentinel car park along an amazing road following the twisting ridge tops.

Hiking Trails The most famous trail is the 10km **Sentinel Hiking Trail**, which commences in Free State and ends in KwaZulu-Natal. The trail starts at the Sentinel car park at an altitude of 2540m and runs for 4km to the top of the Drakensberg plateau, where the average height is 3000m; it's about a two-hour ascent for those of medium fitness. At one point you have to use a chain ladder. Those who find the ladder frightening can take the route up The Gully, which emerges at Beacon Buttress. The reward for the steep ascent is majestic mountain scenery and the opportunity to climb Mont-aux-Sources (3282m). See also the Royal Natal National Park section in the KwaZulu-Natal chapter.

The two-day **Metsi Matsho Hiking Trail** begins at the Witsieshoek Mountain Resort Hotel at 2200m above sea level. From the hotel, it follows the provincial border to Cold Ridge. It then drops, almost in a due northerly direction, to Metsi Matsho (Swartwater) Dam, where there is an overnight hut. Beginning with beautiful views of the mountains, the walk also passes sandstone formations, caves, slopes of proteas and, finally, the dam, where fishing is possible.

Both hikes are free; inquire at Witsieshoek for information on both trails and about other trails that are being developed in the area.

FREE STATE

Places to Stay & Eat

QwaQwa Hotel (☎ 713 0903, fax 713 4989) Singles/doubles R145/155. This hotel in Phuthaditjhaba has packages with meals available. Among the advertised attractions here are beauty contests.

Witsieshoek Mountain Resort Hotel (☎ 713 6361, fax 713 5274) B&B R185 per person. About 25km south of Phuthaditjhaba, this is reputedly South Africa's highest-altitude hotel and is a good source for local hiking information.

There are several fairly ordinary eateries in Phuthaditjhaba including *Da Grill*, which offers snacks and cheap grills. It's basically taxi-rank food served on plates.

Getting There & Away

Minibus taxis from Phuthaditjhaba to Harrismith cost R10; to Bethlehem (usually via Clarens) it's R35.

If you're driving into Phuthaditjhaba from the north, you'll eventually get through the urban sprawl to the tourist information centre (look for a cluster of roofs on the left shaped like Mt Paul). If you're heading for the Witsieshoek Mountain Resort Hotel or the Sentinel Hiking Trail, turn left at the traffic lights at the information centre and keep going.

GOLDEN GATE HIGHLANDS NATIONAL PARK

Golden Gate preserves the unique and spectacular scenery of the foothills of the Maluti Mountains, specifically the beautifully coloured sandstone cliffs and outcrops. The western approach to the park is guarded by immense sandstone cliffs that turn a glowing golden colour in the late afternoon, hence the park's name. There are also quite a few animals, including grey rheboks, blesboks, elands, oribis, Burchell's zebras, jackals, baboons and numerous bird species (see the boxed text 'Bird-watching in Golden Gate').

Winters can be very cold here, with frost and snow; summers are mild but rain falls at this time and cold snaps are possible – if you're out hiking, take warm clothing. There is a shop at the park reception.

Bird-watching in Golden Gate

The bird-watching opportunities in Golden Gate Highlands National Park are particularly good, and more than 140 species have been identified. You may see species such as the rare bearded vulture (*lammergeier*), black eagle, jackal buzzard, southern bald ibis, the endemic orange-throated longclaw (*Macronyx capensis*), the grassbird (*Sphenoaceus afer*) and the ground woodpecker (*Geocolaptus olivaceus*).

Langtoon Dam is a good place to see water birds. Look out for the African black duck (*Anas sparsa*), grey heron (*Ardea cineria*), Egyptian goose (*Alopochen aegyptiacus*) and the very odd-looking hamerkop (*Scopus umbretta*).

Rhebok Hiking Trail

The circular 33km Rhebok Hiking Trail (two days) is a great way to see the park and we've had reports that it has recently been upgraded. The trail takes its name from the grey rhebok, a species of antelope that prefers exposed mountain plateaus, and you will probably see them when hiking. The trail starts at the Glen Reenen Rest Camp, and on the second day the track climbs up to a viewpoint on the side of Generaalskop (2732m), the highest point in the park, from where Mont-aux-Sources and the Malutis can be seen. The return trail to Glen Reenen passes Langtoon Dam.

There are some steep sections so hikers need to be reasonably fit. The trail is limited to 18 people and must be booked through the National Parks Board or **Golden Gate Highlands National Park** *(☎/fax 058-25. 0012)*. There's a fee of R50 per person.

There are also a number of shorter hiking trails in the foothills, ranging from 45 minutes to half a day.

Places to Stay

Book park accommodation through the National Parks Board.

Brandwag Camp Singles/doubles from R180/380, 2-bed self-catering chalet R290. Hotel and self-catering accommodation available at Brandwag; there's also a restaurant here. Camping is not permitted.

Glen Reenen Rest Camp Camp sites R55 (2 people), 3-bed bungalows R190. Glen Reenen is smaller and more basic than Brandwag; the bungalows here have shared ablution facilities.

Getting There & Away
The R712 is a sealed road that runs into the park from Clarens, south of Bethlehem. Minibus taxis run between Bethlehem and Harrismith, via Clarens and Phuthaditjhaba, and go right through the park. Alternatively, with your own vehicle you can approach from Harrismith on the R74 and then the R712.

CLARENS
☎ 058 • postcode 9707
This pretty little town on the junction of the R712 and the R711 (a back road between Bethlehem and Fouriesburg) is well worth a detour from the main drag (the R711 is prettiest between Fouriesburg and Clarens). The town is surrounded by large limestone rocks, such as **Titanic Rock**, and the magnificent Maluti Mountains form a backdrop.

Artists have set up studios in and around Clarens and there are many galleries and craft shops in town. Of course, there's also the usual compact but desperately poor 'township' on the edge of town.

The **information centre** (☎ 256 1542, e clarens@bhm.dorea.co.za; open 9am-1pm & 2pm-5pm daily) has enthusiastic staff.

There's lots of opportunity for **fly fishing** (casting is the trickiest part) in dams and rivers around here. Rainbow and brown trout are usually on offer and it costs around R50 per day including a rod. Inquire at the information centre for details.

Places to Stay & Eat
Bokpoort Holiday Farm & Game Ranch (☎ 256 1181, fax 256 1048) Camp sites R20, dorm beds R40, B&B R135 per person. This place is backpacker-friendly and in a great spot between Clarens and Golden Gate. Horse riding (R95 for two hours) is available and there are mountain-bike trails (but

you must have your own bike). To get here, travel 5km from Clarens on the Golden Gate road, then turn off at the big Bokpoort Holiday Farm sign and drive another 3km along the dirt road.

Clarens Inn (☎ 256 1119) Dorm beds R40. In town, Clarens Inn is a good budget option at the bottom of Van Reenen St (after the Le Roux turn-off) and has braai facilities.

The Thistle Stop B&B (☎/fax 256 1003) Self-catering chalet R65 per person, B&B R110 per person. This is a superb place with huge guest rooms and a private chalet sleeping up to four people.

Berg Cottage (☎/fax 256 1112) Self-catering cottage R70 per person (minimum R280). This rustic little place is north on the road that runs on the eastern side of President Square. Ask the owners about *Strawberry Fayre*, a B&B costing R160 a double.

Street Cafe (☎ 256 1064, Hoof St) Light lunches R15-30. This is a good place for a snack or a meal, and the *pub* next door has live music on weekends.

Getting There & Away
Minibus taxis run between Bethlehem and Harrismith, via Clarens and Phuthaditjhaba.

BETHLEHEM
☎ 058 • postcode 9701
This is one of the more pleasant towns in Free State. Voortrekkers came to this area in the 1840s and Bethlehem was established on the farm Pretoriuskloof in 1864. Devout Voortrekkers gave the name Jordaan to the river that flows through town. Bethlehem is now a large town and the main centre of eastern Free State.

The **tourist office** (☎ 303 5732; open 7.30am-1pm & 2pm-4pm Mon-Fri) is in the civic centre on Muller St, near the corner of Roux St.

Things to See & Do
As usual for this area there are some impressive sandstone buildings, including the **old magistrate's office**, on the corner of Louw and Van der Merwe Sts; and the **NG**

Moederkerk in the town centre. Also right in town is the tiny **Pretoriuskloof Nature Reserve**, *(adult/child R5/2; open 8am-5pm Apr-Sept, 7.30am-6pm Oct-Mar)* on the banks of the Jordaan near the corner of Kerk and Kort Sts.

The easy, two day **Wolhuterskop Hiking Trail** covers a 23km loop through the **Wolhuterskop Nature Reserve** (☎ 303 4056; admission R17/4 for cars/bicycles; open daily), starting just past Loch Athlone Holiday Resort. There is a *hut* on the trail, 18km out, where you can stay overnight, and there is also a *camp site*; a fee of about R25 per person is charged. From the hut it is only a 5km return walk to the resort. There is also a horse trail here (R20 per hour). The overnight, 36km **Houtkop Hiking Trail** begins near Loch Athlone.

Places to Stay

Loch Athlone Holiday Resort (☎/fax 303 4981) Camp site R50, chalets from R80 per person. This resort is about 3km from the town centre and is very popular with families. There are all kinds of activities, including 'super tubing' for the kids, fishing and boating. Day visits are R20 per person.

There are some good B&Bs in the area. The tourist office has a full list including some cheaper places.

Fisant & Bokmakierie Guesthouse (☎ 303 7144, fax 303 1192, 8-10 Thoi Oosthuyse St) Singles/doubles from R195/290. This well-established, acclaimed guesthouse is the best in town and possibly the province. The owners are very friendly and each room is tastefully furnished and has natural lighting. As an indication of their success, the owners bought Bokmakierie next door to the Fisant. If it's full staff will help you find alternative accommodation.

Park Hotel (☎/fax 303 5191, 23 Muller St) Budget singles/doubles R115/145, standard rooms R170/200, superior rooms R220/250. On the corner of High St, the Park Hotel is a lovely old-style hotel built in 1928. Breakfast costs R25 extra and a three-course dinner costs R50.

Royal Hotel (☎ 303 5448, 9 Boshoff St) Singles/doubles R130/150, suites R220. The Royal is reasonable value and has secure parking for an extra R10.

Places to Eat

The *cafe* in Park Hotel is the best place for a quick meal.

Nix Pub on Kerk St, across from the church, is a cosy place for a drink.

Athlone Castle Ship Restaurant (☎ 303 7534) Steaks R40. Located at the Loch Athlone Holiday Resort, the restaurant is shaped like the mail ship *Athlone Castle* and is full of memorabilia. The food isn't bad either.

O'Hagan's (☎ 303 0919, 8 Theron St, Meals R25-50. Above-average pub fare, and definitely the best of the 'chain' pubs, the service here is particularly good.

Getting There & Away

Translux runs to Durban (R150) and Cape Town (R340), as does Greyhound at similar fares. Translux buses stop at Top Grill on Church St and Greyhound stops at Wimpy on the corner of Muller and Hospital Sts.

The weekly *Trans Oranje* (Cape Town–Durban) name train stops here. See under Train in the Getting Around chapter for more details. The station is north of the centre – head up Commissioner St.

The minibus taxi ranks are around the corner of Cambridge and Gholf Sts, north of the town centre on the way to the train station. There are minibus taxis to Harrismith via Clarens.

FOURIESBURG
☎ 058 • postcode 9725

Fouriesburg is 10km north of the Caledonspoort border post for Lesotho. The town is surrounded by mountains, the Witteberge to the west and the Maluti Mountains to the east. Two nearby peaks, Snijmanshoek and Visierskerf, are the highest in Free State.

During the Anglo-Boer War, Fouriesburg town was pronounced the capital of the Free State after the British occupied Bethlehem. There are a number of fine old sandstone buildings in the town including President Steyn's house.

Camelroc Guest Farm (☎ 223 0368, fax 223 0012) Camp sites R20 per person, B&B R120 per person, self-catering chalets R290 (4 people). This farm, with fine views over the Maluti Mountains, has a variety of guest accommodation, as well as hiking trails.

BRANDWATER HIKING TRAIL

The Brandwater *(bookings ☎ 058-223 0050)* offers a 72km, five-day circular walk from the Meiringskloof caravan park, 3km from Fouriesburg, through varied sandstone country offering good views of the Rooiberg, Maluti and Witteberge ranges. Three of the overnight stops are in caves, and a fourth night is in an old sandstone farm building. Most of the walk, the longest in the Free State, is over private land and there's a fee of about R100 per person. You'll need a sleeping bag and your own food. If the Brandwater is too long for you, ask about overnight hikes in the same area, such as the Dikitla and the Ventersberg Trails.

RUSTLER'S VALLEY

This remote valley, in the heart of the conservative Free State, is the vanguard of the dare to be different' movement in the new South Africa. Rustler's attracts a diverse crowd: yuppies from Jo'burg, remnant hippies from all parts of the continent and ideas' people from all over the globe.

You can swim in the pool, wander into the valley, swim or fish in the many dams, walk up onto sandstone escarpments, climb imposing Nyakalesoba (Witchdoctor's Eye), ride into the labyrinthine dongas (gullies) on a placid horse or discuss existential philosophy in the bar with the semipermanent residents of Rustler's.

The Easter **music festival** here is a highlight of the year for alternative South Africans, although in recent years there was a cultural split between the ravers and the rest, and the 'peace and love' was somewhat disturbed.

Rustler's (☎/fax 051-933 3939, **W** *www .rustlers.co.za)* Camp sites R15, dorm beds R40, doubles 160, 2-bed bungalows R200. Rustler's has a variety of mostly inexpen-sive accommodation, including plenty of options for backpackers. Give it a call if you need a lift from Ficksburg (for a small fee).

Getting There & Away

Rustler's does pick-ups for a fee. If you've got your own vehicle, the main turn-off is about 25km south of Fouriesburg on the R26 to Ficksburg. Head west on the dirt road that crosses a train line. From the turn-off it is about 12km to Rustler's. When you reach a prominent crossroads where there are numerous signposts, take the sharp turn to the right (the road to Nebo is behind). A few kilometres further on there is another junction; Rustler's is to the right. You can also reach Rustler's from the south.

FICKSBURG

☎ 051 • postcode 9730

Ficksburg is a pretty place that's a little larger than Ladybrand. It's in sandstone country and there are some fine buildings including the town hall, the NG Kerk and the post office.

Currently tourist information is available in the **library** *(☎ 933 2322)* near Hotel Hoogland.

The mild summers and cold winters of this area (the Maluti Mountains across the river in Lesotho often have snow) are good for growing stone fruits, and Ficksburg is the centre of the Free State's cherry industry. There's a Cherry Festival in November but September and October are the best times to see the trees in bloom. The **Cherry Trail** is a tourist route around the district; there are several orchards to visit, various art and craft shops and guest farms.

There are quite a few **hiking trails** in the area but most are on private property, so you need to book and usually pay a small fee. Check at the library for details.

Places to Stay & Eat

Thom Park (☎ 083-592 1267, Voortrekker St) Sites R30 plus R5 per person. The excellent municipal caravan park, Thom Park, is very green and shady. You can also camp at *Meulspruit Dam*, 5km from town on the R26 to Clocolan.

FREE STATE

Hotel Hoogland (☎ 933 2214) Singles/doubles B&B R160/300. Near Voortrekker St, this is better than many small-town hotels. The facilities are similar to most and the rooms lack air-con but it's a nice place to stay. There are some cheaper rooms with shared bathroom (R240 a double), and weekend specials are offered. There's a restaurant on the upstairs veranda that has fairly standard food (at slightly higher than standard prices) and very good service.

Bella Rosa Guesthouse (☎ 933 2623, 21 Bloem St) Singles/doubles B&B R190/300. This excellent guesthouse does a roaring trade; there's a bar and a restaurant here.

The Pizza Parlour (☎ 933 4792, 64b Piet Retief St) Pizzas R25. Pizza Parlour does pizzas like Mama used to; well, they're almost as good.

The *Bottling Co Pub & Restaurant* (☎ 933 2404, Piet Retief St) is a top little spot for an evening beer in the centre of town.

Getting There & Away
Coming from Jo'burg, you can get to Ficksburg by taking a minibus taxi to Bethlehem. At Bethlehem change minibus taxi for Ficksburg.

LADYBRAND
☎ 051 • postcode 9745
Ladybrand, also on the R26, is the closest South African town to the main border post with Lesotho. It's around 16km from here to Maseru, Lesotho's capital.

The library (☎ 924 0654, Cnr Joubert & Voortrekker Sts) has tourist information.

There are some nice **sandstone buildings** including the town hall and the old magistrate's court. The **Catharina Brand Museum** (☎ 924 0654) has archaeological displays including rock paintings and instruments and tools dating back to the Stone Age. Also housed here is a replica of the fossil *Diathrognatus protozoan*, which was found in a quarry near the town; this important find provides a glimmer of a link between reptile and mammal in the evolutionary process. Ashes taken from an ancient hearth in the **Rose Cottage Cave**, not far from Ladybrand, are 50,000 years old.

About 12km from Ladybrand is one of the most quaint churches you are ever likely to see. **Modderpoort Cave Church**, built in 1869, is nestled under a huge boulder in scenic surroundings.

Places to Stay & Eat
Leliehoek Holiday Resort (☎ 924 0260) Camp sites R50, chalets R150. Located 2km south of the town hall, Leliehoek is a peaceful spot.

Country Lodge (☎ 924 3200, fax 924 2611, 19 Joubert St) Singles/doubles R140/170. Ladybrand's only hotel is a friendly small place with secure parking.

Don's Inn (☎ 924 1316, 13 Joubert St) Singles/doubles B&B R150/239. This is a small motel-style place with good rooms just up the road from the Country Lodge.

Cranberry Cottage (☎ 924 2290, fax 924 1544, 37 Beeton St) Singles B&B R175/205, doubles R280-350. This is perhaps the most interesting B&B in town. It offers luxury accommodation, as well as rooms in the nearby recycled train station – only four trains a week rumble past.

Fort Amity (☎ 924 3131, fax 924 1633, 18 van Riebeeck St) Singles/doubles B&B from R165/330. Despite its name, this isn't a fort, it's a large house, but it's still impressive, and has a tennis court and large gardens.

Impero Romano (☎ 924 1184, 11 Church St) Starters R14-24, mains R19-38. This is the most sophisticated restaurant in this quiet town; the food is excellent and surprisingly reasonable in price.

Getting There & Away
Minibus taxis can be found near the church on Piet Retief St. Most run to nearby areas including Ficksburg (R20). For a wide choice of destinations, take a minibus taxi to Maseru Bridge (at the Lesotho border for R5 and find a long-distance taxi in the big minibus taxi rank there.

ZASTRON
☎ 051 • postcode 9950
Zastron, on the R726, is a quiet little town under the foothills of the Aasvoëlberg and

Maluti Mountains. It's the centre of a rural community and, with Lesotho forming an arc around this section of Free State, Zastron has long-established trading links with the kingdom of Lesotho.

There are some **San paintings** in the area; the best are in the Seekoei and Hoffman Caves. The **Eye of Zastron**, a mildly interesting rock formation with a 9m hole, is best seen from the road to Aliwal North. There are also various walks and climbs that you can do.

Municipal caravan park (☎ 673 1397) Camp sites R40. This park is a few kilometres out of town; it's a nice walk down a wooded gorge.

Maluti Hotel (☎/fax 673 2112) Singles/doubles R137/226. This three-star place in town is rather pleasant and the *Horse & Hound* pub is on site.

The nearest town in Lesotho is Mohale's Hoek, 55km away on a dirt road.

Southern Free State

Southern Free State typifies much of the province: It is dusty, harsh and dry. It's pretty much an area that you'll just transit through, although some of the small old towns are worth a look.

TUSSEN DIE RIVIERE GAME FARM

This 23,000-hectare reserve *(☎/fax 051-763 1114; admission R20 per vehicle; open Sept-Apr)* has more animals than any other reserve in Free State; mostly small mammals and various species of antelope but also white rhinos and hippos. The country is varied, with plains and ridges and a long frontage on the Orange River. For keen hikers, there are the 7km Middelpunt, the 12km Klipstapel and the 16km Orange River hiking trails; water must be carried on all of them.

There are *camp sites* for R30/50 without/with power, and inexpensive two-bed *chalets* for R110 but no food is available. The entrance gate is on the road between Bethulie and Smithfield (R701), about 15km from Bethulie or 65km east of the N1.

There's no public transport, so you'll need your own vehicle.

GARIEP DAM NATURE RESERVE
☎ 051

West of Tussen Die Riviere, on the Orange River, this 13,000-hectare reserve *(☎ 754 0026; admission R20 per vehicle)* surrounds one of the largest dams in South Africa (it used to be called the Hendrik Verwoerd Dam). Be warned, the dam is described in brochures as 'a Mecca for motorboats'. In the flat, arid Karoo grassland, several animal species including Cape mountain zebras, can be seen. There are three *chalets* in the reserve, which cost R200, and you can *camp* for R30.

There's quite a lot of accommodation in the town of Gariep Dam, near the dam wall at the western end. The town was built to house the workers constructing the dam. There are several *B&Bs* charging from R70 per person.

Aventura Midwaters Resort (☎/fax 754 0045) Camp sites R100 (2 people), 2-bed chalets R450. This place is well laid out but the opportunity for water sports here makes it expensive.

Gariep Dam Hotel (☎ 754 0060) Singles/doubles R235/380. This hotel is pricey but comfortable; breakfast is extra.

PHILIPPOLIS
☎ 051 • postcode 9970

On the R717, Philippolis is a beautiful little place; it's the oldest town in Free State, founded in 1823 as a mission station. The Griquas who settled here in 1826 sold the town and then trekked overland, through Lesotho, to settle in Griqualand East (see the Kokstad section in the KwaZulu-Natal chapter). There are a number of interesting buildings in Philippolis, including the NG Kerk, the library and many places built in Karoo style.

If you've ever fancied spending a night in jail, *The Old Jail (☎ 082 550 4421)* is your big chance. The old jail in town has been converted into basic but comfortable accommodation and the 'cells' are virtually soundproof.

FAURESMITH
☎ 051 • postcode 9978

Fauresmith is famous for the train line that runs along the main street. North of town on the Petrusburg road is the 4500-hectare

Kalkfontein Dam Nature Reserve (☎ 722 1441; admission R20 per vehicle), a great place to see the local black population harvesting yellow fish. There are *camp sites* here for R30.

DIANA FRANCES JONES

DIANA FRANCES JONES

KIM WILDMAN

DIANA FRANCES JONES

Lesotho is completely encircled by South Africa. Brace yourself for hikes in remote areas, glimpses of traditional rural life and pony treks offering spectacular views.

Lesotho

Lesotho (le-**soo**-too), duly dubbed 'the kingdom in the sky', is a mountainous kingdom, about the size of Belgium, that is surrounded by South Africa. Its forbidding terrain and the defensive walls of the Drakensberg and Maluti ranges gave both sanctuary and strategic advantage to the Basotho (the people of Lesotho), who forged a nation while playing a key role in the manoeuvres of the white invaders on the plains below.

Lesotho offers the rare opportunity to meet and stay with people living traditional lifestyles. You can do this when hiking or taking one of the well-organised pony treks on offer. Although Lesotho is a poor Third World country, you don't have to rough it – unless you want to, of course. There are good accommodation options in Maseru, and with an ordinary hire car you can see some spectacular scenery and reach at least two of the pony-trekking centres. Public transport is quite good (if uncomfortable) in much of the country, or you can just head off into the mountains and valleys and walk.

After spending time in South Africa, it's a real relief to visit a country that isn't suffering the after-effects of apartheid. You'll meet a lot of friendly, self-assured people who judge you neither by the colour of your skin nor by the details on your passport.

Facts about Lesotho

HISTORY
Before the 19th Century
The mountainous region that makes up modern Lesotho was settled by Basotho peoples comparatively recently, possibly as late as the 16th century.

Early Basotho society was made up of small chiefdoms, which fragmented as groups broke away in search of new land. Cattle and cultivation were the mainstays of the economy, and extensive trade links were

LESOTHO AT A GLANCE

Capital: Maseru
Population: 2,143,141
Time: GMT/UTC + 2
Area: 30,355 sq km
International Dialling Code: ☎ 266
Per Capita GDP: US$2240
Currency: loti (plural maloti), divided into 100 lisente
Languages: South Sotho and English

Lesotho p594

Highlights
• Ride sure-footed Basotho ponies through the rugged and beautiful interior.

• Spend a night in a Basotho village on the edge of townships surrounding Maseru.

• Take up the challenge of wilderness hiking along the top of the Drakensberg range.

• Climb Thaba-Bosiu (Mountain at Night), where King Moshoeshoe the Great established his second mountain stronghold.

• Drive the spectacular road between Leribe and Katse over the Maluti Mountains.

• Follow in the fossilised footsteps of dinosaurs near Quthing (Moyeni).

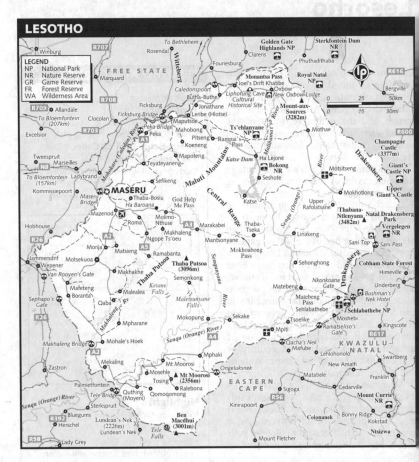

LESOTHO

LEGEND
NP National Park
NR Nature Reserve
GR Game Reserve
FR Forest Reserve
WA Wilderness Area

forged between groups of Basotho. Grain and hides were exported in exchange for iron from the Transvaal area.

The Beginnings of Basotholand

By the early 19th century, white traders were on the scene, exchanging beads for cattle. They were soon followed by the Voortrekkers (literally fore-trekkers or pioneers) and pressure on Basotho grazing lands grew. Even without white encroachment, Basotho society had reached the point where it had expanded as far as it could and would have to adapt to living in a finite territory. On top of this came the disaster of the *difaqane* (forced migration).

The rapid consolidation and expansion of the Zulu state under the leadership of Shaka and later Dingaan, resulted in a chain reaction of turmoil throughout Southern Africa. Huge numbers of people were displaced, their tribes shattered and their land lost, and they, in turn, attacked other tribes. That the loosely organised southern Basotho society survived this period was largely due to the abilities of King Moshoeshoe the Great (pronounced Mo-shwe-shwe but sometimes clipped to Moshesh).

Moshoeshoe began as a leader of a small village and in about 1820 he led his villagers to Butha-Buthe. From this mountain stronghold his people survived the first battles of the difaqane and in 1824 Moshoeshoe began his policy of assisting refugees on the condition that they help in his defence. Later in the same year he moved his people again, to Thaba-Bosiu, a mountain top that was even easier to defend.

From Thaba-Bosiu, Moshoeshoe played a patient game of placating the stronger local rulers and granting protection – as well as land and cattle – to groups of refugees. By 1840 his people numbered about 40,000 and his power base was protected by groups who had settled on his outlying lands and were partially under his authority. These people and others like them were to form Basotholand, which, by the time of Moshoeshoe's death in 1870, had a population exceeding 150,000.

Another factor in Basotholand's emergence and survival was Moshoeshoe's welcoming of Catholic missionaries, and his ability to take their advice without being dominated by them. The first missionaries to arrive in the area, in 1833, were from the Paris Evangelical Missionary Society. Moshoeshoe made one of them his adviser, and the sophisticated diplomacy that had marked his dealings with local chiefs now extended to his dealings with the Europeans. The missions, often situated in remote parts of the kingdom, served as tangible symbols of his authority, and in return for some Christianisation of Basotho customs, the missionaries were disposed to defend the rights of 'their' Basotho against the new threat: British and Boer expansion.

European Aggression & Annexation

The Boers crossed the Senqu (Orange) River in the 1830s, and by 1843 Moshoeshoe was sufficiently concerned by their numbers to ally himself with the British Cape Colony government. The resulting treaties defined his borders but did little to stop squabbles with the Boers, who regarded the grazing rights they'd been granted as title to the land

they occupied, namely the fertile lowveld west of the Mohokare (Caledon) River.

The British residents, installed in Basotholand as a condition of the treaties, decided that Moshoeshoe was too powerful and engineered an unsuccessful attack on his kingdom. In 1854 the British withdrew from the area, having fixed the boundaries of Basotholand. The Boers pressed their claims on the land, and increasing tension led to the 1858 Orange Free State–Basotho War. Moshoeshoe won yet another major battle, and the situation simmered along until 1865 when another Orange Free State–Basotho War erupted. This time Moshoeshoe suffered setbacks and, as a consequence, was forced to sign away much of the western lowlands.

The Boers' hunger for land showed no sign of diminishing and, in 1868, Moshoeshoe again called on the British, this time from the imperial government in London. A high commission was formed to adjudicate the dispute and the result was the loss of more of Basotholand's territory. It was obvious that no treaty between the Boers and the Basotho would hold for long, and continual war between the Orange Free State and Basotholand was bad for British interests. The British solution was simply to annex Basotholand.

After Moshoeshoe the Great

The British, their imperial policy changing yet again, gave control of Basotholand to the Cape Colony in 1871. Moshoeshoe had died the year before and squabbles over succession were dividing the country. The Cape Colony administration exploited this, reducing the powers of chiefs and limiting them to their individual areas.

The Gun War of 1880 began as a protest against the refusal of the Cape Colony administration to allow the Basotho to own firearms, but it quickly became a battle between rebel chiefs on one side and the Cape Colony and collaborating chiefs on the other. The war ended in a stalemate (making it one of the few wars in the area that didn't result in Africans being crushed by Europeans), with the Cape government discredited.

A shaky peace followed, but when another war appeared imminent, the British government again took over direct control of Basotholand in 1884. The imperial British government decided to back strong local leaders rather than rule through its own officers, and this helped to stabilise the country. One unexpected benefit of direct British rule was that, when the Union of South Africa was created in 1910, Basotholand was a British protectorate and was not included in the union. If the Cape Colony had retained control, Lesotho would have become part of South Africa and would then have become a Homeland under the apartheid regime.

Ruling through chiefs might have defused power struggles between rival chiefs, but it did nothing to develop democracy in the country. If anything it created a feudal state more open to abuse than Moshoeshoe's loose confederation of subordinate chiefs.

Home Rule & Independence

In 1910 the Basotholand National Council was formed. This advisory body to the colonial government was composed of members nominated by the chiefs. After decades of allegations of corruption and favouritism, reforms were made in the 1940s to make appointments to the council more democratic.

In the mid-1950s the council requested internal self-government and in 1960, a new constitution was in place and elections were held for a legislative council. Half its members were elected (in a men-only vote) and the other half was made up of chiefs and the appointed representatives of the king.

Meanwhile, political parties had formed. The main contenders were the Basotholand Congress Party (BCP), similar to South Africa's ANC, and the Basotholand National Party (BNP), a conservative party headed by Chief Leabua Jonathan.

The BCP won the 1960 elections and demanded full independence from Britain. This was eventually agreed to and a new constitution was drawn up, with independence to come into effect in 1966. However, at the elections in 1965 the BCP lost power to the BNP and Chief Jonathan became the first prime minister of the new Kingdom of Lesotho. Just why the BCP lost is debatable, but the fact that the BNP promised cooperation with the South African apartheid regime and in turn received massive support from it must have been significant.

As most of the civil service was still loyal to the BCP, Chief Jonathan did not have an easy time. Stripping King Moshoeshoe II of the few powers that the new constitution had left him did not endear Chief Jonathan's government to the people and, in the 1970 election, the BCP regained power.

Chief Jonathan responded by suspending the constitution, arresting then expelling the king and banning opposition parties. The king, after an exile in Holland, was allowed to return, and Chief Jonathan attempted to form a government of national reconciliation. This was partly successful, with several BCP members joining the government. However, some, including the leader Ntsu Mokhehle resisted and attempted to stage a coup in 1974. The coup failed and resulted in the death of many BCP supporters and the jailing or exile of the BCP leadership. Lesotho effectively became a one-party state.

Trouble continued and repressive measures were taken. Chief Jonathan may have continued to cling to power had he not changed his attitude towards South Africa, although this change was partly caused by a need to placate popular opposition to South Africa. He called for the return of land in the Orange Free State that had been stolen from the original Basotholand, and, more seriously from the South African point of view, began criticising apartheid, allegedly offering refuge to ANC guerrillas and flirting with Cuba. Relations soured to the point where South Africa closed Lesotho's borders, strangling the movement of goods and people.

The Lesotho military took action and Chief Jonathan was deposed in 1986. The military council, headed by Major General Lekhanya, restored the king as head of state. This was a popular move, but eventually agitation for democratic reform rose again. In 1990, King Moshoeshoe II was deposed in favour of his son, Prince Mohato Bereng Seeisa (Letsie III). Elections in 1993 resulted in the return of the BCP to government.

In 1995, Letsie III abdicated in favour of his father, and five years after being deposed

Moshoeshoe II was reinstated as king. He restored some calm to Lesotho after a year of unrest. Tragically, less than a year later, in January 1996, he was killed when his 4WD plunged over a cliff in the Maluti Mountains. There are, of course, conspiracy theories about this. Letsie III was again made king.

The BCP was split between those who wanted Prime Minister Ntsu Mokhehle to remain as leader and those who opposed him. Mokhehle formed the breakaway Lesotho Congress for Democracy (LCD) and continued to govern.

Elections & Invasion

Elections were held in 1998, and while international observers agreed that these had been reasonably fair, many people protested that there had been widespread cheating by the LCD, which won in a landslide. Tensions between the public service and the government became acute, and the military was also split.

Following months of protests, the government was losing control. In late September 1998 it called on the Southern African Development Community (SADC) treaty partners, Botswana, South Africa and Zimbabwe, to help restore order. Troops, mainly South African, entered the kingdom. (The acting president of South Africa at the time was Chief Buthelezi as Nelson Mandela was overseas.)

The operation was expected to last 24 hours but rebel elements of the Lesotho army put up strong resistance and there was heavy fighting in Maseru. The fighting was soon over, but order had broken down and many shops and other businesses in Maseru were torched. Foreign-owned businesses have been singled out, presumably by people protesting the invasion, although a lot of plain old-fashioned looting went on as well.

The government had initially agreed to call new elections for 2000, but due to intense political wrangling and lack of preparation, the elections were postponed to early 2001. However, further political disputes, over the composition of the national assembly and the method of voter registration, have again forced the postponement of the long-awaited general elections to early 2002.

GEOGRAPHY

Lesotho's borders are mainly natural and it is completely surrounded by South Africa. The border from its northern tip to its western side, where it juts out almost to the town of Wepener in South Africa, is formed by the Mohokare (Caledon) River. The eastern border is defined by the rugged escarpment of the Drakensberg, and highveld country forms much of the southern border.

All of Lesotho exceeds 1000m in altitude, with peaks of over 3000m in the Central Range and near the escarpment of the Drakensberg. The tourist slogan 'kingdom in the sky' is not far wrong as Lesotho's lowest point is the highest of any country on Earth. The highest mountain in Southern Africa (the highest point south of Mt Kilimanjaro) is the Thabana-Ntlenyana (3482m), near Sani Pass in eastern Lesotho.

CLIMATE

Lesotho's winters are cold and clear. Frosts are common and there are snowfalls in the high country and sometimes at lower altitudes. At other times of the year, snow has been known to fall (especially on the peaks, where the weather is dangerously changeable), but rain and mist are more common bugbears for drivers and hikers. Nearly all of Lesotho's rain falls between October and April, with spectacular thunderstorms in summer – a few people are killed by lightning every year. In the valleys, summer days can be hot, with temperatures over 30°C.

Never go into the mountains, even for an afternoon, without a sleeping bag, tent and sufficient food for a couple of days in case you get fogged in. Even in summer it can be freezing.

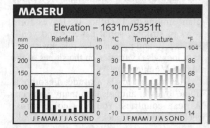

LESOTHO

ECOLOGY & ENVIRONMENT

There are serious environmental concerns about the controversial Highlands Water Project, which will harness Lesotho's abundant water resources to provide water and electricity to a large part of Southern Africa (see the boxed text 'Lesotho Highlands Water Project' later in this chapter).

Traditional Basotho communities have been disrupted, although compensation has been promised. With only around 10% of Lesotho's land suitable for agriculture, the new Mohale Dam (currently under construction about 35km from Katse Dam) will flood some of the most fertile land in the country. Other troubling unknowns include the effects on the ecology of the Senqu (Orange) River and the impact on Namibia, a downstream user with its own water shortage problems.

Other key environmental issues include animal population pressure (which results in overgrazing) and soil erosion. About 18 to 20 tonnes of topsoil per hectare are lost each year and it has been estimated that there will be no cultivatable land left in Lesotho by 2040.

On a brighter note Lesotho and South Africa recently combined forces in a multi-million dollar environment conservation project. Beginning in 2001, the Maluti–Drakensberg Transfrontier Conservation and Development Project aims to protect and develop the alpine ecosystem of the Maluti and Drakensberg mountains, which includes the spiral aloe flower and the rare bearded vulture.

FLORA & FAUNA

The high plains and mountains are home to cape alpine flowers. The national flower, the spiral aloe *(Aloe polyphylla)*, is a strange plant unique to Lesotho. Its leaves form rows of striking, spiral patterns and you'll see its left- and right-handed (clockwise and anticlockwise) varieties on the slopes of the Maluti Mountains.

Due mainly to its altitude, Lesotho is home to fewer animals than many Southern African countries. You may come across rheboks and reedbucks, and in the Drak-

ensberg, elands are still present. Baboons and jackals are reasonably common and there are also mongooses and meerkats.

Lesotho's birdlife is rich, with just less than 300 species recorded. The Drakensberg is an excellent place for bird-watching; bearded vultures and black eagles are found here. Lesotho is also one of the few places you may spot the extremely rare bald ibis.

GOVERNMENT & POLITICS

Lesotho has a hereditary monarchy. The royal family's symbol is the crocodile – a creature that does not occur in Lesotho. The king is the head of state but does not exercise executive power. Under traditional law, the king can be deposed by a majority vote of the College of Chiefs. The current monarch is King Letsie III.

Lesotho's parliament is bicameral, consisting of the national assembly and the senate. The national assembly is made up of 80 members who are elected for five-year terms. There are no elections for the senate, which consists of 22 chiefs and 11 nominated members. Executive power resides in the cabinet headed by the prime minister. The current prime minister is Pakalitha Mosisili of the Lesotho Congress for Democracy (LCD).

ECONOMY

Lesotho is one of the world's poorest countries, with few natural resources other than water. Very little manufacturing takes place in the kingdom and most goods, including much of the country's food, are imported. Given that the economy is almost entirely dependent on subsistence agriculture, the problem of soil erosion (see Ecology & Environment earlier) has major implications.

From the latter half of the 19th century onwards, Lesotho's main export had been labour with approximately 60% of males working in South Africa, mainly in the mining industry. During the 1990s, recession in South Africa resulted in a reduced demand for labourers from Lesotho. The closure of several South African gold mines during 2000 left some 27,000 Basotho miners

Rain-Making Ceremony

Basotho culture is enriched by many customs, some of which are quite light-hearted. This frivolity is evident in the last-resort ceremony for rain-making, which is detailed in the pamphlet *Customs & Superstitions in Basutholand* by Justinus Sechefo.

A first attempt at bringing rain is made by the men of the village, who climb to the top of a nearby mountain and kill every animal they can find. The entrails of the animals are thrown into streams and the men return home, drenched from the heavy rain. If the rain isn't falling, the village calls in a *moroka-pula* (rain-maker). If he fails, it's the turn of the village's young women. Theirs is the ceremony of last resort.

They go to a neighbouring village and the quickest of them enters a hut and steals the *lesokoana*, which can be any wooden cooking utensil. She flees from the village with the lesokoana, raising the alarm herself if she hasn't already been spotted. When the village women run out to reclaim the lesokoana, the young women toss it back and forth, sometimes losing it and sometimes regaining it. This game attracts spectators from both villages and ends when one group makes it back to their village with the lesokoana.

The winners enter the village, their heads and waists bedecked with green leaves, singing joyously. Even if the ceremony still fails to bring rain, at least everyone stops worrying about the drought for a while.

jobless. These massive retrenchments strained the country's already fragile economy and deepened its acute unemployment crisis. Unemployment is now estimated at between 40% and 45%.

In early 2001 both the IMF and the World Bank announced new funding programs for Lesotho totalling over US$47 million. The IMF approved a US$19 million loan help Lesotho alleviate poverty and facilitate economic growth. In addition the World Bank has agreed to provide the Lesotho government with US$28.6 million to improve business infrastructure and attract private investment.

It is also hoped that the ongoing Lesotho Highlands Water Project, which had a beneficial effect on the economy during the late 1990s, might make Lesotho more economically independent (see the boxed text 'Lesotho Highlands Water Project' later in this chapter).

POPULATION & PEOPLE

The 2,143,141 citizens of Lesotho are known as the Basotho people. Culturally, most are Southern Sotho and most speak South Sotho. The melding of the Basotho nation was largely the result of King Moshoeshoe's 19th-century military and diplomatic triumphs; over time, the many diverse subgroups and peoples that he brought together have merged into a homogeneous society. The capital city Maseru, with 170,000 people, is the only population centre larger than a small town.

Traditional culture is still strong despite changes in society and contact with the rest of the world (see the special section 'Peoples of the Region' for information about traditional Basotho culture).

RELIGION

Thanks to the important role that French and Canadian missionaries played in the creation of King Moshoeshoe's Lesotho, most people are at least nominally Christian, with a high percentage of these being Catholic. However, traditional beliefs are still strong in rural areas, probably because the beliefs are tied so closely to both the important and trivial details of everyday life, and seem to coexist with Christianity.

LANGUAGE

The official languages are southern Sotho and English. For some useful words and phrases in South Sotho, see the Language chapter.

LESOTHO

Facts for the Visitor

SUGGESTED ITINERARIES

If you're in Lesotho for a week, there's no need to stop long in Maseru – head south toward Morija where you will find a great museum with displays of Basotho culture. Then continue to Malealea – the 'gem' of Lesotho. Malealea Lodge is the best place in the country to go pony trekking. Depending on time, you could then go down to Quthing (Moyeni) and check out the 180-million-year-old dinosaur footprints.

With two weeks you could add on a visit to Teyateyaneng, north of Maseru, the craft centre of Lesotho. Then after Morija, Malealea and Quthing (Moyeni) you could head to Sehlabathebe National Park, where you can really get away from it all for a few days, before returning to South Africa.

PLANNING
When to Go

Lesotho is worth visiting year round but the weather can determine what you do. In winter be prepared for cold conditions and snow. In summer, rain and mist should be taken into account. In remote areas (a large proportion of the country) roads are often overrun by flooding rivers in summer.

Maps

The **Department of Land, Surveys & Physical Planning** (Lerotholi Rd, PO Box 876, Maseru 100) sells some excellent maps of Lesotho. The 1:250,000-scale map, which covers the whole country (yes, it's that small), is best for driving and costs M30. For trekking or driving in very rugged areas you might want the 1:50,000 series, at about M10 each. The problem with these maps is that they have not caught up with Lesotho's rapid program of road building. Ask the friendly staff at the department for the latest information.

The maps are produced in conjunction with the British government, and you can buy them in the UK from the **Ordnance Survey** (Romsey Rd, Southampton, SO9 4DH, UK). To order maps from Lesotho write to the Department of Land, Surveys & Physical Planning, Ministry of the Interior (see address details above).

TOURIST OFFICES

In Lesotho there's only one **tourist office** (☎ 313760, fax 310108, e ltbhq@ltb.org.ls, informsu@ltb.org.ls, Kingsway, Maseru).

VISAS & DOCUMENTS

The visa situation has changed a couple of times lately and it might have changed again by the time you get to Lesotho.

Citizens of most Western European countries, Japan, Israel, the USA and most Commonwealth countries are granted an entry permit (free) at the border. The standard permitted stay is two weeks, although if you ask for longer you might get it. For a longer stay, apply in advance to the **Director of Immigration & Passport Services** (PO Box 363, Maseru 100, Lesotho).

For those requiring a visa, they can be obtained in South Africa from the **Lesotho High Commission** (☎ 012-460 7648, fax 460 7649, 391 Anderson St, Menlopark, Pretoria; open for visas 9am-12.45pm Mon-Fri). You'll need one passport photo. If you arrive at the Maseru Bridge border crossing without a visa, you might be given a temporary entry permit, which will allow you to go into Maseru and apply for a visa at the Ministry of Immigration. Don't count on this, as it depends on the whim of border officials who are sick of foreigners arriving without visas and demanding to be let in. A single-entry visa costs M30 and a multiple-entry visa costs M50.

Visitors who have travelled through the yellow-fever zone in Africa or South America (including Brazil) must have an international certificate of vaccination against yellow fever.

EMBASSIES & CONSULATES
Lesotho Embassies

In countries without representation, contact the UK representative. Diplomatic representation abroad includes the following:

Belgium (☎ 02-736 3973, fax 736 6770) Blvd General Wahis 45, 1030 Brussels

China (☎ 653-26842, fax 26845) 1–71 Ta Yuan Office Bldg, Choa Yang District, 100600 Beijing

Denmark (☎ 39-62 4343, fax 62 1538) Bogevej 17, 2900 Copenhagen

Germany (☎ 228-308 430, fax 308 4332) Godersberger Alle 50, 53175 Bonn

Italy (☎ 06-854 2199, fax 854 2527) Via Serchio 8, 00198 Rome

South Africa (☎ 012-460 7648, fax 460 7649) 391 Anderson St, Menlopark, Pretoria

UK (☎ 020-7235 5686, fax 7682 4388) 7 Chesam Place, Belgravia, London SW1 8HN

USA (☎ 202-797 5533/4, fax 234 6815) 2511 Massachusetts Ave NW, Washington, DC 20008

Embassies & Consulates in Lesotho

A number of foreign embassies in Lesotho closed or downgraded after South Africa rejoined the international community. The following countries have diplomatic representation in Maseru:

Canada
Consulate: (☎ 316435) 1st floor, Maseru Book Centre Bldg, Kingsway, Maseru

France
Consulate: (☎ 327522) Kingsway, Maseru. The Alliance Française doubles as the French Consulate.

Germany
Consulate: (☎ 314426) 70C Maluti Rd, Maseru West

Ireland
Consulate: (☎ 314068, fax 310028) 2nd floor, Christie House, 2A Orpen Rd. The consulate is open 8am to 12.45pm and 2pm to 4.30pm Monday to Friday.

Netherlands
Consulate: (☎ 312144) Lancer's Inn, Maseru

South Africa
High Commission: (☎ 315758, fax 310128) 10th floor, Lesotho Bank Towers, Kingsway, Maseru. The high commission is open 8.30am to 12.30pm Monday to Friday.

UK
High Commission: (☎ 313961, fax 310120, e hcmaseru@lesoff.co.za) Linare Rd, Maseru. The high commission is open 8am to 1pm Monday to Friday.

USA
Embassy: (☎ 312666, fax 310116, e amles@lesoff.co.za) 254 Kingsway, Maseru. The embassy is open 9am to noon and 2pm to 4pm Monday and Wednesday.

CUSTOMS

Customs regulations are broadly the same as those for South Africa (see Customs in the Facts for the Visitor chapter), but you can't bring in alcohol unless you are arriving from a country other than Botswana, Swaziland and South Africa – and that isn't likely.

MONEY
Currency

The unit of currency is the loti (plural maloti; M), which is divided into 100 lisente.

Exchange Rates

The loti is fixed at a value equal to the South African rand, and rands are accepted everywhere – there is no real need to convert your money into maloti. When changing travellers cheques you can usually get rand notes; this saves having to convert unused maloti. However, when spending rands you will invariably get maloti in change. (For exchange rates, see Money in the Facts for the Visitor chapter.)

Exchanging Money

You can change foreign currency and travellers cheques in Maseru at Lesotho Development Bank, Standard Bank and Nedbank. Banks are open 8.30am to 3pm Monday to Friday (to 1pm Thursday) and 8am to 11am Saturday. There are one or two ATMs in Maseru as well as in Teyateyaneng, Roma, Leribe (Hlotse) and Butha-Buthe, but these are unreliable.

Costs

Lesotho is a cheaper country to travel in than South Africa if you take advantage of the opportunities to stay with local people and to camp in remote areas. Otherwise, hotel prices are about the same as in South Africa. A GST of 10% is added to most transactions. Note that hotels don't usually include the GST when quoting rates.

POST & COMMUNICATIONS

Post offices are open 8am to 4.30pm Monday to Friday and 8am to noon Saturday. Delivery is slow and unreliable.

LESOTHO

The telephone system works reasonably well in Maseru but is less reliable in areas outside the capital. You don't have to go far off the beaten track to be away from the telephone system altogether. There are no area codes within Lesotho; to call Lesotho from South Africa dial ☎ 09 (for international) then ☎ 266 (for Lesotho). To call South Africa from Lesotho dial ☎ 00 then ☎ 27 followed by the South African area code and telephone number.

The cellphone (mobile phone) service is provided by **Vodacom Lesotho** (☎ 212000, fax 311079, ℮ administration@vcl.co.za, ⓦ www.vodacom.co.ls), based in Maseru. The coverage area extends north to Butha-Buthe, south to Quthing (Moyeni) and east to Mohale Dam.

Lonely Planet's eKno Communication Card provides cheap international calls, a range of messaging services and free email; for local calls, you're usually better off with a local card. eKno does not yet cover Lesotho, although it does cover South Africa and new countries are being added all the time. Check the Web site (ⓦ www.ekno.lonely planet.com) for updates; you can join online.

Internet access is limited; there are a few Internet cafes in Maseru.

DIGITAL RESOURCES
Two Web sites that are worth a look before you go to Lesotho are:

African Studies Center – Lesotho Page This is a good page to start your surfing; there are heaps of links to sites about Lesotho. ⓦ www.sas.upenn.edu/African_Studies/ Country_Specific/Lesotho.html
Kingdom in the Sky This is an excellent source of information for planning a trip to Lesotho. ⓦ www.africa-insites.com/lesotho/

BOOKS
If you are keen on walking or hiking, there are some useful books available locally:

A Backpackers Guide to Lesotho by Russell Suchet. This guide, which costs M20, outlines several walks in the country.
Guide to Lesotho by David Ambrose. This is a good guide for hiking.

Hill Walks In & Around Maseru. This publication is available at the local craft shops (M4); although it is worth buying, some walks it describes have been overwhelmed by urban sprawl and are no longer feasible.

NEWSPAPERS
Lesotho has several independent English-language newspapers; these are published weekly and include the *Mirror*, *Mopheme – The Survivor*, the *Sun*, the *Southern Star* and *Public Eye*. All are available in Maseru; distribution outside the capital may take a little longer. South African newspapers are also available in Maseru.

RADIO
If you're a fan of the BBC World Service, Lesotho is the place to be; there's a transmitter and you can pick up the Beeb on short wave, medium wave (1197kHz) and FM.

PHOTOGRAPHY & VIDEO
You're better off bringing your own film into Lesotho and waiting until you're back home before getting it developed.

You are not permitted to take photographs of the palace in Maseru, any government building or Moshoeshoe International Airport – if in doubt ask.

HEALTH
Due to the high altitude and therefore the absence of mosquitoes, there is no malaria in Lesotho. Bilharzia is also not present in Lesotho. You should avoid drinking untreated water taken downstream from a village.

The cold and changeable weather is the greatest threat to your health, and the consequences could be a lot more serious than catching a cold if you're trapped in the highlands without proper clothing. Too much cold can be just as dangerous as too much heat. You should always be prepared for cold, wet or windy conditions.

Hypothermia occurs when the body loses heat faster than it can produce it and the core temperature of the body falls. It is surprisingly easy to progress from very cold to dangerously cold due to a combination of wind, wet clothing, fatigue and hunger, even if the air temperature is above freezing. It is best to dress in layers; silk, wool and some of the new artificial fibres are all good insulating materials. A hat is important, as a lot of heat is lost through the head. A strong, waterproof outer layer (and a 'space' blanket for emergencies) is essential. Carry basic supplies, including food containing simple sugars to generate heat quickly and fluids to drink.

Symptoms of hypothermia are exhaustion, numb skin (particularly toes and fingers), shivering, slurred speech, irrational or violent behaviour, lethargy, stumbling, dizzy spells, muscle cramps and violent bursts of energy. Irrationality may take the form of sufferers claiming they are warm and trying to take off their clothes.

To treat mild hypothermia, first get the person out of the wind and/or rain, remove their clothing if it's wet and replace it with dry, warm clothing. Give them hot liquids – not alcohol – and some high-kilojoule, easily digestible food. Do not rub victims; instead, allow them to slowly warm themselves. This should be enough to treat the early stages of hypothermia. The early recognition and treatment of mild hypothermia is the only way to prevent severe hypothermia, which is a critical condition.

DANGERS & ANNOYANCES
The last Friday of the month is when many people are paid, and by mid-afternoon some towns become like street parties. These can be fun but as the day wears on some of the drunks become over-friendly, boisterous and aggressive.

The return from South Africa of unemployed miners, combined with worsening economic conditions, has led to a marked increase in armed robberies, break-ins and car-jackings. Most assaults have occurred in Maseru, with foreign aid workers and diplomats being targeted – caution is advised. Outside of urban centres, crime is negligible.

If you're hiking without a guide, you might be hassled for money or 'gifts' by shepherds in remote areas. There's a very slight risk of robbery. However, the best way to ensure problems is to greet people with suspicion and show a lack of generosity.

Several lives are lost each year from lightning strikes; remember to keep off high ground during an electrical storm and avoid camping in the open. The sheer ferocity of an electrical storm in Lesotho has to be seen to be believed. With the thunder and torrential rain comes a strong wind, and if you don't have waterproof gear you'll be soaked (and cold) in seconds. The storms don't last long, but they can be frequent.

EMERGENCIES
The contact number for emergency services are: police ☎ 123; and ambulance ☎ 121 (available in Maseru and a few other areas only).

PUBLIC HOLIDAYS
Public holidays include:

New Year's Day	1 January
Moshoeshoe Day	11 March
Hero's Day	4 April
Good Friday	March or April
Easter Monday	March or April
Workers' Day	1 May
Ascension Day	May
King's Birthday	17 July
Independence Day	4 October
Christmas Day	25 December
Boxing Day	26 December

ACTIVITIES
Bird-Watching
About 280 species of bird have been recorded in Lesotho – surprisingly many for a land-locked country. The mountainous terrain provides habitats for many species of raptor (birds of prey). You might see the Cape vulture *(Gyps coprotheres)*, or the rare bearded vulture or lammergeier *(Gypaetus barbtus)*. Good bird-watching places include eyries in the Maluti Mountains and near the eastern Drakensberg escarpment.

Fishing
Trout fishing is very popular in Lesotho. The trout season commences in September and continues until the end of May. There is a minimal licence fee, a size limit and a bag limit of 12 fish. Only rod and line and artificial nonspinning flies may be used. For

more information, contact the **Ministry of Agriculture Livestock Division** (☎ 323986, Private Bag A82, Maseru 100).

The nearest fishing area to Maseru is the Makhaleng River, 2km downstream from Molimo-Nthuse Lodge (a two-hour drive from Maseru). Other places to fish are the Malibamat'so River near Oxbow, 2km below New Oxbow Lodge; the De Beers Dam and the Khubelu and Mokhotlong Rivers near Mokhotlong in the north-east; the Tsoelike River, Park Ponds and Leqooa River near Qacha's Nek; and the Thaba-Tseka main dam.

Hiking

Lesotho offers great hiking in remote areas, with landscapes that are reminiscent of the Tibetan plateau. You can walk just about anywhere in Lesotho as there are no organised hiking trails, just footpaths. Know how to use a compass and get the relevant 1:50,000 scale maps from the map office at the **Department of Land, Surveys & Physical Planning** (Lerotholi Rd, Maseru).

In all areas, and especially in the remote eastern highlands, walking is dangerous if you aren't experienced and prepared. Temperatures can plummet to near zero even in summer, and thunderstorms and thick fog are common. Waterproof gear and plenty of warm clothes are essential. In summer many of the rivers flood, and fords can become dangerous. Be prepared to change your route or wait until the river subsides. By the end of the dry season, good water can be scarce, especially in the higher areas.

There are shops in the towns but these stock only very basic foodstuffs. Bring all you need from Maseru, or from South Africa if you want specialist hiking supplies. There are trout streams in the east – if you don't catch your own fish, buy some from locals.

Hikers should respect the cairns (mounds of stones) that mark graves. However, a mound of stones near a trail, especially between two hills, should be added to by passing travellers, who ensure their good luck by spitting on a stone and throwing it onto the pile. Note that a white flag waving from a village means that local *joala* (sorghum beer) has just been brewed; a yellow flag indicates maize beer, red is for meat and green is for vegetables.

The entire country is good for hiking. The eastern highlands and the Drakensberg's crown in particular attract serious hikers, with the walks between Qacha's Nek and Butha-Buthe offering the best challenge.

Pony Trekking

Lesotho's tough little Basotho ponies can take you to some remote and beautiful places. This is an excellent and popular way of seeing the Lesotho highlands.

The main trekking centres are the Basotho Pony Trekking Centre on God Help Me Pass, Malealea Lodge near the Gates of Paradise and at the isolated Semonkong Lodge. You may be able to join a day ride at these places without booking, but it's a long way to go to be turned away. You don't really need prior riding experience to go pony trekking.

There are basic stores near all these centres but it's better to bring food from Maseru. On an overnight trek you'll need to take food, a sleeping bag and warm, waterproof clothing. You'll also need the usual trekking extras such as sunscreen, a torch (flashlight), a water bottle and water purification tablets.

ACCOMMODATION

Camping isn't really feasible close to towns but away from population centres, you can camp for free anywhere *if* you have local permission. As a local courtesy you may be offered a hut for the night; expect to pay about M20 for this.

There are a couple of hostels in Maseru and one near Butha-Buthe. There are also missions scattered around the country (the 1:250,000 Lesotho map shows them) where you can often get a bed. There are also several agricultural (or farmer) training centres that will provide a bed for about M25.

Maseru has a good range of hotel accommodation. Most towns have small hotels that have survived from the days when Lesotho was a protectorate. These are usually now just run-down bars and liquor stores, but with some persuasion you might get a room.

Just remember that you don't come to Lesotho for high-class accommodation.

SHOPPING

Unfortunately the blanket, Lesotho's all-purpose garment, is usually made outside of the country. Some local production remains, and these colourful wool and mohair rugs and blankets have been transformed into an art form in the internationally acclaimed wall hangings produced by Moteng weavers.

There are plenty of other handicrafts made by the skilled craftspeople of Lesotho to buy, including mohair tapestry and woven-grass products such as mats, baskets and, of course, the Basotho hat (see the boxed text 'The Basotho Hat'). If you're trekking, you might want a sturdy stick; these come plain or decorated and can be found everywhere from craft shops to bus parks (prices start at about M40; bargaining is essential).

In and around the town of Teyateyaneng there are a number of craft shops and cottage industries.

For more information on Lesotho products contact the **Trade Promotion Unit, Ministry of Industry, Trade & Marketing** (☎ *322138, fax 310644,* **e** *tradepu@lesoff .co.ls, PO Box 747, Maseru*).

Getting There & Away

This section contains information about getting to Lesotho from South Africa. See the Getting There & Away chapter for details about getting to South Africa.

AIR

At the time of writing Lesotho Airways was no longer operating, but this situation may have changed by the time you read this.

Lesotho's Moshoeshoe International Airport is 21km from Maseru. South African Airways (SAA) flies daily between Moshoeshoe airport and Johannesburg (Jo'burg) in South Africa. There is an airport departure tax of about M20.

The Basotho Hat

A distinctive feature of Basotho dress is the conical hat with its curious top adornment; it is known to the Basotho as *mokorotlo* or *molianyeoe*.

The style of this hat is taken directly from the shape of a hill near King Moshoeshoe the Great's Thaba-Bosiu fortress. The hill is called Qiloane and it stands proudly alone with a few villages at its base.

These hats can be purchased in Maseru at the Basotho Shield craft shop from the vendors in front of the tourist office and at the border crossings. A large adult-sized hat costs about M40. You'll pay M5 for a tiny one, which could hang from your rear-vision mirror next to those cute FIFA soccer boots. The large hats are highly prized in South Africa; I lost mine to a local angler in an eel-fishing competition in western Transkei.

Jeff Williams

SARAH JOLLY

LESOTHO

LAND

All Lesotho's land borders are with South Africa. Most people enter via Maseru Bridge. The border crossings are shown on the table below.

border crossing	opening hours	nearest Lesotho/South Africa town
Caledonspoort	6am to 10pm	Butha-Buthe/ Fouriesburg
Ficksburg Bridge	24 hours	Maputsoe/ Ficksburg
Makhaleng Bridge	8am to 6pm (Mon to Fri) 8am to 4pm (Sat & Sun)	Mohale's Hoek/ Zastron
Maseru Bridge	24 hours	Maseru/ Ladybrand
Nkonkoana Gate	8am to 4pm	Sehlabathebe/ Bushman's Nek
Peka Bridge	8am to 4pm	Peka/Clocolan
Qacha's Nek	7am to 10pm	Mpiti/Mafube
Ramatseliso's Gate	7am to 5pm	Tsoelike/ Matatiele
Sani Pass	8am to 4pm	Mokhotlong/ Himeville
Sephapo's Gate	8am to 4pm	Mafeteng/ Boesmanskop
Van Rooyen's Gate	6am to 10pm	Mafeteng/ Wepener

Bus & Minibus Taxi

There are no direct buses between major South African cities and Maseru. Take a bus to Bloemfontein or Ladybrand and catch a minibus taxi into Lesotho from there.

Minibus taxis run between Jo'burg and Maseru for M70. Buses from Maseru for places in South Africa leave from the bridge on the South African side of the border.

Car & Motorcycle

The easiest entry points for car and motorcycle are on the northern and western sides of the country. Most of the other entry points in the south and east of the country involve very rough roads. You can't enter Lesotho via Sani Pass unless your vehicle is a 4WD, but you can leave Lesotho via Sani Pass in a conventional 2WD vehicle. Bear in mind, however, that most 2WDs won't have the necessary ground clearance.

Avis (☎ 350328/6) and **Budget** (☎ 316344) have offices in Maseru (see Getting There & Away under Maseru later in this chapter). In Lesotho it is more economical to use a car hired in South Africa; just ensure that you have the written agreement of the hirer. There is a road tax of M2, payable on leaving Lesotho.

Getting Around

AIR

Now that Lesotho Airways no longer operates, it is difficult to get around the country by air. **Mission Aviation** (☎ 325699) may be able to arrange charter flights out of Maseru to various destinations in Lesotho.

BUS & MINIBUS TAXI

There is a good network of buses (albeit slow ones) running to many towns. Minibus taxis are quicker but tend not to run long distances. In more remote areas you might have to arrange a ride with a truck, for which you'll need to negotiate a fare. Be prepared for long delays off the main routes.

You'll be quoted long-distance fares for bus tickets but it's better to just buy a ticket to the next major town, as most passengers will get off there and you'll be stuck waiting for the bus to fill up again, whereas other buses might leave before yours. Buying tickets in stages is only slightly more expensive than buying a direct ticket.

Heading north-east from Maseru you almost always have to change at Maputsoe, although this also sometimes happens on the road into Maputsoe if your bus meets another coming the other way.

TRAIN

Although there are freight-train lines, no passenger trains run in, to or near Lesotho.

CAR & MOTORCYCLE

Driving in Lesotho is getting easier as new roads are built in conjunction with the Highlands Water Project, but once you get off the tar there are still plenty of places where even a 4WD will get into trouble. Apart from rough roads, rivers flooding after summer storms present the biggest problem, and you can be stuck for days. People and animals on the road can also be a hazard.

There are sometimes army roadblocks, usually searching for stolen cars. If you're driving a car hired from South Africa, make sure that you have a letter from the rental agency giving you permission to take the car into Lesotho.

The national speed limit is 100km/h and the speed limit in villages is 50km/h. Petrol is about the same price as in South Africa.

Before attempting a difficult drive, try to get some local knowledge of current conditions; ask at a police station. The sealed roads in the highlands are very good but they are very steep in places. Rain will slow you down and ice or snow make things dangerous. If you're driving an automatic car, you'll be relying heavily on your brakes to get around steep downhill corners.

You must wear a seat belt. You can use any driving licence as long as it's in English or you have a certified translation. As there are occasional police roadblocks there's a chance that your licence will be checked.

ORGANISED TOURS

The tourist office in Maseru sporadically organises day tours to places of scenic and cultural interest for locals. Day tours cost around M75 and there are sometimes weekend trips.

Malealea Lodge, near Mohale's Hoek, organises vehicle safaris and pony trekking. See Malealea later in this chapter.

A few South African operators run tours up Sani Pass and a little way into Lesotho. See Sani Pass in the Easter Lesotho section in this chapter and in the KwaZulu-Natal chapter.

Maseru

pop 170,000 • elevation 1500m

Maseru has been a quiet backwater for much of its history. Kingsway was paved for the 1947 visit by British royals, and remained the capital's only tarred road for some time.

Most of Maseru's population has arrived since the 1970s, but for a rapidly expanding city in a developing country, Maseru remains an easy-going place. Still, it's very much a capital city and a recreation centre for the many foreign aid workers here.

Despite a major city rebuilding program and a mammoth clean up for King Letsie III's wedding, there are still visible scars of the 1998 invasion by troops from SADC member states (see History in the Facts about Lesotho section earlier in this chapter).

Orientation

Maseru's main street, Kingsway, runs from the border crossing at Maseru Bridge right through the centre of town to the Circle, a traffic roundabout and landmark. At the Circle, Kingsway splits to become two important highways: Main North Rd and Main South Rd.

Maps The **Department of Land, Surveys & Physical Planning** (☎ 322376, Lerotholi Rd; open 8am-12.45pm & 2pm-4.30pm Mon-Fri) sells good topographic maps of the country; these are essential if you're hiking. You won't need maps for pony trekking as the guides know the way.

Information

Tourist Offices The **tourist office** (☎ 313 760, fax 310108, ⓔ ltbhq@ltb.org.ls, in formsu@ltb.org.ls, ⓦ www.ltb.org.ls, Kingsway; open 8am-5pm Mon-Fri, 8.30am-1pm Sat) has friendly and helpful staff, but not much in the way of resources. Its guide to accommodation prices around the country and cheap but out-of-date map of Maseru are handy.

For bookings at Sehlabathebe National Park, contact the **Conservation Division** (☎ 323600 ext 30, PO Box 92, Maseru 100, Lesotho) in the Ministry of Agriculture building (look for the 'Bosiu Rural Development Project' sign) on Raboshabane Rd, near the train station.

Money With so many foreigners in town, the banks are used to changing money and there's no hassle except for the short banking

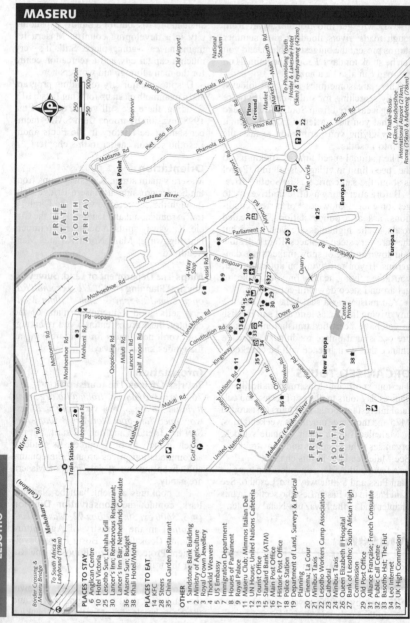

MASERU

To South Africa &
Ladybrand (19km)

Border Crossing &
Maseru Bridge

To South Africa &
Ladybrand (19km)

To Phomolong Youth
Hostel & Lesiba Hotel
(5km) & Teyateyaneng (42km)

To Thaba-Bosiu
(16km); Moshoeshoe
International Airport (21km);
Roma (35km) & Mafeteng (78km)

FREE
STATE
(SOUTH
AFRICA)

FREE
STATE
(SOUTH
AFRICA)

National
Stadium

Sea Point

New Europa

Europa 1

Europa 2

Central
Prison

Quarry

Golf Course

Pitso
Ground

The Circle

Parliament St

4-Way
Stop

Police Station

Train Station

Reservoir

Seputana River

Mohokare (Caledon) River

River
(Caledon)

PLACES TO STAY
6 Anglican Centre
10 Hotel Victoria
25 Lesotho Sun; Lehaha Grill
30 Lancer's Inn; Rendezvous Restaurant;
    Lancer's Inn Bar; Netherlands Consulate
36 Maseru Sun; Budget
38 Khali Hotel/Motel

PLACES TO EAT
14 KFC
28 Steers
35 China Garden Restaurant

OTHER
1 Sandstone Bank Building
2 Ministry of Agriculture
3 Royal Crown Jewellery
4 Thorkild Weavers
5 US Embassy
7 Immigration Department
8 Houses of Parliament
9 Royal Palace
11 Maseru Club; Mimmos Italian Deli
12 UN House; United Nations Cafeteria
13 Tourist Office
15 Standard Bank (ATM)
16 Main Post Office
17 Historic Post Office
18 Police Station
19 Department of Land, Surveys & Physical
    Planning
20 Cinema; La Cour
21 Minibus Taxis
22 Lesotho Workers Camp Association
23 Cathedral
24 Minibus Taxis
26 Queen Elizabeth II Hospital
27 Bank of Lesotho; South African High
    Commission
29 Old Post Office
31 Alliance Française; French Consulate
32 Public Call Centre
33 Basotho Hat; The Hut
34 Leo Internet
37 UK High Commission

LESOTHO

hours: 8.30am to 3pm Monday to Friday (1pm on Thursday) and 8.30am to 11am Saturday. On the last Friday of the month, which is pay day, huge, slow-moving queues wind out of the banks and down the street.

The Bank of Lesotho, Nedbank and Standard Bank are on Kingsway. These are the only places where you can change money. The Standard Bank has an ATM.

Lesotho has a consumption tax that may increase the cost of more formal (restaurant) dining and accommodation options in Maseru.

Post & Communications If you can help it, don't use Maseru as a poste restante address, or you'll join the permanent group of people waiting to complain about missing mail at the **post office** *(open 8am-5pm Mon-Fri, 8am-2pm Sat)*.

To make international phone calls, go to the **public call centre** *(Kingsway, opposite the tourist office; open 8am-4.30pm Mon-Fri, 8am-noon Sat)*. Calls are very expensive – wait until you are back in South Africa if possible.

Leo Internet *(☎ 322772, ⓔ billy@leo.co.ls, ⓦ www.leo.co.ls, Orpen Rd; open 8am-5pm Mon-Fri, 9am-1pm Sat)* is the most reliable Internet cafe in Maseru, charging M20 per half-hour.

Cultural Centres The **Alliance Française** *(☎ 327522, fax 310475, ⓔ maximin@ile sotho.com, Kingsway)* offers South Sothto language lessons for beginners (M250). There is a library at **UN House** *(☎ 313790, fax 310042, ⓔ registry@undp.org, ⓦ www.unlesotho.org.ls, United Nations Rd)*.

Medical Services If you need a doctor or a dentist, contact an embassy; they have lists of recommended practitioners. In an emergency, go to the **Queen Elizabeth II Hospital** *(Kingsway, near the Lesotho Sun Hotel)*. There's also the **Maseru Private Hospital** *(☎ 313260)*.

Emergency For police call ☎ 123 and for an ambulance call ☎ 121.

Dangers & Annoyances Maseru is fairly safe but be on your guard at night, especially off the main street. With the influx into the city of a large number of unemployed miners returning from South Africa, Maseru has seen an increase in personal assaults.

A reader has warned that the area around Hotel Victoria can be dangerous after dark. There have been attacks on expats nearby.

Things to See & Do

There are several good **walks** on the mountain ridges that protrude into the city. One recommended walk begins at the gate of the Lesotho Sun Hotel and takes you up to a plateau where there are great views of Maseru. *Hill Walks In & Around Maseru*, available for M4 at the Basotho Hat and nearby craft shops, describes other walks.

Take some time to go into the 'urban villages' that surround Maseru. You will be welcomed and, if you are lucky, you may be invited to spend the night there. It makes a pleasant change from the Western-style hotels in Maseru.

Places to Stay

As well as the places described here, Thaba-Bosiu, not far from Maseru, also has accommodation options (see Thaba-Bosiu in the Around Maseru section later in this chapter).

Places to Stay – Budget

Hostels Given that there is no camping ground in Maseru, camping would be risky. Still, with a couple of hostels in town, it's possible to find inexpensive accommodation.

Lesotho Work Camps Association *(☎ 314862, 917 Cathedral Rd)* Dorm beds R20. If you are desperate, you could stay at this camp behind the Catholic Cathedral near the Circle at the end of Kingsway. Head down Main North Rd until you come to a garage; nearby is a dirt road where taxis gather. Follow this road until you come to the buildings of the work camp. There is a place to wash and a small kitchen.

Phomolong Youth Hostel *(☎ 332900)* Dorm beds M30. This hostel is not for the claustrophobic; its small rooms are crammed with rickety bunk beds adorned with thin

LESOTHO

mattresses. To get there, head along Main North Rd, go over the bridge and turn right down the Lancer's Gap road. This turn-off is not signposted but on the corner there is a sign reading 'Gold Medal Enterprises'. The hostel, recognisable by the red 'YHA' painted above the front door, is 2.6km farther on. Minibus taxis to Lancer's Gap run past it.

The Anglican Centre (☎ 322046) 2-/4-/5-bed rooms M35 per person. Rooms at the centre are austere but clean. Meals, which smell good, are available if you give notice. The centre is only about 500m north of Kingsway on the bend where Assisi Rd becomes Lancer's Rd, but getting there isn't simple. If you get lost, ask for St James Church, which is next door, or Machabeng High School, which is at least in the area.

Hotels *Lakeside Hotel* (☎ 313646, Bedco St) Singles/doubles M110/150. This hotel, 5km east of the centre off Main North Rd, has simple rooms.

Khali Hotel/Motel (☎/fax 310501) Doubles M200. This large hotel, south of Kingsway, beyond the prison, has reasonable double rooms. It runs an hourly shuttle bus into the centre of town, or you can take a Thetsane minibus on Pioneer Rd, near Lancer's Inn, and get off at the turn-off for the suburb of New Europa.

Places to Stay – Mid-Range & Top End

Hotel Victoria (☎ 312922, fax 310318, Kingsway) Singles/doubles M219/317. Looming high on Kingsway, this place is not exceptional but will do for a night. Its bar and dining room are often busy.

Lancer's Inn (☎ 312114, fax 310223, e lancers-inn@ilesotho.com) Singles/doubles M295/385 B&B. Maseru's best-value accommodation option is a colonial-era hotel with clean comfortable rooms and pleasant self-catering rondavels.

There are two Sun hotels in Maseru, both with casinos.

Maseru Sun (☎ 312434, fax 310158, 12 Orpen Rd) Doubles M594. The modern Maseru Sun is near the river, south-west of Kingsway.

Lesotho Sun (☎ 313111, fax 310104, e agmlesun@adelfang.co.za) Doubles from M556. This indulgent place, on a hillside further east, is more luxury resort than hotel.

Places to Eat

On Kingsway there are **street stalls**, mainly open during the day, selling good grilled meat for about M5. Serves of curry and rice cost M4.

Next to Lancer's Inn, there's a **bakery** selling good pies and cakes – try the freshly baked scones for breakfast.

The indestructible fast-food industry forges on, even in Lesotho; **KFC** and **Steers** are both on Kingsway.

United Nations Cafeteria (☎ 313790, United Nations Rd) Lunch M7. Open 12.30pm-1.30pm Mon-Fri. While only open for a limited time, the cafeteria at UN House serves good cheap lunchtime snacks and is the perfect place to meet expats and aid workers – good sources of information on out-of-the-way places. The downside is that you have to sign in and leave your passport at the gate before entering.

All the hotels have restaurants. The 10% GST has been added to the following price ranges.

Rendezvous (☎ 312114, Lancer's Inn, Kingsway) Mains M22-49.50. Open 7am-10.30pm daily. Rendezvous serves food of a reasonable standard.

China Garden Restaurant (☎ 313915, Orpen Rd) Mains M16.50-27.50. Open noon-2.30pm & 6.30pm-10pm Mon-Sat. China Garden is a big place off Kingsway; the food is OK.

Mimmos Italian Deli (☎ 324979, Maseru Club, United Nations Rd) Mains M20-49.50. Open noon-late daily. New on the scene, Mimmos Italian Deli has quickly become a favourite with the local expat community. It serves delicious authentic-tasting Italian dishes and offers specials on Monday and Tuesday, with pizzas for only M14 and pasta dishes M13.

The Hut (☎ 325102, Basotho Hat, Kingsway) Mains M35.20-65. Open noon-10.30pm daily. The Hut restaurant, upstairs in the newly reopened Basotho Hat, serves a limited menu of seafood and meat dishes. It also has a good bar.

Lehaha Grill (☎ *313111, Lesotho Sun hotel*) Buffet M75, mains M27.50-71.50. Open 6.30pm-late daily. The central feature of the Lesotho Sun's Lehaha Grill is an excellent full-scale three-course meal. An interesting a la carte menu is also available.

Entertainment

Lancer's Inn Bar (☎ *312114*) Open 9am-11.30pm daily. This intimate and friendly bar is a favourite local haunt.

Maseru Club (☎ *326008, United Nations Rd*) is a fine old colonial club with a bar and restaurant and a variety of sports available including squash, tennis and cricket. You can take out temporary membership by the month, but it's easy enough to be signed in as a guest.

Hotel Victoria (☎ *313790, Kingsway*) has good jazz at its bar on weekends. The hotel's disco is in the building to the west of the tower. Many locals come here to dance into the wee hours of the morning and it can be a bit rough.

You can take in a movie at the *cinema*. Coming from the border crossing end of town, turn left off Kingsway onto Parliament St and take the first street to the right; the cinema is on the left. *La Cour*, a bar behind the cinema, often has good live jazz music – however, do not be tempted to visit alone.

Both the Sun hotels have *casinos* and *bars*, and the Lesotho Sun also has *tenpin bowling*.

Shopping

Basotho Hat (☎ *325102, Kingsway*) is a government-run craft shop. It has recently

Crowns, Cows & Wedding Vows

After the tumultuous events of the last decade, the new millennium brought with it plenty of reasons for Lesotho to celebrate. The long-awaited wedding of the country's reigning monarch, King Letsie III, heralded a new era of hope for this tiny mountain kingdom. On 18 February, 2000, the 35-year-old bachelor king finally tied the knot, breaking with tradition to marry Karabo Motsoeneng, a 23-year-old commoner from Leribe (Hlotse) in the country's north. (At the time she was a university student in South Africa, but she has since transferred to the New York–based Columbia University.)

Their special day inevitably turned into a national day of celebration as tens of thousands of well wishers lined the streets of the nation's capital, eager for a glimpse of the couple. A colourful cavalcade headed by the Royal Lesotho Mounted Police in full ceremonial dress made its way through the city, leading King Letsie to the Setsoto Stadium for the open-air ceremony. His bride arrived in an open car escorted by a procession of motorcycles. Motsoeneng looked radiant in a flowing gem-encrusted white gown with a long train and high headdress.

The stadium, filled to capacity, overflowed with euphoria as the couple exchanged their vows. Among the 400 invited guests were the presidents of Botswana, Malawi, Mozambique, Namibia and the then president of South Africa, Nelson Mandela. (The current South African president, Thabo Mbeki, later visited Lesotho to present King Letsie with a cow – a fine the king imposed on Mbeki for his failure to attend the wedding.)

The fairytale wedding marked the beginning of the traditional three days of feasting and dancing that reportedly cost the government M5 million. Despite the cost the royal subjects revelled in national pride, casting aside their woes to rejoice with their king.

A devout Roman Catholic, King Letsie vowed not only to 'love and honour' his beautiful bride, but to never take a second wife as is permitted under customary law. One tradition adhered to, however, was the *lobola* (bride's price), with the king's family paying 40 head of cattle for his new wife.

Following the festivities King Letsie whisked his new queen off to Rome for their honeymoon and to have their union blessed by the Pope.

LESOTHO

been rebuilt, the previous premises having burnt down during the 1998 riots. It's well worth a look, but the prices are generally higher than you'll find in rural areas. If you plan on walking or pony trekking, it's a good idea to buy a horsehair fly whisk here.

Thorkild Weavers (☎ *316858, 226 Moshoeshoe Rd)*, just before Caledon Rd, sells expensive tapestries.

Getting There & Away
Air SA Airlink flies from Jo'burg to Maseru (R700) three times daily.

Bus & Minibus Taxi Buses and long-distance minibus taxis congregate haphazardly in the streets north, east and west of the Circle.

Fares from Maseru include Mafeteng (M10), Basotho Pony Trekking Centre at God Help Me Pass (M12), Mohale's Hoek (M16) and Quthing (M24).

Car Avis (☎ *350328/6)* has an office on Kingsway in the block east of the Bank of Lesotho and **Budget** (☎ *316344)* has its base at the Maseru Sun hotel.

Getting Around
To/From the Airport Moshoeshoe airport is 21km from town, off Main South Rd. A minibus taxi to the airport will cost around M60. The Khali Hotel/Motel's shuttle bus runs to the airport.

Minibus Taxi The standard minibus taxi fare around town is M1.40. There are a few conventional taxi services; try **Moonlite Telephone Taxis** (☎ *312695)*.

Around Maseru

Most towns around Maseru have risen around trading posts or protectorate-era administration centres; none approach Maseru in size or facilities. Most of the larger towns are scrappy, ugly places, of limited interest apart from making transport connections or finding accommodation. It's the tiny villages and countryside that are of real interest.

THABA-BOSIU
King Moshoeshoe the Great's mountain stronghold, first occupied in July 1824, is east of Maseru. Thaba-Bosiu (Mountain at Night), the most important historical site in Lesotho, played a pivotal role in the consolidation of the Basotho nation in the 19th century (see the boxed text 'The Battles for Thaba-Bosiu'). The name may have been bestowed because the site was first occupied at night, but another legend suggests that Thaba-Bosiu, a hill in daylight, grows into a mountain at night-time.

There's a visitor information centre at the base of Thaba-Bosiu where you pay the M5 admission fee and collect a map and a pamphlet. An official guide will accompany you to the top of the mountain, for which you should pay a tip. The guides are generally friendly and knowledgeable, although some of their assertions are dubious. For example, it's highly unlikely that Moshoeshoe held court under the big eucalypt on top of the hill, as the eucalypt hadn't yet been introduced.

There are good views from the summit of Thaba-Bosiu, including the Qiloane hill, which provided the inspiration for the Basotho hat (see the boxed text 'The Basotho Hat' earlier in this chapter). On the summit are the remains of fortifications, Moshoeshoe's grave and parts of the original settlement.

Places to Stay & Eat
Thaba-Bosiu isn't far from Maseru and staying here would definitely be more peaceful and probably more interesting.

Mmelesi Lodge (☎ *852116, fax 314033)* Singles/doubles B&B M170/240. This well-organised lodge is about 2km before the Thaba-Bosiu visitor information centre. The lodge has a conference centre and a terrific a la carte *restaurant*.

Getting There & Away
To get to Thaba-Bosiu, look for a minibus taxi near the Circle; these go as far as the visitor information centre at the base of the mountain (M5). If you're driving, head out on Main South Rd, take the turn-off to Roma and after about 6km (near Mazenod)

The Battles for Thaba-Bosiu

The Basotho stronghold atop Thaba-Bosiu repulsed invaders for nearly 40 years. First, the Ngwane – led by Matiwane – attacked the fortress in 1828. After a fierce battle the attacking regiments were driven off and ceased to be a threat. Early in 1831, the heavily armed Kornnas (Raiders) were driven away. Next, in 1831, from north of the Vaal came the Ndebele led by Mzilikazi. They attacked Thaba-Bosiu at Rafutho's Pass, but were repulsed by defenders hurling spears and rocks from above.

It was then the turn of the British. In 1852, Sir George Cathcart, governor of the Cape Colony, made a punitive attack on King Moshoeshoe's people. On the way to the fortress, about 5km west of Thaba-Bosiu, Cathcart's troops were forced to withdraw by 5000 heavily armed and mounted Basotho warriors.

The Boer republic of the Orange Free State was established in 1854, and the Boers began to encroach upon the territory of Basotholand between the Senqu (Orange) and Mohokare (Caledon) Rivers. There were a number of clashes with the Free State – the most serious started in 1865, when determined Free State *kommandos* (commandoes), led by Commandant Louw Wepener, attempted to storm Thaba-Bosiu. The kommandos were repulsed in what was to be the last attack on Thaba-Bosiu in Moshoeshoe's lifetime. Wepener was killed at Khubedu Pass, today sometimes referred to as Wepener's Pass.

turn off to the left. Thaba-Bosiu is about 10km further along. There's also a shorter route along back roads, but seek local advice about it, as it crosses a riverbed that sometimes floods.

BASOTHO PONY TREKKING CENTRE

On the road between Maseru and Thaba-Tseka is the Basotho Pony Trekking Centre (☎ 314165, 317284), on the top of God Help Me Pass.

Treks range from a two-hour ride (about M30) to a week-long ride (about M405). There are minimum numbers on some of the longer rides, but this is usually only two or four people, so it's easy to get a group together. There are discounts for larger groups. Contact the tourist office in Maseru for details and bookings. (See the boxed text 'The Basotho Pony' later in this chapter for more information about Basotho ponies.)

Accommodation on overnight treks is in villages along the way, which charge about M20 per person a night or M10 if you have a tent. This is not included in the trekking fees, so bring enough money to cover costs. You can't stay at the centre (although travellers have been known to wangle floor space in the past), so if your trek departs early in the morning, you'll have to camp out or stay at Molimo-Nthuse Lodge. The lodge is 3km back down the pass, which means a steep walk the next morning.

Molimo-Nthuse Lodge (☎ 312922) Singles/doubles M160/200. This modern, well-maintained lodge has with accommodation in pleasant garden rondavels. It also has a good restaurant.

Buses to the centre cost M10 from Maseru and take about two hours.

ROMA

The university town of Roma, only 35km from Maseru, is a good place to meet students. There are some attractive sandstone buildings dotted around the town, and the entry to town by the southern gorge is spectacular. To the north is the important Ha Baroana rock-art site.

Trading Post Guest House (☎ 340202/67, fax 340630, e tradingpost@leo.co.ls) Camping M30, bed only/B&B M60/80 per person. The trading post has been here since 1903, as has the Thorn family, which owns the store, grain mill and guesthouse. It's a bustling little place. There is pony riding from M30 per hour, and walks include a 20-minute walk to see dinosaur footprints. There's no restaurant but you can use the

LESOTHO

kitchen. The guesthouse is off the Maseru road before you enter Roma. Take the turn-off signposted 'Manoyane Cash & Carry'; if you get lost ask for 'Thorns'.

Speakeasy Restaurant Meals M10. Open 8am-noon daily. This small restaurant-cum-bar serves basic fare and is popular with locals.

A minibus taxi from Maseru to Roma costs M4.50.

HA BAROANA ROCK ART

Ha Baroana, north of Roma, is an important rock-art site. Although it suffers from neglect and vandalism (including damage done by tourists who spray water on the paintings to produce brighter photos), it's worth seeing.

To get there from Roma, head back to the Maseru road and turn right onto the road heading west to the Basotho Pony Trekking Centre (God Help Me Pass) and Thaba-Tseka. After about 12km, turn off to the left, just after the Ha Ntsi settlement on the Mohlsks-oa-Tuka River.

To get to the site by minibus taxi from Maseru, head for Nazareth and get off about 1.5km before Nazareth. A signpost indicates the way to the paintings, off to the left. Follow this gravel track 3km to the village of Ha Khotso, then turn right at a football field. Follow this track a further 2.5km to a hill top overlooking a gorge. A footpath zigzags down the hillside to the rock shelter where the paintings can be found.

Northern Lesotho

TEYATEYANENG

Teyateyaneng (Place of Quick Sands) is usually known as 'TY'. The town has been developed as the craft centre of Lesotho and there are several places worth visiting.

Some of the best **tapestries** come from Helang Basali Crafts in St Agnes Mission, 2km before Teyateyaneng on the Maseru road. More tapestries are available from Hatooa-Mose-Mosali and **wool products** are available from Setsoto Design, Tebetebeng and Letlotlo Handcrafts.

About 10km north of town beyond the Phutiatsana River, in **Kolonyama** is the largest pottery in Lesotho. Here beautiful stoneware products are fashioned from fine clay and minerals.

Blue Mountain Inn (☎/fax 500362) Camping M60, singles/doubles M154/188. Despite having the monopoly on accommodation in town, the Blue Mountain Inn offers reasonably priced cosy cottages. The hotel's *restaurant* and *nightclub* are popular with locals.

MAPUTSOE

This border town, 86km north of Maseru, is across the Mohokare (Caledon) River from the Free State town of Ficksburg. It has a shopping centre and a few other civic amenities, but its status as a black dormitory suburb of Ficksburg is still apparent – it is very run-down and impoverished. When it rains the streets turn to slippery mud. Still, it is handy to the Ficksburg Bridge border crossing and has good transport connections, especially now that it is a gateway to the Highlands Water Project.

Express Sekekete Hotel (☎ 430789) Singles/doubles M110/170. The hotel is rather run-down, so you're better off staying across the border; see the Ficksburg section in the Free State chapter.

LERIBE

A large town by Lesotho's standards, Leribe (the old name, Hlotse, is still sometimes used) is a quiet village serving as a regional shopping and market centre. It was an administrative centre under the British and there are some old buildings slowly decaying in the leafy streets. **Major Bell's Tower**, on the main street near the market, was built in 1879. A very humble symbol of the might of the British Empire, it spent most of its career as a storehouse for government records.

The Leribe **craft centre**, off the highway between the turn-off to Leribe and the turn-off to Katse Dam, sells woollen goods at reasonable prices.

There are two sets of **dinosaur footprints** near Leribe. The first is a few kilometres south of Leribe at Tsikoane village. Heading north towards Leribe, take the small dirt road going off to the right towards some rocky outcrops. Follow it up to the church and ask someone to direct you to the '*minwane*'. It's a 15- to 20-minute slog up the mountainside to a series of caves. The prints are clearly visible on the ceiling of the rock.

About 10km north of Leribe are the Subeng River dinosaur footprints. There is a signpost indicating the river but not the footprints. Walk down to the river from the road to a concrete causeway (about 250m). The footprints, of at least three species of dinosaur, are about 15m downstream on the right bank. They are fairly worn.

Places to Stay & Eat

It is sometimes possible to stay at the *Catholic Mission*, about 10km past Leribe towards Butha-Buthe.

The Agricultural Training Centre (☎ 400226) Dorm beds M25. While this place is geared more towards farmers than intrepid backpackers, it is possible to bunk here for the night. The centre is just outside town on the old road to Butha-Buthe, just near where it converges with the new road.

Leribe Hotel (☎/fax 400559, Main St) Singles/doubles M147/195. This old-style hotel offers good clean accommodation in the main building or in private rondavels. It has a good tea garden surrounded by well-established trees.

KATSE & THE LESOTHO HIGHLANDS WATER PROJECT

One of the benefits of the Lesotho Highlands Water Project has been the improvement of roads into the interior of the country. From Leribe (Hlotse) you can now take a sealed road all the way to the project headquarters at Katse (pronounced khot-see). Although the dam itself is just a tract of water, the drive is breathtaking, and passes through some remote and beautiful country. It's a must. See Getting There & Away in this section for more details.

Under louring skies, the loch-like arms of the dam and the steep, green mountainsides are like a wilder version of Scotland. The

Lesotho Highlands Water Project

The Lesotho Highlands Water Project (LHWP) is an ambitious scheme developed jointly by Lesotho and South Africa to harness Lesotho's abundant water resources. The project, being implemented in stages, will provide water and electricity for a large tract of Southern Africa. When construction is finished (c. 2020), there will be five major dams, many smaller dams and approximately 200km of tunnels.

Phase 1a includes the already completed 180m-high Katse Dam on the Malibamat'so River, to the north of Thaba-Tseka. A transfer tunnel – 4m in diameter and 45km long – will carry water to a hydroelectric plant at Muela near Butha-Buthe. In 1999 the Muela hydroelectric plant began generating electricity – the first time Lesotho produced its own electricity. From Muela, the water will flow through a 37km tunnel across the border to Clarens and into the Axle River, a tributary of the Vaal. Eventually this water will reach the Vaal Dam, an essential reservoir for Jo'burg.

Construction on Phase 1b of the project, including the Mohale Dam on the Senqu (Orange) River and the Matsoku Diversion Dam on the Matsoku River, is well under way. When complete both dams will be connected by separate transfer tunnels to Katse Dam. The Matsoku Dam and tunnel is due to be completed in 2001, while the Mohale Dam is scheduled for completion by late 2002, with its transfer tunnel to be completed by 2003.

The immediate effect of the development has been improved roads and telecommunications into Lesotho's interior. There are, however, several environmental questions to consider, and critics of the scheme feel that satisfactory answers still have to be provided (see Ecology & Environment earlier in this chapter).

LESOTHO

lives of Lesotho highlands villagers probably aren't very different from the lives of Scottish highlands villagers a hundred years ago either.

For the people living in these remote villages, the new road is a boon, although the billboards in each village warning of AIDS hint at problems caused by easier contact with the outside world and with the labour force building the Highlands Water Project.

When you near the dam, ignore the two turn-offs signposted 'Katse Dam' and keep going until you see signs directing you to Katse village. Here you'll find the information centre (in some blue buildings by the workers' compound) and a viewpoint overlooking the dam wall. You need a permit (which you may not get) to visit the project's headquarters (in the nearby large yellow building with a blue roof) and to get closer to the dam wall.

If you continue further along you'll come to Katse village, which is a rather dreary, modern development housing the project's management.

Places to Stay & Eat

Katse Lodge (☎ *910202, 910004, Katse Ave,* Singles/doubles M240/260, dorm beds M98 Katse Lodge is modern and of a reasonable standard. It can fill up with sightseers on weekends, so book ahead as it is a long drive back. For a decent well-priced meal with good views try the lodge's ***restaurant*** There's also a ***bar*** for a quick nightcap.

Getting There & Away

The distance from Leribe to Katse is only 122km but it takes at least two hours to drive it, longer if you're travelling by bus or taxi The road is excellent (and would be great for a powerful motorcycle), but it is very steep and winding. Be very careful on the down hill sections if it's raining, as the road is quite slick. When icy, it would be pretty scary.

The spectacular road from Leribe to Katse passes the lowland village of Pitseng and climbs over the Maluti Mountains to drop to Ha Lejone, which one day will be at the edge of the dam's lake. It continues south past Mamohau Mission, crosses the

Highlands Parks & Reserves

Capitalising on the interest generated by the impressive Lesotho Highlands Water Project, the Lesotho Highlands Development Authority (LHDA) has created nature reserves and tourist facilities within the project's Phase 1a area. These reserves are part of LHDA's ongoing National Environment and Heritage program, which aims to promote community-based ecotourism and to ensure the protection of these pristine environments for generations to come.

The new facilities and reserves include the Bokong Nature Reserve, the Ts'ehlanyane National Park and the Liphofung Cave Cultural Historical Site. The Muela Environmental Education Centre, near Muela Dam, is still under development. When complete the centre will be situated within an enviro-park where courses in environmental education will be offered.

For bookings and inquiries about these parks and reserves, contact the **Project Officer, Earthplan** (☎ *460723, fax 082-783 5635,* **e** *dave@earthplan.com, PO Box 333, Butha-Buthe 400, Lesotho*).

Bokong Nature Reserve

The Bokong Nature Reserve is situated at the top of Mafika-Liseu Pass (3090m) near the Bokong River, a tributary of the Katse. Among the reserve's many treasures are the fascinating Afro-alpine wetland sponges found in the sources of the Lepaqoa Stream and the Bokong River. It's also home to the bearded vulture, the ice rat (*Otomys sloggettis*) and the vaal rhebuck. The visitor information centre is based in front of a magnificent waterfall created by the Lepaqoa Stream. The reserve has a series of day hiking trails as well as educational walks and an overnight camp site. The reserve is located en route to the Katse Dam.

impressive Malibamat'so Bridge, climbs over another series of hills to the Matsoku Valley, recrosses the Malibamat'so River and ends at Katse. From Katse, you can continue on an improved dirt road to Thaba-Tseka, 45km to the south.

There are minibus taxis from Leribe to Katse (M23) which continue on to Thaba-Tseka (M40), although you might have to change at Pitseng. There's plenty of traffic if you want to hitch.

BUTHA-BUTHE

King Moshoeshoe the Great named this town Butha-Buthe (Place of Lying Down) because it was here that his people first retreated during the chaos of the difaqane. The small town is built alongside the Hlotse River and has the beautiful Maluti Mountains as a backdrop.

Ha Thabo Ramakatane Hostel Beds M30 per person. This hostel is about 3.5km from Butha-Buthe in the village of Ha Sechele. The name means 'Mr Ramakatane's Hostel'. To get there from Butha-Buthe,

turn at the sign to St Paul's primary school, go left after the school, then take the next right. If you get lost ask for the hostel. There are no supplies, so buy food in the village before arriving. There is no electricity; you cook using gas and you fetch your own water just as the villagers do.

Crocodile Inn (☎ 460223, Reserve Rd) Singles/doubles M130/155. The accommodation here is simple but clean, and it's a better place to stay than you might guess by looking at the outside. The *restaurant* here is adequate if you like huge steaks; more importantly, it's probably the only decent place to eat in town.

OXBOW

Oxbow, just over one of the steepest passes you'll ever want to drive, consists of a few huts and a couple of lodges. There's a small shop at New Oxbow Lodge.

South African skiers used to come to Oxbow in winter but the place slowly died as a ski resort. Fortunately this is about to change. The Lesotho government, having

Highlands Parks & Reserves

Ts'ehlanyane National Park

The 5600-hectare Ts'ehlanyane National Park, at the junction of the Ts'ehlanyane and Holomo Rivers, protects a significant portion of the western side of the Maluti Mountains. The reserve contains some of the finest examples of preserved *Leucosidea sericea* (Ouhout or Chi-Chi) woodlands, as well as stands of berg bamboo which host the endangered *Metisella syrinx* butterfly. Although the park abounds with flora, its harsh mountain terrain attracts few large mammals.

The park's facilities include picnic areas, a camp site, trail huts and a number of walks and trails as well as pony rides. There are future plans for the construction of an upmarket lodge.

To reach the park from Butha-Buthe, take the main road south for 6km then following the signs, turn left onto an unsealed road and continue for 32km to the park. En route you'll pass through the village of Khabo.

Liphofung Cave Cultural Historical Site

The Liphofung Cave Cultural Historical Site *(admission M10 per car; open 8.30am-4.30pm Mon-Fri, 9am-3.30pm Sat & Sun)* is 28km from Butha-Buthe, near the foot of Moteng Pass. Liphofung means 'Place of the Eland'. The site's most significant feature is the cave, a large sandstone overhang containing Bushman rock art with historical links dating from the Stone Age up to modern Basotho history. There is also an interesting replica of a traditional Basotho kraal and a small museum through which you can wander. Local guides, happy to share their knowledge, will take you on a free tour of the site.

The site is just off the main road from Butha-Buthe to Oxbow, and a newly constructed road makes the site accessible to all vehicles.

recognised the potential of this beautiful area as a year-round tourist attraction, has begun developing the **Mahlasela Ski Resort** at Oxbow. The first phase of the project resulted in several ski slopes opening for the 2001 winter ski season. Phase two, which includes additional accommodation facilities, restaurants and other amenities, is expected to be completed by winter 2002.

New Oxbow Lodge (☎ 051-933 2247 Free State for bookings, ⓦ www.webscapes.com) Singles/doubles DB&B M205/370. The lodge, on the banks of the Malibamat'so River, is a large ski resort with reasonable accommodation, a cosy bar and an inexpensive restaurant. It's possible to camp near the river. With the creation of the new resort, hotel prices may increase significantly.

A few kilometres further north is a *private chalet* belonging jointly to the Maluti and Witwatersrand University ski clubs. It's possible to sleep here for M25, although winter weekends are crowded. See the caretaker or write to *Club Maluti (PO Box 783308, Sandton 2146, South Africa)*.

Eastern Lesotho

THABA-TSEKA

This remote town is on the western edge of the Central Range, over the sometimes tricky Mokhoabong Pass. It was established in 1980 as a centre for the mountain district.

Farmer Training Centre (☎ 900201) Dorm beds M25. You can usually get a bed in this purpose-built centre, which is on the street behind the post office.

Maluti Guest (☎ 900201, fax 900518, 2km from the main road) M85 per person. The Maluti Guest gives you a unique opportunity to stay within a real Basotho village and experience their culture first hand. If you arrive unannounced, ask for Del Johnson, who can usually be found at the Thaba-Tseka Technical Institute. All meals are included in the price of accommodation.

About four buses a day run from Maseru to Thaba-Tseka (M25). Heading south from Thaba-Tseka to Sehonghong and Qacha's Nek is more difficult – you'll probably have

to negotiate with a truck driver. Minibus taxis also travel along the unsealed road from Thaba-Tseka to Katse (M17), continuing on to Leribe (M40).

MOKHOTLONG

The first major town north of Sani Pass and Sehlabathebe National Park, Mokhotlong (Place of the Bald Ibis) has basic shops and transport to Oxbow and Butha-Buthe. The town, some 270km from Maseru and 200km from Butha-Buthe, has the reputation as being the coldest, driest and most remote place in Lesotho. The horses 'parked' outside the shops give the town a Wild West feel.

The Senqu (Orange) River, the biggest in Lesotho, has its source near Mokhotlong. The town is a good base for walks to the Drakensberg escarpment.

Places to Stay & Eat

Farmer Training Centre Dorm beds M25. The centre has cold-water washing facilities and a kitchen.

Lefu Senqu Hotel (☎ 920330) Singles doubles M130/170. This unappealing hotel 5km from the airport, has adequate rooms.

Molumong Guesthouse & Backpackers (Kwazulu Natal ☎ 033-345 7045, fax 033 355 1122, ⓔ molumong@worldonline.co.za) Camping M30, dorm beds M45, standard beds M60. The guesthouse is 15km south west of Mokhotlong in Upper Rafalotsane village. Follow the signs from the Thaba Tseka turn-off and look for the red-roofed building with 'Molumong' painted in white on its roof. The guesthouse, once a colonial trading post, offers a truly peaceful self catering experience. There is no electricity no TV and no telephones; just the stars. There is a small store next door where you can buy most of your supplies, although you may have to be insistent about what you want as not all items are on the shelves. There are three buses a day to the lodge from Mokhotlong; buses depart from the main street.

Getting There & Away

From Butha-Buthe it's about 170km of sealed road to Mokhotlong. In good weather this takes more than two hours to drive and considerably longer by bus or taxi. There's a long, very steep climb before Oxbow (about 60km from Butha-Buthe) and you cross at least two passes over 3000m above sea level. The road is good but if there's snow or ice the steep hairpin bends are dangerous.

There is one bus a day running between Mokhotlong and Butha-Buthe (M27) and one to Maseru (M34).

SANI PASS

This steep pass is the only dependable road into Lesotho through the Drakensberg range in KwaZulu-Natal. On the KwaZulu-Natal side the nearest towns are Underberg and Himeville.

From Sani Top Chalet at the top of the pass there are several day walks including a long and arduous one to **Thabana-Ntlenyana** (3482m), the highest peak on the continent south of Mt Kilimanjaro. The height of the mountain was only calculated in 1951, and it took another 30 years for this calculation to be confirmed by satellite technology. There is a path, but a guide would be handy. Horses can do the trip so consider hiring one.

Another walk leads to **Hodgson's Peaks**, 6km south, from where you get the benefit of views to Sehlabathebe National Park and to KwaZulu-Natal.

One three-day hike in this area that you could try before attempting something more ambitious is from Sani Top Chalet south along the edge of the escarpment to Sehlabathebe National Park. From here, there's a track leading down to Bushman's Nek in KwaZulu-Natal. As the crow flies, the distance from Sani Top to Nkonkoana Gate is about 45km but the hike is longer than that. Much of this area is over 3000m above sea level and it's remote even by Lesotho's standards: There isn't a horse trail, much less a road or a settlement. Don't try this unless you are well prepared, experienced and in a party of at least three people.

A number of other hikes in this area are outlined in Russell Suchet's *A Backpackers' Guide to Lesotho*. In addition to the hike from Sani Top to Sehlabathebe, he also outlines hikes from Sehonghong to Sehlabathebe (two to three days); and Mokhotlong

to Sani Top via Thabana-Ntlenyana (three to four days). Suchet also suggests the ultimate Lesotho challenge: from Mahlesela Pass in the north near Oxbow Lodge, all the way to Sehlabathebe via Mont-aux-Sources (14 to 20 days). For more details on hiking in Lesotho, see Activities under Facts for the Visitor earlier in this chapter.

Places to Stay & Eat

Sani Top Chalet Camping M30, dorm beds M50, doubles/DB&B M120/180. At a lofty 2874m, this chalet, built right on the edge of the escarpment, boasts the highest bar in Africa. There are cooking facilities for self-caterers but meals are also available. In winter the snow is often deep enough for skiing (there are a few pieces of antique equipment), and pony trekking is available by prior arrangement. Book through *Southern Drakensberg Tours* (☎ 033-702 1158, e drakensberg.info@futurenet.org.za) in KwaZulu-Natal.

The other obvious places to stay are the hostels on the KwaZulu-Natal side of the pass. See the Sani Pass section in the KwaZulu-Natal chapter.

Getting There & Away

The South African border guards won't let you drive up the pass unless you have a 4WD, although you are permitted to come down from Lesotho without one (although this is not recommended). The South African border crossing is open 8am to 4pm daily; the Lesotho border crossing stays open an hour later to let the last vehicles through. Hitching up or down the pass is best on weekends when there is a fair amount of traffic to and from Sani Top.

Hostels at the bottom of the pass on the KwaZulu-Natal side arrange transport up the pass, and various agencies in Himeville and Underberg (KwaZulu-Natal) arrange tours.

There are a few minibus taxis running Basothos down into South Africa (for shopping) that cost much less. You might have to wait a day or so for one of these, though.

Public transport between Sani Top and the rest of Lesotho is sparse but with patience you'll find something.

LESOTHO

SEHLABATHEBE NATIONAL PARK

Lesotho's first national park, proclaimed in 1970, is remote and rugged, and getting there is always an adventure. The park's main attraction is its sense of separation from the rest of the world. Other than a few rare birds such as the Maloti minnow (thought to be extinct but rediscovered on the Tsoelikana River), the bearded vulture and the odd rhebok or baboon, there are relatively few animals here. As well as hikes and climbs, the park has horse riding, with guided horseback tours costing M50.

This is a summer-rainfall area, and thick mist, potentially hazardous to hikers, is common. Winters are clear but cold at night, and there are sometimes light falls of snow.

Close to the nearby village of Sehonghong is **Soai's Cave**. Soai, the last chief of the Maloti San people, was attacked and defeated here by Cape Colony and Basotho forces in 1871.

Places to Stay & Eat

Sehlabathebe Park Lodge Camping M20, singles/doubles M30/50, 4-bed family rooms M100. You can camp in the park, though with the exception of the lodge, there are no facilities (besides plenty of water). You can buy firewood and coal here (M5) but for food (very limited) and petrol or diesel, you'll have to rely on a small store about 5km west of the park entrance and quite a way from the lodge. For bookings contact the **Conservation Division** (☎ *323600 ext 30)*, in the Ministry of Agriculture building in Maseru (see Tourist Offices under Information in the Maseru section earlier).

The Range Management Education Centre Dorm beds M35. This modern well-equipped centre is 1.5km down the Sehonghong road in Sehlabathebe Village. Meals are available.

At the cafe next to the Sehonghong airstrip, there is occasionally *accommodation* available for M25; this is a handy option if you fly in.

Getting There & Away

Sometimes there are charter flights from Maseru to Ha Paulus, a village near the park entrance, and you can arrange to be picked up from there for M40.

Driving into the park can be a problem, as the roads are 4WD tracks that become impassable after the heavy spring and summer rains. Bear in mind that having got to the park, you could be stuck here waiting for a swollen river to go down before you can leave. Still, people usually do make it in and out without too many problems and most agree that the journey was worth it. The road building accompanying the hydroelectric scheme should improve at least some of the routes. Check the situation when you book accommodation.

There are several routes into the park, all of which require a 4WD. The longest is the southern route via Quthing and Qacha's Nek. There's also a route via Thaba-Tseka, then down the Senqu (Orange) River valley, past the village of Sehonghong and over the difficult Matebeng Pass. The park can also be reached from Matatiele, south-east of Qacha's Nek, in the extreme west of KwaZulu-Natal. This route doesn't have as many difficult sections as the other routes but it is less well maintained and sometimes closed; check in Matatiele.

There is a daily bus between Qacha's Nek and Sehlabathebe Village. The relatively short distance takes 5½ hours and costs M19; the bus departs from Sehlabathebe at 5.30am and returns from Qacha's Nek at noon.

Probably the simplest way into the park is to hike the 10km up the escarpment from Bushman's Nek in KwaZulu-Natal. From Bushman's Nek to the Nkonkoana Gate border crossing takes about six hours. You can also take a horse up or down for M50. Ask about horse hire at the lodge (see also Bushman's Nek in the KwaZulu-Natal chapter).

QACHA'S NEK

This pleasant town, with a number of sandstone buildings, was founded in 1888 near the pass (1980m) of the same name. There are Californian redwood trees nearby, some over 25m high.

Farmer Training Centre (☎ *950231)* Dorm beds M25. The centre, just off the main road (turn at the 'Forestry Division' sign), offers the usual standard of accommodation for this type of place.

Nthatuoa Hotel (☎ 950260) Singles/doubles M130/170. The hotel offers adequate accommodation; meals are available. It is within walking distance of the airstrip.

Getting There & Away
Weather permitting (in winter the area can get snowed in), a bus to Sehlabathebe leaves daily at noon (M30). There is more transport between here and Quthing (Moyeni). A bus leaves from both towns at 9am (M30, six hours). It is a spectacular drive.

Southern Lesotho

SEMONKONG
Semonkong (meaning 'Place of Smoke') is a one-horse town that is a good base from which to see the nearby falls. **Maletsunyane Falls**, also known as Lebihan Falls after the French missionary who reported them in 1881, are about a 1½-hour walk from Semonkong. The 192m falls are at their most spectacular in summer and are best appreciated from the bottom of the gorge (where there are camp sites).

The remote **Ketane Falls** (122m) are also worth seeing. The falls are a solid day's ride (30km) from Semonkong or a four-day return horse ride from Malealea Lodge (see the Malealea section later in this chapter).

Places to Stay
You can usually find a bed at the *Roman Catholic Mission* in Semonkong for a small contribution.

Semonkong Lodge (☎/fax 051-933 3106 Free State, e bookings@placeofsmoke.co .ls, w www.placeofsmoke.co.ls) Camping M28, dorm beds M45, singles/doubles with bathroom M167/264. This lodge, on the banks of the Maletsunyane River, is a peaceful place with a good restaurant and bar. Hiking and pony trekking are available; the rates and options are similar to those at Malealea Lodge. Follow the signs from the centre of the town.

Getting There & Away
Semonkong is about 120km south-east of Maseru. Buses between Maseru and Semonkong (M15) leave from either place in the morning and arrive late in the afternoon. By car it's about a three-hour drive due to the rough road. A 2WD vehicle can do it, but a small car might have problems.

MORIJA
In this small village, about 40km from Maseru on the main road south, is where you will find the **Morija Museum & Archives** *(☎ 360308, fax 36001, e info@morijafest .com; admission M5; open 8am-5pm Mon-Sat, noon-5pm Sun)*. The collection includes archives from the first mission to Basotholand; as the missionary was associated with King Moshoeshoe the Great, the collection is of great significance. The museum itself is small but still worth a look, and the staff are very helpful and knowledgeable.

During the last week in September the village hosts the annual **Morija Arts & Cultural Festival**. The three-day celebration highlights the diversity of Basotho culture through dance, music, and theatre and includes horse racing and *moraba-raba* (the African equivalent of chess) competitions. The festival began in 1999 as a means to reunite the people of Lesotho after the turmoil created by the 1998 invasion. For details contact the Morija Museum.

Maeder House crafts centre *(☎ 360487; open 9am-5pm Mon-Sat, noon-5pm Sun)*, near the museum, sells a variety of crafts. **Morija Pony Trekking Association** offers a range of rides, from one hour (M25) to overnight (M140). Book rides through the museum.

Mophato Oa Morija (☎ 360219) Camping M25, beds M62 per person. Mophato Oa Morija, near the museum, is an ecumenical youth centre which offers accommodation. Breakfast/dinner is available for M15/20.

Ha Matela Guest Cottages Beds M80-100 per person. Here you'll find three pleasant self-catering cottages (no minimum number of people is required – it's a good deal). Book through the museum (ask for the curator, Stephen Gill). Breakfast/dinner is available for M15/35.

A minibus taxi to/from Maseru costs M5.

MALEALEA

Malealea is a small village, a shop and a large lodge. This lodge is one of the gems of Lesotho and is appropriately advertised as 'Lesotho in a nutshell'. You can go on a well-organised pony trek from here or wander freely through the hills and villages.

The valleys around here have been occupied for a long time, as shown by the many **San paintings** in rock shelters. The original Malealea trading post was established in 1905 by Mervyn Smith, a teacher, diamond miner and soldier. The owners of the lodge may show you the protected spiral aloe (*Aloe polyphylla*), a plant unique to Lesotho.

The Mafeteng **Children's Choir & Band** practices in the village; just hearing them is worth the trip from Maseru.

Pony Trekking

Malealea is the best place in Lesotho to go pony trekking. These treks offer a good chance to come face to face with Basotho villagers, as well as experience the awesome scenery of the mountains and deep valleys. The treks are conducted by the lodge with the full cooperation of the villagers. In fact they act as guides and provide the ponies, so if you undertake a trek, you are contributing to the local village economy.

The two most-popular treks are those to the Ribaneng Waterfall (two days, one night) and to the Ribaneng and Ketane waterfalls (four days, three nights); however, the lodge will organise a trek to any destination that takes your fancy. You must bring food, a sleeping bag, rainwear, sunscreen, warm clothing, a torch (flashlight) and water purification tablets.

Day rides cost M100 per person and overnight treks cost M135 per person per day. Accommodation in Basotho village huts costs M30 per night.

Walking

Those of tender buttocks who cannot face seven-hour stints on the ponies may elect to go walking. The owners of Malealea Lodge have put together a number of walking options and provide a map. They can also arrange for your packs to be carried on ponies. Day walks include a two-hour return walk to the **Botso'ela Waterfall**; a six-hour return walk to the **Pitseng Gorge** (don't forget your swimwear); an easy one-hour walk along the **Pitseng Plateau**; a walk along the Makhaleng River; and a hike from the **Gates of Paradise Pass** back to Malealea. The scenery along any of these walks is nothing less than stunning and all include visits to the local villages that dot the landscape. Overnight and longer walks can easily be planned.

Driving

Although it is slow going on the dirt roads in this region, there are some very scenic drives. Perhaps the best is the road that forms part of the Roof of Africa Rally; take a right turn at the first junction you come to when leaving Malealea. This road passes through some picturesque villages before crossing the top of the **Botso'ela Waterfall**. A few kilometres on it reaches an impressive lookout over the Makhaleng and Ribaneng Valleys. In a conventional car it takes one hour to reach the viewpoint from Malealea – rally drivers take 20 minutes to cover this same distance!

If you continue north from the lookout to Sebelekoane you can return to Maseru via Roma. This scenic road leads to Basotho villages and missions tucked away in the valleys. Be warned, it is rough in places and the going can be slow; allow three hours from Sebelekoane to Maseru.

Places to Stay & Eat

Malealea Lodge (☎ 051-447 3200 bookings, ☎ 082 552 4215 Free State, e malealea@pixie.co.za, w www.malealea.co.ls, PO Box 12118, Brandhof 9324, Bloemfontein) Camping M30, 2-bed dorm M50, huts M70 per person, rooms M100-150 per person. Malealea Lodge is run by the friendly Mick and Di Jones. There's usually room if you just turn up, but sometimes there are groups that take up the whole place, so you should always book. There's no phone at the lodge (there is a radio), so allow a few days for your booking to go through. The huts have shared facilities while the rooms have private facilities (some even have a kitchen). There's a bar at the lodge, and a fully-stocked shop is nearby. Breakfast/lunch/dinner is available for M30/40/50.

Getting There & Away

Travellers advise that from Maseru, a minibus to Motsekuoa, and from there another to Malealea, is the fastest public transport option (M13).

If you are driving, Maseru to Malealea is 83km. From Maseru, head south on the well-signposted Mafeteng road for 52km to the town of Motsekuoa. Look out for the Golden Rose restaurant, the many taxis and the huddles of potential passengers. Opposite the restaurant, turn left (east) onto a new tar road and follow it for 24km. When you reach the signposted turn-off to Malealea, it is a further 7km along an unsealed road to the lodge. You will pass through the Gates of Paradise Pass and will be rewarded with a stunning view of your destination. The plaque here announces 'Wayfarer – Pause and look upon a gateway of Paradise'. Romantic stuff. Look east from here and you can just make out the Ribaneng Waterfall.

The road to Malealea from the south, via Mpharane and Masemouse, is much rougher. Most drivers take the Motsekuoa road.

It's sometimes possible to arrange transport between Bloemfontein (Free State) and Malealea; inquire when booking. There is also a shuttle-bus service that runs between Malealea and the Amphitheatre backpackers in Kwazulu Natal (see the KwaZulu-Natal chapter for details); fares are M220/350 one way/return.

MAFETENG

The name Mafeteng means 'Place of Lefeta's People'. An early magistrate, Emile Rolland, was known as Lefeta (One who Passes By) to the local Basotho. Nearby is the 3096m Thaba-Putsoa (Blue Mountain), the highest feature in this part of Lesotho.

> ## The Basotho Pony
>
> The Basotho pony is strong and sure-footed and generally docile. Its size and physique are the result of crossbreeding between short Javanese horses and European full mounts.
>
> A few horses were captured from invading Griqua forces by Basotho warriors in the early 19th century, and King Moshoeshoe the Great is recorded as having ridden a Basotho pony in 1830. Since that date, the pony has become an integral part of life in the highlands and the preferred mode of transport for many villagers. In 1983, the Basotho Pony Trekking Centre was set up near God Help Me Pass (at Molimo-Nthuse) in an attempt to prevent dilution of the ponies' gene pool.

There is not much of interest in town, although it is important as a bus and minibus taxi interchange. There's a **memorial** to soldiers of the Cape Mounted Rifles who fell in the Gun War of 1880.

Mafeteng Hotel (☎ 700236, fax 700478) Singles/doubles from M125/150. While not all that appealing, this place offers your standard hotel rooms as well as pleasant garden cottages. There is also a *restaurant*, and its *Las Vegas Disco* is a popular night spot.

MOHALE'S HOEK

This comfortable town is 125km south of Maseru. Mohale, the younger brother of King Moshoeshoe the Great, gave this land to the British for administrative purposes in 1884. It is a much nicer little place than nearby Mafeteng.

Monateng Lodge (☎/fax 785337) Singles/doubles M140/165. If you are on a tight budget this lodge will suffice – its sparsely furnished rooms are clean. However, if you can afford it pay the town's hotel a visit. Breakfast/dinner is available for M25/45.

Hotel Mount Maluti (☎ 785224, fax 785341) Singles/doubles from M163/227. This is perhaps the only pleasant hotel (as opposed to the odd pleasant lodge) in rural Lesotho. There's a large garden with a pool and tennis court. Pony trekking can be arranged. The hotel is down a dirt road

LESOTHO

running off the main through-road, just on the Maseru side of the chaotic main shopping street. Breakfast/dinner is available for M35/39.

QUTHING

Quthing, which is the southernmost major town in Lesotho, is often known as Moyeni (a Sephuthi word meaning 'Place of the Wind'). The town was first established in 1877, abandoned three years later during the Gun War of 1880 and then rebuilt at the present site.

Most of the town is in Lower Quthing; up on the hill overlooking the dramatic Senqu (Orange) River gorge is Upper Quthing, where there is a good hotel, a mission and sundry colonial-era structures. A minibus taxi between Lower and Upper Quthing costs M1.50; you can hitch but you should still pay the driver.

Off the highway, about 5km west of Quthing, is the five-room **Masitise Cave House**. This mission building was built into a San rock shelter in 1866 by Rev Ellenberger. His son Edmund was born in the cave in 1867. Edmund later became the mayor of Bethlehem in the Orange Free State. Inquire at the school about access to the cave house and someone will unlock it for you. There are San paintings nearby.

The **dinosaur footprints** near Quthing are probably the most easily located in Lesotho. To get to these, head up the Mt Moorosi road from Quthing until you reach a thatched-roofed orange building. There is

a short walk to the footprints, which are believed to be 180 million years old.

Between Quthing and Masitise there is a striking, twin-spired sandstone church, which is part of the Villa Maria Mission.

Near Qomoqomong, 10km from Quthing, there is a good collection of San paintings; inquire at the General Dealers store about acquiring a guide for the 20-minute walk to the paintings.

Places to Stay & Eat

Merino Stud Farm 2-bed room without/ with bathroom M25/45 per person. The Merino Stud Farm, 2.5km from Upper Quthing, is the cheapest place to stay. Follow the tar road until it ends; there you'll see a sign pointing to the farm. Breakfast and dinner are available for M10 each.

Orange River Hotel Singles/doubles M150/200. This once-grand hotel, in Upper Quthing, now stands virtually derelict. Its less-than-average rooms have stunning views across the gorge to the bleak hills behind. Breakfast/dinner is available for M25/39.

Mountain Side Hotel (☎ 750257) Singles/ doubles M160/220. The Mountain Side Hotel, in Lower Quthing, is the better of the two hotels in the town. It also has a lively **pub** with a **restaurant**. Breakfast/dinner is available for M25/35.

Getting There & Away

Buses/minibus taxis run from Quthing to Maseru (M25/29) stopping at Mafeteng (M12/14) and Mohale's Hoek (M8/9).

LESOTHO

Swaziland

RICHARD I'ANSON

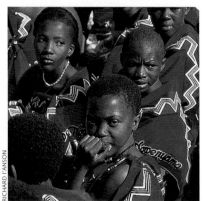

RICHARD I'ANSON

RICHARD I'ANSON

RICHARD I'ANSON

Swaziland offers visitors the best of Africa's landscapes and culture: great national parks; fabulous artwork; and vibrant festivals.

Swaziland

Swaziland comes as a breath of fresh air after travelling through South Africa. Few of the animosities between the races so evident in post-apartheid South Africa are encountered in Swaziland. Swazis are very friendly people and most visitors take away memories of smiling adults and waving children, particularly if they spend any time in the countryside.

Swaziland gives visitors the best of Africa in a neat, compact package. Outside of Mbabane, the capital, and Manzini, the commercial centre, the country is rural and dotted with small villages. It is easy to get from place to place and the distances between points of interest are relatively short.

Swazi handicrafts offer some of the best value in the region and there are places where you can see the craftspeople at work. It's worth tracking down some of the objects that you won't find elsewhere in Southern Africa, such as the colourful Swazi candles and the exquisite, handmade glassware at Ngwenya, to take home.

Swaziland has a short but proud history of nature conservation, and the national parks and nature reserves here are excellent. You can discover these at your leisure, as they are very affordable. For instance, Mkhaya is a superb private game reserve that offers package deals for far cheaper than those offered by the private reserves around Kruger in South Africa. You've possibly a better chance of seeing the endangered black rhino in the wild here than anywhere on the continent.

In addition to seeing the Big Five, there are loads of activities, including some of the finest walking in Southern Africa. There are also some stunning drives around the country that take in spectacular mountain scenery. Between Piggs Peak and Mbabane, for instance, the road goes through the Ngwenya Hills, a stark mountainous range save for a lush, velvet covering of greenery. On an overcast day, this green covering makes the range more reminiscent of the Scottish Highlands than of the rest of Africa.

SWAZILAND AT A GLANCE

Capital: Mbabane
Population: 1.1 million
Time: GMT/UTC + 2
Area: 17,363 sq km
International Dialling Code: ☎ 268
Per Capita GDP: US$4,200
Currency: lilangeni (plural emalangeni; E); the South African rand is also in use
Languages: English, Swati

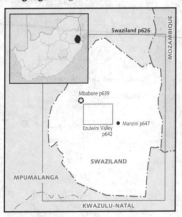

Highlights

- View wildlife in the excellent private Mkhaya Game Reserve.
- Walk around the Malolotja Nature Reserve – one of Africa's most enchanting wilderness areas.
- Witness the spectacular annual Umhlanga (Reed) dance and Incwala ceremony in the Ezulwini Valley, Swaziland's royal heartland.
- Shop for Swazi arts and crafts, including world-famous tapestries.
- Bunk down in a beehive hut in Mlilwane Wildlife Sanctuary.
- Shoot white-water rapids, including a 10m waterfall, on the Usutu River.

SWAZILAND

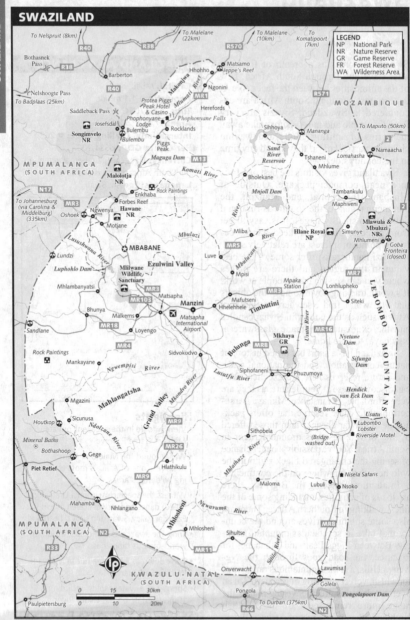

LEGEND

NP	National Park
NR	Nature Reserve
GR	Game Reserve
FR	Forest Reserve
WA	Wilderness Area

Swazis are very proud of their country, and rightly so. They fought long and hard to keep their territory out of the hands of the Boers, the British and the Zulus. It is fortunate that this unique country has kept its independence from South Africa, its much larger neighbour, thereby preserving its cultural heritage very successfully. As one of Africa's monarchies (almost an absolute monarchy at that) there is much evidence of royalty and right royal relationships. The monarchy clings to tradition and there are several chances each year to see cultural spectaculars such as the Incwala ceremony and the Umhlanga (Reed) dance.

Swaziland is small and it's easy to drive around the whole country in a couple of days. But be warned, you'll be disappointed if you spend so little time in this wonderful country. Make the effort to spend at least a week here – you won't regret it.

For more on Swazi arts, society and culture see also the special section 'Peoples of the Region'.

Facts about Swaziland

HISTORY

For a more general history of the region see the Facts about South Africa chapter at the beginning of this book.

Before the 20th Century

The area that is now Swaziland has been inhabited by various groups for a very long time (in eastern Swaziland archaeologists have discovered human remains dating back 110,000 years), but the Swazi people themselves arrived relatively recently.

In the great Bantu migration into Southern Africa, one group, the Nguni, moved down the eastern coast. One clan settled in the area around present-day Maputo in Mozambique, and eventually a dynasty was founded by the Dlamini family. By the mid-18th century increasing pressure from other clans in the area forced the Dlamini king Ngwane III to lead his people south to lands

around the Pongola River, in what is today southern Swaziland and northern KwaZulu-Natal. Today, Swazis consider Ngwane III to have been the first king of Swaziland.

The next king, Sobhuza I, came under pressure from the Zulus. He withdrew to the Ezulwini Valley, which still remains the centre of Swazi royalty and ritual. Trouble with the Zulus continued and there was a further retreat by the next king, Mswazi (or Mswati) – this time as far as the Hhohho area in the extreme north of present-day Swaziland.

However, King Mswazi, with a combination of martial skill and diplomacy, managed to unify the whole kingdom and by the time he died in 1868, a Swazi nation was secure. Mswazi's subjects called themselves people of Mswazi, or Swazis.

From the mid-19th century, Swaziland attracted increasing numbers of European farmers in search of land for their cattle, hunters, traders and missionaries. Mswazi's successor, Mbandzeni, inherited a kingdom rife with European carpetbaggers, and more and more of the kingdom's land was being alienated through leases granted to Europeans. Bribes for the king featured heavily in some of the deals.

The Pretoria Convention of 1881 guaranteed Swaziland's independence and also defined its borders – in the process Swaziland lost large chunks of territory. 'Independence' in fact meant that both the British and the Boers had responsibility for administering their various interests in Swaziland, and the result was chaos. The Boer administration collapsed with the 1899–1902 Anglo-Boer War and afterwards the British took control of Swaziland as a protectorate.

The 20th Century

In the early years of the century, when Swazis were coming to grips with their loss of sovereignty, King Sobhuza II was only a young child. Fortunately Labotsibeni, his mother, ably acted as regent until her son took over in 1921. Throughout the regency and for most of Sobhuza's long reign, the Swazis fought to again become an independent nation and to regain their lands. After

SWAZILAND

petitions and delegations to Britain failed, Labotsibeni encouraged Swazis to buy their land back, and many sought work in the Witwatersrand mines to raise money. Land was gradually returned to the kingdom by both direct purchase and British government action, and by the time of independence in 1968, about two-thirds of the kingdom was again in Swazi control.

Land ownership was not just a political and economic issue: Swazi kings are considered to hold the kingdom in trust for their subjects, and to have a large proportion of the country owned by foreigners threatened the credibility of the monarchy and thus the viability of Swazi culture.

In 1960 King Sobhuza II proposed the creation of a Legislative Council, to be composed of Europeans elected along European lines, and a National Council formed in accordance with Swazi culture. One of the Swazi political parties formed at this time was the Mbokodvo (Grindstone) National Movement, which pledged to both maintain traditional Swazi culture and eschew racial discrimination. When the British finally agreed to elections in 1964, Mbokodvo won a majority. At the next elections in 1967, it won all the seats. Independence, now certain, was achieved on 6 September 1968.

The country's constitution was largely the work of the British, and in 1973 the king suspended it on the grounds that it did not accord with Swazi culture. Four years later the parliament reconvened under a new constitution that vested all power in the king.

Sobhuza II, then the world's longest-reigning monarch, died in 1982, having ensured the continued existence of his country and culture, under threat since his father's reign. He is still referred to as 'the late king'.

The surprising feature of Britain's 66-year rule of Swaziland was the lack of violence with which it was resisted and overthrown.

The then-young Mswati III ascended the throne in 1986 and continues to represent and maintain the traditional Swazi way of life. Although most Swazis seem happy with their political system, there is some political dissent. The main concern of most Swazis, however, is to ensure that their

culture survives in the face of modernisation. Currently, King Mswati III and a small core of advisers (Council of Ministers) run the country.

Opposition parties are illegal. Despite this, there are two main players: Pudemo (People's United Democratic Movement) and Swayoco (Swaziland Youth Congress). Both parties have only minimal support.

The 21st Century

The movement for democratic change in Swaziland picked up pace in 2000 and early 2001. Although most Swazis seem to remain apathetic about change, political tensions have certainly increased. The trade union movement seems to be growing more fearless, with threats of strikes and the blocking of both imported and exported products to and from Mozambique and South Africa.

King Mswati's response has been to place further bans on trade union meetings and reintroduce a 60-day detention law. Undeterred, Swaziland's pro-democracy groups continue to petition for change. They refuse to recognise the Public Order Act, which forbids party politics in the kingdom and requires citizens to obtain police permission for meetings.

A review of the country's constitution ordered by the king in 1996 (due largely to pressure from the United Nations and World Bank) was handed to the king's office in 2000; the office has thus far refused to release the review's findings.

GEOGRAPHY

Swaziland, one of the smallest countries in the southern hemisphere, has a wide range of ecological zones. These range from rainforest in the north-west to savanna scrub in the east.

The western edge of the country is highveld (high-altitude grassland) consisting mainly of short, sharp mountains. It is known as *nkhangala* ('treeless' in Swati), but these days there are large plantations of exotic pine and eucalyptus, especially around Piggs Peak in the north. The mountains dwindle to *middleveld* (middle-altitude area) in the centre of the country, where most people live. The eastern half is scrubby lowveld, (low-altitude area), once lightly populated because of malaria (which is still a risk) and now home to sugar estates. The eastern border with Mozambique is formed by the formidable Lebombo Mountains.

CLIMATE
Swaziland's climate is similar to that of South Africa's eastern lowveld. Summers on the lowveld are very hot, with temperatures often over 40°C in October. Most rain falls in summer, beginning around early December and lasting until April; it usually falls in torrential thunderstorms and mostly in the country's eastern mountains.

May to August are the coolest months, with frosts in June and July. Winter nights on the lowveld are sometimes very cold (and colder still on the highveld).

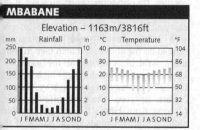

MBABANE

Elevation – 1163m/3816ft

Rainfall | Temperature

FLORA & FAUNA
Although small in size, Swaziland is rich in flora, accounting for 14% of the recorded plant life in Southern Africa. Due to the remote nature of parts of the countryside, there are probably species that have not yet been brought to the attention of botanists. Nature reserves, particularly those administered by the National Trust Commission, have the responsibility of conserving indigenous plants.

Swaziland has about 121 species of mammals, representing a third of (non-marine) mammal species in Southern Africa. These days the larger animals are restricted to the nature reserves and private wildlife farms dotted around the country. Many species (such as elephants, warthogs, rhinos and lions) have been reintroduced. Mon-

gooses and large-spotted genets are common throughout the country, while hyenas and jackals are found in the reserves. Leopards are present, but you'd be lucky to see one.

Nineteen species of bat have been recorded; the most common is the little free-tailed bat, which can be found roosting in houses in the lowveld and middleveld.

For information about the area's wildlife, see the Wildlife Guide.

National Parks & Reserves
The five main reserves in Swaziland reflect the country's geographical diversity. Easiest to get to is Mlilwane Wildlife Sanctuary in the Ezulwini Valley. Mkhaya Game Reserve and Hlane Royal National Park are also well worth visiting. These three reserves are run as part of the Kingdom of Swaziland's Big Game Parks organisation (for contact details see Information under Ezulwini Valley later in this chapter). The National Trust Commission runs Malolotja and Mlawula Nature Reserves (see Malolotja Nature Reserve later in this chapter for contact details). Malolotja Nature Resereve is a western highlands reserve with some good hiking trails. Mlawula is in harsh lowveld country near Mozambique.

GOVERNMENT & POLITICS
Swaziland is governed by a parliament, but final authority (and ownership of much of the country's resources) is vested in the king. The king can dissolve parliament at any time.

There is a Senate as well as a House of Assembly. Half of the 30 senators are elected by the assembly, the other half are appointed by the king. The king also appoints 20 members of the assembly. The other 40 are elected in the constituencies, first by a show of hands and then by ballot. There is no campaigning as such, but each candidate is given a range of subjects to discuss at a controlled meeting. At the secondary elections there will be one successful candidate per constituency.

The real power is vested in the king and the 16-person Council of Ministers. It is fair to say that dilution of the democratic process means that about a quarter of the council actually represent the interests of the average Swazi (not that the average Swazi is demanding rapid change).

ECONOMY

Swaziland is a poor country but it is by no means in crisis and its economy is modestly healthy. The major export is sugar, and forest products are also important. Although most foreign investment in the country is still British, South African investment is extremely important and fluctuations in that country's economy in turn affect Swaziland's.

Nearly 75% of the population works in agriculture, mostly at a subsistence level, but the country is not self-sufficient in food.

POPULATION & PEOPLE

Almost all of Swaziland's 1.1 million citizens are Swazi. The remainder are Zulu, Shangaan-Tsonga and European. There are also Mozambican refugees of both African and Portuguese descent. About 5% of Swazi citizens still live and work in South Africa.

The dominant clan is the Dlamini and you'll meet people with that surname all over the country. It's sometimes felt that ordinary Dlaminis put on unwarranted royal airs and there's a little resentment towards them, usually expressed in the form of friendly jibes. There are a lot of Swazi princes and they come from all walks of life.

See also the special section 'Peoples of the Region' for more on the Swazi people.

RELIGION

Nearly half of all Swazis belong to the Zion Apostolic Church (see the boxed text 'Seven Million Silver Stars' in the Facts about South Africa chapter). While traditional religion is not widely practised, Swazi traditional culture continues strongly and many ceremonies have religious significance.

LANGUAGE

The official languages are Swati and English; English is the official written language. For information on Swati see the Language chapter at the end of this book.

Facts for the Visitor

For more general information see also the Facts for the Visitor chapter near the beginning of this book.

SUGGESTED ITINERARIES

With a week at your disposal, a day in Mbabane is plenty; drop into the Indingilizi Gallery and check out its displays of traditional crafts before moving onto the pretty Ezulwini Valley and Lobamba, its heart. Spend a few days poking around here and make a trip into the Mlilwane Wildlife Sanctuary, where there is excellent walking; you'll probably see zebras, giraffes, hippos, many antelope species and a variety of birds. Try to drop into Malkerns, just south of the Ezulwini Valley, to pick up some excellent crafts, including the unique Swazi candles. If you've time and you want to see the rare black rhino in the wild, continue east past Manzini to Mkhaya Game Reserve.

With two weeks you'd have plenty of time to do the above, and then take in some more wildlife viewing at the extensive Hlane Royal National Park, which has special 'lion' drives, and at the nearby Mlawula Nature Reserve. On your circular route (driving from Hlane Royal National Park along the gravel roads in the north of the country) back to Mbabane, you could stop off at Piggs Peak, located in an area known for its handicrafts and forests, before doing some hiking in Malolotja Nature Reserve, an unspoiled wilderness area with possibly the finest walking in Southern Africa. Note that there is no reason why you can't do the route clockwise, starting in Mbabane and heading north to Malolotja.

PLANNING

Swaziland can get very hot in summer, when there are often quite spectacular thunderstorms; in winter it can get very cold.

The free maps available in various brochures at the tourist office in Mbabane are good enough to get you around this tiny country, although if you're driving you might have to ask directions if you get off the main roads. A good 1:250,000-scale map s available from the Surveyor-General's office at the **Ministry of Works** *(PO Box 58, Mbabane)*. If you're serious about hiking, here are also 1:50,000-scale maps.

An ideal companion to this book is Lonely Planet's *Southern Africa Road Atlas*. Novice travellers and those seeking extra guidance before travelling in the region could consult the excellent trip-planner *Read This First: Africa,* also by Lonely Planet.

TOURIST OFFICES
Local Tourist Offices
The main tourist offices in Swaziland are in Mbabane *(☎ 404 2531, Swazi Plaza)*, and in the Ezulwini Valley *(☎ 416 1136, Mantenga Craft Centre)*.

VISAS & DOCUMENTS
Most people don't need a visa to visit Swaziland. Some nationals of European Union (EU) countries do need visas; these are available free of charge at border posts and the airport. If you do require a visa, contact the UK representative in countries without representation.

Anyone staying for more than 60 days must apply for a temporary residence permit from the **Chief Immigration Officer** *(☎ 404 2941, PO Box 372, Mbabane)*.

Onward Visas for Mozambique
The **Mozambique Embassy** *(open 9am-1pm Mon-Fri)* in Mbabane issues urgent one-month visas for E85 (considerably less than you would pay in Jo'burg) within 24 hours; normally, the processing of visas takes a week and costs E45. You will need two photos. To get to the embassy, head out onto the Manzini road, turn left down the road to the Mountain Inn, turn left onto the dirt road just past the hotel entrance and then left again at the next corner onto Princess Dr. The embassy is 100m or so further on.

Vaccination Certificates
Vaccination certificates are not usually required. The only exception being for those who have recently been in a yellow fever area, who must show have a certificate of vaccination against yellow fever.

EMBASSIES & CONSULATES
Swazi Embassies & Consulates
Countries that have a Swaziland embassy, consulate or high commission include:

Canada
High Commission: (☎ 613-567 1480, fax 567 1058) 130 Albert St, Ottawa, Ontario, KIP 5G4
Germany
Honorary Consulate: (☎ 211-350 866) D4, Dusseldorf 1, Worringer Strasse 59
Kenya
Embassy: (☎ 2-339231, fax 330540) Silopark House, 3rd floor, Mama Ngina St, Nairobi
South Africa
Embassy in Pretoria: (☎ 012-344 1910) 715 Government Ave, Arcadia
UK
High Commission: (☎ 020-7630 6611, fax 7630 6564) 20 Buckingham Gate, London SW1E 6LB
USA
Embassy: (☎ 202-362 6683, fax 244 6059) Suite 3M, 3400 International Dr, Washington, DC 20008

Embassies & Consulates in Swaziland
Diplomatic representation in Swaziland includes:

Denmark & Norway
Consulate: (☎ 404 3547, fax 404 3548) Ground floor, Sokhamlilo Bldg, Johnson St, Mbabane. Open from 9am to 11am Monday to Friday (visas issued during these hours; forms can be collected all day).
France
Embassy: (☎ 404 3667, fax 404 8340) Usutu Rd, Mbabane. Open from 8am to 5.30pm Monday to Friday.
Germany
Embassy: (☎ 404 3174) 3rd floor, Dhlan'ubeka House, Walker (Mhlonhlo) St, Mbabane. Open from 9am to noon Monday to Friday.
Mozambique
Embassy: (☎ 404 3700, fax 404 3692) Princess Dr, Mbabane. Open from 9am to 1pm Monday to Friday.
Netherlands
Embassy: (☎ 404 5178, fax 404 4006) Business Machine House, Gilfillan St, Mbabane. Open from 8.30am to 12.30pm Monday to Friday.
South Africa
High Commission: (☎ 404 4651) The Mall, PO Box 2597, Mbabane. Open from 8.30am to 12.30pm Monday to Friday.

SWAZILAND

UK
High Commission: (☎ 404 2581, fax 404 2586)
Lilunga House, Gilfillan St, Mbabane. Open
from 8am to 4.45pm Monday to Thursday &
8am to 1pm Friday.

USA
Embassy: (☎ 404 6442) 7th floor, Central Bank
Building, Warner St, Mbabane. Open from 8am
to 5pm Monday to Friday.

MONEY
Currency
The unit of currency in Swaziland is the
lilangeni (the plural is emalangeni, abbrevi-
ated 'E'), which is fixed at a value equal to
the rand. Rands are accepted everywhere
and there's no need to change them, although many places will not accept small
denomination South African coins. Emalangeni are difficult to change for other currencies outside Swaziland, so reconvert
these when leaving.

Exchange Rates
The lilangeni is fixed at a rate equal to the
rand. See Money in the Facts for the Visitor
chapter near the beginning of this book for
exchange rates.

Exchanging Money
Standard Chartered Bank, First National
Bank and Nedbank all change cash and
travellers cheques. Rates seem to be about
the same at all three banks, but you may
want to compare commission. At First National Bank a standard E20 commission is
charged, making it more economical to
change your money in large amounts. Credit-
card advances are available at all the banks,
but they'll hit you with a pretty hefty fee
(about E50). Standard Chartered Bank has
branches in Mbabane, Manzini, Nhlangano,
Piggs Peak, Simunye, Tshaneni, Matsapha
and Big Bend. First National also has
branches around the country, but you'll find
Nedbank only in Mbabane, Manzini and
Matsapha.

All banks are open from 8.30am to
2.30pm Monday to Friday, 8.30am to 11am
Saturday. There's a bank at Matsapha International Airport, but it's only open when
flights are scheduled.

The most reliable ATMs are at First National in Mbabane and the Royal Swazi Sun
Hotel & Casino in the Ezulwini Valley. See
the boxed text 'Beating the ATM Scams' in
the Facts for the Visitor chapter near the beginning of this book.

Costs
Costs in Swaziland are similar to those in
South Africa, though food here is a little
cheaper. The game reserves here are particularly good value. Most hotels and restaurants add 8% to 12% VAT to the bill.

POST & COMMUNICATIONS
Swaziland's post offices are open from 8am
to 4pm Monday to Friday and from 8am to
noon Saturday.

There are no telephone area codes within
Swaziland. If you're calling from South
Africa, dial ☎ 09 (for international) then
☎ 268 (for Swaziland). You can make international calls (but not reverse-charge calls)
at the Mbabane post office.

Lonely Planet's eKno Communication
Card provides cheap international calls, a
range of messaging services and free email;
for local calls, you're usually better off with
a local card. The eKno service does not yet
cover Swaziland, although it does cover
South Africa and new countries are being
added all the time. Check the Web site
(W www.ekno.lonelyplanet.com) for updates; you can join on line.

There are plenty of Internet cafes in Mbabane. In the Ezulwini Valley you'll find an
Internet Cafe at the Royal Swazi Sun Hotel &
Casino and a couple of the backpacker hostels have Internet facilities for guests only.

DIGITAL RESOURCES
A couple of sites worth a surf are:

The Ministry of Tourism A site with useful details about Swaziland's hotels, restaurants and
other facilities.
  W www.mintour.gov.sz/szcomplete
Swaziland National Trust Commission A helpful site with information about Malolotja and
Mlawula Nature Reserves as well as Swaziland's
cultural heritage.
  W www.sntc.org.sz

Swaziland Internet Directory Searchable and comprehensive, this Internet gateway site is a good place to start your search for all things Swazi.

W www.directory.sz/internet/

Swazi.com Worth a look for its focus on Swazi media (including *The Times of Swaziland*) and nifty features such as Web cam.

W www.realnet.co.sz/

BOOKS

The *Swaziland Jumbo Tourist Guide* by Hazel Hussey has some useful information between a lot of glossy ads. It's well worth getting a copy if you plan to spend any time in the country.

The Kingdom of Swaziland by D Hugh Gillis is a history of the kingdom (to post-colonial independence) illustrating Swazis' efforts to maintain their traditional way of life in the face of overwhelming European influence.

There is some terrific photography in *All the King's Animals: The Return of Endangered Wildlife to Swaziland* by Cristina Kessler & Mswati III. It's the story of conservationist Ted Reilly and the successful reintroduction of endangered wildlife into the kingdom.

NEWSPAPERS & MAGAZINES

In Swaziland there are two English-language daily newspapers: the *Times of Swaziland* (founded in 1887 by Allister Miller senior) and the *Swazi Observer*.

Look out for the free *What's Happening in Swaziland*, which is aimed at tourists.

PHOTOGRAPHY & VIDEO

Film and photographic accessories are available in Mbabane, the Ezulwini Valley and Manzini.

Be careful about taking photos of soldiers, police, airports and government buildings.

HEALTH

Beware of both bilharzia and malaria. See the Health section in the Facts for the Visitor chapter near the beginning of this book for further information about avoiding contracting these diseases. Since an outbreak of cholera in Lubombo in December 2000, the often fatal disease has spread to most parts of the country. You should seek advice on the current situation and appropriate immunisation before entering the country.

Along with other Southern African countries, Swaziland has a high number of AIDS sufferers. Although actual numbers aren't really known, it was estimated in 1999 that a quarter of the adult population was infected with the HIV virus, the precursor to full-blown AIDS.

Medical assistance is available at the **Mbabane Clinic Service** (☎ 404 2423); the **Mbabane Government Hospital** (☎ 404 2111); the **Raleigh Fitkin Hospital** (☎ 505 2211) in Manzini; and the **Piggs Peak Government Hospital** (☎ 437 1111).

DANGERS & ANNOYANCES

Street crime in Mbabane and Manzini is rising, so take common-sense precautions such as being careful at night and not walking anywhere while drunk.

BUSINESS HOURS

Most businesses are open from 8.30am to 5pm Monday to Friday and 8.30am to 1pm Saturday.

Government offices are closed on weekends and many businesses close for lunch. Supermarkets are often open on Sunday mornings, as are tourist shops.

PUBLIC HOLIDAYS

Good Friday, Easter Monday, Christmas Day, Boxing Day and New Year's Day are all observed in Swaziland. Other holidays include the following:

King Mswati III's Birthday	19 April
National Flag Day	25 April
King Sobhuza II's Birthday	22 July
Umhlanga (Reed) dance	August/September
Somhlolo Day (Independence)	6 September
Incwala ceremony	December/January (exact dates vary each year)

SPECIAL EVENTS

Though Sibhaca dancing only developed fairly recently, it is very popular and there

Swazi Ceremonies

Incwala

The Incwala (sometimes Ncwala) is the most sacred ceremony of the Swazi people. It is a 'first fruits' ceremony, where the king gives permission for his people to eat the first crops of the new year.

Preparation for the Incwala begins some weeks in advance, according to the cycle of the moon. *Bemanti* (learned men) journey to the Lebombo Mountains to gather plants; other bemanti collect water from Swaziland's rivers and some travel across the mountains to the Indian Ocean to skim foam from the waves. Meanwhile, the king goes into retreat.

On the night of the full moon, young men all over the kingdom harvest branches of lusekwane, a small tree, and begin a long trek to the Royal Kraal at Lobamba. They arrive at dawn and their branches are used to build a kraal. If a branch has wilted, it is seen as a sign that the young man bearing it has had illicit sex. Songs prohibited during the rest of the year are sung and the bemanti arrive with their plants, water and foam.

On the third day of the ceremony a bull is sacrificed. On the fourth day, to the pleadings of all the regiments of Swaziland, the king comes out of his retreat and dances before his people. He eats a pumpkin, the sign that Swazis can eat the new year's crops. Two days later there's a ritual burning of all the items used in the ceremony, after which the rains are expected to fall.

Umhlanga (Reed) Dance

Though not as sacred as the Incwala, the Umhlanga (Reed) dance serves a similar function in drawing the nation together and reminding the people of their relationship to the king. It is something like a week-long debutante ball for marriageable young Swazi women, who journey from all over the kingdom to help repair the queen mother's home at Lobamba.

After arriving at Lobamba they spend a day resting, then set off in search of reeds, some not returning until the fourth night. On the sixth day the reed dance is performed as they carry their reeds to the queen mother. The dance is repeated the next day. Those carrying torches (flashlights) have searched for reeds by night; those with red feathers in their hair are princesses.

As the Swazi queen mother must not be of the royal clan, the reed dance is also a showcase of potential wives for the king. As with the Incwala, there are signs that identify the unchaste, a powerful incentive to avoid pre-marital sex.

are national competitions at the Manzini Trade Fair – it's practically a team sport. Local competitions are held frequently; the Mbabane tourist office has details.

The most important cultural events in Swaziland are the Incwala ceremony, held sometime between late December and early January; and the Umhlanga (Reed) dance, held in August or September (see the boxed text 'Swazi Ceremonies'). The venue for both is near Lobamba, in the Ezulwini Valley. Ask at the tourist office next to the Mantenga Lodge in the Ezulwini Valley for exact dates. Photography is not permitted at the Incwala ceremony but it is at the Umhlanga (Reed) dance.

ACTIVITIES

Swazi Trails (for contact details see Organised Tours in the Getting Around Swaziland section) organises all sorts of adventure activities, including **white-water rafting**.

As well as exploring **walking trails** in several parks, especially Malolotja Nature Reserve, you can set out on foot to explore the country, following countless tracks that are generations old. If you have time, this is the best way to see Swaziland.

There are plenty of opportunities to go **horse riding** and a number of stables offer lessons, rides and children's riding camps in areas only accessible by foot or on horseback. In Mlilwane Wildlife Sanctuary, not ar from Mbabane, it is possible to view wildlife on horseback. Guests at some of the country's bigger hotels have access to horse riding and there are also stables at **Nyanza Horse Trails** *(Nyanza Cottages;* ☎ *528 3090,* e *nyanza@africaonline.co.sz,* w *www .africaonline.co.sz/biz/Nyanza)* near Malkerns. Horse riding costs R55 an hour.

Emoyeni Paragliding School *(*☎ *505 7405,* e *airsports@realnet.co.sz, PO Box 1220, Manzini)* has full paragliding courses for E3900.

ACCOMMODATION

There are few designated camp sites outside of the national parks and nature reserves. There's a caravan park in the Ezulwini Valley, 10km from Mbabane.

Away from the few population centres it's usually possible (and safe) to free-camp (camping anywhere), but *always* ask permission from local people, who will probably have to seek permission in turn from their local leader. Be patient. Swazis' hospitality is genuine, but so is their dislike of people imposing on them or disregarding their social structures.

There are backpacker hostels in Mbabane, at Mlilwane Wildlife Sanctuary and near Manzini. If you're stuck for a room in rural areas, you could try the local school, where you'll probably be welcomed.

Many of Swaziland's hotels are geared towards South African tourists and are expensive. A few towns have smaller, public-like places left over from protectorate days that are cheaper.

SHOPPING

Swaziland's handicrafts are worth looking out for. Because of the strength of traditional culture, many items are made for the local market as much as for tourists.

Woven grass ware such as *liqhaga* (grass ware 'bottles' that are so well made they are used for carrying water) and mats are popular, as are wooden items, ranging from bowls to *knobkerries* (traditional African weapons/sticks). The best place to see dyed and woven items is at **Gone Rural** in Malkerns (see Malkerns later in this chapter).

There are also jewellery, pottery, weapons and implements for sale here.

If you come in to Swaziland from the west through the Oshoek border post, you'll find small stalls nearby. There are also several shopping outlets in Mbabane, including a pottery shop. *Mbabane's Swazi Market* is worth visiting to ascertain prices.

In the Ezulwini Valley, there are several craft shops, the biggest being *Mantenga Craft Centre*, off the highway near Mantenga Lodge.

Swazi candles, produced by their namesake in Malkerns (see under Malkerns later in this chapter), are very popular as presents back in South Africa – these are works of art in wax.

The trade fair held in Manzini each year from the end of August is a showcase for handicrafts as well as industrial products.

Getting There & Away

AIR

Most people arrive in Swaziland by land from South Africa or Mozambique, but it is possible to fly – a good option if your time is limited.

Swaziland currently has two major airlines, **Swazi Airlink** *(*☎ *518 6155)* and **Swazi Express Airways** *(*☎ *528 6840,* w *www.swazi express.com)*, which fly to destinations in South Africa and Mozambique.

Swazi Airlink is a joint venture between the Swazi government and SA Airlink in South Africa; it has replaced Royal Swazi Airways as the national carrier.

Swaziland's Matsapha International Airport (often called 'Manzini') is 8km west of Manzini. Swazi Airlink and Swazi Express Airways both operate out of this airport.

Swazi departure tax is E20; there is an additional tax of R127 if you're flying to South Africa (levied by that country).

Flights Within the Region

Swazi Airlink offers only one service, a daily flight to Jo'burg (E430/860 one way/

return; seven-day advance purchase), which connects with SA Airlink flights all over the region.

Swazi Express Airways flies to Maputo in Mozambique (E300, one way) on Tuesday and Thursday; and to Durban in South Africa (E675, one way) on Monday, Thursday, Friday and Saturday.

Swazi Express Airways and sister company **Steffen Air Charters** (☎ 363 6531) also operate private chartered flights within the kingdom and the region.

LAND
Border Crossings
With the exception of the Lomahasha/Namaacha border post in the extreme northeast, which is the entry point to Mozambique, Swaziland's border posts are all with South Africa. Another border post with Mozambique, between Mhlumeni and Goba, is due to open soon. The small posts close at 4pm or 6pm.

The main border posts with South Africa are:

Bulembu (near Josefsdal, Mpumalanga) Open from 8am to 4pm, this post is on the rough dirt road from Piggs Peak to Barberton, Mpumalanga. It is tricky in wet weather.
Lavumisa (near Golela, KwaZulu-Natal) Open from 7am to 10pm. From here it's two hours to the Ezulwini Valley.
Lomahasha (Mozambique) Open from 7am to 8pm. Purchasing visas to Mozambique at the border is an on/off affair, so it's best to get them in advance in Mbabane. See under Visas in the Facts for the Visitor section earlier in this chapter.
Mahamba (near Nhlangano) Open from 7am to 10pm. This is the best border post to use from Piet Retief, Mpumalanga.
Ngwenya (near Oshoek, Mpumalanga) Open from 7am to 10pm. This border post takes most of the traffic, so it can be busy on occasions. It's a good place to pick up lifts.

South Africa & Mozambique
Bus The **Maputo Link** (☎ 404 3750, 604 0137) bus service runs from Jo'burg to Mbabane and on to Maputo (Mozambique). Each leg costs E100. Contact The Chillage hostel in Mbabane for timetable information.

The **Baz Bus** (☎ 021-439 2323 in South Africa) runs from Jo'burg/Pretoria to Durban (R180) via Mbabane and Manzini three times per week, returning the next day.

City to City has buses that are safe, relatively comfortable and rarely crowded. It has two useful routes: Jo'burg to Hlathikulu (R60, 10 hours), via Piet Retief and Nhlangano, which departs Jo'burg at 8am Mondays, Wednesdays and Fridays and returns the same day; and Jo'burg to Mbabane (R60, 10½ hours) via Ermelo, the Ezulwini Valley and Manzini, which departs Jo'burg at 8am on Mondays, Wednesdays and Fridays, returning the same day.

Train There is a passenger train, the *Trans Lubombo*, running between Durban and Maputo (Mozambique), via Swaziland. Unfortunately the service appears to be rather haphazard and was not running at the time of research. To find out if the service has resumed call ☎ 011-773 2944 in South Africa. When it is operating you can pick it up at Mpaka, west of Siteki.

The *Komati* runs north of Swaziland from Pretoria to the Mozambique border at Komatipoort. See under Train in the Getting Around South Africa chapter for details on this service.

Minibus Taxi There are minibus taxis operating directly between Jo'burg and Mbabane (E60), but to get to most places in Swaziland you'll have to take a minibus taxi to the border and another from there to the nearest town, where you'll probably have to change again. This can be a slow process.

Car & Motorcycle There's an E15 road tax for vehicles entering Swaziland. If you're entering Mozambique, your car must have a vehicle breakdown warning triangle, seat belts (even though wearing them is not compulsory) and official papers (eg, permission for rental cars to cross from Swaziland or South Africa into Mozambique).

Hitching If you're hitching into Swaziland, take note that most South Africans enter through the Oshoek/Ngwenya border post. The casinos in the north (near the Matsamo/ Jeppe's Reef border post) and south-west (near the Mahamba border post) attract traffic, especially on weekends. Either of these points can also be good for lifts into/out of the country.

Getting Around

AIR

Swazi Express Airways and Steffen Air Charters operate private chartered flights within Swaziland (see the Getting There & Away section for contact details). If you have the money but not the time, this could be a good way to see wildlife in some of the parks and reserves, as well as take in the spectacular mountain scenery in the north-east and north-west of the country.

BUS & MINIBUS TAXI

There's a good system of buses within Swaziland, including express buses that run infrequently along regular routes. Minibus taxis usually run the same routes, as well as other routes not covered by the buses. These minibus taxis are quicker, although they tend to make frequent stops; their prices are also a little higher than the buses. On some of the longer routes you may have to change taxis.

Minibus taxi routes and fares around Swaziland include:

from	to	one-way fare (E)
Mbabane	Ezulwini Valley	E2
Mbabane	Piggs Peak	E9
Mbabane	Manzini	E4
Mbabane	Oshoek border post	E3.50
Mbabane	Nhlangano	E15
Manzini	Siteki	E8
Manzini	Big Bend	E10
Big Bend	Lavumisa border post	E7
Mahamba border post	Nhlangano	E2
Mahamba border post	Hlathikulu	E6

CAR & MOTORCYCLE

Most roads are quite good and most major routes are now tarred. There are also some satisfyingly rough back roads through the bush. If you're driving between Hlane Royal National Park and Piggs Peak, you'll be on gravel for most of the way, so drive carefully, especially in the wet.

Driving down the Ezulwini Valley in heavy traffic can be slow and dangerous – Malagwane Hill, from Mbabane into the Ezulwini Valley, was once listed in the *Guinness Book of Records* as the most dangerous stretch of road in the world! The road has been greatly improved, but the broken safety railings attest to the fact that driving in bad conditions can still be dangerous.

Road rules are the same as those in South Africa. Away from the population centres and border crossing areas there is very little traffic. The main dangers are people and animals on the road. On narrow gravel roads beware of speeding buses and wandering cattle. Another danger is drunk drivers, as the permitted blood alcohol limit in Swaziland is 0.15%!

Wearing seat belts is compulsory. If an official or royal motorcade approaches, you must pull over and stop. The speed limit is 80km/h on the open road, 60km/h in built-up areas.

Many petrol stations are open 24 hours a day. There are Automobile Association (AA) agents in Mbabane, Manzini and Piggs Peak.

Rental

Swaziland is so small that driving a car around for a few days will give you a good idea of the whole country. Car rental rates are similar to those in South Africa.

Both **Avis** (☎ 518 6226) and **Hertz/Imperial** (☎ 518 4862) are at Matsapha International Airport. Hertz/Imperial also has an agent in Mbabane (☎ 404 1384). The minimum age for hiring a car with either of these companies is 23.

A cheaper option may be **Affordable Car Hire** (☎ 404 9136, fax 404 9137, Swazi Plaza, Mbabane). Its rates start at E159 per day for a small car.

HITCHING

Hitching is easier here than in South Africa, as the colour of the driver and the colour of the hitchhiker aren't the predominant factors in the decision to offer a lift. You might wait a long time for a car on back roads, and everywhere you hitch you'll have lots of competition from locals.

Transport for most people in rural Swaziland is by foot; there are walking trails all over the country.

NONSHARED TAXI

There are private nonshared taxis in Mbabane, the Ezulwini Valley and Manzini. In Mbabane you can usually pick up a taxi near the Swazi Plaza or outside the City Inn. For 24-hour taxis try **Musa's Taxi Service** (☎ 605 8693).

ORGANISED TOURS

Swazi Airlink (☎ 518 6155) is planning to introduce discounted tourist packages into the kingdom from Jo'burg. This will probably be in collaboration with some of the bigger hotels in the Ezulwini Valley, as well as smaller hotels such as The Foresters Arms (which previously had package deals with the former Royal Swazi Airways) in Mhlambanyatsi. There may also be deals available that include accommodation in some of the parks and reserves.

Swazi Trails (☎/fax 416 2180, e tours@ swazitrails.co.sz, w www.swazitrails.co.sz) offers a variety of tours. Some of its day tours are good value if you're short of time or don't have transport. Tours include an in-depth look at Swazi culture, visits to top craft outlets, an historical trip through Swaziland's colourful past and excursions to the big wildlife parks.

Mbabane

pop 50,500

Mbabane (if you say 'ba-baa-nay' you'll be close enough) is the capital of Swaziland, and the second-largest town. There isn't much to see or do here – the adjacent Ezulwini Valley has the attractions – but Mbabane is a relaxing place in a lovely setting in the Dlangeni Hills. The town is growing fast and in recent times has seen a surge in commercial development, a far cry from the basic living in the surrounding countryside.

The hills make Mbabane cooler than Manzini. That's why the British, in 1902, moved their administrative centre here from Manzini.

Orientation

The main street is Allister Miller St. Off Western Distributor Rd is Swazi Plaza, a large, modern shopping mall with most services and a good range of shops; it's also a good landmark. Across Plaza Mall (OK Rd) is The Mall, which is a showpiece of modern architecture.

Information

Tourist Offices The friendly government **tourist office** (☎ 404 2531) is in Swazi Plaza. The free *Swaziland Jumbo Tourist Guide* has loads of information tucked away between advertising. There are several other useful publications available, such as *What's Happening in Swaziland*.

Money There's a **Standard Chartered Bank** (*Allister Miller St*) that changes cash and travellers cheques, but you must have your purchase agreement if changing travellers cheques. **First National Bank** (*Warner St*) changes travellers cheques for a commission of E20; no purchase agreement is required. It also has an ATM that accepts most credit cards. Nedbank in the Swazi Plaza also has a foreign exchange.

Post & Communications You can make international calls, though not reverse-charge calls, at the **post office** (*Warner St (Msunduza); open 8am-4pm Mon to Fri & 8am-noon Sat*). If you're calling from South Africa, dial 09 (for international) then 268 (for Swaziland).

Internet centres are mushrooming in Mbabane and you'll find them at the Omni Centre (open daily); in the post office that is upstairs at the Swazi Plaza; and in The

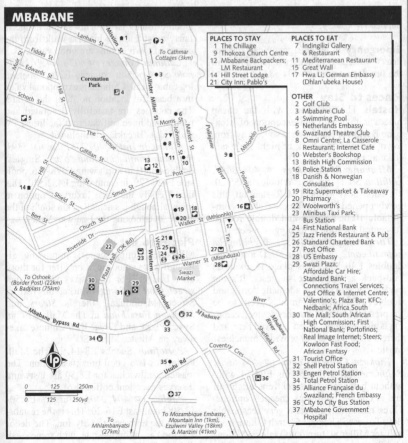

MBABANE

PLACES TO STAY
1 The Chillage
9 Thokoza Church Centre
12 Mbabane Backpackers;
    LM Restaurant
14 Hill Street Lodge
21 City Inn; Pablo's

PLACES TO EAT
7 Indingilizi Gallery
   & Restaurant
11 Mediterranean Restaurant
15 Great Wall
17 Hwa Li; German Embassy
   (Dhlan'ubeka House)

OTHER
2 Golf Club
3 Mbabane Club
4 Swimming Pool
5 Netherlands Embassy
6 Swaziland Theatre Club
8 Omni Centre; La Casserole
   Restaurant; Internet Cafe
10 Webster's Bookshop
13 British High Commission
16 Police Station
18 Danish & Norwegian
    Consulates
19 Ritz Supermarket & Takeaway
20 Pharmacy
22 Woolworth's
23 Minibus Taxi Park;
    Bus Station
24 First National Bank
25 Jazz Friends Restaurant & Pub
26 Standard Chartered Bank
27 Post Office
28 US Embassy
29 Swazi Plaza;
    Affordable Car Hire;
    Standard Bank;
    Connections Travel Services;
    Post Office & Internet Centre;
    Valentino's; Plaza Bar; KFC;
    Nedbank; Africa South
30 The Mall; South African
    High Commission; First
    National Bank; Portofinos;
    Real Image Internet; Steers;
    Kowloon Fast Food;
    African Fantasy
31 Tourist Office
32 Shell Petrol Station
33 Engen Petrol Station
34 Total Petrol Station
35 Alliance Française du
    Swaziland; French Embassy
36 City to City Bus Station
37 Mbabane Government
    Hospital

Mall. Rates are reasonable at around R10 per half hour.

Travel Agencies Connections Travel Services (☎ 404 1954, ⓔ connections@galileo sa.co.za, Swazi Plaza) is a friendly place that can assist with most travel arrangements. It has useful information about flights.

Bookshops There is a Mbabane branch (and several more throughout the country) of the good book chain **Webster's** (120 Johnson St). **Africa South** (Swazi Plaza) stocks a comprehensive range of books. For

second-hand books check out the collection at **Indingilizi Gallery** (see Places to Eat later in this section for contact details).

Cultural Centres The **Alliance Française du Swaziland** (☎ 404 3667) is behind the Ministry of Education; it offers courses in French and Swati.

Medical Services The **Mbabane Government Hospital** (☎ 404 2111) is south of the town centre, among the government offices. There's a **pharmacy** (Allister Miller St) dispensing medical supplies in the centre of town. You could try the **Mbabane Clinic Service** (☎ *404 2423*).

Emergency In an emergency call the **police** (☎ *404 2221*) or in the event of a fire call the **fire department** (☎ *404 3333*).

Places to Stay

Hostels The drawback with the cheap places is that with the exception of Mbabane Backpackers, they are some way from town and walking back at night isn't safe (take a taxi).

Mbabane Backpackers (☎ *404 3097, Gilfillan St)* Dorm beds/doubles E45/120. Upstairs, next to the LM Restaurant, this newly opened hostel offers two clean, comfortable 10-bed dorms and double rooms. Its central location is its biggest asset.

The Chillage (☎ *404 8854,* e *chillage@ hotmail.com, 18 Mission St)* Dorm beds/ doubles E40/130. This place is about as laid-back as the name suggests. It's the perfect place to chill in adequate dorms and doubles (although hammocks seem to be the preferred form of slumber device); camping is also available. Food is served here, and there's a resident DJ to provide 'munchies' music.

Thokoza Church Centre (☎ *404 6681, Polinjane Rd)* 2-bed rooms E94/74 with/ without bathroom. This centre is often full and is one of the town's cheapest options. Three meals daily costs a very reasonable E60. To get to Thokoza Church Centre from Allister Miller St, turn onto Walker (Mhlonhlo) St, cross the bridge at the bottom of the hill, turn left at the police station and head along Polinjane Rd up the hill for about 10 minutes. Taking a taxi from Swazi Plaza to Thokoza costs E8.50.

Hotels & Lodges *City Inn* (☎ *404 2406, fax 404 5855, Allister Miller St)* Singles/ doubles E175/255, standard double room E150. A long-time travellers favourite, this hotel is both central and friendly. Rooms are comfortable and come with TV – there are also more expensive rooms with air-con. The standard doubles are more basic, and are good value for the budget conscious.

Hill Street Lodge (☎ *404 6342, Hill St)* Double rooms E100. This simple lodge is fairly quiet and is a bit of a walk from the centre of town; rooms are good value.

Cathmar Cottages (☎ *602 1364, 167 Lukhalo St)* 4-person cottages E200, 2-person log cabin E150. Cathmar is exceptional value in a beautiful location north of the centre. The cottages are tastefully decorated and roomy and have self-catering facilities, TV and fridge. Breakfast is included.

Mountain Inn (☎ *404 2781, fax 404 5393,* e *mountaininn@realnet.co.sz)* Singles/ doubles B&B in north wing E378/486, poolside E420/529, in south wing E432/540. This inn is easily the most luxurious option in town, although it's actually 1km south of the centre, overlooking the Ezulwini Valley.

Places to Eat

Mbabane's dining scene is improving, although there's not much on offer for those on a budget. For takeaways you can get *street food* at Swazi Market on Warner Street (Msunduza); there's *Steers* and *Kowloon Fast Food* in The Mall; *KFC* in Swazi Plaza; and *Great Wall* Chinese takeaway on Allister Miller St.

Portofinos Snacks E8-14. In The Mall, Portofinos is a good breakfast option. The toasted sandwiches for E8.50 are tasty and it serves excellent coffee (E6).

Pablo's (☎ *404 2406)* Burgers E8.50-12.50, breakfast E16-20. This is the restaurant by the entrance to City Inn. The decor and food are Wimpyesque, with some steak dishes added to the menu. It's a good place for a coffee, breakfast or a pizza.

Indingilizi Gallery & Restaurant (☎ *404 6213,* e *indingi@realnet.co.sz, 112 Johnson St)* Snacks E15-18, curries E35. This relaxed outdoor cafe offers African food and other relatively inexpensive healthy meals (there are also desserts such as carrot cake for E12).

LM (Lourenço Marques) Restaurant (☎ *404 3097, Cnr Gilfillan & Allister Miller Sts)* Starters E30-42, seafood specialities E37-85. LM serves Portuguese food; the chicken *peri peri* (Portuguese-style sauce that ranges from hot to mild) and the king and queen prawns are excellent (E120 &

E95). The diner-like booths give privacy, although sometimes they are too private, as the waiters seem to forget some customers exist!

Hwa Li (☎ 404 5986, Dhlan'ubeka House, Walker St (Mhlonhlo)) Mains E32-50. Open noon-3pm & 6pm-10pm Mon-Sat. A Chinese place seems a bit strange in Mbabane, but this one is well patronised. Hwa Li specialises in spring rolls, chow mein and spicy soups.

Valentino's (☎ 404 7948, Swazi Plaza) Starters E19-23, mains E40-90. Open till late. Valentino's caters for a diverse palate and has a mouth-watering seafood platter for E168. Takeaways are much simpler and cheaper, starting at E15.

La Casserole Restaurant (☎ 404 6426, Omni Centre, Allister Miller St) Mains E35-50. Open 9am-11pm daily. This is one of the city's nicest places, serving Continental food, including some veg dishes, and offering an excellent wine selection. The outside patio is great on a fine day.

Mediterranean Restaurant (☎ 404 3212, Allister Miller St) Mains E40-70. Despite its name, this restaurant is more of an Indian place specialising in curries.

There are supermarkets on Allister Miller St, including *Ritz Supermarket & Takeaway*, which are useful for those self-catering.

Entertainment

Most partying is done in the Ezulwini Valley (see later in this chapter).

Jazz Friends Restaurant & Pub (Cnr Allister Miller & Warner (Mhlonhlo) Sts) This place has a cosy bar where you can have a chinwag with the locals. Snacks such as *bunny chow* (E5; half a loaf of bread hollowed out and filled with curry) are available.

On the river side of Swazi Plaza is the crowded and popular *Plaza Bar*, where you may meet a mixture of locals and travellers.

Shopping

Indingilizi Gallery This gallery has an idiosyncratic collection that's pricey but well worth a look. There is traditional craft, including some interesting old pieces, and excellent art and craftwork by contemporary Swazi artists. See Places to Eat earlier in this section for contact details.

African Fantasy (☎ 404 0205, Shop 11, The Mall) This place offers a great selection of locally made T-shirts and cards.

Getting There & Away

City to City buses leave from the old train station on Coventry Crescent for Jo'burg (via various destinations in Swaziland). Minibus taxis to South Africa leave from the minibus taxi park near Swazi Plaza, where you'll also find buses and minibus taxis to most destinations in Swaziland.

The **Maputo Link** *(☎ 404 3750, 604 0137)* bus service runs from Jo'burg to Mbabane and on to Maputo (Mozambique). Contact The Chillage (see Places to Stay earlier) for timetable information.

The **Baz Bus** *(☎ 021-439 2323 in South Africa)* runs from Jo'burg/Pretoria to Durban via Mbabane and Manzini three times per week, returning the next day.

For more information on getting to and from Mbabane see under Land in the Getting There & Away section earlier in this chapter.

Getting Around

A nonshared taxi from Mbabane to Matsapha International Airport costs about E130.

Nonshared taxis congregate near the bus station by Swazi Plaza. At night you can usually find one near City Inn; alternatively, try ☎ 404 0965/6. For 24-hour taxis try **Musa's Taxi Service** *(☎ 605 8693)*.

Nonshared taxis to the Ezulwini Valley cost at least E45, more to the far end of the valley (at least E60), and still more if hired at night.

Around Mbabane

EZULWINI VALLEY

The Ezulwini Valley begins just outside Mbabane and extends down past Lobamba Village, 18km away. It is known as the Royal Valley as it has always been home to the Swazi royal family. Most of the area's attractions are near Lobamba. It's a pretty valley and there are some spectacular views of the surrounding rocky mountains. Unfortunately, it has metamorphosed into a

SWAZILAND

hotel strip with royal prices to match, the one exception being Mlilwane Wildlife Sanctuary.

Information

The **Ezulwini Tourist Office** (☎ *416 1136, fax 416 1040)* has recently opened at Mantenga Craft Centre. The staff are helpful and supply a decent range of information about accommodation, activities and things to see in the valley and around Swaziland. **Swazi Trails** organises activities and tours all over the kingdom and also has an office at the craft centre (for contact details see Organised Tours in the Getting Around Swaziland section).

The office for **Kingdom of Swaziland's Big Game Parks** (☎ *528 3944, fax 528 3924,* ⓔ *reservations@biggame.co.sz,* ⓦ *www .biggame.co.sz, PO Box 311, Malkerns)*, which used to be at The Mall in Mbabane, is now inconveniently located in the Mlilwane Wildlife Sanctuary, well hidden just behind Sondzela Backpackers Lodge. It must be a much nicer office to trudge into in the morning, but if you want to drop in for some information, it's a hassle to find unless you're staying at the backpackers. Fortunately you

can book accommodation in its parks (Mlilwane Wildlife Sanctuary, Mkhaya Game Reserve and Hlane Royal National Park) by telephone, fax or email. Bookings need to be paid for in advance, which you can do by post (cheques) or by giving them your credit card details by telephone.

Lobamba

This is the heart of Swaziland's Royal Valley, and it has held this position almost since the beginning of the Swazi monarchy. Built by the British, the royal palace, Embo State Palace, isn't open to visitors, and you are not allowed to take photos of it. Swazi kings now live in **Lozitha State House,** about 10km from Lobamba. Embo is a large complex, as it had to house the entire royal (Sobhuza II had 600 children!).

You can see the monarchy in action at the **Royal Kraal** (a hut village surrounded by a stockade) in Lobamba during the Incwala ceremony and the Umhlanga (Reed) dance. The nearby **Somhlolo National Stadium** hosts sports events (mainly soccer) and important state occasions, such as coronations.

The **National Museum** *(adult/student E10/ 3; open 8am-4pm Mon-Fri, 10am-4pm Sat &*

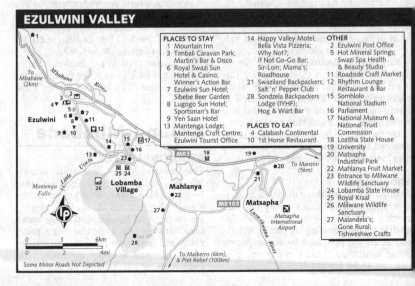

EZULWINI VALLEY

PLACES TO STAY
1 Mountain Inn
3 Timbali Caravan Park; Martin's Bar & Disco
6 Royal Swazi Sun Hotel & Casino; Winner's Action Bar
7 Ezulwini Sun Hotel; Sibebe Beer Garden
8 Lugogo Sun Hotel; Sportsman's Bar
9 Yen Saan Hotel
13 Mantenga Lodge; Mantenga Craft Centre; Ezulwini Tourist Office

14 Happy Valley Motel; Bella Vista Pizzeria; Why Not?; If Not Go-Go Bar; Sir-Loin; Mama's; Roadhouse
21 Swaziland Backpackers; Salt 'n' Pepper Club
28 Sondzela Backpackers Lodge (IYHF); Hog & Wart Bar

PLACES TO EAT
4 Calabash Continental
10 1st Horse Restaurant

OTHER
2 Ezulwini Post Office
5 Hot Mineral Springs; Swazi Spa Health & Beauty Studio
11 Roadside Craft Market
12 Rhythm Lounge Restaurant & Bar
15 Somhlolo National Stadium
16 Parliament
17 National Museum & National Trust Commission
18 Lozitha State House
19 University
20 Matsapha Industrial Park
22 Mahlanya Fruit Market
23 Entrance to Mlilwane Wildlife Sanctuary
24 Lobamba State House
25 Royal Kraal
26 Mlilwane Wildlife Sanctuary
27 Malandela's; Gone Rural; Tishweshwe Crafts

To Mbabane (2km)

Mbabane River

Ezulwini

Little Usutu

Mantenga Falls

Lobamba Village

Mahlanya

MR3

Matsapha

MR103

Matsapha International Airport

Lusushwana River

To Manzini (5km)

To Malkerns (6km), & Piet Retief (100km)

0   3   6km
0   2   4mi
Some Minor Roads Not Depicted

Sun) has some interesting displays of Swazi culture. There's a traditional beehive village and cattle byre beside it. Also here is the **National Trust Commission** (see Malolotja Nature Reserve later in this chapter for contact details), which is the headquarters of the Mlawula and Malolotja Nature Reserves. You can book accommodation for these reserves at the Ezulwini Tourist Office (see Information under Ezulwini Valley earlier in this chapter).

Next to the museum is the **parliament**, which is sometimes open to visitors; if you want to visit, wear neat clothes and use the side entrance. Across the road from the museum is the **memorial** *(adult/concession E10/3; open 8am-4pm Mon-Fri, 10am-4pm Sat & Sun)* to King Sobhuza II, the most revered of Swazi kings.

Mantenga Falls are worth a look, but ask for advice at the nearby Mantenga Lodge or tourist office before you go. The road is steep and sometimes dangerous, and there have been muggings (and worse) here.

About 3km from Mantenga Lodge, near the Umbuluzi River, is **Swazi Cultural Village** *(☎ 416 1178, e mnr@iafrica.sz; adult/concession E25/3)* Accommodation in beehive huts costs E40 per person, E60 Sat & Sun. This place has authentic beehive huts and cultural displays. The Mantenga Nature Reserve is also here and entry is an extra E5 if you take your car in.

The Royal Valley has its own **hot mineral springs** *(☎ 416 1164; admission E5; open 6am-11pm daily)*, which are known affectionately as the 'Cuddle Puddle'. These mineral waters are warm and live up to their name. Nearby is the **Swazi Spa Health & Beauty Studio** *(☎ 416 1164; open 10am-6pm)*. Those in the know will understand what is on offer: aromatherapy steam tube, oxygen multistep and jacuzzi. Just the thing if the puddle isn't enough! It's good value: A massage, sauna and spa bath costs E100; a one-hour massage costs E130; and an aromatherapy massage costs E150.

Mlilwane Wildlife Sanctuary

This sanctuary *(☎ 416 1591; admission E20; open daily)* near Lobamba was the first in Swaziland. It's a private reserve that was created by Ted Reilly on his family farm in the 1950s. Reilly has gone on to open Mkhaya Game Reserve and has supervised the setting up of Hlane Royal National Park. Read about conservation efforts at the reserve (and throughout the kingdom) in the excellent *The Mlilwane Story*, available from the sanctuary. Incidentally, Mlilwane means 'Little Fire', named after the many fires started by lightning strikes in the region.

The reserve is dominated by the precipitous Nyonyane (Little Bird) peak, and there are several excellent walks around it. Animals to be seen include zebras, giraffes, warthogs, many antelope species, crocodiles, hippos and a variety of birds. In summer, black eagles are seen near Nyonyane.

You can walk, cycle or ride a horse through the reserve and there are night drives (E100 for two hours). Bicycles can be rented for E45 per hour, less for longer rides. Horse riding costs E75 per hour, E300 for the four-hour 'Mountain' trail and E600 for the fully catered overnight 'Nyagato' trail.

Note that Mlilwane is very busy during South African school holidays. The entrance is 2km south-east of the Happy Valley Motel on the old Mbabane-Manzini road; it is signposted from the turn-off. At the entrance gate you can get a sanctuary map. Night access is via an alternate gate.

Places to Stay & Eat

All accommodation in the sanctuary can be booked in advance at the Big Game Parks office in Mlilwane Wildlife Sanctuary (for contact details see Information under Ezulwini Valley earlier in this section).

Mlilwane Wildlife Sanctuary Main Camp *Camping, caravanning and beehive huts* Camping and caravanning E35 per person, shared huts from E140 per person. This camp is set in a beautiful location and there are often warthogs snuffling around. There is a small shop and a restaurant here as well as large communal areas for braais (barbecues).

Shonalanga Cottage Per person sharing E160. This spacious (with kitchen) cottage is good for families.

Beehive Village Dorm beds (with bedding) E75, single/twin beehive huts E150/200 with communal bathrooms. For more authentic accommodation, the dorm here is made of timber logs and the huts are in the traditional Zulu style.

Hippo Haunt Breakfast E35 (for kids E17.50), buffet dinner E60. Watching the hippos from the restaurant is great entertainment, especially at feeding time (3pm daily). Readers have also written about the unique spectacle of 'jumping catfish' just outside the window of the restaurant! Were they pulling our leg?

Elsewhere in Mlilwane Wildlife Sanctuary
Sondzela Backpackers (IYHF) Lodge (☎ 528 3117, fax 528 3924, ℮ reservations@biggame.co.sz) Dorm beds E40, camping E35, singles/doubles E70/140. Also in the sanctuary, south of the camp and 2km from Gone Rural in Malkerns, is this luxurious lodge. It calls itself 'Africa's Rolls Royce of Backpacker Hostels'. On seeing this place some backpackers agree. It's spacious with manicured gardens, telephones, a central living area including the *Hog & Wart Bar*, a swimming pool and a large veranda offering great views. There is a 20-minute trail through the reserve to the Hippo Haunt at Main Camp. The pick-up point is at Gone Rural in Malkerns, where the Baz Bus stops; this is about 2km west of the Mahlanya fruit market on the old Manzini-Mbabane road. If you're driving you'll need to use the main Mlilwane Wildlife Sanctuary entrance and drive through the park to reach Sondzela and pay an entry fee.

Nyonyane Camp Singles/doubles E145/290. On the eastern border of the sanctuary, this camp has self-catering cottages with all the facilities. It is a perfect spot if you want to get away from everyone.

Large groups are accommodated in the revamped *Khululeka Lodge,* south of Nyonyane Camp. Rates are about E100 per person.

Reilly's Rock Hilltop Lodge Standard/luxury rooms per person E625/650 (single occupants must pay E165/200 extra). This is undoubtedly Swaziland's most luxurious

accommodation. 'The Rock' has a colourful history. It was the first dwelling in Swaziland to have electric lighting and the original structure was built in exchange for an £80 ox wagon. It has commanding views over the park from the veranda and the building is surrounded by a lovingly tended aloe garden. If only everyone had the money to stay here!

Around the Ezulwini Valley
The camp sites and beehive huts at Mlilwane offer the best budget accommodation in the valley, but there is a range of other places.

Timbali Caravan Park (☎/fax 416 1156) Camp sites per person E25, singles/doubles chalets E120/160 (with communal showers). This park, 10km south of Mbabane, has sites and rooms in chalets and caravans. It's a well-run place and has a swimming pool, a trampoline and a restaurant. Services offered include tent cleaning! There's a supermarket nearby.

Mantenga Lodge (☎ 416 1049, fax 416 2516, ℮ mantenga@iafrica.sz) Singles/doubles B&B in lodge E260/375, in chalets E345/445. This place is off the main valley road, on a wooded hillside near Mlilwane Wildlife Sanctuary. It's relaxed and has an atmosphere nothing like that of the glitzy valley strip. Take the signposted turn-off for the Mantenga Craft Centre; the hotel is 500m along this road.

Happy Valley Motel (☎ 416 1061, fax 416 1050, ℮ happyvalley@iafrica.sz) Singles/doubles B&B E192.50/255. The cost of the comfortable, well-equipped rooms includes free entry to the Why Not? disco and the If Not Go-Go Bar (see Entertainment following).

Yen Saan Hotel (☎ 416 1051) Singles/doubles E80/160. The Yen Saan has been designed in a Chinese style, making its location in the Royal Valley of Swaziland rather incongruous. The hotel is an enormous place with a rather ghostly feel. Most of it has been closed for a while, so it's a bit run down, but recently 34 rooms have reopened and it's a great budget option along this strip of the valley.

At the top of the scale are three of the Sun group's hotels. The rates are always changing, so inquire in advance. All offer weekend specials at some times of the year for about half price and all have restaurants. The buffet lunch includes a selection from the carvery, plus salads and desserts (E70).

Royal Swazi Sun Hotel & Casino (☎ 416 1001, fax 416 1859) Singles/doubles from E929/1010. At Royal Swazi Sun you will find a golf course, casino, tennis courts, Kamp Kwena for kids, Internet cafe and useful ATM that accepts most international credit cards.

Lugogo Sun Hotel (☎ 416 1101, fax 416 1111) Singles/doubles B&B E588/651. This one is in the grounds of the Royal Swazi and is a little less luxurious, with a price tag to match.

Ezulwini Sun Hotel (☎ 416 1201) Singles/doubles E647/710. Across the road from the other two Sun hotels, this complex has the usual international hotel features such as pools and tennis courts.

Calabash Continental (☎ 416 1187) Mains E35-60. Open 12.30pm-2.30pm & 6.30pm-11.00pm daily. Next to Timbali Caravan Park, the Calabash specialises in German and Swiss cuisine.

1st Horse Restaurant (☎ 416 1137) Mains E30-60. Open noon-2pm & 6.30pm-10pm Mon-Sat. Named after an Indian mounted regiment (and probably wishful thinking as it is next to a race-betting agency), this place is on the south side of the road that heads to the Yen Saan Hotel. The curries here are superb, and it also serves seafood, steaks and delightful desserts.

Bella Vista Pizzeria (☎ 416 1061) Meals under E30. Large veg pizzas E25 & hearty seafood pizzas E30. Bella Vista is at Happy Valley Motel. Also here are *Sir-Loin* (a steak and ribs restaurant with mains around E35), *Mama's* coffee shop and an outside *roadhouse* for takeaways.

Good pub meals are available from *Mantenga Lodge* for about E40. Nonguests are welcome.

Entertainment

Why Not? (☎ 416 1061) Admission E20 Mon-Fri, E30 Sat & Sun. The best-known nightspot in the area is this disco-cum-nightclub. The place would have to rate as one of the great incongruities of Swaziland. It looks innocent enough from the outside, but inside it is a veritable den of iniquity and a complete enigma in this conservative country. The Why Not? is a huge auditorium reserved for crowds ogling visiting European strippers, and the dimly lit *If Not Go-Go Bar* (entry to Why Not? includes If Not) has strippers dancing along the bar. In the past questions have been asked in parliament about all this immorality, but they've obviously fallen on deaf ears as the Why Not is as popular as ever.

Sibebe Beer Garden (☎ 416 1201) Meals E45. Open from 7pm Tues. The less voyeuristic will probably enjoy this beer garden at the Ezulwini Sun Hotel. The cost of a meal includes live music.

Sportsman's Bar (☎ 416 1550) Sportsman's at the Lugogo Sun Hotel has a pub night on Wednesday (ladies welcome).

On Friday night there's a live band at *Winner's Action Bar* at the Royal Swazi Sun Hotel. *Martin's Bar & Disco* near the Timbali Caravan Park seems to buzz most nights.

A new place that's recently popped up is the *Rhythm Lounge Restaurant & Bar*. It's an African theme bar that has meals in the evening and bands some nights.

Getting There & Away

Nonshared taxis from Mbabane cost at least E45, and from E60 if you want to go to the far end of the valley. At night you'll have to negotiate a price. During the day you could get on a Manzini-bound minibus, but make sure the driver knows that you want to alight in the valley (even some nonexpress minibuses aren't keen on stopping).

If you're driving from Mbabane, you'll find the views terrific on a clear day, but it's pretty steep and all downhill, making it easy to speed. Make sure you tear your eyes away from the mountains and back onto the road!

MALKERNS

About 7km south of Lobamba on the MR103 is a turn-off to the fertile Malkerns Valley, known for its arts and crafts outlets.

If you need to get wired, **Sigubhu Internet Cafe** will get you connected for E20 per half hour – it also provides tourist information.

Places to Stay & Eat

Nyanza Cottages (Nyanza Horse Trails; ☎ *528 3090,* e *nyanza@africaonline.co.sz,* w *www.africaonline.co.sz/biz/Nyanza)* Caravan E135 plus E35 per person, B&B cottages E200 per person. Set on a working farm with stables, this is a great place to stay. The luxurious cottages sleep four, have a galley-style kitchen, are secluded and overlook pasture land. The kids can help out on the farm and there's horse riding (E55 per hour). Nyanza is next to Baobab Batik. The curious ritual of washing your shoes and hands before entry to the property is to help stop the spread of foot and mouth disease.

Malandela's Homestead (☎ *528 3115)* Starters E13-15, mains E26-50. 1km from the Malkerns turn-off, this is the best restaurant in the region. Good old-fashioned meals might include pork pie (individually E10), fresh carrots, boiled potatoes, Brussels sprouts and pecan pie. If you like seafood, try the grilled trout with almonds (E40). The prawn nights are extremely popular and it is not unusual for 100 dozen prawns to be consumed in an evening. Several English beers are available. The owner, Pete Thorne, is a dab hand – international representative no less – at shove-halfpenny (an English pub game) and is also a noted pumpkin connoisseur.

Shopping

Gone Rural (☎ *528 3439),* where Lutindzi grass is dyed then woven into baskets and mats, is located at Malandela's Homestead. Traditional clay products are also for sale. Also here are *House on Fire (*☎ *528 2001),* which has wood sculptures and a performance area that hosts African theatre, music and films – give it a call to see what's on; *Baobab Too,* offering colourful African batiks; and *Southern Country,* selling handmade leather goods.

Swazi Candles (☎ *528 3219,* e *swazi candles@realnet.co.sz)* is near Malkerns, 7km south from the MR103/Malkerns turn-off; it is well signposted. Its unique candles in the shape of African animals (elephants, rhinos, hippos etc) are absolutely gorgeous and very affordable, starting at about E24. These candles may become decoration on your mantelpiece as it seems such a shame to burn them.

Baobab Batik (☎ *528 3177)* is next to Nyanza Horse Trails, 1km on from Swazi Candles. It's a small place that's worth a poke around, particularly if you're in the market for a wall hanging.

Getting There & Away

The Baz Bus stops at Malandela's Homestead, just outside Gone Rural. This is the pick-up point for Sondzela Backpackers Lodge in Mlilwane Wildlife Sanctuary. Otherwise, you should be able to get a minibus taxi here from the Ezulwini Valley for about E2. As the craft shops and places to stay are spread out, you'll really need a car to get around.

MHLAMBANYATSI

Mhlambanyatsi (meaning 'Watering Place of the Buffaloes') is 27km south-west of Mbabane.

Foresters Arms (☎ *467 4177, fax 467 4051,* e *forestersarms@africaonline.co.sz)* Single/double garden rooms E360/600, poolside rooms E430/720. The popular Foresters Arms is likely to be full of locals on the weekend, as they drift down here from Mbabane for home-made bread and Sunday lunch. You can sail, windsurf or canoe on the nearby Luphohlo Dam, relax in the library or go horse riding. The Foresters Arms is just south of Mhlambanyatsi on the MR18.

Meikles Mount (☎ *604 2826)* Singles/doubles E130/180 (more in high season). Some 6km north of Mhlambanyatsi, on the road to Mbabane, this is a great B&B hideaway. There's horse riding, fishing and bird-watching here.

MANZINI

Today, Manzini is the country's industrial centre, but between 1890 and 1902 it was the combined administrative centre for the squabbling British and Boers. So adversarial

SWAZILAND

was their relationship that during the Anglo-Boer War a renegade Boer *kommando* (commando) burnt the town down! Downtown Manzini isn't large, but it feels like a different country from easy-going rural Swaziland. It features reckless drivers (seemingly confused by the city's perplexing one-way system), city slickers and a hint of menace. Be careful while walking at night.

The market on Thursday and Friday mornings is highly recommended. Get there at dawn if possible when the rural people bring in their handicrafts to sell to retailers.

Places to Stay

Paradise Caravan Park (☎ 518 4935, MR103) Camp sites E20, rondavel/double E75. Paradise is about 12km west of Manzini, just past Matsapha. It's a rough and tumble place, but cheap if you're camping.

Swaziland Backpackers (☎ 518 7225, ✉ swazilandbackpackers@realnet.co.sz) Camp sites E30, dorm beds/doubles E50/

E120. This is a pretty good spot just across from the caravan park and adjacent to the Salt 'n' Pepper Club. It has a fully equipped kitchen (meals are also available), travellers bar, laundry service and email facilities. It's one of the overnight stops for the Baz Bus.

Matsapha Inn (☎ 518 6893, MR103) Singles/doubles E199/268 Sat & Sun, E270/350 Mon-Fri. Also near the caravan park, this inn is rather Spartan-looking, though it's utilitarian enough to satisfy the longings of travelling salespersons, as it is comfortable and clean.

Mozambique Hotel & Restaurant (☎/fax 505 2489, Mahleka St) Singles/doubles E95/160. Mozambique Hotel has a dingy but good bar and a popular restaurant. Rooms are distinctly average. It's not great value, but the place has a lively buzz.

Park Royal Hotel (☎ 505 7423, fax 505 4250, 9 Mancishane St) Singles/doubles B&B E165/205. Moving up the scale, the Park Royal perhaps doesn't deserve the

MANZINI

To Golf Course (500m),
Woza Nawe Hostel (6km),
Hhelehhele (8km) &
Siteki (68km)

Fairview

Mzimnene

To Matsapha International
Airport (8km), Matsapha Inn (11km),
Paradise Caravan Park (12km),
Swaziland Backpackers, Salt 'n' Pepper
Club & Mbabane (31km)

To Sidvokodvo (19km)

Trelawney
Park

Coats Valley

0   200   400m
0   200   400yd

PLACES TO STAY	17 Chicken Licken;	3 Checkers	14 Post Office
6 Mozambique Hotel	King Pie; Steers	5 Bus & Minibus	15 Police Station
& Restaurant	22 Fontana di Trevi	Taxi Park	16 Nedbank
12 Park Royal Hotel	Pizzeria; The Hub	9 Standard	18 Bhunu Mall
		Chartered Bank	19 Library
PLACES TO EAT	OTHER	10 Manzini Club	20 Market
4 OK Restaurant	1 Showgrounds	11 Shell Petrol	21 Total Petrol
7 Gil Vicente Restaurant	2 Manzini Telephone	Station	Station
8 KFC	Exchange	13 First National Bank	23 Club Y2K

'Royal' part of its title, but you can't be fussy in Manzini; rooms have small balconies, air-con, TV and telephones.

Woza Nawe Hostel (Myxo's Place; ☎ 505 8363, 604 4102, ⒠ wozanawe@realnet.co .sz) Dorm beds/doubles E40/140. About 6km out of Manzini on the road to Big Bend is this new backpackers. It's the only Swazi-owned and -run hostel in the country. Readers have raved about this place. There are all types of activities on offer here, including drumming lessons. It's run by a guy called Myxo, who operates cultural tours to his native village, giving visitors the opportunity to gain insight into rural Swazi life (see the boxed text 'The Real Swaziland'). Myxo will pick you up from Manzini. If you're

The Real Swaziland

Many visitors who rush through this beautiful country will probably only remember tacky casinos, sugar cane and speed bumps. There is little tourism that actually exposes them to Swazi village life. Fortunately, an enterprising and charming Swazi named Myxo has blazed a trail enabling travellers to see rural Swazi families in a village environment – he calls his venture Liphupho Lami Camp Holidays (☎ 528 3117, 604 4102).

Myxo drives his distinctive brown truck to Khapunga, his own village, which is 65km south of Manzini. Many travellers come for the day, but wish they had stayed for several once they savour the charm and tranquillity of the place.

You can learn to weave mats, visit the local school, walk in areas of natural beauty, sit around a night fire with locals and stare towards the star-studded heavens, or visit a local homestead and help with ploughing and cattle dipping. A full day's outing (E180), starting at 8am, usually includes a visit to bustling Manzini market. An overnight trip – the preferable option – gives you an opportunity to enjoy a traditional meal (E295 per person, minimum four people).

Remember, rural Swazis are modest and when you enter their domain you should dress appropriately.

driving, the turn-off can be hard to spot: Take the road to Big Bend from Manzini and keep an eye out for the Big Surprise Bottle Store on your left (which is just after Sunnyside Market); follow the signs from here.

Places to Eat

On Louw St in town are a few basic food outlets that are open during the day; the most notable is *OK Restaurant*. Bhunu Mall houses a swag of fast-food places, including *Chicken Licken*, *King Pie* and *Steers*.

Fontana di Trevi Pizzeria (☎ 505 3608, The Hub, Cnr Villiers & Mhlakuvane Sts) Medium pizzas E20-30, burgers E5-26. Open 9am-9pm daily. This place does a little bit of everything at reasonable prices. It's probably the best place in town to get a decent coffee. A full breakfast (E20) is a good way to start the day, salads are cheap at around E12 and the burgers are simple but filling.

Gil Vincente Restaurant (☎ 505 3874, Ilanga Centre, Martin St) Snacks E10-20, Mains E40-60. Open until late. This is a good place for Portuguese food, specialising in prawn dishes.

Mozambique Hotel & Restaurant Starters E10, mains E25-40. This restaurant has a good reputation and serves food all day. It's a great place for Portuguese food and has a good selection of Portuguese and South African wines. See Places to Stay for contact details.

Gobble & Gossip is a rustic place, 8km east of Manzini in Hhelehhele, that usually has a great Sunday braai.

Entertainment

For a wild night out, venture to the *Salt 'n' Pepper Club* near Swaziland Backpackers. It's a good place to swill beer and attempt self-imposed oblivion; it is especially popular on weekends.

Club Y2K (Mhlakuvane St) Admission E20. This disco draws crowds of locals who writhe to the music. Watch out for fights later in the evening.

Getting There & Away

The main bus and minibus taxi park is at the northern end of Louw St. A bus trip up the

Ezulwini Valley to Mbabane costs E2.50. A nonshared taxi to Matsapha International Airport costs around E60.

City to City buses run to South Africa via Mbabane or Hlathikulu and Nhlangano (see South Africa & Mozambique under Land in the Getting There & Away section earlier).

North-West Swaziland

In the north-west of the country you'll find the wild Malolotja Nature Reserve and the cool, pleasant retreats of Piggs Peak and Phophonyane Falls.

HAWANE

Part of the area fringing **Hawane Dam** *(admission free Mon-Fri, E10 per car Sat & Sun)* has been designated a nature reserve, and it's a good spot to observe waterbirds.

Hawane Park *(☎ 442 4335)*, near Hawane Dam, is to the east of the Piggs Peak road and is not far from the Ngwenya-Mbabane road junction. The park was closed at the time of research but was expected to reopen soon. It has beehive huts and chalets.

Hawane African Adventure Trails (☎/fax 442 4109, e *hawane@realnet.co.sz)* DB&B in low/high season per person E225/275, full board in low/high season E495/E545. In Hawane Village, 4km up the Piggs Peak road from the junction of the MR1 and MR3, this place is primarily a horse-riding centre (E60 per hour). Accommodation is in beehive huts, and full board includes four hours' horse riding.

NGWENYA

This town (the name means 'The Crocodile') is 5km east of the Oshoek border post on the road to Mbabane and is inside the Malolotja Nature Reserve.

Ngwenya Glass factory (☎ 442 4053, W *www.ngwenyaglass.co.sz)* Open 7am-4pm Mon-Fri, 9am-4pm Sat & Sun. This place uses recycled glass to create beautiful African animal and bird figures. Miniature/large animals cost E24/79. Nearby is an entrance to

Malolotja Nature Reserve (see following), allowing access to the Ngwenya mine.

Around 1km further up the road is *End-lotane Studios/Phumulanga Tapestries (☎ 442 4196,* W *www.endlotane.com)*, open from 8am to 5pm. Tapestries here are made from mohair and are hung in galleries throughout the world. Small place mats cost around E150, while large tapestries based on San rock paintings cost from E400.

MALOLOTJA NATURE RESERVE

This highveld/middleveld reserve *(☎ 442 4241; admission E15 plus E6 per car; gates open 6am-6pm)* is a true wilderness area, rugged and in the most part unspoiled. It is undoubtedly one of the best walking destinations in Southern Africa. The reserve has mainly antelope species and there are two bull elephants in the Nkomati Valley. More than 280 species of bird (including nesting blue swallows) have been recorded in the reserve, a number of them rare. Southern bald ibises nest on the cliffs near the Malolotja Falls. Wildflowers and rare plants are also attractions in this reserve; several of these plants, including the woolly, Barberton and Kaapschehoop cycads, are found only in this part of Africa. The Komati River cuts a gorge through the reserve and flows east in a series of falls and rapids until it meets the lowveld.

Sadly, the reserve has recently come under threat from mining interests. Until now the matter has see-sawed in parliament, with no firm yes or no being granted. It would be an absolute disgrace if such a wilderness area, one of the continent's finest, was despoiled in such a way. At the time of research the miners were still being held at bay.

Ngwenya mine (see Ngwenya previous) is one of the world's oldest known mines, dating from 41,000 BC. You can visit the mine by vehicle, but a ranger must accompany you; visits should be arranged a day in advance. You can also visit the **Forbes Reef gold mine** in Forbes Reef Forest.

Wildlife drives in the reserve cost E60 per person, plus E30 for the vehicle. There's a minimum of two people per drive (E150).

There are about 200km of **hiking trails**, ranging from short day walks to a week-long trail that extends from Ngwenya in the south to Mgwayiza Range in the north. Shorter walks include Nkomati Viewpoint, the Upper Majolomba River, and Malolotja Falls and Vlei (Swamp). For the extended trails a free permit and map must be obtained from the reserve office at the entrance gate. You'll need to bring all your own food as well as a camp stove, as fires are not permitted outside the base camp.

Accommodation can be booked through the **Ezulwini Tourist Office** (see Information under Ezulwini Valley earlier). For any other inquiries about the reserve contact the **National Trust Commission** (☎ 416 1481, **W** www.sntc.org.sz, Lobamba).

Camping costs E18 at established sites and E15 on the trails. There are fully equipped *cabins* sleeping six for E250 Sunday to Thursday (E350 Friday and Saturday).

The entrance gate is about 35km from Mbabane, on the Piggs Peak road.

PIGGS PEAK

The small town of Piggs Peak was named after a prospector who found gold here in 1884. There was a rush, but only one deep mine ever made much money, and it has been closed for 40 years.

Piggs Peak is in a hilly section of the country and is the centre of the logging industry which is based on the huge pine plantations in the area. There are a couple of petrol stations, a bank or two and a gritty 'frontier' atmosphere.

Highlands Inn (☎ 437 1144) Singles/doubles B&B E157/308. This inn, 1km south of the town centre on the main road, is the only place to stay in town. The rooms are clean and nice enough, but it isn't great value. There's a pleasant garden area with views. The good *Tintsaba Crafts* (☎ 437 1260) is attached to the inn.

Woodcutter's Restaurant (☎ 437 1144) Meals from R15. Open 7.15am-9.15am, noon-2pm & 7pm-9pm daily. This restaurant in the Highlands Inn is probably the best spot – in town at least – for a meal.

The bus and minibus taxi stop is next to the market at the top end of the main street. There are express buses to Mbabane for

about E10. A nonshared taxi to the casino is about E30; to Mbabane it will cost E130.

AROUND PIGGS PEAK

If you're driving between Mbabane and Piggs Peak (or even if you're on public transport) you're in for a treat – the mountain scenery is stunning as you career up and down the winding roads. Cleverly, the local craftspeople have stationed rickety tables full of crafts at every good vantage point along the way! So stopping for a photo may also mean fending off eager sellers. It's touristy, but you'll be hard-pressed to find better mountain viewing in the kingdom.

In addition to the scenery (including the **Phophonyane Falls** about 8km north of town), this area is known for its handicrafts. A good place to check these out is at the newly opened Peak Craft Centre, where you'll find *Ethnic Bound* (☎ 437 3099, **e** lungi@africaonline.co.sz), which specialises in African fabrics; and *Likweti Kraft* (☎ 437 3127), a branch of Tintsaba Crafts, which sells sisal baskets, jewellery and many other Swazi crafts. The Centre is just north of the Protea Piggs Peak Hotel & Casino.

Places to Stay & Eat

Protea Piggs Peak Hotel & Casino (☎ 437 1104, fax 437 1382, **e** sales@proteapiggs peak.sz) Singles/doubles B&B E510/610. About 10km north-east of Piggs Peak, this place is on the road to the Jeppe's Reef border post. It offers midweek specials, which are affordable if gambling is what you seek.

Phophonyane Lodge (☎/fax 437 1319, **e** lungile@phophonyane.co.sz, **W** www.pho phonyane.co.sz) 2-person cottages from E454, 2-person tents E333. Entry to the reserve and therefore the lodge is an additional E10 per person. Day visitors are charged E30 to enter the surrounding reserve. Cooking facilities. North-east of Piggs Peak, this is a serene and beautiful place on a river in its own nature reserve of lush indigenous forest. It's one of the nicest places to stay in Swaziland, and there are walking trails around the river and waterfall. You can also swim in the rock pools. Don't climb on the rocks near the falls as they can be slippery.

Dining Hut Full English breakfast E28, starters E18-23, mains E35-45. Excellent meals are prepared in an informal atmosphere at this hut in Phophonyane Lodge; there is also an interesting collection of masks from Mali here.

To get to Phophonyane Lodge, head north-east from Piggs Peak (towards the casino) and take the signposted turn-off about 1.5km before the casino (minibus taxis will drop you there). Continue down this road until you cross a bridge over a waterfall; the turn-off to the lodge is about 500m further on, to the right. You can arrange with the lodge to be picked up from Piggs Peak; a taxi costs about E35.

Getting There & Away
If you're heading east towards Hlane Royal National Park, the roads are mainly dirt and they're in reasonably rough condition, although a 2WD will handle them OK if you exercise a bit of restraint on the accelerator.

The stretch of dirt road running west from Piggs Peak to Barberton (Mpumalanga) through Bulembu includes some of the roughest tracks in Africa; expect the descent on this shocking road to take two hours. Don't attempt it in wet conditions.

Eastern Swaziland

The north-eastern corner of Swaziland is a major sugar-producing area. It's hot in the arid foothills of the Lebombo Mountains, but the scenery approaches the visions most people have of Africa. Its two gems are Hlane Royal National Park and Mlawula Nature Reserve.

Halfway between the eastern border and Manzini is Mkhaya Game Reserve, one of Swaziland's great treasures.

SIMUNYE
This is the nicest of the sugar-company towns: it's a showpiece and is worth a look. It describes itself as a village, but that's being coy. It's a neat, lush town with great facilities.

Simunye is roughly between Hlane Royal National Park and Mlawula and Mbuluzi

Nature Reserves (see following). Stock up with supplies here before heading off to any of these parks.

Tambankulu Recreational Club (☎ 373 7111) Singles/doubles B&B E170/260. There's a restaurant, swimming pool, gymnasium, tennis court, golf course and places to fish here. Inquire at reception about accommodation in the Mbuluzi Nature Reserve (see following), which adjoins the Mlawula Nature Reserve and is privately owned. This club is north of Simunye and about 8km west of the junction at Maphiveni, off the Tshaneni road.

Simunye Country Club (☎/fax 383 8600, ⓔ dlitschka@simunyeclub.co.sz) Singles/doubles E190/290. This place has air-con rooms, self-catering cottages and a great restaurant. It is intended for the sugar workers, but visitors are welcomed and can use the facilities (swimming pool, golf course, tennis and squash courts) after they become temporary members.

Regular buses run to this region from Manzini and there are also minibus taxis for about E10. There are fewer buses from Piggs Peak. If you're driving here from Piggs Peak, beware of buses, as they speed and hog the gravel road.

HLANE ROYAL NATIONAL PARK
This park (☎ 528 3944, fax 528 3924, ⓔ re servations@biggame.co.sz; admission E20 per person; open 6am-6pm) is near the former royal hunting grounds. The name 'Hlane' means 'Wilderness'. Swaziland's largest protected area, it is home to elephants, lions, cheetahs, leopards, white rhinos and many antelope species.

There are guided walking trails (E15 per person), which afford the opportunity to see lions, elephants and rhinos, as well as two-hour wildlife drives (E100 per person). The entrance gate is about 4km south of Simunye. For more information get a copy of *The History & Significance of Hlane Royal National Park*, which was published to celebrate the return of lions to Swaziland.

Accommodation can be booked through the Kingdom of Swaziland's Big Game Parks office in Mlilwane Wildlife Sanctuary

SWAZILAND

Lions at Large

There are currently 11 lions in Hlane Royal National Park, including two cubs. To see the lions you must hire a guide, as the roads can be confusing and the map of the park, given free at the entrance gate, is next to useless. You can either go on foot, hire a Land Rover or take your own car, but it must be a 4WD with good clearance to get around this area of the park.

If you are in a 2WD you can still drive yourself around some of the park, where you'll have a good chance of seeing rhinos, kudus, giraffes, warthogs, elephants and ostriches, to name a few. To do this turn right just before Ndlovu Camp, coming from the entrance gate. You won't need a guide as it's easy to get around and most roads will lead you back to the camp anyway.

If it's been raining, check with the guides about driving in the park, as some tracks become impassable.

(see Information under Ezulwini Valley earlier in this chapter).

Ndlovu Camp Self-catering rondavels per person E145, E245 single occupancy; larger cottages per person E160; camping and caravanning per person E35. This camp offers excellent accommodation. The small shop here only sells drinks, very basic food items and curios, so stock up in Simunye.

Bhubesi Camp Self-catering rondavels per person E145, E245 single occupancy. Another excellent accommodation choice in the park.

MLAWULA & MBULUZI NATURE RESERVES

These adjoining reserves are in harsh but beautiful country, which take in both plains and the Lebombo Mountains. The turn-off for the entrance gates to the reserves is about 10km north of Simunye; it's signposted. The entrance gate for Mbuluzi is 200m down this road on the left and the gate for Mlawula is a bit further down on the right.

Mlawula Nature Reserve (☎ 416 1136, fax 416 1040; admission E15 plus E6 per car; open 6am-6pm) has antelope species and there are shy hyenas in remote areas. Bird-watching is particularly fruitful here. Activities include two-hour wildlife drives (E40 per person, plus E30 per vehicle), night drives or guided bush walks. You can camp here for E15/6 per adult/child; two-person tented accommodation costs E120. You can also go on an overnight camp-out, which includes a wildlife drive, hiking and basic catering, for E130 per person. Apart from this there is free canoeing and fishing (rods are for hire for E18).

Accommodation can be booked through the Ezulwini Tourist Office at the Mantenga Craft Centre in the Ezulwini Valley (see Information under Ezulwini Valley earlier).

Mbuluzi Nature Reserve (☎ 383 8861, fax 383 8862, e mbuluzi@africaonline.co.sz, w www.mbuluzi.co.za; admission E10 plus E20 per car) is privately owned and managed by Tambankulu Estates. It's a more luxurious option for accommodation than neighbouring Mlawula Nature Reserve, and has the price tag to match. Eight-person cottages cost E715; and the five-person cottage costs E650.

The reserve boasts a range of animals including giraffes, zebras, hippos, antelope species and wildebeests. There have also been over 300 bird species recorded here. Land Rovers are available for wildlife drives at E100, plus E4 per kilometre.

SITEKI

This trading town was originally named when Mbandzeni (great-grandfather of the present king) gave his frontier troops permission to marry – Siteki means 'Marrying Place'.

This town isn't really on the way to anywhere any more, but it's a bit cooler up here in the Lebombo Mountains than it is down on the plains. There are good views on the steep road up here.

Stegi Hotel (☎ 343 4126, 604 4848) DB&B per person E136. The host of this old hotel, Graham Duke, knows lots about the area.

A minibus taxi trip from Manzini costs about E8.

MKHAYA GAME RESERVE

This superb private reserve (☎ 416 1581, e reservations@biggame.co.sz; admission, all-inclusive) is off the Manzini–Big Bend road, near the hamlet of Phuzumoya.

The reserve is on rehabilitated cattle farmland, although the area had always been popular with hunters for its game. Mkhaya takes its name from the *mkhaya* (or 'knobthorn') tree, which abounds on the reserve. Mkhayas are valued not only for their fruit, from which Swazis brew beer, but for the insect and birdlife they support.

Although small, Mkhaya has a wide range of animals, including white and black rhinos (including six black rhinos donated by the Taiwanese government in a gesture of goodwill), roan and sable antelopes, and elephants. The donated black rhinos are breeding well, but numbers are kept secret, for good reason. The reserve's boast is that you're more likely to meet a black rhino in the wild here than anywhere else in Africa. There are also herds of the indigenous and rare Nguni cattle, which make the reserve economically self-supporting.

Day tours are available for E250 including lunch and a wildlife drive; entry to the reserve is included in the cost of day tours and overnight stays. It is worth staying at Mkhaya for at least one night. Note that you can't visit the reserve without having booked (at the Kingdom of Swaziland's Big Game Parks office in the Mlilwane Wildlife Sanctuary; see Information under Ezulwini Valley earlier in this chapter), and even then you can't drive in alone; you'll be met at Phuzumoya at a specified pick-up time, usually 10am or 4pm.

The E730 per person fee for shared self-contained luxury safari tents or stone cottages (single occupants must pay an extra E120) includes three meals, three wildlife-viewing drives and walks, and is better value than many of the private reserves near Kruger National Park in South Africa.

If accommodation described as 'luxury' puts you off, don't worry – here it's full of character and not at all pretentious. Stone Camp, the safari-tent option, is more like a comfortable 19th century hunting camp than

a hotel sitting incongruously in the wilderness. The floors of the tents are raked sand, allowing you to see ant trails and the tracks of the small animals that come in at night.

White-Water Rafting

One of the highlights of Swaziland is rafting the Usutu River (which becomes the Lusutfu River). The river is usually sluggish and quite tame, but near the reserve it passes through the narrow Bulungu Gorge, which separates the Mabukabuka and Bulunga Mountains, generating rapids. Early on, a 10m waterfall has to be portaged. The second half of the day is a sedate trip through scenic country with glimpses of the 'flat dogs' (crocodiles) sunning on the river bank. The crocs haven't devoured anyone recently, hence the claim that rafting here is '…safer than driving through Jo'burg'. The water is Grade IV and not for the faint-hearted, although brave beginners should handle the day easily. The trips, operated by Swazi Trails in two-person 'crocodile rafts', take a full day and cost E390 per person (minimum of two people). All equipment and lunch is included.

Swazi Trails operates many other activities in the country, including mountain biking, caving and hiking. For contact details see Organised Tours in the Getting Around section.

Southern Swaziland

BIG BEND

This is a neat sugar town on, not surprisingly, a big bend in the Lusutfu River just before it joins the Usutu. It's quite a picturesque spot. If you're here during summer you can cool off in the pool at the Bend Inn Hotel (E5 for nonresidents).

Bend Inn Hotel (☎ 363 6725) Singles/doubles B&B E168/201. On a hill just south of town and with good views across the river, this inn is looking a little faded these days. There's a restaurant and a pleasant outdoor bar.

Riverside Motel & Restaurant (☎ 363 6012, fax 363 6032) Singles/doubles B&B

SWAZILAND

E150/200, family room E250. This motel, a 10-minute drive south-east of town on the MR8, is a friendly place. It has a swimming pool, garage (for repairs) and nightclub (for self-wrecking). There's a good restaurant here, open from 7.30am to 10pm daily, with mains from E22 to E45.

Lismore Lodge (☎ 363 6019) Doubles R150. Lismore Lodge has small, comfortable doubles that are good value. The best thing about this place is that it's right next to Lubombo Lobster, making it a short walk for your seafood-stuffed belly after dinner.

Lubombo Lobster (☎ 363 6308) Starters E14-20, mains E35-45. Just south of Big Bend on the MR8, this gem of a place serves possibly the best seafood in this part of the world. The calamari (E35) is superb, you won't taste better. Also recommended is the oven-baked kingklip fish (E45) and the seafood kebabs (E42). Highly recommended is the seafood curry (small E40, large E65) – what do they put in that sauce?! Lubombo Lobster also does crayfish, priced according to size. If you see a tour bus descend on the place, wait for another chance to go there.

Getting There & Away
Most people stop at Big Bend on the way to/from KwaZulu-Natal in South Africa. A minibus taxi to Manzini is E10, and if you're heading the other way to Lavumisa border post, it's about E7.

NSOKO
This town, halfway between Big Bend and the border post of Lavumisa, lies in the heart of sugar-cane country. The region is pleasant enough, with the Lebombo Mountains as a backdrop.

Nisela Safaris (☎ 303 0318, fax 303 0247) Single/double beehive huts E80/100, singles/doubles B&B E200/350. There are plenty of activities here, including game drives (E40 per person, minimum group of six); guided walks (E25); canoeing on the Usutu River (E150); and fly fishing for the fierce tiger fish, florida bass and barbel (E400, breakfast and lunch included). There is also traditional Swazi dancing (E50).

NHLANGANO & HLATHIKULU
Nhlangano is the closest town to the border post at Mahamba, but unless you want to visit the casino, there's no real reason to visit.

Nhlangano Sun Hotel & Casino (☎ 207 8211, fax 207 8402, MR11) Singles/doubles E556/612. The casino is 4km out of town. Rooms are very comfortable.

The City to City bus, which runs from Jo'burg via Ermelo, Piet Retief and Nhlangano terminates further on at Hlathikulu. If you need to stay overnight, the *Assegi Inn (☎ 217 6126, Prince Arthur St, Hlathikulu)* offers doubles for E110. This basic place was closed at the time of research, but should reopen soon.

Language

South African English

English has undergone some changes during its time in South Africa. Quite a few words have changed meaning, new words have been appropriated, and thanks to the influence of Afrikaans, a distinctive accent has developed. Grammar and spelling follow British rather than US practice. In some cases British words are preferred to their US equivalent (eg, 'lift' not 'elevator', 'petrol' not 'gas'). In African English, repetition for emphasis is common. For example, something that burns you is 'hot hot'; fields after the rains are 'green green'; a crowded minibus with no more room is 'full full' and so on.

Afrikaans

Afrikaans has been closely associated with the tribal identity of the Afrikaners but it is also spoken as a first language by many coloureds. Ironically, it was probably first used as a common language by the polyglot coloured community of the Cape and passed back to whites by nannies and servants. Around six million people speak the language, roughly half of whom are Afrikaners and half of whom are coloured.

Afrikaans developed from the High Dutch of the 17th century. It has abandoned the complicated Dutch grammar and has a vocabulary made up of borrowings from French, English, indigenous African languages and even Asian languages (thanks to East Asian slaves). It's inventive, powerful and expressive. It wasn't recognised as one of the country's official languages until 1925; before then it was officially regarded as a dialect of Dutch.

Pronunciation

Afrikaans is phonetically consistent and words are generally pronounced the way they are spelled, with the characteristic guttural emphasis and rolled 'r' of Germanic languages. The following pronunciation guide is not exhaustive, but it includes the more difficult sounds.

a	as the 'u' in 'pup'
e	as in 'hen'
i	as the 'e' in 'angel'
o	as in 'fort', or as the 'oy' in 'boy'
u	as the 'e' in 'angel' but with lips pouted
r	a rolled 'rr' sound
aai	as the 'y' in 'why'
ae	as 'ah'
ee	as in 'deer'
ei	as the 'ay' in 'play'
oe	as the 'oo' in 'loot'
oë	as the 'oe' in 'doer'
ooi	as the 'oi' in 'oil', preceded by 'w'
oei	as the 'ooey' in 'phooey', preceded by 'w'
tj	as the 'ch' in 'chunk'

Greetings & Civilities

Hello.	*Hallo.*
Good morning.	*Goeiemôre.*
Good afternoon.	*Goeiemiddag.*
Good evening.	*Goeienaand.*
Good night.	*Goeienag.*
Please.	*Asseblief.*
Thank you.	*Dankie.*
How are you?	*Hoe gaan dit?*
Good, thank you.	*Goed dankie.*
Pardon.	*Ekskuus.*

Useful Words & Phrases

Yes.	*Ja.*
No.	*Nee.*
What?	*Wat?*
How?	*Hoe?*
How many/much?	*Hoeveel?*
Where?	*Waar?*
Isn't that so?	*Né?*
Do you speak English?	*Praat u Engels?*

Do you speak Afrikaans?	*Praat u Afrikaans?*
I only understand a little Afrikaans.	*Ek verstaan net 'n bietjie Afrikaans.*
Where are you from?	*Waarvandaan kom u?*
from ...	*van ...*
overseas	*oorsee*
sons	*seuns*
daughters	*dogters*
wife	*vrou*
husband	*eggenoot*
mother	*ma*
father	*pa*
sister	*suster*
brother	*broer*
emergency	*nood*
nice/good/pleasant	*lekker*
bad	*sleg*
cheap	*goedkoop*
expensive	*duur*
party/rage	*jol*

Getting Around

arrival	*aankoms*
departure	*vertrek*
one way ticket	*enkel kaartjie*
return ticket	*retoer kaartjie*
to	*na*
from	*van*
travel	*reis*

Around Town

art gallery	*kunsgalery*
at the corner	*op die hoek*
avenue	*laan*
bank	*bank*
building	*gebou*
church	*kerk*
city	*stad*
city centre	*middestad*
enquiries	*navrae*
exit	*uitgang*
information	*inligting*
left	*links*
office	*kantoor*
pharmacy/chemist	*apteek*
police	*polisie*
police station	*polisiestasie*

post office	*poskantoor*
road	*pad, weg*
rooms	*kamers*
right	*regs*
station	*stasie*
street	*straat*
tourist bureau	*toeristeburo*
town	*dorp*
traffic light	*robot*

In the Country

bay	*baai*
beach	*strand*
car	*kar*
caravan park	*woonwapark*
field/plain	*veld*
ford	*drift*
freeway	*vrymaak*
game reserve	*wildtuin*
highway	*snelweg*
hiking trail	*wandelpad*
lake	*meer*
marsh	*vlei*
mountain	*berg*
point	*punt*
river	*rivier*
road	*pad*
track	*spoor*
utility/pick-up	*bakkie*

Food & Drinks

barbecue	*braaivleis/braai*
beer	*bier*
bread	*brood*
cheese	*kaas*
chicken	*hoender*
cup of coffee	*koppie koffie*
dried, salted meat	*biltong*
farm sausage	*boerewors*
fish	*vis*
fruit	*vrugte*
glass of milk	*glas melk*
hotel bar	*kroeg*
meat	*vleis*
pork	*varkvlies*
steak	*biefstuk*
tea	*tee*
vegetables	*groente*
water	*water*
wine	*wyn*

Time & Days

When?	Wanneer?
am	vm
pm	nm
soon	nou-nou
today	vandag
tomorrow	môre
yesterday	gister
daily	daagliks
weekly	weekblad
public holiday	openbare vakansiedag

Monday	Maandag (Ma)
Tuesday	Dinsdag (Di)
Wednesday	Woensdag (Wo)
Thursday	Donderdag (Do)
Friday	Vrydag (Vr)
Saturday	Saterdag (Sa)
Sunday	Sondag (So)

Numbers

1	een
2	twee
3	drie
4	vier
5	vyf
6	ses
7	sewe
8	agt
9	nege
10	tien
11	elf
12	twaalf
13	dertien
14	veertien
15	vyftien
16	sestien
17	sewentien
18	agtien
19	negentien
20	twintig
21	een en twintig
30	dertig
40	veertig
50	vyftig
60	sestig
70	sewentig
80	tagtig
90	negentig
100	honderd
1000	duisend

Ndebele

Ndebele is spoken in the northen border region of Northern Province.

Hello.	Lotsha.
Goodbye.	Khamaba kuhle/ Sala kuhle.
Yes.	I-ye.
No.	Awa.
Please.	Ngibawa.
Thank you.	Ngiyathokaza.
What's your name?	Ungubani ibizo lakho?
My name is ...	Ibizo lami ngu ...
I come from ...	Ngibuya e ...

North Sotho

North Sotho is spoken in the north-eastern provinces of South Africa.

Hello.	Thobela.
Goodbye.	Sala gabotse.
Yes.	Ee.
No.	Aowa.
Please.	Ke kgopela.
Thank you.	Ke ya leboga.
What's your name?	Ke mang lebitso la gago?
My name is ...	Lebitso laka ke ...
I come from ...	Ke bowa kwa ...

South Sotho

South Sotho is one of two official languages in Lesotho (English being the other), and is also spoken by Basotho people in the Free State, North West Province and Gauteng in South Africa. It's useful to know some words and phrases if you're planning to visit Lesotho, especially if you want to trek in remote areas.

Hello.	Dumela.
Greetings father.	Lumela ntate.
Peace father.	Khotso ntate.
Greetings mother.	Lumela 'me.
Peace mother.	Khotso 'me.
Greetings brother.	Lumela abuti.

Peace brother.	*Khotso abuti.*
Greetings sister.	*Lumela ausi.*
Peace sister.	*Khotso ausi.*

There are three ways to say 'How are you?':

How are you?	*O kae?* (sg)
	Le kae? (pl)
How do you live?	*O phela joang?* (sg)
	Le phela joang? (pl)
How did you get up?	*O tsohele joang?* (sg)
	Le tsohele joang? (pl)

The responses are:

I'm here.	*Ke teng.* (sg)
	Re teng. (pl)
I live well.	*Ke phela hantle.* (sg)
	Re phela hantle. (pl)
I got up well.	*Ke tsohile hantle.* (sg)
	Re tsohile hantle. (pl)

These questions and answers are quite interchangeable. Someone could ask you *O phela joang?* and you could answer *Ke teng.*

When trekking, people always ask *Lea kae?* (Where are you going?) and *O tsoa kae?* or the plural *Le tsoa kae?* (Where have you come from?). When parting, use the following expressions:

Stay well.	*Sala hantle.* (sg)
	Salang hantle. (pl)
Go well.	*Tsamaea hantle.* (sg)
	Tsamaeang hantle. (pl)

'Thank you' is *kea leboha* (pronounced 'keya lebowah'). The herd boys often ask for *chelete* (money) or *lipompong* (sweets), pronounced 'dee-pom-pong'. If you want to say 'I don't have any', the answer is *ha dio* (pronounced 'ha dee-oh').

Swati

Swati is one of two official languages in Swaziland (the other is English). It's very similar to Zulu, and the two languages are mutually intelligible. Swati is a tone language (changes of pitch within words determines their meaning), and there are also some clicks to contend with.

Hello. (to one person)	*Sawubona.* (lit: 'I see you')
Hello. (more than one person)	*Sanibona.*
How are you?	*Kunjani?*
I'm fine.	*Kulungile.*
Goodbye. (when leaving)	*Sala kahle.* (lit: 'stay well')
Goodbye. (when staying)	*Hamba kahle.* (lit: 'go well')
Please.	*Ngicela.*
I thank you.	*Ngiyabonga.*
We thank you.	*Siyabonga.*
Yes.	*Yebo.* (also an all purpose greeting)
No.	(click) *Cha.*
Sorry.	*Lucolo.*
What's your name?	*Ngubani libito lakho?*
My name is ...	*Libitolami ningu ...*
I'm from ...	*Ngingewekubuya e ...*
Do you have?	*Une yini?*
How much?	*Malini?*
Is there a bus to?	*Kukhona ibhasi yini leya?*
When does it leave?	*Isuka nini?*

today	*lamuhla*
tomorrow	*kusasa*
yesterday	*itolo*
morning	*ekuseni*
afternoon	*entsambaba*
evening	*kusihlwa*
night	*ebusuku*

Tsonga

Tsonga is spoken in the Mozambique border region north of Hluhluwe in KwaZulu-Natal.

Hello.	*Avusheni.* (morning)
	Inhelekani. (afternoon)
	Riperile. (evening)
Goodbye.	*Salani kahle.*
Yes.	*Hi swona.*
No.	*A hi swona.*

Please.	*Nakombela.*
Thank you.	*I nkomu.*
What's your name?	*U mani vito ra wena?*
My name is ...	*Vito ra mina i ...*
I come from ...	*Ndzihuma e ...*

Tswana

Tswana is widely spoken in South Africa – in the eastern areas of Northern Cape, in the North-West Province and in the western area of the Free State.

Hello.	*Dumela.*
Goodbye.	*Sala sentle.*
Yes.	*Ee.*
No.	*Nnya.*
Please.	*Ke a kopa.*
Thank you.	*Ke a leboga.*
What's your name?	*Leina la gago ke mang?*
My name is ...	*Leina la me ke ...*
I come from ...	*Ke tswa ...*

Venda

Venda is spoken in the north eastern border region of Northern Province.

Hello.	*Ndi matseloni.* (morning) *Ndi masiari.* (afternoon) *Ndi madekwana* (evening)
Goodbye.	*Kha vha sale zwavhudi.*
Yes.	*Ndi zwone.*
No.	*A si zwone.*
Please.	*Ndikho u humbela.*
Thank you.	*Ndo livhuwa.*
What's your name?	*Zina lavho ndi nnyi?*
My name is ...	*Zina langa ndi ...*
I come from ...	*Ndi bva ...*

Xhosa

Xhosa is the language of the Xhosa people. It's the dominant indigenous language in Eastern Cape Province, although you'll meet Xhosa speakers throughout the region.

It's worth noting that *bawo* is a term of respect used when addressing an older man.

Good morning.	*Molo.*
Goodnight.	*Rhonanai.*
Do you speak English?	*Uyakwazi ukuthetha siNgesi?*
Are you well?	*Uphilile na namhlanje?*
Yes, I'm well.	*Ewe, ndiphilile kanye.*
Where are you from?	*Uvela phi na okanye ngaphi na?*
I'm from ...	*Ndivela ...*
When will we arrive?	*Siya kufika nini na?*
The road is good.	*Indlela ilungile.*
The road is bad.	*Indlela imbi.*
I'm lost.	*Ndilahlekile.*
Is this the road to ...?	*Yindlela eya ... yini le?*
Would you show me the way to ...?	*Ungandibonisa na indlela eye ...?*
Is it possible to cross the river?	*Kunokwenzeka ukuwela umlambo?*
How much is it?	*Idla ntoni na?*

day	*usuku*
week	*iveki*
month (moon)	*inyanga*
east	*empumalanga*
west	*entshonalanga*

Zulu

Zulu is the language of the people of the same name. As with several other Nguni languages, Zulu uses a variety of 'clicks', very hard to reproduce without practice. Many people don't try (the 'Kwa' in Kwa-Zulu is a click), although it's worth the effort, if just to provide amusement for your listeners. To ask a question, add *na* to the end of a sentence.

Hello.	*Sawubona.*
Goodbye.	*Sala kahle.*
Please.	*Jabulisa.*
Thank you.	*Ngiyabonga.*

LANGUAGE

Yes.	*Yebo.*	north	*inyakatho*
No.	*Cha.*	south	*iningizumi*
Excuse me.	*Uxolo.*	east	*impumalanga*
Where does this road go?	*Iqondaphi lendlela na?*	west	*intshonalanga*
		water	*amanzi*
Which is the road to ...?	*Iphi indlela yokuya ku ...?*	food	*ukudla*
		lion	*ibhubesi*
Is it far?	*Kukude yini?*	rhino (black)	*ubhejane*
		rhino (white)	*umkhombe*

Glossary

ANC – African National Congress; national democratic organisation formed in 1912 to represent blacks

apartheid – literally 'the state of being apart'; the former South African political system in which people were segregated according to race

AWB – Afrikaner Weerstandsbeweging; Afrikaner Resistance Movement, the Afrikaners' extremist right-wing group

bakkie – utility, pick-up

baie dankie – Afrikaans for 'thank you very much', 'many thanks'

bazaar – market

bilharzia – another name for schistosome, a disease caused by blood flukes, passed on by freshwater snails

black taxi – minibus taxi

bobotie – South African dish of mincemeat with a topping of beaten egg baked to a crust

boerewors – spicy sausage

Bokke – affectionate name for the South African national rugby team, the Springboks

boloi – Basotho term for 'witchcraft'

brandsolder – a layer of clay or brick above the ceiling that protects the house if the thatching catches fire

braai – short for braaivleis, a barbecue at which meat is cooked over an open fire (Afrikaans term)

bredie – traditional Cape Malay dish of lamb, chicken or fish, and vegetables, stewed

broe – Afrikaans for 'brother', equivalent of 'mate' and short for broeder (pronounced brew)

Broederbond – secret society open only to Protestant Afrikaner men; was highly influential under National Party rule

bubblegum – a form of *township* music influenced by Western pop

buck – antelope

buppies – black yuppies

bunny chow – a quarter of a loaf of bread hollowed out and filled with beans or curry stew; a takeaway speciality, especially in Durban

coloureds – although apartheid treated the Indians as a distinct group, separate from the coloureds, generally this term is used to refer to those of mixed-race descent and Indian descent

comma – used and pronounced instead of the decimal point, eg 10,5 (said as 'ten comma five')

dagga – marijuana, also known as 'zol'

diamantveld – diamond fields

difaqane – Basotho for 'forced migration', equivalent to Zulu word *mfecane*

donga – steep-sided gully created by soil erosion

dorp – village or rural settlement where a road crosses a river

drero – traditional African dish, a thick stew

drift – river ford

dzata – Venda term for chief's *kraal*

eisbein – pork knuckle

fanagalo – a pidgin language based on a mixture of English, Afrikaans and Zulu

farm stall – small roadside shop or shelter that sells farm produce

flying squad – emergency response unit of police, originally established to stem interracial violence, now augmented in response to the burgeoning crime rate

free-camp – camping where you want, not in a formal campsite; permission should be sought and money offered

fynbos – literally, 'fine bush', primarily proteas, heaths and ericas

highveld – high-altitude grassland region

Homelands – established for blacks under *apartheid* and considered independent countries by South Africa (never accepted by UN), reabsorbed into South Africa after 1994

IFP – Inkatha Freedom Party; black political

movement, founded around 1975 and lead by Chief Mangosouthu Buthelezi, working against *apartheid*

igqirha – spiritual healer (Xhosa)

impi – warrior

inyanga – medicine man and herbalist who also studies patterns of thrown bones

isicathamiya – a soft-shoe-shuffle style of vocal music from KwaZulu-Natal

isi-danga – Xhosa term for a long turquoise necklace

joala – sorghum beer brewed in Lesotho

jol – party, both noun and verb; also any good time: 'How was Mozambique?' 'Yah, it was a *jol*, man.'

kingklip – an excellent firm-fleshed fish, usually served fried

kloof – ravine

kloofing – canyoning

knobkerry – traditional African weapon, a stick with a round knob at the end, used as a club or missile

koeksesters – small doughnuts dripping in honey, very gooey and figure-enhancing

kopje – small hill

kraal – a hut village, often with an enclosure for livestock; also a Zulu fortified village

kroeg – bar

kwaito – form of *township* music; a mix of mbaqanga, jive, hip-hop, house, ragga and other dance styles

kwela – *township* interpretation of American swing music

KWV – Kooperatieve Wijnbouwers Vereniging; cooperative formed in 1918 to control minimum prices, production areas and quota limits in the wine industry

laager – a defensive circular formation of ox-wagons, used by the Voortrekkers for protection against attack

landdrost – an official acting as local administrator, tax collector and magistrate

lapa – a circular building with low walls and a thatched roof, used for cooking, partying etc

lekker – very good, enjoyable or tasty

lekolulo – a flute-like instrument played by herd boys (Basotho)

location – another word for *township*, usually in rural areas

lowveld – low-altitude area, having scrub vegetation (also called 'bushveld')

mampoer – home-distilled brandy made from peaches and prickly pear

matjieshuis – traditional woven Nama 'mat' huts, similar in shape to Zulu 'beehive' huts (Afrikaans)

mbaqanga – form of *township* music; literally 'dumpling' in Zulu, combining church choirs, doo-wop and sax jive

mealie – an ear of maize (Afrikaans)

mealie pap – maize porridge; the staple diet for rural blacks, served with stew

mfecane – forced migration of many Southern African tribes (Zulu); also known as *difaqane* (Besotho)

muti – traditional medicine of many Ngun peoples

ngxowa yebokwe – goatskin bag carried over the left shoulder on important occasion (Xhosa)

PAC – Pan African Congress; political organisation of blacks founded by Robert Sobukwe in 1959 to work for majority rule and equal rights

peri-peri – spicy Portuguese pepper sauce

pinotage – a type of wine; a cross between pinot noir and hermitage or shiraz

pont – river ferry

Poqo – armed wing of the *PAC*

potjie kos – traditional Afrikaner stew cooked in a poitjie (a three-legged pot)

pronking – strange bouncy leaping by an telope, apparently just for fun

Rikki – an open small van used as public transport in Cape Town

robot – traffic light

rondavel – a round hut with a conical roo

rooibos – literally, 'red bush' (Afrikaans) herbal tea that reputedly has therapeuti qualities

rusks – twice-cooked biscuits usuall served for breakfast or as a snack, and muc better than those given to teething babies

rystafel – Dutch/Afrikaner version of a

Indonesian meal consisting of rice with many accompanying dishes

samp – mix of maize and beans (known as *umngqusho* in Xhosa)
sangoma – traditional witch doctor or herbalist (usually female)
sandveld – dry, sandy belt
setolo-tolo – stringed instrument played with the mouth by men (Basotho)
shebeen – drinking establishment in black *township*; once illegal, now merely unlicensed
slaghuis – butchers
sjambok – short whip, traditionally made from rhino hide; one of the most hated weapons used by apartheid-era police
snoek – firm-fleshed migratory fish that appears off the Cape in June and July; served smoked, salted or curried
sourveld – a type of grassland
spaza – informal shop in a *township*
spruit – shallow river
stad – city centre (Afrikaans); used on road signs
stoep – raised platform, the equivalent of a veranda, a feature of Cape Dutch architecture
strand – beach
sundowner – any drink, but typically alcoholic, that is drunk at sunset
swart gevaar – Afrikaans for 'black threat'

Telkom – government telecommunications company
thkolosi – small, maliciously playful beings (Basotho)
thomo – stringed instrument played by women (Basotho)
tokoloshe – evil spirits (Xhosa)
township – planned urban settlement of blacks and coloureds
Trekboers – first Dutch who trekked off

into the interior of what is now largely Western Cape; later shortened to Boers
tronk – jail (Afrikaans)
tsaba tsaba – a form of music, a forerunner of *kwela* and *township* jive
tsotsi – *township* hoodlum, gangster

Ubuntu – humanity or fellow feeling; kindness (Xhosa and Zulu)
uitlanders – Afrikaans for 'foreigners'; originally the name given by Afrikaners to the immigrants who poured into the Transvaal after the discovery of gold
ukwendisa amasokana – the return of male initiates (Ndebele)
Umkhonto we Sizwe – armed wing of the *ANC*
umngqusho – mix of maize and beans (Xhosa term for *samp*)
umnqombothi – home-brewed beer
umvubo – meal of sour milk and mealie

vaalies – slang name for whites from the former Transvaal region
veld – elevated open grassland (pronounced 'felt')
velskoene – handmade leather shoes
vlei – any low marshy landscape (pronounced flay)
VOC – Vereenigde Oost-Indische Compagnie (Dutch East India Company)
volk – nation of Afrikaners
volkstaal – people's language (Afrikaans)
volkstaat – an independent, racially pure Boer state
Voortrekkers – original Afrikaner settlers of Orange Free State and Transvaal who migrated from the Cape Colony in the 1830s

waaihoek – overnight hut
waterblommetjie bredie – traditional Cape Malay dish; mutton stew with faintly peppery water-hyacinth flowers and white wine

Thanks

Many thanks to the following intrepid travellers who took the time to share their experiences travelling with the last edition of *South Africa, Lesotho & Swaziland*.

Bethan & Claire, Ep Tissing, Hazel Ahrens, Hans Alblas, Nita Andrews, June Arber, Paul Bailey, David Ballantyne, Daniel Barber, Ward Barnes, Eileen Barrett, Jill Barton, Tom Beech, Henk Bekker, Andrew Bergwald, Sebastiaan Biehl, Richard Blyth, Fulia Bonaiuti, Peter Boodell, Steven Bothma, Bob & Anne Bown, Jan Van Den Brand, Leanne Brandis, Craig Brown, Alex Brownlie, Richard Bruce, Debbie Bruk, Ian & Ronnie Buckman, Marcel Busa, Jane Butterfield, Elisabeth Caffyn-Parsons, Beverley Carolan, Melissa Carroll, Jennifer Cassone, Alan & Lynne Charlton, Ann Christian, Caroline Clark, Meg & Al Clark, Jain Close, M & R Cobden, Jo Coley, Janice Comish, Damien Connolly, J Cooper, Dan Coplan, Etelka Corten, Donna Cotter, Emily Cowan, Edward Crean, Kaarina Curtis, Uwe Danapel, Rob Davidowitz, P De Graaf, Zelna de Villiers, Elissa Dennis, William Denton, Andre DeSimone, Sarah Dodson, Jean Dorrell, Cameron Douglas, Lionel Dowler, Michelle Duffield, Anne Easterling, Tami Ebner, Josef Edel, Roderick Eime, Beatrice Elar, Julie Evans, Paula & Marc Feyaerts-Verlinden, Peter Finn, Annika Fjellber, Pamela Flett, Till Francke, J Arthur Freed, Marilynn & Peter Freitag, Erith French, Rob Garner, Audrey Gaughran, Chetan Ghate, Bruce Gilbert, Thomas Goodsim, Mary O Gormau, Tania Gorzkowski, Paul Gowen, Andy Graham, Adin Greaves, Frances Green, MA Greenhalgh, Esther Grovenstein, Erika Grundberg, Marc Grutering, Corinne Gurry, Sue Hall, David Hancock, Phillip Hanson, Mark Harding, Matt Hartley, Taariq Hassan, Steve Hayes, Suzanne Heath, Dr Mag Gottfried Heinisch, H Henrico, Tom Hetley, Rona Hiam, Cherie Hicks, Richard Hill, Manfred Hillberger, Geraldine Hodgkins, Patrick Huddie, Marina Hughes, Sandie Hull, Mark Hunt, Victor Isaac, Benjamin Isgur, Michael Jennings, Paul Jerome, Eric Johnson, Floris Jol, Sabine Joyce, Pablo Juliano, Cynthia Karena, Annie Kennedy, Michael Kilpatrick, SE Kinghorn, Ypie Kingma, Dan Knowles, Karen Kohler, Jopie Kotze, Elsie Kuipers, Noshir Lam, Michael Lambert, Robert Lauwen, John Lavender, Johan Le Roux, Tom Leurquin, Joy Leuthard, Bob Lipske, Andre Lotz, Ansgar Luig, Catarina Lyden, Ronald MacArthur, Jon MacCallum, M J Mackay, Bruce Mackie, Silvia & Stefano Mazzocchio, Roger McEvilly, Elizabeth McSweeney, Sharon Meieran, Martie Meijen, Steve Mendel, Jo Mercuri, A Michaels, Markella Mikkelsen, Lisa Mitchell, Pamela Moffat, Gebhard & Verena Mohr, Kai Monkkonen, Elwyn Morris, Osacr Nagtegaal, Hans-Erik Nobel, Janice Nolan, I D & SE Nosworthy, Anders Noven, Paul S Odendaal, Jean-Yves Ollivier, Aleta O'Meara, Danielle Ompad, Stephen Packer, L & A Pansaru, Dirk Jan Parlevliet, Steve Pearce, Jeff Peires, Giorgio Perversi, Maurice Peters, Patrick Phillips, Pieter Pieterse, Christine Pike, Klaus Piprek, Dan Potter, Jim Potter, Kate Prevedello, James Prior, Julian Quail, Oswald Radford, Helen Randle, J Reid, Marco Reinhoudt, Nancy & Maxim Rice, Anna Rickards, Marion Rimmer, Ian Roberts, Ray Roberts-York, Clare Robinson, Leif Robinson, Robert Romain, Nick Rooker, Kerstin Rosen, Richard & Caroline Rule, Will Sam, Andrew & Pippa Sargent, Thomas Schwarz, Octavia Schweitzer, Greesh Sharma, Nathan Shearing, Reinhardt Slabber, Preston Smith, Stephen Smith, Joost & Conny Snoep, Saskia Soeterbroek, Leng Soo-Tsu, Andy Sparrow, Hilda Srnoy, Nicole Staal, Urs Steiger, David Storey, Bill & Ann Stoughton, Nuna Taras, Janine Taylor, David & Evonne Templeton, Megan Thirey, Chris Thompson, David Thomson, HB Thorpe, Ria Timmerman, Michel Tio, Britta Toll, Johannes van Eeden, Astrid van Leeuwen, Slavica & Jilles van Werkhoven, Marcel van Zonneveld, Harmen Venema, Brandon Vogt, Hedwig Vollers, Jan & Leone Vorster, Veronique Walraven, Patricia Wanzalla, Ian Watson, Alban Weis, Viktor Weisshaupl, Mark Weitz, Claudia Wend, Niels Wennekes, Zane West, Duncan White, NE & BK Whitehead, Vincent Wiegers, Klaas Wiersema, Sanne Wijnhorst, Tim Williams, Jeremy Wills, Jean A Wilsen, Chris Winchester, Wyn Woods, Denis Woodward, Robert Wotton, Mark Wynne, Ian Young, Rodger Young, Laurent Zecha, Julie Zeitlinger, Andrea Zeus.

LONELY PLANET

You already know that Lonely Planet produces more than this one guidebook, but you might not be aware of the other products we have on this region. Here is a selection of titles that you may want to check out as well:

Southern Africa
ISBN 0 86442 662 3

Botswana
ISBN 1 74059 041 4

Cape Town
ISBN 0 86442 759 X

Malawi
ISBN 1 86450 095 6

Mozambique
ISBN 1 86450 108 1

Zambia
ISBN 1 74059 045 7

Read This First: Africa
ISBN 1 86450 066 2

Africa on a shoestring
ISBN 0 86442 663 1

Watching Wildlife Southern Africa
ISBN 1 86450 035 2

Cape Town City Map
ISBN 1 86450 076 X

Southern Africa Road Atlas
ISBN 1 86450 101 4

Healthy Travel Africa
ISBN 1 86450 050 6

Zimbabwe
ISBN 1 74059 043 0

Namibia
ISBN 1 74059 042 2

Available wherever books are sold

LONELY PLANET

ON THE ROAD

Travel Guides explore cities, regions and countries, and supply information on transport, restaurants and accommodation, covering all budgets. They come with reliable, easy-to-use maps, practical advice, cultural and historical facts and a rundown on attractions both on and off the beaten track. There are over 200 titles in this classic series, covering nearly every country in the world.

 Lonely Planet Upgrades extend the shelf life of existing travel guides by detailing any changes that may affect travel in a region since a book has been published. Upgrades can be downloaded for free from **www.lonelyplanet.com/upgrades**

For travellers with more time than money, **Shoestring** guides offer dependable, first-hand information with hundreds of detailed maps, plus insider tips for stretching money as far as possible. Covering entire continents in most cases, the six-volume shoestring guides are known around the world as 'backpackers bibles'.

For the discerning short-term visitor, **Condensed** guides highlight the best a destination has to offer in a full-colour, pocket-sized format designed for quick access. They include everything from top sights and walking tours to opinionated reviews of where to eat, stay, shop and have fun.

CitySync lets travellers use their Palm™ or Visor™ hand-held computers to guide them through a city with handy tips on transport, history, cultural life, major sights, and shopping and entertainment options. It can also quickly search and sort hundreds of reviews of hotels, restaurants and attractions, and pinpoint their location on scrollable street maps. CitySync can be downloaded from **www.citysync.com**

MAPS & ATLASES

Lonely Planet's **City Maps** feature downtown and metropolitan maps, as well as transit routes and walking tours. The maps come complete with an index of streets, a listing of sights and a plastic coat for extra durability.

Road Atlases are an essential navigation tool for serious travellers. Cross-referenced with the guidebooks, they also feature distance and climate charts and a complete site index.

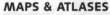

LONELY PLANET

ESSENTIALS

Read This First books help new travellers to hit the road with confidence. These invaluable predeparture guides give step-by-step advice on preparing for a trip, budgeting, arranging a visa, planning an itinerary and staying safe while still getting off the beaten track.

Healthy Travel pocket guides offer a regional rundown on disease hot spots and practical advice on predeparture health measures, staying well on the road and what to do in emergencies. The guides come with a user-friendly design and helpful diagrams and tables.

Lonely Planet's **Phrasebooks** cover the essential words and phrases travellers need when they're strangers in a strange land. They come in a pocket-sized format with colour tabs for quick reference, extensive vocabulary lists, easy-to-follow pronunciation keys and two-way dictionaries.

Miffed by blurry photos of the Taj Mahal? Tired of the classic 'top of the head cut off' shot? **Travel Photography: A Guide to Taking Better Pictures** will help you turn ordinary holiday snaps into striking images and give you the know-how to capture every scene, from frenetic festivals to peaceful beach sunrises.

Lonely Planet's **Travel Journal** is a lightweight but sturdy travel diary for jotting down all those on-the-road observations and significant travel moments. It comes with a handy time-zone wheel, a world map and useful travel information.

Lonely Planet's eKno is an all-in-one communication service developed especially for travellers. It offers low-cost international calls and free email and voicemail so that you can keep in touch while on the road. Check it out on **www.ekno.lonelyplanet.com**

FOOD & RESTAURANT GUIDES

Lonely Planet's **Out to Eat** guides recommend the brightest and best places to eat and drink in top international cities. These gourmet companions are arranged by neighbourhood, packed with dependable maps, garnished with scene-setting photos and served with quirky features.

For people who live to eat, drink and travel, **World Food** guides explore the culinary culture of each country. Entertaining and adventurous, each guide is packed with detail on staples and specialities, regional cuisine and local markets, as well as sumptuous recipes, comprehensive culinary dictionaries and lavish photos good enough to eat.

LONELY PLANET

OUTDOOR GUIDES

For those who believe the best way to see the world is on foot, Lonely Planet's **Walking Guides** detail everything from family strolls to difficult treks, with 'when to go and how to do it' advice supplemented by reliable maps and essential travel information.

Cycling Guides map a destination's best bike tours, long and short, in day-by-day detail. They contain all the information a cyclist needs, including advice on bike maintenance, places to eat and stay, innovative maps with detailed cues to the rides, and elevation charts.

The **Watching Wildlife** series is perfect for travellers who want authoritative information but don't want to tote a heavy field guide. Packed with advice on where, when and how to view a region's wildlife, each title features photos of over 300 species and contains engaging comments on the local flora and fauna.

With underwater colour photos throughout, **Pisces Books** explore the world's best diving and snorkelling areas. Each book contains listings of diving services and dive resorts, detailed information on depth, visibility and difficulty of dives, and a roundup of the marine life you're likely to see through your mask.

LONELY PLANET

OFF THE ROAD

Journeys, the travel literature series written by renowned travel authors, capture the spirit of a place or illuminate a culture with a journalist's attention to detail and a novelist's flair for words. These are tales to soak up while you're actually on the road or dip into as an at-home armchair indulgence.

The range of lavishly illustrated **Pictorial** books is just the ticket for both travellers and dreamers. Off-beat tales and vivid photographs bring the adventure of travel to your doorstep long before the journey begins and long after it is over.

Lonely Planet **Videos** encourage the same independent, tough-minded approach as the guidebooks. Currently airing throughout the world, this award-winning series features innovative footage and an original soundtrack.

Yes, we know, work is tough, so do a little bit of deskside dreaming with the spiral-bound Lonely Planet **Diary** or a Lonely Planet **Wall Calendar**, filled with great photos from around the world.

TRAVELLERS NETWORK

Lonely Planet Online. Lonely Planet's award-winning Web site has insider information on hundreds of destinations, from Amsterdam to Zimbabwe, complete with interactive maps and relevant links. The site also offers the latest travel news, recent reports from travellers on the road, guidebook upgrades, a travel links site, an online book-buying option and a lively travellers bulletin board. It can be viewed at **www.lonelyplanet.com** or AOL keyword: lp.

Planet Talk is a quarterly print newsletter, full of gossip, advice, anecdotes and author articles. It provides an antidote to the being-at-home blues and lets you plan and dream for the next trip. Contact the nearest Lonely Planet office for your free copy.

Comet, the free Lonely Planet newsletter, comes via email once a month. It's loaded with travel news, advice, dispatches from authors, travel competitions and letters from readers. To subscribe, click on the Comet subscription link on the front page of the Web site.

Lonely Planet Guides by Region

Lonely Planet is known worldwide for publishing practical, reliable and no-nonsense travel information in our guides and on our Web site. The Lonely Planet list covers just about every accessible part of the world. Currently there are 16 series: Travel guides, Shoestring guides, Condensed guides, Phrasebooks, Read This First, Healthy Travel, Walking guides, Cycling guides, Watching Wildlife guides, Pisces Diving & Snorkeling guides, City Maps, Road Atlases, Out to Eat, World Food, Journeys travel literature and Pictorials.

AFRICA Africa on a shoestring • Botswana • Cairo • Cairo City Map • Cape Town • Cape Town City Map • East Africa • Egypt • Egyptian Arabic phrasebook • Ethiopia, Eritrea & Djibouti • Ethiopian Amharic phrasebook • The Gambia & Senegal • Healthy Travel Africa • Kenya • Malawi • Morocco • Moroccan Arabic phrasebook • Mozambique • Namibia • Read This First: Africa • South Africa, Lesotho & Swaziland • Southern Africa • Southern Africa Road Atlas • Swahili phrasebook • Tanzania, Zanzibar & Pemba • Trekking in East Africa • Tunisia • Watching Wildlife East Africa • Watching Wildlife Southern Africa • West Africa • World Food Morocco • Zambia • Zimbabwe, Botswana & Namibia
Travel Literature: Mali Blues: Traveling to an African Beat • The Rainbird: A Central African Journey • Songs to an African Sunset: A Zimbabwean Story

AUSTRALIA & THE PACIFIC Aboriginal Australia & the Torres Strait Islands •Auckland • Australia • Australian phrasebook • Australia Road Atlas • Cycling Australia • Cycling New Zealand • Fiji • Fijian phrasebook • Healthy Travel Australia, NZ & the Pacific • Islands of Australia's Great Barrier Reef • Melbourne • Melbourne City Map • Micronesia • New Caledonia • New South Wales • New Zealand • Northern Territory • Outback Australia • Out to Eat – Melbourne • Out to Eat – Sydney • Papua New Guinea • Pidgin phrasebook • Queensland • Rarotonga & the Cook Islands • Samoa • Solomon Islands • South Australia • South Pacific • South Pacific phrasebook • Sydney • Sydney City Map • Sydney Condensed • Tahiti & French Polynesia • Tasmania • Tonga • Tramping in New Zealand • Vanuatu • Victoria • Walking in Australia • Watching Wildlife Australia • Western Australia
Travel Literature: Islands in the Clouds: Travels in the Highlands of New Guinea • Kiwi Tracks: A New Zealand Journey • Sean & David's Long Drive

CENTRAL AMERICA & THE CARIBBEAN Bahamas, Turks & Caicos • Baja California • Belize, Guatemala & Yucatán • Bermuda • Central America on a shoestring • Costa Rica • Costa Rica Spanish phrasebook • Cuba • Cycling Cuba • Dominican Republic & Haiti • Eastern Caribbean • Guatemala • Havana • Healthy Travel Central & South America • Jamaica • Mexico • Mexico City • Panama • Puerto Rico • Read This First: Central & South America • Virgin Islands • World Food Caribbean • World Food Mexico • Yucatán
Travel Literature: Green Dreams: Travels in Central America

EUROPE Amsterdam • Amsterdam City Map • Amsterdam Condensed • Andalucía • Athens • Austria • Baltic States phrasebook • Barcelona • Barcelona City Map • Belgium & Luxembourg • Berlin • Berlin City Map • Britain • British phrasebook • Brussels, Bruges & Antwerp • Brussels City Map • Budapest • Budapest City Map • Canary Islands • Catalunya & the Costa Brava • Central Europe • Central Europe phrasebook • Copenhagen • Corfu & the Ionians • Corsica • Crete • Crete Condensed • Croatia • Cycling Britain • Cycling France • Cyprus • Czech & Slovak Republics • Czech phrasebook • Denmark • Dublin • Dublin City Map • Dublin Condensed • Eastern Europe • Eastern Europe phrasebook • Edinburgh • Edinburgh City Map • England • Estonia, Latvia & Lithuania • Europe on a shoestring • Europe phrasebook • Finland • Florence • Florence City Map • France • Frankfurt City Map • Frankfurt Condensed • French phrasebook • Georgia, Armenia & Azerbaijan • Germany • German phrasebook • Greece • Greek Islands • Greek phrasebook • Hungary • Iceland, Greenland & the Faroe Islands • Ireland • Italian phrasebook • Italy • Kraków • Lisbon • The Loire • London • London City Map • London Condensed • Madrid • Madrid City Map • Malta • Mediterranean Europe • Milan, Turin & Genoa • Moscow • Munich • Netherlands • Normandy • Norway • Out to Eat – London • Out to Eat – Paris • Paris • Paris City Map • Paris Condensed • Poland • Polish phrasebook • Portugal • Portuguese phrasebook • Prague • Prague City Map • Provence & the Côte d'Azur • Read This First: Europe • Rhodes & the Dodecanese • Romania & Moldova • Rome • Rome City Map • Rome Condensed • Russia, Ukraine & Belarus • Russian phrasebook • Scandinavian & Baltic Europe • Scandinavian phrasebook • Scotland • Sicily • Slovenia • South-West France • Spain • Spanish phrasebook • Stockholm • St Petersburg • St Petersburg City Map • Sweden • Switzerland • Tuscany • Ukrainian phrasebook • Venice • Vienna • Wales • Walking in Britain • Walking in France • Walking in Ireland • Walking in Italy • Walking in Scotland • Walking in Spain • Walking in Switzerland • Western Europe • World Food France • World Food Greece • World Food Ireland • World Food Italy • World Food Spain **Travel Literature:** After Yugoslavia • Love and War in the Apennines • The Olive Grove: Travels in Greece • On the Shores of the Mediterranean • Round Ireland in Low Gear • A Small Place in Italy

Lonely Planet Mail Order

onely Planet products are distributed worldwide. They are also available by mail order from Lonely Planet, so if you have difficulty finding a title please write to us. North and South American residents should write to 150 Linden St, Oakland, CA 94607, USA; European and African residents should write to 10a Spring Place, London NW5 3BH, UK; and residents of other countries to Locked Bag 1, Footscray, Victoria 3011, Australia.

INDIAN SUBCONTINENT & THE INDIAN OCEAN Bangladesh • Bengali phrasebook • Bhutan • Delhi • Goa • Healthy Travel Asia & India • Hindi & Urdu phrasebook • India • India & Bangladesh City Map • Indian Himalaya • Karakoram Highway • Kathmandu City Map • Kerala • Madagascar • Maldives • Mauritius, Réunion & Seychelles • Mumbai (Bombay) • Nepal • Nepali phrasebook • North India • Pakistan • Rajasthan • Read This First: Asia & India • South India • Sri Lanka • Sri Lanka phrasebook • Tibet • Tibetan phrasebook • Trekking in the Indian Himalaya • Trekking in the Karakoram & Hindukush • Trekking in the Nepal Himalaya • World Food India **Travel Literature:** The Age of Kali: Indian Travels and Encounters • Hello Goodnight: A Life of Goa • In Rajasthan • Maverick in Madagascar • A Season in Heaven: True Tales from the Road to Kathmandu • Shopping for Buddhas • A Short Walk in the Hindu Kush • Slowly Down the Ganges

MIDDLE EAST & CENTRAL ASIA Bahrain, Kuwait & Qatar • Central Asia • Central Asia phrasebook • Dubai • Farsi (Persian) phrasebook • Hebrew phrasebook • Iran • Israel & the Palestinian Territories • Istanbul • Istanbul City Map • Istanbul to Cairo • Istanbul to Kathmandu • Jerusalem • Jerusalem City Map • Jordan • Lebanon • Middle East • Oman & the United Arab Emirates • Syria • Turkey • Turkish phrasebook • World Food Turkey • Yemen **Travel Literature:** Black on Black: Iran Revisited • Breaking Ranks: Turbulent Travels in the Promised Land • The Gates of Damascus • Kingdom of the Film Stars: Journey into Jordan

NORTH AMERICA Alaska • Boston • Boston City Map • Boston Condensed • British Columbia • California & Nevada • California Condensed • Canada • Chicago • Chicago City Map • Chicago Condensed • Florida • Georgia & the Carolinas • Great Lakes • Hawaii • Hiking in Alaska • Hiking in the USA • Honolulu & Oahu City Map • Las Vegas • Los Angeles • Los Angeles City Map • Louisiana & the Deep South • Miami • Miami City Map • Montreal • New England • New Orleans • New Orleans City Map • New York City • New York City City Map • New York City Condensed • New York, New Jersey & Pennsylvania • Oahu • Out to Eat – San Francisco • Pacific Northwest • Rocky Mountains • San Diego & Tijuana • San Francisco • San Francisco City Map • Seattle • Seattle City Map • Southwest • Texas • Toronto • USA • USA phrasebook • Vancouver • Vancouver City Map • Virginia & the Capital Region • Washington, DC • Washington, DC City Map • World Food New Orleans **Travel Literature:** Caught Inside: A Surfer's Year on the California Coast • Drive Thru America

NORTH-EAST ASIA Beijing • Beijing City Map • Cantonese phrasebook • China • Hiking in Japan • Hong Kong & Macau • Hong Kong City Map • Hong Kong Condensed • Japan • Japanese phrasebook • Korea • Korean phrasebook • Kyoto • Mandarin phrasebook • Mongolia • Mongolian phrasebook • Seoul • Shanghai • South-West China • Taiwan • Tokyo • Tokyo Condensed • World Food Hong Kong • World Food Japan **Travel Literature:** In Xanadu: A Quest • Lost Japan

SOUTH AMERICA Argentina, Uruguay & Paraguay • Bolivia • Brazil • Brazilian phrasebook • Buenos Aires • Buenos Aires City Map • Chile & Easter Island • Colombia • Ecuador & the Galapagos Islands • Healthy Travel Central & South America • Latin American Spanish phrasebook • Peru • Quechua phrasebook • Read This First: Central & South America • Rio de Janeiro • Rio de Janeiro City Map • Santiago de Chile • South America on a shoestring • Trekking in the Patagonian Andes • Venezuela **Travel Literature:** Full Circle: A South American Journey

SOUTH-EAST ASIA Bali & Lombok • Bangkok • Bangkok City Map • Burmese phrasebook • Cambodia • Cycling Vietnam, Laos & Cambodia • East Timor phrasebook • Hanoi • Healthy Travel Asia & India • Hill Tribes phrasebook • Ho Chi Minh City (Saigon) • Indonesia • Indonesian phrasebook • Indonesia's Eastern Islands • Java • Lao phrasebook • Laos • Malay phrasebook • Malaysia, Singapore & Brunei • Myanmar (Burma) • Philippines • Pilipino (Tagalog) phrasebook • Read This First: Asia & India • Singapore • Singapore City Map • South-East Asia on a shoestring • South-East Asia phrasebook • Thailand • Thailand's Islands & Beaches • Thailand, Vietnam, Laos & Cambodia Road Atlas • Thai phrasebook • Vietnam • Vietnamese phrasebook • World Food Indonesia • World Food Thailand • World Food Vietnam

ALSO AVAILABLE: Antarctica • The Arctic • The Blue Man: Tales of Travel, Love and Coffee • Brief Encounters: Stories of Love, Sex & Travel • Buddhist Stupas in Asia: The Shape of Perfection • Chasing Rickshaws • The Last Grain Race • Lonely Planet ... On the Edge: Adventurous Escapades from Around the World • Lonely Planet Unpacked • Lonely Planet Unpacked Again • Not the Only Planet: Science Fiction Travel Stories • Ports of Call: A Journey by Sea • Sacred India • Travel Photography: A Guide to Taking Better Pictures • Travel with Children • Tuvalu: Portrait of an Island Nation

Lonely Planet Mail Order

Index

Abbreviations

Text

Index

Abbreviations

Text

Bold indicates maps.

Boxed Text

---

old indicates maps.

MAP LEGEND

CITY ROUTES

Freeway	Freeway
Highway	Primary Road
Road	Secondary Road
Street	Street
Lane	Lane
	On/Off Ramp

= = = =	Unsealed Road
	One Way Street
	Pedestrian Street
	Stepped Street
= =	Tunnel
	Footbridge

REGIONAL ROUTES

	Tollway, Freeway
	Primary Road
	Secondary Road
	Minor Road

BOUNDARIES

	International
	State
	Disputed
	Fortified Wall

HYDROGRAPHY

	River; Creek
	Canal
	Lake

	Dry Lake; Salt Lake
	Spring; Rapids
	Waterfalls

TRANSPORT ROUTES & STATIONS

	Train
	Underground Train
	Metro
	Tramway
	Cable Car, Chairlift

	Ferry
	Walking Trail
	Walking Tour
	Path
	Pier or Jetty

AREA FEATURES

	Building
	Park; Gardens

	Market
	Sports Ground

	Beach
	Cemetery

	Campus
	Plaza

POPULATION SYMBOLS

CAPITAL	National Capital	
CAPITAL	State Capital	
CITY	City	
Town	Town	
Village	Village	
	Urban Area	

MAP SYMBOLS

	Place to Stay
	Place to Eat
	Point of Interest

Airfield; Airport		Cinema		Museum		Stately Home
Bank		Embassy		National Park		Surfing
Battlefield		Golf Course		Parking		Swimming Pool
Border Crossing		Hindu Temple		Petrol Station		Taxi
Bus Terminal		Hospital		Picnic		Telephone
Camping		Internet Cafe		Police Station		Theatre
Caravan Park		Lighthouse		Post Office		Tourist Information
Cave		Lookout		Pub or Bar		Transport
Chalet/Hut		Monument		Ruins		Winery
Church		Mosque		Shopping Centre		Wildlife Reserve/Zoo

Note: not all symbols displayed above appear in this book

LONELY PLANET OFFICES

Australia
Locked Bag 1, Footscray, Victoria 3011
☎ 03 8379 8000 fax 03 8379 8111
email: talk2us@lonelyplanet.com.au

USA
150 Linden St, Oakland, CA 94607
☎ 510 893 8555 TOLL FREE: 800 275 8555
fax 510 893 8572
email: info@lonelyplanet.com

UK
10a Spring Place, London NW5 3BH
☎ 020 7428 4800 fax 020 7428 4828
email: go@lonelyplanet.co.uk

France
1 rue du Dahomey, 75011 Paris
☎ 01 55 25 33 00 fax 01 55 25 33 01
email: bip@lonelyplanet.fr
www.lonelyplanet.fr

World Wide Web: www.lonelyplanet.com *or* AOL keyword: lp
Lonely Planet Images: lpi@lonelyplanet.com.au